A LEXICON OF MEDIEVAL NORDIC LAW

A Lexicon of Medieval Nordic Law

Edited by *Jeffrey Love, Inger Larsson, Ulrika Djärv,*
Christine Peel, and Erik Simensen

The Royal Swedish Academy of Letters, History and Antiquities, the Magnus Bergvalls Stiftelse and the Stiftelsen Konung Gustaf VI Adolfs fond för svensk kultur have generously contributed to this publication.

Cover image: *Carta marina*, a wallmap of Scandinavia, by Olaus Magnus, 1539, Wikimedia, public domain, https://commons.wikimedia.org/wiki/File:Carta_Marina.jpeg. Cover designer: Anna Gatti

Contents

Introduction

LMNL

A Lexicon of Medieval Nordic Law (LMNL) is a multilingual reference work designed to make terminology from several medieval legal texts more accessible to English-speaking audiences. It contains over 6000 Nordic headwords, more than 9000 English equivalents and approximately 13,200 cross-references. It is intended to function as a general lexicon of medieval Nordic legal terminology in use before the national laws. Where possible the editors have combined related terms in multiple languages under the same headword in order to highlight similarities throughout the Nordic region during the Middle Ages. The LMNL differs from other reference works, and in particular other lexica, by its presentation of related terms from multiple languages within a single entry in a manner similar to the *Kulturhistoriskt lexikon för nordisk medeltid* (KLNM). Around a quarter of the entries feature a brief text articulating how the term fits into the legal landscape. Creation of the LMNL has been made possible in large part due to a generous project grant from the Swedish Research Council (2014–2017) and the gracious cooperation of members of the ongoing Medieval Nordic Laws (MNL) project begun at the University of Aberdeen in 2009. Draft English translations supplied by them, along with a small number of published translations (see table below), form the basis of this lexicon. Additional support was provided by the Royal Swedish Academy of Letters, which supplied funding for translations and revisions of some MNL laws and for the LMNL colloquium held in Stockholm in November 2015.

Material

LMNL is built upon 25 legal texts, mainly provincial laws, written in Old Swedish, Old Icelandic, Old Norwegian, Old Danish, Old Gutnish and Old Faroese. Material for the lexicon was taken from editions used in the latest English translations of the oldest medieval Nordic laws, many of which were produced as part of the Medieval Nordic Laws project. With such a large textual corpus and a relatively short timeframe in which to work, it was deemed most feasible to collect Nordic legal terms and phrases and present them with the English equivalents selected by the translators of the texts in which those terms appear. Modern English equivalents throughout the LMNL are therefore largely taken directly from draft and published translations with minimal interpretation by the editors. Editorial interventions generally consist of minor adjustments in cases where idiomatic translations would be confusing when removed from their contexts. Equivalents in subsequent published translations will possibly vary somewhat from those presented here. Medieval terms have been drawn from editions utilized by the translators. The following table is a list of texts cited, their common abbreviations and bibliographic information on the editions and translations used for the LMNL.

BorgL	Borgartingsloven	Halvorsen, Eyvind Fjeld and Magnus Rindal, eds. 2008. *De eldste østlandske kristenrettene*. Oslo: Riksarkivet. [Version 1, AM 78 4to]
		L. Collinson (draft trans.)
DL	Dalalagen	Schlyter, C. J., ed. 1841. *Codex iuris Vestmannici: Westmanna-lagen*. SSGL. Vol. 5. Lund: Berlingska boktryckeriet.
		I. Larsson (draft trans.)
EidsL	Eidsivatingsloven	Halvorsen, Eyvind Fjeld and Magnus Rindal, eds. 2008. *De eldste østlandske kristenrettene*. Oslo: Riksarkivet. [Longer version, AM 68 4to]
		L. Collinson (draft trans.)

https://doi.org/10.11647/OBP.0188.01

ESjL	Eriks sjællandske lov	Skautrup, Peter, ed. 1936. *Eriks sjællandske lov, text 1–2*. DGL. Vol. 5. Copenhagen: Gyldendal. Tamm, Ditlev and Helle Vogt, trans. 2016. *The Danish Medieval Laws: The Laws of Scania, Zealand and Jutland*. London: Routledge.
FrL	Frostatingsloven	Keyser, R and P. A. Munch, eds. 1846. *Norges gamle Love indtil 1387*. Vol. 1. Christiania: Grøndahl. A. Mindrebø and J. S. Love (draft trans.)
GL	Gutalagen	Pipping, Hugo, ed. 1905–07. *Guta lag och Guta saga jämte ordbok*. Samfund til Udgivelse af gammel nordisk Litteratur 33. Copenhagen: Møller. Peel, Christine, trans. 2015. *Guta Lag and Guta Saga. The Law and History of the Gotlanders*. London: Routledge.
Grg	Grágás	Vilhjálmur Finsen, ed. 1852 (repr. 1974). *Grágás: Konungsbók*. Odense: Odense Universitetsforlag. Dennis, Andrew, Peter Foote and Richard Perkins, trans. 1980–2000. *Laws of Early Iceland: Grágás; The Codex Regius of Grágás with material from other manuscripts*. 2 vols. Winnipeg: Univ. of Manitoba.
GS	Gutasagan	Pipping, Hugo, ed. 1905–07. *Guta lag och Guta saga jämte ordbok*. Samfund til Udgivelse af gammel nordisk Litteratur 33. Copenhagen: Møller. Peel, Christine, trans. 2015. *Guta Lag and Guta Saga. The Law and History of the Gotlanders*. London: Routledge.
GuL	Gulatingsloven	Keyser, R and P. A. Munch, eds. 1846. *Norges gamle Love indtil 1387*. Vol. I. Christiania: Grøndahl. E. Simensen (draft trans.)
HL	Hälsingelagen	Schlyter, C. J., ed. 1844. *Codex iuris Helsingici: Helsinge-lagen*. SSGL. Vol. 6. Lund: Berlingska boktryckeriet. S. Brink (draft trans.)
Jó	Jónsbók	Schulman, Jana K, ed. and trans. 2010. *Jónsbók. The Laws of Later Iceland*. Saarbrücken: AQ-Verlag.
Js	Járnsíða	Haraldur Bernharðsson, Magnús Lyngdal Magnússon and Már Jónsson, eds. 2005. *Járnsíða og Kristinréttur Árna Þorlákssonar*. Reykjavík: Sögufélagið. J. S. Love (draft trans.)
JyL	Jyske lov	Skautrup, Peter, ed. 1933. *Jyske lov, text 1: NkS 295 8o*. DGL Vol. 2. Copenhagen: Gyldendal. Tamm, Ditlev and Helle Vogt, trans. 2016. *The Danish Medieval Laws: The Laws of Scania, Zealand and Jutland*. London: Routledge.
KRA	Kristinréttr Árna Þorlákssonar	Haraldur Bernharðsson, Magnús Lyngdal Magnússon and Már Jónsson, eds. 2005. *Járnsíða og Kristinréttur Árna Þorlákssonar*. Reykjavík: Sögufélagið. J. S. Love (draft trans.)
SdmL	Södermannalagen	Schlyter, C. J., ed. 1838. *Codex iuris Sudermannici: Södermanna-lagen*. SSGL. Vol. 4. Lund: Berlingska boktryckeriet. U. Djärv (draft trans.)
Seyð	Seyðabrævið	Poulsen, Jóhan Hendrik W. and Ulf Zachariasen, eds. Michael Barnes and David R. Margolin, trans. 1971. *Seyðabrævið*. Tórshavn: Føroya Fróðskaparfelag.
SkKL	Skånske kirkelov	Aakjær, Svend and Erik Kroman, eds. 1933. *Skånske lov: Anders Sunesøns parafrase, skånske kirkelov*. DGL Vol. 1, bk. 2. Copenhagen: Gyldendal. Tamm, Ditlev and Helle Vogt, trans. 2016. *The Danish Medieval Laws: The Laws of Scania, Zealand and Jutland*. London: Routledge.

SkL	Skånske lov	Brøndum-Nielsen, Johs and Svend Aakjær, eds. 1933. *Skånske lov, text 1–3.* DGL. Vol. 1, bk. 1. Copenhagen: Gyldendal.
		Tamm, Ditlev and Helle Vogt, trans. 2016. *The Danish Medieval Laws: The Laws of Scania, Zealand and Jutland.* London: Routledge.
SmL	Smålandslagen (Tiohärads lag)	Schlyter, C. J., ed. 1844. *Codicis iuris Smalandici pars de re ecclesiastica: Kristnu-balken af Smålands-lagen.* SSGL. Vol. 6. Lund: Berlingska boktryckeriet.
		S. Fridell (draft trans.)
UL	Upplandslagen	Schlyter, C. J., ed. 1834. *Codex iuris Uplandici: Uplands-lagen.* SSGL. Vol. 3. Stockholm: P. A. Norstedt & Söner.
		C. Peel (draft trans.)
VmL	Västmannalagen	Schlyter, C. J., ed. 1841. *Codex iuris Vestmannici: Westmanna-lagen.* SSGL. Vol. 5. Lund: Berlingska boktryckeriet.
		C. Peel (draft trans.)
VSjL	Valdemars sjællandske lov	Kroman, Erik, ed. 1941. *Valdemars sjællandske lov, ældre og yngre redaktion.* DGL. Vol. 8. Copenhagen: Gyldendal.
		Tamm, Ditlev and Helle Vogt, trans. 2016. *The Danish Medieval Laws: The Laws of Scania, Zealand and Jutland.* London: Routledge.
YVgL	Yngre Västgötalagen	Schlyter, C. J. and H. S. Collin, eds. 1827. *Codex iuris vestrogotici: Westgöta-lagen.* SSGL. Vol. 1. Stockholm: Z. Hæggström.
		T. Lindkvist (draft trans.)
ÄVgL	Äldre Västgötalagen	Schlyter, C. J. and H. S. Collin, eds. 1827. *Codex iuris vestrogotici: Westgöta-lagen.* SSGL. Vol. 1. Stockholm: Z. Hæggström.
		T. Lindkvist (draft trans.)
ÖgL	Östgötalagen	Schlyter, C. J., ed. 1830. *Codex iuris Ostrogotici: Östgöta-lagen.* SSGL. Vol. 2. Stockholm: P. A. Norstedt & Söner.
		J. Benham (draft trans.)

Headword selection

Contents of the LMNL represent only a selection of material from the available medieval legal texts. Four of the editors were given the discretion to determine which terms were legally relevant and merited inclusion in the lexicon. Central legal concepts have been included, as have an expanded set of terms deemed germane to the legal culture of the period. These lists were subsequently brought together to form the core of the lexicon. Not all terms were considered equally necessary by every editor, but all selected terms have been retained in the lexicon with the understanding that some terms may have a more legal significance in one text than in another. Therefore not every term included has been excerpted from all sources used in the LMNL. It is hoped that further material can be included in subsequent editions of the LMNL.

Principles for lemmatization

The LMNL is intended to illustrate how cognate terms function across the breadth of the medieval Nordic region. To accomplish this, closely related terms have often been gathered under a single headword. A distinction has been drawn between words with the same meaning that differ merely in the form of a prefix or suffix (which are gathered under one headword) and those that are a combination of distinct elements forming words with the same meaning (which have been treated separately). Thus *lyte* (ODan) and *áljótr* (ON) are treated together under the headword *lyti* (OSw), while *arvi* (OSw) and *arftaki* (OSw) are kept separate despite both meaning 'heir'. Certain linguistic distinctions, such as nominal gender and verbal prefixes, have been ignored, as with the OGu and ON terms for 'to gamble' (*dufla*), which can be found under *fordoble* (ODan). Extensive cross-references throughout the LMNL ensure that subordinated headword forms and variants remain accessible. Grammatical description has been limited to part of speech for Nordic headwords and in distinguishing homonyms within the English>Nordic section.

Entry content

Each entry contains English equivalents and textual references as found in most dictionaries treating historical languages. The headword line lists forms of the excerpted term, including some of the most common spelling variants. Entries in the lexicon are lemmatized and organized according to the Old Swedish form of the headword, if there is one, as the Old Swedish laws form the bulk of the source material within the LMNL. Otherwise the terms are alphabetized according to the Nordic language abbreviation.

Sample entry

Headword → **lænsmaþer (OSw) lénsmaðr (ON) lænsman (OSw) lænsmander (OSw) noun**

Article {

In the most general sense, a *lænsmaþer* was a representative, proxy or deputy to a higher official. Like *gælkare* (q.v.), the title has been used to translate Lat. *exactor*. In Denmark and Norway a representative of this kind was often called *høvedsmand*.

In the Swedish laws a *lænsmaþer* was often an official of the king (OSw *konungs lænsmaþer*) or bishop (OSw *biskups lænsmaþer*) who saw to local administrative matters and represented their interests at assemblies (OSw *þing*) and collected taxes and fines on their behalf. *Lænsmaþer* also appears to be interchangeable with the term for prosecutor (OSw *soknari*) in YVgL, ÖgL and SmL, all of which appear to have functions similar to the Norwegian *ármaðr* (q.v.). According to UL the *lænsmaþer* had the privilege of convening a panel (OSw *næmd*) which selects judges (OSw *domari*) in each hundred (OSw *hundari*). The *husabyman* (q.v.) in DL may have been the equivalent of a *lænsmaþer* in Dalarna, though the former may have had some slightly different responsibilities or indeed have been subordinate to the *lænsmaþer*. The terms *konungs maþer* and *biskups maþer* in OSw DL and HL may refer to a *lænsmaþer*.

In Denmark and Norway a *lænsmaþer* may also refer specifically to a holder of a fief (ON *lén*, see *læn*) granted by the king (or a bishop, in the case of church estates). As such he operated as governor of an area during the Middle Ages and was permitted to make use of the region's incomes.

In Norway a *lénsmaðr* often referred to a deputy to the sheriff (*sýslumaðr*, see *sysluman*) and acted on his behalf, particularly by serving in court proceedings. He also had the authority to arrest criminals. There were not supposed to be more than two *lénsmenn* in any given district (*fylki*). According to an ordinance issued in 1293, a man who was appointed *lénsmaðr* had to be a householder (*bóndi*, see *bonde*) from a good family. The most important function of a *lénsmaðr* was collecting incomes, namely taxes and fines. He also had police duties and could stand in

for the law-man (*lögmaðr*, see *laghmaþer*). After 1537 the administration system was restructured and a *lénsmaðr* was renamed *bondelensmann*. The title *lensmann* is still used in Norway.

In the Icelandic laws the *lénsmaðr* generally refers to the sheriff and his aides. The term does not appear until amendments began to be made to Jónsbók, though it is used in several medieval Icelandic diplomas thereafter.

administrator **OSw** *YVgL* Kkb, Urb, Tb, Föb, Add
bailiff **OSw** *DL* Mb, Tjdb, Rb, *HL* Mb, Rb   → **Equivalents and Citations**
bishop's administrator **OSw** *UL* Kkb, *VmL* Kkb
deputy **ONorw** *FrL* Mhb 60
king's administrator **OSw** *HL* Rb, *YVgL* Urb, Tb
king's local administrator **OSw** *HL* Rb
local administrator **OSw** *UL* Kgb, Mb, Kmb, Blb, Rb, *VmL* Mb, Kmb, Bb, Rb
official **OSw** *HL* Kkb
representative **OSw** *SdmL* Kkb, Jb, Bb, Kmb, Mb, Tjdb, Rb
sheriff **OSw** *HL* Rb   **Phrases**
Expressions:
biskups lænsmaþer, biskups lænsman, biskops lænsman, biskops man (OSw)   ↗
bishop's administrator **OSw** *UL* Kkb, Äb, Mb *VmL* Kkb
bishop's bailiff **OSw** *DL* Kkb, Rb
bishop's official **OSw** *HL* Kkb
konungs lænsmaþer, konungs man, kunungs lænsman (OSw)
king's administrator **OSw** *DL* Tjdb *UL* Kkb, Mb, Rb *VmL* Mb, Rb   **Cross-references**
king's bailiff **OSw** *HL* Md *DL* Mb, Rb   ↙
See also: *ármaðr, gælkare, husabyman, laghmaþer, læn, sysluman, umbuþsman*
Refs: CV s.v. *lén*; F s.v. *lénsmaðr*; KLNM s.v. *embedsindtægter, høvedsmand, lensmann, soknare* ; LexMA s.v. *Lehen*; NGL s.v. *lénsmaðr*; Schlyter s.v. *lænsmaþer*; SNL s.v. *lensmann*   ← **References**

Headword forms

Normalized headword forms have been adopted from the most comprehensive dictionaries currently available to enable consultation of earlier and ongoing lexicographic efforts. The forms of the Old Swedish and Old Gutnish headwords have been taken more or less directly from Schlyter's *Ordbok till Samlingen af Sweriges gamla lagar*, and Old Danish headwords follow the online *Gammeldansk Ordbog* wherever possible. Old Icelandic, Old Norwegian and Old Faroese entries are listed under the normalized Old Norse (ON) given in the *Dictionary of Old Norse Prose*. Some negative adjective forms are given their own headword (e.g. *ogipter, ólýstr*), and certain participial verbal forms are here treated as adjectives. Some headwords with multiple common forms are listed as alternatives to facilitate easier seaching. Alternative forms were selected by editorial discretion and are not intended to be comprehensive.

Grammar

Grammatical analysis has been limited to part of speech for Nordic headwords. No grammatical information for terms is presented in the English>Nordic section except to distinguish homonyms.

Explanatory articles

Approximately one quarter of the headwords have also been furnished with explanatory articles. They are intended to provide concise supplementary information about the legal concept the term represents, and readers are encouraged to consult the bibliographic references for more detailed analysis. Articles were composed by the LMNL editors with assistance and commentary of external experts. Article content varies in scope depending on the amount of identified scholarship on the term. Certain articles offer brief explanations of the contexts in which a term is found (e.g. ON *halsbók*), while others (e.g. OSw *sökia*) give a preliminary semantic analysis. Still others (e.g. OSw *laghmaþer*) provide historical or comparative background relating to the term as it is used across regions and time periods.

English equivalents

English equivalents are taken more or less directly from published or draft translations without exclusion. In some cases English synonyms have been employed by individual translators to render the same medieval word or phrase, and the parts of speech of the English will not always correspond to those of the Nordic originals. Likewise an English equivalent may be applied to multiple Nordic terms. The editors have elected to leave the majority of these as an accumulation of equivalents in alphabetical order to illustrate the (at times extensive) semantic range of the legal terms (cf. OSw *fæ* and OSw *sak*), and therefore the editors have made minimal attempts to evaluate the choices of the translators. In a few rare cases (e.g. OSw *agnabaker*) the draft translations currently have no English equivalent, and the medieval term is here given within {}.

Phrases/expressions/combinations

Phrases throughout the LMNL have been excerpted at the discretion of the editors with no bound set of criteria beyond legal relevance. Most phrases presented here are set phrases with a technical legal definition or idioms with a meaning specific to legal contexts. Phrases are not a primary focus of LMNL, and those given represent only a selection of possible legal expressions present in the medieval laws. English equivalents and textual references for phrases are presented in the same manner as for individual headwords.

Textual references

Textual references are given for each English equivalent, most of which have been taken verbatim from published or draft translations. Textual references listed beside the equivalents for each headword are intended to be illustrative rather than comprehensive. These textual references have been divided by language grouping; OSw for laws written in Old Swedish, ODan for Old Danish, OFar for Old Faroese, OGu for Old Gutnish, OIce for Old Icelandic and ONorw for Old Norwegian. These are further divided by text and section or chapter number (see abbreviations below). Terms which appear frequently within one or more laws and have a common English equivalent (e.g. OSw *bonde* 'householder') often give only the abbreviation for the work in which the term appears.

See also

In many entries cross-references are given to assist readers in locating synonyms or related terms.

References

A list of references to published works discussing the headword. In most cases author or editor name and year are given and are keyed to the bibliography.

English›Nordic section

The English>Nordic section of the LMNL is a mirror of the Nordic>English section. It is intended as a limited index to give users an overview of the range of medieval terms covered by an individual English equivalent. For instance, the English equivalent 'fine' could represent ON *áfang*, OGu *alagh* and OSw *bot* as well as several similar terms.

Appendices and bibliography

Six appendices have been supplied by the editors to provide information about groups of terms clustering around general medieval Nordic legal concepts. They are intended to give a more meaningful description of the terms together than would be allowed by articles distributed throughout the lexicon. These appendices cover:

    Appendix A: Administrative and judicial divisions
    Appendix B: Agriculture and forestry
    Appendix C: Borders, boundaries and boundary markers
    Appendix D: Currency and weights & measures
    Appendix E: Kinship
    Appendix F: Calendar of Church Feast and Fast Days

A bibliography has also been appended. It is intended to serve as a selective list of primary and secondary works treating the legal texts covered by the LMNL. An emphasis has been placed on recent titles to demonstrate how research has progressed since the publication of the *Kulturhistorisk leksikon*. Many of the works cited are those which informed the explanatory articles throughout the LMNL.

Abbreviations

Many abbreviations for individual sections or books in the laws, particularly Swedish laws, refer to accepted modern titles rather than to the medieval ones, which were often lacking. For example, the abbreviation Rb stands for Sw *Rättegångsbalken*, rather than OSw *þingmalabalker* ('The Legal Procedure Section' in English).

Cited sources

BorgL		The Borgarting Law (Norw *Borgartingsloven*)
DL		The Dala Law (Sw *Dalalagen*, often called *Äldre Västmannalagen* (ÄVmL) 'The Older Västmanna Law')
	Bb	The book concerning building and community (Sw *Byggningabalken*, OSw *bygningabalker*)
	Eb	The book concerning the King's oath (Sw *Edsöresbalken*, OSw *kunungs epsöre*)
	Gb	The book concerning matrimony (Sw *Giftermålsbalken*, OSw *giptninga balker*)
	Kkb	The book concerning Christian law (Sw *Kyrkobalken*, OSw *kristnubalker*)
	Mb	The book concerning personal and property rights (Sw *Manhelgdsbalken*, OSw *manhælghisbalker*)
	Rb	The book concerning the legal process (Sw *Rättegångsbalken*, OSw *þingbalker*)
	Tjdb	The book concerning theft (Sw *Tjuvnadsbalken*, OSw *um þiufnaþ*)
EidsL		The Eidsivathing Law (Norw *Eidsivatingsloven*)
ESjL		Erik's Law of Zealand (Dan *Eriks sjællandske lov*)
FrL		The Frostathing Law (Norw *Frostatingsloven*)
	ArbA	The first book concerning inheritance (Norw *Den fyrste arvebolken*)
	ArbB	The second book concerning inheritance (Norw *Den andre arvebolken*)

	Bvb	The book concerning offences and oaths (Norw *Brotsverksbolken*)
	Intr	Introduction (Norw *Innleiing*)
	Jkb	The book concerning land purchase (Norw *Jordkaupebolken*)
	KrbA	The first book concerning Church Law (Norw *Den fyrste kristendomsbolken*)
	KrbB	The second book concerning Church Law (Norw *Den andre kristendomsbolken*)
	Kvb	The book concerning women (Norw *Kvinnebolken*)
	Leb	The book concerning the naval levy (Norw *Leidangsbolken*)
	LlbA	The first book concerning tenancy (Norw *Den fyrste landsleigebolken*)
	LlbB	The second book concerning tenancy (Norw *Den andre landsleigebolken*)
	Mhb	On inviolability of the person (Norw *Mannhelgebolken*)
	R	Amendments (Norw *Rettarbøter*)
	Rgb	The book concerning the legal process (Norw *Rettargangsbolken*)
	Sab	The book concerning wergild (Norw *Sakøyrebolken*)
	Tfb	The book concerning summons to a thing assembly (Norw *Tingfarebolken*)
	Var	A book on various topics/miscellaneous matters (Norw *Bolk om ymse emne*)
GL		The Law of the Gotlanders (Sw *Gutalagen*)
Grg		'The Grey Goose' Laws of the Icelandic Commonwealth (ON *Grágás*)
	Arþ	Inheritance section (ON *Arfa þáttr*)
	Bat	The wergild ring list (ON *Baugatal*)
	Feþ	Betrothals section (ON *Festa þáttr*)
	Fjl	On hire of property (ON *Um fjárleigur*)
	Hrs	On commune obligations (ON *Um hreppaskil*)
	Klb	Christian Laws section (ON *Kristinna laga þáttr*)
	Lbþ	Land claims section (ON *Landbrigða þáttr*)
	Lrþ	The Law Council section (ON *Lögréttu þáttr*)
	Lsþ	The Lawspeaker's section (ON *Lögsögumanns þáttr*)
	Misc	'Miscellaneous articles'
	Ómb	Dependents section (ON *Ómaga bálkr*)
	Rsþ	Searches section (ON *Rannsókna þáttr*)
	Tíg	On tithe payment (ON *Um tíundargjald*)
	Vís	Treatment of homicide (ON *Vígslóði*)
	Þsþ	Assembly procedures section (ON *Þingskapa þáttr*)
GS		The Saga of the Gotlanders (Sw *Gutasagan*)
GuL		The Gulathing Law (Norw *Gulatingsloven*)
	Arb	The book concerning inheritance (Norw *Arvebolken*)
	Kpb	The book concerning trade (Norw *Kjøpebolken*)

Krb	The Church Law (Norw *Kristendomsbolken*, *Kristenretten*)	
Kvb	The book concerning matrimony (Norw *Kvinnebortgiftingsbolken*)	
Kvr	The rules about whaling (Norw *Kvalretten*)	
Leb	The book concerning the naval levy (Norw *Leidangsbolken*)	
Llb	The book concerning tenancy (Norw *Landsleigebolken*)	
Løb	The book concerning freedmen (Norw *Løysingsbolken*)	
Mhb	On inviolability of the person (Norw *Mannhelgebolken*)	
Reb	Amendments (Norw *Rettarbøter*)	
Sab	The book concerning wergild (Norw *Bjarne Mårssons saktal*)	
Tfb	The book concerning summons to a thing assembly (Norw *Tingfarebolken*)	
Tjb	The book concerning theft (Norw *Tjuvebolken*)	
Trm	The Peace Pledge (Norw *Trygdemålet*)	
Olb	The book concerning redemption of odal land (Norw *Odelsløysingsbolken*)	
HL	The Law of the Hälsingar (Sw *Hälsingelagen*)	
Blb	The book concerning building and community (Sw Byalagsbalken, OSw *viþerbobalker*)	
För	*Praefatio* (Sw *Förord*, OSw 'Praefatio')	
Jb	The book concerning land (Sw *Jordabalken*, OSw *jorþarbalker*)	
Kgb	The King's book (Sw *Konungabalken*, OSw *kunungsbalker*)	
Kkb	The book concerning Church and Christian Law (Sw *Kyrkobalken*, OSw *kirkiubalker*)	
Kmb	The book concerning trade (Sw *Köpmålabalken*, OSw *köpmalabalker*)	
Mb	The book concerning personal and property rights (Sw *Manhelgdsbalken*, OSw *manhælghisbalker*)	
Rb	The book concerning legal process (Sw *Rättegångsbalken*, OSw *þingmalabalker*)	
Äb	The book concerning inheritance (Sw *Ärvdabalken*, OSw *ærfþarbalker*)	
Jó	'Jón's Book' The Laws of Later Iceland (1280) (ON *Jónsbók*)	
Fml	Maritime law (ON *Farmannalög*)	
HT	Of the Holy Faith (ON *Um helga trú*)	
Kab	Trade (ON *Kaupabálkr*)	
Kge	Marriage and inheritance (ON *Kvenna giptingar með erfðum* (includes *Framfærslubálkr* (Maintenance of dependents))	
Lbb	Land claims (ON *Landsbrigðabálkr*)	
Llb	Tenancy (ON *Landsleigubálkr* (includes *Rekabálkr* (Drift rights))	
MagBref	Letter of King Magnús (ON *bréf Magnúss konungs*)	
Mah	Personal rights (ON *Mannhelgi*)	
Sg	Payment of tax (ON *Um skatt greizlu*)	
Þfb	Assembly attendance (ON *Þingfararbálkr*)	
Þjb	Theft (ON *Þjófabálkr*)	

Js			'Ironside' The National Law of Iceland issued in 1271 by King Magnús Lagabætir of Norway (ON *Járnsíða*)
	Ert		The inheritance list (ON *Erfðatal*)
	Kab		Trade section (ON *Kaupabálkr*)
	Kdb		Christianity section (ON *Kristindómsbálkr*)
	Kvg		Marriages (ON *Kvennagiftingar*)
	Lbb		Land-claims section (ON *Landabrigðabálkur*)
	Mah		Personal rights (ON *Mannhelgi*)
	Rkb		Drift rights section (ON *Rekabálkur*)
	Þfb		Assembly procedures section (ON *Þingfararbálkur*)
	Þjb		Theft section (ON *Þjófabálkur*)
JyL			The Law of Jutland (Dan *Jyske lov*)
KRA			The Church Law of Árni Þorláksson (1275) (ON *Kristinréttr Árna Þorlákssonar Skálholtsbiskups*)
SdmL			The Laws of the *Supermæn* (Sw *Södermannalagen*)
	Bb		The village community section (Sw *Byggningabalken*, OSw *bygningabalker*)
	Conf		*Confirmatio* (Sw *Konung Magnus Erikssons stadfästelse*, OSw 'Confirmatio Regis Magni')
	För		*Prologus* (Sw *Förord*, OSw 'Prologus')
	Gb		The marriage section (Sw *Giftermålsbalken*, OSw *giptninga balker*)
	Jb		The land section (Sw *Jordabalken*, OSw *jorþarbalker*)
	Kgb		The King's section (Sw *Konungabalken*, OSw *kunungsbalker*)
	Kkb		The Church section (Sw *Kyrkobalken*, OSw *kirkiubalker*)
	Kmb		The trade section (Sw *Köpmålabalken*, OSw *köpmalabalker*)
	Mb		The personal security section (Sw *Manhelgdsbalken*, OSw *manhælghisbalker*)
	Rb		The assembly procedure section (Sw *Rättegångsbalken*, OSw *þingmalabalker*)
	Till		*Additamenta* (Sw *Tillägg*, OSw 'Additamenta')
	Tjdb		The theft section (Sw *Tjuvnadsbalken*, OSw *þiufnaþabalker*)
	Äb		The Inheritance section (Sw *Ärvdabalken*, OSw *ærfþarbalker*)
Seyð			The Sheep Letter (1298) (OFar *Seyðabrævið*)
SkKL			The Church Law of Scania (Dan *Skånske kirkelov*, Sw *Skånska kyrkrätten*)
SkL			The Law of Scania (Dan *Skånske lov*, Sw *Skånelagen*)
SmL			The Småland Law (Sw *Smålandslagen* or *Tiohärads lag*)
UL			The Law of Uppland (Sw *Upplandslagen*)
		Add	Supplements (OSw 'Additamenta')
		Blb	The village community book (Sw *Byalagsbalken*, OSw *Wiþærbo balkær*)
		För	Foreword (Sw *Förord* OSw 'Praefatio')
		Jb	The land book (Sw *Jordabalken*, OSw *Jorþæ balkær*)

	Kgb	The King's book (Sw *Konungabalken*, OSw *Kununx balkær*)
	Kkb	The Christian book (Sw *Kyrkobalken*, OSw *Kirkiu balkær*)
	Kmb	The trading book (Sw *Köpmålabalken*, OSw *Kiöpmalæ balkær*)
	Mb	The personal security book (Sw *Manhelgdsbalken*, OSw *Manhælghis balkær*)
	Rb	The legal process book (Sw *Rättegångsbalken*, OSw *Þingmalæ balkær*)
	StfBM	King Birger Magnusson's Charter of Ratification (Sw *Konung Birger Magnussons stadfästelsebrev*, OSw 'Confirmatio')
	Äb	The inheritance book (Sw *Ärvdabalken* OSw *Ærfþæ balkær*)
VgL		The Laws of the Västgötar (Sw *Västgötalagen*)
VmL		The Law of Västmanland (Sw *Västmannalagen*)
	Bb	The settlement book (OSw *Bygninga balkær*)
	För	Foreword (Sw *Förord*, OSw 'Praefatio')
	Jb	The land book (Sw *Jordabalken*, OSw *Jorþa balkær*)
	Kgb	The King's book (Sw *Konungabalken*, OSw *Konongs balkær*)
	Kkb	The Christian book (Sw *Kyrkobalken*, OSw *Kristno balkær*)
	Kmb	The trading book (Sw *Köpmålabalken*, OSw *Köpmala balkær*)
	Mb	The personal security book (Sw *Manhelgdsbalken*, OSw *Manhælghis balkær*)
	Rb	The legal process book (Sw *Rättegångsbalken*, OSw *Þingmala balkær*)
	Äb	The inheritance book (Sw *Ärvdabalken*, OSw *Ærfda balkær*)
VSjL		Valdemar's Law of Zealand (Dan *Valdemars sjællandske lov*)
YVgL		The Younger Law of the Västgötar (Sw *Yngre Västgötalagen*)
	Add	*Additamenta* (Sw *Tillägg*, OSw 'Additamenta')
	Drb	The book concerning manslaughter (Sw *Dråparebalken*, OSw *draparibalker*)
	Frb	The book concerning peace (Sw *Fredsbalken*, OSw *friþbalker*)
	Föb	The book concerning illegal appropriation (Sw *Förnämesbalken*, OSw *fornæmisbalker*)
	Gb	The book concerning matrimony (Sw *Giftermålsbalken*, OSw *giptarbalker*)
	Jb	The book concerning land (Sw *Jordabalken*, OSw *jorþarbalker*)
	Kkb	The book concerning the Church (Sw *Kyrkobalken*, OSw *kirkiubalker*)
	Kvab	The book concerning mills (Sw: *Kvarnbalken*, OSw *mylnobolker*)
	Rlb	The book concerning lawlessness (Sw *Rättlösabalken*, OSw *rætlosubolker*)
	Tb	The book concerning theft (Sw *Tjuvabalken*, OSw *þiuvabalker*)
	Urb	Outlaw cases (Sw *Urbotamål*, OSw *urbotamal*)
	Utgb	The book concerning fences (Sw *Utgärdabalken*, OSw *utgærþabolker*)
	Vs	The book concerning accidental wounds (Sw *Balken om vådasår*, OSw *af vaþasarum bolker*)
	Äb	The book concerning inheritance (Sw *Ärvdabalken*, OSw *arvabolker*)

ÄVgL		The Older Law of the Västgötar (Sw *Äldre Västgötalagen*)
	Föb	The book concerning illegal appropriation (Sw *Förnämesbalken*, OSw *fornæmisbalker*)
	Fös	Cases concerning illegal appropriation (Sw *Förnämessaker*, OSw *fornæmissakir*)
	Gb	The book concerning matrimony (Sw *Giftermålsbalken*, OSw *giptarbalker*)
	Jb	The book concerning land (Sw *Jordabalken*, OSw *jorþarbalker*)
	Kkb	The book concerning the Church (Sw *Kyrkobalken*, OSw *kirkiubalker*)
	Kva	How a mill is built (Sw *Huru kvarn skall byggas*, OSw *huru mylnu skal göra*)
	Lek	About a player's rights (Sw *Lekarerätten*, OSw *lekararætter*)
	Md	About manslaughter (Sw *Om mandråp*, OSw *af mandrapi*)
	Rlb	The book concerning lawlessness (Sw *Rättlösabalken*, OSw *rætlosubolker*)
	Slb	The book concerning fighting (Sw *Slagsmålsbalken*, OSw *bardagha*)
	Smb	The book concerning wounds (Sw *Balken om såramål*, OSw *af saramalum bolker*)
	Tb	The book concerning theft (Sw *Tjuvabalken*, OSw *þiuvabalker*)
	Urb	Outlaw cases (Sw *Urbotamål*, OSw *urbotamal*)
	Vs	About wounds by accident (Sw O*m vådasår*, OSw *af vaþasarum*)
	Äb	The book concerning inheritance (Sw *Ärvdabalken*, OSw *ærfþarbalker*)
ÖgL		The Law of the Östgötar (Sw *Östgötalagen*)
	Db	The book of killings (Sw *Dråpsbalken*, OSw *drapabalker*)
	Eb	The king's sworn peace (Sw *Edsöresbalken*, OSw *kunungs eþsöre*)
	Kkb	The church book (Sw *Kyrkobalken*, OSw *kristnubalker*)
	Vm	Cases of accidents and cases of wounds, adultery, rapine and theft (Sw *Vådamålsbalken*, OSw *vaþamal ok saramal, hor, ran ok styld*)

Other Abbreviations

ASun	Liber legis Scaniae Dan: *Anders Sunesens parafrase af Skånske Lov*
Bj	The law for trading places and towns ON: *Bjarkeyjarréttr*
BjR	The law for trading places and towns Sw: *Bjärköarätten*
Dan	Danish
KrL	King Kristoffer's Law of the Realm Sw: *Kristoffers landslag*
MEL	King Magnus Eriksson's Law of the Realm Sw: *Magnus Erikssons landslag*
MESt	King Magnus Eriksson's Town Law Sw: *Magnus Erikssons stadslag*

MLL	King Magnus the Law-Mender's Law of the Realm Norw: *Magnus Håkonsson Lagabøters landslov* ONorw: *Magnus lagabætrs landslög*
Norw	Norwegian
ODan	Old Danish
OFar	Old Faroese
OGu	Old Gutnish
OIce	Old Icelandic
ON	Old Norse
ONorw	Old Norwegian
OSw	Old Swedish
SjKL	The Church Law for Zealand Dan: *Sjællandske kirkelov*
SkSt	The Town Law of Scania Dan: *Skånske stadsret* Sw: *Skånska stadsrätten*
Sw	Swedish
VSjL yr	King Valdemar's Younger Law for Zealand (younger redaction?) Dan: *Valdemars sjællandske lov*
VSjL ær	King Valdemar's Older Law for Zealand (older redaction?) Dan: *Valdemars sjællandske lov*
VSt	The Town Law of Visby Sw: *Visby stadslag*

Further notes

A note on English spelling: All English equivalents of Nordic terms drawn from published and draft translations have been normalized to reflect British spelling conventions, regardless of how they appear in their source. An attempt has been made to standardize language usage and style throughout this work, but various portions have been compiled by multiple authors and reflect their individual preferences.

Medieval Swedish law codes are often referred to by the accepted groupings of Göta laws (*Äldre Västgötalagen, Yngre Västgötalagen, Östgötalagen, Smålandslagen*) and Svea laws (*Dalalagen, Hälsingelagen, Södermannalagen, Upplandslagen, Västmannalagen*).

Alphabetical order of the headwords generally follows the principles of the Dictionary of Old Norse Prose:
a, á, b, c, d, ð, e, é, f, g, h, i, í, j, k, l, m, n, o, ó, p, q, r, s, t, u, ú, v, x, y, ý, z, þ, æ, ö, ø, ǿ

Research group

Principal investigators

Inger Larsson, professor em., Swedish language, Department of Swedish Language and Multilingualism, Stockholm University.

Stefan Brink, Sixth Century Professor of and Chair in Scandinavian Studies at University of Aberdeen,

Editors

Ulrika Djärv, PhD in Scandinavian Languages, Lexicography, Stockholm University. Postdoctoral position at Department of Scandinavian Languages, Stockholm University.

Jeffrey S. Love, PhD in Anglo-Saxon, Norse and Celtic. Corpus Christi College, Cambridge. Postdoctoral position at The Arnamagnæan Institute. Institute for Nordic Research, University of Copenhagen.

Christine Peel, PhD in Scandinavian Studies (Old Gutnish), University College London. LMNL Computer recording system advisor.

Erik Simensen, associate professor (em.), Nordic languages, esp. Norwegian, Department of Linguistics and Scandinavian Studies, University of Oslo. Chief editor of *Norrøn ordbok* [Dictionary of Old Norse], latest edition published in 2008.

Historical consultant

Thomas Lindkvist, professor em., medievalist, Department of Historical Studies, University of Gothenburg.

Nordic to English

https://doi.org/10.11647/OBP.0188.02

abbadís (ON) noun

 abbess **OIce** *Jó* Llb 18, **ONorw** *FrL* LlbA 15

abbet (ODan) **ábóti** (ON) noun

 abbot **ODan** *JyL* 2, **OIce** *Jó* Llb 18,
 Js Kdb 4, **ONorw** *FrL* LlbA 15

abeþas (OSw) **beþas** (OSw) verb

 make demands **OSw** *UL* Jb

aboi (OSw) noun

 Synonymous with *landboe*.

 tenant **OSw** *VmL* Jb

aboliiorþ (OSw) noun

 land of the farm **OSw** *YVgL* Äb

abyrghia (OSw) **ábyrgja** (ON) verb

 leave in custody **OSw** *YVgL* Gb, Tb

 be responsible **OIce** *Grg* Þsþ 54 Ómb 143 Feþ 164
 Lbþ 214, 218, *Jó* Mah 13 Kge 17, 25 Lbb 2 Llb 2, 9
 Þjb 2 Fml 3, *Js* Mah 31 Lbb 1, 3 Kab 11, 17 Þjb 2,
 KRA 26, **ONorw** *FrL* KrbA 2, 12 KrbB 10 Mhb 36

 take care of **ONorw** *EidsL* 35.1

 be valid **ONorw** *FrL* KrbB 22

 See also: *valda*

abyrþ (OSw) **abyr** (OSw) noun

 hidden goods **OSw** *YVgL* Tb

 removal of found corpse **OSw** *YVgL* Add

 secret hiding of a corpse **OSw**
 YVgL Drb, *ÄVgL* Md, Tb

 smuggled stolen goods **OSw** *UL* Mb

 something brought in secret **OSw** *SdmL* Tjdb

 stolen goods (secretly carried into
 someone's house) **OSw** *HL* Mb

advent (OSw) **advent** (ODan) noun

 Advent **ODan** *JyL* 2, **OSw** *YVgL* Kkb

aðalból (ON) noun

A main or primary estate as distinguished from
outlying farms (ON *útjarðir*) (see *utjorth*) or tenant
farms (ON *leiguból*) (q.v.). It was probably connected
to a family, and some have suggested that an *aðalból*
signifies the residence of a landowner. Some degree
of legal protection was afforded to an *aðalból*, as in
Grg Lbþ 172, which states that debt claims must be
paid from other sources before selling the *aðalból*.
Some have argued that the concept dates back to the
settlement period in Iceland, but the earliest known
written evidence for the *aðalból* comes in church
registers dating to the twelfth and thirteenth centuries.
Often thought to be the precursor of the manor house
(ON *höfuðból*) (q.v.) in Iceland mentioned in Jó.

 main estate **OIce** *Grg* Lbþ 172 Fjl 223

 See also: *höfuðból, landboe, leiguból, æt*

Refs: Agnes Arnórsdóttir 2010, 418; Árni Júlíusson
2010; Beck 2011, 217–19; CV s.v. *aðalból*;
GAO s.v. *Odal*; Hastrup 1985, 190–92; KLNM
s.v.v. *jordejendom, odelsrett*; LexMA s.v. *Odal*;
ONP s.v. *aðalból*; Sverrir Jakobsson 2013

aðaltóft (ON) noun

 odal plot **ONorw** *EidsL* 11.4, 11.5

aðilð (ON) noun

The right of being a principal (prosecutor or defendant)
in a case. See *aðili*.

 right of being principal **OIce** *Grg* Vís 94

aðili (ON) noun

The principal plaintiff or defender in a legal case. A
principal had the right (and obligation) to prepare and
present a case or else transfer those responsibilities
to someone else. In most cases it was understood
that the offended party and the one accused of the
offence were to be principals, and Grg Vís 94 provides
guidelines for determining who was principal in cases
where one of these is lacking or incapable. In killing
cases, a freeborn son of legal age (over sixteen) could
be principal. Unmarried women and widows could
also be principals for certain types of cases.

 principal **OIce** *Grg* Klþ 5 Vís 87
 Bat 113 Hrs 234 Tíg 256

 See also: *soknari, væriandi*

Refs: CV; Fritzner; GrgTr I:255; KLNM
s.v. *rettergang*; Miller 1984; ONP

afald (OSw) noun

 killing caused by something falling
 down **OSw** *DL* Mb, *SdmL* Mb

afallsdrap (OSw) noun

 death by accident **OSw** *HL* Mb

 See also: *drap*

afarkostalauss (ON) adj.

 on fair terms **OIce** *Jó* Kab 15

afarkostr (ON) noun

 harsh terms **OIce** *Js* Mah 34

afastr (OGu) adj.

 neighbouring **OGu** *GL* A 25

afbrigð (ON) noun

 deviation **OIce** *Grg* Hrs 235

 transgression **OIce** *KRA* 18

afbrot (ON) noun

 offence **OIce** *KRA* 6, 11

affarefæ (ODan) noun

 lost property **ODan** *ESjL* 3

 See also: *fynd*

afgildi (OSw) noun

   rent **OSw** *SdmL* Jb

   See also: *gildi*, *gælda (1)*

afgipt (OSw) noun

   tenancy payment **OSw** *SdmL* Jb

   See also: *gift*

afgiva (OSw) **afgæva** (OSw) verb

   write off **OSw** *VmL* Rb

afglapa (ON) verb

   balk **OIce** *Grg* Þsþ 58 Vís 94 Lrþ 117 Misc 244

afguþ (OSw) noun

   pagan god **OSw** *HL* Kkb

   See also: *guþ*

afgærþ (OSw) noun

   crime **OSw** *YVgL* Rlb, *ÄVgL* Rlb

afhug (OSw) **afhog** (ODan) **af hagg** (OGu) **afhögg** (ON) **afhogg** (OSw) noun

Many laws regulate the penalty for cutting off, gouging and striking out various body parts such as hands and feet, digits, ears, eyes, nose, teeth and male genitals. ODan laws in particular give detailed lists, but reveal less about the circumstances, whereas OSw laws sometimes state that the victim is lead to a chopping-block, clearly indicating premeditation and rendering it *eþsöre* (q.v.). In OGu GL it appears in connection with *þingfriþr* (see *þingsfriþer*) and *haim friþr* (see *hemfriþer*). In ONorw, it can lead to outlawry (FrL Mhb). The penalty, which could depend on the visibility or permanence of the wound, was based on *manbot* (q.v.), *sarbot* (see *sarabot*) and *lytesbot* (see *lytisbot*) in ODan laws, on *sarabot* (q.v.) and *lytisbot* (q.v.) in OSw laws, and on *mannsgjöld* (see *mangæld*) and *sárbótr* (see *sarabot*) in ONorw laws. Loss of body parts was also used as a punishment, albeit not called *afhug*, most commonly in OSw laws and mainly for theft and adultery, but in ONorw laws only for unfree or freed women stealing and for men committing bestiality, and in ODan JyL for counterfeit. The concept, but not the term, also appears in OIce Grg concerning a slave killing his master. It seems generally assumed that corporal punishments were carried out by the victims, plaintiffs or their relatives.

   chopping off **ODan** *ESjL* 2

   chopping off hand or foot **OSw** *HL* Mb

   cut **OSw** *HL* Kgb, *ÖgL* Vm

   cutting off limbs **ODan** *SkL* 111

   dismemberment **ODan** *ESjL* 3, *JyL* 2, 3, *VSjL* 34, 35, 37, 38, 86, **OSw** *SdmL* Mb

   maiming **OGu** *GL* A 11, 12, **OSw** *UL* Mb, Add. 9, *VmL* Mb, *ÖgL* Db

   mutilation **ODan** *ESjL* 1, **ONorw** *FrL* Mhb 42, *GuL* Mhb, **OSw** *DL* Mb

   See also: *hugga*

   Refs: KLNM s.v.v. *kroppsstraff*, *legemskrænkelse*

afhænda (OSw) **afhænde** (ODan) **afhenda** (ON) verb

   alienate **ODan** *ESjL* 3, *JyL* 1, *SkL* 45, 46, 50, **OSw** *ÄVgL* Jb

   dispense with **ODan** *VSjL* 80

   dispose away **ODan** *VSjL* 5

   dispose of **ODan** *ESjL* 1–3, *JyL* 1–3, *VSjL* 13, 17, **ONorw** *GuL* Mhb

   go from someone's hand **ODan** *ESjL* 3

   hand off **ODan** *ESjL* 3

   part with **OSw** *VmL* Äb

   sell **ODan** *JyL* 1, *SkL* 76

   take away **ODan** *VSjL* 4

   See also: *firihægþa*, *hand*

afi (ON) noun

   man preceding or following across generations **ONorw** *GuL* Olb

afkome (ODan) **afkomende** (ODan) noun

   offspring **ODan** *ESjL* 1, *JyL* 1, *VSjL* 1, 20

afkænnuþing (OSw) **affkiænnoþing** (OSw) noun

A *þing* 'assembly' held at the home of one who refused to appear at the regular *þing*, or one from whom due fines, etc., were to be exacted.

   extraordinary thing assembly **OSw** *UL* Jb, Rb, *VmL* Rb

   See also: *laghþing*, *urþinga*, *þing*, *þingariþ*, *þingfastar (pl.)*, *þinglami*

   Refs: Schlyter s.v. *afkænnu þing*

afl (ON) noun

   majority **OIce** *Grg* Lrþ 117 Misc 244

   strength of numbers **OIce** *Grg* Þsþ 35

aflag (ON) noun

   unlawfully **OIce** *Jó* Þfb 6 Kge 26, *Js* Þfb 5, **ONorw** *FrL* Intr 14

aflagha (OSw) adj.

Appears in the phrase *aflagha eþer*, an oath given on a day when swearing was not allowed, or given by a thrall, minor or outlaw.

   illegal **OSw** *YVgL* Kkb, Add

   See also: *lagha*

   Refs: Schlyter s.v. *aflagha*

afli (ON) noun

   income **ONorw** *FrL* Intr 12

   interest **OIce** *Jó* Kge 18

   provision **OIce** *KRA* 10

aflima (ON) verb

    dismember **OIce** *Js* Mah 18

afling (OSw) aflung (OSw) noun

    Property, particularly land, acquired in other ways than inheritance, such as purchase, gift or clearing, and which could be sold without restrictions in contrast to heritable lands labelled *ærfþaiorþ* (OSw) or *oþal* (OSw).

    acquired property **OSw** *HL* Kkb

    foetus **OSw** *HL* Äb

    Refs: Brink forthcoming; Schlyter s.v.v. *afling, aflinga iorþ*

aflingaiorþ (OSw) æflingaiorþ (OSw) noun

    acquired land **OSw** *SdmL* Kkb, Jb, *UL* Kkb, Jb, Add. 1, *VmL* Kkb, Jb

    See also: *afling, aldaoþal, jorþ, ærfþaiorþ*

aflæggia (OSw) verb

    abandon **OSw** *UL* StfBM

    make amends **OSw** *VmL* Mb

    settle **OSw** *UL* StfBM

afneyzla (ON) noun

    expense **OIce** *Jó* Fml 22

afnæma (OSw) verb

    exclude **OSw** *DL* Bb

    See also: *afnæmning*

afnæmning (OSw) af næfning (OSw) affnæmpning (OSw) noun

    exception **OSw** *SdmL* Jb

    exception to a purchase **OSw** *DL* Bb

    exclusion **OSw** *UL* Jb, *VmL* Jb

afradskarl (OSw) noun

    tenant **OSw** *DL* Bb

    See also: *afraþ, landboe*

afrapalas (OSw) noun

    Obligatory transportation of paupers between householders for support.

    pauper-burden **OSw** *HL* Kmb

    See also: *almosa*

    Refs: Brink forthcoming; KLNM s.v. *fattigvård*; Schlyter s.v. *afrapa las*

afraþ (OSw) afráð (ON) affræþ (OSw) avræþ (OSw) noun

    In ON, dues paid in kind. In OSw, annual rent, paid in coin or in kind, for tenanted land.

    annual rent **OSw** *DL* Bb, Rb, *HL* Jb, *UL* Kkb, Jb, Rb, *VmL* Kkb, Äb, Jb, Rb

    dues **ONorw** *FrL* Reb 1

    rent **OSw** *HL* Jb, *SdmL* Jb

    See also: *landskyld*

    Refs: ONP s.v. *afráð*; Schlyter s.v. *afraþ*

afraþalaus (OGu) adj.

    saleable without being subject to a kinsman's portion **OGu** *GL* A 28

    See also: *byrþ*

afraþr (OGu) noun

    kinsman's portion **OGu** *GL* A 28

afraþsdagher (OSw) noun

    day for the annual rent to be paid **OSw** *HL* Jb

    See also: *afraþ*

afreþa (OSw) verb

    free **OSw** *DL* Rb

    See also: *friþer*

afréttardómr (ON) noun

    A court held to settle disputes concerning communal pastures; similar to an *engidómr* (q.v.). These courts were held at the location under contest. It is supposed that matters unresolved at an *afréttardómr* could be taken up at the relevant quarter court (ON *fjórðungsdómr*) at the General Assembly.

    communal pasture court **OIce** *Grg* Lbþ 202

    See also: *domber, engidómr*

    Refs: CV; Finsen III:607; Fritzner; KLNM s.v. *dómr*; ONP; Strauch 2011, 231

afréttarfé (ON) noun

    animals in communal pasture **OIce** *Jó* Llb 53

afréttarmaðr (ON) noun

    communal pasture owner **OIce** *Grg* Lbþ 206

afréttr (ON) afrétt (ON) noun

    Communal pasture owned by two or more men, sometimes by a whole commune.

    communal pasture **OIce** *Grg* Klþ 2, 12 Lbþ 174, 201 Fjl 225, *Jó* Lbb 6 Llb 46, 51, *Js* Lbb 2, 21

    See also: *almænninger, hagamark, haghi, haglendi, mark (3)*

    Refs: Lýður Björnsson 1972–79, I:44–45, CV s.v. *afréttr*

afrækt (OSw) noun

    damage **OSw** *HL* Blb

afrøkja (ON) verb

    neglect **OIce** *Jó* Sg 3, Mah 21, Llb 12, **ONorw** *EidsL* 36.2

afsifja (ON) verb

    To transfer property away from one's family.

    give **OIce** *Jó* Kge 22

    Refs: CV s.v. *afsifja*; Fritzner s.v. *afsifja*; ONP s.v. *afsifja*

afsighia (OSw) **aff sighia** (OSw) **afsæghia** (OSw) verb
  evict **OSw** *UL* Jb
  terminate an agreement **OSw** *UL* Jb
  withdraw **OSw** *UL* Jb, *VmL* Jb

afskyld (OSw) noun
  profit **OSw** *UL* Jb

afsætia (OSw) verb
  set aside **OSw** *UL* Kkb

aftaka (ON) noun
  execution **ONorw** *FrL* Intr 1
  killing **ONorw** *FrL* Intr 8
  slaying **OIce** *Js* Mah 7

aftakin (OGu) adj.
  abolished **OGu** *GL* A 24, 24a, 65
  prohibited **OGu** *GL* A 61

aftersaghn (ODan) noun
  defence **ODan** *ESjL* 3

aftrfǿrsla (ON) noun
  restitution **OIce** *Jó* Llb 15, **ONorw** *FrL* LlbA 17

aftrlausnarjörð (ON) noun
  redemption land **ONorw** *BorgL* 8.12

aftækt (OSw) **afftekte** (OSw) noun
  confiscated item(s) **OSw** *SdmL* Bb, *UL* Blb, *VmL* Bb
  confiscation **OSw** *SdmL* Bb, *UL* Blb, *VmL* Bb
  damage **OSw** *HL* Blb
  See also: *agriper*

aftæktavitne (OSw) noun
  witness concerning confiscated items **OSw** *SdmL* Bb
  See also: *aftækt*, *vitni*

aftökisfæ (OSw) noun
  Possibly an illegal deal over what to exclude when selling or trading something. This exclusion was presumed to remain unclaimed if revealed, and would then pass to the king.
  exclusion **OSw** *SdmL* Bb
  See also: *fæ*
  Refs: Schlyter s.v. *aftökisfæ*

afvita (OSw) **atvita** (OSw) **avita** (OSw) adj.
  defective **OSw** *UL* Mb, *VmL* Mb
  lost one's senses **OSw** *DL* Mb, *SdmL* Mb
  See also: *galin*, *vitvillinger*, *ørr*

afvöxtr (ON) noun
  A decrease in value or loss. The opposite of ON *ávöxtr*.
  loss **ONorw** *FrL* ArbB 22
  See also: *avaxter*
  Refs: ONP

afærþ (OSw) noun
  damage **OSw** *HL* Blb, *SdmL* Bb
  illegal activity **OSw** *UL* Blb
  See also: *aværkan*

aganga (OSw) noun
  dispute **OSw** *HL* Blb
  hostile act **OSw** *ÖgL* Db
  trespass **OSw** *HL* Blb
  See also: *bothegang*, *garthgang*, *hemsokn*, *hærværk*, *landnám*

agnabaker (OSw) **aghnbak** (ODan) noun
  Etymologically disputed, but presumably 'husk back', used as a derogatory term for a grain thief.
  corn theft **OSw** *HL* Mb
  corn thief **OSw** *YVgL* Tb
  grain thief **ODan** *VSjL* 87, **OSw** *SdmL* Mb, *UL* Mb {*agnabaker*} **OSw** *HL* Mb
  Refs: Lund s.v. *agnbak*; Ney 1998, 113; Schlyter s.v. *agnabaker*; Wennström 1936, 37–40

agnesmessa (ON) noun
  St Agnes's Day **OIce** *Grg* Klþ 13

agr (OGu) noun
  fen sedge **OGu** *GL* A 25

agriper (OSw) **agripr** (OGu) **af griper** (OSw) **agreper** (OSw) **agræper** (OSw) noun
  confiscated item(s) **OSw** *DL* Kkb, Bb, Tjdb, *SdmL* Gb, Tjdb, *VmL* Mb
  confiscation **OSw** *VmL* Mb
  stolen goods **OGu** *GL* Add. 8 (B 55)
  stolen property **OSw** *DL* Tjdb
  See also: *þiufnaþer*

agripslaus (OGu) adj.
  in the absence of material evidence **OGu** *GL* Add. 8 (B 55)

agærþ (OSw) noun
  difference **OSw** *YVgL* Jb, *ÄVgL* Jb

ahænda (OSw) verb
  retrieve from **OSw** *UL* Mb

ainloypr (OGu) **einhleypr** (ON) adj.
  single **OIce** *Jó* Kab 9, *Js* Kab 7, **ONorw** *FrL* KrbA 33, *GuL* Kpb
  unmarried **OGu** *GL* A 20a, **OIce** *KRA* 18
  See also: *drengmaðr*

ainsyri (OGu) noun
  self-witness **OGu** *GL* A 19
  See also: *eneþer*

aka (OSw) verb

cart OSw *HL* Kkb, *SdmL* Kkb, Jb

aka (OSw) noun

carting OSw *UL* Kkb, *VmL* Kkb (E: text)

carting-job OSw *HL* Kkb

transport OSw *VmL* Kkb

akallan (OSw) noun

suit OSw *YVgL* Add

aker (OSw) aker (ODan) akr (OGu) akr (ON) akær (OSw) noun

This term refers to cultivated land, as opposed to meadow (OSw *æng*) and wood (OSw *skogher*). In Denmark, *akær* also refers to a strip field, corresponding to OSw *tegher* and ON *teigr*. The distribution of certain types of place names indicates that Denmark had largely been settled by the Viking Age (ca. 800–1050). During this period, settling was extended, partly through extension of earlier settlements (esp. names in *-torp*), partly through clearance of wood by the so-called slash-and-burn method. The gradual extension of arable land is reflected in many place names, e.g. *-ager*, *-bod*, *-rød* and *-torp* (Denmark); *-hult*, *-mala*, *-ryd*, *-säter*, and *-torp* (Sweden); *-brandr*, *-rud*, and *-váll* (Norway). In Denmark and Scania, a major improvement in agriculture was achieved by the introduction (probably in the Viking Age) of the heavy wheeled iron plough, which led to a more intense exploitation of the soil. This new equipment made it possible to plough deeper furrows and turn the sod in long strips. These strips gradually became long, gentle ridges, with channels for drainage of surplus water between them. The land was exploited in a wide variety of patterns of crop rotation also known elsewhere in Europe, but the efficient three-field-system was probably not introduced until about 1300. Crops consisted primarily of rye, with barley (important in beer brewing) and oats ranking second, and wheat very rare. The parcelling out of arable land, buying and selling, and the coordination of work (ploughing, sowing, and reaping) led to regulation, measuring, and the use of boundary marks. Measuring was performed with ropes in Denmark or a *mælistang* 'measuring pole' in SdmL and ÖgL.

arable field OSw *DL* Tjdb, *HL* Blb, *UL* Kkb, Mb, Jb, Blb, *VmL* Kkb, Mb, Jb, Bb

arable land OIce *Grg* Klþ 2 Þsþ 48, 62 Vís 109a (add. 131) Feþ 166 Lbþ 198 Fjl 222 Hrs 234, *Jó* Mah 2 Llb 2, 4 Kab 20 Fml 27, *Js* Mah 11 Lbb 11, *KRA* 11, ONorw *FrL* Leb 26, OSw *HL* Mb, Blb

cornfield ONorw *FrL* LlbA 2 Bvb 5

crop-fields OIce *Grg* Lbþ 180

cropland OIce *Jó* Lbb 3

field ODan *JyL* 3, *SkKL* 3, *SkL* 174, OGu *GL* A 3, 10, 47, ONorw *BorgL* 14.5, *EidsL* 11.5, *GuL* Krb, Llb, Olb, Leb, OSw *DL* Kkb, Bb, Gb, Tjdb, *HL* Mb, Jb, Blb, *SdmL* Kkb, Jb, Bb, *SmL*, *UL* Rb (E-text only), *YVgL* Kkb, Äb, Jb, Kvab, Föb, Utgb, *ÄVgL* Kkb, Äb, Jb, Kva, Fös, Föb, *ÖgL* Kkb, Eb, Vm

land OFar *Seyð* 2

strip ODan *ESjL* 2, *JyL* 3, *SkL* 76, 86, 168, 169, 175, 179, 181, 183, 186, 187, 189, 206, *VSjL* 79, 80

Expressions:

enka aker (OSw)

Land in a village other than the one in which the householder using the land lives.

separate field OSw *YVgL* Kkb, Äb

See also: *akerskifte*, *attunger*, *bol*, *famn*, *fiarþunger*, *hiorþvalder*, *mælistang*, *rep*, *skogher*, *tegher*, *træþi*, *vreter*, *æng*

Refs: DMA s.v. *Denmark, land and people*; Helle 2001, 109–10; KLNM s.v.v. *ager*, *bol*, *bymark*, *fornåkrar*, *græsmarksbrug*, *jordbruk*, *odlingssystem*, *svedjebruk*, *sædeland*, *tovangsbrug*, *trevangsbrug*; LexMA s.v. *Dänemark*. F. Wirtschafts-, Verfassungs- und Sozialgeschichte

akerdeld (OSw) akra deld (OSw) noun

A strip field in a *gærþi* (OSw) (q.v.) or in arable land generally.

field allotment OSw *SdmL* Bb

See also: *aker*, *akrlandadeild*, *deld*, *gærþi*

Refs: Schlyter s.v. *aker deld*

akerfrith (ODan) noun

Protection of growing crops. Any theft, however small, of crops from fields was punished, except when committed by itinerants who were allowed restricted grazing in the fields (JyL).

harvest peace ODan *SkL* 184

peace in the field ODan *JyL* 3

See also: *aker*, *friþer*

akergjald (ODan) noun

payment for damage to a field ODan *SkL* 168

See also: *aker*, *korngjald*

akergærþi (OSw) akergærthe (ODan) akragerði (ON) akrgerði (ON) akra gærþi (OSw) noun

enclosed field ONorw *GuL* Kpb

fence between tofts ODan *SkL* 187

fencing of strips ODan *JyL* 3

field ONorw *FrL* LlbA 20, OSw *YVgL* Jb, *ÄVgL* Jb

See also: *aker*, *gærþi*

akerhirthe (ODan) noun

    shepherd **ODan** *JyL* 3

    See also: *aker*

akerland (ODan) **akrland** (ON) noun

    In Icelandic laws it refers to arable land or cropland in general. In Danish laws to strip fields.

    arable land **OIce** *Grg* Lbþ 197

    cropland **OIce** *Jó* Lbb 4

    field **ODan** *JyL* 1

    strip **ODan** *JyL* 1

    See also: *aker*

    Refs: CV s.v. *akrland*; Hoff 1997, 142–49; ONP s.v. *akrland*

akerlas (OSw) noun

    load from a field **OSw** *YVgL* Kkb

akermal (OSw) noun

    arable field plot **OSw** *UL* Blb

akern (ODan) noun

    acorn **ODan** *SkL* 207

    See also: *aldin, bok (2), ek, gisningaskogher*

akernam (OSw) noun

    cattle taken in custody **OSw** *YVgL* Föb, Add, *ÄVgL* Fös

    taking another man's animals to his field **OSw** *YVgL* Kkb

    See also: *aker, nam*

akerran (ODan) noun

    Secret taking of crops from a field.

    field rapine **ODan** *JyL* 2

    See also: *aker, ran*

akerskifte (ODan) noun

    Common strip field.

    common strip **ODan** *JyL* 1

    See also: *aker, skipti, vang*

    Refs: Hoff 1997, 142–149

akerspjal (ODan) noun

    damage to a field **ODan** *SkL* 168, 169

    See also: *aker*

akkeri (ON) noun

    anchor **ONorw** *GuL* Leb

akkerissát (ON) **akkerissæti** (ON) noun

    anchorage **OIce** *Grg* Feþ 166 Misc 248, *Jó* Fml 16

aklæþi (OSw) noun

    bedspread **OSw** *UL* Äb, *VmL* Äb

akoma (OSw) **ákoma** (ON) **ákváma** (ON) noun

    bodily injury **OIce** *Js* Mah 34, **OSw** *DL* Mb, *UL* Mb, Rb, *VmL* Mb, Rb, *ÖgL* Vm

    harm **OSw** *DL* Eb, Mb

    injury **OSw** *DL* Mb, *SdmL* Kgb, Gb, Bb, Mb, *YVgL* Add, *ÖgL* Kkb, Eb

    mark **OSw** *YVgL* Rlb

    physical injury **OIce** *Jó* Mah 16

    wound **OSw** *HL* Mb

akralaghi (OSw) noun

    fellow field owners **OSw** *DL* Bb

    See also: *aker*

akrlandadeild (ON) noun

    division of arable land **OIce** *Grg* Lbþ 197

    See also: *akerdeld*

akrlandaskifti (ON) noun

    division of arable land **OIce** *Grg* Lbþ 197

akrtíund (ON) noun

    field-tithe **ONorw** *EidsL* 48.9

akta (ON) verb

    weigh a decision **OIce** *Jó* Kge 29

ala (ON) verb

    give board **OIce** *Grg* Klþ 1, 2 Ómb 129

    house **ONorw** *FrL* Mhb 41

    sustain **ONorw** *FrL* Mhb 41

    See also: *vist*

alaðsfestr (ON) noun

    According to Grg Þsþ 51 a pledge given by someone convicted of lesser outlawry (*fjörbaugsgarðr*) at a confiscation court (*féránsdómr*) to avoid a sentence of full outlawry (*skóggangr*). The pledge was to be one *eyrir* of the 'life ring' (*fjörbaugr*). It has been suggested that the root term comes from an obsolete word *alaðr* meaning 'alimentum', which may be present in a runic inscription on a gold bracteate from Trollhättan (Axboe & Källström 2013, 166), but it has also been thought to be a manuscript variant of the more common *aðal-* ('main').

    sustenance pledge **OIce** *Grg* Þsþ 51, 67

    See also: *féránsdómr, fjörbaugr*

    Refs: Axboe & Källström 2013; CV; Konráð Gíslason 1882; ONP

alagh (OSw) **alag** (OGu) **álag** (ON) **alagha** (OSw) noun

    An additional payment or fine issued as a penalty. Additional fines could be assessed for several reasons, including charging excessive interest (Grg Fjl 221), failure to take charge of a dependent at the appointed time (Grg Ómb 130) or withholding tithes (Grg Tíg 259, KRA 15). There appears to have been some overlap in usage between this term and OSw *alagha* (ON *álaga*).

duty **OSw** *SdmL* Till

fine **OGu** *GL* Add. 8 (B 55)

penalty payment **OIce** *Grg* Ómb 130
Fjl 221, 222 Tíg 259, *KRA* 15

See also: *handsalsslit, harðafang*

Refs: CV s.v. *álag*; Fritzner s.v. *álag*; GrgTr
II:39 n. 72; Hertzberg s.v. *álag, álaga*; ONP
s.v. *álag, álaga*; Schlyter s.v. *alagh, alagha*

alda (OSw) noun

acorn bearer **OSw** *UL* Blb, *VmL* Bb

aldaoþal (OSw) **allda oþal** (OSw) **aldaeðli** (ON) noun

Literally, 'family land from ancient times'. The word
occurs only in UL, DL and VmL referring to land
considered to belong within a family as of right from
time immemorial. Schlyter relates the first element
not to the pronoun *alder*, 'all', but to the noun *ald*,
'age' and the translation in SL UL reflects this. It is
linked there with the expression *fasta fæþerni* and the
two together seem to form a synonymic parallelism,
stressing that newly acquired land is specifically
omitted from the provision. The meaning is the same as
other combinations with *oþal* (q.v.) and the expression
gambli byrþ used elsewhere (e.g. OSw HL). This
latter phrase emphasises the birthright nature of the
land. The sale of such land could only be made under
certain conditions and to certain people. In specified
circumstances, purchased land could be converted
to family land as of right, if it were exchanged for a
parcel of family land of equal value, for example.

ancestral land from time immemorial
OSw *UL* Jb, Blb, *VmL* Bb

Expressions:

at aldaeðli (ON)

permanently **OIce** *Grg* Ómb 133, 134

See also: *arver, byrþ, forn, fæþerni, gamal, oþal*

Refs: KLNM s.v. *odelsrett*; ONP s.v. *aldaeðli*;
Schlyter 1877, s.v. *alda oþal*; SL UL, 178

alder (OSw) noun

Appears in several expressions for age of maturity,
such as *kome til alders* 'come of age' (ODan ESjL 2,
3; JyL 1), *kome til alders oc witz* 'come of age and to
wits' (ODan ESjL 1), *lagha alder* 'legal age' (OSw DL
Tjdb). The expressions for this varied, as did the age.

Expressions:

um aldr ok ævi (ON)

forever and ever **OIce** *Jó* Mah 4

See also: *maghandi*

aldin (OSw) noun

Food for pigs was an important economic resource,
which is reflected in some OSw laws regulating the
pasture in woodland and the felling of trees. *Aldin* may
refer to several species, such as acorns, beechnuts,
hazelnuts and apples.

acorn **OSw** *SdmL* Bb, *UL* Blb, *VmL* Bb, *ÄVgL* Fös

oak wood where pannage is permitted **OSw** *VmL* Bb

tree fruit **OSw** *UL* Mb

See also: *akern, ek, gisningaskogher*

Refs: KLNM s.v. *løvtræer*

aldinbær (OSw) adj.

with acorns **OSw** *YVgL* Utgb, *ÄVgL* Föb

See also: *ek*

aldinkarl (OSw) noun

*owner of the oak wood where pannage
is permitted* **OSw** *UL* Blb, *VmL* Bb

aldinlegha (OSw) noun

acorn lease **OSw** *SdmL* Bb

See also: *gisningaskogher*

aldinviþer (OSw) noun

acorn tree **OSw** *YVgL* Jb

tree with acorn **OSw** *YVgL* Föb, Add, *ÄVgL* Fös

See also: *aldin, ek, undirviþer*

aldra hælghuna dagher (OSw) noun

All Saints' Day **OSw** *VmL* Kkb

See also: *hælghunamæssudagher*

aleiga (ON) noun

everything one owns **OIce** *Jó* Þjb 10

aleigumál (ON) noun

A case involving all property owned by an individual.
Also refers to the goods confiscated in such a case.

case involving all property **ONorw** *FrL* Intr 8

confiscation of all property **OIce** *Jó* Þjb 22

Refs: CV s.v. *aleiga*; ONP

algildi (ON) noun

full compensation **OIce** *Jó* Llb 35, 40

algildisvitni (ON) noun

valid testimony **ONorw** *FrL* ArbB 10

alheilagr (ON) adj.

altogether holy **ONorw** *FrL* KrbA 31

alin (OSw) **alen** (ODan) **elin** (OGu) **eln** (OGu) **alin**
(ON) **öln** (ON) **aln** (OSw) noun

ell **ODan** *JyL* 1, **OFar** *Seyð* 5, **OGu** *GL* A 19, 20,
26, **OIce** *Grg* passim, *Jó* Kab 5, *KRA* 14, 26, **ONorw**
BorgL 12.3, *FrL* KrbA 8 LlbA 21, *GuL* Løb, Kvr,
Mhb, Leb, **OSw** *HL* Kkb, Mb, Blb, Rb, *SdmL* Bb,
UL Blb, *VmL* Bb, *YVgL* Jb, *ÄVgL* Jb, *ÖgL* Db

{*alin*} **OSw** *DL* Kkb, Bb, Rb

allhelagher (OSw) adj.

completely holy **OSw** *YVgL* Add

fully holy **OSw** *YVgL* Add

Refs: Schlyter s.v. *allhelagher*

allherjarlög (pl.) (ON) noun

The laws of the nation. *Allsherjarlög* is a rare term appearing only once in the Icelandic laws (Grg ch. 392 in Staðarhólsbók). Both there and in *Njáls saga* it is employed in the formula *at alþingismáli ok allsherjarlögum* ('in accordance with the formalities laid down by the General Assembly and the laws of the nation').

Refs: CV; GrgTr II:294

allraheilagramessa (ON) noun

All Saints' Day **OIce** *Grg* Klþ 13, **ONorw** *GuL* Krb

See also: *hælghunamæssudagher*

allramannafasta (ON) noun

All Men's Fast **ONorw** *BorgL* 6.2

almannaleþ (OSw) noun

public waterway **OSw** *HL* Mb, Blb, *SdmL* Bb

almenniligr (ON) adj.

common **OIce** *Jó* Kab 6

almenningsfar (ON) noun

public ferry **OIce** *Jó* Llb 45

almenningsgata (ON) noun

common highway **OIce** *Jó* Llb 44

almenningshvalr (ON) noun

whale in waters where common rights exist **OIce** *Jó* Llb 70

almoghe (OSw) **almúgi** (ON) noun

inhabitants **OFar** *Seyð* 0

peasantry **OSw** *HL* För

people **OFar** *Seyð* 0, **OSw** *SdmL* Till

almosa (OSw) **almuse** (ODan) **ölmusa** (ON) noun

In OIce, the size, number and dates of alms were regulated, and mainly consisted of food for the poor. ODan JyL mentions alms for orphans, and OSw YVgL that alms, intended for the poor, must not be taken by the priest.

alms **ODan** *ESjL* 3, **OFar** *Seyð* 3, **OIce** *KRA* 13, 30, **OSw** *YVgL* Kkb

charity **OIce** *Jó* Mah 29, *Js* Mah 27

See also: *afrapalas*

Refs: KLNM s.v.v. *eleemosyne, fattigvård*

almosomaþer (OSw) noun

In OSw YVgL, a poor man entitled to alms was shown lenience if stealing food. Similar provisions, albeit not with this word, exist in OIce (e.g. Js).

man of alms **OSw** *YVgL* Tb

See also: *almosa*

Refs: KLNM s.v. *fattigvård*

almænni (OSw) noun

public **OSw** *SdmL* För, Rb

almænnigsbonde (OSw) noun

common householder **OSw** *YVgL* Föb

See also: *almænninger, bonde*

almænnigslandboe (OSw) noun

tenant farmer *on common land* **OSw** *YVgL* Kkb

almænninger (OSw) **almænning** (ODan) **almenning** (ON) **almenningr** (ON) **almænningia** (OSw) noun

Refers to uncultivated land (wood, heath etc.) open to common use for all men, esp. for grazing cattle during the summer months. As the first element of compounds (*almænnings-*) it indicated that the word referred to facilities (bridges, roads etc.), areas or arrangements open to the general public and economic assets such as grazing, forests and fishing open to landowners of a particular area (i.e. village, district). In a more abstract sense ('common to all men') ON *almenningr* also had the meaning 'mobilization' (for the levy). OSw *almænningsgæld* meant general duty.

area where common rights exist **OIce** *Grg* Misc 239, 240, *Jó* Llb 59, 66

common **ODan** *SkL* 211, **ONorw** *GuL* Tfb, Kvr

common area **OIce** *Jó* Llb 59

common land **ODan** *SkL* 71, **OIce** *Grg* Klþ 2, *Jó* Llb 49, 59 Þjb 14, *Js* Rkb 2, **ONorw** *FrL* LlbA 13 LlbB 7, **OSw** *HL* Mb, Blb, *UL* Mb, Blb, *VmL* Mb, Bb, *YVgL* Jb, Kvab, Föb, Utgb, *ÄVgL* Jb, Kva, Föb

common pasture **ONorw** *FrL* Intr 19

common wood **ODan** *JyL* 1

general levy **OIce** *Grg* Misc 248

mobilization **ONorw** *GuL* Leb

waters where common rights exist **OIce** *Jó* Llb 70

Expressions:

hæræþs almænninger (OSw)

common land of the district **OSw** *YVgL* Föb

lands almænninger (OSw)

common land of the province **OSw** *YVgL* Föb

See also: *hæraþ, mark (3), skogher, svinavalder*

Refs: Helle 2001, 111–14; Hertzberg s.v. *almenningr*; Hoff 1997, 255–62; Holmbäck 1920; KLNM s.v.v. *alminding, beite, bergsregale, envangsbrug, hvalfangst, häradsallmänning, jordejendom, landnám II, regale*; Porsmose 1988, 298–301; Rosén 1949, 36 f.; Schlyter s.v. *almænninger*

almænningsbro (OSw) noun

common bridge **OSw** *YVgL* Föb

See also: *almænninger*

almænningsbrun (ODan) noun

   common well **ODan** *SkL* 100

   See also: *almænninger*

almænningsgæld (OSw) noun

   general duty **OSw** *YVgL* Urb

   See also: *almænninger*

almænningsiorþ (OSw) noun

   common land **OSw** *YVgL* Kkb, Äb, Add

   See also: *almænninger*

almænningsköp (OSw) noun

   general/common purchase **OSw** *YVgL* Add

   See also: *almænninger*

almænningsskogh (ODan) noun

   common wood **ODan** *SkL* 201, 208

   See also: *almænninger*

almænningsthing (ODan) noun

   Appears as a venue for public announcements of land conveyance.

   ordinary assembly **ODan** *ESjL* 2

   See also: *almænninger*, *þing*

   Refs: Tamm and Vogt, eds, 2016, 301

almænningstorgh (OSw) noun

   public square **OSw** *DL* Mb

   See also: *almænninger*

almænningsvatn (OSw) almænningsvatn (ODan) noun

   common water **ODan** *SkL* 211, 213, **OSw** *YVgL* Kvab, *ÄVgL* Kva

   See also: *almænninger*

almænningsvægher (OSw) almanna vægher (OSw) noun

   common road **OSw** *YVgL* Föb

   public road **OSw** *DL* Bb, *HL* Blb, *SdmL* Bb, Kmb

   See also: *almænninger*

almænningsöre (OSw) noun

   A tax of a half or one *öre* paid annually in coin by all men, i.e. all landowning householders.

   {*almænningsöre*} **OSw** *YVgL* Föb

   See also: *almænninger*

   Refs: KLNM s.v. *skatter*; Lindkvist 2011, 270; Schlyter s.v. *almænningsöre*

alnarborð (ON) noun

   plank one ell long **ONorw** *GuL* Leb

alstýfingr (ON) noun

   crop-eared sheep **OIce** *Grg* Fjl 225

alsýkn (ON) adj.

   Completely reprieved; acquitted. Grg Vís 110 stipulates that certain types of outlaw could have his sentence ameliorated by dispatching other outlaws or by having someone do so on his behalf. The outlaw's punishment was reduced for each outlaw killed up to three, at which point he became *alsykn*. A nominal form of the term (ON *alsykna*) appears once in the Staðarhólsbók version of Grg in the section on betrothals (cf. Grg tr. II:282–83). In one later usage from 1466 (DN X nr. 235) *alsykn* is employed as a synonym of ON *sykn* in the sense of 'free, ordinary' as opposed to a holiday.

   completely reprieved **OIce** *Grg* Vís 110

   Refs: CV s.v. *alsýkn*; Fritzner s.v. *alsykn*; Hertzberg s.v. *alsykn*

alsætti (ON) alsætt (ON) noun

   complete satisfaction **ONorw** *FrL* Intr 3

   full agreement **ONorw** *FrL* Var 2–6

   reconciliation **OIce** *Js* Mah 3, 20

altarabyrþ (OSw) noun

   altar gift **OSw** *SdmL* Kkb

   See also: *altaralæghi*, *altaraværning*

altaraklæþi (OSw) noun

   altar cloth **OSw** *UL* Kkb, *VmL* Kkb

altaralæghi (OSw) noun

   altar donations **OSw** *ÖgL* Kkb

   altar gift **OSw** *SmL*

   gift on the altar **OSw** *YVgL* Kkb

   See also: *altarabyrþ*, *altaraværning*

altaraværning (OSw) noun

   altar donations **OSw** *ÖgL* Kkb

   See also: *altarabyrþ*, *altaralæghi*

alyrkr (ON) adj.

   working **ONorw** *FrL* KrbB 19

alþingi (ON) noun

   The Icelandic General Assembly held annually at Þingvellir in the Southwestern part of the island. According to *Íslendingabók* it was instituted by Ulfljótr in 930, taking over the regional assembly at Kjalarnes. Afterwards the courts of the General Assembly, the Quarter Courts (ON *fjórðungsdómar*) and the Fifth Court (ON *fimmtardómr*), functioned as the highest courts in Iceland. All chieftains (ON *goðar*) were required to attend the General Assembly, and each could demand the presence of one ninth of all householders in his assembly group as well. Until 1271 the General Assembly was also the legislative seat of government in the form of the Law Council (ON *lögrétta*). Afterwards the assembly was administered by royal officials. The *alþingi* was abolished in (1798? – LexMA; the nineteenth century? – CV; the first decades of the eighteenth century? – KLNM) but subsequently reformed as the modern Icelandic parliament in Reykjavík. The Faroese General Assembly is also called *alþingi* in Seyð and presumably refers to the precursor to the Faroese *Løgting*.

general assembly **OFar** *Seyð* 1, **OIce** *Grg* Klþ 6, 8 Þsþ 25, *Jó* Þfb 1 Llb 37, *Js* Þfb 1, 2, Lbb 5, Rkb 1

See also: *goði, Lögberg, lögrétta, lögsögumaðr, vapntak, varþing, þing, þingbrekka*

Refs: CV; Fritzner; GAO s.v. *Ding*; KLNM s.v. *alþingi*; LexMA s.v. *Allthing*; MSE s.v. *alþingi*

alþingisdómr (ON) noun

General Assembly court **OIce** *Grg* Þsþ 50, 58

alþingisför (ON) noun

journey to the General Assembly **OIce** *Js* Þfb 4

alþingislof (ON) noun

leave of the General Assembly **OIce** *Grg* Vís 98 Bat 113

alþingismaðr (ON) noun

member of the General Assembly **OIce** *Jó* Þfb 1

alþingismál (ON) noun

formalities of the General Assembly **OIce** *Grg* Þsþ 57

General Assembly regulation **OIce** *Grg* Misc 246

alþingisnefna (ON) noun

nomination at the General Assembly **OIce** *Grg* Lrþ 117

alþingisreið (ON) noun

attendance at the General Assembly **OIce** *Grg* Vís 99

alþingissáttarhald (ON) noun

keeping a General Assembly settlement **OIce** *Grg* Arþ 126

alþýða (ON) noun

common people **OIce** *Js* Kdb 7

general public **OIce** *Grg* Lrþ 117

ambat (OSw) **ambut** (ODan) **ambatn** (OGu) **ambátt** (ON) **ambot** (OSw) **ambut** (OSw) noun

A female slave, a bondwoman, usually serving as a housekeeper or a housemaid. This was the common Nordic word for a female slave, the equivalent of *þræl(l)* for a male slave. There were, however, other words in use, particularly collectively: *hemakona, huskona*. The ON *þý* appears in GL in the words *þybarn, þydotir*, and *þysun* (q.v.) in reference to the children of slave women, usually those fathered by the householder. The *ambat* did the indoor work on a farm and despite their low status they appear to have been given time off after childbirth (ÄVgL Gb 6 §3). In GL (chapter 6) it states that if a slave (male or female) worked on a Holy day, the master of the slave was fined and the slave had their period of slavery extended by three years, which seems excessively harsh. It does indicate, however, that lifetime slavery was disappearing and that slavery was perhaps viewed more as a punishment for crime, a means of supporting oneself by voluntary subjugation, or a way of discharging a debt, rather than a 'state', although domestic slavery does not seem to have disappeared from Sweden until the beginning of the fourteenth century (Karras, 138–40). The *deghia* (q.v.) was the most senior female slave in the household with special duties and rights, the female equivalent of the *bryti* (q.v.).

bondmaid **OIce** *Grg* Rsþ 229

bondwoman **OIce** *Grg* Vís 111, **ONorw** *FrL* Mhb 5 Rgb 47 Kvb 20 Bvb 8, *GuL* Krb, Løb, Mhb, Tjb

female slave **OGu** *GL* A 2, 6, **ONorw** *EidsL* 7, **OSw** *UL* Mb, Kmb, *VmL* Mb

female thrall **OSw** *YVgL* Äb

slave **ONorw** *FrL* KrbA 1

slave-woman **OIce** *Grg* Feþ 144, 156, **ONorw** *EidsL* 50.5, **OSw** *SdmL* Mb, *ÄVgL* Äb

thrall woman **OSw** *YVgL* Gb, Rlb, Tb, Add, *ÄVgL* Gb, Rlb

unfree servant **ODan** *VSjL* 86

{ambat} **OSw** *ÄVgL* Tb

See also: *bryti, deghia, fostra, friþlös, frælsgiva, hemakona, hion, huskona, ofræls, sætesambut, þræl, þybarn*

Refs: Hertzberg, s.v. *ambátt*; Karras 1988; KLNM, s.v.v. *kvinnearbeid, træl*; Nevéus 1974, 26; Peel 2015, 120 note 16/23–26; Schlyter 1877, s.v. *ambat*; SL GL, 260–61 note 11 to chapter 16; SL UL, 125 note 93; SL VmL, 98–99 note 128; Stuard 1995, 4, 15, 16

ambáttarbarn (ON) noun

child of a bondswoman **ONorw** *FrL* KrbA 6

ambrósiusmessa (ON) noun

St Ambrose's Day **OIce** *Grg* Klþ 13

amerki (OGu) noun

over-branding **OGu** *GL* A 46, B 64 (correcting A 46)

See also: *mærki*

amia (OSw) noun

A French loan word used as a milder insult than *skökia* 'whore'.

mistress (2) **OSw** *HL* Mb

See also: *arinelja, frilla, meinkona, sløkefrithe*

Refs: SL HL, 346, note 73

anbol (OGu) noun

building material **OGu** *GL* A 25

andmarki (OSw) **andmarki** (ON) **annmarki** (ON)
anmarki (OSw) noun

damage **OSw** *ÄVgL* Kva

defect **OIce** *Grg* Feþ 144 Fjl 224

andreasmessa (ON) noun

St Andrew's Day **OIce** *Grg* Klþ 13

St Andrew's Mass (30 November) **ONorw** *GuL* Krb

andverþa (OGu) verb

answer for **OGu** *GL* A 26

be answerable for **OGu** *GL* A 26

andvirði (ON) noun

expense **ONorw** *FrL* ArbB 23

money **OIce** *Jó* Kab 11

payment **OIce** *Js* Kab 9

andvirki (ON) noun

crops **ONorw** *FrL* LlbA 13, *GuL* Llb

hay **OIce** *Jó* Llb 34

haystores **OIce** *Grg* Lbþ 200

stores **OIce** *Grg* Klþ 8

andvitni (ON) noun

Norwegian law allowed contradictory testimony in a number of cases, such as, e.g., matters related to inheritance (GuL ch. 127). On the other hand, it was forbidden in such cases as home summons witness, witness to summons to the assembly, witness to a demand for surrender of odal land, and witnesses to quarrels at drinking-parties (GuL chs 59, 60, 268). The purpose of counter-witnesses was to show that the allegation of the opposite party was not true and therefore to make his (or her) witnesses appear as false witnesses. Iceland law (Grg) was more restrictive. A panel verdict at odds with testimony offered by witnesses, or testimony at odds with a verdict (testimony had to precede panel verdict in the procedure) was inadmissible contrary testimony and subject to penalty.

contradictory evidence **OIce** *Jó* Þfb 4

contrary testimony **OIce** *Grg* Þsþ 37, *Js* Kab 2

counter-witness **ONorw** *GuL* Løb, Mhb

counter-witnessing **OIce** *Jó* Kab 2

See also: *vitni, vætti*

Refs: KLNM s.v. *vitne*; Laws of Early Iceland I, 243

anfriþer (OSw) noun

The harvest peace lasted from the end of June (HL) or July (SdmL, UL, VmL) until the end of September, during which time lawsuits were prohibited and certain rules applied concerning taking and taking back draft animals (HL).

harvest immunity **OSw** *UL* Rb, *VmL* Rb

harvest peace **OSw** *DL* Rb, *SdmL* Rb

harvest sanctity **OSw** *HL* Rb

See also: *friþer, høsthælgh, önn (pl. annir), varfriþer*

Refs: Schlyter s.v. *anfriþer*

angerløs (ODan) adj.

blameless **ODan** *JyL* 1–3

ankostir (pl.) (OSw) noun

farm equipment **OSw** *UL* Blb, *VmL* Bb

anlaþi (OSw) noun

barn with barley or hay **OSw** *DL* Bb

annarrabróðra (pl.) (ON) **annarrabróðri** (ON) noun

third cousins **OIce** *Grg* Bat 113 Ómb 143

annkostr (ON) noun

Expressions:

fyrir önnkostr (ON)

on purpose **OIce** *Grg* Þsþ 64

annöþogher (OSw) **anøthigh** (ODan) **ánauðigr** (ON) adj.

Used of unfree people. It is not stated what constituted this particular lack of freedom in terms of e.g. conditions or status.

enslaved **OIce** *Grg* Rsþ 229, **ONorw** *FrL* KrbA 28

hired **ODan** *SkL* 152

servant **ODan** *VSjL* 43

slave **ODan** *ESjL* 3

slavery **OSw** *ÄVgL* Äb

thrall **OSw** *YVgL* Drb, Rlb, *ÄVgL* Md, *ÖgL* Db

unfree **ODan** *ESjL* 3, *SkL* 62, 105, 122, 126, 128, 135, *VSjL* 56, 69, 86, **ONorw** *BorgL* 5.2 14.4, **OSw** *YVgL* Gb, *ÄVgL* Gb, *ÖgL* Vm

unfree servant **ODan** *VSjL* 86

See also: *ambat, deghia, fostra, fostre, frælsgiva, frælsgivi, hion, huskona, man, sætesambut, þræl*

Refs: Brink 2012, 125–26; Tamm and Vogt, eds, 2016, 313

annöþogherdomber (OSw) **anøthighdom** (ODan) noun

servitude **ODan** *SkL* 130, 132

slavery **ODan** *ESjL* 3

thralldom **OSw** *YVgL* Äb

unfree servant **ODan** *SkL* 129

anværkdagher (OSw) **andrum dæghi** (OSw) noun

working day **OSw** *ÄVgL* Fös

See also: *önn (pl. annir)*

apeldgarth (ODan) noun

apple garden **ODan** *JyL* 3

orchard **ODan** *JyL* 3

aplöghia (OSw) noun

ploughing in another man's land **OSw** *YVgL* Kkb, Add

apostlamæssudagher (OSw) noun
  Day of the Apostles **OSw** *YVgL* Kkb
  See also: *petersmessa*

ar (1) (OSw) **ár** (ON) noun
  Literally 'oar'. *Ar* is supposed to have been the lowest administrative taxation district in the naval defence system in UL. Its existence and role has been much debated and even questioned, as there are few traces of it. On the other hand Andersson (2014, 15) regards *ar* as synonymous with *hamna* (q.v.) and *har* (see *har* (2)).
  oar **ONorw** *GuL* Kvr, Mhb, Leb
  oarsman **OSw** *UL* Kgb
  See also: *hamna, har (2), hasæti, skiplagh, manngerð*
  Refs: Andersson 2014, 15; Hafström 1949a, Lundberg 1972, 11, 16, 178–79; Schlyter s.v.v. *ar, har, hamna*; SL UL, 61 note 52

ar (2) (ODan) noun
  Expressions:
  ar ok dagh (ODan)
  a year and a day **ODan** *JyL* 1

arath (ODan) noun
  ambush **ODan** *JyL* 3
  attack **ODan** *ESjL* 2, 3, *VSjL* 35–37, 46, 47, 60, 86
  fight **ODan** *ESjL* 3

arf (OSw) **ör** (ON) noun
  This term (etymologically a cognate of English arrow) occurred in two senses in ON: 1) a weapon (used with a hand-bow), 2) a message baton. The latter sense does not occur in OSw laws. The arrow usually had a point of metal and a shaft of wood. A message baton in the form of an arrow was used to summon people to the thing assembly in the case of murder, or to give warning against an approaching enemy. These functions are attested in several chapters of the GuL, esp. in the *Mannhelgarbölkr* (151, 160, 181), but also elsewhere (32, 314). On the fairway along the coast, the arrow had to be of iron when war was expected, otherwise wood. It was required by law to pass the message baton on. If this was neglected the culprit might in some cases be fined. Exempted from this duty were tenants who were about to move their household (GuL ch. 73). A message baton might be stopped temporarily where it came to a night quarter, or if it could not be passed on for reasons of emergency (GuL ch. 131). If anyone was not at home to receive the message baton the bearer had to cut three notches into the doorpost or the casing and set the baton in the lintel above the door (ibid.).
  arrow **ONorw** *GuL* Kvr, Leb, **OSw** *HL* Blb, Rb, *SdmL* Mb
  message baton **ONorw** *GuL* Krb, Mhb, Leb
  Expressions:
  skera ör (ON)
  cut an arrow **OIce** *Jó* Mah 10 *Js* Mah 10, 17 **ONorw** *FrL* Mhb 6, 23
  Refs: Hertzberg s.v. *ör*; KLNM s.v.v. *budstikke, landvärn, lendmann, pil* II, *ǫrvarþing*

arfa (ON) noun
  heiress **ONorw** *GuL* Olb
  See also: *arvi*

arfgænger (OSw) **arfgengr** (ON) adj.
  born a lawful heir **OIce** *Grg* Vís 94 Arþ 118 Ómb 137 Feþ 144 Misc 253
  eligible to inherit **ONorw** *EidsL* 22.3
  entitled to inherit **OIce** *Jó* Kge 21, **ONorw** *GuL* Kvb, Arb
  with a right to inherit **ONorw** *FrL* ArbB 1
  with the right to inherit **OSw** *DL* Gb

arfkaup (ON) noun
  price paid for an inheritance **OIce** *Grg* Arþ 123

arfsal (ON) **arfsala** (ON) noun
  A transfer of inheritance rights; an agreement by which one person, with the consent of his heirs, gave up his property in exchange for lifelong maintenance. According to Grg Arþ 127 an arfsal had to be witnessed by five neighbours and result in an official (written?) agreement (*máldagi*). Saga evidence suggests that these types of transfers allowed the rights seller to retain his estates until he dies, at which time they would pass on to the protector (cf. Miller 1990). *Arfsal* has been viewed as a type of care for the elderly (cf. Hoff 2011), but in the sagas it was also a tool to ensure protection against aggressors (cf. Miller 1990, 348, 362). In the former case *arfsal* bears similarity to the Norwegian *branderfð* (q.v.), Danish *flatføring* (q.v.) and other forms of lifelong maintenance, such as retiring to a monastery. In several medieval diplomas *arfsal* is referred to as *próventa*.
  inheritance sale **OIce** *Jó* Kge 30
  inheritance trade **OIce** *Grg* Arþ 127 Ómb 128, *Jó* Kge 23
  Expressions:
  seljask arfsali [e-m] (ON)
  to trade inheritance **OIce** *Jó* Kge
  See also: *arfskot, branderfð, flatføring, omaghi*
  Refs: CV; Fritzner; GAO s.v. *Armenrecht*; GrgTr II:26; Hoff 2011, 220; KLNM s.v.

alderdom, branderfð, próventa; Miller
1984; Miller 1990, 249, 348, 362; ONP

arfskifti (ON) **arfskipti** (ON) **arfsskifti** (ON) noun

division of inheritance **ONorw** *GuL* Arb

inheritance division **OIce** *Jó* Kge 20,
Js Ert 2, **ONorw** *FrL* KrbB 11

See also: *arver*

arfskot (ON) noun

Inheritance fraud; the selling of property with the intent
of defrauding someone's heirs. Grg Arþ 127 specifies
lesser outlawry or loss of property as the penalty for
someone committing *arfskot* by giving or receiving
'friendship gifts' (*vingjöf*) deemed fraudulent by the
heir. Heirs of someone trading away their inheritance
for maintenance (*arfsal*) could also claim *arfskot*.

dispossession of heirs **OIce** *Grg* Arþ 127

See also: *arfsal, arfsvik*

Refs: CV; F; KLNM s.v. *förskingring*;
Miller 1990; ONP

arfsókn (ON) **arfssókn** (ON) noun

inheritance claim **ONorw** *FrL* ArbB 29

suit for inheritance **OIce** *Jó* Kge 19,
ONorw *FrL* ArbA 17, *GuL* Arb

arfsvik (ON) noun

fraud in matters of inheritance **OIce**
Jó Kge 12, 22, **ONorw** *GuL* Løb

inheritance fraud **ONorw** *FrL* KrbB 13 Jkb 4

arftak (ON) noun

inheritance **ONorw** *FrL* ArbB 6

taking on by inheritance trade **OIce**
Grg Ómb 128, 135, *Jó* Kge 13

arftaka (ON) noun

inheritance taking **OIce** *Grg* Rsþ 229 Misc 249

arftaki (OSw) **arvtake** (ODan) **arftaki** (ON) noun

heir **ODan** *ESjL* 1, 3, *SkL* 166, **OIce** *Jó* Kge
23, **ONorw** *GuL* Mhb, **OSw** *ÖgL* Kkb

heritor **ODan** *ESjL* 1, **OSw** *YVgL* Add

inheritor **ODan** *ESjL* 1

one who shall take the inheritance **ODan** *ESjL* 3

See also: *arvi, arvingi, erfðarmaðr*

arftakin (OSw) adj.

inherited **OSw** *YVgL* Rlb, Jb, Add, *ÄVgL* Jb

arftaksómagi (ON) noun

inheritance-trade dependent **OIce** *Grg* Ómb 135

arftökumaðr (ON) noun

heir **OIce** *Grg* Klþ 2 Þsþ 39, 68 Vís
95, 96 Ómb 129, 130 Misc 248

See also: *arvi, arvingi*

arfván (ON) noun

inheritance prospect **OIce** *Grg* Arþ 122,
Jó Kge 30, **ONorw** *FrL* ArbB 11

argafas (ON) noun

cowardly assault **OIce** *Js* Mah
22, **ONorw** *FrL* Mhb 18

cowardly attack **OIce** *Jó* Mah 14, 22

ari (OSw) noun

Only appearing in OSw HL, where it was obsolete
already when the law was written down, and
possibly influenced by ONorw *ármaðr* (q.v.). A
representative of the king, and possibly archbishop,
for all of Hälsingland, where he managed royal
estates, collected taxes and the king's fines, convened
assemblies and was responsible for overseeing the
accounts of sheriffs.

emissary **OSw** *HL* Kgb

Refs: Brink 2010b, 129–30; Brink 2013a,
441; Tegengren 2015, 142–43

arinelja (ON) noun

concubine **ONorw** *GuL* Krb

See also: *amia, frilla, meinkona, sløkefrithe*

arsfæsta (OSw) noun

entry fee for one year **OSw** *YVgL* Äb, *ÄVgL* Äb

arvabot (OSw) noun

compensation to the heirs **OSw** *YVgL* Drb, *ÄVgL* Md

fine to an heir **OSw** *SdmL* Äb, Mb

See also: *arvi, bot*

arvbet (ODan) adj.

If two spouses received an inheritance each, both
inheritances, irrespective of their worth, were
passed on to the household. In ESjL and VSjL all
inheritances received by one spouse were passed on
to the household if the other spouse received at least
one inheritance. Similar concepts, albeit not the word,
appear in OSw laws.

inheritance chase **ODan** *SkL* 29

inheritance chased on both sides **ODan** *SkL* 7

inheritance on both sides **ODan** *SkL* 29

See also: *arvbit, arver*

Refs: Lund s.v.v. *arfbetær, betæ, bitæ*; Schlyter s.v.v.
arfbeter, beta, bita; Tamm and Vogt, eds, 2016, 306

arvbit (ODan) noun

biting inheritance **ODan** *ESjL* 1

See also: *arvbet, arver*

arvebitning (ODan) noun

inheritence that bites inheritance **ODan** *VSjL* 2

arvedele (ODan) noun

disagreement over inheritance **ODan** *ESjL* 3

division of inheritance **ODan** *ESjL* 1

arvemal (ODan) noun

inheritance case **ODan** *VSjL* 12

See also: *arver*

arver (OSw) **arv** (ODan) **arf** (OGu) **arfr** (ON) **arf** (OSw) **ærf** (OSw) noun

In the Swedish laws, this word carried several meanings: land (as a possession); possessions left by a deceased person; inheritance (as a concept); birthright (esp. in land). Inheritance was based on a division of the deceased person's property and not on primogeniture. In general, male descendants received twice that of their female counterpart, but this was not universal. Illegitimate descendants could inherit, in some instances, but this was subject to certain conditions. Slaves had the right to inherit from each other when brought up in the same household. This type of inheritance was called lesser inheritance (*litla erfð*, see GuL chs 65 and 114). In GL, the laws of inheritance were extremely complex and interpreting them is not aided by the use of the words *lindagyrt* (q.v.) and *gyrþlugyrt* (q.v.), which are open to conflicting translations.

birthright **OSw** *UL* Äb, *VmL* Äb

heritage **OSw** *DL* Gb

inheritance **ODan** *ESjL* 1, 3, *JyL* 1, 2, *SkL* 2, 3, 7, 29–34, 36, 38, 59–61, *VSjL* passim, **OGu** *GL* A 20, **OIce** *Grg* Þsþ 50 Arþ 118 Ómb 128 Misc 247, *Jó* MagBref Mah 2, 4 Kge 2, 7 Llb 47, *Js* Mah 8 Kvg 3 Ert 13, **ONorw** *FrL* KrbB 10, 11 ArbA 1, *GuL* Krb, Kpb, Kvb, Løb, Arb, Mhb, **OSw** *DL* Gb, *HL* Kgb, Äb, Mb, *SdmL* Äb, Mb, *SmL*, *UL* Kkb, Äb, Mb, Jb, Add. 7, *VmL* För, Kkb, Äb, Mb, Jb, *YVgL* Kkb, Äb, Jb, Add, *ÄVgL* Äb, Jb, Lek, *ÖgL* Eb, Db

Expressions:

alinn til arfs (ON)

born a lawful heir **OIce** *Grg* Vís 95

arf ok orf (OSw)

inheritance **OSw** *HL* Äb

bite arv (ODan)

bite inheritance **ODan** *ESjL* 1 *VSjL* 1, 2, 7, 8

leiða til arfs (ON)

adopt **OIce** *Jó* Kge 7-2

See also: *arvbet, arvbit, byrþ, ærfþ*

Refs: Hertzberg s.v. *arfr*; Holmbäck 1919; KLNM s.v.v. *adoption, alderdom, arveret, festermål, foster, gangarv, gæld, husbonde, husfru, lejermål, medgift,* *morgongåva, mundr, odelsrett, oäkta barn, spolierett, straff, syn, testament, ætt, ættleiing*; ONP s.v. *arfr*

arvfælagh (ODan) noun

inheritance had together **ODan** *ESjL* 1

arvi (OSw) **arve** (ODan) **arfi** (OGu) **arfi** (ON) **arve** (OSw) noun

A son inherited twice as much as a daughter. See GuL ch. 103.

heir **ODan** *ESjL* 1, 3, *JyL* 1, *SkKL* 5, *SkL* passim, *VSjL* 9, 19, 21, 22, **OGu** *GL* A 19, **OIce** *Grg* Ómb 118, *Jó* Sg 1 Mah 8 Kge 1, 2 Fml 23, *Js* Mah 8, 20 Kvg 1, 2 Kab 8, **ONorw** *FrL* KrbA 1 Mhb 6, 10 Var 2–6 ArbA 1, *GuL* Kpb, Løb, Arb, Mhb, **OSw** *DL* Bb, Gb, Rb, *HL* Kkb, Kgb, Mb, Jb, *SdmL* Kkb, Kgb, Äb, Jb, Mb, Tjdb, Rb, *SmL*, *UL* Kkb, Kgb, Äb, Mb, Jb, Rb, *VmL* Kkb, Kgb, Äb, Mb, Jb, Rb, *YVgL* Kkb, Frb, Drb, Äb, Gb, Rlb, Tb, Jb, Add, *ÄVgL* Md, Slb, Äb, Jb, Tb, *ÖgL* Kkb, Eb, Db

relative **OSw** *HL* Mb

See also: *arftaki, arftökumaðr, arver, arvingi, erfðarmaðr*

Refs: KLNM, s.v.v. *arveret, medgift, odelsrett, oäkta barn, ættleiing*

arvibol (OSw) noun

hereditary farm **OSw** *HL* Äb

arvingi (OSw) **arving** (ODan) **ærving** (ODan) **erfingi** (OGu) **erfingi** (ON) **ærffwingi** (OSw) **ærvingi** (OSw) noun

heir **ODan** *ESjL* 1–3, *JyL* 1–3, *VSjL* 3, 5, 21, **OGu** *GL* A 14, **OIce** *Grg* Klþ 2, 5 Þsþ 50, 54 Bat 114 Ómb 135 Feþ 153, 170 Fjl 221 Misc 247 Tíg 268, *Jó* Þfb 9 Mah 1, 4 Kge 3, 6 Lbb 1 Llb 28 Kab 8, 16 Þjb 16 Fml 23, *Js* Mah 3, 12 Kvg 2 Kab 3, 6, *KRA* 9, 11, **ONorw** *BorgL* 8.12 9.14, *FrL* Intr 4 KrbB 14, 17 Mhb 7, *GuL* Krb, Kpb, Kvb, Løb, Llb, Arb, Mhb, Olb, **OSw** *DL* Kkb, Mb, Gb, *HL* Kkb, Äb, *SdmL* Kkb, Jb, Mb, *UL* Äb, Mb, Jb, Rb, *YVgL* Drb, *ÄVgL* Md

inheritor **ONorw** *EidsL* 50.9

relative **OSw** *HL* Mb

See also: *arftaki, arftökumaðr, arver, arvi, erfðarmaðr*

arvstathe (ODan) adj.

according to how much a person is to inherit **ODan** *ESjL* 1

arvuþi (OSw) **ærvethe** (ODan) **arviþi** (OSw) **ærvoþi** (OSw) **ærwþi** (OSw) noun

effort **ODan** *SkL* 41, **OSw** *UL* Kkb, Blb, *VmL* Bb

labour **ODan** *SkL* 56

trouble **ODan** *JyL* 3

work **ODan** *JyL* 1, 2, *SkKL* 3, **OSw** *YVgL* Äb

arþer (OSw) **arðr** (ON) noun

A more archaic agricultural implement for preparing the soil than a plough; an *arþer* not turning the turf over. Both were used in medieval Scandinavia, but only *arþer* occurs in the laws.

plough **ONorw** *GuL* Olb

plough share **OSw** *DL* Bb

See also: *krok*

Refs: KLNM s.v.v. *ager, plov*; Myrdal 2011, 82

asaka (OSw) verb

Related to the noun *sak* '(legal) case' and the verbs *sækia* (q.v.) and *sækta* (q.v.) from which the usage is indistinguishable.

prosecute **OSw** *DL* Mb

asighling (OSw) **ásigling** (ON) noun

ramming **OSw** *SdmL* Kgb

sailing upon someone **ONorw** *GuL* Mhb

asker (OSw) noun

spear **OSw** *UL* Mb, *VmL* Mb

askilia (OGu) verb

disagree **OGu** *GL* A 32

dispute **OGu** *GL* A 28

askuoþensdagher (OSw) noun

Ash Wednesday **OSw** *SdmL* Rb

aslata (OSw) noun

harvesting of hay or corn in another man's land **OSw** *YVgL* Kkb, Λdd

asokn (OSw) noun

case having been brought to trial **OSw** *DL* Tjdb

prosecuting the case **OSw** *VmL* Mb

prosecution **OSw** *DL* Tjdb

See also: *sokn*

asyn (OSw) **asjun** (ODan) **asyn** (OGu) noun

bruise **OSw** *HL* Kgb

enquiry **OSw** *YVgL* Jb

estimate **ODan** *SkL* 95, 122

examination **OSw** *YVgL* Jb, *ÄVgL* Jb

eyewitness **OGu** *GL* A 25

inspection **ODan** *SkL* 44, 105, *VSjL* 24, **OGu** *GL* A 25, **OSw** *HL* Blb

mark **OSw** *DL* Eb, *UL* Kgb, *VmL* Kgb, Mb

observation **OSw** *DL* Mb

opinion **ODan** *VSjL* 12

survey **OSw** *YVgL* Kvab, *ÄVgL* Kva

visible mark **OSw** *DL* Mb, Bb, *SdmL* Kgb, Gb

visible score **OSw** *DL* Bb

Expressions:

hæraþs asyn (OSw)

examination of the district **OSw** *YVgL* Jb

survey of the district **OSw** *YVgL* Kvab

lands asyn (OSw)

examination at the province level **OSw** *YVgL* Jb

asyun aldræ mannæ (ODan)

opinion of older men **ODan** *VSjL* 12

gothæ mæns asyun (ODan)

good men's inspection **ODan** *VSjL* 24

See also: *handaværk, hæraþ*

asöreseþer (OSw) **asvareeth** (ODan) **asøreseth** (ODan) **assvarueþ** (OSw) noun

An oath about the guilt of an accused sworn by the victim of a crime. ODan SkL 149 dictates the wording of such an oath.

oath **ODan** *SkL* 147

oath of guilt **ODan** *SkL* 156, 180

oath of substantiation **OSw** *VmL* Kkb

oath of/to a person's guilt **ODan** *SkL* 121, 147, 149, 161, 177, 226, 230, **OSw** *SdmL* Kkb

See also: *brista, eþer, fælla, sværia*

atakin (OSw) adj.

caught in the act **OSw** *DL* Bb

See also: *taka*

atala (OSw) **atalan** (OSw) verb

Literally 'to speak to/against', specifically of starting legal proceedings. Also appearing as *tala a*.

bring a case (against) **OSw** *UL* Kkb, *VmL* Kkb

bring an action against **OSw** *SdmL* Kkb, Jb

prosecute **OSw** *DL* Mb, *YVgL* Add

See also: *tiltala*

atala (OSw) noun

prosecution **OSw** *YVgL* Add

suing **OSw** *YVgL* Drb, Add

aterbryta (OSw) **atterbryta** (OSw) **attærbryta** (OSw) verb

judge invalid **OSw** *UL* Kkb, Rb, *VmL* Rb

See also: *aterganga, atergangs, ogilder*

aterdöma (OSw) verb

disallow **OSw** *ÖgL* Kkb

aterfang (OSw) **atær fang** (OSw) noun

recovered property **OSw** *UL* Mb

value of the property **OSw** *UL* Mb

See also: *agriper, fyli, þiufnaþer, þiuft*

aterfylla (OSw) verb

 make good OSw *UL* Kkb, *VmL* Kkb, Äb

 pay back OSw *UL* Äb, *VmL* Äb, Jb

aterganga (OSw) **atterganga** (OSw) **attærganga** (OSw) verb

 deem invalid OSw *UL* Rb, *VmL* Kkb, Rb

 be dismissed OSw *SdmL* Kkb, Rb

 be judged as invalid OSw *YVgL* Add

 return OSw *UL* Jb, Kmb, *VmL* Äb

 revert OGu *GL* A 7, OSw *UL* Kkb, Jb, Blb, *VmL* Kkb, Jb, Bb

 See also: *aterbryta*, *atergangs*, *ganga*, *ogilder*

atergangs (OSw) **attergangs** (OSw) **attirgans** (OSw) **attærgangs** (OSw) adj.

 invalid OSw *UL* Kkb, *VmL* Kkb

 See also: *aterbryta*, *ateranga*, *ogilder*

atergangseþer (OSw) noun

 Literally an oath that goes back, i.e. is invalid for various reasons, such as oaths by minors, false oaths or several oaths sworn by one person on the same day.

 dismissed oath OSw *HL* Kkb, *SdmL* Kkb, Rb, Till

atergildi (OSw) **atergæld** (OSw) noun

 compensation OSw *UL* Blb, *VmL* Mb, Bb

 recompense OSw *YVgL* Rlb

 replacement OSw *UL* Blb

 return OSw *UL* Mb

atergælda (OSw) **atergialda** (OSw) **attærgælda** (OSw) **ættargælda** (OSw) verb

 make restitution OSw *UL* Kkb, Äb, Mb, Blb, *VmL* Äb, Bb

 pay back OSw *UL* Jb, Kmb, Rb, *VmL* Bb

 pay compensation OSw *UL* Blb, *VmL* Bb

 See also: *aterfylla*, *gælda (1)*, *varþa*

aterköpsfastaeþer (OSw) noun

 oath of transactions witnesses for repurchases OSw *SdmL* Jb

aterköpsfastar (pl.) (OSw) noun

 repayment {fastar} OSw *HL* Jb

 transaction witnesses for a repurchase OSw *SdmL* Jb

 {fastar} at repayment OSw *HL* Jb

aterlæggia (OSw) **atterlæggia** (OSw) **attærlæggia** (OSw) verb

 allow to lie fallow OSw *UL* Blb, *VmL* Jb

 leave blocked OSw *UL* Blb

 See also: *aterlægha*, *fyrna*, *lata*, *liggia*, *træpi*

aterlægha (OSw) **atterlægha** (OSw) **attærlægha** (OSw) noun

 abandoned field OSw *SdmL* Bb

 fallow land OSw *UL* Blb, *VmL* Bb

 uncultivated land OSw *VmL* Bb

 See also: *aterlæggia*, *lata*, *liggia*, *træpi*

aterlösa (OSw) **ater loysa** (OGu) **atrloysa** (OGu) **atterlösa** (OSw) verb

 make repayment OSw *VmL* Kkb

 ransom OGu *GL* A 28

 redeem OGu *GL* A 30, 44, 45, Add. 8 (B 55), OSw *DL* Rb, *HL* Jb, *SdmL* Kkb, Jb, Bb, *SmL*, *UL* Kkb, Äb, Jb, Kmb, Blb, Rb, *VmL* Kkb, Jb, Kmb, Bb, Rb, *YVgL* Kkb

 release OSw *YVgL* Utgb

 return OGu *GL* Add. 8 (B 55)

atersighia (OSw) verb

 relinquish OSw *UL* Jb

aterstaþa (OSw) **attærstaþa** (OSw) noun

 shortfall OSw *VmL* Kgb

atertæppa (OSw) verb

 obstruct OSw *UL* Blb, *VmL* Bb

 See also: *svintæppa*, *tæppa*

atfarardómr (ON) **atfaradómr** (ON) noun

 judgement of distraint ONorw *FrL* KrbB 20

atferð (ON) noun

 The implementation of a judgment; the carrying out of a sentence. Used especially with reference to the seizure of goods.

 execution OIce *Jó* Mah 21

 See also: *atferli*, *atför*

 Refs: CV s.v. *atferð*; Fritzner s.v. *atferð*; ONP s.v. *atferð*

atferli (ON) noun

 procedure OIce *Grg* Feþ 167 Lbþ 174, *KRA* 1

atför (ON) noun

 distraint OIce *Js* Mah 14, ONorw *FrL* Mhb 7

 seizure OIce *Jó* Mah 10 Llb 15, 34, ONorw *FrL* Mhb 50 Rgb 24 LlbA 11

athelbarn (ODan) noun

 legitimate child ODan *ESjL* 1

 See also: *aþal*

athelbit (ODan) noun

 owner's lot ODan *JyL* 2

 See also: *aþal*

athelbonde (ODan) noun

 One who owned inherited land and remained in an old village, as opposed to one moving to a new village located by the fields. Mostly appearing as *otholbondæ* (cf. *oþal*) and often in the phrase *mæþ tyltær eþ oþolbondæ* 'with an oath of twelve land-owning men' (SkL).

landowner **ODan** *JyL* 2

landowning man **ODan** *SkL* passim

real householder **ODan** *JyL* 2

See also: *aþal*

Refs: Andersen 2014, 23; Tamm
and Vogt, eds, 2016, 307

athelbondebarn (ODan) noun

child of a husband **ODan** *JyL* 1

See also: *aþal, aþalkonubarn*

athelby (ODan) noun

main village **ODan** *JyL* 1

See also: *aþal*

athelkonedotter (ODan) noun

wife's daughter **ODan** *ESjL* 1

See also: *aþal*

athelvægh (ODan) noun

main road **ODan** *JyL* 1, 2, *SkL* 68, 70, *VSjL* 74

See also: *aþal, vægher*

atkvæði (ON) noun

decree **OIce** *KRA* 18

statement **OIce** *Grg* Rsþ 227

atløp (OSw) athlaup (ON) noun

assault **OIce** *KRA* 8, **OSw** *ÖgL* Vm

attack **ONorw** *FrL* KrbA 10

threatening behaviour **ONorw** *GuL* Mhb

atmeli (OGu) noun

year **OGu** *GL* A 13, 20, 26, 28, Add. 7 (B 49)

See also: *jamlangi*

attundidagher (OSw) noun

Eighth Day of Christmas **OSw** *YVgL* Kkb

attunger (OSw) atting (ODan) áttungr (ON) noun

Literally 'eighth' of something. In SkL VSjL, and ÖgL the *attunger* was primarily a land assessment unit and an administrative district in the organization of the military levy system, *leþunger*. 'Most probably the original purpose of the taxation was to create an adequate base for the military levy system [i.e. in ÖgL, eastern Småland and Närke]. Several indications show that the *attunger* originally corresponded to one family's normal holding of land. The usefulness of the *attunger* for other purposes was soon realized. Besides taxes it also became the base for tenant's land rent, tithes to a particular hospital (*domus Sancti Spiritus*), compensation for plowing of fallow fields but also for the subdivision of common fields on a pro rata basis. The right to an easement could also be connected to the *attunger*. At the same time a subdivision of the *attunger* unit in several fractions was created which facilitated the trading of landed property.' (Ericsson

2007, Abstract). In the Västgöta laws and Svea laws (SdmL, UL) *attunger* was an administrative district on a low level. In the Svea laws area the land assessment unit was the *markland* (q.v.) around the late thirteenth century. The *attunger* in DL denotes an eighth of a legally divided village. In Norwegian laws it was used about an eighth of a *fylki* (q.v.), but in some laws it was an important unit in the organization of the *leiðangr* (see *leþunger*).

descendant within the third degree
OSw *UL* Kmb, *VmL* Äb

eighth **ODan** *SkL* 73, 75, 76, *VSjL* 78–80,
ONorw *FrL* Mhb 8, **OSw** *DL* Bb, *SdmL*
Kkb, Kgb, Bb, *YVgL* Jb, *ÄVgL* Jb

eighth of a village **OSw** *DL* Bb

eighth of a {fylki} **ONorw** *GuL* Krb, Leb

eighth of a {hundari} **OSw** *UL* Kgb, Blb, Rb, Add. 4

eighth of the inhabitants of an area **ONorw** *GuL* Krb

{attunger} **OSw** *YVgL* Kkb, Jb, Föb, *ÄVgL* Jb

Expressions:

halver attunger (OSw)

descendant within the fourth degree **OSw** *VmL* Äb

See also: *fiarþunger, hundari,
hæraþ, markland, þriþiobyrþ*

Refs: Dovring 1947b; Ericsson 2007, Abstract and passim; Ericsson 2012, 181–82, 329–41 and passim; KLNM s.v.v. *attung, bol, byamål, hundare, jordmått, jordskatter, leidang, markland, sogn, öresland, örtugland*; Lindkvist 1995, 20–21; Lundberg 1972, 92–93; Schlyter, s.v. *attunger*

attungsbro (OSw) noun

bridge of an eighth **OSw** *SdmL* Bb

See also: *attunger*

atvik (ON) noun

circumstance **OIce** *Jó* Mah 13, 20
Kge 29 Llb 30 Kab 7 Þjb 16

atvinna (ON) noun

means of livelihood **OFar** *Seyð* 7

subsistence **OIce** *Js* Ert 22

atvist (OSw) noun

Case concerning presence at, but not active participation in, a crime.

case of {atvist} accomplice **OSw** *ÄVgL* Md

Refs: Schlyter s.v.v. *atvist, atvistarmaþer*

atvistarmaþer (OSw) noun

A man in company with perpetrators of violent crimes, who was punished whether actively participating or not.

accomplice **OSw** *ÄVgL* Md

man present at the deed **OSw** *YVgL* Drb

See also: *fylghi, haldbani, laghsman, umstaþumæn (pl.)*

atvígi (ON) noun

attack **OIce** *Jó* Mah 20, *Js* Mah 16, **ONorw** *FrL* Mhb 22

wound **ONorw** *GuL* Mhb

auðhófi (ON) **auðæfi** (ON) **auðófi** (ON) noun

goods **ONorw** *GuL* Løb

resources **OIce** *Grg* Ómb 136 Lbþ 174

wealth **OIce** *Grg* Klþ 3

auðn (ON) noun

destitution **OIce** *Grg* Þsþ 39

penury **OIce** *Grg* Ómb 130, 143

uncultivated land **ONorw** *GuL* Llb

uninhabited farm **OIce** *Jó* Kge 29

uninhabited land **ONorw** *FrL* Intr 17, 18

wasteland **OIce** *Js* Lbb 21, **ONorw** *FrL* Intr 17

See also: *eyðijörð*

auðr (ON) adj.

Expressions:

auð jörð (ON)

uncultivated land **ONorw** *GuL* Llb

auga (OGu) **auga** (ON) noun

eye **OGu** *GL* A 19, 22, **ONorw** *GuL* Mhb

augnaskot (ON) noun

measuring with the eye **ONorw** *GuL* Llb

See also: *álburðr*

auralag (ON) noun

This referred to money value and rate of exchange. The relation between pure silver and silver in coin was often determined by relating them to some standard article of trade, such as ells of wadmal. An *eyrir* worth six ells was usual, and the ONorw laws also mention an *eyrir* worth ten ells (GuL), twelve ells, and nine ells (EidsL). The money value had to be considered especially in some cases of fines and business transactions. See GuL ch. 170 and FrL Jkb.

money value **ONorw** *FrL* Jkb 1, *GuL* Mhb

Refs: KLNM s.v. *auralag*

aurastefna (ON) noun

meeting for payment **ONorw** *FrL* Jkb 4

aurataka (ON) noun

receipt of money **ONorw** *GuL* Olb

austker (ON) noun

scoop **ONorw** *GuL* Kvr, Mhb

austmaðr (ON) noun

man from overseas **OIce** *Grg* Misc 249

austr (ON) noun

bailing water out of a boat **ONorw** *GuL* Leb

austr (ON) adv.

overseas **OIce** *Grg* Þsþ 54

auvirði (ON) noun

detriment **OIce** *Grg* Fjl 224

auvislabót (ON) **uslabót** (ON) noun

compensation for damages **OIce** *Grg* Feþ 165 Lbþ 181 Fjl 225 Misc 241, **ONorw** *FrL* LlbA 21

See also: *bot*

auvislagjald (ON) **auslagjöld** (ON) noun

compensation for damages **OIce** *Jó* Llb 21, 33

See also: *aværkan*

auvisli (ON) **ausli** (ON) **usli** (ON) noun

compensation for damages **OIce** *Jó* Llb 32, 33

damages **OIce** *Grg* Lbþ 183 Rsþ 230, *Jó* Llb 31, **ONorw** *FrL* LlbA 21

avaxter (OSw) **ávöxtr** (ON) **afvæxter** (OSw) **avæxter** (OSw) noun

harvest **ONorw** *GuL* Krb

income **OIce** *Jó* Kge 14

increase **OIce** *Jó* Kge 8 Kab 15

interest **OIce** *Jó* Kge 26 Fml 22, 23, *KRA* 9, 35

yield **OSw** *YVgL* Äb, *ÄVgL* Äb

avisning (OSw) noun

referral **OSw** *UL* Jb, Blb, *VmL* Jb, Bb

aviti (OSw) **aviti** (OGu) noun

fines **OGu** *GL* A 6, **OSw** *UL* Jb, *VmL* Jb

avugher (OSw) **avigh** (ODan) **öfugr** (ON) adj.

Literally, 'backwards'. The principal use of this word is in speaking of enemies of the king, those who were hostile to him. It alludes to the fact that shields facing the king, or 'backwards', were those of an enemy. Several other expressions, however, include this word. In the expression *ganga avugh or ætt sinni*, referring to a free woman marrying a slave, it implies that she is 'backing out' of her inheritance. The word also appears in the expression *elda afgum brandum* (literally 'start a fire with backward firebrands'), referring to an inheritance that takes a step, or throws a glance, backwards (i.e. makes a reversion to ascendant inheritance) in the case in which there are no direct or co-lateral heirs. The ascendant inheritance would go right back as far as to a maternal aunt. The closest single relative took the full inheritance. If there were no living relatives of that order, the inheritance was divided equally between the paternal and maternal kin — the nearest on each side taking an equal share. The rules about the precise division of the inheritance are complex and not entirely consistent. In some cases, the division was according to the distance from the deceased, but in others, this did not apply.

backwards **OSw** *UL* Äb, *VgL* Äb

of the butt side of a weapon **ONorw** *GuL* Mhb

deformed **ONorw** *EidsL* 5

hostile **OSw** *UL* Mb

Expressions:

avugher skiolder (OSw) avighskjold (ODan)

averse shield **OSw** *SdmL* Mb

hostile shield **OSw** *HL* Mb *UL* Mb

shield-brandishing **ODan** *ESjL* 2

elda afgum brandum (OSw)

take a step backwards **OSw** *VmL* Äb

ganga avugh or ætt sinni (OSw)

relinquish her birthright **OSw** *UL* Äb *VmL* Äb

See also: *arver, bakarf, brander, fiærþungsmaþer, skiolder, æt*

Refs: KLNM s.v. *arveret*; Schlyter 1877, s.v.v. *avugher, brander, skiolder*; SL DL, 87 note 33; SL VmL, 61–62 notes 67–71; Tamm and Vogt, eds, 2016, 313

avund (OSw) **avend** (ODan) **öfund** (ON) **avond** (OSw) noun

In ODan, appearing in the context of preventing biased witnesses or others acting at, for example, the *thing* 'assembly' or a *ransak* 'house search'. Also used of premeditated, violent deeds; in OSw often contrasted to deeds done in sudden rage (*vreþe*), and appearing in the context of *eþsöre* 'the king's (sworn) peace'. In ON, referring to physical damage to persons or objects, including illegal use of other people's property, offences which had to be compensated.

enmity **ODan** *JyL* 2, **OSw** *DL* Eb, *HL* Kgb, *SdmL* Kgb, *UL* Kgb, *VmL* Kgb, *YVgL* Add, *ÖgL* Eb

evil intent **ONorw** *GuL* Tfb, Mhb

hatred **ODan** *SkL* 121, 149

malice **OIce** *Jó* Llb 36, *Js* Mah 34

premeditated harm **ONorw** *GuL* Mhb

Expressions:

avund ok ilder vili (OSw) avend ok ilvilje (ODan)

hate or ill will **ODan** *SkL* 149

malignancy and wrath **OSw** *YVgL* Rlb

fæ, vild æller avend (ODan)

gain, favour or hatred **ODan** *SkL* 121

See also: *fegþ*

aværkan (OSw) **áverk** (ON) **áverki** (ON) **aværk** (OSw) noun

compensation for an assault **ONorw** *FrL* Var 9

compensation for damages **OIce** *Jó* Mah 2 Llb 18, 20

damage **ONorw** *FrL* LlbA 11, **OSw** *HL* Blb, *UL* Jb, *VmL* Jb

illegal products **ONorw** *GuL* Llb

illegal work **ONorw** *FrL* LlbA 26

illicit use **OSw** *UL* Kkb, Jb, Blb, *VmL* Bb

injury **OIce** *Grg* Vís 86, 87 Feþ 159, 167 Misc 238, 242, **ONorw** *FrL* Var 7

misuse **OSw** *UL* Jb, Blb

produce of the land **OIce** *Jó* Llb 31, **ONorw** *FrL* LlbA 1

reparation mulct **OIce** *Grg* Feþ 165 Lbþ 199, 204

tools or fruits of unauthorized labour **ONorw** *GuL* Llb

unlawful usage of arable land **OSw** *SdmL* Kkb, Jb

unlawful use **OIce** *Jó* Llb 26

wounding **OIce** *Jó* Llb 39

See also: *afærþ, auvislagjald*

ax (OSw) noun

ears of grain **OSw** *UL* Mb, Blb, *VmL* Mb, Bb

ayrkia (OSw) noun

work in another man's land **OSw** *YVgL* Add

aþal (OSw) **aþal** (OGu) adj.

Literally, 'true, genuine'. A closely related word, originally meaning 'ancestry', came in later medieval Swedish to signify 'the nobility' (cp. *frælse*), but *aþal* in the medieval Nordic laws carried the connotations: 'true-born', 'legitimate', 'proper' and, of land, 'cultivated' (as opposed to woodland, marsh, etc.). An *aþalkona/-man* was thus a wedded wife or husband, as opposed to a concubine or lover; an *aþal dotir* (OGu GL) was a legitimate daughter, as opposed to one born out of wedlock; a man who was *aþal gutnisker* was a native-born Gotlander, as opposed to a foreigner. In GL, cultivated land was *aþal jorþ* and the proximity of this class of land in someone's ownership was considered to be more valid in determining the ownership of disputed land than woodland or marsh owned by another. More obscurely, *aþalköps fastar* (OSw UL) were *fastar* (q.v.) present at an unconditional land purchase (the *aþal fæst*, 'confirmation of unconditional purchase', in ÖgL), as opposed to *væþiafastar* (q.v.), who were present for the mortgaging or pledging of land. *Aþal værknaþer* (OSw UL, VmL) was (heavy) work that was done on a working day (as opposed to that permitted on a Sunday). In DL the otherwise unrecorded *aþalbogher* (q.v.) is interpreted as the percentage (99%) of an inheritance that, in the case of ascendant inheritance, passed to the father or mother who alone survived the deceased, the remaining 1% passing to the maternal or paternal kin respectively. It was the 'major branch' of the inheritance. The prefix *aþal-/adel-* occurs as an alternative to *oþal-/oþol-* in words related to ancestral land and it also takes the meaning 'main, principal' in relation to settlements and roads.

cultivated **OGu** *GL* A 25

legitimate **OGu** *GL* A 20

proper **OSw** *UL* Kkb, *VmL* Kkb

trueborn **OGu** *GL* A 20, 20a

Expressions:

aþal dotir (OGu)

legitimate daughter **OGu** *GL* A 20

aþal gutnisker (OGu)

trueborn Gotlander **OGu** *GL* A 20, 20a

aþal iorþ (OGu)

cultivated land **OGu** *GL* A 25

aþal værknaþer (OSw)

proper labour **OSw** *UL* Kkb *VmL* Kkb

See also: *arver*, *fræls*, *oþal*, *væþiafastar (pl.)*

Refs: Peel 2015, 139 note 20/93; Schlyter 1877, s.v. *aþal-*

aþalbogher (OSw) noun

part of an inheritance **OSw** *DL* Gb

See also: *aþal*

aþalkona (OSw) **athelkone** (ODan) noun

lawful wife **ODan** *JyL* 1, *SkL* 13, 215

wife **ODan** *ESjL* 1, *VSjL* 1, 2, 51, 52, **OSw** *YVgL* Äb, *ÄVgL* Äb

See also: *aþal*, *frilla*, *husfrugha*, *kona*, *sløkefrithe*

aþalkonubarn (OSw) **athelkonebarn** (ODan) **aþall kono barn** (OSw) noun

child (born) of a legitimate wife **ODan** *ESjL* 1

child by/with a lawful wife **ODan** *SkL* 59, 60, 63, 64, **OSw** *UL* Äb, *VmL* Äb

child of a lawfully wedded wife/woman **OSw** *YVgL* Gb, Add, *ÄVgL* Gb

child of a married woman **OSw** *SdmL* Äb

lawful-married woman's child **OSw** *HL* Äb

lawfully wedded woman's child **OSw** *YVgL* Äb

legally married wife's child **OSw** *DL* Gb

legitimate child **ODan** *ESjL* 1, *JyL* 1, *SkL* 60, 63, *VSjL* 68–70, **OSw** *UL* Äb, *VmL* Äb

legitimate offspring **OSw** *UL* Äb, *VmL* Äb

See also: *aþal*, *aþalkona*, *barn*, *frillubarn*, *horbarn*

aþalkonusun (OSw) **athelkonesun** (ODan) noun

legitimate son **ODan** *JyL* 3

son of a lawfully married woman **OSw** *YVgL* Äb, *ÄVgL* Äb, *ÖgL* Db

son of a legitimate wife **ODan** *ESjL* 2

son of a wife **ODan** *ESjL* 1

See also: *aþal*, *slokifrilluson*

aþalköp (OSw) noun

unconditional sale or purchase **OSw** *UL* Jb

See also: *aþal*

aþalman (OSw) noun

husband **OSw** *HL* Äb

lawful spouse **OSw** *UL* Äb, *VmL* Äb

See also: *aþal*, *bonde*, *husbonde*

á (ON) noun

stream **ONorw** *GuL* Løb, Llb, Mhb

Expressions:

mið á (ON)

middle of the stream **ONorw** *GuL* Llb

See also: *vatn*

áauki (ON) noun

profit **OIce** *KRA* 35

áberi (ON) noun

plaintiff **OIce** *Jó* Llb 27

See also: *sakaráberi*

ábúð (ON) noun

actual possession **ONorw** *GuL* Olb

householding period **OIce** *Grg* Tíg 266

tenancy **OIce** *Jó* Llb 14, **ONorw** *FrL* LlbA 1

tenancy agreement **OIce** *Jó* Llb 28

ábyrgð (ON) noun

responsibility **OIce** *Grg* Þsþ 76, *Jó* passim, *Js* Mah 8 Kab 5 Þjb 2, *KRA* 11, **ONorw** *BorgL* 3, *EidsL* 11.5 36.4, *FrL* KrbA 12 KrbB 24 Mhb 12, 32, *GuL* Kpb, Løb, Arb

áfall (ON) noun

sentence **OIce** *Grg* Þsþ 41

áfang (ON) noun

A fine for the illegal use of another's property. Often incurred for misusing a means of transport (horse, ship) belonging to someone else.

fine **OIce** *Jó* Þjb 17 Fml 28

illegal use of another man's property **ONorw** *FrL* Rgb 43 LlbA 10

seizure mulct **OIce** *Grg* Feþ 164, 165

Refs: Fritzner; Lúðvík Ingvarsson 1970, 272–73; ONP

áhöfn (ON) noun

cargo **OIce** *Jó* Fml 1

ákvæðisverk (ON) noun

piecework **OIce** *Jó* Kab 25, *Js* Kab 19

álburðr (ON) noun

Measuring of land, if requested, could not be denied. Such measuring might often (but not exclusively) be made with a rope (*ál*, usually of leather).

measuring of land with a rope **ONorw** *GuL* Llb

See also: *augnaskot*

Refs: KLNM s.v.v. *rebning, reip*

áljótseyrir (ON) noun

fine for serious bodily injury **ONorw** *FrL* Mhb 45

áljótsráð (ON) noun

Conspiring to commit a serious bodily injury (*áljótr*). The term seems to appear exclusively in Grg, which devotes an entire chapter to the subject (Vís 108). Plots to disfigure included ambushes and traps, and they carried a penalty of lesser outlawry even when unsuccessful.

plot to disfigure **OIce** *Grg* Vís 108

See also: *lyti, ráþ*

Refs: ONP

álykð (ON) noun

A final judgment made at an assembly. These decisions were reported at subsequent assemblies.

decision **OIce** *Js* Þfb 5

Refs: CV s.v. *álykt*; Fritzner s.v. *álykt*; ONP s.v. *álykð*

ámálga (ON) verb

make a claim **OIce** *Jó* Llb 20

ánauð (ON) noun

slavery **OIce** *Grg* Rsþ 229

ánauðga (ON) verb

enslave **OIce** *Jó* HT 2

árborinn (ON) adj.

freeborn **OIce** *Jó* Mah 2, **ONorw** *FrL* Mhb 45 ArbB 10 LlbA 15 LlbB 10

ármaðr (ON) noun

The *ármaðr* (pl. *ármenn*) originally designated a king's steward or bailiff who managed royal estates in Norway and those of *jarls* in the Orkneys. *Ármenn* were expected to house the king and bishop during their journeys and were in charge of almost the entire local administration. Over time he assumed functions as the king's local representative, endowed with the power to act on behalf of the king in administrative and judicial affairs. In these latter functions he was also called *erendreki* (see *ørendreki*) in GuL, though this may refer to a separate official in FrL (LlbB 7). There may also have been some overlap in the duties of an *ármaðr* and those of the *umboðsmaðr* (see *umbuþsman*) or *lénsmaðr* (see *lænsmaþer*). Bishops and provosts later had *ármenn* to operate on their behalf. In FrostL (11.2) one of the tasks of a bishop's *ármaðr* was the recovery of fines owed to the bishop. *Ármenn* of the king may have collected taxes and other revenues on his behalf as well. Another responsibility assigned to the *ármaðr* was the construction of buildings for the king, a duty which may previously have been performed by local farmers. There may have been one *ármaðr* for each *fylki* (q.v.) in Norway. According to FrL (Þfb 2), one of the duties of an *ármaðr* from each *fylki* was to enclose the Law Council (*lögrétta*) (q.v.) with boundary ropes (*vébönd*) (q.v.) during assemblies. According to GuL (ch. 311), the *ármaðr*, along with men given land by the king (*lendir menn*) (see *lænder*) was responsible for sending around a summons to assemble for war. According to GuL (ch. 37), *ármenn* were not permitted to attend judgments at an assembly, though they could be represented by delegates (*nefndarmenn*) (see *næmdarmaþer*). An *ármaðr* was generally someone of lower birth and was brought into the service of the king, similar to the *bryti* (q.v.) or *lænsmaþer* (q.v.) in the Old Swedish laws. It has been suggested that *ármenn* were slaves, though this is a matter of some debate, as there is little evidence available. Regardless they, along with the *lendir menn*, were often in conflict with local nobility whose interests rivaled those of the king or bishop. During the fourteenth and fifteenth centuries *ármenn* were gradually replaced by the more esteemed and higher-ranked sheriffs (*sýslumenn*) (see *syslyman*) and by deans (*provaster*) (q.v.) for church business. The position had vanished entirely by the sixteenth century.

king's official **ONorw** *FrL* KrbA 29 Mhb 10, 22

king's representative **ONorw** *FrL* Intr 12, 19 Mhb 22 Var 13 Rgb 3 LlbB 7 Bvb 5 Reb 1

official **ONorw** *FrL* KrbA 46

representative **ONorw** *EidsL* 30.5 32.6, *FrL* KrbA 1, 2, *GuL* Krb, Kpb, Løb, Llb, Tfb, Mhb, Olb, Leb

steward **OIce** *KRA* 36, 39, **ONorw** *FrL* KrbB 3 Leb 2

See also: *ari, bryti, lænsmaþer, næmdarmaþer, provaster, sysluman, umbuþsman, ørendreki*

Refs: Bagge 1991; Bagge 2010; Bolton 2009; Brink 2008a; Brink 2010b; CV; F; Helle 2001; KLNM, s.v.v. *bryde, embedsindtægter, lendmann, lensmann, official, sysselmann, tomte, årmann*; Krag 2008; LexMA s.v.v. *Bauer, Bauerntum*; NGL V s.v. *ármaðr*; ONP; Orning 2008; Strauch 2012 s. v. *Ármaðr*

ármannsréttr (ON) noun

right of the king's representative **ONorw** *GuL* Mhb

ármenning (ON) noun

office **ONorw** *FrL* Mhb 57

árofi (ON) noun

   redemption witness **ONorw** *GuL* Olb

áta (ON) noun

   shoal of herring **ONorw** *GuL* Kvr

átan (ON) noun

   eatables **ONorw** *GuL* Krb

   See also: *óátun*

átt (ON) noun

   family **OIce** *Grg* Ómb 128

   kindred **OIce** *Grg* Vís 102

áttandi dagr jóla (ON) átti dagr jóla (ON) noun

   Eighth Day of Christmas **ONorw** *GuL* Krb

áttarmót (ON) noun

   family link **OIce** *Grg* Feþ 147

áttungskirkja (ON) noun

   eighth church **ONorw** *GuL* Krb

átuþýfi (ON) noun

   theft of food **OIce** *Grg* Rsþ 228

átölulauss (ON) adj.

   without dispute **OIce** *Jó* Llb 26

ávaxtalauss (ON) adj.

   without interest **OIce** *Grg* Arþ
118 Ómb 129, *Jó* Kge 27

ávaxtartíund (ON) noun

   crop tithe **ONorw** *BorgL* 11.1

áverkabót (ON) noun

   compensation for damage **OIce** *Jó* Llb 18

   See also: *bot*

áverkadrep (ON) noun

   blow classed among injuries **OIce** *Grg* Vís 86

áþyngð (ON) noun

   burden **OIce** *Js* Kdb 2

bainheil (OGu) adj.

   whole in bone **OGu** *GL* Add. 8 (B 55)

   See also: *brustheil*

bait (OGu) noun

   pasture **OGu** *GL* A 35

   See also: *haghi*

bakarf (OSw) bak arver (OSw) noun

   ascendant inheritance **OSw** *UL* Äb

   inheritance from descendants **OSw** *DL* Gb

   reversionary inheritance **OSw** *HL* Äb, *YVgL* Äb

bakhærbærghi (OSw) noun

   bake-house **OSw** *YVgL* Kkb

bakkastokkar (pl.) (ON) noun

   building berth **ONorw** *GuL* Mhb, Leb

bakmæli (ON) noun

   Back-speech, backbiting, slander. Described in Grg Misc 237 as a situation where two men slander each other with no witnesses and subsequently one of them boasts of this. The penalty for backbiting was lesser outlawry.

   backbiting **OIce** *Grg* Misc 237

   See also: *fjölmæli*, *níð*, *rógja*

   Refs: CV; ONP

bakvaþi (OSw) noun

   accidental killing through a backwards blow **OSw** *UL* Mb, *VmL* Mb

bal (OSw) noun

   pyre **OSw** *HL* Blb

   stake **OSw** *SdmL* Mb

balker (OSw) noun

   Most significantly used of a part of a law relating to a specific subject, often subdivided into chapters (cf. *flokker*). Mostly, and in ON only, appearing in compounds (cf. ON *-bölkr*, OSw *-balker*).

   book **OSw** *HL* För

   section **OSw** *UL* Blb, *VmL* Bb

   section of a fence **OSw** *YVgL* Kkb, Utgb, *ÄVgL* Kkb

   {balker} **OSw** *HL* Blb

ban (OSw) ban (ODan) bann (OGu) bann (ON) bann (OSw) noun

   ban **ODan** *SkL* 121

   excommunication **ODan** *SkKL* 6, 7, 11, **OGu** *GL* A 7–9, **OIce** *KRA* 6, 31, **ONorw** *GuL* Krb, **OSw** *DL* Kkb, *SdmL* Kkb, *UL* Kkb, *VmL* Kkb, *YVgL* Add, *ÖgL* Kkb

   prohibition **ONorw** *FrL* Leb 1, *GuL* Leb

   See also: *bansatter*, *forbuþ*

banaman (OSw) noun

   slayer **OSw** *SdmL* Mb, Tjdb

   See also: *bani*, *haldbani*, *raþsbani*

banaorþ (OSw) banorþ (OSw) noun

   case of killing **OSw** *YVgL* Drb

   crime **OSw** *YVgL* Drb, *ÄVgL* Md

   homicide **OSw** *ÄVgL* Md

   killing **OSw** *YVgL* Drb, *ÄVgL* Md

   murderer **OSw** *DL* Mb

   See also: *bani*

banaráð (ON) noun

   advice leading to death **OIce** *Jó* Mah 11

banasak (OSw) banesak (ODan) noun

   accusation of homicide **OSw** *ÄVgL* Slb

   accusation of killing **OSw** *YVgL* Frb

case of killing **ODan** *SkL* 118, 119, 121

homicide case **ODan** *JyL* 2

See also: *bani*

banavapn (OSw) noun

   killing-weapon **OSw** *SdmL* Mb

See also: *bani*, *vapn*

band (OSw) band (ODan) band (OGu) noun

Appears in legally significant phrases such as ODan *band ok stok* 'ropes and iron' and *bast ok band* 'ropes and bonds' of lawful or unlawful detention, and OSw YVgL Add *binda fullum bandum* 'bind someone with full ropes' of violent abduction in breach of the king's peace.

binding **ODan** *JyL* 2

binding relationship **OSw** *UL* Kkb, *VmL* Kkb

bond **OSw** *UL* Mb, *VmL* Mb

bonds **ODan** *ESjL* 3

captive **OSw** *HL* Mb

leash **OGu** *GL* A 19

pair **OGu** *GL* A 65

rope **ODan** *SkL* 136, 163

strap **ODan** *VSjL* 87

Expressions:

band hail (OGu)

   having unbroken ties **OGu** *GL* A 26

band ok stok (ODan)

   ropes and iron **ODan** *SkL* 138

bast ok band (ODan)

   bonds and ropes **ODan** *JyL* 2 *SkL* 144

   tied and bound **ODan** *SkL* 112

binda fullum bandum (OSw)

   bind someone with full ropes **OSw** *YVgL* Add

See also: *basta*, *binda*, *valdføra*

banda (OGu) noun

The literal meaning seems to be one of an enclosure (see *vebönd*). In GL, however, it was a defined area of protection (*griþ*, q.v.): the 'circle of peace' or 'security circle' that a killer could draw to shield himself from revenge. The killer had to go and stay in the rectory or churchyard of one of the three asylum churches (at Fardhem, Tingstäde or Atlingbo) for forty days, together with his closest male relatives (father, son and brother). These would presumably have also been under suspicion. They would have been protected from attack by the imposition of a wergild (*vereldi*) (see *værgæld*) of forty marks in coin (ten marks of silver), just under half a full wergild. The killer was then to draw up a circle in which he was immune from revenge attacks, encompassing three farms, with the permission of the owners, and a church. This temporary circle (*vatubanda*, q.v.) was converted to a permanent one during the general period of peace and security next after Easter. During the following year, others were to negotiate compensation with the wronged family, making the offer annually over three years. If not accepted, the offer was placed with the assembly and the accused was free to go, with full wergild now payable for his life. If no offer was made, or the killer left his circle (other than to go on pilgrimage), he was outlawed, unless he paid full wergild (twenty-four marks in silver) and an extra twelve marks in silver. A Gotlander killed in his circle was compensated with half a wergild (twelve marks in silver). The exact provisions in GL seem to be unique in Scandinavian laws, but the later town law of Visby shows similarities in respect of asylum, which may be the result either of direct influence or of a common concept and there are similar provisions in Grg, in particular for outlaws attempting to leave the country. Despite being outlaws, they had asylum at certain homesteads, roads and docks. On roads it is prescribed that, when passing other parties, they are to move off the road 'to such a distance that they could not be hit by the point of a spear'. A parallel, although not necessarily a precursor, is to be found in the Mosaic laws as exhibited in the Pentateuch (Exodus 21 v. 13; Num. 35 vv. 6–8, 11–15; Deut. 4 vv. 41–43, 19 vv. 2–4) and it was thus a very old concept, which seems to have been retained as a relic in GL. For example, the Oklunda inscription in Östergötland, dated to the ninth or tenth century, indicates that a particular killer sought refuge in a holy place (*vi*, q.v.) prior to making a settlement over the killing. In ÖgL there is a reference to a killer being protected from attack by the killer's relatives in a churchyard and as early as ÄVgL killing in a church is recorded as a despicable crime, so the protection offered by holy places seems to have been a continuum.

The *bandavereldi* (q.v.) was the particular man price payable for killing someone within their circle of peace.

peace circle **OGu** *GL* A 9, 13, 14

See also: *fjörbaugsgarðr*, *griþ*, *vatubanda*, *vébönd* (pl.), *værgæld*

Refs: Hasselberg 1953, 277; KLNM s.v. *drab*; Olsen 1966, 64–65; Peel 2015, 111–13 notes to 13/7–13/23–24; Ruthström 1988, 64–75; Schlyter 1877, s.v. *banda*; SL GL, 254–58; Wennström 1946, 188

bandavereldi (OGu) banduvereldi (OGu) noun

   wergild within the peace circle **OGu** *GL* A 16

See also: *banda*, *værgæld*

bandhail (OGu) adj.
   fully tied **OGu** *GL* A 26
bandi (OGu) noun
   band (of withy) **OGu** *GL* A 26
banesar (ODan) **banasár** (ON) noun
   death wound **OIce** *Grg* Vís 107
   mortal wound **OIce** *Jó* Llb 58, *KRA* 26
   wound **ODan** *SkL* 119
   See also: *bani, sar*
bani (OSw) **bane** (ODan) **bani** (OGu) **bani** (ON) noun
   assassin **OSw** *HL* Mb
   cause of death **ODan** *JyL* 2, **ONorw** *EidsL* 26.1
   death **OGu** *GL* A 14, 17, 18, **ONorw**
   GuL Krb, Llb, Mhb, **OSw** *DL* Mb, *HL*
   Mb, *UL* Mb, *VmL* Mb, *YVgL* Urb
   execution **ONorw** *GuL* Mhb
   executioner **ONorw** *GuL* Mhb, Tjb
   homicide **OSw** *YVgL* Add
   being killed **ODan** *JyL* 2, **OSw** *YVgL*
   Kkb, Rlb, Add, *ÄVgL* Kkb, Md, Rlb
   killer **ODan** *JyL* 2, *SkL* 121, **OGu** *GL* A 16, **OIce**
   Jó Mah 9, *Js* Mah 19, **ONorw** *FrL* Mhb 5, 7, *GuL*
   Mhb, **OSw** *DL* Mb, Bb, *HL* Mb, *SdmL* Mb, *UL*
   Mb, *VmL* Mb, *YVgL* Drb, *ÄVgL* Md, Slb, *ÖgL* Db
   killing **OGu** *GL* A 14, **OSw** *UL* Mb
   lethal wound **OSw** *YVgL* Drb, *ÄVgL* Md
   slayer **OSw** *YVgL* Frb
   Expressions:
   fa bana af (OSw)
   be killed **OSw** *YVgL* Kkb, Drb, Rlb, Add
   See also: *drap, drapari, mansbani*
banliusa (OSw) verb
   excommunicate **OSw** *DL* Kkb, *SdmL* Kkb
   See also: *ban, lysa*
banna (ON) verb
   ban **OIce** *Grg* Þsþ 52 Feþ 151, *Js* Mah 19 Lbb 4
   deny **ONorw** *GuL* Llb
   forbid **OIce** *Jó* Llb 56
bannfóra (ON) verb
   excommunicate **OIce** *KRA* 18
bannsetning (ON) noun
   excommunication **OIce** *KRA* 9, **ONorw** *FrL* KrbB 21
bansatter (OSw) **bansat** (ODan) **bansætter** (OSw) adj.
   excommunicated **ODan** *SkKL* 11,
   OSw *SmL, UL* Kkb, *VmL* Kkb
   See also: *ban, bansætia, banzmal*
banslætter (OSw) noun
   absolution **OSw** *SmL*
   See also: *ban*

bansætia (OSw) **bannsetja** (ON) verb
   excommunicate **OIce** *KRA* 5, 11, **ONorw**
   FrL KrbB 21, **OSw** *HL* Kkb, *SmL*
   sentence to greater excommunication **OSw** *HL* Kkb
   See also: *ban*
banzmal (OSw) **banzmall** (OGu) noun
   This word is used in the provincial laws of Sweden
   and Gotland to refer to a crime subject to full
   excommunication (*ban*) (q.v.) from the Christian
   community, sometimes for a specific period, until
   sufficient penance had been done, or the prescribed fine
   paid. It also refers to the procedure of pronouncing the
   excommunication, for which the rural dean or bishop
   was paid an amount by the excommunicate varying
   between the laws. While the person was under this ban,
   their very presence in the church during Mass could
   force the immediate abandonment of the proceedings.
   Simply being in the company of an excommunicate
   could also render one liable for punishment. The
   crimes that resulted in such exclusion were those that
   were aggravated by being committed on a holy day
   or on church premises, particularly killings or actions
   against a cleric. Such crimes were considered to have
   harmed the Church body itself. In DL the punishment
   is served in particular on men who committed
   bestiality and women who practised witchcraft. In GL
   excommunication was the punishment for Sabbath
   breaking. The word *banzmal* occurs in VmL, but in a
   passage that differs between the various manuscripts
   and is the subject of a number of later emendations in
   the main manuscript. It seems in this instance to be an
   error for a word meaning 'spiritual case', one relating
   to moral laxity, where the punishment was usually a
   fine rather than excommunication.
   case of ban **OSw** *YVgL* Urb
   case of excommunication **OSw** *YVgL* Kkb, *ÖgL* Kkb
   excommunication **OSw** *DL* Kkb
   excommunication case **OSw** *DL* Kkb,
   HL Kkb, *SdmL* Kkb, *UL* Kkb
   pronouncing excommunication
   OGu *GL* A 8, **OSw** *UL* Kkb
   See also: *ban, banliusa, banna, bannfóra,*
   bannsetning, bansatter, banslætter,
   bansætia, forbuþ, páfabann

Refs: KLNM s.v.v. *excommunicatio og interdict,*
kommunion, kyrkobalkar, kyrkostraff, sacrilegium;
Lexikon des Mittelalters s.v. *bannum;* Peel 2015, 104
note 8/17–19; Schlyter 1877, s.v. *banzmal;* SL DL, 20
notes 76 and 77; SL GL, 252 notes 8 and 9 to chapter
8; SL UL, 39 note 54, 40 notes 67 and 68, 41 note 83;
SL VmL, 29 notes 76 and 77; SL ÖgL, 30 note 65

bardaghaböter (OSw) noun

   compensation of blows **OSw** *YVgL* Äb, *ÄVgL* Äb

   See also: *bardaghi*, *bot*

bardaghi (OSw) **bardaghe** (ODan) **bardagi** (ON) noun

   assault **ODan** *ESjL* 3

   beat **OSw** *YVgL* Add

   beating **ODan** *ESjL* 2, *VSjL* 43, **OIce** *Grg* Vís 111

   blow **ODan** *ESjL* 2, **OSw** *DL* Mb, *ÄVgL* Slb

   bruise **ODan** *ESjL* 2

   fight **ODan** *VSjL* 47, **ONorw** *GuL* Mhb, **OSw** *DL* Mb, Gb, *SdmL* Gb

   fighting **OSw** *SdmL* Kmb, Mb, *ÄVgL* Slb, *ÖgL* Kkb

   injury **ODan** *SkL* 96, 111, 114, 122, *VSjL* 48

   staff-blow **ODan** *JyL* 3, *SkKL* 7, *VSjL* 41, 42, 63, 86

   violence **ONorw** *BorgL* 18

   Expressions:

   slagh ok bardaghi (OSw)

   blows and battle **OSw** *UL* Kmb

   See also: *barsmið*, *bæria*, *lysta (1)*

barð (ON) noun

   stem (1) **ONorw** *GuL* Llb, Tfb

barka (OSw) verb

   strip bark from trees **OSw** *UL* Blb, *VmL* Bb

   Expressions:

   barka ok blika (OSw)

   carve marks in the barks of trees **OSw** *UL* Blb

barlike (ODan) adv.

   openly **ODan** *ESjL* 2

   See also: *openbarlika*

barliþ (OSw) noun

   open passage **OSw** *SdmL* Bb

   unprotected opening **OSw** *UL* Kkb, Blb

   See also: *liþ (1)*

barn (OSw) **barn** (ODan) **barn** (ON) noun

   child **ONorw** *GuL* Krb, Kvb, Løb, Arb, Tfb, Mhb, Olb, Leb

   childbirth **ODan** *JyL* 2, **OSw** *HL* Kkb, *ÄVgL* Gb

barnagoþs (OSw) noun

   children's property **OSw** *HL* Äb, *UL* Äb, Jb, *VmL* Äb, Jb

   children's inheritance **OSw** *HL* Äb

barnamorþ (OSw) noun

   infanticide **OSw** *UL* Rb, *VmL* Rb

barnbærr (ON) adj.

   capable of bearing children **ONorw** *GuL* Mhb

barnfar (OGu) noun

   labour **OGu** *GL* A 2

   See also: *barnsot*

barnfóstr (ON) noun

   fostering a child **OIce** *Grg* Ómb 141, *Jó* Mah 30

barnfóstri (ON) noun

   foster-father **ONorw** *FrL* Rgb 14

barnfóstrlaun (ON) **barnfóstrslaun** (ON) noun

   payment or reward for fostering children **ONorw** *GuL* Arb, Olb

barnfulga (ON) noun

   payment for maintenance of a child **ONorw** *GuL* Løb

barnlauss (ON) adj.

   childless **ONorw** *GuL* Kvb, Sab

barnmynd (ODan) noun

   The right of a husband to dispose over, though not sell, his wife's ancestral lands and movables brought to the household; and to inherit a lot in her property at her death, if they had mutual, legitimate children.

   entitlement by the birth of a child **ODan** *ESjL* 3, *SkL* 7, 8, 29, *VSjL* 1

   lot in property through the birth of a child **ODan** *ESjL* 1

   Refs: Tamm and Vogt, eds, 2016, 303

barnskírn (ON) noun

   baptism of a child **OIce** *Grg* Tíg 261, *KRA* 1

barnsot (OSw) noun

   childbirth **OSw** *UL* Äb, Mb, *VmL* Äb, Mb

barsmíð (ON) noun

   beating **OIce** *Grg* Hrs 235

   fight **ONorw** *GuL* Mhb

   See also: *bardaghi*, *dela*, *vingretta*

bartholomeusmessa (ON) noun

   St Bartholomew's Day (24 August) **OIce** *Grg* Klþ 13

   St Bartholomew's Mass (24 August) **ONorw** *GuL* Krb

barún (ON) noun

   baron **OIce** *Jó* Llb 18

bas (OSw) noun

   box trap **OSw** *HL* Blb

   byre **OSw** *VmL* Mb

bast (ON) noun

   bast **ONorw** *GuL* Kvr

   Expressions:

   bast ok band (ODan)

   bonds and ropes **ODan** *SkL* 144

   rope and bonds **ODan** *JyL* 2

   tied and bound **ODan** *SkL* 112

   See also: *band*, *basta*, *binda*

basta (OSw) verb

Expressions:

basta ok binda, basta ok i band föra, basta æller binda, binda ok basta (OSw)

accuse **OSw** *HL* Mb

bind **OSw** *YVgL* Tb

bind (and put) in bonds **OSw** *UL* Kkb, Mb, Blb *VmL* Mb, Bb

fetter and imprison **OSw** *HL* Kgb

fetter or bind **OSw** *HL* Kgb

put in fetters and bonds **OSw** *HL* Mb

tether or tie up **OSw** *DL* Eb; *UL* Kgb *VmL* Kgb

tie and violate **OSw** *HL* Blb

tie up and bind **OSw** *SdmL* Kgb, Mb, Tjdb

See also: *band, bast, binda*

bataleþ (OSw) **batæ leþ** (OSw) noun

shipping lane **OSw** *SdmL* Bb, *UL* Blb, *VmL* Bb

bater (OSw) **batr** (OGu) noun

boat **OGu** *GL* A 36, **OSw** *SdmL* Bb, *UL* Äb, Blb, *VmL* Äb, Mb, *ÄVgL* Fös

See also: *byrthing, farkoster, floti, kaupskip, myndrikkia, skip*

batsfarmber (OSw) **baz farm** (OSw) noun

boatload **OSw** *UL* Blb, *VmL* Bb

baugamaðr (ON) **baugamenn** (ON) noun

man who shares the ring payment **ONorw** *GuL* Mhb

ring-man **ONorw** *FrL* Sab 2

baugatal (ON) noun

The 'ring list' of wergild payments found in Grg *Baugatal* gives detailed instructions concerning the proportion of homicide payments each group of family members should pay or receive.

wergild ring list **OIce** *Grg* Þsþ 80 Bat 113

See also: *bauggildi, bogher, manbot, nefgildi, vígslóði*

Refs: Clover 1986; CV s.v. *baugr*; Fritzner; KLNM s.v. *straff*; ONP

baugband (OGu) noun

A strap or rope fastened around the wrist (*baugliþer*) (see *baugliþr*) of a captured felon, in particular a slave accused of theft. It could have been simply a type of restraining handcuff, or else a form of minor torture. This latter theory is supported partly by the fact that torture is specifically mentioned just previously in the text, and partly by the fact that the accuser who applied the *baugband* had to pay compensation if there was no material evidence to implicate the slave upon whom they were inflicted, whether he was found to be innocent or confessed. The word occurs only in the B-text of GL, the synonym *ærmaband* (q.v.) being used elsewhere in the mainland Swedish laws.

wristband **OGu** *GL* Add. 8 (B 55)

See also: *basta, binda, ærmaband*

Refs: Peel 2015, 198–99 note to Addition 8/18; Schlyter 1877, s.v. *baugband*; SL GL, 284 note 10

baugbót (ON) noun

ring-atonement **OIce** *Grg* Bat 113

See also: *bot*

baugbótandi (ON) noun

payer of the ring **OIce** *Grg* Bat 113

bauggildi (ON) noun

compensation to be paid or received by kinsfolk on the father's side **ONorw** *GuL* Olb

father's side **ONorw** *FrL* ArbB 8, *GuL* Olb

ring payment **OIce** *Grg* Bat 113, **ONorw** *FrL* Sab 11 ArbA 8

See also: *nefgildi*

bauggildismaðr (ON) noun

Means 'agnate', a near kinsman on the father's side and in the male line. The agnatic kinsman received and paid the larger payments in the *manbot* (q.v.). The circle of agnatic kinsmen included relatives up to and including first cousins.

agnate **OIce** *Js* Mah 13, 34 Kab 2

agnate kinsman **ONorw** *FrL* Mhb 7, 9 ArbB 20

agnate who has to pay or receive {bauggildi} **ONorw** *GuL* Kpb, Løb, Tfb, Mhb, Olb

kinsman on the father's side **ONorw** *FrL* Var 9 ArbB 1 Kvb 9 Jkb 4

See also: *bogher, höfuðbarmr, höfuðbarmsmaðr, karlsvift, lindagyrt, nefgildismaðr*

Refs: KLNM s.v.v. *böter, mansbot, straff, værge I*; RGA2 s.v. *ringgeld*; Robberstad 1981, 343

baugliþr (OGu) noun

wrist **OGu** *GL* A 23

See also: *baugband*

baugrýgr (ON) **baugrygr** (ON) noun

A 'ring-woman'. An only daughter or sister, unmarried, who accepted and paid compensation in the absence of male relatives. According to GuL a *baugrýgr* was also entitled to inherit allodial land.

ring-lady **OIce** *Grg* Bat 113, **ONorw** *FrL* Sab 4

sole heiress **ONorw** *GuL* Olb

Refs: CV s.v. *baugrygr*; F; KLNM s.v. *odelsrett*

baugshelgi (ON) noun

A ring (*bauger*) (see *bogher*) was a fine to the king if a slave was insulted when accompanying his master to public places.

protection of a ring **ONorw** *GuL* Mhb

Refs: Hertzberg, s.v. *baugshelgi*

baugsskapþótandi (ON) noun

proper ring payer **OIce** *Grg* Bat 113

baugþak (ON) noun

supplement **OIce** *Grg* Bat 113

baugþiggjandi (ON) noun

receiver of the ring **OIce** *Grg* Bat 113

baþstova (OSw) bastugha (OSw) bastuva (OSw) bazstuwa (OSw) noun

bath house **OSw** *HL* Mb, *SdmL* Mb, *UL* Mb

beiðask (ON) verb

claim **ONorw** *GuL* Tfb, Sab

See also: *biþia*

beingjald (ON) noun

bone payment **ONorw** *FrL* Mhb 49

beini (ON) noun

help **OIce** *Grg* Klþ 1

hospitality **OIce** *KRA* 1

See also: *liþ (2)*

beita (ON) verb

graze **ONorw** *GuL* Llb

beitarmaðr (ON) noun

man who owns grazing **OIce** *Jó* Llb 23

beititeigr (ON) noun

grazing plot **OIce** *Grg* Lbþ 194, *Jó* Llb 22

See also: *tegher*

ben (1) (ODan) bein (ON) noun

bone **ODan** *SkL* 117, **ONorw** *GuL* Kvr, Mhb

Expressions:

bain heil (OGu)

whole in bone **OGu** *GL* Add 8 (B 55)

See also: *brustheil*

benbæria (OSw) verb

crush someone's legs **OSw** *YVgL* Urb

benedictusmessa (ON) noun

St Benedict's Day (21 March) **OIce** *Grg* Klþ 13

benhog (ODan) noun

kick with a leg **ODan** *SkL* 98

kicking with a leg **ODan** *JyL* 3

strike with bone **ODan** *ESjL* 2

benjaváttr (ON) noun

mortal-wound witness **OIce** *Grg* Vís 87

benlösning (OSw) noun

bone extraction **OSw** *UL* Mb

taking of bones (out of a wound) **OSw** *DL* Mb

berendi (ON) noun

female animal **ONorw** *GuL* Mhb

berg (ON) noun

cliff **ONorw** *GuL* Krb, Kpb, Mhb

betrfeðrungr (ON) betrfeðringr (ON) noun

man better than his father **ONorw** *FrL* Rgb 47

beþroyta (OGu) bedroyta (OGu) noun

bed-wetting **OGu** *GL* Add. 7 (B 49)

bi (OSw) bi (ODan) noun

Bees appear as an important, and seemingly often disputed, resource, sometimes natural and sometimes privately owned. Regulations include determining who had the right to bees found in woodland or in other places, how properly to announce such finds, what to do with swarming and potentially aggressive bees, and how to protect bees and domestic animals from each other. Particularly detailed regulations are found in ODan SkL.

bee **ODan** *ESjL* 3, *JyL* 3, *SkL* 196–201, **OSw** *SdmL* Bb, *YVgL* Utgb

Refs: Miller and Vogt, 2015, 55–56

bigarth (ODan) noun

bee garden **ODan** *JyL* 3

biltugher (OSw) biltogher (OSw) byltugher (OSw) adj.

This adjective is used to describe someone who was outlawed on what was effectively a temporary basis, with the prospect of returning under the rule of law if fines or compensation were paid in time, and the king had granted him his peace. The fine payable to the king was usually 40 *marker* in addition to the compensation payable to the victim and the confiscation of property. The crimes for which this punishment was prescribed were those that fell under the category of *eþsöris brut* 'crimes against the King's Peace' such as attacks in the home, and it was in connection with this law that the term first came into use in its legal sense. According to the relevant laws of Sveland and Götaland, the person concerned had to leave the realm until he had discharged his outlawry. It is possible that this was not initially a requirement, although by the time of the national laws, this was clearly the case. The fact that exile was not always essential is exhibited in the fact that an outlaw was seemingly permitted to attend church services (as opposed to excommunicates, whose presence would force the priest to abort the Mass) and could not be dragged out of the church (VmL, UL). There were penalties for sheltering such a person beyond a month after he has been declared outlawed. In this particular statute in VmL and UL it seems that the outlawed person was expected to leave the kingdom, although the text is ambiguous and it might simply mean that he was to leave the province, which perhaps reflects two different forms of outlawry. This latter interpretation is supported by statutes relating to inheritance in which it refers to a child born to an outlawed man who has fled the province (*land* (q.v.) rather than *riki* (q.v.)) with his wife, whether that child was conceived before or after he had fled. Only if his child were born in the province could it inherit, and then only if it were conceived either before he was outlawed, or outside the province during his outlawry. An outlawed man could not claim an inheritance himself, even after discharging his outlawry. If he killed someone while outlawed, he was to pay the appropriate compensation after his outlawry had been discharged. According to Schlyter, the punishment was not initially for a fixed term, although this has at times been assumed. It is worth noting that both UL and VmL state that no woman or minor might be outlawed (literally 'forced to flee from the King's Peace'), although the word *biltugher* is not used in this instance. Schlyter considers a derivation from a presumed OSw verb *bila*, 'to lack' (found independently in ON in the meanings 'fail, break, give way') with the ending *-ugher*, but cannot himself find a link. It seems, however, that the person concerned is 'wanting the King's Peace', or the rule of law, so such a derivation is not unreasonable. It could also be related to a noun *bil*, 'a short time', also found in ON. SAOB, however, considers all attempts at an etymology unsatisfactory.

outlaw **OSw** *YVgL* Drb

outlawed **OSw** *DL* Eb, *HL* Kgb, Äb, *SdmL* Kgb, Äb, Mb, *SmL*, *UL* Kkb, Kgb, Äb, Mb, Jb, Add. 3, *VmL* Kkb, Kgb, Äb, Mb, Jb, *YVgL* Add, *ÖgL* Eb

See also: *eþsöre*, *flya*, *friþlös*

Refs: Ekholst 2009; KLNM s.v. *fredlöshed*; Lexikon des Mittelalters s.v. *bannum*; SAOB s.v. *biltog*; Schlyter 1877, s.v. *biltugher*

binda (OSw) **binde** (ODan) **binda** (ON) verb

Literally 'to bind, to tie'. In legal contexts most significantly bringing certain criminals — particularly thieves — to justice, physically restrained during the transportation to, or while waiting for, the *þing*

'assembly'. On the other hand, illegally apprehending or physically restraining an innocent free person was severely punished. Most often appears as *baste ok binde* (ODan), *basta ok binda* (OSw), but also *binda a bak* (OSw), (see below), which might be interpreted as tying the hands, or possibly the stolen goods, to the back of the thief. Occasionally, there is a more abstract legal interpretation of tying something to someone, often in the phrase *binda a* (OSw), literally 'tie to', which might be translated as 'to claim', 'to refer', 'to substantiate' or 'to attribute' for instance a crime to a person.

bind **ODan** *ESjL* 3, *JyL* 2, *SkL* 136, 151, 159, 184, *VSjL* 59, 60, **ONorw** *GuL* Llb,Tjb, Olb
confirm **OSw** *HL* Jb
contract **OSw** *VmL* Kkb
fetter **OSw** *HL* Mb
link **OSw** *HL* Mb
prove **OGu** *GL* A 18
tie up **ODan** *VSjL* 59, 86, 87, **OSw** *SdmL* Bb
Expressions:
basta ok binda, basta ok i band föra, basta æller binda, binda ok basta (OSw)
accuse **OSw** *HL* Mb
bind **OSw** *YVgL* Tb
bind (and put) in bonds **OSw** *UL* Kkb, Mb, Blb *VmL* Mb, Bb
fetter and imprison **OSw** *HL* Kgb
fetter or bind **OSw** *HL* Kgb
put in fetters and bonds **OSw** *HL* Mb
tether or tie up **OSw** *DL* Eb *UL* Kgb *VmL* Kgb
tie and violate **OSw** *HL* Blb
tie up and bind **OSw** *SdmL* Kgb, Mb, Tjdb
binda a (OSw)
claim **OSw** *UL* Jb *VmL* Jb
refer to **OSw** *UL* Jb *VmL* Jb
OSw *UL* Jb, Kmb, Blb *VmL* Jb, Kmb, Bb
support **OSw** *UL* Jb *VmL* Jb
binda a bak (OSw) **binde a bak** (ODan)
bind to the back **ODan** *JyL* 2
pinion **OSw** *YVgL* Drb, Tb *ÄVgL* Md, Tb
binda fullum bandum (OSw)
bind someone with full ropes **OSw** *YVgL* Add
binda æller basta æller i fiætur sætia (OSw)
accuse **OSw** *HL* Mb
See also: *band*, *bast*, *basta*, *baugband*, *vinna*
Refs: Kjus 2011; KLNM s.v.v. *frihedsberøvelse*, *fængelse*

biorn (OSw) bjorn (ODan) björn (ON) noun

Bears appear in the laws as a threat to people and domestic animals, and in some laws the hunting of bears was either an obligation or done with impunity (ONorw GuL, OSw HL, UL, VmL). In OSw ÄVgL and YVgL, bears are seen as *ofæfli* ('superior force') if they kill domestic animals in one's care, in contrast to attacks by wolves, which were occasionally seen as neglect. In ODan, predators — bears, wolves and hawks — only appear as domestic animals, for which the owner was responsible if they attacked somebody.

bear **ODan** *SkL* 104, **ONorw** *GuL* Krb, Kpb, Løb, Llb, **OSw** *HL* Blb, *YVgL* Rlb, Utgb, *ÄVgL* Rlb, Föb

See also: *ofæfli*

Refs: KLNM s.v.v. *björnejakt, jakt, vilda djur*

biskopsnævning (ODan) noun

Two men from each parish or quarter appointed for one year to deal with certain violations of the Church.

men nominated by the bishop **ODan** *JyL* 2

Refs: KLNM s.v. *nämnd*

biskuper (OSw) biskop (ODan) biskup (ON) byskup (ON) biskoper (OSw) noun

archbishop **ODan** *SkKL* Prol

bishop **ODan** *ESjL* 1, 2, *JyL* Fort, 1, 2, *SkKL* 1–3, 6, 9, 11–13, *VSjL* 5, 73, **OFar** *Seyð* 0, **OIce** *Grg* Bat 114 Lrþ 117 Arþ 118 Feþ 149 Hrs 235 Tíg 260, 261, *Jó* MagBref HT 2 Llb 18, *Js* Mah 26, *KRA* 1, 2 passim, **ONorw** *BorgL* 5.7 passim, *EidsL* 2.2 3.3 passim, *FrL* KrbA 1, 2 KrbB 1, 2 LlbA 15, *GuL* Krb, Mhb, Leb, **OSw** *DL* Kkb, Eb, Mb, Rb, *HL* Kkb, Äb, Mb, *SdmL* Conf, Kkb, Kgb, Gb, Kmb, Mb, Rb, Till, *SmL*, *YVgL* Kkb, Äb, Gb, Rlb, Jb, Add, *ÄVgL* Kkb, Äb, Gb, Rlb, Jb, *ÖgL* Kkb, Db, Vm

bishop's representative **ONorw** *GuL* Krb

Expressions:

biskups ørendreki (ON)

bishop's representative **ONorw** *GuL* Krb

biskups længsmaþer, biskups længsman, biskops længsman (OSw)

bishop's administrator **OSw** *UL* Kkb, Äb, Mb *VmL* Kkb

bishop's bailiff **OSw** *DL* Kkb, Rb

bishop's official **OSw** *HL* Kkb

biskups umbuþsman (OSw)

representative of the bishop **OSw** *YVgL* Kkb

See also: *prester, ærchibiskuper, ørendreki*

biskupsdöme (OSw) noun

bishopric **OSw** *YVgL* Kkb

diocese **OSw** *SdmL* Till

biskupsfærþ (OSw) noun

journey that is incumbent on the bishop **OSw** *HL* Kkb

biskupsgarþer (OSw) biskopsgarth (ODan) noun

bishop's farm **OSw** *SdmL* Jb

bishop's manor **ODan** *ESjL* 3

See also: *biskuper, kirkiubol, konongsgarþer, præstastuva*

biskupsmaþer (OSw) biskopsman (ODan) noun

bishop's man **ODan** *JyL* 2, **OSw** *DL* Mb, *HL* Mb

biskupsnæmd (OSw) noun

A *næmd* 'panel' dealing with adultery, offences in church or on holy days (SmL and ÖgL), sins and breaches of church penance (SmL), perjury and manslaughter not repented (ÖgL). OSw ÖgL (Kkb 16) prescribed a functional division between *hæraþsnæmd* (q.v.) (formal aspects) and *biskupsnæmd* (q.v.) (facts).

bishop's jury **OSw** *ÖgL* Kkb

bishop's panel **OSw** *SmL*

See also: *biskuper, næmd*

biskupsrætter (OSw) biskopsræt (ODan) noun

bishop's due **ODan** *ESjL* 1–3, *VSjL* 23, 73

bishop's fine **OSw** *HL* Mb, *ÖgL* Kkb

bishop's right **OSw** *SmL*, *ÖgL* Kkb

right of a bishop **OSw** *YVgL* Kkb

See also: *biskuper, konungsrætter*

biskupssak (OSw) noun

bishop's case **OSw** *ÖgL* Kkb

bishop's cause **OSw** *SmL*

case with compensation to the bishop **OSw** *YVgL* Kkb

fine to the bishop **OSw** *HL* Kkb

See also: *biskuper, sak*

bismari (OSw) noun

steelyard **OSw** *YVgL* Föb

bistokker (OSw) noun

bee-hive **OSw** *SdmL* Bb

bisvarm (ODan) noun

swarm of bees **ODan** *JyL* 3, *SkL* 196

bita (OGu) bíta (ON) verb

bite **OGu** *GL* A 17, 34, **ONorw** *GuL* Krb, Llb, Tfb

condemn **OGu** *GL* A 37

Expressions:

bita a (OSw)

be valid **OSw** *UL* Rb

bestow **OSw** *VmL* Jb

eat into **OSw** *UL* Rb

seize upon **OSw** *UL* Jb *VmL* Jb

support **OSw** *VmL* Jb

biti (ON) noun

 girder **ONorw** *GuL* Llb

biuþa (OSw) biauþa (OGu) bjóða (ON) byþa (OSw) verb

 adjure **OSw** *UL* StfBM

 announce **OSw** *DL* Kkb

 ask **ONorw** *GuL* Kpb, Llb

 authorize **ONorw** *GuL* Kpb

 bid for **OSw** *ÄVgL* Gb

 call out **OSw** *UL* Kgb, Mb, Rb, *VmL* Kgb, Mb, Rb

 declare **OGu** *GL* A 6

 demand **OSw** *UL* Blb

 enforce **OSw** *UL* Kkb, Kmb, *VmL* Kkb, Kmb

 give **ONorw** *GuL* Llb

 instigate **OSw** *UL* Kgb, *VmL* Kgb

 invite **OGu** *GL* A 24, **OSw** *UL* Kmb, Rb, *VmL* Kmb

 offer **OGu** *GL* A 13, 14, 16, 44, Add. 1 (B 4), **ONorw** *GuL* Krb, Kpb, Løb, Llb, Mhb, Tjb, Olb, Leb, **OSw** *DL* Gb, *SdmL* Jb, *UL* Kkb, Mb, Jb, Blb, Rb, *VmL* Mb, Jb, Kmb, Bb, Rb, *YVgL* Kkb, Frb, *ÄVgL* Kkb, Jb

 offer one's land **OSw** *DL* Gb

 prescribe **OSw** *YVgL* Kkb

 summon **OGu** *GS* Ch. 4, **OSw** *UL* Kgb, Rb, *VmL* Kgb, Rb

 See also: *dul, lagh, raþa*

biþia (OSw) biðja (ON) beþas (OSw) verb

 ask **OSw** *UL* Kkb, *VmL* Kkb, *ÖgL* Kkb, Eb

 ask for **OSw** *UL* Kkb, Äb, Mb, *VmL* Kkb, Äb, Mb

 demand **OSw** *UL* Äb, *VmL* Äb, Mb, Rb

 plead **OSw** *DL* Eb, *HL* Kgb, *SdmL* Kgb, *ÖgL* Eb

 summon **ONorw** *GuL* Mhb, Olb

 See also: *beiðask*

bjalki (ON) noun

 beam **ONorw** *GuL* Llb

bjargkviðr (ON) noun

 clearing verdict **OIce** *Grg* Klþ 9 Þsþ 25, 27 Víg 89, 90 Ómb 130, 137 Feþ 144

bjargleysi (ON) noun

 lack of care **OIce** *Jó* Kge 26

bjargráð (ON) noun

Advice given to assist someone in getting out of a situation. In Grg Vís 110 this refers specifically to a prohibition against assisting outlaws.

 saving advice **OIce** *Grg* Vís 110

 Refs: CV s.v. *bjargráð*; Fritzner s.v. *bjargráð*; ONP s.v. *bjargráð*

bjarkeyjarréttr (ON) noun

A general name for town or municipal laws during the Middle Ages in the North, particularly in Norway and Sweden. It has been speculated that the name likely derived from a lost set of laws from a particular Bjarkey ('birch island'), one candidate being Birka in Lake Mälaren. Two of the most cited *bjarkeyjarréttir* are the so-called 'Elder Bjarkey Law' for Trondheim/ Niðarós and the 'Younger Bjarkey Law' for Bergen and subsequently other Norwegian towns.

 Bjarkey law **OIce** *Grg* Misc 248, **ONorw** *FrL* Rgb 32

 See also: *rætter*

 Refs: CV s.v. *bjarkey-*; Fritzner; GAO s.v. *Bjarkörecht*; Hagland & Sandnes 1997:XII; Hertzberg; KLNM s.v. *bjärköarätt*; LexMA s.v. *Björkö, Ding*; ONP

bjarneggjun (ON) bjarneggjan (ON) noun

Incitation to a fight might be compared to baiting a bear. The instigator of a fight, if injured, had no right to compensation. See GuL ch. 216.

 incitation to a fight **ONorw** *GuL* Mhb

 Refs: KLNM s.v. *björnejakt*

bjarnveiðr (ON) noun

 hunting of bears **ONorw** *GuL* Llb

bjóðandi (ON) noun

 bidder **OIce** *Grg* Lbþ 193

björg (ON) noun

 assistance **OIce** *Grg* Vís 87 Feþ 161, *Jó* Mah 6, *Js* Mah 13

 means to support **OIce** *Grg* Arþ 122 Ómb 134

 provision **OIce** *Jó* Kge 23

bladragning (OGu) noun

 wall coverings of black or blue cloth **OGu** *GL* A 24a, 65

 See also: *skarlaþ*

blak (ON) noun

 slap **OIce** *Jó* Mah 22

blami (OSw) noun

 bruise **OSw** *YVgL* Add

 bruising **OSw** *VmL* Kkb, Mb

blandask (ON) verb

 have sexual intercourse with **ONorw** *GuL* Krb

blasa (OSw) verb

 Expressions:

 blasande munne, blasændæ munni (OSw)

 blowing on the flames **OSw** *UL* Blb *VmL* Bb

bláfeldr (ON) noun

Cloak of fur (of black sheep) was accepted as a legal means of payment.

cloak of fur **ONorw** *GuL* Mhb

Refs: Falk 1919, 174–75; Hertzberg 1889, 231–32

blea (OSw) noun

Expressions:

bulster ok blea (OSw)

bolster and sheet **OSw** *HL* Mb

Bloody beddings appear as proof in cases of killings in conjunction with adultery.

blekoblandaþer (OSw) adj.

fraudulently adulterated **OSw** *UL* Kmb, *VmL* Kmb

blokhogg (OSw) noun

severe blow with a blunt object **OSw** *SdmL* Mb

blot (OGu) **blót** (ON) noun

heathen practice **ONorw** *BorgL* 16.9

sacrifice **OGu** *GL* A 4, **ONorw** *EidsL* 24.1, *FrL* KrbB 15, *GuL* Krb

See also: *blot, blotan, guþ, lunder, sten*

blota (OSw) **blóta** (ON) **blota** (OGu) verb

To worship and sacrifice to heathen gods was strictly forbidden; see e.g., GL ch. 4. Human sacrifice was not unknown: 'They sacrificed their sons and daughters' (GS ch. 1).

hallow **OIce** *Grg* Bat 115

sacrifice **OGu** *GS* Ch. 1, **ONorw** *FrL* KrbB 15, **OSw** *HL* Kkb, *UL* Kkb

worship **OIce** *Grg* Klþ 7, **ONorw** *GuL* Krb

See also: *blotan*

Refs: KLNM s.v.v. *alv, blot, diser, hov og horg, kult, magi, offer, stalli, þorri, år och fred*

blotan (OGu) noun

sacrifice **OGu** *GL* A 4, *GS* Ch. 1, 3

See also: *blot, blota*

bloþ (OSw) **bloþ** (OGu) **bloþer** (OSw) noun

blood **OGu** *GL* A 24e, **OSw** *UL* Mb, *VmL* Kkb, Mb

blood relative **OGu** *GL* A 20

bloodshed **OSw** *DL* Kkb

descendant **OGu** *GL* A 20

kin **OGu** *GL* A 20

bloþlæti (OSw) noun

bloodshed **OSw** *HL* Kkb, Kgb, Mb, *SdmL* Mb

drawing of blood **OSw** *UL* Mb

injury that draws blood **OSw** *UL* Mb

See also: *bloþsar, bloþviti*

bloþsar (OSw) **bloþsæri** (OSw) noun

bleeding wound **OSw** *SdmL* Mb

blood wound **OSw** *HL* Md

injury that draws blood **OSw** *UL* Mb

See also: *bloþlæti, bloþviti*

bloþugher (OSw) adj.

Expressions:

blar æller bloþugher, blat ok bloþugt (OSw)

blue or bloody **OSw** *SdmL* Kgb *YVgL* Frb, Rlb, Add *ÄVgL* Slb

bruised or bloody **OSw** *DL* Mb *SdmL* Mb

bruises and bloodshed **OSw** *HL* Kkb

bloþviti (OSw) **blothvite** (ODan) noun

blood fine **ODan** *JyL* 1, 2

blood injury **OSw** *DL* Eb

blood payment **ODan** *ESjL* 3

bloodletting **OSw** *DL* Eb

bloodshed **ODan** *JyL* 2, **OSw** *HL* Kgb, Mb, *SdmL* Kgb, *YVgL* Add, *ÖgL* Eb, Vm

drawing of blood **OSw** *HL* Kgb, Mb, *UL* Kgb, *VmL* Kgb

injury that draws blood **OSw** *UL* Kgb, *VmL* Kgb

blótskapr (ON) **blótsskapr** (ON) noun

heathen practice **ONorw** *BorgL* 16.9

bo (OSw) **bo** (ODan) **bo** (OGu) **bú** (ON) **bö** (OSw) noun

Literally 'dwelling' with many separate meanings in the laws: 1) a farm, group of farms, or a village; 2) the houses themselves and the function of the dwelling as an economic unit, sometimes including the people living and working there; 3) the belongings representing a substantial part of its value including livestock; and 4) an administrative unit of an unknown function in ÄVgL (not in the translated laws).

assets **OSw** *SdmL* Jb

capital in a household **OIce** *Grg* Þsþ 81

cattle **OSw** *YVgL* Rlb, Add, *ÄVgL* Urb

common property **OSw** *YVgL* Frb

court (2) **ONorw** *GuL* Mhb

estate **ODan** *ESjL* 3, *SkL* 7, 141, 146, 152, **ONorw** *GuL* Llb, **OSw** *DL* Eb, *UL* Kgb, Äb, *VmL* Kgb, Äb

farm **OGu** *GL* A 6, **OIce** *Grg* Vís 89, *Jó* Llb 10, *KRA* 14, 15, **ONorw** *BorgL* 5.13, *FrL* KrbA 33, *GuL* Krb, Mhb, Olb, **OSw** *ÄVgL* Äb

farmstead **OIce** *Jó* Kab 15

goods **OSw** *YVgL* Rlb

home **ODan** *ESjL* 2, **OSw** *DL* Tjdb, *HL* Äb, *SdmL* Kgb, Mb, Tjdb, *YVgL* Urb, Äb, Gb, Tb, Jb, Add, *ÄVgL* Slb, Äb, Gb, Rlb, Jb, *ÖgL* Kkb, Db *house* **ODan** *ESjL* 1, *JyL* 3, *SkL* 5, **OGu** *GL* A 10

household **ODan** *ESjL* 1, 3, *JyL* 2, 3, *VSjL* 1, 12, **OIce** *Grg* Þsþ 27, 81 Vís 97 Fjl 225, *Jó* Sg 1 Kge 14, 21, *KRA* 26, **ONorw** *BorgL* 8.5, *EidsL* 41.3, *GuL* Arb, Leb, **OSw** *SdmL* Gb, *UL* Äb, Rb, *VmL* Äb, Rb

household stock **OIce** *Grg* Þsþ 81, *Js* Mah 7, Kab 1

land **ONorw** *FrL* KrbB 20

manor **ODan** *SkL* 228

movables **OSw** *SdmL* Kmb

property **ODan** *ESjL* 1, *VSjL* 3, **OSw** *DL* Eb, *HL* Kkb, Kgb, *UL* Kgb, Mb, Jb, Add. 5, *VmL* Kgb, Mb, Jb, *YVgL* Äb, Rlb, Tb, *ÄVgL* Äb, *ÖgL* Eb, Db

residence **ODan** *ESjL* 2

stock animals **ONorw** *EidsL* 19.1

Expressions:

bregða búi (ON)

give up householding **OIce** *Grg* Þsþ 80

eiga í búi (ON)

own a share in a household **OIce** *Grg* Feþ 152

gera bú (ON)

start householding **OIce** *Grg* Tíg 259

See also: *bol, bolagh, bonde, bryti, byr, egn, fæ, garþer, goþs, husaby, hæraþ, inviþi, jarl, konongsgarþer, oþal, öþer*

Refs: Árni Júlíusson 2010, 8; CV s.v. *bú*; KLNM s.v. *bo, kronogods*; Miller 1990, 115; ONP s.v. *bú*; Schlyter s.v. *bo*; Wiktorsson 2011:II, 160–65

boandi (OSw) adj.

settled **OSw** *ÄVgL* Jb, *ÖgL* Eb, Db

See also: *bofaster*

bodræt (OSw) noun

Literally, 'dragging from the house'. It describes (incitement to commit) a crime of the type that would now be called 'an inside job', especially when the instigator was himself outside the household. The related *bospænd* (q.v.) occurs only in VmL and seems to describe specifically the act of theft by household members instigated by others, as it is followed by an expression meaning incitement to something. Schlyter and Wennström differ over whether two different crimes are being described. The latter believes that there is a difference, especially as VmL includes two separate statutes, one relating to *bodræt* and one to *bospænd*. He considers the latter to refer to the crime of incitement to theft and the former to the theft by household members whether resulting from incitement by outsiders or on their own initiative. These crimes are not mentioned in the laws of Götaland, GL or DL and Wennström argues that the relatively freer nature of household members in Svealand meant that they could be subject to fines and other punishments that were not relevant in Götaland.

house theft **OSw** *HL* Mb, *SdmL* Tjdb

theft by incitement within the household **OSw** *UL* Mb, *VmL* Mb

See also: *bospænd, ransaka*

Refs: Schlyter 1877, s.v. *bodræt, bospænd*; SL SdmL, 215 note 68; SL UL, 129 note 166; SL VmL, 102 note 179; Wennström 1936, 90–91

bodsæti (OSw) noun

A category of dependent people, who lived in somebody else's household, and who may have paid rent. They are mentioned in the laws concerning their reduced obligation to pay the priest an annual sum.

croft household **OSw** *DL* Kkb

boðburðr (ON) noun

forwarding summons **OIce** *Jó* Kge 29 Llb 7

forwarding the message baton **ONorw** *GuL* Llb

message baton **ONorw** *FrL* Intr 17

route for forwarding messages **OIce** *Jó* Kge 31

token duty **ONorw** *EidsL* 11.4

boðfall (ON) noun

dropping the summons **OIce** *Jó* Kge 32

boðgreizla (ON) noun

duty of forwarding the summons **OIce** *Jó* Kge 33

boðleið (ON) noun

The path a message or token (cf. *buþ, buþkafli*) should take in order to reach all members of a community. Also called *boðferð* in some sources. The route ran from a farm to the nearest neighboring farm. According to Jó Kge 29 the same route was used for housing and transporting impoverished members of the community.

proclamation route **ONorw** *BorgL* 13.2, 13.3, *EidsL* 10.1

summons route **OIce** *Jó* Kge 29

token-path **ONorw** *EidsL* 11.4

token-route **ONorw** *EidsL* 11.5

See also: *boðburðr, boðfall, buþ, skæra (2)*

Refs: CV s.v. *boðleið*; Fritzner s.v. *boðleið*; Hertzberg; KLNM s.v. *budstikke*; ONP s.v. *boðleið*

boðorð (ON) noun

commandment **OIce** *KRA* 12

edict **OIce** *KRA* 30

boðskurðr (ON) noun

summoning baton **ONorw** *FrL* KrbB 19

boðslöttr (ON) noun

uninvited guest **OIce** *Jó* Mah 28

boðsváttr (ON) noun

witness to a bid **ONorw** *FrL* Jkb 4

bofaster (OSw) **bofast** (ODan) adj.

resident **OSw** *SdmL* Mb, *YVgL* Rlb, Tb, *ÄVgL* Tb

settled **ODan** *ESjL* 3

See also: *boandi, bolfaster*

bofæ (ODan) **búfé** (ON) noun

animals **OIce** *Jó* Kab 16, **ONorw**
FrL Intr 11 KrbA 27

cattle **OIce** *Jó* Kab 17

household movables **ODan** *ESjL* 1

livestock **OIce** *Grg* Klþ 4, 6 Lbþ 174 Fjl
221, 224, *Jó* Kge 4 Llb 7, *Js* Kvg 3 Lbb 18
Kab 12, *KRA* 15, 26, **ONorw** *FrL* KrbB 18,
GuL Krb, Kpb, Llb, Tfb, Mhb, Olb, Leb

movable goods **ODan** *ESjL* 1

movables **ODan** *JyL* 1, 2, *VSjL* 68

boghaböter (OSw) noun

{bogha} fines **OSw** *HL* Mb

See also: *bogher*

bogher (OSw) **baugr** (ON) noun

The term *baugr*, 'ring' (of gold and silver), appears in numerous medieval Germanic languages, and it was a multipurpose item used in various, often legal, contexts. People swore oaths on rings or ring-swords, and rings were visible signs of political networking and honourable gifts.

The medieval Nordic laws show that rings, or bits of rings, were used as payment, esp. of compensation for manslaughter and fines, primarily to the king. In this case, a *baugr* in Norway equalled 12 *aurar* (1 1/2 *mörk*). OSw *bogher* only appears in HL, where it also equalled 12 *örar* (revealing a close connection with ONorw law). In Iceland the *baugar* were calculated in ounces of silver.

The plural form (ON) *baugar* usually referred to wergild, the sum of compensation a killer had to pay to the kin of the killed person. In ONorw laws three classes of *baugar* were distinguished: *höfuðbaugr* (q.v.), *bróðurbaugr* (q.v.), and *bróðrungsbaugr* (q.v.), reflecting the distance in degree of kinship to the killed person. The people belonging to one such class were called *baugamenn* (see *baugamaðr*). The group of people entitled to (paying or receiving) compensation for manslaughter was called *bauggildi* (q.v.).

The term *ránbaugr* (q.v.) referred to unlawful seizure or holding of property; *slanbaugr* (q.v.) was what a person had to pay when he or she was watching an assault without interfering.

A famous example of this system of compensation is found in the OIce *Baugatal* ('The Wergild Ring List') in Grágás, which contains rules for compensation for manslaughter as far as to fourth cousins, which one kindred paid to another (see Laws of Early Iceland: Grágás I, 175). Various components made up the compensation, the silver *baugr* and smaller units were referred to as *baugþak* (q.v.) and *þveiti* (q.v.). Similar complex and extensive tariffs appear in the FrL and GuL (Norway) and in the HL (Sweden).

The reliability of the *Baugatal* as a historical source has been disputed, but recent scholarship (Christoph Kilger, Peter Foote) views it as credible, at least in its fundamental features.

The latter element of the *baugþak* is derived from the verb *þekja*, which means 'to increase a sum by adding to it' or 'to contribute to a price or fine'. *Baugþak* may therefore refer to the smaller pendant rings that are found linked around larger rings. *Þveiti* means 'piece' or 'fragment', and possibly also 'fragmented silver', and it is also mentioned in the earliest ONorw laws (see Hertzberg, 750).

At the assembly (ON *þing*) the compensation rings of silver were checked for weight and tested, and *Baugatal* stipulated that the rings should be '... standing up to the test of a nick, and of one quality inside and out'. The *baugr* denoted a fine to the king, not only for manslaughter, but also for infringements of other kinds, such as letting one's cattle go grazing on other people's pasture (GuL ch. 81).

The importance of the concept *bauger* is also revealed by the number of compounds. In addition to those mentioned above, we find *baugrygr* (q.v.) (a woman entitled to a main part of the wergild), *baugshelgi* (q.v.) (degree of personal protection amounting to a fine of a *bauger* to the king in case of injury or insult), *bauggildr* (protected by a fine of a *bauger*), *bauggildismaðr* (q.v.) (a male relative on the father's side), *baugaskipti* (the distribution of fines and compensation among the persons involved), and *fjörbaugsgarðr* (the lesser outlawry). The last concept is known from the Grágás. The only OSw compound *þiufbogher* (q.v.) (compensation/fine for theft) appears in HL.

ring **OIce** *Js* Lbb 19, **ONorw** *FrL* Mhb 52
Sab 2, *GuL* Kpb, Løb, Llb, Mhb, Sab

wergild **OIce** *Grg* Bat 113, **ONorw** *FrL* Mhb 13, 18

wergild ring **OIce** *Grg* Bat 113,
ONorw *FrL* Var 7 Rgb 24 Jkb 4

{bogher} **OSw** *HL* Mb

See also: *bauggildismaðr, bot, gæld,
mangæld, nefgildismaðr*

Refs: Brink 2010b, 127–28; Engeler 1991, 86;
Hedeager 2011, 12–13; Hertzberg s.v.v. *baugamaðr,
baugaskipti, bauggildi, bauggildismaðr, bauggildr,
baugrygr, baugshelgi, baugr, bróðurbaugr,
bróðrungsbaugr, höfuðbaugr, ránbaugr,
slanbaugr*; Kilger 2008, 282; KLNM s.v.v. *böter,
edsformular, hov og horg, hälsingelagen, mansbot,
odelsrett, straff*; Riisøy 2016; Schlyter s.v.v.
bauger, bogher 2 b; Vogt 2010, 120–21, 146

boghi (OSw) **bogi** (ON) **bughi** (OSw) noun

A weapon included among *folkvapn* (q.v.), *hamnuvapn*
(q.v.) and *morþvapn* (q.v.). In OSw HL, also a man
with a bow, used as a unit of taxation.

bow ONorw *GuL* Mhb, Leb, **OSw**
HL Kgb, Äb, Rb, *SdmL* Mb

Refs: Förvaltningshistorisk ordbok s.v. *båge*;
Hansen 2011, 314–15; KLNM s.v. *båge*

bok (1) (OSw) **bok** (ODan) **bók** (ON) noun

Referring to law-books (OSw HL Kkb, Rb; SdmL
Conf, För; ODan JyL Fort; OIce Js Kdb 3) and parts of
such books (passim, cf. *balker*) as well as to liturgical
books (OSw ÖgL Kkb; YVgL and ÄVgL Kkb; SdmL
Kkb). Books also appear in certain oath procedures;
commonly (including the prepositional phrase *við
bók*, see below) in OIce concerning, for instance,
defamation and the location of an accused (Js), as well
as in ONorw concerning bestiality, drunken quarrels
and liberation of slaves (GuL). Only rarely in OSw,
concerning theft (DL), paternity (HL) and shepherd
duties (ÄVgL), as well as in a new king's oath of
allegiance which should be sworn holding both a book
and holy relic (SdmL). It seems generally assumed
that the book on which an oath was sworn was the
bible or a liturgical book, which might be supported
by statements of a 'holy book' in OIce Js, for
instance concerning the appointment of men for the
alþingi 'General Assembly' and an ODan occurrence
concerning the oaths of a *nævning* (see *næmpning*)
(JyL 2:42). ODan SkL 113 explicitly states that a
levelling oath (ODan *javnetheeth*, see *jamnaþereþer*)
should be sworn on a book, not on holy relics (ODan
helaghdom, see *hælghidomber*), while SkL 147 and
226 state that swearing should be done by joining
hands, and not on a book (see *handtak*).

bible/lawbook/book **OSw** *DL* Tjdb

book **ODan** *JyL* Fort, 1, 2, *SkL* 113, 147,
226, **ONorw** *GuL* Krb, Kpb, Løb, Tfb, Mhb,
OSw *HL* Äb, *SdmL* Conf, För, Till, *YVgL*
Kkb, Äb, *ÄVgL* Kkb, Rlb, *ÖgL* Kkb

law-book **OSw** *HL* Kkb, Rb

National Law **OFar** *Seyð* 7, 8

Expressions:

landzens bok (OSw)

law-book of the land **OSw** *HL* Rb

við bók (ON)

by oath on a book **OIce** *Grg* Þsþ 63, Vís
109b (add. 132), Arþ 122, Ómb 128, Feþ
164, Lbþ 172, 178, Tíg 266 *Js* Lbb 6

See also: *hælghidomber*

Refs: KLNM s.v. *edsformular*

bok (2) (ODan) noun

beech nut **ODan** *SkL* 207

See also: *akern*

bokarl (OSw) noun

resident **OSw** *ÄVgL* Kkb

boklærder (OSw) adj.

book-learned **OSw** *ÄVgL* Kkb

bokumbel (OSw) noun

livestock brand **OSw** *UL* Blb (table of contents only)

bol (OSw) **bol** (ODan) **bol** (OGu) **ból** (ON) noun

Literally 'dwelling' and by extension referring to a
farm including its farmland. In Danish laws *bol* refers
to a certain part of the village land and the rights and
obligations that followed, but may also be used as a
land assessment unit. A specifically judicial use of *bol*
in Norwegian laws was as a farming unit of a certain
size, which was originally the basis for calculating
the lease and later the taxation, and usually specified
as to the unit measure, i.e. *marker* (see *mark*(2)) or
mánaðarmatr (q.v.). There are several, sometimes
conflicting, ideas of the nature of the *bol* in the
Swedish laws. In Scandinavian texts in Latin *bol* is
rendered by *mansus*, but the possible links between
the uses of *bol* in Scandinavia and of the *mansus* in
post-Roman Europe have not been explored.

cultivated land ONorw *GuL* Arb, **OSw** *DL* Bb

dwelling house **OSw** *HL* Rb

farm OGu *GL* A 3, 13, 28, **OIce** *Grg* Lbþ 206 Fjl
225, **OSw** *DL* Bb, *UL* Kkb, Jb, Rb, *VmL* Kkb,
Jb, Bb, Rb, *YVgL* Kkb, Jb, *ÄVgL* Kkb, Jb

farmland OGu *GL* A 47

farmstead **ODan** *SkL* 238, **OIce** *Jó* Llb 14,
OSw *YVgL* Äb, Jb, Föb, Add, *ÄVgL* Äb

homestead **OSw** *SdmL* Kkb

land **OSw** *ÄVgL* Jb

village unit **ODan** *ESjL* 2, *JyL* 1,
3, *SkL* 73, 74, *VSjL* 78

Expressions:

sa bool aff sæthom (OSw)

Used of householders who own
farms in several villages.

sowing land that is separated from the cultivator's residence **OSw** *YVgL* Kkb

See also: *attunger, bo, bolstaþer, byamal, bygning, fiarþunger, garþer, kirkiubol, mánaðarmatr, ornume, oþoliorþ, rep, urfiælder*

Refs: Andersson 2014, 24; Christensen 1983; Ericsson 2012, 22, 24, 28, 270; Hoff 1997, 197; KLNM s.v. *bol*; ONP s.v. *ból*; Porsmose 1988, 234–36; Rahmqvist 1996, 29; Schlyter 1877, s.v. *bol*; Tamm & Vogt 2016, 25; Venge 2002, 8, 173, 283; Åström 1897, 193–98

bolagh (OSw) noun

This word is used in several different ways, all closely related. At the simplest level, it means a partnership, but it can also simply mean a common household, or by transference to the property shared in the partnership or household. The *bolaghsmaþer* (q.v.) was someone who owned a part of the farm as a partner, often for a stipulated period, as opposed to a *bryti* (q.v.) who was a paid member of staff. The word carries the same meanings as the ODan word *fælagh* (q.v.), which also appears in YVgL, and the ON *félag*. It is worth noting that in VmL the church and parishioners are involved in the setting up of a partnership, whereas in UL, of which in many respects VmL is a close copy, no mention is made of the church and the semi-official term *fastar* (q.v.) is used of the witnesses to the formation of a partnership.

There is an ON equivalent (*búlag*), occurring in legal texts not excerpted for the current work, defined as 'household partnership (on a farm), joint householding' or 'agreed tariff for agricultural produce and services'. An apparently synonymous (and even less common) term is *búalag*. There is also a relatively obscure late medieval legal text called *búalög*.

aggregated property **OSw** *HL* Äb

common household **OSw** *UL* Äb, *VmL* Äb

partnership **OSw** *DL* Bb, *HL* Jb, *SdmL* Jb, *UL* Äb, Jb, *VmL* Äb, Jb

See also: *bo, fastar (pl.), félagi, fæ, fælagh, maþer, stæmna*

Refs: KLNM, s.v. *félag;* Schlyter 1877, s.v.v. *bolagh, fælagh*

bolaghsfastar (pl.) (OSw) noun

partnership fastar **OSw** *UL* Äb, Jb, *VmL* Äb

transaction witnesses of a partnership **OSw** *SdmL* Jb

bolaghsfæ (OSw) **bolax fæ** (OSw) noun

goods in common **OSw** *DL* Rb

property in common **OSw** *UL* Rb, *VmL* Rb

property owned in partnership **OSw** *HL* Jb

See also: *bolagh, fæ*

bolaghsmaþer (OSw) **bolaghsman** (OSw) noun

partner **OSw** *UL* Rb

partnership man **OSw** *ÖgL* Db

See also: *bryti*

bolaghsstæmpna (OSw) **bolagsstæmna** (OSw) **bolax stæmpna** (OSw) noun

period of lease **OSw** *VmL* Jb

period of partnership **OSw** *UL* Jb

time limit of a partnership **OSw** *SdmL* Jb

See also: *giftastæmna, stæmna*

bolamb (OGu) noun

tame sheep **OGu** *GL* A 42

See also: *lamb*

boland (OGu) **búland** (ON) noun

Inhabited land, agricultural land on a farm incl. grazing area.

farm land **OIce** *Grg* Lbþ 202, *Jó* Llb 51

inhabited land **OGu** *GS* Ch. 1

Refs: CV s.v. *búland*; ONP s.v. *búland*; Schlyter s.v. *bo land*; Zoega s.v. *búland*

bolatækkia (OSw) noun

tenancy period **OSw** *SdmL* Jb

bolbyr (OSw) **bolby** (OSw) noun

parcelled land **OSw** *SdmL* Äb, *UL* Äb, *VmL* Äb

boldiur (OSw) noun

poor creature **OSw** *SmL*

See also: *bol, diur*

bolfaster (OSw) **bolfast** (ODan) **bolfastr** (OGu) adj.

This word, frequently used in the expression *bolfaster man*, means literally 'land-tied (man)'. In the translation 'resident', it occurs both as an adjective and as a noun. The implication is that the man concerned is a resident of the area with a fixed abode, as opposed to a *löskamaþer* (see *löska*), an itinerant. The translation 'resident' employed in UL and VmL is intended to include both those who own land and those who do not own land, but who are permanent residents. Such people were permitted to give evidence as witnesses of character or fact and to take part in the watch. Their status seems to overlap with that of *bonde* in the meaning 'householder'. In GL the translation 'landowning man' perhaps limits the cohort too much, but is intended to indicate the status of the person referred to, especially as the concept of an itinerant does not appear in GL and the word might be considered to distinguish landowning from tenant farmers (*laigulenninger*, the OGu word for OSw *landboe*). Since tenants could move from one parish to another when their tenancy ended, they might not have been regarded as 'residents' in the full sense of the word for legal purposes. This distinction equates to the translation in SkL. There seems to be no discernible difference between the meaning of this word and that of *bofaster* (q.v.).

landowning **OGu** *GL* A 14, 18, 19

resident **OGu** *GL* A 20a, **OSw** *HL* Kgb, Mb, *SdmL* Kgb, Kmb, *UL* Kkb, Kgb, Mb, Jb, Kmb, Blb, Rb, *VmL* Kkb, Mb, Kmb, Bb, Rb, *YVgL* Tb, Add

resident farmer **OSw** *HL* Äb

with a fixed abode **ODan** *SkL* 118

See also: *bofaster, bol, bolstaþsmaþer, bonde, jorþeghandi, karl, löska, værnalaghi*

Refs: Schlyter 1877, s.v.v. *bofaster, bolfaster*

bolfæ (ODan) noun

movables **ODan** *SkL* passim

See also: *bol, fæ*

bolgarþer (OSw) noun

fence around a village plot **OSw** *YVgL* Utgb, *ÄVgL* Föb

See also: *bol, garþer*

bolköp (OSw) noun

Presumably synonymous with *siængaköp* (q.v.).

purchase into the household **OSw** *UL* Äb

purchase to the home **OSw** *HL* Äb

See also: *siængaköp*

Refs: Schlyter s.v. *bolköp*; SL HL, 315–16, note 57

bolsbrygþi (OSw) noun

fence **OSw** *YVgL* Utgb

bolsmærki (OSw) noun

brand **OSw** *HL* Blb

farm brand **OSw** *UL* Blb, *VmL* Bb

owner's mark **OSw** *SdmL* Bb

bolstaþabro (OSw) noun

farmland bridge **OSw** *SdmL* Bb

See also: *byabro*

bolstaþaskæl (OSw) noun

farmland boundary **OSw** *SdmL* Bb

bolstaþer (OSw) **bólstaðr** (ON) noun

Village or farmstead in a village or the area around the dwelling on a farm. Also used of farming land delineated by boundary markers as being part of a specific village.

farm **OIce** *Grg* Klþ 2, 4 Feþ 144, 152 Lbþ 172, 179 Tíg 258, *Jó* Llb 41, **OSw** *HL* Blb

farmland **OSw** *SdmL* Kkb, Jb, Bb, Mb, *UL* Jb, Blb, *VmL* Mb, Bb

farmstead **OIce** *Grg* Lbþ 175, 177 Rsþ 230, *KRA* 11, **OSw** *DL* Bb, *UL* Blb, *VmL* Kkb, Bb

farmstead or village **OSw** *DL* Kkb

land **OSw** *DL* Bb

village **OSw** *DL* Mb, Tjdb, *UL* Blb, *VmL* Mb, Bb

village property **OSw** *UL* Blb, *VmL* Bb

villager **OSw** *DL* Bb

Expressions:

by ok bolstaþer (OSw)

Alliterative expression for a village and the related farmland, which might be translated alternatively as 'village and environs'.

village and farmland **OSw** *UL* Jb *VmL* Bb

See also: *bygning, byr, garþer, skæl*

Refs: CV s.v. *bólstaðr*; Gammeltoft 2001, 15; KLNM s.v. *bolstadh*; ONP s.v. *bólstaðr*; Schlyter s.v. *bolstaþer*; Zoega s.v. *bólstaðr*

bolstaþsmaþer (OSw) **bolstaz man** (OSw) **bolstaþsman** (OSw) noun

landowner **OSw** *DL* Kkb, Mb, Bb, *SdmL* Bb, Mb, Rb, *VmL* Mb

See also: *bolfaster, bonde, jorþeghandi, karl, værnalaghi*

bolæggia (OSw) verb

make a partnership **OSw** *DL* Bb

make an agreement on partnership **OSw** *DL* Bb

See also: *bolagh*

bolöþsla (OSw) noun

neglect of farm(stead) **OSw** *YVgL* Föb, Add

bonaþer (OSw) noun

repair **OSw** *UL* Kkb

bondaby (OSw) noun

householder's village **OSw** *SdmL* Jb

bondakona (OSw) **bondekone** (ODan) **bóndakona** (ON) noun

householder's wife **ODan** *JyL* 2, **OSw** *YVgL* Kkb, *ÄVgL* Kkb

wife of a householder **OIce** *Jó* Kab 24

See also: *bonde, kona*

bondalagh (OSw) noun

Literally 'householder's' or 'farmer's law'. In the context in which the term is used, it seems that this is by comparison with Canon (church) law, the equivalent of *lekmannalagh* (see *lekman*). The context in UL and VmL is that of land put in surety to the church, presumably against a monetary consideration. If it could not be redeemed before the agreed date, the matter was to be pursued according to *bondelagh* as recorded in the Land Book of those laws. The translation 'civil law' has been used as conveying the distinction intended. The translation 'community of householders' in a different context, comparable to *værnalagh* (q.v.) elsewhere, reflects the ambiguity/ vagueness of the literal meaning of *lagh* (q.v.).

civil law **OSw** *UL* Kkb, *VmL* Kkb

community of the householders **OSw** *YVgL* Kkb

farmers' law **OSw** *HL* Blb

law of householders **OSw** *ÄVgL* Md

See also: *bolagh*, *bonde*, *fælagh*, *gislingalagh*, *jorþalagh*, *köplagh*, *lagh*, *værnalagh*

Refs: Schlyter 1877, s.v. *bonda lagh*; SL UL, 40 note 64; SL VmL, 29 note 74

bondasun (OSw) **bondesun** (ODan) **bóndasonr** (ON) noun

farmer's son **OSw** *SmL*

householder's son **ODan** *JyL* 1, 2, *SkL* 5, **OIce** *Jó* Mah 2, *Js* Mah 11, **OSw** *YVgL* Kkb, Äb, Gb, Rlb, Tb, Föb, *ÄVgL* Kkb, Gb, Rlb, Fös

husband's son **ODan** *JyL* 3

See also: *bonde*

bondatal (OSw) noun

Number of householders as the basis for taxation and other obligations, viz. building a church.

taxation **OSw** *HL* Kkb, *SdmL* Kkb

See also: *bonde*

Refs: Brink forthcoming

bonde (OSw) **bonde** (ODan) **bondi** (OGu) **bóndi** (ON) **búandi** (ON) noun

As indicated by the last form the noun *bonde* (pl. *bönder*) is derived from the present participle of the verb (OSw) *boa*/(ON) *búa* in the sense 'live, dwell'. The term *bóndi/búandi* was used to denote a man fixed to a location (as opposed to *göngumaðr*, q.v.) and usually married (cf. Beck 1975, 64). Düwel (1975, 190–92 (citing Hjärne)) defines *bonde* as a free, weapon-bearing man who has a fixed abode where he can be lawfully summoned.

In general, the *bonde* was a farmer and landowner, and head of a household. However, not all farmers were landowners; many were tenants (OSw *landboar*, ODan *garthsæter*, *landboer*, ON *landbúar*, *leiglendingar*, *leiguliðar*) (see *landboe*, *garthsæte*, *laigulenningr*, *leiguliði*). In WNorway (the province of the Gulathing law) there were thus two kinds of free *bönder*. In Mid and Northern Norway (the province of the Frostathing law) three kinds of *bönder* were distinguished: *hauldr* (see *hölðr*), *árborinn maðr*, and *reksþegn* (q.v.) (see below). There were also two classes of landowners: (1) farmers who had purchased

their land (ON *kauplendingar* (see *kauplendingr*)), and (2) farmers who owned their land by hereditary (odal) right. The latter category, in ONorw called a *hauldr* or *óðalborinn maðr*, was considered the normal man with respect to legal and social status. He was to be preferred as witness, and he set the standard for the system of compensation and fines (*bótr* (see *bot*)) and *sektir* (see *sækt*) (see Helle 2001, 117). This system was graded according to the rank of the person(s) insulted, whether they had a higher or a lower status than a *bonde*. Only landed men (*lendir men*, see below), the king's marshal (*stallari*), the earl (*jarl*), the bishops and the king had a higher rank, tenants and freedmen (*frjálsgjafar*, *leysingjar*) had a lower standing. Slaves had no personal rights whatsoever. The social stratification of the Norwegian society was also reflected in the gravesites: the higher the rank of the deceased, the closer to the church this person was buried.

Peculiar to the FrL was the *reksþegn*, a *bonde* whose legal rights were half of those of the *hauldr*. He was ranked between the freeborn man (the *árborinn maðr*), and the freedman and each of their descendants. The former had at least four generations of free men as ancestors, but he could not match the *hauldr* because he lacked odal rights. He either was a tenant or owned purchased land.

It should be noted that the tenant, although inferior to the *hauldr* in social status, enjoyed the same personal rights (*réttr*) as the *bonde* with respect to fines and compensations.

In the OSw provincial laws and in the law of Gotland, the peasantry was less hierarchically structured, the main distinction being that of the free versus the unfree man. The latter group consisted of the slaver (*þrælar*). An exception to this pattern occurs in the VgL, where the landed man (the *lænder maþer*) enjoyed a higher social status than the *bonde*. On the other hand, the *bonde* was ranked above the landed man, the bishop, and the king with respect to the *vitsorþ* (q.v.), which probably refers to the right of possessing land. A parallel may be found in the ÖgL, which supports the *bonde* against the king in disputes about the *vitsorþ*. In Norway, the landed men have been considered a special higher class of *bönder* who owned extensive lands themselves or possessed lands as grants from the king. It is doubtful whether this is the case in the VgL, despite Norwegian influence (see Lindkvist 2009a, 63 with further references).

An example of a hierarchically inferior *bonde* may be seen in the HL, where the messenger of the king (the *kunungs ari*) enjoyed a special protection when travelling in Hälsingland. If insulted he was entitled to a compensation double that of a *bonde*.

In the GL the landowners (*bönder*) and the tenants (*laigulenningar, landboar*) were equal before the law, except in their function as witnesses. In this and in several other respects there was a distinction between Gotlanders, non-Gotlanders, and slaves, with falling degrees of status. See, e.g., GL A 15, 17, 20, 20a, 24.

In Sweden, as well as in Denmark, the *bonde* belonged to a commune. He was part of the village (*byr*) and the parish (*sokn*). As such, he was responsible for the building and upkeep of churches, roads, and bridges. The priest was legally on a par with the *bonde*. He was a member of the village, sharing the same obligations as the *bönder*. The importance of a *bonde* as a free man, implying a designation of respect, is evident in the laws of Västergötland. Here it is stated that a bishop and a judge (*laghmaþer*) have to be sons of *bönder*.

The ODan provincial laws indicate that most farmers were freeholders, but the number of tenants was increasing, esp. in Zealand. There were small differences between the two classes and mainly of a legal nature: Only freeholders were allowed as *nævninger* (nominated men, members of judicial panels, see *næmpning*) in Jutland and compurgators in Scania in disputes about property. Within the group of tenants, there was a distinction between the *landbo* and the *garthsæte*. The latter was a smallholder, more dependent on his landlord. He was allowed to till a small piece of land for himself in return for compulsory labour for the landlord. The class of *garthsæter* was greatly increased by the liberation of slaves.

OIce law distinguished between freeholders, tenants, and smallholders (*búðsetumenn*). Only the freeholders visited the assembly (the *þing*). This implied that they had to be wealthy, because they were obliged to pay a fee for travelling to the assembly, the so-called *þingfararkaup* (q.v.). After the union with Norway had been established they were called *skattbóndr*. In contrast, the *bonde* who lived on land belonging to the church was called *kirkjubóndi*. These two terms were peculiar to Iceland.

adult man **OSw** *SmL*

farmer **OFar** *Seyð* 8, 9, **OGu** *GL* A 5, 7, 10, 17, 28, 48, 56, 56a, Add. 1 (B 4), **ONorw** *BorgL* 4.2 5.2 passim, *EidsL* 8.3 10.5 passim, *FrL* Intr 12 Tfb 1 KrbA 22, **OSw** *DL* Tjdb, *HL* Kkb, Kgb, Äb, Mb, Jb, Kmb, Blb, Rb, *SmL*

freeholder **ONorw** *FrL* Intr 1, 15

head of the household **ONorw** *GuL* Kjb, Tjb, Leb

householder **ODan** *ESjL* 1–3, *JyL* 1–3, *SkKL* 1–3, 7, 9, 12, 13, *SkL* passim, *VSjL* 1, 24, 32, 52, 57–59,

64–66, 84, 85, 87, **OIce** *Grg* Klþ passim Þsþ 23, 27, 35, 59 Vís 97 Lsþ 116 Arþ 120 Fjl 225 Rsþ 230 Hrs 234 Misc 251 Tíg 255, *Jó* Sg 1 Mah 2, 3 Kge 17, 24 Llb 18 Kab 25 Þjb 2, 6 Fml 2, 12, *Js* Mah 11, 14 Kab 1, *KRA* 1, 4 passim, **ONorw** *FrL* Intr 12, 19, 20 KrbA 2, 18 KrbB 19 passim Mhb 4, 7 Var 1, *GuL* Krb, Kpb, Kvb, Løb, Llb, Arb, Tfb, Mhb, Tjb, Olb, Leb, **OSw** *DL* Kkb, Eb, Mb, Bb, Gb, Tjdb, Rb, *SdmL* Kkb, Kgb, Gb, Äb, Jb, Bb, Kmb, Mb, Tjdb, Rb, Till, *SmL*, *UL* passim, *VmL* passim, *YVgL* passim, *ÄVgL* Kkb, Md, Smb, Vs, Slb, Äb, Gb, Rlb, Jb, Tb, Fös, Föb, *ÖgL* Kkb, Eb, Db, Vm

husband **ODan** *JyL* 1, 3, *SkL* 8, 10, 23, *VSjL* 1, 61, **OGu** *GL* A 20, **OIce** *Grg* Þsþ 81 Vís 89, 95 Arþ 118 Ómb 143 Misc 248, *Jó* Mah 2, 30 Kge 5 Kab 24, *Js* Mah 9 Kvg 2, *KRA* 17, **ONorw** *BorgL* 3.5, 17.3, *EidsL* 23.1, *FrL* KrbA 3 KrbB 7 Mhb 35 Kvb 5, *GuL* Krb, Kvb, Løb, Arb, Mhb, **OSw** *DL* Kkb, Mb, Gb, *HL* Kkb, Äb, *SdmL* Kkb, Gb, Äb, Mb, *SmL*, *UL* Kkb, Äb, Mb, Jb, Rb, *VmL* Kkb, Äb, Mb, Jb, Rb, *YVgL* Äb, *ÄVgL* Äb, Gb, *ÖgL* Db

man **ODan** *SkL* 22, 57, 161, 162, **OSw** *DL* Kkb, Mb

master **ODan** *SkL* 131, **OFar** *Seyð* 7, **OSw** *HL* Mb

neighbour **OIce** *Grg* Fjl 223

parishioner **OSw** *SmL*

peasant **OSw** *ÄVgL* Kkb

See also: *aþalman, bolfaster, bolstaþsmaþer, husbonde, jorþeghandi, karl, kona, maþer, værnalaghi*

Refs: Beck 1975, 64; Düwel 1975, 190–92; Helle 2001, 117; KLNM s.v.v. *bonde, böter, gärd, hauld, husbonde, husmand, leiglending, rekstegn, stænder, þegn*; Lindkvist 2009a

bondeman (ODan) noun

landowning man **ODan** *ESjL* 2

bopænningar (pl.) (OSw) noun

common money **OSw** *YVgL* Äb

borafóli (ON) noun

Stolen goods put into another man's house in order to create suspicion.

hidden stolen goods **ONorw** *FrL* Bvb 8

stolen goods **ONorw** *GuL* Tjb

See also: *stungafóli*

Refs: Hertzberg s.v. *borafoli*; KLNM s.v.v. *nyckelbärare, rannsakning, tyveri*; ONP s.v. *borafóli*

borð (ON) noun

board **ONorw** *GuL* Krb, Arb, Mhb, Leb

plank **ONorw** *GuL* Leb

See also: *tré*

borgh (OSw) noun

  stronghold **OSw** *SdmL* Till

borgha (OSw) borghe (ODan) verb

  guarantee **OSw** *DL* Bb, *SdmL* Kmb

  make a guarantee **OSw** *ÖgL* Eb

  make a security **OSw** *YVgL* Add

  pay bail **OSw** *HL* Kmb

  stand surety **OSw** *DL* Bb

  vouch **ODan** *JyL* 2

borghan (OSw) borghen (ODan) burgan (OGu)
burghan (OSw) noun

This noun and the associated verb, *borgha*, is used in a number of associated ways as is shown by the translations and instances listed below. It can refer simply to a guarantee of someone appearing at a certain time (to answer a charge, for instance), an early form of recognisance or bail, but can also involve other sorts of guarantee or surety, even in some instances the submission of a hostage. It can also mean the obtaining of credit (cf. ModEng cognate, 'borrow'). This was specifically forbidden in GL in certain circumstances, although permitted in UL, VmL and ÖgL.

  bail **OSw** *DL* Bb, *HL* Kmb

  credit **OGu** *GL* A 65, Add. 9 (B 81),
OSw *UL* Kmb, *VmL* Kmb

  guarantee **OSw** *DL* Rb, *SdmL*
Kmb, Mb, *UL* Mb, *VmL* Mb

  security **OSw** *YVgL* Tb, *ÄVgL* Tb

  surety **ODan** *JyL* 2

  See also: *fæsta, hemuld, nam, panter, tak, varzla, varþnaþer, væþ*

  Refs: KLNM s.v.v. *borgen, gidsler, kreditväsen*; Peel 2015, 191 note 65/17−19; Schlyter 1877, s.v. *borghan*

borghanaman (OSw) borgaz man (OSw) borghaman
(OSw) borghandæman (OSw) borghansman
(OSw) borghaþaman (OSw) noun

  guarantor **OSw** *SdmL* Kmb, *VmL* Rb

  See also: *fangaman, fastar (pl.), hemulsman, skuli, taki*

borghare (OSw) noun

  guarantor **OSw** *ÖgL* Eb

  surety **OSw** *YVgL* Add

bosbrigþ (OSw) bosbrigh (OSw) noun

  livestock taking **OSw** *VmL* Mb

  See also: *bosran*

boskaper (OSw) boskap (ODan) noun

  cattle and household goods **OSw** *HL* Kkb

  chattels **OSw** *ÖgL* Db

  farm **OSw** *SdmL* Kmb

  household **OSw** *VmL* Jb

  household effects **OSw** *VmL* Mb

  movable goods **ODan** *JyL* 1

  movables **ODan** *JyL* 1

  See also: *bo, inviþi*

boskipti (OSw) boskipt (OSw) noun

  division **OSw** *ÄVgL* Jb

  division of home **OSw** *YVgL* Frb, Add, *ÄVgL* Slb

  partition of home **OSw** *YVgL* Äb, *ÄVgL* Äb

  partition of property **OSw** *ÖgL* Eb

  portion of a property **OSw** *VmL* Jb

  property division **OSw** *UL* Kgb,
Äb, *VmL* Kgb, *ÖgL* Db

  See also: *bo, skipti*

bosloter (OSw) boslot (ODan) noun

  Synonymous with *hovoþloter* (q.v.).

  capital lot **ODan** *JyL* 2

  lot in a household **ODan** *JyL* 2

  part **OSw** *ÄVgL* Gb

  part of the home **OSw** *YVgL* Gb

  See also: *bo, hovoþloter, luter*

bospænd (OSw) noun

  household theft **OSw** *VmL* Mb

  See also: *bodræt*

bosran (OSw) boran (ODan) búrán (ON) noun

  burglary **ONorw** *FrL* Var 14

  house rapine **ODan** *JyL* 2

  livestock rustling **OSw** *VmL* Mb

  property rapine **ODan** *JyL* 2

  robbery **OSw** *ÄVgL* Gb

  robbery at home **OSw** *YVgL* Gb

  theft **ONorw** *FrL* Var 13

  theft of livestock **OIce** *Jó* Llb 34

  See also: *bo, bosbrigh, ran*

bot (OSw) bot (ODan) bøter (ODan) bot (OGu) bót
(ON) böter (OSw) noun

Both *bot* and the derived verb *böta* refer to payment of two different kinds: (1) compensation to private persons for injury, insult or damage; and (2) fines to the king or the church for crimes or violations of ecclesiastical regulations. In this latter case the fine was called *sekt* (see *sækt*). Several OSw laws (ÄVgL, YVgL, ÖgL, HL, DL) conceive *böter* as a means of reconciliation between families (*ættir*, see *átt* and *æt*). This was also the purpose of ODan laws (e.g. SkL) concerning *böter*. For this reason, *böter* were paid not only to the aggrieved person(s), but also to the family (the *æt*). *Böter* to public authorities were paid partly to the king, partly to society (*land* (q.v.), *hæraþ* (q.v.) etc.) or to the church.

Both compensation and fines were often stipulated in terms of *baugar* ('rings', or parts of rings), the values of which were expressed in monetary units (*mark, öre* etc.), and frequently paid in domestic animals or goods like clothes and weapons; the amount varying with the scope and seriousness of the offence in question. Some fines also implied fasting (see *fasta* v.).

For very serious offences or crimes, such as murder, *værgæld* 'wergild' had to be paid by the killer and his kin to the killed person's kin, as well as a fine to the king. Some crimes, the so-called *óbótamál/ orbodemál*, were considered too grave to be atoned for by compensation. The punishment for such crimes was usually outlawry.

There was no uniform system of fines and compensation in the Nordic countries. However, fines and compensation were graded in two respects: on the one hand according to the nature, scope, and harmful effects of the offence, on the other hand according to the social standing and personal rights (ON *réttr*) of the aggrieved person. All free persons were entitled to compensation when insulted, and OSw provincial laws considered all free men equal in this respect. The only social gradation known in OSw law was the so-called *þokkabot* (q.v.). In ONorw laws social gradation was the rule (except for cases of insult in church, at the assembly, or in parties, see FrL Mhb, ch. 58). In Western and Mid-Norway the freeholder (the *hauldr*) set the standard of comparison. Payments were stipulated in fixed relations to him. He was entitled to 3 *merkr*, an ordinary farmer (one without odal rights) the half of this (12 *aurar*), a freedman 6 *aurar*. Higher up on the scale were the landed men and the *stallari* (6 *merkr* each), earls and bishops (12 *merkr*). The highest fine to the king might amount to 40 *merkr*. Otherwise, the standard fine to the Norwegian king was 12 *aurar* (1 1/2 *mörk*). For minor offences, publicly known, the standard fine was 3 *aurar*. For bodily harm the Norw laws have very detailed and explicit provisions. For violations of church law fines were paid to the bishop.

As indicated above the culprit had in some cases, e.g. when *værgæld* was involved, to make payments both to the king and to private persons. A division of the fine is also found in ONorw law, when both the king and society (the householders) received fines for breach of justice (see Helle 2001, 94). Not only active offences were fined, but also disregard of decisions or judgements from a court (*dómrof*).

There were two calculation systems in use: (1) the duodecimal system, based on 3 *merkr* or multiples of 3 (6, 9, and 12), and (2) the 40 *merkr*-system ('den store bod'), 40 *merkr* or multiples of 40. It is disputed which system is the older, the 3 *merkr*-series or the 40 *merkr*-series. In Sweden and Denmark the 3 *merkr*-series is considered to be the older one; in Norway the 3 *merkr*-system seems to have prevailed.

atonement **OIce** *Grg* Vís 94

compensation **ODan** *ESjL* 1–3, *JyL* 1–3, *SkL* passim, *VSjL* 23, 48, 49, 52, 53, 55, 65, 69, 86, **OGu** *GL* A 13–19, Add. 1 (B 4), **OIce** *Grg* Þsþ 60 Feþ 156 Misc 249, *Jó* Mah 1, 8 Kge 26 Fml 17, *Js* Mah 4, 28, **ONorw** *FrL* Intr 4 Var 9 Sab 1, *GuL* Sab, **OSw** *DL* Mb, *HL* Kgb, Mb, *UL* Äb, Mb, Jb, Blb, Rb, *VmL* Äb, Mb, Bb, Rb, *YVgL* Frb, Drb, Äb, Gb, Tb, Föb, Add, *ÄVgL* Md, Smb, Slb, Tb, *ÖgL* Kkb, Eb, Db, Vm

fine **ODan** *ESjL* 1, *SkL* 226, *VSjL* 40, 49, 86, **OGu** *GL* A 7, 11, 12, 14, 16, 19, 23, Add. 2 (B 17), **ONorw** *BorgL* 5.2, *FrL* Intr 5 KrbB 8, *GuL* Løb, **OSw** *DL* Kkb, Eb, Mb, Bb, Gb, Rb, *HL* Kkb, Kgb, Äb, Mb, Blb, *SdmL* Kkb, Kgb, Gb, Äb, Jb, Bb, Kmb, Mb, Tjdb, Rb, Till, *UL* Kkb, Kgb, Äb, Mb, Jb, Kmb, Blb, Rb, *VmL* Kkb, Kgb, Äb, Mb, Jb, Kmb, Bb, Rb

means to pay fines **OSw** *DL* Kkb

payment **ODan** *ESjL* 2, 3, *JyL* 2, *SkL* 43, 97, 118, *VSjL* 41, 50

recompense **OGu** *GL* A 37

remedy **OSw** *UL* StfBM

repair **OSw** *SdmL* Kkb

Expressions:

fulder bot, fulder bruta, full bot, fullar böter (OSw)

full compensation **OSw** *UL* Mb, Rb *VmL* Mb, Rb

full fines **OSw** *VmL* Mb

See also: *auvislagjald, aværkan, bogher, bóndaréttr, bóta, fulder, fullrétti, fæbot, gæld, lögréttr, manhælghi, rætter, skaðabót, vaþabot, vígsbót*

Refs: Helle 2001, 94; Hertzberg s.v.v. *bót, réttr*; KLNM s.v.v. *byfred, böter, dómrof, hämnd, kroppsstraff, kyrkostraff, legemskrænkelse, leidang, lejermål*; Schlyter s.v. *bot*

botebuth (ODan) noun

compensation **ODan** *VSjL* 50

offer of payment **ODan** *ESjL* 3

See also: *bot*

botefæ (ODan) *bótafé* (ON) noun

compensation **ODan** *ESjL* 3, **ONorw** *FrL* Var 10

See also: *bot, fæ*

botefæstning (ODan) noun

agreement of compensation **ODan** *ESjL* 2

agreement of payment **ODan** *ESjL* 2

agreement to pay a compensation **ODan** *VSjL* 41

promise of compensation **ODan** *ESjL* 3, *VSjL* 50, 53

See also: *bot*, *fæsta*

botemal (ODan) noun

compensation case **ODan** *ESjL* 2, *JyL* 3

See also: *bot*, *mal (1)*

botestævne (ODan) noun

payment for a summons **ODan** *SkKL* 11

See also: *bot*, *stæmna*

botevirthning (ODan) noun

value of a compensation **ODan** *VSjL* 86

See also: *bot*

bothegang (ODan) noun

trespassing **ODan** *ESjL* 2

See also: *aganga*, *garthgang*, *hemsokn*, *hærværk*, *landnám*

botmark (OSw) noun

fine-mark **OSw** *HL* Kkb, Kgb

See also: *bot*, *mark (2)*

botulfsmæssa (OSw) bótolfsmessa (ON) noun

Saint Botulf's Mass (17 June) **ONorw** *GuL* Krb, **OSw** *DL* Bb, *HL* Blb, Rb

See also: *varfriþer*

boþ (OSw) both (ODan) búð (ON) noun

booth **ODan** *ESjL* 2, **OIce** *Grg* Klþ 10 Þsþ 23, 25 Vís 100 Arþ 120 Ómb 130 Hrs 234

hut **OIce** *Grg* Þsþ 53 Misc 240

shed **ODan** *JyL* 2

shelter **OIce** *Grg* Þsþ 53

storehouse **OSw** *YVgL* Tb, *ÄVgL* Tb

See also: *torgh*

boþakarl (OSw) noun

companion in the fishing colony **OSw** *UL* Äb

bóka (ON) verb

Literally 'to book'; used figuratively of swearing on a book, usually thought to be a gospel or some other type of holy book. Testimony sworn on a book could be referred to as *bókarvitni* (q.v.), and several fourteenth- and fifteenth-century diplomas attest to oaths on books (ON *bókareið*).

swear on a book **OIce** *Jó* Mah 9, *Js* Mah 11, **ONorw** *FrL* Rgb 25

See also: *bókarvitni*, *eþer*, *halsbók*

Refs: CV; Fritzner; ONP; Páll Vídalín s.v. *bókarvitni*

bókarvitni (ON) noun

testimony with an oath sworn on the holy book **OIce** *Jó* Llb 40

See also: *vitni*

bólfesta (ON) noun

rented land **OIce** *Jó* Llb 14

bóndafé (ON) noun

Funds gathered by a community of householders used to make joint payments, such as provisions for a bishop at a church consecration (EidsL 34.3).

wealth of farmers **ONorw** *EidsL* 34.3

Refs: CV s.v. *bóndafé*; Fritzner s.v. *bóndafé*; ONP s.v. *bóndafé*

bóndalega (ON) noun

burial-place for farmers **ONorw** *BorgL* 9.3

bóndaréttr (ON) noun

The *bóndaréttr* — as opposed to the *konungs réttr* and the *kristinn réttr* — was the personal right of the *bóndi* (see *bonde*) (in the broader sense of the term) to compensation in case of insult, graded in accordance with his legal and social status. This *réttr* 'right' had three levels. The lowest level was that of the *bóndi* or *bóndi árborinn* (freeborn *bóndi*) who had purchased his land or tilled it as a tenant. In the GuL (chs 91 and 200) his *réttr* was stipulated to half of what was fixed for the *hauldr* (see *hölðr*), in the FrL (Rgb ch. 34) one third. On the intermediate level stood the freeholder/householder (the *hauldr* or *hauldr óðalborinn*). When entitled to *fullrétti* (full compensation) he received three *merkr* (FrL Rgb ch. 34, GuL Mhb ch. 200). The top level consisted of chieftains, esp. *lendir menn* (see *lænder*), *ármenn* (see *ármaðr*) and *stallarar* (see *stallari*). This tripartite division is found in the FrL and GuL. The BorgL and EidsL seem to recognize only two levels, the *hauldsmaðr* and the *bóndi*, although this cannot be stated with certainty because only the Church Laws have been preserved.

According to the FrL (KrbB ch. 2) the *bóndaréttr* set the standard of fines for a number of offences, such as (e.g.) fornication, the eating of flesh before taking part in the Holy Communion, paying inadequate tithes, violation of the church peace, neglect of providing saddle horses for the bishop, and failure to send forth a message concerning this duty. A later addition states that these fines had to be paid in burnt silver (FrL Rgb ch. 35).

farmers' law **ONorw** *FrL* KrbB 2

householder's right **ONorw** *GuL* Mhb

See also: *bonde*, *leysingi*

Refs: Hertzberg s.v. *bóndaréttr*; KLNM s.v. *böter*; RGA2 s.v. *hǫlðr*

bónhús (ON) noun

oratory **OIce** *Grg* Tíg 263

bótalauss (ON) adj.

requiring no compensation **OIce** *Jó* Mah 13

bótamaðr (ON) noun

   compenser **OIce** *Js* Mah 29

   man with a legal right to atone by paying compensation **OIce** *Jó* Mah 1

brander (OSw) noun

   fire **OSw** *HL* Blb

   Expressions:

   brander mæþ wiliæ wærkiæ (OSw)

   arson **OSw** *HL* Blb

branderfð (ON) noun

The *branderfð*, 'foster inheritance', was the foster father's right to inherit from a foster son. The right was not reciprocal.

   foster inheritance **ONorw** *GuL* Arb, Olb

   Refs: KLNM s.v.v. *branderfð*, *bålferd*, *kår*; Robberstad 1981, 359–60

brandstuþ (OSw) **brænnestuth** (ODan) noun

Collective compensation to victims of accidental fire paid in coin or kind by local householders in the *hæraþ* (q.v.) or *hundari* (q.v.) or part thereof depending on the damages caused. Similar responsibilities, albeit not the word, appear in OIce Grg.

   compensation for fire **OSw** *DL* Bb

   fire compensation **ODan** *SkL* 225, 226

   Refs: KLNM s.v. *brandstod*

brandvaþa (OSw) noun

   accidental fire **OSw** *UL* Kkb, *VmL* Kkb

   See also: *vaþabrænna*, *vaþaelder*

brauthöfn (ON) noun

An abduction; illicit transport from the country. Used of abducting women and the removal of property.

   carrying off **OIce** *Grg* Arþ 126 Feþ 151 Misc 250

   Refs: CV s.v. *brotthöfn*; Fritzner s.v. *brotthöfn*; ONP s.v. *brauthofn*

bráð (ON) noun

   carcass **ONorw** *GuL* Tjb

bref (OSw) **brev** (ODan) **bref** (OGu) **bréf** (ON) noun

Written documents appear from the bishop (*biskups bref* OSw YVgL), king (*konungs bref* ODan, OSw, *konungs opit bref* OSw), *lykt bref miþ kunungs insigli* (GS ch. 4) and dean (*provastar bref* OSw), and both to and from the pope (*pava bref* OSw). Occasionally referring to their purpose, such as interdictions (*forbuþa bref* OSw) and ordination to the priesthood (*vigsla bref* OSw).

   charter **OSw** *DL* Kkb

   document **OFar** *Seyð* 0, **OIce** *Jó* Kab 12, **OSw** *DL* Gb

   letter **ODan** *ESjL* 3, *JyL* 2, **OGu** *GS* Ch. 4, **OSw** *HL* Rb, *SdmL* Kkb, Kgb, Äb, Kmb, Rb, *SmL*, *YVgL* Kkb, Äb, Gb, *ÄVgL* Gb

   writ **OIce** *Jó* Mah 2

   Refs: Larsson 2001, 229–42

bregþa (OGu) **bregða** (ON) verb

   abuse **OGu** *GL* A 39

   See also: *brigþa*

brek (ON) noun

   deceit **OIce** *Grg* Lbþ 192

brekboð (ON) noun

   deceitful bid **OIce** *Grg* Lbþ 192

breklauss (ON) adj.

   without deceit **OIce** *Grg* Þsþ 73 Fjl 221

breksekð (ON) noun

A legal stratagem whereby someone is prosecuted for outlawry by two separate plaintiffs, one of whom only brings the case to ruin that of the other prosecutor. The benefits of this are not explicitly stated in Grg, but it seems likely that the one committing *breksekð* is somehow allied with the outlaw, thus preventing his goods from being confiscated by another party.

   deceptive outlawry **OIce** *Grg* Þsþ 60

   See also: *sækt*

   Refs: CV s.v. *breksekð*; Fritzner s.v. *breksekt*

brennustaðr (ON) noun

The location of a burnt building; an arson site.

   burnt place **OIce** *Grg* Vís 109

   Refs: CV s.v. *brennustaðr*; ONP s.v. *brennustaðr*

brennuvargr (ON) noun

There is no mention of a fatal outcome for the crime committed by a *brennuvargr*. According to GuL the punishment could be outlawry and loss of all property.

   arson-wolf **ONorw** *EidsL* 50.13

   arsonist **OIce** *Jó* Llb 30

   fire-wolf **ONorw** *GuL* Llb

   Refs: KLNM s.v. *mordbrand*; ONP s.v. *brennuvargr*

brethøks (ODan) **breiðøx** (ON) noun

   broad-axe **ODan** *ESjL* 3, **ONorw** *GuL* Leb

brettifumessa (ON) noun

   Feast of St Brictiva (11 January) **ONorw** *GuL* Krb

brevafæ (OSw) noun

   letter fee **OSw** *UL* Kkb

bréfagerð (ON) noun

   letter-writing **OIce** *Jó* Kab 12

brigðandi (ON) noun

   man asserting a claim **OIce** *Grg* Lbþ 176

person who reclaims **ONorw** *FrL* Jkb 8

See also: *brigþa*

brigðarmaðr (ON) **brigðamaðr** (ON) noun

allodial owner **ONorw** *FrL* Jkb 8

See also: *brigþa*

brigíðarmessa (ON) noun

St Brigid's Day **OIce** *Grg* Klþ 13

brigsl (OGu) **brigzli** (ON) noun

dispute **OGu** *GL* A 25, Add. 7 (B 49)

ownership claim **OGu** *GL* Add. 7 (B49)

taunt **OIce** *Grg* Misc 237

brigþ (OSw) **brigð** (ON) noun

Related to the verb *brigþa* 'to dispute; to claim; to
reproach'. Used of disputed land as well as the right
to claim the disputed land and the legal procedure for
the claim.

challenge to landholding **OSw** *VmL* Jb

disputed property **OSw** *UL* Kmb, *VmL* Kmb

redemption of land **ONorw** *FrL* Jkb 7

redemption process **ONorw** *GuL* Olb

right to claim **OIce** *Jó* Lbb 1

right to reclaim **OIce** *Js* Lbb 1

See also: *qvælia*

Refs: ONP s.v. *brigð*

brigþa (OGu) **brigþas** (OGu) **brigða** (ON) verb

annul **OIce** *Js* Þfb 5

assert a claim **OIce** *Grg* Arþ 126, *Jó* Lbb
1, 11, *Js* Lbb 1, 8, **ONorw** *FrL* Jkb 6

claim **OGu** *GL* Add. 7 (B 49), **ONorw** *GuL* Arb

declare oneself free of something **ONorw** *GuL* Løb

dispute **OGu** *GL* A 25

dispute about **OGu** *GL* A 25

disregard **OIce** *Jó* Þfb 6

redeem **ONorw** *GuL* Kpb, Olb

See also: *bregþa, brigðandi, brigðarmaðr, dela*

brista (OSw) **briste** (ODan) verb

break **OSw** *SmL, UL* Kkb, Blb, *VmL* Kkb, Bb

be convicted **ODan** *ESjL* 3

crack **OSw** *UL* Kkb, *VmL* Kkb

fail **ODan** *ESjL* 3, *JyL* 1, 2, *SkL* 78, 86, 140,
144, 147, 170, 230, **OSw** *SmL, ÖgL* Eb

be wanting **OSw** *UL* Kkb, Äb, Blb,
Add. 14, *VmL* Äb, Bb

Expressions:

brista at eþi (OSw)

fail in an oath **OSw** *UL* Kkb, Äb,
Mb, Blb *VmL* Kkb, Mb, Bb

See also: *eþer, eþsöre, fælla*

brík (ON) noun

bench boards **ONorw** *GuL* Llb

bro (OSw) **bro** (ODan) **brú** (ON) noun

bridge **ODan** *JyL* 1, **ONorw** *GuL* Llb, **OSw** *DL* Bb,
HL Blb, *SdmL* Kkb, Jb, *UL* Kgb, Blb, Add. 14, *VmL*
Kgb, Bb, *YVgL* Kkb, Jb, Utgb, Add, *ÄVgL* Jb, Föb

bridge or causeway **OSw** *UL* Kkb, Blb, *VmL* Kkb

See also: *gata, vægher*

broa (OSw) **broa** (OGu) verb

make roads good **OGu** *GL* A 52,
OSw *UL* Blb, *VmL* Bb

broabot (OSw) noun

A fine paid by the community (*attunger* (q.v.),
fiarþunger (q.v.), *hundari* (q.v.)) to the king for
neglecting to build or maintain bridges.

bridge fine **OSw** *SdmL* Bb

See also: *bot*

broafall (OSw) noun

neglect of bridges **OSw** *SdmL* Bb

broafiol (OSw) **brofjal** (ODan) **bro fiæl** (OSw) **brofial**
(OSw) **brofiol** (OSw) noun

Literally, 'bridge plank'. In DL and VmL, an
administrative unit referring to a quarter of a *hundari*
(q.v.) (VmL) or of a *þriþiunger* (q.v.) (DL). The exact
meaning is obscure. In ODan, it refers to a part of the
home.

bridge-plank **ODan** *ESjL* 3

quarter of a Thing assembly area **OSw** *DL* Rb

threshold **ODan** *ESjL* 3, *SkL* 142

{broafiol} **OSw** *VmL* Rb

See also: *hundari, þriþiunger*

Refs: Schlyter, s.v. *broafiol* (2); Schück 1949,
17; SL DL, 112 note 42; SL VmL, 175 note 5

broaflokker (OSw) noun

chapter on bridges **OSw** *SdmL* Bb

broasyn (OSw) **broar syn** (OSw) noun

bridge inspection **OSw** *DL* Bb

brok (OGu) noun

trousers **OGu** *GL* A 19

broþursluter (OSw) noun

brother's lot **OSw** *SdmL* Jb

bróðurbaugr (ON) noun

brother's ring **ONorw** *GuL* Mhb

See also: *bróðrungsbaugr*

bróðurkván (ON) noun

brother's wife **ONorw** *FrL* Mhb 39

brudsæta (OSw) **bruþsæta** (OSw) noun

bride's dresser **OSw** *DL* Gb

matron of honour **OSw** *VmL* Äb

See also: *bruþframma, bruþmaþer, bruþtugha*

brullöp (OSw) **bryllaup** (OGu) **brúðhlaup** (ON)
brúðlaup (ON) **brudlop** (OSw) **brudlöpi** (OSw)
bruþlöp (OSw) **bruþlöpi** (OSw) **brydlöp** (OSw)
bryllöp (OSw) noun

wedding **OGu** *GL* A 24, **OIce** *Grg* Þsþ 81
Arþ 118 Feþ 144, 148, *Jó* Mah 19 Kge 1, *Js*
Kvg 1, *KRA* 16, 17, **ONorw** *FrL* KrbB 1,
GuL Krb, **OSw** *DL* Gb, *SdmL* Gb, *UL* Äb,
VmL Äb, *YVgL* Kkb, Drb, Gb, *ÄVgL* Md

wedding feast **OGu** *GL* A 24, **OSw** *UL* Äb, *VmL* Äb

See also: *brúðkona, bruþmaþer, gifta, giftarmal,
giftaröl, kvánfang, kvennagifting, vighning, vigsl*

bruni (ON) noun

arson **ONorw** *GuL* Tfb

See also: *brænna*

brustheil (OGu) adj.

whole in breathing **OGu** *GL* Add. 8 (B 55)

See also: *bainheil*

brut (OSw) **brut** (ODan) **brot** (ON) **brot** (OSw) **brott**
(OSw) noun

act **ODan** *SkKL* 8

breaking (a bone) **OSw** *VmL* Mb

broken ends of bone **OSw** *VmL* Mb

crime **ODan** *JyL* 2, *SkL* 126, **OSw** *DL* Mb,
HL För, Kkb, Mb, *SdmL* Kkb, Kgb, Jb, Kmb,
Mb, Tjdb, *UL* Kkb, Mb, Jb, Kmb, Blb, Rb,
VmL Kkb, Mb, Jb, Kmb, Bb, Rb, *YVgL* Add

damage **OIce** *Grg* Vís 100 Rsþ 230, *Jó* Þjb 6

distribution **OSw** *SdmL* Jb, Bb

fine **OSw** *HL* Mb

misdemeanour **OSw** *UL* Kgb, Blb, *VmL* Bb

offence **ODan** *ESjL* 1, *JyL* 2, *SkKL* 2,
3, **OSw** *HL* Äb, Mb, *UL* Kkb, Mb

punishment **OSw** *UL* Mb, Kmb, Rb, *VmL* Kmb, Rb

violation **OSw** *HL* Äb

wrongdoing **OSw** *YVgL* Äb

Expressions:

brut ok byamal, brut ok byæ mal (OSw)

village measurement and distribution **OSw** *UL* Blb

brut ok tomtamal (OSw)

part of the village measurement **OSw** *VmL* Jb

See also: *afbrot, brauthöfn, brutliker, bunkebrut,
byabrut, byamal, dombrut, epsörisbrut,
föstuafbrot, friþbrut, gislingabrut, husbrut,
hælghebrut, hælghebrutsak, hælghudaghabrut,
kirkjufriðbrot, kristinsdómsbrut, kynsæmesbrut,
lögbrot, oþulbrut, saköriesbrut, skipbrotsmaðr,*

*skipbrut, skriptabrut, solskipt, tegher, tiældrubrut,
tomtamal, ubrutliker, vitherlæghisbrut*

brutliker (OSw) **brotlikær** (OSw) adj.

criminal **OSw** *HL* Kgb, *SdmL* Kgb

felonious **OSw** *DL* Eb, *UL* Kgb, *VmL* Kgb

guilty **OSw** *DL* Rb, *UL* Rb, *VmL* Rb

bruþ (OSw) **brúðr** (ON) noun

bride **OIce** *Grg* Klþ 10, **OSw** *DL*
Gb, *HL* Äb, *SdmL* Gb

bruþasæti (OSw) noun

bridal seat **OSw** *SdmL* Gb

bruþbænker (OSw) noun

bridal bench **OSw** *HL* Äb

bruþframma (OSw) noun

bridesmaid **OSw** *HL* Äb

matron of honour **OSw** *UL* Äb

See also: *brudsæta, bruþtugha*

bruþfærd (OSw) **brúðför** (ON) **brudfærd** (OSw) noun

bridal journey **OSw** *ÄVgL* Gb

bride's journey **OSw** *DL* Gb

wedding journey **OIce** *Grg* Feþ 164, *Jó* Llb 36

bruþgome (OSw) **brúðgumi** (ON) noun

bridegroom **OIce** *Grg* Klþ 10, **OSw**
DL Gb, *HL* Äb, *SdmL* Gb

bruþkalla (OSw) noun

bride's swains **OSw** *DL* Gb

See also: *bruþmaþer*

bruþlöpsgærþ (OSw) **brúðhlaupsgerð** (ON) **brölöpis
gærþ** (OSw) **brullöps gærþ** (OSw) **brydlöps gærþ**
(OSw) **bryllöps gærþ** (OSw) noun

holding a wedding **OIce** *KRA* 16, 19

wedding **ONorw** *FrL* KrbB 9, **OSw** *HL* Äb

wedding celebration **OSw** *UL* Äb, *VmL* Äb

wedding provisions **OSw** *SdmL* Gb

See also: *brullöp, gærþ*

bruþlöpstimi (OSw) **brúðhlaupstími** (ON) noun

time of marriage **OSw** *HL* Äb

wedding-time **ONorw** *BorgL* 7, **OSw** *SdmL* Gb

bruþmaþer (OSw) **brúðmaðr** (ON) **bruþmæn** (pl.)
(OSw) noun

bridal men **OSw** *SdmL* Gb, *YVgL* Gb, *ÄVgL* Gb

bridal pages **OSw** *HL* Äb

bridesman **ONorw** *GuL* Kvb, Arb

supporter (of the bride) **OSw** *UL* Äb, *VmL* Äb

See also: *brudsæta, brullöp*

bruþmessa (OGu) noun

nuptial mass **OGu** *GL* A 24

bruþtugha (OSw) **bryttuga** (OGu) noun
chief bridal attendant **OGu** *GL* A 24
matron of honour **OSw** *VmL* Äb
See also: *brudsæta*, *bruþframma*
bruþvaþir (pl.) (OSw) noun
bridal cloths **OSw** *YVgL* Gb, *ÄVgL* Gb
brúarhald (ON) noun
maintenance of bridges **OIce** *Jó* Llb 45
brúðkaup (ON) noun
wedding celebration **OIce** *Grg* Arþ 118
brúðkaupsvitni (ON) noun
witness to a wedding **OIce** *Jó* Kge 4
See also: *vitni*
brúðkona (ON) noun
bridesmaid **ONorw** *GuL* Kvb, Arb
See also: *brullöp*
brúðstóll (ON) noun
bridal chair **ONorw** *FrL* Sab 4
bryllöpsdagher (OSw) **bröþlöpes dagher** (OSw) noun
legal marriage day **OSw** *YVgL* Gb
See also: *brullöp*
brynia (OSw) noun
coat of mail **OSw** *HL* Rb
brystarf (OSw) noun
direct inheritance **OSw** *UL* Äb, *VmL* Äb
inheritance by direct heirs **OSw** *HL* Äb, *SdmL* Äb
bryta (OSw) **bryte** (ODan) **briauta** (OGu) verb
breach **OSw** *HL* Kgb, Rb, *ÖgL* Eb, Db, Vm
break **OGu** *GL* A 8, 24, 26, Add. 8 (B 55),
OSw *UL* Kkb, Kgb, Mb, Jb, Blb, Rb, *VmL* Kkb,
Kgb, Mb, Jb, Bb, Rb, *YVgL* Kkb, *ÄVgL* Rlb
break out **OGu** *GL* A 33
commit a crime/offence **ODan** *ESjL* 1,
OSw *UL* Kkb, Kgb, Mb, Rb, *VmL* Kkb,
Kgb, Äb, Mb, Rb, *YVgL* Kkb
cultivate **OSw** *UL* Blb, *VmL* Bb
damage **OSw** *VmL* Mb
desecrate **OGu** *GL* A 8
distribute **OSw** *SdmL* Bb, *UL* Blb, *VmL* Bb
divide **OSw** *UL* Blb, *VmL* Bb
fail (to observe or fulfil something)
OSw *UL* Kkb, Kgb, *VmL* Kkb
forfeit **ODan** *JyL* 2
infringe against **OGu** *GL* A 28, 31, 59, 65
injure **OSw** *UL* Blb, *VmL* Bb
offend **ODan** *JyL* 2, *VSjL* 86, **OSw**
DL Eb, *HL* Kkb, Äb, *ÖgL* Eb
violate **ODan** *SkKL* 3, **OSw** *HL* Kkb,
Kgb, Mb, *SdmL* Kkb, *VmL* Kkb

Expressions:
bryta hus (OSw) **bryte hus** (ODan)
break into a house **OSw** *HL* Kgb
SdmL Kgb **ODan** *JyL* 2
bryte hælgh (ODan)
commit sacrilege **ODan** *JyL* 2
bryte skip (ODan)
to be shipwrecked **ODan** *JyL* 3 *SkL* 165
See also: *bröta*, *ryva*
brytefælagh (ODan) noun
partnership with a bailiff **ODan** *ESjL* 1
See also: *fælaghsbryte*
bryti (OSw) **bryte** (ODan) **bryti** (ON) **brytia** (OSw)
noun
This word is derived from the verb (ON) *brytja* in the senses 'chop, divide, apportion, distribute' (namely food and labour). The word is used in ODan, Old West Norse and OSw laws and can be traced back to pre-Christian times, at least to the Viking Age. In Norway and parts of Sweden (Östergötland) the *bryti* ('overseer', Lat. *villicus*) was the foreman among the slaves and distributed work between them. In his function as an overseer, he was also (in the FrL) called a *verkhúsbryti*. If insulted he was entitled to a higher compensation than the other servants were.

In Denmark, the situation was different. The *bryte* was not a slave (see Ulsig 1981, 142). Although originally landless (see Vogt 2010), he was later (in Christian times) usually a free man. Socially he ranked above the tenant in so far as he was in the service of the landowner, but he was not leasing the latter's land (as the tenant did).

The ODan provincial laws distinguished between two types of *bryter*, on the one hand the so-called *fælaghsbryte* (q.v.), who enjoyed some kind of partnership with the landowner, on the other hand the ordinary *bryte*, who was just a manager or steward. See Ulsig 1981, 142–45; 2011, 125, 129. Although the tenant was more independent, the *bryte* often managed far larger farms than the tenant did (see Ulsig 1981, 145; 2011, 129–30). As a steward or manager of royal estate — sometimes the word *bryte* is used synonymous with *ármaðr* (q.v.) — he might assume higher administrative functions as well, e.g. the collecting of taxes and fines. In the ESjL the word *bryte* is also used synonymously with ombudsman (*umbuthsman*, see *umbuþsman*). He might even have responsibilities of command in military expeditions.

During the twelfth century the relationship between these two social classes changed, because the tenants were taken into the service of the estate owners (see Ulsig 1981, 146). Later (in the thirteenth century) the great lords (*herremæn*, see *hærraman*) were allowed (by the JyL II 76) to keep for themselves the three marks' fines incurred by the *bryte*, fines that would otherwise have accrued to the king. E. Ulsig has argued (1981, 155–56; 2011, 97) that the great lords took advantage of this to redefine many of their tenants as *bryter*. This seems to have expanded the nobility's grip on the resources of their dependents (see Ulsig 2011, 141).

In the late Middle Ages the *bryte* seems to disappear as a particular social group, probably an effect of the abandoning of large-scale demesne farming during the late medieval agrarian crisis after 1350. The examples of the word *bryte* in sixteenth-century sources (see Kalkar s.v. *bryd(j)e*) suggest that the word was then used synonymously for 'tenant' (Danish *fæster*).

In Västergötland the *bryti* often became a *lænsmaþer* (q.v.).

bailiff **ODan** *ESjL* 2, 3, *JyL* 1, 2, *SkL* 59, 163, 171–73, 226–31, *VSjL* 68, 87

farm administrator **ODan** *ESjL* 2

official **ODan** *ESjL* 3

overseer **ONorw** *FrL* Mhb 10 Kvb 21, *GuL* Løb, Mhb, Tjb, **OSw** *UL* Mb, Rb, *VmL* Mb

steward **OIce** *Jó* Kge 32, **OSw** *SdmL* Mb, Tjdb, Rb, *YVgL* Drb, Äb, Rlb, Tb, Föb, Utgb, *ÄVgL* Äb, Tb, *ÖgL* Kkb, Db

{*bryti*} **OSw** *ÄVgL* Tb

See also: *bolaghsmaþer*, *deghia*, *halzmaþer*

Refs: Brink 2008c, 3–6; 2012, 45, 139–45, 258; 2014b; Hertzberg s.v.v. *bryti*, *verkhúsbryti*; Iversen 1997, 119, 120, 124, 153; Kalkar s.v. *bryd(j)e*; KLNM s.v.v. *befalingsmand*, *bryde*, *embedsindtægter*, *kyrkogods*, *landgilde*, *tyende*, *årmann*; Lund [1877] 1967 s.v. *bryti*; Nevéus 1974, 26, 28, 141, 162; RGA2 s.v. *bryte*; Schlyter s.v. *bryti*; Tamm & Vogt, eds, 2016, 5, 21–22; Ulsig 1981, 141, 142–46, 155–56; 2011, 97, 125, 129–30, 141; Vogt 2010, 54

brytjun (ON) **brytjan** (ON) noun

catering **OIce** *Grg* Þsþ 78

brytstokker (OSw) **brusthogh** (OSw) **brutstok** (OSw) noun

Possibly a hollowed out piece of timber used as a moneybox, and as such referring to the household economy.

household **OSw** *YVgL* Äb, *ÄVgL* Äb

Refs: Schlyter s.v. *brytstokker*

brænna (OSw) **brænne** (ODan) **brenna** (ON) **brinna** (ON) **brinna** (OSw) **brenna** (ON) verb

Trans and intrans. Legally significant uses include arson and accidental fires, clearing of woodland for agriculture, and being burned by irons as an ordeal.

burn **ODan** *SkL* 225, **ONorw** *GuL* Leb, Llb, **OSw** *DL* Bb, *HL* Kgb, Mb, Blb, *UL* Kgb, Äb, Mb, Jb, Kmb, Blb, *VmL* Kkb, Äb, Mb. Kmb, Bb, *YVgL* Föb, Utgb, Add

burn down **ODan** *JyL* 3, **OSw** *UL* Kkb

be burned **ODan** *SkL* 161

set on fire **ONorw** *GuL* Leb, Llb, Mhb

Expressions:

brenna inni (ON)

burn (someone) inside a house **OIce** *Grg* Vís 102 *Jó* Mah 2

See also: *bruni*

brænna (OSw) noun

arson **OIce** *Jó* Llb 30, **ONorw** *GuL* Llb

burning **OIce** *Grg* Vís 109

fire **OSw** *DL* Bb, *YVgL* Add

bræþavitni (OSw) **breþa vitni** (OSw) noun

Probably a witness — a person or a testimony — of a crime done in public with eyewitnesses, that was to be called upon immediately in connection with the deed. In YVgL, the scene of the crime was the assembly itself, but in UL these witnesses could be used whenever a killer, attacker or thief was caught in the act.

quick witness **OSw** *YVgL* Urb

witness of a sudden act **OSw** *UL* Rb

See also: *vitni*

Refs: Schlyter s.v. *bræþa vitni*

bræþe (OSw) noun

anger **OSw** *VmL* Mb

See also: *hand*, *vreþe*

bröta (OSw) verb

cultivate **OSw** *UL* Blb, *VmL* Bb

See also: *bryta*

brötartak (OSw) **brautartak** (ON) noun

home surety **ONorw** *FrL* Rgb 31

security **ONorw** *GuL* Llb

security of stolen goods given on the road **OSw** *YVgL* Tb, *ÄVgL* Tb

See also: *tak*

bröþrungi (OSw) **bræðrungr** (ON) **bróðrungar** (pl.) (ON) **bróðrungr** (ON) **bröllungi** (OSw) **bryllungi** (OSw) noun

A *bróðrungr* is specified as 'first male cousin' in Grg (Bat 113), but it is defined variously in dictionaries as a son of a paternal uncle or any child of a paternal uncle (male/female cousin) or agnate cousin, as well as a female second cousin (the paternal grandfathers being brothers). The term is also used more generally to designate a male agnate cousin, i.e. male children of siblings on the paternal side. F also notes that *bróðrungr* is sometimes used to mean a paternal uncle's daughters instead of *bræðrung* or *bræðrunga*. This and other kinship notations in the Nordic laws are often misleading to modern interpreters, as they do not necessarily refer to ego.

brothers' daughters **OSw** *YVgL* Urb, *ÄVgL* Gb

brothers' sons **OSw** *YVgL* Urb, Gb, *ÄVgL* Gb

daughter of father's brother **OSw** *YVgL* Urb

first cousin **OIce** *Grg* Bat 113, **ONorw** *FrL* KrbB 1, 8

male first cousin **ONorw** *GuL* Mhb, Sab

nephew **OSw** *DL* Mb, Gb

paternal cousin **OSw** *SdmL* Äb, *UL* Äb, Jb

son of a paternal uncle **OIce** *Grg* Feþ 162

sons of father's brothers **OSw** *YVgL* Add

Expressions:

bræðrungar eða systrungar (ON)

daughters of brothers or sisters **OIce** *Grg* Feþ 162

first cousin (on father's & mother's side) **OIce** *KRA* 20, 37

See also: *systrunger*

Refs: CV s.v. *bræðrungr*; F s.v. *bræðrungr*; Vestergaard 1988; Z s.v. *bræðrungr*

bróðrabarn (pl.) (ON) **bræðrabarn** (ON) noun

Defined alternately in CV as agnate cousins and in ONP as brothers' children (cousins) and children of paternal uncle(s). F expands this to children of siblings on the paternal side.

male first cousins **OIce** *Jó* Kge 7-10, **ONorw** *GuL* Sab

Refs: CV s.v. *bróðir*; F s.v. *bræðrabörn*; ONP; Vestergaard 1988

bróðradótr (pl.) (ON) **bróðurdóttir** (ON) noun

brothers' daughters **OIce** *Js* Ert 5, 8, **ONorw** *FrL* ArbA 9

daughters of a father's brothers **OIce** *Jó* Kge 7-6, 7-11

bróðrasynir (pl.) (ON) **bróðursonr** (ON) noun

brothers' sons **OIce** *Js* Ert 5, 8, **ONorw** *FrL* ArbA 9, 15 Sab 2, 10

male first cousins **ONorw** *GuL* Arb, Mhb, Sab

son of a father's brother **OIce** *Jó* Kge 7-6

bróðrungsbarn (ON) noun

second cousin **ONorw** *GuL* Mhb, Sab

bróðrungsbaugr (ON) noun

first cousin's ring **ONorw** *GuL* Mhb

See also: *bróðurbaugr*

bukker (OSw) **bukkr** (OGu) noun

billy-goat **OGu** *GL* A 45, **OSw** *UL* Blb, *VmL* Mb, Bb

bulki (ON) noun

cargo **OIce** *Grg* Arþ 125

bunkabrytari (OSw) **bunkabitær** (OSw) noun

pirate **OSw** *YVgL* Urb, Add, *ÄVgL* Urb

bunkebrut (ODan) noun

Piracy was considered a *hærværk*, a 'gang crime'.

boarding a ship **ODan** *VSjL* 64

breaking into a ship **ODan** *VSjL* 64

crime on a ship **ODan** *ESjL* 2

See also: *bunkabrytari*, *hærværk*

Refs: Tamm and Vogt, eds, 2016, 303

bursven (ODan) noun

A male servant.

head of the household **ODan** *SkKL* 1

burtomt (OSw) noun

Literally, 'house plot'. This referred specifically to the parcel of land designated for the owner's dwelling house and other buildings. It was subject to certain protections against encroachment and is what we would now call the curtilage. It could be excluded from a property sale, for example. This word occurs only in DL and VmL and this meaning is conveyed elsewhere in the word *tom(p)t* alone. It is clear from the context, however, in DL, VmL and UL that certain instances of *tompt* refer to this building land of the owner and not to the agricultural land, which is referenced later in the same chapter. The division of the agricultural land in the village was based on the amount and siting of curtilage that the householder owned.

building plot **OSw** *DL* Bb

curtilage **OSw** *VmL* Jb

See also: *brut*, *byamal*, *tompt*

Refs: KLNM, s.v. *tomt;* Schlyter 1877, s.v. *burtomt;* SL UL, 189 note 21; SL VmL, 152 note 23

buthhelagh (ODan) adj.

prescribed holy **ODan** *SkKL* 9

Expressions:

buthhelagh dagh (ODan)

prescribed holy day **ODan** *SkKL* 9

buþ (OSw) **buth** (ODan) **buþ** (OGu) **boð** (ON) **boþ** (OSw) **bud** (OSw) noun

behest **OSw** *YVgL* Föb

call **OSw** *YVgL* Kkb, *ÄVgL* Slb

command **ODan** *ESjL* 2, *JyL* 3, *VSjL* 43, **OFar** *Seyð* 0, **ONorw** *FrL* Tfb 3 Leb 1, **OSw** *HL* Rb, *YVgL* Add

commandment **ONorw** *FrL* KrbB 17, **OSw** *UL* Kkb, *VmL* Kkb

edict **OSw** *HL* Rb

message **ONorw** *EidsL* 15.2, **OSw** *HL* Rb,
UL Kkb, Kgb, Rb, *VmL* Kkb, Kgb, Rb, *YVgL*
Kkb, Tb, Föb, Add, *ÄVgL* Kkb, Tb, Föb

message baton **ONorw** *GuL* Tfb, Mhb, Llb

messenger **ODan** *JyL* 1

mission **OSw** *UL* StfBM

notice **OSw** *HL* Kkb, Kgb, *ÄVgL* Smb

notification **ODan** *ESjL* 3

offer **OGu** *GL* A 16, Add. 1 (B 4),
OSw *UL* Mb, Kmb, Blb

order **ODan** *JyL* 3, **OSw** *SdmL* Conf, Kkb,
Kgb, Kmb, Mb, Rb, Till, *UL* Kgb, *VmL* Kgb

representative **OSw** *UL* Kgb, Mb

request **ODan** *VSjL* 86, **OSw** *YVgL* Kkb

right to command **ONorw** *GuL* Leb

right to redeem land **ONorw** *GuL* Olb

summons **OGu** *GS* Ch. 4, **OIce** *Jó* Kge 31,
ONorw *FrL* Intr 21, **OSw** *UL* Kkb, Kmb, Rb,
VmL Kkb, Kmb, Rb, *YVgL* Kkb, *ÖgL* Kkb, Db

summons baton **ONorw** *BorgL* 17.5

tokens **OIce** *Jó* Llb 59 Fml 3,
ONorw *EidsL* 11.2 15.1

word **OGu** *GL* A 20a, **OSw** *SmL*

Expressions:

skera (upp) boð (ON)

carve a summons baton **ONorw** *BorgL* 17.5

send forth tokens **OIce** *Jó* Llb 59, Fml 3

See also: *arf*, *buþkafli*, *kross*, *stæmna*, *umbuþ*

buþa (OSw) verb

summon **OSw** *YVgL* Utgb

buþkafli (OSw) **buþkafli** (OGu) **boþkafli** (OSw) noun

The *buþkafli*, derived from OSw *kafli* 'long piece of wood', is variously translated as 'message baton', 'message scroll', 'summoning baton', and 'summons baton'. It was the usual instrument for sending out official information, calls, or orders in civil, ecclesiastical, or military matters. It was cut in such a way that it indicated the content and nature of the message. Shaped as a cross (see GuL ch. 19) it announced church services, shaped as an arrow it ordered the apprehension of a criminal, summons to an assembly, or warning against enemies and mobilization for the defence of the country. In this last case, the message baton had to be made of iron (see *arf*). The FrL shows that people could be summoned to road work by a message baton sent out by the bishop's representative. According to the GuL (chs 308, 309, 311) the king's representative or a landed man (ON *lendr maðr*, see *lænder*) had to send out a message baton to prepare people for service in the

military defence. The duty to send out a message baton depended on the purpose of the message. In Sweden, matters concerning the assemblies required the district principal (OSw *hæraþshöfþingi* or *fiarþungshöfþingi*) or the lawman to be responsible. In cases of murder or serious mistreatment, the aggrieved party was entitled to send out the message baton. It was usually carried from one farm to the next and seems to have followed regular routes; it was not to be stopped except in case of emergency (see *arf*). There was also a fixed procedure to be followed when a person was not at home to receive the message baton (ibid.)

message scroll **OSw** *ÖgL* Db

summoning baton **OGu** *GS* Ch. 4, **OSw** *DL* Rb,
SdmL Mb, Rb, *UL* Kgb, Rb, *VmL* Mb, Rb, *YVgL* Rlb

summons baton **OSw** *HL* Rb

Refs: KLNM s.v.v. *budstikke*, *bystævne*, *landvärn*, *lendmann*, *naboforhold*, *vägvisare*, *ǫrvarþing*; Schlyter s.v. *buþkafli*

buþsiorþ (OSw) noun

Land that, when sold, had to be offered to the kin first, and which could be reclaimed by them, unless it was donated to the church.

land that has been offered **OSw** *YVgL* Kkb

See also: *laghbiuþa*

Refs: Lindkvist forthcoming; Schlyter s.v. *buþsiorþ*

buþskaper (OSw) noun

order **OSw** *SdmL* Rb

summons **OSw** *DL* Rb

búa (ON) verb

be a householder **OIce** *Grg* Feþ 153,
164 Fjl 225 Rsþ 231, *Js* Ert 17

live **OIce** *Grg* passim, *Jó* Lbb 1, **ONorw** *FrL* Rgb 4

búakviðr (ON) noun

panel of neighbours **OIce** *Grg* Þsþ 27,
58 Vís 87 Ómb 137 Lbþ 172, 176

búakvǫð (ON) noun

neighbour-calling **OIce** *Grg* Þsþ 27 Vís 89

búandakirkjugarðr (ON) noun

householder's churchyard **OIce** *Grg* Vís 110
Lsþ 116 Ómb 130 Feþ 147 Lbþ 215 Fjl 222

búðakviðr (ON) noun

booth-panel **OIce** *Grg* Vís 101

búðargagnaleiga (ON) noun

hut-utensil hire **OIce** *Grg* Feþ 166

búðarrúm (ON) noun

booth-space **OIce** *Grg* Misc 251

búðarstaðr (ON) noun

dwelling-place **ONorw** *BorgL* 5.15

búðfastr (ON) adj.
  booth-resident **OIce** *Grg* Þsþ 25
búðunautr (ON) noun
  booth-mate **OIce** *Grg* Klþ 2 Þsþ 26, 27
  hut-mate **OIce** *Grg* Klþ 1, 2
búferill (ON) noun
  household **OIce** *Grg* Misc 248
búfjárgangr (ON) noun
  range grazed by livestock **OIce** *Grg*
  Feþ 164, *Jó* Lbb 6 Llb 59
búfjárleiga (ON) noun
  rent of livestock **ONorw** *GuL* Kpb
búhögg (ON) noun
  cattle slaughter **ONorw** *FrL* Leb 23
búi (ON) noun
  neighbour **OIce** *Grg* Klþ 1 Þsþ
  22, 27 Arþ 118, *KRA* 1
  See also: *heimilisbúi*
búlauss (ON) adj.
  without a fixed household **OIce** *Jó* Sg 1
búmissa (ON) noun
  payment for loss of stock **OIce** *Jó* Llb 34
búnaðarbölkr (ON) noun
  agricultural law **OFar** *Seyð* 0
búnuðr (ON) búnaðr (ON) noun
  household **OIce** *Jó* Sg 1 Llb 15, **ONorw** *BorgL* 17.1
búr (ON) noun
  storehouse **ONorw** *GuL* Mhb (Intr)
búrekstr (ON) noun
  managing a farm **OIce** *Jó* Llb 3
búrshurð (ON) noun
  door to storehouse **ONorw** *GuL* Llb
búsafleif (ON) noun
  left-over household stores **OIce** *Grg* Ómb 143
búsbúhlutr (ON) noun
  equipment **OIce** *Jó* Sg 1
  household implements **OIce** *Grg*
  Vís 89 Lbþ 220, *Jó* Llb 6
búslitsmaðr (ON) noun
  A person who has left a farm and has no fixed
  household residence.
  homeless person **ONorw** *FrL* LlbA 1
  Refs: CV s.v. *búslitsmaðr*; Fritzner s.v. *búslitsmaðr*;
  KLNM s.v. *jordleige*; ONP s.v. *búslitsmaðr*
búsútlausn (ON) noun
  redemption of livestock **OIce** *Jó* Llb 34

búþegn (ON) noun
  householder **ONorw** *FrL* Intr 1
byabolstaþer (OSw) noun
  farmland of a village **OSw** *SdmL* Bb
  See also: *byaland*
byabro (OSw) noun
  village bridge **OSw** *SdmL* Bb
  See also: *bolstaþabro*
byabrut (OSw) noun
  village distribution **OSw** *SdmL* Jb, Bb, Till
  village measurement **OSw** *UL* Blb
  See also: *brut*, *byamal*
byaland (OSw) noun
  village land **OSw** *SdmL* Bb, *UL* Blb, *VmL* Bb
  See also: *byabolstaþer*
byamal (OSw) bymal (OSw) noun
  Literally, 'village measurement'. It refers both to the
  individual's allocation of land in a village and the
  whole village area, including unallocated land. The
  system of measurement varied between the different
  provinces of Sweden. It was the basis of the levy
  commitment and also governed inheritance law.
  village measurement **OSw** *SdmL*
  Jb, Bb, *UL* Blb, *VmL* Bb
  Expressions:
  brut ok byamal, brut ok byæ mal (OSw)
  village measurement and distribution **OSw** *UL* Blb
  See also: *brut*, *burtomt*, *byabrut*, *byr*,
  solskipt, *tompt*, *tomtamal*
  Refs: KLNM, s.v.v. *byamål*, *bymark*;
  Schlyter 1877, s.v. *byamal*; SL UL, 188
  note 11; SL VmL, 151 note 13
byaman (OSw) byamaþr (OGu) býjarmaðr (ON)
  byman (OSw) bymaþer (OSw) noun
  man of a village **OSw** *SdmL* Jb, Bb, Rb
  resident **OSw** *SdmL* Kmb
  town dweller **OGu** *GL* A 65, Add. 9
  (B 81), **OSw** *VmL* Kmb, Rb
  townsman **OIce** *Grg* Misc 248
  villager **OSw** *DL* Mb, Bb, Tjdb, *HL* Blb,
  UL Kgb, Mb, Jb, Blb, *VmL* Jb, Bb
  See also: *bygdamæn (pl.)*, *granni*, *nagranni*
byamark (OSw) bymark (ODan) noun
  field of a village **ODan** *JyL* 3
  land of a village **OSw** *YVgL* Rlb, Jb, *ÄVgL* Rlb, Jb
  village field **ODan** *ESjL* 2, 3, *JyL* 1, 3, *SkL* 178, 184
  See also: *byr*, *mark (3)*

byarfriþer (OSw) noun

The village peace appears in the context of potential conflicts between neighbours concerning fences, roads, bridges etc, which should be handled by nominated men (OSw *næmd*).

peace of a village **OSw** *YVgL* Utgb

See also: *byr, friþer, torghfrith*

Refs: Schlyter s.v. *byarfriþer*

byarskogher (OSw) noun

village woodland **OSw** *SdmL* Bb

byaskæl (OSw) noun

village boundary **OSw** *SdmL* Till

byavarþer (OSw) noun

village guard **OSw** *SdmL* Kgb

byfaster (OSw) adj.

resident **OSw** *SdmL* Kmb

bygd (OSw) **bygth** (ODan) **byggð** (ON) **bygð** (ON) **byghþ** (OSw) noun

Inhabited area or district sometimes including the inhabitants and the cultivated land.

area **ODan** *ESjL* 1–3, *JyL* 1–3, *SkKL* 11, *SkL* 72, **OIce** *Jó* Þfb 7

community **ONorw** *FrL* Intr 12, **OSw** *SdmL* Jb, Bb

district **OIce** *Jó* Llb 12

farm **ONorw** *FrL* Intr 12, *GuL* Tfb

habitation **ONorw** *BorgL* 5.14

home district **ONorw** *FrL* KrbA 43

inhabited area **ONorw** *BorgL* 14.12

inhabited place **OIce** *Grg* Lbþ 210

place **ODan** *ESjL* 3

settlement (2) **ODan** *ESjL* 3, *SkL* 69, *VSjL* 72, 75, **OIce** *Js* Þfb 6, **ONorw** *EidsL* 15.2 29.3

village **ODan** *JyL* 2, *SkL* 240

village surroundings **ODan** *ESjL* 3

Refs: CV s.v. *bygð*; Hertzberg s.v. *bygð*; KLNM s.v. –*bygd*; ONP s.v. *byggð*; Schlyter 1877 s.v. *bygd*; Zoega s.v. *bygð*

bygdamæn (pl.) (OSw) **bygthemæn** (pl.) (ODan) **bygþamæn** (pl.) (OSw) noun

men of the area **ODan** *JyL* 2

men of the community **OSw** *SdmL* Mb, *UL* Blb, *VmL* Bb

See also: *byaman, granni, nagranni*

bygdfaster (OSw) adj.

resident **OSw** *SdmL* Äb, Jb, Bb, Kmb, Tjdb, Rb

See also: *bolfaster*

byggðfleyttr (ON) adj.

settlement-sent **ONorw** *EidsL* 41.1

byggia (OSw) **byggja** (ON) verb

grant tenancy **OIce** *Grg* Hrs 234

lease **OIce** *Jó* Llb 28 Þjb 16 Fml 13, **OSw** *VmL* Jb

let out **ONorw** *FrL* KrbA 19 LlbB 8

occupy **OSw** *UL* Jb, *VmL* Jb

rent out **OIce** *Jó* Llb 1 Kab 15, **ONorw** *FrL* Jkb 2

See also: *leghia, sitia*

bygning (OSw) noun

building **OSw** *UL* Kkb, Blb, *VmL* Kkb, Bb

cultivated land **OSw** *DL* Bb

farmhouse **OSw** *DL* Bb

farmland **OSw** *UL* Jb, *VmL* Jb

settlement (2) **OSw** *UL* För, *VmL* För, Bb

tenancy **OSw** *UL* Jb, Blb

See also: *bolstaþer*

bygningabalker (OSw) noun

book concerning building and community **OSw** *DL* Bb

village community section **OSw** *SdmL* För, Bb

See also: *balker*

bygningaræter (OSw) noun

village community regulation **OSw** *SdmL* Bb

bygningavitni (OSw) noun

tenancy witness **OSw** *UL* Jb, Blb, Rb, *VmL* Bb

See also: *bygþaskæl, vitni*

bygþaskæl (OSw) noun

Probably refers to proof of tenancy.

legal form for building **OSw** *SdmL* Rb

See also: *bygningavitni*

Refs: Schlyter s.v. *bygþa skæl*

bylia (OSw) verb

culvert **OSw** *UL* Blb, *VmL* Bb

plank over **OSw** *UL* Mb

Expressions:

bylia ok umhylia, bylia æller umhylia, ombylia ok hylia, ombylia ok omhylia, ombylia ællær omhylia (OSw)

plank over and protect **OSw** *UL* Mb *VmL* Mb

byr (OSw) **by** (ODan) **byr** (OGu) **by** (ON) **býr** (ON) **bær** (ON) **bør** (ON) noun

This word has several different but associated meanings. At the lowest level, it can be a synonym for OSw *bolstaþer* ('farmstead'), then it can mean 'village' (comprising a number of farmsteads forming a community) or habitation in general and finally it can mean a 'town' (as opposed to the countryside). The first two meanings are the most common. Used in the expression *by ok bolstaþer* or the compound *byabolstaþer* to mean 'village and the related farmland'.

farm **OIce** *Grg* Tíg 258, *Jó* Kge 32 Lbb 1, 3 Þjb 12, **ONorw** *EidsL* 10.6 11.4, *FrL* KrbA 23 Mhb 4 Rgb 4, *GuL* Llb, Tfb, **OSw** *HL* Blb, *SdmL* Bb, *YVgL* Utgb, *ÄVgL* Föb

farmstead **OIce** *Jó* Mah 10 Lbb 5 Llb 15, 42, *Js* Mah 14 Lbb 1, 18, *KRA* 4, 11, **ONorw** *GuL* Krb, Llb, **OSw** *UL* Äb, Mb, Jb, Blb, *VmL* Äb, Mb, Jb, Bb

habitation **OGu** *GL* A 22

hamlet **OSw** *HL* Kgb, Jb, Kmb, Blb

homestead **OSw** *DL* Tjdb

house **OIce** *Grg* Þsþ 77, *Js* Mah 5

town **OSw** *VmL* Rb

village **ODan** *ESjL* 2, 3, *JyL* 1–3, *SkKL* 11, *SkL* passim, *VSjL* 60, 71, 72, 75–78, 80, **OSw** *DL* Kkb, Eb, Mb, Bb, Tjdb, Rb, *HL* Mb, Blb, Rb, *SdmL* Kkb, Kgb, Jb, Bb, Kmb, Mb, Tjdb, Rb, Till, *UL* Kkb, Kgb, Äb, Mb, Jb, Kmb, Blb, Rb, *VmL* Kkb, Kgb, Äb, Mb, Jb, Kmb, Bb, Rb, *YVgL* passim, *ÄVgL* Kkb, Md, Äb, Gb, Rlb, Jb, Kva, Tb, *ÖgL* Db

Expressions:

by ok bolstaþer (OSw)

village and farmland **OSw** *UL* Jb *VmL* Bb

See also: *bolstaþer, byabro, byabrut, byaland, byamal, byaman, byamark, byarfriþer, byarskogher, byaskæl, byavarþer, byfaster, heimili*

Refs: CV s.v. *bær*; KLNM, s.v.v. *landsby, stad*; Miller 1990, 115; Schlyter s.v. *byr*

byria (OGu) verb

Expressions:

byria halda (OGu)

commence **OGu** *GL* A 31

byrthing (ODan) **byrþingr** (OGu) noun

cargo vessel (of the smaller type) **OGu** *GL* A 36

merchant vessel **ODan** *ESjL* 3

See also: *bater, farkoster, floti, kaupskip, myndrikkia, skip*

byrþ (OSw) **byrth** (ODan) **byrþ** (OGu) **byrd** (OSw) noun

Literally, 'burden'. In several instances, it is used in the sense, 'birth, family' or in a wider sense, 'kinship', particularly degree of kinship in cases of incest. Frequently, however, it means 'birthright', 'birthright land' or 'ancestral land'. These latter distinguished such inherited land from that which had been bought in the lifetime of the owner and which could more freely be disposed of by sale or bequest, described as *afraþalaus* in GL.

The birthright redemption was a payment offered by the previous owner of birthright land in order to reclaim it from the purchaser. Subject to certain time constraints, this offer could be made but if it were not made within these constraints, the purchaser kept the land.

ancestral land **OSw** *UL* Jb, *VmL* Jb

birth **OGu** *GL* Add. 1 (B 4)

birthright **OSw** *SdmL* Kkb, Äb, *UL* Äb, Jb, *VmL* Äb, Jb

birthright inheritance **OSw** *DL* Bb

birthright land **OSw** *DL* Bb, *SdmL* Jb, *UL* Kkb, Jb, Add. 10, *VmL* Kkb, Jb

degree (of kinship) **ODan** *JyL* 1, **OSw** *DL* Kkb

generation **OSw** *DL* Gb

inheritance **OSw** *DL* Bb

inherited land **OSw** *HL* Jb

kin **ODan** *JyL* 1, *VSjL* 6, **OSw** *SdmL* Äb, Jb

kinship **ODan** *SkL* 92, **OSw** *VmL* Kkb, Äb

kinsman **ODan** *SkL* 219

lineage **OSw** *HL* Jb

nativity **OSw** *UL* StfBM

patrimony **OSw** *HL* Kkb

related **ODan** *JyL* 3, *SkL* 36, *VSjL* 1, 20

testimony **OSw** *HL* Rb

Expressions:

biuþa till byrþ (OSw)

offer birthright redemption **OSw** *VmL* Jb

offer to the kin **OSw** *SdmL* Äb

See also: *afraþalaus, aldaoþal, arver, bolbyr, forn, gamal, æt*

Refs: KLNM, s.v. *bördsrätt;* Schlyter 1877, s.v. *byrþ* (3–7); SL UL, 145 preamble and note 2; SL VmL, 31–32 note 108

byrþa (OSw) verb

claim a birthright portion **OSw** *UL* Blb

Expressions:

byrþa sik (OSw)

claim one's birthright portion **OSw** *UL* Blb

confirm one's birthright **OSw** *UL* Äb, Jb

byrþaluter (OSw) noun

kin's lot **OSw** *SdmL* Jb

byrþaman (OSw) **byrtheman** (ODan) **byrþamaþer** (OSw) **byrþarman** (OSw) noun

descendant **OSw** *DL* Bb

direct descendant **OSw** *UL* Jb, *VmL* Jb

kinsman **ODan** *SkL* 34, **OSw** *DL* Bb, Rb, *SdmL* Kkb, Jb *relative* **OSw** *HL* Jb

See also: *siængaralder, sængaslæt*

byrþaþer (OSw) adj.

entitled by birth **OSw** *SdmL* Gb

byrþi (OSw) **byrde** (OGu) **byrþ** (OGu) **byrðr** (ON) **burþi** (OSw) **byrþe** (OSw) noun

burden **OGu** *GL* A 6, **ONorw** *GuL* Llb, **OSw** *UL* Äb, Blb, *VmL* Äb, Mb

byskupan (ON) noun

confirmation **OIce** *KRA* 3

See also: *ferming*

byskupsfundr (ON) noun

meeting with a bishop **OIce** *Grg* Feþ 150

byskupsríki (ON) **biskupsríki** (ON) noun

bishopric **OIce** *Js* Kdb 4

diocese **ONorw** *GuL* Krb

byskupssekð (ON) noun

episcopal fine **ONorw** *BorgL* 16

byskupssonr (ON) noun

bishop's son **ONorw** *GuL* Mhb

byskupsstóll (ON) **biskupsstóll** (ON) **byskupstóll** (ON) noun

bishop's seat **ONorw** *EidsL* 31

cathedral establishment **OIce** *Jó* Kge 30

diocese **OIce** *KRA* 15

byskupstíund (ON) noun

bishop's tithe **OIce** *Grg* Tíg 257, *KRA* 15

byvirthning (ODan) noun

village assessment **ODan** *JyL* 1

bælgmord (OSw) **bælgmorþ** (OSw) noun

abortion **OSw** *DL* Kkb, *VmL* Kkb

bælskin (OSw) noun

Tax paid in animal skin, and contrasted to other skin-taxes, *leþungsskin* (q.v.) and *vighramannaskin* (q.v.).

{bälg}-tax **OSw** *DL* Rb

Refs: KLNM s.v. *skinnskatt*; Schlyter (bihang) s.v. *bælskin*

bæn (OSw) **ben (2)** (ON) **bæn** (ON) noun

mortal wound **OIce** *Grg* Vís 86, 87, *Js* Mah 34, **ONorw** *FrL* Var 45

wound **ONorw** *EidsL* 37.1, *GuL* Krb, Mhb

lethal wound **OSw** *YVgL* Drb

See also: *sar*

bændil (OSw) **bændel** (OSw) noun

cord **OSw** *VmL* Mb

bæra (OSw) **bera** (ON) **bera** (OSw) **biæra** (OSw) verb

substantiate **OSw** *VmL* Mb

Expressions:

bera kvið (ON)

give a (panel) verdict **OIce** *Grg* Þsþ 35

bera út (ON)

expose a child **ONorw** *GuL* Krb

bærgvarþer (OSw) noun

hill-guard **OSw** *HL* Kgb

bæria (OSw) **barther** (ODan) **bærje** (ODan) **beria** (OGu) **berias** (OGu) **berja** (ON) **berjask** (ON) **barþer** (OSw) verb

beat **ODan** *ESjL* 1, 2, *JyL* 2, 3, *SkL* 122, 124, 219, *VSjL* 40–43, 48, 49, 56, 63, 86, **OIce** *Grg* Vís 88, *Jó* Mah 3, 30 Llb 39, **ONorw** *FrL* Intr 24, **OSw** *HL* Blb, *SdmL* Mb, *YVgL* Frb, Utgb, Add, *ÄVgL* Slb, Lek, *ÖgL* Eb

fight **ODan** *JyL* 2, **OGu** *GL* A 19, **ONorw** *GuL* Krb, Arb, Mhb, Leb, **OSw** *DL* Kkb, *HL* Kkb, *SdmL* Kkb, *UL* Kkb, *VmL* Kkb, *YVgL* Frb, *ÖgL* Kkb

strike **ODan** *JyL* 3, **OGu** *GL* A 9, 12, 18, **ONorw** *GuL* Krb, Tfb, Kvb, **OSw** *DL* Mb, *VmL* Kkb, Mb

thresh **OGu** *GL* A 3, **OSw** *VmL* Kkb

wound **OGu** *GL* A 19

See also: *bardaghi, lysta (1)*

bæsingr (ON) noun

A 'cribling'; an illegitimate child born to a mother under penalty of full outlawry (a child born to an outlawed father was known as a *vargdropi*).

cribling **OIce** *Grg* Arþ 118

See also: *hornungr, hrísungr, laungetinn, vargdropi*

Refs: CV; Fritzner; GrgTr II:7; ONP; KLNM s.v. *oäkta barn*

bætring (ODan) noun

compensation **ODan** *ESjL* 2

bölvun (ON) noun

heathen cursing **ONorw** *BorgL* 16.9

bön (OSw) noun

prayer **OSw** *YVgL* Add

right to plead **OSw** *DL* Eb

böta (OSw) **bøte** (ODan) **byta** (OGu) **bæta** (ON) **bóta** (ON) verb

atone **OFar** *Seyð* 1, **OGu** *GL* A 13, **OIce** *Grg* Klþ 2 Vís 112 Bat 113 Feþ 154, **ONorw** *FrL* KrbB 3, 9

compensate **ODan** *ESjL* 2, 3, *JyL* 2, *SkL* 56, 214, *VSjL* 13, 69, **OGu** *GL* A 15, **OIce** *Grg* passim, *Jó* Mah 8 Llb 1 Kab 16 Þjb 16 Fml 2, *Js* Mah 4, 7 Kab 1, 11 Þjb 7, *KRA* 2, 6 passim, **ONorw** *FrL* Mhb 17 LlbA 1, **OSw** *DL* Mb, Bb, Gb, *HL* Mb, *SdmL* Kkb, Kgb, Gb, Bb, Mb, Tjdb, *YVgL* passim, *ÄVgL* Kkb, Md, Smb, Vs, Slb, Gb, Rlb, Jb, Tb, Fös, Föb *be compensated* **OSw** *DL* Kkb

extract **OSw** *UL* Kkb, Äb,, *VmL* Äb

fine **OSw** *DL* Rb, *ÄVgL* Smb

be fined **OGu** *GL* A 2, 4– 9, 11, 12, 14, 18, 19, 22, 26, 46, 50, 59, Add. 1–5 (B 4, 17, 19, 19, 20), **OSw** *DL* Kkb, Bb, *HL* Kgb, Äb, Blb, *UL* Kkb, Kgb, Mb, Blb, Rb, *VmL* Kkb, Mb, Jb, Kmb

give **ODan** *SkL* 77

improve **OIce** *Grg* Tíg 266, *Jó* Kge 9, *Js* Kdb 5, **ONorw** *GuL* Tfb, Løb

have a liability **OGu** *GL* A 62

be liable to (pay) a fine **OGu** *GL* A 26, 60, 61, 63, 65, Add. 8 (B 55)

make good **OFar** *Seyð* 2, **OIce** *Grg* Tíg 266

make up the difference **OIce** *Jó* Lbb 1

mend **OIce** *Jó* Llb 6, 9, **ONorw** *BorgL* 18.4, **OSw** *UL* Kkb

pay **ODan** *ESjL* 1–3, *JyL* 1–3, *SkKL* 2–4, 7–9, 11, 12, *SkL* passim, *VSjL* passim, **OGu** *GL* A 2, 6, 16–19, 21, 23, 24, 26, 31, 35, 51, 59, Add. 6, 8 (B 33, 55), **ONorw** *BorgL* 3.3 5.14, *EidsL* 41.2, *FrL* Intr 3, 5 KrbA 2, 10, **OSw** *HL* Kkb, Mb, Kmb, Blb, Rb, *UL* Äb, *ÄVgL* Kkb, Md, *ÖgL* Kkb, Eb, Db, Vm

pay a fine **ODan** *ESjL* 2, **OGu** *GL* A 4, 7, 8, 16, 19, 20a, 28, 31, 36–39, 52, 57, Add. 2, 8 (B 17, 55), **ONorw** *GuL* Krb, Kpb, Mhb, **OSw** *DL* Kkb, Eb, Mb, Bb, Tjdb, Rb, *HL* Kkb, Kgb, Äb, Mb, Jb, Kmb, Blb, Rb, *SdmL* Kkb, Kgb, Gb, Äb, Jb, Bb, Kmb, Mb, Tjdb, Rb, Till, *SmL* *UL* Kkb, Kgb, Äb, Mb, Jb, Kmb, Blb, *VmL* Kkb, Kgb, Äb, Mb, Jb, Kmb, Bb, *ÖgL* Kkb, Eb

pay compensation **ODan** *ESjL* 2, *SkL* 61, 62, 66, 187, 188, 193, 195, 202, 224, 225, **OGu** *GL* A 15–19, Add. 1 (B 4), **ONorw** *GuL* Kpb, Kvb, Løb, Tjb, Llb, Mhb, Sab, Trm, **OSw** *DL* Bb, Gb, Tjdb, *UL* Mb, Blb, *VmL* Mb, *ÄVgL* Kkb, Md, Slb, Äb, Gb, *ÖgL* Kkb, Eb, Db

pay damages **OIce** *Jó* Mah 11, 15 Llb 16

do penance **OIce** *Jó* Kge 29, **ONorw** *FrL* KrbA 5, 38, *GuL* Krb, Løb, **OSw** *YVgL* Urb

redress **OIce** *Grg* Bat 115

repair **OSw** *UL* Kkb, *VmL* Kkb

restore **OIce** *Jó* Llb 9

Expressions:

bøte ut (ODan)

return **ODan** *SkL* 110

litla böta (OSw)

pay a small fine **OSw** *HL* Kgb

See also: *bot, fulder, gælda (1), liggia, vaþabot*

bötavarþer (OSw) noun

beacon guard **OSw** *SdmL* Kgb

bølesak (ODan) noun

harrassment **ODan** *JyL* 2

børnevirthning (ODan) noun

Children within a *fælagh* (q.v.) were to be treated equally financially.

making even between children **ODan** *ESjL* 1

Refs: Tamm and Vogt, eds, 2016, 312

bónahald (ON) noun

recitation of prayers **OIce** *Jó* HT 1, *Js* Kdb 1, *KRA* 11

ceciliomessa (ON) noun

St Cecilia's Day **OIce** *Grg* Klþ 13

chirographum (ON) noun

A chirograph, a document on which the same text is written twice (or more) and subsequently divided and given to multiple parties as proof of a transaction. Chirographs are well attested in medieval Europe, in particular in England, whence this type of document likely spread to the Nordic countries. The oldest attested chirograph from Norway dates to 1225 (DN I nr. 8), and several others survive from Sweden, Norway, Denmark and Iceland, mostly from the later Middle Ages.

chirograph **OIce** *Jó* Kab 12

Refs: Beal 2008 s.v. *chirograph*; KLNM s.v. *chirographum*; LexMA s.v. *chirograph*

crucismisse (ODan) noun

Cross Mass **ODan** *ESjL* 3

Exaltation of the Cross **OIce** *Grg* Klþ 13

Invention of the Cross **OIce** *Grg* Klþ 13

See also: *crucisuke, krossmessa um haustit, krossmessa um várit*

crucisuke (ODan) noun

Cross week **ODan** *SkKL* 9

See also: *crucismisse, krossmessa um várit*

dagakaup (ON) noun

day wages **OIce** *Grg* Þsþ 78, 80

dagher (OSw) noun

Expressions:

miðr dagr, miðdagr (ON)

midday (twelve o'clock) **ONorw** *GuL* Krb

taka af daghum (OSw)

kill **OSw** *YVgL* Drb

put to death **OSw** *ÄVgL* Md

take from the day **OSw** *ÖgL* Db

See also: *hælghidagher*

daghsværksspjal (ODan) noun

labour lost **ODan** *SkL* 122, *VSjL* 86

lost labour **ODan** *SkL* 105

See also: *dagsværki*

dagleið (ON) noun

full day's journey **OIce** *Grg* Ómb 133

dagríki (ON) noun

holiness of the day **ONorw** *BorgL* 6.4 13.4

dagsværki (OSw) **daghværke** (OSw) **daxuærki** (OSw) noun

Mainly referring to the householders' obligation to participate in the building of the church. In SdmL Bb also the obligations of hired workers towards their employer.

day's work **OSw** *HL* Kkb, *SdmL* Kkb, Bb, *SmL*

See also: *fearnyt*

dailumal (OGu) noun

matter of conflict **OGu** *GS* Ch. 3

See also: *dela*

danaarver (OSw) **dana arf** (OSw) **dana arff** (OSw) noun

An unclaimed inheritance, usually after a foreigner, that was passed on to the king or the bishop.

unclaimed inheritance **OSw** *SdmL* Kgb, Mb, Till {*danaarver*} **OSw** *DL* Gb, *HL* Mb, *UL* Kgb, Mb (table of contents only), *VmL* Mb, *ÄVgL* Äb

Refs: Brink forthcoming; KLNM s.v. *danefæ*; SAOB s.v. *danaarf*; Schlyter s.v. *dana arver*; Söderwall s.v. *dana arver*

danefæ (ODan) **dánarfé** (ON) noun

dead man's property **OIce** *Grg* Arþ 125, 126

treasure trove **ODan** *ESjL* 3

dansker (OSw) **dænsker** (OSw) adj.

Appears in connection with varying punishments for killing men of different nationality. Also in the phrase *dönsk tunga* lit. 'dansih tongue' (OIce Grg Þsþ) of the common language of the North or of Danish specifically.

Danish **OSw** *YVgL* Drb, *ÄVgL* Md

daufiorþ (OGu) noun

infertile land **OGu** *GL* A 25

deghia (OSw) **deghje** (ODan) **deigja** (ON) noun

Literally, 'dough maker'. This derivation is reflected in similar words in other Germanic languages (Hellquist) and the English word 'lady' has a similar derivation.

Her function in the household seems to be the female equivalent of a *bryti* (q.v.) or overseer. It was a person who was herself a slave or serf, but who had the responsibility for the other slaves or serfs in the household and who had the confidence of the householder and might even be in partnership with them. In GuL she was the highest-ranked of the female slaves. With the abolition of slavery, the role of the *bryti* became that of a steward of a household or estate. In Norway, *deigja* seems, in certain circumstances, to have been the designation used for the housekeeper (perhaps the best description of this female role) and possibly, for the concubine of a priest.

female steward **OSw** *YVgL* Äb, *ÄVgL* Äb

housekeeper **ODan** *ESjL* 3, **ONorw** *FrL* Kvb 21, *GuL* Mhb, **OSw** *SdmL* Tjdb, *UL* Mb, *VmL* Mb

See also: *ambat*, *annöþogher*, *bryti*, *fostra*, *frælsgiva*, *hion*, *lavarþer*, *seta*, *sætesambut*

Refs: Brink 2005; Hellquist [1948] 1964, s.v. *deja*; KLNM s.v.v. *bryde*, *kvinnearbeid*, *slegfred*, *tyende*; ODEE 1986, s.v. *lady*; Schlyter 1877, s.v. *deghia*; SL UL, 129 note 163; SL VmL, 103 note 209a

dela (OSw) **dele** (ODan) **daila** (OGu) **deila** (ON) **delæ** (OSw) **dele** (ODan) **daila** (OGu) **deila** (ON) verb

Literally 'to divide'. To express differing opinions in legal matters (translated as 'to disagree', 'to dispute', 'to contest', 'to argue', 'to quarrel', 'to fight'). Also to bring this disagreement to court, that is to start legal proceedings (translated as 'take action', 'raise a claim/complaint', '(lawfully) sue', 'press charges').

appeal **OSw** *YVgL* Föb

argue **OSw** *HL* Kkb, Äb, Jb

claim **ODan** *JyL* 1

deal with **ODan** *ESjL* 2

decide **ODan** *JyL* 2, *SkKL* 6

disagree **OGu** *GL* A 32, **OSw** *DL* Bb, Rb, *UL* Kkb, Äb, Jb, Blb, Rb, *VmL* Kkb, Äb, Mb, Jb, Kmb, Bb, Rb, *YVgL* Kvab, *ÄVgL* Kva, *ÖgL* Kkb

discuss **ONorw** *GuL* Llb

dispute **ODan** *ESjL* 3, *JyL* 1, 3, **OSw** *DL* Mb, Bb, Gb, Tjdb, Rb, *HL* Äb, Mb, Jb, Blb, Rb, *SdmL* Kkb, Kgb, Jb, Bb, Kmb, Rb, *UL* Kgb, Äb, Jb, Blb, Rb, *VmL* Jb, Rb, *YVgL* Kkb, Äb, Jb, Add, *ÄVgL* Jb

divide **OSw** *HL* Blb

lawfully sue **ODan** *JyL* 2

press charges **OSw** *HL* Mb

quarrel **ONorw** *GuL* Mhb, **OSw** *HL* Kkb, Äb, Blb

raise a claim **ODan** *ESjL* 3, *JyL* 2, 3

raise a complaint **ODan** *JyL* 2

sue **ODan** *JyL* 1–3

take action **ODan** *JyL* 2, 3

See also: *skilia*, *barsmíð*, *dailumal*, *deld*, *vingretta*

Refs: Fritzner s.v. *deila*; Gammeldansk ordbog s.v. *dele*; Hertzberg s.v. *deila*; ONP s.v. *deila*; SAOB s.v. *dela*; Schlyter s.v. *dela*

dela (OSw) noun

    case **ODan** *JyL* 1–3

    claim **ODan** *JyL* 2

    contest **ODan** *ESjL* 3

    disagreement **ODan** *ESjL* 2, 3, **OGu** *GL* A 32

    dispute **ODan** *ESjL* 2, 3, *JyL* 2, *SkL* 26,
    VSjL 1, **OGu** *GL* A 32, *GS* Ch. 3, **OSw**
    HL Jb, *UL* Kkb, Jb, *VmL* Jb, Rb

    quarrel **ONorw** *GuL* Løb, Mhb, **ODan** *ESjL* 1

deld (OSw) deld (ODan) noun

    In the Danish laws and Svea laws (except HL), *deld*
    refers to a part of the village land, sometimes a strip
    field in a *gærþi* (q.v.) (OSw) or *vang* (q.v.) (ODan).

    allotment **OSw** *SdmL* Bb

    cultivated field **ODan** *JyL* 1

    field plot **OSw** *DL* Bb, Tjdb

    fight **ONorw** *GuL* Mhb

    meadow plot **OSw** *VmL* Bb

    part of the village land **ODan** *JyL* 1

    plot (1) **OSw** *UL* Blb, *VmL* Bb

    quarrel **OIce** *Jó* Kab 2, **ONorw** *GuL* Løb, Mhb

    See also: *akerdeld, dela, gærþi, tegher, tompt, vang*

    Refs: Hoff 1997, 204; Schlyter s.v. *deld*

delejorth (ODan) noun

    disputed land **ODan** *JyL* 2

deleman (ODan) noun

    counterpart **ODan** *JyL* 2

    opponent **ODan** *JyL* 1

delobroþir (OSw) noun

    antagonist **OSw** *UL* Kkb

deyddr (ON) deyðr (ON) adj.

    deserving of death **OIce** *Js* Mah 7

deyðandi (ON) adj.

    deserving of death **OIce** *Jó* Mah 2, 14

dirfas (OGu) verb

    presume **OGu** *GL* A 25

disaþing (OSw) noun

    Literally, 'assembly of the Disir'. This was a festival
    and market held in February in pre-Christian Svealand,
    presumably in honour of the Disir, a group of pagan
    female divine beings. The event had legal significance
    and actually incorporated a number of separate
    assemblies. An attempt was made after the conversion
    to re-name it *Kyndilþing* (Candlemas Assembly), but
    this did not succeed. Candlemas (2 February) was the
    day upon which the levy was summoned. There was
    also a period of immunity from prosecution at that
    time, which lasted through two market days, probably
    eight days in all. Candlemas was one of the festivals

of obligation in the church, in that the priest had to
celebrate them. These were also the days upon which
parishioners were obliged to make offerings to the
church.

    disthing **OSw** *UL* Rb

    See also: *kyndilmæssa, þing*

    Refs: KLNM s.v. *disting*; Schlyter 1877,
    s.v. *disaþing*; SL UL, 211 note 91

disker (OSw) noun

    Expressions:

    disker ok duker (OSw)

    board and lodging **OSw** *UL* Kkb *VmL* Kkb

diunga (OSw) verb

    beat **OSw** *YVgL* Urb, *ÄVgL* Slb

    See also: *bardaghi, lysta (1)*

diur (OSw) djur (ODan) dýr (ON) noun

    animal **ODan** *SkL* 104, 205, **ONorw**
    GuL Llb, **OSw** *HL* Blb

    game **OSw** *UL* Mb, *VmL* Mb

    non-domestic animal **OSw** *UL* Mb, *VmL* Mb

    wild animal **ODan** *SkL* 205, **OSw**
    SdmL Bb, *YVgL* Utgb, *ÄVgL* Föb

    See also: *fæ, fælaþi, griper, ortasoyþr, söþer*

djakn (ODan) diakn (ON) djákn (ON) noun

    deacon **ODan** *JyL* 1, **OIce** *KRA* 17, **ONorw**
    EidsL 47.5, *FrL* Leb 17, *GuL* Leb

dobblare (OSw) doblare (OSw) noun

    gambler **OSw** *SmL*

domalöst (OSw) domælöst (OSw) adv.

    without judgement **OSw** *UL* Jb, Rb, *VmL* Rb

    See also: *skælalöst*

domarapænningar (pl.) (OSw) noun

    It is not stated who should pay this, presumably
    annual, fee to the judge.

    payment to a judge **OSw** *SdmL* Till

    Refs: Schlyter s.v. *domara pænningar*

domari (OSw) domeri (OGu) dómari (ON) noun

    A general designation for a judge; someone with the
    authority to pass judgment. In the Norwegian and
    Icelandic laws the terms *dómandi* (q.v.) and *dæmandi*
    are also used, both seemingly synonymous with ON
    dómari. Multiple judges served on a panel (ON *kvið*),
    and their collective decision constituted a judgment
    (ON *dómr*) on a case. In some instances (e.g. Js Mah
    34 and Jó Mah 16) a *dómari* is appointed to punish an
    offender.

    In the Svea laws a judge (OSw *domari*)
    had the additional responsibility of organizing
    legal proceedings in conjunction with the king's

representative (OSw *lænsmaþer*). In medieval Gotland each assembly district (OGu *þing*) was administered by a *domari*.

judge **OGu** *GL* A 19, 61, **OIce** *Jó* Mah 16 Kab 12 Þjb 24, *Js* Mah 34, *KRA* 33, **OSw** *DL* Eb, Rb, *SdmL* Jb, Bb, Kmb, Tjdb, Rb, Till, *UL* StfBM, Kkb, Äb, Mb, Jb, Blb, Rb, Add. 17, 18, *VmL* Kgb, Mb, Jb, Bb, Rb, *YVgL* Kkb, Add, *ÖgL* Kkb

Expressions:

högsti domari (OSw)

supreme judge OSw *YVgL* Föb

kalla sik vndir högre domara (OSw)

submit one's case to a higher judge OSw *YVgL* Kkb

See also: *dómandi, domber, hærapshöfþingi, laghmaþer, landsdomari, rættari*

Refs: CV; Fritzner; GAO s.v. *domare*; Hertzberg; KLNM s.v. *domare, rettergang*; ONP; von See 1964, 44

domber (OSw) **dom** (ODan) **dombr** (OGu) **dómr** (ON) **dom** (OSw) **dombær** (OSw) noun

A court; a judgment issued by a court. Medieval Nordic *dómar* have been described as instruments of arbitration (Sunde 2014, 143), as they typically serve to resolve disputes between two private parties. Such courts usually did not have a judge but rather a panel or jury who issued a judgment for a case based on evidence provided by a prosecutor and defendant. In Iceland *dómar* always dealt only with the facts of a case. Points of law were taken up in the Law Council (ON *lögrétta*).

In compounds –*dómr* often denotes a state or condition, e.g. ON *heiðindómr* ('heathendom'). A rare usage of the term denotes an object in the phrase *heilagr dómr* ('relic').

conviction **OSw** *DL* Rb

court (1) **OIce** *Grg* Þsþ 20, *Jó* Þfb 8, *Js* Þfb 6 Ert 25 Kab 1, **ONorw** *FrL* Intr 16 Var 46 Sab 1, *GuL* Krb, Kpb, Løb, Llb, Arb, Mhb, Olb

court meeting **ONorw** *FrL* KrbA 1

court-sitting **OIce** *Grg* Hrs 234

decision **ODan** *ESjL* 2, *JyL* Fort, 2, *VSjL* 58, 87, **OSw** *ÄVgL* Md

judge **OSw** *SdmL* Rb, *VmL* Kkb

judgement **ODan** *ESjL* 2, 3, *JyL* 1–3, *SkL* 188, 241, *VSjL* 52, 58, **OFar** *Seyð* 2, 5, **OGu** *GL* A 31, **OIce** *Grg* passim, *Jó* Kab 1 Fml 25, *Js* passim, *KRA* 18, 34, **ONorw** *FrL* Var 7, 46, *GuL* Krb, Kpb, Mhb, Olb, **OSw** *DL* Rb, *HL* Kkb, Rb, *SdmL* Conf, Kkb, Jb, Bb, Kmb, Mb, Tjdb, Rb, *UL* StfBM, Kkb, Mb, Jb, Blb, Rb, *VmL* Kkb, Mb, Jb, Bb, Rb, *YVgL* Drb, Tb, Jb, Add, *ÄVgL* Jb, *ÖgL* Kkb, Eb, Vm

judicial power **OSw** *HL* Rb

permission **ODan** *ESjL* 3, *SkL* 162, 233

right to judge **OSw** *HL* Kkb

sentence **ODan** *SkL* 163, 233, **ONorw** *GuL* Mhb, **OSw** *DL* Tjdb

verdict **OIce** *Jó* Þfb 3, **ONorw** *FrL* ArbB 7, **OSw** *DL* Bb, Gb, Rb, *HL* Kkb, Mb, Rb, *YVgL* Add

Expressions:

dómar eru úti (ON)

courts are sitting OIce *Grg* Vís 105

domber ok skæl, mæþ domom och full skælom (OSw)

excuse OSw *VmL* Mb

legal grounds OSw *HL* Rb

legal procedures OSw *UL* Blb *VmL* Mb, Bb

heiðinn dómr (ON)

heathendom ONorw *GuL* Krb

heilagr dómr (ON)

relic OIce *Js* Kdb 5

rísa ór dómi (ON)

to withdraw (to recuse onself?) OIce *Grg* Þsþ 25

See also: *döma, forfall, skæl*

Refs: CV s.v. *dómr*; F s.v. *dómr*; GAO s.v. *Urteil*; Gunnar Karlsson 2005; KLNM s.v. *dómr*; LexMA s.v. *Domen*; NGL V s.v. *dómr*; Sunde 2014; Z s.v. *dómr*

dombrut (OSw) noun

breach of a judgement **OSw** *SdmL* Rb

disregard of the judgement **OSw** *UL* Rb

domvilla (OSw) **domwilla** (OSw) noun

miscarriage of justice **OSw** *UL* Kkb

unjust verdict **OSw** *HL* Kkb

dómandi (ON) **dǿmandi** (ON) noun

See *domari*.

judge **OIce** *Grg* Þsþ 28, 29 Lrþ 117 Lbþ 176 Fjl 221, 223 Hrs 234, *Jó* Lbb 1, *Js* Lbb 1, *KRA* 7, **ONorw** *FrL* Jkb 8, *GuL* Llb, Olb, Trm

member of a court **ONorw** *FrL* Rgb 14

dómaútførsla (ON) **dómaútfærsla** (ON) noun

moving out courts **OIce** *Grg* Þsþ 24, 58

dómfesta (ON) noun

appeal to a court **ONorw** *FrL* Rgb 17

dómflogi (ON) noun

A *dómflogi* ('defaulter') was literally 'one who flees from the court'. A man might default either by failing to attend the hearing of his case or by violating the accepted rules of court procedure.

defaulter **ONorw** *GuL* Kpb, Olb

runaway from court **ONorw** *FrL* Rgb 12

Refs: Helle 2001, 154; Hertzberg s.v. *dómflogi*; Robberstad 1981, 344

dómhringr (ON) noun

A circle of judges or judgment circle. In Grg Þsþ 47 this refers to an area where judges dismissed from the Fifth Court are to sit during the proceedings of a case. It has been suggested that the *dómhringr* was the area surrounded by a *vébönd* (q.v.) as portrayed in the description of Gulaþing in *Egils saga*. Saga evidence further depicts the *dómhringr* as the location where the person on trial stood (*Eyrbyggja saga*) or where human sacrifices took place (*Landnámabók*), though most now consider the latter unlikely. Some confusion has arisen between the term *dómhringr* and the Early Modern Swedish appellation *domarring*, which has been used to denote a variety of stone circles identified through archaeological investigations. These circles have been attributed a variety of purposes, including burial, ritual and legal usage.

circle of judges **OIce** *Grg* Þsþ 47

See also: *vébönd (pl.)*

Refs: CV s.v. *dómhringr*; Fritzner s.v. *dómhringr*; GAO s.v. *Domarring, Menschenopfer*; KLNM s.v. *dómhringr*; Olsen 1966, 194–97; ONP s.v. *dómhringr*

dómnefna (ON) noun

court nomination **OIce** *Grg* Þsþ 45

nomination of judges **OIce** *Grg* Lbþ 202

dómrof (ON) noun

disregard of judgement **OIce** *Jó* Þfb 5, 8 Mah 21, **ONorw** *FrL* Rgb 13

judgement breaking **OIce** *Grg* Klþ 6 Þsþ 51, 75

dómruðning (ON) noun

challenging a court **OIce** *Grg* Þsþ 25

dómsetning (ON) noun

opening of a court meeting **ONorw** *FrL* Rgb 14

dómsmaðr (ON) noun

judge **OIce** *Jó* Kab 13

dómstaðarbúi (ON) noun

neighbour of the court-place **OIce** *Grg* Feþ 167

dómstaðr (ON) **dómsstaðr** (ON) noun

court-place **OIce** *Grg* Lbþ 176, 202 Fjl 223 Hrs 234, **ONorw** *FrL* Rgb 11 Jkb 8

dómstaurr (ON) noun

A 'court pole' or 'judgment stake'. Refers to witnesses who testified from outside of the official court circle (ON *vébönd*).

court bar **ONorw** *FrL* Rgb 15 Jkb 8

Refs: CV s.v. *dómstaurr*; Fritzner s.v. *dómstaurr*; KLNM s.v. *dombrev*; ONP s.v. *dómstaurr*

dómstefna (ON) noun

court-meeting **OIce** *Grg* Lbþ 202 Hrs 234

request for judicial decision **ONorw** *GuL* Olb

See also: *stæmna*

dómsuppsöguváttr (ON) noun

witness of the anouncement of judgement **OIce** *Grg* Þsþ 48 Lsþ 116

dómsuppsöguvætti (ON) noun

testimony of the announcement of judgement **OIce** *Grg* Þsþ 49 Feþ 158

dómsætr (ON) adj.

eligible to sit in court **ONorw** *GuL* Olb

having a seat in court **OIce** *Grg* Þsþ 40

dómvarzla (ON) noun

court guarding **OIce** *Grg* Þsþ 41

dómvörzlumaðr (ON) noun

court-guard **OIce** *Grg* Þsþ 41

drap (OSw) **drap** (ODan) **drap** (OGu) **dráp** (ON) **dræp** (OSw) noun

A killing that was publicly announced and admitted, and as such contrasted to *morþ* 'murder'. Both could, however, be punished by death or outlawry, as well as fines/compensation.

case of killing **OSw** *HL* Mb

execution **OIce** *Jó* Þjb 2, *Js* Þjb 2

homicide **ODan** *ESjL* 3, *VSjL* 53, 86

killing **ODan** *ESjL* 2, *JyL* 3, **OSw** *DL* Eb, Mb, Rb, *HL* Kgb, Äb, Mb, *SdmL* Kkb, Kgb, Äb, Mb, Tjdb, Rb, *UL* För, Kkb, Kgb, Äb, Mb, Rb, *VmL* För, Kgb, Äb, Mb, Rb, *YVgL* Drb, Add, *ÄVgL* Md, Urb, *ÖgL* Kkb, Eb, Db, Vm

manslaughter **OGu** *GL* A 5, **OSw** *DL* Gb, *HL* Mb, Rb, *YVgL* Add, *ÖgL* Eb

See also: *bani, döpsdrap, dræpa, dulghadrap, morþ*

Refs: Ekholst 2009, 155–58; KLNM s.v.*drab*; Maček 2009; SAOB s.v. *dråp*

drapabalker (OSw) noun

book of killings **OSw** *ÖgL* Db

See also: *balker, drap*

drapamal (OSw) noun

book of manslaughter **OSw** *YVgL* Add

case of manslaughter **OSw** *ÖgL* Eb

See also: *drap, mal (1)*

drapari (OSw) **dræpari** (OSw) noun

assassin **OSw** *HL* Mb

killer **OSw** *SdmL* Mb, *UL* Mb, Add. 8, 9, *VmL* Mb, *YVgL* Drb, Add, *ÖgL* Eb, Db

murderer **OSw** *DL* Mb

slayer **OSw** *YVgL* Add

See also: *bani*, *drap*, *dræpa*

draparibalker (OSw) noun

book about killing **OSw** *YVgL* Drb

See also: *balker*, *drapari*

drekkulaun (ON) noun

This concept refers to land granted as a reward from the king. Such land was considered equal to odal land. See GuL ch. 270.

gift in reward for hospitality **ONorw** *GuL* Olb

Refs: Hertzberg s.v. *drekkulaun*; KLNM s.v. *kongegåve*

drengmaðr (ON) noun

soldier **ONorw** *FrL* Leb 13

unmarried man **ONorw** *GuL* Kpb, Leb

See also: *ainloypr*

drep (ON) noun

beating **ONorw** *GuL* Mhb

blow **OIce** *Grg* Vís 88

drepráð (ON) noun

plot to strike **OIce** *Grg* Vís 108

drinkare (OSw) noun

drinker **OSw** *SmL*

drivari (OSw) noun

vagrant **OSw** *DL* Tjdb

drotin (OGu) **dróttinn** (ON) noun

Derived from *drótt* (ON) 'household' especially 'the king's bodyguard'. Used of any lord or master.

lord **OIce** *Jó* HT 1, **ONorw** *BorgL* 14.5, *FrL* KrbA 31 Mhb 57

master **OGu** *GL* A 2, 6, 16, 22, Add. 8 (B 55), **OIce** *Grg* Vís 102, 110, **ONorw** *FrL* KrbA 2, 6 Mhb 61 Rgb 40 LlbB 10, *GuL* Krb, Løb, Llb, Mhb, Tjb

See also: *skapdróttinn*

Refs: Cleasby and Vigfusson s.v. *drótt*

drozsieti (OGu) noun

wedding host **OGu** *GL* A 24

See also: *gerþamaþr*, *reþuman*

dróttinssvik (ON) noun

high treason **OIce** *Jó* Mah 4

dróttinssvikari (ON) **dróttinssviki** (ON) noun

lord-cheater **ONorw** *EidsL* 50.13

traitor **OIce** *KRA* 11

traitor to the king **ONorw** *GuL* Krb

dróttning (ON) noun

The lady or mistress of a house, estate, etc.

mistress (1) **OIce** *Grg* Vís 102, 110

dryghe (ODan) verb

prove **ODan** *ESjL* 2

drænger (OSw) noun

farm hand **OSw** *UL* Blb, *VmL* Bb

farm-hand **OSw** *SdmL* Bb

worker **OSw** *YVgL* Utgb

young man **OSw** *SmL*

See also: *maþer*

dræpa (OSw) **dræpe** (ODan) **dræpin** (ODan) **drepa** (OGu) **drepa** (ON) **dræpin** (OSw) verb

beat **ONorw** *FrL* Mhb 7

kill **ODan** *ESjL* 1–3, *JyL* Fort, 1–3, *SkL* passim, *VSjL* 23, 50, 51, 53–55, 63, 69, 86, **OGu** *GL* A 8, 9, 11–16, 28, **OIce** *Grg* Vís 110 Bat 113 Rsþ 230, *Jó* Mah 2 Llb 39 Kab 16 Þjb 2 Fml 9, *Js* Mah 6, 9 Þjb 2, *KRA* 6, **ONorw** *BorgL* 8.5, *FrL* Intr 1, 5 Mhb 4, 10 LlbB 12, *GuL* Krb, Mhb, Tjb, **OSw** *DL* Kkb, Eb, Mb, Bb, Gb, Rb, *HL* Kkb, Kgb, Äb, Mb, Blb, *SdmL* Kkb, Kgb, Gb, Äb, Bb, Tjdb, *UL* Kkb, Kgb, Äb, Mb, Blb, *VmL* Kkb, Kgb, Äb, Mb, Bb, *YVgL* Kkb, Frb, Urb, Drb, Äb, Rlb, Tb, Add, *ÄVgL* Kkb, Md, Slb, Urb, Äb, Gb, Rlb, *ÖgL* Kkb, Eb, Db, Vm

slaughter **OSw** *UL* Mb

slay **ODan** *JyL* 2, **OSw** *DL* Eb, *HL* Äb, *YVgL* Kkb, Drb, Add

strike **OIce** *Grg* Vís 86, 101, *Jó* Mah 22, *KRA* 8, **OSw** *SdmL* Kgb, Gb

Expressions:

döþan ok dræpnan (OSw)

person done to death **OSw** *VmL* Mb

See also: *drap*, *myrþa*, *sla*, *vigh*

dræpr (ON) adj.

'Killable', describing someone who has no legal immunity and whose heirs would have no right to compensation. The commission of certain serious offenses, such as refusing to leave the country when convicted of outlawry (Grg Þsþ 53), running off with another man's wife (Js Mah 7) or theft (Js Þjb 1), resulted in becoming *dræpr*.

to be killed **OIce** *Jó* Þjb 1, **ONorw** *FrL* Mhb 10

who may be killed with impunity **OIce** *Grg* Þsþ 53, *Jó* Mah 2, 14, *Js* Mah 7, 31 Þjb 1, **ONorw** *GuL* Tjb

Expressions:

dræpr ok deyddr (ON)

should be put to death **OIce** *Jó* Mah 2

may be killed or put to death **ONorw** *FrL* Intr 9

See also: *deyddr*, *friþlös*, *sækt*, *útlagi*

Refs: CV; F; NGL V; ONP

dufl (OGu) **dubl** (ON) **dufl** (ON) noun

gambling **OGu** *GL* A 61, **OIce** *Jó* Þjb 18

See also: *fordoble*

dul (OSw) **dyl** (OSw) noun

acquittal **OSw** *YVgL* Utgb

denial **OSw** *DL* Rb, *HL* Mb, *SdmL* Tjdb, *UL* Mb, Jb, Kmb, Blb, *VmL* Mb, Bb

denial by oath **OSw** *SmL*

hiding **OSw** *ÄVgL* Föb

legal defence **OSw** *UL* Jb, Kmb, Blb, *VmL* Kkb, Jb, Mb, Rb

right to defend with an oath **OSw** *HL* Rb

Expressions:

dul biuþa (OSw)

deny by/on oath **OSw** *UL* Mb

See also: *biuþa, dylia, ne, neka*

duleiðr (ON) **dulaeiðr** (ON) **dulareiðr** (ON) noun

An umbrella term for oaths given by a defendant and his associates, the latter being witnesses rather than simply compurgators as in a *jafnaðareiðr* (cf. Js Mah 37) (see *jamnaþareþer*). In Iceland these oaths usually included one, three, six or twelve men depending on the severity of the charge. At least one scholar has equated the *duleiðr* to the process of acquittal (ON *undanfœrsla*, see *undanfórsla*).

oath of denial **OIce** *Js* Mah 37

See also: *eneþer, eþer, jamnaþareþer, undanfórsla*

Refs: CV s.v. *duleiðr*; Fritzner s.v. *duleiðr*; KLNM s.v.v. *edgärdsman, värjemål* ; Imsen 2009; ONP s.v.v. *dulaeiðr, duleiðr*

dulghadrap (OSw) noun

Literally, 'hidden killing'. This word is used of the situation in which someone is killed outside a locked house and the killer is not discovered. If the body was found in a locked house, the owner of the property was liable for the compensation. As the custom was normally to declare a killing, the non-disclosure made the crime more serious. Compensation at about a third of that normal for a killing went to the relatives of the dead person (provided they identified themselves within a year and a day) or to the king in the case of DL. This was provided by the landowners of the land where the body was discovered (DL and VmL) or by the whole *hundari* (q.v.) (if the body was discovered on common land and in every case in UL). The members of the community, or the *hundari* as appropriate, also had the responsibility for seeking the real culprit. If the relatives did not come forward, within a year and a day, the compensation went to the king. The difference between *dulghadrap* and *morþ* (q.v.) is far from clear but to equate *morþ* with *dulghadrap* is not justified by the sources available.

hidden homicide **OSw** *HL* Mb

hidden killing **OSw** *SdmL* Kgb, Mb, Till

hidden-homicide fine **OSw** *HL* Mb

undeclared killing **OSw** *UL* Kgb, Mb, *VmL* Mb

undetected murder **OSw** *DL* Mb

See also: *bot, drap, dræpa, dylia, flugumaðr, gæld, mandrap, morþ*

Refs: KLNM, s.v.v. *drab, dulgadråp, mord;* Schlyter 1877, s.v. *dulghadrap*; SL DL, 42 note 29; SL UL, 53 note 13; 118 note 26, 121–22 not 53

dulsak (OSw) noun

cause where one shall defend oneself by oath **OSw** *SmL*

See also: *dul, sak*

dylia (OSw) **dylje** (ODan) **dula** (OGu) **dula** (ON) **dylja** (ON) verb

attest **OSw** *HL* Kkb

confirm **OSw** *YVgL* Rlb, Föb, Add

confirm not guilty **OSw** *YVgL* Add

defend **OSw** *HL* Blb, Rb

defend one's position **OSw** *HL* Äb

deny **ODan** *ESjL* 1–3, *JyL* 2, 3, *SkKL* 3–7, 9, 11, *SkL* passim, *VSjL* passim, **OGu** *GL* A 2, 18, 37, 39, **OIce** *Jó* Fml 25, *Js* Ert 20, **OSw** *DL* Gb, Rb, *HL* Äb, Mb, Blb, Rb, *SdmL* Kkb, Gb, Äb, Jb, Bb, Kmb, Mb, Tjdb, Rb, *UL* Kkb, Äb, Mb, Jb, Kmb, Blb, Rb, *VmL* Äb, Mb, Kmb, Bb, *YVgL* Kkb, Add, *ÄVgL* Kkb, *ÖgL* Kkb, Eb, Db, Vm

deny by/on oath **OSw** *SmL*

deny responsibility **OSw** *HL* Mb

dissemble **OIce** *Grg* Þsþ 35

not recognize **ODan** *ESjL* 2

prove **OSw** *HL* Kgb, Äb, Mb, Kmb, Blb

prove one's innocence **OSw** *HL* Kgb, Mb, Kmb, Blb, Rb

refuse **OSw** *HL* Äb, Blb

refute **OSw** *UL* Mb, *VmL* Mb

strengthen **OSw** *HL* Blb

strengthen one's case **OSw** *HL* Blb

substantiate a denial **OSw** *DL* Eb, *UL* Kkb, Kgb, Äb, Mb, Jb, Kmb, Blb, Rb, *VmL* Kkb, Kgb, Äb, Mb, Kmb, Bb, Rb

substantiate one's denial **OSw** *DL* Eb

See also: *dul, ne, neka, vita*

dylkas (OSw) verb

be contumacious **OSw** *DL* Rb

dylsbot (OSw) noun
  fine for hiding OSw *DL* Mb
  fine for hiding a crime OSw *DL* Mb
  See also: *bot*, *dylia*

dymbilvika (OSw) noun
  Holy week OSw *ÖgL* Kkb

dynter (OSw) noun
  blow OSw *YVgL* Föb

dyrr (ON) noun
  door ONorw *GuL* Kpb, Olb

dýrgarðr (ON) noun
  animal fence ONorw *FrL* LlbB 9

dýrveiðr (ON) noun
  deer hunting ONorw *GuL* Llb

döfviþer (OSw) **döfwiþær** (OSw) **döviþer** (OSw)
döþwiþer (OSw) noun
  firewood OSw *UL* Blb, *VmL* Bb
  non-fruit bearing tree OSw *UL* Blb, *VmL* Bb

döma (OSw) **døme** (ODan) **dyma** (OGu) **dæma** (ON)
dóma (ON) **dömba** (OSw) verb
  adjudge ODan *ESjL* 2, *VSjL* 50, 84, OIce *Grg* Tíg
  255, *Jó* Lbb 1, *Js* Ert 25, *KRA* 7, ONorw *FrL* Sab
  2, OSw *SdmL* Jb, *YVgL* Jb, *ÄVgL* Jb, *ÖgL* Eb
  adjudicate ODan *ESjL* 3, ONorw *GuL* Løb, Arb
  award OIce *Jó* Sg 3, *Js* Lbb 1, ONorw *GuL* Kpb,
  Olb, Arb, Leb, OSw *DL* Bb, *UL* Jb, Blb, *VmL* Mb, Jb
  call OSw *SdmL* Jb
  commit OGu *GL* A 38
  condemn OSw *UL* Kkb, Mb, *VmL*
  Kkb, Mb, Jb, *YVgL* Tb
  convict OIce *KRA* 11, ONorw *EidsL* 50.13
  decide ODan *ESjL* 2, *JyL* 2, *SkL* 136, 138, 139, 145,
  156, 170, 184, OFar *Seyð* 12, OIce *Jó* Þfb 4, ONorw
  BorgL 14.5, OSw *YVgL* Drb, Äb, Jb, *ÄVgL* Slb, Jb
  declare OSw *HL* Kkb, *YVgL* Tb
  deem OGu *GL* A 2, 13, ONorw *GuL* Tjb, OSw
  DL Rb, *UL* Kkb, Kgb, Äb, Mb, Jb, *VmL* Kkb, Jb,
  YVgL Rlb, *ÄVgL* Md, Smb, Slb, Tb, *ÖgL* Eb
  deem appropriate OIce *Jó* Mah 14
  denounce ODan *VSjL* 87
  deprive by court judgement ONorw *GuL* Arb
  doom OSw *ÄVgL* Rlb
  give a verdict OIce *Jó* Mah 13
  give an opinion OIce *Jó* Kab 13
  give judgement ODan *JyL* Fort, OSw *HL* Rb
  grant ODan *JyL* 2, *SkL* 83
  have a decision ODan *JyL* 2
  impose ONorw *GuL* Sab, OSw *HL* Rb

  judge ODan *ESjL* 2, 3, *VSjL* 41, 50, 87, OGu *GL*
  A 31, OIce *Grg* passim, *Jó* Þfb 5 Sg 3, *Js* Mah 7,
  KRA 29, 33, ONorw *EidsL* 25, *FrL* Tfb 2, OSw
  DL Bb, *SdmL* Kkb, Gb, Tjdb, Rb, Till, *UL* Kkb,
  Kgb, Mb, Blb, Rb, *VmL* Kkb, Mb, Rb, *YVgL* Kkb,
  Frb, Drb, Rlb, Tb, Jb, Add, *ÄVgL* Md, Slb, Jb, Tb
  make a judgement ODan *ESjL* 2
  order ODan *JyL* 2, *VSjL* 87
  pass judgement ONorw *GuL* Mhb,
  Trm, OSw *DL* Rb, *ÖgL* Eb
  permit ODan *SkL* 233
  pronounce OSw *HL* Kkb, *SdmL* Kgb, Add
  sentence ODan *SkL* 151, 163, 184, 226, OIce *Jó*
  Llb 39, OSw *DL* Kkb, Mb, Rb, *HL* Kkb, *SdmL*
  Kkb, Kgb, Bb, Mb, *YVgL* Drb, *ÄVgL* Md
  settle OSw *ÄVgL* Md, Smb
  submit OSw *UL* Kkb, *VmL* Kkb
  Expressions:
  fram döma (OSw)
    accept a statement OSw *UL* Jb
    See also: *domber*, *fælla*, *laghbinda*,
    laghvinna, *læggia*, *vinna*, *viþerbinda*

döpa (OSw) **døpe** (ODan) **deyfa** (ON) **deypa** (ON)
verb
  baptize ODan *JyL* 1, ONorw *BorgL* 2.2,
  OSw *DL* Kkb, *HL* Kkb, Äb, *SdmL* Kkb,
  SmL, *YVgL* Kkb, Add, *ÄVgL* Kkb
  See also: *kristna*

döpilse (OSw) noun
  baptism OSw *DL* Kkb, *SmL*, *YVgL* Add

döþsdrap (OSw) **döz drap** (OSw) **dozdrap** (OSw)
noun
  killing OSw *HL* Kgb, *SdmL* Mb, *UL* Mb, *VmL* Mb
  manslaughter OSw *HL* Mb
  See also: *drap*

døthelot (ODan) noun
  dead man's lot ODan *SkL* 21

edgilder (OSw) adj.
  Of a person who is allowed to swear an oath.
  with the right to swear an oath OSw *DL* Rb
  See also: *eþer*, *gilder*
  Refs: Schlyter s.v. *eþganger*

eftirbróðrasynir (pl.) (ON) **eftirbræðrasonr** (ON)
noun
  second cousins in the agnatic line ONorw *FrL* Sab 2

eftirför (ON) **eptirför** (ON) noun
  pursuit ONorw *GuL* Tjb

eftirkomandi (ON) noun

successor **OFar** *Seyð* 0, 11

eftirsýnarmaðr (ON) noun

'One who looks after'. The person responsible for collecting compensation and pledges following an outlawry case.

prosecutor **ONorw** *FrL* Mhb 41

Refs: CV s.v. *eftirsýnarmaðr*;
ONP s.v. *eftirsýnarmaðr*

eftirætlandi (ON) noun

one who intends to prosecute **ONorw** *FrL* Mhb 23

egðir (pl.) (ON) noun

people from Agder **ONorw** *GuL* Leb

eggver (ON) noun

nesting grounds **OIce** *Jó* Llb 32, 57

right to gather eggs **OIce** *Jó* Llb 6, *Js* Lbb 13

eghere (ODan) noun

landowner **ODan** *JyL* 1, 2

owner **ODan** *JyL* 3

eghereman (ODan) noun

owner **ODan** *JyL* 3

egn (OSw) **eghn** (ODan) **aign** (OGu) **eign** (ON) **eghn** (OSw) **eign** (OSw) **æghn** (OSw) **æighn** (OSw) noun

belongings **ODan** *SkL* 58, 76, 221, 222

common property **OSw** *YVgL* Jb

estate **ODan** *SkL* 1, 41

land **OGu** *GL* A 20, 24f (64), 25, 26, 27, 28, 48, **OIce** *Jó* Mah 1 Llb 52, **ONorw** *FrL* Intr 2 KrbA 35, **OSw** *DL* Bb, *UL* Jb, *VmL* Jb, *YVgL* Äb, Kvab, Föb, Utgb, *ÄVgL* Föb, *ÖgL* Kkb, Eb, Db

landed property **OIce** *Js* Mah 4,
OSw *SdmL* Gb, Äb, Jb

ownership **OGu** *GL* A 31, **OSw** *VmL* Jb

ownership of land **OSw** *DL* Bb

piece of land **OSw** *SmL*

private property **OSw** *YVgL* Jb

property **ODan** *ESjL* 1, 3, *JyL* 1–3, *SkKL* 5, *SkL* 112, 121, 226, *VSjL* 3, 4, 13, 15, 20, 21, 65, 67, **OGu** *GL* A 7, 13, 25, 28, 53, B 44 (correcting A 28), **OIce** *Jó* Llb 17, 27 Fml 25, *Js* Mah 2 Kab 16, *KRA* 4, 11, **ONorw** *FrL* Intr 2, 4 LlbB 2, *GuL* Kpb, Olb, **OSw** *VmL* Kkb, *YVgL* Utgb, *ÄVgL* Jb, Kva, *ÖgL* Kkb, Db

property in the form of land **OSw** *UL* Äb, *VmL* Äb

right to ownership **OIce** *Jó* Lbb 3

title **OIce** *Jó* Llb 26

See also: *bo, fæ, goþs, jorþ, kununger, tompt, ægha*

egningarkviðr (ON) noun

A panel or verdict resulting from goads or incitements. Appears only once in Grg Þsþ 35 where it is defined as a panel verdict irrelevant to the case at hand. The party which calls for a verdict on irrelevant matters loses their case. The name *egningarkviðr* suggests that these types of panel verdicts are incited by third parties.

baiting verdict **OIce** *Grg* Þsþ 35

See also: *glafseþer, skroksak*

Refs: CV; Fritzner; GrgTr I:75;
Maurer 1910, 561; ONP

eiðalið (ON) noun

oath helpers **ONorw** *FrL* KrbA 45 Mhb 23

eiðasekð (ON) noun

fine for the wrong oath **ONorw** *FrL* ArbB 10

eiðastefna (ON) noun

deadline for oaths **ONorw** *GuL* Krb

See also: *eþer*

eiðavandr (ON) adj.

painstaking in oath-taking **ONorw** *EidsL* 3.2

eiðbróðir (ON) noun

A man allied with another in a relationship of mutual rights and obligations. The relationship did not require kinship, and was probably established through some ritual. In GuL an *eiðbróðir* could receive compensation if the other was killed.

sworn brother **ONorw** *GuL* Mhb

Refs: KLNM s.v. *fostbrorskap*

eiðfall (ON) noun

failing in one's oath **ONorw** *GuL* Krb, Løb, Tfb, Mhb

oath-lapse **OIce** *Grg* Tíg 255, *KRA* 36, **ONorw** *FrL* KrbB 3 Mhb 8

eiðfóra (ON) **eiðfæra** (ON) verb

deliver by oath **OIce** *Grg* Ómb 129, 143

eiðfórsla (ON) **eiðfærsla** (ON) noun

delivering by oath **OIce** *Grg* Ómb 129

eiðlauss (ON) adj.

without oaths **OIce** *Grg* Klþ 6 Tíg 255, *KRA* 14

eiðrof (ON) **eiðarof** (ON) noun

oath-breaking **OIce** *KRA* 22, **ONorw** *FrL* KrbB 16

eiðrofi (ON) **eiðrofa** (ON) adj.

oath-breaking **OIce** *KRA* 22

Eiðsifaþing (ON) noun

Eiðsiva assembly **ONorw** *EidsL* 10.2

See also: *þing*

eiðspjall (ON) noun

oath-taking **OIce** *Grg* Þsþ 30, 31, 38, 46

eiðstafr (ON) eiðsstafr (ON) noun

There are only a few occurrences in the laws of a term for oath formulas. ON *eiðstafr* occurs e.g. concerning land sales (ONorw FrL) and swearing in nominated men for the *alþingi* 'General Assembly' and *lögrétta* 'Law Council' (OIce Js). Various oath formulas in the laws typically invoke the Christian God or, in OSw ÄVgL, pagan gods collectively.

oath-formula **OIce** *Jó* Þfb 1, 3, *Js* Þfb 1, 3 Mah 37, **ONorw** *FrL* KrbA 29

words to swear an oath **ONorw** *FrL* Jkb 1

Refs: ONP s.v. *eið(s)stafr*

eiðstefnudagr (ON) noun

oath-summons day **ONorw** *FrL* Mhb 8

eiðunning (ON) noun

oath-swearing **OIce** *Grg* Þsþ 35

eiginkona (ON) eiginkvinna (ON) eignarkona (ON) noun

lawful wife **OIce** *KRA* 16, 17

wedded wife **ONorw** *FrL* Kvb 12

wife **OIce** *Jó* Mah 2 Kge 5, *Js* Mah 7, **ONorw** *BorgL* 17.2, *FrL* Intr 10 KrbB 6, *GuL* Krb

eiginmaðr (ON) noun

lawful husband **OIce** *KRA* 18

eiginorð (ON) noun

marriage **OIce** *Grg* Þsþ 81 Arþ 118 Feþ 144, 160

ownership **OIce** *Grg* Lbþ 176, 215 Fjl 225, *Jó* Llb 67

See also: *hjúskapr, kvánfang*

eigna (ON) verb

belong to **ONorw** *GuL* Llb, Kvr

eignarmaðr (ON) noun

owner **OIce** *Jó* Kab 23

eignarskifti (ON) eignaskifti (ON) noun

right to ownership **OIce** *Jó* Lbb 5 Llb 19, 20 Kab 20

eignarvitni (ON) noun

witness to the right of ownership **OIce** *Jó* Lbb 1

See also: *vitni*

eindaga (ON) verb

appoint **ONorw** *GuL* Kpb, Llb, Tjb

set a date **OIce** *Grg* Klþ 2 Þsþ 56 Ómb 133 Fjl 221 Misc 250, *Jó* Kge 1 Llb 1 Kab 4, *Js* Kvg 1 Lbb 10 Kab 5

See also: *endaghi*

einfyndr (ON) adj.

as a finder entitled to the whole **ONorw** *GuL* Kvr

owning alone **ONorw** *FrL* LlbB 10

einganga (ON) noun

walking alone (in a pasture) **OFar** *Seyð* 5

einhleypr (ON) adj.

unmarried and without a fixed household **OIce** *Jó* Sg 1 Kab 9, *Js* Kab 7, **ONorw** *FrL* Leb 11 Rgb 26

See also: *göngumaðr, húsgangsmaðr*

einkaleyfi (ON) noun

special leave **OIce** *Grg* Feþ 161

einkalof (ON) noun

special leave **OIce** *Grg* Lrþ 117

einkamál (ON) noun

provision **OIce** *Js* Mah 7, 29

special right **ONorw** *FrL* Var 44

einkunn (ON) noun

ownership **OFar** *Seyð* 5

ownership mark **OIce** *Grg* Fjl 225

einkynna (ON) verb

To place a mark of ownership on something, usually livestock.

mark **OIce** *Grg* Lbþ 208 Fjl 225, *Jó* Llb 47

See also: *marka*

Refs: CV s.v. *einkenna, einkynna*; Fritzner s.v. *einkynna*; ONP s.v. *einkenna, einkynna*

einlát (ON) noun

desertion **OIce** *Grg* Arþ 118

einmánaðarsamkváma (ON) noun

commune meeting in the last month of winter **OIce** *Jó* Llb 54

einmánuðr (ON) einmánaðr (ON) noun

'Single-month'; the sixth and final month of winter beginning on a Tuesday between 10 and 16 March. According to Páll Vídalín it might once have been called *Óðinsmánuðr*.

single month **OIce** *Grg* Þsþ 84 Lbþ 193

See also: *tvímánuðr*

Refs: Árni Björnsson 1995, 108–09; CV s.v. *einmánuðr*; GAO s.v.v. *Misseristal, Monate*; GrgTr I:137; Hastrup 1985, 40; Janson 2011; ONP s.v. *einmánuðr*; Páll Vídalín 1854 s.v. *tvímánuður*

einræði (ON) noun

own decision **ONorw** *FrL* Var 43

einvirki (ON) einyrki (ON) noun

An *einvirki* was a man who ran his farm alone without the help of hired labour.

farmer who has no help **OIce** *Jó* Kge 29, 34

lone farmer **ONorw** *BorgL* 12.2

single worker **ONorw** *GuL* Tfb, Leb

single-handed farmer **OIce** *Grg* Þsþ 35, 77 Vís 89 Feþ 166, **ONorw** *FrL* Leb 7

See also: *ainloypr, drengmaðr*

Refs: KLNM s.v.v. *bonde, enörkne män, våpensyn*; RGA2 s.v. *bonde*

ek (OSw) noun

Oaks appear in some OSw laws (SdmL, UL, VmL, YVgL, ÄVgL) regulating their felling due to their economic importance providing food for pigs and material for construction.

oak **OSw** *YVgL* Utgb, *ÄVgL* Fös, Föb

See also: *akern, aldin, gisningaskogher*

ekia (OSw) **eke** (ODan) **eikja** (ON) noun

A small boat made of oak.

river boat **ONorw** *FrL* LlbA 10

skiff **OSw** *SdmL* Bb, *ÄVgL* Fös

small boat **ODan** *ESjL* 3

ekrugerði (ON) noun

fence around fields **ONorw** *FrL* Rgb 2

elder (ON) noun

arson **ONorw** *FrL* Mhb 4

fire **ONorw** *GuL* Llb, Mhb, Tjb, Leb

See also: *bruni, brænna*

eldhus (ODan) **eldhus** (OGu) noun

dwelling house **ODan** *JyL* 3

kitchen **OGu** *GL* A 50

eldhúshurð (ON) noun

It was forbidden for a tenant to remove or damage a kitchen door. See GuL ch. 75.

kitchen door **ONorw** *GuL* Llb

Refs: KLNM s.v.v. *eldhus, skåle, stuehus*

elði (ON) noun

Generally 'lodging, boarding'. Possibly also in a more strict usage, obligation for those in the *hreppr* 'district' paying *þingfararkaup* (a fee related to attendance at the *þing* 'assembly') to, relative to their resources, support paupers, including those labelled *úmagi* (see *omaghi*).

boarding **OIce** *Grg* Hrs 234

maintenance for the poor **OIce** *Jó* Kge 34

sustenance **OIce** *Grg* Vís 98

Refs: Cleasby and Vigfusson s.v. *eldi*; Gerhold 2002, 188–203; KLNM, s.v. *tiggar*; ONP s.v. *elði*

enböte (OSw) **enböti** (OSw) noun

single compensation **OSw** *DL* Eb, *UL* Mb, *VmL* Mb

single fine **OSw** *DL* Rb, *SdmL* Gb, Mb, Tjdb

See also: *bot, böta*

endaghi (OSw) **eindagi** (ON) **ændaghi** (OSw) noun

The expiration of a time limit concerning judicial matters, often payment. Also the legal meeting summoned in such matters.

appointed day **ONorw** *GuL* Krb, Kpb, Llb, Tjb

day for a hearing **OIce** *Jó* Þjb 4

day specified for payment **OIce** *Jó* Þfb 8 Llb 1 Kab 4

one-day **OSw** *YVgL* Drb, Äb, Gb, Jb, Add, *ÄVgL* Md, Smb, Slb, Gb, Rlb, Jb

settling day **OIce** *Grg* Þsþ 51 Vís 110 Lsþ 116 Fjl 221 Tíg 257, *Jó* Kab 16, *Js* Lbb 22 Kab 5, 17 Þjb 3, *KRA* 15, **ONorw** *FrL* Var 46

term **OSw** *YVgL* Föb

See also: *eindaga, fæmt, siunættinger, þrenættinger*

Refs: Brink 2011b, 150–51; ONP s.v. *endaghi*

endimark (ON) noun

border **OIce** *Grg* Bat 114

rule **OIce** *Jó* HT 2

See also: *mærki*

eneþer (OSw) **enethe** (ODan) **eineiði** (ON) **einseiði** (ON) noun

oath of one **ODan** *ESjL* 3, **OIce** *Jó* Þfb 6 Mah 7, 8 Kge 2 Llb 11 Kab 7 Þjb 21 Fml 15, *Js* Mah 8 Kvg 1, 4 Þjb 11, *KRA* 1, **ONorw** *FrL* KrbA 32 KrbB 12 Rgb 48 Kvb 14 LlbB 1

one oath alone **ODan** *ESjL* 3

one single oath **ODan** *ESjL* 3

one's own oath **ONorw** *FrL* KrbA 15

only one's own oath **OSw** *YVgL* Föb, *ÄVgL* Fös

personal oath **ONorw** *BorgL* 11.4

See also: *ainsyri, eþer*

enfæ (OSw) noun

business **OSw** *VmL* Bb

exclusive property **OSw** *SdmL* Gb

own business **OSw** *DL* Bb, Gb

See also: *ensak*

engidómr (ON) noun

A meadowland court where disputes concerning property and grazing rights were resolved. A rare term, but it is the subject of the entire paragraph in Grg Lbþ 176. The court was held at the location of the disputed meadowland and was similar to a communal pasture court (ON *afréttardómr*).

meadowland court **OIce** *Grg* Lbþ 176

See also: *afréttardómr*

Refs: CV s.v. *engidómr*; Fritzner s.v. *engidómr*; KLNM s.v. *dómhringr*

engimark (ON) **engjamark** (ON) noun

meadow boundaries **OIce** *Jó* Llb 22, 37

meadow bounds **OIce** *Grg* Lbþ 188

See also: *æng*

Refs: CV s.v. *engimark*; Hertzberg s.v. *engimark*

engiskiftisbúi (ON) noun

    meadowland division **OIce** *Grg* Lbþ 198

engiteigr (ON) noun

    meadowland **OIce** *Jó* Lbb 4

engiverk (ON) noun

    outfield haymaking **OIce** *Grg* Klþ 17 Þsþ 78

engivöxtr (ON) noun

    what grows on meadowland **OIce** *Jó* Llb 24

engjabrigð (ON) noun

    meadowland claim **OIce** *Grg* Lbþ 176

engjamerki (ON) noun

    meadowland boundary mark **OIce** *Grg* Lbþ 175

    See also: *mærki*

    Refs: CV s.v. *engjamerki*

engjaskifti (ON) noun

    division of meadowlands **OIce** *Jó* Llb 15

    Refs: CV s.v. *engjaskipti*; Hertzberg s.v. *engjaskipti*

eniorþ (OSw) noun

    land of a man **OSw** *YVgL* Rlb

enkøp (ODan) noun

    Land that was bought and privately owned, and was excluded from land division.

    single buy **ODan** *JyL* 1

    See also: *særkøp*

enløpkona (OSw) **enløp kone** (ODan) noun

    single woman **ODan** *SkL* 219

    unmarried woman **OSw** *YVgL* Gb, *ÄVgL* Gb

    See also: *kona*

enløpman (ODan) **einhleypismaðr** (ON) noun

    single man **ONorw** *FrL* KrbA 18, 32 KrbB 20 Leb 7

    unmarried man **ODan** *ESjL* 3

ennætþing (OSw) noun

    Etymologically disputed, but referring to a þing 'assembly' dealing with serious cases, such as killings, that could forego the usual requirement of several summonses.

    one-night assembly **OSw** *ÖgL* Db

    single assembly **OSw** *SdmL* Till

    See also: *þing*

    Refs: Schlyter s.v. *ennæt þing*; SL SdmL, 258, note 91; SL ÖgL, 67–68, note 14

ensak (OSw) **ensokn** (OSw) **ænsak** (OSw) noun

    This refers to a procedure, fines or responsibility that fall to a single person (or sometimes a number of specified people) to follow, receive or take in charge. In a number of the laws, it refers to fines or cases that are to be referred to the king, but in other instances it simply indicates who is to take up the matter.

    affair **OSw** *HL* Mb

    case **OSw** *HL* Rb

    exclusive right **OSw** *SdmL* Kkb, Kgb, Gb, Jb, Bb, Kmb, Mb, Tjdb, Rb, Till

    fine belonging to one party **OSw** *DL* Kkb

    for himself **OSw** *HL* Kkb

    matter **OSw** *DL* Mb

    own business **OSw** *DL* Tjdb, Rb

    own case **OSw** *ÖgL* Eb, Db

    own matter **OSw** *UL* Kkb, Kgb, Mb, Jb, *VmL* Mb, Jb, Bb

    particular to **OSw** *YVgL* Add

    Expressions:

    biskups ensak (OSw)

    bishop's own matter **OSw** *UL* Kkb

    bondans ensak (OSw)

    householder's (i.e. landowner's) own matter **OSw** *UL* Jb *VmL* Mb, Jb

    byamanna ensak (OSw)

    villagers' own matter **OSw** *UL* Kgb *VmL* Bb

    konungs ensak

    king's affair **OSw** *HL* Mb

    king's cases **OSw** *HL* Rb

    king's own matter **OSw** *UL* Kgb

    matter for the king **OSw** *DL* Mb

    til ensak (OSw)

    on his own account in the matter **OSw** *UL* Mb

    See also: *bot, enfœ, sak*

    Refs: Schlyter 1877, s.v. *ensak*

envaldugher (OSw) adj.

    omnipotent **OSw** *SdmL* För

erfðafé (ON) noun

    inherited property **OIce** *Grg* Arþ 127 Feþ 150

erfðamark (ON) noun

    inherited ownership mark **OIce** *Grg* Fjl 225, *Jó* Llb 47, 48

erfðarmaðr (ON) noun

    heir **OIce** *Js* Mah 18, **ONorw** *GuL* Mhb

    See also: *arftaki, arvi, arvingi*

erfðarómagi (ON) **erfðaómagi** (ON) noun

    A dependent being maintained by a man who stood to inherit from him. The term appears only in Grg and is specifically used to distinguish him from a more closely related heir who did not have the means to maintain the dependent. Previously thought to refer to an inherited dependent in Grg Þsþ 68, but see glossary note and corrigenda in GrgTr II.

    dependent from whom one stands to inherit **OIce** *Grg* Þsþ 68 Ómb 129

See also: *omaghi*

Refs: CV s.v. *erfð*; Fritzner s.v.
erfðarúmagi; GrgTr II:373

erfðaskipun (ON) **erfðaskipan** (ON) noun
order of inheritance **ONorw** *GuL* Arb

erfðatal (ON) noun
being entitled to inheritance **ONorw** *GuL* Arb
inheritance chapter **OIce** *Jó* MagBref
inheritance list **OIce** *Js* Ert 24
inheritance section **OIce** *Jó* Kge 7

erfðaölðr (ON) **erfðaöldr** (ON) noun
inheritance ale **ONorw** *GuL* Krb

erfi (ON) noun
wake **ONorw** *EidsL* 49.1

erfilytia (OGu) noun
heiress **OGu** *GL* A 20

erfingjasátt (ON) noun
agreement of heirs **OIce** *Grg* Tíg
268, **ONorw** *FrL* ArbB 17

erfisgierþ (OGu) noun
funeral feast **OGu** *GL* A 24a

eriksgata (OSw) noun
Possibly derived from the name Erik or a corresponding appellative meaning 'omnipotent ruler' or the noun *eþer* 'oath'; the second element is *gata* 'travel; road, street'. A newly chosen king of Sweden should ride with an entourage starting and ending in the province of Uppland, passing through and exchanging hostages in the central provinces, where, at specified places, the king and the *laghmaþer* 'lawman' of the province swore mutual oaths. The origin of the procedure is disputed, but there are parallels in Norway and elsewhere in Europe. In the laws, a completed *eriksgata* was required for the king to be legally accepted. *Eriksgata* is not to be confounded with travels connected with an itinerant kingship.
Erik's street **OSw** *ÖgL* Db
king's route **OSw** *SdmL* Kgb, Till
royal progress **OSw** *UL* Kgb
Refs: Blomkvist 2011, 180–84; Hellquist s.v.
eriksgata; Holmblad 1993; Imsen 2014, 46; KLNM
s.v. *eriksgata*; Schlyter s.v. *eriksgata*; Scovazzi 1971

etarmannaskra (OGu) noun
genealogical table **OGu** *GL* A 20
See also: *skra*

etarmen (pl.) (OGu) noun
family members **OGu** *GL* A 28
See also: *skyldarman*

ethe (ODan) verb
give an oath **ODan** *JyL* 2
swear **ODan** *JyL* 2
take an oath **ODan** *JyL* 2

ethelagh (ODan) noun
oath **ODan** *ESjL* 3

etja (ON) verb
graze off **ONorw** *GuL* Llb

eyðijarðarboðburðr (ON) noun
summons to a deserted farm **OIce** *Jó* Kge 33

eyðijörð (ON) noun
deserted farm **OIce** *Jó* Llb 41
See also: *aterlægha*, *auðn*, *ödmark*, *ökn*, *öþebol*

eykjafóðr (ON) noun
Horse fodder was stipulated to be one cartload of hay and two of straw, which was the amount of fodder that a tenant might take away with him when leaving rented land. See GuL ch. 74.
horse fodder **ONorw** *GuL* Llb

eyrisbót (ON) noun
atonement of one ounce-unit
OIce *Grg* Þsþ 80 Bat 113
See also: *bot*

eyrr (ON) noun
sandbank **ONorw** *GuL* Llb

eyzlueyrir (ON) noun
disposable funds **OIce** *Jó* Kge 16

eþabuþ (OSw) noun
offering of oaths **OSw** *SdmL* Kmb

eþafylli (OSw) noun
oath-taker **OSw** *DL* Rb

eþamæn (pl.) (OSw) noun
oath-takers **OSw** *DL* Rb
oathsmen **OSw** *HL* Rb

eþarvitni (OSw) noun
witness to an oath **OSw** *DL* Rb
See also: *eþer*, *vitni*

eþataki (OSw) **eþar taki** (OSw) noun
guarantor for an oath **OSw** *DL* Rb
oath trustee **OSw** *SdmL* Rb
oath-receiver **OSw** *HL* Rb
oath-taker **OSw** *ÖgL* Kkb
oath-taking **OSw** *HL* Rb
pledge man for an oath **OSw** *HL* Rb

eþer (OSw) **eth** (ODan) **aiþr** (OGu) **eiðr** (ON) **eþ**
(OSw) noun
An oath was sworn to confirm loyalty and obedience; and it was a frequent way of proving one's innocence

when faced with an accusation of crime. In this latter case it was often taken with some form of compurgation, with two others (a three-man oath, ON *lýrittareiðr*), five others (a six-man oath, ON *séttareiðr*), or eleven others (a twelve-man oath, ON *tylftareiðr, see tylftareþer*); OSw laws also allow for other numbers of compurgators. In general, the person taking an oath was to swear by God or Christ, in heathen times by the gods (ÄVgL Kkb 12 and passim). After the introduction of Christianity, he laid his hand on the Bible or another holy book (*bókareiðr*).

According to VmL, a local administrator could challenge a householder saying that he had been robbed. The householder had to agree that this was the case and was then granted leave to pursue the thief. Once he had denied that he had been robbed, however, he could not later retract, and he was *orþlös ok eþlös* ('without grounds and without an oath') and could not pursue the case.

oath **ODan** *ESjL* 2, 3, *JyL* 1, 3, *SkKL* 12, *SkL* passim, *VSjL* 40, 66, 81, **OGu** *GL* A 2, 3, 4, 13, 14, 16, 18, 19, 20a, 22, 25, 26, 31, 32, 39, **OIce** *Grg* Þsþ 31 Vís 87 passim, *Jó* passim, *Js* passim, *KRA* 2, 14, **ONorw** *BorgL* 5.7, *EidsL* 3.2 7 passim, *FrL* Intr 13, 16 KrbA 1, 18 KrbB 3 Mhb 5 Bvb 1 passim, *GuL* Krb, Kpb, Løb, Llb, Tfb, Mhb, Tjb, Leb, **OSw** *DL* Kkb, Eb, Mb, Bb, Gb, Tjdb, Rb, *HL* Kkb, Kgb, Äb, Mb, Jb, Kmb, Blb, Rb, *SdmL* Kkb, Kgb, Gb, Äb, Jb, Bb, Kmb, Mb, Tjdb, Rb, Till, *SmL*, *UL* Kkb, Kgb, Äb, Mb, Jb, Kmb, Blb, Rb, *VmL* Kkb, Kgb, Äb, Mb, Jb, Kmb, Bb, Rb, *YVgL* passim, *ÄVgL* Kkb, Rlb, Jb, Tb, *ÖgL* Kkb, Eb, Db
promise **OIce** *Jó* Kge 32, **ONorw** *FrL* Mhb 8
testimony **OSw** *DL* Bb

Expressions:

brista at eþi (OSw)
fail in an oath **OSw** *UL* Kkb, Äb, Mb, Blb *VmL* Kkb, Mb, Bb

falla at eþi (OSw)
convict in respect of an [invalid] oath **OSw** *VmL* Kkb
fail in an oath **OSw** *UL* Kkb, Äb, Mb, Jb, Kmb, Blb, Rb *VmL* Kkb, Äb, Mb, Kmb, Bb, Rb

fela undir eið (ON)
hang (something) upon an oath **OIce** *Grg* Lrþ 117

ganga eþ (OSw)
swear an oath **OSw** *UL* Mb *VmL* Kkb, Bb

orð ok eiðr (ON)
pledge and promise **ONorw** *GuL* Krb, Kpb, Tfb

orþlös ok eþlös (OSw)
without grounds and without an oath **OSw** *VmL* Mb

rangr eiðr (ON)
false oath **OIce** *Js* Þjb 9 **ONorw** *FrL* KrbB 46
perjury **OIce** *Jó* Þjb 22

siattæ manz eþ (ODan)
oath of six men **ODan** *SkL* 77

þriþiæ manz eþ (ODan)
oath of three men **ODan** *SkL* 77

tolf manna eþer (OSw)
oath of twelve men **OSw** *YVgL* Gb, Rlb

tylftær eþer (OSw) **tylftær eþe** (ODan)
oath of twelve men **ODan** *SkL*
OSw *YVgL*, *ÄVgL*, *ÖgL*

See also: *asöreseþer, brista, eiðastefna, eneþer, eþsöre, fimmtareiðr, fælla, lagh, lýrittareiðr, munhaf, orþ, séttareiðr, sexmannaeiðr, tveggjamannaeiðr, tylft, tylftareþer, væria, þriggjamannaeiðr*

Refs: Bagge 2010, 189, 212–14; Helle 2001, 103–04; KLNM s.v.v. *edgärdsman, edsformular, gæld, rettergang, vitne, värjemål*; Robberstad 1981, 331, 363; Schlyter s.v. *eþer*

eþlös (OSw) adj.

Expressions:

orþlös ok eþlös (OSw)
without grounds and without an oath **OSw** *VmL* Mb

eþsorþ (OSw) noun
content of an oath **OSw** *HL* Rb
oath **OSw** *DL* Rb

eþsöre (OSw) **ezöre** (OSw) noun
Literally, 'oath swearing' (a compound of *eþer* 'oath' and form of *sværia* 'swear'). This can refer prosaically to the swearing of any oath. More frequently it refers to the oath sworn by the king of Sweden and his highest nobility to uphold the law of the land (the 'rule of law'), to keep civil order in the kingdom and to protect the rights of the common people to peace and protection, particularly in respect of certain grave crimes, which they had agreed upon. The crown, in return, took a portion of any fine payable in respect of such crimes. This oath first came into force in the time of Birger (often given the soubriquet jarl) (d. 1266) and his son, King Magnus Birgersson (Ladulås) (1240–90), and is interpreted as the King's Oath [of Peace], or simply the King's Peace, sworn at the king's coronation. It was the king's promise to uphold peace in the realm and anyone who went against that consequently became the enemy of the king personally. This is laid out in the foreword to UL.

The word *eþsöre* is also used as an abbreviation for *eþsörisbrut*, 'crime against the King's Peace', or for the penalty for such crimes, *eþsörisböter*. In addition to a fine, frequently consisting of his entire movables, the perpetrator was usually exiled from the kingdom, rather than just the province. If the plaintiff or the family of the injured party pleaded on behalf of the exiled person, then, according to, for example, UL Kgb 9, VmL Kgb 6 and ÖgL Eb 10, they could be 'returned under the King's Peace' against a sum of 40 *marker* being paid to the crown.

Originally, breach of the King's peace was such a crime as was considered to be against the realm as a whole, which effectively made the king your personal enemy, and with fines payable to the king rather than the local community or the injured party. The intention or consequence was that personal vendetta was discouraged and the power of the crown increased, leading eventually to the establishment of kingdom-wide rather than provincial law. It was limited to very serious offences (murder, rape, illegal revenge, etc.), as exhibited in the Nordic laws. Such crimes were elsewhere designated *niþingsværk* (q.v.) or *urbotamal* (q.v.). These terms appear only occasionally in the law texts that have statutes covering *eþsöre*. It is clear from some of the statutes that women were not treated in the same way as men if they committed the equivalent crimes — banishment was in several laws specifically excluded as a punishment applicable to women.

It is worth noting that *eþsöre* is not mentioned in ÄVgL nor in GL. In the latter, the king is not referred to at all, even though he is mentioned in GS in the context of the levy and trade. In ÄVgL, the concept of *urbotamal* might be considered a parallel covering the same group of crimes, but there is no equivalent concept in GL.

breach of the king's sworn peace **OSw** *SdmL* Kgb
King's Oath **OSw** *UL* Kgb, *VmL* För, Kgb
King's Peace **OSw** *HL* Kgb, *UL* För,
Kkb, Kgb, Rb, *VmL* Kgb
king's sworn peace **OSw** *SdmL* Kgb
sworn peace **OSw** *ÖgL* Kkb, Db
sworn peace day **OSw** *ÖgL* Kkb
{*eþsöre*} **OSw** *HL* Kgb, *YVgL* Frb, Urb, Add
Expressions:
kunungs eþsöre (OSw)
book concerning the king's oath **OSw** *DL* Eb
breach of the king's peace **OSw** *HL* Kgb
crime against the king's peace **OSw** *DL* Eb
crimes against the king's oath of peace **OSw** *DL* Eb
edsöre of the king **OSw** *YVgL* Urb, Add
king's peace **OSw** *DL* Eb *UL* Rb
king's sworn peace **OSw** *ÖgL* Eb, Db

violations of the king's peace **OSw** *HL* Kgb
See also: *asöreseþer, brista, eþer, friþer, friþlös, fælla, griþ, konungsþing, kununger, kunungsræfst, niþingsværk, sværia, urbotamal*
Refs: Ekholst 2009, 59–66; KLNM, s.v. *konungs edsöre*; Schlyter 1877, s.v. *eþsöre*; von See 1964, 56–57; SL DL, 25–26; SL UL, 54 note 15

eþsörisbrut (OSw) noun
breach of the king's sworn peace **OSw** *SdmL* Kgb
intentional crime **OSw** *DL* Mb
See also: *eþer, eþsöre, sværia*

eþsörisböter (OSw) noun
fines for breaching the king's peace **OSw** *HL* Kgb
fines for breaking the king's sworn peace **OSw** *SdmL* Kgb
See also: *bot, eþer, eþsöre, sværia*

eþsörismal (OSw) noun
case concerning the king's sworn oath **OSw** *SdmL* Bb
Expressions:
kunungs eþsörismal (OSw)
case of the king's peace **OSw** *HL* Kgb

eþsörisrætter (OSw) noun
law of the king's peace **OSw** *HL* Kgb

eþsört (OSw) **eþfört** (OSw) adj.
Of a day when swearing an oath was allowed.
allowed to swear an oath **OSw** *YVgL* Kkb, Add
lawful for swearing oaths **OSw** *DL* Rb
legal to provide an oath **OSw** *DL* Mb
permitted to take an oath **OSw** *HL* Äb
sworn peace day **OSw** *ÖgL* Kkb
Refs: Schlyter s.v. *eþsört*

eþviti (OSw) **eþwiti** (OSw) noun
oath-takers **OSw** *UL* Kkb, Rb
oath-witness **OSw** *SdmL* Jb
oathsman **OSw** *HL* Kkb
See also: *eþer*

falbyr (OSw) **falz byr** (OSw) noun
Appears in the context of buying infected cattle and bringing the disease to one's neighbours.
village where the plague is present **OSw** *YVgL* Utgb, *ÄVgL* Föb
See also: *byr*

fald (ODan) noun
fold **ODan** *JyL* 2, 3

falda (OGu) **falling** (OGu) noun
bedcover **OGu** *GL* A 20
See also: *aklæþi*

fall (OSw) **fald** (OSw) noun

case **OSw** *UL* Rb, *VmL* Rb, *YVgL* Kkb

conviction **OSw** *ÖgL* Kkb

decay **OSw** *UL* Jb, *VmL* Jb

nature **OSw** *UL* Mb

neglect **OSw** *DL* Bb, *SdmL* Jb, Till

situation **OSw** *UL* StfBM

See also: *mal (1)*, *sak*

falr (ON) noun

socket (of a spear) **ONorw** *GuL* Llb

falr (ON) adj.

for sale **OIce** *Js* Lbb 5

fals (OSw) **fals** (ODan) **fals** (ON) noun

counterfeit **OSw** *HL* Kmb, *SdmL* Kmb

falsehood **OSw** *UL* Kmb, *VmL* Kmb

faulty goods **OSw** *UL* Kmb, *VmL* Kmb

forgery **ODan** *JyL* 3

fraud **OIce** *Jó* Kab 11 Fml 2, *Js* Lbb 9 Kab 9

something faulty **OSw** *UL* Kmb, *VmL* Kmb

See also: *flærþ*

falsa (ON) verb

forge **OIce** *Jó* Mah 2

falsere (ODan) noun

forger **ODan** *JyL* 3

falsvitni (OSw) noun

false witness **OSw** *SdmL* Rb

See also: *ljúgvitni*

falzeþer (OSw) noun

invalid oath **OSw** *YVgL* Add

See also: *glafseþer*, *meneþer*

famn (OSw) **faghn** (ODan) **faðmr** (ON) **fampn** (OSw) noun

cord **OSw** *YVgL* Jb, *ÄVgL* Jb

fathom **ODan** *JyL* 1, **OIce** *Grg* Lbþ 181, *Jó* Llb 2, 23, **OSw** *HL* Blb, *SdmL* Bb, *UL* Mb, *VmL* Bb

fang (OSw) **fang** (ODan) **fang** (ON) noun

Lawful ways to acquire property, particularly land, often appearing in the phrase *lagha fang* (OSw) 'legal acquisition'. These were purchase, exchange, gift and pledge, and sometimes including, other times contrasted to inheritance. Also used of anything acquired in general, in particular from the forest, such as building material and firewood. In one instance, used as a synonym to *fangaman* (q.v.) (UL Mb). Moreover, a unit of measure.

acquired land **ODan** *ESjL* 1

acquisition **ODan** *VSjL* 13, **OSw** *YVgL* Gb, Jb

assignor **OSw** *UL* Mb

bundle **OSw** *UL* Kgb, *VmL* Kgb

fuel and timber **OSw** *ÄVgL* Md

land **ODan** *ESjL* 2

legal acquisition **OSw** *UL* Äb, Mb, Jb, *VmL* Jb

means **OIce** *KRA* 30

movables **ONorw** *FrL* Intr 23

timber **OSw** *YVgL* Drb, Kvab, *ÄVgL* Kva, Fös

wood (2) **OSw** *YVgL* Jb, Föb, Utgb, *ÄVgL* Jb, Fös, Föb

See also: *fangaman*

Refs: G. B. Larsson 2010; Schlyter s.v. *fang*

fanga (OSw) verb

capture **OSw** *UL* Kmb, *VmL* Kmb

Expressions:

fangin meþ/viþ, fingin (OSw)

captured **OSw** *SdmL* Bb, Mb *YVgL* Gb *ÄVgL* Gb

caught in the (very) act **OSw** *YVgL* Tb

taken **OSw** *YVgL* Add

See also: *taka*

fangaman (OSw) noun

One from whom an object was acquired (bought, given, traded). Appears in the context of accusations of theft.

assignor **OSw** *DL* Bb, *UL* Jb, Kmb, *VmL* Mb, Jb, Kmb

guarantor **OSw** *HL* Mb

legal acquirement **OSw** *HL* Jb

one who says he has acquired something **OSw** *HL* Jb

trader **OSw** *SdmL* Bb, Tjdb

See also: *borghanaman*, *fang*, *fastar (pl.)*, *hemulsman*, *skuli*, *taki*

fangaváttr (ON) noun

oath helper **OIce** *Jó* Þjb 19, 21

witness selected at random **OIce** *Js* Þjb 9, **ONorw** *FrL* Rgb 32

freely selected witness **ONorw** *GuL* Tfb

fangejorth (ODan) noun

acquired land **ODan** *ESjL* 1, *VSjL* 1

fanginfæst (OSw) adj.

captured **OSw** *YVgL* Gb, Add

fangtíð (ON) noun

taking-time **ONorw** *BorgL* 7.5

far (ON) noun

passage **ONorw** *GuL* Tfb

See also: *fartekja*

fara (ON) **fara** (OSw) **fare** (ODan) verb

be itinerant

Expressions:

fare æfter (ODan)

pursue a case **ODan** *SkL* 136, 158, 201, 223

farareyrir (ON) noun

travel expenses **OIce** *Jó* Þfb 2

See also: *þingfararkaup*

farargreiðabót (ON) noun

conveyance repair **OIce** *Jó* Llb
20, **ONorw** *FrL* LlbA 10

See also: *bot*

fararkaup (ON) noun

wages for sailors **ONorw** *GuL* Leb

farartalmi (ON) noun

travel delay **OIce** *Jó* Llb 45

fardagher (OSw) **fardagh** (ODan) **fardagr** (ON) noun

The *fardaghar*, 'moving days', was the usual term for coming into possession of a farm, for payment in trade or leasing, assessment of land, payment of fines, etc. These were also the days when the tenant's right to remain on the land expired. According to the ÄVgL there were four *fardaghar*, all in the latter half of winter: the twelfth day of Christmas, Candlemas (2 February), Sunday before Lent, and Mid-lent. The ÖgL mentions only one: Mid-lent. The DL has no provisions about *fardaghar*, but two terms are mentioned for lease agreement: the winter nights (around 14 October) and Easter. In the SdmL and VmL the corresponding terms are Martinmas (11 November) and Whitsun. The VmL mentions three *afraþsdaghar* ('days for the annual rent to be paid') which coincide with the three last *fardaghar* of the VgL, It is therefore possible that these *afraþsdaghar* were also *fardaghar*.

Most ODan provincial laws do not mention *fardagh*. The only exception (no date is given) is that the SkL ch. 238. Ch. 239 indicates one such day: the first Mass of the Virgin Mary (15 August).

The FrL knows only one *fardagr*, the first weekday (not holy day) after the thirteenth day of Christmas (6 January). The tenant was nevertheless allowed to keep half of the houses and, in addition, one fourth of the hay until the first day of summer (14 April), if he was homeless. In the GuL the *fardagar* was a period of nine days after 'summer day' (23 April). If the tenant could not move all his property within that period, he might keep half of the houses for another nine days.

In OIce law the *fardagar* began on Thursday in the seventh week of summer, i.e. in the week beginning 21–27 May, and expired in the night before the following Monday.

moving day **ODan** *SkL* 238, **ONorw** *GuL*
Llb, Olb, **OSw** *YVgL* Äb, *ÄVgL* Äb

moving days **OIce** *Grg* Klþ 6, 8 Þsþ 22, 78
Vís 89, 104 Ómb 128 Lbþ 172, 220 Fjl 224
Hrs 234 Misc 246, *Jó* Þfb 9 Sg 1 Kge 14 Lbb
1, 7 Llb 1, 7 Kab 4 Þjb 23, *Js* Lbb 3, 10 Kab
11, *KRA* 14, 26, **ONorw** *FrL* LlbA 1

Refs: Helle 2001, 120–22; Hertzberg
s.v. *fardagr*; KLNM s.v.v. *fardag,
skiftedag*; Schlyter s.v. *fardagher*

fargalter (OSw) noun

travelling boar **OSw** *UL* Blb

See also: *galter*

farhirðir (ON) noun

ferryman **OIce** *Jó* Llb 45

farkoster (OSw) **farkost** (ODan) **farkostr** (ON) noun

boat tackle **OSw** *VmL* Mb

goods **ODan** *JyL* 2

vessel **ONorw** *GuL* Leb, **OSw** *SdmL* Bb, *VmL* Mb

See also: *bater, byrthing, floti,
kaupskip, myndrikkia, skip*

farliþ (OSw) noun

driving passage **OSw** *SdmL* Bb

gate **OSw** *DL* Bb

right of way **OSw** *UL* Blb, *VmL* Bb

See also: *farvægher*

farlög (ON) noun

Maritime law; the law for traders and sailors. Thought to be synonymous with *farmannalög* (q.v.) though both terms appear only rarely in ON.

maritime law **OIce** *Grg* Feþ 166

See also: *bjarkeyjarréttr, farmannalög*

Refs: CV; F; GrgTr II:90

farmaðr (ON) noun

trader **OIce** *Grg* Klþ 10 Feþ 167, *KRA* 26

farmannabúð (ON) noun

traders' hut **OIce** *Grg* Klþ 2

farmannalög (ON) noun

Maritime law; law for traders and sailors. Provincial laws of medieval Iceland and Norway do not much emphasize maritime law, though a thirteenth century fragment of the younger *Bjarkeyjarréttr* (q.v.) does mention *farmannalög*. In the later thirteenth century this area of law started to become more prominent as evidenced by chapters in Jó for Iceland and an appendix to MLL in Norway. The chapter on *farmannalög* in Jó is chiefly based on King Magnús Hákonarson's 'younger' Bjarkey Law or Municipal law of 1276.

maritime law **OIce** *Jó* MagBref Fml 1, 20

See also: *bjarkeyjarréttr, farlög, leþunger*

Refs: GrgTr II:90; KLNM s.v. *farmannsloven, sjörätt*

farmr (ON) noun

   cargo **OIce** *Grg* Feþ 165 Lbþ 220, *Jó*
   Fml 2, **ONorw** *GuL* Krb, Leb

farning (ON) noun

   passage from the country **OIce** *Grg* Þsþ 55 Ómb 132

fartekja (ON) noun

   contract of affreightment **OIce** *Jó* Fml 1

   taking passage in a ship **ONorw** *GuL* Tfb

   See also: *far*

farunöti (OSw) **förunautr** (ON) **faronöte** (OSw) noun

   fellow traveller **OSw** *UL* Kkb, *VmL* Mb

   journey companion **OIce** *Grg* Klþ 1

   travel companion **OIce** *KRA* 1

   See also: *flokker, fylghi, hærværk*

faruskiaut (OGu) noun

   draught animal **OGu** *GL* A 25

   See also: *skiut*

farvitenævning (ODan) noun

   Synonymous with *skipsnævning* (q.v.).

   nominated penalty men **ODan** *JyL* JyL 3

farvægher (OSw) **farvegr** (OGu) noun

   highway **OSw** *DL* Bb, *SdmL* Bb, *UL* Blb, *VmL* Bb

   right of way **OGu** *GL* A 24f (64)

   road **OSw** *DL* Bb

   travellers' pathway **OGu** *GL* A 24f (64)

   See also: *vægher*

fasta (OSw) **faste** (ODan) **faste** (ODan) **fasta** (OGu)
fasta (ON) verb

The Church ordered people to fast, i.e. to abstain from particular kinds of food, mainly meat, on certain weekdays and in certain periods of the year (esp. during Lent); see *fasta* n. The purpose was to subjugate the powers of the flesh and to deliver the mind from distractions with respect to the teachings of the church.

The weekdays in question were Wednesday (only mentioned in the OIce laws) and Friday. Fasting was also obligatory on Ember Days (ON *imbrudagar*, see *imbrudagr*), periods of three days four times a year; on Rogation Days (ON *gangdagar*, see *gangdagher*), i.e. 25 April (OSw *litli gangdagher*) and the three days preceding Ascension Day; and on the days preceding many of the greater feasts such as e.g. Whitsun, *jónsmessa*, *maríumessuaptann*, *ólafsmessuaptann*, and three weeks preceding Christmas. The FrL (Tfb) also states that men were to go fasting to the assembly.

The most severe form of fasting was (ON) *fasta við salt ok brauð*, i.e. only water, salt, and bread were allowed. On the other hand, the rules of fasting were sometimes eased: meat was never allowed, but milk products, fish, and eggs were permitted. On some fasting days, one meal was allowed, on some others two meals, or one had to fast until noon (three o'clock). The punishment for violations of the fasting rules varied, ranging from fines to outlawry; but dispensations were granted, e.g. to manual labourers, to travellers, to the poor, and to the infirm. Sick and old people, persons under the age of twelve (in Iceland: fourteen), pregnant women, and persons in a state of emergency — when the eating of flesh was necessary for survival — were exempted.

Fasting was a usual penitential exercise, sometimes consisting in a diet of water and bread for a period of six weeks. In the OSw DL and SdmL, fasting was combined with fines in cases of illegitimate oaths, as well as in cases of multiple participants in killings in SdmL and the ODan ESjL.

For further details, see the Christian Law section (*kristinn réttr*) of the various provincial laws.

   fast **ODan** *ESjL* 1, 3, **OSw** *HL* Kkb, *SdmL*
   Mb, Till, *SmL*, *ÖgL* Kkb, Eb, Db

   observe the fast **OSw** *DL* Kkb

   do penance **OSw** *DL* Mb, *UL* Äb, *VmL* Äb

   See also: *fasta, skript, skæra (1),*
   fasta, karina, skript, skæra (1)

   Refs: DMA s.v. *fasting, Christian*; KLNM s.v. *fasta*

fasta (OSw) noun

   church penalty **OSw** *DL* Kkb, Rb

   fast **ODan** *ESjL* 2, *JyL* 2, *SkKL* 9, **OIce** *Js* Kdb 1,
   KRA 24, **ONorw** *GuL* Krb, **OSw** *HL* Äb, *YVgL* Kkb

   fasting **OSw** *SdmL* Kkb, Tjdb, Rb, *VmL* Kkb

   Lent **OGu** *GL* A 8, **ONorw** *GuL* Krb, Kpb, Olb,
   OSw *UL* Mb, Jb, Rb, *VmL* Jb, *YVgL* Kkb

fastaeþer (OSw) noun

   oath by {fastar} **OSw** *HL* Jb, Rb

   oath of transaction witnesses **OSw** *SdmL* Jb, Till

fastar (pl.) (OSw) **fasti** (OSw) noun

Etymologically related to the adjective *faster* 'fastened, fixed'. Additional witnesses to transactions, particularly of landed property and in relation to betrothals, in OSw HL also to *bolagh* 'partnership' and settlements of killing. The number of *fastar* varied between seven and twenty-four, sometimes depending on the value of that being handled. *Fastar* of land transactions were normally local landowners (who according to the later MEL were to be named in written documents of the deal). *Fastar* of other arrangements usually represented the two parties in equal numbers. *Fastar* also appeared in medieval diplomas from the

Norwegian province of Jämtland, albeit not in the laws, presumably under Swedish influence.

purchase witnesses **OSw** *DL* Bb

transaction witnesses **OSw** *DL* Bb, *SdmL* Gb, Jb

witnesses **OSw** *DL* Bb

{*fastar*} **OSw** *DL* Bb, *HL* Kkb, Äb, Mb, Jb, *UL* Kkb, Äb, Jb, Add. 5, *VmL* Kkb, Äb, Jb

See also: *borghanaman, fangaman, fullskæl, hemulsman, skuli, taki*

Refs: Brink forthcoming; Fritzner s.v. *fasti*; KLNM, s.v. *fastar*; Larsson 2009, 160–61, 167–68; Schlyter s.v. *fastar*

fastehælgh (ODan) noun

fast day **ODan** *SkL* 157

fast holiday **ODan** *ESjL* 2

faster (ON) **fastr** (ON) adj.

bound by debt **ONorw** *GuL* Løb

Expressions:

faster ok fullder, fastr oc fulldr, fastær ok fuldær (OSw)

in total and for good **OSw** *UL* Kkb *VmL* Kkb

valid **OSw** *UL* Kkb, Jb, Kmb, Rb *VmL* Kkb, Jb, Kmb, Rb

fastr á fótum (ON)

stuck where he stands **OIce** *Grg* Rsþ 229

fastna (ON) verb

betroth **OIce** *Grg* Λrþ 118 Feþ 144

fastnandi (ON) noun

A 'fastener'; one who betrothes a woman to another.

betrother **OIce** *Grg* Feþ 144 Misc 253

Refs: CV s.v. *fastnandi*; Fritzner s.v. *fastnandi*; ONP s.v. *fastnandi*

fastr (OGu) adj.

uncastrated **OGu** *GL* A 17, 43, 44

fastudagher (OSw) **föstudagr** (ON) noun

fast-day **ONorw** *GuL* Krb, **OSw** *DL* Kkb, Rb, *HL* Kkb, *SdmL* Kkb, *YVgL* Kkb, Add

Lent **OSw** *ÖgL* Kkb

fastuganger (OSw) noun

beginning of the fast **OSw** *HL* Jb

fatöker (OSw) **fatøk** (ODan) **fátækr** (ON) **fátókr** (ON) **fateker** (OSw) **fatigher** (OSw) **fatugher** (OSw) adj.

indigent **OIce** *Jó* Kge 29

poor **ODan** *JyL* Fort, 1, 2, *SkL* 41, 76, *VSjL* 21, **OIce** *Jó* Kge 35 Llb 69 Kab 16, *Js* Kab 11, *KRA* 28, **OSw** *HL* Jb, Kmb, *SdmL* Kkb, Till, *SmL*, *UL* För, Kkb, Kmb, *VmL* För, Kkb, Kmb, *YVgL* Kkb, Tb, *ÖgL* Kkb, Eb

Expressions:

fatökra manna loter (OSw)

A part of the tithes kept by the householder as compensation for care of the poor.

share of the poor **OSw** *YVgL* Kkb

fatökt (OSw) **fátókð** (ON) noun

poverty **OIce** *Jó* Mah 4, *KRA* 28, **OSw** *SdmL* Jb

faþghar (pl.) (OSw) **feþgar** (pl.) (OGu) **feðgar** (pl.) (ON) **feðgi** (ON) **feþgar** (pl.) (OSw) noun

father and son **OGu** *GL* A 20, **OIce** *Grg* Þsþ 77, *Jó* Kab 2, *Js* Mah 8, **ONorw** *FrL* Mhb 31, *GuL* Løb, **OSw** *YVgL* Tb, *ÄVgL* Gb, Tb

fár (ON) noun

fraud **ONorw** *GuL* Kpb

mischief **OIce** *Grg* Þsþ 36

See also: *flærþ, fox, kaupfox*

fársótt (ON) noun

dangerous disease **ONorw** *GuL* Løb

fátókramannaflutningr (ON) **fátækramannaflutningr** (ON) noun

Obligatory transportation of paupers between householders for support.

transportation of poor people **ONorw** *FrL* Intr 17

Refs: Hertzberg s.v. *fátækr*

fearkraf (OGu) **fjarkröf** (ON) noun

claim for money **OGu** *GL* A 32

pecuniary claim **ONorw** *GuL* Kpb

See also: *krafa*

fearnyt (OSw) noun

The basis for deciding the householders' obligation to provide food in conjunction with church building. Appears as a parallel to *mantal* (q.v.) and *ökiaafl* (q.v.) which concerned the corresponding obligation to provide labour and transport respectively.

yield of cattle **OSw** *SmL*

See also: *dagsværki, fæ*

Refs: SL SmL, 436, note 4

feartaki (OSw) noun

money trustee **OSw** *SdmL* Rb

pledge man for money **OSw** *HL* Rb

taking of money **OSw** *HL* Rb

See also: *fæ*

feðgin (ON) noun

father and daughter **OIce** *Jó* Sg 1

parents **OIce** *KRA* 21

fegher (OSw) **fegh** (ODan) **faigr** (OGu) **fegh** (OSw) adj.

condemned to death **OSw** *UL* Mb, *VmL* Mb

doomed **OGu** *GS* Ch. 2

without hope **ODan** *VSjL* 87

fegþ (OSw) noun

enmity **OSw** *VmL* Mb

See also: *avund*

fela (ON) verb

place **ONorw** *GuL* Kpb, Løb

prevent from being seen **ONorw** *GuL* Mhb

put into care **OIce** *Grg* Þsþ 80, 81 Ómb 132

felling (ON) noun

knocking down **OIce** *Grg* Vís 87

ferfóttr (ON) adj.

four-footed **ONorw** *GuL* Tjb

ferja (ON) verb

ferry **OIce** *Grg* Klþ 12

ferjandi (ON) adj.

who may be given passage **OIce** *Grg* Þsþ 52 Vís 110

ferjuhald (ON) noun

maintenance of ferries **OIce** *Jó* Llb 45

ferma (OSw) **ferma** (ON) **fyrma** (OSw) **færma** (OSw) verb

confirm **OIce** *KRA* 3, 21, **ONorw** *BorgL* 10.5 15.12, *EidsL* 32.7, **OSw** *ÖgL* Kkb

confirm the baptism **OSw** *SmL*, *YVgL* Kkb

fermidregill (ON) noun

This ribbon was worn across the forehead to protect the holy oil. It should be taken off and burnt three days after the confirmation.

white ribbon worn at confirmation **ONorw** *GuL* Krb

Refs: KLNM s.v. *kyrktagning*

ferming (ON) noun

confirmation **OIce** *KRA* 3

fertugr (ON) adj.

forty years old **ONorw** *GuL* Kvb, Mhb, Leb, Sab

festardómr (ON) noun

private judgement **ONorw** *FrL* Var 8

festarhæll (ON) noun

mooring stakes **OIce** *Grg* Þsþ 78 Misc 250

pylon on the pier **OIce** *Jó* Fml 15

festarmál (ON) **festamál** (ON) noun

betrothal **ONorw** *GuL* Kvb

engagement **ONorw** *FrL* KrbB 22

See also: *fæstning*, *fæstningamal*

festaváttorð (ON) noun

betrothal witness **OIce** *Grg* Feþ 144

festaváttr (ON) noun

betrothal witness **OIce** *Grg* Feþ 153

See also: *festaváttorð*

festavætti (ON) noun

betrothal witness **OIce** *Grg* Feþ 150

festuaiga (OGu) **festueyga** (OGu) noun

land held in pledge **OGu** *GL* A 63, Add. 9 (B 81)

féboð (ON) noun

offer of a bribe **OIce** *Grg* Þsþ 44

féfang (ON) **féföng** (pl.) (ON) noun

booty **ONorw** *GuL* Mhb

féhirðir (ON) noun

herdsman **ONorw** *GuL* Kpb

fékaup (ON) noun

object of bargaining **ONorw** *GuL* Krb

félagaerfð (ON) noun

partner's inheritance **ONorw** *GuL* Arb

félagi (ON) noun

partner **OIce** *Grg* Vís 97 Arþ 120 Misc 247, 249, *Jó* Kge 17

trade partner **ONorw** *GuL* Arb, Mhb

See also: *fælagh*

félagsgerð (ON) noun

entrance into co-ownership **ONorw** *GuL* Kvb

félagslagning (ON) noun

partnership making **OIce** *Grg* Feþ 150

félagsskapr (ON) **félagksapr** (ON) noun

partnership **OIce** *KRA* 16

félagsvætti (ON) noun

partnership witness **OIce** *Grg* Feþ 150

félauss (ON) adj.

penniless **OIce** *Jó* Kge 16

poor **ONorw** *GuL* Arb

without means **OIce** *Grg* Feþ 149, 154, *Jó* Kge 25

féleysi (ON) noun

poverty **OFar** *Seyð* 12

félítill (ON) adj.

Of little value. Frequently appears in the superlative (*féminnstr*).

worth the least **OIce** *Jó* Fml 10

Refs: CV s.v. *félítill*; Fritzner s.v. *félítill*; Hertzberg s.v. *félítill*

fémál (ON) noun

suit concerning money **OIce** *Grg* Þsþ 49, 62

fémætr (ON) adj.

having cash value **OIce** *Jó* Llb 62, 71 Þjb 14

fénýta (ON) verb

make use of **ONorw** *FrL* Rgb 39

profit **OIce** *Grg* Vís 111, **ONorw** *EidsL* 45.5

féprettr (ON) noun

A ploy; a ruse designed to trick someone out of their property.

money-trick **ONorw** *FrL* Intr 12

Refs: CV s.v. *féprettr*; Fritzner s.v. *féprettr*; Hertzberg s.v. *féprettr*

férán (ON) noun

robbery **ONorw** *FrL* Intr 23

See also: *fjárrán*

féránsdómr (ON) noun

A process by which the property of an outlaw was seized according to medieval Icelandic law. The *féránsdómr* was held at the home of the outlaw a fortnight after the assembly at which the accused was convicted. Proceedings were handled by a group of twelve men and overseen by a *goði* (q.v.), who received a set fee for his services. Property was distributed to the outlaw's wife, if she could prove what was hers, as well as creditors who could provide evidence of debts, and the remainder was divided between the person who successfully prosecuted the outlaw and community of the quarter or region in which the case was prosecuted. Communal property was held by the prosecutor and then distributed at the next spring assembly (*várþing*) for maintaining dependents or itinerants attached to the assembly (cf. Grg Þsþ 49). Confiscation courts were held for both lesser outlaws (*fjörbaugsmaðr*) and full outlaws (*skógarmaðr*).

A process similar to the *féránsdómr* took place in Sweden and was called the *afkænnuþing* (cf. LexMA; appears [with alt. spelling] in UL & VML).

confiscation court **OIce** *Grg* Þsþ 48, 49 Arþ 126 Ómb 142 Feþ 148, 158

See also: *afkænnuþing*, *domber*, *skuldadómr*

Refs: KLNM s.v. *féránsdómr*; LexMA s.v. *Haus/-formen - Rechts- und Verfassungsgeschichte - Skandinavien*

fésekð (ON) noun

fine **ONorw** *FrL* KrbB 20

penalty **OIce** *Jó* Sg 3

fésekr (ON) adj.

under money penalty **OIce** *Grg* Fjl 222

féskifti (ON) noun

division of property **OIce** *Jó* Mah 19

fésök (ON) noun

case concerning property **OIce** *Grg* Þsþ 75 Tíg 259

fétaka (ON) noun

acceptance of a bribe **OIce** *Grg* Þsþ 44

receipt of money **OIce** *Grg* Þsþ 75

taking property **OIce** *Grg* Klþ 4

févél (ON) noun

device against one's property **ONorw** *GuL* Løb

févíti (ON) noun

cash penalty **OIce** *Grg* Fjl 225 Hrs 234 Tíg 259

money penalty **OIce** *Grg* Bat 113 Feþ 144 Lbþ 177, 220

fiandi (OGu) noun

devil **OGu** *GL* A 13

fiarþunger (OSw) **fjarthing** (ODan) **fiarþungr** (OGu) **fjórðungr** (ON) **fiorþongr** (OSw) **fiorþunger** (OSw) **fiærþunger** (OSw) **fiærþungær** (OSw) noun

Literally a 'fourth' of something. A lower judicial and administrative district in OSw JyL, VgL, ÖgL, SdmL, UL, VmL, and the Norwegian laws GuL and FrL. In ODan ESjL and SkL it is used in land-distribution.

In the Icelandic laws the *fjórðungr* was the largest administrative district beneath *land* (q.v.). According to *Íslendingabók* Iceland was divided into four *fjórðungr* (north, east, south and west) during the tenth century.

couplet **OIce** *Grg* Misc 238

fourth **OSw** *ÄVgL* Smb

quarter **ODan** *ESjL* 2, *JyL* 2, 3, *SkL* 73, 75, 76, *VSjL* 78–80, **OGu** *GL* A 24c, **OIce** *Grg* passim, *Jó* Þfb 9 Sg 2 Kge 1, 18, *Js* Ert 25, Kab 3, **OSw** *SdmL* Kgb, Bb, Kmb, Rb, Till, *UL* Kgb, Äb, Mb, Kmb, Blb, Rb, *VmL* Kkb, Kgb, Äb, Mb, Jb, Kmb, Bb, Rb, *ÖgL* Db

quarter of a {fylki} **ONorw** *GuL* Krb, Kpb, Løb, Llb, Llb, Olb, Leb

quarter stanza **OIce** *Jó* Mah 26, *Js* Mah 25

quarter-share **OIce** *Grg* Lbþ 215, *Jó* Llb 62

See also: *attunger*, *fylki*, *hundari*, *hærað*, *land*

Refs: Hafström 1949b, 58–59; KLNM s.v. *fjerding*; Lundberg 1972, 78–80

fiarþungsbro (OSw) noun

bridge of a quarter **OSw** *SdmL* Bb

See also: *fiarþunger*

fiarþungsnæmd (OSw) noun

A *næmd* 'panel' dealing with witchcraft (ÄVgL), adultery, unatonable crimes, violent robbery, theft, forest fire, arson (YVgL) and an entire quarter's association with an outlaw (ÖgL). The expression *lukt* (literally 'closed/locked') *fiarþungsnæmd* (YVgL Add) may indicate unanimity, confidentiality or something else.

nominated men of the fourth **OSw** *YVgL* Kkb, Urb, Rlb, Tb, Föb, Utgb, Add, *ÄVgL* Slb

quarter-district jury **OSw** *ÖgL* Db

See also: *fiarþunger*, *næmd*

Refs: Lindkvist forthcoming; Åqvist 1989, 283

fikia (OSw) **fikiæ** (OSw) verb
use **OSw** *UL* Blb
Expressions:
fara æller fikia (OSw)
utilize or use **OSw** *UL* Blb *VmL* Bb

fila (ON) noun
thin board **ONorw** *GuL* Mhb

filungr (ON) noun
deal hewer **ONorw** *GuL* Leb

fimmnættingr (ON) noun
A legal meeting, presumably synonymous with ON *fimt* (see *fæmt*).
assembly with five days' notice **ONorw** *FrL* Intr 15
See also: *fæmt*
Refs: Cleasby and Vigfusson s.v. *fimmnættungr*

fimmtardómr (ON) **fimtardómr** (ON) noun
'The Fifth Court' established in 1005 at the General Assembly in Iceland. Served as a type of appeals court for cases which were not resolved within one of the four Quarter Courts (ON *fjórðungsdómr*). The *fimmtardómr* also had jurisdiction for certain types of cases, such as perjury or bribery occurring at the General Assembly. Decisions within The Fifth Court were made by simple majority by a panel of 48 judges. The Fifth Court was abolished when Iceland came under the control of the Norwegian king during the second half of the thirteenth century. The term may also refer to a judgment given after five-day notice period as suggested in GuL.
Fifth Court **OIce** *Grg* Þsþ 41, 43
See also: *domber*, *fæmt*
Refs: CV s.v. *fimt*; Fritzner s.v. *fimtardómr*; GAO s.v. *Ding, domare*; Hertzberg s.v. *fimtardómr*; KLNM s.v. *dómr*, *fimtardómr*; Miller 1984; Miller 1990, 18; MSE s.v. *althingi*

fimmtardómseiðr (ON) **fimtardómseiðr** (ON) noun
Fifth Court oath **OIce** *Grg* Þsþ 45, 46 Feþ 167
See also: *eþer*

fimmtardómssök (ON) noun
case for the Fifth Court **OIce** *Grg* Klþ 4

fimmtareiðr (ON) **fimtareiðr** (ON) noun
oath of five **ONorw** *FrL* Bvb 8
See also: *eþer*

fimmtargrið (ON) **fimtargrið** (ON) noun
five-days' grace **ONorw** *BorgL* 5.15 16.7
legal protection for five days **ONorw** *GuL* Krb
See also: *grið*

fimmtarnafn (ON) noun
five-day notice **ONorw** *GuL* Olb
See also: *fimmtarstefna*, *fimmtarþing*, *fæmt*

fimmtarstefna (ON) **fimtarstefna** (ON) noun
assembly with a five-day notice **ONorw** *FrL* ArbA 16 Var 13
five nights' summons **ONorw** *GuL* Mhb
five-day moot **ONorw** *FrL* Var 8, 13 LlbA 1
five-days-notice summons **OIce** *Jó* Mah 10, 19 Llb 1, 4, *Js* Ert 23 Lbb 15, *KRA* 29, **ONorw** *FrL* KrbB 20
respite of five days **ONorw** *GuL* Llb, Leb
See also: *fimmtarnafn*, *fimmtarþing*, *fæmt*, *stæmna*

fimmtarþing (ON) **fimmtaþing** (ON) **fimtarþing** (ON) **fimtaþing** (ON) noun
A 'fifth assembly'; a type of extraordinary assembly held after five days' notice, usually following an arrow assembly (ON *örvarþing*). A fifth assembly was convened in response to serious offenses, such as injury or homicide.
assembly with a five-day notice **ONorw** *FrL* Mhb 7 Var 7
fifth assembly **OIce** *Jó* Mah 10, *Js* Mah 14, 20
five-day assembly **ONorw** *GuL* Mhb
See also: *fimmtarnafn*, *fimmtarstefna*, *fæmt*, *örvarþing*, *þing*
Refs: CV s.v. *fimtarþing*; Fritzner s.v. *fimtarþing*; Hertzberg s.v. *fimtarþing*; KLNM s.v. *ting*, *ǫrvarþing*

fimmtungr (ON) noun
fifth **ONorw** *GuL* Mhb, Olb

fimmtungsfall (ON) noun
reduction by a fifth **ONorw** *GuL* Olb

fingr (ON) noun
finger **ONorw** *GuL* Mhb

finnandaspik (ON) noun
finder's blubber **OIce** *Grg* Lbþ 217, *Jó* Llb 66, **ONorw** *FrL* LlbB 10, *GuL* Kvr

finnför (ON) noun
Sámi-seeking **ONorw** *BorgL* 16.3

fiorlæsting (OSw) noun
lethal wound **OSw** *ÄVgL* Rlb

firðir (pl.) (ON) noun
people from Fjordane **ONorw** *GuL* Leb

firibiera (OGu) verb
forfeit (by carrying) **OGu** *GL* A 37

firifara (OSw) **fyrirfara** (ON) **fore fara** (OSw) verb
forfeit **OIce** *Js* Ert 23, *KRA* 29, **ONorw** *FrL* KrbA 14, 18 KrbB 6 Mhb 2, 8 ArbB 29, **OSw** *UL* Blb
See also: *firigiva*, *firigæra*, *firiköpa*

firiganga (OSw) **firiganga** (OGu) **fore ganga** (OSw)
verb
appear at the Thing and defend oneself **OSw** *DL* Gb
defend **OSw** *ÄVgL* Gb
forfeit by abandoning **OSw** *UL* Blb
forfeit by wandering **OGu** *GL* A 44

firigielda (OGu) verb
pay **OGu** *GL* A 28

firigiva (OSw) **firi giefa** (OGu) verb
forfeit **OGu** *GL* A 28
forgive **OSw** *SdmL* Gb

firigæra (OSw) **forgøre** (ODan) **firi giera** (OGu)
fyrirgera (ON) **fyrirgöra** (ON) **firigiora** (OSw)
foregöra (OSw) **forgöra** (OSw) verb
Used of any disposal of property, often as a result of
criminal activity, and including phrases referring to
the punishment of losing one's skin, i.e. to be flogged.
Also of a killing, particularly through witchcraft or
poisoning, whose clandestine nature made it *morþ*
'murder' and which was often associated with female
offenders.
alienate **ODan** *ESjL* 3
bewitch **OSw** *UL* Rb, *VmL* Rb
confiscate **OSw** *DL* Eb
do damage **ODan** *SkL* 124, 125
demolish **OSw** *YVgL* Frb
destroy **OSw** *YVgL* Frb, Urb, Äb,
Rlb, Add, *ÄVgL* Slb, Äb
destroy/damn **OSw** *ÄVgL* Rlb
embezzle **OSw** *HL* Äb
expend **OSw** *DL* Gb, *UL* Äb, *VmL* Äb
forfeit **ODan** *ESjL* 1–3, *JyL* 1–3, *SkKL* 3, 10, *VSjL*
62, 86, 87, **OGu** *GL* A 22, 29, 63, **OIce** *Jó* Þfb 5, 8
Mah 1, 10 Llb 30 Þjb 1 Fml 9, *Js* Þfb 4 Mah 1, 14 Þjb
1, *KRA* 11, 15, **ONorw** *BorgL* 3.2 4.2 passim, *EidsL*
52.2, *FrL* KrbA 10, 38 KrbB 3 Mhb 1, *GuL* Krb,
OSw *DL* Eb, Gb, *HL* Kgb, Äb, Mb, Blb, *SdmL* Kgb,
Gb, Mb, *UL* Kgb, Äb, Jb, Mb, Kmb, Blb, *VmL* Kgb,
Äb, Kmb, Bb, *YVgL* Urb, Äb, Rlb, *ÄVgL* Urb, Äb
forsake **ODan** *JyL* 2
misappropriate **OGu** *GL* A 63
spoil **ONorw** *GuL* Kvb
use **OGu** *GL* A 24d
Expressions:
fyrirgera fé ok friði (ON)
forfeit property and peace **OIce** *Jó* Þfb 8 *Js* Þfb 4
fyrirgera landi ok lausum eyri (ON)
forfeit land and chattels **OIce** *Jó* Mah 4

See also: *firiköpa, foreföra, forestanda,*
forgærning, forlöpa, forværka, troldomber
Refs: Ekholst 2014, 139–50

firihægþa (OSw) **forhæfþa** (OSw) **forhægþa** (OSw)
verb
part with **OSw** *UL* Äb
squander **OSw** *UL* Äb, *VmL* Äb
See also: *afhænda*

firikomas (OSw) **fore komas** (OSw) verb
miscarry **OSw** *UL* Äb, *VmL* Äb
See also: *spilla*

firiköpa (OSw) **fore köpa** (OSw) **forköpa** (OSw) verb
forfeit **OSw** *UL* Mb, *VmL* Mb
See also: *firigæra, foreföra,*
forestanda, forlöpa, forværka

firilata (OSw) **forlate** (ODan) **fyrirláta** (ON) verb
condone **ODan** *ESjL* 2
forgive **ODan** *ESjL* 2, **OIce** *Js* Kdb 1, **OSw** *HL* Äb

firistiæla (OSw) **firistiela** (OGu) **fyrirstela** (ON) verb
forfeit **OIce** *Jó* Þjb 1
forfeit by stealing **OIce** *Js* Þjb 1
forfeit through theft **OGu** *GL* Add.
8 (B 55), **OSw** *DL* Tjdb

firnari (ON) adj.
Expressions:
firnari menn (pl.) (ON)
remoter kin **OIce** *Grg* Arþ 122,
Ómb 137 **ONorw** *GuL* Mhb

firnarorþ (OSw) noun
shameful word **OSw** *YVgL* Rlb, *ÄVgL* Rlb
See also: *oqvæþinsorþ*

firnarværk (OSw) noun
act of abomination **OSw** *YVgL* Kkb, *ÄVgL* Gb
case of abomination **OSw** *YVgL* Urb, *ÄVgL* Gb
crime of abomination **OSw** *YVgL* Add

firrask (ON) verb
avoid **ONorw** *GuL* Løb, Mhb
decrease **ONorw** *GuL* Mhb

fiskeleker (OSw) noun
spawning ground (for fish) **OSw** *SdmL* Bb
spawning season (for fish) **OSw**
UL Kkb, Blb, *VmL* Kkb, Bb

fisketol (OSw) **fiskiatol** (OSw) **fisktol** (OSw) noun
fishing tackle **OSw** *UL* Blb, *VmL* Bb
fishing tool **OSw** *SdmL* Bb

fiskhelgr (ON) noun
Literally 'fish-sanctity'. A unit for measuring distance;
the distance at which cod fish could still be seen in the

water from land. This indicated the space between the coast and the limit in open waters to which the fishing and drift rights of the landowner extended. Beyond the *fiskhelgr* were common waters (ON *almenningr*, see *almænninger*).

distance from land where the caught fish belongs to the owner of the shore **OIce** *Jó* Llb 65

See also: *almænninger, rekamark*

Refs: Gísli Pálsson and E. Durrenberger 1987; idem 1996; GrgTr II:369; Hastrup 1992; KLNM s.v. *hvalfangst*

fiski (ON) noun

fishing **OIce** *Grg* Þsþ 78, **ONorw** *GuL* Krb

fiskiahus (OSw) noun

fishing construction **OSw** *HL* Blb

fiskigarþer (OSw) **fiskegarth** (ODan) noun

fish garth **ODan** *SkL* 212

fish trap **ODan** *JyL* 1, **OSw** *SdmL* Bb

fishery **OSw** *YVgL* Kvab, Utgb, *ÄVgL* Kva, Föb

fishing place **OSw** *YVgL* Drb, *ÄVgL* Md

fiskigjöf (ON) noun

contribution of fish **ONorw** *FrL* Reb 2

fiskiskáli (ON) noun

fishing hut **OIce** *Grg* Þsþ 79

fiskiværk (OSw) noun

fishery **OSw** *ÄVgL* Kva

fiskja (ON) verb

fish **ONorw** *GuL* Krb

fiskr (ON) noun

fish **ONorw** *GuL* Krb, Llb

fiskveiðr (ON) noun

fishing rights **OIce** *Grg* Lbþ 220, *Jó* Llb 6, *Js* Lbb 13

fit (ON) noun

skin of the feet of animals **ONorw** *GuL* Løb

fiti (OSw) noun

deck **OSw** *DL* Kkb

fiurmænninger (OSw) **fermenningr** (ON) **fjórmenningar** (ON) **fioþermæningi** (OSw) noun

people related to the fourth degree **OIce** *Jó* Mah 3, 7 Kab 2

third cousin **OIce** *Jó* Kge 23, **OSw** *DL* Kkb, Mb, *HL* Mb

fiælder (OSw) noun

enclave **OSw** *SdmL* Kkb, Bb

See also: *flutfiælder, urfiælder*

fiærþungsmaþer (OSw) **fjarthingsman** (ODan) **fjórðungsmaðr** (ON) **fiorþongs maþer** (OSw) **fiorþungs maþer** (OSw) noun

Literally, 'man of the quarter'. In JyL (2 §56) it occurs in the context of the nomination of a replacement

(*nævning*, see *næmpning*) for one of the pair of men from a quarter of a district who were to form part of the adjudication panel of eight for that district. Those making the nomination would seem to include to all the qualified men from that quarter. In FrL, Grg and Js, it refers more generally to the inhabitants of a quarter, an administrative district in Norway and Iceland. The word has two different meanings in VmL. The first meaning relates to the levy and refers to a man or the men of the quarter of the *skiplagh* (q.v.) (presumably the population division called elsewhere the *hundari* (q.v.)) from whom the troops in the levy are drawn. The second meaning relates to reversion inheritance and refers to ascendants two generations removed from the deceased person, who were thus entitled to one quarter of the inheritance each according to the laws of inheritance set out in VmL.

man entitled to a quarter **OSw** *VmL* Äb

man of a quarter **ODan** *JyL* 2

man of the quarter **OIce** *Grg* Þsþ 49, 50 Ómb 138, 143 Misc 240, *Js* Rkb 2, **ONorw** *FrL* KrbA 7, **OSw** *VmL* Kgb

See also: *arver, avugher, fiarþunger, leþunger, næmpning, skiplagh*

Refs: KLNM, s.v. *fjerding*; Schlyter 1877, s.v.v. *fiærþungs maþer, skiplagh, skiplæghi*; SL VmL, 41 note 24, 42 note 26, 62 note 71

fiærþungsþing (OSw) **fjórðungsþing** (ON) noun

A *þing* 'assembly' of the judicial district *fiarþunger* (OSw)/*fjórðungr* (ON). In ONorw, appearing in the context of appealing a case from one type of *þing* to another. In OSw YVgL, appearing in the context of seeking compensation for fornication, alternatively at the *hærapsþing* (q.v.) and prior to the *landsþing* (q.v.).

assembly of the fourth **OSw** *YVgL* Gb, Add

quarter thing assembly **ONorw** *GuL* Kpb, Olb

See also: *fiarþunger, þing*

Refs: KLNM s.v. *ting*

fiæt (OSw) **fiat** (OSw) **fæt** (OSw) noun

foot **OSw** *HL* Blb, *UL* Blb, *VmL* Bb

trail **OSw** *UL* Kgb, Mb, *Jb*, *VmL* Mb

{fiæt} **OSw** *DL* Bb

fiætra (OSw) verb

fetter **OSw** *UL* Äb, *VmL* Äb

fiætur (OSw) **fjöturr** (ON) **fiatur** (OSw) **fiædher** (OSw) noun

fetters **OSw** *UL* Mb, *VmL* Mb

shackle **ONorw** *GuL* Llb, Mhb

fjallganga (ON) noun

going up to the mountain to gather sheep **OIce** *Jó* Llb 49

fjallhagi (ON) noun
  mountain pasture **OIce** *Jó* Llb 23
fjallnár (ON) noun
  mountain-corpse **OIce** *Grg* Bat 113
fjara (ON) noun
  foreshore **OIce** *Grg* Klþ 8, *Js* Lbb 13, *KRA* 26
  shore **OIce** *Jó* Þjb 2
fjándboð (ON) noun
  ridiculous bid **ONorw** *GuL* Llb
fjárdóming (ON) fjárdæming (ON) noun
  judgement in a payment suit **OIce** *Grg* Fjl 222
fjáreign (ON) noun
  property ownership **OIce** *KRA* 15
  wealth **OIce** *Grg* Þsþ 77
  See also: *öþer*
fjárfar (ON) noun
  money affairs **ONorw** *FrL* Kvb 5
  state of means **OIce** *Grg* Feþ 154
fjárfélag (ON) noun
  trade partnership **OIce** *Jó* Fml 22, 23
fjárgjöf (ON) noun
  gift of property **OIce** *Grg* Hrs 236
fjárhald (ON) noun
  administration of money **ONorw** *FrL* ArbB 22
  care of property **OIce** *Jó* Kge 3, 15, *Js* Kvg 4 Ert 24, **ONorw** *FrL* Mhb 9 Kvb 9
  guardianship **ONorw** *GuL* Arb
  See also: *halzmaþer*
fjárhaldsmaðr (ON) noun
  guardian **ONorw** *FrL* Mhb 38 Var 19 ArbB 22, *GuL* Arb
  man who has care of the property **OIce** *Jó* Kge 14 Kab 8, *Js* Ert 20, 24 Kab 11
  manager **ONorw** *GuL* Løb
  person in charge of property **ONorw** *FrL* Jkb 2
  person who keeps property **ONorw** *FrL* ArbB 7
  See also: *fjárvarðveizlumaðr*, *halzmaþer*
fjárheimta (ON) noun
  claim for payment **OIce** *Grg* Misc 250
fjárheimting (ON) noun
  claim **OIce** *Grg* Feþ 150 Hrs 236
  property claim **OIce** *Grg* Tíg 259
fjárhlutr (ON) noun
  estate **OIce** *Jó* Kge 5
  goods **OIce** *Jó* Þjb 14
  means **ONorw** *FrL* LlbB 5
  possessions **OIce** *Js* Kvg 4, 5, *KRA* 8
  property **ONorw** *FrL* KrbA 35 Kvb 11

property share **ONorw** *BorgL* 16.8
fjárlag (ON) fjárlóg (ON) noun
  case of the disposal of property **OIce** *Grg* Arþ 127
  standard value **OIce** *Grg* Misc 246, *Jó* Kab 1 Kab 6
fjárlát (ON) noun
  expense **ONorw** *FrL* Intr 12
fjárleiga (ON) noun
  hire of property **OIce** *Grg* Fjl 221
  hiring stock **OIce** *Grg* Fjl 224
  interest **ONorw** *GuL* Kpb
  See also: *legha*
fjármegin (ON) fjármagn (ON) fjármegn (ON) noun
  amount of property **OIce** *Js* Mah 29 Kvg 2 Ert 19
  claim **OIce** *Jó* Þfb 8
  claim size **OIce** *Jó* Þjb 5
  financial ability **OIce** *Jó* Kge 7-1
  fortune **ONorw** *FrL* Var 46
  value of wares **OIce** *Jó* Fml 10
  wealth **ONorw** *GuL* Krb, Arb
fjárrán (ON) noun
  seizure of goods **OIce** *Grg* Misc 244
fjárreiða (ON) noun
  money matters **OIce** *Grg* Feþ 151
fjárskaði (ON) noun
  loss **OIce** *Grg* Rsþ 230
  loss of money **OIce** *Jó* Llb 20 Fml 13
fjárskilorð (ON) noun
  conditions and means of payment **ONorw** *GuL* Mhb
fjárskuld (ON) noun
  money debt **ONorw** *FrL* Var 42 Rgb 24
fjársókn (ON) noun
  case concerning property **OIce** *Js* Þfb 5
  legal action **ONorw** *FrL* KrbA 35
  legal proceedings **OIce** *Jó* Þfb 5 Kab 1
  money claim **OIce** *Jó* Þfb 6, **ONorw** *FrL* Var 46 Rgb 24
  parish **ONorw** *GuL* Krb
  prosecution for property **OIce** *Js* Ert 23 Lbb 10, *KRA* 29
  suit concerning property **ONorw** *FrL* KrbB 20 ArbB 29
  See also: *kirkiusokn*
fjártaka (ON) fjártekja (ON) noun
  case for taking property **OIce** *Grg* Rsþ 227, 231
fjártala (ON) noun
  sum **OIce** *Grg* Feþ 154
fjártöpun (ON) noun
  property loss **ONorw** *FrL* Intr 1

fjárupptekð (ON) noun

property seizure **OIce** *Jó* Kab 1, *Js* Kab 1

fjárvarðveizla (ON) noun

care of property **OIce** *Grg* Arþ 118, 122
Feþ 161 Fjl 223, *Jó* Lbb 1, *KRA* 15

fjárvarðveizlumaðr (ON) noun

guardian of the estate **OIce** *Js* Lbb 1
man who has care of others' property **OIce**
Grg Lbþ 195 Misc 244, *Jó* Kge 14 Lbb 1

fjorðingi (ON) noun

A person who has resided in a location for a year.

resident since the previous year **ONorw** *FrL* Leb 11

Refs: CV s.v. *fjörðingi*; Fritzner s.v.
fjörðingi; ONP s.v. *fjorðingi*

fjórðungamót (ON) noun

quarter boundary **OIce** *Grg* Vís 99

fjórðungavætt (ON) noun

quarter weight **OIce** *Jó* Kab 26

fjórðungsdómr (ON) noun

A Quarter Court. Four of these were held, one for
each quarter, at the annual General Assembly in
Iceland. Quarter Courts served as higher courts in
which unresolved cases from district assemblies
were judged. Cases which remained disputed after
having been tried in a Quarter Court moved on to the
Fifth Court (ON *fimmtardómr*). They had original
jurisdiction over cases in which the two parties were
residents of different quarters of the country. All cases
concerning injury (ON *áverk*) were also to be heard
at the Quarter Courts (cf. Grg Vís 99). The Quarter
Courts, along with the Fifth Court, were abolished
when Iceland came under Norwegian rule during the
thirteenth century.

Quarter Court **OIce** *Grg* Þsþ 20, 21 Vís
99, 110 Feþ 159 Lbþ 172, 176 Fjl 223

See also: *alþingi, domber, fimmtardómr, varþing*

Refs: CV s.v. *fjórðungr*; Fritzner; KLNM s.v.
alþingi, dómr; MSE s.v. *althingi, Iceland*

fjórðungsgjald (ON) noun

A quarter payment. According to Js Mah 3 it is paid
from the property of a killer sentenced to outlawry
to the kinsmen of the slain. It is unclear whether the
'quarter' is meant as one fourth of the wergild payment
as suggested by Hertzberg, as this would suggest
the remaining three quarters would be paid from
elsewhere or not at all. Alternatively it could mean that
the victim's kinsmen were entitled to a quarter of the
outlaw's remaining property. The equivalent passage
in FrL Intr 3 states that the outlaw's kinsman is to pay

a quarter of the payment from his (i.e. the outlaw's)
property (ON *böti ... fíórðung giallda*).

quarter payment **OIce** *Js* Mah 3

See also: *gæld*

Refs: Hertzberg s.v. *fjórðungsgjald*

fjórðungsgjöf (ON) noun

According to Jó (Kge 22) one was permitted to give
away up to a quarter of one's property as a legal
gift. This referred only to acquired property and not
inherited property, of which one could only legally
give a tenth (ON *tíundargjöf*). Gifts in excess of this
amount were considered to be defrauding one's heirs.
In FrL (e.g. FrL ArbB 18) the term *fjórðungr* is thought
to be equivalent to *fjórðungsgjöf*. This is supported by
the full term appearing in the table of contents of a
variant manuscript (cf. NGL II:510).

quarter-gift **OIce** *Jó* Kge 22

See also: *gæf, tíundargjöf*

Refs: CV s.v. *fjórðungr*; Fritzner s.v.
fjórðungsgjöf; KLNM s.v. *donasjon*

fjórðungskirkja (ON) noun

quarter church **ONorw** *GuL* Krb

fjórðungsómagi (ON) noun

quarter dependent **OIce** *Grg* Hrs 234

fjós (ON) noun

byre **OIce** *Grg* Klþ 11

fjölbrú (ON) noun

board-bridge **ONorw** *BorgL* 5.8

fjölði (ON) **fjöldi** (ON) noun

assembled men **ONorw** *GuL* Kpb,
Kvb, Løb, Llb, Mhb, Olb

fjölkynngi (ON) **fjölkyngi** (ON) noun

magic **OIce** *Grg* Klþ 7, 17

fjölmæli (ON) noun

Generally gossip, loose talk, slander; a broad category
of defamatory speech which could be prosecuted. No
specific list of such terms is given in the laws, but a
1313 amendment issued by King Hákon Magnússon
states that calling someone the son of a whore (ON
pútusonr eða hórkonusonr) constituted *fjölmæli*, and
at least two manuscripts of Bj stipulate that saying a
man is 'womanish' (ON *ragr*) is considered *fjölmæli*.
It has been suggested that *fjölmæli* is equivalent
to 'unspeakable words' (ON *ókvæðisorð*, see
oqvæþinsorþ).

defamation **OIce** *Jó* Mah 24

slander **OIce** *Js* Mah 24, **ONorw** *GuL* Tfb

See also: *fullréttisorð, mansöngr, níð,*
oqvæþinsorþ, ragr, róg, tréníð, tunguníð, ýki

Refs: CV s.v. *fjölmæli*; Ebel 1993,163; Fritzner;
Hagland & Sandnes 1997, 106; Hertzberg
s.v. *fjölmæli*; KLNM s.v. *ærenkrænkelse*

fjölmælismaðr (ON) noun

slanderer **OIce** *Jó* Mah 26, *Js* Mah
25, **ONorw** *FrL* KrbB 15

fjölskyldi (ON) noun

effort **OIce** *Grg* Arþ 127

fjörbaugr (ON) noun

A 'life ring'. A mark of legal tender given to the
chieftain (ON *goði*) who appoints a confiscation court
(ON *féránsdómr*). This mark is paid by a lesser outlaw
(ON *fjörbaugsmaðr*) in order to avoid a sentence of
full outlawry (ON *skóggangr*).

life ring **OIce** *Grg* Þsþ 51, 52, 67

See also: *alaðsfestr*, *bogher*, *féránsdómr*

Refs: CV s.v. *fjörbaugr*; Finsen 1883, 609;
Fritzner s.v. *fjörbaugr*; KLNM s.v. *fredløshed*

fjörbaugsgarðr (ON) noun

Lesser outlawry; one of two types of outlawry or
banishment prescribed in Grg. It has been suggested
that this penalty was an Icelandic invention (Riisøy
2014, 123 [following van Houts]), and its absence in
Js and Jó suggests that the practice was discontinued
by the time Iceland fell under Norwegian rule in
second half of the thirteenth century.

Lesser outlawry was the penalty for a wide range
of crimes in Grg, such as being ignorant of the baptism
ritual, abusing the power of a *goði* (q.v.), practicing
sorcery and numerous other offenses. Anyone judged
a lesser outlaw (*fjörbaugsmaðr*) was forced to leave
the country for three consecutive summers, and the
outlaw's property was confiscated. Prior to departing
the country a lesser outlaw retained his legal immunity
at three declared 'homes' (*heimili*) (cf. Grg Þsþ 52).

lesser outlawry **OIce** *Grg* Klþ 1, 4 Þsþ 23, 25 Vís
88, 98 Bat 113 Lrþ 117 Arþ 118, 126 passim

See also: *féránsdómr*, *skóggangr*

Refs: CV s.v. *fjörbaugr*; GAO s.v.
Friedlosigkeit; KLNM s.v. *fredløshed*; Lúðvík
Ingvarsson 1970, 140–55; Riisøy 2014

fjörbaugsmaðr (ON) noun

lesser outlaw **OIce** *Grg* Klþ 4 Þsþ
32, 41 Arþ 118 Ómb 142

fjörbaugssekð (ON) noun

lesser outlawry **OIce** *Grg* Þsþ 60

fjörbaugssök (ON) noun

lesser outlawry case **OIce** *Grg* Klþ 16, 17 Misc 243

lesser outlawry offence **OIce** *Grg* Þsþ 52

fjörlöstr (ON) noun

Loss of life.

Expressions:

gera fjörlöst (ON)

take the life (of a person) **OIce** *Grg* Misc 249

fjörráð (ON) noun

death plot **OIce** *Jó* Mah 11

scheming **ONorw** *FrL* Mhb 37

fjörskaði (ON) noun

bodily injury **ONorw** *FrL* Mhb 37

fjörumaðr (ON) noun

owner of drift rights **OIce** *Jó* Llb 61, 63

See also: *rekamaðr*

fjörumark (ON) noun

shore-bounds **OIce** *Grg* Lbþ 213, *Jó* Llb 62

fjörvél (ON) noun

design against one's life **ONorw** *GuL* Løb

flannfluga (ON) noun

runaway from her betrothed man **ONorw** *GuL* Kvb

flat (OSw) **flat** (ODan) **flæt** (OSw) noun

bench **OSw** *YVgL* Jb, *ÄVgL* Jb

house **ODan** *ESjL* 1, *VSjL* 1, 2, **OSw** *YVgL* Add

house-led **ODan** *JyL* 1

partnership **ODan** *VSjL* 2, 10

Expressions:

fara a flat, flytta til flæt (OSw)

*move from the high settle to the
bench* **OSw** *YVgL* Jb *ÄVgL* Jb

move to another's house **OSw** *YVgL* Add

See also: *flatföring*

flatfara (OSw) verb

move to another's house **OSw** *YVgL* Add

flatføre (ODan) verb

house-lead **ODan** *ESjL* 1, 2, *JyL* 1,
3, *SkL* 42, 43, *VSjL* 21, 22

See also: *flatføring*

flatføring (ODan) noun

Support of the old and disabled, primarily by relatives
who became their guardians in return for their
property. Also the person supported in this way, who
gave up their property and legal status.

house-leading **ODan** *ESjL* 1, *JyL* 1

house-led **ODan** *ESjL* 1, *JyL* 1, *SkL* 44, *VSjL* 23, 24

See also: *sytning*

Refs: KLNM s.v.v. *fattigvård*, *flatföring*; Vogt 2008

flatr (ON) adj.

flat **ONorw** *GuL* Mhb

fleyðr (ON) noun

   rafter **ONorw** *GuL* Leb

flís (ON) noun

   sliver **ONorw** *GuL* Llb

fljóta (ON) verb

   be vacant **ONorw** *GuL* Leb

fljúga (ON) verb

   fall over a cliff **ONorw** *GuL* Llb

   fight **ONorw** *GuL* Llb

flokkaatvígi (ON) noun

   attack of a crowd **ONorw** *FrL* Mhb 23

flokker (OSw) **flokkr** (ON) **flukker** (OSw) noun

Etymologically disputed, but usually referring to a collection of something. In OSw, notably used of law chapters. Also appearing in phrases such as *i flok ok farunöti* 'in the party of fellow travellers', *i flok ok fylghi* 'in a group and a gang' (OSw) often referring to those in company with perpetrators of violent crimes, in ONorw GuL (ch. 154) defined as at least five men, who were punished whether participating or not (cf. *fylghi*).

   band of men **ONorw** *GuL* Tfb, Mhb

   chapter **OSw** *HL* Kkb, Kgb, Äb, Mb, Jb, Kmb, Blb, Rb, *SdmL* För, Kgb, Gb, Äb, Jb, Bb, Kmb, Mb, Tjdb, Rb, *UL* passim, *VmL* passim, *YVgL* passim, *ÖgL* Kkb, Eb, Db, Vm

   cohort **OSw** *UL* Äb, *VmL* Äb

   collection **OSw** *UL* StfBM

   company **OSw** *SdmL* Kkb, Kgb, Gb, Bb, Till

   fellowship **OSw** *UL* Kkb, *VmL* Mb

   flock **OSw** *YVgL* Add

   group **ONorw** *FrL* Mhb 23, *GuL* Tfb, Mhb

   party **OIce** *Grg* Vís 99, **OSw** *UL* Mb

   side **OIce** *Grg* Vís 86

See also: *farunöti*, *fylghi*, *hærværk*

Refs: ONP s.v. *flokkr*; SAOB s.v. *flock*

flokksvíg (ON) noun

   killing in a group fight **ONorw** *GuL* Mhb

flothemal (ODan) **flóðarmál** (ON) **flæðarmál** (ON) noun

   foreshore **ONorw** *GuL* Krb

   high water mark **OFar** *Seyð* 8, **OIce** *Grg* Klþ 8, *Js* Lbb 13, *KRA* 26

   high-water line **OIce** *Grg* Lbþ 209, *Jó* Llb 6, 60

   stemming up water **ODan** *JyL* 1

floti (OSw) **fluti** (OGu) **flotæ** (OSw) noun

   raft **OSw** *UL* Blb, *VmL* Bb

   small boat **OGu** *GL* Add. 8 (B 55)

See also: *bater*, *byrthing*, *farkoster*, *kaupskip*, *myndrikkia*, *skip*

flórfili (ON) noun

   loose boards in the stable **ONorw** *GuL* Llb

flugumaðr (ON) noun

A *flugumaðr* was a man who let himself be hired to perform a manslaughter of which he had no personal interest. Such a man was to be treated as an *óbótamaðr* (evildoer). See, e.g., GuL ch. 32.

   assassin **OIce** *Jó* Mah 2, *Js* Mah 6, *KRA* 11, **ONorw** *FrL* Var 45

   fly-man **ONorw** *EidsL* 50.13

   hired bandit **ONorw** *GuL* Krb

Refs: Hertzberg s.v. *flugumaðr*

flut (OGu) noun

   boat (i.e. afloat) **OGu** *GL* Add. 8 (B 55)

   flotsam at sea **OGu** *GL* A 49

flutfiælder (OSw) noun

   transfer enclave **OSw** *SdmL* Jb

See also: *fiælder*, *urfiælder*

flutning (ON) **flutningr** (ON) noun

   crossing **OIce** *Jó* Llb 45

   salvage **OIce** *Grg* Lbþ 211, *Jó* Llb 61, 66

   transport **OIce** *Jó* Kge 31 Fml 26

   voyage **OIce** *Jó* Fml 8

flutningshvalr (ON) **flutningarhvalr** (ON) noun

   salvaged whale **OIce** *Jó* Llb 65

flya (OSw) **flyje** (ODan) **flya** (OGu) **flýja** (ON) verb

   avoid **ONorw** *GuL* Kvb, Mhb

   flee **ODan** *ESjL* 2, *JyL* 2, 3, *SkL* 126

Expressions:

flya frip (OSw)

   be forced to flee from the King's Peace **OSw** *UL* Kgb *VmL* Kgb

See also: *friþer*, *land*

flytja (ON) verb

   give testimony **ONorw** *FrL* Var 7

   plead **OIce** *Js* Þfb 5

flærþ (OSw) **flærð** (ON) noun

   counterfeit **OSw** *HL* Kmb

   deceit **OIce** *Js* Kab 9

   forgery **OSw** *SdmL* Kmb

   fraudulent goods **OSw** *UL* Kmb, *VmL* Kmb

   fraudulent thing **ONorw** *GuL* Kpb

   worthless goods **OIce** *Jó* Kab 11

See also: *fals*, *far*, *fox*, *kaupfox*

flærþaköp (OSw) flærþæ köp (OSw) noun
   deception encountered when buying **OSw** *HL* Kmb
   fraud in purchase **OSw** *UL* Kmb, *VmL* Kmb
   fraud in trading **OSw** *UL* Kmb, *VmL* Kmb
   See also: *fals*

flærþsala (OSw) noun
   selling of forgeries **OSw** *SdmL* Kmb

fløghelas (ODan) noun
   wood load **ODan** *SkL* 191

foghati (OSw) noun
   An official who, together with the *hærapshöfþingi* (q.v.), controlled lawful measurements. Presumed to have had a complementary function to the *lænsmaþer* (q.v.). Later in the Middle Ages, and in other sources, fairly common as an official of the king, the church, towns, etc, with duties primarily as a tax-collector and policeman.
   sheriff **OSw** *YVgL* Föb
   Refs: Förvaltningshistorisk ordbok s.v. *fogde*; KLNM s.v. *fogde*; Schlyter s.v. *foghati*

folk (OSw) fulk (OGu) fulk (OSw) noun
   people **OSw** *YVgL* Rlb, *ÄVgL* Kkb, Rlb
   population **OGu** *GS* Ch. 1

folkfræls (OSw) adj.
   free-folk **OSw** *ÖgL* Db
   See also: *fræls*

folkland (OSw) fulkland (OSw) noun
   The highest judicial and administrative district in UL, which mentions three *folkland*: Tiundaland, Attundaland and Fjädrundaland, divided into *hundari* (q.v.), and Roden (the historical region along the coast of Uppland), which was divided in *skiplagh* (q.v.). When *folkland* appears in VmL and SdmL this is considered to be copied from UL or to reflect an older administrative division.
   province **OSw** *SdmL* Kgb, Till, *VmL* Kmb, Bb
   {folkland} **OSw** *UL* StfBM, Kgb, Mb, Jb, Kmb, Blb, Rb
   See also: *hundari, land, skiplagh*
   Refs: Brink 1998, 298; KLNM, s.v. *folkland*; Lundberg 1972, 74–76, 82–86; Schlyter, s.v. *folkland*; Schück 1949 p. 8, 25–50; SL 1:xxxviii f.; SL UL, 52 note 1; SL VmL, 104 note 225

folklandsnæmd (OSw) noun
   A *næmd* 'panel' with members from the entire *land* 'province' dealing with appeals concerning disputed land and borders (SdmL).
   provincial panel **OSw** *SdmL* Till
   Refs: Schlyter s.v. *folklands næmd*

folklandsþing (OSw) noun
   The *þing* assembly of the *folkland* (q.v.). The relationship between the *landsþing* (q.v.) and the *folklandsþing* in the OSw UL is unclear. In VmL, *folkland* refers to 'province'.
   provincial thing assembly **OSw** *VmL* Mb
   thing assembly of the folkland **OSw** *UL* Mb, Jb, Blb
   See also: *folkland, land, þing*
   Refs: KLNM s.v. *folkland*; Schlyter 1877 s.v. *folkland*; SL 1:xxxviii f.

folkvapn (OSw) folkevapn (ODan) fulkvapn (OGu) folkvápn (ON) noun
   Literally 'folk weapons, people's weapons' or perhaps 'battle weapons' where *folk* refers to 'troops, army'. *Folkvapn* were the prescribed weapons of men in combat, though it is unclear whether it was considered a privilege to own these weapons or a requirement; possibly both. The term appears in several Swedish, Danish and Norwegian laws, though the number and type of weapons varied.
   In ÖgL three *folkvapn* are named: shield sword and *kittelhatt* (iron hat?), while in HL every man capable of fighting was required to have five, probably for levy service: a sword or axe, an iron hat, a shield, a mailcoat or *musu* (coif?) and a bow with three dozen arrows. In HL *folkvapn* could be inherited by sons of concubines (*frillosonr*). Four *folkvapn* are listed in SdmL, but three — a carving knife, a food knife and arrows — are listed as murder weapons. There also seems to have been some overlap between *folkvapn* and 'sea warrior district weapons' (*hamnu vapn*) in SdmL. In the Swedish laws, the ability to bear *folkvapn* may also have distinguished free men from those of lesser status, i.e. slaves, or even sons of householders — someone who was 'folk-free' (*folkfri*) had the right to bear *folkvapen* and go to war. In HL all men capable of bearing arms over 18 (higher than the age of majority) were required to have *folkvapn*.
   In JyL (3.4) the captain of a ship was required to have a crossbow, three dozen arrows and a man who could fire it (if not himself). All householders on a ship were meant to have a shield and three *folkevapn*: a sword, iron hat and spear.
   In FrL (VIII.13 & 15) all unmarried men were supposed to own *folkvapn*, namely a shield, spear and sword or axe. For the levy (*leiðungr*) every other man (one per bench on a ship) had to provide a bow while the other was to supply two dozen arrows.
   In GL the *folkvapn* formed part of the inheritance given to illegitimate sons when they left home, along with three marks in coin, a variety of bedclothes and fifteen ells of broadcloth for outdoor clothes. There is

no description of what they consisted of. Daughters received a cow instead, so they must have been quite valuable.

A citation from a text on *lögfræði* and a later canon law statue stipulate that clerics should not bear *folkvápn* (without necessity).

battle weapon **OGu** *GL* A 20, **OSw** *UL* Mb

folk weapon **ODan** *SkL* 88, *VSjL* 56, **ONorw** *FrL* Intr 21, *GuL* Leb, **OSw** *HL* Äb, Rb, *SdmL* Gb, Mb

See also: *hamnuvapn*, *leþunger*, *morþvapn*

Refs: Brink forthcoming; SL ÖgL/UL 71; Larsson 1988; KLNM s.v. *folkvapen*; NGL V s.v. *folkvápn*; Schlyter s.v. *folkvapn*; Tamm and Vogt, eds, 2016, 35

for (OSw) noun

Furrow; also boundary between strip fields.

furrow **OSw** *SdmL* Bb

raid **OIce** *Grg* Feþ 160

Refs: Schlyter s.v. *for*.

forað (ON) noun

dangerous place **ONorw** *GuL* Løb, Mhb

perilous place **OIce** *Grg* Misc 241

foráttalaust (ON) adv.

without good cause **OIce** *Grg* Þsþ 80

See also: *forfallalöst*, *nauðsynjalauss*, *ørendlauss*

forbiuþa (OSw) **forbjuthe** (ODan) **fyrirbjóða** (ON) verb

evict **OSw** *UL* Jb

exclude **ODan** *SkKL* 11

forbid **ONorw** *GuL* Krb, Llb, **OSw** *UL* Kkb, *VmL* Kkb

prevent **ODan** *SkL* 165

put in prohibition **OSw** *HL* Kkb, Kmb

forbuþ (OSw) **forbuth** (ODan) **forbuþ** (OGu) **forboð** (ON) noun

Literally, 'prohibition'. It is used generally to mean that something is prohibited (e.g. trade in certain commodities in the case of GS) or that a person is prevented from doing something (e.g. retaining use of land in UL). In particular it referred to a form of lesser excommunication (*forbuþ*, *interdictum locale*), where only the sacrament of Mass (together with other church services) was withheld for a short period. This was common to all medieval Nordic laws, in contrast to the *banzmal* (q.v.), where the person was subject to permanent excommunication, and which occurs only in GL and a number of the OSw laws. This lesser punishment could be escalated to full excommunication if the fine imposed were not paid within a year and a day. It appears from the texts of UL and VmL that, if the culprit did not redeem himself within a further

year and a day, he was to pay for it with his life and that punishment was to be administered by the king. He was to be buried outside the churchyard, although his heirs could retain their share of his property.

ban **OSw** *YVgL* Kkb

eviction **OSw** *UL* Jb

interdict **OIce** *Js* Kdb 4, *KRA* 7, 11, **ONorw** *EidsL* 50.13, **OSw** *YVgL* Kkb

interdiction **OSw** *DL* Kkb, *SdmL* Kkb, *SmL*

lesser ban **ONorw** *GuL* Krb

minor excommunication **OSw** *UL* Kkb, *VmL* Kkb

objection **ODan** *JyL* 1

prohibition **ODan** *SkKL* 3, 6, *SkL* 74, *VSjL* 66, 78, **OGu** *GS* Ch. 2, **OIce** *Jó* Sg 3, **OSw** *HL* Kkb, *UL* Blb, *YVgL* Jb, Kvab, *ÄVgL* Jb, *ÖgL* Kkb

See also: *ban*, *banzmal*, *forbiuþa*

Refs: KLNM, s.v.v. *excommunicatio og interdict*, *kommunion*, *kyrkobalkar*, *kyrkostraff*, *sacrilegium*; Lexikon des Mittelalters, s.v. *bannum*; Peel 2015, 104 note 8/17–19; Schlyter 1877, s.v. *forbuþ*; SL DL, 20 notes 76 and 77; SL UL, 39 note 54, 40 notes 67 and 68, 193 note 87; SL ÖgL, 30 note 65

forbuþa (OSw) **forboða** (ON) verb

ban **OSw** *YVgL* Kkb

excommunicate **OSw** *YVgL* Kkb

forbid **OSw** *UL* Kkb, *VmL* Kkb, *YVgL* Kvab

interdict **OSw** *SdmL* Kkb

put in ban **OSw** *YVgL* Kkb

put under interdict **OIce** *KRA* 7, **OSw** *YVgL* Kkb

fordath (ODan) noun

spell **ODan** *SkKL* 7

See also: *forgærning*

fordeþskepr (OGu) **fordeþskiepr** (OGu) **fordæsskapr** (ON) **fordæðuskapr** (ON) noun

black sorcery **OIce** *Grg* Klþ 7, *Js* Mah 6, 25

sorcery **ONorw** *FrL* Var 45, *GuL* Krb

undeed **ONorw** *EidsL* 41.1

witchcraft **OGu** *GL* A 39, **OIce** *Jó* Mah 2, 26

witchcraft-paraphernalia **ONorw** *BorgL* 16.7

See also: *fordæða*, *gærning*

fordoble (ODan) **dufla** (OGu) **dubla** (ON) **dufla** (ON) verb

gamble **OGu** *GL* A 61, **OIce** *Jó* Þjb 18

gamble away **ODan** *ESjL* 1

See also: *dobblare*, *dufl*, *fordrikke*

fordrikke (ODan) verb

drink away **ODan** *ESjL* 1

See also: *fordoble*

fordæða (ON) noun

    sorcerer **ONorw** *GuL* Mhb

    witch **ONorw** *BorgL* 5.15 16.6

    See also: *fordeþskepr, gærning*

fordøme (ODan) verb

    condemn **ODan** *JyL* 2

foreföra (OSw) verb

    forfeit **OSw** *VmL* Äb

    See also: *firigæra, firiköpa,*
    forestanda, forlöpa, forværka

forehalda (OSw) verb

    pay for **OSw** *UL* Kkb

forestanda (OSw) **forestanda sik** (OSw) **forstanda sik**
(OSw) verb

    forfeit **OSw** *UL* Jb, Blb, *VmL* Kkb

    See also: *firigæra, firiköpa,*
    foreföra, forlöpa, forværka

foreþer (OSw) noun

    An oath sworn by witnesses — in SdmL usually the
plaintiff or defendant, possibly alone — prior to the
compurgators, who were to support it with their oaths.

    oath **OSw** *ÄVgL* Tb

    pre-oath **OSw** *SdmL* Kkb, Äb, Till, *YVgL* Tb, Add

    Refs: Schlyter s.v. *foreþer*

foreþismaþer (OSw) noun

    man who swears first **OSw** *ÖgL* Kkb

forfall (OSw) **forfal** (ODan) **forfall** (OGu) **forfall** (ON)
forfald (OSw) noun

    Typically referring to a circumstance, such as illness
or service to the king, preventing the performance of a
duty. Often appearing with the same meaning, 'lawful
excuse', in the phrase *lagha forfall* in OSw and as the
compound *lagheforfal* in ODan (which, however, has
been dealt with as a phrase here). Also of impediments
to marriage. Partly synonymous with *nöþsyn* (q.v.)
(OSw).

    absence **ODan** *ESjL* 3, *SkKL* 11, *SkL*
72, 83, *VSjL* 50, 77, 84, 87

    excusal **OSw** *UL* Mb, Rb, *VmL* Mb, Rb

    excuse **ODan** *ESjL* 2, 3, *JyL* 1, 2, *SkKL* 7, *VSjL* 84,
OSw *DL* Kkb, Rb, *HL* Kgb, Mb, Rb, *SdmL* Kkb,
Kgb, Gb, Tjdb, Rb, *SmL, UL* Kkb, Kgb, Mb, Jb,
Add. 18, *VmL* Kkb, Kgb, Jb, *YVgL* Kkb, Gb, Rlb,
Tb, Föb, Add, *ÄVgL* Kkb, Gb, *ÖgL* Kkb, Db

    hindrance **OSw** *SdmL* Kkb, *UL* Äb, *VmL* Kkb, Äb

    impediment **OSw** *SmL, UL* Kkb, *VmL* Kkb

    lawful absence **ODan** *SkL* 146, 147

    lawful excuse **ODan** *JyL* 2, **OSw** *HL* Kkb

    legal excuse **ODan** *ESjL* 3

    necessity **OIce** *Jó* Þfb 2

    neglect **OSw** *SmL*

    obstacle **OSw** *DL* Kkb, *HL* Äb

    prevention **ODan** *ESjL* 3

    reasonable excuse **OFar** *Seyð* 10

    reasons **OGu** *GS* Ch. 4

    rightful absence **ODan** *SkL* 147

    See also: *domber, menföre, skæl*

    Refs: Gammeldansk ordbog s.v. *lagheforfal*

forfallalöst (OSw) **forfallalauss** (ON) adv.

    not hindered **OIce** *Js* Þfb 1

    without excuse **OSw** *YVgL* Kkb, *ÄVgL* Kkb

    without legal cause **OFar** *Seyð* 1, **OIce** *Jó* Þfb
1, *Js* Þfb 2, *KRA* 14, **ONorw** *BorgL* 17.1

    without legitimate hindrance **OIce** *KRA* 16

    without valid excuse **OIce** *Jó* Þfb 2, 9
Sg 1 Llb 8, 21 Kab 4, 24 Fml 3

    See also: *foráttalaust, forfall*

forfallseþer (OSw) noun

    oath of validity **OSw** *ÖgL* Kkb

forfallsvitni (OSw) noun

    excuse witness **OSw** *SdmL* Rb, Till

    See also: *forfall, vitni*

forfiski (OSw) noun

    encroachment on another persons
fishing rights **OSw** *DL* Bb

forgift (ON) noun

    payment for keep **OFar** *Seyð* 9

forgærning (OSw) **forgiærning** (OSw) noun

    killing by witchcraft **OSw** *SdmL* Mb

    poisoning **OSw** *HL* Mb

    spell **OSw** *UL* Mb, *VmL* Mb

    witchcraft **OSw** *UL* Mb, *VmL* Mb, Rb (rubric only)

    See also: *firigæra, fordath, gærning*

forhugsun (ON) **forhugsan** (ON) noun

    intention **OIce** *Jó* Þjb 24

forhæfþi (OSw) noun

    paternal inheritance **OSw** *DL* Bb

    See also: *fæþerni*

forhæfþiseþer (OSw) noun

    oath of paternal inheritance **OSw** *DL* Bb

forhæghthe (ODan) verb

    lose **ODan** *ESjL* 1

    sell away **ODan** *ESjL* 3

    spoil **ODan** *VSjL* 67

    squander **ODan** *SkL* 58, 85

forhælgþ (OSw) **forheld** (OSw) **forhælgh** (OSw)
forhælghþ (OSw) noun

day of preparation for a feast day
OSw *UL* Kkb, Rb, *VmL* Kkb

eve of a holy day **OSw** *HL* Äb

vigils **OSw** *SdmL* Kkb, *YVgL* Kkb

forköp (OSw) noun

detrimental purchase **OSw** *SdmL* Kmb

forlag (ON) noun

maintenance **OIce** *Js* Ert 24

See also: *forlagseyrir*

forlagseyrir (ON) noun

Money for one's support, particularly the support of a
specified number of children of impoverished relatives
in proportion to one's assets. Also the obligation to
pay this.

maintenance **ONorw** *FrL* Kvb 11, *GuL* Arb

maintenance money **OIce** *Jó* Kge 15, 23, *Js* Ert 24

means of subsistence **ONorw** *FrL* Var 13 ArbB 22

See also: *innstóðueyrir*

Refs: Fritzner s.v. *forlagseyrir*; Hertzberg
s.v. *forlagseyrir*; KLNM s.v. *fattigvård*

forligje (ODan) **fyrirliggja** (ON) verb

To 'for-lie'; to forfeit (property, status) due to sexual
misconduct.

commit adultery **ONorw** *FrL* ArbB 16 Kvb 14

lie (2) **ODan** *JyL* 2

See also: *liggia*

Refs: CV s.v. *fyrirliggja*; Fritzner s.v.
fyrirliggja; GDO s.v. *forligje*

forlægje (ODan) verb

ban **ODan** *JyL* 3

forlækisværk (OSw) noun

irreparable harm **OSw** *DL* Mb

forlöpa (OSw) **fore löpa** (OSw) verb

forfeit **OSw** *VmL* Kkb

See also: *firigæra*, *firiköpa*, *foreföra*,
forestanda, *forværka*

formal (ODan) noun

absolution **ODan** *JyL* 3

formali (OGu) noun

agreement **OGu** *GL* Add. 7 (B 49)

forman (OSw) **forman** (ODan) noun

Generally, a leader or supervisor of a group of people,
such as household servants. Particularly, the supervisor
of a parish priest to whom he was referred if he failed
in his duty in some way or committed a crime against a
layman. The same person is referred to as the arbiter in
the context of the breaking of a betrothal, the validity
of oaths, the inheritance rights of a child conceived
at home but born abroad following the mother being
captured. This person would presumably have been
the rural dean or the bishop himself. The same word is
used of the person appointed by the king to act in his
stead in respect of the provision of moorings for the
levy. The relationship between the person referred to
by this title and the person(s) referred to as *lænsmaþer*
is unclear. It is possible that the former was a cleric (in
the case of Church matters) or a member of the nobility
(in the case of the levy), whilst the latter were laymen
(such as the *biskops lænsman* a bishop's official) or
simply government appointees respectively.

foreman **ODan** *JyL* 2

leader **OSw** *ÖgL* Db

overseer **OSw** *HL* Blb

supervisor **OSw** *HL* Kkb, *SdmL* Kkb,
Kgb, *UL* Kkb, Kgb, Äb, *VmL* Kkb

See also: *lænsmaþer*, *umbuþ*

Refs: Schlyter 1877, s.v. *forman*; SL UL, 40 note 56

forn (OSw) **forn** (ON) adj.

ancient **OSw** *UL* StfBM, Blb, *VmL* Bb

old **ONorw** *GuL* Llb

Expressions:

fornt ok gamalt (OSw)

from time immemorial **OSw** *UL* Jb

See also: *byrþ*, *fyrnska*, *gamal*, *aldaoþal*

fornhæfþ (OSw) noun

ancient possession **OSw** *SdmL* Jb, Bb

fornæmi (OSw) **fornam** (ODan) **fornæmi** (ON) noun

Defined in *Jó* Þjb 7 as taking away an item belonging
to someone else in the presence of the owner. Along
with hand-seizure (*handrán*) *fornæmi* was considered
a lesser form of theft. In the Norwegian laws the
term was often used for unlicensed, temporary use of
another's transport, such as a horse or boat (e.g. FrL
Rgb 42).

conversion **OIce** *Jó* Llb 45 Þjb 7, 16

illegal appropriation **OSw** *ÄVgL* Fös

illegal land use **OSw** *UL* Jb

plundering **ONorw** *FrL* Rgb 42

taking **ODan** *ESjL* 2

See also: *áfang*, *görtóki*, *handran*,
hvinska, *misfangi*, *ran*

Refs: CV; F; Hertzberg; KLNM s.v. *lån*, *tyveri*;
LexMA (Diebstahl > C. Rechte einzelner
Länder > IV. Skandinavische Rechte)

fornæmisbalker (OSw) noun

book about illegal appropriation **OSw** *YVgL* Föb

See also: *balker*, *fornæmi*

fornæmissak (OSw) noun

case of illegal appropriation **OSw** *YVgL* Föb

forraþa (OSw) **firi raþa** (OGu) **firi raþa** (OSw) verb

betray **OGu** *GL* A 37, **OSw** *SdmL* Mb

forráð (ON) **forræði** (ON) noun

authority **OIce** *Grg* Þsþ 24, *Jó* Mah
2 Kge 26, *Js* Mah 29, *KRA* 4

*being entitled to make decisions about
marriage* **ONorw** *GuL* Krb

charge (2) **OIce** *Grg* Vís 88, 94 Rsþ 228, *Jó* Þjb 4

custody **OIce** *Js* Mah 6

decision-making **ONorw** *EidsL* 22.6

disposal **OIce** *Jó* Kge 2

guardianship **ONorw** *FrL* Var 45

management **OIce** *KRA* 4

responsibility **ONorw** *FrL* KrbB 22

forráðandi (ON) noun

administrator **OIce** *Grg* Feþ 156

See also: *lögráðandi*

forræðismaðr (ON) noun

authority **OIce** *KRA* 8

guardian **ONorw** *FrL* Kvb 1

man in charge **ONorw** *FrL* KrbA 10 KrbB 1

forsagnarvitni (ON) noun

testimony of a declaration **OIce** *Js* Kab 2

*witness to a demand for the surrender
of odal land* **OIce** *Jó* Þfb 4

See also: *vitni*

forsat (OSw) **forsæti** (OSw) noun

ambush **OSw** *DL* Eb, *HL* Kgb, *SdmL* Kgb,
Mb, *UL* Kgb, Mb, *VmL* Kgb, Mb, *ÖgL* Vm

trap **OSw** *DL* Eb

forseaman (OSw) noun

overseer **OSw** *HL* Blb

forsighia (OSw) verb

forfeit **OSw** *UL* Jb

forsjá (ON) noun

oversight **OIce** *KRA* 7

supervision **ONorw** *GuL* Krb

forskialamaþer (OSw) noun

Men who spoke for or dictated the oath to specific witnesses known as *fastar* (q.v.) in certain cases of killing settlements (HL) and morning gifts (SdmL). Only appearing in the plural.

oath-spellers **OSw** *HL* Mb, *SdmL* Gb

Refs: Schlyter s.v. *forskialamaþer*

forskæl (OSw) **forskiel** (OGu) noun

conditions **OGu** *GS* Ch. 3, **OSw** *YVgL* Gb

full use of one's senses **OGu** *GL* A 19

specifications **OSw** *YVgL* Äb

forstaða (ON) noun

hindrance **ONorw** *GuL* Arb, Mhb

forstjóri (ON) noun

overseer **OIce** *KRA* 6

forsværje (ODan) verb

forswear **ODan** *JyL* 2

forsögn (ON) noun

notice of redemption **ONorw** *GuL* Olb

forsölujörð (ON) noun

mortgaged estate **ONorw** *FrL* ArbB 22

mortgaged land **ONorw** *FrL* Jkb 2

forsölumáli (ON) noun

mortgage agreement **ONorw** *FrL* Jkb 2

forta (OSw) **forta** (ODan) noun

Communal open space where building was prohibited, located between the individual ground plots (OSw *tompt*) and the village road.

village passage **ODan** *SkL* 67

village space **ODan** *JyL* 1, 3

{*forta*} **OSw** *YVgL* Kvab, *ÄVgL* Kva

Refs: Lindkvist forthcoming; Schlyter s.v. *forta*; Tamm and Vogt, eds, 2016, 315–16

fortaka (OSw) **fore taka** (OSw) verb

forfeit **OSw** *UL* Mb

hinder **OSw** *UL* Blb, *VmL* Bb

forveði (ON) **forveða** (ON) **forveðja** (ON) adj.

forfeit **OIce** *Grg* Lbþ 192, *Js* Kab 17

unpledged **ONorw** *EidsL* 48.8

forvegr (ON) noun

footprints **ONorw** *GuL* Tjb

forverk (ON) noun

work of labourers **ONorw** *FrL* Leb 7

forverksmaðr (ON) noun

labourer **OIce** *Jó* Þfb 1, *Js* Þfb 1

forvé (ON) noun

Unhallowed ground; the area outside of consecrated ground (ON *vé*, see *vi*).

unhallowed ground **ONorw** *BorgL* 1.2

Refs: CV s.v. *forve*; Fritzner s.v. *forve*; Hertzberg s.v. *forvé*; Lawing 2013

forvinna (OSw) verb

convict **OSw** *DL* Rb, *SdmL* Till

forvist (OSw) noun

    aiding **OSw** *ÖgL* Db

    See also: *hema, husa, samvist, samværa, viþervist*

forværka (OSw) **firiværka** (OSw) **fore værka** (OSw) verb

    forfeit **OSw** *HL* Äb, *UL* Äb (table of contents only), Mb, *VmL* Äb, *YVgL* Add, *ÖgL* Kkb, Eb, Db

    See also: *fìrigæra, fìriköpa, foreföra, forestanda, forlöpa*

forvæþia (OSw) **forveðja** (ON) **forvæthje** (ODan) adj.

    forfeit **OSw** *YVgL* Jb, *ÄVgL* Jb

    forfeited **ONorw** *GuL* Kpb, **ODan** *SkL* 183

foryftalaust (ON) adv.

    without cause **ONorw** *GuL* Kvb

forældre (ODan) noun

    ancestors **ODan** *ESjL* 3, *SkL* 76

    parents **ODan** *JyL* 1, 2, *SkL* 72, *VSjL* 80

foster (OSw) **fóstr** (ON) noun

    care **OIce** *Jó* Kge 28

    foster-home **OIce** *Grg* Ómb 141

    foster-kin **OIce** *Grg* Vís 102

    fostering **OIce** *Grg* Klþ 4 Ómb 141, *Js* Lbb 9, **ONorw** *GuL* Løb

    maintenance **OIce** *Jó* Lbb 12

    support **OFar** *Seyð* 7, **OIce** *Jó* Þjb 1, *Js* Þjb 1

    youngstock **OSw** *UL* Kkb

    See also: *framförsla*

fosterland (OSw) noun

    fatherland **OSw** *YVgL* Äb, *ÄVgL* Äb

    home province **OSw** *YVgL* Drb

    See also: *land*

fosterløn (ODan) **fóstrlaun** (ON) noun

    fostering **ODan** *SkL* 58

    fostering payment **ODan** *JyL* 1

    payment for maintenance of a child **ONorw** *GuL* Løb, Arb

fostermoþer (OSw) noun

    wet-nurse **OSw** *UL* Äb, *VmL* Äb

fostra (OSw) **fóstra** (ON) **folstra** (OSw) noun

    foster-daughter **OIce** *Grg* Vís 90

    foster-mother **OIce** *Grg* Vís 90 Ómb 141

    home born female thrall **OSw** *YVgL* Gb

    home born slave woman **OSw** *ÄVgL* Äb, Gb

    home born thrall woman **OSw** *YVgL* Gb

    See also: *ambat, annöþogher, deghia, fostre, frælsgiva, hion, huskona*

fostre (OSw) **fóstri** (ON) noun

In ON, a foster-father or -son, while in OSw it is traditionally presumed to refer to a male slave (born and) raised within a household. The seemingly contradictory usages may reflect an earlier continuum of incorporation in the household, as the social complexity of the institution in ON is known from the sagas, and a *fostre* in OSw laws enjoyed a relatively high status with certain legal rights and responsibilities.

    foster-father **OIce** *Grg* Ómb 141, **ONorw** *FrL* ArbB 17

    foster-son **ONorw** *FrL* ArbB 17

    home born slave **OSw** *ÄVgL* Äb

    home-born thrall **OSw** *ÖgL* Db, Vm

    home-bred slave **OSw** *VmL* Mb

    See also: *ambat, annöþogher, fostra, frælsgivi, hemahion, hemakona, hion, ofræls, þiþborin, þræl*

    Refs: Brink 2012, 149–50; KLNM s.v.v. *fostre, fostring*

foter (OSw) **fótr** (ON) noun

    foot **OIce** *Js* Lbb 22, **ONorw** *GuL* Løb, Mhb, Leb, **OSw** *SdmL* Bb

fox (ON) noun

    counterfeit goods **OIce** *Jó* Kab 11

    false thing **ONorw** *GuL* Kpb

    See also: *far, flærþ, kaupfox*

foþerfæ (OSw) noun

    cattle taken for foddering **OSw** *YVgL* Utgb, *ÄVgL* Föb

    See also: *fulgumáli, fulgunaut, fæ*

fóðr (ON) noun

    fodder **ONorw** *GuL* Kpb

fólagjald (ON) **fólagjöld** (ON) noun

    theft payment **OIce** *Grg* Þsþ 49, 62

fóstbróðir (ON) noun

A man allied with another in a relationship of mutual rights and obligations. The relationship did not require kinship, and was established through joint upbringing (or through some ritual as suggested by sagas). In GuL, a *fóstbróðir* could receive compensation if the other was killed.

    foster-brother **ONorw** *GuL* Løb, Mhb

    See also: *barnfóstr, eiðbróðir, foster, fostre, fælagh*

    Refs: Fritzner s.v. *fóstbróðir*; KLNM s.v. *fostbrorskap*

framarve (ODan) noun

    descendant **ODan** *SkL* 34, 36

framburðr (ON) noun

    delivery **OIce** *Grg* Þsþ 32

framflytja (ON) verb

    give an oath **OIce** *KRA* 33

    swear **OIce** *Jó* Þjb 24

framförsla (ON) **framfærsla** (ON) noun

Obligatory support — potentially in the form of slavery — of paupers by relatives depending on degree of kinship and assets, or, if needed, by the community (the householders in the *hreppr* (q.v.), *fjórðungr* (see *fiarþunger*) or *land* (q.v.)).

  maintenance **OIce** *Grg* Þsþ 22, 39 Arþ 118, 122 Ómb 128, 135 Rsþ 229 Hrs 234, 235, *Jó* Lbb 12, *Js* Lbb 9

  See also: *arfsal, fiarþunger, flatføring, foster, gæfþræl, hreppr, land, omaghi, sytning*

  Refs: CV s.v. *framfærsla*; Gerhold 2002, 77–80, 173–88; KLNM, s.v. *framfærsla*

framförslubölkr (ON) **framfærslubálkr** (ON) noun

  section on the maintenance of dependents and indigent people **OIce** *Jó* Kge 23

framförslulauss (ON) **framfærslulauss** (ON) adj.

  having no means of maintenance **OIce** *Jó* Kge 31

  without maintenance **OIce** *Grg* Hrs 235

framförslumaðr (ON) **framfærslumaðr** (ON) noun

  person who maintains a dependant **OIce** *Jó* Kge 31

framsaga (ON) noun

  presentation **OIce** *Grg* Þsþ 30, 31

framsæld (OSw) noun

  presentation procedure **OSw** *UL* Mb

frangipter (OSw) adj.

  married **OSw** *DL* Mb

  See also: *gifter*

frankumin (OGu) adj.

  related **OGu** *GL* A 25

frelsingr (ON) noun

A freed slave or a free man as opposed to a slave.

  free man **OIce** *Grg* Klþ 9

  See also: *leysingi*

  Refs: Fritzner s.v. *frelsingi*; ONP s.v. *frelsingr*

frelsisgjöf (ON) noun

  manumission of a slave **ONorw** *GuL* Løb

  See also: *frelsisöl, frælsa*

frelsisöl (ON) noun

  freedom ale **ONorw** *FrL* ArbB 10 Rgb 35, *GuL* Kvb, Løb, Leb

  See also: *frelsisgjöf, leysingi*

fresta (OGu) verb

  torture **OGu** *GL* Add. 8 (B 55)

frétt (ON) noun

  inquiry **OIce** *Grg* Þsþ 27

friðhelga (ON) verb

  make one legally immune **OIce** *Jó* Mah 20

friðluborinn (ON) adj.

  illegitimate **OIce** *Jó* Kge 7-13, 23

friðludóttir (ON) noun

  concubine's daughter **OIce** *Jó* Kge 7-4, *Js* Ert 7

  illegitimate daughter **ONorw** *GuL* Arb

  See also: *slokefrithedotter*

friðlulífi (ON) noun

  concubinage **OIce** *KRA* 34

friðmenn (pl.) (ON) noun

Men who are at peace; friends, allies (of the king).

  men at peace **ONorw** *FrL* Leb 25, 27

  Refs: CV s.v. *friðmenn*; Fritzner s.v. *friðmaðr*; Hertzberg s.v. *friðmaðr*

frilla (OSw) **friðla** (ON) noun

A (free) woman living with a man without them being married. The church acted against these relationships (OSw YVgL). The woman could gain status of legal wife after 20 years (ONorw GuL). Children were not called *horbarn* ('children born in adultery') and there existed varying rights to mutual paternal inheritance.

  concubine **ONorw** *FrL* KrbB 11, *GuL* Arb, **OSw** *UL* Äb, *VmL* Äb, *YVgL* Kkb

  mistress (2) **ONorw** *FrL* KrbB 13

  See also: *amia, arinelja, aþalkona, husfrugha, kona, meinkona, slokefrithe*

  Refs: Dübeck 2012; Ebel 1993; KLNM s.v. *slegfred*; ONP s.v. *friðla*

frillubarn (OSw) **frillabarn** (OSw) **fræellobarn** (OSw) noun

  concubine's child **OSw** *SdmL* Kkb, Äb, *YVgL* Kkb, Äb, Add, *ÄVgL* Äb

  illegitimate child **OSw** *HL* Äb, *UL* Äb, *VmL* Äb

  See also: *aþalkonusun, slokifrilluson*

frillubroþir (OSw) noun

  illegitimate brother (a concubine's) **OSw** *DL* Gb

frillusun (OSw) **friðlusonr** (ON) noun

  concubine's son **OIce** *Js* Ert 6, 7, **OSw** *YVgL* Äb

  illegitimate **ONorw** *FrL* ArbA 8

  son by/with a concubine **OSw** *ÖgL* Db

  son of a mistress **ONorw** *FrL* ArbA 15

frillusystir (OSw) noun

  illegitimate sister **OSw** *DL* Gb

frithkøp (ODan) **friðkaup** (ON) noun

Payment to the king by an offender sentenced to outlawry for the return of his *friþer* (q.v.).

  offer of payment to get the peace back **ODan** *VSjL* 53

  paying for the peace **ODan** *ESjL* 3

  payment to get the peace back **ODan** *JyL* 2

purchase of peace **OIce** *Jó* Mah 4

See also: *friþer, köp*

Refs: Fritzner s.v. *friðkaup*; Olesen 2000, 19

frithløsen (ODan) noun

payment to keep the peace **ODan** *ESjL* 3

See also: *friþer, lösn*

frithløsmal (ODan) noun

case of loss of peace **ODan** *JyL* 3

See also: *friþer, mal (1)*

friþa (OSw) **frithe** (ODan) **frida** (OSw) verb

absolve **OSw** *UL* Kkb, Mb, Blb,
Rb, *VmL* Kkb, Mb, Rb

let in peace **ODan** *JyL* 2

protect **OSw** *SdmL* Till

See also: *friþer*

friþbalker (OSw) noun

book about peace **OSw** *YVgL* Frb

See also: *balker, friþer*

friþbot (OSw) noun

peace fine **OSw** *DL* Eb, *HL* Mb

See also: *bot, friþer*

friþbrut (OSw) **frithbrut** (ODan) **friðbrot** (ON) noun

breach of the peace **OIce** *Jó* Fml 14,
ONorw *GuL* Mhb, **OSw** *YVgL* Kkb

breaking the peace **ODan** *SkL* 91, **OSw** *UL* Add. 2

broken peace **OSw** *ÄVgL* Kkb

peace crime **OSw** *SdmL* Kgb, Mb

peace fine **OSw** *HL* Mb

violation **OSw** *HL* Kkb

violation of the sanctity **OSw** *HL* Kkb

See also: *brut, friþer*

friþer (OSw) **frith** (ODan) **friþr** (OGu) **friðr** (ON) noun

Legal protection of people and property; also occasionally protection of wild plants (OSw SdmL) and animals (OSw HL). Referring both to the state and to the time of protection. Breach of *friþer* was considered more serious the closer to home and the private sphere that it was done (OSw UL), and this concept also appears under other terms, such as *hemsokn* (OSw HL). Including, but not restricted to, the protection by the king, in OSw known as *eþsöre*, and, like this, occasionally translated as 'king's peace'. Losing this protection was a punishment mainly for killings (OSw *friþlös*), and when referring to the return of *friþer*, occasionally translated as 'pardon' or 'rule of law'. Numerous types of *friþer* appear in the laws specifying the times, places, events or persons

enjoying it. During such *friþer*, restrictions concerning for example the right to prosecute could apply (OSw HL, SdmL, UL). Breach of such a specific *friþer* was sometimes considered an unatonable crime (OSw *urbotamal*) but could at other times result in high fines to the king, bishop or the community depending on the violation. When referring to matters of the church, occasionally translated as 'sanctity' or 'sanctuary'. Also of exemption from certain obligations, such as taxes, and occasionally translated as 'freedom'. There is considerable overlap between usages and translations.

asylum **OSw** *HL* Kkb

freedom **OGu** *GS* Ch. 2, **OIce** *Jó* Mah 14,
OSw *DL* Eb, *UL* Kgb, Äb, *VmL* Kgb, Äb

immunity **OSw** *UL* Äb, Rb, *VmL* Äb, Rb

inviolability **OSw** *HL* Kgb

King's Peace **OSw** *DL* Eb, *UL* Kgb, Mb, *VmL* Kgb

pardon **OSw** *HL* Äb

peace **ODan** *ESjL* 2, 3, *JyL* Fort, 2, 3, *SkKL* 3, *SkL* 90, 118, 121, *VSjL* 50, 53, 54, 87, **OGu** *GL* A 1, 13, *GS* Ch. 2, **OIce** *Jó* Mah 1 Þjb 24, *Js* Þfb 4 Mah 4, *KRA* 8, 17, **ONorw** *BorgL* 3.2 passim, *FrL* Intr 1, 5 KrbA 5, 10 KrbB 24 Mhb 4 passim, *GuL* Krb, Reb, Leb, **OSw** *HL* Kgb, Äb, Mb, Blb, *SdmL* Kkb, Kgb, Gb, Äb, Bb, Mb, Tjdb, Rb, Till, *SmL*, *UL* För, Kkb, Kgb, Rb, *VmL* För, Kgb, Rb, *YVgL* Kkb, Frb, Urb, Drb, Äb, Gb, Rlb, Utgb, Add, *ÄVgL* Kkb, Md, Smb, Slb, Urb, Äb, Gb, Rlb, *ÖgL* Kkb, Eb, Db, Vm

peace (or rule of law) **OSw** *DL* Eb

peace for the outlawed **OSw** *HL* Kgb

period of peace and protection **OSw**
DL Mb, *UL* Kkb, Mb, *VmL* Mb

period of peace and security **OGu** *GL* A 8–10, 13

period of sanctity **OSw** *HL* Rb

protection **OSw** *SdmL* Bb, Till, *UL* Mb, *VmL* Mb

right to inviolability **OSw** *HL* Äb

rights **OSw** *UL* Kgb (ch. 6 title),
VmL Kgb (ch. 3 rubric)

rule of law **OSw** *UL* Kgb, Äb, *VmL* Äb, Mb

sanctity **OGu** *GL* A 9–12, **OSw** *HL* Kkb, Rb, *UL* Kkb

sanctuary **OSw** *HL* Mb, *UL* Kkb, Mb

time of peace **OSw** *HL* Mb

truce **OIce** *Jó* MagBref

Expressions:

flya friþ, flyæ friþ, friþ flya (OSw)

be outlawed **OSw** *HL* Kgb

be forced to flee from the King's Peace **OSw** *UL* Kgb *VmL* Kgb

guþs ok the hælgha kirkiu friþer (OSw)

God's and the Holy Church's sanctity **OSw** *HL*Kkb

See also: *eþsöre, flya, friþbrut, griþ, hemfriþer, hælgh, manhælghi, sielfsvald, trygth, varfriþer, þingsfriþer*

Refs: Cleasby and Vigfusson s.v. *friðr*; Fritzner s.v. *friðr*; Hertzberg s.v. *friðr*; ONP s.v. *friðr*; Schlyter s.v. *friþer*

friþgærþi (OSw) noun

protected field **OSw** *YVgL* Föb, *ÄVgL* Fös

See also: *friþer*

friþhelagher (OSw) **friðheilagr** (ON) adj.

declared in peace **OSw** *YVgL* Add

inviolate **ONorw** *FrL* Intr 6 Mhb 1, 5 Var 45

protected by law **OIce** *Js* Mah 1, 11 Kab 4, *KRA* 6, **ONorw** *GuL* Krb, Kpb, Arb, Mhb

retaining legal immunity **OIce** *Jó* Mah 1, 2 Kge 19 Llb 34 Kab 3

See also: *friþer*

friþkallaþer (OSw) adj.

protected **OSw** *VmL* Mb

See also: *friþer, værnkallaþer*

friþlös (OSw) **frithløs** (ODan) **friþlaus** (OGu) **friðlauss** (ON) adj.

Someone being declared *friþlös* usually implied that the person concerned was outlawed because of the crime that he had committed (usually a killing) and that the injured party or his agents could kill him, without penalty. Exceptionally in KRA 20, it is used to describe a man who has committed incest, considered an *ódáðaverk* (q.v.), and his state of being 'without peace' persists until the parties undergo penance issued by the bishop. In GL the killer was only outlawed if he refused to offer appropriate compensation within three years. If the offer was made three times but refused, the killer escaped the penalty. If the person were outlawed, his family was forbidden from taking revenge for his death and hence the law seemed to be intended to put a halt to blood feuds. According to ÄVgL, both an outlaw and an excommunicate could be driven out of the church if the parishioners wished, but this provision was dropped in YVgL, presumably because it was not considered appropriate that lay people should extract church punishments. The outlaw was driven out of the community to the uncultivated woodland and this punishment could even be extracted for failure to pay compensation for wounding someone. In the laws of Götaland, it is clear that a woman may, under certain circumstances be declared outlawed, but in SdmL it is specifically stated that women and minors might not be outlawed. The concept of being 'outside the King's Peace' was one that in most of the laws of Svealand was covered chiefly by the adjective *biltugher* (q.v.) and the concept of having to *flya friþ*, that is 'be forced to flee the King's Peace'; the word *friþlös* does not figure in UL, HL, DL or VmL.

having lost one's peace **ODan** *ESjL* 2, 3, *SkL* 90

outlawed **OGu** *GL* A 13, **ONorw** *GuL* Krb, **OSw** *YVgL* Föb, Add, *ÄVgL* Kkb, *ÖgL* Db

without peace **ODan** *JyL* 2, 3, *VSjL* 87, **OIce** *KRA* 20, **OSw** *SdmL* Kgb, Mb, *YVgL* Drb, Gb, Rlb, Add, *ÄVgL* Md, Slb, *ÖgL* Eb

See also: *banda, biltugher, friþer, friþlösa, griþ*

Refs: Ekholst 2009; KLNM, s.v. *fredløshed*; Lexikon des Mittelalters, s.v.v. *acht, friedlosigkeit*; Peel 2015, 115 note 13/58–65; Riisøy 2014; Schlyter 1877, s.v. *friþlös*; SL GL 257–58 note 19 to chapter 13; SL SdmL, 59 note 33; SL YVgL, 290 note 29, 301 note 22; SL ÄVgL, 22 note 72, 36–37 notes 28, 31, 66 note 16; SL ÖgL, 46–47

friþlösa (OSw) **frithløse** (ODan) noun

lose one's peace **ODan** *SkL* 145

being outside the peace **OSw** *ÖgL* Eb, Db

being without peace **OSw** *YVgL* Add

See also: *friþer*

friþsökia (OSw) verb

seek a person's peace **OSw** *ÖgL* Db, Vm

See also: *friþer, sökia*

friþvakn (OSw) noun

peace weapon **OSw** *HL* Rb

See also: *friþer, vapn*

friþviter (OSw) **friþ vetr** (OGu) adj.

Literally, 'known to be free'. It is used a number of times, in various law texts, but only in seemingly tautological parallelisms such as *frælsir mæn ok friþvitir* (pl.) 'free and freeborn men', where it is intended to strengthen the requirement for witnesses, etc., to be free men or, in the case of GL, to distinguish female victims who were free (*frels ok friþvet*) from those who were not. This had the possible implication that they were to be free born and not simply freed slaves, about whose free status there could be some dispute. Although the word *frælse* (q.v.) later came to refer collectively to those who were free from taxes in one way or another, that is not the implication here: it is merely a distinction between those in slavery and those not.

freeborn **OGu** *GL* A 23, **OSw** *UL* Rb, *VmL* Rb

known to be free **OSw** *SdmL* Rb

See also: *árborinn, frelsingr, friþer, friþætta, fræls, frælsboren, fullkyniaþer, ætborin*

Refs: KLNM, s.v. *frälse*; Peel 2015,
150−51 note 23/32; Schlyter 1877, s.v.
friþviter; SL GL, 273 note 10

friþætta (OSw) **fiuþætigher** (OSw) **friþætigher** (OSw)
adj.

   freeborn **OSw** *VmL* Kkb

   See also: *friþer*, *friþviter*

fríðr (ON) adj.

   in livestock **OIce** *Grg* Þsþ 71 Arþ 118

frjádagr (ON) noun

   Friday **ONorw** *GuL* Krb

frjánátt (ON) noun

   night before Friday **ONorw** *GuL* Krb

Frostuþing (ON) noun

   Frostaþing **ONorw** *FrL* Var 46 Rgb 31

   See also: *þing*

Frostuþingsbók (ON) noun

   Frostathing book **ONorw** *FrL* Intr 2, 25

frostuþingslög (ON) noun

   Frostathing law **ONorw** *FrL* Intr 25

frue (ODan) noun

   wife **ODan** *VSjL* 1−3, 6, 7, 9

   woman **ODan** *VSjL* 20, 62, 69

frumgagn (ON) **frumgögn** (ON) noun

   *formal means of proof in an original
suit* **OIce** *Grg* Þsþ 35 Lbþ 202

frumhlaup (ON) noun

   assault **OIce** *Grg* Vís 86, 87

   See also: *hlaup*

frumhlaupsmaðr (ON) noun

   assailant **OIce** *Grg* Vís 86

frumkviðr (ON) noun

   *panel (verdict) for an original
suit* **OIce** *Grg* Þsþ 26, 35

frumsök (ON) noun

   original suit **OIce** *Grg* Þsþ 22 Vís 89 Feþ 156

frumváttr (ON) noun

A witness who was present at an event and can give
testimony to it. Usually refers to a witness who is ill
or otherwise unable to travel and give testimony when
needed. In such a case the testimony of an indisposed
frumváttr could be taken by two other men who then
presented the original testimony at court.

   original witness **OIce** *Grg* Misc 252,
Js Kab 2, **ONorw** *GuL* Løb, Olb

   See also: *vatter*

Refs: CV s.v. *frumváttr*; Fritzner s.v.
frumváttr; Hertzberg s.v. *frumváttr*

fryghtheorth (ODan) noun

   threat **ODan** *JyL* 3

frýja (ON) verb

   challenge **OIce** *Js* Þfb 5

   complain **OIce** *Jó* Þfb 6

   question **ONorw** *FrL* Var 46

   See also: *ryþia*

fræls (OSw) **fræls** (ODan) **frels** (OGu) **frjáls** (ON)
frelse (OSw) adj.

Etymologically a compound of words meaning 'free'
and 'neck', supposedly referring to the absence of
the neck ring of slaves, or potentially to the neck,
metonymically for 'life', and its inviolability (Neckel
1916). Used of many aspects of freedom, from the
lack of physical restraints to the exemption from taxes,
many of which are legally significant, albeit perhaps
none more so than that applied to people, non-slaves,
enjoying some independence as manifested in their
legal status, including, but not exclusive to, those born
free.

   available **OIce** *Jó* Sg 3

   exempt **OSw** *HL* Kgb, *SdmL* Gb, Bb

   free **ODan** *ESjL* 2, 3, *JyL* 1, 3, *SkL* 76, 105, 118,
122−25, 128, 130, 132, *VSjL* 28, 42, 43, 50, 56, 59,
61, 80, 86, **OGu** *GL* A 2, 6, 19, 23, **OIce** *Grg* Þsþ
20 Vís 111 Feþ 155, 156 Misc 237, 248, *Jó* Mah 5
Llb 29 Kab 10, 25, *Js* Mah 14, 23 Lbb 15, 25 Kab 8,
19, *KRA* 9, 10, **ONorw** *BorgL* 14.4, *EidsL* 3.2 12.4,
FrL KrbA 1, 28 Mhb 5, 7 Var 15 LlbB 10, *GuL* Løb,
Tjb, Kpb, Llb, Tfb, Leb, **OSw** *DL* Kkb, *HL* Kkb,
SdmL Äb, Bb, Kmb, Mb, Tjdb, Rb, *UL* Äb, Mb,
Kmb, Rb, *VmL* Kkb, Äb, Mb, Kmb, Rb, *YVgL* Drb,
Gb, Rlb, Tb, Add, *ÄVgL* Kkb, Rlb, *ÖgL* Db, Vm

   freeborn **ONorw** *FrL* KrbA 2

   tax free **OSw** *SdmL* Kkb, *UL* Kkb, Kgb, *VmL* Kkb

   unfettered **ODan** *VSjL* 52

   unhindered **OGu** *GS* Ch. 2

Expressions:

frjáls ok fulltíða (ON)

   free and of age **OIce** *JKs* Kab 8

fræls fød (ODan)

   born free **ODan** *ESjL* 3

   See also: *frelsingr*, *friþviter*

Refs: CV s.v. *frjáls*; Fritzner s.v. *frjáls*;
Hellquist s.v. *frälsa*; Neckel 1916, 405

frælsa (OSw) **frælse** (ODan) **frelsa** (ON) verb

   free **ODan** *JyL* 3, **OSw** *SdmL* Till

   give freedom **ONorw** *GuL* Løb

   See also: *frelsisgjöf*

frælsboren (ODan) **frjálsborinn** (ON) adj.

born free **ODan** *SkL* 126

freeborn **ODan** *SkL* 129, **OIce** *Grg*
Vís 94, 96 Arþ 118, 119 Feþ 144

See also: *árborinn, friþer*

frælsgiva (OSw) noun

A woman released from slavery.

freedwoman **OSw** *YVgL* Gb, Add

See also: *ambat, annöþogher, deghia, fostra,
fræls, frælsgivi, gæfþræl, leysingi, þræl*

frælsgivi (OSw) **frælsgive** (ODan) **frjálsgjafi** (ON)
noun

For details concerning usage, see *leysingi*.

freed slave **ONorw** *BorgL* 9.6 12.7

freedman **ODan** *SkL* 127, **ONorw** *FrL*
ArbB 13, **OSw** *YVgL* Vs, Frb, Drb, Äb, Gb,
Rlb, *ÄVgL* Md, Smb, Vs, Slb, Gb, Rlb

freedom-giver **OIce** *Grg* Vís 96 Arþ
119, 127 Ómb 137 Rsþ 229

part-freed slave **ONorw** *EidsL* 50.4

Expressions:

frælsgiva bot (OSw)

compensation for a freed man **OSw** *YVgL* Frb

See also: *fræls, leysingi, æt, þræl*

frælsi (OSw) **frælse** (ODan) **frelsi** (OGu) **frelsi** (ON)
noun

freedom **ODan** *ESjL* 1, 3, *JyL* 1, 2, *SkL* 62, 126,
128, 130, 131, 135, *VSjL* 69, 86, 87, **OGu** *GL* A 16,
OIce *Grg* Vís 112 Arþ 118 Ómb 128, 137 Feþ 156
Rsþ 229, *Jó* MagBref, **ONorw** *FrL* Mhb 55 ArbA 8,
GuL Krb, Løb, Arb, Leb, **OSw** *SdmL* Till, *ÖgL* Kkb

liberty **ODan** *JyL* Fort

frælsmansbot (OSw) noun

fine of a free man **OSw** *VmL* Kkb

free man's compensation **OSw** *UL* Rb, *VmL* Mb, Rb

See also: *bot, böta, þiængsgæld*

frælst (OSw) adv.

freely **OSw** *UL* Rb

frændatjón (ON) noun

loss of kinsmen **ONorw** *FrL* Intr 1

frændbót (ON) **frændbætr** (ON) noun

Compensation paid by the kinsmen of a killer to
the equivalent kinsmen of the victim. This type of
compensation was abolished in Norway in MLL
(IV.12; X.2) in Iceland in Js (Mah 29).

compensation **OIce** *Jó* Mah 1

kin-compensation **OIce** *Js* Mah 29,
ONorw *FrL* Sab 11, 18

wergild to the kinsmen **ONorw** *GuL* Mhb

See also: *baugatal, bauggildi, nefgildi*

Refs: CV s.v. *frændbætr*; Fritzner; Hertzberg;
Jørgensen 2014; KLNM s.v. *böter*; Riisøy 2009, 65

frænderfð (ON) noun

inheritance among kinsmen **ONorw** *GuL* Arb

frændeth (ODan) noun

men of one's kin **ODan** *JyL* 2

oath of kinsmen **ODan** *JyL* 2

frændi (OSw) **frænde** (ODan) **frænder** (ODan) **frendi**
(OGu) **frændi** (ON) noun

kin **ODan** *JyL* 1, 2, *SkL* 51, 92, 127, 128, *VSjL* 15,
23, 32, 50, 86, **OSw** *DL* Mb, Gb, *SmL*, *UL* Kkb,
Äb, Mb, Jb, Rb, Add. 6, *VmL* Kkb, Äb, Mb, Jb, Rb

kinfolk **OSw** *YVgL* Add

kinsfolk **ONorw** *GuL* Krb, Kvb, Løb, Arb, Mhb, Olb

kinsman **ODan** *ESjL* 1–3, *JyL* 1–3, *SkKL* 6,
SkL passim, *VSjL* 1, 13, 19, 20, 67, **OGu** *GL*
A 20a, 21, 24, 24d, 28, **OIce** *Grg* passim, **OSw**
UL Äb, *YVgL* Äb, Rlb, Jb, *ÄVgL* Äb, *ÖgL* Db

relative **ONorw** *EidsL* 22.7, **OSw** *DL* Gb,
Tjdb, *HL* Äb, Mb, Jb, Rb, *SdmL* Kkb,
Gb, Äb, Jb, Mb, *SmL*, *YVgL* Äb

See also: *frændsimi, kné, kyn, niþi, skyldarman*

frændkona (OSw) **frændkone** (ODan) **frændkona**
(ON) **frænka** (OSw) **frænkona** (OSw) noun

kinswoman **ODan** *ESjL* 1, 3, *SkKL* 6, 11, *SkL*
131, **OIce** *Jó* Sg 3 Mah 2 Kge 1, *Js* Mah 6, *KRA*
20, **ONorw** *BorgL* 15.3, *EidsL* 30.1, *FrL* Var
45, *GuL* Krb, Olb, **OSw** *YVgL* Kkb, *ÖgL* Kkb

related woman **ONorw** *FrL* KrbB 1

frændlauss (ON) adj.

without kin **OIce** *Grg* Vís 97 Misc 249

frændleif (ON) **frændleifar** (pl.) (ON) noun

kinsman's widow **ONorw** *BorgL* 15.3, *EidsL* 30.1

widow of a kinsman **ONorw** *GuL* Krb

widow of a relative **ONorw** *EidsL* 30.3

frændmø (ODan) noun

maiden **ODan** *ESjL* 1

frændsemistala (ON) noun

enumeration of kinship **OIce** *Grg*
Þsþ 25 Ómb 130, 136 Feþ 147

frændsimi (OSw) **frændsæme** (ODan) **frændsemi**
(ON) **frenseme** (OSw) **fræncimi** (OSw) **frændsim**
(OSw) **frændsæmi** (OSw) **frænsim** (OSw)
frænzæme (OSw) noun

consanguinity **OSw** *UL* Kkb, Äb, *VmL* Kkb, Äb

kin **ODan** *ESjL* 1

kinship **ODan** *ESjL* 3, **OIce** *Grg* Klþ 18 Þsþ
25, 35 Vís 89, 97 Bat 113 Arþ 118 [Add. 140]
Ómb 130, 136 Feþ 144, 147 passim, *Jó* Mah
3, 7 Kge 17 Kab 2, *Js* Ert 6, **ONorw** *BorgL*
15.8, *EidsL* 30.2, *FrL* KrbB 1 Var 9, *GuL* Krb,
Mhb, Olb, **OSw** *YVgL* Kkb, Gb, *ÄVgL* Gb

kinsman **ODan** *ESjL* 1

relatives **OSw** *HL* Mb

See also: *frændi, guþsivi, kné, mægð*

frændsimisspiæl (OSw) **frændsemisspell** (ON) noun

crime in kinship **OSw** *YVgL* Kkb

incest **OIce** *Grg* Feþ 156, *Jó* Kge 7-6,
KRA 34, **ONorw** *EidsL* 52, **OSw** *DL*
Kkb, *HL* Kkb, *SdmL* Kkb, Äb

violation of kinship rules (incest) **OSw** *HL* Kkb

See also: *kynsæmesbrut*

frændstævne (ODan) noun

meeting for the kinsmen **ODan** *ESjL* 3

fræst (OSw) **frest** (OGu) **frest** (OSw) noun

grace **OGu** *GL* A 26, 32, Add. 7, 9 (B 49, 81)

lawful time **OGu** *GL* A 39

legal time **OGu** *GL* A 30

period **OGu** *GL* A 13, 32, *GS* Ch. 4,
OSw *UL* Mb, *VmL* Mb, Jb

probation **OSw** *DL* Bb

respite **OGu** *GL* A 13, *GS* Ch. 4

specified time **OGu** *GS* Ch. 4, **OSw** *VmL* Kkb

fræstmark (OSw) **frestmark** (OSw) noun

period of grace **OSw** *UL* Kmb, *VmL* Kmb

time limit for repurchase **OSw** *SdmL* Kmb

fræstning (OSw) noun

period **OSw** *YVgL* Äb

probation **OSw** *HL* Kmb

frölön (OSw) noun

payment for seed **OSw** *YVgL* Kkb

frøsgjald (ODan) noun

worth of one's seed **ODan** *JyL* 2

fuðflogi (ON) noun

runaway from his betrothed woman **ONorw** *GuL* Kvb

fuglaren (OSw) **fughlæ ren** (OSw) noun

field margin **OSw** *UL* Blb

fuglveiðr (ON) noun

fowling rights **OIce** *Grg* Lbþ 220, *Jó* Llb 6, *Js* Lbb 13

fuglverð (ON) noun

value of a bird **OIce** *Jó* Llb 57

ful (OSw) **ful** (OGu) **fúll** (ON) adj.

condemned **OGu** *GL* A 2

convicted **OSw** *ÄVgL* Md

foul **ONorw** *EidsL* 43.3

found guilty (in trial by ordeal) **ONorw** *GuL* Krb

guilty **OGu** *GL* A 2

unclean **ONorw** *BorgL* 5.15

fulaldre (ODan) adj.

of full age **ODan** *ESjL* 1, 3, *VSjL* 1, 13, 53, 61, 67

fully of age **ODan** *ESjL* 2

fulder (OSw) **ful** (ODan) adj.

The literal meaning 'full', as opposed to only a part,
might be illustrated by *fulder luter* 'full lot' and *full
manbot* 'full man's compensation'. A *fulder þiuver*
'full thief', committing *fulder þiufnaþer* 'full theft',
had stolen valued at or above a certain amount and
was punished more severely. A *fullr bóndi* (ONorw
BorgL 12.2) is interpreted as a farmer with workers
(as opposed to an *einvirki*), possibly an earlier form
of *bóndi*. A *fulder byr* 'full village' was a village of
a specified size that could be dated back to pagan
times, but it is not clear what this status entailed
(OSw *YVgL* Jb; *ÄVgL* Jb). Other usages are even
less clear as to what constituted the fullness; certain
injuries entitled a wounded person to higher fines, if
the injury was *fulder* as in *full sar* 'full wound' (OSw
DL Mb; *SdmL* Kkb; *ÖgL* Eb, Vm). When applied
to certain officeholders, functions or rights, *fulder*
can be understood as 'authorized' or 'legal' as in *fult
umbuþ* 'authorized agent' (OSw *SdmL* Kgb), *fulder
vitnismaþer* 'full witness' (OSw *ÄVgL/YVgL* Rlb),
full iorthæværn 'full right to defend land' (ODan *ESjL*
3:3).

authorized **OSw** *SdmL* Kgb

binding **OSw** *YVgL* Kvab

convicted **OSw** *HL* Äb

full **ODan** *ESjL* 1–3, *JyL* 1–3, *SkL* 5, 23, 64, 73,
87, 93, 103, 116, 129, 130, *VSjL* passim, **OSw**
DL Kkb, Mb, Bb, Tjdb, *HL* Kkb, Kgb, Mb, Blb,
SdmL Conf, Kkb, Kgb, Gb, Jb, Bb, Kmb, Mb,
Tjdb, Rb, Till, *YVgL* Urb, Drb, Gb, Rlb, Tb, Föb,
Add, *ÄVgL* Rlb, Tb, Fös, *ÖgL* Kkb, Eb, Vm

fully competent **OSw** *YVgL* Rlb

real **OSw** *ÄVgL* Tb

serious **OSw** *DL* Eb

valid **ODan** *ESjL* 2

Expressions:

**faster ok fullder, fastr oc fulldr,
fastær ok fuldær** (OSw)

in total and for good **OSw** *UL* Kkb *VmL* Kkb

valid **OSw** *UL* Kkb, Jb, Kmb, Rb
VmL Kkb, Jb, Kmb, Rb

fulder bot, fulder bruta, full bot, fullar böter (OSw)

full compensation **OSw** *UL* Mb, Rb *VmL* Mb, Rb

full fines **OSw** *VmL* Mb

fulder þiufnaþer (OSw)

full theft **OSw** *UL* Mb *VmL* Mb

See also: *bot, böta, gælda (1), sander, vaþabot, þiufnaþer*

Refs: Miller 1990, 333 n. 9

fulga (ON) **fúlga** (ON) noun

charge for keep **OIce** *Grg* Þsþ 77, 79 Arþ 122 Ómb 128, 136 Feþ 156 Fjl 225 Hrs 234, *Jó* Llb 50, *Js* Kab 12, *KRA* 2

foddering by contract **ONorw** *GuL* Kpb

maintenance **OIce** *Jó* Kge 24

support **OIce** *Jó* Kge 13

fulgufé (ON) **fúlgufé** (ON) noun

Cattle foddered by contract.

animals **OIce** *Jó* Llb 11

kept stock **OIce** *Grg* Fjl 226, *Jó* Kab 17

Refs: Hertzberg s.v. *fulgufé, fulgubúfé*; JB tr. p. 183

fulgumáli (ON) **fúlgumáli** (ON) noun

agreement on keep **OIce** *Grg* Fjl 226, *Jó* Kab 17, *Js* Kab 12

charge for keep **OIce** *Grg* Fjl 224

contract about foddering **ONorw** *GuL* Kpb

See also: *foþerfæ, fulgunaut*

fulgunaut (ON) **fúlgunaut** (ON) noun

cattle foddered by contract **ONorw** *GuL* Kpb

cattle taken to keep **OIce** *Jó* Kab 17, *Js* Kab 12

See also: *foþerfæ, fulgumáli*

fulgærþabondi (OSw) noun

fully taxable man **OSw** *HL* Kkb

fulkome (ODan) verb

pursue **ODan** *JyL* 2

fulla (OSw) **fylle** (ODan) verb

compensate **ODan** *ESjL* 1, *VSjL* 56, **OSw** *DL* Gb

confirm **OSw** *ÄVgL* Gb

pursue **ODan** *SkL* 121

substantiate **OSw** *VmL* Mb

See also: *fylla*

fullbyr (OSw) noun

A village of a specified size that could be dated back to pagan times, but it is not clear what this status entailed (OSw *YVgL* Jb; *ÄVgL* Jb).

full village **OSw** *YVgL* Jb, *ÄVgL* Jb

See also: *byr, fulder*

fulljuse (ODan) verb

fully make public **ODan** *ESjL* 1

See also: *lysa*

fullkyniaþer (OSw) **fullkyniaþær** (OSw) adj.

freeborn **OSw** *VmL* Kmb

fullliða (ON) adj.

fully manned **OIce** *Js* Lbb 15

having men enough **ONorw** *GuL* Llb, Arb

fullrétti (ON) noun

An action, usually of a defamatory nature, which entitled the offended party to receive full personal compensation. Also refers to the compensation paid for such actions. The amount constituting full compensation varied depending on time and region. A fine of 48 ounces is listed in Grg Misc 237, whereas in GuL and FrL compensation amounts differed according to the social class of the aggrieved party. Types of offenses requiring the payment of full compensation also varied but were generally associated with breaches of honour, such as verbal insults (ON *fullréttisorð*; Grg Misc 237) and sexual offenses, such as intercourse with another man's bride prior to the wedding (FrL KrbB 13). Minor breaches may instead require payment of half compensation (ON *halfrétti*).

damages **OIce** *Jó* Mah 3

full compensation **OIce** *Jó* Mah 14, 20 Llb 36 Kab 3 Þjb 6 Fml 25, **ONorw** *FrL* KrbB 13 Mhb 17 Var 15 ArbB 10 Rgb 34 Kvb 1, *GuL* Mhb

full personal compensation **OIce** *Grg* Þsþ 80 Vís 111 Misc 237, *Jó* Kge 1, *Js* Mah 22, 23

personal atonement **OFar** *Seyð* 1, 5

See also: *halfrétti, manbot, réttarfar*

Refs: CV; Fritzner; Hertzberg; KLNM s.v. *fullrétti, straff, ærekrænkelse*

fullréttisorð (ON) noun

Verbal insults; defamation which required the offender to pay full personal compensation (ON *fullrétti*) to the injured party. In Iceland this type of insult carried a penalty of lesser outlawry in addition to a fine (cf. Grg Misc 237).

defamatory word **ONorw** *GuL* Mhb

insulting words for which one should be compensated **OIce** *Jó* Mah 24

words requiring full personal compensation **OIce** *Grg* Misc 237, **ONorw** *FrL* Rgb 35

See also: *bakmæli, fjölmæli, háðung, mansöngr, níð, oqvæþinsorþ, skáldskaparmál, ýki*

Refs: CV s.v. *fullréttisorð*; Fritzner s.v.
fullréttisorð; Hertzberg s.v. *fullréttisorð*;
KLNM s.v. *fullrétti, ærekrænkelse*

fullréttisskaði (ON) noun

*damage for which full compensation
is to be paid* OIce *Jó* Fml 25

fullréttisverk (ON) noun

act requiring full compensation OIce *Jó*
Mah 19, *Js* Mah 11, ONorw *FrL* Intr 6

See also: *fullrétti*

fullskæl (OSw) noun

legal formalities OSw *UL* Kkb, Äb,
Jb, *VmL* Kkb, Äb, Mb, Jb

See also: *fastar (pl.), skæl*

fullsæri (OSw) **full sar** (OSw) **fulsari** (OSw) **fulsæri**
(OSw) **fulzære** (OSw) noun

Literally, 'full wound'. This concept seems to have
applied only in the Swedish laws and designated a
wound subject to maximum compensation. It was also
called a *fult sar*. The fines for such wounds varied
greatly, however, from 3 *örar* to 40 *marker*, depending
on circumstances, with the most serious cases being
treated as crimes against the King's Peace (ÖgL and
YVgL). The highest fines were applied if the wound
were inflicted during a period or in a place of peace
and security, *friþer* (HL). In this latter case the fine was
payable to the king (or the bishop if the wound were
inflicted on a church festival). In SdmL and ÄVgL the
term is applied to injuries where medical treatment
was required. In HL, UL and VmL, although there is
no formal definition of the concept (in comparison to
SdmL and ÄVgL) one is able to deduce the meaning
from the context and it was up to the doctor to confirm
the status of the wound. The fine for such a wound was
40 *marker* in UL. In VmL the fine is only 20 *marker*.
DL uses the equivalent expression *fulder sar*.

full wound OSw *HL* Mb, *SdmL* Mb, *YVgL*
Add, *ÄVgL* Smb, *ÖgL* Kkb, Eb

wound subject to full compensation
OSw *UL* Mb, *VmL* Kkb, Mb

See also: *bot, fulder, sar*

Refs: KLNM, s.v. *legemskrænkelse*;
Schlyter 1877, s.v. *fullsæri*; SL UL, 126
note 115; SL VmL, 96 note 97

fullt (OSw) **fult** (OSw) adv.

in full (e.g. of compensation) OSw *UL* Kkb, Kgb,
Äb, Jb, Blb, Rb, *VmL* Kkb, Äb, Mb, Jb, Bb

fullveðja (ON) adj.

with full security ONorw *FrL* ArbB 5

fullvirði (ON) noun

full value OIce *Js* Lbb 4

fulnaþer (OSw) **fulneth** (ODan) **fulldnaþ** (OSw)
fulnæþ (OSw) noun

equivalent to the rest ODan *VSjL* 87

obligation OSw *SmL*

payment ODan *ESjL* 3, OSw *UL*
Kkb, Kgb, *VmL* Kkb

fultiþa (OSw) **fulltíða** (ON) **fulltíði** (ON) adj.

adult OIce *Jó* Mah 29 Llb 29, *Js* Mah
11, 27 Lbb 1, 25 Kab 8, *KRA* 1, 10

of age OIce *Grg* Klþ 1 Vís 94, 95 Bat 113 Misc
244, *Jó* Mah 9 Kge 32 Lbb 1 Kab 8, 10 Þjb 19, *Js*
Kvg 4 Ert 16 Þjb 9, *KRA* 10, ONorw *FrL* KrbA 41

of full age ONorw *GuL* Løb, Arb, Tjb, Leb

full-grown ONorw *FrL* Mhb 5,
38 ArbB 1, OSw *HL* Mb

fulvaksen (ODan) adj.

adult ODan *ESjL* 3, *JyL* 1

fully grown ODan *JyL* 1, 2

grown-up ODan *SkL* 50

fygla (ON) verb

hunt birds ONorw *GuL* Krb

fylghessak (ODan) noun

case of being in company ODan *SkL* 118

See also: *fylghi*

fylghi (OSw) **fylghe** (ODan) noun

Those in company with perpetrators of violent crimes,
whether participating or not, were punished. Appears
in phrases such as *i færth ok fylghe* (ODan) 'in
accompanying and following', *i flok ok i fylghi* and
i fylghi eller faranöti (OSw) 'in a group and a gang'.

being together ODan *ESjL* 3

companions ODan *VSjL* 57

escort OSw *HL* Kkb

following ODan *ESjL* 2, 3, *VSjL* 53, 56, 57, 59, 61,
64, OSw *DL* Eb, *HL* Rb, *SdmL* Kkb, Kgb, Gb, Bb

gang ODan *SkL* 86, 87

See also: *atvistarmaþer, farunöti, flokker, haldbani,
hærværk, laghsman, umstaþumæn (pl.)*

Refs: Tamm and Vogt, eds, 2016, 300

fylghia (OSw) **fylgi** (OGu) noun

This was one of a number of words used to designate
the marriage portion given by the parents to their
son or daughter on marriage. It occurs only in this
unqualified form in VmL and in later manuscripts of
this and UL is replaced by *fylghþ*. A more frequent
alternative was *hemfylghþ* (q.v.). The word could also
refer specifically to the amount given to a bride by her

marriage agent (*giftomaþer*), but otherwise applied equally to both sexes. The portion could consist of both land and movables and was at the time of the provincial laws treated as an advance on inheritance (Kock 1926) so that when the time came for the father's estate to be divided, any such portion was deducted from what was due to the heir(ess) according to the normal allocation.

dowry **OGu** *GL* A 65

marriage portion **OSw** *VmL* Äb

See also: *gift, heimangerð, hemfylghþ, hemfærth, hemgæf, hindradagsgæf, morghongæf, munder, mæþfylghþ, tilgæf, vingæf*

Refs: KLNM, s.v. *medgift*; Kock 1926; Peel 2015, 137 note 20/54–56, 164–65 notes 28/37–38, 28/38, 190 note 65/9–11; Schlyter 1877, s.v.v. *fylghþ, hemfylghþ*; SL UL, 83 notes 30, 31, 279 note 12

fylgja (ON) noun

support **OIce** *Grg* Misc 251

fyli (OGu) **fóli** (ON) noun

stolen goods **OGu** *GL* A 37, Add. 8 (B 55), **OIce** *Grg* Rsþ 230, *Jó* Þjb 2, 6, *Js* Mah 19 Þjb 2, 5, **ONorw** *FrL* Mhb 30 LlbB 12, *GuL* Tjb

See also: *þiufnaþer*

fylki (ON) noun

In Western Norway and Trøndelag (Mid-Norway) the law districts were subdivided into provinces called *fylki*, a unit corresponding roughly to the Anglo-Saxon shire. The Gulathing consisted of six *fylki*. In Western Norway (except Agder and Sunnmøre) these provinces were further divided into quarters (*fjórðungar*, see *fiarþunger*) and eighths (*áttungar*, see *attunger*). A smaller unit was the *herað (see hæraþ)*, corresponding roughly to the Anglo-Saxon hundred. ONorw *fylki* as a smaller unit of land was used similarly to ODan *bygth* (see *bygd*) (cf. von See).

county **OIce** *Js* Kdb 7, **ONorw** *FrL* Tfb 4 Mhb 24

province **ONorw** *GuL* Krb, Kpb, Kvb, Løb, Llb, Arb, Tfb, Mhb, Tjb, Olb, Leb

region **OIce** *Grg* Ómb 143

See also: *attunger, fiarþunger*

Refs: Helle 2001, 76–79; Hertzberg s.v. *fylki*; KLNM s.v. *fylke*; Sunde 2011a, 58; von See 1964, 191

fylkiskirkja (ON) noun

A primary church for an entire district (*fylki*) according to GuL, but there are two *fylkiskirkjur* per district in BorgL and three in EidsL. It may be synonymous with a *höfuðkirkja* (q.v.) or *stórkirkja*. It has at times been equated to a burial church (*graptarkirkja*) as well, but this assumption is probably inaccurate. It was the duty

of the bishop and the king to decide which churches were to be designated as a *fylkiskirkja*. All other churches in the *fylki* would then be subordinate to it. Bishops confirmed children and led services once a year at the *fylkiskirkja*.

A *fylkiskirkja* has also been identified as a type of church which replaced the heathen *höfuðhof* ('chief temple') during the early stages of conversion to Christianity. Thereafter it became the mother church for all *høgendiskirkjur, heraðskirkjur, fjórðungskirkjur* and *áttungskirkjur* in each *fylki*.

Tradition states that Olaf Tryggvason commanded the *fylkiskirkjur* to be built, and his order was carried out during the reign of St. Olaf. In *Ólafs saga helga* it is recorded that a mark of weighed silver was to be paid to the *fylkiskirkja* each year from the church's estates. This was to be used for the maintenance of the *fylkisprestr* (q.v.). According to FrL KrbA 45, ordeals were performed at the *fylkiskirkja*. The priest of a *fylkiskirkja*, his wife and his dean were exempt from the levy (*leiðangr*, see *leþunger*) according to FrL Leþ 17.

Brink (2013b, 34–35) equates *fylkiskirkjur* and *höfuðkirkjur* with the Swedish *hundareskirkior*. These churches served a large area with no defined territorial boundaries and functioned as a kind of early stage of church hierarchy in the North during the eleventh and twelfth centuries.

county church **ONorw** *BorgL* 8, *FrL* KrbA 7

{fylkis} church **ONorw** *GuL* Krb

See also: *heraðskirkja, höfuðkirkja*

Refs: Brink 2013b; F s.v. *fylkiskirkja*; NGL V s.v. *fylkiskirkja*; Maurer 1908; RGA s.v. *Kirchenverfassung, Pfründe*; Skre 2007, 394–95.

fylkismaðr (ON) noun

man belonging to a {fylki} **ONorw** *GuL* Krb, Olb

man of the county **ONorw** *FrL* Tfb 1 KrbA 2 Var 43 Bvb 16

fylkisprestr (ON) noun

county priest **ONorw** *FrL* KrbA 14

fylkisþing (ON) noun

A *þing* 'assembly' of the administrative/judicial district *fylki*. Appears in the context of appealing a case from one type of assembly to another.

county assembly **ONorw** *FrL* Intr 23 Mhb 30 Rgb 3 Jkb 4

{fylkis} assembly **ONorw** *GuL* Kpb, Olb

See also: *fiærþungsþing, folkland, fylki, hundarisþing, hæraþsþing, landsþing, skipreiðuþing, soknaþing, syselthing, þing*

Refs: Fritzner s.v. *fylkisþing*, Hertzberg s.v. *fylkisþing*

fylla (OSw) **fylle** (ODan) verb

appoint **OSw** *UL* Jb

confirm **OSw** *HL* Äb, Mb

execute **OSw** *UL* Kkb, Äb, Mb, Jb, Kmb, Blb, Rb, *VmL* Kkb, Äb

fulfil **OSw** *SdmL* Kgb

make good **OSw** *UL* Kkb, Äb, Mb, Kmb, *VmL* Kkb

pay **OSw** *UL* Kkb, Mb

prove **ODan** *SkL* 147, **OSw** *HL* Mb

provide **OSw** *UL* Mb, Jb, Blb, *VmL* Jb

pursue **OSw** *HL* Mb

satisfy **OSw** *UL* Mb, Blb, *VmL* Mb, Bb

strengthen with an oath **OSw** *HL* Rb

substantiate **OSw** *UL* Kgb, Äb, Mb, Blb, Rb, *VmL* Kgb, Äb, Mb, Bb, Rb

succeed **OSw** *UL* Kkb

testify **OSw** *HL* Äb

See also: *fulla*

fylling (ODan) noun

compensation **ODan** *JyL* 1

full compensation **ODan** *JyL* 1

full payment **ODan** *JyL* 1

fylsmærke (ODan) noun

Literally 'foal mark', referring to an owner's mark on disputed home born domestic animals, not only horses, and appearing in the context of accusations of theft.

possession mark **ODan** *JyL* 2

See also: *fylsvat*, *hemaföder*

fylsvat (OSw) noun

An oath of twelve men, sometimes with the additional testimony of two others, confirming that disputed domestic animals were born at the home of the one claiming ownership, and thus not stolen.

oath about a foal **OSw** *YVgL* Tb, *ÄVgL* Tb

oath that someone bred a foal **OSw** *ÄVgL* Tb

See also: *fylsmærke*, *hemaföder*, *hemagiorþer*, *hemefødvitne*, *hemföþoeþer*, *sumartenlunger*

Refs: Schlyter s.v. *fylsvat*

fynd (OSw) **fund** (ODan) **fundr** (ON) **fyndr** (ON) **find** (OSw) noun

find **ONorw** *GuL* Llb, Tfb, Mhb, **OSw** *DL* Bb, *HL* Md, *SdmL* Tjdb

lost property **ODan** *JyL* 2

meeting **OIce** *Grg* Þsþ 32 Fjl 225, *Js* Lbb 7, **ONorw** *EidsL* 22.7, *GuL* Krb, Mhb

See also: *affarefæ*, *samqvæmd*

fyndalön (OSw) **fundar laun** (OGu) noun

reward **OGu** *GL* Add. 8 (B 55), **OSw** *SdmL* Bb

See also: *fyndarluter*, *lön*

fyndarluter (OSw) noun

finder's lot **OSw** *SdmL* Bb, Tjdb

reward for finding **OSw** *SdmL* Bb, *ÖgL* Bb

See also: *fyndalön*

fyrirmæla (ON) verb

harm with words **OIce** *Js* Kvg 2

spoil by word **ONorw** *GuL* Kvb

See also: *fyrirrǿgja*

fyrirnemask (ON) verb

neglect **ONorw** *GuL* Krb, Leb

fyrirrǿgja (ON) **fyrirrægja** (ON) verb

ruin with slander **OIce** *Js* Mah 26

spoil by slander **ONorw** *GuL* Tfb

fyrirskjóta (ON) verb

forfeit **OIce** *Jó* Kge 19

become invalid **ONorw** *EidsL* 11.1

lose **ONorw** *GuL* Arb

fyrirtaka (ON) verb

lose (e.g. a case) **ONorw** *FrL* LlbA 23

fyrirvega (ON) verb

forfeit by killing **OIce** *Js* Ert 13, **ONorw** *GuL* Mhb

fyrma (1) (OSw) verb

To observe a type of fast.

observe the {fyrma} **OSw** *DL* Kkb

Refs: Schlyter s.v. *fyrma*

fyrma (2) (OSw) verb

maltreat **OSw** *DL* Bb

fyrna (OSw) **fyrna** (ON) **fyrnask** (ON) verb

become useless with age **OIce** *Jó* Llb 45

go out of date **OIce** *Grg* Rsþ 227

hinder by letting lie fallow **OSw** *VmL* Jb

become time-barred **ONorw** *GuL* Kpb

See also: *aterlæggia*

fyrning (OSw) **fyrning** (ODan) noun

ancestral rights **OSw** *UL* Jb

oath about inherited land **OSw** *HL* Jb

the old way **ODan** *ESjL* 2

fyrnska (OGu) **fyrnska** (ON) noun

decay **ONorw** *GuL* Leb

old customs **OGu** *GL* A 4

the past **ONorw** *GuL* Llb, Tfb, Leb

See also: *forn*

fæ (OSw) **fæ** (ODan) **fe** (OGu) **fé** (ON) **fe** (OSw) noun

This word has two groups of meanings, both amply attested in Medieval Nordic laws: 1) cattle, livestock, 2) goods, money, payment; property. The original meaning, as indicated by the Latin cognate *pecus*, was 'cattle'. The extension of meaning is easily understandable in view of the fact that cattle constituted a large part of a man's or institution's property. Cattle might also be used as a means of payment.

Some words with *fæ-/fé-* occur in both senses: OSw *leghofæ*, ON *leigufé* (1) 'leased cattle', 2) 'leased thing, money or property'); ON *féhirðir* (1) 'herdsman, shepherd', 2) 'treasurer').

The ODan *danæt fæ* referred to valuables found in the ground without a legal owner or heir to claim them; they went to the Crown. Such treasure troves, perhaps specifically connected to pagan burials, have been found in Denmark. The idea is contrasted to contemporary Icelandic ideas of property ownership/buried property in Miller & Vogt 2015, 45.

amount **ONorw** *EidsL* 8.3

animal **ODan** *JyL* 2, 3, *SkL* 170, 171, 175–77, 180, 181, 189, 190, **OSw** *DL* Kkb, Mb, Bb, *HL* Mb, Blb, Rb, *SdmL* Bb, Mb, *UL* Kkb, Mb, Blb, *VmL* Kkb, Mb, Bb, *YVgL* Rlb, Tb, Föb, Utgb, *ÄVgL* Rlb

animals **OIce** *Grg* Fjl 225, *Jó* Lbb 4

beast **OSw** *DL* Kkb, *UL* Kkb, Mb, Blb, *VmL* Kkb, Kgb, Mb, Bb, *ÄVgL* Fös

belongings **ODan** *SkL* 241, **ONorw** *FrL* Intr 9, **OSw** *DL* Tjdb

cash **OIce** *Grg* Vís 96 Bat 115

cattle **ODan** *ESjL* 3, *JyL* 2, *SkL* 83, 136, 160, 169, 172, 173, 188, 195, 203, **ONorw** *EidsL* 11.6, *GuL* Llb, **OSw** *DL* Bb, *HL* Blb, *ÄVgL* Rlb

chattels **ODan** *ESjL* 2, *VSjL* 1, 87, **OIce** *Jó* Mah 1

creature **OSw** *DL* Bb, *SmL*, *ÄVgL* Föb

domestic animal **ODan** *JyL* 2, 3, *SkL* 105, **OSw** *HL* Mb, *UL* Mb, Kmb, Blb, *VmL* Mb, Kmb, Bb

fine **OIce** *Grg* Feþ 147, **ONorw** *BorgL* 3.3, *FrL* KrbA 10

funds **OIce** *Jó* Llb 45, **ONorw** *BorgL* 8.13

gain **ODan** *SkL* 72, 121

goods **ODan** *ESjL* 3, *JyL* 2, *SkL* 85, 112, 122, 135, 230, 231, 233, 240, *VSjL* 2, 13, 18, **OIce** *Grg* Bat 114, *Jó* Þfb 7 Þjb 1, **ONorw** *FrL* Intr 22, **OSw** *DL* Bb, Gb, *HL* Mb, Kmb, *YVgL* Urb, Drb, Äb, Gb, Rlb, Tb, Add, *ÄVgL* Md, Äb, Gb, Rlb, Tb

home **OSw** *ÄVgL* Gb

livestock **ODan** *ESjL* 2, 3, *SkL* 115, **OIce** *Grg* Vís 112, *Jó* Llb 2, **ONorw** *FrL* Intr

23, **OSw** *HL* Mb, Kmb, Blb, *SdmL* Bb, *UL* Kkb, Kgb, Blb, *VmL* Bb, *YVgL* Tb

means **OIce** *Grg* Feþ 149 Tíg 260, **ONorw** *GuL* Løb

money **OFar** *Seyð* 2, **OGu** *GL* A 2, 13, 14, 21, 28, Add. 8 (B 55), **OIce** *Grg* Þsþ 51 Vís 110, *Jó* Þfb 2, *Js* Þfb 2 Mah 2, *KRA* 6, 31, **ONorw** *BorgL* 3.5 12.14, *EidsL* 31.2, *FrL* KrbB 23, *GuL* Mhb, Olb, Leb, Krb, Kpb, Løb, Trm, **OSw** *UL* Kkb, Mb, Blb, Rb, *VmL* Kkb, Äb, Bb

movable goods **ODan** *ESjL* 3

movables **ODan** *ESjL* 1–3, *JyL* 1, *SkL* 6, 23, 29, 40, *VSjL* 1, 87, **ONorw** *FrL* Intr 2 KrbB 21

payment **OGu** *GL* Add. 1 (B 4), **OIce** *Grg* Tíg 258

possessions **ONorw** *FrL* KrbA 5

price **ODan** *ESjL* 3

property **ODan** *ESjL* 3, **OGu** *GL* A 19, 28, **OIce** *Grg* passim, *Jó* passim, *Js* passim, *KRA* 1, 7 passim, **ONorw** *BorgL* 3.2 4.2 passim, *FrL* Intr 1, 3 KrbA 10, 18 KrbB 3 passim, *GuL* Arb, Kpb, Leb, Trm, Krb, Llb, Mhb, **OSw** *HL* Kkb, *UL* Mb, Rb, *VmL* Mb, Rb, *YVgL* Äb, Jb, *ÄVgL* Jb, *ÖgL* Db

ransom **OSw** *YVgL* Äb

reward **ODan** *VSjL* 87

stock (2) **OIce** *Grg* Lbþ 178

sum **OIce** *Grg* Klþ 4

wealth **ONorw** *EidsL* 24.6 passim, *FrL* KrbB 17

Expressions:

danæt fæ (ODan)

treasure trove (lit. 'dead man's property') **ODan** *ESjL* 3

ihald fear (OSw)

animals in another man's enclosure **OSw** *YVgL* Kkb

animals within another man's fences **OSw** *YVgL* Till

inlaght fæ (OSw)

deposited goods **OSw** *DL* Bb, Rb

goods left in custody **OSw** *YVgL* Äb *ÄVgL* Äb

See also: *bo, danefæ, egn, fæarganger, fæbot, fægarþer, fæhus, fælaþi, fælöt, fæmark, fæmune, goþs, inviþi, kúgildi, orf, pænninger*

Refs: Hertzberg s.v.v. *fé, fé-, fjár-*; KLNM s.v. *danefæ*; Lund [1877] 1967 s.v.v. *fæ, fæ-, -fæ*; Miller & Vogt 2015, 45; ONP s.v. *fé*; Schlyter s.v.v. *fæ, fæ-, fear-, fæar-*

fæarföling (OSw) **fearföling** (OSw) **föiærfölengh** (OSw) **fæiærföling** (OSw) noun

crime of hiding a dead animal **OSw** *ÄVgL* Rlb

hiding of cattle **OSw** *ÄVgL* Rlb

hiding of killed animal **OSw** *YVgL* Rlb

fæarganger (OSw) **fægang** (ODan) **fjárganga** (ON)
fæganger (OSw) noun

The grazing of cattle, or a passage or path used by the
cattle (ODan, OIce).

passage **ODan** *JyL* 1

pasture **OSw** *YVgL* Drb, Jb, *ÄVgL* Jb

sheep-walk **OIce** *Jó* Llb 47

See also: *sauðagangr*

Refs: CV s.v. *fé*; Lund s.v. *fægang*;
Schlyter 1877 s.v. *fæar ganger*

fæarlæstir (pl.) (OSw) noun

damage of livestock **OSw** *YVgL* Rlb

fæbot (OSw) **febytr** (OGu) **fébót** (ON) **fébætr** (ON)
fébótr (ON) **feabot** (OSw) noun

atonement payment **OIce** *Grg* Feþ 154

cash compensation **OGu** *GL* A 23

fine **OSw** *SmL*, *ÖgL* Kkb

fines **OSw** *VmL* Kkb

monetary fine **OSw** *DL* Kkb, Rb, *HL* Rb,
SdmL Kkb, Bb, Rb, *UL* Rb, Mb, *VmL* Rb

money as compensation **OIce** *Grg* Tíg 266

payment of financial compensation **ONorw** *GuL* Mhb

See also: *bot, bóta, fæ, fægæld*

fægarþer (OSw) **fægarth** (ODan) noun

cattle pen **OSw** *HL* Mb

cattle-yard **ODan** *VSjL* 53

stable **ODan** *VSjL* 57

fægæld (OSw) **fégjald** (ON) **fjárgjald** (ON) **fea giald**
(OSw) noun

fine **OIce** *Jó* Mah 16, **OSw** *ÖgL* Kkb

monetary debt **OSw** *DL* Bb, *SdmL*
Kkb, *UL* Kkb, *VmL* Kkb

money fine **OIce** *KRA* 7

payment **OIce** *Grg* Feþ 167

payment of money **OIce** *Js* Mah 34

See also: *fæbot*

fæhus (OSw) **fæhus** (ODan) **fjárhús** (ON) noun

byre **OSw** *DL* Kkb, *SdmL* Kkb, *UL* Kkb, *VmL* Kkb

cattle shed **ODan** *VSjL* 57

stable **OIce** *Js* Lbb 11

stock shed **OIce** *Jó* Llb 3

fælagh (OSw) **fælagh** (ODan) **félag** (ON) noun

The *fælagh* was a form of co-ownership or jointly
held property. The provincial laws distinguished
between two kinds of *fælagh*: 1) co-ownership, union
of properties within the family; and 2) partnership in
trade.

1) Co-ownership could be established by
agreement between spouses (GuL ch. 53); if no such
agreement was reached, the properties of husband and
wife were kept separate. However, after twenty years'
marriage (in the FrL twelve months), co-ownership
was established automatically if it did not exist
already. In Swedish households, the properties of
husband and wife were kept more strictly apart.
According to the JyL *fælagh* implied co-ownership
between husband and wife only. The SkL and ESjL
included the whole (extended) family in the *fælagh*.
This meant that children got their part when they
married, i.e. before their parents died. This *fælagh*
was abolished in Denmark in 1547 and replaced by
the marriage *fælagh*. In Sweden, both types continued
to exist during the Middle Ages.

2) Partnership was the usual form for cooperation
in order to equip end finance commercial travels and
to secure the profit. Each partner (ON *félagi*) had
to take care of the interests of his other partner(s) if
necessary (e.g. in cases of accident or death).

goods in partnership **ODan** *JyL* 2

household **ODan** *JyL* 2, *SkL* 16, 18

household community **OSw** *YVgL* Äb

marital co-ownership **ONorw** *GuL* Kvb, Arb

partnership **ODan** *ESjL* 1–3, *JyL* 1–3, *SkL* 5,
6, 20, 21, 230, 240, *VSjL* 1–3, 6–13, 18, 70,
OIce *Grg* Arþ 120, 125 Ómb 128 Feþ 150,
153, *Jó* Kge 3, 7 Fml 22, *Js* Kvg 2 Ert 19

trade partnership **ONorw** *FrL* Intr 20

See also: *félagi*

Refs: Bagge 2010, 220, fn.140, Dübeck
2003, 81; Helle 2001, 141–42; KLNM s.v.v.
*bergenshandel, félag, formuefællesskab;
kompaniskap*; Robberstad 1981, 351

fælaghlagh (ODan) noun

agreed partnership **ODan** *VSjL* 2

agreement over partnership **ODan** *ESjL* 1

See also: *fælagh*

fælaghsbryte (ODan) noun

bailiff in partnership **ODan** *JyL* 2

fælaghsfæ (ODan) noun

movables in a partnership **ODan** *ESjL* 2

fælath (ODan) noun

cattle land **ODan** *SkL* 185

common land **ODan** *JyL* 3

commons **ODan** *ESjL* 2, 3, *JyL* 3

fælaþi (OSw) **fileþi** (OGu) **fælædhe** (OSw) noun

animal **OSw** *DL* Bb

cattle **OSw** *DL* Bb, *SdmL* Bb

creature **OGu** *GL* A 46

domestic animal **OSw** *DL* Bb

livestock **OGu** *GL* A 40, **OSw** *VmL* Bb

fælla (OSw) falle (ODan) fælle (ODan) fella (OGu)
felz (OGu) fella (ON) falla (OSw) fallas (OSw)
fiollas (OSw) fællas (OSw) verb

Apart from the literal felling and falling of people
and things, three main usages with legal significance
can be discerned, albeit with some overlap: 1) To fail
or neglect to perform a duty (or something similar),
which is reflected in translations such as 'fail',
'neglect', 'decline', often referring to a person or
a group of people failing to make transports, build
fences, maintain bridges etc. 2) To fail to achieve
(wanted) result — particularly of an oath — reflected
in translations such as 'fail (an oath)', and possibly 'be
annulled', 'dismiss', 'overthrow', 'default', usually
referring to a defendant's failure to produce the
stipulated number of oath-helpers, or to be supported
by the men nominated to determine the case. In this
usage, often appearing in the passive and as participles.
3) Presumably influenced by both a sense 'to fell,
defeat; to fall, to be defeated' and from the usage
'to fail (an oath)', meaning 'to convict', and hence
'to pass judgment', which is reflected in translations
such as 'convict', 'find guilty', 'condemn', 'sentence',
'judge'. The conviction, which could be reached
through an *eþer* 'oath', could be issued by witnesses,
occasionally other men involved in the dealings at
hand, sometimes other actual eye-witnesses or other
local men assumed to have knowledge of the facts of
the case, or a group of nominated men, sometimes
referred to as a *næmd*. The verbs appear in numerous
phrases and expressions and a few citations can
illustrate the usage and translations: *fællær han at
loghum* 'if the oath fails for him' (ODan JyL 3:35),
fals han at laghum 'if he fails the oath' (OSw ÄVgL
Äb 11), *værþær han fælþær* 'if he is found guilty'
(OSw ÄVgL Gb 7, Fös 5), *þa wærin fældir* 'then it
becomes invalid' (OSw HL Rb 8), *tha ær han fældær
at the sac* 'then he is at fault in the cases' (ODan ESjL
3:65), *döma (man) fældan* 'judge (someone) guilty'
(OSw YVgL Till).

accuse **OSw** *DL* Kkb

be annulled **OSw** *DL* Rb

attack **ODan** *SkL* 200

build a fence **ONorw** *GuL* Llb

cancel **OSw** *VmL* Rb

charge (someone) with (something) **OGu** *GL* A 20

condemn **OGu** *GL* A 2, **OSw** *DL* Kkb, Bb, *UL* Kkb, Kgb, Äb, Mb, Kmb, Blb, Rb, *VmL* Äb, Mb, Kmb, Bb, Rb, *ÄVgL* Slb

convict **ODan** *ESjL* 2, 3, *JyL* 2, 3, *VSjL* 87, **OSw** *DL* Eb, Rb, *HL* Kkb, Kgb, Äb, Mb, Blb, Rb, *SdmL* Kkb, Kgb, Gb, Bb, Kmb, Mb, Tjdb, Rb, Till, *SmL*, *UL* Kkb, Äb, Mb, Kmb, Blb, Rb, *VmL* Kkb, Kgb, Äb, Mb, Jb, Kmb, Bb, Rb, *YVgL* Kkb, Frb, Äb, Gb, Rlb, Tb, Add, *ÄVgL* Slb, Jb, Tb, *ÖgL* Kkb, Eb, Db

be convicted **ODan** *JyL* 2, **OSw** *HL* Kgb, Äb, *SdmL* Bb, *YVgL* Drb, Föb

decline (to do something) **OSw** *UL* Blb, *VmL* Kmb, Bb

dismiss **OSw** *YVgL* Add

fail **ODan** *JyL* 3, *SkL* 155, 218, 226, *VSjL* 87, **OSw** *DL* Kkb, Bb, Tjdb, *HL* Kkb, Kgb, Mb, Jb, Blb, Rb, *SdmL* Gb, Äb, Jb, Bb, Kmb, Mb, Tjdb, Rb, *YVgL* Drb, Tb, Jb, Föb, Add, *ÄVgL* Md, Äb, Rlb, Tb, *ÖgL* Db

fail (to observe or fulfil something) **OGu** *GL* A 20a, **OSw** *UL* Kkb, Kgb, Mb, Jb, Blb, Rb, Add. 14, *VmL* Mb

fail an oath **OSw** *YVgL* Kkb, Rlb, Utgb, *ÄVgL* Fös

fail one's case of defending **OSw** *YVgL* Add

fall **OGu** *GL* A 20, 23, 24e, **OSw** *HL* Kgb, *UL* Kkb, Äb, Mb, Blb, *VmL* Kkb, Äb, Mb, Bb

fell **OSw** *ÄVgL* Md

find guilty **OSw** *DL* Bb, Rb, *HL* Kkb, *UL* Kkb, Kgb, Äb, Mb, Kmb, *VmL* Kkb, Kgb, Äb, Bb, Rb, *YVgL* Add, *ÄVgL* Gb, Fös

be found guilty **OGu** *GL* A 20, **OSw** *UL* Kkb, Mb, *VmL* Kkb

go against **ODan** *SkL* 146

be guilty and fined **OSw** *DL* Bb

hinder **ONorw** *GuL* Krb

judge **OSw** *YVgL* Föb

be lawfully convicted **ODan** *JyL* 2

make at fault **ODan** *ESjL* 3

make invalid **OSw** *HL* Rb

neglect **OSw** *DL* Rb, *HL* Kkb, Kgb, Mb, Blb, Rb, *SdmL* Kkb, Kgb, Bb, Rb, *SmL*

overthrow **OSw** *YVgL* Add

pass away **OSw** *UL* StfBM, Äb, *VmL* Kkb, Äb

push **ONorw** *GuL* Mhb

be reduced **OSw** *UL* Äb, *VmL* Äb

reject **OSw** *HL* Kkb

sentence **OSw** *HL* Äb, *SmL*, *YVgL* Frb, Föb

be slain **OSw** *UL* Kgb, Mb, *VmL* Kgb, Mb

be void **OSw** *DL* Rb

write off **OGu** *GL* A 17

Expressions:

falla/fals at eþe (OSw)

convict in respect of an oath OSw *VmL* Kkb

fail in an oath OSw *UL* Kkb, Äb, Mb, Jb, Kmb, Blb, Rb *VmL* Kkb, Äb, Mb, Kmb, Bb, Rb

fælla til næs (OSw)

sentence to defence by oath **OSw** *SmL*

niþer fælla (OSw) **falla niðr** (ON)

to be abolished OIce *Jó* Mah 1

to lapse OIce *Grg* Klþ 2

leave unused OSw *UL* Blb

to be negligent OSw *UL* Kkb, Blb *VmL* Kkb

See also: *brista, eþer, eþsöre, laghvinna, vinna, viþerbinda, þingfall*

Refs: Andersen 2010, 47–48; Hellquist s.v. *fälla*; Hertzberg s.v.v. *falla, fella*; KLNM s.v. *rettergang*; SAOB s.v. *fälla*; Schlyter s.v.v. *falla, fælla*

fælöt (OSw) noun

pasture ground **OSw** *YVgL* Jb, *ÄVgL* Jb

See also: *fæ, löt*

Refs: Schlyter s.v. *fæ löt*

fæmark (OSw) **fear mark** (OSw) noun

Common pasture land of a village.

pastureland **OSw** *YVgL* Jb, *ÄVgL* Jb

Refs: Schlyter s.v. *fæ mark*

fæmt (OSw) **fimt** (ODan) **fimmt** (ON) **fimt** (ON) noun

This word — derived from the numeral *fæm/fimm* — was the usual term for a summons to appear in a certain place after five days, and for the meeting or gathering held at the expiration of five days. The *fæmt* was the usual notice, summons, or time limit in relation to judicial matters.

It is known from several Nordic provincial laws and even elsewhere (e.g. the Faroes). OSw *fæmt* was held five days after an assembly and fulfilled a function similar to a home summons (*heimstefna*, see *hemstæmpnung*) in Norway, where debts could be settled. In Iceland, this concept appears in Js and Jó.

There are reasons to believe that the *fæmt* was the length of a week in early Medieval Norway, and probably in all mainland Scandinavia. This rests, *inter alia*, on the length of the month, which was six weeks in the GuL (see Sunde 2011b, 224–25). It is not clear when the seven-day week was introduced in Scandinavia, but this probably took place before the introduction of Christianity. Nevertheless, the five-day week continued in use, esp. in matters of law and public business.

fifth **ODan** *JyL* 1, **OSw** *ÖgL* Kkb, Eb, Db

five day term **ODan** *ESjL* 3

five day's notice summons OIce *Jó* Llb 13, *KRA* 29, **ONorw** *FrL* KrbB 20 LlbB 4, *GuL* Llb, Olb

five days **ODan** *ESjL* 3, *SkL* 142, **OIce** *Jó* Llb 15, *KRA* 11, **ONorw** *FrL* Mhb 33

five-day deadline **ONorw** *EidsL* 32.6

five-day grace period **ONorw** *EidsL* 38.2

five-day interval **ODan** *ESjL* 2, 3

five-day time limit **ONorw** *BorgL* 11.3, *EidsL* 8.2 17.3

gathering **OSw** *SmL*

grace **OSw** *SmL*

notice **OFar** *Seyð* 10

period of five days **ONorw** *GuL* Krb, Kpb, Llb, Mhb, Tjb, Leb, Olb

term of five days **ODan** *ESjL* 2, 3, *JyL* 2, 3, *SkL* 71

within five days **ODan** *JyL* 2

See also: *endaghi, fimmtarnafn, fimmtarstefna, mél, siunættinger, þrenættinger*

Refs: Helle 2001, 185–86; Hertzberg s.v. *fimt*; KLNM s.v.v. *fimtarstefna, gravøl, termin, vecka*; LexMA s.v.v. *Haus, -formen, C, Rechts- und Verfassungsgeschichte. II: Skandinavien*; Schlyter s.v. *fœmt*; Sunde 2011b, 223–29

fæmta (OSw) **fimte** (ODan) verb

sue **OSw** *ÖgL* Eb

take away a house after five days **ODan** *ESjL* 2

fæmune (ODan) noun

movable goods **ODan** *VSjL* 14

movables **ODan** *ESjL* 1

fænaþer (OSw) **fénaðr** (ON) **fénuðr** (ON) noun

animal **OFar** *Seyð* 8, **OIce** *Jó* Mah 23, **OSw** *YVgL* Tb

beast **OSw** *YVgL* Vs, *ÄVgL* Vs

cattle **OIce** *Jó* Þjb 16

livestock **ONorw** *BorgL* 5.6, *EidsL* 2.2, *GuL* Mhb

See also: *fæ*

færsauðr (ON) noun

sheep **ONorw** *GuL* Mhb

fæsak (OSw) noun

cause of fine **OSw** *SmL*

fæshoveth (ODan) noun

cattle **ODan** *ESjL* 3

fæst (OSw) **festr** (ON) noun

betrothal OIce *Grg* Feþ 144, **OSw** *YVgL* Kkb, Gb, *ÄVgL* Gb

confirmation **OSw** *YVgL* Gb, *ÄVgL* Gb

mooring **ONorw** *GuL* Leb

rope **ONorw** *GuL* Kvr

state of engagement **OSw** *HL* Äb

testimony **OSw** *YVgL* Jb

witness **OSw** *YVgL* Jb, Kvab, Add, *ÄVgL* Jb, Kva

See also: *fæstning*, *fæstningamal*, *rep*, *snóri*

fæsta (OSw) **fæste** (ODan) festa (OGu) festa (ON)
fæste (ODan) festa (OGu) festa (ON) verb

Literally, 'fasten'. This word is used in a considerable
number of different ways. On the one hand, it might
have a meaning similar to *biuþa* in the more general
sense of 'offer' or 'pledge' and similar concepts.
The thing offered or promised could be fines, an
oath or surety, a tenancy or loan agreement, a sale,
property division or exchange as well as a contract of
employment or marriage. In the context of marriage,
it means specifically to pledge or offer to be married
to someone. This usually involved the passing of
a betrothal gift or price, the *fæstnaþa fæ*, or *vingæf*
(q.v.), to the designated *giftarmaþer* (q.v.).

accept **OSw** *HL* Rb

accept a conviction **OSw** *HL* Rb

accept fines **OSw** *HL* Rb

agree **ODan** *ESjL* 2, *JyL* 2, 3, *SkL* 66,
97, 192, 227, 228, 239, *VSjL* 39, 41

announce **OSw** *YVgL* Add

betroth **ODan** *SkKL* 6, **OIce** *Jó* Mah 30 Kge
5, 6, *Js* Mah 36 Ert 14, *KRA* 16, **ONorw**
FrL KrbB 22 Kvb 1, **OSw** *DL* Gb, *HL* Kkb,
Äb, *SdmL* Gb, *UL* Kkb, Äb, *VmL* Kkb, Äb,
YVgL Kkb, Äb, Gb, Add, *ÄVgL* Äb, Gb

bind **OSw** *HL* Äb

confirm **OIce** *Grg* Rsþ 230, **OSw** *HL* Jb

convict **OSw** *HL* Rb

espouse **ONorw** *BorgL* 15.8

fasten **ONorw** *GuL* Krb, **OSw** *HL* Kkb, Äb

formally agree **ODan** *ESjL* 3, *VSjL* 81

hire **OSw** *YVgL* Utgb, *ÄVgL* Föb

marry **ODan** *ESjL* 1, **OIce** *KRA* 16

offer **OSw** *HL* Mb, *UL* Kkb, Mb,
Jb, Rb, Add. 8, *VmL* Rb

pay **ONorw** *FrL* KrbA 22, **OSw** *UL* Blb

pay a fine **OSw** *HL* Rb

pledge **OGu** *GL* A 28, 63, **ONorw** *GuL* Kvb,
OSw *UL* Jb, Blb, Rb, *VmL* Jb, Rb, *ÖgL* Kkb, Eb

pledge to swear **OIce** *Jó* Llb 30

promise **ODan** *ESjL* 2, 3, *JyL* 2, 3, *SkL*
77, *VSjL* 55, 65, 87, **OSw** *DL* Rb, *HL* Rb,
SdmL Jb, Mb, Rb, *VmL* Rb, *ÖgL* Db

rent **ODan** *JyL* 3, *SkL* 238, 239

set **OSw** *ÖgL* Eb

submit to something **ONorw** *GuL* Kpb

give surety **OIce** *Js* Mah 20

swear **OIce** *Jó* Þjb 5, **ONorw** *FrL* KrbB 3 Mhb 8

take in pledge **OGu** *GL* A 20

take into one's service **ONorw** *GuL* Løb

Expressions:

festa í vist (ON)

hire **OIce** *Jó* Kge 24

fæsta lagh (OSw) **festa lög** (ON)

place a ban **OIce** *Jó* Llb 52

promise an oath **OSw** *UL* Rb *VmL* Kkb, Rb

fæstu aiga (OGu)

land held in pledge **OGu** *GL* A 63, Add 9

See also: *biuþa*, *fæstning*, *giftarmaþer*, *lagh*, *vingæf*

Refs: KLNM, s.v.v. *bröllop*, *fastar*, *festermål*,
morgongåva; Korpiola 2004; Peel 2015, 188
note 63/9–11; Schlyter 1877, s.v. *fæsta*; SL
GL, 278 note 4 to chapter 28; SL UL, 41
notes 72–73, 78–79, notes 8–11; SL VmL,
29 notes 82–84, 57 note 11; Vogt 2010

fæsta (OSw) **fæste** (ODan) festa (OGu) noun

acceptance **OSw** *HL* Rb

bail **ONorw** *FrL* Tfb 1

betrothal **OGu** *GL* A 21, **OSw** *SdmL*
Gb, *UL* Kkb, *VmL* Kkb

farm rent **ODan** *JyL* 3

promise **ONorw** *FrL* Var 2-6,
OSw *SdmL* Rb, *VmL* Kkb

promise of an oath **OSw** *HL* Rb

surety **OIce** *Js* Mah 20

term **OSw** *YVgL* Äb, *ÄVgL* Äb

fæstakona (OSw) festarkona (ON) **fæstikona** (OSw)
noun

betrothed woman **OIce** *Grg* Feþ 160, **ONorw** *FrL*
KrbB 1, 12 Rgb 38 Kvb 1, *GuL* Krb, Kvb, Mhb,
OSw *HL* Äb, *SdmL* Gb, *YVgL* Gb, *ÄVgL* Gb

fiancée **OSw** *UL* Äb, *VmL* Äb

fæstamaþer (OSw) **fæsteman** (ODan) festarmaðr
(ON) **fæstaman** (OSw) **fæstimaþer** (OSw) **fæstnaþa
maþer** (OSw) noun

betrothed **ODan** *ESjL* 1

betrothed man **OIce** *Grg* Feþ 160, *Js* Kvg
1, **ONorw** *FrL* KrbB 12 Rgb 38, *GuL* Kvb,
OSw *HL* Äb, *YVgL* Gb, *ÄVgL* Gb

fiancé **OIce** *Jó* Kge 1, **ONorw** *FrL* KrbB 22

fæstaruf (OSw) noun

    broken betrothal **OSw** *ÄVgL* Gb

fæster (OSw) adj.

    announced/promised **OSw** *YVgL* Add

fæstipæninger (OSw) **fæstipænninger** (OSw) noun

    contract money **OSw** *DL* Bb, *HL* Blb

    contract payment **OSw** *UL* Blb, *VmL* Bb

    down payment **OSw** *SdmL* Bb, Kmb

fæstnaþafæ (OSw) **fæstænæfæ** (OSw) noun

    betrothal price **OSw** *UL* Äb, *VmL* Äb

    See also: *fæstningafæ*

fæstnaþarstæmna (OSw) **fæstnaþastæmna** (OSw) **fæstnæþæstæmpna** (OSw) noun

    meeting of betrothal **OSw** *YVgL* Gb, *ÄVgL* Gb

    See also: *fæsta, fæstningastæmpna, stæmna*

fæstning (OSw) **fæstning** (ODan) **festing** (ON) noun

    betrothal **OIce** *Js* Ert 14, *KRA* 16, 17, **OSw** *DL* Gb, *HL* Äb, *UL* Äb, *VmL* Äb

    formal agreement **ODan** *ESjL* 3

    See also: *festarmál, fæsta, fæstningamal*

fæstningafæ (OSw) **fæstingafæ** (OSw) **fæstningæfæ** (OSw) noun

    betrothal payment **OSw** *HL* Äb

    betrothal price **OSw** *HL* Äb, *UL* Äb

    {*fæstingafæ*} **OSw** *HL* Kkb

    See also: *fæstnaþafæ*

fæstningamal (OSw) noun

    betrothal **OIce** *Grg* Arþ 118 Misc 253, **ONorw** *GuL* Kvb

    betrothal agreement **OIce** *Grg* Feþ 153

    betrothal case **OSw** *YVgL* Add

    engagement **ONorw** *FrL* KrbB 22

    See also: *festarmál, fæst, fæstning*

fæstningaran (OSw) noun

    robbery of betrothal **OSw** *YVgL* Add

fæstningastæmpna (OSw) **festingarstefna** (ON) **fæstningastæmna** (OSw) **fæstningæstæmpna** (OSw) noun

    betrothal meeting **ONorw** *EidsL* 22.7, **OSw** *DL* Gb, *HL* Äb, *UL* Äb, *VmL* Äb, *ÖgL* Db

    See also: *fæstnaþarstæmna*

fæthrenelot (ODan) **fætherns lot** (ODan) noun

    paternal lot **ODan** *VSjL* 8

fæthreneærvth (ODan) noun

    paternal inheritance **ODan** *VSjL* 7

fæþerni (OSw) **fæthrene** (ODan) **feþrni** (OGu) **faðerni** (ON) **fæþrini** (OSw) noun

Literally, 'paternal'. The meaning extended to cover the whole of the paternal side of the family, the paternal inheritance (as opposed to the maternal) and the ancestral land inherited from the father, although the expression *fæþernis jorþ* was frequently written in full. Sometimes the same word was employed with more than one of these meanings in the same sentence. In the possessive case, *fæþerni* was used adjectivally to mean 'paternal', to relate to other specific parts of an inheritance, e.g. ancestral home, movables. The word also appears in connection with the question of how the children of mixed marriages between Gotlanders and non-Gotlanders were treated in respect of wergild. This is the subject of some ambiguity in the text, but it seems that the father's family was taken as the yardstick. ON *faðerni* is often used in a sense quite similar to modern 'paternity' and could be the cause for a legal case (*sækja til faðernis*, Grg Feþ 158).

    ancestral home **OGu** *GL* A 20

    father's **ODan** *VSjL* 15

    father's family **OGu** *GL* A 15

    father's part **ODan** *SkL* 2, 23

    father's side **ODan** *ESjL* 3, *JyL* 2, *SkL* 57, 223, **ONorw** *FrL* Var 9, **OSw** *DL* Gb

    what is from the father **ODan** *JyL* 1

    father-line **ONorw** *EidsL* 30.5

    fathering **OIce** *Grg* Þsþ 50, 62 Ómb 142 Feþ 156 Tíg 264

    paternal **ODan** *ESjL* 1, 3, *SkL* 5, 22, 26, 27, 59, 85, 92, 128, *VSjL* 1, 15, **OSw** *HL* Äb

    paternal belongings **ODan** *SkL* 54, 64

    paternal goods **ODan** *ESjL* 1, *JyL* 1

    paternal inheritance **ODan** *ESjL* 1, *SkL* 19, 37, **OGu** *GL* A 20, 24e, **OSw** *DL* Bb, Gb, *HL* Jb, *SdmL* Gb, Jb, *UL* Äb, Jb, Blb, *VmL* Äb, Bb, *YVgL* Äb, Rlb, *ÄVgL* Äb

    paternal kin **OSw** *DL* Gb

    paternal land **ODan** *ESjL* 3, *JyL* 1, *SkL* 27, *VSjL* 4, **OSw** *UL* Jb, *VmL* Jb, *YVgL* Jb, *ÖgL* Eb

    paternal property **OSw** *HL* Jb

    paternal side **ODan** *JyL* 2, *SkL* 57, **OSw** *SdmL* Gb, Äb, *UL* Äb, *VmL* Äb, *YVgL* Drb, Äb, Add, *ÄVgL* Md, Äb

    paternity **OIce** *KRA* 2, **ONorw** *GuL* Løb

    patrimony **ODan** *ESjL* 1

Expressions:

fæþernis frændi (OSw)

    father's kinsman **ODan** *ESjL* 3 *JyL* 1 *SkL* 2

kinsman of the father **ODan** *ESjL* 2 *JyL* 1

kinsman of the father's side **ODan** *SkL* 57, 233

paternal kin **ODan** *JyL* 2 *SkL* 128
VSjL 15 **OSw** *DL* Gb

paternal kinsman **ODan** *ESjL* 1, 2, 3
JyL 1 *SkL* 85, 92, 128 **OSw** *DL* Bb

paternal relative **OSw** *DL* Rb *SdmL* Gb, Äb

See also: *byrþ*, *forhæfþi*, *gyrþlugyrt*,
lindagyrt, *möþerni*

Refs: ONP s.v. *faðerni*; Peel 2015, 119 note
15/6–12, 134 note 20/36–37; Schlyter 1877, s.v.v.
fæþernis, *fæþernis iorþ*; SL UL, 86 note 68

fæþerniseþer (OSw) noun

oath of paternal inheritance **OSw** *SdmL* Jb

fæþernisiorþ (OSw) **fæthrenejorth** (ODan) noun

ancestral land **OSw** *UL* Jb, *VmL* Jb

paternal land **ODan** *JyL* 1, *SkL* 5, 22,
VSjL 1, **OSw** *DL* Rb, *VmL* Bb

fæþringar (pl.) (OSw) noun

relatives on the paternal side **OSw** *SmL*

föðurarfr (ON) noun

inheritance from a father **OIce** *Js* Ert 20

paternal inheritance **ONorw** *FrL* ArbB 7

föðurfrændi (ON) noun

kinsman on the father's side **ONorw**
FrL Intr 4 ArbB 22 Kvb 9

paternal kinsmen **OIce** *Grg* Ómb
137, *Js* Kvg 4 Ert 24

föðurgarðr (ON) noun

father's home **OIce** *Jó* Kge 7

father's house **OIce** *KRA* 10

föðurleifð (ON) noun

inheritance **ONorw** *FrL* Intr 16

föðurætt (ON) noun

paternal kin **OIce** *Js* Kvg 3

förning (OSw) **fyrning** (OGu) **fyrning** (OSw) noun

betrothal gift **OSw** *UL* Äb, *VmL* Äb

gift **OSw** *HL* Äb

guest's contribution to a meal **OGu** *GL* A 24

förumannaflutningr (ON) noun

poor person **OIce** *Jó* Kge 29 Llb 7

See also: *afrapalas*, *göngukona*, *göngumaðr*,
húsgangr, *húsgangsmaðr*, *hæraþspiækker*, *stafkarl*

förumannaförsla (ON) noun

indigent person **OIce** *Jó* Kge 33

See also: *afrapalas*, *göngukona*, *göngumaðr*,
húsgangr, *húsgangsmaðr*, *hæraþspiækker*, *stafkarl*

föruneyti (ON) noun

armed escort **OIce** *Jó* Mah 20

föstuafbrigð (ON) noun

neglecting a fast **OIce** *KRA* 30

föstuafbrot (ON) noun

fast infraction **OIce** *KRA* 30

föþa (OSw) **fyþa** (OGu) **fyþa** (OGu) **fózla** (ON) verb

bear **OGu** *GL* A 2, 20a, **OSw** *UL* StfBM,
Kkb, Äb, Mb, Rb, *VmL* Kkb, Äb, Mb, Rb

bring up **OGu** *GL* A 20a

feed **OGu** *GL* A 42, 56a, **OSw** *UL* Kmb, *VmL* Kmb

give birth to **OSw** *UL* Kkb

keep **OSw** *UL* Jb, *VmL* Jb

provide for **OSw** *UL* Jb, *VmL* Jb

raise **OGu** *GL* A 20a, **OSw** *UL* Äb, Mb, *VmL* Äb, Mb

support **OGu** *GL* A 20

See also: *uppihalda*

föþa (OSw) noun

fodder **OSw** *UL* Jb, *VmL* Jb

food **OGu** *GL* A 20, **ONorw** *GuL* Krb,
Mhb, **OSw** *UL* Äb, *VmL* Äb

maintenance **ONorw** *GuL* Krb, Mhb

upkeep **OSw** *UL* Kkb, Äb, Jb, Kmb,
VmL Kkb, Äb, Jb, Kmb

fóra (ON) verb

Expressions:

fóra aftr (ON)

make restitution **OIce** *Jó* Llb 15

fóra fram (ON)

announce **OIce** *Js* Kvg 2

maintain **OIce** *Grg* Þsþ 39 Vís 111 *Js* Lbb 9 *KRA* 14

fórask undan (ON)

to acquit oneself of a charge **OIce** *Js*
Mah 11 Þjb 9 *Jó* Mah 9 *KRA* 2

to clear oneself **OIce** *Jó* Þjb 19

to free oneself **ONorw** *FrL* KrbA 1

fóri (ON) **færi** (ON) noun

means **OIce** *Grg* Þsþ 39

fórr (ON) adj.

seaworthy **ONorw** *GuL* Tfb, Leb

gagn (ON) **gögn** (ON) noun

Proof, evidence; the men who give such proof during
legal proceedings. A definition of what constitutes
proof is not given in any of the Icelandic or Norwegian
laws, but throughout Grg it seems to refer to formal
oaths sworn by neighbors or witnesses to an event.
However in Js, *KRA* and Jó the term is employed in
the phrase *vitni ok gögn* ('testimonies and proofs')

suggesting that other types of proof may have been admissible.

evidence **ONorw** *FrL* Jkb 2, *GuL* Løb, Arb, Olb

formal means of proof **OIce** *Grg* Þsþ 23, 31 Vís 106, 107 Arþ 125 Feþ 149, 167 Lbþ 176, 202 Fjl 221, 223 Misc 238, *Jó* Þfb 4 Kge 19, *Js* Kab 2, *KRA* 34

See also: *vatter*, *vitni*

Refs: CV; F; ONP

gagnagagn (ON) **gagnagögn** (ON) noun

attestation that formal means of proof have been produced **OIce** *Grg* Þsþ 58, 59

gagngjald (ON) noun

The *gagngjald* or *tilgjöf* ('bridal gift', 'husband's gift') was given by the bridegroom to the bride as a 'donatio propter nuptias' (lit. 'gift because of marriage'). The size of the *gagngjald* was to be in a fixed relation to the size of the *heimanfylgja* (see *hemfylghþ*).

bridal gift **OIce** *Jó* Kge 13, *Js* Ert 19, **ONorw** *GuL* Kvb, Arb

husband's gift **ONorw** *GuL* Kvb, Arb

See also: *hemfylghþ*, *tilgæf*

Refs: Helle 2001, 139; Hertzberg s.v. *gagngjald*; KLNM s.v.v. *enke, festermål, medgift, ægteskab*; Robberstad 1981, 348, 361

gagnkvöð (ON) noun

A counter-summons. Mentioned in Grg Vís 104 in the context of two parties to a case summoning the same neighbors. Fritzner has interpreted this as a method by which one party can weaken or nullify the summons of the opposition party.

counter-calling **OIce** *Grg* Vís 104

See also: *kvöð*

Refs: CV s.v. *gagnkvöð*; Fritzner s.v. *gagnkvöð*

gagnsök (ON) noun

counter-suit **OIce** *Grg* Tíg 259

galdr (ON) **galdrar** (pl.) (ON) noun

sorcery **ONorw** *GuL* Krb

spell **OIce** *Grg* Klþ 7

See also: *gærning*

galghi (OSw) noun

Etymologically '(flexible) branch' and closely related to a word meaning 'pole'. An implement for execution by hanging appearing in the expression *galghæ ællr gren* 'gallows or branch'. The construction consisted of up to three posts with horizontal beams.

gibbet **OSw** *UL* Mb, *VmL* Mb

Refs: Ambrius 1996, 38–39; Bjorvand and Lindeman 2000, s.v. *galge*; Hellquist s.v. *galge*; KLNM s.v.v. *dødsstraf, galge o. galgbacke*

galgnár (ON) noun

gallows-corpse **OIce** *Grg* Bat 113

galin (OSw) **galen** (ODan) adj.

insane **ODan** *ESjL* 3

mad **ODan** *ESjL* 2, **OSw** *HL* Mb, *SdmL* Mb, *YVgL* Drb, *ÄVgL* Md

See also: *afvita*, *örr*

galter (OSw) **galtr** (OGu) noun

boar **OGu** *GL* A 17, **OSw** *VmL* Mb, Bb

See also: *fargalter*

gamal (OSw) **gambli** (OSw) adj.

customary **OSw** *UL* Mb, Blb, *VmL* Bb

Expressions:

fornt ok gamalt (OSw)

from time immemorial OSw *UL* Jb

See also: *byrþ, forn, aldaoþal*

ganga (OSw) **ganga** (OGu) **gangas** (OGu) **ganga** (ON) **gangas** (OSw) verb

execute (e.g. an oath) **OSw** *UL* Kkb, Jb, Blb, Rb, *VmL* Mb, Jb, Bb, Rb

go **ONorw** *GuL* Kpb

present **OGu** *GL* A 25, **OSw** *UL* Mb

satisfy **OSw** *UL* Kkb

take (e.g. an oath) **OGu** *GL* A 2

be taken **OSw** *UL* Kkb, Mb, Jb, Rb

become a vagrant **OIce** *Grg* Ómb 128, 143 Hrs 234

be without sons **OGu** *GL* A 20

Expressions:

ganga atr (OGu)

abandon **OGu** *GL* A 2

ganga undan, ganga ondan (OSw)

defend oneself **OSw** *VmL* Mb, Bb

ganga viþr (OGu, OSw)

admit **OGu** *GL* A 2, 19 **OSw** *UL* Äb, Mb, Kmb, Blb *VmL* Mb, Kmb, Blb

confess **OGu** *GL* A 37

See also: *fylla, gangare, standa*

ganganzfoter (OSw) noun

livestock **OSw** *DL* Bb, Rb

ganganzfæ (OSw) noun

livestock **OSw** *DL* Bb, *HL* Rb

gangare (OSw) noun

ambler **OSw** *VmL* Bb

gangdagahelgr (ON) noun

Rogation Days **ONorw** *GuL* Krb

See also: *gangdagher, helgavika*

gangdagher (OSw) gangdaghar (pl.) (OGu) gangdagr (OGu) gangdagar (pl.) (ON) gangdagr (ON) noun
Rogation Day **OIce** *KRA* 24, **ONorw** *FrL* KrbA 31
Rogation Days **OGu** *GL* A 8, **ONorw** *GuL* Krb, Kpb
Expressions:
gangdagher litli (OSw)
minor walking day **OSw** HL *Rb*
See also: *gangdagahelgr*

gangearv (ODan) noun
common inheritance **ODan** *ESjL*
1, *SkL* 34, 36, *VSjL* 1, 20

gangfempni (OGu) noun
ability to walk **OGu** *GL* B 19

gangklepi (OGu) noun
walking-clothes **OGu** *GL* A 20
See also: *ivirklæpi*

gangr (OGu) noun
path **OGu** *GL* A 27
See also: *gata*

gangsilfr (ON) noun
circulating silver **OIce** *Jó* Kge 18

garðafar (ON) noun
fencing **ONorw** *FrL* LlbA 18

garðbrjótr (ON) noun
fence-breaker **OIce** *Jó* Llb 31, *Js*
Lbb 20, **ONorw** *GuL* Llb

garðfóðr (ON) noun
fodder from the farm **ONorw** *GuL* Llb

garðlag (ON) noun
walling work **OIce** *Grg* Lbþ 177, *Jó* Llb 54

garðlagsstefna (ON) noun
appointed times for walling work **OIce** *Jó* Llb 54
See also: *stæmna*

garðlauss (ON) adj.
without a fence **ONorw** *GuL* Krb

garðsbóndi (ON) noun
landlord **OIce** *Jó* Kge 18

garðskifti (ON) garðskipti (ON) noun
partition by a fence **ONorw** *GuL* Llb
wall division **OIce** *Js* Lbb 22

garðsmögull (ON) adj.
crawling through fences **ONorw** *GuL* Llb

garðstaurr (ON) noun
fence post **ONorw** *GuL* Llb, Mhb
See also: *staurgulf*

garðönn (ON) noun
walling work-season **OIce** *Grg* Lbþ 181, *Jó* Llb 54

garthgang (ODan) noun
farm-trespassing **ODan** *ESjL* 3
trespass **ODan** *ESjL* 2
See also: *aganga*, *bothegang*, *hemsokn*, *hærværk*, *landnám*

garthsæte (ODan) noun
tenant **ODan** *JyL* 1, *VSjL* 87
See also: *landboe*

garþadeld (OSw) noun
fence allotment **OSw** *SdmL* Bb

garþafall (OSw) noun
neglect of fences **OSw** *SdmL* Jb
neglected maintenance of fences **OSw** HL Blb

garþasyn (OSw) garþar syn (OSw) noun
fence inspection **OSw** *DL* Bb

garþaviti (OSw) noun
compensations for fences **OSw** *YVgL* Utgb

garþer (OSw) garth (ODan) garþr (OGu) garðr (ON) gærþer (OSw) noun
It is often unfeasible to distinguish between the main meanings, 'fence, barrier' and 'enclosed land', which is an ambiguity that can be traced back to the etymological origin of *garþer*. By extension *garþer* also may refer to the houses themselves — of various size and stature — and/or to the open space enclosed by those houses.
dam **OIce** *Jó* Llb 56
enclosure **OGu** *GL* A 24f (64), 25, **OIce** *Grg* Rsþ 230, **ONorw** *BorgL* 9.1, *EidsL* 38.2
estate **OIce** *Jó* Kge 13, *Js* Ert 19, *KRA* 15, **ONorw** *GuL* Arb
farm **ODan** *ESjL* 2, 3, *JyL* 2, 3, *SkL* 6, *VSjL* 56, 65, 86, **OGu** *GL* A 12, 13, 16, 17, 20, 27, 37, 39, 50, 56, 65, Add. 7, 8 (B 49, 55), *GS* Ch. 3, **OIce** *Jó* Mah 3, **ONorw** *EidsL* 27.6, *GuL* Mhb, **OSw** *DL* Eb, Gb, Rb, *HL* Kkb, Kgb, Äb, Mb, Jb, Kmb, Blb, Rb, *SdmL* Kgb, Gb, Bb, Kmb, Mb, Tjdb, Rb, *SmL*, *UL* Kgb, Äb, Mb, Kmb, Blb, Rb, *VmL* Kgb, Äb, Mb, Jb, Kmb, Bb, Rb, *YVgL* Kkb, Äb, Gb, Tb, Föb, Add, *ÄVgL* Slb, Äb, Gb, Jb, Tb, *ÖgL* Eb, Db
farm estate **OGu** *GL* A 20
farm unit **ODan** *JyL* 3
farmstead **ODan** *ESjL* 2, **OSw** *YVgL* Tb, Add, *ÖgL* Eb, Db
farmyard **OSw** *DL* Eb, Mb, *UL* Kgb, Mb, Blb, *VmL* Kgb, Mb, Jb
fence **ODan** *ESjL* 2, 3, *JyL* 1, 3, *SkL* 167, 186, *VSjL* 58, 74, **OGu** *GL* A 7, 9, 24f (64), 25, 26, 35, 63, **OIce** *Jó* Mah 2 Lbb 3, **ONorw** *FrL* KrbA 13 Rgb 41 LlbA

2, *GuL* Krb, Kpb, Llb, Tfb, Kvr, Mhb, Tjb, Olb, **OSw**
DL Bb, Tjdb, *HL* Jb, Blb, *SdmL* Kkb, Jb, Bb, Till, *UL*
Kkb, Mb, Jb, Blb, *VmL* Kkb, Mb, Jb, Bb, *YVgL* Kkb,
Urb, Rlb, Jb, Föb, Utgb, Add, *ÄVgL* Rlb, Jb, Fös, Föb

hay-yard **OIce** *Jó* Llb 9

home **ONorw** *GuL* Tfb

home field **OFar** *Seyð* 5

homestead **OIce** *Jó* Kab 9, **OSw**
DL Eb, Mb, Bb, Gb, Rb

house **ODan** *ESjL* 2, *JyL* 1–3

manor **ODan** *SkL* 172

place **ODan** *ESjL* 2

plantation **OSw** *VmL* Kkb, Bb

premises **OIce** *Grg* Arþ 125, *Jó* Kge 18

residence **OSw** *UL* Jb, *VmL* Jb

trap **OSw** *SdmL* Bb

wall **OIce** *Grg* Þsþ 48 Lbþ 175 Fjl 222 Hrs 234, *Jó*
Lbb 3 Llb 31 Þjb 6, *Js* Lbb 22, **ONorw** *EidsL* 38.1

yard **OIce** *Grg* Rsþ 230, *Js* Lbb 22 Þjb 5, **ONorw**
FrL LlbA 1, *GuL* Krb, Olb, **OSw** *HL* Mb, *SdmL* Mb

Expressions:

lagha garþer (OSw)

Defined as to the construction and size with
differences for those surrounding an OSw *aker*
('field') or an OSw *æng* ('meadow') (cp. *laghegarth*).

legal fence **OSw** *HL* Blb

miþal garþr (OGu)

fence between fields or meadows **OGu** *GL* A 25

See also: *bo, bol, byr, garthgang, garþsliþ,
gærþi, haghi, hemsokn, humbli, jorþ,
staur, tompt, túnvöllr, værn, þorp*

Refs: Adams 1976, s.v. *settlement*; CV s.v.
garðr; Helle 2001, 106–16; Hellquist [1948]
1964, s.v. *gård*; KLNM s.v. *gård*; Pellijeff
1967; Schlyter 1877, s.v. *garþer*.

garþsliþ (OSw) garthslith (ODan) garðahlið (ON)
garöshlið (ON) noun

border of a farm **OSw** *YVgL* Add

farm **ODan** *ESjL* 3

farmgate **ODan** *VSjL* 86, **OSw** *DL* Eb

farmstead **OSw** *YVgL* Drb, *ÖgL* Eb

fence of a farm **ODan** *ESjL* 3, **OSw** *YVgL* Add

gate **ONorw** *GuL* Llb

gate of a farm's fence **OSw** *YVgL* Kkb, *ÄVgL* Kkb

gate of a farmstead **ODan** *ESjL* 2,
OSw *YVgL* Drb, *ÄVgL* Md

gate to a house **ODan** *JyL* 2

See also: *garþer, grind, hyrnustokker, liþ (1)*

garþsvirki (OGu) garzvirki (OGu) noun

fencing wood **OGu** *GL* A 26

See also: *troþr*

gas (OSw) gas (OGu) noun

goose **OGu** *GL* A 26, **OSw** *UL* Kkb,
Kgb, Blb, *VmL* Kkb, Bb

gassaglópr (ON) noun

goose's crime **ONorw** *GuL* Mhb

gata (OSw) gate (ODan) gata (OGu) gata (ON) noun

gauntlet **ONorw** *GuL* Tjb

highway **OIce** *Jó* Llb 44 Þjb 14

path **OGu** *GL* A 19, 24f (64), **OIce** *Jó* Llb 58

road **ODan** *ESjL* 2, *VSjL* 71, **OGu** *GL* A 19,
26, 27, **OIce** *Grg* Þsþ 52, *Jó* Llb 21 Þjb 12,
Js Lbb 19, **ONorw** *FrL* Rgb 16 LlbB 15,
GuL Llb, Tfb, Mhb, **OSw** *DL* Mb, *UL* Mb,
Blb, *VmL* Mb, Bb, *YVgL* Jb, *ÄVgL* Jb

street **ODan** *ESjL* 2, *SkL* 67, **ONorw** *GuL* Løb

track **OGu** *GL* A 27, **OIce** *Grg* Misc 239

See also: *broa, eriksgata, farvægher,
sörgata, ta, vægher, þjóðvegr*

gatelith (ODan) noun

street gate **ODan** *ESjL* 2

See also: *gata*

gatestævne (ODan) noun

village assembly **ODan** *SkL* 82

village meeting **ODan** *ESjL* 2, *SkL* 148

See also: *gata, stæmna*

gatnamót (ON) noun

crossroads **ONorw** *GuL* Mhb

geil (ON) noun

gauntlet **ONorw** *FrL* LlbB 12

geirskaft (ON) geirskapt (ON) noun

spearshaft **ONorw** *GuL* Llb

See also: *spjótskaft*

geldfé (ON) noun

dry stock **OIce** *Jó* Llb 53

non-milking stock **OIce** *Grg* Lbþ 203

geldfjárrekstr (ON) noun

managing pasture for dry stock **OIce** *Jó* Llb 46

geneþer (OSw) noun

counteroath **OSw** *SdmL* Till, *YVgL* Add

genfasta (OSw) gagnfasta (ON) noun

See *fasta* (noun).

pre-fast day **OSw** *HL* Rb

*preparatory fast (beginning at
Septuagesima)* **ONorw** *GuL* Krb

gengærþ (OSw) **gingerþ** (OGu) **gengiærþ** (OSw)
gingærþ (OSw) noun

Originally a collective contribution of food for the
support of a visiting king, bishop or official and their
following, which was transformed into a permanent
tax.

billeting **OSw** *UL* Kmb, *VmL* Kmb,
YVgL Kkb, Föb, *ÄVgL* Kkb

hospitality **OSw** *HL* Rb, *SmL*, *ÖgL* Kkb

payment in kind **OGu** *GS* Ch. 3, **OSw** *UL* Kkb

provision of food **OSw** *SdmL* Kkb, Kgb, Kmb

See also: *gengöra*, *gærþ*, *gæstning*,
matgærþ, *stuþ*, *utgærþ*, *væzla*

Refs: Förvaltningshistorisk ordbok, s.v.
gengärd; KLNM, s.v.v. *gengärd*, *gärder*,
gästning; Lindkvist 2011, 270

gengöra (OSw) verb

give billeting **OSw** *YVgL* Jb

provide hospitality **OSw** *SmL*

See also: *gengærþ*

genmæli (OSw) **ginmeli** (OGu) noun

denial **OSw** *YVgL* Rlb

dissent **OSw** *UL* StfBM

excuse **OGu** *GL* A 56a

See also: *ginmela*

gerðarmark (ON) noun

made-up mark **OIce** *Jó* Llb 48

See also: *kaupamark*

gerþamaþr (OGu) **gierþamaþr** (OGu) **gerðarmaðr**
(ON) noun

arbitrator **OIce** *Grg* Misc 244

master of the feast **OGu** *GL* A 24

See also: *drozsieti*, *reþuman*

gesterfð (ON) noun

guest's inheritance **ONorw** *GuL* Arb

gestfeðri (ON) noun

Refers specifically to someone who has died while
lodging with someone else and has no known heirs. A
person who was a *gestfeðri* was permitted to give away
their property before they died or through a testament
(*gjaferð*), but if no such testament was made, the
householder would be entitled to inherit the property
of the deceased up to a certain amount (six *eyrir*
according to Js Ert 17 and FrL ArbB 5). If the heirless
person owned more property than this, it was to be
split into equal shares between the householder and
the king. Regardless the householder was obligated to
wait for three years in case an heir was made known.

The same procedure was applicable to a person who
has died on another's land or ship.

The term *gestfeðri* and related nomenclature
appears only infrequently in the laws, so it is unclear
whether it refers to a specific type of person or a
description of an individual. Earlier dictionaries class
it as a noun, whereas the ONP has elected to identify
it as an adjective.

heirless man **OIce** *Js* Ert 17

person with no heirs **ONorw** *FrL* ArbB 3

See also: *gesterfð*, *gjaferð*

Refs: Brandt 1880; CV; F; NGL
V s.v. *gestfeðra*; ONP

get (OSw) **gait** (OGu) **geit** (ON) noun

goat **ONorw** *GuL* Mhb, **OSw** *UL*
Mb, Blb, *VmL* Mb, Bb

nanny-goat **OGu** *GL* A 45, **OSw** *UL* Blb, *VmL* Bb

geymslufé (ON) noun

goods in storage **OIce** *Jó* Þjb 15

giefa (OGu) verb

exchange **OGu** *GL* A 65

leave **OGu** *GL* A 7

pay **OGu** *GL* A 3

gieldeti (OGu) noun

debt **OGu** *GL* A 17, 30

See also: *gæld*

gift (OSw) **gift** (ODan) **gift** (ON) **gipt** (OSw) noun

dowry **OSw** *HL* Äb

gift **ODan** *ESjL* 1, **OSw** *ÄVgL* Kkb

income **ONorw** *BorgL* 10.4

marriage **ODan** *SkL* 46, 219, **OSw**
YVgL Äb, Gb, Add, *ÄVgL* Gb

oblation **ONorw** *BorgL* 12.12

tenancy **OSw** *HL* Jb, *SdmL* Jb

tenancy payment **OSw** *SdmL* Jb, *UL* Jb, *VmL* Äb, Jb

wedding **OSw** *YVgL* Kkb

See also: *fylghia*, *gæf*, *hemfylghþ*, *mæþfylghþ*

gifta (OSw) **gifte** (ODan) **gipta** (OGu) **gifta** (ON) **gipta**
(OSw) **gipta** (OGu) **gipta** (OSw) verb

give **OSw** *YVgL* Kkb

give as wife **OSw** *ÄVgL* Gb

give in marriage **OGu** *GL* A 20,
OSw *DL* Gb, *UL* Äb, *VmL* Äb

marry **ODan** *JyL* 1, *VSjL* 1, **OGu** *GL* A 20, 21,
28, 65, **OIce** *Js* Kvg 1, 3, *KRA* 17, **ONorw** *EidsL*
22.3 23.1, *FrL* KrbB 22 Kvb 2, **OSw** *HL* Äb,
SdmL Gb, Äb, *UL* Äb, Mb, Jb, *VmL* Äb, Mb,
YVgL Kkb, Äb, Gb, Add, *ÄVgL* Äb, Gb, *ÖgL* Eb

marry away **ODan** *ESjL* 1

marry off **ODan** *ESjL* 1, 3

put out to tenancy **OSw** *SdmL* Jb, *UL* Jb, *VmL* Jb

take tenancy **OSw** *SdmL* Jb

Expressions:

gifta undan (OSw)

release to someone's detriment **OSw** *DL* Bb

See also: *ainloypr, ogipter, brullöp, giftarmal, vighning, vigsl*

gifta (OSw) noun

marriage **OGu** *GL* A 65, **OSw** *DL* Gb, *HL* Äb, *SdmL* Gb, *UL* Äb, *VmL* Äb, *YVgL* Äb, *ÄVgL* Äb

wedding **OGu** *GL* A 24d

giftarmal (OSw) giftemal (OSw) giftningamal (OSw) giptar mal (OSw) noun

marriage **OSw** *HL* Äb, *SdmL* Gb, *UL* För, Kkb, Äb, *VmL* För, Kkb, Äb, *YVgL* Gb, Add

marriage ceremony **OSw** *HL* Äb

matrimony **OSw** *UL* Äb, *VmL* Äb, *YVgL* Add

See also: *giftarorþ, giptning*

giftarmaþer (OSw) giftingarmaðr (ON) gifftarman (OSw) giftarman (OSw) giptarmaþer (OSw) giptninga maþer (OSw) noun

This was the man or woman in the woman's family circle responsible for organizing her marriage. He or she was her 'marriage agent', a matchmaker, in fact, receiving the *fæstnaþa fæ* ('betrothal price') in return. Usually her father, it would be a close family member if he were dead. According to UL and VmL, the right passed to her mother, then brothers, then sisters and so on, according to the inheritance rules. That the 'marriage-man' had to be the father or mother (or else nearest paternal, then maternal kinsman) is also specified in OIce law (Jó Kge 1). In ONorw law, FrL (Kvb 2), however, a third person (i.e. not the parents), the *giftingarmaðr*, had to be present at the instigation of a marriage agreement. A detailed exposition of the proceedings is given in VmL, although similar procedures and stipulations are recorded in ONorw and OIce laws as well as other OSw provincial laws. The *giftarmaþer* had to resist the temptation to accept payment from more than one suitor. In this case, it seems that the giver of the price paid a fine, although the text is unclear. He certainly paid a fine if he paid the price to his intended wife and she had not obtained permission for the betrothal. If the betrothal were broken by the woman (or presumably her side of the relationship), the price had to be returned, together with any other gifts received from the fiancé. If, on the other hand, the man broke the betrothal, he forfeited the betrothal price and any gifts he had given. In addition, there was a compensation payment to be made, even in situations where the betrothal had been broken after the Church had judged the betrothal to be unlawful (either due to consanguinity or other kinds of forbidden relationships). Fines pertaining to the marriage-man are similarly mentioned in FrL KrbB 1 (three marks for accepting property during a pending case of hindrances to marriage). If an unmarried woman was seized and taken out of the province by force, the *giftarmaþer* had the power to bring the offender back under the rule of law (UL, VmL). If an unmarried woman entered into a betrothal or marriage without that person's permission, she lost her inheritance and might be subject to other strictures. In that case, her parents and not the *giftarmaþer* were entitled to forgive her, if they wished. This seems to confirm that in certain cases, even if her parents were alive, someone else might act as a woman's *giftarmaþer* (but this is not clarified in UL or VmL). If someone unauthorised gave her away in marriage, that person was subject to a fine as punishment for the loss of the betrothal price to the *giftarmaþer* (UL). If, when the bridegroom went to claim his bride, he were refused, the *giftarmaþer* could incur a fine, as well as paying the groom's expenses. In addition, it seems that, certainly in the OIce laws, the *giftingarmaðr* was responsible for the woman's dowry, as the passage quoted above prohibits the heir of the *giftingarmaðr* from rescinding the dowry (also supported by a 1294 amendment to Jó stipulating that women who marry without consent forfeit their dowry from the *giftingarmaðr*). The concept of someone 'giving the bride away' for a sum of money or other consideration seems to hint at marriage by purchase referring back to a pre-Christian practice.

betrothal man **OSw** *HL* Äb, *ÖgL* Vm

man authorized to give away a woman **ONorw** *FrL* Kvb 2

marriage agent **OSw** *UL* Kgb, Äb, *VmL* Kgb, Äb

marriage guardian **OSw** *SdmL* Kkb, Kgb, Gb, Äb, *YVgL* Kkb, Add

marriage man **OIce** *Jó* Kge 1, *Js* Kvg 1, 3, **ONorw** *FrL* KrbB 1, **OSw** *HL* Kgb

right person to give the bride away **OSw** *DL* Gb

See also: *forrædismaðr, fæsta, fæstning, hömtaman, vingæf*

Refs: KLNM s.v.v. enke, festermål, forskiliaman, Ægteskab; Korpiola 2004; Lexikon des Mittelalters, s.v. ehe; Schlyter 1877, s.v. giftarmaþer; SL UL, 77–78 notes 2–4; SL VmL, 56 note 5; Vogt 2010.

giftarorþ (OSw) **gifterorth** (ODan) **giptarorþ** (OSw)
noun

marriage **ODan** *ESjL* 1, *JyL* 2,
OSw *SdmL* Gb, *VmL* Äb

See also: *giftarmal*, *giptning*

giftaröl (OSw) **giptar öl** (OSw) noun

marriage beer **OSw** *YVgL* Drb, *ÄVgL* Md

See also: *brullöp*, *gifta*, *öl*

giftastæmna (OSw) **gifftarstæmna** (OSw)
giftarstæmna (OSw) **giptastæmna** (OSw)
giptostæmna (OSw) noun

tenancy period **OSw** *UL* Jb, *VmL* Jb

See also: *bolaghsstæmpna*, *stæmna*

giftasæng (OSw) **giptasæng** (OSw) noun

marriage **OSw** *DL* Gb

marriage bed **OSw** *VmL* Äb

See also: *gifta*, *siang*

gifter (OSw) **gift** (ODan) adj.

married **ODan** *SkL* 60, **OSw** *HL* Kkb, Äb, *SdmL*
Kkb, *SmL*, *YVgL* Kkb, Äb, Add, *ÄVgL* Äb, *ÖgL* Vm

giftingardagr (ON) noun

wedding day **OIce** *Jó* Kge 3, *Js* Kvg 2

gilda (OSw) verb

be compensated **OSw** *DL* Mb, *ÖgL* Eb

be responsible for upkeep **OSw** *DL* Bb

be subject to compensation **OSw** *DL* Tjdb

value for fines **OSw** *SdmL* Mb

gilder (OSw) **gild** (ODan) **gildr** (ON) adj.

Etymologically related to the verb *gælda* 'to pay (for);
to be worth'. The many translations might be summed
up as '(worth) being paid (for) or used as payment and
thus (legally) approved'. Used of 1) (the worth/value
of) the victim's — or their damaged possession's —
right to) compensation; and 2) (the worth/value of) the
criminal's obligation to pay (a fine/compensation); as
well as of 3) the status of being in accordance with
the law, specifically concerning inanimate objects. A
possible grouping, with some overlap, is thus 1) used
of victims receiving compensation in translations
such as 'compensated', 'entitled to compensation/
payment', 'valued (for fines)', (and possibly
'permitted to be revenged'); 2) used of criminals
paying a fine or compensation 'valued (for fines)'; and
3) used of inanimate objects, fences, houses etc., in
translations such as 'valid', 'adequate', 'satisfactory',
'serviceable', 'useable', 'binding', 'in accordance
with law', 'legal(ly qualified)'.

adequate **OSw** *DL* Bb

as good as **OSw** *DL* Bb

binding **OSw** *UL* Blb, *VmL* Bb

compensated **ONorw** *FrL* Var 14, **OSw**
DL Mb, *HL* Blb, *UL* Kkb, Mb, Blb,
VmL Kkb, Mb, Bb, *ÖgL* Kkb, Db

entitled to compensation **OSw** *DL* Mb

entitled to payment **ODan** *SkL* 170

in a good state **OSw** *HL* Blb

in accordance with law **OIce** *Jó* Llb 32

in good repair **OSw** *YVgL* Kkb

in order **OSw** *YVgL* Jb, Föb, Utgb

legal **OSw** *DL* Rb

legally qualified **OSw** *HL* Jb

obliged to pay compensation **OSw** *ÖgL* Eb

permitted to be revenged **OSw** *DL* Eb

satisfactory **ONorw** *GuL* Llb

serviceable **OSw** *UL* Blb, *VmL* Bb

usable **OSw** *ÄVgL* Kkb

valid **OIce** *Grg* Fjl 221, *Js* Lbb 20, **ONorw** *FrL* LlbA
21, **OSw** *DL* Mb, Rb, *HL* Kkb, Jb, Rb, *SdmL* Äb, Bb,
Kmb, Rb, Till, *UL* Jb, Kmb, Rb, Add. 1, *VmL* Äb,
Mb, Kmb, Bb, Rb, *YVgL* Drb, Jb, Add, *ÄVgL* Jb, Föb

valued **OSw** *SdmL* Kkb, Kgb, Äb, Bb, Mb

valued at **OIce** *Grg* Vís 102

valued for fines **OSw** *SdmL* Mb

worth a certain payment in fine **OSw** *HL* Kkb

See also: *liggia*, *ogilder*

Refs: Clcasby and Vigfússon s.v. *gildr*; Fritzner,
s.v.v. *gildr*, *gjalda*; Hellquist s.v.v. *gill*, *giltig*,
gäld, *gälla*; Hertzberg s.v. *gildr*; Ruthström 1990;
OED s.v. *yield* (verb); SAOB s.v.v. *gill*, *gilla*,
gälda, *gälla*; Schlyter s.v. *gilda*, *gilder*, *gælda*

gildi (OSw) noun

compensation **OSw** *DL* Bb, *ÖgL* Db

value **OSw** *SdmL* Kgb, Gb, Bb, Mb

gildingr (ON) noun

In a legal context only appearing in Grg, where it
is understood to refer to an object of sufficient size
and value. In Grg Lbþ 211 and Grg Lbþ 216 the term
applies to fish. In Grg Lbþ 211 the *gildingr* seems
to have been considered as a unit of measurement
for considering the range of offshore fishing rights.
Dufeau (forthcoming) suggests that the term implies
an object of great value and therefore a nascent
concept of commercial fishing in Iceland.

item of full value **OIce** *Grg* Lbþ 211, 216

See also: *fiskhelgr*

Refs: CV s.v. *gildingr*; Dufeu forthcoming;
Fritzner s.v. *gildingr*; GrgTr II:142

gildra (OSw) **gildra** (ON) verb

contrive deceitfully **OIce** *Grg* Vís 108

lay a trap **OSw** *DL* Bb

set a trap **OSw** *SdmL* Bb

trap **ONorw** *FrL* LlbA 7

gildri (OSw) **gildre** (ODan) **gildri** (OGu) **gildra** (ON) noun

gin (trap) **OGu** *GL* A 58, **OSw** *UL* Blb, *VmL* Mb, Bb

trap **ODan** *SkL* 205, **ONorw** *GuL* Llb, **OSw** *HL* Blb, *SdmL* Bb, Mb

See also: *stilli*

gilia (OSw) verb

seduce **OSw** *DL* Gb

gilzl (OSw) noun

Safe conduct and peace to, during and from the *þing* 'assembly'. Alternatively interpreted as a form of *gisli* 'hostage', which in OSw appears in the context of *eriksgata* (q.v.).

security **OSw** *SmL*

See also: *gisli*, *griþ*

Refs: Dovring 1947a; Fridell forthcoming; Hasselberg 1948; SL SmL 423; Schlyter s.v. *gisli*

ginmela (OGu) verb

refuse **OGu** *GL* A 56a

giolsæmi (OSw) noun

adultery **OSw** *DL* Mb

See also: *hor*

giptarbalker (OSw) **gipta balker** (OSw) **giptninga balker** (OSw) noun

book about marriage **OSw** *YVgL* Gb, *ÄVgL* Gb

book concerning matrimony **OSw** *DL* Gb

marriage section **OSw** *SdmL* För, Gb

See also: *balker*, *gifta*

giptareþer (OSw) noun

marriage oath **OSw** *SdmL* Till

giptning (OSw) **gifting** (ON) noun

marriage **OIce** *Jó* Kge 1, *Js* Kvg 1, 4, **ONorw** *FrL* Kvb 2, **OSw** *DL* Gb, *SdmL* Gb, *VmL* Äb

See also: *giftarmal*, *giftarorþ*

gisli (OSw) **gísl** (ON) noun

The concept of hostage occurred in three contexts: 1 a) when war was imminent, and b) in wartime or war-like situations; 2) when guarantors were needed to secure payment of debts etc.; 3) in connection with royal elections.

1 a) According to the Leb of GuL (ch. 312) the king was allowed to take some of his men as hostages when war was imminent and he had reason to doubt the loyalty of his men. If a man refused to let himself be taken as hostage he was *eo ipso* guilty of treason (GuL ibid.). However, if people remained loyal and provided good defence, the king had to return the hostages unhurt, at the latest when a hostile fleet had been out of sight for five nights.

b) If people had been taken prisoners they were often treated as hostages, who could only be released by ransom (see, e.g., GuL ch. 201). The size and character of the ransom varied and was the subject of discussion, including questions about who was to pay, and how, etc. See the lengthy description in GL (A 28).

2) The OSw laws contained provisions about *borghan* and *gilzl* (bail, security, etc.). A person functioning as a hostage was to guarantee that certain obligations were met, be it offences, deals, or debts. An offender had to provide hostages to secure the execution of punishment (personal, social or economic) if he himself was not capable of paying the penalty. If a man had contracted debts, he was in his capacity as debtor also a hostage. Hostages enjoyed a special protection by the law (cf. OSw *gislingabrut*, 'captives' crime', and *gislingalagh*, 'law of captives') against abduction. On hostages in law texts, see Olsson 2016, 35−36, 206−09, 281−88, 347−68.

3) The procedure prior to royal elections in Sweden implied the use of hostages. On his journey through the central provinces, the so-called *eriksgata*, the prince who was to be elected king had to be escorted by four men, chosen anew from one province to another, so as to secure that the right person was elected king.

hostage **ONorw** *GuL* Leb, **OSw** *SdmL* Kgb, *UL* Kgb, Mb, *YVgL* Rlb, *ÄVgL* Rlb

See also: *gilzl*, *gísla*

Refs: KLNM s.v.v. *borgen*, *eriksgata*, *gisslan*; Olsson 2016; RGA2 s.v.v. *bürgschaft*, *geisel*; Schlyter s.v.v. *gisli*, *gislingabrut*, *gislingalagh*

gislingabrut (OSw) noun

captives crime **OSw** *ÖgL* Db

gislingalagh (OSw) noun

law of captives **OSw** *ÖgL* Db

gisningaek (OSw) noun

acorn oak **OSw** *SdmL* Bb

gisningaskogher (OSw) noun

acorn woodland **OSw** *SdmL* Bb

See also: *akern*, *aldin*, *ek*

giva (OSw) verb

Expressions:

viþ givas (OSw)

concern oneself with **OSw** *UL* Jb

See also: *kæra*, *sak*, *sökia*, *tiltala*

gísla (ON) verb

take or give as hostages **ONorw** *GuL* Leb

See also: *gisli*

gjafamark (ON) noun

given mark **OIce** *Jó* Llb 48

See also: *erfðamark, kaupamark*

gjaferfð (ON) noun

inheritance by gift **ONorw** *GuL* Arb

gjaldandi (ON) noun

debtor **OIce** *Jó* Kab 23

payer **OIce** *Grg* Fjl 221

gjalddagi (ON) noun

payment day **OIce** *Grg* Klþ 2, 5 Arþ 122 Lbþ 172, 192 Misc 244, 249, *Jó* Lbb 11 Kab 23

gjaldgengr (ON) adj.

valid as a form of payment **OIce** *Grg* Misc 246

gjavstuth (ODan) noun

An additional gift that the king's *bryte* (ODan) 'bailiff' could ask for — but not demand — when collecting legal taxes (*laghæ stuth*). Failing to provide this gift could render the householder without the support of the *bryte* if needed.

gift **ODan** *ESjL* 3

See also: *bryti, muta, stuþ, umbuþsman*

Refs: Tamm and Vogt, eds, 2016, 303

glafseþer (OSw) noun

An oath that did not result in a judgment. Those swearing such an oath were fined.

gossip oath **OSw** *SdmL* Till

See also: *falzeþer, hægume, jæva, ljúgkviðr, ljúgvitni, meneþer, skruk, tvætala, væna*

glepja (ON) verb

balk **OIce** *Grg* Þsþ 38 Vís 89, 99 Hrs 234 Misc 244

glófi (ON) noun

glove **ONorw** *GuL* Kpb

glömska (OSw) noun

negligence **OSw** *UL* Mb, *VmL* Mb

glöp (ON) noun

A flaw or irregularity in legal proceedings.

balking **OIce** *Grg* Lrþ 117

Refs: CV s.v. *glap*; Fritzner s.v. *glap*; ONP s.v. *glǫp*

glópa (ON) **glæpa** (ON) verb

seduce **ONorw** *FrL* KrbB 14

glópr (ON) **glæpr** (ON) noun

A sinful or wicked deed.

crime **OIce** *Js* Kvg 5

sin **OIce** *Jó* Kge 5, **ONorw** *FrL* KrbB 24

Refs: CV s.v. *glæpr*; Fritzner s.v. *glæpr*; ONP s.v. *glópr*

goðakviðr (ON) noun

A panel of twelve chieftains (ON *goðar*, see *goði*); a verdict given by such a panel. Thought to be synonymous with a *tolftarkviðr* (q.v.).

chieftain's panel **OIce** *Grg* Þsþ 85 Feþ 156

See also: *tolftarkviðr*

Refs: CV s.v. *goðakviðr*; Fritzner s.v. *goðakviðr*

goðalýrittr (ON) **goðalýrit** (ON) **goðalýritr** (ON) **goðalýritt** (ON) noun

A chieftain's veto. Appears only rarely in Grg and seems to have been used exclusively for prohibiting judgment on cases in which a summons was issued to a man from outside the assembly district (ON *útanþingsmaðr*).

chieftain's veto **OIce** *Grg* Þsþ 58, 59

See also: *lýrittr*

Refs: CV; Finsen III:641−42; Fritzner; KLNM s.v. *lýrittr*

goði (ON) noun

A leader or chieftain in Iceland during the commonwealth. As a secular chieftain, it has been suggested that the *goði* was the Icelandic equivalent of a *hersir* ('local chief, lord') or *jarl* (q.v.) elsewhere in Scandinavia. The title of *goði* appears almost exclusively in Iceland, but toponyms and evidence from runestones suggest that they may once have existed throughout the Nordic lands. Prior to the advent of Christianity *goðar* are thought to have served as a type of priest.

In Grg the power of a *goði* stemmed from ownership of a *goðorð* (q.v.) A *goði* had a variety of administrative duties and was required to attend public assemblies. They sat as members of the legislative Law Council (ON *lögrétta*), inaugurated assemblies, served as foremen of certain courts (such as the Confiscation Court [ON *féránsdómr*]) and occasionally delivered verdicts (ON *goðakviðr*) or issued vetoes (ON *goðalyrittr*). Evidence from sagas suggests that *goðar* also provided limited police functions within their home districts.

From about the year 930 the number of *goðar* in Iceland was fixed at 36. This was subsequently raised to 39 and then 48. The position was abolished with the institution of Js in 1271.

chieftain **OIce** *Grg* Klþ 10, 17 Þsþ 20, 22 Vís 96, 110 Lrþ 117 Arþ 118 passim

See also: *höfþingi, jarl, þingsmæn (pl.)*

Refs: CV s.v. *goði*; Fritzner s.v. *goði*; GAO s.v.
Gode, Godentum; KLNM s.v. *goði og goðorð*;
LexMA s.v. *Gode*; MSE s.v. *Goði*; Riisøy 2013

goðorð (ON) noun

The power or authority of a *goði* ('chieftain') in
Iceland during the commonwealth; the office which
empowered a *goði* to handle legal affairs. The office
was not tied to a specific geographic area, but there
were a limited number of them in each of the four
quarter districts (ON *fjórðungr*, see *fiarþunger*). A
goðorð could be held by multiple people, though only
one person could use it at a given time. It was also
inheritable and could be bought, sold or traded. By the
mid-thirteenth century almost all of the 48 offices were
held by five powerful families. The institution of the
goðorð was abolished in 1271 with the introduction of
Js in Iceland.

chieftaincy **OIce** *Grg* Þsþ 20, 22 Lrþ 117 Arþ
122, 126 Feþ 152, 169 Fjl 223 Tíg 255

Expressions:

fara með goðorð (ON)

to act in a chieftaincy **OIce** *Grg*
Klþ 10 Þsþ 23, 81 Lrþ 117

vera ór goðorði (ON)

to forfeit a chieftaincy **OIce** *Grg* Þsþ 36

See also: *alþingi, goði, leið, varþing*

Refs: CV s.v.v. *goði, goðorð*; GAO s.v. *Gode,
Godentum*; KLNM s.v. *goði og goðorð*;
LexMA s.v. *Gode*; MSE s.v. *goði*

gorbötir (pl.) (OSw) noun

fines for injury to animals **OSw** *VmL*
Bb (table of contents only)

See also: *bot, böta*

gornithing (ODan) noun

One who inflicted a bleeding wound to a domestic
animal of another.

gore villain **ODan** *JyL* 3

See also: *niþinger*

Refs: Tamm and Vogt, eds, 2016, 316

gornithingsværk (ODan) noun

villainy goring **ODan** *SkL* 176

gorvargher (OSw) noun

One who killed somebody else's domestic animal;
appearing in a list of *urbotamal* (OSw), i.e. crimes
that could not be redeemed by paying a fine or
compensation.

{*gorvargher*} **OSw** *ÄVgL* Urb

See also: *brennuvargr, kasnavargher,
morðvargr, urbotamal, vargher*

gorþiuver (OSw) noun

cattle thief **OSw** *YVgL* Tb

gore thief **OSw** *ÖgL* Vm

goþer (OSw) **góðr** (ON) adj.

Literally 'good'. People referred to as *goþer* served
legal functions such as to inspect, give valuations,
appear as witnesses, give advice, and are often
difficult to delimit from other representatives of the
local community with similar functions.

of higher social standing **ONorw** *GuL* Kvr

highest ranked **OIce** *Jó* Llb 19

of the highest social standing **ONorw** *GuL* Llb

worthy **OSw** *UL* Kmb, *VmL* Mb

Expressions:

goth bonde (ODan)

good householder **ODan** *ESjL* 2

gothe kone (pl.) (ODan)

These could give testimony of
pregnancy and childbirth.

good women **ODan** *ESjL* 1 *JyL* 1 *SkL* 1

goþer drænger (OSw)

Occurring once of a man, presumably a pilgrim,
who is re-baptized in the river Jordan.

good man **OSw** *SmL*

goþir mæn (OSw) **gothe mæn**
(ODan) **góðir menn (pl.)** (ON)

In ON, a more or less well defined group of men
acting as advisors to and representatives of the king,
but also more generally referring to all upstanding
citizens defended by the king and the bishop. In
ODan, sometimes with another adjective such as
ræt 'just' or *san* 'true', usually of a group of men
who testified or inspected something. In OSw,
men taking part in the *eriksgata* (q.v.) (SdmL).

good men **OSw** *SdmL* Till **ODan** *ESjL* 2, 3
JyL Fort, 1–3 *SkL* 44, 95, 105, 231 *VSjL* 24
OIce *Jó* Þfb 8, HT 2 *Js* Mah 4 *KRA* 16

reliable men **ODan** *JyL* 3

trustworthy men **ODan** *VSjL* 75, 82

gömin ok goþer (OSw)

careful and caring **OSw** *UL* Äb

göþa ok goþan göra (OSw)

*suggest and substantiate someone's free
status* **OSw** *UL* Kmb *VmL* Mb

Refs: Helle 1972, 19–102; KLNM, s.v. *drengskapr*;
Lindow 1976, 106–12; SAOB s.v. *god* (2c),
godeman; Sawyer and Sawyer 2002; SL SmL,
443, note 6; Tamm and Vogt, eds, 2016, 309

goþs (OSw) **goths** (ODan) **góz** (ON) **goz** (OSw) noun

goods **ODan** *ESjL* 1, *JyL* 1, 2, **OIce** *Jó* Kab 15, **OSw** *DL* Gb, Rb, *ÖgL* Eb, Db

property **ODan** *JyL* 1, **OSw** *DL* Gb, Tjdb, Rb, *HL* Kkb, Mb, Jb, *SdmL* Kkb, Kgb, Äb, Jb, Kmb, Mb, Tjdb, Till, *UL* Kkb, Äb, Mb, Jb, Kmb, Blb, Rb, *VmL* Kkb, Äb, Mb, Jb, Kmb, Bb, Rb, *YVgL* Kkb, Äb, Gb, Rlb, Add, *ÖgL* Eb

See also: *bo, egn, fæ, inviþi*

goþvili (OSw) **gothvilje** (ODan) noun

agreement **OSw** *UL* Kkb, Äb, Kmb, *VmL* Kkb (C-, D- and E-texts), Äb, Kmb

approval **OSw** *HL* Äb, *SdmL* Kkb, Jb, Bb, Kmb, Tjdb, Till

consent **OSw** *DL* Gb, *HL* Kkb, Blb, *SdmL* Kkb, *SmL* Kkb

good will **ODan** *ESjL* 2, 3

well disposed **ODan** *ESjL* 3

See also: *lof, vili*

graðr (ON) adj.

not castrated **ONorw** *GuL* Mhb

graf (OSw) noun

trapping pit **OSw** *UL* Mb, *VmL* Mb

grafgangsmaðr (ON) noun

An impoverished man, typically a freed slave, who was put in an open grave with his family; the one who lived the longest was saved and supported by the former master.

gravegoer **ONorw** *GuL* Løb, Leb

pauper freedman **ONorw** *GuL* Løb, Leb

Refs: KLNM s.v. *fattigvård*

grafnár (ON) noun

grave-corpse **OIce** *Grg* Bat 113

graftarkirkja (ON) **greftarkirkja** (ON) noun

burial church **OIce** *Grg* Klþ 2, *KRA* 6, 11, **ONorw** *BorgL* 10.4

graftarkirkjuþór (ON) noun

church-farm where burial is permitted **OIce** *Grg* Klþ 4

gramunk (ODan) noun

grey monk **ODan** *JyL* 3

granbragð (ON) noun

lips twitching (in pain) **ONorw** *GuL* Mhb

granbragðseyrir (ON) noun

A fine for an injury which causes the victim to grimace.

grimacing fine **ONorw** *FrL* Mhb 49

Refs: CV s.v. *granbragðseyrir*; Fritzner s.v. *granbragðseyrir* (suppl.); Hertzberg s.v. *granbragðseyrir*

granda (ON) verb

damage **OIce** *Jó* Fml 17, *KRA* 28

injure **ONorw** *GuL* Tfb

grannaeþer (OSw) **granzla eþer** (OSw) noun

neighbour oath **OSw** *SdmL* Bb

oath together with all neighbours **OSw** *DL* Tjdb

grannekone (ODan) **grankuna** (OGu) **grannkona** (ON) noun

female neighbour **OGu** *GL* A 2

neighbour woman **ODan** *JyL* 2, **ONorw** *BorgL* 3.1

See also: *granni, kona*

grannestævne (ODan) **grannastefna** (ON) noun

meeting of neighbours **OIce** *Jó* Llb 31

village meeting **ODan** *ESjL* 2

See also: *gatestævne, granni, stæmna*

granni (OSw) **granne** (ODan) **granni** (OGu) **granni** (ON) noun

Those living close by, possibly restricted to landowners or householders, ranging from next door neighbours to fellow villagers or others living in the area (*bygd*). The rights and obligations of the villagers were regulated concerning fencing, harvesting, grazing, building etc, but *grannar* could also be called on to act as legally required witnesses to various dealings in the community such as summons, house searches (OSw *ransak*) and paternity matters.

man of the village **OSw** *UL* Jb, Blb, *VmL* Mb, Jb, Bb

neighbour **ODan** *ESjL* 2, 3, *JyL* 2, 3, *SkKL* 11, *SkL* 67, 68, 76, 100, 140, 159, 169, 181, 188, 189, *VSjL* 71, 72, 77, 80, 87, **OGu** *GL* A 26, 37, **OIce** *Jó* Kge 32 Lbb 8 Llb 6 Kab 17 Þjb 2, 6, *Js* Lbb 5, **ONorw** *BorgL* 5.6, *FrL* KrbA 15 LlbA 20 Bvb 8, *GuL* Krb, Llb, Mhb, Tjb, **OSw** *DL* Kkb, Mb, Bb, Gb, Tjdb, *HL* Kkb, Mb, Jb, Blb, *SdmL* Kkb, Jb, Bb, Kmb, Mb, *UL* Kkb, Äb, Mb, Jb, Blb, *VmL* Kkb, Mb, Kmb, Bb (ch. 12 rubric only), *YVgL* Kkb, Drb, Rlb, Tb, Jb, Kvab, Föb, Utgb, Add, *ÄVgL* Md, Rlb, Jb, Kva, Tb, Föb

villager **OSw** *HL* Blb

See also: *byaman, bygdamæn (pl.), nagranni*

Refs: KLNM s.v. *naboforhold*

gras (ON) noun

grass **ONorw** *GuL* Kpb, Llb

grasgarðr (ON) noun

fenced area **ONorw** *FrL* LlbB 9

graskin (OSw) noun

squirrel pelt **OSw** *UL* Kkb

See also: *ikorni*

grasnautn (ON) **grasnaut** (ON) noun

right to use grass **OIce** *Grg* Lbþ 175, *Jó* Llb 4

grasrán (ON) noun

grass robbery **OIce** *Js* Lbb 19

stealing grass **ONorw** *GuL* Llb

unlawful grazing **OIce** *Jó* Llb 42

grasránsbaugr (ON) noun

compensation for stealing grass **ONorw** *GuL* Llb

grass robbery ring **OIce** *Js* Lbb 19

grasverð (ON) noun

value for the grass **OIce** *Jó* Llb 15, 42, *Js* Lbb 18

value of grass **ONorw** *GuL* Llb

gravarbakki (OSw) **griptar bakki** (OSw) noun

burial ground **OSw** *SdmL* Mb

churchyard **OSw** *HL* Äb, Mb

grefleysingr (ON) noun

Literally a 'hoe-freedman'. A former slave who had been granted freedom but whose freedom had not yet been announced at an assembly and therefore possessed a liminal legal status. The term appears only once in Grg Vís 112. The name *grefleysingr* has been variously interpreted as referring to someone permitted only to be armed with a hoe as a weapon (as opposed to the *folkvápn* (see *folkvapn*) born by free men) or as someone relieved from the more onerous tasks performed by slaves, such as digging.

spade-freedman **OIce** *Grg* Vís 112

See also: *folkvapn, leysingi, þræl*

Refs: CV; F; GAO s.v. *Freigelassene*; Grg I:174 n. 171; KLNM s.v. *leysingi*

greftarrán (ON) noun

grave robbery **ONorw** *BorgL* 12.16

gregoriusmessa (ON) noun

St Gregory's Day **OIce** *Grg* Klþ 13

greiða (ON) verb

pay **OIce** *Jó* Þfb 5, 8 Mah 1, 10 Lbb 2 Fml 2, 13, *Js* Mah 4 Kvg 3 Ert 24 Kab 4, *KRA* 14, **ONorw** *FrL* Intr 2, 5 Var 9

pay back **OIce** *Jó* Kge 18

grein (ON) noun

decree **OFar** *Seyð* 4

gren (OSw) noun

Literally 'branch', for details on usage, see *galghi*.

gallows **OSw** *UL* Mb, *VmL* Mb

grennd (ON) **grend** (ON) **grenn** (ON) noun

neighbourhood **OIce** *Js* Lbb 19, **ONorw** *GuL* Llb

vicinity **OIce** *Jó* Llb 35

grevadöme (OSw) noun

county **OSw** *SdmL* Till

grey (ON) noun

bitch **ONorw** *GuL* Mhb

greyping (ON) noun

If a tenant broke bench boards that were mortised together, he had to bring them back and pay 3 *merkr*. See GuL ch. 75.

mortise joint **ONorw** *GuL* Llb

griðamál (ON) noun

truce speech **OIce** *Grg* Bat 114

griðarof (ON) noun

truce-breaking **OIce** *Grg* Bat 114

griðastaðr (ON) noun

place of asylum **OIce** *Jó* Mah 20

place of truce **OIce** *Jó* Mah 19

griðastefna (ON) noun

summons for truce **ONorw** *FrL* Var 9

griðatími (ON) noun

time of truce **OIce** *Jó* Mah 19

griðbítr (ON) noun

truce-ravener **OIce** *Grg* Bat 114

griðfang (ON) noun

legal domicile **OIce** *Grg* Þsþ 22

See also: *heimilisfang, löggrið*

griðmaðr (ON) noun

free male servant **ONorw** *GuL* Tjb

household man **OIce** *Grg* Klþ 9 Þsþ 27, 35 Vís 101 Ómb 128 Feþ 166 Lbþ 176, 216 Hrs 234 Misc 237, 251 Tíg 255, *Jó* Llb 66 Fml 3, *KRA* 14

See also: *griþkuna*

griðsala (ON) noun

granting of security **ONorw** *FrL* Var 2-6, 9

truce-guarantee **OIce** *Js* Mah 20

griðtaka (ON) noun

household-joining **OIce** *Grg* Þsþ 80

grimumaþer (OSw) **grímumaðr** (ON) noun

Literally a masked man. In ON, one who beats and robs a householder at his home, and who could, as a result, himself be killed or outlawed. In OSw, one living in the forest where he robs someone, and who, if killed, was not compensated.

man in disguise **ONorw** *FrL* Mhb 62

robber in the forest **OSw** *YVgL* Drb

See also: *grímueiðr*

Refs: Schlyter s.v. *grimumaþer*

grind (OSw) **grind** (ON) noun

gate **ONorw** *GuL* Llb, **OSw** *DL* Bb, *SdmL* Bb

See also: *garþsliþ*

grindastolpi (OSw) grindastulpi (OSw) noun

    gatepost **OSw** *UL* Kgb, *VmL* Kgb

    See also: *garþer*

gripa (OSw) verb

    Expressions:

    gripa til (OSw)

    appeal to **OSw** *UL* Mb

    claim **OSw** *UL* Mb, Jb, Kmb, Rb

    invoke **OSw** *UL* Mb, Jb, Blb, Rb *VmL* Mb, Jb, Rb

gripalán (ON) noun

    loan of valuables **ONorw** *FrL* Kvb 4

gripatak (ON) noun

    taking articles **OIce** *Grg* Rsþ 231

gripdeild (ON) noun

    robbery **OIce** *Js* Kab 1

    taking the law into one's own
    hands **ONorw** *GuL* Kpb

    theft **OIce** *Jó* Kab 1

    See also: *mistekja*

griper (OSw) gripr (OGu) gripr (ON) noun

    A valuable piece of property; an object with trade value.

    animal **OSw** *YVgL* Tb, Föb, *ÄVgL* Tb, Lek

    article **OIce** *Grg* Fjl 223, *Jó* Kge 13, *Js* Kvg 3

    beast **OSw** *ÄVgL* Fös

    domestic animal **OSw** *ÄVgL* Tb

    horse **OSw** *YVgL* Tb

    item **OIce** *Jó* Þjb 13

    object of value **OIce** *Grg* Þsþ 71 Arþ 122, 127 Feþ 164 Lbþ 192 Hrs 234 Misc 239, *Jó* Kge 2, 22 Lbb 9 Kab 11, 20 Þjb 16, *Js* Kvg 1 Ert 19 Kab 14, *KRA* 15, **ONorw** *FrL* Rgb 6

    property **OIce** *Jó* Þjb 4, **OSw** *YVgL* Tb

    something taken **OGu** *GL* Add. 8 (B 55)

    valuable **ONorw** *FrL* Kvb 4

    See also: *agriper, diur, fæ*

    Refs: CV s.v. *gripr*; Fritzner s.v. *gripr*; ONP s.v. *gripr*

gripr (OGu) noun

    assault **OGu** *GL* A 23

gript (OSw) grift (OSw) noun

    grave **OSw** *UL* Kkb, *VmL* Kkb

gris (OSw) gris (OGu) noun

    pig **OGu** *GL* A 26, **OSw** *UL* Kkb, Kgb, *VmL* Kkb

    piglet **OSw** *UL* Blb

    See also: *svin*

griþ (OSw) grith (ODan) gruth (ODan) grið (ON) grid (OSw) grud (OSw) gruþ (OSw) noun

The most frequently occurring meaning of this word, which is in certain instances considered to be in the plural form, is that of 'protection, sanctuary, truce'. The protection granted under this concept was one limited in time and/or place, as opposed to *trygth* (q.v.), which implied a permanent peace settlement and a promise not to take revenge. *Griþ* could be granted to someone and accepted by him (*griðasetning*), or it could be self-imposed (*sjalfsettr*). The truce was usually granted for a limited period during which the killer or other criminal could not be attacked. After that he had to satisfy certain conditions, otherwise he would again be in jeopardy. The granting of asylum in churches came relatively late into Icelandic law, although it appears to have been current earlier. In ÄVgL, the word is used in the context of disputes over a promised marriage arrangement. Meetings between the parties were governed by *griþ*, translated as 'peace', but in fact more in the nature of 'safe conduct' (as translated in YVgL). The dispute was to be resolved, in other words, without recourse to violence. Similar provisions are apparent in ÖgL, translated as 'promise of immunity' and the concept can perhaps be traced to pre-Christian times (e.g. on the Oklunda inscription). Breaking of a truce or promise of immunity was a *niþingsværk* (q.v.), and later became a crime against the King's Peace (*eþsörisbrut*). The various truce speeches (ON *griðamál*) to be found in Icelandic sources seem, from the wording, to have originated in Norway and are notable for their complex grammatical structure. The legal framework behind truce speeches appears also in the laws of medieval Denmark.

A subsidiary meaning refers to the relationship that a person without their own household had to the household in which they lived, were employed and to which they were attached for legal purposes. In Grg in particular, it is stated that a person must have a 'legal domicile'. Being a member of a household in this way brought with it rights, but also responsibilities. There was the responsibility to respond to summonses and sometimes to act as the householder's legal substitute. The word also appears in GuL. A *griðmaðr* (Grg and GuL) was a free man in a household and in GuL, BorgL and GL the word *griþkuna* seems to refer to the female equivalent, who could sometimes be treated like a daughter or sister. In GuL, it seems just to have referred to a free female servant as opposed to an enslaved servant; someone who could be called as a witness. In BorgL and in GL it refers specifically to a woman who had to be present at a birth, together with a female neighbour, in order to confirm that a child was born dead, or had died naturally just thereafter, and had not been killed deliberately. In the Danish and Low German translations of GL, words referring to midwives are used. Although it is possible that this is the result of a misunderstanding and that it was merely any unrelated female household member that was intended, Wessén thinks that it is probable that the OGu word acquired the meaning 'midwife' under the influence of an unrecorded OGu *graiþa, 'help, speed' at the birth (cf. ON greiða). It is in any case likely that one of the female members of the household would have been particularly skilled in this respect. The relationship between this meaning of griþ and the meanings related to 'truce' might not be obvious, but the protection offered by being a legal member of a household might be seen as a general form of protection and the other meanings as more narrow forms of the same. The concept of 'household attachment' is not present in the mainland Swedish or Danish laws nor are the designations griþmaðr or griþkona.

asylum OIce *Jó* Mah 2, 19

concord OSw *YVgL* Add

household attachment OIce *Grg* Þsþ 78 Misc 237, ONorw *GuL* Mhb

legal protection ONorw *GuL* Krb, Mhb

lodging ONorw *FrL* ArbB 5

peace OIce *Jó* Mah 1, ONorw *FrL* Tfb 5 KrbA 10 Mhb 30, OSw *YVgL* Urb, Drb, *ÄVgL* Md, Slb, Urb, Gb

period of grace ONorw *EidsL* 43.4

promise of immunity OSw *DL* Eb, SdmL Kgb, UL Kgb, VmL Kgb

safe conduct ODan *ESjL* 2, OSw *SmL*, UL Kgb, *YVgL* Gb, *ÖgL* Db

security OSw *HL* Kgb, *ÄVgL* Tb

truce ODan *ESjL* 2, *VSjL* 55, OIce *Grg* Bat 114 Rsþ 230, *Jó* MagBref Þfb 5, 8 Mah 2, *Js* Þfb 4 Mah 4, 19, *KRA* 6

Expressions:

a grudh ok göræ sæt (OSw)

against given security and completed settlement OSw *HL* Kgb

fá/taka sér grið (ON)

find a household to join OIce *Grg* Þsþ 78

fara til griðs (ON)

move into a household OIce *Grg* Þsþ 78

ganga á grið (ON)

break a truce OIce *Js* Þfb 4

forfeit one's right to truce OIce *Jó* Þfb 8

ganga/koma í grið/koma til griðs (ON)

enter a household OIce *Grg* Þsþ 78

griþær at beþas (OSw)

ask for peace OSwe *ÄVgL* Md

hafa grið (ON)

be attached to a household OIce *Grg* Þsþ 78

varðveita grið (ON)

maintain a household attachment OIce *Grg* Þsþ 78

vera á griði (ON)

be in a household attachment OIce *Grg* Þsþ 78

See also: *banda, fimmtargrið, friþer, griðamál, griðarof, griðastaðr, griðastefna, griðatími, griðbítr, griðfang, griðmaðr, griðsala, griðtaka, griþkuna, gruthe, gruthnithing, gruþspiæl, hemahion, hion, örvarþing, spekð, tryggðamál, trygth, vatubanda, þræl*

Refs: Helgi Þorláksson 2005; KLNM, s.v.v. *drab, grið, griðamál og trygðamál, jordejendom, kvinnearbeid, lejde, landsvist, trygd, tyende*; Laws of early Iceland: Grágás I 2000, 247; Peel 2015, 90–91 note 2/5; Ruthström 1988, 64–75; Schlyter 1877, s.v.v. *griþ, griþkuna, gruþ*; SL GL, 245 note 3 to chapter 2; SL HL, 294 note 3; SL ÄVgL, 33 note 7; Söderwall 1884–1973, s.v. *gruþ*

griþkuna (OGu) **griðkona** (ON) noun

free female servant ONorw *GuL* Mhb

midwife OGu *GL* A 2

servant-woman ONorw *BorgL* 3.1

See also: *griðmaðr*

grímueiðr (ON) noun

mask oath ONorw *GuL* Sab

grun (OSw) noun

suspicion OSw *YVgL* Tb, *ÄVgL* Tb

See also: *humamal, jæva, vanesak, væna*

gruthe (ODan) verb

grant truce ODan *ESjL* 2

See also: *griþ*

gruthnithing (ODan) **griðníðingr** (ON) noun

breaker of a truce ODan *ESjL* 2

peace-breaker ONorw *EidsL* 50.13

truce-breaker OIce *KRA* 11

See also: *griþ*

gruþspiæl (OSw) noun

breach of safe conduct OSw *ÖgL* Db

See also: *griþ*

græsgjald (ODan) noun

Compensation paid by the owner of an escaped domestic animal for illegal grazing on commons.

payment for grass **ODan** *ESjL* 3

See also: *fælath, hemaföder, lysning*

græsspæri (OSw) **græspari** (OSw) noun

One who illegally gains or uses pasture.

grass snatcher **OSw** *YVgL* Jb, *ÄVgL* Jb

Refs: Lindkvist forthcoming; Schlyter s.v.v. *græsspæri, græsspari*

græssæti (OSw) noun

Servants without land, who lived in somebody else's household and may have paid rent, are mentioned in the laws for not being allowed grazing since they did not own part of fences or fields.

unlanded servant **OSw** *YVgL* Utgb, *ÄVgL* Föb

See also: *bodsæti, flatføring, hion, hussætisfolk, hussætumaþer, innestkone, innisfolk, innismaþer, landboe, sytning*

Refs: KLNM s.v. *husmand*; Schlyter s.v. *græssæti*

græsvægher (OSw) noun

grass road **OSw** *YVgL* Jb, *ÄVgL* Jb

See also: *vægher*

gröftr (ON) **gröptr** (ON) noun

burial **ONorw** *GuL* Krb

grønir (pl.) (ON) noun

people from Grenland (Lower Telemark) **ONorw** *GuL* Leb

guðsgæfi (ON) noun

God's gift **ONorw** *GuL* Llb, Kvr

guðsifjavörnun (ON) noun

abstention from spiritual kinswomen **ONorw** *FrL* KrbB 8

guðskírsl (ON) noun

ordeal **ONorw** *EidsL* 42.2, *FrL* ArbB 10

See also: *jarnbyrþ, skærsl*

Gulaþing (ON) noun

Gulathing assembly **ONorw** *GuL* Krb, Kpb, Mhb

See also: *þing*

Gulaþingsbók (ON) noun

Gulathing Law **ONorw** *GuL* Krb

Gulaþingslög (ON) noun

Gulathing law district **ONorw** *GuL* Krb

gulaþingsmenn (pl.) (ON) noun

delegates to the Gulathing **ONorw** *GuL* Krb

gulfæste (ODan) verb

bind by gold **ODan** *SkL* 60

gull (OSw) **gul** (ODan) **gull** (ON) noun

gold **ODan** *ESjL* 3, *JyL* 2, 3, *SkL* 30, **ONorw** *GuL* Kpb, Mhb, Olb, Sab, **OSw** *HL* Kmb, *SdmL* Äb, Kmb, *YVgL* Äb, Gb, Jb, *ÄVgL* Äb, Gb, Jb

See also: *væghin*

gullaþ (OGu) **gullat** (OGu) noun

golden headdress **OGu** *GL* A 65

gullsmiþer (OSw) **gulsmith** (ODan) noun

goldsmith **ODan** *JyL* 3, **OSw** *HL* Kmb, *SdmL* Kmb

gulvirthning (ODan) noun

valuation in gold **ODan** *JyL* 3

guthshus (ODan) noun

church **ODan** *JyL* 2

God's house **ODan** *JyL* 1

house of God **ODan** *ESjL* 1

guthsthjanesteman (ODan) noun

servant of god **ODan** *JyL* Fort

gutnalþing (OGu) noun

This is one of a number of words and phrases used to refer to the general assembly of the Gotlanders or more particularly its membership as a whole. Other, more common, ones are *allir lyþir (see lyþir), allir menn (see maþer), landar allir* and *land alt (see land)*. The word itself occurs only in GS in the context of the Swedish king or his *jarl* (q.v.) sending a message to the Gotlanders to collect tax, and not in GL, which does not refer to the Swedish king or *jarl*. The form of the word is problematic and in both Schlyter's glossary and in SL GL it is suggested that it should be 'Guta alþing'. The linguistic aspects are discussed in Peel, 2015 and Myrberg, 2009. The site of the *Gutnalþing* was thought to be Roma, in the central third (*þriþiungr*) of the island. Roma was the site of the Cistercian monastery of Beata Maria de Gutnalia, established on 9 September 1164. It is not certain, however, that there was a general assembly held at Roma before the founding of the monastery, since the place-name is only mentioned in the German translation of GS. Myrberg offers a different interpretation of the history of the general assembly on Gotland and proposes a different site for the earlier general assembly, although conceding that the later medieval assembly might have been held near the monastery.

Gotlanders' general assembly **OGu** *GS* Ch. 2

See also: *land, lyþir (pl.), maþer, þing, þriþiunger*

Refs: KLNM s.v. *ting på Gotland*; Myrberg 2009; Peel 2015, 295 note 2/22; Schlyter 1877, s.v. *gutnal þing*; SL GL, 306 note 23; Steffen 1945, 246

guþ (OSw) **guð** (ON) **gud** (OSw) noun

Christian God **ONorw** *GuL* Krb

pagan god **ONorw** *GuL* Krb, **OSw** *ÄVgL*
Kkb, Md, Smb, Vs, Gb, Rlb, Jb

See also: *afguþ*, *hult*

guþfaþir (OSw) **guthfather** (ODan) **guðfaðir** (ON)
noun

   godfather **ODan** *SkL* 3, **ONorw** *EidsL* 17.2, **OSw**
DL Kkb, *SdmL* Kkb, *YVgL* Kkb, *ÄVgL* Kkb

guþmoþir (OSw) **guthmother** (ODan) **guðmóðir** (ON)
noun

   godmother **ODan** *SkL* 3, **OIce** *KRA*
37, **ONorw** *EidsL* 17.2, **OSw** *DL* Kkb,
SdmL Kkb, *YVgL* Kkb, *ÄVgL* Kkb

guþsivalagh (OSw) noun

   spiritual affinity **OSw** *DL* Kkb, *UL* Kkb, *VmL* Kkb

   spiritual kinship **OSw** *HL* Kkb, *YVgL* Kkb

guþsivalaghspiæl (OSw) noun

   spiritual incest **OSw** *SdmL* Kkb

   violation of spiritual kinship rules **OSw** *HL* Kkb

guþsivi (OSw) **guðsifjar** (pl.) (ON) **guzcifvi** (OSw)
guzzivi (OSw) noun

   godparent **ONorw** *BorgL* 2, *EidsL* 1.3,
FrL KrbA 5, **OSw** *DL* Kkb, *SmL*

   kin in God **OSw** *SmL*

   spiritual affinity **OSw** *UL* Kkb, *VmL* Kkb

   spiritual kinship **OIce** *Grg* Þsþ 25, 35
Vís 89 Feþ 144, 156, *KRA* 1, 21, **ONorw**
BorgL 15.9, *EidsL* 53, *GuL* Krb

See also: *frændsimi*, *mansivi*, *mægð*

guþsivia (OSw) **guðsifja** (ON) noun

   religious kinswoman **ONorw** *EidsL* 30.1

   spiritual kinswoman **ONorw** *BorgL*
15.13, *FrL* KrbB 8, *GuL* Krb

   woman in spiritual affinity **OSw** *DL* Kkb

guþslikami (OSw) **guzlikami** (OSw) noun

   Holy Communion **OSw** *SdmL* Kkb, *SmL*

   Host of the sacrament **OSw** *UL* Kkb, *VmL* Kkb

See also: *rebskaper*

gylfin (ON) noun

   werewolf **ONorw** *GuL* Tfb

gylning (OGu) noun

   gilding **OGu** *GL* A 65

See also: *gullaþ*

gyrþlugyrt (OGu) adj.

Literally, 'girt with a girdle'. In the context of GL, it
refers to either the male inheritance side or the female
inheritance side. Schlyter and others argue for the
former, while Pipping and SL GL argue for the latter.
Both arguments are supported by examples from other
texts where the context seems either to favour one

interpretation or the other. Peel has followed Pipping
in translating this as the female (side). The equivalent
English translation would be 'distaff side'. The word
more commonly used in the Swedish provincial laws
is *möþerni* (q.v.).

   female **OGu** *GL* A 20

See also: *fæþerni*, *lindagyrt*, *möþerni*, *snælda*

Refs: KLNM s.v. *gördel och gördelmakare*;
Peel 2015, 133–34 note 20/24–26;
Pipping 1904, 7–10; Schlyter 1877, s.v.
gyrþlugyrt; SL GL, 266–67 note 12

gæf (OSw) **gáfa** (ON) **gjöf** (ON) **gief** (OSw) **gif** (OSw)
giæf (OSw) noun

   gift **ONorw** *GuL* Kvb, Arb, Reb, Mhb,
OSw *HL* Kkb, Äb, *SdmL* Tjdb, *SmL*,
YVgL Äb, Rlb, Add, *ÄVgL* Äb, Rlb

gæfþræl (OSw) **giæff þræl** (OSw) noun

A person given as a slave, referring to a form of slavery
that could last indefinitely or for a limited time, as a
means of support or to settle a debt.

   bondsman **OSw** *SdmL* Kmb

   gift thrall **OSw** *ÖgL* Db

   slave in payment of a debt **OSw** *UL* Kmb

See also: *ambat*, *annöþogher*, *deghia*,
flatføring, *fostra*, *fostre*, *frælsgivi*, *hemakona*,
hion, *huskona*, *man*, *skuldarmaðr*, *sven*,
sytning, *sætesambut*, *þjónn*, *þræl*

Refs: Schlyter s.v. *gæfþræl*

gæld (OSw) **gjald** (ODan) **gield** (OGu) **gjald** (ON)
giald (OSw) **gield** (OSw) noun

   compensation **ODan** *ESjL* 1, **OIce** *Jó* Mah
2, *Js* Mah 9, **ONorw** *FrL* Mhb 35, *GuL* Krb,
Løb, Tjb, **OSw** *HL* Mb, Blb, *UL* Äb, Mb,
Rb, *VmL* Mb, Bb, *YVgL* Rlb, *ÖgL* Kkb

   confiscation **OSw** *VmL* Rb

   debt **ODan** *ESjL* 2, 3, *JyL* 1, 2, **OGu** *GL* A
10, 20, 29, Add. 2, 9 (B 17, 81), **OSw** *DL*
Rb, *HL* Kkb, Äb, Rb, *SdmL* Äb, Kmb, Rb,
UL Kkb, Äb, Kmb, *VmL* Kkb, Äb, Kmb

   fine **OIce** *Jó* Kge 5, **ONorw** *GuL* Krb, Mhb,
OSw *DL* Mb, *HL* Mb, *UL* Mb, *VmL* Mb

   indemnity **OIce** *Grg* Lbþ 199, 207

   payment **ODan** *ESjL* 3, *SkL* 8, 9, 120, 179,
180, 226, 233, 234, **OIce** *Grg* Hrs 234, Vís
109a (add. 131), 110 Arþ 122, *Js* Mah 6 Rkb
1 Þjb 7, *KRA* 8, **ONorw** *FrL* Sab 4, *GuL* Arb,
OSw *HL* Rb, *SdmL* Kgb, Rb, Bb, Kmb, Mb

   recompense **OSw** *UL* Kgb, *YVgL*
Äb, Rlb, *ÄVgL* Äb, Rlb

   sum **ONorw** *FrL* Intr 4

wergild **OIce** *Jó* Mah 5, **ONorw** *FrL* Intr 3
KrbA 10, *GuL* Løb, Llb, Mhb, Olb, Sab

See also: *bogher*, *bot*, *rætter*, *uppnám*

gælda (1) (OSw) **gielda** (OGu) **gjalda** (ON) **gialda**
(OSw) **gielda** (OSw) **giælda** (OSw) **guldin** (OSw)
verb

To pay fines, compensations, debts, fees, etc., including
phrases referring to paying with one's life or limbs
as punishment. Additionally 'to cost' reflected in the
translation 'to be worth' and in the closely related 'to
be valid'. Often appearing with various prepositions
and adverbs.

atone **OSw** *VmL* Kkb

buy **OSw** *YVgL* Tb

compensate **OSw** *DL* Kkb, Bb, *HL* Mb, Blb, *YVgL*
Äb, Add, *ÄVgL* Kkb, Äb, Rlb, Tb, Fös, Föb, *ÖgL* Kkb

exchange **OSw** *DL* Bb

be fined **OIce** *Jó* Þfb 5 Mah 10, **OSw**
DL Kkb, *UL* Kkb, Mb, *VmL* Mb

forfeit **OGu** *GL* A 28, **OSw** *UL* Mb

make good **OSw** *UL* Kkb, *VmL* Kkb

make reparation **OSw** *VmL* Kkb

owe **ONorw** *EidsL* 32.5

pay **OGu** *GL* A 20, 25, 51, 54, Add. 7, 8 (B 49, 55),
OIce *Grg* Þsþ 63 [and elsewhere possibly] Vís 89
passim, *Jó* Sg 1 Mah 1 Lbb 1 Fml 15, *Js* Lbb 11 Kab
2, *KRA* 1, 6 passim, **ONorw** *BorgL* 14.5, *EidsL* 3.4,
FrL Intr 16 Tfb 1 KrbA 2 KrbB 4, *GuL* Krb, Kpb,
Arb, Leb, **OSw** *DL* Mb, Bb, Tjdb, *HL* Kkb, Äb, Mb,
Jb, Blb, *SdmL* Kkb, Kgb, Äb, Jb, Bb, Kmb, Mb, Rb,
SmL, *UL* Kkb, Kgb, Mb, Jb, Kmb, Blb, Rb, *VmL*
Kkb, Kgb, Äb, Mb, Jb, Kmb, Bb, Rb, *YVgL* Kkb,
Äb, Rlb, Föb, Add, *ÄVgL* Kkb, Rlb, Tb, *ÖgL* Db

pay a fine **OGu** *GL* A 16, 24, **OSw**
DL Mb, *HL* Mb, Kmb, *UL* Rb

pay compensation **ONorw** *GuL* Løb, Llb,
Tfb, Mhb, **OSw** *UL* Mb, *VmL* Mb, Bb, Rb

pay out **OGu** *GL* A 29

proffer **OIce** *Grg* Fjl 221

purchase **OSw** *HL* Rb

put down **OGu** *GL* A 28

recompense **OSw** *YVgL* Tb, Rlb, Föb

redress **OGu** *GL* A 25

remit **OIce** *Jó* Kge 14

repay **OIce** *Jó* Kge 15, **OSw** *HL* Rb, *UL* Äb, Kmb

replace **OSw** *VmL* Kkb

requite **OSw** *SmL*

return **OSw** *ÄVgL* Rlb

tender in payment **OIce** *Jó* Kab 6

be valid **OSw** *UL* Kmb, Blb

be worth **OGu** *GL* A 47, **OSw** *SdmL* Bb,
UL Äb, Jb, Kmb, Blb, *VmL* Kkb, Jb

Expressions:

gielda eptir (OGu)

pay for **OGu** *GL* A 65

gielda firi sik (OGu)

pay for **OGu** *GL* A 65

ransom oneself **OGu** *GL* A 28

See also: *bot*, *böta*, *fulder*, *vaþabot*

gælda (2) (OSw) **gelda** (ON) verb

Appears in the context of castrating a man.

castrate **OIce** *Grg* Vís 86, **ONorw** *GuL* Krb, Mhb

geld **OSw** *YVgL* Urb

spay **OSw** *ÄVgL* Smb

See also: *fastr*, *hovethlim*, *ofödder*,
oskabarn, *sar*, *skap*, *snöpa*

gældruf (OSw) noun

reclaiming of sold goods **OSw** *DL* Bb

gælkare (OSw) **gjaldkyri** (ON) **giælkyræ** (OSw) noun

The king's treasurer or steward. The *gjaldkyri* has been
suggested as a Nordic equivalent of the Lat. *præfectus
urbis* or *exactor* or a justice of the peace in medieval
England. The *gjaldkyri* appears in Scandinavia from
the twelfth century, most frequently in Norway. The
term itself possibly of foreign origin, though it might
also be a combination of ON *gjald* 'payment' and
-keri/-kyri from ON *kjósa* in the sense of 'to acquire'.

The *gjaldkyri* was in charge of city affairs and served
as the king's agent in market towns (ON *kaupangar*,
see *köpunger*), where he was responsible for collecting
fees, maintaining order and the administration of
justice. According to Bj and *Morkinskinna*, the
gjaldkyri was also obligated to collect land dues (ON
landeyrir, see *landaurar*), had to report news from
a legal assembly (ON *lögþing*, see *laghþing*) and
declared outlaws. He may have had an obligation
to jail criminals and to assign members of the night
watch. A *gjaldkyri* might have been synonymous with
a *sýslumaðr* (see *sysluman*), or at least the two seem to
have worked together closely. Following amendments
during the late thirteenth century, the *gjaldkyri* was
one of the few men permitted to bear arms in a city.
The Swedish *gælkare* in VmL appears to have had
the same responsibilities as the Norwegian *gjaldkyri*.
The rarely attested Danish *gælkere* probably initially
held these duties as well before eventually receiving
an expanded set of powers as the king's governor of
Skåne.

In Norway the *gjaldkyri* was initially elected by the population of a city, but he was later joined by the *sýslumaðr* and *lögmaðr* (see *laghmaþer*), all appointed by the king. These three, along with the councilmen (ON *ráðsmenn*, see *raþman*) made up the city council. After the fourteenth century they were gradually replaced by the *foguti* (in Norway: *byfogd*), an official borrowed from the German administrative tradition.

Gjaldkyri remains in use in modern Icelandic to refer to an organization's treasurer or bursar.

paymaster **OIce** *Jó* Kge 28

town sheriff **OSw** *VmL* Mb

treasurer **ONorw** *FrL* Leb 8 Reb 2

See also: *foghati, laghmaþer, laghþing, lænsmaþer, raþman, sysluman*

Refs: Bayley 1990; CV s.v. *gjaldkeri*; Fritzner s.v. *gjaldkeri*; Hertzberg s.v. *gjaldkeri*; KLNM s.v. *gældker, vapenförbud*; NF s.v. *gjaldkere*

gælmaþer (OSw) noun

A man guilty of illicit sexual relations.

guilty man **OSw** *DL* Gb

See also: *horkarl*

gælskaper (OSw) **giolskapær** (OSw) **giælskaper** (OSw) noun

illicit relations **OSw** *UL* Äb, *VmL* Äb

gærning (OSw) **gærning** (ODan) **giarning** (OGu) **gerning** (ON) **gerningr** (ON) **görning** (ON) **gerning** (OSw) **giarning** (OSw) noun

Literally 'deed', particularly criminal deeds. Appears in numerous expressions referring to encountering someone in incriminating circumstances, exemplified below.

act **ODan** *ESjL* 2, 3, *JyL* 2, *SkL* 43, 103, *VSjL* 35, **OSw** *DL* Mb, *UL* Kgb, Mb, Kmb, Blb, Rb, *VmL* Kgb, Mb, Kmb, Rb, *YVgL* Kkb, Drb

act of violence **OSw** *HL* Kgb, *UL* Kgb, Kmb

action **ODan** *SkL* 8, 15, 17, 18, 61, 62, 118, 126, 127, 132, *VSjL* 35

crime **OSw** *DL* Eb, *HL* Kgb, Mb, *SdmL* Bb, *YVgL* Drb

deed (1) **ODan** *ESjL* 2, 3, *JyL* 2, 3, *VSjL* 23, 43, 46, 53, 57, 63, 69, 86, **OGu** *GL* A 1, **OSw** *DL* Eb, *HL* Kgb, Mb, *SdmL* Kgb, Gb, Äb, Kmb, Mb, Till, *SmL*, *UL* Kkb, Kgb, Mb, Add. 3, *VmL* Kkb, Kgb, Mb, *YVgL* Drb, Add, *ÖgL* Eb

evil deed **OSw** *YVgL* Add

misdeed **OSw** *ÖgL* Eb

offence **OSw** *UL* Kgb, Mb

poison **OSw** *SdmL* Mb

sorcery **ONorw** *FrL* KrbB 15

violence **OSw** *YVgL* Add

violent act **OSw** *DL* Rb

violent deed **OSw** *SdmL* Kgb

witchcraft **OIce** *Grg* Klþ 7, **ONorw** *BorgL* 16.7, *GuL* Krb

work by an artisan **OSw** *UL* Kkb, Kmb, *VmL* Kmb

Expressions:

braþ gærning (OSw)

spur of the moment **OSw** *HL* Kgb

sudden action **OSw** *DL* Eb

fa a færski gærning (OSw)

catch in the act **OSw** *UL* Kgb, Kmb *VmL* Kgb, Kmb

gerningar illar (ON)

sorcery **ONorw** *GuL* Krb

gærning göra, gærning gjora (OSw)

commit (a crime or offence) **OSw** *UL* Kkb, Kgb, Mb, Kmb, Rb *VmL* Kkb, Kgb, Mb, Kmb, Rb

takin ok gripin a faersko gaerning (OSw)

apprehended redhanded **OSw** *HL* Kgb

caught and apprehended in the very act **OSw** *SdmL* Kgb, Kmb

takin ælla fangin a samu gærning (OSw)

caught or captured in the act **OSw** *DL* Eb

See also: *brut, firigæra, fordeþskepr, fordæða, forgærning, galdr, gærningisman, gærþ, illgærningisman, innitakin, ovitagærning, taka, valdsgærning, vathegærning, viliagærning, værk*

gærningisman (OSw) **gerningarmaðr** (ON) **gjörningamaðr** (ON) **giærnings man** (OSw) **gærninga man** (OSw) noun

artisan **OSw** *DL* Kkb, *UL* Kkb, *VmL* Kkb

sorcerer **OIce** *Js* Mah 6, **ONorw** *FrL* Var 45

See also: *gærning*

gærsala (OSw) noun

illegal sale **OSw** *UL* Jb, *VmL* Jb

unlawful sale **OSw** *DL* Bb

gærsemi (OSw) **gørsæme** (ODan) **gersemi** (OGu) **giersemi** (OGu) **görsimi** (OSw) **gærsimi** (OSw) noun

additional compensation **ODan** *JyL* 3

extra payment **ODan** *JyL* 2, 3

precious object **OSw** *YVgL* Äb

valuable **OGu** *GL* A 53

gærthsle (ODan) noun

fence **ODan** *JyL* 3

gærþ (OSw) **gerð** (ON) **gierþ** (OSw) **giærþ** (OSw) **gærd** (OSw) noun

act of violence **OSw** *DL* Eb, *HL* Kgb

arbitration **OIce** *Grg* Hrs 235 Misc 244 Tíg 263

attack **OSw** *HL* Kgb

contribution **ONorw** *GuL* Krb, Leb

crime **OSw** *HL* Kgb, *UL* Kkb, Mb

deed (1) **OSw** *SmL*, *UL* Kgb, Mb, *YVgL* Urb, Add, *ÖgL* Eb, Db

offence **OSw** *HL* Äb, Mb

settlement (1) **OIce** *Grg* Misc 244

wound **OSw** *DL* Eb, *UL* Kgb

See also: *gærning*

gærþa (OSw) **gærthe** (ODan) **gierþa** (OGu) **gerða** (ON) **gierþa** (OSw) **giærtha** (OSw) verb

build a fence **ONorw** *FrL* LlbA 9

care for a fence **OSw** *DL* Bb

create grazing enclosure **OGu** *GL* A 24f (64)

enclose **OGu** *GL* A 25, **ONorw** *EidsL* 11.6, **OSw** *UL* Jb, Blb, *VmL* Jb, Bb

erect a fence **OGu** *GL* A 26, **OSw** *UL* Kkb, Jb, Blb, *VmL* Kkb, Jb, Bb

fence **ODan** *ESjL* 2, *SkL* 185, 188, 189, **OGu** *GL* A 24f (64), **ONorw** *GuL* Llb, **OSw** *SdmL* Kkb, Jb, Bb, *SmL*, *YVgL* Urb, Jb, Utgb, *ÄVgL* Kkb

fence in **OFar** *Seyð* 2

make a fence **OSw** *SdmL* Bb, *ÄVgL* Jb

put up fence **ODan** *JyL* 3

set up fence **ODan** *SkL* 188

See also: *garþer*, *gærþi*

gærþi (OSw) **gærthe** (ODan) **gierþi** (OGu) **gerði** (ON) **gierþi** (OSw) **giærþi** (OSw) noun

Derived from *garþer* referring both to a fence and to a fenced in piece of land, usually an arable field or a meadow, since the land in need of protection from grazing animals was fenced in, rather than the animals. The form of the fences varied considerably across Scandinavia and also over time depending on available building material, and the laws mention a wide variety of different types of fences, however the numerous general words for fences (such as *garþer*, *gærþning*, *gærthsle*, *hæghnaþer*) do not appear to reflect any inherent difference in meaning. The laws specify — with different terms for the fences — the areas to be fenced in, the dates for achieving this and, with the exception of Danish laws, the criteria for legal fences. Fencing was an important part of communal village life. Inadequate fences, and the resultant damages of crops, appear to have been a frequent source of conflict between villagers, since provisions concerning the obligations to fence constituted a substantial part of the sections of the laws dealing with communal village life, occasionally even forming an

entire section of a law (*utgærþa bolker* in the Swedish YVgL).

In the Swedish laws, the large individual cultivated field in a field rotation system was called *gærþi*. Each farm had at least one strip field (*tegher* (OSw), *teigr* (ON), *aker* (ODan)) in each field (*gærþi* (OSw), *vang* (ODan)).

enclosed wood(land) **OGu** *GL* A 26, **OSw** *SdmL* Bb

enclosure **OGu** *GL* A 24f (64), **OSw** *UL* Blb, *VmL* Bb

fence **ODan** *ESjL* 2, *SkL* 70, 187, **OSw** *DL* Bb, *YVgL* Rlb

field **ONorw** *FrL* LlbA 20, **OSw** *DL* Bb, *YVgL* Utgb, *ÄVgL* Föb

grazing (within the enclosed part of the village) **OGu** *GL* A 24f (64)

land **OSw** *DL* Bb

See also: *balker*, *garþer*, *gærthsle*, *gærþa*, *gærþning*, *hæghnaþer*, *staur*, *vang*, *værn*, *værnalaghi*

Refs: Hellquist [1948] 1964, s.v. *gärda*; Hoff 1997, 142–49; KLNM s.v.v. *gärde, hegn, odlingssystem, envangsbrug, teig, teiglag, tovangsbrug, trevangsbrug, vang*; Myrdal 1999a, 19–109; 2011, 77–95; SAOB, s.v. *gärde*; Schlyter s.v. *gærþi;* Widgren 1997

gærþning (OSw) **gerðing** (ON) **gærdning** (OSw) noun

fence **OSw** *DL* Bb

fencing **ONorw** *FrL* LlbA 18, *GuL* Llb

wall building **OIce** *Js* Lbb 22

gæsta (OSw) verb

lodge **OSw** *SdmL* Kmb

See also: *gæstning*

gæster (OSw) **gæst** (ODan) noun

guest **ODan** *JyL* 2, 3, **OSw** *DL* Mb, *HL* Mb, *SdmL* Kmb, Mb, *YVgL* Kkb, Add, *ÄVgL* Kkb

hospitality **OSw** *ÖgL* Eb

gæstning (OSw) **gisting** (ON) noun

Obligation to lodge and feed travellers for payment, and paupers for free if required.

hospitality **OSw** *UL* För, Kmb, *VmL* För, Kmb

lodging **OIce** *Grg* Klþ 9 Þsþ 53, 82 Bat 113 Hrs 234, *Jó* Kge 34, *KRA* 26, **OSw** *SdmL* Kmb

procuration **OSw** *HL* Kmb

See also: *gengærþ*, *koster*, *vist*, *væzla*

Refs: KLNM s.v. *gästning*

gæta (ON) **gieta** (OGu) verb

look after **ONorw** *GuL* Kpb

maintain **ONorw** *GuL* Llb

observe **ONorw** *GuL* Krb, Kpb

protect **OIce** *Js* Þfb 4, **ONorw** *GuL* Krb

take (care of) **OGu** *GL* A 18, 26

gætsla (OSw) **gætsle** (ODan) **gezla** (OGu) **gæzla** (ON) noun

care **OGu** *GL* A 18, 36, **OIce** *Jó*
Kab 16, **ONorw** *GuL* Kpb

custody **OIce** *Jó* Kab 7, **OSw** *YVgL* Rlb, *ÄVgL* Rlb

keeping **OIce** *Grg* Þsþ 76, *Js* Kab 11

protector **ODan** *JyL* Fort

tending **OIce** *Grg* Þsþ 80 Lbþ 220

gætsleman (ODan) **gæzlumaðr** (ON) noun

herdsman **OIce** *Jó* Llb 37

protector **ODan** *JyL* 1

See also: *gætsla*

gættitré (ON) noun

door-frame **ONorw** *GuL* Llb

göma (OSw) **gøme** (ODan) verb

look after **OSw** *UL* Äb, *VmL* Äb, Bb

retain **OSw** *UL* Mb

shield **OSw** *UL* Kgb, Mb

summon **ODan** *JyL* 2

take (care of) **OSw** *UL* För, Kkb

take in custody **ODan** *JyL* 1, **OSw** *YVgL* Tb

tend to **OSw** *UL* Mb

uphold **OSw** *UL* För, *VmL* För

Expressions:

gömin ok goþer (OSw)

careful and caring **OSw** *UL* Äb

göma (OSw) noun

custody **OSw** *YVgL* Add

göngukona (ON) noun

vagrant woman **OIce** *Grg* Feþ 156

göngumaðr (ON) noun

A pauper supported by the community. It was illegal for able-bodied persons to beg, and certain forms of support for illegal beggars was punishable. An illegal *göngumaðr* could be enslaved by anyone.

vagrant **OIce** *Grg* Klþ 2 Þsþ 82 Ómb 131 Feþ 156 Hrs 234, 235 Misc 254

See also: *einhleypr*, *húsgangsmaðr*

Refs: Dennis, Foote and Perkins 1980, 382; Dennis, Foote and Perkins 2000, 40; Gerhold 2002, 82–93; Hertzberg, s.v. *göngumaðr*; KLNM s.v.v. *fattigvård*, *tiggar*

göngumannafat (ON) noun

vagrant's baggage **OIce** *Grg* Klþ 8

görræði (ON) noun

Expressions:

taka at görræði (ON)

to appropriate **OIce** *Grg* Feþ 165

görtóki (ON) **görtæki** (ON) noun

A lesser form of theft only mentioned in Grg. According to Grg Rsþ 227 people who took items worth between one *penningr* and half an *eyrir* were to be prosecuted for *görtóki* ('appropriation') rather than theft. The penalty was double the value of the item taken and a three mark fine. In some instances (e.g. Grg Fjl 224) the prosecutor had a choice between charging someone with *görtóki* or outright theft.

appropriation **OIce** *Grg* Lbþ 186, 198 Lbþ 215 Fjl 221, 224 Rsþ 227

appropriation mulct **OIce** *Grg* Lbþ 215 Fjl 224

See also: *fornæmi*, *hvinska*, *ran*

Refs: CV s.v. *görtæki*; F s.v. *görtæki*; KLNM s.v. *förskingring*, *tyveri*

görtókissök (ON) noun

appropriation case **OIce** *Grg* Rsþ 227

götar (pl.) (OSw) noun

Expressions:

allir götar (pl.) (OSw)

all Götar **OSw** *YVgL* Drb, Rlb, Tb, Kvab *ÄVgL* Md, Slb, Rlb, Kva, Tb

göþa (OSw) **gyþa** (OGu) verb

fertilize **OSw** *VmL* Jb

obtain the right **OGu** *GL* A 20

substantiate **OSw** *UL* Kmb, *VmL* Mb

Expressions:

göþa ok goþan göra (OSw)

suggest and substantiate someone's free status **OSw** *UL* Kmb *VmL* Mb

göþning (OSw) **gödning** (OSw) noun

set-aside **OSw** *UL* Blb, *VmL* Bb

set-aside area **OSw** *UL* Blb, *VmL* Bb

göþsl (OSw) noun

compensation **OSw** *SdmL* Bb

göþslueþer (OSw) noun

oath of confirmation **OSw** *ÖgL* Kkb

gørsæmefisk (ODan) noun

Fish to be handed over to the king if found.

valuable fish **ODan** *ESjL* 3

See also: *gærsemi*

góði (ON) **gæði** (ON) noun

natural resource **OIce** *Jó* Lbb 6, *Js* Lbb 2

haf (ON) noun

    The sea.

    Expressions:

    mitt haf (ON)

    middle of the sea **ONorw** *GuL* Arb

hafna (ON) verb

    renounce **ONorw** *GuL* Løb

    waive a claim **OIce** *Jó* Kab 25

hafnarrán (ON) noun

    berth theft **OIce** *Jó* Fml 15, 16

hafnartollr (ON) noun

    landing-place toll **OIce** *Grg* Feþ 166

hafnarvitni (ON) noun

    witness to the right to live on the land **ONorw** *FrL* LlbA 23

hafnbit (ON) noun

    grazing ground **ONorw** *GuL* Kpb

hafning (ON) noun

    baptism **ONorw** *BorgL* 2.1 4.1

hafrek (OGu) hafrek (ON) noun

    shipwreck **OGu** *GL* A 49

    things drifting ashore **ONorw** *GuL* Tfb

haft (ON) noun

    fetter **ONorw** *GuL* Løb

hafþatal (OGu) noun

    number **OGu** *GL* A 20

    Expressions:

    at hafþatali (OGu)

    according to their numbers **OGu** *GL* A 20

    See also: *mantal*

hagabeit (ON) noun

    pastureland grazing **OIce** *Grg* Lbþ 175, 198

hagamark (ON) noun

    Pasture boundary/border area, possibly referring to 'where different pasture lands meet'.

    pasture boundary line **OFar** *Seyð* 10

    See also: *afréttr, haghi, haglendi, markreina*

    Refs: Hertzberg s.v. *hagamark*

hagaskipti (ON) noun

    parcelling out pastureland **ONorw** *GuL* Llb

hagfastr (ON) adj.

    grazing constantly **OFar** *Seyð* 5, 10

hagh (OSw) noun

    fence **OSw** *UL* Blb

haghi (OSw) haghe (ODan) hagi (OGu) hagi (ON) noun

    Enclosed area, in particular a fenced in pasture. Often in compounds such as *hagabeit* (ON) 'pastureland

grazing'; *húshagi* (ON) 'home pasture'; *hema haghi* (OSw) 'home pasture'; *hagamark* (ON) 'pasture boundary'; *hagfastr* (ON) 'grazing constantly'; *haglendi* (ON) 'pasture'; *fjellhagi* (ON) 'mountain pasture'.

    enclosure **ODan** *VSjL* 57, 58, **OGu** *GL* A 24f (64), **OSw** *HL* Blb

    hedge **ODan** *ESjL* 2, 3

    hunting ground **ODan** *SkL* 204

    land **OFar** *Seyð* 1, 4, **ONorw** *GuL* Krb

    pasture **ONorw** *GuL* Llb, Olb

    pastureland **OFar** *Seyð* 5, **OIce** *Grg* Klþ 2, 8 Þsþ 59 Feþ 164, 166 Lbþ 175, 180, *Jó* Lbb 4 Llb 3, 6 Fml 5, *Js* Lbb 11, *KRA* 26, **ONorw** *FrL* Rgb 43 LlbA 11 LlbB 3

    See also: *afréttr, bait, garþer, hagamark, haglendi*

    Refs: CV s.v. *hagi*; KLNM s.v. *beite*; ONP s.v. *hagi*; Schlyter s.v. *haghi*

haglendi (ON) noun

    pasture **OFar** *Seyð* 1–3, 5

    See also: *afréttr, hagamark, haghi*

    Refs: Hertzberg s.v. *haglendi*

hagri (OGu) noun

    oats **OGu** *GL* A 56a

haildir (pl.) (OGu) noun

    damages **OGu** *GL* A 25

haimþorp (OGu) noun

    farm **OGu** *GL* A 13

    homestead **OGu** *GL* A 13

    See also: *burtomt, tompt*

haizl (OGu) noun

    invocation **OGu** *GL* A 4

    See also: *heta*

hald (ON) noun

    possession **ONorw** *GuL* Kpb

halda (OSw) halda (OGu) halda (ON) hallda (OSw) verb

    abide by **OGu** *GL* A 61

    be binding **OIce** *Grg* Klþ 4

    confiscate **OGu** *GL* A 6

    consider **OGu** *GL* A 6

    enforce **OGu** *GL* A 48

    hold **OGu** *GL* A 19, 31, Add. 7 (B 49), **OSw** *UL* Äb, Mb, *VmL* Mb

    keep **OGu** *GL* A 20, **OSw** *UL* Kkb, Kgb, Äb, Jb, Blb, *VmL* Kkb, Äb, Mb, Jb, Bb

    keep to **OGu** *GL* A 13, **OSw** *UL* Äb, *VmL* Äb

    lift **OGu** *GL* A 19

    maintain **OSw** *UL* Blb, *VmL* Bb

observe **OGu** *GL* A 9, **OSw** *UL* Kkb, *VmL* För, Kkb

protect **OGu** *GL* A 9, 13, 14, *GS* Ch. 2

retain **OGu** *GL* A 28, *GS* Ch. 4, **OSw**
UL Kkb, Jb, *VmL* Kkb, Äb, Jb

shelter **OSw** *UL* Kmb, *VmL* Kmb

suffer **OSw** *UL* Mb, Jb

supply **OSw** *UL* Kmb, Blb, *VmL* Kkb, Bb

support **OGu** *GS* Ch. 1, **OSw** *UL* Äb, *VmL* Äb, Rb

transfer **OSw** *VmL* Rb

uphold **OGu** *GL* A 1

withhold **OIce** *Grg* Þsþ 58

Expressions:

halda firi, firihalda (OGu)

cover **OGu** *GL* A 19

halda qvarran (OSw)

retain **OSw** *VmL* Kkb, Äb

shelter **OSw** *UL* Kmb *VmL* Kmb

halda saman (OSw)

agree **OSw** *UL* Kkb

hold in common **OSw** *UL* Jb *VmL* Jb

halda uppi (OGu)

answer for **OGu** *GL* A 54

be able to **OGu** *GL* A 16

confirm **OGu** *GL* A 14

provide oneself with **OGu** *GL* A 54

substantiate **OGu** *GL* A 39

support **OGu** *GS* Ch. 1

See also: *uppihalda*

haldandi (ON) noun

A 'holder'; the person currently in possession of a piece of property as opposed to the claimant (ON *brigðandi*) for that property.

man in possession **OIce** *Grg* Lbþ 176

Refs: Fritzner s.v. *halda*

haldbani (OSw) **halbani** (OSw) **haldsbani** (OSw) **halfbani** (OSw) **halssbani** (OSw) noun

An accessory who participated in a killing by holding the victim.

accomplice **OSw** *UL* Mb, *VmL* Mb, *ÄVgL* Md

killer's accomplice **OSw** *SdmL* Mb

killer's aide **OSw** *HL* Mb

man holding the victim **OSw** *YVgL* Drb

restrainer **OSw** *ÖgL* Db

See also: *atvistarmaþer, bani, forman, fylghi, höfþingi, hovoþsmaþer, hærværk, laghsman, raþsbani, sanbani, umstaþumæn* (pl.)

haldbænd (OSw) **haldsbænd** (OSw) noun

case of restraining **OSw** *ÖgL* Db

case of {haldbænd} accomplice **OSw** *ÄVgL* Md

men holding the victim **OSw** *YVgL* Drb

haldsböter (OSw) noun

Compensation paid by the person restraining the victim in violent crimes.

restrainer's compensation **OSw** *ÖgL* Db

haldsfæ (ODan) noun

fungible loan **ODan** *ESjL* 3, *SkL* 236, 237

halfbróðrungr (ON) **halfbræðrungr** (ON) noun

children of a father's half-brother **OIce** *Js* Ert 6

halfgarþer (OSw) **halvgarth** (ODan) noun

half fence **ODan** *JyL* 3, **OSw** *YVgL* Jb, *ÄVgL* Jb

See also: *garþer*

halfgierþi (OGu) noun

shared fences **OGu** *GL* A 26

halfgildi (OSw) **halfgildi** (ON) noun

half compensation **OIce** *Jó* Llb 35, 40, **OSw** *ÄVgL* Rlb

half recompense **OSw** *YVgL* Rlb

half wergild **ONorw** *GuL* Mhb

See also: *tvægildi*

halfgildr (ON) adj.

half-compensated **ONorw** *FrL* Var 18

halfhundarisbro (OSw) noun

bridge of half a {hundari} **OSw** *SdmL* Bb

See also: *hundari*

halfrétti (ON) noun

half personal compensation **OIce** *Grg* Þsþ 80 Vís 111 Misc 237, *Js* Mah 22, **ONorw** *FrL* Mhb 16 Rgb 35

halfréttiseiðr (ON) noun

An oath submitted by a defendant charged with an offense carrying a penalty of half personal compensation.

oath for half personal compensation **ONorw** *BorgL* 17.10

Refs: CV s.v. *hálfréttiseiðr*; Fritzner s.v. *halfréttiseiðr*; Hertzberg s.v. *halfréttiseiðr*

halfréttismaðr (ON) noun

A person who pays and receives half compensation for grievances. Children between the ages of 12 (or 8) and 15 were considered *halfréttismenn* (cf. GuL ch. 190 and FrL IV.36) as were unwelcome guests (Js Mah 33).

man entitled to half compensation **OIce** *Jó* Mah 28, *Js* Mah 33

man of half personal right **ONorw** *GuL* Mhb

See also: *rætter*

Refs: CV s.v. *hálfréttismaðr*; F; KLNM s.v. *úmagi*

halfrými (ON) noun

This was the place of a rower on a warship.

half room **ONorw** *GuL* Leb

See also: *hamla*

Refs: Hertzberg s.v. *halfrými*

halfsmánaðarstefna (ON) noun

summons to appear within half a month **OIce** *Jó* Kab 3

See also: *stæmna*

halfvirði (ON) noun

half value **OIce** *Jó* Fml 21

halfþrítugr (ON) adj.

twenty-five **ONorw** *GuL* Leb

See also: *skip*

hali (ON) noun

tail **ONorw** *GuL* Kpb, Llb, Mhb

hallvarðarmessa (ON) noun

Feast of St Hallvard (15 May) **ONorw** *EidsL* 9.1, *FrL* KrbA 24, *GuL* Krb

halmlaþa (OSw) noun

hay barn **OSw** *HL* Mb

halmr (ON) noun

straw **ONorw** *GuL* Llb

hals (OSw) **hals** (ODan) **hals** (OGu) **halsar** (pl.) (ON) noun

Literally 'neck', appears in several expressions for execution, presumably referring to beheading, possibly also to hanging, or, if understood metonymically as 'life', to other methods. It seems generally assumed that capital punishments were carried out by the plaintiffs, but in ODan JyL 3 it is specified that the king is responsible for the execution of highwaymen and for those breaking settled cases. Other cases concerning the *hals* were treason (OSw HL, SdmL), grain theft and moving boundary markers (OSw SdmL), marriage by force without the family's permission and misappropriating land (OGu GL). Appearing in expressions such as *firigera hals* (OSw) 'forfeit one's life' and *ganga a hals* 'lose one's neck'. In ONorw, in the plural, hooding ends for ships in the navy; neglect to provide these was punished with a fine of half a *mörk* (GuL ch. 306).

hooding ends **ONorw** *GuL* Leb

life **OSw** *HL* Mb

neck **ODan** *JyL* 2, 3, **OGu** *GL* A 21, 63, **OSw** *SdmL* Bb, Mb

See also: *halshugga, halslausn, hængia, liflat, sværþ*

Refs: Hertzberg s.v. *hals*; KLNM s.v. *dødsstraf*; Schlyter s.v. *hals*

halsbók (ON) **hálsbók** (ON) noun

Possibly a 'neck-book' or a 'health-book'. The Old English cognate *heálsbóc* has been identified as the latter, a protective amulet or phylactery. A *halsbók* may have been a small book containing prayers for private use. In Grg Þsþ 42 it is specified that when swearing on a book, it must be larger than a *halsbók*.

prayer book **OIce** *Grg* Þsþ 42, 46 Ómb 129

See also: *bok (1)*

Refs: Bosworth & Toller s.v. *heálsbōc*; CV s.v. *hálsbók*; Fr; GrgTr I:82–83; Páll Vídalín 1854 s.v. *háls-bók*

halshugga (OSw) verb

Beheading, presumably by sword when it was the king who was responsible for the execution in cases of excommunication over a year (cf. *sværþ*). In the beheading of hostage takers, however, executioner and weapon were unspecified.

behead **OSw** *ÖgL* Eb, Db

cut someone's head off **OSw** *ÖgL* Kkb

Refs: KLNM s.v. *dødsstraf*

halslausn (ON) noun

'Neck-loosing'; a payment given by the slave to his master as part of the ceremony in which the slave was freed.

neck-payment **ONorw** *FrL* ArbB 12

Refs: CV s.v. *hálslausn*; Fritzner s.v. *halslausn*; Hertzberg s.v. *halslausn*; KLNM s.v. *leysingi*

halvbrother (ODan) noun

half-brother **ODan** *ESjL* 1, *SkL* 35, 92, *VSjL* 19

halvhelagh (ODan) adj.

half holy **ODan** *SkKL* 9

halvsystken (ODan) noun

half sibling **ODan** *ESjL* 1, *JyL* 1

halzmaþer (OSw) **haldsmaðr** (ON) **haldsmaþer** (OSw) noun

A guardian or keeper (cf. ON *hald* 'custody'), especially someone who manages someone else's property. Responsibilities of a *haldsmaðr* appear to have been similar to several other designations, such as a *vörzlumaðr* (q.v.) or a *fjárvarðveizlumaðr* (q.v.). A *haldsmaðr* could be designated in a variety of situations, including watching over an inheritance until an heir comes of age and maintaining property while the owner is abroad. According to Gul Arb 115 women were permitted to be *haldsmenn*.

agent **ONorw** *GuL* Olb

custodian **OSw** *VmL* Mb

guardian **ONorw** *GuL* Kpb, Arb, Olb

herdsman **OIce** *Jó* Kab 17, **ONorw** *GuL* Kpb

property caretaker **OIce** *Jó* Kge 14, *Js* Ert 25 Kab 12

representative **ONorw** *GuL* Kpb

See also: *bryti, fjárhaldsmaðr, fjárvarðveizlumaðr, forræðismaðr, gætsleman, malsmaþer, uphaldsman, vörzlumaðr*

Refs: CV s.v. *haldsmaðr*; Fritzner s.v. *haldsmaðr*; Hertzberg s.v. *haldsmaðr*

halzörar (pl.) (OSw) noun

goods in custody **OSw** *YVgL* Äb, *ÄVgL* Äb

hamarr (ON) noun

butt of an axe **ONorw** *GuL* Mhb

hamarskipt (OSw) **hamar skifte** (OSw) noun

Older land division system than *solskipt* 'sun division'. It is mentioned in SdmL, VmL and UL only. The exact meaning is still obscure. According to an older explanation the term might refer to uncultivated and stony land available for reclamation and cultivation on the village common land. Another explanation suggests that it was an individually based cultivation and reclamation of land in common meadows and pastures.

hammer division **OSw** *SdmL* Bb

{hamarskipt} **OSw** *UL* Blb, *VmL* Bb

See also: *solskipt*

Refs: Brink 1991, s.v. *–hammare;* Hafström 1951, 104–56; Schlyter s.v. *hamar*

hamblan (OSw) noun

mutilation **OSw** *HL* Kgb, *SdmL* Kgb, *UL* Kgb (table of contents only), *VmL* Kgb (rubric only)

hamla (ON) noun

oar bench **ONorw** *GuL* Leb

oar-grummet **ONorw** *GuL* Mhb, Leb

oarsman **ONorw** *GuL* Leb

See also: *halfrými*

hamle (ODan) verb

mutilate **ODan** *JyL* 2, *SkL* 124

See also: *hamblan*

hamna (OSw) **havne** (ODan) **hampna** (OSw) noun

An administrative district in the naval defence organization. Originally, a man and equipment were to be provided, but by the time that the Swedish laws were written down in the form that we know them today, these obligations were being transformed into yearly taxes. Whether Östergötland was divided into *hamna* (and *har*, q.v.) has been debated (Ericsson 2007, 113 and passim). Ericsson suggests that a *hamna* might have consisted of eight *attungar* (see *attunger*), but its very existence has also been questioned (Söderlind 1989, 16–17).

area which pays due for military tax **ODan** *JyL* 3

military tax **ODan** *JyL* 3

sea warrior district **OSw** *SdmL* Kgb, Rb, Till

seat **ODan** *ESjL* 3

{hamna} **OSw** *UL* Kgb, Rb, *VmL* Kgb, Mb, Rb

See also: *ar (1), har (1), leþunger, skiplagh, manngerð*

Refs: Andersson 2014, 14; Ericsson 2007, 113 and passim; Hafström 1949a, 26, 87–127; KLNM s.v. *hamna*; Lindkvist 1995, 17–21; Lund 1967 s.v. *hafn*; Lundberg 1972, 76–78; Söderlind 1989, 16–17

hamnumæn (pl.) (OSw) noun

men of a sea warrior district **OSw** *SdmL* Kgb

See also: *hamna*

hamnuvapn (OSw) noun

In SdmL each *hamna*, a district in the naval defence organization, had to supply their man with a set of weapons, consisting of shield, sword, spear and iron hat, as a parallel to the individual *folkvapn* (q.v.). The *hamna* also had to provide some sort of armour as well as a bow and arrows.

weapons of the sea warrior district **OSw** *SdmL* Till

See also: *hamna, vapn*

Refs: Schlyter s.v. *hamnu vapn*; SL SdmL, 241

hanaótta (ON) noun

cockcrow **ONorw** *GuL* Krb

hand (OSw) **hönd** (ON) noun

hand **OIce** *Grg* passim, **ONorw** *GuL* Krb, Løb, Tfb, Kpb, Arb, Llb, Mhb, Olb, Sab

side **ONorw** *GuL* Krb, Tfb, Mhb

Expressions:

á hönd, á hendr (ON)

against **ONorw** *GuL* Krb, Løb

hafa hönd at (ON)

be in the possession of **ONorw** *GuL* Olb

handar mair (OGu)

higher up **OGu** *GL* A 23

harms hand (OSw)

anger **OSw** *UL* Mb, Blb *VmL* Mb, Bb

leþa i hænder (OSw)

trace to someone's possession **OSw** *VmL* Kkb

leþa sik av handom (OSw) **laiþas a hand** (OGu)

confirm **OGu** *GL* A 4

trace provenance from oneself **OSw** *UL* Mb *VmL* Mb

mæþ harms hændi (OSw)

in anger **OSw** *UL* Mb, Blb *VmL* Mb, Bb

See also: *hershendr (pl.)*

handalestr (OGu) noun

deformity in the hand **OGu** *GL* A 19

handamællum (OSw) **handa mellum** (OSw)
handamællom (OSw) adv.

entrusted with **OSw** *UL* Kkb, Äb,
Mb, Kmb, *VmL* Kkb, Äb, Kmb

in possession of **OSw** *UL* Mb, Blb, *VmL* Mb, Bb, Rb

handaværk (OSw) **handaverk** (OGu) **handaverk**
(ON) **handavirke** (OSw) **handaværki** (OSw)
handvirki (OSw) **handværk** (OSw) **handværki**
(OSw) noun

deed (1) **OSw** *ÄVgL* Rlb

doings of one's hands **ONorw** *GuL* Mhb

hand **OGu** *GL* A 2

handiwork **OSw** *UL* Blb, *VmL* Mb, *ÖgL* Eb

handmark **ONorw** *EidsL* 3.1

injury caused by a human hand **OSw** *HL* Mb

intended action **OSw** *UL* Mb (table of
contents only), Kmb, Blb, *VmL* Mb, Bb

man-made harm **OSw** *SdmL* Mb

manipulation **OSw** *SdmL* Bb

mark of violence **OSw** *DL* Mb

marks of violence **OSw** *UL* Mb, *VmL* Mb

visible wound **OSw** *HL* Mb

work of a man **OSw** *ÄVgL* Rlb

See also: *vaþi, vili, viliagærning, viliandis, viliaværk*

handgenginn (ON) adj.

Expressions:

handgenginna menn (pl.) (ON)

king's retainers **OIce** *Jó* Kge 35

liegemen **OIce** *Js* Kdb

sworn retainers of the king **OIce** *Jó* Þfb 2

handgærning (ODan) noun

action **ODan** *SkL* 235

handla (ON) verb

capture **OIce** *Js* Mah 13

Expressions:

illa handla, handla illa (OSw)

abuse **OSw** *UL* Blb *VmL* Bb

See also: *misfyrma*

handlagh (ODan) **handlag** (ON) noun

hand giving **ODan** *ESjL* 3

hand-oath **ODan** *ESjL* 3

handshake **OIce** *Jó* Llb 1

swearing by taking hands **ODan** *ESjL* 3

See also: *handtak*

handleggja (ON) verb

catch **ONorw** *FrL* Mhb 10

handnuminn (ON) adj.

caught **ONorw** *GuL* Mhb

found in someone's hands **OIce** *Grg* Rsþ 230

handpundari (ON) noun

handheld steelyard **OIce** *Jó* Kab 26

handran (OSw) **handran** (ODan) **handrán** (ON) noun

Forcefully, though without weapons, taking
something, including disputed property, from another
person's hands or custody. The punishment for this
offence could be relative to the value of the goods.

forcible seizure from someone's grasp
OIce *Grg* Vís 86, 87, *Jó* Llb 44

hand rapine **ODan** *ESjL* 2, *JyL* 2, *SkL* 167, *VSjL* 65

hand-robbery **ONorw** *GuL* Llb,
Tfb, **OSw** *YVgL* Rlb, Add

hand-seizure **OIce** *Grg* Rsþ 228, *Jó* Þjb 7, 16

robbery from a person's hands **OSw** *ÄVgL* Rlb

See also: *ran*

Refs: Hertzberg s.v. *handrán*; KLNM
s.v. *ran*; Schlyter s.v. *handran*

handsal (ON) **handssal** (ON) noun

Joining hands (ON *handarband* or *handsal*) was a
common way of confirming an agreement, a contract
or the conclusion of a transaction. The corresponding
verbs were (ON) *handsala, handselja,* or *leggja/taka
hendr saman.* When both parties of an agreement
joined hands they or a designated third person had to
pronounce the content of the agreement, framed within
a set of fixed formulae. (In Icelandic law (Grg) this
last requirement was waived in cases regarding debts.)
These words and the corresponding action had to be
seen and heard by at least two witnesses in order to
be accepted as legally binding. Some agreements even
had to be made public in front of a gathering of men,
either at a thing assembly, in a church or alehouse, or
on board a fully manned ship. A breach of agreement
was called (ON) *handsalsslit* or *handsalsrof* and
implied compensation to the aggrieved party.

formal guarantee **OIce** *Grg* Klþ 2 Þsþ 49 Arþ
122 Feþ 152, 158 Tíg 255, *Js* Lbb 16, *KRA* 14

handshake **OIce** *Jó* Kab 11, 25

Refs: Hertzberg s.v.v. *handsal, handsala,
handsalsband, handsalsrof, handsalsslit, handselja;*
KLNM s.v.v. *bröllop, handarband; handsal;*
Schlyter s.v.v. *handsalder, handsalu fæ*

handsala (ON) **handssala** (ON) verb

agree on with a handshake **OIce**
Jó Kge 5 Lbb 6 Kab 11

confirm by handshaking **ONorw** *GuL* Kpb, Løb

formally agree **OIce** *Grg* Klþ 2 Þsþ 48, 51 Ómb 130 Lbþ 174, 192 Fjl 221 Hrs 235 Misc 244 [passim?], *Jó* Lbb 9 Kab 25, *Js* Lbb 2, 5 Kab 9

formally guarantee **OIce** *Grg* Klþ 2 Feþ 164

formally transfer **OIce** *Jó* Lbb 6

See also: *handsalsslit*

handsalsband (ON) noun

transaction with shaking hands **ONorw** *FrL* Rgb 28

handsalsmaðr (ON) noun

man who formally agreed to accept a settlement **OIce** *Grg* Misc 244

handsalsslit (ON) noun

breach in the transference of title **OIce** *Jó* Llb 1

breach of contract **ONorw** *GuL* Kvb, Llb, Tfb

breach-of-agreement payment **OIce** *Grg* Feþ 166 Lbþ 194, 219 Fjl 221, *Js* Lbb 10 Kab 20

See also: *handsala*

handsalufæ (OSw) noun

entrusted goods **OSw** *YVgL* Äb, *ÄVgL* Äb

handselja (ON) verb

confirm by handshaking **ONorw** *GuL* Kpb

formally guarantee **OIce** *Js* Lbb 2

See also: *handsala*

handtak (ODan) noun

ODan SkL requires swearing by joining hands, not on a book, in cases of disputed land, a man's lawful absence and fire compensation (ODan *brandstuth*).

joining of hands **ODan** *SkL* 83

taking hands **ODan** *SkL* 147, 226

See also: *handlagh*

handtaka (ON) verb

stipulate **ONorw** *FrL* Intr 22

handvömm (pl.) (ON) **handvamm** (ON) noun

Negligence could in some cases lead to liability for compensation. See GuL chs 36, 43.

carelessness **ONorw** *FrL* KrbA 12

mishandling **OIce** *Grg* Þsþ 76, *Js* Kab 5, 11

negligence **OIce** *Jó* Llb 62 Kab 4, 16, **ONorw** *GuL* Kpb

hang (ODan) noun

hanging **ODan** *SkL* 151, *VSjL* 87

See also: *hængia*

hanga (ON) verb

be joined **ONorw** *GuL* Mhb

hankagjald (ON) noun

A fine for failure to supply rope pulleys for ships at the levy.

pulley-payment **ONorw** *FrL* Leb 4

Refs: Fritzner s.v. *hankagjöld*; Hertzberg s.v. *hankagjöld*

hanki (ON) noun

strap **ONorw** *GuL* Leb

har (1) (OSw) **har** (ODan) **hár** (ON) noun

Hair appears in the laws mainly in the context of honour. Pulling someone's hair was a punishable offence in ODan, OGu, ONorw and OSw laws. A woman could have her hair cut as a penalty for adultery (OSw SdmL, UL). Cutting a man's hair was punished both as a defect (OSw *læst*) and a wound (OSw *sar*) (OSw ÄVgL Smb). Accusing a woman of being seen with loose hair was in insult (OSw ÄVgL, YVgL). The possession of cut hair (and nails) also appears as evidence of witchcraft (OSw SmL).

hair **ODan** *VSjL* 25, 45, 86, **ONorw** *GuL* Mhb, **OSw** *ÄVgL* Smb

Expressions:

horn ok har (OSw)

nails and hair **OSw** *SmL*

taka i har (OSw, OGu) **take i har** (ODan)

lug by the hair **OSw** *YVgL* Kkb *ÄVgL* Kkb

pull the hair **ODan** *VSjL* 86

take by the hair **OGu** *GL* A 8, 11, 19

take in the hair **ODan** *ESjL* 2

See also: *hardræt, hargrip, tutten*

Refs: Carlsson 1934, 130–31; KLNM s.v.v. *hår, skamstraff, trolldom*

har (2) (OSw) noun

Har is supposed to have been the lowest administrative taxation district in the naval defence system in HL and possibly in ÖgL. Its existence and role in ÖgL has been much debated and even questioned, as there are few traces of it. Andersson (2014, 15) regards *har* as synonymous with *hamna* (q.v.) and *ar* (see *ar* (1)).

{*har*} **OSw** *HL* Kgb

See also: *ar (1), hamna, skiplagh, manngerð*

Refs: Andersson 2014, 15; Brink 1994, 146

hardræt (ODan) noun

pulling of hair **ODan** *ESjL* 3

harðafang (ON) noun

This term (lit. meaning 'that which is difficult to get') refers to the mulct which a debtor had to pay to his creditor if the latter required distraint.

distraint **ONorw** *GuL* Kpb

recovery mulct **OIce** *Grg* Feþ 164 Fjl 221, *Js* Kab 4

Refs: Hertzberg s.v. *harðafang*; KLNM s.v.v. *execution, handarband; handsal, straff*; Laws of early Iceland 2000, 391; Lúðvík Ingvarsson 1970, 266–72; RGA2 s.v. *zwangsvollstreckung*

hargrip (ODan) noun

pulling of hair **ODan** *SkL* 98

seizing of hair **ODan** *JyL* 3

harmber (OSw) **harm** (ODan) noun

anger **ODan** *ESjL* 2, **OSw** *HL* Mb

Expressions:

mæþ harms hændi (OSw)

in anger **OSw** *UL* Mb, Blb *VmL* Mb, Bb

harund (OGu) noun

skin **OGu** *GL* A 19

hasæti (OSw) **háseti** (ON) **hásæti** (ON) **assæti** (OSw) **asæti** (OSw) **asættare** (OSw) noun

crewman **OIce** *Grg* Þsþ 53, *Jó* Fml 2, 9, **ONorw** *FrL* Leb 19, *GuL* Leb

member of the ship's company **OIce** *Grg* Ómb 132 Feþ 156, 166 Misc 243, 250

oarsman **OSw** *SdmL* Kgb, *UL* Mb, *VmL* Mb

rowing bench **OSw** *UL* Kgb

See also: *hamla, liþ (2)*

hathkone (ODan) noun

A woman who had been raped — abducted and/or violated — and kept against her will.

woman in shame **ODan** *JyL* 2

See also: *kona, vald*

Refs: Tamm and Vogt, eds, 2016, 316

haukastulðr (ON) noun

theft of falcons **OIce** *Jó* Þjb 9

haukr (ON) noun

hawk **ONorw** *GuL* Llb, Tjb

hausttíund (ON) noun

autumn tithe **OIce** *Grg* Tíg 260

havandi (OSw) adj.

pregnant **OSw** *YVgL* Äb, Gb, *ÄVgL* Äb

havnebonde (ODan) noun

householder in a recruiting area **ODan** *JyL* 3

See also: *hamna*

havnebrother (ODan) noun

recruiting unit brother **ODan** *JyL* 3

há (ON) noun

aftermath **ONorw** *GuL* Llb

háðung (ON) noun

defamation **OIce** *Jó* Mah 26

disgrace **OIce** *Grg* Klþ 16 Rsþ 227, *Js* Mah 22, 25, **ONorw** *FrL* Var 21

mockery **OIce** *Grg* Misc 237, 238

háleygir (pl.) (ON) noun

people from Hålogaland **ONorw** *FrL* Reb 2, *GuL* Leb

hátíð (ON) noun

holiday **OIce** *KRA* 26

hátíðahald (ON) noun

observance of festivals **OIce** *Grg* Klþ 14

hegnan (OGu) noun

protection **OGu** *GS* Ch. 2

hegning (ON) noun

castigation **OIce** *KRA* 7

punishment **ONorw** *FrL* KrbB 2

See also: *ræfsing*

heiðlaunaðr (ON) adj.

Expressions:

heiðlaunað jörð (ON)

land given as mark of honour **ONorw** *GuL* Olb

heiðr (ON) noun

heath **ONorw** *BorgL* 5.6

moorland **OIce** *Grg* Feþ 164 Misc 239

heift (ON) noun

enmity **OIce** *Js* Mah 22, 34, **ONorw** *FrL* Var 21

hate **OIce** *Jó* Llb 36

heiftugr (ON) **heiptugr** (ON) adj.

Usually used in the expression *heiftugri hendi* ('with a malicious hand') to indicate hostile intent.

hostile **OIce** *Jó* Mah 20, 22, *Js* Mah 16, *KRA* 5, 6

with evil intent **ONorw** *GuL* Llb, Mhb

Refs: CV s.v. *heiptugr*; Fritzner s.v. *heiptugr*; Hertzberg s.v. *heiptugr*

heilagra manna messa í Selju (ON) **heilagra manna í Selju** (ON) noun

Saints' Mass of Selja (8 July) **ONorw** *GuL* Krb

heilagradagasókn (ON) noun

legal proceedings on holy days **OIce** *Jó* Kab 10

heill (ON) adj.

unhurt **ONorw** *GuL* Kpb, Mhb

heilspenaðr (ON) adj.

with unhurt teats **ONorw** *GuL* Kpb

heilund (ON) noun

brain wound **OIce** *Grg* Vís 86, 88

heilvita (ON) adj.

having a healthy mind **ONorw** *FrL* KrbA 41

heimaland (ON) noun

home field **OIce** *Jó* Llb 53

heimamaðr (ON) noun

A person who has established residence within another's household. Often a servant or labourer.

home-man **OIce** *Grg* Ómb 143, *KRA* 13, **ONorw** *FrL* Rgb 17

household man **OIce** *Grg* Feþ 164

Refs: CV s.v. *heimamaðr*; Fritzner s.v. *heimamaðr*; Hertzberg s.v. *heimamaðr*

heimanferð (ON) noun

dowry **ONorw** *FrL* Kvb 10

heimangerð (ON) **heimangörð** (ON) noun

dowry **OIce** *Grg* Feþ 154

See also: *hemfylghþ*

heimankvöð (ON) noun

local calling **OIce** *Grg* Þsþ 56, 77 Vís 104

heimaseta (ON) noun

Remaining at home; refusal to appear when summoned.

staying at home **OIce** *Grg* Þsþ 32 Vís 89

Refs: CV s.v. *heimaseta*; Fritzner s.v. *heimaseta*; Hertzberg s.v. *heimaseta*

heimilðartaka (ON) noun

claim **ONorw** *GuL* Tjb

exchange of legal title **OIce** *Jó* Kab 11 Þjb 4

transfer of warranty **OIce** *Js* Þjb 3

heimilðarváttr (ON) **heimildarváttr** (ON) noun

warranty witness **OIce** *Grg* Lbþ 202

heimili (ON) noun

A man's home, including his entire farm (OSw, ODan *bo*, ON *bú*), was considered inviolate. Its sacrosanct character is clearly borne out by the term (OSw) *hemfriþer* (q.v.), attested in the GL, YVgL, SdmL, and UL. The concept seems also to occur in the HL and VmL. Corresponding provisions are found in the FrL (Mhb). Violating the *hemfriþer* was called (OSw) *hemsokn*, (ON) *heimsókn* (q.v.). The home was the correct place for receiving official summonses, etc. See, e.g., FrL Rgb ch. 3, GuL chs 46, 98, 102, and 266.

home **OIce** *Grg* Þsþ 32, 33 Lsþ 116 Arþ 122 Ómb 128, *Jó* Þfb 5 Mah 19 Kge 17 Kab 9, *Js* Þfb 4 Mah 14 Kab 7, **ONorw** *FrL* Tfb 5 Mhb 5, 8 Rgb 3, *GuL* Kpb, Llb, Olb

homestead **OIce** *Jó* Sg 1

house **OIce** *Jó* Llb 8, *Js* Mah 11

place of residence **OIce** *Jó* Kab 9

See also: *byr*

Refs: KLNM s.v.v. *fridlagstiftning, gård, hærværk*; RGA2 s.v.v. *hausfrieden, haussuchung, vermögenseinziehung*; Strauch 2016, 72, 481

heimiliga (ON) adv.

with warranty **OIce** *Js* Lbb 10

heimilisbúi (ON) noun

neighbour **OIce** *Grg* Klþ 1, 4 Þsþ 20, 28 Vís 89 Bat 113 Lrþ 117 Arþ 118 Ómb 128

See also: *búi*

heimilisfang (ON) noun

residence **OIce** *Grg* Þsþ 22, 48

See also: *griðfang*

heimilisfastr (ON) adj.

having a settled home **OIce** *Grg* Þsþ 20, 35 Vís 89 Feþ 155 Fjl 221 Hrs 234, *KRA* 15

heimiliskviðarvitni (ON) noun

evidence from a verdict given by homestead neighbours **OIce** *Jó* Mah 22, 24

testimony of a verdict from homestead neighbours **OIce** *Js* Mah 24, 25, *KRA* 18, 23, **ONorw** *FrL* KrbB 5, 15 Mhb 7, 24

See also: *vitni*

heimilismaðr (ON) noun

home-man **OIce** *Grg* Þsþ 77

heimskr (ON) adj.

foolish **OIce** *Jó* Llb 39

Expressions:

heimskr maðr (ON)

simpleton **OIce** *Grg* Arþ 118

heimsóknarvitni (ON) noun

home attack testimony **OIce** *Js* Mah 11, 14

witness to an attack **ONorw** *FrL* Mhb 5

See also: *vitni*

heimstefnuváttr (ON) noun

A witness to the issue of a home summons (ON *heimstefna*, see *hemstæmpnung*).

witness at someone's home **ONorw** *FrL* Rgb 3

Refs: CV s.v. *heimstefnuváttr*; Fritzner s.v. *heimstefnuváttr*; Hertzberg s.v. *heimstefnuváttr*

heimstefnuvitni (ON) noun

testimony of a home summons **OIce** *Js* Kab 2, **ONorw** *FrL* Rgb 2

witness to a home summons **OIce** *Jó* Þfb 4, **ONorw** *GuL* Kpb, Løb

See also: *stefnuvitni, vitni*

heimsvist (ON) noun

dwelling-place **ONorw** *EidsL* 48.12

heimta (ON) verb

claim **OIce** *Grg* Þsþ 51 Vís 109a (add. 131) Feþ 144 passim, *Jó* Kge 16 Kab 20, *Js* Mah 6 Lbb 14 Kab 4, 16, *KRA* 15

collect **OIce** *Grg* Þsþ 49, **ONorw** *BorgL*
11.4, *EidsL* 48.8, *FrL* Tfb 1

demand **OIce** *Jó* Mah 2, 30 Lbb 2
Þjb 24, **ONorw** *FrL* Var 9

fetch **ONorw** *EidsL* 33.1

See also: *telja*

heimta (ON) noun

claim **OIce** *Jó* Llb 28

right to claim recompense **OIce** *Jó* Llb 37

heimtandi (ON) noun

debtor **OIce** *Jó* Kab 23

heimting (ON) noun

claim **OIce** *Grg* Þsþ 54, 78 Vís 95 Bat 113 Arþ
118 Ómb 131 Lbþ 192, 215 Rsþ 233, *Js* Lbb 4

right of claim **OIce** *Grg* Misc 244, *Jó* Llb 64 Þjb 4

heit (ON) noun

promise **OIce** *Grg* Arþ 127

vow **OIce** *KRA* 12, 13

helagher (OSw) hailigr (OGu) heilagr (ON) helægher
(OSw) hælagher (OSw) hælægher (OSw) adj.

This word is used in at least three distinct ways. Firstly,
it is translated as 'holy' or 'sacred', in such expressions
as *helga land*, 'the Holy Land' (GL), *heilög orð*,
'sacred words' (Grg). In referring to persons it is used
as a designation of holy people as a class (that is those
connected to the church), or the saints in general or the
particular, Secondly, it refers to 'holy' days as opposed
to working days: Sundays, saints' days, church
festivals, etc. Thirdly, it is translated as protected in
some way. The related noun, *hælgh* (q.v.), and all its
derivatives are used with similar implications and
the noun appears in the concept, *manhælghþ*. In the
translations 'immune' and 'protected', the word is
related to the concept of *hemfriþer*, the protection
that one had in one's own home against attack. The
concept is very closely connected with that of *friþer*
(q.v.) and being 'under the King's Peace', with all the
protection that the rule of law supplied.

The original meaning of the word, as opposed to
the translations employed, has been much disputed,
and the history of this is reflected in the references.
The discussion is the more interesting as it is a word
carrying concepts of great importance in the Norse
and wider Germanic sources, both legal and literary.

holy **OGu** *GL* A 6, 8, 9, 60, **OIce** *Grg* Feþ 166
Lbþ 181, *Jó* HT 2, *KRA* 7, 9, **ONorw** *BorgL*
14.2, *FrL* KrbA 29, 31 LlbA 25, **OSw** *UL* Kkb,
Äb, *VmL* Kkb, **ONorw** *GuL* Krb, Kpb, Olb

immune **OIce** *Grg* Þsþ 52, 53 Misc
240, *Js* Rkb 2, **OSw** *DL* Gb

inviolate **ONorw** *FrL* Mhb 22

protected **OGu** *GL* A 37, 59, Add. 1 (B 4)

protected by law **OIce** *Jó* Llb 59

sacred **OGu** *GL* A 6, 8

sanctified **OGu** *GL* A 8

hallowed **ONorw** *GuL* Krb

immune by the law **ONorw** *GuL* Mhb

without guilt **ONorw** *GuL* Olb

Expressions:

heilagt vatn (ON)

hallowed water **ONorw** *GuL* Krb

heilög jörð (ON)

hallowed earth **ONorw** *GuL* Krb

heilagr dagr (ON)

In general, most kinds of work, the eating of meat
and fish, prosecutions and sexual intercourse were
forbidden during holy days and the preceding
night. See, e.g., GuL chs 16–18, 20, 27 and 266.

holiday **ONorw** *GuL* Krb, Kpb, Olb

heilagr dómr (ON)

relic **OIce** *Js* Kdb 5

See also: *friþer*, *friþhelagher*, *friþkallaþer*,
friþlös, *hemfriþer*, *hælgh*, *hælghe*, *hælghidagher*,
manhælghi, *ohailigr*, *saker*, *skóggangr*, *varþnaþer*

Refs: Bætke 1942; Calissendorff 1964, 119–20;
Heggstad, Leiv, Finn Hødnebø, and Erik
Simensen 2012, s.v.v. *helga, helgi*; KLNM s.v.v.
*helgener, helgi, helligbrøde, kalendarium II,
vilodagar*; Lexikon des Mittelalters s.v. *friede*;
Peel 2015, 172 note 37/7–9; Schlyter 1877, s.v.v.
helagher, hælgh; Sundkvist 2015, 119–20

helbryghþu (OSw) adj.

fit **OSw** *UL* Äb, *VmL* Äb

helgavika (ON) noun

Rogation Week **OIce** *Grg* Þsþ 56, 58

See also: *gangdagahelgr*

helgihald (ON) noun

keeping of holy days **ONorw** *BorgL* 14

heli (OGu) noun

sanctuary **OGu** *GL* A 13

helmingr (ON) noun

half share **OIce** *Jó* Llb 64

helsótt (ON) noun

Expressions:

liggja í helsótt (ON)

to lie on one's deathbed **OIce** *Grg* Arþ 126

helvænn (ON) adj.

expected to die **OIce** *Jó* Llb 64

hema (OSw) verb

provide home **OSw** *HL* Kgb

Expressions:

husa ok hema, hysa ok hema, husa ællær
hema (OSw) **hysa eþa haima** (OGu)

house and shelter **OSw** *SdmL* Kgb

give shelter or lodging **OSw** *UL*
Kgb, Kmb *VmL* Kgb, Kmb

shelter or house **OGu** *GL* A 2

See also: *forvist, husa, samvist, samværa, viþervist*

hemaföder (OSw) **hemefød** (ODan) **hemfödder** (OSw)
adj.

Born at the home of the one claiming ownership.
Applied to both disputed animals, everything from
bees to horses, and to people, i.e. slaves (explicitly
in OSw ÄVgL and YVgL) concerning accusations of
theft.

born at home **OSw** *YVgL* Tb, *ÄVgL* Tb

domesticated **OSw** *YVgL* Drb

home born **ODan** *SkL* 142

home bred **ODan** *ESjL* 3, *JyL* 2, *SkL*
197, **OSw** *YVgL* Vs, Drb

See also: *fylsmærke, fylsvat*

hemagiorþer (OSw) adj.

Used of items made at the home of the one claiming
ownership when disputed by accusations of theft.

home made **OSw** *SdmL* Tjdb

See also: *hemaföder*

hemahion (OSw) noun

Literally, 'home people'. Although this is commonly
perceived to designate slaves (cf. *hemakona*), the
translation 'household serfs' is suggested because it
was not wholly clear if their status was identical to
that of *þrælar* (see *þræl*). They do seem, however, to
have been treated in some respects as property in UL
and VmL. In UL they are grouped with other 'poor
people' who did not have to buy their own candles
for the churching of women and who did not have to
give a specific amount to the church for the service.
In VmL they were permitted to undertake a purchase
of up to an *örtugh*, which would seem to indicate a
certain amount of autonomy not expected for a full
slave. No such permission is granted in UL, however.
It can perhaps be inferred that 'slave' and 'free' were
not binary states, but a continuum, not uniquely
determined by birth, but sometimes by circumstances
beyond a person's control, or as a result of their
(criminal) actions.

household serf **OSw** *UL* Kkb, Äb,
Mb, *VmL* Äb, Mb, Kmb

See also: *griþ, hemakona, hion,*
leghohion, ofræls, þræl

Refs: KLNM s.v. *tyende*; Nevéus 1974; Schlyter
1877, s.v. *hema hion*; SL UL, 38 note 46, 82
note 20, 157 note 12; SL VmL, 127 note 12

hemakona (OSw) noun

Possibly synonomous with *huskona* (q.v.).

female slave **OSw** *VmL* Kkb, Mb

See also: *ambat*

hembuþ (OSw) **heimboð** (ON) noun

reprimand **OSw** *HL* Blb

warning **ONorw** *GuL* Llb

hemefødvitne (ODan) noun

A testimony, usually consisting of an oath of twelve
men supported by two others, confirming that a
disputed domestic animal was born at the home of the
one claiming ownership, and thus not stolen.

proof of home birth **ODan** *JyL* 2

See also: *fylsmærke, fylsvat, hemaföder*

hemegjald (ODan) noun

carrying a loss for oneself **ODan** *JyL* 1, 3

no compensation **ODan** *JyL* 1

hemfriþer (OSw) **haim friþr** (OGu) **haima friþr**
(OGu) **heimafriðr** (ON) noun

Peace at home, often in a wide sense including fields,
etc., for instance in OIce Js, which also explicitly
includes travelling to and from home. Whether
originating in pre-Christian or Christian tradition is
disputed. In OSw, part of the king's peace laws. Violent
attacks at home resulted in additional fines, to either
the king, community, victim or all three, however
only for the highest-ranking victim in OGu GL. OIce
Js prescribed outlawry if the victim survived. The
home peace, understood as asylum, did not apply to
convicted thieves (OSw SdmL, UL).

home peace **OIce** *Jó* Mah 19, *Js* Mah
11, **OSw** *SdmL* Mb, Tjdb, Till

homestead sanctity **OGu** *GL* A 12, **OSw** *UL* Mb

offence against the peace of the home **OSw** *YVgL* Urb

peace of home **OSw** *YVgL* Add

See also: *friþer*

Refs: KLNM s.v. *fridslagstiftning*;
NE s.v. *fridslagstiftning*

hemfylghia (OSw) verb

give as a marriage gift **OSw** *YVgL* Äb, *ÄVgL* Äb

See also: *hemfylghþ*

hemfylghþ (OSw) **haim fylgi** (OGu) **heimanfylgja**
(ON) **hemfylghia** (OSw) **hemfylgia** (OSw) noun

A gift from parents, or the other closest relative, to
a child — particularly a daughter — on marriage.
Likely to be the personal property of the woman and
typically consisted of textiles and tools for textile
making, but also other movables and immovables,
reflecting the resources of the giver. In OSw, an
advance of the inheritance, in some laws compulsory
while in others voluntary, and to be returned for
redistribution at the death of the giver. In ÖgL, also
the gift given by the groom to the bride. In ONorw,
a substitution for inheritance of daughters, and could
not be redistributed among her siblings. Although the
term is not attested in Danish laws, wedding gifts to
daughters are presumed to have been given, albeit
with no specification as to them being her personal
property.

advance of inheritance **OSw** *HL* Äb

dowry **OGu** *GL* A 20, 28, 46, **OIce** *Grg* Þsþ 62 Arþ
118 Feþ 144, 150 Fjl 223, *Jó* Mah 30 Kge 1, 13, *Js*
Mah 36 Kvg 1, 3 Ert 19, *KRA* 18, **ONorw** *FrL* KrbB
7, 17 ArbB 19 Kvb 2, **OSw** *YVgL* Äb, *ÄVgL* Äb

endowment **OIce** *KRA* 4

marriage gift **OSw** *DL* Gb, *YVgL*
Äb, Jb, *ÄVgL* Äb, Jb

marriage portion **ONorw** *GuL* Arb, **OSw** *SdmL* Gb,
UL Äb (table of contents only), *VmL* Äb (rubric only)

See also: *fylghia*, *gift*, *heimangerð*,
hemfærth, *mæþfylghþ*

Refs: KLNM s.v. *medgift*; Kock 1926; SAOB, s.v.
hemföljd; Schlyter s.v.v. *fylghþ*, *haim fylgi*, *hemfylghþ*

hemfærth (ODan) noun

dowry **ODan** *JyL* 1

hemföþa (OSw) noun

A disputed domestic animal born at the home of the
one claiming ownership, and thus not stolen.

animal that is home bred **OSw** *SdmL* Tjdb

livestock born at home **OSw** *DL* Bb

See also: *hemaföder*

hemföþoeþer (OSw) noun

An oath confirming that a disputed domestic animal,
or a slave, was born at the home of the one claiming
ownership, and thus not stolen.

oath about birth at home **OSw** *YVgL* Add

See also: *fylsvat*, *hemaföder*

hemgiva (OSw) verb

give as a marriage gift **OSw** *YVgL* Äb, *ÄVgL* Äb

hemgæf (OSw) **heimangjöf** (ON) noun

dowry **OIce** *Jó* Kge 2, **OSw** *YVgL* Add

marriage gift **OSw** *YVgL* Jb, *ÄVgL* Jb

morning gift **OSw** *YVgL* Kkb

See also: *gæf*, *hemfylghþ*

hemgærþ (OSw) **hemgiærþ** (OSw) noun

homemade **OSw** *UL* Mb, *VmL* Mb

See also: *hemagiorþer*

hemsokn (OSw) **hemsokn** (ODan) **haim sokn** (OGu)
heimsókn (ON) noun

Literally, 'home attack'. Breaking into a man's house,
assaulting him and his household in their home, were
severely punished. This crime is described at length
in HL, where it was punished harder the closer to
the home it was committed, culminating with the
compensation/fine for *hemsokn* committed in the
man's bed. In UL and VmL the crime is handled in
the King's Book, where the most serious crimes were
listed, those that broke the King's Peace (*eþsöre*). In
ÖgL, UL and VmL it is stated that it was not *hemsokn*
if someone came to the residence on friendly terms but
hostilities broke out in the course of the visit, even if
they led to violence. If, on the other hand, the visitor
went away and returned with armed companions,
then it was considered to be *hemsokn*. There are
stipulations in the laws concerning the extent of a
householder's protection from his dwellings, often
given in alliterative phrases.

In Denmark such crimes were often gang crimes,
which were more severely punished (graded according
to the number of gang members) than crimes
committed by individuals acting on their own.

In GL the word is used only for penalty, not the
crime itself. Killing the householder usually elicited
triple compensation.

Also in Norway, *heimsókn* was considered to be
a serious crime, normally leading to outlawry for the
culprit, but he might be released by paying a very high
compensation/fine, forty *merkr*, half of this to the king
in case of killing (*dráp*, see *drap*). See GuL chs 142,
178, 242.

assault on someone in his home **ONorw** *GuL* Mhb

attack at/in one's home **ODan** *VSjL* 64,
OSw *DL* Eb, *SdmL* Kgb, *UL* Kgb, *VmL*
Kgb, *YVgL* Urb, *ÄVgL* Md, *ÖgL* Eb

*distance as far away the peace (for
a man) goes* **OSw** *HL* Mb

fine for an attack in the home **OGu** *GL* A 12

home attack **OIce** *Jó* Mah 19

*serious trespassing (in someone's
home)* **OSw** *HL* Kgb

theft in someone's home **OSw** *HL* Blb

trespassing in someone's home **OSw** *YVgL* Drb, Add

See also: *aganga, bothegang, garthgang, hærværk, landnám*

Refs: KLNM s.v. *hærværk*; Peel 2015, 108–09 notes 12/2, 12/3–5, 12/9–10; Schlyter s.v. *hemsokn*; SL GL, 254 note 2 to chapter 12; SL UL, 54 note 19, 123 note 70; SL VmL, 39 note 5, 92–94 notes 64, 66–68; SL ÖgL, 46–47

hemstæmpna (OSw) **heimstefna** (ON) verb

call someone at his farm OSw HL Rb

sue a person at his home OSw HL Rb

summon somebody home **ONorw** GuL Kpb, Kvb, Løb, Arb

summon to be at home OIce *Grg* Lbþ 193, *Jó* Lbb 10

hemstæmpnung (OSw) **heimstefna** (ON) noun

The *hemstæmpnung* was an official summoning served at one's home, a legal action where the plaintiff bade the accused before witnesses to be at his home on a set day.

home summons OIce *Jó* Kge 19, 26 Kab 9, **ONorw** GuL Kpb, Arb, Tjb, Olb

summoning a person at his home OSw HL Rb

summons to be at home OIce *Grg* Lbþ 181, **ONorw** *FrL* Rgb 2

See also: *stæmna*

Refs: Hagland & Sandnes 1997, 108; KLNM s.v. *rettergang*

hemul (OSw) **heimul** (OGu) **heimill** (ON) **hemol** (OSw) adj.

at one's free disposal **ONorw** GuL Kvb, Olb

authenticated in legal ownership OSw UL Jb

confirmed (ownership of goods) OSw HL Mb

having a warrantable right OIce *Grg* Tíg 260

legitimate **ONorw** *FrL* Kvb 16

possessing a legal right OIce *Jó* Llb 2, 3 Þjb 16 Fml 28

responsible OSw HL Kmb

rightful (ownership) OGu GL Add. 7 (B 49)

warrantable OIce *Grg* Feþ 144, *Js* Kvg 3, *KRA* 15

See also: *hemula, ohemul*

hemul (OSw) adv.

by law OSw UL Mb

hemula (OSw) **hemle** (ODan) **heimila** (ON) verb

act as guarantor OSw UL Jb

defend OSw ÖgL Kkb

defend the claim of ownership OSw UL Kkb, VmL Kkb

entitle ODan JyL 2, VSjL 82, 83

give a right **ONorw** *FrL* LlbA 1

give title **ODan** ESjL 3, JyL 1, **OIce** *Jó* Lbb 6, 11 Llb 1 Kab 23 Þjb 4, **OSw** SdmL Bb

give warrantable title **ODan** SkL 81, 82

guarantee a sale OSw UL Jb

have title **ODan** ESjL 3

have warrantable rights OIce *Grg* Feþ 151

warrant **ODan** SkL 233

warrant a title OIce *Grg* Lbþ 175 Rsþ 228, *Js* Lbb 2

warrant one's ownership OSw HL Jb

See also: *hemuld*

hemuld (OSw) **hemlen** (ODan) **heimild** (ON) **heimilð** (ON) **hemold** (OSw) **hemul** (OSw) **hemult** (OSw) noun

Related to the noun *hem* (OSw) 'home'. A seller's (or donor's etc.) authority to release property (landed or not) to a buyer (or other recipient), as well as his responsibility to prove this authority; i.e. essentially evidence of being the rightful owner.

authentication OSw UL Mb, Jb, Ad. 12, VmL Mb

consent **ONorw** GuL Løb

legal right to something **ONorw** GuL Llb

legal title OIce *Jó* Llb 1, 71 Þjb 4

right **ONorw** *FrL* LlbB 3

title **ODan** ESjL 3, JyL 2, VSjL 82, **OSw** SdmL Bb

warrant **ODan** ESjL 3, SkL 233

warranty OIce *Grg* Lbþ 172, 174 Rsþ 227, *Js* Lbb 10, 15 Rkb 1 Þjb 3

Expressions:

i hemuld standa (OSw)

stand guarantor OSw UL Mb, Jb VmL Mb, Jb

See also: *borghan, fang, fangaman, hemulsman*

hemulsman (OSw) **heimildarmaðr** (ON) **heimilðarmaðr** (ON) **hemolman** (OSw) noun

guarantor OSw UL Jb, Add. 12

guarantor of ownership OSw UL Mb, Jb, VmL Mb, Jb

man who holds the title OIce *Jó* Þjb 4

person who promised or leased out OSw HL Blb

warranty man OIce *Grg* Lbþ 172, 174, *Jó* Lbb 1 Llb 26, **ONorw** *FrL* Rgb 25 LlbA 26, GuL Tjb, **OSw** SdmL Jb, Tjdb

See also: *borghanaman, fangaman, fastar (pl.), hemuld, skuli, taki*

heptalaun (OGu) **heptalauns** (OGu) noun

redemption fine OGu GL A 43

See also: *hæfta, lösn, þinglaun*

heraðsdómr (ON) noun

district court OIce *Grg* Þsþ 59 Feþ 167 Hrs 234

See also: *hreppadómr*

heraðsfleyttr (ON) adj.

district-sent **ONorw** *EidsL* 41.1

rumoured in the district **ONorw** *GuL* Krb

heraðskirkja (ON) noun

district church **ONorw** *BorgL* 8, 12.1

parish church **ONorw** *GuL* Krb

heraðskona (ON) noun

woman from the district **ONorw** *FrL* Kvb 23

heraðsprestr (ON) noun

district priest **ONorw** *BorgL* 11.1

heraðssókn (ON) noun

district prosecution **OIce** *Grg* Hrs 234, *Js* Kab 8

legal proceedings before a district court **OIce** *Jó* Kab 10

heraðstakmark (ON) noun

district limit **OIce** *Grg* Feþ 167

herbergja (ON) verb

house **OIce** *Jó* Kge 29

herfang (ON) noun

booty **OIce** *Jó* Mah 2

herfloti (ON) noun

hostile fleet **ONorw** *GuL* Leb

herhlaup (ON) noun

assembling for war **ONorw** *GuL* Leb

See also: *hersaga, hær*

hernuðr (ON) **hernaðr** (ON) noun

plunder **ONorw** *BorgL* 8.5

raid **OIce** *Jó* Mah 3, **ONorw** *BorgL* 8.5

raiding **ONorw** *GuL* Leb

hernuminn (ON) adj.

taken captive **ONorw** *GuL* Kvb

hersaga (ON) noun

report of an impending attack **OIce** *Jó* Mah 4

reports of war **ONorw** *GuL* Mhb, Leb

See also: *herhlaup, hær*

hershendr (pl.) (OGu) **hershendr** (pl.) (ON) noun

hands of an enemy **ONorw** *GuL* Mhb

taken hostage **OGu** *GL* A 28

hertogadómr (ON) noun

dukedom **OFar** *Seyð* 0

hes (ON) noun

swivel **ONorw** *GuL* Kpb

hespa (ON) noun

hank **OIce** *Grg* Klþ 8 Tíg 255

hestfórr (ON) **hestfærr** (ON) adj.

able to ride a horse **OIce** *Jó* Kge 21

capable of riding a horse **ONorw** *GuL* Arb

heta (OSw) **hete** (ODan) **haita** (OGu) **heita** (OGu) verb

Verbal sanctions against certain convicted criminals legitimized the use of invectives that otherwise would have been considered defamation, a criminal offence. The frequently occurring statement that a convicted criminal should 'be known as a thief' or 'be called a whore', etc., in connection with other penalties, suggests that such verbal sanctions could be seen as part of the punishment. Certain non-criminal circumstances also caused the laws to stipulate that individuals publicly 'be known as the child's father' or 'be called a lawfully gotten wife', etc. Exceptionally in GL, it refers to heathen worship.

be called **ODan** *ESjL* 3, *JyL* 3, *SkKL* 3, 9, *SkL* 201, 209, **OGu** *GL* A 23, *GS* Ch. 1, 4, **OSw** *DL* Kkb, Bb, Tjdb, Rb, *HL* Mb, *UL* Äb, Mb, Blb, Rb, *VmL* Äb, Mb, Kmb, Bb, Rb, *YVgL* Äb, Rlb, Tb, Jb, *ÄVgL* Äb, Gb, Rlb, Jb, *ÖgL* Kkb, Db

be considered to be **OSw** *DL* Gb

be declared **OSw** *UL* Mb, Kmb, *VmL* Mb, Kmb

be held to be **OSw** *UL* Äb, *VmL* Äb

be known as **OSw** *SdmL* Kkb, Gb, Äb, Bb, Kmb, Mb, Tjdb

be looked upon **OSw** *HL* Äb

be named **OSw** *YVgL* Drb, Tb, *ÄVgL* Vs

pray to **OGu** *GL* A 4

See also: *fullréttisorð, haizl, kalla, lysa, níð, oqvæþinsorþ, upphaita, upphaizlusoypr, vanvirðing, þokki*

Refs: Inger 2011, 72; KLNM s.v. *ærekrænkelse*; Ney 1998

heygjald (ON) noun

hay price **OIce** *Grg* Lbþ 198

heyja (ON) verb

belong to an assembly **OIce** *Grg* Klþ 4

hold an assembly **OIce** *Grg* Þsþ 84

participate in an assembly **OIce** *Grg* Þsþ 49, 56

heykaup (ON) noun

purchase of hay **OIce** *Jó* Llb 12

heyrendr (pl.) (ON) noun

witnesses outside the court **ONorw** *GuL* Olb

See also: *hörœngi*

heysala (ON) noun

sale of hay **OIce** *Jó* Llb 11, 12

heysdeild (ON) noun

division of hay **OIce** *Grg* Lbþ 198

heytaka (ON) noun

theft of hay **ONorw** *FrL* LlbB 15

heyverð (ON) noun

hay price **OIce** *Jó* Llb 11

See also: *heygjald*

heþin (OSw) **hethen** (ODan) **haiþin** (OGu) **heiðinn** (ON) **hedin** (OSw) **hæþin** (OSw) adj.

In the early Middle Ages, when Christianity was relatively new in Norway, traces of heathen cult and practice were heavily punished. See, e.g., GuL ch. 28. In OSw and ODan laws the word *heþin* was often used of children in the sense 'unbaptized'. Leaving a child unbaptized was not allowed. According to ODan law unbaptized children could not inherit, and OSw law punished priests who neglected to baptize. Killing unbaptized children was a criminal act. Emergency christening was allowed when a priest was not available. Gotlanders agreed to follow the Swedish king in crusades against heathen countries, but not against Christian ones (GS ch. 4).

heathen **ODan** *VSjL* 6, **OGu** *GL* A 4, *GS* Ch. 1, 2, 3, 4, **ONorw** *GuL* Krb, Løb, **OSw** *UL* För, Kkb, *VmL* Kkb

pagan **OSw** *SdmL* Kkb, Mb, *SmL*

unbaptized **OSw** *HL* Kkb, *SmL*, *UL* Mb, *VmL* Mb, *ÖgL* Kkb

unchristian **OSw** *HL* Kkb

Expressions:

heiðinn dómr (ON)

heathendom **ONorw** *GuL* Krb

Refs: KLNM s.v. *trosskiftet*

heþna (OSw) **haiþna** (OGu) **heiðni** (ON) noun

heathendom **ONorw** *GuL* Krb

pagan times **OSw** *YVgL* Jb, *ÄVgL* Jb

paganism **OGu** *GL* A 1

See also: *heþin*

héralinn (ON) adj.

of native birth **ONorw** *GuL* Tjb

hiernskal (OGu) noun

skull **OGu** *GL* A 19

hindardags (ON) adv.

on the following day **ONorw** *GuL* Olb

hinder (OSw) noun

hindrance **OSw** *UL* Kkb

hindradagher (OSw) noun

day after the wedding **OSw** *SdmL* Gb

hindradagsgæf (OSw) noun

bride price **OSw** *UL* Äb

morning gift **OSw** *YVgL* Frb, Äb, Gb, *ÄVgL* Slb, Äb, Gb, *ÖgL* Eb

wedding gift **OSw** *HL* Äb

See also: *gæf*, *morghongæf*

hindrvitni (ON) noun

superstition **OIce** *Grg* Klþ 7

hinna (OGu) noun

membrane **OGu** *GL* A 19

Expressions:

himin eþa hinna (OGu)

membrane **OGu** *GL* A 19

hion (OSw) **hjon** (ODan) **hjón** (ON) **hjóna** (ON) **hjún** (ON) noun

Derived from a PGmc word meaning 'family', and etymologically related to *hirð* (q.v.) and other similar words, it might mean 'household members' or 'servants', or 'folk' in general, and in the context of marriage refer to the married or betrothed couple as an entity. In all the meanings exhibited there is a sense of 'belonging', whether between people or between a person and a household. The compounds formed from the word as a prefix tend to refer to aspects of marriage, whereas when used as a suffix, the word tends to specify a type of servant, which illustrates the two separate meanings.

betrothed couple **OSw** *DL* Kkb

couple **ONorw** *BorgL* 3.4 17.1, **OSw** *DL* Gb, *SdmL* Kkb, Gb, Mb, *UL* Kkb, Äb, Mb, *VmL* Kkb, Äb, Mb, *YVgL* Kkb

domestic servant **OSw** *DL* Kkb, Eb, Bb

engaged couple **OSw** *HL* Kkb

folk **OSw** *UL* Kmb, *VmL* Kmb

household **ONorw** *EidsL* 12.2, *FrL* Mhb 5, **OSw** *ÖgL* Kkb, Eb, Db

household member **ONorw** *BorgL* 5.2 14.5, **OSw** *SdmL* Kgb, Till, *UL* Kgb, Äb, *VmL* Kgb, Mb

household members **OIce** *Js* Mah 11, *KRA* 13, **ONorw** *EidsL* 12.3, *FrL* Rgb 3 Bvb 6

household servant **OSw** *HL* Kgb

household servants **OFar** *Seyð* 3, 7

man and wife **OIce** *Grg* Arþ 125 Tíg 259, *Jó* Kge 3, *Js* Kvg 3, 5, **ONorw** *FrL* Kvb 5, **OSw** *DL* Gb

married couple **OIce** *Jó* Kge 7, 13, *KRA* 15, **ONorw** *EidsL* 4

member of a household **OSw** *DL* Eb, *HL* Kgb

people belonging to the household **ONorw** *GuL* Kvb, Mhb, Tjb, Leb

people of the household **OIce** *Jó* Llb 4

servant **ODan** *ESjL* 1–3, *JyL* 2, 3, *SkL* 62, 122, 126,131–135, 152, *VSjL* 56, 69, **OSw** *HL* Kkb, *SdmL* Kkb, *SmL*, *UL* Kkb, Kmb, Blb, *VmL* Kmb, Bb, *YVgL* Kkb, Drb, Rlb, Tb, Add, *ÄVgL* Kkb, Rlb, Tb, *ÖgL* Eb *slave* **ODan** *ESjL* 3

spouse **ODan** *ESjL* 1, *JyL* 1, *SkL* 7, **OIce**
KRA 18, **ONorw** *BorgL* 17, **OSw** *HL* Äb,
SmL, *YVgL* Äb, Gb, Jb, *ÄVgL* Äb, Gb, Jb

unfree servant **ODan** *VSjL* 86

See also: *ambat, annöpogher, fostra, fostre,
frælsgiva, frælsgivi, griþ, gæfþræl, hemahion,
hemakona, hionafælagh, hionalagh, hionamali,
hionaspan, hionavighning, hjónalið, hjú, husfolk,
huskona, husþiauþ, hælghhion, leghohion,
man, repohion, varþnaþahion, þræl*

Refs: Brink 2005; Brink 2012; Hellquist
[1948] 1964, s.v. *hjon*; Korpiola 2004;
SAOB s.v. *hjon*; Schlyter 1877, s.v. *hion*

hionafælagh (OSw) **hjónafélag** (ON) noun

The economic partnership between married
spouses. Rarely attested as a compound noun and
possibly the same as OSw *hionalagh*/ON *hjónalag*.
An entire chapter in Jó Kge 3 outlines the rights
and responsibilities of each spouse in this kind of
partnership. A similar description exists in Grg
Feþ 153. According to ÖgL Kb 28 the bishop was
empowered to establish or dissolve such partnerships.

community property **OIce** *Jó* Kge 3

marriage **OSw** *ÖgL* Kkb

See also: *fælagh, hionalagh*

Refs: Agnes Arnórsdóttir and Thyra Nors 1999;
ONP s.v. *hjónafélag*; Schlyter s.v. *hionafælagh*

hionalagh (OSw) **hjonelagh** (ODan) **hjónalag** (ON)
hionælagh (OSw) noun

conjugality **OSw** *YVgL* Kkb

connubial union **OSw** *HL* Kkb

couple **OSw** *HL* Kkb

intercourse **OSw** *HL* Kkb

marital intercourse **OSw** *UL* Kkb, *VmL* Kkb

marriage **ODan** *ESjL* 3, *SkKL* 11, **OSw** *SmL*,
UL Kkb, Jb, *VmL* Kkb, Jb, *YVgL* Äb

marriage contract **OSw** *DL* Kkb

marriage union **OSw** *SdmL* Kkb

married couple **OSw** *SmL*

matrimony **OSw** *SdmL* Kkb, *YVgL* Kkb

relationship **OSw** *UL* Kkb, *VmL* Kkb

union **ONorw** *BorgL* 3.4 15.4

See also: *giftarmal*

hionamali (OSw) noun

servant's payment **OSw** *HL* Kkb

hionaspan (OSw) **hionaspanan** (OSw) noun

enticing servants to steal **OSw** *HL* Mb

hionavighning (OSw) **hionæwighneng** (OSw) noun

marriage **OSw** *HL* Kkb, *SdmL* Kkb

wedding **OSw** *UL* Kkb, *VmL* Kkb

See also: *vighning*

hiorþ (OSw) **hjorth** (ODan) noun

In ODan, defined as twelve bovines. JyL considered
intentional illegal grazing by a *hjorth* a gang crime
(ODan *hærværk*), which was severely punished.
Contrasted to damage made by stray or single animals.

cattle herd **ODan** *JyL* 3

herd **ODan** *ESjL* 2, *JyL* 3, *SkL*
168, 169, **OSw** *SdmL* Bb

See also: *stoth, vrath*

hiorþlöt (OSw) noun

pastureland **OSw** *SdmL* Bb, *UL*
Mb, Blb, *VmL* Mb, Bb

See also: *fælöt, hiorþvalder, löt*

Refs: Schlyter s.v. *hiorþlöt*

hiorþvalder (OSw) **hiorþvalla** (OSw) **hiorþvalle**
(OSw) noun

common grazing land **OSw** *UL* Blb, *VmL* Bb

grazing land **OSw** *SdmL* Bb

pasture **OSw** *UL* Blb, *VmL* Bb

See also: *aker, hiorþlöt, svinavalder, valder, æng*

Refs: Schlyter s.v. *hiorþvalder*

hirð (ON) noun

A lord's, including a king's, retinue.

bodyguard **ONorw** *FrL* Bvb 1

king's bodyguard **ONorw** *GuL* Krb

king's court **OIce** *Jó* Mah 2

retinue **OIce** *Js* Kdb 4, **ONorw** *FrL* Mhb 4

See also: *hirðstjóri, hær*

Refs: Cleasby and Vigfusson s.v. *hirð*

hirða (ON) verb

hide **ONorw** *GuL* Leb

keep **ONorw** *GuL* Løb, Olb, Leb

hirðhestr (ON) noun

bodyguard's horse **ONorw** *FrL* Rgb 44

hirðskip (ON) noun

bodyguard's ship **ONorw** *FrL* Rgb 44

hirðstjóri (ON) noun

The most senior representative of the Norwegian king
in Iceland from the late thirteenth century until the end
of the fifteenth century. A *hirðstjóri* is occasionally
referred to as a *lénsmaðr* (see *lænsmaþer*). Usually
there was only a single *hirðstjóri* present in Iceland,
but anywhere between one and four could be
active at a given time. The *hirðstjóri* had a range of

responsibilities including the collection of royal fines from sheriffs (ON *sýslumenn*, see *sysluman*) and managing royal property in Iceland. They also carried out a number of judicial duties, such as presenting royal ordinances at the General Assembly and occasionally appointing judges.

In Iceland the title was replaced by the *höfuðsmaðr* ('headman, leader') or *fógeti* (see *foghati*) (the latter of which was unfortunately also at times used to refer to the *hirðstjóri*'s agent) by the end of the fifteenth century.

In Norway the *hirðstjóri* must once have had some connection to the king's retinue (*hirð*), but the term ceased to be used there by around the 1390s (cf. Wærdahl 2011, 258). They may have held a kind of military rank similar to captain, and it is in this capacity that they appear in the Church Law of GuL.

captain **OIce** *Js* Kdb 4, 6

officer of the King's bodyguard **ONorw** *GuL* Krb

See also: *hirð*, *jarl*, *merkismaðr*, *sysluman*

Refs: CV s.v. *hirðstjóri*; Fritzner s.v. *hirðstjóri*; Hertzberg s.v. *hirðstjóri*; Imsen 2014; Jón Viðar Sigurðsson 2014; KLNM s.v.v. *embedsindtægter*, *hirðstjóri*, *lensmann*; Wærdahl 2011

hirzla (ON) noun

safekeeping **OIce** *Jó* Þjb 15 Fml 26

storage shed **OIce** *Jó* Þjb 15

hirþe (OSw) **hirthe** (ODan) **hirþingi** (OSw) noun

shepherd **ODan** *ESjL* 2, *JyL* 3, **OSw** *YVgL* Frb, Rlb, Föb, Utgb, *ÄVgL* Rlb, Föb

hirþgarþer (OSw) noun

farm of a lord's retinue **OSw** *ÖgL* Db

hirþman (OSw) **hirthman** (ODan) **hirðmaðr** (ON) noun

A member of the king's retinue.

king's man **ODan** *JyL* 3

man of the king's guard **OSw** *SdmL* Kmb

retainer **OIce** *Js* Mah 5

Refs: Tamm and Vogt, eds, 2016, 307

hittas (OSw) verb

fight **OSw** *SdmL* Gb

híð (ON) noun

A bear caught in a lair belonged to the man who owned the ground where the lair was found (GuL ch. 94). Hired slaves were not to be sent to bears' lairs (GuL ch. 69).

lair **ONorw** *GuL* Løb, Llb

Refs: KLNM s.v.v. *björnejakt*, *jakt*

hjalm (ODan) **hjalmr** (ON) noun

barn **ODan** *JyL* 1

stack **ONorw** *GuL* Llb

hjalmróður (pl.) (ON) noun

stack supports **ONorw** *GuL* Llb

hjáfélag (ON) noun

trade partnership **OIce** *Jó* Fml 22

hjoneleghe (ODan) noun

payment of servants **ODan** *JyL* 1

hjones (ODan) verb

marry **ODan** *ESjL* 3

See also: *hion*

hjónalið (ON) noun

household helpers **OIce** *Grg* Þsþ 80

See also: *hion*, *hjú*

hjónaskilnuðr (ON) noun

separation of man and wife **OIce** *Grg* Feþ 149

hjónaskírn (ON) noun

baptism by a couple **ONorw** *EidsL* 4

hjónskapsslit (ON) noun

dissolution of marriage **ONorw** *FrL* KrbB 10

hjul (ODan) noun

An implement for capital punishment in the form of a wheel on which arsonists, church burglars and murderers could be broken. It was not specified who was to act as executioner.

wheel **ODan** *ESjL* 2, *SkL* 151

See also: *galghi*, *hang*, *huþstryka*, *hængia*, *morþ*, *sten*, *stæghl*, *sværþ*

Refs: KLNM s.v. *dødsstraf*

hjú (ON) noun

household people **OIce** *Grg* Klþ 10 Lbþ 181, 219 Hrs 234, *Jó* Llb 3, 13, *Js* Mah 11, *KRA* 4

man and wife **OIce** *Grg* Ómb 128, 143 Feþ 149 Tíg 259

married couple **OIce** *KRA* 15

See also: *hion*, *hjónalið*

hjúskaparhald (ON) noun

observance of marriage **OIce** *KRA* 18

hjúskaparráð (ON) noun

marriage **OIce** *Grg* Klþ 18

hjúskapr (ON) **hjónskapr** (ON) **hjúnskapr** (ON) noun

marriage **OIce** *Jó* Mah 27, *Js* Kvg 5, *KRA* 1, **ONorw** *EidsL* 22.1, *GuL* Krb

matrimony **OIce** *KRA* 16, **ONorw** *FrL* KrbB 6

relations **ONorw** *EidsL* 4

wedlock **OIce** *Jó* MagBref

See also: *eiginorð*, *kvánfang*

hland (ON) noun
  urine **ONorw** *GuL* Løb
hlaup (ON) noun
  assault **OIce** *Grg* Vís 86
  rush **ONorw** *GuL* Mhb
  See also: *frumhlaup*
hlunnar (pl.) (ON) noun
  rollers **ONorw** *GuL* Kpb, Llb, Leb
hlunnendi (ON) noun
  emolument **OIce** *Js* Kdb 7
hlunnroð (ON) noun
  This word is a compound of *hlunnr* 'roller' and *-roð* 'reddening' (namely by blood) and refers to an accident whereby a man was squeezed between the ship and the rollers.
  being killed under a ship **ONorw** *GuL* Mhb
  See also: *hlunnar (pl.)*
hlutfall (ON) noun
  A procedure for distribution of land and inheritance, as well as a means of resolving disputes about property.
  drawing lots **OIce** *Grg* Þsþ 29, 46, *Jó* Llb 13
  See also: *lotfal*, *lutfal*
hlýða (ON) verb
  pay attention to **ONorw** *GuL* Krb
hnekkja (ON) verb
  drive away **ONorw** *GuL* Kvr
hneyksli (ON) hnexyli (ON) noun
  dishonour **OIce** *Js* Mah 25
  shame **OIce** *Jó* Mah 26
hnúfa (ON) noun
  female thief whose nose has been cut off **ONorw** *GuL* Tjb
  See also: *stúfa*
hnykkja (ON) verb
  jerk **OIce** *Jó* Mah 22
hofþa (OSw) høvthe (ODan) höfþa (OSw) verb
  Derived from a noun meaning 'head'. In ODan, used of participation in an oath sworn by many, such as an entire village (SkL). In OSw, used of swearing a pre-oath (that was to be confirmed by fellow oath-takers) by the defendant (DL), by witnesses concerning marriage (SdmL) and by the *hæraþshöfþingi* 'district principal' concerning cases of *eþsöre* 'the king's (sworn) peace' (YVgL). Also of paying compensation in killing-cases (DL).
  begin an oath **OSw** *DL* Rb
  dictate an oath **OSw** *SdmL* Till, *YVgL* Add
  give an oath **ODan** *SkL* 72
  participate in an oath **ODan** *VSjL* 77
  pay **OSw** *DL* Mb
  prescribe an oath **OSw** *YVgL* Add
  swear **ODan** *VSjL* 76
  See also: *eiðstafr*, *eþer*, *foreþer*, *hæraþshöfþingi*, *munhaf*, *stava*
  Refs: Schlyter s.v. *hofþa*
hogsbot (ODan) noun
  compensation for cutting **ODan** *VSjL* 55
  fine for a blow **ODan** *VSjL* 30
  See also: *bot*
hogsl (OGu) noun
  This word occurs chiefly in the phrase *hogsl ok iþ*, translated 'consolation and provision'. In GL it states that this was what a widow was entitled to from her husband's estate. The amount involved is not stated. It is clear that the two elements of the expression do not refer to the same thing, since the word *hogsl* alone is used to designate the amount of compensation that an unmarried mother had a right to receive from the father of her child. The meaning of *hogsl* put forward by Schlyter and Pipping covers both situations. The word *iþ*, which does not occur independently in the East Norse laws, means 'work, occupation, diligence' and seems to have had a transferred meaning to the payment and reward for the effort that a wife put into the upkeep of the family and property during her marriage. Wessén suggests that *hogsl ok iþ* together were the equivalent of the *morghongæf* (q.v.) that the husband gave the bride elsewhere in the provincial laws, since there is no mention of this in GL and the widow retained this even if she married again. A certain amount was also granted to her from the estate for each year after being widowed that she was unmarried and in charge of her family, quite separately from the *hogsl ok iþ*.
  consolation **OGu** *GL* A 20, 20a
  See also: *hogsla*, *iþ*, *morghongæf*
  Refs: Holmbäck 1919, 221–22; KLNM, s.v.v. *enke*, *lejermål*, *morgongåva*; Peel 2015, 137–38 notes 20/54–56 to 20/66–70, 143 notes to 20a/24–31, 20a/27–28; Pipping 1905–07, cxii; Schlyter 1877, s.v.v. *hogsl*, *iþ*; SL GL, 268 notes 31 and 32 to chapter 20, 270 note 63 and 271 notes 67 and 71 to chapter 20a
hogsla (OGu) verb
  give/pay consolation **OGu** *GL* A 20, 21
  See also: *hogsl*

holmsköp (OSw) noun

　　{holmsköp} **OSw** *ÄVgL* Jb

　　See also: *holmstompt, köp*

holmstompt (OSw) noun

Presumably a new settlement on outlying land which gave the owner limited rights in the village.

　　{holmstompt} **OSw** *YVgL* Jb

　　Refs: Lindkvist forthcoming; Schlyter s.v. *holms tompt*

holund (ON) noun

　　internal wound **OIce** *Grg* Vís 86, 88

holunda (ON) adj.

　　wounded internally **ONorw** *FrL* Mhb 47

holundarsár (ON) noun

　　internal wound **OIce** *Grg* Vís 86

hor (OSw) **hor** (ODan) **hor** (OGu) **hór** (ON) noun

Appears in ecclesiastical, marriage, inheritance and criminal law sections. Mainly seen as a violation of the honour of the husband — and in ONorw other male guardians — whose wife, or in ONorw other dependent women, engaged in extramarital activities. In OSw, one of a few legitimate reasons for calling an extraordinary *þing* 'assembly', connected to the right to take the law into one's own hands. Generally, an offended man could kill the male adulterer if caught in the act, and in some laws his right extended to killing his wife too. In OSw UL and VmL the offended woman had the right to kill the adulteress but not her own cheating husband; although the latter may have been possible in OSw HL. Both the man and the woman could be fined, and in addition the woman could be rejected by her husband and lose all of her property, her wedding gifts as well as her legal part of the mutual property of the married couple. In ODan SkL, both the rejected wife and the offended husband were prohibited from remarrying while their spouse was still alive. In GL, a married woman committing adultery with an unmarried man received no consolation, while any man caught in the act with a married woman was heavily penalized (wergild equivalent or death), and with an unmarried woman, he was placed in the stocks and risked losing a hand or foot unless he or his kin redeemed it with six *marker*.

　　adultery **ODan** *ESjL* 2, *JyL* 1, **OGu** *GL* A 21, **ONorw** *GuL* Krb, Løb, Mhb, **OSw** *DL* Kkb, *HL* Kkb, Äb, *SdmL* Kkb, Gb, *UL* Kkb, Äb, Rb, *VmL* Kkb, Äb, *YVgL* Kkb, Gb, *ÄVgL* Gb, *ÖgL* Kkb, Vm

　　case concerning adultery **OSw** *DL* Kkb

　　Expressions:

enfalt hor (OSw)

Adultery where only one of the adulterers was married.

　　single adultery **OSw** *HL* Kkb *YVgL* Kkb

tvefalt hor (OSw)

Adultery where both adulterers were married.

　　double adultery **OSw** *YVgL* Kkb

　　twofold adultery **OSw** *HL* Kkb

　　See also: *giolsæmi, hordomber, hormal*

　　Refs: Agnes Arnórsdóttir and Thyra Nors 1999; Ekholst 2009, 228–35; KLNM s.v. *ægteskabsbrud*

horbarn (OSw) **horbarn** (ODan) **hórbarn** (ON) noun

Children conceived in adultery were distinguished from children conceived in other types of pre- and extramarital relations. The definition differed, but the parents were generally in a clandestine relation or had some prerequisite of a legal marriage missing. In OIce and OSw, they could be legitimatized if their parents married. Their right to parental inheritance varied; in OIce they were far down the line of prospective heirs, and in ODan they were explicitly excluded from paternal inheritance, while in OSw laws they were excluded from any inheritance.

　　bastard **OSw** *YVgL* Äb, *ÄVgL* Äb

　　child born in adultery **ODan** *JyL* 1, **OSw** *UL* Äb

　　child of adultery **OSw** *HL* Äb

　　illegitimate child **OIce** *Jó* Mah 17

　　See also: *barn, hor*

　　Refs: Agnes Arnórsdóttir and Thyra Nors 1999; KLNM s.v. *oäkta barn*; Tamm and Vogt, eds, 2016, 301

horbot (ODan) noun

　　compensation for adultery **ODan** *ESjL* 2

　　See also: *bot, hor*

hordomber (OSw) **hordom** (ODan) **hordombr** (OGu) **hórdómr** (ON) noun

　　adultery **ODan** *VSjL* 52, **OGu** *GL* A 39, **OIce** *Jó* Kge 7-6, *KRA* 18, 34, **ONorw** *BorgL* 17, *FrL* KrbA 46, **OSw** *SdmL* Kkb, Äb, *UL* Kkb, Äb, *VmL* Kkb, Äb

　　See also: *hor*

hordomssak (ODan) noun

　　adultery **ODan** *SkL* 221, 222

horkarl (ODan) noun

　　adulterer **ODan** *ESjL* 2, *SkL* 215, 216, *VSjL* 51, 52

　　See also: *gælmaþer*

horkona (OSw) **horkone** (ODan) noun

　　adulteress **ODan** *JyL* 1, *VSjL* 51

　　whore **OSw** *YVgL* Kkb

　　See also: *hor, hóra, kona*

hormal (OSw) noun

   adultery **OSw** *HL* Kkb, *SmL*

   adultery case **OSw** *SmL*, *ÖgL* Kkb

   case of adultery **OSw** *UL* Kkb, *VmL* Kkb

   See also: *hor*, *mal (1)*

hormalsbot (OSw) noun

   fine for an adultery case **OSw** *SdmL* Kkb

   See also: *bot*, *hor*, *mal (1)*

horn (ON) noun

   A damaged horn was considered a flaw, which reduced the value of the cow (GuL ch. 223) and gave rise to a demand for compensation (GuL ch. 41).

   horn on a cow **ONorw** *GuL* Kpb, Llb, Mhb

horna (ON) noun

   female nookling **ONorw** *FrL* ArbA 8

hornband (OGu) noun

   horn hobble **OGu** *GL* A 26

hornstafr (ON) noun

   corner post **ONorw** *GuL* Krb

   See also: *hyrnustokker*

hornungr (ON) noun

   One of several types of illegitimate child mentioned in the medieval Icelandic and Norwegian laws. According to Grg Arþ 118, a *hornungr* was specifically the illegitimate child of a free woman and a slave whom the woman frees. In GuL (Arb, ch. 104) a *hornungr* is the child of two free parents living together openly, but where the mother has not been given her bride price (ON *mundr*). It has been suggested that these 'nooklings', along with 'scrublings' (ON *hrísungr*) held free status, while other types of illegitimate children, such as those labelled *þyborinn*, were unfree.

   nookling **OIce** *Grg* Arþ 118, **ONorw** *FrL* ArbA 8 Rgb 47, *GuL* Løb, Arb

   See also: *bæsingr*, *hrísungr*, *laungetinn*, *vargdropi*

   Refs: Clunies Ross 1985; CV s.v. *hornungr*; Fritzner s.v. *hornungr*; GAO s.v.v. *Geschlechtsleite*, *Kinder*; GrgTr II:7; Hertzberg s.v. *hornungr*; KLNM s.v. *oäkta barn*; ONP s.v. *hornungr*

horsak (OSw) **horsak** (ODan) noun

   adultery **ODan** *SkKL* 9, **OSw** *YVgL* Gb, Add

   case of adultery **ODan** *JyL* 3, **OSw** *ÖgL* Kkb, Vm

   See also: *hor*, *sak*

horsiang (OSw) **horsjang** (ODan) **horsiæng** (OSw) **horsæng** (OSw) noun

   adulterous bed **OSw** *DL* Kkb, *UL* Äb (table of contents only), *VmL* Äb (rubric only)

   adultery **OSw** *DL* Kkb

   adultery bed **ODan** *JyL* 3

   bed of adultery **OSw** *ÖgL* Kkb, Eb

   fornication **OSw** *HL* Äb

horstakka (OSw) noun

   When a married woman was found guilty of adultery then, according to VmL, she could have her nose or ears cut off, or her clothing shredded upon discovery (it is not stated by whom), without any compensation being payable. In SdmL, the status of the adulteress is not mentioned, but the person allowed to take revenge was the wife who had been supplanted. The latter was to be paid three *marker* by the adulteress According to both VmL and UL, but not SdmL, she would then be taken to the assembly for judgement. If she were found guilty by twelve men, she was then to be subject to a 40-mark fine. If she were unable to pay then, according to UL, her nose and ears were to be cut off, together with her hair. Since she was unlikely to be able to pay, as she had forfeited her bride price by committing the offence, the mutilation or hair cutting was probably a frequent consequence. Short hair was possibly the sign of a prostitute, or at least a rebellious woman, in medieval society, following one of the interpretations of an obscure passage in 1 Corinthians 11. What happened if the accused woman had been mutilated and later found innocent is not stated — either regarding payment of compensation, or punishment of the mutilator.

   mutilated whore **OSw** *SdmL* Gb, *UL* Äb, *VmL* Äb

   See also: *hor*, *stækkia*, *yfirhor*

   Refs: KLNM s.v. *ægteskabsbrud;* Peel 2015, 144 note to chapter 21; Schlyter 1877, s.v. *horstakka;* SL UL, 82 note 22; SL VmL, 58 note 28

hortuta (OSw) **hortugha** (OSw) noun

   whore **OSw** *YVgL* Rlb, *ÄVgL* Rlb

   See also: *hor*

hovethlim (ODan) noun

   A man's nose, tongue or penis, if cut off, resulted in a full man's compensation.

   principal limbs **ODan** *ESjL* 2

hovethsak (ODan) noun

   main case **ODan** *ESjL* 2, 3

   main claim **ODan** *SkKL* 11

hovethtoft (ODan) noun

   capital toft **ODan** *ESjL* 2

   See also: *tompt*

hovoþloter (OSw) **hovethlot** (ODan) **hafuþ lutr** (OGu) **hafuþluti** (OGu) **huvuþ luter** (OSw) noun

   A person's share in a piece of property, such as an inheritance, proportionate to the number of owners or heirs.

capital lot **ODan** *ESjL* 1, 3, *JyL* 1–3, *SkKL* 5, *SkL* 6, 38, 40, 41, 141, 226, *VSjL* 1–8, 14, 21, 50, 53, 87, **OSw** *ÖgL* Kkb

head share **OSw** *SmL*

per capita share **OGu** *GL* A 20

personal share **OGu** *GL* A 7, 28, Add. 1 (B 4)

principal parcel **OSw** *YVgL* Add

principal part **OSw** *YVgL* Kkb, Add

See also: *bosloter, luter*

Refs: ODS s.v. *hovedlod*; Tamm and Vogt, eds, 2016, 308

hovoþsmaþer (OSw) **hovethsman** (ODan) **hovuþs man** (OSw) **huvuþs man** (OSw) **huvuþs maþer** (OSw) **huwzman** (OSw) **huwzmander** (OSw) noun

culprit/headman **OSw** *HL* Mb

instigator **OSw** *UL* Kgb, Mb, Rb, *VmL* Kgb, Mb, *ÖgL* Kkb, Db

leader **ODan** *VSjL* 53, 56, 60

principal **OSw** *DL* Eb, Mb, Tjdb, Rb, *HL* Kkb, *SdmL* Kgb, Till

responsible (man) **OSw** *HL* Kgb, *YVgL* Urb, Föb, Add

See also: *raþsbani, raþsbænd*

hovoþsynd (OSw) noun

capital sin **OSw** *YVgL* Kkb, *ÄVgL* Kkb

See also: *synd*

hovoþtiunda (OSw) verb

deliver capital tithe **OSw** *ÄVgL* Kkb

See also: *tiund, tiunda*

hovoþtiundi (OSw) **höfuðtíund** (ON) noun

Tithes consisting of a tenth of a person's total assets (it has been debated whether this included land or not) paid primarily at the consecration of a church, potentially also at other occasions such as inheritance, or marriage.

capital tithe **OIce** *KRA* 10, **OSw** *YVgL* Kkb, *ÄVgL* Kkb

greater tithe **ONorw** *FrL* KrbA 17

main-tithe **ONorw** *EidsL* 48.9

See also: *tiund*

Refs: Fritzner s.v. *höfuðtíund*; Förvaltningshistorisk ordbok s.v. *huvudtionde*; Hertzberg s.v. *höfuðtíund*; KLNM s.v. *tiend*; Runer 2012; Schlyter s.v. *hovoþtiundi*

hovuþduker (OSw) **hofþoduker** (OSw) **hovudduker** (OSw) **huvuþduker** (OSw) **huwþduker** (OSw) noun

coif **OSw** *UL* Äb, *VmL* Äb

hoysletr (OGu) noun

haymaking **OGu** *GL* A 47

hófr (ON) noun

If a horse caused a man's death, the owner was to dispose of the animal or pay a compensation to the kinsfolk of the killed man. See GuL ch. 165.

hoof **ONorw** *GuL* Llb, Mhb

See also: *hæster*

hóra (ON) verb

betray **ONorw** *FrL* Kvb 13

be unfaithful **ONorw** *FrL* KrbB 7

whore **OIce** *KRA* 17, 18

See also: *horkona*

hóra (ON) noun

whore **ONorw** *GuL* Mhb

hóran (ON) noun

whoring **OIce** *KRA* 5

hreðjar (pl.) (ON) noun

sex organs **ONorw** *GuL* Mhb

hreiðr (ON) noun

nest **ONorw** *GuL* Tjb

hreppadómr (ON) noun

A court convened to deal with matters of the commune (ON *hreppr*). A *hreppadómr* handled cases involving care of the poor. Prosecutions for failure to meet obligations toward the poor were held at the residence of the defendant. Case procedures are outlined in Grg Hrs 234. In Grg Feþ 167 it is stated that certain infractions concerning trade should also be prosecuted at the *hreppadómr*, but it is thought that this instance actually refers to a district court (ON *heraðsdómr*).

commune court **OIce** *Grg* Hrs 234

district court **OIce** *Grg* Feþ 167

See also: *domber, heraðsdómr*

Refs: CV s.v. *hreppr*; Fr; GAO s.v. *hreppr*; GrgTr II:93; KLNM s.v. *dómr*; Lýður Björnsson 1972–79, I:48–49; Miller 1990, 19

hreppamál (ON) noun

The articles or rules established within a commune (ON *hreppr*). These pertained mostly to the care of the poor and the treatment of itinerants and vagrants. May also refer to specific cases concerning a commune and resolved within it.

commune rules **OIce** *Grg* Hrs 234, 235

See also: *fynd, mal (1), samqvæmd*

Refs: CV s.v. *hreppamál*; Finsen III:625; Fritzner s.v. *hreppamál*; KLNM s.v. *hreppr*

hreppamót (ON) noun

> *boundary between communes* **OIce** *Grg* Hrs 234

hreppaskil (ON) noun

> *commune business* **OIce** *Jó* Kge 34
>
> *commune obligations* **OIce** *Grg* Hrs 234

hreppatal (ON) noun

> *commune list* **OIce** *Grg* Hrs 234

hreppr (ON) noun

A commune; the designation for the smallest administrative district in medieval Iceland, though Grg Hrs 234 states that a *hreppr* could be further divided into thirds or quarters. It is unknown when the division of the country into communes occurred, but a general consensus places it prior to Christianization in the year 1000. According to Grg Hrs 234 and Jó Kge 31 a commune had to have at least twenty householders capable of paying assembly attendance dues (*þingfararkaup*), but the precise number of extant *hreppar* is unknown prior to 1703. It has been suggested that the term referred to personal properties prior to becoming geographic districts (cf. Hoff 2012, 26) and that the *hreppar* were a type of medieval guild (cf. Sv. Jakobsson 2013, 275).

Each *hreppr* was governed by a group of five councilmen (*hreppstjóri*; also called [*hrepp*]*sóknarmenn*). Communes were allotted one quarter of annual tithes, and these funds were dedicated to the maintenance of the poor and to serve as insurance in the event members of the commune suffered a disastrous fire or loss of livestock. The insurance aspect however seems to have vanished by the time Norwegian rule began in Iceland, as there is no mention of it in Jó. Communes were also involved in the process of spring sheep drives. Maintenance of the poor by the *hreppr* is thought to predate the tithe system introduced to Iceland in 1097.

In England, particularly in Sussex, the term *hreppr* was co-opted as *rape* and referred to an administrative division between a hundred and a shire. In Norwegian dialects and place names it refers to a settlement or group of estates, while in Sweden it was part of a church parish, but the term never took on any legal or political strength as in Iceland. However a manuscript variant in MLL indicates that a *hreppr* might have been an older administrative district in Norway as well. The term *hreppr* has been equated with *sogn* in Norway.

> *commune* **OIce** *Grg* Klþ 2 Ómb 132 Fjl 225 Hrs 234 Tíg 255, 256, *Jó* Þfb 9 Kge 31 Llb 69 Þjb 2, *Js* Kab 3, 7, *KRA* 14, 15

> See also: *fjarþunger*, *hærap*

Refs: CV; Gunnar Karlsson 2005; Hoff 2012; KLNM s.v. *hreppr*; LexMA s.v. *hrepp*, *Armut (Armenfürsorge, Sonderformen in Skandinavien, Island)*; Lýður Björnsson 1972–79, I:9–32, I:55–66; ONP; Svavar Sigmundsson 2003; Sverrir Jakobsson 2013

hreppsfundarboð (ON) noun

> *commune-meeting message* **OIce** *Grg* Hrs 234

> See also: *hreppsfundr*

hreppsfundr (ON) **hreppfundr** (ON) noun

A meeting of householders belonging to a commune (ON *hreppr*). It is thought that this refers to a special meeting of the members convened to deal with communal issues, such as determining who was responsible for maintaining a dependent. Might also refer to a guild meeting (ON *gildisfundr*).

> *special commune meeting* **OIce** *Grg* Hrs 234

> See also: *gatestævne*, *grannestævne*, *samqvæmd*, *þing*

Refs: CV; Fritzner; GAO s.v. *hrepp*; Grg II:371–72; Jón Jóhannesson 2006, 88; Lýður Björnsson 1972–79: I:47–48, 58–59

hreppsmaðr (ON) noun

> *man of the commune* **OIce** *Grg* Klþ 13 Ómb 129, 132 Hrs 234, 235 Tíg 255, *Jó* Kge 31
>
> *man of the district* **OIce** *Jó* Llb 12

> See also: *hærapsmaþer*

hreppsókn (ON) noun

> *commune prosecution* **OIce** *Grg* Hrs 235

hreppsóknarmaðr (ON) noun

> *commune prosecutor* **OIce** *Grg* Hrs 235

hreppstjóri (ON) noun

A leader or councilman within an Icelandic commune (ON *hreppr*). Five of them governed a commune, and they were elected annually. Possibly the same as a *hreppsóknarmaðr* (q.v.), the designation being replaced over the course of the twelfth century. The position was unpaid, but according to early fourteenth-century documents, holders of the post were entitled to a portion of certain fines, such as penalties for failing to uphold decisions passed by the *hreppstjórar* (DI II nr. 182, 1305). In addition to administering duties assigned to the commune, such as maintenance for the poor, a *hreppstjóri* was, according to Gamli sáttmáli, also responsible for delivering tax payments to the king's representative.

> *commune councilman* **OIce** *KRA* 15
>
> *commune leader* **OIce** *Grg* Ómb 143

> See also: *hirðstjóri*, *hreppsóknarmaðr*

Refs: CV; F; Hertzberg s.v. *reppstjóri*; Jón Viðar Sigurðsson 2011b; KLNM s.v.

embedsindtægter, *hreppr*; LexMA s.v. *hrepp*;
Lýður Björnsson 1972–79, I:50, 59–64

hreppstjórn (ON) noun

commune council **OIce** *Jó* Kge 34 7

hreppstjórnarmaðr (ON) noun

See *hreppstjóri*

commune councilman **OIce** *Jó* Kge 29, 34 Llb 69

hreppstjórnarþing (ON) noun

A *þing* 'assembly' held in autumn dealing with local affairs of the judicial/administrative district at the lowest level, the *hreppr* ('commune'), where all householders were obliged to participate.

commune assembly **OIce** *Jó* Kge 31

See also: *hreppr*, *hreppstjórn*, *þing*

Refs: Hertzberg s.v. *reppstjórnarþing*;
KLNM s.v. *ting*

hreppsvist (ON) noun

lodging in a commune **OIce** *Grg* Ómb 143

hreysi (ON) **hreys** (ON) noun

stony place **OIce** *Jó* Llb 2, *Js* Lbb 11

hrífa (ON) verb

scratch **OIce** *Jó* Mah 22

hrísa (ON) noun

female scrubling **ONorw** *FrL* ArbA 8

hrísungr (ON) noun

A derogatory term for a son of a free man and a, later freed, slave woman (OIce), or a son conceived secretely by free parents (ONorw), probably alluding to a conception in the forest. OIce *hrísungr* was not entitled to any inheritance, in contrast to a *hornungr* (q.v.) who was acknowledged by the father.

scrubling **OIce** *Grg* Arþ 118, **ONorw**
FrL ArbA 8 Rgb 47, *GuL* Løb, Arb

See also: *hornungr*

Refs: Clunies Ross 1985, 16; KLNM s.v. *oäkta
barn*; Ney 1998, 107–08; Schlyter s.v. *rishofþe*

hrísungserfð (ON) noun

scrubling's inheritance **ONorw** *GuL* Arb

hrjóstr (ON) noun

stony ground **OIce** *Jó* Llb 22

hrjóta (ON) verb

fly out **ONorw** *GuL* Mhb

hrossakjöt (ON) noun

The eating of horse flesh was forbidden (GuL ch. 20), but this ban was not equally strict throughout the Nordic countries. See Kværness 1996, 79–81, 84, 156.

horse flesh **ONorw** *GuL* Krb

See also: *rus*

Refs: KLNM s.v. *hästkött*; Kværness 1996

hrosslán (ON) noun

horse loan **OIce** *Jó* Þjb 17

hruðning (ON) **ruðning** (ON) noun

challenge **OIce** *Grg* Þsþ 25, 35 Vís 89, 102
Lbþ 176, 202 Fjl 223 Hrs 234 Tíg 259

hruðningarmál (ON) **ruðningarmál** (ON) noun

words of challenge **OIce** *Grg* Þsþ 25, 35

hrufa (ON) noun

scab **ONorw** *GuL* Mhb

hryggr (ON) noun

back **ONorw** *GuL* Kvr, Mhb

hrækja (ON) verb

spit **ONorw** *GuL* Krb

hrør (ON) noun

Expressions:

at hreyrum (ON)

in terms of attachment **OIce** *Grg* Vís add.
57(ii), 101 Feþ 166 Lbþ 176, 218

huaifibain (OGu) noun

larger bone splinter **OGu** *GL* A 19

hug (OSw) **hog** (ODan) **hagg** (OGu) **högg** (ON) noun

beating **ONorw** *GuL* Krb, Kvb, Løb, Mhb

blow **ODan** *ESjL* 2, 3, *VSjL* 34, 54, **OGu** *GL*
A 19, Add. 1 (B 4), **OSw** *UL* Mb, *VmL* Mb

cut **ODan** *JyL* 2, *SkL* 116

dismemberment **ODan** *VSjL* 86

felling of trees **OSw** *YVgL* Jb, Föb

stabbing **OSw** *SdmL* Mb

stroke **ODan** *ESjL* 2

wounding **OSw** *DL* Eb

hugga (OSw) **hogge** (ODan) **hagga** (OGu) **höggva**
(ON) **hogga** (OSw) verb

chop **ODan** *ESjL* 2, *JyL* 2, *VSjL* 29,
OSw *HL* Mb, *UL* Blb, *VmL* Bb

cut **ODan** *JyL* 2, 3, *SkKL* 4, *SkL* 99, 116, 122, 191,
193–196, 204, *VSjL* 26–28, 31, 33–35, 55, 86,
ONorw *GuL* Llb, Mhb, Leb, **OSw** *DL* Eb, Mb,
HL Kgb, Mb, *SdmL* Kgb, Mb, *UL* Kgb, Mb, Blb,
VmL Kgb, Mb, Bb, *YVgL* Drb, Rlb, Add, *ÄVgL*
Smb, Vs, Urb, Föb, *ÖgL* Kkb, Eb, Db, Vm

cut (down) wood **OGu** *GL* A 26, 63

cut down **OSw** *UL* Blb, *VmL* Bb

cut off **OGu** *GL* A 19, 20a, Add. 5 (B 20)

fell **OGu** *GL* A 7, 25, **OSw** *SdmL* Bb,
Mb, *UL* Mb, Blb, *VmL* Mb, Bb

hew **ONorw** *GuL* Llb, **OSw** *SmL*,
YVgL Add, *ÄVgL* Fös, Föb

hit **ODan** *ESjL* 3, **OSw** *ÄVgL* Lek

punch **ODan** *VSjL* 30

slay **ONorw** *FrL* Mhb 9

smash **OSw** *YVgL* Rlb, *ÄVgL* Rlb

stab **OSw** *SdmL* Mb, *SmL*, *YVgL* Utgb

strike **ODan** *ESjL* 2, **ONorw** *GuL* Mhb, **OSw** *UL* Kgb, Mb, *VmL* Mb

wound **OSw** *DL* Mb, Rb, *VmL* Mb

hugvakn (OSw) noun

cutting weapon **OSw** *HL* Äb

See also: *vapn*

huifr (OGu) noun

wimple **OGu** *GL* A 23

See also: *tuppr*

hulsar (OSw) **hulsar** (ODan) **hulseri** (OGu) **holsár** (ON) **holsaar** (OSw) noun

internal wound **ODan** *SkL* 89, 96, 116

perforation **ODan** *ESjL* 2, *JyL* 3, *SkL* 89, *VSjL* 36

wound **OSw** *HL* Mb

wound in the cavities **ONorw** *GuL* Mhb

wound in the trunk **OSw** *DL* Mb, *SdmL* Mb, *UL* Mb, *VmL* Mb

wound that has penetrated the abdominal or breast cavity **OGu** *GL* A 19

hult (OGu) **holt** (ON) noun

grove **OGu** *GL* A 4, **ONorw** *GuL* Olb

wooded lot **OIce** *Jó* Llb 17, 26

woods **ONorw** *FrL* LlbA 14 LlbB 3

See also: *guþ*

humamal (OSw) noun

suspected case **OSw** *ÖgL* Kkb

See also: *grun, jæva, vanesak, væna*

humblagarþer (OSw) noun

garden of hops **OSw** *HL* Mb

hop-garden **OSw** *DL* Kkb, Bb, *HL* Blb, *SdmL* Kkb

humbli (OSw) **humbli** (OGu) noun

hop **OGu** *GL* A 3, **OSw** *UL* Kkb, Kgb, *VmL* Kkb, Bb

hun (OSw) **hun** (OGu) noun

bar **OGu** *GL* Add. 8 (B 55), **OSw** *VmL* Kkb

See also: *hæl (1)*

hund (ODan) **hundr** (ON) noun

dog **ONorw** *GuL* Krb, Llb, Tfb, Mhb

hundari (OSw) **hunderi** (OGu) noun

An administrative and judicial district in the Svea laws and GL. The size of a *hundari* is not stated.

hundred **OGu** *GL* A 19, 28, 31, Add. 8 (B 55)

{hundari} **OSw** *DL* Mb, Bb, Tjdb, Rb, *SdmL* Kkb, Kgb, Gb, Äb, Jb, Bb, Kmb, Mb, Tjdb, Rb, *UL* passim, *VmL* passim

See also: *attunger, fiarþunger, hamna, hæraþ, skiplagh*

Refs: Andersson 1982a, 52–66; Andersson 1999, 5–12; Andersson 2014, 12–14; KLNM s.v. *hundare*; Lindkvist 1995, 49–53; Lundberg 1972, 78–81; Peel 2015, 14–16, 248–49, 286 note 1/18; SL 2, xx–xxiii; Tegengren 2015

hundarisbro (OSw) noun

bridge of a {hundari} **OSw** *SdmL* Bb

See also: *hundari*

hundarisnæmd (OSw) noun

A *næmd* 'panel' dealing with unjust revenge (DL, SdmL), rape and bridges and roads (SdmL).

panel from/of the {hundari} **OSw** *DL* Eb, *SdmL* Kgb, Bb

See also: *hundari, næmd*

hundarissyn (OSw) noun

inspection by a {hundari} **OSw** *SdmL* Till

See also: *hundari*

hundarisþing (OSw) noun

A *þing* 'assembly' of the judicial district *hundari* (q.v.), appearing as the venue for announcing madmen.

assembly of the hundari **OSw** *SdmL* Mb

See also: *fiærþungsþing, fylkisþing, hundari, hæraþ, hærapsþing, landsþing, þing*

hunderismenn (pl.) (OGu) noun

men of the hundred **OGu** *GL* A 28

hundrað (ON) noun

hundred **OIce** *Grg* Hrs 234, *Jó* Þfb 2 Kge 15, 31

hurð (ON) noun

door leaf **ONorw** *GuL* Llb

hus (OSw) **hus** (ODan) **hús** (ON) noun

building **ODan** *ESjL* 3, **OSw** *HL* Mb, Rb

castle **OSw** *SdmL* Till

family **OSw** *DL* Rb

house **ODan** *ESjL* 2, *JyL* 1–3, *SkL* 1, 29, 87, 190, 199, 218, 224, 226, 239, *VSjL* 53, 56–58, 86, **OSw** *DL* Kkb, Mb, Bb, Rb, *HL* Kkb, Mb, Jb, Kmb, Blb, *SdmL* Kkb, Jb, Bb, Kmb, Mb, Tjdb, Till, *SmL*, *YVgL* Kkb, Urb, Rlb, Tb, Jb, Föb, Add, *ÄVgL* Äb, Rlb, Jb, Tb

household **ODan** *VSjL* 3

movables **ODan** *VSjL* 12

Expressions:

bryta hus (OSw) **bryte hus** (ODan)

break into a house **ODan** *JyL* 2 **OSw** *SdmL* Kgb

See also: *bryta, husbrut*

husa (OSw) huse (ODan) hysa (OSw) verb

Sheltering an outlaw was illegal. Similar concepts could be expressed in terms of feeding and meeting with them. Keeping stolen goods in one's home was another offence occasionally expressed with this verb (ODan SkL).

accommodate **OSw** *UL* Blb, *VmL* Bb

house **ODan** *SkL* 141, **OSw** *HL* Kgb, *SdmL* Kgb

provide house **OSw** *HL* Kgb

shelter **ODan** *JyL* 2, **OSw** *UL* Kgb, Kmb, *VmL* Kgb, Kmb

Expressions:

husa ok hema, hysa ok hema, husa ællær hema (OSw) hysa eþa haima (OGu)

house and shelter **OSw** *SdmL* Kgb

give shelter or lodging **OSw** *UL* Kgb, Kmb *VmL* Kgb, Kmb

shelter or house **OGu** *GL* A 2

See also: *forvist, hema, samvist, samværa, viþervist*

husaby (OSw) noun

Presumably a royal estate (king's farm) providing living for a royal administrator. A *husaby* is mentioned only in HL, which is not what would be expected since the king's estates were called *konungsgarþer* (q.v.) in the north of Sweden and *husaby* in the south. The function of a *husaby* as an administrative unit has been much debated, the historical material is very limited and no definite answers to its function have yet been published.

Husaby appears as a place-name in Sweden, Denmark and Norway although most of them are situated in central Sweden and around Viken in Norway. Stefan Brink claims that in Uppland they constitute *bona regalia*, and were part of the royal administration, but calls for more research into their function in the rest of Scandinavia.

A *husabyman* (q.v.) is mentioned only in DL, where he is a representative of the king with certain judicial rights on the local administration level beside the *lænsmaþer* (q.v.), or under him.

king's farm **OSw** *HL* Rb

See also: *konongsgarþer, öþer*

Refs: Brink 2000b, 65–73; KLNM s.v. *husaby*; Pettersson 2000, 49–65; Schlyter s.v.v. *husaby, husabyman*

husabyman (OSw) noun

In DL a representative of the king on the local administration level beside the *lænsmaþer* (q.v.) with certain judicial rights.

local administrator **OSw** *DL* Mb, Tjdb, Rb

See also: *husaby, lænsmaþer*

Refs: Brink 2000b, 65–73; KLNM s.v. *husaby*; Pettersson 2000, 49–65; Schlyter s.v.v. *husaby, husabyman*

husbonde (OSw) husbonde (ODan) husbondi (OGu) húsbóndi (ON) noun

Occasionally synonymous with *bonde* 'householder', but often with stronger emphasis on authority in relation to tenants, slaves, servants, members of the household etc.

employer **OGu** *GL* A 56, **OSw** *DL* Tjdb

householder **ODan** *ESjL* 1–3, *JyL* 1, 2, *SkKL* 9, *SkL* 231, *VSjL* 86, **OFar** *Seyð* 3, **OGu** *GL* A 12, 24, 36

husband **ODan** *JyL* 3, **OGu** *GL* A 14, **OIce** *Jó* Kab 24, **OSw** *UL* Äb

man **ONorw** *FrL* KrbA 5

master **OSw** *SdmL* Mb, *YVgL* Add

master of a house **OIce** *Grg* Þsþ 78

owner **ODan** *SkL* 161, 162

patron **OSw** *YVgL* Kkb

See also: *aþalman, bonde*

Refs: Cleasby and Vigfusson s.v. *húsbóndi*; Fritzner s.v. *húsbóndi*; Hertzberg s.v. *húsbóndi*; Schlyter s.v. *husbonde*

husbrut (OSw) husbrut (ODan) húsbrot (ON) noun

Breaking or breaking into someone's house. In OIce and ONorw regarding removal of parts of the building, particularly doors and their attachments, when moving away from a house. In ODan and OSw in connection with illegally entering someone's home, considered an offence against the king's sworn peace (OSw *hemsokn, eþsöre*) or a gang crime (ODan *hærværk*).

damage to a building **ONorw** *GuL* Llb

housebreaking **ODan** *JyL* 2, **OIce** *Jó* Llb 9, *Js* Lbb 12, **OSw** *SdmL* Kgb, *ÖgL* Eb

See also: *bryta, hus*

Refs: Fritzner s.v. *húsbrot*; Hertzberg s.v. *húsbrot*

husetoft (ODan) noun

house toft **ODan** *SkL* 56, 67, 75, 76, *VSjL* 71, 79, 80

land around the house **ODan** *SkL* 240

See also: *hus, tompt*

husfolk (OSw) noun

dependents **OSw** *SdmL* Tjdb

husfrugha (OSw) husfrue (ODan) husfroyia (OGu) húsfreyja (ON) húspreyja (ON) hosprea (OSw) husfru (OSw) husfrua (OSw) husfruha (OSw) husprea (OSw) hustro (OSw) hustru (OSw) noun

The wife of a householder. She was in charge of lock and key, but she had limited freedom in matters of trade and business compared to her husband. The limits were varying. In Norway she was not allowed to engage in economic transactions worth more than half of the amount that was allowed to the householder. See BorgL II Till. 9 and GuL ch. 56. According to certain OSw and ODan laws she had full disposition of her heritage.

housewife **ODan** *ESjL* 1, 3, *JyL* 1, *VSjL* 6, **OGu** *GL* A 36, **ONorw** *GuL* Krb, Arb, Tjb, Olb, **OSw** *SdmL* Kkb, Gb, Äb, Kmb, Mb, Tjdb, *SmL*, *UL* Äb, *VmL* Äb

lady of the house **OIce** *Jó* Kge 32

mistress (1) **ODan** *JyL* 1

mistress of the house **ODan** *SkL* 141, **OIce** *Grg* Þsþ 80

spouse **OSw** *YVgL* Tb, Add, *ÄVgL* Äb

wife **ODan** *ESjL* 1, 3, *JyL* 1–3, **OGu** *GS* Ch. 3, **ONorw** *BorgL* 12.17, *FrL* KrbA 32, 33, *GuL* Krb, Arb, Tjb, Olb, **OSw** *DL* Kkb, Mb, Mb, Gb, Rb, *HL* Kkb, Äb, Mb, Kmb, *SdmL* Äb, Jb, Mb, *SmL*, *UL* Kkb, Äb, Mb, Jb, Kmb, Rb, *VmL* Kkb, Äb, Mb, Jb, Kmb, Rb, *YVgL* Urb, Äb, Tb, Add, *ÄVgL* Tb, *ÖgL* Eb, Db, Vm

wife of a householder **OIce** *Jó* Sg 1

woman **OSw** *ÖgL* Kkb

See also: *aþalkona*, *bonde*, *frilla*, *kona*, *kærling*, *leghokona*, *sløkefrithe*

Refs: KLNM s.v.v. *husbonde*, *husfru*, *nyckelbärare*

huskona (OSw) **huskone** (ODan) noun

Several compounds beginning with *hus* 'house' or *hem* 'home' refer to people of varying status and degree of dependence serving at or managing a house(hold). A *huskona* appears to have been an unfree woman serving in a household. In OSw *ÄVgL* and *YVgL* her status was so low that she was used in an illustration of humiliation.

female servant **ODan** *SkL* 220

female slave **OSw** *YVgL* Utgb

servant-woman **ODan** *SkL* 62, *VSjL* 69

slave-woman **OSw** *ÄVgL* Gb, Lek

thrall woman **OSw** *YVgL* Gb

See also: *ambat*, *annöpogher*, *deghia*, *fostra*, *frælsgiva*, *gæfþræl*, *hion*, *hus*, *kona*, *sætesambut*

husl (OSw) noun

Holy Communion **OSw** *YVgL* Kkb, Äb, *ÄVgL* Kkb, Äb

See also: *guþslikami*

husla (OSw) **húsla** (ON) verb

administer Holy Communion **OSw** *YVgL* Kkb, *ÄVgL* Kkb, Föb

give communion **OSw** *YVgL* Utgb

housel **ONorw** *EidsL* 47.4

See also: *husl*

hussætisfolk (OSw) **hussætu folk** (OSw) noun

A category of people without landed property, possibly living permanently in somebody else's household. They may have paid rent (UL Mb) or been labourers. Appearing in a list of poor people (UL Kkb) and dealt with concerning their responsibilities if they had keys to the farm where they lived (VmL Mb).

lodgers **OSw** *UL* Kkb, Mb, *VmL* Kkb, Mb

See also: *hussætumaþer*

Refs: KLNM s.v. *husmand*

hussætumaþer (OSw) **hussætisman** (OSw) noun

The male equivalent of *hussætisfolk* (q.v.) appears concerning his obligation to pay the priest at Easter (SmL, UL Kkb).

cottager **OSw** *SmL*

lodger **OSw** *UL* Kkb

See also: *hussætisfolk*

Refs: KLNM s.v. *husmand*

husþiauþ (OGu) noun

household servants **OGu** *GL* A 55

See also: *hion*

huvuþsar (OSw) noun

head wound **OSw** *SdmL* Mb

wound in the head **OSw** *DL* Mb

huþ (OSw) **huth** (ODan) **húð** (ON) noun

Two senses are to be distinguished: 1) skin of human beings, and 2) hides, skin of animals. 1) Referring to human skin concerns corporal punishment, i.e. flogging (whipping), mainly for theft, including illicit barking of another's tree (OSw SdmL, VmL) and use of another's horse (ODan ESjL), as well as for sending a hired man in one's place for military duty (ODan JyL). It was rarely specified who was to effect the punishment, but the plaintiff (OSw SdmL) as well as officials such as *lænsmaþer* (OSw VmL, YVgL) and *umbuthsman* (ODan SjL) were mentioned. 2) Hides were needed as material for cordage in the fleet of conscripted warships. See GuL ch. 308. They were also articles of payment and trade.

hide **ONorw** *GuL* Leb

hide whipping **ODan** *VSjL* 87

skin **ODan** *ESjL* 2, *SkKL* 10, *SkL* 151, 160, 161, **OSw** *SdmL* Tjdb, *YVgL* Tb

skin of animals **ONorw** *GuL* Krb, Kpb

skin of human beings **ONorw** *GuL* Krb, Tjb

whip **ODan** *SkL* 162

whipping **ODan** *VSjL* 87

Expressions:

mista huþ ok öron (OSw)

lose skin and ears **OSw** *YVgL* Tb

See also: *hjul, huþstryka*

Refs: KLNM s.v. *hudlag*

huþstryka (OSw) **huthstryke** (ODan) **hustryka** (OSw)
huþstrika (OSw) **huþstruka** (OSw) verb

flog **OSw** *SdmL* Bb, *UL* Blb, *VmL*
Bb, *YVgL* Frb, Tb, Utgb

whip **ODan** *SkL* 161, 184

See also: *hjul, huþ*

huþsverf (OSw) noun

skin-scratch **OSw** *SdmL* Mb

húðafang (ON) noun

number of hides **ONorw** *GuL* Leb

húðarlausn (ON) noun

hide-ransom **ONorw** *BorgL* 14.5

See also: *huþ*

húfr (ON) noun

strakes **ONorw** *GuL* Leb

húnn (ON) noun

square piece of a whale's blubber **ONorw** *GuL* Kvr

húsaskifti (ON) noun

division of houses **OIce** *Jó* Llb 13

húsaupphald (ON) noun

upkeep of buildings **ONorw** *GuL* Llb

húsbeða (ON) noun

Interpreted as 'house bed'; ground which lies beneath
a house, site for a house.

house site **ONorw** *FrL* LlbA 1

Refs: Hertzberg s.v. *húsbeða*

húsbúandi (ON) noun

householder **OIce** *Grg* Misc 248, **ONorw** *FrL* Bvb 7

See also: *husbonde*

húseigandi (ON) noun

house owner **ONorw** *BorgL* 14.5

húsfastr (ON) adj.

House-fixed. Refers to men who owned or rented
property for at least half a year in a (Norwegian)
town. According to Magnus the Lawmender's City
Law (VII.16), those who met this requirement were
required to take part in town meetings (ON *mót*).

owning or renting **OIce** *Grg* Arþ
125 Misc 248, *Jó* Kge 18

See also: *bonde, mot*

Refs: CV s.v. *húsfastr*; Fritzner s.v. *húsfastr*; GrgTr
II:18 n. 102; Hagland and Sandnes 1997, 108;
Hertzberg s.v. *húsfastr*; KLNM s.v. *borgare, husleige*

húsgangr (ON) noun

begging **ONorw** *GuL* Arb

house-to-house vagrancy **OIce** *Grg* Ómb 143

húsgangsmaðr (ON) noun

A vagrant beggar. ONorw FrL exhibits lenience
towards them and their family if caught stealing
herring or fishing nets. It was illegal for able-bodied
persons to beg, and certain forms of support for illegal
beggars was punishable.

beggar **ONorw** *FrL* KrbA 16 Rgb 39 Bvb 6

tramp **OIce** *Grg* Þsþ 82

See also: *einhleypr, göngumaðr*

Refs: Dennis, Foote and Perkins 1980, 246; Dennis,
Foote and Perkins 2000, 399; KLNM s.v. *tiggar*

húsgerð (ON) noun

construction of houses **OIce** *Js* Lbb 11

obligation to build a house **ONorw** *GuL* Llb

húshagi (ON) noun

home pasture **OIce** *Jó* Llb 42

húskarl (ON) noun

Several compounds beginning with *hus* 'house' or *hem*
'home' refer to people of varying status and degree
of dependence serving at or managing a house(hold),
and a *karl* was a grown man, potentially a warrior.
Thus, a man performing service, including military, at
the house or in the retinue of another, usually high-
ranking, man, or possibly woman.

hired man **OIce** *Jó* Fml 3

man-servant **ONorw** *FrL* Var 43

retainer **OIce** *Grg* Misc 238

servant **OFar** *Seyð* 8

serving man **OIce** *Grg* Klþ 3, 5 Vís 89 Feþ 164, 166

Refs: Brink 2012, 151−54; Fritzner s.v.
húskarl; Hertzberg s.v. *húskarl*; KLNM
s.v. *hird*; von See 1964, 167

húskarlserfð (ON) noun

housecarl's inheritance **ONorw** *GuL* Arb

húsrúm (ON) noun

house-room **OIce** *Grg* Klþ 1 Feþ 166

húsverð (ON) noun

cost of a house **OIce** *Js* Lbb 11

value of a house **OIce** *Jó* Llb 2

hval (ODan) **hvalr** (ON) noun

In ODan, appearing in the context of the right to
beached whales; the king was to be informed of the
find, but the finder also had the right to a part.

whale **ODan** *ESjL* 3, *JyL* 3, **ONorw** *GuL* Kvr

Refs: Tamm and Vogt, eds, 2016, 31

hvalflutningr (ON) noun

whale salvaging **OIce** *Grg* Lbþ 213, 216

hvalflystri (ON) noun

pieces of whale **OFar** *Seyð* 11

hvalfundr (ON) noun

whale finding **ONorw** *FrL* LlbB 10

hvalreki (ON) noun

whale drift rights **OIce** *Grg* Lbþ 214

hvalrétti (ON) noun

law on whaling **ONorw** *GuL* Kvr

hvalréttr (ON) noun

whale rights **OIce** *Grg* Lbþ 215

hvalsverð (ON) noun

whale-price **OIce** *Grg* Lbþ 215

hvannastulðr (ON) noun

theft of angelica **OIce** *Jó* Þjb 11

hvanngarðr (ON) noun

angelica garden **OIce** *Js* Þjb 8,
ONorw *FrL* LlbA 2, *GuL* Llb

hvardagsklæþi (OSw) noun

The only possessions an adulteress could take when made to leave the home.

daily clothes **OSw** *YVgL* Gb, *ÄVgL* Gb

hvin (OSw) **hvinn** (ON) noun

A petty thief, a pilferer; one who commits a minor theft (cf. *hvinska*).

petty larcener **OSw** *YVgL* Tb

pilferer **ONorw** *FrL* LlbB 12

See also: *hvinska, snattan, þiuver*

Refs: CV s.v. *hvinnr*; Fritzner s.v. *hvinn*; Hertzberg s.v. *hvinn*; ONP s.v. *hvinn*

hvinska (OSw) **hvinnska** (ON) noun

Pilfering, petty larceny. In some Nordic laws *hvinnska* is given as the lowest degree of theft. In Seyð and Jó (Þjb 1) thefts of goods valued at less than one *eyrir*, and less than one *þveit* (q.v.) in FrL (XIV.12), were considered *hvinnska*. Penalties for *hvinnska* were severe but appear to have lessened over time. In YVgL (Tb 13) the punishment for *hvinska* is a large cash payment or corporal punishment in the form of flogging and clipped ears. *Hvinnska* in FrL (XIV.12) incurred a loss of rights. In the later MLL and Jó (Þjb 1) *hvinnska* incurs a fine of three *øre*, and the perpetrator is to be called 'a lesser man' (ON *maðr at verri*). *Snattan* (q.v.), or its subsequent fine, *snattan-* or *snattarabot* (q.v.), is a corresponding offense listed in ÖgL, some Svea laws and GL.

petty larceny **OIce** *Jó* Þjb 1, **OSw** *YVgL* Tb, Add

petty theft **OIce** *Jó* Mah 26, *Js* Mah 25

pilfering **OFar** *Seyð* 5

See also: *fornæmi, görtóki, hvin, misfangi, ran, snattan, þiufnaþer, þiuver*

Refs: CV s.v. *hvinnska*; Fritzner s.v. *hvinnska*; KLNM s.v.v. *rättlösa, tyveri*; ONP s.v. *hvinnska*

hvitisunnudagher (OSw) noun

first Sunday in Lent **OSw** *SdmL* Rb, Till

hvítaváðir (pl.) (ON) noun

This robe was worn by the child at baptism and taken off one week later.

white robes **ONorw** *GuL* Krb

hyndask (ON) verb

rise to half a hundred (i.e. sixty) **ONorw** *GuL* Kpb

hyrnustokker (OSw) noun

Appears as a border in the context of *hemsokn* 'attack in the home'; killing an intruder at the *hyrnustokker* was considered self-defence.

corner of a house **OSw** *YVgL* Drb, *ÄVgL* Md

See also: *garþsliþ, hemsokn, hornstafr, staver*

hýbýli (ON) **híbýli** (ON) noun

home **OIce** *Js* Ert 21, **ONorw** *FrL* ArbB 9

house **OIce** *Jó* Kge 29

place where people live **OIce** *Grg* Rsþ 231

hýða (ON) verb

flog **OIce** *Grg* Hrs 235, *KRA* 30, **ONorw** *BorgL* 14.5, *FrL* KrbA 2 Rgb 40, *GuL* Krb, Tjb

hýðing (ON) noun

flogging **OIce** *Grg* Hrs 235, **ONorw** *BorgL* 14.5

hývíg (ON) noun

servant killing **OIce** *Grg* Vís 111

hæfta (OSw) **hepta** (OGu) **hæpta** (OSw) **hæfte** (ODan) **hæfti** (OSw) **hæpta** (OSw) verb

Apprehension of certain criminals, particularly those caught in incriminating circumstances, and bringing them to justice, including waiting for the *þing* 'assembly'. There is no mention of prisons as a means of punishment. In GL also used of animals put in a hobble.

be captive **OGu** *GL* A 20a

confine **OSw** *VmL* Mb

detain **OSw** *YVgL* Gb, *ÄVgL* Gb

put a fetter on **OSw** *HL* Blb

restrain **OSw** *ÖgL* Db

tether **OGu** *GL* A 26

Refs: KLNM s.v.v. *frihedsberøvelse, fängelse*

hæfta (OSw) noun

arrest **ODan** *VSjL* 60

confinement **OSw** *DL* Mb, *UL*
Kkb, Mb, *VmL* Kkb, Mb

fetter **OSw** *HL* Blb

fetterlock **OSw** *HL* Mb

jail **OSw** *DL* Rb

locking-up **ODan** *ESjL* 3, **OSw** *HL* Mb

restraint **OSw** *ÖgL* Db

tether **ODan** *JyL* 3

hæfþ (OSw) **hævth** (ODan) noun

Derived from a verb meaning 'to have'. Possession of, in particular, land. One who used land for cultivation, buildings etc. for a stipulated period, often three years, without being challenged, gained legal ownership. Occasionally appearing in phrases such as *lagha hæfþ* (OSw), *laghhævth*, *ræt hæfth* (ODan) 'legal possession'. Also of sexual relations resulting in incest or paternity matters, but not rape.

acquisition **OSw** *YVgL* Add

consuetude **OSw** *HL* Blb

cultivation **OSw** *UL* Jb

lawful possession **ODan** *ESjL* 2, *SkL* 82

possession **ODan** *ESjL* 1–3, *JyL* 1–3, *SkL* 37, 49, 53, 59, 72, 75, 76, 78, 80, 84, 135, 136, 141, *VSjL* 1, 68, 76, 79, 80, 82, 83, 85, **OSw** *ÖgL* Kkb

property **ODan** *ESjL* 2

sexual intercourse **OSw** *SdmL* Kkb

See also: *brigþ, fang, fornhæfþ, hæfþa, illa, jorþ, jorþaklandan, klanda, klutra, laghhæfþa, moþnahæfþ, oklandaþer, oklutraþer, oqvalder, qvælia, uilsketh, uilter*

Refs: Schlyter s.v. *hæfþ*; Tamm and Vogt, eds, 2016, 312

hæfþa (OSw) **hævthe** (ODan) verb

farm **OSw** *DL* Bb

lie with **OSw** *UL* Kkb, *VmL* Kkb

possess **ODan** *VSjL* 80

take into possession **ODan** *JyL* 2, **OSw** *SdmL* Jb

use **OSw** *DL* Kkb, *SdmL* Bb, *UL* Blb, *VmL* Bb

hæghna (OSw) **hæghne** (ODan) **hegna** (OSw) verb

defend **ODan** *JyL* 1

fence **OSw** *YVgL* Jb, *ÄVgL* Jb

protect **ODan** *ESjL* 2, **OSw** *ÄVgL* Slb, Äb

hæghnaskogher (OSw) noun

enclosed wood(land) **OSw** *DL* Bb

hæghnaþer (OSw) **hæghneth** (ODan) noun

enclosing **ODan** *ESjL* 2

enclosure **ODan** *JyL* 3, *SkL* 185, **OSw** *SdmL* Bb

fence **ODan** *JyL* 3

hægume (ODan) noun

Appears in the context of false accusations of theft.

loose talk **ODan** *SkL* 137

See also: *glafseþer, jæva, ljúgkviðr, ljúgvitni, meneþer, skruk, tvætala, væna*

hæl (1) (OSw) **hell** (OGu) noun

bolt **OGu** *GL* Add. 8 (B55), **OSw** *VmL* Kkb

See also: *hun*

hæl (2) (OSw) noun

Expressions:

hæl æller hugher (OSw)

death or mind **OSw** *YVgL* Frb, Gb, Jb *ÄVgL* Slb, Gb

See also: *dræpa, sla*

hæla (ON) verb

kick with the heel **ONorw** *FrL* Mhb 17

hælgh (OSw) **hælgh** (ODan) **helg** (OGu) **helgi** (ON) **helgr** (ON) **hælghþ** (OSw) **hælgþ** (OSw) noun

holiday **ODan** *ESjL* 2, *SkL* 157

holy day **OSw** *HL* Rb, *ÖgL* Kkb

holy peace **ODan** *SkKL* 5

holy period **OIce** *KRA* 24

holy time **ONorw** *EidsL* 16

immunity **OIce** *Grg* Vís 90 Misc 241, *Js* Mah 14, **ONorw** *FrL* Mhb 61

observance **OSw** *UL* Kkb, *VmL* Kkb

peace **ODan** *SkKL* 9

period of peace **ODan** *SkKL* 8

personal rights **ONorw** *FrL* Mhb 7

protection **OGu** *GL* A 8

safety **OGu** *GL* A 13

sanctity **OGu** *GL* A 8

sanctuary **OGu** *GL* A 8, 13

Expressions:

bryte hælgh (ODan)

commit sacrilege **ODan** *JyL* 2

See also: *friþer, hælghidagher, manhælghi*

hælghe (ODan) **helga** (OGu) **helga** (ON) verb

consecrate **OIce** *Js* Kdb 1, *KRA* 30

establish immunity **OIce** *Grg* Lbþ 191, *Js* Mah 16, 24

free **ODan** *ESjL* 2

inaugurate formally **OIce** *Grg* Klþ 19 Þsþ 56, 61 Vís 99

protect **OGu** *GL* A 24f (64), **ONorw** *GuL* Mhb

See also: *helagher, hælgh*

hælghebrut (ODan) **helgisbrut** (OGu) noun

breaking the peace **ODan** *SkKL* 9, 10

fine for Sabbath-breaking **OGu** *GL* A 6, 8

Sabbath-breaking **OGu** *GL* A 6, 8

sacrilege **ODan** *JyL* 2

See also: *hælgh, hælghe, hælghidomber*

hælghebrutsak (ODan) noun

case of sacrilege **ODan** *JyL* 2

hælghhion (OSw) noun

domestic servants with immunity **OSw** *DL* Gb

hælghidagher (OSw) **helaghdagh** (ODan)

hælghadaghar (OSw) noun

feast day **ODan** *SkKL* 11, **OSw** *UL* Kkb, *VmL* Kkb

holiday **OSw** *YVgL* Kkb

holy day **ODan** *JyL* 2, **OSw** *DL* Kkb, Mb, Bb, Rb, *HL* Kkb, *SdmL* Kkb, Tjdb, *UL* Kkb, *VmL* Kkb, Rb, *YVgL* Kkb, Add, *ÖgL* Kkb

See also: *dagher, hælgh*

hælghidomber (OSw) **helaghdom** (ODan) noun

Holy objects appear in certain oath procedures concerning disputed borders between *land* (q.v.) and *hærab* (q.v.) and disputed land transactions (OSw YVgL) as well as in the new king's oath of allegiance, which should be sworn holding both a book and holy relic (OSw SdmL). According to ODan SkL 113 a levelling oath (ODan *javnetheeth*, see *jamnaþareþer*) should be sworn on a book, not on holy relics. The word also occurs referring to places of pilgrimage (ODan SkL 83, 124) and relics in a church (ODan SkKL 1).

holy object **ODan** *SkKL* 1, *SkL* 113

holy place **ODan** *SkL* 83, 146

holy relic **OSw** *SdmL* Till, *YVgL* Jb, Add

See also: *bok (1), eþer, halsbók, hælghebrut, hærab, jamnaþareþer, kununger, land, pilegrim, pilægrimsfærþ, sværia, vitni, vætti*

hælghisbot (OSw) noun

wergild compensation **OSw** *ÄVgL* Md

See also: *bot, manhælghi*

hælghiþorsdagher (OSw) noun

Holy Thursday (Ascension Day) **OSw** *SdmL* Rb, *UL* Kkb, Blb, Rb, *YVgL* Kkb, Jb, Utgb, *ÄVgL* Jb, Föb

See also: *uppstigningardagr*

hælghudaghabrut (OSw) noun

offence on a holy day **OSw** *ÖgL* Kkb

Sabbath-breaking **OSw** *UL* Kkb, *VmL* Kkb

violation of a holy day **OSw** *HL* Kkb, *SdmL* Kkb

See also: *hælghebrut*

hælghunamæssudagher (OSw) **helgunamessa** (OGu) noun

All Saints' Day **OGu** *GS* Ch. 3, **OSw** *DL* Kkb, *SdmL* Kkb, *SmL*, *UL* Kkb, Blb, *YVgL* Kkb

See also: *aldra hælghuna dagher, allraheilagramessa*

hælmninger (OSw) noun

armed attendants **OSw** *VmL* Mb

Expressions:

hær ok hælmninger (OSw)

armed men and attendants **OSw** *VmL* Mb

hælraþ (OSw) **hælræþ** (OSw) noun

death **OSw** *ÄVgL* Md

incited killing **OSw** *YVgL* Drb

See also: *raþa*

hæmd (OSw) **hævnd** (ODan) **hemd** (OGu) **hefnd** (ON) noun

Revenge was mainly allowed in cases of killing, other bodily injury and adultery (the latter supposedly the only legal cause for revenge in ODan). In OIce Grg and ONorw FrL it also applied to insults. Only an actual offender could be the legal target of revenge (OIce Js; OSw DL, HL, SdmL, UL, VmL, ÖgL), and OGu GL and OSw ÖgL allowed revenge on women, which was explicitly prohibited, along with 'learned men', in ODan JyL. Revenge was prohibited when breaching a promise of immunity or an agreed settlement (ODan JyL; ONorw FrL; OSw DL, HL, SdmL, UL, VmL, YVgL, ÄVgL, ÖgL), an oath, a testimony or a legal indictment (OSw HL, SdmL, UL, VmL, ÖgL). It was also prohibited for avoidance of a legal punishment or compensation (ODan ESjL, JyL; OSw YVgL, ÄVgL, ÖgL), and as an act of enmity (OSw SdmL, VmL) or for accidents (OSw YVgL), or if death occurred later than a year after a wounding (OSw SdmL, VmL). Most OSw laws explicitly described these acts of revenge as violations of the king's sworn peace (OSw *eþsöre*), the peace (OSw *friþer*) or as an unatonable crime (OSw *urbotamal*). OIce Js and ONorw FrL state that anyone who took vengeance for an unatonable criminal became themselves an unatonable criminal. The injured party was sometimes allowed to choose between revenge and fine/compensation (OSw HL, SdmL, UL, VmL), while ODan JyL explicitly denied the victim of theft the possibility of hanging his own thief. Occasionally *hæmd* referred to a legal punishment by the king (OSw SdmL, UL). Although there are more attestations of the word from East Norse laws, revenge is presumed to have been more widespread, in the West than in the East, and the examples above include provisions expressed with the verb *hævne* (ODan)/*hefna* (ON)/*hæmna* (OSw).

revenge **ODan** *ESjL* 3, *JyL* 2, *VSjL* 86, **OGu**
GL A 11, 14, **OSw** *HL* Kgb, *SdmL* Conf, Kgb,
UL StfBM, Kgb (table of contents only), *VmL*
Kgb (table of contents only), *YVgL* Add

vengeance **ODan** *ESjL* 2, **OIce** *Jó* Mah 21

Refs: KLNM s.v. *hämnd*

hæmna (OSw) **hævne** (ODan) **hemna** (OGu) **hefna**
(ON) verb

avenge **ODan** *ESjL* 3, *JyL* 2, **OIce** *Grg* Vís 86 Misc
237, 238, *Jó* Mah 2, 21, *Js* Mah 6, 7, **ONorw** *FrL*
Intr 5 Var 45 Rgb 35, **OSw** *YVgL* Urb, Add, *ÖgL* Db

revenge **OSw** *YVgL* Add, *ÄVgL* Urb

take revenge **ODan** *ESjL* 2, *JyL* 2, 3, *VSjL* 52,
OGu *GL* A 14, 17, Add. 1, 2 (B 4, 17), **ONorw**
GuL Krb, Tfb, Mhb, **OSw** *DL* Eb, *HL* Kgb, Mb,
SdmL Kgb, Mb, *UL* Kgb, Mb, *VmL* Kgb, Mb

take vengeance **OSw** *ÖgL* Eb, Db

hængia (OSw) **hængje** (ODan) **hengja** (ON) verb

Hanging may have been the most common form of
capital punishment, although the method was rarely
explicitly mentioned in OIce and ONorw laws.
Hanging was considered dishonourable and was
mainly used in cases of theft exceeding a certain value,
and when the thief was caught in the act. Women
were not to be hanged with the explicit exception of
cases of witchcraft in OSw ÄVgL Tb. In ODan JyL
2:87 the hanging was to be carried out by the king's
official, but otherwise it seems generally assumed that
the plaintiffs could act as executioners of the death
sentence issued by the *þing* 'assembly'; a preceding
sentence was, however, not required in OIce and
ONorw laws. Often appears with the adverb/particle
up.

hang **ODan** *JyL* 2, *SkL* 151, 162, 184, 226,
VSjL 86, 87, **OIce** *Grg* Bat 113, **OSw** *DL*
Tjdb, *SdmL* Tjdb, *YVgL* Tb, *ÄVgL* Tb

See also: *galghi, gren, hals, hang, þing*

Refs: Gade 1986, 159–68; KLNM s.v.
dødsstraf; Schlyter s.v. *up hængia*

hær (OSw) **hær** (ODan) **herr** (ON) noun

army **ODan** *ESjL* 2, **ONorw** *GuL* Kvb,
Leb, **OSw** *SdmL* Kgb, Äb, Mb, *ÖgL* Eb

enemy force **OIce** *Grg* Misc 248, **OSw** *UL* Kgb

group of armed men **OSw** *VmL* Mb

Expressions:

hær ok hælmninger (OSw)

armed men and attendants **OSw** *VmL* Mb

See also: *herhlaup, hirð*

hærap (OSw) **hæreth** (ODan) **herað** (ON) noun

The highest judicial and administrative district in the
Danish laws and the Göta laws. Each *hærap* had its
own assembly, *hærapsþing* (q.v.). In the Icelandic
laws, a *herað* was a lower-level administrative district.
In Norwegian laws, *herað* refers to the local court
district and an administrative and ecclesiastical unit
(a parish). It was to be distinguished from the town
(*kaupangr*, see *köpunger*), which had a separate law.

commune **OIce** *Grg* Klþ 5

countryside **ONorw** *FrL* KrbA 45

district **ODan** *ESjL* 1–3, *JyL* 1–3, *SkL* 80, 145,
147, 225, *VSjL* 82, 87, **OIce** *Grg* Klþ 2, 4 Þsþ
22, 58, *Jó* Þfb 6, 9 Mah 6, 9 Kge 24 Lbb 6 Llb
47 Kab 2, 6 Þjb 5, 13, *Js* Mah 13, 14 Lbb 11
Kab 2, 7 Þjb 4, *KRA* 15, **ONorw** *EidsL* 33.1 45.3
47.1 passim, *FrL* Intr 20 Mhb 7, 30 Var 46 Rgb
31 Kvb 23 LlbA 10, **OSw** *YVgL* passim, *ÄVgL*
Kkb, Md, Smb, Slb, Jb, Tb, *ÖgL* Kkb, Eb, Db

home district **ONorw** *GuL* Krb, Arb, Tfb, Mhb, Leb

Expressions:

hæræþs almænninger (OSw)

common land of the district **OSw** *YVgL* Föb

hæraþs asyn (OSw)

examination of the district **OSw** *YVgL* Jb

survey of the district **OSw** *YVgL* Kvab

See also: *almænninger, asyn, attunger, fiarþunger,
heraðstakmark, hreppr, hundari, hærapshöfþingi,
hærapsrætter, hærapsþing, land, sysel*

Refs: Andersson 1982a, 52–66; 1984, 90–100;
Andersson 2014; Brink 1998; Dalberg and
Kousgård Sørensen 1984, 76–89; Hagland
and Sandnes 1997, 98 note 2; KLNM s.v.
herred; Tamm and Vogt 2016, 5–7

hærapshöfþingi (OSw) noun

The *hærapshöfþingi* was the ordinary judge at the
hærapsþing (q.v.); he also had some executive
obligations.

district principal **OSw** *YVgL* Kkb, Frb, Drb,
Tb, Jb, Föb, Utgb, Add, *ÄVgL* Md, Slb, Tb
{*hærapshöfþingi*} **OSw** *ÖgL* Eb, Db

See also: *domari, höfþingi, hærap,
hærapsþing, laghmaþer, þing*

Refs: KLNM s.v. *häradshövding*

hærapsmannamal (OSw) noun

office as district principal **OSw** *YVgL* Add

See also: *hærap*

hæraþsmaþer (OSw) **hærethsman** (ODan)
heraðsmaðr (ON) **hæraþsmæn (pl.)** (OSw) noun

district men **ODan** *ESjL* 3, **OSw** *ÖgL* Db

local man **OIce** *Grg* Klþ 6

man of the district **ODan** *ESjL* 3, *JyL* 2, *SkL* 69, *VSjL*
32, 58, 72, **OIce** *Grg* Fjl 225, *Jó* Kge 32 Lbb 3 Llb
42 Þjb 6, *Js* Þjb 5, **ONorw** *GuL* Llb, Tjb, Arb, Leb

See also: *hreppsmaðr*, *hæraþ*

hæraþsnæmd (OSw) **hærethsnævnd** (ODan) noun

A *næmd* 'panel' with, according to ODan JyL, three
members from each *fjarthing* 'quarter' (see *fiarþunger*)
of the *hæreth* 'district' (see *hæraþ*). It dealt with
cases of, for instance, forgery, arson, highwaymen
(ODan JyL), referrals from the king concerning sins
(OSw SmL), contradictory oaths, infanticide, unjust
revenge, rape, chasing off opponents, association
with outlaws, breaching the king's sworn oath,
killings and a *hærapshöfþingi* failing to heed a call
from a householder (OSw ÖgL). OSw ÖgL (Kkb 16)
prescribed a functional division between *hæraþsnæmd*
(formal aspects) and *biskupsnæmd* (q.v.) (facts).
Appears in OSw ÄVgL and YVgL in the expression
lukt (lit. 'closed, locked') *hæraþsnæmd*, which
indicated unanimity, confidentiality or something else.

district jury **OSw** *ÖgL* Kkb, Eb, Db

men of a district **ODan** *JyL* 3

nominated men of the district **OSw** *YVgL*
Frb, Drb, Äb, Rlb, Add, *ÄVgL* Slb, Äb

panel from the {hæraþ} **OSw** *SmL*

See also: *hæraþ*, *næmd*

Refs: Andersen 2014; Lindkvist forthcoming;
SL ÄVgL, 69 note 33; Åqvist 1989, 283

hæraþspiækker (OSw) noun

Literally 'district hare' used of a vagrant, possibly a
beggar. There is no mention of an organization within
the *hæraþ* to care for them.

district beggar **OSw** *ÖgL* Db

See also: *förumannaflutningr*,
förumannaförsla, *göngumaðr*, *húsgangr*,
húsgangsmaðr, *hæraþ*, *stafkarl*

Refs: KLNM s.v. *fattigvård*; SL ÖgL, 71, note 54

hæraþsræfst (OSw) noun

Used of a specific decision to protect woodland.
Breaching it was punished with higher fines than other
illegal felling.

protection of the district **OSw** *YVgL* Föb, *ÄVgL* Fös

See also: *hæraþ*

Refs: Lindkvist forthcoming;
Schlyter s.v. *hærapsræfst*

hæraþsrætter (OSw) **heraðsréttr** (ON) noun

district law **ONorw** *GuL* Arb

right of the district **OSw** *YVgL* Kkb

See also: *hæraþ*

hæraþsþing (OSw) **hærethsthing** (ODan) **heraðsþing**
(ON) noun

A *þing* 'assembly' of the administrative/judicial district
hæraþ in its various usages. The highest assembly of
the *hæraþ* (q.v.) in the Göta laws. Dealing mostly
with local matters, and the venue for interactions
with representatives of king and bishop. According to
ODan laws, held every fortnight (every eight days in
SkL). In OSw YVgL held twice a year and led by the
hæraþshöfþingi (q.v.), but in ODan laws apparently
without a formal leader. In OIce Grg, *herað* was
synonymous with *hreppr* (q.v.), but the *heraðsþing*
was an assembly of the quarter (ON *fjórðungr*, see
fiarþunger).

assembly in the district **ODan** *JyL* 1

assembly of the district **OSw** *YVgL* Gb, Föb, Add

district assembly **ODan** *ESjL* 2, 3, *JyL* 2, *SkL* 17,
19, 71, 73, 139, 145, 188, 214, 226, *VSjL* 32, 68, 69,
78, 87, **OIce** *Jó* Lbb 8 Llb 39, *Js* Mah 19 Rkb 2

See also: *hæraþ*, *landsþing*, *þing*

Refs: Andersen 2011, 242−313; KLNM s.v.
herredsting, *ting*; Tamm and Vogt, eds, 2016, 301

hærbuþ (OSw) noun

summons for military service **OSw** *HL* Kgb

hærbærghi (OSw) **hærbærghe** (ODan) **herbergi**
(OGu) **herbergi** (OSw) **hærbyrghe** (OSw) noun

board and lodging **OGu** *GL* A 20

house **OSw** *DL* Kkb

place **ODan** *JyL* 2

room **ODan** *ESjL* 3

shelter **ODan** *ESjL* 2, *VSjL* 86

sleeping quarters **OSw** *DL* Bb, *VmL* Mb, Bb

storehouse **OSw** *SmL*

hærethsskjal (ODan) noun

boundary between districts **ODan** *JyL* 2

See also: *hæraþ*, *markarskæl*, *skæl*

hærethsthingsvitne (ODan) noun

witness from the district assembly **ODan** *SkL* 145

hærethsvitne (ODan) noun

district witness **ODan** *ESjL* 2

witness from the district **ODan** *VSjL* 87

hærethsvægh (ODan) noun

road of a district **ODan** *JyL* 1

hærfangin (OSw) adj.

war captive **OSw** *SdmL* Jb

hærfærþ (OSw) **herferþ** (OGu) **herferð** (ON) **herferþ**
(OSw) noun

campaign **OIce** *Grg* Misc 248

military expedition **OGu** *GS* Ch. 4

war expedition **OSw** *YVgL* Add

warfare **OSw** *SdmL* Till

hæria (OSw) **hærje** (ODan) **herja** (ON) verb

destroy **ODan** *SkL* 57

devastate **ODan** *ESjL* 2

go on raids **OIce** *Jó* Mah 3

harry **OSw** *ÖgL* Eb

raid **ONorw** *FrL* Mhb 4, *GuL* Leb

ravage **OSw** *HL* Kgb, *SdmL* Kgb,
YVgL Urb, *ÄVgL* Urb

violate **OSw** *ÄVgL* Urb

hærjende (ODan) noun

destroyer **ODan** *ESjL* 1

hærlænsker (OSw) **hérlenzkr** (ON) adj.

from the province **OSw** *YVgL* Drb

in the province **OSw** *YVgL* Tb

native **ONorw** *GuL* Tjb

See also: *utlændsker*

hærman (OSw) noun

warrior **OSw** *SdmL* Kmb

hærop (OSw) noun

alarm **OSw** *SdmL* Kgb

hærra (OSw) **hærre** (ODan) **herra** (ON) **herra** (OSw)
noun

Prominent men on various positions in society: the
king and his knights and other noble men of the realm
or those in charge of parts of/districts in the realm,
as well as a master or lord. Also used as a title. OSw
UL *lænshærra* refers specifically to the king's highest
official in a *hundari* (q.v.), and the superior of the
lænsmaþer (q.v.).

lord **OFar** *Seyð* 0, 1, **OSw** *DL* Eb, *HL* Mb, *SdmL*
Kgb, Kmb, Mb, Tjdb, Rb, Till, *UL* Kgb, Mb, Jb, Rb,
VmL Kkb, Kgb, Mb, *YVgL* Urb, Rlb, Jb, *ÖgL* Db, Vm

lord or master **OSw** *HL* Mb

master **ODan** *SkL* 173, **OSw** *UL*
Mb, Jb, Kmb, *VmL* Mb, Kmb

nobleman **OSw** *HL* Kgb, *UL* Kmb, *VmL* Kmb

Our Lord **OSw** *UL* StfBM

Sir **OSw** *SdmL* Conf, Till, *UL* StfBM

Expressions:

hærra garþer (OSw)

lord's farm **OSw** *SdmL* Rb

See also: *hundari, hæraþ, hærraman,
kununger, leþunger, lænsmaþer, riddari*

Refs: KLNM s.v. *herretitel*; Olesen
2000, 16–17; Schlyter s.v. *hærra*

hærraman (OSw) **hærreman** (ODan) noun

In ODan, a man obliged to perform military service at
his own expense in return for tax-exemption. In OSw,
presumably synonymous with *hærra*.

lordsman **ODan** *JyL* 3

nobleman **OSw** *UL* Kmb, *VmL* Kmb

See also: *hærra*

Refs: Tamm and Vogt, eds, 2016, 308

hærskip (OSw) noun

warship **OSw** *YVgL* Urb, *ÄVgL* Urb

hærskjold (ODan) **herskjöldr** (ON) noun

armed gang **ODan** *SkL* 226

Expressions:

fara með herskildi (ON)

to harry (*a land*) **ONorw** *FrL* Reb 1

hærstræte (ODan) noun

highroad **ODan** *JyL* 1

hærtaka (OSw) **hærtake** (ODan) verb

abduct **OSw** *HL* Äb

take in battle **ODan** *SkL* 129

hærtughi (OSw) **hærtugh** (ODan) **hertogi** (ON)
hærtugh (OSw) noun

duke **ODan** *JyL* Fort, **OFar** *Seyð* 0, 1, **OIce** *Jó* Llb
18, **OSw** *SdmL* Conf, För, Till, *UL* Rb, *ÖgL* Db, Vm

hærvirkesmal (ODan) noun

gang crime case **ODan** *ESjL* 3

hærværk (ODan) **hærvirke** (ODan) noun

Generally and originally a crime, typically violent,
committed by at least five offenders, but in JyL also by
one offender as well as by larger numbers of animals.

gang crime **ODan** *ESjL* 2, 3, *JyL* 2, 3,
SkL 87, 218, *VSjL* 35, 56, 64, 86

See also: *aganga, bothegang, farunöti, flokker,
fylghi, garthgang, hemsokn, landnám*

Refs: Tamm and Vogt, eds, 2016, 305

hærværksak (ODan) noun

case of gang crime **ODan** *ESjL* 2

See also: *hærværk*

hæskaper (OSw) **hæskap** (ODan) **hiskepr** (OGu) noun

estate **ODan** *ESjL* 3, *SkL* 227

house **OSw** *YVgL* Utgb, *ÄVgL* Föb

household **ODan** *VSjL* 6, **OGu** *GS* Ch. 3,
OSw *YVgL* Tb, *ÄVgL* Tb, *ÖgL* Db

marriage **OSw** *YVgL* Äb, *ÄVgL* Äb

property **ODan** *JyL* 1, 3

See also: *hionalagh*

hæsteleghe (ODan) noun

Payment to *sannendemæn* (ODan) 'men of truth' (see *sannindaman*) for their transport in connection with cases they were to handle at the *thing* (ODan) 'assembly'.

horse rent **ODan** *JyL* 2

See also: *legha*, *sannindaman*, *þing*, *þingfararkaup*

Refs: Andersen 2010, 100; Tamm and Vogt, eds, 2016

hæster (OSw) **hestr** (OGu) **hestr** (ON) noun

There were numerous regulations concerning horses in various laws. In Norway, for example, the bishop was only allowed to bring with him a limited number of horses (11, in some cases 30, in summer; 6, in some cases 15, in winter) when travelling in his diocese (EidsL 32.11, 34. 3). Horses were a valid means of payment (GuL ch. 223). As articles of trade, they had to be free of flaws: they must not be blind or deaf, ruptured or restive, lame, epileptic or spastic (FrL Rgb ch. 48). A number of other requirements are listed in GuL (ch. 223) and in GL (A 34). If flaws were discovered within five days (three days in GL) after a horse was bought, the bargain could be reversed (FrL ibid.). Horses might not be used without the consent of the owner (GuL ch. 92; GL A 35). If they were injured or caused damage, this was to be compensated (GuL chs 96, 97, 147).

horse **OGu** *GL* A 6, 10, 17, 34–36, *GS* Ch. 3, **ONorw** *EidsL* 32.11, 34.3, *GuL* Krb, Kp, Llb, Arb, Tfb, Mhb, **OSw** *UL* Äb, Mb, Kmb, Blb, *VmL* Kkb, Äb, Mb, Kmb, Bb

See also: *hófr*, *rus*, *skiut*

Refs: KLNM s.v.v. *hestehandel*, *husdyrsygdomme*, *häst*, *jakt*, *kløv*, *kvægavl*, *trækdyr*

hæsthus (OSw) noun

stable **OSw** *DL* Kkb

hætte (ODan) **heita** (ON) verb

declare **ODan** *JyL* 2

have as surety **ODan** *ESjL* 1,3, *JyL* 2

pledge **ODan** *ESjL* 1, *JyL* 2

provide surety **ODan** *JyL* 1

give surety **ODan** *JyL* 1

take responsibility **ODan** *SkL* 126

vow **OIce** *KRA* 12

hæzla (OSw) noun

gift **OSw** *HL* Kkb

Expressions:

hælgha mans hæzla (OSw)

gift to saints **OSw** *HL* Kkb

hö (OSw) **hey** (ON) noun

hay **ONorw** *GuL* Llb, **OSw** *YVgL* Kkb, Jb, Utgb, *ÄVgL* Jb, Föb

höfn (ON) noun

landing place **OIce** *Grg* Feþ 166

höfuð (ON) noun

Injuries to a man's head were severely punished, see, e.g., GuL chs 238, 241, 242. On the other hand, a slave should be punished for theft by having his head cut off (ch. 259).

head of animals **ONorw** *GuL* Kvr, Leb

head of human beings **ONorw** *GuL* Mhb, Tjb

höfuðbarmr (ON) noun

male side **ONorw** *GuL* Arb

See also: *bauggildismaðr*, *höfuðbarmsmaðr*, *karlsvift*

höfuðbarmsmaðr (ON) **höfuðbarmsmenn (pl.)** (ON) noun

paternal kinsman **OIce** *Js* Kvg 2

paternal relative **ONorw** *GuL* Kvb

See also: *bauggildismaðr*, *höfuðbarmr*, *karlsvift*

höfuðbaugr (ON) noun

capital ring **ONorw** *FrL* Sab 3

head ring **ONorw** *GuL* Mhb

main ring **OIce** *Grg* Bat 113

höfuðból (ON) noun

A man's home farm seems to have enjoyed a special legal status (on a par with that of the *heimili*, q.v.), esp. in relation to the division of odal land. See GuL ch. 87.

home farm **ONorw** *GuL* Llb

land on which the main house is **OIce** *Jó* Kge 7 Lbb 5

Refs: KLNM s.v.v. *hovedgård*, *odelsrett*

höfuðkirkja (ON) noun

high church **ONorw** *FrL* Leb 26

main church **ONorw** *EidsL* 32.7, *GuL* Krb

höfuðprestr (ON) noun

main priest **ONorw** *EidsL* 10.1, 47.6

höfþingi (OSw) **høvthing** (ODan) **höfðingi** (ON) noun

Derived from a noun meaning 'head', and used of any leader ranging from leaders of the realm (*kununger*) and various districts (*hæraþshöfþingi* (q.v.) and *fiarþungxs höfþinganum af hæraþinu* (OSw), *væreldshøvthing* (q.v.) (ON)), to principals in violent (gang) crimes.

chieftain **OIce** *Jó* MagBref HT 2 Mah 1, *Js* Kdb 2, **ONorw** *FrL* Intr 5 Mhb 62

leader **ODan** *SkL* 87, **OIce** *Jó* Þjb 6, **ONorw** *FrL* Var 14, *GuL* Kpb, Olb, **OSw** *SdmL* Till, *ÖgL* Db

lord **ODan** *JyL* Fort

höggskógr (ON) noun

Cutting woodland; a scarce and therefore valuable resource in medieval Iceland. Usually mentioned in contrast with scrubland (ON *rifhrís*). A *höggskógr* is broadly defined as a wooded area which can be cut down more quickly than pulled up in Jó Llb 24. Ownership regulations concerning trees which became sufficiently thick to qualify as cutting woodland are given in Grg Lbþ 190.

cutting woodland **OIce** *Grg* Lbþ 181, *Jó* Llb 24, 32

See also: *rifhrís*, *skogher*

Refs: CV s.v. *höggskógr*; Fritzner s.v. *höggskógr*; Hertzberg s.v. *höggskógr*

höghabyr (OSw) noun

village with a mound **OSw** *YVgL* Jb, *ÄVgL* Jb

See also: *byr*, *heþna*

högtiþisdagher (OSw) noun

commemoration day **OSw** *SdmL* Kkb

hölaþa (OSw) noun

hay barn **OSw** *HL* Mb

hölðborinn (ON) adj.

freeholder-born **ONorw** *BorgL* 12.4

See also: *hölðmaðr*, *hölðr*

hölðmaðr (ON) **hauldmaðr** (ON) **höldsmaðr** (ON) noun

freeholder **ONorw** *FrL* Rgb 35, *GuL* Llb, Arb, Mhb

yeoman **ONorw** *EidsL* 48.2, 50.2

See also: *hölðr*

hölðmannsréttr (ON) noun

compensation of a freeholder **ONorw** *FrL* Mhb 60

freeholder's right **ONorw** *GuL* Mhb

See also: *hölðmaðr*, *hölðr*, *hölðsréttr*

hölðr (ON) **hauldr** (ON) noun

A Norwegian class of landowners who possessed allodial land. The concept was borrowed in England and became OE *hold*. A *hölðr* has been compared to the slightly later 'statesman', a type of landowner in Northern and Eastern England and to the modern Norwegian *odelsbonde*. In GuL a *hölðr* is also referred to as an *óðalborinn maðr* and in BorgL as an *árborinn maðr*. The legal status of a *hölðr* according to Gul was between a landed man (*lendr maðr*, see *lænder*) and a householder (*bóndi*, see *bonde*). The primary distinction between a landed man and a *hölðr* was that the former had received land from the king whereas the latter had not. A *hölðr* was entitled to double wergild (as compared to a householder), and they could pass on twice as much property to an illegitimate son. In Gul and the LandsL a *hölðr* had the right to be an *einfyndr*

(i.e possessor of sole rights) when coming upon a drift whale of a certain size. Moreover they, along with householders, were permitted more prestigious burial plots than freed men and thralls. Some earlier commentators have viewed the *hölðr* as a type of landed aristocrat. In LandsL a *hölðr* is strictly defined as someone who has inherited allodial land from both his father and mother, and it has been suggested that this criterion meant that there were relatively few *hölð* and that they became increasingly fewer as the Middle Ages progressed.

According to Bj, everyone in the Niðaros township was accorded the rank of *hölðr*. In GuL this notion of 'freeholder's rights' (*hauldsrett*) is expanded to include all free men in places where strangers came together, such as cities, fishing areas and trade stations. In FrL the king's page (*skutilsveinn*) also holds the rank of *hölðr*, as do the king's goldsmith and the captains of his ships. In GuL (ch. 200) Icelanders on trading voyages to Norway were granted the rights of a *hölðr* for three years, but those of other countries only the rights of a *bóndi*. A similar law attributed to St Olaf decreed that Icelanders should hold the rank of *hölðr* when visiting Norway (DI i.65.2). The term is not otherwise used in Iceland, and in JB it has been substituted with *riddari* (q.v.). The term is not found in the Danish or Swedish provincial laws, but it does appear in some Danish place names.

In courts, a *hölðr* was preferred for serving on jury panels, but they could be replaced by householders if necessary (cf. FrL). Their importance declined sharply in the later Middle Ages as their property was absorbed by the nobility and the church, and the number of tenant farmers (*leiglendinger*, see *laigulenningr*) increased.

freeholder **ONorw** *FrL* Mhb 8, 49 ArbB 17 Rgb 34 LlbA 15 LlbB 7 Bvb 11, *GuL* Kvr, Mhb

See also: *hölðmannsréttr*, *hölðmaðr*, *maþer*, *óðalborinn*, *riddari*

Refs: CV s.v. *hölðr*; F s.v. *hölðr*; Hagland 2011; KLNM s.v. *bonde*, *bøter*, *hauld*, *stænder*; LexMA s.v. *bauer*, *bauerntum*, *odal*; NF s.v. *bonde*; ONP; Phillpotts 1913; Pons Sanz 2007; RGA s.v. *odal*; Riisøy 2005; Vogt 2010

hölðsréttr (ON) **hauldsréttr** (ON) noun

freeholder's rights to compensation **ONorw** *FrL* Mhb 60, Kvb 21, *GuL* Mhb

See also: *hölðmannsréttr*

hölfuþing (ON) **hálfuþing** (ON) noun

half-district assembly **ONorw** *FrL* LlbB 7

See also: *þing*

hölkn (ON) **helkn** (ON) noun
>*rocky ground* **OIce** *Jó* Llb 22, 67, *Js* Lbb 11
>*stony ground* **ONorw** *GuL* Llb
>*uninhabited place* **OIce** *Jó* Llb 2

hömlufall (ON) noun
>*illegal breaking* **ONorw** *GuL* Leb
>
>See also: *hamla*

hömlumaðr (ON) noun
>*oarsman* **ONorw** *GuL* Leb
>
>See also: *hasæti*

hömtaman (OSw) noun
>*person who has the right to give the bride away* **OSw** *DL* Gb
>
>See also: *giftarmaþer*

hörðar (pl.) (ON) noun
>*people from Hordaland* **ONorw** *GuL* Leb

hörgr (ON) noun
>*stone altar* **ONorw** *GuL* Krb, Mhb (Intr)
>
>See also: *høgh*

hörundfall (ON) noun
>The *hörundfall* was considered as an obstacle to marriage. See GuL ch. 51. It has been understood as referring to impotence (Fritzner, CV).
>*impotence* **ONorw** *GuL* Kvb
>
>See also: *sinfallinn*
>
>Refs: KLNM s.v. *impotens*

hörzkr (ON) adj.
>*from Hordaland* **ONorw** *GuL* Løb

hörængi (OSw) **heyringjar (pl.)** (ON) **hörængiar (pl.)** (OSw) noun
>*auditory man* **OSw** *ÄVgL* Slb
>*witnesses outside the court* **ONorw** *GuL* Kpb
>
>See also: *heyrendr (pl.)*

höstþing (OSw) noun
>A *þing* 'assembly' held in autumn, appearing, alongside *varþing* ('assembly held in spring'), in the context of refusal to fence, suggesting that it dealt with local village matters. The *höstþing* could also function as a *ræfsingaþing* (literally 'punishment assembly') which could be held at a *hærapsþing* (q.v.) or a *fiærþungsþing* (q.v.).
>*autumn assembly* **OSw** *YVgL* Utgb, Add
>
>See also: *fiærþungsþing*, *hærapsþing*, *leið*, *leiðarþing*, *ræfsingaþing*, *varþing*, *þing*

höta (OSw) **hóta** (ON) verb
>*threaten* **OSw** *DL* Eb, *HL* Kgb, *SdmL* Kgb, Mb, *YVgL* Add, *ÖgL* Eb

hötning (OSw) noun
>*threatening* **OSw** *SdmL* Mb

hötsl (OSw) noun
>*threat* **OSw** *YVgL* Add, *ÖgL* Eb
>
>See also: *höta*

høgh (ODan) **haugr** (OGu) **haugr** (ON) noun
>*burial mound* **ODan** *JyL* 2
>*hill* **ONorw** *GuL* Part X Intr
>*howe* **OGu** *GL* A 4
>*mound* **ONorw** *GuL* Krb
>
>See also: *hörgr*, *ætahögher*

høghe (ODan) verb
>*be a case for* **ODan** *VSjL* 47

høgheman (ODan) noun
>A pagan child, i.e. one who had not been baptized; these could not inherit.
>*barrow man* **ODan** *SkL* 3
>
>See also: *høghabyr*
>
>Refs: Tamm and Vogt, eds, 2016, 301

høretoft (ODan) noun
>*outer toft* **ODan** *ESjL* 2
>
>See also: *tompt*

høsthælgh (ODan) noun
>*harvest holiday* **ODan** *ESjL* 2
>*harvest peace* **ODan** *SkKL* 9
>
>See also: *anfriþer*, *önn (pl. annir)*, *varfriþer*

høgendiskirkja (ON) **høgendakirkja** (ON) noun
>A *høgendiskirkja* ('proprietary church') was an annex church or a private church, as well as a church built for comfort/convenience (*høgindi*) for a portion of a parish (distinguished from a *heraðskirkja* (q.v.) and a *fjórðungskirkja* (q.v.)). An individual man was allowed to build a private church when the journey to another church was considered (too) long and strenuous. The private churches were gradually included in the parish organisation; they were used by other people in the surrounding areas and even obtained the right to receive tithes. In this way, they formed the basis of a new parish organisation, which from the second half of the twelfth century onwards partly replaced the one of the regional laws.
>*comfort-church* **ONorw** *EidsL* 39.1
>*ease-church* **ONorw** *EidsL* 40.2
>*private chapel* **ONorw** *FrL* KrbA 10, 13, *GuL* Krb
>*private church* **ONorw** *BorgL* 8
>*proprietary church* **ONorw** *BorgL* 8.11 10.5
>
>Refs: Bagge 2010, 232; Hagland and Sandnes 1997, 108; Helle 2001, 201–04; KLNM s.v.v.

kirkegård, kyrkans finanser, privatkirke, sogn; Robberstad 1981, 326; Skre 1995, 198; Wood 2006, 85 (with further refs.), 918

hógendisprestr (ON) noun

private chaplain **ONorw** *FrL* KrbA 17, 45

iðra (ON) verb

repent **OIce** *Grg* Klþ 2, **ONorw** *EidsL* 50.12

iðranarmark (ON) noun

mark of repentance **OIce** *KRA* 11

iðrun (ON) **iðran** (ON) noun

repentance **OIce** *Jó* HT 1, *Js* Kdb 1

ifalauss (ON) adj.

doubt-free **OIce** *Grg* Rsþ 227

ifasök (ON) noun

doubtful case **OIce** *Grg* Þsþ 44

ikorni (OSw) **ikorni** (OGu) **ekorni** (OSw) **ykorni** (OSw) noun

squirrel **OGu** *GL* A 57, **OSw** *UL* Blb, *VmL* Bb

See also: *graskin*

illa (OSw) **ille** (ODan) **ilske** (ODan) **illa** (ON) verb

Related to words meaning 'evil' or 'bad'. Mainly used in connection with disputed land, boundaries and other property such as domestic animals, but also with other legally reprehensible behaviour, such as not sending a message in due time. When the one complaining is the rightful owner of a disputed object, sometimes translated as 'to claim'. Expresses a complaint that could be dealt with at the *þing* 'assembly', and possibly to be understood as a formal start of legal proceedings.

challenge **ODan** *VSjL* 82, 84

charge **OSw** *YVgL* Kkb

claim **ODan** *SkL* 79, 80, 83, 143, 144, 150, *VSjL* 77, **OSw** *YVgL* Tb, *ÄVgL* Jb, Tb

complain **ONorw** *GuL* Løb, **OSw** *YVgL* Tb, Jb, *ÄVgL* Jb, Tb

demand **ODan** *SkL* 37

dispute **ODan** *SkL* 72, **OSw** *YVgL* Jb

lay claim **ODan** *SkL* 78

make a complaint **ODan** *SkL* 80

See also: *uilter*

illa (OSw) adv.

Expressions:

illa handla, handla illa (OSw)

abuse **OSw** *UL* Blb *VmL* Bb

illaviliaþer (OSw) **illa viliaþær** (OSw) adj.

malicious **OSw** *VmL* Bb

illgirni (ON) noun

malice **OIce** *Grg* Þsþ 64

illgærningisman (OSw) **illgiærningis man** (OSw) **illgærnings man** (OSw) noun

malefactor **OSw** *HL* För

miscreant **OSw** *UL* Kkb

scoundrel **OSw** *HL* Kkb

See also: *skaþamaþer*

illmæli (ON) noun

malicious speech **OIce** *Grg* Vís 86 Misc 238

slander **OIce** *Grg* Rsþ 227

illska (ON) **illzka** (ON) noun

ill will **ONorw** *GuL* Krb

illvirki (ON) noun

malicious damage **OIce** *Grg* Þsþ 64

See also: *spellvirki*

ilvilje (ODan) noun

malice **ODan** *SkL* 175

iviljes (ODan) verb

be a dispute **ODan** *VSjL* 11

imbrudagaboð (ON) noun

proclamation of ember days **ONorw** *BorgL* 13

imbrudagr (ON) noun

Ember Days **ONorw** *BorgL* 6.3 7.6 passim, *EidsL* 10.1 27.1

ingæld (OSw) noun

income **OSw** *SdmL* Till

ingærþis (OSw) adv.

Refers to land 'within enclosure'. Cultivated fields, meadows and some areas used for grazing would be fenced in. The use of this land in Sweden was characterized by annual cropping and intensive use. The main part of the food supply originated in the land 'within enclosure'.

within enclosures **OSw** *SdmL* Bb

within the enclosure **OSw** *VmL* Kkb

See also: *garþer*, *gærþi*, *staur*

Refs: KLNM s.v. *ager* col. 37–38; Myrdal 1999a, 125–30

inlaghsfæ (OSw) **inlax fæ** (OSw) noun

deposited property **OSw** *HL* Jb, *SdmL* Jb, Rb

property in trust **OSw** *UL* Jb

property placed in safe keeping **OSw** *UL* Rb, *VmL* Kmb (ch. 8 rubric only), Rb

inleþa (OSw) verb

church **OSw** *SmL*

inleþning (OSw) **inlezning** (OSw) **inleþsla** (OSw) **inleþsn** (OSw) noun

churching **OSw** *HL* Kkb, *SdmL* Kkb, *SmL*, *UL* Kkb, *VmL* Kkb, *YVgL* Kkb *first church attendance of a newly-married couple* **OSw** *HL* Kkb

payment for churching **OSw** *SmL*

See also: *kirkiuleþer*

inlænder (OSw) **ílendr** (ON) adj.

being allowed to stay in the country **ONorw** *GuL* Leb

entered into a land **OSw** *ÄVgL* Rlb

See also: *land*

inlænding (OSw) noun

A collective tax of 40 *marker* from each *hæraþ* (q.v.) given to a newly elected king arriving in the province (possibly only Östergötland) on his journey through the realm (OSw *eriksgata*).

provincial tax **OSw** *ÖgL* Db

Refs: KLNM s.v. *eriksgata*; Schlyter s.v. *inlænding*

inlændinger (OSw) noun

man from the provinces **OSw** *SdmL* Till

man of the province **OSw** *ÖgL* Db

inlændis (OSw) **inlændes** (ODan) adv.

in the land **OSw** *HL* Äb

in the province **ODan** *SkL* 90, 91, **OSw** *SdmL* Äb, Jb, Mb, *UL* Äb, Mb, *VmL* Äb, Mb

inlændsker (OSw) adj.

from the province **OSw** *DL* Rb, *SdmL* Mb

inna (ON) verb

pay **OIce** *Jó* Llb 6, *Js* Lbb 10, **ONorw** *FrL* LlbA 3

innam (ODan) noun

The taking of animals grazing without permission on somebody else's land; taken by the wronged landowner as security. Also the animal taken.

right to seize **ODan** *ESjL* 2

seized cattle **ODan** *SkL* 167

seizure **ODan** *ESjL* 2, *SkL* 169, 170, 182, 206

seizure of animals **ODan** *SkL* 171

See also: *nam*

Refs: Lund s.v. *innam*

innanfjórðungsmaðr (ON) noun

man within the quarter **OIce** *Grg* Rsþ 233

innanheraðsmaðr (ON) noun

man of the district **OIce** *Grg* Feþ 167

innanhreppsmaðr (ON) noun

man from inside the commune **OIce** *Grg* Klþ 8 Hrs 234 Tíg 259, *KRA* 26, 32

innankonungsrikismaþer (OSw) noun

man from the realm **OSw** *YVgL* Drb

innanlands (OSw) **innenlands** (ODan) **innanlands** (OGu) adv.

at home **OGu** *GL* Add. 1 (B 4)

within the province **ODan** *JyL* 2, *SkL* 90, 133, 146, *VSjL* 86, 87, **OSw** *YVgL* Urb, Tb

See also: *land*, *utanlands*

innansoknafulk (OGu) noun

parishioners **OGu** *GL* A 24a

innanþingsmaðr (ON) noun

man of the same assembly **OIce** *Grg* Þsþ 58, 64

See also: *þingunöti*

inne (ODan) noun

A duty of householders to work for the king, and later a tax replacing this labour, contrasted to the duty to perform military service.

labour **ODan** *SkL* 75

public labour **ODan** *VSjL* 79

work **ODan** *SkL* 238

See also: *inna*, *leþunger*, *stuþ*

Refs: KLNM, s.v. *inne*; Olesen 2000, 22–23; Tamm and Vogt, eds, 2016, 280, 307; Venge 2002, 283

innebonde (ODan) noun

ordinary householder **ODan** *JyL* 3

innestkone (ODan) noun

The female equivalent of the male *innestman* (see *innismaþer*) appears concerning her responsibility for stolen goods found behind locks, to which she, presumably, had the keys.

tenant's wife **ODan** *JyL* 2

innihafnir (pl.) (ON) noun

harbouring **OIce** *Grg* Klþ 4, Þsþ 44, Feþ 144

innihús (ON) noun

dwelling house **OIce** *Grg* Lbþ 219, *Jó* Llb 3

innisfolk (OSw) noun

Presumably a collective equivalent of the male *innismaþer* (q.v.) and female *innestkone* (q.v.). Appears concerning their obligation to pay *sialagift* 'soulgift'.

in-dwellers **OSw** *SdmL* Kkb

innismaþer (OSw) **innestman** (ODan) noun

Presumably a free man without land living in somebody else's house or on their property. Appears concerning his obligations in communal society regarding hunting, and his responsibilities towards the landlord regarding fire and stolen goods found behind locks, to which he, presumably, had the key.

in-dweller **ODan** *SkL* 226

tenant **ODan** *JyL* 2

unlanded man **OSw** *YVgL* Föb

Refs: Schlyter s.v. *innismaþer*; Tamm and Vogt, eds, 2016, 306

innitakin (OSw) innitakin (OGu) inne takin (OSw) adj.

    caught in the (very) act **OSw** *DL* Rb, *SdmL* Kkb, *SmL*, *YVgL* Kkb

    caught red-handed **OSw** *DL* Kkb

    discovered in the act **OGu** *GL* A 20a

    found in flagrante delicto **OGu** *GL* A 20

    taken in flagrante delicto **OGu** *GL* A 20a, 21, **OSw** *UL* Kkb, *VmL* Kkb, Äb, Rb

    See also: *gærning, taka*

innsigli (ON) noun

    seal (1) **OFar** *Seyð* 0, **OIce** *Grg* Klþ 6, *Jó* Mah 2 Kab 12, **ONorw** *FrL* Mhb 4 Bvb 1

innstóða (ON) innstóði (ON) noun

    capital **OIce** *Grg* Arþ 118, 122 Lbþ 172, *Jó* Kge 14 Fml 22

    main sum **OIce** *Grg* Ómb 141 Lbþ 218 Fjl 222 Misc 249 Tíg 259

    principal **OIce** *KRA* 35

innstóðueyrir (ON) innstæðueyrir (ON) noun

    capital for maintenance **OIce** *Jó* Kge 16, **ONorw** *GuL* Arb

    principal capital **OIce** *Js* Ert 25

    See also: *forlagseyrir*

innviðartré (ON) noun

    rib (in a ship) **ONorw** *GuL* Leb

innþróndr (ON) noun

    someone from inner Trondelag **ONorw** *FrL* Mhb 56

innþrónzkr (ON) adj.

    of inner Trondelag **ONorw** *FrL* Mhb 54

inrikis (OSw) innenrikes (ODan) innanrikis (OSw) adv.

    in the realm **OSw** *SdmL* Till, *UL* Mb, Jb, *YVgL* Drb, Add

    inside the country **ODan** *ESjL* 2

    inside the realm **ODan** *VSjL* 19

    within the country **ODan** *ESjL* 2, **OSw** *HL* Mb

    within the realm **ODan** *JyL* 2, *VSjL* 1, 87

    See also: *land, riki*

intaka (OSw) noun

    enclosed land **OSw** *YVgL* Jb, *ÄVgL* Jb

intækiuman (OSw) noun

The king's official collecting taxes. It is not clear whether referring to a specific office or one of the functions of some other official.

    tax collector **OSw** *SdmL* Kgb

    Refs: Schlyter s.v. *intækiuman*

intækt (OSw) intekt (OGu) noun

    discovery of illicit intercourse **OGu** *GL* B 29 rubric

    seized property **OSw** *SdmL* Bb

    seizure **OSw** *SdmL* Bb

intæktefæ (ODan) noun

    domestic animals taken up **ODan** *JyL* 3

    taking out domestic animals **ODan** *JyL* 3

invarþer (OSw) noun

    inland guard **OSw** *SdmL* Kgb

invistar (pl.) (OSw) noun

    chattels **OSw** *HL* Jb

invistarhus (OSw) noun

    provision house **OSw** *YVgL* Tb, *ÄVgL* Tb

inviþi (OSw) inuiþer (OSw) inviþer (OSw) noun

    household effects **OSw** *UL* Äb, *VmL* Äb

    movables **OSw** *DL* Rb, *VmL* Äb

    See also: *bo, boskaper, egn, fæ, goþs*

invræka (OSw) verb

    drive in **OSw** *UL* Blb, *VmL* Bb

    See also: *vræka*

invænge (ODan) noun

    taking in to cultivated fields **ODan** *ESjL* 2

    See also: *vang*

invængje (ODan) verb

    enclose in strip **ODan** *ESjL* 2

    See also: *vang*

iorþaign (OGu) noun

    property in the form of land **OGu** *GL* A 7

istaþamaþer (OSw) noun

    man in an oath **OSw** *YVgL* Add

ivinaxlaþer (OSw) överaxlaþer (OSw) adj.

    bareheaded **OSw** *UL* Mb, *VmL* Mb

ivirklæþi (OSw) yfirkleþi (OGu) noun

    gown **OSw** *UL* Äb

    outer garments **OGu** *GL* A 19

    See also: *gangkleþi*

iþ (OGu) noun

    provision **OGu** *GL* A 20

    See also: *hogsl, morghongæf*

ílit (ON) noun

    scar **ONorw** *GuL* Mhb

    visible mark **OIce** *Grg* Misc 241

ísetuarfr (ON) noun

    inheritance by right of occupancy **ONorw** *FrL* ArbA 17

íslendingr (ON) noun

He had the same personal rights as a *hauldr* (see *hölðr*) for three years, when trading in Norway. See GuL ch. 200.

Icelander **ONorw** *GuL* Mhb

Refs: KLNM s.v.v. *Island, islandshandel*

ítak (ON) noun

rights **OIce** *Grg* Lbþ 172

ítala (ON) noun

calculation of quotas **OIce** *Grg* Lbþ 177, 201, *Jó* Lbb 4 Llb 46

ívist (ON) noun

stay **ONorw** *GuL* Llb

jafnborinn (ON) adj.

of equal birth **OIce** *Jó* Mah 2, *Js* Mah 5

of equal rank **ONorw** *FrL* Mhb 4

of the same social class **ONorw** *FrL* Bvb 1

of the same social standing **ONorw** *FrL* Kvb 7

of the same social status **ONorw** *FrL* Rgb 36

jafndýrr (ON) adj.

as holy **ONorw** *BorgL* 14.1, *FrL* KrbA 24

costing the same **OIce** *Grg* Klþ 2

entitled to equally big compensation **ONorw** *GuL* Løb

worth as much **ONorw** *BorgL* 15.9

jafnfullr (ON) adj.

just as valid **OIce** *Jó* Kab 2, *Js* Kab 2, **ONorw** *FrL* Mhb 56 ArbA 19

jafnheilagr (ON) adj.

as holy **ONorw** *EidsL* 9.3 20.6

equally holy **ONorw** *GuL* Krb

having the same immunity **OIce** *Grg* Þsþ 53

jafnheimill (ON) adj.

equally available **OFar** *Seyð* 1

equally warrantable **OIce** *Js* Kvg 1

possessing the same legal right **OIce** *Jó* Kge 2 Llb 13, 64 Fml 26, **ONorw** *FrL* Kvb 4 Jkb 4

restored to its former condition **ONorw** *GuL* Llb

usable by all **ONorw** *FrL* LlbB 8

jafnmikill (ON) adj.

as much **ONorw** *GuL* Arb

jafnmæli (ON) noun

fair agreement **OIce** *Grg* Þsþ 50 Arþ 127 Ómb 135 Feþ 153

jafnnáinn (ON) adj.

equally close to inheritance **ONorw** *GuL* Arb

jafnrétti (ON) noun

equality of rights and social standing **ONorw** *GuL* Løb, Tfb

See also: *jafnréttismaðr*

jafnréttismaðr (ON) noun

man enjoying the same rights as anybody else **ONorw** *GuL* Løb, Tfb

See also: *jafnrétti*

jafnréttr (ON) adj.

as rightful **OIce** *Grg* Þsþ 56

having the same validity **OIce** *Grg* Þsþ 24

jafnræði (ON) noun

equal match **OIce** *Grg* Feþ 144, *Jó* Kge 1

jafnsekr (ON) adj.

equally guilty **OIce** *Jó* Þjb 1

under the same penalty **OIce** *Grg* Þsþ 63, Vís 93

jafnútlagr (ON) adj.

equally outlawed **ONorw** *FrL* Mhb 4

jakobsmessa (ON) noun

St James's Day **OIce** *Grg* Klþ 13

St James's Mass (25 July) **ONorw** *GuL* Krb

jamföri (OSw) **iæmföri** (OSw) noun

equal division **OSw** *SdmL* Bb

equitable allocation **OSw** *UL* Blb, *VmL* Bb

jamka (OSw) verb

set off **OSw** *ÖgL* Kkb

jamkunder (OSw) adj.

equally close in kin **OSw** *YVgL* Äb

See also: *jamnskylder*

jamkyrnismæn (pl.) (OSw) noun

Men who assisted in inheritance divisions.

agents **OSw** *YVgL* Add

arbiters **OSw** *YVgL* Add

Refs: Schlyter s.v. *jamkyrnismæn*

jamlangadagher (OSw) **jamlangedagh** (ODan) noun

anniversary **OSw** *ÖgL* Kkb

within a year **OSw** *YVgL* Äb, *ÄVgL* Äb

year and a day **ODan** *ESjL* 3

year and a day from **ODan** *ESjL* 2

the yearly day **ODan** *VSjL* 87

jamlangaoffer (OSw) noun

annual sacrifice **OSw** *DL* Kkb

jamlangaþing (OSw) noun

Thing assembly held within one year **OSw** *DL* Rb

See also: *jamlangi, þing*

jamlangi (OSw) **jamlange** (ODan) **iemlangi** (OGu)
iamlangde (OSw) **iæmlange** (OSw) noun

Literally 'equal length', meaning one year, or
sometimes possibly one year and six weeks.
Frequently occurring in expressions such as *dagh*
('day') *ok iamlangi* and *nat* ('night') *ok iamlangi* and
used for time limits concerning, for example, an heir's
right to claim inheritance under certain circumstances
and the healing of certain wounds with consequence
for their compensation.

after one year **OSw** *SmL*, *ÄVgL* Smb

course of a year **OSw** *UL* Äb, *VmL* Äb

during a year **OSw** *YVgL* Äb

in a year **OSw** *ÄVgL* Äb

one year **ODan** *SkKL* 11, **OSw**
SdmL Kkb, Gb, Jb, Bb

same time the following year **OGu** *GL* A 14

year **ODan** *ESjL* 3, *JyL* 2, 3, **OSw** *UL* Kkb, Mb,
Jb, Blb, *VmL* Kkb, Äb, Mb, Jb, *ÖgL* Kkb, Db

year and a day **ODan** *ESjL* 2, 3, **OGu** *GL* A 19

Expressions:

dagh ok iamlangi (OSw) **dagh oc iamling** (ODan)

a year and a day **ODan** *VSjL* 1,
19, 20, 83, 87 **OSw** *HL* Mb

nat ok iamlangi (OSw)

a night and a year **OSw** *YVgL* Frb, Äb, Föb

a year and a day **OSw** *HL* Mb *YVgL* Kkb

See also: *atmeli*

Refs: KLNM s.v.v. *termin, år og dag;* Lund
s.v.v. *dagh, iamlinge;* Schlyter s.v. *jamlangi;*
Tamm and Vogt, eds, 2016, 316

jamna (OSw) **javne** (ODan) verb

divide equally **OSw** *YVgL* Add

even out **ODan** *ESjL* 1–3, *JyL* 1, *SkL* 97

make equal **ODan** *SkL* 67, **OSw** *YVgL* Add

make even **ODan** *ESjL* 1, *SkL* 56,
73, 74, *VSjL* 17, 71, 78

share **OSw** *HL* Kgb

treat in the same way **ODan** *ESjL* 1

Expressions:

jafnask orðum (ON)

consider oneself somebody's equal **ONorw** *GuL* Løb

jamnarva (OSw) **javnearve** (ODan) adj.

equal in inheritance **OSw** *SdmL* Äb

equally near as heirs **ODan** *ESjL* 3

*with the right to equal portions of
inheritance* **OSw** *YVgL* Äb, *ÄVgL* Äb

See also: *arver*

jamnaþareþer (OSw) **javnetheeth** (ODan)
jafnaðareiðr (ON) noun

An oath establishing the equal status of both parties at a
settlement. It was an assurance given by the offending
party to the aggrieved party that, if the circumstances
of the case had been reversed, they would accept an
identical settlement. In Iceland these were banned
with the introduction of Js (Mah 37).

levelling oath **ODan** *ESjL* 3, *SkL* 113–115

oath of equality **OSw** *YVgL* Vs, *ÄVgL* Vs

oath of equity **OIce** *Js* Mah 37

See also: *duleiðr, eþer, trygth*

Refs: CV s.v. *eiðr;* Fritzner s.v. *jafnaðareiðr;* GAO
s.v. *Selbsurteil;* Hagland and Sandnes 1997, 108;
Hertzberg s.v. *jafnaðareiðr;* KLNM s.v. *böter,
drab;* Miller 1988; Tamm and Vogt 2016, 310

jamnskylder (OSw) **jafnskyldr** (ON) adj.

equally close in kin **OSw** *YVgL* Äb,
Gb, Add, *ÄVgL* Md, Äb

equally closely related **OSw** *HL* Äb

equally obliged **OIce** *Js* Mah 8

equally related **OIce** *Jó* Kge 7-4 Kab 2, *Js*
Ert 15 Kab 2, **ONorw** *FrL* Sab 9 ArbA 15,
GuL Løb, Mhb, Sab, **OSw** *SdmL* Jb

equally required **OIce** *Grg* Hrs 234, *KRA* 32

required in the same way **OIce** *Jó* Llb 62

of the same kinship **ONorw** *FrL* Mhb 31

See also: *jamkunder, skylder (2)*

jamskiala (OSw) **iamskila** (OSw) **iomskila** (OSw) adj.

equally justified **OSw** *SdmL* Kkb, Jb

equally strong in evidence **OSw** *VmL* Kkb

jarðabrigð (ON) **jarðarbrigði** (ON) noun

redemption of land **ONorw** *FrL* Jkb 6

jarðarhöfn (ON) noun

landholding **OIce** *Jó* Llb 13, 32

jarðarleiga (ON) **jarðleiga** (ON) noun

ground rent **ONorw** *GuL* Arb

land rent **OIce** *Jó* Kge 16, *Js* Ert 25

jarðarmegin (ON) noun

plot size **OIce** *Jó* Kge 33, *Js* Lbb 20

size of land **ONorw** *FrL* KrbA 23, *GuL* Llb

size of the share **OIce** *Jó* Llb 19

jarðarskeyting (ON) noun

conveyance of land **ONorw** *GuL* Olb

jarðarspell (ON) noun

damages to the land **OIce** *Jó* Llb 56 Þjb 14

jarðarvígsla (ON) noun

ground consecration **ONorw** *BorgL* 18.1

jarðarþjófr (ON) noun

land thief **ONorw** *GuL* Llb

jarðfé (ON) noun

buried property **OIce** *Grg* Feþ 171

jarl (OSw) **ierl** (OGu) **jarl** (ON) noun

A title of rank used at various points throughout the Nordic lands. It was a common Germanic title (cf. OE *eorl*) and probably corresponded to a continental *comes*, *dux* or *præfectus*. Older sources (e.g. sagas and poetry) suggest that a *jarl* was a type of sovereign chief, but in the Norwegian and Swedish provincial laws a *jarl* was subservient to the king. In the Norwegian laws a *jarl* was placed above a landed man or baron (ON *lendr maðr* (see *lænder*); cf. GuL ch. 200), and in several places he was entitled to compensation at the same level as a bishop (cf. GS ch. 2; FrL LlbA 15). In Sweden the title of *jarl* ceased being used around 1250, possibly replaced by the title of duke (OSw *hærtughi*). A Norwegian ordinance issued in 1308 forbade anyone other than the sons of the Norwegian king and the ruler of the Orkneys from holding the title of *jarl*. In Iceland the *jarl* was a short-lived title given to the official appointed by the Norwegian king to govern the entire island.

Earl **OIce** *Jó* Llb 18, **ONorw** *FrL* ArbA 16 LlbA 15, *GuL* Krb, Llb, Mhb, **OSw** *SdmL* Kgb, Mb, *ÖgL* Db

jarl **OGu** *GS* Ch. 2, **OIce** *Js* Mah 26, **ONorw** *FrL* KrbA 5 Mhb 51

See also: *hirð, hölðr, hærtughi, kununger, lænder, maþer*

Refs: Crawford 2013, 83–84; CV; Fritzner; GAO s.v. *Adel, jarl*; KLNM s.v. *hirðstjóri, jarl*; LexMA s.v. *jarl*; ONP

jarlsjörð (ON) noun

earl's farm **OIce** *Grg* Vís 112

jarlssonr (ON) noun

earl's son **ONorw** *GuL* Mhb

See also: *jarl*

jarn (OSw) **jarn** (ODan) noun

Mostly referring to ordeals (see *jarnbyrþ*), but occasionally to constraints: in OSw DL concerning the rights of an official, *lænsmaþer* (q.v.), to constrain certain criminals.

carrying iron **ODan** *SkL* 121

hot iron **ODan** *SkKL* 7

iron **ODan** *ESjL* 2, *SkKL* 5, 7, 9, *SkL* 86, 88, 89, 121, 137, 139, 145, 147, 154, 156, 157, 161, **OSw** *ÖgL* Eb

irons **OSw** *DL* Rb

jarnbyrþ (OSw) **járnburðr** (ON) noun

The bearing of a hot iron, a trial by iron, an ordeal. A trial of hot iron was prescribed for men in certain situations which called for an ordeal (*skírsl*, see *skærsl*). Ordeals for women usually involved boiling water (*ketiltak*), but in SkL a woman could be forced to undergo an ordeal by hot iron in cases of suspected adultery. The trial of hot iron may have been imported to Danish-ruled Estonia for a time during the thirteenth century (cf. Vogt 2013, 240–41).

iron-bearing **ONorw** *EidsL* 45.3, *FrL* ArbA 16

ordeal **ONorw** *FrL* KrbA 45 Mhb 5, 23, *GuL* Krb, Mhb, Leb

ordeal of hot iron **OSw** *ÖgL* Eb

test of the red iron **OSw** *HL* Äb

trial by iron **ONorw** *EidsL* 3.3

See also: *jarn, skær, skæra (1), skærsl, vitni*

Refs: KLNM s.v. *gudsdom*; LexMA s.v. *Ehebruch*; NGL V s.v. *járnburðr*; Nilsson 2001

jarnbyrþamal (OSw) noun

case of the test of the red iron **OSw** *HL* Äb

jarnhatter (OSw) noun

iron hat **OSw** *HL* Rb

jartighni (pl.) (OSw) **jartekn** (ODan) **jartegn** (ON) **jarteign** (ON) **iartigne** (OSw) **iartækn** (OSw) **iærtekn** (OSw) noun

characteristics **ODan** *JyL* 2

identifying features **OSw** *UL* Mb, *VmL* Mb

proof **ONorw** *FrL* ArbA 16, *GuL* Mhb, Tjb

sign **ODan** *VSjL* 19

token **ONorw** *FrL* Mhb 41

jather (ODan) noun

Literally 'border'. Used regarding heirs inside or outside the household.

farm **ODan** *VSjL* 68

farmstead **ODan** *VSjL* 65, 69

house **ODan** *SkL* 59, 63, 64

javneth (ODan) **jafnaðr** (ON) **jöfnuðr** (ON) noun

equal division **ODan** *VSjL* 2

equal share **ODan** *JyL* 3

equal share or proportions **ONorw** *GuL* Arb, Leb

equalisation **ODan** *VSjL* 17, 18

evened out **ODan** *ESjL* 2, 3

regulation **ODan** *ESjL* 2

jaxl (ON) noun

In a case of dishonourable killing, the injury to a cheek or beard that led to a loss of teeth, had to be compensated with an *eyrir* for each molar. See GuL ch. 238.

molar **ONorw** *GuL* Mhb

járnsaumr (ON) noun

iron nail **ONorw** *GuL* Leb

járnspöng (ON) noun

Three such clasps were part of the minimum requisites on a man's shield. See GuL ch. 309.

iron clasp **ONorw** *GuL* Leb

Refs: KLNM s.v. *sköld*

járnör (ON) noun

iron arrow **ONorw** *GuL* Leb

játa (ON) **játta** (ON) verb

agree **ONorw** *GuL* Olb

consent **OIce** *Grg* Þsþ 33, **ONorw** *GuL* Kvb, Løb

grant **ONorw** *GuL* Løb, Leb

promise **ONorw** *GuL* Krb, Leb

want **ONorw** *GuL* Krb

jáyrði (ON) noun

consent **OIce** *KRA* 16

jorthdrotten (ODan) noun

landowner **ODan** *SkL* 238–240

jorthebit (ODan) noun

bit of land **ODan** *VSjL* 87

non-living movables **ODan** *ESjL* 3

piece of land **ODan** *VSjL* 87

jorthefang (ODan) noun

acquired land **ODan** *ESjL* 3

jorthemal (ODan) noun

land-division **ODan** *ESjL* 1

jortheværn (ODan) noun

defence of land **ODan** *SkL* 83

right to defend land **ODan** *ESjL* 3

jorthhog (ODan) noun

beat someone to the ground **ODan** *VSjL* 46

throwing to the earth **ODan** *ESjL* 2

jorthskuv (ODan) noun

pushing to the ground **ODan** *SkL* 98

throwing to the ground **ODan** *JyL* 3

jorþ (OSw) **jorth** (ODan) **iorþ** (OGu) **jörð** (ON) **iord** (OSw) noun

This word has several but related meanings: 1) earth, 2) ground, soil, land used for a specific purpose, 3) immovables, property.

arable land **OSw** *HL* Jb

building site **ONorw** *GuL* Krb, Leb

earth **OIce** *Grg* Bat 114, *Jó* HT 1, **ONorw** *GuL* Krb, **OSw** *DL* Mb

estate **OIce** *Jó* MagBref Kge 4

field **OSw** *HL* Blb

ground **OGu** *GL* A 23, **OIce** *Grg* Feþ 170, *Js* Lbb 2, **ONorw** *EidsL* 38.1, *GuL* Krb, Løb, Llb, Leb, **OSw** *DL* Eb, *UL* Kkb, Kgb, Mb, *VmL* Kkb, Kgb, Mb

land **ODan** *ESjL* 1–3, *JyL* 1–3, *SkL* passim, *VSjL* passim, **OFar** *Seyð* 2, 8, **OGu** *GL* A 20, 25, 28, **OIce** *Jó* MagBref Kge 4, *Js* Mah 1 Kvg 3, **ONorw** *FrL* Mhb 22, **OSw** *DL* Eb, Bb, Rb, *HL* Kgb, Mb, Jb, Blb, Rb, *SdmL* Kkb, Gb, Äb, Jb, Bb, Mb, *UL* För, Kkb, Kgb, Äb, Mb, Jb, Blb, Rb, Add. 1, 5, 10, 11, *VmL* För, Kkb, Kgb, Äb, Mb, Jb, Bb, Rb, *YVgL* Kkb, Äb, Gb, Rlb, Jb, Kvab, Föb, Add, *ÄVgL* Urb, Äb, Gb, Jb, Kva, *ÖgL* Kkb, Eb

landed property **ONorw** *GuL* Llb, Arb, Mhb, Leb, Kvr, Olb, Tjb, Reb, Kpb, **OSw** *HL* Kkb, Äb

plough **OSw** *SmL*

property **OSw** *DL* Bb

real estate **OSw** *DL* Gb

soil **ONorw** *GuL* Llb, **OSw** *YVgL* Kkb

Expressions:

auð jörð (ON)

uncultivated land **ONorw** *GuL* Llb

dauf iorþ (OGu)

infertile land **OGu** *GL* A 25

heiðlaunað jörð (ON)

land given as mark of honour **ONorw** *GuL* Olb

See also: *bo, egn, fæ, goþs, inviþi, land, tompt*

Refs: CV *jörþ*; Hertzberg s.v. *jörþ*; Lund s.v. *iorþ*, Schlyter s.v. *jorþ*

jorþaaværkan (OSw) noun

unlawful usage of arable land **OSw** *HL* Kkb

jorþadela (OSw) **jorthedele** (ODan) noun

dispute over land **ODan** *VSjL* 82

dispute regarding arable land **OSw** *HL* Kkb

division of land **ODan** *ESjL* 1

land dispute **OSw** *HL* Jb, *SdmL* Kkb, Jb, *ÖgL* Kkb

jorþafastar (pl.) (OSw) noun

{fastar} at land purchase **OSw** *HL* Jb

jorþaklandan (OSw) noun

land challenge **OSw** *SdmL* Jb

jorþaköp (OSw) **jorthkøp** (ODan) noun

land for sale **ODan** *ESjL* 3

land purchase **OSw** *HL* Jb, *SdmL* Jb

jorþalagh (OSw) noun

laws of land **OSw** *SmL*

See also: *jorþ, lagh*

jorþalösn (OSw) noun

land ransom **OSw** *HL* Jb

jorþapanter (OSw) noun

    land pledge **OSw** *HL* Kmb

jorþaran (OSw) jorthran (ODan) noun

    Illegally taking something, such as animals, crops or wood, from someone else's land.

    land rapine **ODan** *JyL* 2, *VSjL* 66, **OSw** *ÖgL* Vm

jorþarbalker (OSw) iorþa balker (OSw) noun

    book concerning land **OSw** *HL*
    För, Jb, *YVgL* Jb, *ÄVgL* Jb

    land section **OSw** *SdmL* För, Jb

    See also: *balker*, *jorþ*

jorþaskifti (OSw) jorthskifte (ODan) jarðarskifti (ON) jarðaskifti (ON) jarðaskipti (ON) noun

    division of land **OIce** *Jó* Lbb 3, 5 Fml 25, **ONorw** *FrL* LlbB 4, *GuL* Llb

    exchange of land **ODan** *ESjL* 3, **OSw** *HL* Jb

    land exchange **OSw** *SdmL* Jb

jorþaværþ (OSw) jorthværth (ODan) jarðarverð (ON) noun

    land value **ONorw** *FrL* Jkb 2

    purchase sum **OSw** *YVgL* Jb

    worth of the land **ODan** *JyL* 1, **ONorw** *GuL* Olb

jorþavæþsætning (OSw) noun

    pawning of land **OSw** *HL* Jb

    See also: *væþ*

jorþeghandi (OSw) jortheghende (ODan) jarðeigandi (ON) iorþæghandi (OSw) noun

    landowner **OSw** *DL* Eb, *HL* Jb, *SdmL* Conf, Kkb, Jb, Till, *SmL*, *UL* Kkb, Jb, Blb, *VmL* Kkb, Jb, Bb, *YVgL* Kkb, Jb, Föb, Utgb, Add, *ÄVgL* Kkb, Jb, *ÖgL* Eb

    landowning **ODan** *VSjL* 87

    landowning man **ODan** *ESjL* 2

    the one who has the land **ODan** *SkL* 239

    owner of the land **OIce** *Jó* Llb 10, 24 Þjb 14

    See also: *bolfaster*, *bolstaþsmaþer*, *bonde*, *jorþ*, *karl*, *landeigandi*, *værnalaghi*, *æghandi*

jorþægha (OSw) noun

    landed property **OSw** *SdmL* Kkb

jóhannesmessa (ON) jóansmessa (ON) noun

    St Jón's Day (Ögmundarson) **OIce** *Grg* Klþ 13

jóladagr (ON) noun

    Christmas Day (and the days following) **OIce** *Grg* Klþ 11

jólagjafir (pl.) (ON) noun

    Christmas gifts **ONorw** *GuL* Reb

jólahelgr (ON) noun

    Christmas **ONorw** *GuL* Krb

jólanátt (ON) noun

    Christmas Eve **ONorw** *GuL* Krb, Kpb, Løb, Olb, Leb

    See also: *jul*, *julaapton*, *náttin helga*

jónsmessa (ON) jóansmessa (ON) noun

    Feast of St John the Baptist **OIce** *KRA* 32, 33, **ONorw** *FrL* LlbB 11, *GuL* Krb

    See also: *jónsvaka*

jónsvaka (ON) noun

    Feast of St John the Baptist **ONorw** *GuL* Krb

    See also: *jónsmessa*

jul (OSw) jul (ODan) jól (ON) noun

    Christmas **ODan** *ESjL* 2, *JyL* 2, **ONorw** *GuL* Krb, Olb, **OSw** *DL* Kkb, *HL* Kkb, Jb, *SdmL* Kkb, Rb, *SmL*, *YVgL* Kkb, Föb, *ÖgL* Kkb

    Yule **OSw** *HL* Rb

    Yule time **OSw** *HL* Blb

julaapton (OSw) julaaptan (OSw) noun

    Christmas Eve **OSw** *UL* Rb, *VmL* Rb

julafriþer (OSw) noun

    Beginning on Christmas Eve (in HL, nine days earlier) and ending twenty days after it. During this time, lawsuits were forbidden.

    Christmas peace **OSw** *SdmL* Rb, *UL* Rb, *VmL* Rb

    peace at Christmas **OSw** *ÖgL* Kkb

    peace of Christmas **OSw** *YVgL* Kkb

    Yule sanctity **OSw** *HL* Rb

    See also: *friþer*, *jul*

    Refs: KLNM s.v. *jul*

julehælgh (ODan) noun

    Christmas peace **ODan** *SkKL* 9

junkhærre (ODan) noun

    lord **ODan** *JyL* Fort

    See also: *hærra*

jæmnaþahænder (OSw) javnethehand (ODan) noun

    Impartial holding of a disputed object until a matter is resolved.

    impartial hands **ODan** *JyL* 2, *VSjL* 19, **OSw** *DL* Gb, *UL* Äb, Mb, *VmL* Äb, Mb

    Refs: Gammeldansk ordbog s.v. *javnethehand*; Schlyter s.v. *jæmnaþa hænder*

jæmpnaþaarf (OSw) iæmpnaþa arf (OSw) jamnarf (OSw) noun

    equable inheritance **OSw** *HL* Äb

jæva (OSw) æve (ODan) iefa (OGu) iava (OSw) verb

    To challenge the validity of a legal claim, particularly relating to children and inheritance: if a child was born alive and the mother had the right to inherit (OSw HL), if a child had been baptized (OSw UL, VmL) and if a deceased man was the father of his widow's child (ODan ESjL).

dispute **ODan** *ESjL* 3

doubt **ODan** *ESjL* 1, 2, **OSw** *HL* Äb, *UL* Kkb, *VmL* Kkb

have a suspicion about **OGu** *GL* A 37

kafli (OSw) **kaffli** (OSw) noun

portion **OSw** *UL* Mb

rolling pin **OSw** *HL* Mb

See also: *buþkafli*

kaldakol (ON) noun

Literally 'cold coals'; an extinguished hearth fire. Used to refer to an abandoned farm, especially one which was inhabited by a tenant who left it before his lease had expired at the moving days (cf. Jó Llb 7).

desertion of a farm **OIce** *Jó* Llb 7

leaving too early **ONorw** *FrL* LlbA 2

letting the hearth fire go out **OIce** *Jó* Llb 7

See also: *eyðijörð*, *fardagher*, *landboe*, *öþebol*

Refs: CV; Fritzner; Hertzberg; Páll Vídalín 1854 s.v. *kaldakol*

kalfr (ON) noun

calf **ONorw** *GuL* Kpb, Løb

kalgarth (ODan) noun

cabbage garden **ODan** *JyL* 3

vegetable garden **ODan** *JyL* 3

kalla (OSw) **kalle** (ODan) **kalla** (ON) verb

Literally 'to call'. Often used in reference to public announcements, such as convening assemblies, identifying offenders, and publicly declaring criminal activity or legal responsibility (cf. *heta*). Within legal proceedings, *kalla* often takes on more specific meanings, such as 'to complain' and 'to sue'. Occasionally suggesting entitlement, reflected in translations such as 'to claim'. There is considerable overlap between usages and translations.

announce **OSw** *HL* Äb

assert **ONorw** *GuL* Arb

call **ODan** *ESjL* 1–3, *JyL* 1, *SkL* 131, 158, 159, *VSjL* 8–10, 66, 87, **ONorw** *GuL* Arb, Tfb, Leb, **OSw** *HL* Äb, Mb, *SdmL* Kkb, Kgb, Bb, Mb, Rb, *YVgL* Rlb, *ÖgL* Kkb

call by a nickname **ONorw** *GuL* Mhb

call upon **ODan** *ESjL* 2, **OSw** *ÄVgL* Tb

claim **ODan** *ESjL* 1–3, *JyL* 1, 2, *SkL* passim, *VSjL* 1, 12, 16, 18, 20, **ONorw** *GuL* Løb, Arb, **OSw** *YVgL* Drb, Rlb, Jb, Föb, *ÄVgL* Äb, Jb, Kva

complain **ODan** *VSjL* 5

deem **ONorw** *GuL* Leb

demand **ODan** *SkL* 8, 9, 235

make a claim **ODan** *ESjL* 1–3, *SkL* 13

name **OSw** *YVgL* Frb, Äb, Rlb, Tb, Add, *ÄVgL* Vs, Slb, Äb, Rlb, Tb

proclaim **ODan** *VSjL* 68

raise a claim **ODan** *ESjL* 1–3, *JyL* 1, 2, *SkL* 51, 56, *VSjL* 1, 17

raise a complaint **ODan** *VSjL* 5

raise a demand **ODan** *ESjL* 3, *JyL* 2, *VSjL* 71, 77, 78, 82, 83

sue **ODan** *JyL* 2

summon **ODan** *ESjL* 1–3, *JyL* 2, *SkL* 18, 19, 71, 140, *VSjL* 87, **ONorw** *GuL* Leb, **OSw** *DL* Bb, Rb, *HL* Rb, *YVgL* Tb, Föb, Utgb, *ÄVgL* Kkb, Rlb, Tb, *ÖgL* Kkb

take action **ODan** *JyL* 2

See also: *heta*

kambstaðr (ON) noun

scar on the head **ONorw** *GuL* Mhb

kampr (ON) noun

beard **ONorw** *GuL* Mhb

kanceler (ON) noun

Chancellor; a high-ranking official in the king's court. Known in Norway from at least the beginning of the thirteenth century until the death of the last named chancellor in 1679. Duties of the *kanceler* are outlined in *Hirðskrá*, but they changed over time. Among these were the responsibilities of *seglbevarer* ('keeper of the [royal] seal'), overseer of royal dispatches (including letters for *landsvist* 'the right to reside in a realm or province' and keeping copies of outgoing missives), management of royal incomes and registration of royal estates. For a time the *kanceler* was also head of the royal chapel clerics, though the position gradually lost its ecclesiastical duties after the Reformation. While most members of the chancery were stationary, the *kanceler*, as bearer of the royal seal, accompanied the king's ambulatory court. After 1380, when Norway was ruled by foreign monarchs, the chancellor's duties diminished and consisted mostly of issuing letters of peace (*gridsbrev*) and pardons (*landsvistsbrev*). From 1314 the Norwegian chancery operated primarily from Mariakirken in Oslo.

In Denmark the figure of chancellor first appears around the end of the twelfth century; in Sweden not until the end of the thirteenth century.

chancellor **OFar** *Seyð* 0

See also: *landsvist*

Refs: Kongsrud 2011; MSE s.v. *chancery*; ONP s.v. *kanceler*

kapellan (OSw) kapellan (ODan) noun
  chaplain **ODan** *SkKL* 1, **OSw** *SmL*
kardinali (ON) kardinal (ON) noun
  cardinal **OIce** *KRA* 27, 28, **ONorw** *FrL* KrbB 17
karina (OSw) noun
  penance by fasting **OSw** *DL* Rb
  See also: *fasta*
karl (OSw) karl (ODan) karl (OGu) karl (ON) kall
  (OSw) noun
  The normal meaning of this word is '(old) man', or as
  an alternative to *bonde* (q.v.), meaning man in general,
  householder, husband, or as 'common man', as
  opposed to the king, but in GL it is used in two specific
  instances, firstly to mean 'grandfather' in particular
  and secondly to mean 'the head of the family' in
  general. If a man's son dies leaving daughters, they
  were to be adopted by their grandfather in a more or
  less formal manner. In UL and VmL, it is used as a title,
  signifying the 'representative of the *hundari*' and this
  title has been retained in the respective translations.
  It has not been excerpted in the OIce laws, being in
  general rather than particular usage.
  grandfather **OGu** *GL* A 20
  head of the family **OGu** *GL* A 20
  householder **ONorw** *FrL* Intr 19, **OSw**
  DL Tjdb, *UL* Blb, *VmL* Jb, Bb
  husband **ONorw** *FrL* Intr 24
  man **ODan** *SkL* 34, 36, **OGu** *GL* A 20, **ONorw**
  GuL Løb, Arb, Mhb, Olb, **OSw** *DL* Bb, *HL*
  Kkb, Äb, *SdmL* Kgb, Gb, *SmL*, *UL* Kkb,
  Äb, *VmL* Kkb, Äb, Jb, *YVgL* Drb, Tb
  representative of the hundari **OSw** *UL*
  Äb, Mb, Blb, Rb, *VmL* Bb, Mb, Rb
  See also: *bolfaster, bolstaþsmaþer,*
  bonde, jorþeghandi, kærling, maþer,
  skötsætubarn, værnalaghi
  Refs: Peel 2015, 132 note 20/16; Schlyter 1877,
  s.v. *karl*; SL GL, 266 note 5 to chapter 20
karlaskr (ON) noun
  man's measure **OIce** *Jó* Kab 26
karldyrr (ON) noun
  main doorway **OIce** *Grg* Klþ 2, 4, *KRA* 15
  principal door **ONorw** *GuL* Olb
karlerfðir (pl.) (ON) noun
  inheritance on the male side **ONorw** *GuL* Arb
karlgilder (OSw) kalgilder (OSw) kralgilder (OSw)
  adj.
  of silver **OSw** *UL* Äb, Mb, Blb
  See also: *köpgilder*

karlklæði (ON) noun
  men's clothes **ONorw** *GuL* Mhb, Tjb
karlsvift (ON) karlsift (ON) noun
  kinship traced through men **OIce** *Grg* Bat 113
  male side **ONorw** *GuL* Mhb, Sab
  See also: *bauggildismaðr, höfuðbarmr*
karlsviftarmaðr (ON) noun
  kinsman on the male side **ONorw** *GuL* Mhb
karnaðr (ON) noun
  bedfellow **OIce** *Grg* Vís 112
kasnavargher (OSw) kasnavargr (OGu)
  kaxnavargher (OSw) noun
  Literally presumably 'kindling-evildoer', referring
  to an arsonist. In ÖgL it appears among the *kunungx*
  eþzsöre (see *eþsöre*), crimes against the King's Peace,
  and is defined as an arsonist with the intent to kill, who
  could be punished by being himself burned alive and
  losing all property. The same punishment applied in
  UL and VmL, if the arson resulted in a killing, which,
  however, did not define a *kasnavargher*. DL and
  YVgL did not require deadly outcome, but the arsonist
  was still severely punished, in DL forty marker and
  in YVgL forfeiture of land (meaning perhaps the
  right to live in the province or realm, or on his landed
  property) and movables. In GL used exclusively as a
  punishable insult.
  fire-wolf **OSw** *ÖgL* Eb
  homicidal arsonist **OSw** *DL* Bb, *UL*
  Blb, *VmL* Bb (rubric only)
  murdering arsonist **OGu** *GL* A 39
  tinder-wolf **OSw** *YVgL* Rlb
  See also: *brennuvargr, bruni, brænna, elder,*
  eþsöre, gorvargher, morðvargr, vargher
  Refs: Elmevik 1967, 9ff; KLNM, s.v. *mordbrand*;
  Lexikon des Mittelalters, s.v. *brandstiftung*; Peel
  2015, 175 note 39/3; Schlyter 1877, s.v. *kasna*
  vargher; SL GL, 285 note 1 to chapter 39; SL
  ÖgL, 51 note 50; Wennström 1936, 270–74, 301
kast (ON) noun
  throw **ONorw** *GuL* Mhb
katrinamæssa (OSw) noun
  Saint Katrin's Mass **OSw** *DL* Bb
kaupabölkr (ON) kaupabálkr (ON) noun
  book on trade **ONorw** *GuL* Kpb
  chapter on trade **OIce** *Jó* MagBref Kab 1 Fml 25
kaupamark (ON) noun
  bought mark **OIce** *Grg* Fjl 225, *Jó* Llb 48
  See also: *erfðamark*

kaupandi (ON) noun
> buyer **OIce** *Grg* Lbþ 174, 175

kaupangrslög (ON) noun
> town law **ONorw** *GuL* Arb

See also: *kaupangrsréttr*

kaupangrsréttr (ON) noun
> town law **ONorw** *GuL* Arb

See also: *kaupangrslög*

kaupfox (ON) noun
> fraud **OIce** *Jó* Kab 14, *Js* Kab 10, **ONorw** *GuL* Kpb
> worthless trade **OIce** *Jó* Kab 14

See also: *far, flærþ, fox*

kaupför (ON) noun
> trading journey **ONorw** *GuL* Mhb

See also: *köpfærþ*

kauplauss (ON) kaupalauss (ON) adj.
> free **ONorw** *FrL* KrbA 17
> without payment **ONorw** *EidsL* 47.2

kauplaust (ON) adj.
> without payment **ONorw** *GuL* Krb

kauplendingr (ON) noun
> one who lives on purchased land **ONorw** *FrL* LlbA 25

kauplöstr (ON) noun
> flaw in a bargain **ONorw** *GuL* Mhb

kaupmannaskylda (ON) noun
> merchants' duties **OIce** *Jó* Fml 4

kaupmáli (ON) noun
> contract **OIce** *Grg* Arþ 127, *Jó* Fml 1

See also: *kaupskil*

kaupreina (ON) kauprein (ON) noun
> location where a deal was concluded **OIce** *Js* Kab 7
> place where a bargain or contract was made **ONorw** *GuL* Kpb, Llb
> place where a contract was made **OIce** *Jó* Kab 9
> place where business is transacted **OIce** *Jó* Kab 9

kaupskil (ON) noun
> dealing **OIce** *Jó* MagBref

See also: *kaupmáli*

kaupskip (OGu) kaupskip (ON) noun
> merchant ship **OGu** *GL* A 36, **ONorw** *GuL* Llb, Arb, Tfb, Leb

See also: *bater, byrthing, farkoster, floti, myndrikkia, skip, snækkia*

kaupstefna (ON) noun
> market **OIce** *Jó* Kab 24 Fml 6, *Js* Kab 18, **ONorw** *FrL* Leb 27

See also: *stæmna*

kaupsvætti (ON) noun
> purchase witness testimony **OIce** *Grg* Lbþ 176

kaupváttr (ON) kaupsváttr (ON) noun
> purchase witness **OIce** *Grg* Lbþ 172, **ONorw** *FrL* Rgb 28

keisari (ON) noun
> emperor **OIce** *KRA* 9

kelda (ON) noun
> marshland **OIce** *Grg* Lbþ 182, *Jó* Llb 42

kelfa (ON) verb
> calve **ONorw** *GuL* Kpb

kennandi (ON) noun
> identifier **OIce** *Grg* Fjl 225, *Jó* Llb 47

kenndr (ON) adj.
> charged **OIce** *Jó* Kge 5 Þjb 1
> identified **OIce** *Jó* Mah 2 Kab 7 Þjb 1
> recognized **OIce** *Jó* Þfb 5

kennimaðr (ON) noun
> cleric **OIce** *KRA* 7, 11, **ONorw** *BorgL* 1.1 7.7, *EidsL* 31.4
> priest **OIce** *Grg* Klþ 16, **ONorw** *FrL* KrbA 11 LlbB 3, *GuL* Krb

See also: *prester*

kennsl (ON) kensl (ON) noun
> accusation **ONorw** *FrL* Bvb 9, *GuL* Tjb
> evidence **ONorw** *FrL* Var 9

kennslumál (ON) kennslamál (ON) noun

A case involving evidence. The term is used in Js Mah 37 and MLL (NGL II:70), both of which specify that only oaths from witnesses will be acceptable, such as those in a *kennslamál* or an oath of denial (ON *duleiðr*), rather than oaths of equity (ON *jafnaðareiðr*, see *jamnaþareþer*) given by compurgators. In *Kjalnesinga saga* it is stated that oaths were to be sworn on a silver ring for all *kennslamál*.

> evidence case **OIce** *Js* Mah 37

See also: *duleiðr, jamnaþareþer, kænna, mal (1), væna, vænslamal*

Refs: CV s.v. *kennslamál*; Fritzner s.v. *kenslamál*; Hertzberg s.v. *kenslamál*

kerldi (OGu) noun
> male **OGu** *GL* A 14, 20, Add. 1 (B 4)
> man **OGu** *GL* A 20, 28

kerra (OGu) noun
> cart **OGu** *GL* A 26

See also: *vagn*

kinn (ON) noun
> cheek **ONorw** *GuL* Mhb

kirkia (OSw) **kirkje** (ODan) **kirkja** (ON) **kyrkia** (OSw) noun

church **ODan** *ESjL* 1–3, *JyL* 1–3, *SkKL* 1–3, 5, 8, 11, *SkL* 3, 97, 148, *VSjL* 5, **ONorw** *GuL* Krb, Løb, Tfb, Leb, **OSw** *DL* Kkb, Eb, Mb, Bb, Gb, *HL* Kkb, Kgb, Mb, Jb, Blb, Rb, *SdmL* Kkb, Kgb, Äb, Jb, Bb, Mb, Tjdb, Till, *SmL*, *YVgL* Kkb, Frb, Urb, Drb, Rlb, Tb, Jb, Add, *ÄVgL* Kkb, Slb, Urb, Rlb, Jb, Tb, *ÖgL* Kkb, Eb, Db

Expressions:

af kirkiu sætia (OSw)

sentence to lesser excommunication **OSw** *HL* Kkb

kirkiuna rætter (OSw)

right of the church **OSw** *YVgL* Kkb

kirkiubalker (OSw) noun

book concerning Church or Christian law **OSw** *HL* För, Kkb

church section **OSw** *SdmL* För, Kkb

See also: *balker*, *kirkia*

kirkiubol (OSw) **kirkjuból** (ON) **kyrkiu bol** (OSw) noun

church farm **OSw** *YVgL* Kkb, *ÄVgL* Kkb, *ÖgL* Kkb

church-farm **OIce** *Grg* Tíg 266

farm **OSw** *HL* Kkb

glebe **OSw** *SmL*

glebe land **OSw** *UL* Kgb, Kkb, *VmL* Kkb

vicarage **OSw** *HL* Kkb, Rb, *SdmL* Kkb

See also: *bol*, *kirkia*, *kirkiubyr*, *kirkiugarþer*, *prestgarþer*, *præstastuva*

kirkiubolsgarþer (OSw) noun

vicarage building **OSw** *SdmL* Kkb

kirkiubro (OSw) noun

church bridge **OSw** *SdmL* Bb

kirkiubrytare (OSw) **kirkjebrytere** (ODan) noun

church thief **OSw** *SmL*

man who has broken into the church **ODan** *SkL* 151

kirkiubyr (OSw) **kirkjubær** (ON) **kirkjubór** (ON) noun

church village **OSw** *YVgL* Kkb, *ÄVgL* Kkb

church-farm **OIce** *Grg* Klþ 1 Tíg 258, *KRA* 15

See also: *byr*, *kirkia*

kirkiudroten (OSw) noun

church warden **OSw** *SmL*, *YVgL* Kkb, *ÄVgL* Kkb

See also: *kirkia*

kirkiudyr (OSw) **kirkjudyrr** (ON) noun

The location for certain legally binding actions, such as emergency baptism (OSw SmL), and suing in specified legal cases (OSw ÖgL Kkb).

church door **ONorw** *GuL* Krb, Tfb, **OSw** *HL* Kkb, *SmL*, *YVgL* Kkb, *ÄVgL* Kkb, *ÖgL* Kkb

doorway to the church **OSw** *HL* Kkb

See also: *kirkia*

kirkiufriþer (OSw) **kirkjufriðr** (ON) noun

The church peace covered the church itself as well as the churchgoers; in OSw including their journey to and from church. Asylum in church is explicitly mentioned in OIce KRA and OSw HL and SdmL (as well as in OGu GL, albeit without this word). Some OSw laws relate the church peace to the king and *eþsöre* (q.v.) (DL, HL, SdmL) or considers breaching it an unatonable crime (YVgL).

church peace **OSw** *DL* Eb, *SdmL* Kkb, Kgb, Mb, Tjdb, Till, *UL* Kgb, *VmL* Kgb

church sanctity **OSw** *HL* Kkb, Kgb, *UL* Kkb, Mb

peace of the church **OIce** *KRA* 8, **ONorw** *FrL* KrbA 10, **OSw** *YVgL* Add

See also: *friþer*, *kirkia*, *kirkjugrið*

Refs: KLNM s.v. *fridslagstiftning*; s.v. Schlyter s.v. *kirkiufriþer*

kirkiufæ (OSw) **kirkjufé** (ON) noun

church property **OIce** *KRA* 7

goods of the church **OSw** *ÖgL* Kkb

property of the church **OSw** *ÖgL* Kkb

kirkiuganga (OSw) **kirkiuganger** (OSw) noun

churching **OSw** *ÖgL* Kkb

kirkiugarþer (OSw) **kirkjegarth** (ODan) **kirkiugarþr** (OGu) **kirkjugarðr** (ON) **kyrkiugarþer** (OSw) noun

Commiting a crime in the churchyard was an aggravating factor. Certain criminals were prohibited from being buried in the churchyard.

church enclosure **ONorw** *EidsL* 50.5

church fence **ONorw** *GuL* Krb

churchyard **ODan** *ESjL* 2, *JyL* 2, 3, *SkKL* 3, 5, 8, *SkL* 215, 216, *VSjL* 51, 53, **OGu** *GL* A 8, 13, **OIce** *Grg* Klþ 1, *KRA* 5, 8, **ONorw** *BorgL* 1.3 9.2 passim, *EidsL* 2.2 6 passim, *FrL* KrbA 10 KrbB 2, *GuL* Krb, Løb, **OSw** *DL* Kkb, Eb, *HL* Kkb, Äb, Mb, *SdmL* Kkb, Gb, Mb, Tjdb, *SmL*, *UL* Kkb, Mb, *VmL* Kkb, Mb, *YVgL* Kkb, *ÄVgL* Kkb, *ÖgL* Kkb, Eb

churchyard fence **ONorw** *FrL* KrbA 7, **OSw** *SdmL* Kkb, *YVgL* Kkb, *ÄVgL* Kkb, Jb

fence around the churchyard **OSw** *HL* Kkb

fence of a churchyard **OSw** *YVgL* Jb

See also: *garþer*, *kirkia*

Refs: Riisøy 2015

kirkiugif (OSw) noun

funeral fee **OSw** *SdmL* Conf

kirkiugoþs (OSw) **kirknagóz** (ON) noun
　　church goods **OIce** *KRA* 34
　　church property **OSw** *YVgL* Kkb
kirkiugærþ (OSw) **kirkiugerþ** (OGu) **kirkjugerð**
　　(ON) **kirkiogærdh** (OSw) noun
　　building of churches **ONorw** *GuL* Krb, **OSw** *SmL*
　　church-building **OGu** *GL* A 3
kirkiugömari (OSw) noun
　　church warden **OSw** *ÖgL* Kkb
kirkiuiorþ (OSw) **kirkjejorth** (ODan) **kirkjujörð**
　　(ON) noun
　　church ground **ONorw** *EidsL* 39.7
　　church land **ODan** *JyL* 3, **ONorw** *FrL* LlbB 3
　　land of the church **OSw** *YVgL* Kkb
kirkiuklæþi (OSw) noun
　　church clothes **OSw** *SdmL* Kkb
　　churchgoing clothes **OSw** *UL* Äb, *VmL* Äb
　　See also: *gangklepi*
kirkiuleþer (OSw) adj.
　　brought to church **OSw** *DL* Rb
　　See also: *inlepning*
kirkiumæn (pl.) (OGu) noun
　　parishioners **OGu** *GL* A 2–4, 6, 8, 20, 26, 59
　　See also: *soknamaper*
kirkiunykil (OSw) noun
　　key of the church **OSw** *YVgL* Kkb, *ÖgL* Kkb
kirkiupræster (OSw) **kirkjuprestr** (ON) noun
　　The owner of a church could finance the education
　　of a priest who became a *skuldarmaðr* (q.v.) and was
　　obliged to serve at that church for life.
　　church-priest **OIce** *KRA* 11, **OSw** *HL* Mb
　　Refs: Mundal 2016
kirkiupænningar (pl.) (OSw) noun
　　money of the church **OSw** *YVgL* Kkb
kirkiuran (OSw) **kirkjeran** (ODan) noun
　　church rapine **ODan** *SkKL* 3, 5, 7, 8, **OSw** *ÖgL* Kkb
　　rapine from churches **ODan** *SkKL* 3
kirkiurum (OGu) noun
　　place in church **OGu** *GL* A 63
kirkiurætter (OSw) noun
　　canon law **OSw** *UL* StfBM, För
　　church regulation **OSw** *SdmL* Conf
kirkiuskuld (OSw) noun
　　debt of the church **OSw** *YVgL* Kkb

kirkiusokn (OSw) **kirkjesokn** (ODan) **kirkiusokn**
　　(OGu) **kirkjusókn** (ON) noun
　　church attendance **OIce** *Grg* Tíg 257
　　church congregation **OSw** *HL* Mb
　　church gathering **OIce** *Grg* Feþ 164 Fjl 225
　　church parish **ODan** *JyL* 1–3, *SkKL* 3, 5, 7, 11, 12,
　　VSjL 73, **OSw** *SdmL* Kkb, Jb, *YVgL* Add, *ÖgL* Eb
　　church-goers **OSw** *HL* Jb
　　gathering at church **ONorw** *GuL* Løb
　　parish **ODan** *ESjL* 3, *SkL* 70, **OGu** *GL* A 3,
　　6, 13, **OIce** *KRA* 11, **ONorw** *FrL* KrbA 22
　　LlbB 3, **OSw** *HL* Äb, Mb, Jb, *UL* Mb, Jb
　　See also: *kirkia*, *sokn*
kirkiuvægher (OSw) **kirkjevægh** (ODan) noun
　　church road **ODan** *ESjL* 3, *VSjL* 73, **OSw** *DL*
　　Bb, *HL* Kkb, Kgb, Blb, *SdmL* Kgb, *YVgL* Föb
　　road to the church **ODan** *SkL* 70, *VSjL*
　　73, **OSw** *DL* Eb, *YVgL* Add
　　way to church **OSw** *DL* Eb, *ÖgL* Eb
　　See also: *kirkia*, *kirkiufriper*, *vægher*
kirkiuværiandi (OSw) **kirkjeværjende** (ODan) noun
　　church warden **ODan** *JyL* 1, **OSw** *HL* Kkb, *SdmL*
　　Kkb, Till, *UL* Kkb, Kgb, *VmL* Kkb, *YVgL* Kkb
kirkiuþiuver (OSw) noun
　　church theft **OSw** *HL* Mb
　　church thief **OSw** *SdmL* Tjdb
kirkjeaker (ODan) noun
　　field of a church **ODan** *SkKL* 3
kirkjelyse (ODan) verb
　　make public at church **ODan** *ESjL* 3
　　See also: *kirkia*, *lysa*
kirkjeman (ODan) noun
　　churchman **ODan** *ESjL* 2
　　man of a parish **ODan** *JyL* 1, 2
　　parish man **ODan** *SkKL* 3, 11
kirkjeskogh (ODan) noun
　　church's wood **ODan** *SkKL* 4
kirkjestuv (ODan) noun
　　land given to the church **ODan** *JyL* 1
　　See also: *kirkia*, *stumn*
kirkjestævne (ODan) noun
　　church assembly **ODan** *ESjL* 2
　　church meeting **ODan** *SkL* 148
kirkjudagr (ON) noun
　　church consecration day **OIce** *KRA* 4, 24

kirkjueign (ON) noun

    church property **OIce** *Jó* Llb 58

kirkjufrelsi (ON) noun

    church privilege **OIce** *KRA* 34

kirkjufriðbrot (ON) noun

    not respecting the peace of the
    church **ONorw** *FrL* KrbB 2

kirkjugarðsniðrfall (ON) noun

    disrepair of a church enclosure **ONorw** *BorgL* 9

kirkjugrið (ON) noun

    peace of the church **ONorw** *FrL* KrbA 10

    See also: *kirkiufriþer*

kirkjugrófr (ON) **kirkjugræfr** (ON) adj.

    having the right to a church burial **OIce** *Js*
    Kdb 4, *KRA* 1, **ONorw** *FrL* KrbA 10

    who can be buried at a church **ONorw** *GuL* Krb

    See also: *kirkjulægr*

kirkjulægr (ON) adj.

    having the right to a church burial **OIce** *Grg* Vís 90

    See also: *kirkjugrófr*

kirkjumáldagi (ON) noun

An agreement or contract for a certain church containing a register of its properties, rights and obligations. When property was endowed to a church, these agreements were drawn up by the heirs of the property owner and the bishop. An announcement of the terms had to be made at the General Assembly or the spring assembly.

    agreements on church endowment **OIce** *Grg* Tíg 268

    See also: *máldagi*

    Refs: Cederschiöld 1887; CV; Fritzner

kirkjusóknarmaðr (ON) **kirkjusóknarmenn** (pl.)
(ON) noun

    member of a church **OIce** *KRA* 6

    parishioner **ONorw** *GuL* Krb

    person of the parish **ONorw** *FrL* KrbA 10

kirkjusóknarþing (ON) noun

A *þing* 'assembly' of the parish, possibly, at least in part, corresponding to *soknaþing* (q.v.) in OSw HL.

    parish assembly **OIce** *Jó* Llb 34

    See also: *þing*

kirkjutíund (ON) **kirknatíund** (ON) noun

The church-tithe. Signifies the one quarter of the annual tithes in Iceland which went to churches. Of the remaining three quarters, one quarter each was apportioned to the poor, the bishop and priests.

    tithe for churches **OIce** *Grg* Tíg 258, *KRA* 15

    See also: *tiund*

    Refs: CV; Fritzner; Hertzberg

kirkjuvígsla (ON) noun

    consecration of a church **OIce** *KRA* 5, 8,
    ONorw *EidsL* 34.3, *FrL* KrbA 10, *GuL* Krb

kirkmæssa (OSw) **kirkiumæssa** (OSw) noun

    Church Dedication Mass **OSw** *UL* Kkb, *VmL* Kkb

    Church Dedication Mass Day **OSw**
    DL Kkb, *SdmL* Kkb, Till

    Church Mass Day **OSw** *SmL*, *YVgL* Kkb

    day of church mass **OSw** *YVgL* Kkb

kirkmæssudagher (OSw) **kirkiumæssudagher** (OSw)
noun

    Church Dedication Mass Day **OSw** *VmL* Kkb

kirkmæssufriþer (OSw) noun

Peace within a parish on the commemoration of the inauguration of its church. Breaching this peace was punished with fines to the bishop.

    peace of church mass **OSw** *YVgL* Kkb

    {kirkmæssufriþer} **OSw** *ÖgL* Kkb

    See also: *friþer*, *kirkmæssa*

    Refs: Schlyter s.v. *kirkmæssu friþer*

kirkmæssuhælgþ (OSw) noun

    festival **OSw** *ÖgL* Kkb

kiste (ODan) **kista** (ON) noun

    chest **ODan** *ESjL* 3, *JyL* 2, 3, *VSjL*
    87, **ONorw** *GuL* Løb

    coffin **ONorw** *GuL* Krb

kiurtil (OSw) **kurtil** (OGu) **kiortel** (OSw) noun

    kirtle **OGu** *GL* A 19, **OSw** *UL* Äb, *VmL* Äb

    See also: *gangklæþi*, *ivirklæþi*, *likvari*, *serkr*, *stæniza*

kjölr (ON) noun

    keel **ONorw** *GuL* Leb

kjöt (ON) noun

    flesh **ONorw** *GuL* Krb

klafi (ON) noun

    halter **ONorw** *GuL* Krb, Kpb

klanda (OSw) **klanda** (OGu) verb

Literally 'to complain', and hence to state one's complaint to an opponent or to court, particularly concerning disputed land and other property. Expresses a complaint that could be dealt with at the *þing* 'assembly', possibly as a formal start of legal proceedings. The participle, *oklandaþer* (q.v.), appears in several adjective phrases, often concerning land that has not been subject to a legal challenge and therefore can be lawfully used.

    allege **OSw** *YVgL* Föb

    blame **OGu** *GL* A 6

challenge **OSw** *DL* Bb, *SdmL* Jb, Bb,
Kmb, Tjdb, *UL* Kkb, Äb, Mb, Jb, Kmb,
Blb, *VmL* Kkb, Äb, Mb, Jb, Kmb, Bb

claim **OSw** *YVgL* Föb, Utgb, *ÄVgL* Föb

complain **OSw** *HL* Mb, *ÄVgL* Fös

conduct a prosecution **OSw** *DL* Bb

dispute **OSw** *DL* Bb, *UL* Mb

make a demand **OSw** *DL* Bb

raise a challenge **OSw** *DL* Bb, Tjdb

See also: *uilter*

klandalöst (OSw) adv.

Expressions:

klasalöst ok klanda (OSw)

undisputedly **OSw** *DL* Bb

klandan (OSw) **kland** (ON) **kland** (OSw) noun

challenge **OSw** *SdmL* Tjdb, *UL* Mb (table
of contents only), *VmL* Mb (rubric only)

objection **ONorw** *FrL* KrbB 1

reprobation **OSw** *HL* Mb

klappa (OGu) verb

cut off **OGu** *GL* A 25

klámhögg (ON) noun

Literally 'a foul strike'; a blow shameful to the person
struck. A *klámhögg* is a strike from behind across the
buttocks and was probably considered a kind of sexual
attack intended to shame the victim. It is described in
saga literature in *Hrólfs saga kraka* and *Hrólfs saga
Gautrekssonar*. In Grg Víg 86 it is classified as a major
wound, and the victim had the right to vengeance up
until the General Assembly, after which the attacker
could be prosecuted and outlawed.

shame-stroke **OIce** *Grg* Vís 86

See also: *níð*

Refs: CV; F; KLNM s.v. *ærenkrænkelse*;
Jochens 2001; Miller 1990, 63; Z

klementsmessa (ON) **clemensmessa** (ON) noun

Feast of St Clement (23 November) **ONorw** *GuL* Krb

St Clement's Day **OIce** *Grg* Klþ 13

klerker (OSw) **klærk** (ODan) **klerkr** (ON) **klærker**
(OSw) noun

clergyman **OSw** *HL* Kkb, Mb

cleric **ODan** *JyL* 2, **OIce** *KRA* 7, 34, **ONorw**
GuL Leb, **OSw** *SdmL* Conf, Kkb, Äb, Mb,
Till, *YVgL* Kkb, *ÄVgL* Kkb, *ÖgL* Kkb

kliaufa (OGu) verb

cut **OGu** *GL* A 25

klippa (OGu) verb

shear **OGu** *GL* A 43, 44

See also: *fastr*

klokkaragiald (OSw) noun

sexton's remuneration **OSw** *ÖgL* Kkb

klokkari (OSw) **klukkari** (OSw) noun

bell ringer **OSw** *HL* Kkb

church clerk **OSw** *HL* Kkb

parish clerk **OSw** *HL* Kkb, *YVgL* Kkb, *ÄVgL* Kkb

sexton **OSw** *DL* Kkb, *SdmL* Kkb, *SmL* Kkb,
UL Kkb, Mb, *VmL* Kkb, *ÖgL* Kkb

kloknaoþensdagher (OSw) noun

Bell Wednesday **OSw** *YVgL* Kkb

kloster (OSw) **kloster** (ODan) **klaustr** (ON) noun

abbey **ODan** *ESjL* 1, *JyL* 1–3, *SkL* 38, 39

monastery **ODan** *VSjL* 4, 5, 13, **OIce** *KRA*
10, **OSw** *DL* Gb, *SdmL* Kkb, Mb, Till, *SmL*,
YVgL Äb, Add, *ÄVgL* Äb, *ÖgL* Kkb

nunnery **OSw** *SmL*

nunnery and monastery **OSw** *HL* Mb

See also: *munk*, *nunna*

klosterlöpare (OSw) noun

monastery escaper **OSw** *SmL*

klosterman (ODan) **klaustramaðr** (ON) noun

monk **ODan** *ESjL* 2, *JyL* 1–3, **OIce** *KRA* 7, 10

See also: *kloster*

kló (ON) noun

cleat **ONorw** *GuL* Leb

eyelet **ONorw** *GuL* Leb

klutra (OSw) verb

complain **OSw** *SdmL* Jb

complain (about something) **OSw** *UL* Jb, *VmL* Jb

See also: *klanda*

klyf (OSw) **klyf** (ON) noun

packhorse **OSw** *YVgL* Tb

klýpa (ON) verb

pinch **OIce** *Jó* Mah 22

klæðaspell (ON) noun

compensation for clothes **ONorw** *FrL* Mhb 16

klæþi (OSw) **klæthe** (ODan) **kleþi** (OGu) **klæði** (ON)
noun

Cloth and clothes appear in many contexts regarding,
for instance, inheritance, liturgical objects, habits of
monks and nuns (ODan ESjL 1:31, JyL 2:23). Torn
clothes also appear as evidence in accusations of rape
(OSw YVgL Add). Trade in cut cloth *skapat klæþi*
(OSw ÄVgL), *skorit klæþi* (OSw DL), *skapeth klæthe*
(ODan ESjL, JyL) and uncut cloth *oskapat klæþi*
(OSw YVgL, ÄVgL), *oskorit klæþi* (OSw SdmL),
uskapeth klæthe (ODan SkL) is regulated particularly
in the context of accusations of theft.

bedclothes **OGu** *GL* A 18

broadcloth **OGu** *GL* A 20

cloth **ODan** *ESjL* 3, *JyL* 2, *SkL* 143, **OSw** *SdmL*
Äb, *UL* Kmb, *YVgL* Gb, Rlb, Tb, *ÄVgL* Gb, Tb

clothes **ODan** *JyL* 2, 3, **OGu** *GL*
A 24a, **OSw** *YVgL* Add

clothing **ODan** *JyL* 2, **OGu** *GL* A 19, **ONorw**
GuL Mhb, **OSw** *UL* Mb, Blb, *VmL* Äb, Mb, Bb

garment **OGu** *GL* A 23

habit **ODan** *ESjL* 1

woollen cloth **OSw** *DL* Tjdb

See also: *aklæþi*, *gangklæþi*, *ivirklæþi*,
kirkiuklæþi, *mæssuklæþi*, *sengaklæþi*

klöftroþ (OSw) noun

cattle path **OSw** *YVgL* Jb, *ÄVgL* Jb

knapi (ON) noun

attendant **OIce** *Js* Kdb 4

kné (ON) noun

degree in relationship or lineage
ONorw *GuL* Krb, Arb

knee (body part) **ONorw** *GuL* Mhb

See also: *frændi*, *frændsimi*

knérunnr (ON) noun

A method of reckoning kinship by 'knees' used in Grg.
Grg Arþ 118 states that kinship is to be counted from
brothers and sisters (ON *systkin*), which has led to
the interpretation that first cousins made up the first
'knee'.

branch of a family **OIce** *Grg* Þsþ 25 Vís 94
Arþ 122, 125 Ómb 129, 143 Arþ 147

Expressions:

hverfa í knérunna (ON)

*to be divided among the branches of the
family* **OIce** *Grg* Vís 94, Bat 113, Arþ 118

See also: *frændsimi*, *æt*

Refs: CV; Finsen III:628; Fritzner;
Hastrup 1985, 78; KLNM s.v. *ætt*

knéskot (ON) noun

shift in the order of inheritance **ONorw** *GuL* Arb

knifslagh (OSw) noun

knife wound **OSw** *DL* Mb, *HL* Rb

kniver (OSw) **kniv** (ODan) **knífr** (ON) noun

Unique for GuL (ch. 56) was the provision that the
only article that a slave was allowed to buy was a
knife.

knife **ODan** *JyL* 3, **ONorw** *GuL* Kvb, **OSw** *DL*
Mb, *YVgL* Add, *ÄVgL* Urb, *ÖgL* Db, Vm

Refs: KLNM s.v. *kniv*

knútsmessa (ON) noun

Feast of St Knut (10 July) **ONorw** *GuL* Krb

kolder (OSw) **kul** (ODan) **koller** (OSw) **kulder** (OSw)
noun

batch **OSw** *HL* Äb

brood **ODan** *ESjL* 1, 3, *JyL* 1, *VSjL* 1, 20, **OSw**
DL Gb, *UL* Äb, *VmL* Äb, *YVgL* Äb, Add

brood of children **OSw** *YVgL* Äb

group of full siblings **ODan** *SkL* 24

group of siblings **ODan** *ESjL* 1, *VSjL*
15, **OSw** *YVgL* Drb, *ÄVgL* Md, Äb

kin **ODan** *ESjL* 3

side of the family **ODan** *ESjL* 3

kolfr (ON) noun

blunt, heavy arrow **ONorw** *GuL* Mhb

kollararf (OSw) **kullar arf** (OSw) noun

inheritance between broods **OSw** *SdmL* Äb

*inheritance from siblings and half-
siblings* **OSw** *HL* Äb

See also: *kolder*

kollaskipti (OSw) noun

division between broods **OSw** *YVgL* Add

See also: *kolder*

kolumbamessa (ON) noun

St Columba's Day **OIce** *Grg* Klþ 13

kona (OSw) **kone** (ODan) **kuna** (OGu) **kona** (ON)
kuna (OSw) **qvinna** (OSw) noun

bride **OSw** *DL* Gb

spouse **OSw** *YVgL* Frb, Äb, Gb, Tb, *ÄVgL* Äb, Gb

wife **ODan** *ESjL* 1–3, *JyL* 1, 3, *SkKL* 6, 9, 11,
SkL passim, *VSjL* 2, 3, 15, 20, 52, 86, 87, **OGu**
GL A 15, 21, 63, *GS* Ch. 1, 2, **OIce** *Grg* Þsþ 49,
78, **ONorw** *GuL* Krb, Kvb, Løb. Arb, Mhb, Intr
to Book X, Leb, **OSw** *DL* Kkb, Gb, *HL* Äb, Mb,
SdmL Gb, Jb, *SmL*, *UL* Kkb, Äb, Mb, Jb, Rb,
VmL Kkb, Äb, Mb, Jb, Rb, *YVgL* Frb, Drb, Äb,
Jb, *ÄVgL* Md, Slb, Äb, Gb, Tb, *ÖgL* Kkb, Eb

wife/woman **OSw** *ÄVgL* Äb

woman **ODan** *ESjL* 1, 3, *JyL* 1–3, *SkKL* 7, *SkL* 3,
34, 36, 37, 41, 60, 128, 132, 219, 224, *VSjL* 1, 61,
62, 88, **OGu** *GL* A 2, 6, 14, 15, 18–20, 20a, 21–23,
24d, 39, 65, **ONorw** *GuL* Krb, Kpb, Kvb, Løb, Mhb,
Olb, Leb, Arb, Sab, Tfb, Tjb, **OSw** *DL* Kkb, Eb,
Mb, Gb, *HL* Kkb, Kgb, Äb, Mb, Jb, Blb, Rb, *SdmL*
Kkb, Kgb, Gb, Äb, Bb, Kmb, Mb, Rb, Till, *SmL*,
UL Kkb, Kgb, Äb, Mb, Jb, Blb, Rb, *VmL* Kkb, Kgb,
Äb, Mb, Jb, Bb, Rb, *YVgL* Kkb, Frb, Urb, Äb, Gb,

Rlb, Tb, Jb, Föb, Utgb, Add, *ÄVgL* Md, Vs, Slb, Urb, Äb, Gb, Rlb, Jb, Tb, Fös, *ÖgL* Kkb, Db, Vm

See also: *aþalkona, bondakona, bonde, frilla, husfrugha, kærling, leghokona, sløkefrithe*

konongsgarþer (OSw) **kunungsgarth** (ODan) **konungsgarðr** (ON) noun

Farms managed by the king's representative, which contributed to the incomes of the crown and functioned as stops on the king's journeys and as the king's treasury. In OSw, presumably part of *upsala öþer* (farms of the Swedish Crown, see *öþer*) together with *husabyar* (see *husaby*), and in ONorw related to the institution of *veizla* (see *væzla*). Appears in the laws as the occasional place for announcements (see *lysning*) (ODan ESjL) or for deposits of disputed purchase sums (OSw SdmL), but more often mentioned as the recipient of certain fines or compensations (OIce KRA, ONorw FrL, GuL) and valuable finds (ODan ESjL, SkL). Most often, though, in ODan ESjL, VSjL, SkL, ONorw FrL, GuL and OSw ÄVgL, YVgL, a place to which certain criminals could be sentenced, in ODan SkL explicitly called slavery.

king's court **ONorw** *GuL* Mhb

king's estate **ODan** *VSjL* 87, **OIce** *KRA* 8

king's farm **OSw** *SdmL* Jb, *YVgL* Tb, *ÄVgL* Tb

king's household **ONorw** *FrL* KrbA 10 Var 13

king's manor **ODan** *ESjL* 3, *SkL* 130, 133, 151, 164

See also: *biskupsgarþer, garþer, husaby, kununger, öþer*

Refs: Cleasby and Vigfusson s.v. *konungsgarðr*; Hertzberg s.v. *konungsgarðr*; KLNM s.v.v. *kronogods, kungsgård*; Nevéus 1974, 71; Schlyter s.v. *konongsgarþer*; Tamm and Vogt, eds, 2016, 36

konongsriki (OSw) **kunungerike** (ODan) **konungsríki** (ON) **kunungsriki** (OSw) noun

king's realm **ODan** *SkL* 146, 166

kingdom **ODan** *SkL* 133, **OIce** *Jó* Mah 1 Kge 17, **OSw** *DL* Gb, *SdmL* Till, *ÄVgL* Gb

realm **OSw** *YVgL* Add, *ÄVgL* Md

realms belonging to the king **OIce** *Jó* Llb 18

See also: *konungsveldi, kununger, riki*

konubú (ON) noun

household led by a woman **OIce** *Grg* Vís 89

See also: *ænkjebo*

konunám (ON) noun

abduction of a woman **OIce** *Grg* Feþ 160

konungsbréf (ON) noun

king's letter **OIce** *Jó* Kge 34

konungsefni (ON) noun

The title born by the person next in the line of succession between the death of a king and the presumptive heir's coronation.

crown prince **OIce** *Js* Kdb 4

Refs: CV s.v. *konungsefni*; Fritzner s.v. *konungsefni*; Hertzberg s.v. *konungsefni*

konungsfé (ON) noun

royal property **ONorw** *GuL* Krb

konungsjörð (ON) noun

king's farm **OIce** *Grg* Vís 112

king's land **ONorw** *GuL* Olb, Leb

konungsman (OSw) **kunungsman** (ODan) **konungsmaðr** (ON) noun

king's man **ODan** *JyL* 2, **ONorw** *GuL* Krb, **OSw** *HL* Kgb, Äb, Mb, Rb, *SdmL* Mb, *ÖgL* Db, Vm

king's official **ONorw** *FrL* KrbB 24

lordsman **ODan** *JyL* 2

konungsmörk (ON) noun

Forested land belonging to the king (of Norway). In Grg Misc 248 it is stipulated that Icelanders had the right to cut wood in these forest for any purpose. According to the later *Bjarkeyjarréttr* (q.v.) (III.2, NGL II:199–200), The King's Forest was to be used as a resource for building ships for national defense.

king's forest **OIce** *Grg* Misc 248

See also: *mark (3), skogher, viþer*

Refs: CV s.v. *konungsmörk*; Fritzner s.v. *konungsmörk*; Hertzberg s.v. *konungsmörk*

konungsrætter (OSw) **kunungsræt** (ODan) **konungsréttr** (ON) **konongsrætter** (OSw) noun

fine to the king **ODan** *SkL* 85

king's due **ODan** *ESjL* 1–3, *JyL* 1, 2, *SkL* 43, 57, 67, 69, 72, 108, 137, 145, *VSjL* 23, 32, 51, 66, 71, 82, 84, 86, 87

king's fine **ODan** *SkL* 144, 145, 147, 148, **OSw** *HL* Mb

king's rights **OIce** *Jó* Þjb 3, **OSw** *YVgL* Kkb, Add

payment to the king **ODan** *SkL* 102, 108

right of the king **OSw** *YVgL* Rlb, Add

See also: *biskupsrætter, kununger*

konungssteði (ON) noun

An anvil; a stithy; the minting of money. Used in Jó in the phrase *konungs steðja* to refer to a royal mint.

king's coin **OIce** *Jó* Mah 2

king's mint **OIce** *Jó* Kge 18

Refs: CV; F; NGL V s.v. *steði*

konungsvald (ON) noun

   king's authority OIce *Jó* Þjb 22, *Js* Þjb 1

   royal authority OIce *Jó* Þjb 1

konungsveldi (ON) konungaveldi (ON) noun

   kingdom OIce *Grg* Vís 97, *Jó* Kge 28,
   ONorw *FrL* KrbA 4 Mhb 34, *GuL* Tjb

   realms of the king OIce *Grg* Vís 94
   Arþ 118, 127 Ómb 143 Misc 248

   See also: *konongsriki, lagh, riki*

konungsþing (ON) noun

   An assembly summoned by the king.

   king's assembly ONorw *GuL* Tfb

   See also: *eþsöre, kunungsræfst, þing*

   Refs: KLNM s.v.v. *högmålsbrott,
   konungsräfst, nämnd, rettergang, ting*

konungsørendi (ON) konungserindi (ON) noun

   king's business OIce *Jó* Þfb 2 Llb 28

koppofunder (OSw) noun

   bee-swarm OSw *ÄVgL* Föb

korn (OSw) korn (OGu) korn (ON) noun

   barley OGu *GL* A 6, 20, OSw *UL* Kgb

   corn OGu *GL* A 56a, OSw *VmL* Kkb

   crop OSw *UL* Kkb, Blb, *VmL* Kkb, Bb

   grain ONorw *GuL* Mhb, Leb, OSw *UL*
   Kkb, Kgb, Mb, Jb, Kmb, Blb, Rb, *VmL*
   Kkb, Kgb, Mb, Jb, Kmb, Bb, Rb

   See also: *ax, spannamali, sæþ*

kornband (OGu) noun

   ban against trade in corn OGu *GS* Ch. 2

korngjald (ODan) noun

   damage for crop ODan *SkL* 172, 175, 181

   payment for crop ODan *ESjL* 3, *SkL* 182

   payment for damaged crop ODan *SkL* 169

   See also: *akergjald*

kornhærbærghi (OSw) noun

   grain house OSw *YVgL* Tb

   grain store OSw *UL* Kkb

   granary OSw *SdmL* Kkb

kornlaþa (OSw) noun

   corn barn OSw *HL* Mb

kornskæmma (OSw) kornskamma (OSw) noun

   grain house OSw *ÄVgL* Tb

   See also: *matskamma, symnskæmma*

kornspell (ON) noun

   corn damage OFar *Seyð* 2

korntiund (OSw) korntiunt (OGu) korn tyund (OSw)
noun

   corn tithe OGu *GL* A 3, OSw *HL*
   Kkb, *UL* Kkb, *VmL* Kkb

koste (ODan) verb

   pay ODan *SkL* 129

kostebuthseth (ODan) noun

   voluntary oath ODan *JyL* 3

   See also: *eþer*

koster (OSw) kost (ODan) noun

   belongings OSw *DL* Tjdb, *SdmL* Jb

   board OSw *SdmL* Kkb, Jb, Kmb,
   Till, *UL* Kkb, *VmL* Kkb

   cost ODan *JyL* 1, 3, OSw *UL* Kkb,
   Äb, Jb, *VmL* Kkb, Äb, Jb

   expense OSw *HL* Kkb, *UL* Kkb, Jb,
   Kmb, *VmL* Kkb, Jb, Kmb

   fare OSw *HL* Kkb, *YVgL* Äb

   food OSw *YVgL* Kkb, Add

   goods ODan *ESjL* 1–3, *JyL* 2, 3, *SkL* passim,
   VSjL 56, 65, 87, OSw *YVgL* Rlb, Tb

   goods and chattels OSw *HL* Kmb

   hospitality OSw *UL* Jb, Kmb, *VmL* Jb, Kmb

   legal right OSw *SmL*

   maintenance ODan *JyL* 1, OSw *YVgL* Kkb

   manner OSw *UL* Äb, Blb, *VmL* Äb

   movable goods ODan *.JyL* 1, 2

   possessions OSw *UL* Kkb, Kgb, Jb,
   VmL Kkb, Kmb (rubric only), Rb

   property ODan *SkL* 137, 140, OSw *HL* Äb

   provisions OSw *UL* Kkb, Kmb,
   VmL Kkb, Kmb, *YVgL* Jb

   representation ODan *ESjL* 2

   valuable property OSw *ÄVgL* Rlb

   See also: *föþa*

kostningsgjald (ODan) noun

   money for expenses ODan *JyL* 1

kostnuðr (ON) kostnaðr (ON) noun

   expense OIce *Grg* Ómb 130, *Jó* Þfb 6, 9 Mah 8,
   30 Kge 3, 28 Llb 8, 62 Þjb 8 Fml 6, 23, *Js* Þfb
   2, 5, *KRA* 16, ONorw *EidsL* 36.1, *FrL* Intr 23

kot (ON) noun

   croft OFar *Seyð* 7

kotsæte (ODan) noun

   cabin ODan *VSjL* 86

kórsbróðir (ON) noun

   canon ONorw *FrL* KrbA 40

krafa (ON) noun

   claim **ONorw** *GuL* Kpb, Løb

   See also: *fearkraf, krævia*

krafarvereldi (OGu) noun

   wergild subject to claim **OGu** *GL* A 17

krapti (ON) noun

   If the man responsible for providing the knee timber (on a ship in the *leþunger* (q.v.)) failed to do his duty, he had to pay a fine. See GuL ch. 306.

   knee timber on a ship **ONorw** *GuL* Leb

   Refs: Hertzberg s.v. *krapti*

kristin (OSw) **kristen** (ODan) **kristinn** (ON) adj.

   christened **ONorw** *GuL* Krb, **OSw** *ÖgL* Eb

   Christian **ODan** *JyL* 1, **OSw** *SdmL* Kkb, Kmb, *SmL*, *ÄVgL* Kkb

kristindomber (OSw) **kristendom** (ODan) **kristindómr** (ON) noun

   baptism **OSw** *DL* Gb, *SdmL* Kkb

   Christendom **ODan** *ESjL* 2, *SkL* 2–4, *VSjL* 6, **OSw** *ÄVgL* Äb

   christening **ODan** *JyL* 1, **OSw** *SmL*, *YVgL* Kkb

   Christianity **ODan** *ESjL* 1, *JyL* 1, **OIce** *KRA* 11, **ONorw** *GuL* Krb

   Christianity/cases concerning Christianity **OIce** *Js* Kab 8

   church law **ONorw** *GuL* Kpb

   Expressions:

   kristendoms logh (ODan)

   Christian law **ODan** *JyL* 1

kristindómsbölkr (ON) **kristindómsbálkr** (ON) **kristinsdómsbölkr** (ON) noun

   Christian law **ONorw** *BorgL* 1

   Christian laws chapter **OIce** *Jó* MagBref

   ecclesiastical law **OFar** *Seyð* 0

kristinréttr (ON) noun

   Christian law **OIce** *KRA* 29, **ONorw** *BorgL* 18.4, *FrL* KrbA 1

   church law **ONorw** *FrL* KrbB 20

kristinsdómsbrot (ON) noun

   violation of Christian law **ONorw** *GuL* Krb

kristinsdómshald (ON) noun

   observance of Christianity **ONorw** *GuL* Krb

kristna (OSw) **kristne** (ODan) **kristna** (ON) verb

   baptize **ONorw** *BorgL* 1.2, *FrL* KrbA 1, **OSw** *UL* Kkb, *VmL* Kkb

   christen **ODan** *ESjL* 1, *JyL* 1, *SkL* 3, **OSw** *DL* Kkb, *SdmL* Kkb, *SmL*, *YVgL* Kkb, *ÄVgL* Kkb, *ÖgL* Kkb

   christianize **OSw** *ÄVgL* Kkb

   See also: *döpa*

kristna (OSw) noun

   baptism **OSw** *HL* Kkb

   christening **OSw** *YVgL* Kkb, *ÄVgL* Kkb

   Christian faith **OSw** *YVgL* Kkb, *ÄVgL* Kkb

   Christian times **OSw** *YVgL* Jb, *ÄVgL* Jb

   Christianity **OSw** *ÖgL* Kkb

kristning (OSw) noun

   christening **OSw** *HL* Kkb, *SdmL* Kkb

kristnubalker (OSw) noun

   book concerning Christian law **OSw** *DL* Kkb

   Christianity book **OSw** *SmL*

   church book **OSw** *ÖgL* Kkb

   See also: *balker, kristna*

krok (ODan) noun

   plough **ODan** *SkL* 239

   See also: *arþer*

kroklokarl (OSw) **krökiokarl** (OSw) noun

   old man on crutches **OSw** *DL* Mb, *VmL* Mb

krona (OSw) **krúna** (ON) verb

   crown **OSw** *SdmL* Till

krona (OSw) noun

   the Crown **OSw** *HL* Kkb, Kgb, Mb, *SdmL* Kkb, Mb, Till

   tonsure **OIce** *Grg* Klþ 6

kross (ON) noun

   cross **OIce** *KRA* 24, 25

   sign of the cross **ONorw** *GuL* Krb

   token of seizure **ONorw** *GuL* Llb

   Expressions:

   skera krossa (ON)

   cut cross-tokens **OIce** *Grg* Þsþ 84 Hrs 234 Misc 240 *Js* Rkb 2

   prepare a cross **ONorw** *FrL* KrbA 22

   See also: *skæra (1)*

krossmessa hin øfri (ON) noun

   Exaltation of the Cross **ONorw** *GuL* Krb

krossmessa um haustit (ON) noun

   Exaltation of the Cross **ONorw** *FrL* KrbA 25

   See also: *crucismisse, krossmessa um várit*

krossmessa um várit (ON) noun

   Finding of the Holy Cross (3 May) **ONorw** *GuL* Krb

   See also: *crucismisse, crucisuke, krossmessa um haustit*

krossskurðr (ON) noun

   The cutting of a cross to be used as a message token.

   cross cutting **ONorw** *FrL* KrbA 22

   Refs: CV s.v. *krossskurðr*; Hertzberg s.v. *krossskurðr*

krossvíti (ON) noun

cross fine **ONorw** *GuL* Krb

krókspjót (ON) noun

barbed spear **ONorw** *GuL* Mhb

krævia (OSw) krævje (ODan) krefia (OGu) krefja
(ON) verb

Literally 'to demand', usually payment, such as an
inheritance or a compensation. Also construed as
a verb for starting legal proceedings, reflected in
translations such as 'to raise a case'.

accuse **ODan** *SkL* 226

ask **OSw** *UL* Äb, *VmL* Kkb, Äb

ask for **OSw** *UL* Blb, *VmL* Kkb, Bb

claim **ONorw** *GuL* Krb, Kpb, Kvb,
Løb, Llb, Arb, Mhb, Leb, Olb

demand **OGu** *GL* A 17, Add. 2 (B17), **OSw**
UL Kgb, Äb, Mb, Jb, *VmL* Kkb, Äb, Mb, Jb

put a case **OSw** *VmL* Jb

raise a case **OSw** *UL* Äb, *VmL* Äb

Expressions:

krævia æptir fæþær (OSw)

raise a paternity case **OSw** *UL* Äb *VmL* Äb

See also: *kveðja*

kunder (OSw) kun (ODan) kunnr (ON) adj.

related **ODan** *SkL* 53, 85, 86, 113,
OSw *SmL*, *UL* Äb, *VmL* Äb

Expressions:

kunnr ok sannr (ON)

identified and convicted **OIce** *Jó* Þfb 3 Mah 25
Llb 30 Þjb 22 **ONorw** *GuL* Krb, Løb, Llb

See also: *sander*

kununger (OSw) kunung (ODan) konungr (ON)
konunger (OSw) noun

king **ODan** *ESjL* 1–3, *JyL* Fort, 1–3, *SkL* passim,
VSjL passim, **OFar** *Seyð* 0, 1, 2, 3, 5, **OIce** *Grg*
Bat 114 Ómb 139 Misc 238 Misc 247, *Jó* passim,
Js Þfb 2, Kdb Mah 5 passim, *KRA* 1, 6 passim,
ONorw *BorgL* 8.11, *EidsL* 8.3 25, *FrL* passim,
GuL Krb, Kpb, Løb, Arb, Tfb, Reb, Kvr, Mhb, Tjb,
Olb, Leb, **OSw** *DL* Kkb, Eb, Mb, Bb, Gb, Tjdb, Rb,
HL För, Kkb, Kgb, Mb, Blb, Rb, *SdmL* Conf, För,
Kkb, Kgb, Gb, Äb, Jb, Bb, Kmb, Mb, Tjdb, Rb,
Till, *SmL*, *YVgL* passim, *ÄVgL* Kkb, Md, Smb, Slb,
Äb, Gb, Rlb, Jb, Tb, Fös, *ÖgL* Kkb, Eb, Db, Vm

Expressions:

konungs ægha (OSw)

king's property **OSw** *HL* Rb

konungs borþ (OSw)

king's table **OSw** *HL* Mb

kóróna konungs (ON)

king's crown **ONorw** *GuL* Krb

See also: *egn, eþsöre, lanardroten, ægha, ørendreki*

kunungsbalker (OSw) noun

king's book **OSw** *HL* För, Kgb

king's section **OSw** *SdmL* För, Kgb

See also: *balker, kununger*

kunungsdömi (OSw) konungdómr (ON)
konungsdómr (ON) noun

the Crown **OFar** *Seyð* 0, 11, **ONorw** *FrL* Intr 21

king **ONorw** *FrL* Intr 21

kingdom **ONorw** *FrL* Intr 2, **OSw**
SdmL Kgb, Till, *UL* Kgb

kunungsnæmd (OSw) noun

king's commission **OSw** *DL* Rb

king's jury **OSw** *ÖgL* Kkb

kunungsræfst (OSw) noun

king's inquest **OSw** *ÖgL* Eb

See also: *eþsöre, konungsþing*

kurtilbonaþr (OGu) noun

underskirt decorations **OGu** *GL* A 65

kuska (OSw) verb

force **OSw** *ÖgL* Eb

kuskan (OSw) noun

force **OSw** *ÖgL* Eb

kúgildi (ON) noun

The *kúgildi* may have represented an early standard
of legal currency (*lögeyrir*, q.v.) in Iceland, namely
one based on cattle. This standard was later replaced
by cloth and subsequently by fish. It is thought that
cattle served as a currency standard throughout
Scandinavia from the prehistoric period up into the
Middle Ages, and the term *kúgildi* persisted for some
time after cows ceased to be physically exchanged. A
cow which was *kúgildi* is defined in Grg Misc 246; it
had to be medium-sized, aged between three and ten
winters, horned, without blemish and in milk. Interest-
bearing loans could be assessed in *kúgildi*. Values of
other animals could be expressed in *kúgildi*, such as
twelve one-year-old sheep being worth one *kúgildi*,
though some fluctuations on this standard are attested.
The money equivalent of *kúgildi* was set at spring
assemblies (*várþing*) and therefore could have a
different value in various parts of Iceland. This lasted
until the late twelfth century, when, in comparison with
the later cloth standard, *kúgildi* became equivalent to
120 ells of homespun cloth (*vaðmál*) or its equivalent
in silver from 1186, if not earlier.

The *kúgildi* was used particularly for larger
transactions, such as farmsteads or land. As such,

kúgildi and its compounds appear frequently in medieval diplomas. It has been suggested that *kúgildi* might also refer to a plot of land required to maintain a cow. Alternatively, it may have been a unit measuring an amount needed to sustain one person for a year.

Kúgildi was in common use until at least the sixteenth century and was used sporadically well up into the modern period. The value of a *kúgildi* in relation to other goods, in particular butter, changed over the years, especially from Erik Magnússon's 1294 amendment and later.

In the Norwegian laws *kúgildi* has been compared to *kýrlag*, which appears in numerous diplomas. *Kýrlag* is defined in GuL (ch. 223), though the term itself does not appear there.

Between c. 1100 and 1300 a *kúgildi* was worth at least 2–2.5 *aurar* of pure silver (cf. Gelsinger 1981, 195).

cow equivalent **OIce** *Grg* Lbþ 202, 220, *Jó* Sg 1 Llb 51

cow value **ONorw** *FrL* Var 14

cow's worth **ONorw** *FrL* KrbA 27

price of a cow **OIce** *Grg* Þsþ 77 Vís 89 Misc 246, *Jó* Kab 6, 15, **ONorw** *FrL* Bvb 10

See also: *fæ*, *kýrverð*, *lögeyrir*, *málnytukúgildi*, *vaðmal*

Refs: Einzig 1966; Finnur Jónsson 1936; Gelsinger 1981, 36–38; Hastrup 2006; Helgi Þor. 1991, 93–97, 523–26; KLNM s.v. *byamál*, *hundrað*, *kýrlag*; RGA s.v. *kúgildi*; Strauch 2013a; Þorvaldur Thoroddsen 1908–22, III: 43–58

kúgildisskaði (ON) noun

damage equivalent to the price of a cow **OIce** *Grg* Þsþ 64

kúgildr (ON) adj.

having the value of a cow **ONorw** *FrL* Leb 23 LlbA 21

kvaðarváttr (ON) noun

calling witness **OIce** *Grg* Þsþ 32

kvánarmundr (ON) noun

bride price **OIce** *Grg* Arþ 118

kvánfang (ON) noun

marriage **OIce** *Grg* Klþ 1, 18, *KRA* 16, **ONorw** *EidsL* 22.6, *GuL* Kvb, Løb

See also: *brullöp*, *eiginorð*, *hjúskapr*, *kvennagifting*

kvánga (ON) verb

marry **OIce** *Grg* Þsþ 80 Arþ 118, *Jó* Kge 7, 26, **ONorw** *EidsL* 22.3

See also: *kvænes*

kveða (ON) verb

state **OIce** *Js* Lbb 2

kveðja (ON) verb

call **OIce** *Grg* passim

claim **ONorw** *GuL* Kpb, Olb

present a claim **ONorw** *FrL* Rgb 6

See also: *krævia*

kvenaskr (ON) noun

woman's measure **OIce** *Jó* Kab 26

kvengjafir (pl.) (ON) noun

gifts to women **ONorw** *GuL* Mhb

kvenklæði (ON) noun

woman's clothes **ONorw** *GuL* Mhb

kvennagifting (ON) **kvennagift** (ON) **kvennagiptir** (ON) noun

marriage of women **OIce** *Jó* MagBref Kge 1 Kab 12, **ONorw** *BorgL* 7.1, *GuL* Kvb

women's marriage **ONorw** *GuL* Kvb

See also: *brullöp*, *kvánfang*

kvennalegorð (ON) noun

case concerning intercourse with women **OIce** *Js* Þfb 6, *KRA* 34

case concerning the seduction of women **OIce** *Jó* Þjb 16, **ONorw** *FrL* Var 46

seduction of women **OIce** *Jó* Þfb 8

See also: *legorð*

kvennamál (ON) noun

illicit sexual intercourse **ONorw** *FrL* KrbB 2

kvensift (ON) **kvennsift** (ON) noun

kinship traced through women **OIce** *Grg* Bat 113

kvensvift (ON) **kvennsvipt** (ON) noun

feminine side **ONorw** *GuL* Arb, Mhb, Sab

See also: *nefgildismaðr*

kviðburðr (ON) noun

verdict-giving **OIce** *Grg* Þsþ 35, 36

kviðja (ON) verb

forbid **ONorw** *GuL* Krb

kviðmaðr (ON) noun

panel member **OIce** *Grg* Lbþ 202 Hrs 234

kviðr (ON) noun

verdict **OIce** *Grg* Klþ 2 Þsþ Vís passim

Expressions:

bera kvið (ON)

give a (panel) verdict **OIce** *Grg* Þsþ 35

See also: *kvöð*

kvikvendi (ON) noun

domestic animal **ONorw** *GuL* Tfb, Mhb

kvinnetakt (ODan) noun

  rape **ODan** *JyL* 2

  rape of women **ODan** *JyL* 2

  See also: *kona, vald*

kvæfa (ON) verb

  choke **ONorw** *BorgL* 3.2

kvænes (ODan) verb

  marry **ODan** *ESjL* 1, *JyL* 1

  See also: *kvánga*

kvöð (ON) **kvaða** (ON) noun

When the merits of a dispute were not known (when the claimant had no legal witnesses to his claim), the claimant proceeded with a *kvaða*, a formal demand for restitution, a request that his counterpart (the defendant) should follow a certain procedure in the matter. The defendant must then either comply with the request (e.g. to pay his debt) or agree to have the complaint heard and considered by a court of arbitration.

  claim **OIce** *Grg* Þsþ 33, *Js* Kab 5, **ONorw** *FrL* Rgb 4

  demand **ONorw** *GuL* Kpb, Arb, Olb

  See also: *kviðr*

  Refs: Hertzberg s.v. *kvaða, kvöð*; Robberstad 1981, 343

kvöðudómr (ON) noun

  court for settling a claim **ONorw** *FrL* Rgb 11

kvöðuváttr (ON) noun

  appointed witness **ONorw** *FrL* Rgb 2

  witness to a claim **ONorw** *GuL* Olb

  See also: *kvöðuvitni*

kvöðuvitni (ON) noun

  testimony of a claim **OIce** *Js* Kab 2, **ONorw** *FrL* Rgb 2

  witness to a claim **ONorw** *GuL* Løb, Olb

  witness to a formal claim **OIce** *Jó* Þfb 4

  See also: *kvöðuváttr, vitni*

kyn (OSw) **kyn** (ODan) **kynne** (ODan) **kyn** (OGu) **kyn** (ON) **kön** (OSw) **kun** (OSw) noun

  family **OGu** *GL* A 5, Add. 1 (B 4)

  kin **ODan** *ESjL* 2, *JyL* 1, *SkKL* 7, *SkL* 2, **OIce** *Grg* Ómb 140, **ONorw** *GuL* Løb, Arb, Mhb, Leb, **OSw** *SmL*

  kinship **OSw** *UL* Äb, *VmL* Äb

  kinsman **ODan** *JyL* 2, *SkL* 219

  relationship **ODan** *SkL* 92, 97, **OSw** *DL* Gb

  See also: *frændi, niþi, skyldarman, skylder (1), æt*

kyndilmæssa (OSw) **kyndilsmessa** (ON) **quindilmæssa** (OSw) noun

  Candlemas **ONorw** *GuL* Krb, **OSw** *DL* Kkb, *SdmL* Kkb, Bb, *UL* Kkb, Kgb, *VmL* Kkb, Jb, *YVgL* Kkb, Add

  See also: *mariumæssa*

kynsarv (ODan) noun

  inheritance between kin **ODan** *VSjL* 20

kynseth (ODan) noun

An oath sworn by kinsmen, possibly in a *kynsnævnd* (q.v.).

  men of the kin **ODan** *JyL* 3

kynsnævnd (ODan) noun

A *nævnd* (ODan) 'nominated men' consisting of twelve of the defendant's kinsmen in the region, and nominated by the plaintiff, possibly a reduced form of defence in cases where the plaintiff lacked important evidence. Appearing mostly in cases of inheritance but occasionally also concerning violent crimes without witnesses. The concept, albeit not the word, also appears in SkL.

  men named from the kin **ODan** *JyL* 1

  men of one's kin **ODan** *JyL* 1, 2

  men of the kin **ODan** *JyL* 3

  Refs: Andersen 2010, 92, 103–05; Tamm and Vogt, eds, 2016, 307

kynsæme (ODan) noun

  kinship **ODan** *SkKL* 6, 7

kynsæmesbrut (ODan) noun

  offences as to kinship relations **ODan** *SkKL* 8

  See also: *frændsimisspiæl*

kyrking (ON) noun

  throttling **OIce** *Grg* Vís 87

kyrkja (ON) verb

  strangle **OIce** *Js* Kab 12, **ONorw** *BorgL* 3.2, *GuL* Krb, Kpb

  throttle **OIce** *Grg* Vís 88

kyrr (ON) adj.

  quiet **ONorw** *GuL* Llb, Olb, Leb

kyrra (ON) verb

  tame **OFar** *Seyð* 5, 10

kýr (ON) noun

  cow **ONorw** *GuL* Krb, Kpb, Løb, Llb, Mhb, Leb

kýrverð (ON) noun

  value of a cow **OIce** *KRA* 35

kæfsir (OSw) **kæpsir** (OSw) noun

  concubinal man of a slave woman **OSw** *ÄVgL* Gb

  thrall woman's concubinal man **OSw** *YVgL* Gb

kælkadræt (OSw) noun

sledge dragging rights **OSw** *UL* Jb, *VmL* Jb

kænna (OSw) **kænne** (ODan) **kenna** (OGu) **kenna** (ON) **kiænna** (OSw) verb

Essentially, to make someone or something known, mainly concerning responsibility in legal matters. When referring to oneself translated as 'to confess', 'to admit', 'to acknowledge' (mostly appearing as *kænna sik, kænnas* and often with a particle *viþ(er)*). When referring to somebody else: to make a suspected criminal known ('to accuse', 'to charge'), or, for example, to make the father of a child known ('to identify', 'to attribute'). Also to make a convicted criminal known ('to be found guilty'). When referring to an object: to make ownership known of, for instance, missing domestic animals ('to identify', 'to recognize', 'to claim'). There is considerable overlap between usages and translations.

accuse **OFar** *Seyð* 1, **OIce** *Jó* Mah 20 Þjb 5, *KRA* 20, **ONorw** *BorgL* 16.8, *EidsL* 7 41.1, *FrL* KrbB 15 Mhb 4 Bvb 1, *GuL* Krb, Mhb, Tfb, Tjb, Leb, **OSw** *UL* Mb, Blb, Rb, *VmL* Kkb, Äb, Mb, Bb, Rb

blame **ODan** *SkL* 44

bring a complaint against **OIce** *Jó* Mah 8

charge **OGu** *GL* Add. 8 (B 55), **OIce** *Grg* Vís 87, *Jó* Mah 2 Þjb 19, *Js* Mah 5 Kvg 5 Þjb 1, 4, *KRA* 2

claim **ONorw** *GuL* Tjb

find **ODan** *SkL* 145

be found guilty **ONorw** *FrL* Intr 10

identify **ODan** *SkL* 159, 230, **OIce** *Jó* Mah 2, 9 Kab 7, *Js* Þjb 3, **ONorw** *FrL* Mhb 5

recognize **ODan** *SkL* 136, 142, 144, 150, 157, **OIce** *Jó* Þjb 3 Fml 21, **OSw** *YVgL* Tb

Expressions:

kenna sak (OGu)

accuse **OGu** *GL* A 2

kænna sik (OSw) **kenna sér** (ON)

admit to **OSw** *UL* Mb

claim **OSw** *UL* Jb, Blb

profess to own **OIce** *Grg* Rsþ 228

kænna(s) viþ (OSw) **kænne(s) vither** (ODan)

accuse **ODan** *SkL* 161 **OSw** *DL* Bb *ÖgL* Eb, Db

accuse of having committed a misdemeanour **OSw** *DL* Kkb

acknowledge **OSw** *SdmL* Mb, Tjdb, Rb *ÖgL* Kkb

attribute **OSw** *SdmL* Kkb, Gb, Bb, Mb

claim **ODan** *SkL* 140, 142 **OSw** *SdmL* Jb, Kmb, Mb, Tjdb

make a claim **ODan** *SkL* 13

See also: *sak, viþerkænnas*

kænneland (ODan) noun

Agricultural land that was not farmed jointly.

land marked separately **ODan** *JyL* 3

Refs: Gammeldansk ordbog s.v. *kænneland*; Tamm and Vogt, eds, 2016, 307

kæra (OSw) **kære** (ODan) **kera** (OGu) **kæra** (ON) **kære** (ODan) verb

Literally 'to complain'. When used of the injured party's declaration of having been wronged often referring to the initiation of a legal procedure (at the *þing* 'assembly'), and translated as for example 'bring a case (before the Thing assembly)', 'prosecute', 'sue', 'take action'. Sometimes focusing on the identification of an alleged culprit ('accuse', 'charge'), or on the request for justice ('claim', 'demand', 'petition'). The right to *kæra* typically belonged to the injured party (including the bishop's *lænsmaþer* (q.v.) as the representative of the Church when it was considered the injured party).

accuse **ODan** *ESjL* 2, **OSw** *HL* Rb, *ÖgL* Kkb 18:2

bring a case (against) **OSw** *DL* Kkb, Bb, Gb, Rb, *ÖgL* Eb

bring a case before the Thing assembly **OSw** *DL* Tjdb

bring a complaint **ODan** *SkL* 226

bring a prosecution **OSw** *UL* Mb, Rb, *VmL* Mb, Rb

challenge **ODan** *JyL* 2

charge **ODan** *ESjL* 3, *SkL* 98

claim **ODan** *SkL* 51, 67, 83, **OSw** *YVgL* Jb, Föb, Utgb, *ÄVgL* Jb

complain **ODan** *ESjL* 1, *JyL* 1, 2, *SkL* 15, 44, 49, 75, 187, 214, *VSjL* 24, 71, **OSw** *DL* Tjdb, *HL* Kkb, Äb

conduct a prosecution **OSw** *DL* Rb

demand **ODan** *JyL* 2

lay a complaint **OGu** *GL* A 23

make a claim **ODan** *ESjL* 2, 3

make a complaint **ODan** *ESjL* 2, **OSw** *UL* Kkb, Äb, Mb, Jb

make an accusation **OGu** *GL* A 22, **OSw** *UL* Kgb

make charges **ODan** *ESjL* 3

petition **OSw** *YVgL* Föb, *ÖgL* Kkb

plead **OGu** *GL* Add. 1 (B 4)

present a claim **ONorw** *FrL* Intr 15

prosecute **OSw** *DL* Kkb, Mb, Bb, *HL* Kkb

pursue **ODan** *ESjL* 2, 3

raise a claim **ODan** *JyL* 1, *SkL* 14, **OSw** *ÖgL* Eb, Db

raise a complaint **ODan** *ESjL* 3, *JyL* 1, 2, *SkKL* 3, *SkL* 8, 173, *VSjL* 18, 25, 78

start accusation **ODan** *ESjL* 2

sue **OSw** *HL* Mb, *SdmL* Kkb, Kgb, Äb, Bb,
Kmb, Mb, Rb, *YVgL* Add, *ÖgL* Kkb, Eb

take action **ODan** *JyL* 2

Expressions:

kæra fyrir (ON)

to bring an action before **OIce** *Jó* Sg 3, Mah 21

kæra sik (ON)

bring an action **OIce** *Jó* Sg 1

kæra til, kæra til, til kæra (OSw)

prosecute **OSw** *UL* Kkb, Kgb, Mb, Blb
VmL Kkb, Kgb, Mb, Jb, Bb, Rb

kæra æptir (OSw)

bring a prosecution **OSw** *UL* Mb, Rb

raise an objection **OSw** *UL* Blb *VmL* Jb

See also: *giva, sak, sökia, tiltala*

Refs: Hellquist s.v. *kära*; Schlyter s.v. *kæra, sökia*

kæra (OSw) noun

action **ODan** *ESjL* 2, *JyL* 2

case **ODan** *ESjL* 2

claim **ODan** *ESjL* 2

complaint **ODan** *JyL* 1, 3

suit **OSw** *SdmL* Till

kærande (OSw) **kærandi** (OSw) noun

plaintiff **OSw** *HL* Kgb, *UL* Kmb, Blb, *VmL* Kmb, Bb

suitor **OSw** *SdmL* Bb, Kmb

See also: *malsæghandi*

kærasunnudagher (OSw) noun

*fifth Sunday in Lent — Passion
Sunday* **OSw** *UL* Mb, Rb

kærling (OSw) noun

wife **OSw** *HL* Kkb, *UL* Kkb, *VmL* Kkb

See also: *bonde, husfrugha, karl, kona, leghokona*

kæromal (OSw) noun

complaint **OSw** *YVgL* Add

suit **OSw** *SdmL* Till

kæti (OSw) **kiæti** (OSw) noun

amusement **OSw** *UL* Mb, *VmL* Mb

köp (OSw) **køp** (ODan) **kaup** (ON) noun

The many translations reflect the ambiguity of the verb *köpa* (OSw) *køpe* (ODan) *kaupa* (ON) 'to settle affairs', i.e. both 'to buy' and 'to sell' etc., from which this noun is derived. Appears in many legally significant compounds and some derivations.

agreement **OIce** *Jó* Kge 30, **ONorw** *FrL* Intr 17

arrangement **ONorw** *FrL* Intr 18

bargain **ONorw** *FrL* Rgb 48

buying **ODan** *SkL* 12, 30, 72, 77, *VSjL* 81

buying and selling **OIce** *Grg* Feþ 152

contract **OIce** *Jó* Llb 6, **ONorw** *FrL* Jkb 1

deal **OIce** *Grg* Arþ 127, *Jó* Kab 11, *Js* Kab 9

pay **OIce** *Grg* Þsþ 78, *Jó* Kab 25

purchase **ODan** *ESjL* 2, 3, *JyL* 2, *SkL* 50, **OSw**
DL Bb, *HL* Kkb, Äb, Mb, Jb, Kmb, Blb, Rb, *SdmL*
Kkb, Jb, Kmb, Tjdb, *YVgL* Tb, Jb, *ÄVgL* Jb, Tb

purchase agreement **OSw** *DL* Bb

sale **ODan** *SkL* 48, 81, *VSjL* 82, **OFar** *Seyð* 5,
OIce *Grg* Arþ 126, *Jó* Lbb 6, **OSw** *DL* Gb

selling **ODan** *VSjL* 82

trade **OIce** *Jó* Kab 11 Fml 5, **ONorw** *GuL*
Kpb, Kvb, Løb, Llb, Arb, Tjb, Olb

transaction **OIce** *Jó* Kab 12

wages **OIce** *Grg* Þsþ 80, *Js* Kab 19

See also: *legha, verkakaup*

köpa (OSw) **køpe** (ODan) **kaupa** (ON) verb

Originally 'to settle affairs', i.e. both 'to buy' and 'to sell' etc.

buy **ODan** *ESjL* 1–3, *JyL* 1–3, *SkL* 30, 47, 50, 51,
75, 77, 80, 129, 152, 239, *VSjL* 50, 79, 81, **OIce** *Grg*
Arþ 123, *Jó* Kab 11, **ONorw** *GuL* Krb, Kpb, Kvb,
Løb, Arb, Tfb, Tjb, Olb, Leb, **OSw** *DL* Bb, *HL* Kkb,
Äb, Mb, Jb, Kmb, *SdmL* Jb, Kmb, Tjdb, *SmL*, *YVgL*
Äb, Tb, Jb, Kvab, Föb, Add, *ÄVgL* Äb, Tb, Föb

contract to pay **OIce** *Grg* Þsþ 78

deal **OIce** *Grg* Arþ 125

exchange **OSw** *YVgL* Jb

gain **ONorw** *EidsL* 11.6

make a deal **OIce** *Js* Lbb 2

make a purchase **ODan** *JyL* 2, **OSw** *YVgL* Tb

purchase **ODan** *ESjL* 1, 2, **OSw**
DL Bb, *ÄVgL* Jb, Kva

redeem **ONorw** *GuL* Leb, Mhb

release **ONorw** *GuL* Mhb

seal a bargain **OIce** *Jó* Lbb 6

sell **OSw** *YVgL* Jb

trade **ONorw** *FrL* Rgb 48, **OSw** *SdmL* Kmb

Refs: Schlyter s.v. *köpa*

köpavin (OSw) noun

friend at purchases **OSw** *YVgL* Tb

köpfastar (pl.) (OSw) noun

transaction witnesses for a purchase **OSw** *SdmL* Jb

köpfærþ (OSw) **køpfærth** (ODan) **kaupferð** (ON) noun

business travel **ODan** *JyL* 1

merchant journey **OSw** *YVgL* Äb, *ÄVgL* Äb

trade voyage **OIce** *Jó* MagBref Fml 2, 6

trading journey **ONorw** *FrL* Intr 20

See also: *kaupför*

köpfæst (OSw) noun

confirmation of purchase **OSw** *YVgL* Jb, *ÄVgL* Jb
purchase **OSw** *ÄVgL* Jb
witness of purchase **OSw** *YVgL* Add

köpgilder (OSw) kiöpgilder (OSw) adj.

negotiable (i.e. in coin) **OSw** *UL* Äb, Mb, Blb

See also: *karlgilder*

köpi (OSw) køpe (ODan) kaupi (ON) köpe (OSw) noun

buyer **ONorw** *GuL* Olb
purchaser **OSw** *YVgL* Jb, *ÄVgL* Jb
salesman **ODan** *SkL* 139, 144
seller **ODan** *JyL* 2, 3, *SkL* 144

köplagh (OSw) noun

laws of trading **OSw** *SmL*

See also: *lagh*

köpmalabalker (OSw) noun

book concerning trade **OSw** *HL* För, Kmb
trade section **OSw** *SdmL* För, Kmb

See also: *balker, köp, mal (1)*

köpman (OSw) kaupmaþr (OGu) kaupmaðr (ON) noun

merchant **OGu** *GS* Ch. 3, **OIce** *Jó* Fml 5, 14,
ONorw *FrL* ArbB 13, **OSw** *UL* Kmb (table of contents only), *VmL* Kmb (rubric only)
salesman **OSw** *SdmL* Jb

köpoiorþ (OSw) køpejorth (ODan) kaupajörð (ON) noun

Bought land could be sold without the restrictions that applied to inherited land. In ODan SkL often appearing in the phrase *køpejorth ok bolfæ* 'bought land and movables' in the context of inheritance. In ONorw GuL appearing as a non-acceptable means of payment of fines.

bought land **ODan** *ESjL* 1, 3, *JyL* 1, 3, *SkL* 1, 5, 7, 22, 24–26, 30, *VSjL* 1, 3, 14
land which one buys **OSw** *HL* Blb
purchased land **ONorw** *GuL* Mhb,
OSw *YVgL* Äb, Rlb, Jb

See also: *aldaoþal, ærfþaiorþ*

Refs: Tamm and Vogt, eds, 2016, 307

köpruf (OSw) kauprof (ON) noun

breach of bargain **ONorw** *FrL* Jkb 4
breach of purchase **OSw** *YVgL* Jb, *ÄVgL* Jb
suspension of purchase **OSw** *DL* Bb

köpskatter (OSw) køpskat (ODan) kiöpskatter (OSw) noun

bought goods **ODan** *SkL* 230

wares **OSw** *UL* Jb

köpstaþer (OSw) kaupstaðr (ON) noun

It is unclear how the use of *köpstaþer* differed from that of *köpunger* (q.v.) and *torgh* (q.v.). When contrasted to the surrounding countryside (OSw SdmL, UL, VmL), it presumably referred to a market town. In SdmL appearing in the context of correct procedure for trade regarding specific witnesses and oaths to avoid accusation of theft or forgery, not least in the trade with objects such as weapons, horses and cattle, cloth, silver and gold. In UL and VmL appearing in the context of land exchange and in UL concerning a very specific killing. In OIce Jó (Kge) it refers to market towns as the home of foreign fathers of illegitimate children in Iceland, and in the context of benchmarks for pricing lost merchandise (Fml).

market town **OIce** *Jó* Kge 28 Fml 10, **OSw** *SdmL* Jb, Kmb, Mb, *UL* Mb, Jb, Kmb, *VmL* Mb, Jb, Kmb, Bb

See also: *köpunger*

köpstaþsman (OSw) noun

market town-dweller **OSw** *SdmL* Kmb, Tjdb

köpuman (OSw) köpa man (OSw) noun

purchaser **OSw** *DL* Bb

köpunger (OSw) køping (ODan) kaupungr (OGu) kaupangr (ON) noun

A trading center, market-place or town. As a proper noun Kaupangr refers to several place names throughout the North, the best known of which is perhaps Kaupang in Skiringssal west of Oslo. There is some semantic overlap with other designations for trading areas, such as *bær* (see *byr*), *kaupstaðr* (see *köpstaþer*), *bjarkey* and *torg* (see *torgh*). In FrL (e.g. KrbB 24) a *kaupangr* is often contrasted with a *herað* ('district', see *hæraþ*), as the summons process varied slightly between urban and rural areas. Dansih and Swedish and laws (e.g. JyL, UL) associate these trading areas with major roads, and infractions occurring there could incur additional fines similar to breaches of law committed at an assembly.

market town **ONorw** *FrL* Leb 11,
OSw *UL* Blb, *VmL* Bb
marketplace **OGu** *GL* A 6, 13,
OSw *UL* Mb, *VmL* Mb
town **ODan** *JyL* 1–3, *SkL* 69, **ONorw** *FrL* KrbA 10, 37 KrbB 24 Rgb 31 Kvb 23, *GuL* Arb
township **OIce** *Grg* Misc 248, **ONorw** *FrL* KrbB 20

See also: *bjarkeyjarréttr, byr, hæraþ, köpstaþer*

Refs: CV s.v. *kaupangr*; Fritzner s.v. *kaupangr*; GAO s.v. *kaupang*; Hertzberg s.v. *kaupangr*; KLNM s.v.v. *handelsplasser, köping, marked,*

stad, torvevæsen; ONP s.v. *kaupangr*; Skre
2007; Tamm & Vogt, eds, 2016, 46, 315

köpvitni (OSw) **kaupsvitni** (ON) **köpavitni** (OSw)
noun

purchase witness **OSw** *SdmL* Tjdb, Rb

testimony about purchase **OSw** *YVgL* Jb

testimony of purchase **OSw** *ÄVgL* Jb

witness to a sale **ONorw** *FrL* LlbB 2

See also: *kaupváttr, köp, vin, vitni*

köpþingafriþer (OSw) noun

The peace of the market held in the town of Strængnæs
in spring.

market peace **OSw** *SdmL* Rb

See also: *friþer, köpstaþer, köpunger, torgh, þing*

kötsunnudagher (OSw) noun

Shrove Sunday (meat Sunday) **OSw** *YVgL* Jb

köpingsman (ODan) **kaupangrsmaðr** (ON)
kaupangsmaðr (ON) noun

townsman **ODan** *JyL* 2, **ONorw**
FrL Leb 11, *GuL* Arb

lafrinzmæssa (OSw) **laurentiusmessa** (ON)
laurinzardagher (OSw) noun

Feast of St Lawrence **OSw** *UL* Kkb

Saint Lawrence's Day **OIce** *Grg*
Klþ 13, **OSw** *YVgL* Kkb

St Lawrence's Mass (10 August) **ONorw**
GuL Krb, **OSw** *ÖgL* Kkb

lagaafbrigði (ON) **lagaafbrigð** (ON) noun

deviation from the law **OIce** *Grg* Lbþ 220 Tíg 255

lagabeizla (ON) noun

lawful claim **OIce** *Jó* Llb 26

lagaboð (ON) noun

lawful offer of compensation **OIce** *Jó* Mah 17

lagabót (ON) noun

lawful compensation **ONorw** *FrL* Sab 1

lagafrest (ON) noun

legal deferral **OIce** *KRA* 29, **ONorw** *FrL* KrbB 20

lagagift (ON) noun

legal oblation **ONorw** *BorgL* 12

lagainnsetning (ON) noun

Legal provisions for the enclosure of livestock.

legal shutting in **OIce** *Jó* Llb 33

lagakaup (ON) noun

legal bargain **OIce** *Jó* Kab 25, **ONorw** *GuL* Løb

legal sale of land **OIce** *Jó* Lbb 6

legal trade **ONorw** *FrL* Rgb 48

lagakefli (ON) **lagarkefli** (ON) noun

law-stick **ONorw** *FrL* ArbB 30
Rgb 11 LlbA 23 LlbB 11

lagaleiga (ON) noun

legal amount of rent **ONorw** *FrL* Jkb 2

lagalöstr (ON) noun

lawbreaking **OIce** *Grg* Vís 86, 87

lagaórskurðr (ON) noun

A legal decision or verdict presented at the outcome
of a case. According to Jó (Mah 2 and Kab 21) this
decision was delivered by the law-man (ON *lögmaðr*,
see *laghmaþer*).

legal decision **OIce** *Jó* Mah 2 Kab 21

See also: *domber, órskurðr, skipan*

Refs: CV s.v. *lagaúrskurðr*; F s.v.
lagaorskurðr; Hertzberg

lagarefsing (ON) noun

*punishment in accordance with the
law* **OIce** *Jó* MagBref Mah 16

See also: *ræfsing*

lagaréttr (ON) noun

legal compensation **OIce** *Jó* Mah 30, *Js* Mah 36

lagasekð (ON) noun

legal fine **ONorw** *FrL* KrbA 27

lagasetning (ON) noun

The establishment of law; legislation.

law **ONorw** *FrL* Intr 16

Refs: CV s.v. *lagasetning*; Fritzner s.v.
lagasetning; Hertzberg s.v. *lagasetning*

lagaskilorð (ON) noun

legal provision **OIce** *Js* Mah 29, 31

provision of the law **OIce** *Jó* Mah 1, 14

lagasókn (ON) noun

lawful action **OIce** *Jó* Þfb 6

laggiertr (OGu) adj.

lawfully acceptable **OGu** *GL* A 25, 26

lagh (OSw) **logh** (ODan) **lag** (OGu) **lag** (ON) **lög** (ON)
logh (OSw) noun

Usually plural. Literally 'something laid', most
commonly in the general meaning 'law', with varying
degree of specificity (reflected in translations such as
'rule', 'law of the land', 'right' and 'legislation'). Also
the jurisdiction of a law (translated as 'jurisdiction',
'law district', 'legal district'), and various means to
obtain what is right, such as 'oath' and 'proof'. In the
singular occasionally more concrete, such as a defined
group of people (reflected in the translation 'guild').

agreement **ODan** *VSjL* 1, 2, 7

ban **OIce** *Jó* Llb 15

guild **ODan** *JyL* 2

jurisdiction **ONorw** *FrL* LlbB 1

law **ODan** *ESjL* 2, 3, *JyL* Fort, 1–3, *SkKL* 3, 13, *SkL* passim, *VSjL* 1, 13, 51, 58, 79, 84, 87, **OFar** *Seyð* 1, 4, **OGu** *GL* A 1, 7, 8, 19, 20, 23, 24f (64), 28, 36, 61, Add. 7 (B 49), **OIce** *Grg* passim, *Jó* passim, *Js* Mah 7 [passim possibly], *KRA* 6, 7 passim, **ONorw** *BorgL* 1.1 10.4, *EidsL* 22.1 30.4, *FrL* Intr 1, 7 KrbA 1, 27 KrbB 6 Mhb 7 passim, *GuL* Krb, Kpb, Kvb, Løb, Llb, Arb, Tfb, Mhb, Olb, Leb, **OSw** *DL* Mb, Bb, Gb, Tjdb, Rb, *HL* För, Kkb, Äb, Mb, Blb, Rb, *SdmL* För, Kgb, Gb, Äb, Jb, Bb, Kmb, Mb, Rb, Till, *SmL*, *UL* StfBM, För, Kgb, Äb, Mb, Jb, Kmb, Blb, Rb, *VmL* För, Kgb, Äb, Mb, Jb, Kmb, Bb, Rb, *YVgL* passim, *ÄVgL* Kkb, Md, Slb, Äb, Gb, Rlb, Jb, Tb, Föb, *ÖgL* Eb, Db

law district **ONorw** *FrL* Var 44, *GuL* Krb, Løb, Llb, Olb, Leb

law of the land **OSw** *HL* Blb

lawful proof **ODan** *JyL* 1

legal district **ONorw** *FrL* KrbA 39 ArbB 28

legislation **OGu** *GL* A 38

oath **ODan** *ESjL* 1–3, *JyL* 1–3, *SkKL* 6, 11, *SkL* passim, *VSjL* passim, **OGu** *GL* A 32, **OSw** *DL* Kkb, Mb, Bb, Tjdb, Rb, *HL* Kkb, Kgb, Mb, Rb, *SdmL* Conf, Kkb, Kgb, Mb, Tjdb, Rb, *UL* Kkb, Kgb, Mb, Rb, *VmL* Kkb, Kgb, Mb, Bb, Rb, *YVgL* Kkb, Gb, Rlb, Tb, Jb, Add, *ÄVgL* Äb, Jb, Kva, Tb, *ÖgL* Kkb

partnership **OIce** *Grg* Vís 97

person's share **ODan** *JyL* 3

place **OGu** *GL* A 23

proof **ODan** *JyL* 1, 2, *SkL* 75, 200, 203, *VSjL* 18, 39, 49, 57, 85, 87

proving **ODan** *JyL* 2

reason **ODan** *ESjL* 3

right **ODan** *ESjL* 3, *JyL* 1, **OSw** *YVgL* Jb, Kvab

right to prove **ODan** *ESjL* 3

rule **ODan** *ESjL* 1, 3, **OSw** *HL* Blb

standard value **OIce** *Grg* Feþ 167

stipulated fine **OGu** *GL* A 8

Expressions:

at lagum (OGu) **at lögum** (ON)

in accordance with the law **OIce** *Grg* Þsþ 25

lawfully **OGu** *GL* A 26

biuþa lagh (OSw)

offer a defence **OSw** *UL* Kkb

offer an oath **OSw** *UL* Kgb, Rb

eftir lögum (ON)

in accordance with the law **OFar** *Seyð* 1

fæsta lagh (OSw)

promise an oath **OSw** *UL* Rb *VmL* Kkb, Rb

ganga lagh (OSw)

swear an oath **OSw** *UL* Mb *VmL* Kkb, Bb

guþs lagh (OSw)

God's law **OSw** *SmL* *ÄVgL* Äb

kristendoms logh (ODan)

Christian law **ODan** *JyL* 1

lagh ok landsræt, lagh ok lanzræt (OSw)

law and custom of the province **OSw** *UL* Äb *VmL* Äb

mæþ logh, mæþ lohum (ODan) **mæþ laghum, miþ lagum** (OGu)

lawfully **ODan** *SkL* 8, 66, 152, 180 *VSjL* 58 **OGu** *GL* A 37

according to the law **ODan** *SkL* 60

mæþ rætum lohum (ODan)

lawfully **ODan** *SkL* 7

uæræ uiþær loh (ODan)

prove **ODan** *SkL* 75

uæræ i lohum mæþ (ODan)

swear with **ODan** *SkL* 78

See also: *biuþa, eþer, fæsta, rætter, vinna*

Refs: Cleasby and Vigfusson s.v. *lag*; Fritzner s.v. *lög*; Hertzberg s.v. *lög*; ONP s.v. *lag*; Schlyter s.v. *lagh*

lagha (OSw) **lagh** (ODan) **laga** (OGu) *adj.*

In OSw appearing in many phrases corresponding to compounds with ODan and ON nouns *lagh-/lög-* 'law-'. Examples are *lagha forfall* 'lawful excuse', *lagha domber* 'lawful judgment', *lagha rætter* 'right law', *lagha stæmna* 'legal meeting', *lagha thing* 'lawful assembly', *lagha alder* 'legal age', *lagha hus* 'prescribed houses', *lagha garth* 'lawful fence', *lagha mæn* 'prudent men', *lagha tompt* 'rightful/legal ground'. It is rarely defined what makes a certain object or action legal.

according to the law **OSw** *DL* Bb

lawful **ODan** *ESjL* 2, 3, *JyL* 1–3, *SkKL* 7, *SkL* 49, 78, 83, *VSjL* 10, 60, 82–84, **OGu** *GL* A 24f (64), 39, **OSw** *DL* Eb, *HL* Kkb, Kgb, Äb, Mb, *SmL*, *UL* Kkb, Kgb, Äb, Mb, Blb, *VmL* Kkb, Kgb, Äb, Mb, Bb, *YVgL* Gb, Rlb, Tb, Jb, *ÄVgL* Kkb, Gb, Tb, *ÖgL* Kkb, Eb, Db, Vm

legal **ODan** *ESjL* 1, 3, *JyL* 1, **OGu** *GL* A 11, 12, 20, 30, Add. 7 (B 49), **OSw** *DL* Eb, Mb, Gb, Tjdb, Rb, *HL* Mb, Jb, Blb, *SdmL* Conf, Kkb, Kgb, Gb, Jb, Bb, Mb, Tjdb, Rb, *UL* StfBm, Kkb, Kgb, Äb, Mb, Jb, Blb, Rb, *VmL* Kkb, Kgb, Äb, Mb, Jb, Bb, Rb, *YVgL* passim, *ÄVgL* Smb, Slb, Gb, Jb, Tb, Föb *prescribed* **OSw** *SmL*, *ÄVgL* Gb

prudent **ODan** *SkKL* 7

regular **ODan** *ESjL* 3

right **OSw** *YVgL* Tb, *ÄVgL* Tb

rightful **OSw** *YVgL* Jb

stipulated **OSw** *SdmL* Kkb

valid **OSw** *DL* Rb, *ÄVgL* Kkb

See also: *laghlika*, *laghliker*

laghabalker (OSw) noun

law section **OSw** *SdmL* För

See also: *balker*, *lagh*

laghabötir (pl.) (OSw) **lögbót** (ON) noun

lawful fines **OSw** *HL* Kkb, Kgb

See also: *bot*

laghagærþ (OSw) **lagh gærþ** (OSw) noun

oath-taking **OSw** *VmL* Kkb, Jb

laghakland (OSw) noun

legal claim **OSw** *YVgL* Utgb, Add

laghaloter (OSw) noun

legal part **OSw** *YVgL* Föb, Add, *ÄVgL* Föb

laghalös (OSw) **laghløs** (ODan) adj.

freed from proof **ODan** *JyL* 1

illegal **OSw** *YVgL* Tb, *ÄVgL* Tb

laghaskillinger (OSw) **laghskillinger** (OSw) noun

legal sum **OSw** *SdmL* Bb, *UL* Blb, *VmL* Bb

laghastæmna (OSw) **laghestævne** (ODan) **lagastefna** (ON) **lögstefna** (ON) noun

agreed day **ODan** *SkL* 188

day decided **ODan** *SkL* 83, 188, 231

fixed day **ODan** *SkL* 183

lawful summons **OIce** *Jó* Þjb 5

legal meeting **OSw** *YVgL* Add

legal summons **OIce** *Grg* Þsþ 31 Fjl 221 Tíg 256, *Jó* Þfb 9 Llb 54, *Js* Kab 2 Þjb 4

legal time limit **ONorw** *BorgL* 4.1 17.1

provided day **ODan** *SkL* 183

summons at the assembly **ONorw** *GuL* Løb, Llb, Tjb, Olb

summons to the assembly **ONorw** *FrL* LlbA 26

See also: *laghdagh*, *stæmna*

laghasökning (OSw) noun

legal prosecution **OSw** *SdmL* Tjdb

laghbinda (OSw) verb

lawfully convict **OSw** *UL* Mb, Rb, *VmL* Rb

See also: *vinna*

laghbiuþa (OSw) **laghbjuthe** (ODan) verb

Land that was to be sold had to be offered to the legal heirs first.

follow the law **OSw** *HL* Rb

lawfully offer **ODan** *ESjL* 3, *JyL* 1, **OSw** *UL* Jb, Add. 10

legally bid **OSw** *YVgL* Add

legally offer **OSw** *SdmL* Jb

legally offer to the kin **OSw** *HL* Jb

notify **ODan** *VSjL* 22

offer a legal option **OSw** *VmL* Jb

offer according to the law **OSw** *YVgL* Jb, Add, *ÄVgL* Jb

offer legally **OSw** *YVgL* Jb, Add

offer with a purchase option to one's kin/offer legal option on ownership **OSw** *DL* Bb

publicly offer **ODan** *SkL* 42, 51, *VSjL* 21

See also: *buþsiorþ*

laghbok (OSw) **laghbok** (ODan) **lögbók** (ON) noun

law **OSw** *HL* För

law code **OFar** *Seyð* 1

law-book **ODan** *JyL* 3, **OIce** *Jó* MagBref Þfb 4, 9 Sg 1 Mah 4 Kge 9 Llb 20, *Js* Þfb 3 Mah 15, 35, **ONorw** *EidsL* 10.2, *FrL* Intr 9, 21 Tfb 2, **OSw** *DL* Rb, *SdmL* Conf, Till, *YVgL* Add, *ÄVgL* Kkb, *ÖgL* Kkb

National Law **OFar** *Seyð* 10

See also: *bok (1)*, *lagh*

laghbundin (OSw) adj.

lawfully caught **OSw** *HL* Mb

laghböta (OSw) verb

compensate according to the law **OSw** *ÄVgL* Tb

See also: *böta*, *lagh*

laghdagh (ODan) noun

day decided **ODan** *JyL* 3, *SkL* 19, 67

day set by the assembly **ODan** *JyL* 2

fixed day/date **ODan** *JyL* 1

lawful day **ODan** *ESjL* 2, *JyL* 2, *VSjL* 22, 71

lawful day set by the assembly **ODan** *JyL* 2

set day **ODan** *SkL* 42

laghdele (ODan) verb

complete a lawful case **ODan** *JyL* 2

lawfully pursue **ODan** *JyL* 2

laghdeling (ODan) noun

lawful pursuit **ODan** *ESjL* 2

laghdöma (OSw) verb

deem right **OSw** *YVgL* Jb, Kvab

legally judge **OSw** *SdmL* Mb

laghe (ODan) noun

    assault **ODan** *JyL* 3

laghealder (ODan) noun

    legal age **ODan** *JyL* 1, 2

laghedom (ODan) lagadómr (ON) lögdómr (ON) noun

A private court established in the way prescribed by the law.

    lawful court **OIce** *Grg* Þsþ 20, 45, *Jó* Þfb 8, **ONorw** *FrL* Var 46, *GuL* Krb

    lawful judgement **ODan** *ESjL* 2, *VSjL* 58, **OFar** *Seyð* 1

    legal decision **OIce** *Jó* Kge 29

    legal judgement **OIce** *Jó* Mah 11 Kge 26 Llb 26, 30 Þjb 6 Fml 16

    verdict **ONorw** *FrL* Jkb 8

See also: *skiladómr*

lagheeghere (ODan) noun

    lawful owner **ODan** *JyL* 2

laghegarth (ODan) löggarðr (ON) noun

A wall built to legal specifications. Defined in Grg Lbþ 181 and Js Lbb 22 as being the height of an average-sized man's shoulder and five feet thick at the base and three at the top. Probably synonymous with OSw *lagha garth(er)* (see *garþer*). According to the Icelandic laws, legal walls could only be built between work seasons during the summer.

    lawful fence **ODan** *JyL* 3

    legal wall **OIce** *Grg* Lbþ 181, 188, *Jó* Llb 22, 23, *Js* Lbb 22

See also: *garþer*

Refs: CV s.v. *löggarðr*; Hertzberg s.v. *löggarðr*; KLNM s.v. *hegn*

laghegift (ODan) noun

    lawful reward **ODan** *VSjL* 86

lagherep (ODan) noun

    lawful roping **ODan** *JyL* 2

See also: *lagha, rep*

laghesar (ODan) noun

    wound covered by the law **ODan** *ESjL* 2

lagheskip (ODan) noun

    regular ship **ODan** *ESjL* 3

laghestævnedagh (ODan) noun

    fixed day **ODan** *SkL* 214

laghevæth (ODan) lögveð (ON) noun

A legal pledge. A legal pledge, or a right of preemption (ON *lögmáli*), could be placed upon land or an object of value by the person selling it. Legal pledges could be sold or inherited.

    lawful pledge **ODan** *JyL* 3

    legal pledge **OIce** *Grg* Lbþ 192, *Jó* Lbb 9, *Js* Lbb 6

See also: *laghmal, væþ*

Refs: CV s.v. *lögveð*; Fritzner s.v. *lögveð*; Hertzberg s.v. *lögveð*; Hoff 2012, 191–92; KLNM s.v. *pant*; Páll Sigurðsson 2016, 39–40

laghfangen (OSw) adj.

    legally acquired (land) **OSw** *UL* Add. 10, *YVgL* Gb, Add

laghfast (ODan) adj.

    prudent **ODan** *ESjL* 1–3, *JyL* 3, *SkKL* 4–7, 9, 11, 12, *SkL* 19, 29, 51, 53, *VSjL* 76, 79, 82, 87

laghfylghia (OSw) verb

    bring a case lawfully **OSw** *UL* Mb

laghfylla (OSw) verb

    lawfully convict **OSw** *UL* Mb, *VmL* Mb

See also: *laghbinda, laghfælder*

laghfælder (OSw) laghfæld (ODan) lagfeldr (OGu) adj.

    lawfully convicted **ODan** *JyL* 2, 3, **OSw** *UL* Rb, *VmL* Rb

    lawfully dismissed **OGu** *GL* A 31

    legally convicted **OSw** *HL* Rb

    sentenced **OSw** *YVgL* Add

See also: *fælla, laghfylla, laghvinna*

laghfæstning (ODan) lögfesting (ON) noun

    promise of oaths **ODan** *ESjL* 2

    right to place a ban **OIce** *Jó* Llb 17

See also: *lýrittr*

laghgifter (OSw) laggiptr (OGu) adj.

    lawfully married **OGu** *GL* A 21, 22, **OSw** *SdmL* Gb, *UL* Äb

    lawfully wedded **OSw** *ÖgL* Db

    legally married **OSw** *YVgL* Äb

laghgive (ODan) verb

    lawfully marry **ODan** *VSjL* 69

laghgæld (OSw) laghagæld (OSw) noun

    legal rate **OSw** *UL* Blb

    legal restitution **OSw** *UL* Blb, *VmL* Bb

laghhæfþa (OSw) verb

    have legal possession of something **OSw** *ÖgL* Kkb

laghkallaþer (OSw) adj.

    lawfully announced **OSw** *HL* Äb

    lawfully summoned **OSw** *ÖgL* Kkb, Db

    legally summoned **OSw** *HL* Rb

laghklanda (OSw) verb

    claim **OSw** *ÄVgL* Föb

See also: *klanda, lagh*

laghkrævje (ODan) verb

demand **ODan** *JyL* 3

laghlika (OSw) **loghlike** (ODan) **laglika** (OGu) **lögliga** (ON) adv.

according to the law **ODan** *JyL* 1, **ONorw** *FrL* Intr 16

in law **OSw** *UL* Kgb, Äb, *VmL* Äb

lawfully **ODan** *ESjL* 1–3, *JyL* 1, 2, *SkL* 83, *VSjL* 69, 84, **OGu** *GL* A 26, 28, *GS* Ch. 4, **OIce** *Jó* Mah 1, 3 Þjb 2 Fml 1, 25, *Js* Kab 3, *KRA* 4, 9, **OSw** *DL* Eb, Bb, *HL* Äb, *SdmL* Kkb, Kgb, Gb, Jb, Bb, Kmb, Mb, Tjdb, Till, *UL* Kkb, Kgb, Äb, Mb, Jb, Blb, Rb, *VmL* Kkb, Kgb, Äb, Mb, Jb, Bb, Rb, *YVgL* Drb, Tb, *ÖgL* Kkb, Eb, Db

legally **ODan** *SkL* 50, 226, **OSw** *DL* Kkb, *HL* Äb, Mb, Jb, Blb, Rb, *UL* Äb, Mb, Jb, Add. 18, *VmL* Äb, Mb, Jb, *YVgL* Kkb, Add

See also: *lagha*, *laghliker*

laghliker (OSw) **laglikr** (OGu) **lögligr** (ON) adj.

lawful **OFar** *Seyð* 12, **OGu** *GS* Ch. 4, **OIce** *Jó* MagBref Þfb 1, 2 HT 2 Mah 2 Kab 8 Fml 1, *Js* Þfb 1 Kdb 2 Mah 18 Kvg 2, *KRA* 7, 10, **ONorw** *FrL* Intr 4, **OSw** *SdmL* Till

legal **OSw** *HL* Blb

legitimate **OSw** *YVgL* Kkb

See also: *lagha*, *laghlika*, *lögfullr*, *rætter*

laghlysa (OSw) verb

announce lawfully **OSw** *DL* Bb

lawfully proclaim **OSw** *HL* Mb

legally announce **OSw** *SdmL* Bb, Mb, Tjdb, *YVgL* Tb

See also: *lysa*, *thingljuse*

laghlysning (OSw) noun

lawful announcement **OSw** *ÖgL* Db

laghmal (OSw) **laghmal** (ODan) **lagamál** (ON) **lögmál** (ON) **laghamal** (OSw) noun

That which is prescribed by, handled by or decided according to the law (mainly secular but occasionally ecclesiastical).

article of the law **OIce** *Grg* Klþ 4, 18 Þsþ 76 Lrþ 117 Lbþ 219, *Jó* Llb 17, 26, *KRA* 9, **ONorw** *FrL* KrbB 13

case **ODan** *JyL* 2

case in which a defendant defends himself with an oath **OSw** *HL* Rb

commandment **OIce** *Jó* HT 2, *Js* Kdb 2

lawful case **ODan** *ESjL* 2

legal case **OIce** *Jó* MagBref, **OSw** *SdmL* Conf

See also: *laghevæth*

Refs: Cleasby and Vigfusson s.v. *lögmál*; Fritzner s.v. *lögmál*; Hertzberg s.v. *lögmál*; Schlyter s.v. *laghmal*

laghmansdöme (OSw) noun

lawman's jurisdiction **OSw** *SdmL* Kmb, Add

lawmanship **OSw** *YVgL* Add

laghmanspænningar (pl.) (OSw) noun

A fee, presumably annual, to the lawman. It is not stated who was to pay.

payment to a lawman **OSw** *SdmL* Till

Refs: Schlyter s.v. *laghmans pænningar*

laghmaþer (OSw) **lögmaðr** (ON) **laghman** (OSw) **laghmandr** (OSw) noun

One of the king's officials; a royal judge. The *laghmaþer* was a prominent judicial figure throughout the Nordic lands during the medieval period. In most areas one of the prime responsibilities of the *laghmaþer* was the organization of assemblies (*þing*). *Lagmenn* were paid from a combination of public funds and royal grants.

In Sweden the term *laghmaþer* probably originally referred to a man learned in law who advised during assemblies. A *laghmaþer* was of particular import in Sweden, as he was placed over an entire province by the king. He led assemblies, suggested and framed judgments, recited law at assemblies annually from memory, presented official notices and legally recognize newly elected kings ahead of the *eriksgata* (q.v.), assessor in the ?provincial tax committee (? Sw *beskattningsnämnd*). Initially *laghmæn* were legislators in Sweden, but from the late thirteenth century on they were almost exclusively judges. In HL the *laghmaþer* seems to refer almost exclusively to judges. According to a charter dated to 1270, the *laghmaþer* in Västergötland was the recipient of a tax called *lagmanskyld* in the sum of fifty cattle every four years. In both Sweden and in Norway the *laghmaþer* had the right to demand hospitality from householders on the way to and from assemblies (cf. e.g. UL Kmb 10). After MEL was promulgated in Sweden, and perhaps even before, the *laghmaþer* had the power to convene extraordinary assemblies. One of most important duties of the *laghmaþer* in MEL was to hold four 'land' assemblies (*landsþing*) every year. The *laghmaþer* was also in charge of the general assembly for the areas governed by the Göta laws (*aldra göta þing*). ÄVgL (Rlb 3) stipulates that a *laghmaþer* must be the son of a householder (*bonde*, q.v.) and be elected by 'all householders' for life. The post was not hereditary, but it often fell to magnate families and later to members of the landed nobility. *Laghmæn* were commonly among the king's council and were appointed by him and the bishop up until the sixteenth century, when it became a noble privilege to select *lagmenn* until 1668. In Sweden the office of *laghmaþer* was not abolished until 1849.

In Norway a *lögmaðr* could refer to anyone knowledgeable in legal matters as well as an official title. They remained legal councilors until the late twelfth century when a *lögmaðr* became a royal official. In the mid-thirteenth century they were given judicial powers and control of the *lagting*. As an official he was entitled to a portion of certain fines (cf. FrL Intr 1). Besides these a portion of royal estate was set aside for their maintenance (cf. FrL Intr 16). In later amendments *lögmenn* also received a fee from attendees at assemblies. A *lögmaðr* in Norway was required to 'recite the law', i.e. announce judgments which occurred at assemblies. Like the Icelandic Lawspeaker (*lögsögumaðr*, q.v.), the Norwegian *lögmaðr* was also responsible for dictating the law to the general public (cf. EidsL 1.10 and FrL Rgb 1). During the twelfth century the position of *lögmaðr* was absorbed into the royal sphere and became one of the king's officials. He was also charged with prosecuting certain cases, such as those in which were illicitly resolved outside of a court. Occasionally several *lögmenn* were assembled to decide on a case. As in Sweden, the *lögmaðr* eventually became a type of judge in Norway and is referred to as such in e.g. MLL. Likewise in MLL the *lögmaðr* was responsible for setting up the boundaries (*vébönd*, q.v.) around the assembly and around the Law Council (*lögrétta*, q.v.). Early on *lögmenn* were drawn from among the *hersir* ('local chiefs, lords') and then from the landed men (*lendir menn*, see *lænder*). The office of *lagmann* was not abolished in Norway until 1797, and it was subsequently revived in 1890 as a new type of official.

In Iceland the *lögmaðr* replaced the *lögsögumaðr* after the Commonwealth Period. The term appears first in Js and subsequently in Jó and numerous charters. In Iceland the *lögmenn* were appointed by the king, and from 1277–83 there were two of them. They directed the General Assembly (*alþingi*, q.v.) and chaired the Law Council (*lögrétta*), which by this time was now a court rather than a legislative body. According to an ordinance issued in 1294 a *lögmaðr* in Iceland had to be a member of a chieftain's (*góði*, q.v.) family. In later sources the term *lögmaðr* is often applied to earlier persons who did not bear such a title at the time. Icelandic *lögmenn* continued to be appointed until 1800 when the General Assembly was dissolved.

Macek (2009, 242) makes a distinction between the *lögmaðr* and one of its translations: lawyer. Where the latter is a profession involving formal education and practice, the former, she states, was a relative or friend to whom one turned for legal assistance.

lawman **OFar** *Seyð* 0, **ONorw** *EidsL* 30.11 44, *FrL* Intr 1, **OSw** *HL* Kkb, Rb, *SdmL* Conf, Kkb, Kgb, Kmb, Rb, Till, *UL* StfBM, För, Kkb, Kgb, Mb, Kmb, Rb, Add. 18, *VmL* Kmb (correction), Rb, *YVgL* Äb, Gb, Rlb, Tb, Jb, Föb, Add, *ÄVgL* Rlb, Tb, *ÖgL* Kkb, Db
legal expert **OIce** *Grg* Lsþ 116 Lrþ 117, *Js* Mah 7, 29
magistrate **OIce** *Js* Þfb 2, 3 Lbb 5
presiding judge **OIce** *Jó* MagBref Þfb 2, 3 Sg 3 Mah 2
See also: *domari, hærapshöfþingi, lagh, landsdomari, lögsögumaðr, maþer, sysluman*
Refs: CV s.v. *lögmaðr*; Einar Arnórsson 1945, 170–90; F s.v. *lögmaðr*; FJ s.v. *lagman*; Jón Víðar Sigurðsson 2011a; KLNM s.v.v. *Allra Göta thing, embedsindtægter, häradshövding, lagman, lagting, rettarting, rettargang, stadsstyrelse*; Lindkvist 2007; Schulmann 2010; SNL s.v. *lagmann*

laghmæla (OSw) verb
legally address **OSw** *SdmL* Kmb

laghmæli (OSw) **laghmæle** (ODan) noun
claim **ODan** *ESjL* 3
law **OSw** *YVgL* Äb, Jb, *ÄVgL* Äb, Jb

laghsagha (OSw) **lögsaga** (ON) noun
Literally, 'law speaking' or 'law saying', which might be a translational borrowing of the Latin, *jurisdiction*. This word is used in three distinct meanings. The closest to the literal meaning is the formal recitation of the law by a lawman, for example in the OIce Grg, also including the office of the man who does the recitation. The second is the written manifestation of the law — the legislation itself, and the third is the jurisdiction over which a particular version of the law is relevant; this last could be a grouping of a number of provinces, a single province or a smaller division thereof. In the third meaning, the word is often coupled with *land* (q.v.) in an alliterative expression that seems to be synonymic. A distinction is drawn in UL between *hundari* (q.v.), *folkland* (q.v.), and *laghsagha* in such a way that it is evident that increasing areas of authority are referenced. Wessén clearly equates *laghsaga* with 'landskap', province.
jurisdiction **OSw** *SdmL* Tjdb, Till, *UL* Mb, Jb, Rb, *VmL* Mb, Jb, *ÖgL* Eb, Db
law-speaking **OIce** *Grg* Klþ 19
Lawspeakership **OIce** *Grg* Lsþ 116
legal district **OSw** *DL* Bb
legislation **OSw** *UL* För
recitation of the law **OSw** *SdmL* Rb, *SmL*, *UL* Rb, *VmL* Rb

statement of the law **OSw** *SmL*

See also: *folkland*, *hundari*, *lagh*,
laghmaþer, *lögsögumaðr*

Refs: KLNM, s.v. *lagsaga*; Schlyter 1877,
s.v. *laghsagha*; SL VmL, 103 note 198

laghsighia (OSw) verb

lawfully relinquish **OSw** *UL* Jb

laghskila (OSw) noun

judgement **OSw** *UL* Mb

legal district **OSw** *DL* Bb

laghskipta (OSw) verb

divide according to law **OSw** *YVgL* Kvab, *ÄVgL* Kva

legally divide **OSw** *DL* Bb

parcel legally **OSw** *YVgL* Add

See also: *lagh*, *skipta*

laghskipter (OSw) adj.

lawfully divided **OSw** *ÖgL* Db

See also: *laghskipta*

laghslit (OSw) noun

breach of the law **OSw** *SdmL* Mb

contempt of the law **OSw** *HL* Kgb

fine **OSw** *HL* Mb

penalty **OSw** *UL* Mb

laghsman (ODan) noun

followers **ODan** *SkL* 88

See also: *atvistarmaþer*, *fylghi*,
haldbani, *umstaþumæn (pl.)*

laghstandin (OSw) adj.

legally set **OSw** *SdmL* Jb

legally valid **OSw** *VmL* Jb

stood for a lawful period **OSw** *UL* Add. 10

laghstæmna (OSw) verb

lawfully sue **OSw** *YVgL* Add

legally summon **OSw** *SdmL* Till

laghsökia (OSw) **laghsøkje** (ODan) verb

lawfully sue **ODan** *JyL* 2, **OSw** *ÖgL* Db

legally prosecute **OSw** *SdmL* Mb, Tjdb

sue **ODan** *JyL* 2, **OSw** *HL* Rb

take action **ODan** *JyL* 2, 3

laghtakin (OSw) **lögtekinn** (ON) adj.

according to the law **OSw** *YVgL* Gb

included in the law **OIce** *Grg* Klþ 15, 18

lawfully claimed **OSw** *UL* Äb, *VmL* Äb

lawfully taken **OSw** *HL* Äb, *SdmL* Gb

laghvaksen (ODan) adj.

of age **ODan** *SkL* 49, 50

laghvara (OSw) **laghvarna** (OSw) verb

lawfully claim **OSw** *ÖgL* Kkb

lawfully tell **OSw** *ÖgL* Kkb

legally inform **OSw** *SdmL* Kkb, *UL* Kkb, *VmL* Kkb

tell according to the law **OSw** *YVgL* Föb

laghvardnaþer (OSw) noun

safeguard **OSw** *HL* Kgb

See also: *lagh*, *varþnaþer*

laghvinna (OSw) **laghvinne** (ODan) verb

find guilty **OSw** *UL* Mb, *VmL* Mb

lawfully convict **OSw** *DL* Kkb, *UL*
Äb, Mb, Rb, Add. 9, *VmL* Äb

legally convict **OSw** *SdmL* Äb, *YVgL* Add

legally decide **OSw** *ÖgL* Kkb

legally recognize **OSw** *HL* Kgb

proceed **ODan** *ESjL* 3

prove in law **OSw** *UL* Äb, *VmL* Äb

try and lawfully convict **OSw** *HL* Mb

See also: *fælla*, *lagh*, *læggia*, *vinna*, *viþerbinda*

laghværje (ODan) verb

lawfully defend **ODan** *ESjL* 3

laghværn (OSw) noun

legal fencing **OSw** *SdmL* Bb

laghþing (OSw) **laghthing** (ODan) **lögþing** (ON)
lögþingi (ON) **laghaþing** (OSw) noun

A *þing* 'assembly' that 1) was legal, i.e. held at the
right time and place etc., 2) upheld and sanctioned
the law, 3) covered the ONorw administrative/judicial
district *lög* (see *lagh*) and was held once a year for
those nominated from each *fylki* (q.v.). It is unclear
whether the OSw phrase *lagha þing* was synonymous
with the OSw compound.

assembly **ODan** *ESjL* 3, *JyL* 2

legal assembly **OIce** *Jó* Þfb 1, 4, *Js* Þfb
1, **OSw** *SdmL* Jb, Bb, Kmb, Mb, Rb

legal thing assembly **ONorw** *GuL* Krb,
OSw *DL* Gb, Rb, *UL* Äb, Mb, Jb, Blb, Rb,
Add. 12, 15, *VmL* Äb, Mb, Jb, Bb, Rb

See also: *afkænnuþing*, *lagh*, *urþinga*, *þing*,
þingariþ, *þingfastar (pl.)*, *þinglami*

Refs: Cleasby and Vigfusson s.v. *lögþing*; Fritzner
s.v. *lögþing*; Hertzberg s.v. *lögþingi*; KLNM s.v.
lagting; Lund s.v. *laghthing*; Schlyter s.v. *laghþing*

laghþinga (OSw) verb

prosecute at a legal thing **OSw** *HL* Mb

summon to legal assemblies **OSw**
UL Äb, Rb, *VmL* Kgb, Äb

See also: *þing*

lagkauptr (OGu) adj.

legally purchased **OGu** *GL* A 28

lagreka (OGu) verb

lawfully secure **OGu** *GL* Add. 8 (B 55)

lagryþia (OGu) verb

lay a legal claim **OGu** *GL* A 10, 17, Add. 2 (B 17)

lagsmaðr (ON) noun

companion **OIce** *Grg* Rsþ 230, *Jó*
Llb 66, **ONorw** *GuL* Leb

laigi (OGu) noun

This refers to land worth a certain amount in rent. The word was originally used in connection with the rent to be paid by a tenant farmer. The expression *marka laigi* came later to be used in reference to any area of land that would fetch a mark of silver in annual rent, if tenanted, in the context of inheritance, dowry and punishment for misappropriation of land. This usage seems to have continued into the eighteenth century in Gotland. It is not clear how the rental value was calculated and all the numerical evidence comes from a much later period. According to Schlyter's glossary, it was the equivalent of *markland* (q.v.) in UL and elsewhere in the Svea laws, giving for comparison the passage in UL Jb 1. Here it is stated that rent is one twenty-fourth of the freehold value of the land. If the same relationship (ignoring the actual value of a *mark*) applied on Gotland a *mark laigi* would have been land to the freehold value of twenty-four *marker* of silver or three *marker* of gold. The basis for land taxation was freehold value, but this could also be expressed in acreage, varying from district to district depending on the fertility of the soil.

land bringing/valued at/worth (a specified amount) in rent **OGu** *GL* A 20, 28, 63

See also: *attunger, landboe, legha, leghia, markland*

Refs: KLNM s.v. *jordleige*; Peel 2015, 138−39 note 20/91; Schlyter 1877, s.v. *laigi*; SL GL, 269 note 39

laigulenningr (OGu) **leiglendingr** (ON) noun

The word used in GL for a tenant, particularly a tenant farmer. The word is not known from Swedish or Danish sources, but is found in Norwegian and Icelandic sources. The sense is the same as *landboe*, 'someone living on or using another's land on payment of a lease'. Wessén considers that the word is derived from the combination *leigu-land*, 'land put out to lease'.

tenant **OFar** *Seyð* 2, **OGu** *GL* A 3,
OIce *Grg* Klþ 4 Lbþ 220, *Jó* Llb 42, *Js*
Lbb 11, 13, **ONorw** *FrL* LlbB 3

See also: *aboi, afradskarl, garthsæte, innismaþer, laigi, landboe, leghia, leghomaþer, leiguliði*

Refs: KLNM s.v.v. *landbo, leiglending*; Peel 2015, 96 note 3/18; Schlyter 1877, s.v. *laigulenninger*; SL GL, 247 note 7

laika (OGu) verb

Expressions:

laika at (OGu)

assault **OGu** *GL* A 19

lamabarning (ON) noun

crippling beating **OIce** *Grg* Vís 111

lamb (OSw) **lamb** (OGu) **lamb** (ON) noun

lamb **ONorw** *GuL* Llb, Kvr, Tjb,
OSw *UL* Kkb, Kgb, *VmL* Kkb

sheep **OGu** *GL* A 42, 43, 65

See also: *bolamb*

lan (OSw) **lan** (ODan) **lán** (ON) noun

loan **ODan** *ESjL* 3, *JyL* 2, 3, *SkL* 234, **OIce** *Grg*
Fjl 221, *Jó* Kab 21 Þjb 1, 16, *Js* Lbb 1 Kab 16,
OSw *DL* Bb, *SdmL* Kmb, Mb, Tjdb, *UL* Mb, Kmb,
VmL Mb, *YVgL* Kkb, Rlb, Tb, *ÄVgL* Rlb, Tb

lana (OSw) **lane** (ODan) **læne** (ODan) **læna** (OSw)
verb

borrow **OSw** *DL* Bb

lend **ODan** *ESjL* 1−3, *JyL* 2, 3, *SkL* 234, **OSw**
SdmL Kmb, *YVgL* Kkb, Rlb, Add, *ÄVgL* Rlb

See also: *lan*

lanardroten (OSw) **lánardróttinn** (ON) **landroten**
(OSw) **landsdroten** (OSw) **lönar droten** (OSw)
noun

landowner **ONorw** *GuL* Llb, Arb,
OSw *YVgL* Äb, *ÄVgL* Äb

liege lord **ONorw** *GuL* Krb

lord **OSw** *YVgL* Add

master **OSw** *ÄVgL* Urb

See also: *kununger*

land (OSw) **land** (ODan) **land** (OGu) **land** (ON) noun

1) arable land, 2) province, kingdom, 3) ground, 4) shore, 5) property, 6) countryside as opposed to town and 7) parcel of land. As a place-name element, it means 'large island or peninsula' for example Öland, Langeland, Lolland.

authorities **OGu** *GL* A 4, 13, 21, 24,
28, 37, 63, 65, Add. 6 (B 49)

country **OGu** *GL* A 28, *GS* Ch. 3, 4, **OIce**
Grg passim, *Jó* Kab 10, *Js* Mah 1, 28 Kab 3,
ONorw *GuL* Krb, Kpb, Kvb, Løb, Llb, Arb,
Tfb, Reb, Mhb, Tjb, Olb, Leb, **OSw** *DL* Kkb,
HL Rb, *SdmL* Kgb, *UL* Jb, *ÄVgL* Md

countryside **ODan** *JyL* 2, **OSw** *SdmL* Jb, Kmb, *UL* Mb, Jb, *VmL* Jb, Kmb

estate **OIce** *Grg* Tíg 266

island **OGu** *GS* Ch. 1, 3

islanders **OGu** *GS* Ch. 3

kingdom **ONorw** *FrL* Rgb 3 LlbB 5

land **ODan** *JyL* Fort, *SkKL* 3, **OGu** *GL* A 49, Add. 8 (B 55), *GS* Ch. 1, 3, **OIce** *Grg* Bat 114 Arþ 122, *Jó* Þfb 5 Mah 2, *Js* Mah 5, **ONorw** *BorgL* 9.3, *GuL* Krb, Tfb, Leb, Mhb, Kvr, **OSw** *DL* Bb, *HL* För, Kkb, Kgb, Blb, Rb, *SdmL* Äb, *UL* Kgb, Mb, Jb, Blb, *YVgL* Urb, Rlb, Kvab, *ÄVgL* Urb, Kva

landed property **ONorw** *GuL* Mhb, Krb

people of the island **OGu** *GS* Ch. 1, 2, 3

people of the land **OSw** *HL* Rb

province **ODan** *ESjL* 1–3, *JyL* 2, 3, *SkKL* 11, *SkL* 139, 217, *VSjL* 16, 87, **OGu** *GL* A 1, 2, 8, 53, **OSw** *DL* Kkb, Bb, Gb, Tjdb, Rb, *SdmL* Äb, Kmb, Tjdb, Rb, Till, *SmL* Äb, *UL* Kgb, Äb, Mb, Jb, Kmb, Rb, *VmL* För, Kgb, Äb, Mb, Kmb, Bb, Rb, *YVgL* passim, *ÄVgL* Urb, Äb, Gb, Rlb, Tb, *ÖgL* Eb, Db, Vm

provincial assembly **ODan** *VSjL* 50

shore **ODan** *JyL* 3

Expressions:

flya land (OGu)

go into exile **OGu** *GL* A 2

innan lands (OSw, ODan, OGu)

at home **OGu** *GL* Add 1 (B 4)

within the province **OSw** *YVgL* Urb, Tb **ODan** *JyL* 2 *SkL* 90, 133, 146 *VSjL* 86

land allt, land alt (OGu)

This phrase is used exceptionally in GL to refer to the general assembly in particular, as opposed to lower level assemblies, rather than simply 'all men', where fines are concerned. It is cited in reference to the escalating levels of fines that could be imposed by these various bodies.

general assembly **OGu** *GL* A 31

landar allir, landi allir (OGu)

general assembly **OGu** *GL* A 2, 4, 9, 12, Add 1 (B 4)

lands syn, lanz syn (OGu)

sight of land **OGu** *GL* A 49, Add 8 (B 55)

See also: *flya, folkland, fosterland, jorþ, landnám, lyþir (pl.), maþer, utanlands*

Refs: Brink 1998; Brink 2008b, 99, 106; CV *land*; Hertzberg s.v. *land*; KLNM s.v. *-land*; Lund s.v. *land*; Peel 2015, 167–68 note 31/12; Ruthström 2002, 118–28; Schlyter s.v. *land*; SL GL, 281 note 5

landamæri (OSw) noun

Boundary or border/border area between provinces. In OIce it refers to border land or border marker.

border **OSw** *SdmL* Till

border marker **OSw** *YVgL* Tb

boundary marks between lands **OSw** *HL* Rb

boundary of the province **OSw** *DL* Bb, *VmL* Mb

See also: *land, landamærki*

Refs: CV s.v. *land-*; KLNM s.v. *rigsgrænse*; Schlyter s.v. *landamæri*

landamærki (OSw) **landamerki** (ON) **landsmerki** (ON) noun

Border marker between provinces in VgL. In OIce sometimes between estates.

border marker of the province **OSw** *ÄVgL* Tb

boundary **OIce** *Jó* Llb 16

boundary mark **OIce** *Grg* Lbþ 175, *Js* Lbb 25

land boundary **OIce** *Jó* Lbb 6

See also: *land, landamæri, mærki*

Refs: CV s.v. *land-*; Schlyter s.v. *landamærki*

landasak (OGu) noun

fine to the general assembly **OGu** *GL* A 7, 8

landaurar (pl.) (ON) **landeyrir** (ON) noun

This was a toll exacted by Norwegian kings, paid by Icelanders (and by Norwegians engaged in the Icelandic trade except c. 1022–c. 1030) when entering Norway (before c. 1022 when leaving Norway); after c. 1022 payable instead in the Shetlands or Orkneys if visited prior to arrival in Norway. It consisted of either six ells of wadmal and six cloaks or 1/2 *mörk* of impure silver. The duty to pay *landaurar* was abolished for Norwegians in the beginning of the twelfthcentury. When Iceland came under Norwegian rule in 1262, Icelanders were also exempted from the *landaurar*.

land dues **OIce** *Grg* Misc 248, **ONorw** *FrL* Reb 1, *GuL* Reb

Refs: Gelsinger 1981, 195–96; KLNM s.v.v. *handelsafgifter, hundrað, islandshandel, stadsskatter*

landboe (OSw) **landbo** (ODan) **landboi** (OGu) **landbúi** (ON) **landbo** (OSw) noun

The corresponding ON word is *leiglendingr* (see *laigulenningr*). A person who cultivated farmland he didn't own himself, and paid a yearly rent for (*landskyld* OSw/ON, ODan *landgilde*). The landowner would be the king, the church, the nobility or some other magnate. The legal and social status of the *landboe* is regulated in detail in most of the laws. Formally, he had the right to farm the land for an agreed period of time, which differed between provinces/laws. The contract is described in most laws as a mutual agreement between the landowner and the *landboe*. The *landboe* was a free man of equal status with the landowner, except for Denmark where certain landowners had a jurisdiction over the *landboe*. Most often, he would have been an allodial peasant who for various reasons had been forced to sell his land.

neighbour of the land **OIce** *Grg* Lbþ 174

tenant **ODan** *JyL* 2, *SkL* 76, **OGu** *GL* A 47, **OIce** *Grg* Lbþ 215, *Jó* Llb 62, **ONorw** *FrL* LlbA 1 LlbB 3, **OSw** *DL* Eb, *HL* Kgb, Jb, *SdmL* Kkb, Kgb, Jb, Kmb, Rb, Till, *UL* Kkb, Kmb, Jb, Kmb, Rb, *VmL* Kkb, Kgb, Jb, Kmb, Rb

tenant farmer **ODan** *ESjL* 2, *JyL* 1–3, *SkL* 238–241, *VSjL* 80, 87, **OSw** *YVgL* Kkb, Äb, Föb, Utgb, Add, *ÄVgL* Kkb, Äb, *ÖgL* Eb

See also: *bonde, garthsæte, laigulenningr, land, landgilde, landskyld, leghomaþer, leiguliði*

Refs: KLNM s.v. *landbo, landgild, leiglending*; Lindkvist 1979

landbrigðaþáttr (ON) noun

land-claims section **OIce** *Grg* Lbþ 172

landeigandi (ON) **landseigandi** (ON) noun

landowner **OIce** *Grg* Klþ 2, 3 Þsþ 81 Vís 89 Arþ 118 Ómb 143 Feþ 166 Lbþ 177, 190 Fjl 223, 225 Hrs 234 Misc 237, *Jó* Llb 61, *Js* Lbb 13 Rkb 1, *KRA* 4

See also: *jorþeghandi*

landeign (ON) noun

land **OIce** *Jó* Llb 49

realm **ONorw** *GuL* Krb, Tjb

landerfð (ON) noun

land inheritance **ONorw** *GuL* Arb

landfrith (ODan) noun

peace of the land **ODan** *JyL* 3

See also: *friþer, land*

landgilde (ODan) noun

land rent **ODan** *SkL* 239, 241

rent **ODan** *SkL* 240, 241

landhreinsun (ON) **landhreinsan** (ON) noun

cleansing of the country **ONorw** *GuL* Krb

cleansing of the land **OIce** *Js* Mah 6

expulsion in order to purify the land **OIce** *Jó* Mah 2

landi (OSw) **allandæ** (OSw) **lænder** (OSw) noun

man of a province **OSw** *YVgL* Rlb, Tb, *ÄVgL* Rlb, Tb

See also: *land*

landkaup (ON) noun

land deal **OIce** *Grg* Lbþ 174, 194

purchase of land **ONorw** *FrL* KrbB 21

landnám (ON) noun

fine for trespass **OIce** *Jó* Llb 1, 6 Þjb 16 Fml 5, 26, *Js* Lbb 10, 13, **ONorw** *FrL* LlbA 1 LlbB 1 Bvb 5 Reb 1

trespass and compensation for this **ONorw** *GuL* Llb, Kvr

See also: *aganga, bothegang, garthgang, hemsokn, hærværk*

landnámlaust (ON) adv.

without fine for trespass **OIce** *Jó* Llb 20, 45

landnámstaka (ON) noun

receiving of the fine for trespass **OIce** *Jó* Llb 19

landráð (ON) noun

Landráð 'high treason' was one of the most serious crimes, on a par with murder and pledge breaking. See GuL ch. 132.

betrayal against one's land **OIce** *Jó* Mah 4

high treason **OIce** *Js* Mah 5, **ONorw** *GuL* Tfb, Leb

treason **OIce** *Jó* Mah 2, 24 Þjb 19, **ONorw** *FrL* KrbA 46 Mhb 4 Bvb 1

Refs: KLNM s.v.v. *edgärdsman, fredløshed, konfiskation, majestätsförbrytelse*

landráðamaðr (ON) noun

traitor **OIce** *Js* Kdb 4

landráðasök (ON) noun

treason **OIce** *Jó* Þjb 3

landsala (ON) **landssala** (ON) noun

land-sale **OIce** *Grg* Lbþ 194

landsbók (ON) noun

National Law **OFar** *Seyð* 0

landsbrigð (ON) **landabrigði** (ON) **landbrigð** (ON) noun

land-claim **OIce** *Grg* Lbþ 172, *Jó* MagBref, *Js* Lbb 1

landsbrigðabölkr (ON) **landsbrigðabálkr** (ON) noun

chapter on land claims **OIce** *Jó* Lbb 1

landsbú (ON) noun

common weal **OIce** *Grg* Þsþ 45

landsbyggð (ON) noun

tenantry **OIce** *Grg* Hrs 234

landsdeild (ON) noun

division of land **OIce** *Grg* Lbþ 177

landsdomari (OGu) **lanzdomari** (OGu) noun

district judge **OGu** *GL* A 19

landsdróttin (ON) **landdróttinn** (ON) noun

landlord **OFar** *Seyð* 2, **OIce** *Grg* Lbþ 219, *Js* Lbb 10, 14, **ONorw** *FrL* Mhb 24 Kvb 15 LlbB 3 Bvb 5 Reb 1

owner of the land **OIce** *Jó* Llb 1, 2 Fml 26, **ONorw** *FrL* LlbA 1 LlbB 1

landsendi (ON) noun

Land's End **ONorw** *GuL* Leb

landsfolk (ON) noun

people of the land **OIce** *Jó* HT 2, *Js* Kdb 2

landshlutr (ON) noun

land share **OIce** *Jó* Llb 66

landshærra (OSw) noun

lord of the land/province **OSw** *YVgL* Kkb, Föb

See also: *hærra*

landskap (OSw) **landsskap** (OSw) noun

province **OSw** *SdmL* Tjdb, *UL* Mb

See also: *land*

landskyld (OSw) **landskyld** (ON) **landsskyld** (ON) noun

Annual rent for land, which ensured the tenant's right to the crops.

land rent **ONorw** *FrL* Kvb 15

rent **OFar** *Seyð* 2, **OIce** *Jó* Mah 1 Kge 8, 16 Llb 4, 5, *Js* Mah 4, *KRA* 29, **ONorw** *FrL* Intr 5 KrbB 20 LlbA 1 LlbB 2, **OSw** *YVgL* Föb

tax **ONorw** *FrL* Intr 16

See also: *legha*

Refs: Hagland and Sandnes 1997, 109; KLNM s.v.v. *landgilde*, *landskyld*

landskyldarlykð (ON) noun

paying rent **ONorw** *FrL* LlbA 1

landslagabók (ON) noun

book of the law of the land **OIce** *Jó* Fml 29

landslagh (OSw) **landslogh** (ODan) **landslög** (ON) **lanzlagh** (OSw) noun

country's law **ONorw** *FrL* Intr 9 KrbB 10

law of the country **ONorw** *GuL* Krb

law of the land **ODan** *JyL* 2, **OIce** *Jó* Kge 4, *Js* Kvg 3, *KRA* 9, 13, **OSw** *HL* Kkb, Äb, Mb, Rb

law of the province **OSw** *DL* Eb, Mb, Bb, *UL* Kkb, Kgb, Äb, Mb, Blb, Rb, *VmL* Kkb, Äb, Mb, Rb, *YVgL* Add, *ÖgL* Kkb, Eb

provincial law **OSw** *SdmL* Conf, För, Kgb, Äb, Bb, Mb, Rb, Till

public law **OIce** *Jó* Kge 6

See also: *landsrætter*

landslaigha (OGu) **landzlaiga** (OGu) **lanzlaiga** (OGu) **landaleiga** (ON) **landsleiga** (ON) noun

land rent **OGu** *GL* A 28, **OIce** *Grg* Arþ 122 Lbþ 196, **ONorw** *FrL* Kvb 5 Jkb 2 LlbA 1

landsleigubölkr (ON) **landsleigubólkr** (ON) noun

book on tenancy **ONorw** *GuL* Llb

chapter on tenancy **OIce** *Jó* MagBref Llb 1

landsmaþer (OSw) **landsmaðr** (ON) **landsman** (OSw) **landsmæn** (pl.) (OSw) **lanzmaþær** (OSw) noun

country-dweller **OSw** *VmL* Kmb, Rb

countryman **OIce** *Jó* Sg 3, *KRA* 15

inhabitant **OIce** *Grg* Misc 247

man **OIce** *Jó* Kab 5

man from the province **OSw** *HL* Kkb, *SdmL* Conf, Till

man of the country **OIce** *Grg* Hrs 235

man of the land **OSw** *HL* Blb

rural men **OSw** *SdmL* Kmb

landsmáli (ON) noun

The right of redemption, or preemption, of land. When sold, a condition could be placed upon land whereby the original seller was allowed to purchase it back when the land went on sale again, if he were willing to match the highest bid. These rights could be passed on to heirs (cf. Grg Lbþ 192).

pre-emption rights on land **OIce** *Grg* Lbþ 192, 193, *Jó* Llb 9, *Js* Lbb 7

See also: *málaland*, *viðrbjóðandi*, *væþ*

Refs: CV s.v. *landsmáli*; Fritzner s.v. *landsmáli*; GrgTr II:392; Hertzberg s.v. *landsmáli*

landsnyt (ON) noun

Resources, yield from land, including non-agricultural benefits such as found property and drift.

land benefit **OIce** *Grg* Lbþ 192, *Jó* Lbb 7, *Js* Lbb 3

Refs: CV s.v. *landsnytjar*; Fritzner s.v. *landsnytjar*; Hertzberg s.v. *landsnytjar*

landsnæmd (OSw) noun

A *næmd* 'panel', presumably representing the entire *land* 'province', dealing with appeals.

province's commission **OSw** *DL* Rb

landsofringi (ON) noun

vagabond **OIce** *Grg* Arþ 118

landsrætter (OSw) **landræt** (ODan) **lanzræter** (OSw) noun

assembly of a province **ODan** *ESjL* 2

custom of the province **OSw** *UL* Äb, *VmL* Äb

province rights **OSw** *DL* Gb

Expressions:

lagh ok landsræt, lagh ok lanzræt (OSw)

law and custom of the province **OSw** *UL* Äb *VmL* Äb

See also: *landslagh*

landssyn (OGu) **lanz syn** (OGu) noun

sight of land **OGu** *GL* A 49, Add. 8 (B 55)

landstjórnarmaðr (ON) noun

A high-ranking official. Appears only rarely in the earliest laws. *Landstjórnarmenn* are mentioned in Js Mah 31 as men who decide whether some legal necessity precipitated the use of illegal daggers. Given the rarity of the term it is difficult to say whether a *landstjórnarmaðr* was a fixed post or whether it was a more general term covering multiple officials.

governor **OIce** *Js* Mah 31

See also: *hirðstjóri, laghmaþer*

Refs: F; NGL V s.v. *landsstjórnarmaðr*

landsverð (ON) noun

land price **OIce** *Grg* Lbþ 192

land value **OIce** *Jó* Lbb 9, *Js* Lbb 6

landsvirðing (ON) noun

land-valuing **OIce** *Grg* Þsþ 49, 62

landsvist (OSw) **landsvist** (ON) **lanzwist** (OSw) noun

The right to reside in a realm or province. Such a right was possessed by every free person (ON *friðheilagr maðr*) but could be lost via the commission of a serious crime. Exile was usually part of the penalty for particularly heinous crimes which could not be mitigated with compensation (*óbótamál*, see *urbotamal*).

In the Norwegian and Icelandic laws, *landsvist* seems to have carried some additional meanings. There it may refer specifically to a letter in which a king grants this right to someone proven guilty of a crime which would incur a sentence of exile, such as murder. *Landsvist* seems to have been granted specifically for homicide cases in which some mitigating circumstances became apparent. In order to be granted *landsvist* the defendant had to procure a letter outlining these circumstances (ModNorw *provsbrev*) and pay a fine to the king (ON *friðkaup*; also called *landkaup* or *skógarkaup*) as well as compensation to the kin of the slain. The actual *landsvist* letter was then issued by the king's chancellor (ON *kanceler*).

Since *landsvist* is not present in GuL, it has been suggested that the concept was an innovation of the thirteenth century as part of the growing centralized power of the monarchies in the Nordic countries.

leave to remain in the country **OIce** *Jó* Mah 1, 2, *Js* Mah 4, **ONorw** *FrL* Intr 5 KrbB 24

leave to remain in the kingdom **ONorw** *FrL* Mhb 41

right to live in the land **OSw** *HL* Kgb

right to live in the province **OSw** *SdmL* Kkb, Kgb, *UL* Kgb, *VmL* Kgb, *ÄVgL* Urb

right to remain in the land **ONorw** *EidsL* 28.2

See also: *frithkøp, inlænder, land, urbotamal*

Refs: CV s.v. *landsvist*; Fritzner s.v. *landsvist*; Imsen 2009; Kadane and Næshagen 2013; Kjus 2011, 81–88; KLNM s.v. *fredløshed, landsvist, landsvistbrev, niddingsværk;* Kongsrud 2011; LexMA s.v. *Treuga Dei*

landsvægher (OSw) **landsvægh** (ODan) noun

highway **ODan** *ESjL* 2

main road **OSw** *YVgL* Föb

road over land **ODan** *ESjL* 3

See also: *vægher*

landsþing (OSw) **landsthing** (ODan) noun

A *þing* 'assembly' of the highest administrative/judicial district *land* 'province' in ODan and OSw laws. There may, however, have been more ODan *landsthing* than *land*, at least understood as the provinces with separate law codes (i.e. Jylland, Sjælland and Skåne). The ODan *landsthing* were held every two weeks and dealt with certain cases relating to inheritance (often with the *hærethsthing* (see *hæraþsþing*) as an alternative), land disputes, killings, theft, and occasionally as an appeals court (explicitly stated in ESjL 2:40). Less is known of the OSw *landsþing*, but in YVgL it dealt with incompliance with a decision from or summonses to another thing, and in SdmL it was as a venue for announcing new laws. The relationship between the *landsþing* and the *folklandsþing* (q.v.) in OSw UL is unclear. *Landsþing* presumably corresponded to OGu *gutnalþing* (q.v.), OIce *alþingi* (q.v.) and the four ONorw provincial assemblies/law districts.

assembly of the province **OSw** *YVgL* Kkb, Gb, Föb, Add

provincial assembly **ODan** *ESjL* 2, 3, *JyL* 1, 2, *SkL* 17, 19, 59, 71, 73, 118, 121, 139, 145, *VSjL* 32, 50, 51, 53, 58, 68, 69, 78, 87, **OSw** *SdmL* Conf

thing of the land **OSw** *HL* Rb

See also: *hæraþsþing, land, þing*

Refs: Andersen 2011, 314–42; KLNM s.v.v. *landsting, ting*; Tamm and Vogt, eds, 2016, 301

landværn (OSw) **landværn** (ODan) **landvörn** (ON) noun

defence of the country **ONorw** *GuL* Leb

defence of the land **OSw** *HL* Kgb

military due **ODan** *JyL* 2

military tax **ODan** *JyL* 2, 3

See also: *leþunger*

landværr (ON) adj.

having the right to be in the country **OIce** *Grg* Arþ 125

langafasta (ON) noun

Lent **ONorw** *GuL* Krb, Kpb

langafredagher (OSw) langafrjádagr (ON)
   langafreadagher (OSw) noun
   Good Friday **ONorw** *GuL* Krb,
   OSw *YVgL* Kkb, *ÄVgL* Kkb

langfeðgar (pl.) (ON) langfeðr (ON) noun
   ancestor **ONorw** *FrL* Jkb 4
   ancestors on the father's side **ONorw** *GuL* Olb
   forefathers **ONorw** *GuL* Olb

langskip (ON) noun
   longship **ONorw** *GuL* Leb

langviðr (ON) noun
   long log **ONorw** *GuL* Mhb, Leb
   See also: *timber*, *verkviðr*

langþili (ON) noun
   floor planks running lengthwise **ONorw** *GuL* Llb

lansvitni (OSw) noun
   loan witness **OSw** *SdmL* Rb
   See also: *vitni*

las (OSw) las (ODan) láss (ON) noun
   lock **ODan** *ESjL* 3, *JyL* 2, *SkL* 141, *VSjL* 87, **ONorw**
   GuL Tjb, **OSw** *SdmL* Bb, *YVgL* Tb, *ÄVgL* Tb

lass (OSw) las (ODan) lass (OGu) hlass (ON) noun
   cart-load **ODan** *ESjL* 2, 3, *SkL*
   164, **ONorw** *GuL* Kpb, Llb
   load **ODan** *ESjL* 2, *SkL* 191, 227, *VSjL* 66, **OGu**
   GL A 6, 47, **OSw** *DL* Kkb, Bb, Rb, *HL* Blb, *SdmL*
   Kkb, Jb, Bb, *UL* Blb, *VmL* Kkb, Bb, *YVgL* Kkb,
   Jb, Föb, Utgb, Add, *ÄVgL* Jb, Föb, *ÖgL* Kkb
   wagon-load **OSw** *HL* Kkb

lasta (OGu) verb
   dispute **OGu** *GL* A 13

lastalaus (OGu) lastalauss (ON) adj.
   free of defects **OIce** *Grg* Misc 246, *Jó* Kab 6
   without defect **OGu** *GL* A 19

laster (OSw) lastr (OGu) lestr (OGu) löstr (ON) noun
   damage **OGu** *GL* A 19, Add. 2 (B 17), **OSw** *UL* Mb
   defamation **OIce** *Grg* Misc 238
   defect **OIce** *Grg* Ómb 140, *Jó* Kab 18, **ONorw**
   GuL Kpb, Løb, Mhb, **OSw** *HL* Mb, Kmb
   disability **OGu** *GL* A 19
   fault **OGu** *GL* A 33, 33a, 34, Add. 7 (B
   49), **OSw** *UL* Kmb, *VmL* Äb, Kmb
   injury **OIce** *Jó* Kab 16
   maiming **OGu** *GL* A 17
   Expressions:
   laster æller lyti, laster æller liute (OSw)
   fault or failing OSw *VmL* Äb

leynandi löstr (ON)
   hidden flaw **ONorw** *GuL* Kpb, Løb
   See also: *lyti*, *læst*, *ókostr*, *vamm*

lastmæli (ON) noun
   defamation **OIce** *Grg* Misc 238

lat (OSw) noun
   loss **OSw** *UL* Mb, Kmb, Blb, Rb, Add. 14, *VmL* Mb

lata (OSw) lata (OGu) láta (ON) verb
   allow **OGu** *GL* A 13, **OSw** *UL* Kkb,
   Kgb, Äb, Mb, *VmL* Kkb, Äb, Mb
   bring **OSw** *UL* Jb
   cause **OGu** *GL* A 20a, **OSw** *UL*
   StfBM, Kkb, Kmb, *VmL* Kmb
   claim **OGu** *GL* A 22
   fail **OSw** *UL* Kgb
   force **OGu** *GL* A 19
   give **OSw** *UL* Äb, Jb, *VmL* Kkb, Kgb, Äb, Mb, Jb, Rb
   grant **OSw** *UL* Jb, *VmL* Jb
   leave **OGu** *GL* A 13, **OSw** *VmL* Kkb
   let **OGu** *GL* A 25, 40, **OSw** *UL* Jb,
   Kmb, Blb, Rb, *VmL* Kmb, Bb, Rb
   lose **OSw** *UL* Mb, Rb, *VmL* Mb
   permit **OGu** *GL* Add. 8 (B 55)
   be place for **OGu** *GL* A 19
   put to (cultivation) **OGu** *GL* A 48
   release **OGu** *GL* A 26, **OSw** *UL* Mb, Kmb
   surrender **OIce** *Js* Þfb 4
   take **OSw** *UL* Mb, Kmb, Blb, *VmL* Mb
   Expressions:
   lata liggia (OGu)
   allow to lie fallow **OGu** *GL* A 47
   lata löst, laust lata (OGu)
   release **OGu** *GL* A 44
   lata sik (OSw)
   allow **OSw** *UL* Kkb
   til lata (OSw)
   supply **OSw** *UL* Kkb *VmL* Kkb
   See also: *aterlæggia*, *aterlægha*,
   lös, *sea*, *slæppa*, *træþi*

lathegarth (ODan) noun
   barn **ODan** *VSjL* 53

launbarn (ON) noun
   If a slave had a natural child, the one who sold the
   slave was to provide for the child. See GuL ch. 57.
   illegitimate child **OIce** *Grg* Feþ 158
   natural child **ONorw** *GuL* Løb
   See also: *lönd*
   Refs: KLNM s.v. *oäkta barn*

laungetinn (ON) adj.

> *illegitimate* **OIce** *Grg* Vís 94 Bat 113 Arþ
> 118, 127 Ómb 143 Feþ 146, *Js* Ert 7

laupr (OGu) noun

> This was a measure of capacity apparently equating
> to approximately a bushel or a quarter of a barrel,
> although Schlyter does not suggest this. It was also
> the basket in which the grain to be sown was carried.
> The word is not used in the OSw laws.
>
> *bushel* **OGu** *GL* A 20
>
> See also: *laupsland, skæppa*
>
> Refs: KLNM s.v. *laup*; Peel 2015,
> 136 note 20/47–48; Schlyter 1877,
> s.v. *löper*; SL GL, 268 note 28

laupsland (OGu) noun

> An area equivalent in size to one quarter of an acre,
> or in metric units 1/10 hectare or 1,000 square metres.
> The obsolete English term for this is a decare, while the
> modern Swedish equivalent of an acre is a *tunnland*.
> It was the area on which one would sow a quarter of a
> barrel of seed corn.
>
> *bushel-land* **OGu** *GL* A 47, 48, 56a
>
> See also: *laupr, markland, öresland,
> örtoghaland, spannaland*
>
> Refs: KLNM s.v. *laup*; Peel 2015, 181 note
> 47/7; Schlyter 1877, s.v. *laupsland* (under
> 'löp-'); SL GL, 286 note 3 to chapter 47

lausafé (ON) noun

> *chattels* **OIce** *Jó* Mah 1 Kge 4 Þjb 1
>
> *goods* **OIce** *Grg* Bat 114
>
> *movables* **OIce** *Js* Mah 2, 4, **ONorw** *FrL* Intr 2, 4
>
> *property* **ONorw** *FrL* Intr 2
>
> See also: *lösöre*

lausakør (ON) noun

> *floating options* **OIce** *Grg* Arþ 127

lauss eyrir (ON) -

> *chattels* **OIce** *Grg* Klþ 4 Arþ 122 [and elsewhere
> possibly] Tíg 255, *Jó* MagBref Þfb 5 Mah 1 Kge
> 22 Þjb 1, *Js* Mah 2, 9 Kvg 3 Þjb 1, *KRA* 14, 15,
> **ONorw** *BorgL* 3.2 4.2, *FrL* Mhb 2, 12, *GuL* Mhb
>
> *movable property* **ONorw** *GuL* Krb
>
> *movables* **ONorw** *FrL* Tfb 5 LlbB 12, *GuL* Llb

lausungarorð (ON) noun

> *unreliable report* **OIce** *Jó* Fml 6

lavarþer (OSw) noun

> An OE borrowing, literally 'bread warden' referring to
> a master of slaves.
>
> *lord* **OSw** *YVgL* Rlb, *ÄVgL* Rlb
>
> Refs: Brink 2008c, 7–9; von See 1964, 16–17

laxá (ON) noun

> *salmon stream* **ONorw** *GuL* Llb

laþa (OSw) **lathe** (ODan) **hlaða** (ON) **laða** (ON) noun

> *barn* **ODan** *JyL* 2, 3, **ONorw** *GuL* Llb, Tjb, **OSw** *DL*
> Kkb, *SdmL* Kkb, Bb, *SmL*, *YVgL* Kkb, Tb, *ÄVgL* Tb

lánfé (ON) noun

> *borrowed chattels* **OIce** *Jó* Kab 4
>
> *borrowed thing* **ONorw** *GuL* Kpb, Tfb, Olb
>
> *lent property* **OIce** *Js* Kab 5
>
> See also: *leghofæ*

látr (ON) noun

> *rookery* **OIce** *Jó* Llb 68
>
> *sealing ground* **ONorw** *GuL* Llb

lefssufl (OSw) **lefs sughl** (OSw) **lefsufghl** (OSw)
lefsufl (OSw) noun

> *food to eat with a loaf of bread* **OSw** *VmL* Kkb

legha (OSw) **leghe** (ODan) **laigha** (OGu) **leiga** (ON)
noun

> *contract* **OSw** *HL* Blb
>
> *employment* **OSw** *DL* Bb, *SdmL* Bb, *UL* Blb, *VmL* Bb
>
> *fee* **OSw** *VmL* Kmb, *YVgL* Add
>
> *hire* **ODan** *ESjL* 3, *JyL* 3, **OGu** *GL* A 56, **OSw** *UL*
> Kmb, *VmL* Kmb, *YVgL* Urb, Utgb, *ÄVgL* Föb
>
> *hire charge* **OIce** *Grg* Misc 246
>
> *interest* **OIce** *Grg* Arþ 122 Ómb 130 Lbþ 192
> Fjl 221 Misc 249, **ONorw** *GuL* Kpb, Arb
>
> *lease* **ODan** *JyL* 3, **OSw** *DL* Bb, *SdmL* Bb,
> Kmb, Tjdb, *UL* Mb, Jb, Blb, *VmL* Bb
>
> *passage money* **OIce** *Grg* Feþ 166
>
> *payment* **ODan** *SkL* 165, **OIce** *Jó* Llb 45,
> **OSw** *HL* Kmb, *UL* Kmb, *VmL* Kmb
>
> *rent* **ODan** *JyL* 2, **OFar** *Seyð* 2, 5, **OIce** *Grg*
> Lbþ 183, *Jó* Kge 16 Llb 1, 4 Kab 16 Þjb 16 Fml
> 1, 2, *Js* Lbb 10, 21 Kab 13, *KRA* 35, **ONorw**
> *FrL* LlbB 1, *GuL* Kpb, Olb, **OSw** *HL* Blb
>
> *rental* **OSw** *VmL* Kmb, Bb
>
> *salary* **OIce** *Jó* Kab 25, **OSw** *HL* Kkb
>
> *wages* **OSw** *SdmL* Bb, *UL* Blb, *VmL* Bb
>
> *yield* **OIce** *Grg* Lbþ 218
>
> See also: *fjárleiga, köp, landskyld,
> lön, mali, verkakaup*

leghemal (ODan) **leigumál** (ON) **leigumáli** (ON) noun

> *contract* **ONorw** *GuL* Kpb, Llb
>
> *hire agreement* **OIce** *Grg* Fjl 224
>
> *lease* **ODan** *JyL* 2
>
> *legal agreement* **OIce** *Jó* Kab 16
>
> *tenancy agreement* **OIce** *Grg* Lbþ 219, *Js*
> Lbb 10 Kab 11, **ONorw** *FrL* LlbA 4
>
> See also: *legha*

legheværk (ODan) noun

salaried work **ODan** *ESjL* 1

leghia (OSw) **leghe** (ODan) **laigia** (OGu) **leiga** (ON)
leigja (ON) verb

borrow **ONorw** *GuL* Kpb, **OSw** *HL* Kmb

employ **OSw** *DL* Bb

hire **OIce** *Grg* Arþ 122 Feþ 164 Fjl 224, *Jó* Llb 37,
ONorw *FrL* Rgb 10, *GuL* Kpb, Løb, **OSw** *DL* Bb,
HL Blb, *SdmL* Bb, Till, *UL* Kkb, Äb, Kmb, Blb, *VmL*
Kkb, Äb, Kmb, Bb, *YVgL* Rlb, *ÄVgL* Rlb, *ÖgL* Eb

lease **OIce** *Jó* Llb 1 Fml 13, **ONorw** *GuL*
Llb, **OSw** *DL* Bb, *SdmL* Bb, Kmb

pay interest **ONorw** *GuL* Kpb

pay rental **OSw** *UL* Blb, *VmL* Bb

rent **ODan** *JyL* 2, *SkL* 235, **OGu** *GL* A 3,
OIce *Grg* Lbþ 183, 219, *Jó* Llb 3, *Js* Lbb
10, 11, **ONorw** *FrL* Kvb 23, **OSw** *HL* Blb,
UL Kkb, Mb, *VmL* Mb, *YVgL* Add

take against rent **OSw** *UL* Kkb, *VmL* Kkb

See also: *byggia, laigulenningr, sitia*

leghodrænger (OSw) **leghedræng** (ODan)
læghudrængær (OSw) noun

farm-hand **OSw** *HL* Kkb

hired man **OSw** *DL* Kkb, Mb, *SdmL* Mb, *UL*
Kkb, Kgb, Mb, *VmL* Kkb, Mb, *ÖgL* Db

hired servant **ODan** *JyL* 2

worker **OSw** *YVgL* Add, *ÖgL* Kkb

leghofæ (OSw) **leigufé** (ON) noun

hired cattle **OSw** *YVgL* Utgb, *ÄVgL* Föb

hired livestock **OSw** *YVgL* Rlb

hired stock **OIce** *Grg* Fjl 224, *Jó* Kab 15

leased thing **ONorw** *GuL* Kpb

See also: *fæ, lánfé, legha, leigukýr*

leghohion (OSw) **leghehjon** (ODan) **leghu hion** (OSw)
noun

hired servant **ODan** *JyL* 2, 3, *SkL* 152, **OSw** *HL*
Blb, *SdmL* Bb, *UL* Kkb, Mb, Blb, *VmL* Mb, Bb

hireling **OSw** *HL* Mb

servant **OSw** *YVgL* Add

See also: *hemahion, hion, legha*

leghokona (OSw) **leghukona** (OSw) **leghukuna** (OSw)
noun

farm-maid **OSw** *HL* Kkb

hired woman **OSw** *DL* Kkb, Bb, *HL* Blb, *SdmL*
Mb, Till, *UL* Kkb, Mb, Blb, *VmL* Kkb, Mb

See also: *bonde, husfrugha, kona, kærling*

leghomaþer (OSw) **legheman** (ODan) **leigumaðr** (ON)
noun

hired man **ODan** *JyL* 3, **OIce** *Jó* Kab
25, **OSw** *DL* Bb, *SdmL* Add

hired worker **OSw** *YVgL* Föb, Utgb, Add, *ÄVgL* Föb

labourer **OIce** *Js* Kab 19

tenant **OIce** *Grg* Vís 89 Lbþ 172, 214, *Jó* Lbb
7 Llb 6, *Js* Lbb 3, 13, **OSw** *YVgL* Kkb

workman **ONorw** *GuL* Løb

See also: *hion, laigulenningr,
landboe, legha, leiguliði*

leghosven (OSw) noun

hired servant **OSw** *YVgL* Tb

leghuruf (OSw) noun

breach of employment **OSw** *SdmL* Bb

breaching of a work contract **OSw** *DL* Bb, *HL* Blb

breaking of an employment contract
OSw *UL* Blb, *VmL* Bb

leghustæmpna (OSw) **leghostæmna** (OSw) noun

employment period **OSw** *DL* Bb, *SdmL* Bb

period of employment **OSw** *UL* Blb, *VmL* Bb

See also: *stæmna*

legkaup (ON) **legrkaup** (ON) noun

burial fee **ONorw** *EidsL* 47.7 48.1, *GuL* Krb

grave fee **OIce** *Grg* Klþ 2 Lbþ 218

legorð (ON) noun

Sexual misconduct, adultery, fornication. A case
involving such infractions.

adultery **ONorw** *GuL* Krb, Løb, Mhb

intercourse **OIce** *Grg* Vís 90 Feþ 149, 155

Refs: CV s.v. *legorð*; Fritzner s.v.
legorð; Hertzberg s.v. *legorð*

legorðssekð (ON) noun

punishment for sexual intercourse
ONorw *FrL* KrbB 4

legorðssök (ON) noun

case of seduction **OIce** *Jó* Fml 22

intercourse case **OIce** *Grg* Þsþ 57 Feþ
144, 145 Misc 254, *Jó* Mah 27 Kge 5

legvita (OGu) noun

under-blanket **OGu** *GL* A 20

leið (ON) noun

autumn meeting **OIce** *Grg* Klþ 2, 6 Þsþ
49, 54 Vís 100 Lbþ 202, *Js* Þfb 5

meeting on the autumn assembly site **OIce** *Jó* Þfb 7

leiðangrsfar (ON) noun

levy journey **ONorw** *FrL* Leb 26

leiðangrsferð (ON) noun

levy expedition duty **ONorw** *FrL* Leb 8

leiðangrsfé (ON) noun

levy provisions **ONorw** *FrL* Leb 19

leiðangrsgerð (ON) leiðangrgerð (ON) noun

levy preparation duty **ONorw** *FrL* Leb 8, 12

leiðangrsmaðr (ON) noun

man of the levy **ONorw** *FrL* Leb 23

leiðangrsskip (ON) noun

levy ship **ONorw** *FrL* Leb 19 Bvb 11

leiðangrsvist (ON) noun

levy provisions **ONorw** *FrL* Leb 8

leiðangrsvíti (ON) noun

fine for neglecting the levy **ONorw** *GuL* Leb

levy fine **ONorw** *FrL* Leb 14

leiðarmál (ON) noun

autumn meeting matters **OIce** *Grg* Þsþ 61

leiðarvöllr (ON) noun

autumn meeting place **OIce** *Grg* Klþ 2

leiðarþing (ON) noun

A *þing* 'assembly' held in autumn in each OIce district known as *sýsla* (ON) (see *sysel*), where its leader (ON *sýslumaðr*, see *sysluman*), informed the inhabitants of events at the preceding *alþingi* (ON) 'General Assembly'.

autumn assembly **OIce** *Jó* Þfb 7

See also: *leið*, *þing*

Refs: Jón Viðar Sigurðsson 2015; KLNM s.v. *leið*

leiðrétta (ON) verb

compensate **ONorw** *FrL* Rgb 48

make redress **OIce** *KRA* 11

leiðsögumaðr (ON) noun

guide **OIce** *Jó* Fml 7

leiglendingaþáttr (ON) noun

tenants' section **OIce** *Grg* Lbþ 219

leiguból (ON) noun

tenant farm **OIce** *Grg* Lbþ 172, *Jó* Lbb 1

See also: *leiguland*

leiguburðr (ON) noun

amount paid in rent **OIce** *Jó* Llb 14 Fml 1

leigufall (ON) noun

salary reduction **OIce** *Jó* Kab 25

wage reduction **OIce** *Js* Kab 19

leigufénuðr (ON) noun

rented livestock **OIce** *Jó* Kab 16

leigujörð (ON) noun

land **OIce** *Jó* Llb 4

leased land **OIce** *Js* Lbb 17, **ONorw** *GuL* Llb

rental farm **OIce** *Jó* Llb 1

See also: *leiguland*

leigukýr (ON) noun

hired cow **ONorw** *GuL* Kpb

See also: *leghofæ*

leiguland (ON) noun

tenant land **OIce** *Grg* Lbþ 183, 192, *Js* Lbb 13

See also: *leiguból*

leigulandsfjara (ON) noun

shore of tenant land **OIce** *Jó* Llb 6

leigulauss (ON) adj.

rent free **OIce** *Jó* Kab 4

untenanted **OIce** *Grg* Lbþ 219

without interest **OIce** *Grg* Feþ 154 Lbþ 192

See also: *óleigis*, *vaxtalauss*

leiguliðaskifti (ON) noun

division made by tenants **OIce** *Jó* Llb 14

leiguliði (ON) noun

tenant **OIce** *Jó* Llb 1, 3, *Js* Lbb 10, **ONorw** *FrL* Kvb 15, *GuL* Llb

See also: *laigulenningr*, *landboe*, *leghomaþer*

leirblót (ON) noun

clay-sacrifice **ONorw** *EidsL* 24.3

lekararætter (OSw) noun

{lekararætter} **OSw** *ÄVgL* Lek

lekari (OSw) noun

jester **OSw** *ÄVgL* Lek

wandering minstrel **OSw** *ÖgL* Db

lekisskepr (OGu) noun

medical treatment **OGu** *GL* A 19

lekman (OSw) leikmaðr (ON) legman (OSw) noun

layman **OIce** *KRA* 4, 34, **ONorw** *EidsL* 2, **OSw** *HL* Kkb, Mb, Jb, *SdmL* Kkb, Mb, *SmL*, *YVgL* Kkb

Expressions:

lekmanna lagh (OSw)

law of laymen **OSw** *SmL*

lekmannething (ODan) noun

Presumably a non-ecclesiastical *thing* 'assembly', appearing in the context of learned men's limited rights there.

layperson's assembly **ODan** *JyL* 1

See also: *þing*

lemð (ON) lemd (ON) noun

injury **ONorw** *GuL* Løb, Mhb

See also: *lemja*

lemja (ON) verb

  disable **OIce** *Grg* Vís 88

  prevent **ONorw** *GuL* Leb

  See also: *lemð*

lemstrarsár (ON) noun

  disabling wound **OIce** *Jó* Þfb 5 Mah 19, 22

lend (OGu) noun

  loin **OGu** *GL* A 23

lenda (ON) verb

  provide with land **OFar** *Seyð* 7

lendsmannsgarðr (ON) noun

  house of a landed man **ONorw** *FrL* Rgb 9

lendsmannskona (ON) noun

  wife of a baron **OIce** *Jó* Kab 24

lerþrmaþr (OGu) noun

  priest **OGu** *GL* A 2, 3, 6, 21, Add. 1 (B 4), *GS* Ch. 3

lest (ON) noun

  cargo **OIce** *Jó* Fml 10

lestatal (ON) noun

  weight of cargo **OIce** *Jó* Fml 10

leta (OSw) verb

  inquire into **OSw** *UL* Kkb, Jb, Blb, *VmL* Kkb

  search **OSw** *UL* Mb, *VmL* Mb

  seek **OSw** *UL* Äb, Mb, Jb, Kmb, Blb, *VmL* Äb, Bb

lethingshælgh (ODan) noun

  peace during the military duty **ODan** *ESjL* 2

  See also: *leþunger*

leyfa (ON) verb

  give permission **OIce** *Jó* Llb 19

leyfislaust (ON) adv.

  without permission **OIce** *Jó* Llb 13
  Fml 17, **ONorw** *FrL* LlbB 11

leysingi (ON) leysingr (ON) noun

A freed slave was a person whose freedom was limited or imperfect. The man was variously termed *frælsgivi* (OSw), *frælsgive* ODan) and *frjálsgjafi* (ONorw) (freed slave, freedman), the woman *frælsgiva* (OSw) and *frjálsgjafa* (ONorw) (freed woman, freedwoman). It should be added that the word *frjálsgjafi* in OIce (Grg) means 'freedom-giver'. A different set of terms was *leysingi* and *leysingja*. Among free men, *frjálsgjafar* and *leysingjar* occupied the lowest rank in society with respect to personal rights and social status. The difference between the two categories was marked by the *frelsisøl* (freedom ale). The *frjálsgjafi* (OIce *grefleysingr*) was a person whose manumission had been granted, but not confirmed (made public). Until he had given his freedom ale, he ranked below the *leysingi*. (This terminological distinction was not always strictly observed: the word *leysingi* was sometimes used to denote *frjálsgjafi* as well.) Nevertheless, *frjálsgjafi* and *leysingi* belonged to the same class with respect to the system of compensation for insults etc. (*bótr*, see *bot*).

The *leysingi* could attain a practically free status either by giving his freedom ale or by other means (e.g. through performing extra work, or having his freedom granted by others). In ODan and OSw laws — with the exception of ESjL — manumission presupposed that the slave to be freed was adopted into a free kin. Still a freedman had a lower status in society. With respect to compensation for offences, whether suffered or performed, he was worth less than a (completely) free man. Although his master had to provide him with a place where he could live, the master inherited the *frælsgivi* and could decide whom the latter was allowed to marry. When he got old, he had to rely on the care of the church. In any case, the act of manumission had to be confirmed by oath and later announced in public, either at the assembly or in the church.

ON laws also show that the freedman was not entirely free from dependence on his master. His disability in this respect was inherited in the form of special loyalty commitments (*þyrmslir*) (which might end after twenty years). His freedom was also restricted in other respects. He could not leave his *fylki* (q.v.) without his master's permission (GuL ch. 67). If he had not given his freedom ale he could not make any bargain that exceeded the worth of one *ertog*, i.e. 1/3 *eyrir* (GuL ch. 56), in the FrL 6 counted *aurar* (Kvb ch. 23); his master made decisions about his marriage (GuL ch. 63) and inherited from him. The children of a freedman could not inherit from him, unless the freedman was married to a freedwoman and they had both given their freedom ale (GuL ch. 65). The master was also responsible for his freedman's contribution to the levy, if the latter could not pay (GuL ch. 296).

His right to compensation (in case of injury) was 6 *aurar* (GuL ch. 200), half of what the *bóndi* (householder) could claim. According to the BorgL he was buried in the quarter *leysingjalega*, which was farther from the church than (and inferior in rank to) the quarter where the householder was buried. The EidsL (I 50) has a similar provision.

The system of slavery implied in this terminology was gradually abolished. The GuL (Krb ch. 4) states that the assembly each year had to give one slave his freedom, and slavery seems to have disappeared in Norway towards the end of the twelfth century. In Sweden, slavery disappeared gradually under the influence of the church and the king. An important step in this direction was marked by the Skara stadga (1335). In Denmark slavery disappeared in the thirteenth century. In Iceland slavery was never officially abolished, but seems to have disappeared in the twelfth century.

freed slave **ONorw** *EidsL* 48.3

freedman **OIce** *Grg* Vís 96 Bat 113 Arþ 119, 127 Ómb 128, 134 Feþ 146, **ONorw** *FrL* Mhb 4, 49 ArbB 10 Rgb 35 LlbA 15 Bvb 1, *GuL* Krb, Kvb, Løb, Llb, Arb, Mhb, Leb

fully freed slave **ONorw** *BorgL* 9.5 12.6, *EidsL* 50.3

See also: *bóndaréttr*, *bonde*, *bot*, *frelsisöl*, *frælsgiva*, *frælsgivi*, *fylki*, *grefleysingr*, *leysingja*, *ættleiðing*, *þyrmsl*

Refs: Helle 2001, 125–32; Hertzberg s.v.v. *frjálsgjafi*, *leysingi*; Iversen 1997, 41–43, 190–91, 199–204, 210–28, 235–40, 258–65, 281–84; KLNM s.v.v. *böter*, *leysingi*, *stænder*, *årboren mann*; Nevéus 1974, 46–50, 80–86, 102–05, 128–31, 150–56, 162, 165; RGA2 s.v. *freigelassene*; Robberstad 1981, 348; Strauch 2008b, 250–53; 2016, 35–37

leysingja (ON) **leysing** (ON) noun

freedwoman **OIce** *Grg* Arþ 119 Feþ 146, **ONorw** *FrL* ArbB 11, *GuL* Løb, Mhb, Tjb

See also: *leysingi*

leysingjabarn (ON) **leysingsbarn** (ON) noun

children of fully freed slaves **ONorw** *BorgL* 9.5

freedman's child **OIce** *Grg* Arþ 119

leysingjakaup (ON) noun

purchase by a freedman **ONorw** *FrL* Kvb 23

leysingjavitni (ON) noun

witness to the freeing process **ONorw** *FrL* Jkb 8

leysingjaætt (ON) noun

family of freedmen **ONorw** *FrL* ArbB 11

leysingsaurar (pl.) (ON) noun

freedman's purchase money **ONorw** *GuL* Arb

ransom fee **ONorw** *GuL* Løb

See also: *værþörar (pl.)*

leysingserfð (ON) noun

freedman's inheritance **ONorw** *GuL* Arb

leysingskona (ON) noun

freedman's wife **OIce** *Grg* Feþ 156

leysingskyn (ON) noun

family of a freedman **ONorw** *GuL* Arb

leysingslög (ON) noun

Freedman's Law **ONorw** *GuL* Løb

leysingssonr (ON) **leysingjasonr** (ON) noun

son of a freedman **ONorw** *GuL* Arb

son of a fully freed slave **ONorw** *BorgL* 12.5

leþa (OSw) **laiþa** (OGu) **leiða** (ON) verb

confirm **OSw** *YVgL* Add

find guilty **OSw** *YVgL* Föb

lead **OSw** *YVgL* Tb, *ÖgL* Kkb, Eb

present **ONorw** *GuL* Kpb

prove **OGu** *GL* A 4

take **ONorw** *GuL* Krb

trace **OSw** *SdmL* Kkb, Bb, Kmb, Tjdb

leþsn (OSw) **laizn** (OGu) **ledsn** (OSw) **lezn** (OSw) **læzn** (OSw) noun

The obligation and ability to trace a disputed object to one who could prove that it was legally acquired, potentially back through several transactions.

finding a guarantor **OSw** *HL* Mb

proof of provenance **OSw** *UL* Mb, *VmL* Mb

provenance **OSw** *UL* Mb, Rb, *VmL* Mb

tracing **OSw** *SdmL* Tjdb, *YVgL* Tb

tracing to an assignor **OSw** *DL* Bb, Tjdb

warrant for ownership **OGu** *GL* A 37

Expressions:

ræna taks ok leþsnar, ræna taks ok leznar (OSw)

deprive of the right to put matters into the hands of a surety man and permit proof of provenance **OSw** *VmL* Mb

Refs: Schlyter s.v. *leþsn*

leþsnafall (OSw) **leznu fall** (OSw) noun

failure to trace proof of provenance **OSw** *UL* Mb, *VmL* Mb (rubric only)

neglect concerning tracing **OSw** *SdmL* Tjdb

See also: *leþsn*

leþsnaforfall (OSw) noun

excuses concerning tracing **OSw** *SdmL* Tjdb

See also: *forfall*, *leþsn*

leþsnavitni (OSw) noun

tracing witness **OSw** *SdmL* Rb

See also: *leþsn*, *vitni*

leþsund (OSw) noun

navigable sound **OSw** *UL* Blb (E text), *VmL* Bb

waterway sound **OSw** *SdmL* Bb

leþunger (OSw) **lething** (ODan) **laiþingr** (OGu) **leiðangr** (ON) **leþonger** (OSw) noun

The *leþunger* was the military service connected to the system of naval defence, and the dues and taxes that the subjects owed to this service. When mobilised, the soldiers were obliged to stand at the king's disposal in order to protect the country, esp. the coastal areas, against attacks from enemies. There is evidence of its existence in all Danish laws, in *ÖgL*, and all Svea laws except DL, and in the Norwegian FrL and GuL as well as in the appendix to GL (Guta saga, GS). By the time that the Swedish laws were written down in the form we know them today, these obligations had been transformed into yearly taxes in times of peace.

levy **OGu** *GS* Ch. 4, **OSw** *HL* Kgb, *SdmL* Kgb, Mb, Rb, Till, *UL* Kgb, Mb, Rb, *VmL* Kgb, Mb

levy duty **ONorw** *FrL* Leb 9

military due **ODan** *ESjL* 3, *JyL* 2, *SkL* 75

military duty **ODan** *ESjL* 2, 3, *JyL* 2, 3

military service due **ODan** *JyL* 3

military tax **ODan** *JyL* 3

naval levy **ONorw** *GuL* Kpb, Leb

tax **ONorw** *FrL* Intr 17

warfare **ODan** *VSjL* 79

{leþunger} **OSw** *HL* Kgb

See also: *ar (1)*, *hamna*, *har (1)*, *landværn*, *leþungslami*, *skiplagh*

Refs: Bagge 2010, 72–80 and passim; Hafström 1949a; Helle 2001, 32–34, 158–75; Hertzberg s.v. *leiðangr*; Hjärne I, 1980, 263; KLNM s.v.v. *folkvapen, frälse, hamna, håndverkslovgivning, landvärn, ledungslama, leidang, lide, nefgildi, proviantering, skatter, stadens skepp, styresmann, årmann*; Lindkvist 1995, 56–64; Lund 1967; Lönnroth 1940, 62–72; Robberstad 1981, 389–93; Tamm and Vogt 2016, 37–38

leþungslami (OSw) **laiþingslami** (OGu) **leþongslami** (OSw) noun

A tax levied replacing military duty in the naval defence organization.

levy tax **OGu** *GS* Ch. 4, **OSw** *UL* Kgb, *VmL* Kgb

{leþungslami} **OSw** *HL* Kgb

See also: *leþunger*

Refs: Ericsson 2012, 139 f.; Hafström 1949, 63–65; KLNM, s.v. *leidang*; Lindkvist 1995, 56–64; Peel 2015, 314 note 4/14; Schlyter, s.v. *leþungslami*; SL GL, 321 note 68

leþungsskin (OSw) noun

A tax paid in animal skin replacing military duty in the naval defence organization, and contrasted to the other skin-taxes *bælskin* (q.v.) and *vighramannaskin* (q.v.).

{leþungs}-tax **OSw** *DL* Rb

See also: *boghi, bælskin, leþunger, leþungslami, skin, vighramannaskin*

Refs: Schlyter s.v. *leþungsskin*

liðförr (ON) **liðfærr** (ON) adj.

sufficiently manned **OIce** *Jó* Fml 6

liðskostr (ON) noun

assistance **OIce** *Jó* Mah 16, *Js* Mah 34

lif (OSw) noun

life **OSw** *SdmL* Tjdb, *ÖgL* Eb

liflat (OSw) **livslat** (ODan) noun

life-threatening wound **OSw** *HL* Mb

loss of life **ODan** *JyL* 2, **OSw** *YVgL* Tb

lifspund (OSw) noun

lispound **OSw** *UL* Kgb

liftapilse (OSw) noun

loss of life **OSw** *HL* För

lifvakn (OSw) noun

protective weapon **OSw** *HL* Äb

See also: *vapn*

liggia (OSw) **ligje** (ODan) **liggia** (OGu) **liggja** (ON) verb

lie (1)

sleep with **ONorw** *GuL* Krb

Expressions:

lata liggia sik (OSw) **late ligje (sik)** (ODan)

allow someone to fornicate with **OSw** *HL* Äb

allow someone to lie with **ODan** *ESjL* 3

lata liggia (OGu)

allow to lie fallow **OGu** *GL* A 47

liggia i (OSw)

be entitled to **OSw** *UL* Äb, Mb, Blb *VmL* Mb

be subject to **OSw** *UL* Mb, Blb, Rb *VmL* Mb

liggia viþ (OSw) **ligje vither** (ODan) **liggia viþr** (OGu)

compensate **OSw** *ÄVgL* Md

be compensated **OSw** *YVgL* Drb

fine applies **OGu** *GL* A 13

be a fine **OGu** *GL* A 8

be fined **OGu** *GL* A 2, 6, 7, 8, 13

be liable for **OGu** *GL* A 21

be (liable) to pay a fine **OGu** *GL* A 7

be payable **OGu** *GL* A 23

pay **ODan** *SkL* 69, 70, 72 *VSjL* 73, 82

liggia i hæl (OSw)

overlie **OSw** *ÖgL* Eb

See also: *aterlæggia, aterlægha, böta, forligje, gilder, træþi*

lighra (OSw) **læghra** (OSw) verb

seduce **OSw** *DL* Gb

sleep with **OSw** *YVgL* Gb

lighri (OSw) **læghri** (OSw) noun

seduction **OSw** *UL* Äb, *VmL* Äb

sexual intercourse **OSw** *DL* Gb

state of ownership (in a village) **OSw**
DL Bb, *UL* Blb, *VmL* Jb, Bb

See also: *lægher*

lighrisbot (OSw) **læghre bot** (OSw) noun

compensation for seduction **OSw** *UL* Äb, *VmL* Äb

See also: *bot, böta*

lighrisvilla (OSw) noun

Concerns illegal moving of boundary markers.

changed position **OSw** *DL* Bb

confusion in the state of land ownership **OSw** *VmL* Jb

likran (OSw) noun

robbery from a corpse **OSw** *HL* Mb, *SdmL* Mb

liksvitni (OGu) **ligsvitni** (OGu) noun

evidence of neighbours **OGu** *GL* A 25

See also: *vitni*

likvari (OGu) noun

undergarments **OGu** *GL* A 19

See also: *gangklepi, ivirklæpi, serkr, stæniza*

likvægher (OSw) **ligvægher** (OSw) noun

road for dead bodies **OSw** *YVgL* Jb, *ÄVgL* Jb

See also: *vægher*

limalastr (OGu) noun

disability **OGu** *GL* A 19, Add. 3 (B 19)

See also: *limalyti*

limalyti (OGu) noun

maiming **OGu** *GL* A 16, Add. 2 (B 17)

See also: *limalastr*

limber (OSw) **lim** (ODan) noun

Appears in expressions for corporal punishment, such as *liif æth limmæ* (ODan JyL 2), *lif æller limi* (OSw SdmL Mb) 'life or limbs' and *döma af hanum huþ ællær annær slikæn lim* 'sentence him to lose his skin or another such limb' (ODan SkL 151).

limb **ODan** *JyL* 2, 3, *SkL* 94, 95,
151, 153, **OSw** *SdmL* Tjdb

limheill (ON) adj.

sound in limb **ONorw** *GuL* Tjb

lindagyrt (OGu) adj.

male **OGu** *GL* A 20

See also: *bauggildismaðr, fæþerni, gyrþlugyrt, möþerni*

lindebot (ODan) noun

Presumed to mean that all possessions but the belt should be paid in fines by a poor person.

belt-fine **ODan** *SkL* 126, 127

See also: *bot, lindi*

Refs: Tamm and Vogt, eds, 2016, 301

lindi (ON) noun

Expressions:

søkja til lindalags (ON)

claim one's last penny **ONorw** *FrL* ArbB 23

A symbolic gesture of insolvency.

See also: *lindebot*

Refs: CV s.v. *lindi*

litvan (OGu) noun

facial defect **OGu** *GL* A 19

liugha (OSw) **ljúga** (ON) verb

lie (3) **OIce** *Grg* Þsþ 27 Vís 86,
OSw *DL* Rb, *ÄVgL* Slb

liughari (OSw) noun

liar **OSw** *SdmL* Mb

liuta (OSw) **liauta** (OGu) **hljóta** (ON) **lyta** (OSw) verb

get or be assigned by lot **ONorw**
GuL Kvb, Llb, Arb, Olb, Leb

deal **ONorw** *FrL* Leb 24

get **ONorw** *GuL* Arb

inherit **OGu** *GL* A 14, 20, 24e, 28, Add. 1 (B 4)

suffer **OGu** *GL* A 27, **OSw** *UL* Kkb, Mb,
Kmb, Blb, Rb (E text), *VmL* Bb

take a share **OGu** *GL* A 26

win by lot **ONorw** *GuL* Kpb

Expressions:

liauta ater (OGu)

revert **OGu** *GL* A 20

liuþ (OSw) noun

hearing **OSw** *UL* Äb, *VmL* Äb

liþ (1) (OSw) **liþ** (OGu) noun

The meaning of *liþ* in this instance is, basically, 'gap' and has no connection with *liþ2*. As well as several related meanings, it also forms part of a number of combinations, all of them relating in some way to a link between two things — hand and arm, outside and inside a house, two fields, two villages, etc.

gap **OGu** *GL* A 24f (64), **OSw** *UL* Kkb, Blb

gate **OSw** *YVgL* Kkb, Jb, Add, *ÄVgL* Jb

passage **OSw** *SdmL* Bb

path **OSw** *YVgL* Utgb

slip rail **OSw** *UL* Blb, *VmL* Bb

track **OSw** *YVgL* Utgb

wicket-gate **OSw** *HL* Kkb

See also: *barliþ, baugliþr, farliþ, garþsliþ, gatelith, liþsmeli, liþstarkr, liþstukkr*

Refs: Schlyter 1877, s.v. *liþ* (first entry)

líþ (2) (OSw) **lið** (ON) **lidh** (OSw) **lith** (OSw) noun

The word *líþ* in this instance has the basic meaning 'company', a group of people supporting another, as well as a particular significance when linked with the word *leþunger* (q.v.), in which case it refers to the official fighting force taken by the king on the levy. It is, perhaps, simply part of an alliterative tautological expression (parallelism). It occurs in this context in the Swedish laws UL, VmL and SdmL. In the Norwegian laws, it occurs in this context in GuL; elsewhere other words are used for the same concept.

assistance **ONorw** *GuL* Llb, Mhb, Tjb, Olb, Leb

crew **ONorw** *GuL* Mhb, Leb

escort **OSw** *SmL*

fighting force **OSw** *SdmL* Kgb, Mb

help **OIce** *Grg* Vís 86, 99, *Jó* Mah 20

party **OIce** *Grg* Rsþ 230

service **OIce** *Grg* Ómb 141

support **OIce** *Grg* Þsþ 46, *Js* Mah 30

troop **OSw** *UL* Kgb, *VmL* Kgb

See also: *beini*, *flokker*, *leþunger*, *liþstæmpna*, *væzla*

Refs: KLNM, s.v.v. *leidang, lide*; Schlyter 1877, s.v. *liþ* (second entry); SL UL, 55–58 notes 30, 31; SL VmL, 40 note 16

liþer (OSw) **lith** (ODan) **liðr** (ON) noun

degree in relationship or lineage **ONorw** *GuL* Krb

joint **ODan** *ESjL* 2, **OSw** *UL* Mb

See also: *baugliþr*, *liþstarkr*

liþsmeli (OGu) **lizmeli** (OGu) **liþzmeli** (OGu) noun

gap to drive through **OGu** *GL* A 26

See also: *líþ (1)*

liþstarkr (OGu) adj.

stiffened **OGu** *GL* A 19

See also: *liþer*

liþstukkr (OGu) noun

entrance pillar **OGu** *GL* A 17

See also: *líþ (1)*

liþstæmpna (OSw) **liþstemna** (OGu) noun

mobilization **OGu** *GS* Ch. 4, **OSw** *UL* Kgb

See also: *stæmna*

liþugher (OSw) **lidugher** (OSw) **liþogher** (OSw) adj.

free **OSw** *SdmL* Kkb, Bb, Tjdb, *UL* Kkb, Kgb, Blb

freed **OSw** *SdmL* Rb

lík (ON) noun

corpse **ONorw** *GuL* Krb, Mhb

líkagröftr (ON) noun

burial **OIce** *Grg* Tíg 267

líkamslosti (ON) noun

sexual intercourse **ONorw** *GuL* Krb

líksíma (ON) noun

bolt-rope **ONorw** *GuL* Leb

líksöngr (ON) noun

burial service **OIce** *Grg* Tíg 262, 267

funeral service **OIce** *Grg* Klþ 1, 2 Arþ 125, *KRA* 11, **ONorw** *GuL* Krb

postmortem rites **ONorw** *BorgL* 12.13

líksöngskaup (ON) noun

burial service fee **OIce** *Grg* Lbþ 218

funeral fee **ONorw** *GuL* Krb

See also: *líksöngr*

líkþrár (ON) adj.

leprous **ONorw** *GuL* Leb

ljúgkviðr (ON) noun

A false verdict could be prosecuted, and was severely punished.

false verdict **OIce** *Grg* Þsþ 35, 37

Refs: Dennis, Foote and Perkins, trans., 1980, 76-77

ljúgvitni (ON) noun

Both a *vitni* (ON) 'testimony' and a *kviðr* (ON) 'verdict' that was either false or refused to be given, which was severely punished.

false witness **OIce** *Grg* Þsþ 25, 32

See also: *falsvitni*, *vitni*

Refs: Finsen 1883, III:640

ljúgvætti (ON) noun

false witness **OIce** *Grg* Þsþ 32, 58

lof (OSw) **lov** (ODan) **luf** (OGu) **lof** (ON) **loff** (OSw) **luf** (OSw) noun

confirmation **OSw** *YVgL* Add

consent **OSw** *HL* Jb, *YVgL* Kkb

leave **OGu** *GL* A 57, **OSw** *SmL*, *UL* Jb, Blb, *VmL* Bb

licence **OIce** *Grg* Lrþ 117

permission **ODan** *ESjL* 2, 3, *SkKL* 3, *SkL* 178, 196, 204, 210, 211, 240, **OGu** *GL* A 6, 24, 55, **OIce** *Grg* Þsþ 59, *Jó* Þfb 3, **OSw** *DL* Bb, *HL* Kkb, Blb, *SdmL* Kkb, Bb, Kmb, Till, *UL* Kkb, Äb, Kmb, Blb, *VmL* Kkb, Äb, Kmb, Bb, *YVgL* Kkb, Gb, Tb, Jb, Utgb, *ÄVgL* Kkb, Gb, Föb, *ÖgL* Kkb

promise **OSw** *HL* Blb

lofi (OGu) noun

flat of the hand **OGu** *GL* A 19, 62, Add. 5 (B 20)

lofliker (OSw) adj.

permissible **OSw** *ÖgL* Kkb

lofsvitni (OSw) **loff vitni** (OSw) **lufvitni** (OSw) noun

permission witness **OSw** *SdmL* Rb

witness as to permission **OSw** *UL* Jb,
Blb, Rb (E, F texts), *VmL* Bb

witness that one has permission **OSw** *DL* Bb

See also: *lof, vitni*

lok (ON) noun

cover **ONorw** *GuL* Tjb

lokurán (ON) noun

Lock-robbery. Refers to a specific situation in which
a landowner whose property has been damaged by
cattle belonging to someone else has penned in the
animals until damages are settled. Passages in Jó and
MLL relate that a charge of lock-robbery is incurred
when the owner attempts to take back his livestock
without paying for the damaged property.

burglary **OIce** *Jó* Llb 33

See also: *ran*

Refs: CV s.v. *loka*; Fritzner; Jó tr.:225

lom (OSw) noun

disability **OSw** *HL* Kkb

lotfal (ODan) noun

Possibly a procedure for distribution of land and
inheritance, as well as a means of resolving disputes
about property.

lot **ODan** *SkL* 55

See also: *luta, luter, hlutfall, lutfal*

Refs: KLNM s.v.v. *arveskifte, gudsdom,
jordejendom, lutkasting*

lotkafli (OSw) noun

A baton used for drawing lots at distributions.

lot baton **OSw** *SdmL* Mb

See also: *buþkafli, luter, skipta, kafli*

lotran (OSw) **lut ran** (OSw) noun

*robbery of goods which shall be divided
by lots* **OSw** *HL* Mb, *SdmL* Mb

lottakari (OSw) noun

participant **OSw** *YVgL* Tb, *ÄVgL* Tb

See also: *luter*

loyfa (OGu) verb

leave **OGu** *GL* A 3, 20, 24f (64), 26, 35, 48

pay back **OGu** *GL* A 56

loyfi (OGu) **leyfi** (ON) noun

licence **OIce** *Grg* Lrþ 117

permission **OGu** *GL* A 13, **OIce** *Jó* Llb 19, 26 Fml 9

privilege **OIce** *KRA* 27, 28

See also: *lof*

loyski (OGu) noun

bald patch **OGu** *GL* A 19, 62, Add. 5 (B 20)

lóð (ON) noun

crop **OFar** *Seyð* 2, **OIce** *Js* Lbb 26, **ONorw** *GuL* Llb

produce from the land **OIce** *Jó* Llb 10, 32

lufa (OGu) **lofa** (ON) verb

give leave **OGu** *GL* A 25

give permission **OGu** *GL* A 6

grant **OGu** *GS* Ch. 1

permit **OGu** *GL* A 7, 65, **OIce** *Jó*
Þjb 11, **ONorw** *EidsL* 26.1

promise **OGu** *GL* A 28, *GS* Ch. 1

luka (OSw) **lúka** (ON) **loka** (OSw) verb

compensate **OSw** *ÄVgL* Äb

disburse **OIce** *Js* Kvg 5 Ert 24, *KRA* 15

discharge **OIce** *Jó* Kab 23, *Js* Kab 4, 18, *KRA* 31

pay **OIce** *Jó* Mah 4 Kge 6 Llb 11, 49, **ONorw**
BorgL 11.3, *FrL* Rgb 24, *GuL* Kvb, Løb,
OSw *YVgL* Kkb, Vs, Frb, Äb, Gb, Rlb, Tb,
Jb, Utgb, *ÄVgL* Kkb, Slb, Äb, Jb, Tb, Föb

redeem **OSw** *ÄVgL* Jb

settle **ONorw** *BorgL* 11.2, *GuL* Kpb

lukahagg (OGu) noun

*blow that does not cause blood
to be spilt* **OGu** *GL* A 19

lukka (OGu) verb

seduce **OGu** *GL* A 21

lunder (OSw) noun

Appears as a place of pagan worship.

grove **OSw** *HL* Kkb

See also: *sten*

lunnendi (OSw) **lum** (OSw) **lumminu** (OSw) noun

Disputed form, alternatively interpreted as an
otherwise not recorded *lum*.

property **OSw** *HL* Kgb

Refs: Brink forthcoming

lurker (OSw) noun

beggar **OSw** *ÖgL* Db

luta (OSw) **lote** (ODan) **hluta** (ON) verb

assign by lots **OSw** *YVgL* Add

cast lots **ODan** *ESjL* 1, *JyL* 1, *SkL* 55,
OIce *Grg* Þsþ 22, *Jó* Kge 25 Lbb 5 Llb
13 Kab 20 Fml 6, 25, *Js* Kab 15

draw lots **OIce** *Grg* Þsþ 25, **ONorw** *GuL* Kpb,
Kvb, Llb, Arb, Leb, **OSw** *YVgL* Jb, *ÄVgL* Jb

See also: *luter*

lutadagr (OGu) noun

day of division **OGu** *GL* A 26

luter (OSw) **lot** (ODan) **luti** (OGu) **lutr** (OGu) **hluti** (ON) **hlutr** (ON) **loter** (OSw) **lytir** (OSw) noun

allotment **OSw** *YVgL* Add

case **ONorw** *GuL* Kvb, Olb

inheritance **OGu** *GL* A 20

instalment **ODan** *SkL* 43

land **ONorw** *GuL* Llb, Tjb

line (of inheritance) **OGu** *GL* A 20

lot **ODan** *ESjL* 1–3, *JyL* 1, 3, *SkL* passim, *VSjL* passim, **OIce** *Jó* Lbb 5, **ONorw** *EidsL* 32.1, *GuL* Llb, Arb, **OSw** *DL* Kkb, *HL* Kgb, Äb, Mb, Blb, *SdmL* Kkb, Kgb, Gb, Äb, Jb, Bb, Kmb, Mb, Tjdb, *UL* Äb, Mb, Blb, *VmL* Bb, *YVgL* Kkb, Jb, Add, *ÄVgL* Kkb, Jb, *ÖgL* Kkb, Eb, Db

monetary value **OGu** *GL* A 20

part **ODan** *JyL* 2, **OGu** *GL* A 3, 7, 8, 17, 25, Add. 8 (B 55), **OSw** *DL* Kkb, Mb, Bb, Gb, Tjdb, Rb, *HL* Mb, *SmL*, *UL* Kkb, Kgb, Mb, Jb, Blb, *VmL* Kkb, Kgb, Mb, *YVgL* passim, *ÄVgL* Slb, Rlb

portion **OGu** *GL* A 3, 20, 24d, 29, **OSw** *DL* Eb, *UL* Kkb, Kgb, Äb, Mb, Jb, Blb, Rb, *VmL* Kkb, Kgb, Äb, Mb, Jb, Bb, Rb

respect **OGu** *GL* A 5

section **OSw** *UL* Blb, *VmL* Bb

share **ODan** *JyL* 3, **OGu** *GL* A 26, **ONorw** *GuL* Kvb, Løb, Llb, Arb, Mhb, **OSw** *HL* Kgb, Äb, *UL* Rb, *VmL* Jb, Rb, *YVgL* Gb, Utgb, *ÄVgL* Äb

thing (2) **OGu** *GL* A 3

third **OSw** *UL* Äb, *VmL* Äb, Jb

See also: *arver*, *hiorþlöt*, *hovoþloter*

lutfal (OSw) noun

Outlying land, a piece of land separated from the lands of the village.

enclave **OSw** *DL* Bb

See also: *lotfal*, *urfiælder*, *hlutfall*

Refs: KLNM s.v.v. *gränsläggning*, *hump*, *urfjäll*

lutlös (OSw) **lotlös** (OSw) adj.

impartial **OSw** *HL* Mb, Blb, Rb

not involved **OSw** *HL* Blb

without share **OSw** *HL* Kkb

See also: *luter*

lutskipter (OSw) adj.

divided into lots **OSw** *ÖgL* Db

lyf (ON) noun

An herb; medicine. Refers particularly to plants involved with healing or sorcery.

herb **ONorw** *EidsL* 45.4

Refs: CV s.v. *lyf*; Fritzner s.v. *lyf*; ONP s.v. *lyf*

lygð (ON) noun

lie **OIce** *Jó* Fml 6

See also: *liugha*

lykil (OSw) **lykel** (ODan) **nykil** (OSw) noun

Keys appear in contexts of legal responsibility of stolen goods found in houses and containers (ODan JyL 2; OSw HL Mb; UL Mb; YVgL Kkb), theft from churches (OSw DL, SdmL), the care of ships (GL A 36), and women's legal status (ODan ESjL 1; OSw UL Äb; YVgL Gb, Add).

key **ODan** *ESjL* 1, 3, *JyL* 2, *VSjL* 87, **OSw** *DL* Kkb, *HL* Mb, *SdmL* Kkb, *YVgL* Kkb, Gb, Tb, Add, *ÄVgL* Äb, Tb

Expressions:

las ok lykil (OSw)

lock and key **OSw** *HL* Äb

See also: *las*

Refs: Carlsson 1942

lykkia (OGu) **lykia** (OGu) verb

seal **OGu** *GS* Ch. 4

lyktaran (OSw) noun

robbery of confiscated goods **OSw** *UL* Rb

lyktarvitni (OSw) **ályktarvitni** (ON) **álykðarvitni** (ON) **lyktar** (OSw) noun

conclusive testimony **OIce** *Jó* Kab 2, *Js* Kab 2, **ONorw** *GuL* Løb

final witness **OSw** *SdmL* Kkb

sworn testimony concerning final judgement **OSw** *VmL* Kkb

See also: *vitni*

lyktrygguar (pl.) (OGu) **littrygg** (OGu) **lyktryggiar (pl.)** (OGu) noun

expiry period **OGu** *GL* A 63

lypta (OGu) **lyfta** (OGu) verb

take **OGu** *GL* A 31

See also: *liuta*

lyptinger (OSw) **lypting** (OSw) noun

poop deck **OSw** *UL* Mb, *VmL* Mb

lysa (OSw) **ljuse** (ODan) **lysa** (OGu) **lýsa** (ON) **liusa** (OSw) verb

announce **OIce** *Jó* Þfb 5 Lbb 3 Llb 50 Kab 9 Þjb 5, 13 Fml 21, *Js* Mah 14 Kvg 2 Lbb 5 Þjb 4, *KRA* 15, 16, **ONorw** *FrL* Mhb 7 ArbB 5, *GuL* Kvb, Løb, Llb, Arb, Tfb, Mhb, Olb, Leb, **OSw** *DL* Mb, Bb, Tjdb, *HL* Kkb, Mb, *SdmL* Conf, Kkb, Bb, Kmb, Mb, Tjdb, *YVgL* Kkb, Drb, Gb, Tb, Jb, Föb, Add, *ÄVgL* Md, Smb, Slb, Jb, Tb, Fös

announce lawfully **OSw** *DL* Tjdb

dawn **OGu** *GL* A 8

declare **ODan** *ESjL* 3, *VSjL* 87, **OGu** *GL*
A 28, **OIce** *Jó* Mah 10 Llb 34, **ONorw** *FrL*
Mhb 23, **OSw** *UL* Kkb, Äb, Mb, Kmb, Blb,
VmL Kkb, Kgb, Mb, Kmb, Bb, Rb

make a declaration **OGu** *GL* A 3

make a public declaration **ODan** *ESjL* 3

make known **OIce** *Jó* Kge 9, **ONorw** *EidsL* 33.4

make public **ODan** *ESjL* 1–3, *JyL* 1–3, *SkKL*
11, *SkL* 17, 41, 42, 52, 59, 63, 64, 148, 166,
170, *VSjL* 22, 68, 70, 86, 87, **OSw** *HL* Mb

make public at the assembly **ODan** *ESjL* 3

prescribe **OSw** *YVgL* Add

proclaim **OGu** *GL* Add. 8 (B 55), *GS* Ch. 2,
OSw *UL* StfBm, *YVgL* Rlb, *ÄVgL* Rlb

publicly declare **ODan** *SkL* 59

publish **OIce** *Grg* passim, *Jó* Mah 6 Kge 3 Lbb 5

read the banns **OSw** *UL* Kkb, *VmL* Kkb

report **OIce** *Jó* Mah 10 Þjb 9

See also: *laghlysa*, *thingljuse*, *þing*

lysning (OSw) **ljusning** (ODan) **lýsing** (ON) noun

The purpose of an announcement (*lysning*) was to call
certain facts to the attention of assembled men, usually
at church, at an ale feast, or at the assembly (see *þing*).
Such notice had to be given to validate certain acts and
to keep alive certain rights, such as the right to redeem
odal land.

announcement **ONorw** *GuL* Arb, Olb,
OSw *DL* Mb, *HL* Mb, *SdmL* Bb, Tjdb

announcing **OIce** *Jó* Fml 21, *KRA* 16,
ONorw *FrL* KrbB 19 Kvb 5

declaration **OSw** *UL* Mb, Rb, *VmL* Mb

publication **ODan** *ESjL* 2

publishing **OIce** *Grg* Þsþ 21, 57 Vís 87

See also: *löglýsing*, *næmni*

Refs: KLNM s.v.v. bröllop, hittegods, hämnd,
lysing, termin, ægteskab, ættleiing

lysningavitni (OSw) noun

announcement witness **OSw** *SdmL* Tjdb, Rb

witness that something was announced
OSw *DL* Mb, *HL* Mb

witness to an announcement of a crime **OSw** *DL* Mb

See also: *vitni*

lysta (1) (OSw) **liausta** (OGu) **ljósta** (ON) **lustin** (OSw)
verb

beat **ONorw** *FrL* KrbA 10 Mhb 22, *GuL* Løb,
Mhb, **OSw** *YVgL* Kkb, Frb, *ÄVgL* Kkb, Slb

cut **OSw** *ÄVgL* Smb

harpoon **ONorw** *GuL* Llb

hurt **ONorw** *GuL* Mhb

strike **OGu** *GL* A 19, **OIce** *Grg* Vís
111, *Js* Mah 16, 17, *KRA* 8

See also: *bardaghi*, *bæria*, *diunga*

lysta (2) (OSw) verb

wish **OSw** *UL* Kkb, Blb

lyte (ODan) verb

maim **ODan** *JyL* 3, *SkL* 94, *VSjL* 30

lytessar (ODan) noun

maiming wound **ODan** *VSjL* 36

lytesvirthning (ODan) noun

valuation of maiming **ODan** *VSjL* 32

lyti (OSw) **lyte** (ODan) **áljótr** (ON) **lýti.** (ON) **liute**
(OSw) **lysti** (OSw) noun

blemish **OIce** *Grg* Misc 238

damage **ODan** *JyL* 3

deformity **ODan** *ESjL* 2, **OSw** *HL* Mb, *UL* Mb

disadvantage **ODan** *ESjL* 2

disfigurement **OIce** *Grg* Misc 237, 244,
OSw *SdmL* Mb, *UL* Mb, Blb, *VmL* Mb

failing **OSw** *VmL* Äb

injury **ODan** *VSjL* 33, 86

maiming **ODan** *ESjL* 2, 3, *JyL* 3, *SkL* 94, 95, 105,
122, *VSjL* 27, 32, 34, 36–38, 41, 44, 46, 49, 86

Expressions:

laster æller lyti, laster æller liute (OSw)

fault or failing **OSw** *VmL* Äb

See also: *laster*

lytisbot (OSw) **lytesbot** (ODan) noun

compensation for maiming **ODan** *ESjL* 2, *VSjL* 33

disfigurement fine **OSw** *DL* Mb, *SdmL* Mb, *VmL* Mb

fine for maiming **ODan** *VSjL* 46

maiming compensation **OSw** *ÖgL* Vm

maiming-fine **ODan** *VSjL* 36

payment for maiming **ODan** *SkL* 105

See also: *bot*, *lyti*

lytter (OSw) **lytr** (OGu) adj.

damaged **OGu** *GL* A 19, Add. 4 (B 19)

defective **OSw** *YVgL* Frb

maimed **OSw** *HL* Mb

lyznuvarþer (OSw) noun

listening guard **OSw** *SdmL* Kgb

lyþbiskuper (OSw) **ljóðbyskup** (ON) noun

A suffragan bishop beneath the archbishop; the term
has been used to translate Medieval Lat. *suffraganeus*
('subordinate'). A *ljóðbyskup* still refers to a
subordinate bishop in Modern Icelandic. Thought to
be derived from OE *leoð-byscop* ('people-bishop').
As such it can also refer to a bishop of an entire area

or people, including an archbishop. In Iceland the Archbishop of Níðarós confirmed the election of a *ljóðbiskup* and performed his consecration.

The term *lyþbiskuper* was also used to designate missionary bishops who preached the gospel among the 'gentiles', including the Nordic peoples. A *lyþbiskuper* has also been identified as a type of rural bishop (*korbiskop*) who was responsible for a district of countryside until at least the sixth century and possibly as late as the ninth. These were bishops without a fixed see and who assisted with consecrations and acted on the behalf of the ordinary bishops when the latter were unavailable.

bishop **ONorw** *FrL* Intr 1

people's bishop **OSw** *SdmL* Kgb

suffragan bishop **OIce** *Js* Kdb 3 Mah 7

See also: *biskuper*

Refs: Brink 2010a; CV s.v. *ljóðbiskup*; Fritzner s.v. *ljóðbiskup*; Hertzberg s.v. *ljóðbiskup*; Keyser 1856, 142; KLNM s.v. *ærkebiskop*; Magnús Már Lárusson 1956; NF s.v. *korbiskopar*; ODS s.v. *lydbiskop*; Rietz 1962 s.v. *löid*; SAOB s.v. *lyd*; von See 1964, 60

lyþir (pl.) (OSw) noun

people **OSw** *SdmL* Mb

Expressions:

allir lyþir (pl.) (OGu)

all the people **OGu** *GL* A 13, 14, Add. 1 (B 4)

everyone **OGu** *GL* A 28

general assembly **OGu** *GL* A 2

þing fyri alla lyþi, þing firi alla lyþi (OGu)

all the people at the general assembly **OGu** *GL* Add. 1 (B 4)

general assembly **OGu** *GL* Add. 1 (B 4)

See also: *land, maþer, þing*

lyðskylda (ON) noun

homage **OIce** *Js* Kdb 3, 7

See also: *þegnskylda*

lyðskærr (ON) adj.

Carve-able by the people. Refers to the practice of allowing free men to flense for themselves portions of certain types of whale.

which everyone has a right to carve **ONorw** *FrL* LlbB 10

Refs: CV s.v. *lyðskærr*; Fritzner s.v. *lyðskærr*; Hertzberg s.v. *lyðskærr*

lyrittareiðr (ON) **lyritareiðr** (ON) noun

folk-law-oath **ONorw** *EidsL* 45.6

oath of three **OIce** *Jó* Mah 22 Kge 20, 32 Llb 19, 39 Kab 14 Þjb 3, 21, *Js* Mah 12, 22 Rkb 1

Kab 10 Þjb 6, *KRA* 2, 18, **ONorw** *FrL* KrbB 3, 5 Mhb 15 Var 9 Leb 3 Bvb 11 Reb 2

three-man oath **ONorw** *FrL* KrbA 1, 35

See also: *eþer, þriggjamannaeiðr*

lyrittarvörn (ON) noun

veto-ban **OIce** *Grg* Lbþ 174, 185

lyritti (ON) **lyriti** (ON) noun

Three boundary stones marking divisions between properties. According to Jó Lbb 3 (and MLL VI.3) these are also called *marksteinar* (see *marksteinn*). Associated with the power of 'veto' (ON *lyrittr*). It has been suggested that these stones serve as a type of witness and derive their name from the legal term for a three-man oath (ON *lyrittareiðr*), though at least one scholar has argued that the stones predate the oath (cf. Páll Vídalín 1854 s.v. *lyrittar*).

boundary stone **OIce** *Jó* Lbb 3

See also: *mark (3), marksteinn, mærki, tiældrusten, þræstene*

Refs: Fritzner s.v. *lyrittarstein, lyritti*; Hertzberg s.v. *lyriti, lyrittarstein*; KLNM s.v. *jordejendom, lyrittr*; Páll Vídalín 1854 s.v. *lyrittar*

lyrittnæmr (ON) noun

Expressions:

lyrittnæm sök (ON)

case conferring rights of veto **OIce** *Grg* Þsþ 80 Bat 113

lyrittr (ON) **lyrit** (ON) **lyritr** (ON) **lyritt** (ON) noun

A prohibition or veto. These could be issued in a variety of circumstances during private cases, such as prohibiting a man thought to be deserting dependents from leaving the country (Grg Ómb 132) or forbidding owners of pasture land from grazing when boundaries were not properly established (Grg Lbþ 175). A similar, and probably related, term is used to indicate stone boundary markers (q.v. *lyritti*). Hoff (2012, 329) suggests that ON *lyrittr* parallels the concepts of *actio auctoritatis* or *actio finium regundorum* in Roman Law. One commonly accepted etymology of *lyrittr* is *lyð* ('people') and *réttr* ('rights') which yields an interpretation of 'the law of the people, the law of the land' as in GuL Løb and Jó Llb 26.

law **ONorw** *GuL* Løb

laws of the people **OIce** *Jó* Llb 26

veto **OIce** *Grg* Klþ 4 Þsþ 25, 37 Bat 113 Lrþ 117 Ómb 128, 132 Feþ 144, 158 Lbþ 174, 183 Misc 250, **ONorw** *FrL* Rgb 6

Expressions:

verja lyritti (ON)

to forbid by veto **OIce** *Grg* Þsþ 58

See also: *lögfesta*

Refs: CV s.v. *lyritr*; Finsen III:641–43; GrgTr II:400; Hertzberg; Hoff 2012, 329; KLNM s.v. *lýrittr*; ONP; von See 1964, 57–63; de Vries 2000 s.v. *lyréttr*

lýsistollr (ON) noun

light toll **OIce** *KRA* 13, 15

læa (OSw) **ljá** (ON) **lea** (OSw) verb

lend **OIce** *Grg* Klþ 5 Ómb 131 Feþ 164 Fjl 225, *Js* Kvg 1 Kab 16, *KRA* 1, 3, **ONorw** *FrL* Rgb 45, *GuL* Kpb, Løb, **OSw** *DL* Bb

loan **OIce** *Jó* Kge 2 Llb 47 Þjb 16 Fml 28

rent **ONorw** *FrL* Intr 18

Expressions:

læa sik til (OSw)

intend **OSw** *UL* Mb *VmL* Mb

læande (OSw) noun

lender **OSw** *UL* Kmb, *VmL* Kmb

lægarth (ODan) noun

depository **ODan** *VSjL* 57

storehouse **ODan** *VSjL* 53

læggia (OSw) **leggja** (ON) **laggher** (OSw) **lagher** (OSw) **lagþær** (OSw) verb

declare **OSw** *UL* Kgb, *VmL* Kgb, Äb, Bb

decree **OSw** *UL* Kgb, *VmL* Kgb

Expressions:

leggja á (ON)

incur a fine **OIce** *Jó* Llb 9 *Js* Lbb 12

leggja til (ON)

endow **OIce** *Grg* Klþ 4

leggja við (ON)

to charge (with a crime) **OIce** *Jó* Kab 14

læggia fram/niþer/in (OGu, OSw)

deposit **OSw** *DL* Bb

lay in custody **OSw** *HL* Rb

leave **OGu** *GL* Add. 1 (B4)

See also: *laghvinna*

lægher (OSw) **lægher** (ODan) noun

fornication **OSw** *YVgL* Gb, Add, *ÄVgL* Gb

sleeping with **ODan** *SkL* 217

See also: *hor, löskalæghi, lønlæghe*

lægherbarn (OSw) noun

child of fornication **OSw** *YVgL* Add

læghersbot (OSw) noun

compensation for fornication **OSw** *YVgL* Gb, Add

fine for adultery **OSw** *HL* Äb

See also: *bot, lægher*

lægherstaþer (OSw) noun

burial place **OSw** *YVgL* Kkb, *ÄVgL* Kkb

grave **OSw** *SmL*

læghervite (ODan) noun

illegal intercourse **ODan** *JyL* 2

lying with a woman **ODan** *JyL* 1

lægþorætter (OSw) noun

right of land tenancy **OSw** *VmL* Mb

lækersbot (OSw) **lækisbot** (OSw) noun

doctor's fee **OSw** *DL* Mb, *YVgL* Mb

See also: *bot*

lækir (OSw) noun

doctor **OSw** *HL* Mb

physician **OSw** *SdmL* Mb

lækirsgæf (OSw) **lækesgave** (ODan) **lækesgift** (ODan) noun

leech's fee **ODan** *VSjL* 86

medical expenses **ODan** *JyL* 3, *SkL* 105, 122

physician's fee **OSw** *YVgL* Vs, *ÄVgL* Smb, Vs

See also: *gæf, lækningarkaup, lækærisfæ*

lækningarkaup (ON) noun

physician's fee **ONorw** *GuL* Mhb

See also: *lækærisfæ*

lækærisfæ (OSw) **læknisfé** (ON) noun

doctor's fee **OIce** *Jó* Mah 8, *Js* Mah 8

doctor's payment **OSw** *HL* Mb

leech money **ONorw** *FrL* Mhb 11, 12

See also: *lækirsgæf, lækningarkaup*

læn (OSw) **læn** (ODan) **lén** (ON) noun

Literally 'loan'. Granted by a superior to a subordinate, and may refer to the area granted, the revenue from this area, the office controlling it, and it is not always clear which of the senses is intended. Most of the regulations deal with restrictions on the fief-holder's rights, and with causes for him to lose his fief. In OIce *Jó* referring to the king's sheriff in charge of a district.

area of an office **ODan** *JyL* 2

charge of a district **OIce** *Jó* Fml 14

county **OSw** *UL* Kgb, Kmb, Rb, *VmL* Kmb

enfeoffment **OSw** *SdmL* Kgb, Kmb, Till

fief **OSw** *YVgL* Urb, Add

office **ODan** *JyL* 2, 3

See also: *lænsmaþer*

Refs: Cleasby and Vigfusson s.v. *lén*; Fritzner s.v. *lén*; Gammeldansk ordbog s.v. *læn*; Hertzberg s.v. *lén*; KLNM s.v. *län*; Schlyter s.v. *læn*; Schlyter Bihang s.v. *læn*

lænder (OSw) **lendr** (ON) adj.

The landed man (*lænder maþer, lendr maðr*, so called because he had been endowed with land from the king) was a local magnate who acted as the king's highest representative in his district. He was a royal vassal, attached to the king by an oath of fealty and service. He was ranked below an earl, but above a freeholder. With respect to personal rights, his status (in the FrL and GuL) was equal to that of the *stallari* (q.v.), i.e. twice as high as that of a freeholder. He belonged to the group of the king's most important advisers. In the king's retinue (*hirð*) he was counted among the officers. If the son of a landed man was not endowed with land by the king before he was 40 years old, he was not counted as a landed man.

Men holding this title were called barons after 1277, and they were granted the right to use the title *herra* (see *hærra*).

In Sweden the concept of *lænder maþer* is only known from the VgL. He seems to have been an aristocrat. His functions are unknown.

Expressions:

lænder maþer (OSw) **lendr maðr,**
lendir menn (pl.) (ON)

baron **OIce** *Jó* Kab 1 Þjb 3

landed man **ONorw** *EidsL* 48.1; 50.1 *FrL* Intr 1 Mhb 10, 52 Var 43 Leb 8 Rgb 8 LlbA 15 Reb 2 *GuL* Krb, Kpb, Kvb, Løb, Llb, Arb, Tfb, Mhb, Tjb, Ulb, Leb **OIce** *Js* Kdb 3 Mah 7, 29

länderman **OSw** *YVgL* Jb *ÄVgL* Jb

See also: *jarl, merkismaðr, riddari*

Refs: Andrae 1960, 77 ff.; Bagge 2010, 53, 80, 119, 233; DMA s.v. *Scandinavia: Political and legal organization*; Helle 2001, 149–52, 154–55, 159–60; Hertzberg s.v. *lendr maðr*; KLNM s.v.v. *baron, befalingsmand, edsformular, hird, jarl, lendmann, stænder, årmann*; Lindkvist 2009a, 62–63; Nilsson 2012, 207–09; Robberstad 1981, 378; SL 5, 143; Wærdahl 2011, 51; 2013, 96

lænsmaþer (OSw) **lénsmaðr** (ON) **lænsman** (OSw) **lænsmander** (OSw) noun

In the most general sense, a *lænsmaþer* was a representative, proxy or deputy to a higher official. Like *gælkare* (q.v.), the title has been used to translate Lat. *exactor*. In Denmark and Norway a representative of this kind was often called *høvedsmand*.

In the Swedish laws a *lænsmaþer* was often an official of the king (OSw *konungs lænsmaþer*) or bishop (OSw *biskups lænsmaþer*) who saw to local administrative matters and represented their interests at assemblies (OSw *þing*) and collected taxes and fines on their behalf. *Lænsmaþer* also appears to be interchangeable with the term for prosecutor (OSw *soknari*) in YVgL, ÖgL and SmL, all of which appear to have functions similar to the Norwegian *ármaðr* (q.v.). According to UL the *lænsmaþer* had the privilege of convening a panel (OSw *næmd*) which selects judges (OSw *domari*) in each hundred (OSw *hundari*). The *husabyman* (q.v.) in DL may have been the equivalent of a *lænsmaþer* in Dalarna, though the former may have had some slightly different responsibilities or indeed have been subordinate to the *lænsmaþer*. The terms *konungs maþer* and *biskups maþer* in OSw DL and HL may refer to a *lænsmaþer*.

In Denmark and Norway a *lænsmaþer* may also refer specifically to a holder of a fief (ON *lén*, see *læn*) granted by the king (or a bishop, in the case of church estates). As such he operated as governor of an area during the Middle Ages and was permitted to make use of the region's incomes.

In Norway a *lénsmaðr* often referred to a deputy to the sheriff (*sýslumaðr*, see *sysluman*) and acted on his behalf, particularly by serving in court proceedings. He also had the authority to arrest criminals. There were not supposed to be more than two *lénsmenn* in any given district (*fylki*). According to an ordinance issued in 1293, a man who was appointed *lénsmaðr* had to be a householder (*bóndi*, see *bonde*) from a good family. The most important function of a *lénsmaðr* was collecting incomes, namely taxes and fines. He also had police duties and could stand in for the law-man (*lögmaðr*, see *laghmaþer*). After 1537 the administration system was restructured and a *lénsmaðr* was renamed *bondelensmann*. The title *lensmann* is still used in Norway.

In the Icelandic laws the *lénsmaðr* generally refers to the sheriff and his aides. The term does not appear until amendments began to be made to Jónsbók, though it is used in several medieval Icelandic diplomas thereafter.

administrator **OSw** *YVgL* Kkb, Urb, Tb, Föb, Add
bailiff **OSw** *DL* Mb, Tjdb, Rb, *HL* Mb, Rb
bishop's administrator **OSw** *UL* Kkb, *VmL* Kkb
deputy **ONorw** *FrL* Mhb 60
king's administrator **OSw** *HL* Rb, *YVgL* Urb, Tb
king's local administrator **OSw** *HL* Rb
local administrator **OSw** *UL* Kgb, Mb, Kmb, Blb, Rb, *VmL* Mb, Kmb, Bb, Rb
official **OSw** *HL* Kkb
representative **OSw** *SdmL* Kkb, Jb, Bb, Kmb, Mb, Tjdb, Rb
sheriff **OSw** *HL* Rb

Expressions:

biskups lænsmaþer, biskups lænsman, biskops lænsman, biskops man (OSw)
bishop's administrator **OSw** *UL* Kkb, Äb, Mb *VmL* Kkb
bishop's bailiff **OSw** *DL* Kkb, Rb
bishop's official **OSw** *HL* Kkb
konungs lænsmaþer, konungs man, kunungs lænsman (OSw)
king's administrator **OSw** *DL* Tjdb *UL* Kkb, Mb, Rb *VmL* Mb, Rb
king's bailiff **OSw** *HL* Md *DL* Mb, Rb
See also: *ármaðr, gælkare, husabyman, laghmaþer, læn, sysluman, umbuþsman*

Refs: CV s.v. *lén*; F s.v. *lénsmaðr*; KLNM s.v. *embedsindtægter, høvedsmand, lensmann, soknare* ; LexMA s.v. *Lehen*; NGL s.v. *lénsmaðr*; Schlyter s.v. *lænsmaþer*; SNL s.v. *lensmann*

lænspræster (OSw) noun
deputy priest **OSw** *YVgL* Kkb, *ÄVgL* Kkb
See also: *prester*

lærder (OSw) lærth (ODan) lerþr (OGu) lærþer (OSw) adj.
cleric **ODan** *ESjL* 2
learned **ODan** *JyL* 1–3, **OSw** *SmL*, *UL* Jb, *ÄVgL* Äb
ordained **OGu** *GL* A 5, Add. 1 (B 4)

læript (OSw) lerept (OGu) léreft (ON) lérept (ON) noun
Used as currency.
linen **OGu** *GL* A 65, **OIce** *Grg* Arþ 125, *Jó* Kab 6 Þjb 23, **OSw** *DL* Kkb, *HL* Kgb
linen cloth **ONorw** *GuL* Mhb

læsa (OSw) verb
harvest **OSw** *VmL* Bb
read **OSw** *ÄVgL* Kkb

læst (OSw) læst (ODan) noun
defect **OSw** *SdmL* Kmb, *YVgL* Vs, *ÄVgL* Smb, Vs
disfigurement **OSw** *UL* l, *VmL* Mb
mutilation **ODan** *JyL* 3
See also: *lyti*

læsta (OSw) læste (ODan) lesta (OGu) lesta (ON) verb
damage **OGu** *GL* A 19, **OIce** *Jó* Fml 11, *KRA* 4, **OSw** *DL* Bb, *ÄVgL* Smb
incapacitate **OGu** *GL* A 19
injure **ODan** *ESjL* 2, **OIce** *Jó* Kab 16
maim **OGu** *GL* A 17, **OSw** *YVgL* Rlb, *ÄVgL* Rlb
mutilate **OSw** *YVgL* Frb
See also: *spilla, styva*

læstemal (ODan) noun
mutilation case **ODan** *VSjL* 33

læstisbot (OSw) noun
compensation for defect **OSw** *ÄVgL* Smb
deformity fine **OSw** *HL* Mb
disfigurement **OSw** *DL* Mb
disfigurement compensation **OSw** *UL* Mb, *VmL* Mb
See also: *bot, læst*

löfvirkinger (OSw) noun
vagrant **OSw** *YVgL* Drb
See also: *lösvittinger*

lögarfi (ON) noun
legal heir **OIce** *Jó* Llb 28

lögbaugr (ON) noun
A 'legal ring'. Four types of legal ring are outlined in Grg Bat 113, which recounts the division of wergild among the victim's family members. In FrL *lögbaugar* are a fine submitted to the king by the perpetrator of certain types of injures. These fines are in addition to wound compensation (ON *sárbót*) and doctor's fees paid to the injured person. Bj (NGL I:306) stipulates that injuries committed by multiple persons at a marketplace (ON *kaupangr*, see *köpunger*) required *lögbaugar* to be paid both to the king and the men of the town. [CV equates *lögbaugr* with *höfuðbaugr*, but this does not appear to be correct? In Grg Bat 113 a *höfuðbaugr* is called the 'main ring' and refers to the first category of *lögbaugar*, i.e. the three-mark rings.]
ring (wergild) fixed by law **OIce** *Grg* Bat 113, **ONorw** *FrL* Mhb 16, 17
wergild **ONorw** *FrL* Mhb 11
See also: *baugatal, baugþak, bogher, höfuðbaugr, sarabot, þveiti*

Refs: CV s.v. *baugr*; F; Finsen III:588; Hagland and Sandnes 1997, 109; Hertzberg; Hoff 2012, 185; KLNM s.v. *legemskrænkelse, mansbot*

lögbeiðing (ON) noun
legal request **OIce** *Grg* Þsþ 25, 58 Lrþ 117 Misc 244

Lögberg (ON) noun
The Law-Rock; part of the Icelandic General Assembly (ON *alþingi*) during the Commonwealth. The Law-Rock was the seat of the lawspeaker (ON *lögsögumaðr*) and was the location for announcements, such as new laws. It fell out of use after Js was introduced in 1271. The actual site of the Law-Rock at Þingvellir is unknown, though several places have been suggested.
Law Rock **OIce** *Grg* Vís 99 Lsþ 116
See also: *þingbrekka*

Refs: CV; F; GAO s.v. *Þingvellir*;
KLNM s.v. *lögberg*; Z s.v. *lǫgberg*

lögboð (ON) noun

legal offer **OIce** *Grg* Arþ 122 Lbþ
192, **ONorw** *GuL* Olb

lögbrot (ON) noun

breach of law **OIce** *Jó* Llb 56

See also: *brut*

lögeiðr (ON) noun

A lawful oath. In Grg Þsþ 49 this kind of oath is
sworn on a book, though in several instances a
cross is stipulated (e.g. Grg Þsþ 25). A passage in
Landnámabók in which lawful oaths are sworn on
rings suggests that the practice predates the Christian
period.

lawful oath **OIce** *Grg* Þsþ 25, 41 Ómb 129
Lbþ 178 Tíg 255, **ONorw** *FrL* Rgb 24

See also: *eþer*

Refs: CV; Fritzner; Hertzberg; KLNM
s.v. *edsformular, kors*; RGA s.v. *Eid*

lögeindagi (ON) noun

legal settling day **OIce** *Grg* Fjl 221

lögeyrir (ON) noun

lawful money **ONorw** *GuL* Mhb, Olb

legal tender **OIce** *Grg* Klþ 6 Þsþ 51, 78
Vís 88, 102 Bat 113 Arþ 122 Feþ 148 Lbþ
193 Fjl 221, 222 Hrs 234, *Jó* Kab 5

lögfardagar (pl.) (ON) **lögfaradagar (pl.)** (ON) noun

legal moving days **OIce** *Grg* Klþ 2 Tíg 255

lögfasta (ON) noun

established fast **OIce** *Grg* Klþ 16, 17 Feþ 148

legal fast **OIce** *KRA* 26

lögfastr (ON) adj.

legally resident **OIce** *Grg* Klþ 1, 2 Vís 87,
89 Ómb 143 Rsþ 228 Misc 238, *KRA* 1

lögfesta (ON) verb

claim **ONorw** *FrL* ArbA 16

place a ban on **OIce** *Jó* Llb 4, 15

secure by law **ONorw** *FrL* ArbB 28

lögfesta (ON) noun

ban **OIce** *Jó* Llb 26, 52

lawful prohibition **ONorw** *FrL* LlbB 7

legal ban **ONorw** *FrL* Leb 26

lögfé (ON) noun

legal payment **ONorw** *BorgL* 17.14

lögfóstr (ON) noun

legal fostering **OIce** *Grg* Vís 89

lögfóstri (ON) noun

legal foster-son **OIce** *Grg* Vís 89

lögfrétt (ON) noun

legal information **OIce** *Grg* Þsþ 27

lögfullr (ON) adj.

lawful **OIce** *Jó* Þfb 9, *Js* Þfb 6 Lbb 1

See also: *laghliker, rætter*

lögföstnun (ON) noun

legal betrothal **OIce** *Grg* Feþ 144

löggjöf (ON) noun

gift allowed by law **OIce** *Jó* Kge 22

löggrið (ON) noun

legal domicile **OIce** *Grg* Þsþ 22, 78

See also: *griðfang*

löggrind (ON) noun

legal gate **OIce** *Jó* Llb 32

lögheilagr (ON) adj.

Expressions:

lögheilagr dagr (ON)

established holy day **OIce** *Grg* Feþ 148 Lbþ 185,
198 Fjl 221 Tíg 265 *Jó* Llb 3, 69 *Js* Lbb 11 *KRA* 30

lögheimili (ON) noun

legal home **OIce** *Grg* Klþ 4, 6 Þsþ 27, 78 Feþ 156 Fjl
221, 222 Hrs 235 Misc 251, 252 Tíg 255, *KRA* 15

löghlið (ON) noun

established gateway **OIce** *Grg* Klþ 8

legal gateway **OIce** *Grg* Lbþ 206, *KRA* 26

löghreppr (ON) noun

established commune **OIce** *Grg*
Klþ 5 Feþ 156 Hrs 234, 235

legal commune **OIce** *Jó* Kge 31

lögkaup (ON) noun

legal fee **OIce** *Grg* Klþ 6 Tíg 265

legal pay **OIce** *Grg* Þsþ 78

lögkominn (ON) adj.

lawfully entitled **OIce** *Jó* Kge 9

lögkvöð (ON) **lagakvöð** (ON) noun

legal calling **OIce** *Grg* Þsþ 26 Lbþ
177, 199, **ONorw** *FrL* Rgb 6

löglangr (ON) adj.

of lawful length **OIce** *Jó* Fml 24

lögleið (ON) noun

established autumnal meeting **OIce** *Grg* Klþ 6

lögleiga (ON) noun

interest at a legal rate **OIce** *Grg* Arþ 122, 126 Fjl 221

legal rent **OIce** *Jó* Kab 15

löglengð (ON) noun

   lawful length **OIce** *Jó* Fml 24

lögleysa (ON) noun

   contempt of law **OIce** *Jó* Llb 15,
   ONorw *GuL* Kpb, Olb

löglýrittr (ON) noun

   legal veto **OIce** *Grg* Þsþ 58 Ómb 132

löglýsing (ON) noun

   legal publishing **OIce** *Grg* Þsþ 21,
   39 Vís 88 Lbþ 172 Tíg 259

   See also: *lysning*

lögmannsinnsigli (ON) noun

   seal of the presiding judge **OIce** *Jó* Kab 12

lögmark (ON) noun

   lawful mark **OIce** *Grg* Fjl 225, *Jó* Llb 57, 60, *KRA* 26

lögmálaland (ON) noun

   land subject to a right of lawful pre-emption **OIce** *Grg* Lbþ 193

lögmáli (ON) noun

   right of lawful pre-emption **OIce** *Grg*
   Lbþ 192, *Jó* Lbb 8, *Js* Lbb 5

lögmet (ON) noun

   legal valuation **ONorw** *GuL* Olb

lögmetandi (ON) noun

   lawful valuer **OIce** *Grg* Þsþ 51, 67
   Fjl 221 Hrs 234 Misc 246

lögmætr (ON) adj.

   deemed by law **OIce** *Grg* Vís 86, 88

lögpundari (ON) noun

   lawful steelyard **OIce** *Grg* Rsþ 232

lögráðandi (ON) noun

   legal administrator **OIce** *Grg* Klþ 4 Þsþ 81 Feþ
   144, 152 Misc 238 Tíg 259, *Js* Lbb 4, 8, *KRA* 15

   See also: *forráðandi*

lögrán (ON) noun

   denial of legal right **ONorw** *GuL* Olb

lögrengð (ON) noun

   rejection at law **OIce** *Grg* Þsþ 20, 25

lögrétt (ON) noun

An enclosure for livestock gathered together following the summer grazing season. Landowners were required to drive all animals found on their land to these enclosures so that they could be sorted and collected by their owners through identification of lawful ownership marks (ON *lögmark*). Locations for lawful enclosures were determined by the men of the district (ON *heraðsmaðr*, see *hæraþsmaþer*), or possibly men of the commune (ON *hreppsmaðr*).

   lawful fold **OIce** *Grg* Fjl 225

   sheep gathering **OIce** *Jó* Llb 49

   See also: *fjallganga*, *rétt*

   Refs: CV s.v. *lögrétt*; Fritzner; Hertzberg s.v. *lögrétt*; KLNM s.v. *fåreavl*, *hreppr*

lögrétta (ON) noun

This institution was peculiar to Norw and Ice law. The word is derived from the expression *rétta lög*, i.e. to provide a valid explanation and interpretation of what the law says about a given case (see Hertzberg, s.v. *lögrétta*; KLNM, s.v. *lagting*). In Iceland, this expression had a wider meaning (see below).

In Norway the *lögrétta* was a panel or tribunal under the provincial assembly (the *lagþing*, see *laghþing*). Originally it seems to have consisted of 36 men, authorized together with the law-speaker to explain the law, pass judgements or sentences, or give verdicts. To be legally binding, the decisions of the *lögrétta* had to be approved by the assembly.

The size of the *lögrétta* is a moot question in Norw legal history. An older group of scholars thought that the *lögrétta* was composed of three tribunals only, each consisting of twelve men. Later scholars tend to believe that it was constituted by the whole body of delegates to the provincial assembly, which in the *Frostuþing* consisted of four hundred men.

Whether large or small, its function as a judicial power and ultimate court of law seems certain as far as the provincial laws are concerned, until the introduction of King Magnus the Law-Mender's Law of the Realm (the 'ML landslov') 1274 (see Strauch 2016, 115, 153, 168).

In Iceland the *lögrétta* (the Law Council) was originally a body under the *alþingi*. The expression *rétta lög* was here also taken to mean 'formulating or passing laws' (see KLNM, s.v. *lögrétta*). In the period 930–ca. 965 it seems to have been composed of the law-speaker and 36 *goðar* (see *goði*), each accompanied by two ordinary members of the *alþingi* 'General Assembly'. Around 965 additional members were appointed, and from 1106 onwards, Iceland's two bishops joined the *lögrétta*. The total number of members then amounted to 147 persons. As already indicated, the Icel *lögrétta* mainly functioned as a legislature, it decided what was law or should be law (see KLNM, s.v. *rettergang* (vol. XXI, col. 299)). It also elected the law-speaker, it granted licences and exemptions from the law, and it had the right to pardon. In other words, it was in some ways an administrative body (see Laws of Early Iceland, Grágás I, 249; RGA 2, s.v. *lögrétta*; Strauch 2016, 40, 218).

With Iceland's submission to Norway in 1262/64, the *lögrétta* was remodelled on the pattern of Norw law. Járnsíða (1271) and Jónsbók (1281) transformed it into a higher court of law, consisting of 36 men, 3 from each of the 12 new administrative districts (*sýslur*, see *sysel*), plus two Icelandic bishops. It was from now on a superior court and a court of appeal (see KLNM, s.v. *lögrétta*; Strauch 2016, 238).

Law Council **OIce** *Grg* Klþ 4 Þsþ 43 Feþ 144, 147 Lbþ 184 Fjl 225 Hrs 235 Tíg 268, *Jó* Þfb 3 Llb 64 Þjb 13, *Js* Þfb 3, 5, **ONorw** *FrL* Var 46 Rgb 30

ultimate court of law **ONorw** *GuL* Olb

Refs: Gunnar Karlsson 2005, 504; Hagland and Sandnes 1994, xxvii–xxviii; Helgi Þorláksson 2005, 142, 151; Helle 2001; Hertzberg s.v. *lögrétta*; KLNM s.v.v. *alþing, lagting, lögrétta, rettergang, ting*; Laws of Early Iceland, Grágás I; Sandvik and Jón Viðar Sigurðsson 2005, 236–37; Strauch 2016, 40–41, 119, 153, 158, 218–20, 223, 234, 236, 238, 240, 242, 246; Sveaas Andersen 1977, 259–60

lögréttr (ON) noun

personal compensation fixed by law **OIce** *Grg* Vís 94

lögréttufé (ON) noun

Funds at the disposal of the Law Council in Iceland. It is unclear how these funds were generated. Grg Feþ 147 states that payments for licenses to marry someone who was too closely related were paid as *lögréttufé*, and it is possible that other forms of license generated revenue as well. The lawspeaker (ON *lögsögumaðr*) was annually paid two hundreds of homespun cloth from Law Council money (cf. Grg Lsþ 116). Presumably these payments ceased to be collected when Iceland fell under Norwegian rule and the Law Council lost its legislative powers.

Law Council money **OIce** *Grg* Feþ 147

Law Council's funds **OIce** *Grg* Lsþ 116

See also: *fæ, lögrétta*

Refs: CV; Fritzner; GrgTr I:188 n.7; KLNM s.v. *embedsindtægter, lögrétta*

lögréttumaðr (ON) noun

man of the Law Council **OIce** *Grg* Þsþ 43 Lsþ 116 Feþ 158, *Jó* Þfb 2, 3, *Js* Þfb 3, 5, **ONorw** *FrL* Var 46

lögréttuseta (ON) noun

seat on the Law Council **OIce** *Grg* Lsþ 116 Lrþ 117

lögréttuþáttr (ON) noun

law council section **OIce** *Grg* Lrþ 117

lögræna (ON) verb

take **OIce** *Jó* Þjb 8

lögsamðr (ON) **lögsamdr** (ON) adj.

lawfully pronounced **OIce** *Js* Þfb 6, **ONorw** *GuL* Krb

legal **OIce** *Jó* Þfb 8

legally set **ONorw** *FrL* Var 46

lögsegjandi (ON) noun

lawful reporter **OIce** *Grg* Vís 87

lögsekð (ON) noun

A general designation for legal outlawry in Iceland. Grg Þsþ 60 stipulates that there are three types of legal outlawry: a full outlaw (ON *skógarmaðr*), a lesser outlaw (ON *fjörbaugsmaðr*) and lesser outlawry with permanent exile (ON *fjörbaugssekð*).

type of legal outlawry **OIce** *Grg* Þsþ 60 Feþ 158

See also: *fjörbaugsgarðr, skóggangr, sækt, útlagi*

Refs: CV s.v. *lögsekt*; Fritzner s.v. *lögsekt*

lögsekr (ON) adj.

under legal penalty **OIce** *Grg* Vís 91

See also: *útlægr*

lögsilfr (ON) noun

legal silver **OIce** *Grg* Bat 113 Fjl 221

lögsjándi (ON) noun

lawful eyewitness **OIce** *Grg* Vís 87

lawful viewer **OIce** *Grg* Fjl 221 Misc 246

lögskifti (ON) noun

legal division **OIce** *Grg* Feþ 166 Lbþ 177, 178 Fjl 225, *Jó* Lbb 4

lögskil (ON) noun

legal business **OIce** *Grg* Hrs 234

legal duties **OIce** *Grg* Þsþ 23, 35 Vís 89 Lrþ 117 Lbþ 202 Fjl 223 Hrs 234 Tíg 255, *KRA* 14

legal formalities **OIce** *Grg* Lbþ 176

lögskilnuðr (ON) **lögskilnaðr** (ON) noun

legal separation **OIce** *Grg* Feþ 151

lögskuld (ON) noun

A type of servitude imposed upon those who could not pay their debts. Bounden debtors held limited rights in some sections of Grg, but their legal status returned to normal once their debt was discharged. Dependents of a man condemned to slavery for theft could also be placed into legal debt-bondage (cf. Grg Rsþ 229). Outside of Grg *lögskuld* may also refer to legal debt rather than debt-bondage.

legal debt-bondage **OIce** *Grg* Arþ 118 Ómb 128 Rsþ 229

See also: *gæfþræl, gæld, skuldarkona, skuldarmaðr, skuldfastr, skyld, skæl*

Refs: CV; Fritzner; Guth 2002–03; GrgTr II:369

lögskuldarkona (ON) noun

A 'legal debt woman'; a woman in legal debt-bondage. Presumably held the same status as a *lögskuldarmaðr* (q.v.).

woman in legal debt-bondage **OIce** *Grg* Feþ 156

See also: *lögskuldarmaðr, skuldarkona, skuldarmaðr*

Refs: CV s.v. *lögskuldarkona*; Fritzner

lögskuldarmaðr (ON) noun

A 'man of legal debt'; a bounden debtor. A person who was legally obligated to work for another in order to pay off a debt. Along with the *leysingi*, the *lögskuldarmaðr* occupied a social status between householders and slaves. This type of debtor also existed in medieval Sweden (cf. SdmL Mb 14:2), albeit without a specific designation.

bounden debtor **OIce** *Grg* Vís 96 Arþ 118

See also: *lögskuldarkona, skuldarmaðr*

Refs: CV s.v. *lögskuldarmaðr*; Fritzner; RGA s.v. *Gesellschaft, Island*

lögskyldr (ON) **lögskyldugr** (ON) adj.

legally required **OIce** *Grg* Klþ 15, 18 Ómb 143, *KRA* 13, 26

lögsókn (ON) noun

prosecution at law **OIce** *Grg* Vís 88, *Jó* Kge 2, *Js* Kvg 3, **ONorw** *FrL* Kvb 16

lögspurning (ON) noun

legal asking **OIce** *Grg* Þsþ 22, 26 Vís 89

lögstakkgarðr (ON) noun

legal stackyard **OIce** *Grg* Lbþ 191

lögsögn (ON) noun

law-speaking **OIce** *KRA* 34

legal decision **OIce** *Jó* Mah 2

lögsögumaðr (ON) noun

The office of Lawspeaker present in Iceland from ca. 930 until 1262/71. The primary responsibility of the Lawspeaker was to recite a third of the law each year at the General Assembly (ON *alþingi*). He was elected by the Law Council (ON *lögrétta*) and is often cited as the only governmental official in Iceland during the commonwealth period. This position was eventually replaced by the office of *lögmaðr* (see *laghmaþer*) when Iceland fell under Norwegian rule.

Lawspeaker **OIce** *Grg* Klþ 19 Þsþ 21, 24 Lsþ 116 Lrþ 117 Arþ 127 Lbþ 172

See also: *alþingi, laghmaþer, lögrétta*

Refs: KLNM s.v. *embedsindtægter, lǫgsǫgumaðr*; LexMA s.v. *Rechtssprecher*

lögsögumannsrúm (ON) noun

the Lawspeaker's seat **OIce** *Grg* Þsþ 24

lögsögumannsþáttr (ON) noun

lawspeaker's section **OIce** *Grg* Lsþ 116

lögtíðir (pl.) (ON) noun

established services **OIce** *Grg* Þsþ 80

lögtíund (ON) noun

legal tithe **OIce** *Grg* Klþ 4 Tíg 255, *KRA* 14

lögunautr (ON) **lögunautar (pl.)** (ON) noun

man belonging to the same law district **ONorw** *GuL* Krb

member of a jurisdiction **ONorw** *FrL* KrbB 17 Mhb 53 Reb 1

lögváttr (ON) noun

lawful witness **OFar** *Seyð* 10

See also: *vatter*

lögvilla (ON) noun

deception at law **OIce** *Grg* Þsþ 22

lögvörn (ON) noun

legal defence **OIce** *Grg* Þsþ 32, 34 Ómb 130, 139 Lbþ 172 Hrs 235

lögvöxtr (ON) noun

yield at the legal rate **OIce** *Grg* Arþ 122

lögþáttr (ON) noun

section of the law **OIce** *Grg* Lsþ 116

lön (OSw) **laun** (OGu) **laun** (ON) noun

fee **OGu** *GL* A 42, 43

pay **OSw** *SdmL* Kmb, Till

return **OIce** *Grg* Arþ 127

wages **OSw** *UL* Jb, *VmL* Jb

See also: *heptalaun, legha, mali, þinglaun*

löna (OSw) **launa** (ON) verb

make a return **OIce** *Grg* Ómb 141

pay **ONorw** *GuL* Leb

present **OSw** *ÄVgL* Rlb

requite **ONorw** *GuL* Arb

lönd (OSw) **løn** (ODan) **lønd** (ODan) **loyndir (pl.)** (OGu) **lynd** (OGu) **laun** (ON) **lön** (OSw) noun

Used in the plural for 'private parts'.

private part **OGu** *GL* A 23

Expressions:

getinn á laun (ON)

begotten secretly **ONorw** *GuL* Arb

i lön, i löndum (OSw) **i løn, i lønd** (ODan)

secretly **OSw** *SdmL* Bb **ODan** *ESjL* 3 *JyL* 2, 3 *SkKL* 6 *VSjL* 62, 69

surreptitiously **ODan** *SkL* 60, 219, 223, 224

læggia lön a, læggia lön at (OSw)

lægje løn a (ODan)

hide **OSw** *SdmL* Bb **ODan** *JyL* 2

See also: *openbarlika*

löndaskript (OSw) noun

private church penalty **OSw** *DL* Kkb

private church penance **OSw** *SdmL* Kkb

{löndaskript} **OSw** *ÖgL* Kkb

löpiseþer (OSw) noun

Oath sworn by someone without the right to do so.

precipitate oath **OSw** *YVgL* Add

Refs: Schlyter s.v. *löpiseþer*

löpstigher (OSw) **løpstigh** (ODan) **laupstigr** (OGu) **hlaupstígr** (ON) noun

Appears in phrases such as OSw *i löpstighum*, ODan *a løpstigi* of fugitive criminals and slaves. In GL there are detailed provisions relating to the actions of a slave declared to be 'on the run'.

fled **ODan** *SkL* 133

road of escape **OSw** *YVgL* Tb, *ÄVgL* Tb

run **OGu** *GL* Add. 8 (B 55)

run away **ODan** *SkL* 162

running away **ONorw** *GuL* Løb

Refs: Peel 2015, 199−200

lös (OSw) **løs** (ODan) **lauss** (ON) adj.

deprived of something **ONorw** *GuL* Arb

free **ODan** *JyL* 2, *SkL* 159, **OSw** *UL* Mb, *YVgL* Tb

loose **OSw** *UL* Kkb

null and void **OIce** *Jó* Kge 23

released **OIce** *Grg* Misc 244, **OSw** *UL* Mb, *YVgL* Tb, *ÄVgL* Tb

unbound **OIce** *Jó* Kab 7, **ONorw** *GuL* Kpb, Løb

vacant **OSw** *YVgL* Äb

See also: *lata*

lösa (OSw) **løse** (ODan) **loysa** (OGu) **leysa** (ON) verb

absolve **OSw** *ÖgL* Kkb

buy **ODan** *SkL* 135, *VSjL* 50

discharge **OIce** *Grg* Misc 252

dissolve **OSw** *UL* Kkb, *VmL* Kkb

free **ODan** *JyL* 2, *SkKL* 11, **OGu** *GL* A 14, **OSw** *DL* Tjdb, *HL* Mb, *UL* Kmb, *ÄVgL* Äb, *ÖgL* Kkb

get back **ODan** *SkL* 142, 144

get back against payment **ODan** *SkL* 182

give absolution **OGu** *GS* Ch. 3

give back **ODan** *SkL* 83

grant **ODan** *SkL* 128

pay **ODan** *SkL* 90, 133, 150, 159, 161, 162, 166, 183, **OSw** *HL* Kgb

pay a fee **OGu** *GS* Ch. 3

pay back **OSw** *DL* Rb

pay for one's life **OSw** *DL* Kkb

ransom **OGu** *GL* A 28

redeem **ODan** *ESjL* 2, 3, *JyL* 3, *SkL* 126, 130, 157, 170, 171, 179, **OGu** *GL* A 28, 63, **OIce** *Jó* Mah 1 Llb 10, 33 Kab 20, 22 Þjb 1 Fml 21, *Js* Kab 17, *KRA* 6, **OSw** *DL* Eb, Tjdb, Rb, *HL* Rb, *SdmL* Kkb, Kgb, Äb, Rb, Bb, Kmb, Mb, Tjdb, *YVgL* Urb, Rlb, Tb, Jb, Föb, Add, *ÄVgL* Rlb, Jb, Tb, Fös, *ÖgL* Eb, Db

release **ODan** *SkL* 131, 139, 233, **ONorw** *FrL* Mhb 55, **OSw** *YVgL* Äb, Tb, *ÄVgL* Äb, Tb

resolve **OSw** *DL* Bb

settle **OSw** *YVgL* Jb, *ÄVgL* Jb

solve **ODan** *ESjL* 2, **OSw** *HL* Kmb, *ÄVgL* Tb

take back **ODan** *SkL* 197

unbind **ODan** *SkL* 156

unchain **OSw** *HL* Mb

Expressions:

lösa sik (OSw) **loysa sik** (OGu)

redeem oneself **OGu** *GL* A 22 *UL* Kgb, Mb, Blb *VmL* Kgb, Mb

loysa ut, loysa undan (OGu)

redeem **OGu** *GL* A 20, 20a, 26

See also: *aterlösa*

lösgiurþer (OSw) **laus gyrtr** (OGu) **lausgyrðr** (ON) **losgyrþer** (OSw) adj.

In house-searches, those doing the search had to show that they did not have anything hidden under their clothing in order to plant it on the premises and thus incriminate the householder. They also had to have their hoods thrown back and so be bareheaded.

loosely girded **OGu** *GL* A 37, **OSw** *DL* Tjdb, *UL* Mb, *VmL* Mb

with belts undone **OSw** *SdmL* Tjdb

with loose girdle **OSw** *YVgL* Rlb, Tb, *ÄVgL* Tb

without a belt **ONorw** *GuL* Tjb

See also: *ransaka*

Refs: Schlyter s.v. *lösgiurþer*; SL GL, 283, note 2 to chapter 37

löska (OSw) **lösker** (OSw) adj.

Expressions:

löska kona (OSw)

unmarried woman **OSw** *YVgL* Gb, Add *ÖgL* Vm

löska maþer, lös maþer, löska man, lösker man, lösker maþer (OSw)

impecunious man **OSw** *HL* Kmb

itinerant **OSw** *DL* Bb *UL* Kkb, Kgb *VmL* Kkb, Mb *ÖgL* Db

unmarried man **OSw** *SmL* *VmL* Äb *YVgL* Kkb

vagrant **OSw** *HL* Kgb, Mb *SdmL* Kgb *YVgL* Drb

See also: *bolfaster, stafkarl*

löskalæghi (OSw) **lönskalæghe** (OSw) noun

Literally 'secret laying' referring to illegal sexual relations between unmarried people. The man had to compensate the woman's kin, with the woman herself receiving nothing. In OSw YVgL, a criminal offence only if the woman got pregnant, or if the wrongdoers were caught in the act, and it was explicitly a violation of ecclesiastical law, demanding confession and penance on top of the compensation paid. OSw HL made no real distinction between *löskalæghi* and *hor* (q.v.); any man who seduced another man's mother or daughter was to pay compensation to the aggrieved party as well as a fine to the king and to the community.

fornication **OSw** *HL* Äb, *SdmL* Äb, *YVgL* Kkb

illicit relationship **OSw** *DL* Gb, *UL* Kkb, Äb, Mb, *VmL* Äb

See also: *hor, lægher, lønlæghe*

Refs: Hertzberg s.v. *legorð*; KLNM s.v.v. *lejermål, ægteskabsbrud*; Schlyter s.v. *löskalæghi*

lösn (OSw) **løsn** (ODan) **launs** (OGu) **lausn** (OGu) **lausn** (ON) **lösning** (OSw) noun

Payment for the release of property, such as sold land, slaves used as bonds and stolen or lost goods, under certain circumstances. Also of slaves buying their freedom and of killers paying for their crime. In ON occasionally of the right to such release.

compensation **OSw** *HL* Mb

compensation to the captor **OSw** *HL* Mb

fee **OGu** *GS* Ch. 3

payment **OIce** *Jó* Fml 21

payment for freedom **OSw** *YVgL* Tb

ransom **OSw** *HL* Mb

redemption **ODan** *VSjL* 86, **OIce** *KRA* 6, 7 passim, **ONorw** *GuL* Olb, **OSw** *SdmL* Jb, Bb, Tjdb

reward **OSw** *DL* Bb, *UL* Mb, *VmL* Mb

right of redemption **OIce** *Grg* Fjl 221, *Jó* Mah 1, *Js* Mah 2, **ONorw** *FrL* Jkb 1

Refs: Cleasby and Vigfusson s.v. *lausn*; Fritzner s.v. *lausn*; Hertzberg s.v. *lausn*; ONP s.v. *lausn*; Schlyter s.v. *lösn*

lösvittinger (OSw) noun

vagrant **OSw** *ÄVgL* Md

See also: *löfvirkinger*

lösörapanter (OSw) noun

pledge concerning movable property **OSw** *HL* Kmb

See also: *lösöre, panter*

lösöre (OSw) **lösore** (OSw) noun

chattels **OSw** *HL* Rb

goods **OSw** *DL* Gb

movable goods **OSw** *YVgL* Äb, Jb, Add, *ÄVgL* Urb, Äb, Jb

movable property **OSw** *HL* Kkb, Äb, *YVgL* Urb, Rlb, *ÖgL* Kkb

movables **OSw** *SdmL* Kkb, Gb, Jb, *SmL*, *UL* För, Kkb, Äb, Jb, Kmb, Rb, *VmL* För, Kkb, Äb, Jb. Kmb, Rb, *ÖgL* Eb

personal goods **OSw** *DL* Gb

See also: *lausafé, öre*

löt (OSw) noun

Pasture, 'green grass-ground', 'level field' and a direct synonym of ON *vall/völlr* (pl. *vellir*) in Brink 2004, 210.

pasture **OSw** *UL* Blb, *VmL* Bb

pastureland **OSw** *SdmL* Mb, *ÄVgL* Tb

See also: *fælöt, hiorþlöt, valder*

Refs: Brink 2004b, 210

løne (ODan) verb

conceal **ODan** *SkL* 121

cover up **ODan** *VSjL* 87

hide **ODan** *JyL* 2

be secret **ODan** *JyL* 2

withhold **ODan** *SkL* 229

lønlike (ODan) adv.

secretly **ODan** *JyL* 2, *SkKL* 12

See also: *openbarlika*

lønlæghe (ODan) noun

Illegal sexual relations between unmarried people. The woman's kin prosecuted and her guardian received any fines, which could only be taken once.

intercourse in secrecy **ODan** *JyL* 2

See also: *löskalæghi*

løpe (ODan) **hlaupa** (ON) verb

run away **ODan** *VSjL* 86, **ONorw** *GuL* Løb, Leb

run off **ODan** *VSjL* 86, 87

magaraiþ (OGu) noun

ride of the relatives **OGu** *GL* A 24

See also: *vagniklaferþ*

magararfi (ON) noun

heir to a son **ONorw** *FrL* ArbA 7

See also: *maghararf*

maghandi (OSw) **magandi** (OGu) **moghandi** (OSw) adj.

Usually appears in expressions such as *koma til maghandi alder* or *vara a maghandi ar* (OSw) 'be/become of age' (for example DL Bb, SdmL Jb). The expression for this varied, as did the age.

adult **OSw** *SdmL* Tjdb, *UL* Kkb, Kgb, Mb, *VmL* Mb, *YVgL* Kkb, Frb, Rlb, Add, *ÄVgL* Slb

of age **OGu** *GL* A 20, **OSw** *UL* Jb, *VmL* Kkb, Äb, Jb

of full age **OSw** *YVgL* Tb, *ÄVgL* Tb, *ÖgL* Db

grown **OGu** *GL* A 20

mature **OSw** *SdmL* Jb

See also: *omaghi, vit*

maghararf (OSw) noun

son's inheritance **OSw** *HL* Äb, *UL* Äb

See also: *magararfi*

magher (OSw) **magh** (ODan) **magr** (OGu) **mágr** (ON) noun

These refer to a male person related by marriage.

The usual meaning in Medieval Nordic legal texts is 'son-in-law', attested in ODan ESjL, but also other meanings (some of them more comprehensive) occur: 'brother-in-law' (OSw DL; OIce Jó), 'kinsman' (ODan ESjL), 'kinsman by marriage' (ONorw GuL), and 'relative' (OGu GL).

The plurality of the meanings of this term in the medieval Nordic languages can be compared to the similar ambiguity of the kinship terms *gener* ('male in-law') and *nepos* (i.a. 'grandchild', 'nephew', 'niece') in medieval Latin.

brother-in-law **OIce** *Jó* Kab 2, **OSw** *DL* Mb

in-law **OGu** *GL* A 63, Add. 6 (B 33)

kinsman **ODan** *ESjL* 2

kinsman by marriage **ONorw** *GuL* Sab

relative **OGu** *GL* A 24

son-in-law **ODan** *ESjL* 1, **OGu** *GS* Ch. 3

See also: *mögr*

Refs: Bjorvand 2007, 772; KLNM s.v. *ætt*; Latham and Howlett s.v.v. *gener, nepos*; Niermeyer and van de Kieft s.v.v. *gener, nepos*

magnúsmessa (ON) noun

Feast of St Magnus **ONorw** *EidsL* 9.2, *FrL* KrbA 25

St Magnus's Day **OIce** *Grg* Klþ 13

mak (OGu) noun

benefit **OGu** *GL* A 28

convenience **OGu** *GL* A 3

makeskifte (ODan) noun

exchange of land **ODan** *JyL* 1

exchange of real property **ODan** *JyL* 1

makt (OSw) noun

power **OSw** *SdmL* Till

mal (1) (OSw) **mal** (ODan) **mal** (OGu) **mál** (ON) noun

Etymologically 'congregation', specifically a legal one, and hence the speaking at this ('language', 'speech', 'tale', 'talk'), the matters dealt with ('case', 'dispute', 'matter', 'procedure', '(law)suit', 'crime', 'offence') and the agreements made ('contract', 'lease').

affair **OIce** *Grg* Þsþ 23, 35

agreement **OIce** *Grg* Ómb 135

appeal **OSw** *DL* Rb

arrangement **OIce** *Grg* Þsþ 78, *Js* Kvg 5

article of law **OIce** *Grg* Hrs 235 Tíg 263

bargain **ONorw** *GuL* Kpb

business **OIce** *Grg* Þsþ 81

case **ODan** *ESjL* 2, 3, *JyL* 2, 3, *SkKL* 7, *SkL* 83, 87, 101, 108, 112, 145, 146, 150, 217, *VSjL* 15, 50, 86, 87, **OGu** *GL* A 2, 21, 28, 31, 37, Add. 1 (B 4), **OIce** *Grg* Lrþ 117, *Jó* Þfb 9, *Js* Þfb 3 passim, *KRA* 7, **ONorw** *BorgL* 17.5, *FrL* Intr 16 Tfb 2 KrbA 1, 29 KrbB 2 Mhb 4 passim, *GuL* Krb, Kpb, Løb, Mhb, Llb, Tfb, Leb, Arb, **OSw** *DL* Eb, Rb, *HL* Kkb, Kgb, Äb, Mb, Jb, Blb, Rb, *SdmL* Conf, Kkb, Kgb, Jb, Bb, Mb, Rb, Till, *UL* Kkb, Kgb, Äb, Mb, Jb, Blb, Rb. Add. 16, *VmL* Kkb, Kgb, Äb, Mb, Jb, Bb, Rb, *YVgL* passim, *ÄVgL* Md, Smb, Äb, Gb, Jb, Föb, *ÖgL* Kkb, Eb, Db

cause **OSw** *VmL* Bb

charge (1) **OGu** *GL* A 2, **OSw** *UL* Mb

contract **OIce** *Grg* Arþ 127

crime **OGu** *GL* A 2, **OSw** *DL* Eb, *UL* Rb

dispute **OSw** *DL* Rb

language **OGu** *GS* Ch. 1

lawsuit **OIce** *Jó* Þfb 4

lease **OSw** *DL* Bb

matter **OGu** *GL* A 20a, **OIce** *Grg* Þsþ 58, *Jó* MagBref, *KRA* 16, **ONorw** *BorgL* 17, **OSw** *UL* StfBM, Kkb, Äb, Mb, Jb, Kmb, Blb, *VmL* Kkb, Jb, Kmb, Rb

offence **OSw** *UL* Kkb, *YVgL* Urb, *ÖgL* Kkb, Eb, Db

procedure **ONorw** *FrL* Intr 7

reason **OSw** *DL* Rb

section of the law **OIce** *Grg* Lbþ 220

situation **OIce** *Jó* Kge 31 Þjb 15

speech **OSw** *ÄVgL* Smb

suit **OSw** *UL* Mb

tale **OSw** *UL* Mb

talk **OGu** *GL* A 19, **OIce** *Grg* Lsþ 116

wages **ODan** *JyL* 3

Expressions:

koma lykt viþer mal (OSw)

conclude a case **OSw** *UL* Rb *VmL* Rb

mat ællær mal (OSw)

food and rent **OSw** *HL* Blb

See also: *brut*, *fall*, *gærning*, *mæla (1)*, *sak*, *sokn*

Refs: Hellquist s.v. *mål 2*; ONP
s.v. *mál*; Schlyter s.v. *mal*

mal (2) (OSw) **mal** (ODan) **mal** (OGu) noun

measurement **OSw** *UL* Blb

measuring **ODan** *VSjL* 71

time (point) **OGu** *GL* A 14

malakarl (OSw) noun

hireling **OSw** *UL* Kkb

malaruf (OSw) noun

breach of agreement **OSw** *YVgL* Föb

malaþing (OGu) noun

betrothal meeting **OGu** *GL* A 28

mali (OSw) **mali** (OGu) **máli** (ON) noun

agreement **OIce** *Js* Kab 19, **ONorw** *FrL* LlbA 2

claim **OIce** *Jó* Kge 13, *Js* Ert 19

conditions **OGu** *GL* Add. 7 (B 49)

mortgage **ONorw** *GuL* Olb

payment in coin **OSw** *UL* Kkb, *VmL* Kkb

portion **ONorw** *GuL* Arb

pre-emption right **OIce** *Grg* Lbþ
192, *Jó* Lbb 8, *Js* Lbb 5

time of slavery **OGu** *GL* A 2, 6, 16

tithe **OSw** *HL* Kkb

wages **OSw** *UL* Blb, *VmL* Bb

See also: *legha*, *lön*, *málajörð*, *tillagha*

malsmaþer (OSw) **malsman** (OSw) noun

guardian **OSw** *YVgL* Gb, Add, *ÖgL* Kkb, Db

spokesman **OSw** *SdmL* Mb

malstævne (ODan) noun

deliberation at a meeting **ODan** *SkKL* Prol

malsæghandi (OSw) **malsaigandi** (OGu) **malsatti**
(OSw) **malseghandi** (OSw) noun

appellant **OSw** *UL* Add. 15, *VmL* Bb

claimant **OSw** *UL* Mb, *VmL* Mb

complainant **OGu** *GL* A 21, 35,
OSw *UL* Kkb, *VmL* Kkb

injured party **OGu** *GL* A 25, 26, **OSw** *DL* Kkb,
Eb, Mb, Bb, Gb, Tjdb, Rb, *UL* Kmb, *VmL* Kmb

person aggrieved **OSw** *YVgL* Add

plaintiff **OGu** *GL* A 13, **OSw** *DL* Rb, *HL* Kkb,
Kgb, Äb, Mb, Blb, Rb, *SdmL* Kkb, Kgb, Gb, Äb,
Jb, Bb, Kmb, Mb, Tjdb, Rb, Till, *UL* Kkb, Kgb,
Mb, Jb, Blb, Rb, *VmL* Kkb, Kgb, Mb, Jb, Bb, Rb,
YVgL Urb, Tb, Föb, Utgb, *ÖgL* Kkb, Eb, Db, Vm

See also: *kærande*

malt (ON) noun

Malt was a necessary part of the subsistence allowances
to the delegates in the *Gulaþing* (q.v.).

malt **ONorw** *GuL* Krb

Refs: KLNM s.v.v. *brygging*, *kornhandel*,
malt och malthandel, *øl*, *ölhandel*

malþing (OSw) noun

A *þing* 'assembly' handling lawsuits at the lower
levels of judicial districts, *hæraþ* (q.v.) and *fiarþunger*
(q.v.) as opposed to the provincial assembly (OSw
landsþing).

local assembly **OSw** *ÖgL* Db

Refs: Schlyter s.v. *lionga þing*, *malþing*

man (OSw) **man** (ON) noun

Often used collectively of 'people', particularly
'household members', or of unspecified slaves.

household members (as a group)
ONorw *GuL* Løb, Leb

slave **OIce** *Grg* Fjl 221, **ONorw**
GuL Krb, Llb, Olb, Leb

thrall **OSw** *YVgL* Gb

See also: *annöþogher*, *hion*, *mansmaðr*, *þjónn*, *þræl*

Refs: Fritzner s.v. *man*; Hertzberg s.v.v
man, *mansmaðr*; Schlyter s.v. *man*

manbot (OSw) **manbot** (ODan) **mannbót** (ON)
mannbætr (ON) **mansbot** (OSw) noun

man's compensation **ODan** *ESjL* 2,
JyL 2, 3, *SkL* 43, 87, 93, 95, 103, 126,
128–130, *VSjL* 23, 26–31, 33–35, 38

man's fine **OSw** *HL* Mb, *SdmL* Mb

wergild **OIce** *Js* Mah 29, **OSw** *YVgL* Add

See also: *bot*, *mannsgjald*

mandrap (OSw) **mandrap** (ODan) **manndrap** (OGu)
manndráp (ON) noun

Literally, 'man killing'. This crime was specifically
one in which the killer was known, and had admitted
to the killing. The killing was also one that was not
aggravated by other circumstances (cf. *dulghadrap*,
morþ). The word appears as an alternative to *drap*
in the laws of Denmark and Götaland, in GL and
in SdmL but is absent from most of the laws of
Svealand, where *drap* (q.v.) with different qualifying
prefixes appears throughout. The contrast with the
crime of *morþ* ('murder') seems to be more in the
context of the admission to the killing and the lack
of concealment than in the nature of the killing itself,
although there are instances in the laws of Götaland in
which breach of trust is an element in the classification
of the crime. This being the case, the translations
'killing', 'homicide' and 'slaying' are probably nearer

in meaning to the original than 'manslaughter', which carries with it the connotation of a reckless or violent act, likely to cause or intending injury, but devoid of a prime intent to kill.

case of homicide **ODan** *ESjL* 2, *JyL* 3

case of killing **ODan** *SkL* 114

homicide **ODan** *ESjL* 2, 3, *JyL* 2, **OIce** *Js* Mah 7

killing **ODan** *SkL* 92, **ONorw** *FrL* Intr 1, 7 KrbA 46, **OSw** *SdmL* Mb

killing of a man **ODan** *SkL* 17, 85

manslaughter **OGu** *GL* A 13, **OSw** *YVgL* Drb, Äb, *ÄVgL* Md, Äb, *ÖgL* Kkb

See also: *drap, dræpa, dulghadrap, mandrapare, mandraplogh, mandrapsmal, maþer, morþ*

Refs: KLNM, s.v. *drab*; Peel 2015, 110 preamble to notes to chapter 13; Schlyter 1877, s.v. *mandrap*; SL GL, 254 preamble to notes to chapter 13

mandrapare (OSw) **manndrápari** (ON) noun

Although translated 'murderer' in Jó (Þfb 5), the more general 'manslayer' is perhaps preferable. Appears in SmL in the context of who may be appointed a priest. These requirements are stated in alliterating, to some extent synonymic, pairs: *han scall ey wara moorthare eller mandrapære. ey kirkiu brytære eller kloster løpære. ey doblare eller drinkare. ey puto mather eller portkunw.* ("He must neither be a murderer nor a manslayer, neither a church thief nor a monastery escaper, neither a gambler nor a drinker, not a man who visits whores or harlots.") The paragraph may in fact be inspired by a letter from the pope Alexander III to the archbishop of Uppsala, written around 1170, where he issues a warning against recruiting criminal priests.

manslayer **OSw** *SmL*

murderer **OIce** *Jó* Þfb 5

See also: *drap, drapari, morðvargr*

Refs: Fridell forthcoming; Schlyter 1877, s.v. *mandrapare*; SL SmL, 438

mandraplogh (ODan) noun

An oath of defence in cases for which a full man's compensation was to be paid.

oath for homicide **ODan** *ESjL* 2

See also: *drap, lagh*

Refs: Tamm and Vogt, eds, 2016, 305

mandrapsmal (ODan) noun

case of killing **ODan** *SkL* 85

See also: *mal (1), mandrap*

mangæld (OSw) **manngjald** (ON) **mannsgjöld** (ON) noun

damages **OIce** *Jó* Mah 20

fine for manslaughter **OSw** *HL* Mb

wergild **OIce** *Jó* Þfb 8 Mah 2, **ONorw** *GuL* Olb

See also: *bogher, manbot*

manhælghi (OSw) **manhælgh** (ODan) **mannhelg** (OGu) **mannhelgi** (ON) **mannhelgr** (ON) **manhælghþ** (OSw) noun

Literally 'sanctity of man', these two forms are used as synonyms in the medieval Nordic laws. A translation, or rather a modern interpretation, suggested in private correspondence by Helle Degnbol of Copenhagen University, was 'human rights'. These rights applied to free men and women, but not to slaves, under the law. The books in the law that are entitled *manhælghisbalker* (q.v.) cover those aspects of the law that we would today call criminal law (as opposed to civil law, family law, land law, ecclesiastical law, etc. Sometimes, however, these statutes are split over a number of different books in the law, covering theft, killing, wounding and in some law texts there are no divisions into books at all. Crimes against *manhælgi* include cases in which the personal security and liberty of an individual are breeched in situations ranging from murder to petty theft. In GL, and elsewhere, the word is used particularly in connection with periods in which greater security was granted to people — times of church festivals, harvest, etc. — times that were called -*friþer*, '-peace', with a prefix specifying of the period in question. The link between *manhælghi* and the concept of 'peace' is therefore very close. From there the link to *hemfriþer* (q.v.), the sanctity of the home, can be made and by extension to the grave crime of *hemsokn* (q.v.) — an attack upon a man in his own home.

book of personal rights **ONorw** *FrL* Mhb 45

crime against the personal peace **OSw** *YVgL* Add

individual's right to peace and security **OGu** *GL* A 8

individual's right to protection **OGu** *GL* A 9

inviolability of the person **ONorw** *GuL* Krb

man's personal peace **OSw** *ÖgL* Vm

personal and property rights **OSw** *DL* Mb

personal liberty **OSw** *DL* Mb

personal peace **ODan** *ESjL* 2, 3, *JyL* 2, 3, *VSjL* 41, 65, 87, **OSw** *SdmL* Kkb, Gb, *ÄVgL* Slb

personal rights **OGu** *GL* A 8 (rubric only), **OIce** *Jó* MagBref Mah 1 Llb 30 Þjb 3, 16, *KRA* 29, **ONorw** *FrL* Intr 7 KrbB 20 Mhb 1, **OSw** *DL* Mb

personal security or liberty **OSw** *UL* Kkb, Mb, *VmL* Äb, Mb

violation of someone's personal liberty **OSw** *DL* Mb
violation of someone's personal rights **OSw** *DL* Mb
See also: *bot, friþer, helagher, hemfriþer, hemsokn, manhæliæsbot, maþer, rætter*
Refs: KLNM s.v. *manhelgd*; Peel 2015, 102–03 note 8/2, 106 note 9/10–11; Schlyter 1877, s.v.v. *manhælghi, manhælghþ*; SL DL, 38 note 1; SL GL, 252 note 1 to chapter 8; SL UL, 117; SL ÖgL, 96 note 6

manhælghisbalker (OSw) noun
book concerning personal and property rights **OSw** *DL* Mb, *HL* För, Äb, Mb
personal rights section **OSw** *SdmL* För, Mb
See also: *balker*

manhælghismal (OSw) **manhælghþamal** (OSw) noun
breach of personal peace **OSw** *ÖgL* Kkb
case concerning personal and property right **OSw** *HL* Mb
case for a man's personal peace **OSw** *ÖgL* Vm

manhæliæsbot (OSw) **manhælghisbot** (OSw) noun
compensation for wergild **OSw** *YVgL* Drb
See also: *bot, hælghisbot, manhælghi*

manløs (ODan) adj.
unmarried **ODan** *SkL* 58
without a husband **ODan** *VSjL* 67

manndrápsþing (ON) noun
A *þing* 'assembly' summoned at killings, presumably at a *þing* location close to the scene of the killing or to the home of the accused. All householders receiving a summons were obliged to participate.
assembly held on account of a murder **ONorw** *GuL* Tfb
manslaughter assembly **OIce** *Jó* Kge 34
See also: *þing*
Refs: KLNM s.v. *ting*; Jón Viðar Sigurðsson, 2015

manne (ODan) verb
get a man **ODan** *SkL* 58
marry **ODan** *JyL* 1, *SkL* 46, *VSjL* 67

mannelði (ON) **mannaelði** (ON) noun
people for boarding **OIce** *Grg* Hrs 234, *Jó* Kge 34

mannfrelsi (ON) noun
freeing of slaves **OIce** *Grg* Vís 112, **ONorw** *FrL* KrbB 19

manngerð (ON) noun
The levy district called *manngerð* was the area that had to equip one man for naval service, usually 2–3 farms.
levy district **ONorw** *GuL* Krb, Leb

See also: *leþunger, hamna, har (2), ar (1), skiplagh*
Refs: Helle 2001, 35, 170–71; Hertzberg s.v. *manngerð*; KLNM s.v.v. *leidang, manngjerd*; Robberstad 1981, 324

manngerðarmenn (pl.) (ON) noun
men belonging to the same levy district **ONorw** *GuL* Krb

mannmergð (ON) noun
number of people **OIce** *Jó* Fml 10, 15

mannsgildi (ON) noun
wergild **ONorw** *EidsL* 3.4

mannsgjald (ON) noun
wergild **ONorw** *EidsL* 3.4

mannskaði (ON) noun
bloodshed **OIce** *Js* Mah 34
killing **OIce** *Jó* Mah 16

mannsverk (ON) noun
full farm **ONorw** *GuL* Llb
man's work **OIce** *Jó* Kab 25, **ONorw** *GuL* Løb

mannsöfnuðr (ON) **mannsafnaðr** (ON) noun
gathering **OIce** *Grg* Bat 114

manntalseiðr (ON) noun
census oath **ONorw** *FrL* Leb 8

manntalsþing (ON) noun
An assembly held to number the men available for service in the naval levy, and to prepare the muster lists. It was held each year, probably at some time between 15 May and 15 June.
levy census assembly **ONorw** *FrL* Leb 8
mustering thing **ONorw** *GuL* Tfb, Leb
spring county meeting **ONorw** *FrL* Intr 17
See also: *mantal, þing*
Refs: Helle 2001, 83; Jón Viðar Sigurðsson 2015, 17–24; KLNM s.v. *ting*; Robberstad 1981, 394

mannvilla (ON) noun
false identification **OIce** *Grg* Feþ 158

mannæta (ON) noun
maneater **ONorw** *GuL* Krb

mansal (ON) noun
sale of a slave **ONorw** *GuL* Løb

mansbani (OSw) **mannsbani** (ON) noun
killer **OIce** *Jó* Mah 1, 8, *Js* Mah 8, 19, *KRA* 32, **ONorw** *FrL* Intr 2, 4 KrbB 15 Mhb 30, *GuL* Mhb, Leb, **OSw** *SdmL* Mb
See also: *bani*

mansivi (OSw) **manzcifvi** (OSw) noun
kin in blood **OSw** *SmL*
See also: *guþsivi*

mansleiga (ON) noun

hiring slaves **ONorw** *FrL* Rgb 31

mansmaðr (ON) noun

A compound presumably made up of *man* (ON) — used collectively of household members, particularly slaves — and of *maðr* (ON) 'man', 'human', i.e. 'slave-person'.

bondsman **OIce** *Grg* Ómb 138

slave **OIce** *Grg* Klþ 4, **ONorw** *FrL* Mhb 44 Kvb 21, *GuL* Løb, Leb

See also: *man, þjónn, þræl*

Refs: Fritzner s.v. *man*; Hertzberg s.v.v. *man, mansmaðr*; Schlyter s.v. *man*

mansöngr (ON) noun

Literally 'maiden-song'. The first element *man* is thought to be an old word for a maid or female servant similar to an *ambátt* (see *ambat*). There is some disagreement among scholars over what constitutes a *mansöngr*, but from the context of Grg Misc 238 it has been interpreted by many as defamatory love poetry or erotic libel. This specifically legal usage of obscene love poetry has been identified in certain literary texts, such as *Vatnsdæla saga* and *Jóns saga helga*. Others have interpreted *mansöngr* more broadly as love poetry inspired by French troubadour literature and German Minnesang, and it is in this context that they appear in late medieval Icelandic *rímur*.

love-verse **OIce** *Grg* Misc 238

See also: *ambat, fjölmæli, illmæli, níð, skáldskapr, snápr*

Refs: Bjarni Einarsson 2003; CV s.v. *mansöngr*; Fritzner s.v. *mansöngr*; GAO s.v. *Liebesdichtung*; KLNM s.v. *kjærlighetsdiktning*; Marold 2007

mantal (OSw) **mantal** (ODan) **manntal** (ON) noun

A count or number of men, particularly concerning certain obligations, such as to participate in the levy (ONorw GuL), build a church (OSw SmL), take an oath (OSw YVgL), pay a murder fine (OSw ÖgL), or concerning certain rights, such as to receive an inheritance (ODan SkL, VSjL; OSw YVgL).

count **OIce** *Grg* Þsþ 41 Lbþ 217

headcount **OSw** *UL* Kgb

muster **ONorw** *GuL* Leb

number **ODan** *SkL* 34

number of men **ONorw** *GuL* Krb, **OSw** *SmL, YVgL* Äb, Add, *ÖgL* Db

number of people **OIce** *Jó* Llb 13

number of persons **ODan** *VSjL* 1

See also: *bondatal, haffatal, leþunger, manntalsþing, ökiaafl, tal, vighramannatal*

Refs: Cleasby and Vigfusson s.v. *manntal*; Fritzner s.v. *manntal*; Hertzberg s.v. *manntal*; Schlyter s.v. *mantal*; SL SmL, 436, note 4; Tamm and Vogt, eds, 2016, 312

mantul (OSw) **mantol** (OSw) noun

cloak **OSw** *YVgL* Gb

gown **OSw** *VmL* Äb

Expressions:

særk ok mantel (ODan)

shift and mantle **ODan** *ESjL* 2

manvæt (ODan) noun

homicide **ODan** *SkKL* 8

marbakki (ON) noun

sea bank **OIce** *Jó* Llb 68

mariumæssa (OSw) **mariemisse** (ODan) **mariumessa** (OGu) **maríamessa** (ON) **maríumessa** (ON) noun

Various feasts of the Blessed Virgin Mary

Purification of the Blessed Virgin Mary **OIce** *Grg* Klþ 13

Expressions:

maríumessa (ON)

Purification of the Blessed Virgin Mary **OIce** *Grg* Klþ 13

mariumæssa fyrra (OSw) **maríumessa fyrri** (ON)

earlier St Mary's Mass (15 August) **ONorw** *GuL* Krb

Feast of the Assumption (15 August) **OSw** *UL* Kkb

first Mass of the Virgin Mary **ODan** *SkL* 239

mariumæssa öfra (OSw) **maríumessa øfri** (ON)

Feast of the Nativity of Our Lady (8 September) **ONorw** *GuL* Krb **OSw** *UL* Blb *VmL* Kkb

Nativity of Mary **OIce** *Grg* Klþ13

mariumessa i fastu (OGu) **maríumessa í fǫstu** (ON)

Annunciation (25 March) **OGu** *GL* A 3, 47, 57, 58 **ONorw** *GuL* Krb

See also: *kyndilmæssa, varafrudagher*

mark (1) (ON) noun

boundary mark **OIce** *Grg* Lbþ 174, Lbþ 199, **ONorw** *FrL* LlbB 7

mark (of ownership) **OIce** *Grg* Fjl 221, 225, *Jó* Llb 6, 47, *Js* Lbb 13

See also: *mærki*

Refs: Bjorvand 1994, 79–80, 158–59; 2007, 722; KLNM s.v. *rågång*; Schlyter s.v. *mark* [3]

mark (2) (OSw) **mark** (ODan) **mark** (OGu) **mörk** (ON) noun

Unit of weight and coinage.

mark (a unit of the weight and monetary system) **ODan** *ESjL* passim, *JyL* passim, *SkKL* passim,

OFar *Seyð* 1, OGu *GL* A 2–4, 7–20, 20a, 21–26,
28, 31, 32, 35–39, 46–48, 50, 52, 55, 57, 58,
60–63, 65, Add. 1, 3– 6, 8, 9 (B 4, 19, 19, 20,
33, 55, 81), *GS* Ch. 2, 3, 4, OIce *Grg* passim,
Jó passim, *Js* passim, *KRA* 1, 2 passim, ONorw
BorgL 3.5 5.2, *EidsL* 3.4, *FrL* Intr 12, 16 Tfb 1
KrbA 1 passim, *GuL* passim, OSw *DL* passim,
HL passim, *SdmL* passim, *SmL*, *UL* passim, *VmL*
passim, *YVgL* passim, *ÄVgL* passim, *ÖgL* passim

See also: *karlgilder*, *köpgilder*,
öre, *örtogh*, *pænninger*

Refs: CV s.v. *mörk*; Fritzner s.v.v. *mörk*, *mǫrk*;
KLNM s.v. *mark*; Schlyter s.v. *mark* [2]

mark (3) (OSw) mark (ODan) mörk (ON) noun

field ODan *ESjL* 2, 3, *JyL* 1–3, *SkL* 87, 178, 202,
203, 211, 218, *VSjL* 57, 58, ONorw *FrL* LlbA 10

forest ONorw *FrL* LlbA 10, *GuL* Llb, Leb

land ODan *SkL* 205, ONorw *FrL* Mhb 24,
OSw *YVgL* Drb, Rlb, Jb, *ÄVgL* Md, Rlb, Jb

See also: *byamark*

Refs: Bjorvand 1994, 79–80, 158–59; 2007,
722; Brink 2008b; CV s.v. *mörk*; KLNM s.v.v.
–*mark*, *utmark*; Schlyter s.v. *mark* [1]

marka (ON) verb

mark OFar *Seyð* 5, OIce *Grg* Fjl 225,
Jó Llb 57, *Js* Lbb 13, *KRA* 26

See also: *einkynna*

markabro (OSw) noun

bridge OSw *YVgL* Föb

markarskæl (OSw) markeskjal (ODan) noun

Boundary between villages or provinces or, in
Denmark, between fields.

boundary ODan *ESjL* 2, *JyL* 2, *SkL* 72,
VSjL 75, OSw *YVgL* Jb, *ÄVgL* Jb

boundary between fields ODan
ESjL 2, *JyL* 2, *VSjL* 76, 77

field boundary ODan *JyL* 2

See also: *mark (3)*, *skilia*, *skæl*

Refs: KLNM s.v.v. *gränsläggning*, *rågång*;
Lund s.v. *markæskial*; Schlyter s.v. *markar skæl*;
Tamm and Vogt 2016 s.v. *markeskjal* p. 332

markarspell (ON) noun

damages done to the woodland OIce
Jó Llb 19, ONorw *FrL* LlbA 12

See also: *skógarspell*

markatal (OSw) markatal (OGu) noun

value in {marker} OGu *GL* A
53, OSw *UL* Jb, *VmL* Jb

markavægher (OSw) noun

road OSw *YVgL* Föb

See also: *vægher*

markeran (ODan) noun

Stealing crops from fields.

field rapine ODan *JyL* 2

See also: *ran*

markland (OSw) markaland (OSw) noun

Land assessment unit in SmL, VgL and the Svea laws.

{markland} OSw *SdmL* Bb, *SmL*, *UL* Kkb,
Kgb, Blb, *VmL* Mb, Bb, *YVgL* Kkb

See also: *attunger*, *laigi*, *legha*, *ploghsærje*

Refs: Dovring 1947b; Ericsson 2007,
9–10; Hafström 1949, 193–228; KLNM
s.v. *markland*; Schlyter s.v. *markland*

markrá (ON) noun

marked boundary ONorw *FrL* LlbA 19

markreina (ON) markrein (ON) noun

boundary line OFar *Seyð* 10, ONorw *GuL* Llb

See also: *hagamark*, *merkigarðr*, *mærki*

Refs: CV s.v. *markreina*

marksteinn (ON) noun

boundary stone OIce *Jó* Þjb 10, *Js*
Lbb 26, ONorw *GuL* Llb, Tjb

See also: *mærki*, *sten*

Refs: CV s.v. *marksteinn*

markteigr (ON) noun

forest lot ONorw *GuL* Llb

marreinsbakki (ON) noun

edge of the shore ONorw *GuL* Kpb, Llb, Mhb, Olb

martinsmæssa (OSw) marteinsmessa (ON) noun

Martinmas (11 November) OIce *Grg* Klþ
13, ONorw *GuL* Krb, OSw *SdmL* Bb,
Till, *UL* Jb, Blb, *VmL* Bb, *YVgL* Föb

See also: *sancta martens dagher*

matarverð (ON) noun

price for food OIce *KRA* 1

value of food OIce *Jó* Kab 25, *Js* Kab 19

matban (ODan) noun

Prohibition against feeding a criminal.

food-ban ODan *SkL* 145

food-ban decision ODan *SkL* 145

See also: *ban*

Refs: Tamm and Vogt, eds, 2016, 304

matblót (ON) noun

food-sacrifice ONorw *EidsL* 24.3

matgerðarmaðr (ON) noun

cook **ONorw** *GuL* Leb

matgjald (ON) noun

Food gifts for the poor from householders with specified minimum assets.

food payment **OIce** *Grg* Hrs 234

Refs: KLNM s.v. *matgjald*

matgjöf (ON) noun

Food gifts handed out four times a year by householders to needy persons.

food gift **OIce** *Grg* Hrs 234 Tíg 255, *Jó* Kge 31, *KRA* 13, 14

Refs: Gerhold 2002, 210–14; Lýður Björnsson 1972–79, I:85–86

matgærþ (OSw) noun

Obligation to provide food for the *leþunger* 'levy'.

food provision **OSw** *SdmL* Jb, Rb

matkniver (OSw) noun

Listed as a *morþvapn* 'murder weapon' as opposed to a *folkvapn* (presumably 'battle weapon').

table knife **OSw** *SdmL* Mb

See also: *kniver*

matlaunarmaðr (ON) **matlaunamaðr** (ON) noun

A person who earned his food, but got no wages. According to GuL ch. 115 he had to be at least twelve years old to be counted as a *matlaunarmaðr*.

man who works for his living **ONorw** *GuL* Arb

man who works for his meals **OIce** *Jó* Kge 16

matlauni (ON) noun

one who can earn his food **OIce** *Grg* Vís 89, *Js* Ert 25

matnaþr (OGu) noun

food **OGu** *GL* A 6

See also: *mielkmatr*

matr (OGu) **matr** (ON) noun

food **OGu** *GL* A 2, 4, Add. 8 (B55), *GS* Ch. 1, **ONorw** *GuL* Krb, Løb, Mhb, Leb

Expressions:

hvítr matr (ON)

foods made from milk **OIce** *Grg* Klþ 12, 15, 16

mat ællær mal (OSw)

food and rent **OSw** *HL* Blb

matskamma (OSw) noun

food house **OSw** *ÄVgL* Tb

See also: *kornskæmma*, *symnskæmma*

matskut (OSw) **matskot** (OSw) noun

Support for the priest paid in bread and butter, or something else of the same value, by every householder three times per year.

food contribution **OSw** *HL* Kkb

Refs: KLNM s.v. *matskott*

matskutsfredagher (OSw) noun

Day for offering food to the poor. It is stated specifically that the priest is to have none of it.

Friday of providing food **OSw** *YVgL* Kkb

Refs: Schlyter s.v. *matskutsfredagher*

mattéimessa (ON) **mattéusmessa** (ON) **matthaeusmessa** (ON) noun

St Matthew's Day **OIce** *Grg* Klþ 13

St Matthew's Mass (21 September) **ONorw** *GuL* Krb

mattíasmessa (ON) **matthiasmessa** (ON) noun

Feast of St Matthias (24 February) **ONorw** *GuL* Krb

St Matthias's Day **OIce** *Grg* Klþ 13

matþrota (ON) adj.

running out of food **ONorw** *GuL* Leb

maþer (OSw) **man** (ODan) **maþr** (OGu) **man** (OSw) noun

Appears *passim* — including in numerous compounds — and is also used as a pronoun. Also with more specific reference to a farmer, householder, husband, subordinate or even slave, depending on the context.

farmer **OSw** *HL* Mb

generation **OGu** *GL* A 20

householder **OSw** *YVgL* Frb

husband **ODan** *ESjL* 1, 3, **OSw** *DL* Gb, *HL* Kkb, Mb, *UL* Äb, Jb, *VmL* Äb, Jb, *ÖgL* Eb

man **ODan** *ESjL* 1–3, *JyL* Fort., 1, 2, *SkL* passim, **OGu** *GL* passim, *GS* passim, **OSw** *DL* Kkb, Eb, Mb, Bb, Gb, Tjdb, Rb, *HL*, *SdmL* Conf, Kkb, Kgb, Gb, Äb, Jb, Bb, Kmb, Mb, Tjdb, Rb, *SmL*, *UL* passim, *VmL* passim, *YVgL* Kkb, Vs, Frb, Urb, Drb, Äb, Gb, Rlb, Tb, Jb, Kvab, Föb, Utgb, Add, *ÄVgL* Kkb, Md, Smb, Vs, Slb, Urb, Äb, Gb, Rlb, Jb, Kva, Tb, Fös, Föb, Lek, *ÖgL* Kkb, Eb, Db, Vm

one **ODan** *SkL* 225, *VSjL* 9, 37, 56, 82, **OSw** *HL*, *SdmL* Conf, Bb, Rb, *ÄVgL* Kva, Fös

slave **OGu** *GL* A 32a (rubric), Add. 7, 8 (B 49, 55)

somebody **OSw** *DL* Eb, Mb, Bb

someone **OSw** *DL* Kkb, Eb, Mb, Bb, *HL*

you **ODan** *ESjL* 2, 3, *JyL* 1–3, *SkL* 226, *VSjL* 65, 66

Expressions:

allir mæn (pl.) (OSw) **alle mæn** (pl.) (ODan)

The inhabitants of a district (*land*, *hæraþ* etc.) with collective rights and obligations, such as to receive part of numerous fines and compensations, to decide over the location of the assembly (ODan ESjL 2) and to maintain bridges, roads and ferries (OSw HL Blb).

all men **OSw** *DL* Kkb, Eb, Mb, Bb, Gb, Tjdb, Rb *HL* Kkb, Kgb, Äb, Mb, Blb, Rb *SdmL* Mb *YVgL* Kkb, Drb, Gb, Rlb, Utgb *ÄVgL* Gb, Rlb, Tb, Fös *ÖgL* Kkb, Eb **ODan** *JyL* Fort, 1, 3 *SkKL* 12 *SkL* 187

dauðr maðr (ON)

dead man **ONorw** *GuL* Mhb

firnari menn (ON)

remoter kin **OIce** *Grg* Arþ 122, Ómb 137

mans man (OGu) **maðr manns** (ON)

man (servant or slave) of a man **ONorw** *EidsL* 36.4, 50.5 *BorgL* 9.7, 12.8

someone's slave **OGu** *GL* A 32a (rubric), Add. 7, 8 (B 49, 55)

nærri menn (ON)

men of closer kin **OIce** *Grg* *Jó* Kge 1, 18 *Js* Kvg 1 **ONorw** *FrL* Mhb 8

ungr maðr (ON)

Lit. 'young man'.

ward **OIce** *Grg* Misc 249

See also: *bonde, karl, lýþir (pl.)*

málaefni (ON) **málefni** (ON) noun

circumstances of a case **OIce** *Jó* Llb 26

substance of a case **OIce** *Grg* Þsþ 47

málajörð (ON) noun

The *máli* (ON, 'contract') was a term for mortgage contract, which meant conveyance of property by debtor to creditor as security for debt, with the provision that the seller might redeem the property when he wanted, if he gave notice of this half a year in advance. In ONorw *málajörð* was a term for mortgaged land. In OIce (Grg, Js, Jó) *málajörð* (*málaland*) implied a right to purchase land when resold with no sense of credit or debt.

land given in mortgage **ONorw** *GuL* Llb, Olb

land subject to pre-emption right **OIce** *Jó* Lbb 10, *Js* Lbb 17

See also: *mali*

Refs: Helle 2001, 118; Hertzberg s.v.v. *málajörð, máli*; KLNM s.v.v. *jordleige, pant*; Robberstad 1981, 385–89

málakona (ON) noun

A married woman who retained legal ownership of her own property. When married a *málakona* and her husband stipulated an agreement (ON *máli*) concerning which property was to remain hers. This type of property ownership during marriage was an alternative to the more common practice of joint-ownership between spouses (ON *félag*).

wife **OIce** *Jó* Kge 13

See also: *gagngjald, hemfylghþ*

Refs: CV s.v. *máli*; Fritzner; Guðrún Ása Grímsdóttir 2015; KLNM s.v. *festermål*; Páll Vídalín 1854 s.v. *prioritas dotis*

málaland (ON) noun

Land upon which a right of preemption (ON *máli*) had been placed. The holder of this right had the opportunity to match the offer of the highest bidder or purchase the land at a pre-arranged price when it was put up for sale again.

land subject to pre-emption right **OIce** *Grg* Lbþ 192, 196, *Jó* Lbb 11, *Js* Lbb 7, 8

See also: *landsmáli, lögmálaland, málajörð*

Refs: CV s.v. *máli*; Fritzner; GrgTr II:392; Hertzberg

málalandsbrigð (ON) noun

land claim where there is a right of pre-emption **OIce** *Jó* Lbb 11

málalauss (ON) adj.

free of pre-emption right **OIce** *Grg* Lbþ 193, *Jó* Lbb 10, *Js* Lbb 7

málamaðr (ON) noun

owner of a pre-emption right **OIce** *Grg* Lbþ 192

málamundi (ON) noun

agreement **OIce** *Grg* Þsþ 78

málavöxtr (ON) noun

circumstances of a case **OIce** *Jó* Mah 1, 7, *Js* Mah 13, 29, *KRA* 16, 34, **ONorw** *FrL* KrbA 17 Mhb 35

máldagi (ON) noun

A general term for an agreement or contract, but often refers specifically to a written document or register detailing the terms of the agreement. Frequently used for church inventories (*kirkjumáldagi*) from the end of the twelfth century onwards. This sort of *máldagi* was kept updated and could include, among other things, land deeds, incomes, number of priests, granted rights or privileges, lists of books and registers of church equipment. New *máldagar* were supposed to be read aloud at the General Assembly (ON *alþingi*) and then annually at the church where the document was kept.

agreement **OIce** *Grg* Klþ 4 Þsþ 80 Arþ 125 Ómb 133 Feþ 144 Fjl 223 Misc 251, *Jó* Lbb 11 Llb 1, *KRA* 4, **ONorw** *GuL* Krb

arrangement **OIce** *Jó* Kge 18, *Js* Kvg 1

endowment agreement **OIce** *Grg* Tíg 268

register **OIce** *KRA* 15

terms **OIce** *Jó* Kge 1

See also: *kirkjumáldagi*

Refs: CV; KLNM s.v. *donasjon, máldagi* ; LexMA s.v. *máldagi*; NGL V s.v. *máldagi*

málnyta (ON) noun

dairy stock **OIce** *Grg* Klþ 8 Þsþ 81

málnytukúgildi (ON) noun

animal equivalent to one milk cow **OIce** *Jó* Kab 15

málsafglöpun (ON) noun

balking an affair **OIce** *Grg* Misc 244

málsmatr (ON) noun

meal **ONorw** *GuL* Krb, Leb

máltryggva (ON) **máltryggja** (ON) verb

plan with security **ONorw** *FrL* ArbB 10

mánaðarmatr (ON) noun

The amount of food which one man needed for one month, when he served in the levy. Usually provided as butter (7.7 kg) and meal (24.7 kg).

month's food **ONorw** *GuL* Krb, Mhb, Leb

Refs: Helle 2001, 69; Hertzberg s.v. *mánaðarmatr*; KLNM s.v. *månadsmat*

mánaðarstefna (ON) noun

one-month time limit **ONorw** *BorgL* 8.1

summons with one month notice **OIce** *KRA* 36

meiða (ON) verb

damage **OIce** *Grg* Feþ 165, 166, *Jó* Fml 25

hurt **ONorw** *FrL* Rgb 26

maim **OIce** *Grg* Vís 110, *Js* Mah 9, **ONorw** *FrL* Mhb 35

mutilate **OIce** *Jó* Mah 2

meiðing (ON) noun

maiming **ONorw** *FrL* Mhb 43

meinbugalaust (ON) adv.

without impediment **OIce** *KRA* 16

meinbugr (ON) noun

impediment **OIce** *KRA* 16

meinkona (ON) noun

concubine **ONorw** *GuL* Krb

See also: *amia, arinelja, frilla, sløkefrithe*

meinlauss (ON) **meinalauss** (ON) adj.

not prevented **OIce** *Grg* Klþ 4 Þsþ 24 Feþ 144

meinleiki (ON) noun

impediment **OIce** *Jó* Kge 6, *Js* Kvg 5

legally acceptable reason **ONorw** *FrL* Kvb 14

meinsóri (ON) **meinsæri** (ON) noun

A false oath given as a deliberate lie.

perjury **OIce** *Jó* Þjb 19, *KRA* 2, 23

See also: *meneþer*

meinsórismaðr (ON) **meinsærismaðr** (ON) noun

perjurer **OIce** *Jó* Kab 2

men (OSw) **men** (ODan) **main** (OGu) **mein** (ON) noun

damage **OIce** *Jó* Llb 43

harm **OGu** *GL* A 7, **OIce** *Grg* Vís 88, 108 Lbþ 184, 203 Fjl 225 Rsþ 230, *Js* Mah 30 Lbb 21, *KRA* 8, 16

hindrance **OIce** *Grg* Feþ 164, *Jó* Llb 9

inconvenience **ONorw** *GuL* Llb

injury **OIce** *Jó* Mah 13, 23 Llb 29, **ONorw** *GuL* Kvb

perjury **ODan** *ESjL* 3, *JyL* 2, *SkL* 78

wound **ONorw** *FrL* KrbA 10

Expressions:

ren ok eig men (OSw)

pure oath and not perjury **OSw** *YVgL* Add

See also: *meneþer*

mena (OSw) **mene** (ODan) **meina** (ON) verb

bar **ODan** *JyL* 1

forbid **OSw** *VmL* Kkb

object **OFar** *Seyð* 10

prevent **ODan** *JyL* 2

meneþer (OSw) **meneth** (ODan) **meineiðr** (ON) noun

In OSw ÖgL, an oath given on a day when swearing was not allowed; otherwise not defined, even when contrasted to other illegal oaths, *afflagha ethar* (YVgL) and *skrokvitni* (ÖgL), or when graded (HL). In ODan VSjL, probably an oath given as a deliberate lie (as with *men* in SkL, ESjL and JyL). In ON, not defined.

false oath **OIce** *KRA* 34, **ONorw** *FrL* KrbB 2

perjury **ODan** *VSjL* 82, **OSw** *HL* Kkb, *SmL, YVgL* Kkb, *ÖgL* Kkb

See also: *falzeþer, glafseþer, men, osvurin, skrokvitni, meinsóri*

menföre (OSw) noun

hindrance **OSw** *UL* Blb, *VmL* Bb

See also: *forfall*

mergund (ON) **mergunda** (ON) noun

marrow wound **OIce** *Grg* Vís 86, 88

mergundaðr (ON) **mergunda** (ON) adj.

wounded to the marrow **ONorw** *FrL* Mah 47, *GuL* Mhb

merkia (OGu) **merkja** (ON) verb

brand **OGu** *GL* A 17 (B-text), 40, 41

mark **OGu** *GL* A 38, **OIce** *Jó* Llb 6

See also: *amerki*

merkiá (ON) noun

boundary river **OIce** *Grg* Lbþ 208

merkibjörk (ON) noun

Birch trees which served as a boundary marker between land plots in Iceland.

boundary birch **OIce** *Grg* Lbþ 199, *Jó* Llb 19, 21

See also: *mark (3)*

Refs: CV s.v. *merkibjörk*; KLNM s.v. *gränsläggning*; NGL V s.v. *merkibjörk*

merkigarðr (ON) noun

boundary fence **ONorw** *GuL* Llb

boundary wall **OIce** *Jó* Llb 31, *Js* Lbb 22

See also: *markreina*

merkióss (ON) noun

boundary rivermouth **OIce** *Grg* Lbþ 209, *Jó* Llb 60

merkismaðr (ON) noun

A standard-bearer. The term appears in numerous saga sources referring to a person who bore a standard, especially during battle. By the late thirteenth century it is thought to have been primarily an honorific title, albeit a significant one with a rank equivalent to a chancellor (ON *kanceler*) or marshal (ON *stallari*). According to *Hirðskrá*, a *merkismaðr* held the same rights as a landed man (ON *lendr maðr*, see *lænder*). After an ordinance issued in 1302, the *merkismaðr* was one of four men responsible for daily governance of Norway during a king's minority. The *merkismaðr* became the highest official in the Norwegian royal retinue (ON *hirð*) once the post of *stallari* ceased to be used during the reign of King Hákon V. The title of *merkismaðr* seems to have vanished in Norway during the fourteenth century as part of the union with Sweden and Denmark.

standard bearer **OIce** *Jó* Llb 18

See also: *hirð*, *lænder*, *stallari*

Refs: CV; Fritzner; GAO s.v. *Feldzeichen*; Imsen 2015; KLNM s.v. *baner*, *merkesmann*

merkivatn (ON) noun

boundary stream **OIce** *Grg* Lbþ 191, *Jó* Llb 24

merkjaganga (ON) noun

boundary walk **OIce** *Grg* Lbþ 174, 175

merkjasýning (ON) noun

boundary showing **OIce** *Grg* Lbþ 175

merkrskaði (ON) noun

one mark worth of damage **ONorw** *FrL* Bvb 11

merr (ON) noun

mare **ONorw** *GuL* Mhb

messudagaboð (ON) noun

proclamation of feast days **ONorw** *BorgL* 13

messudagr (ON) noun

feast day **OIce** *Grg* Klþ 4, **ONorw** *EidsL* 10.1

mass-day **ONorw** *GuL* Krb, Kpb

messuprestr (ON) noun

mass-priest **ONorw** *GuL* Krb, Leb

messusöngr (ON) noun

mass chant **ONorw** *GuL* Krb

metandi (ON) noun

assessor **ONorw** *GuL* Trm

valuer **OIce** *Grg* Bat 115

See also: *mætsmæn (pl.)*

metfé (ON) noun

stock whose value is open to assessment **OIce** *Grg* Fjl 221 Misc 246, *Jó* Kab 6

mél (ON) noun

notice **OIce** *Grg* Þsþ 56, 57 Arþ 122 Feþ 144

See also: *fæmt*

miðskipsár (ON) noun

This oar was used as a measure of how big a part of a whale the finder was allowed to keep for himself. See GuL ch. 150.

midship oar **ONorw** *GuL* Kvr

miðuppnám (ON) noun

middle group of payers or receivers of wergild **ONorw** *GuL* Mhb

mielkmatr (OGu) noun

dairy produce **OGu** *GL* A 6

See also: *matnaþr*

mielkstulin (OGu) adj.

lacking in milk **OGu** *GL* A 33a

mikialsdagher (OSw) noun

Saint Michael's Day **OSw** *YVgL* Kkb

See also: *sancta mikials dagher*

mikialsmæssa (OSw) **mikjalsmisse** (ODan) **mikjálsmessa** (ON) noun

Michaelmas **ODan** *JyL* 3, *SkKL* 9, **OIce** *Grg* Klþ 13, **OSw** *HL* Rb, *SdmL* Kkb, Bb, Rb, *UL* Rb, *VmL* Kkb, Kgb, Bb, *YVgL* Utgb, *ÄVgL* Föb

St Michael's Mass (29 September) **ONorw** *GuL* Krb

mikialsmæssodagher (OSw) noun

Michaelmas Day **OSw** *UL* Rb, *VmL* Rb

minni (OGu) noun

toast **OGu** *GL* A 24, 63, Add. 6 (B 33)

minnung (OSw) **minnungi** (OSw) noun

evidence of long-standing possession **OSw** *HL* Jb

long-standing possession **OSw** *HL* Jb

oath of inheritance from ancient times **OSw** *HL* Jb

testimony of old holding **OSw** *HL* Blb

testimony of old possession **OSw** *HL* Blb

minnungamæn (pl.) (OSw) noun

Men who verified ownership, particularly of land and boundary markers between villages, probably as a reminiscence of an old oral legal custom.

men with good memory **OSw** *HL* Kkb, Jb, Blb

men with memory **OSw** *HL* Jb

Refs: Brink 2010b, 132; Brink
2014a; SL HL, 280 note 39

misbjóða (ON) verb

misproclaim **ONorw** *BorgL* 13.1

proclaim wrongly **ONorw** *GuL* Krb

misbundinn (ON) adj.

unlawfully bound **ONorw** *GuL* Tjb

See also: *réttbundinn*

misdauði (ON) noun

death at different times **ONorw** *GuL* Arb

dying at different times **OIce** *Jó* Kge 5, 6

misdeila (ON) verb

quarrel inappropriately **ONorw** *GuL* Mhb

misdeild (ON) noun

inappropriate quarrel **ONorw** *GuL* Mhb

misdómi (ON) noun

misjudgement **ONorw** *GuL* Olb

miseta (ON) verb

eat improperly **ONorw** *EidsL* 15.1

misfall (OSw) noun

misdemeanour **OSw** *ÖgL* Kkb

misfangi (ON) noun

mistake **OIce** *Grg* Rsþ 231, *Jó* Þjb 13

misfara (ON) verb

abuse **OIce** *Jó* Kab 21

be damaged **ONorw** *GuL* Kpb

misfyrma (OSw) misfirma (OGu) misfirma (OSw)
verb

abuse **OGu** *GL* A 63, Add. 6 (B 33)

assault **OSw** *SdmL* Gb, *YVgL* Drb

injure **OSw** *DL* Gb, *UL* Äb, *VmL* Äb

insult **OSw** *VmL* Rb

mistreat **OSw** *HL* Äb

See also: *bregþa, handla*

misfyrmilse (OSw) noun

assault **OSw** *SdmL* Gb

misganga (ON) noun

misconduct **ONorw** *GuL* Mhb

misgerning (ON) noun

crime **OIce** *Jó* Mah 17

misgrafinn (ON) adj.

misburied **ONorw** *EidsL* 50.15

misgörr (ON) adj.

wrongfully conducted **ONorw** *BorgL* 17.5

misgøre (ODan) misgera (ON) verb

act wrongly **OIce** *Js* Mah 22, **ONorw** *BorgL* 17.7

do something inappropriate **ONorw** *GuL* Krb

do harm **ODan** *SkL* 98

offend **ODan** *SkKL* 2

perpetrate a crime **OIce** *Jó* Mah 21

wrong **ONorw** *BorgL* 17.4, *FrL* Intr 6

mishaldinn (ON) adj.

treated unfairly **OIce** *Jó* Sg 3

mishægha (OSw) verb

mismanage **OSw** *YVgL* Äb

mishælde (ODan) noun

maltreatment **ODan** *SkKL* 8

offence **ODan** *SkKL* 7

mishöggva (ON) verb

wound by accident **ONorw** *FrL* Mhb 26

miskun (OSw) miskund (OSw) noun

grace **OSw** *YVgL* Gb, *ÄVgL* Gb

See also: *naþir*

miskunnakona (OSw) misskonna kona (OSw) noun

woman at the mercy of (someone) **OSw** *UL* Äb

woman dependent on compassion **OSw** *HL* Äb

See also: *naþakona*

miskunnarmaþer (OSw) noun

man in state of mercy towards another
OSw *YVgL* Äb, *ÄVgL* Äb

misleti (OGu) noun

disfigurement **OGu** *GL* A 16

See also: *lyti, læst*

mismarka (ON) verb

incorrectly mark **OFar** *Seyð* 5, **OIce** *Jó* Llb 48

misróða (ON) misræða (ON) noun

wrongful (sexual) intercourse
OIce *Grg* Vís 90 Feþ 155

misseramót (ON) noun

The *misseramót* was a usual time for workmen to
begin or leave service.

end of a half-year **ONorw** *GuL* Løb

Refs: KLNM s.v. *året och dess indelning*

misseri (ON) noun

The bipartite division of the year was dependent on
the climate and the organization of labour (e.g. length
of service time for workmen). See *misseramót*.

half of a year **OFar** *Seyð* 7

half-year **ONorw** *GuL* Kpb

season **OIce** *Grg* Klþ 6, 8 Vís 89
Ómb 128, *Js* Lbb 3, *KRA* 26

six months **ONorw** *FrL* KrbB 12

Refs: Janson 2011; KLNM s.v.
tideräkning, året och dess indelning

misseristal (ON) noun

calendar **OIce** *Grg* Þsþ 61 Lsþ 116

misskifta (ON) verb

divide in an unfair way **ONorw** *GuL* Arb

divide incorrectly **OIce** *Jó* Kge 20

missverja (ON) verb

perjure oneself **ONorw** *GuL* Løb

mistaka (ON) verb

take by mistake **OIce** *Grg* Rsþ 231

mistekja (ON) noun

unlawful seizure **ONorw** *GuL* Kpb

See also: *gripdeild*

mistroa (OGu) verb

disbelieve **OGu** *GL* A 2, 28

suspect **OGu** *GL* A 25

See also: *væna*

misverja (ON) verb

fail to defend successfully **ONorw** *GuL* Olb

misverki (ON) noun

misdeed **OIce** *Grg* Feþ 154, *Jó* Kge 5

misvinna (ON) verb

work wrongfully **ONorw** *EidsL* 12.5 15.1

misvígi (ON) noun

dishonourable killing **ONorw** *GuL* Mhb

misþyrma (ON) verb

mistreat **OIce** *Js* Kvg 2, *KRA* 7

misþyrmsl (ON) noun

violation **OIce** *KRA* 34

misæti (ON) noun

mis-eating **ONorw** *EidsL* 29.3

miþfasta (OSw) **miðfasta** (ON) noun

Mid-Lent was an important date for the settlement of certain transactions regarding odal land. See GuL chs 266 and 267.

mid-Lent **ONorw** *GuL* Olb, **OSw** *SdmL* Jb, Rb

Refs: KLNM s.v. *ting*

miþsumar (OSw) **mithsumer** (ODan) noun

midsummer **ODan** *JyL* 2, **OSw** *HL* Rb, *YVgL* Kkb

miærþi (OSw) **miarþi** (OSw) **miarþri** (OSw) **miærdi** (OSw) **miærþri** (OSw) **mærdri** (OSw) **mærþi** (OSw) **mærþri** (OSw) noun

osier fish basket **OSw** *UL* Blb, *VmL* Bb

mjöl (ON) noun

meal **ONorw** *GuL* Krb, Kpb

mogi (OGu) noun

community **OGu** *GL* A 12, 19, 25, 26, 31, 35

mold (ON) noun

sod **ONorw** *GuL* Olb

See also: *torf*

moldran (OSw) noun

land theft **OSw** *HL* Blb

theft of land **OSw** *HL* Blb

molka (OSw) **mulka** (OGu) verb

Appears in the context of illegal milking.

milk **OGu** *GL* A 33a, **OSw** *HL* Blb, *SdmL* Bb, *UL* Blb, *VmL* Mb, Bb, *ÄVgL* Fös

morðseiðr (ON) noun

murder oath **ONorw** *GuL* Mhb

morðvargr (ON) noun

A murderer was outlawed and could not be buried in hallowed earth.

murder-wolf **ONorw** *EidsL* 50.13

murderer **OIce** *Grg* Vís 102, **ONorw** *GuL* Krb

See also: *mandrapare*, *morþingi*

Refs: KLNM s.v. *fredløshed*

morghongæf (OSw) **morghon gieff** (OSw) **morghon giæf** (OSw) noun

Literally, 'morning gift'. This was the gift that the groom gave to his wife on the morning after their marriage. Carlsson maintains that this was to be interpreted as the price for her virginity (*pretium virginitatis*), following early Germanic law. Later writers, however, Kopiola and Ekholst, point out that there is no direct indication of this interpretation in the Swedish medieval laws, even if its origin might have been such. Ekholst believes that it was merely a culmination of the preceding acts in the marriage process. The giving of the *morghongæf* might thus simply be confirmation that the marriage was valid and indissoluble. The importance of consummation to a marriage was that, if it had not been consummated, it could be dissolved leaving both parties free to marry again. This was the only way in which a marriage could be ended under the Catholic Church, unless it was incestuous or entered into under duress. Although widows sometimes did not receive a *morghongæf*, or the equivalent, if they married a second time, this was not always the case. The equivalent gift is called the *hindradagsgæf* ('following day gift') in HL, UL, ÄVgL and ÖgL. This gift, which could be in land or movables, was the bride's to keep, unlike the dowry (*hemfylghþ*) that came with the bride as an advance on inheritance and had to be returned to her family estate if she were widowed. It was thus clearly intended to support her if she became widowed, especially as the gift returned to the husband's estate should she die before him. It could, however, be forfeited if she committed adultery. A completely different system applied in GL and no mention is made of any gift to his wife by a man while he lives, but only of what she is to receive on and after his death, which included everything that she took to the farm at her marriage, as well as the *hogsl ok iþ* (see *hogsl*). This implies that in this case her dowry was not returnable. The *morghongæf* does not figure in Nordic countries apart from Sweden.

bride price **OSw** *UL* Äb, *VmL* Äb

morning gift **OSw** *DL* Gb, *HL* Äb, *SdmL* Gb, *YVgL* Gb, Add

wedding gift **OSw** *HL* Äb

See also: *gagngjald, gift, heimanferð, heimangerð, hemfylghþ, hemfærth, hemgæf, hindradagsgæf, hogsl, iþ, omynd, tilgæf*

Refs: Carlsson 1965; Ekholst 2009; Holmbäck 1919; KLNM s.v. *morgongåva*; Korpiola 2004; Lexikon des Mittelalters s.v. *ehe*; SAOB s.v. *morgongåva*; Schlyter 1877, s.v.v. *bröllop, hindradags gæf; husfru, morghongæf, vängåva, ægteskab*; SL UL, 82 note 21; SL VmL, 58 note 24; Vogt, Helle 2010

morthbrand (ODan) noun

An act of deliberately and secretly setting fire to another's house. It was not stated that the deed had to have fatal outcome. In JyL 3:12, an arsonist caught in the act could be burned alive.

arson-murder **ODan** *JyL* 3

murderous arson **ODan** *JyL* 3

See also: *morþ*

morþ (OSw) **morth** (ODan) **morð** (ON) noun

A secret killing — i.e. when the offender failed to make an announcement (*lysning*) of the deed, was unknown, denied the killing or hid the body (the latter, presumably, the original meaning) — or one committed as breach of loyalty, i.e. killing between spouses or servants killing their master. A crime characterized by its lack of openness and honourability and contrasted to *drap* (q.v.) and *vigh* (q.v.). All these types of killing could, however, be punished by death or outlawry, or fine/compensation.

foul murder **ONorw** *GuL* Krb, Tfb, Mhb

murder **ODan** *ESjL* 3, **OIce** *Grg* Klþ 2 Vís 87, 88, *Jó* Mah 2, 10, *Js* Mah 6, 14, **ONorw** *BorgL* 3.2, *EidsL* 3.2 7, *FrL* Mhb 4 Var 45 Bvb 4, **OSw** *DL* Mb, *HL* Mb, *SdmL* Mb, *SmL*, *UL* Mb, Rb, *VmL* Mb, Rb, *YVgL* Add, *ÖgL* Eb

See also: *döþsdrap, drap, niðingsvíg*

Refs: Ekholst 2009, 180–82; KLNM s.v. *mord*; Maček 2009; SAOB s.v. *mord*; Schlyter s.v. *morþ*; Tamm and Vogt, eds, 2016, 309

morþari (OSw) **morthere** (ODan) **mordari** (OSw) **morþare** (OSw) noun

killer **OSw** *HL* Mb

murderer **ODan** *JyL* 2, *SkL* 151, **OSw** *HL* Mb, *SdmL* Mb, *SmL*, *UL* Mb, *VmL* Mb, *ÖgL* Db

See also: *drapari, morþ, morþingi, stæghla*

morþgæld (OSw) **mordgæld** (OSw) **morgiald** (OSw) **morþgiald** (OSw) **morþgælld** (OSw) noun

compensation for murder **OSw** *DL* Mb, *SdmL* Mb, *UL* Äb, Mb, *VmL* Äb, Mb

murder fine **OSw** *ÖgL* Db

See also: *gæld, morþ, sporgæld*

morþingi (OGu) **morðingi** (ON) noun

murderer **OGu** *GL* A 39, **OIce** *Jó* Mah 10, *Js* Mah 14, *KRA* 11, **ONorw** *BorgL* 3.2, *FrL* Mhb 1, 7 Var 20, *GuL* Mhb

See also: *morþ, morþari*

morþraþ (OSw) noun

death by chastening **OSw** *SdmL* Mb

See also: *morþ, raþ*

morþvapn (OSw) noun

Using a *morþvapn* was more severely punished than using a *folkvapn* (q.v.). The specific weapons may have varied, but SdmL lists table knife, carving knife, and bow and arrow; the latter is sometimes classified as a *folkvapn*, but its simultaneous status as *morþvapn* seems to be confirmed by DL and HL.

murder weapon **OSw** *DL* Mb, *SdmL* Mb

See also: *folkvapn, morþ, vapn*

Refs: Brink forthcoming; KLNM s.v. *vapenförbud*; Schlyter s.v. *morþvapn*; SL DL, 45 note 61; SL HL, 407 note 104

Mostrarþing (ON) **monstrarþing** (ON) noun

The assembly that met at Moster in Sunnhordland (SW Norway) (probably) 1024. At this meeting, the Christian church was officially established in Norway.

Moster assembly **ONorw** *GuL* Krb

See also: *þing*

Refs: Helle 2001, 46, 177–80, 201–04; Robberstad 1981, 325

mot (OSw) **mot** (OGu) **mót** (ON) noun

assembly **OGu** *GL* A 19

town-meeting **OIce** *Grg* Misc 248

motstukkr (OGu) noun

Literally, 'meeting post'. Most probably one of the posts used to mark out the site of the assembly. In

GL, stray cattle and ponies were to be tied up within sight of these, but a distance away, presumably so that they were not confused with animals belonging to the people attending the assembly. It is possible that the assembly was in a natural hollow and that by having the animals a distance away the men holding them could see the posts over the heads of others at the assembly, or alternatively that potential claimants could see the beasts.

assembly-site pole **OGu** *GL* A 45a

See also: *vébönd (pl.)*

Refs: Peel 2015, 180 note 45a/10–11; Schlyter 1877, s.v. *motstukker*; SL GL, 286 note 2 to chapter 45a

moþghur (pl.) (OSw) noun

mother and daughter **OSw** *ÄVgL* Gb

moþnahæfþ (OSw) noun

intercourse with mother or daughter **OSw** *SmL*

móðurarfr (ON) noun

inheritance from a mother **OIce** *Js* Ert 21, **ONorw** *FrL* ArbB 9

móðurfrændi (ON) noun

kinsman on the mother's side **ONorw** *FrL* Intr 4 ArbB 22 Kvb 9

maternal kinsmen **OIce** *Js* Kvg 4

móðurætt (ON) noun

kin on mother's side **ONorw** *FrL* ArbB 26

maternal kin **OIce** *Js* Kvg 3

mother's family **OIce** *Grg* Ómb 128

mun (ODan) noun

goods **ODan** *VSjL* 7, 14

means **ODan** *ESjL* 1

movables **ODan** *ESjL* 1

valuables **ODan** *VSjL* 6, 53

munder (OSw) **mundr** (ON) noun

A bride-price paid by the bridegroom, which originally was a requirement for a legal marriage and was added to the personal property of the woman as a counterpart to her portion (in ONorw laws at least 12 *aurar* (GuL ch. 51)). A woman married off in this way, *mæþ mund ok mæþ mæli* 'with payment and measurement' (OSw ÄVgL, YVgL), was a legally married woman (*mundgipt* or *mundi keypt* 'paid and bought').

bridal gift **OSw** *YVgL* Äb, Gb

bride price **OIce** *Grg* Þsþ 62 Arþ 118 Feþ 144, 150 Fjl 223, *Js* Kvg 5, **ONorw** *FrL* KrbB 13 Kvb 14, *GuL* Krb, Kvb, Løb, Arb

See also: *mynde*

Refs: Agnes Arnórsdóttir and Thyra Nors 1999; Helle 2001, 138–40; Hertzberg s.v. *mundr*;

KLNM s.v.v. *arveskifte, brudköp, bröllop, festermål, konkurs, lejermål, morgongåva, mundr, vängåva, ægteskab*; Lindkvist forthcoming; RGA s.v. *mund*; Robberstad 1981, 346–48

mundgipt (OSw) adj.

legally married **OSw** *ÄVgL* Äb

See also: *kona*

mundr (OGu) noun

thumb-nail's breadth **OGu** *GL* A 19

mundriði (ON) noun

handle of a shield **ONorw** *GuL* Leb

mungat (OGu) noun

ale **OGu** *GL* A 19, *GS* Ch. 1

feast **OGu** *GL* A 18

See also: *öl*

mungatstiþir (pl.) (OSw) noun

Presumably a communal feast day when, among other things, wedding days were decided.

feasts **OSw** *ÄVgL* Gb

times for feasts **OSw** *YVgL* Gb

See also: *ölstæmna*

Refs: Schlyter s.v. *mungats tiþir*

munhaf (OSw) **munhav** (ODan) **munhævthe** (ODan) noun

There are only a few occurrences in the laws of a term for oath formulas. OSw *munhaf* and ODan *munhav*, *munhævthe* occur, among other things, concerning land disputes and roping (ODan VSjL and SkL), wounding and levelling oaths (ODan SkL), and illegitimate children and perjury (OSw YVgL). Various oath formulas in the laws typically invoke the Christian God, but in OSw ÄVgL pagan gods collectively.

formula **ODan** *VSjL* 76

statement **ODan** *JyL* 2

wording **ODan** *JyL* 2, *SkL* 72, 114, **OSw** *YVgL* Drb, Add

wording of an oath **ODan** *VSjL* 76

Refs: Lindkvist forthcoming

munk (ODan) **munkr** (OGu) noun

monk **ODan** *JyL* 2, 3, **OGu** *GL* A 7

See also: *kloster, nunna*

musa (OSw) noun

armour **OSw** *HL* Rb

muslegumaþr (OGu) noun

fugitive **OGu** *GL* Add. 8 (B 55)

muta (OSw) **múta** (ON) noun

A bribe. Related to Gothic *mōta* ('toll'). At some point *múta* meant a business transaction fee or gift, a sense

retained in ÄVgL, where it is described as a gift of
moveable goods. In the *Gammal Norsk Homiliebok*,
mútufé ('bribe') is listed among the deadly sins.

bribe **OIce** *Jó* Mah 17 Kge 18, *Js* Kvg 4, **ONorw**
FrL Kvb 9, **OSw** *SdmL* Kmb, *YVgL* Add

gift **OSw** *ÄVgL* Äb, Kva

See also: *væghsel*

Refs: CV s.v. *múta*; Fritzner s.v. *múta*;
Haubrichs 2014; KLNM s.v. *huvudsynd*;
Lindkvist forthcoming; Schlyter s.v. *muta*

myllari (OSw) **möllari** (OSw) noun

miller **OSw** *YVgL* Föb

mylna (OSw) **mylne** (ODan) noun

mill **ODan** *ESjL* 3, *JyL* 1, *SkL* 211, 214,
226, *VSjL* 57, **OSw** *HL* Blb, *YVgL* Kvab,
Utgb, *ÄVgL* Md, Äb, Kva, Föb

mylnobolker (OSw) noun

book about mills **OSw** *YVgL* Kvab

mylnustaþer (OSw) noun

millrace **OSw** *UL* Blb, *VmL* Bb

mynde (ODan) **mynda** (ON) verb

dispose of a lot after the wife **ODan** *SkL* 45

be entitled to a man's lot **ODan** *SkL* 23

have a right by a child **ODan** *VSjL* 3

*have a right to take something by the
birth of a child* **ODan** *ESjL* 3

pay a dowry **OIce** *Jó* Kge 2, *Js* Kvg 1

pay the bride price ({munder}) **ONorw** *GuL* Kvb

take a lot after the wife **ODan** *SkL* 23

See also: *barnmynd, munder*

mynding (ODan) **mynding** (ON) noun

In ODan, a lot or portion of a spouse's property, if they
had mutual children. In ON, the balancing, or possibly
joining, of bride price and portion.

paying the bride price ({munder}) **ONorw** *GuL* Kvb

right by a child **ODan** *VSjL* 2

See also: *munder, mynde*

Refs: Gammeldansk ordbog s.v. *mynding*; Hertzberg
s.v. *mynding*; Tamm and Vogt, eds, 2016, 333

myndrikkia (OGu) noun

small vessel **OGu** *GL* A 36

See also: *bater, byrthing, farkoster,
floti, kaupskip, skip*

myntere (ODan) noun

mint-master **ODan** *JyL* 3

myr (OGu) noun

marshland **OGu** *GL* A 25

myrþa (OSw) **myrða** (ON) verb

kill **OSw** *YVgL* Rlb

murder **OIce** *Grg* Vís 88, *Jó* Mah 2, *Js* Mah
5, **ONorw** *EidsL* 7, *GuL* Mhb, **OSw** *DL* Mb,
HL Mb, *SdmL* Mb, *UL* Mb, *VmL* Mb, *YVgL*
Urb, Gb, *ÄVgL* Gb, Rlb, *ÖgL* Kkb, Eb

See also: *dræpa, morþ*

mægð (ON) **mægðir** (ON) noun

kinship by marriage **OIce** *Grg* Þsþ
25, 35, *Jó* Mah 7, 10 Kab 2

marriage relations **ONorw** *GuL* Sab

See also: *frændsimi, guþsivi*

mæghen (ODan) noun

power **ODan** *VSjL* 52

mægjask (ON) verb

enter into marriage relations **ONorw** *GuL* Krb

mæla (1) (OSw) **mæla** (ON) verb

Derived from the noun *mal* (1). A basic, albeit not
original, meaning ('to speak') is reflected in several
translations relating to various stages of legal
proceedings (as 'appoint', 'order', 'respond', 'agree',
'decide', 'declare'), particularly relating to the start
of legal proceedings ('summon', 'prosecute', 'take
action', 'pursue'). Also used in numerous phrases and
compounds.

agree **ONorw** *GuL* Krb, Løb

make a claim **OSw** *ÄVgL* Md

order **ONorw** *GuL* Krb

plead **OSw** *ÄVgL* Äb

promise **ONorw** *GuL* Kpb, **OSw** *YVgL* Gb, Utgb

prosecute **OSw** *YVgL* Drb, Tb,
ÄVgL Kkb, *ÖgL* Kkb, Eb

See also: *mal (1)*

Refs: Bjorvand and Lindeman 2000, s.v. *mål*

mæla (2) (OSw) **mæle** (ODan) verb

measure **OSw** *SdmL* Bb

assess **ODan** *SkL* 168, 169

mælandi (ON) noun

advocate **ONorw** *FrL* Var 43

spokesman **OIce** *Grg* Vís 94

mælikerald (ON) noun

measuring vessel **OIce** *Jó* Kab 26

mælir (ON) noun

measure **ONorw** *FrL* ArbB 12 Bvb 13

measure of capacity, ca. 1/2 bushel
ONorw *GuL* Krb, Løb

mælistang (OSw) noun

measuring pole **OSw** *SdmL* Bb

See also: *rep, stangfall, vaþstang*

mærki (OSw) **mærke** (ODan) **merki** (OGu) **merki**
(ON) **merki** (OSw) noun

A 'landmark' of any kind. When meaning boundary
marker it is often preceded by a qualification: *ra-*
'stake' *rör-* 'cairn of stones', *skogha-* 'forest', *skogs-*
'forest', *sokna-* 'parish', *sten-* 'stone', *træ-* 'wooden'.
When meaning a livestock brand it can be preceded
by *bols-* 'farm'. Also used to mean a general means of
identification.

boundary **OIce** *Grg* Klþ 2 Lbþ 174, 181, *Jó* Lbb
6, *Js* Lbb 2, **ONorw** *GuL* Llb, **OSw** *UL* Mb

boundary land **OGu** *GL* A 25

boundary mark **OSw** *HL* Blb

boundary marker **OIce** *Jó* Llb 43,
OSw *YVgL* Jb, *ÄVgL* Jb

brand **OGu** *GL* A 44, **OSw** *HL* Blb,
UL Mb, Blb, *VmL* Mb, Bb

dividing mark **OSw** *HL* Blb

identification **OSw** *UL* Mb, *VmL* Mb

indication **ODan** *JyL* 2

mark **ODan** *ESjL* 3, *JyL* 2, **OSw** *SdmL* Bb

markbrand **OSw** *HL* Blb

visible indication **OIce** *Grg* Tíg 262

See also: *bol, engjamerki, landamærki,*
mark (1), markreina, merkigarðr

Refs: CV s.v. *merki*; Schlyter s.v. *mærki*

mæssufall (OSw) **messufall** (OGu) **mæssofall** (OSw)
mæssufal (OSw) noun

cancelled mass **OSw** *HL* Kkb

case of (breach of) mass (peace) **OSw** *ÖgL* Kkb

failure to say mass **OGu** *GL* A 60,
OSw *UL* Kkb, *VmL* Kkb

neglect of the mass **OSw** *SdmL* Kkb

mæssuklæþi (OSw) **mæsso klæþi** (OSw) noun

mass vestments **OSw** *UL* Kkb, *VmL* Kkb

See also: *klæþi*

mæssuskruþer (OSw) noun

mass vessels and vestments **OSw** *UL* Kkb

mæt (OSw) noun

assessment **OSw** *DL* Rb, *UL* Rb

confiscation **OSw** *DL* Rb, *UL* Rb, *VmL* Rb

scale of measurement **OSw** *DL* Gb

seizure **OSw** *HL* Rb

seizure process **OSw** *HL* Rb

set value **OSw** *DL* Gb

mæta (OSw) **meta** (ON) **miæta** (OSw) verb

assess **ONorw** *GuL* Mhb, Olb, **OSw** *DL*
Bb, *SdmL* Kkb, Jb, Bb, Kmb, Tjdb, Rb,
UL Kmb, Blb, *VmL* Mb, Bb, Rb

confiscate **OSw** *DL* Rb, *UL* Rb, *VmL* Rb

consider **ONorw** *GuL* Kpb

decide **ONorw** *GuL* Arb, Mhb, Olb

deem **OIce** *Grg* Vís 93, **ONorw** *GuL* Olb

determine **ONorw** *GuL* Arb

estimate **ONorw** *GuL* Olb, **OSw** *YVgL* Add

examine **OSw** *YVgL* Add

extract **OSw** *UL* Kgb

measure **ONorw** *FrL* LlbA 1, **OSw** *HL*
Blb, *YVgL* Vs, Gb, Jb, *ÄVgL* Vs, Gb

seize **OSw** *HL* Rb

send bailiffs (to someone) **OSw** *UL* Rb

value **ONorw** *GuL* Kvb, Løb, **OSw**
DL Bb, *HL* Mb, *VmL* Kmb, Bb

Expressions:

mæta ut (OSw)

distrain **OSw** *HL* Rb

See also: *ofsökia, utmæta*

mætansorþ (OSw) **metorð** (ON) noun

assessment **OIce** *Grg* Fjl 221, **ONorw** *FrL* Rgb 29

investigators' decision **OSw** *YVgL* Add

words of investigators **OSw** *YVgL* Add

mætr (ON) adj.

valid **OIce** *Grg* Þsþ 41

mætsmæn (pl.) (OSw) **miætans mæn** (pl.) (OSw)
miætsmæn (pl.) (OSw) **mætansmæn** (pl.) (OSw)
mættens men (pl.) (OSw) **mæzmæn** (pl.) (OSw)
noun

Literally 'measuring men'. Combined the function of
surveyors, assessors and collectors. Often appear in
the plural, which implies that they worked in pairs or
groups, but nothing seems to be known of their status
or appointment.

assessors **OSw** *DL* Bb, Rb, *SdmL* Bb,
Kmb, Tjdb, *UL* Mb, Blb, *VmL* Mb, Bb

bailiffs **OSw** *UL* Rb, *VmL* Rb

evaluators **OSw** *YVgL* Add

measure men **OSw** *HL* Blb

measurers **OSw** *HL* Rb

measuring men **OSw** *HL* Blb

See also: *metandi, mæta*

Refs: Brink, forthcoming, KLNM s.v. *mätisman*;
SAOB s.v. *mätesman*; Schlyter s.v. *mætans mæn*

mæþfylghþ (OSw) noun

This was one of a number of words used to designate
the marriage portion given by the parents to their son
or daughter on marriage. This form occurs only in UL

and in VmL, where *fylghia* (q.v.) is also used in one instance. The more commonly used form is *hemfylghþ* (q.v.).

marriage portion **OSw** *UL* Äb, *VmL* Äb

See also: *fylghia, gift, heimanferð, heimangerð, hemfylghþ, hemfærth, hemgæf, hindradagsgæf, morghongæf, munder, tilgæf, vingæf*

Refs: KLNM, s.v. *medgift*; Schlyter 1877, s.v.v. *fylghþ, hemfylghþ*

mö (OSw) **mø** (ODan) **mær** (ON) noun

girl **OIce** *Grg* Arþ 118, **ONorw** *FrL* Rgb 36, *GuL* Arb, Olb

maid **ODan** *JyL* 2, **ONorw** *GuL* Kvb, **OSw** *YVgL* Gb, Add, *ÄVgL* Gb

maiden **ODan** *ESjL* 1–3, *JyL* 1, 2, *VSjL* 1, **OIce** *Jó* Llb 19, **OSw** *HL* Äb, *SdmL* Gb, *SmL*

spinster **OSw** *DL* Gb

unmarried sister **OSw** *DL* Gb

unmarried woman **OIce** *Grg* Þsþ 78 Vís 94, *Js* Mah 36 Kvg 3, 4, **ONorw** *FrL* Sab 4

virgin **ODan** *SkL* 218

mögr (ON) noun

son **OIce** *Grg* Bat 115

See also: *magher*

möiaralder (OSw) noun

virginity **OSw** *UL* Äb, *VmL* Äb

mötunautr (ON) noun

messmate **OIce** *Grg* Vís 97 Arþ 120 Misc 249, *Jó* Kge 18 Fml 9, **ONorw** *GuL* Mhb

mötuneyti (ON) noun

eating in common **ONorw** *GuL* Krb, Tjb

möþerni (OSw) **møthrene** (ODan) **myþrni** (OGu) **móðerni** (ON) **möþrini** (OSw) **moþærni** (OSw) **mæþærni** (OSw) noun

Literally, 'maternal'. The meaning extended to cover the whole of the maternal side of the family, the maternal inheritance (as opposed to the paternal) and the ancestral land inherited from the mother, although the expression *möþrinis jorþ* in full does occur. Sometimes the same word was employed with more than one of these meanings in the same sentence. The noun in the possessive case was also used adjectivally to mean 'maternal', to relate to other specific parts of an inheritance, e.g. ancestral home, movables.

maternal **ODan** *ESjL* 1, 3, *JyL* 2, *SkL* 24, 26, 27, 85, 92, 223, *VSjL* 1, **OSw** *HL* Äb

maternal goods **ODan** *VSjL* 1

maternal inheritance **ODan** *SkL* 37, **OGu** *GL* A 20, 24e, **OSw** *DL* Bb, Gb, *SdmL* Gb, Jb, *UL* Äb, *VmL* Äb, *YVgL* Rlb, *ÄVgL* Äb

maternal kin **OSw** *DL* Gb

maternal land **ODan** *ESjL* 3, *SkL* 23, 27, 45, *VSjL* 1, 4, **OSw** *UL* Jb, *VmL* Jb, *YVgL* Jb

maternal part **OSw** *YVgL* Äb

maternal side **ODan** *SkL* 57, 223, **OSw** *SdmL* Gb, Äb, *UL* Äb, *VmL* Äb, *YVgL* Drb, Äb, Add, *ÄVgL* Md, Äb

mother's **ODan** *VSjL* 15

mother's side **ODan** *ESjL* 1, 3, *JyL* 2, *SkL* 57, **ONorw** *EidsL* 30.5, *FrL* Var 9, **OSw** *DL* Gb

what is from the mother **ODan** *JyL* 1

Expressions:

möþernis frændi (OSw)

kinsman of the mother **ODan** *ESjL* 2 *JyL* 1

kinsman on the mother's side **ODan** *SkL* 57

maternal kinsman **ODan** *ESjL* 1–3 *JyL* 1 *SkL* 85, 92 **OSw** *DL* Bb

maternal relative **OSw** *DL* Rb *SdmL* Gb, Äb

mother's kinsman **ODan** *ESjL* 3 *JyL* 1

möþernis jorþ (OSw)

maternal land **ODan** *SkL* 23, 45 *VSjL* 1 **OSw** *DL* Rb

See also: *fæþerni, gyrþlugyrt, lindagyrt*

Refs: Peel 2015, 134 note 20/36–37; Schlyter 1877, s.v.v. *möþerni, möþrinis iorþ*

möþringar (pl.) (OSw) noun

mother's side **OSw** *ÖgL* Eb, Db

relatives on the maternal side **OSw** *SmL*

mørir (pl.) (ON) noun

people from Sunnmøre **ONorw** *GuL* Leb

nafnbót (ON) noun

rank **OIce** *Jó* Llb 18 Þjb 16

naglfastr (ON) adj.

fastened with a nail **ONorw** *GuL* Llb

nagli (ON) noun

If a nail needed for the building of a church or a warship was missing, the person(s) responsible had to pay a fine. See GuL chs 10, 306.

nail (of tree or metal) **ONorw** *GuL* Krb, Leb

Refs: KLNM s.v.v. *nagle, sud, tak*

nagranni (OSw) **nágranni** (ON) **næorw** **næranni** (OSw) **nærgranni** (OSw) noun

Neighbour, possibly other than the closest one, who appears as a legally required witness to various events in the community, such as *nam* 'seizure', fires and funerals. Often in the phrase *granni ok/æller nagranni* (OSw).

close neighbour **OSw** *DL* Kkb, Gb, *HL* Kkb, Blb
man of the area **OSw** *UL* Blb, *VmL* Mb, Bb
near neighbour **OSw** *DL* Bb, *SdmL* Kkb, Bb, Mb, *UL* Kkb, Äb, Jb, *VmL* Kkb
neighbour **OFar** *Seyð* 10

See also: *byaman*, *bygdamæn (pl.)*, *granni*

Refs: KLNM s.v. *naboforhold*; SAOB s.v. *någranne*

nam (OSw) **nam** (ODan) noun

Literally 'taking'. Movable goods taken by a creditor or plaintiff as surety for due compensation or fine. In ODan, *nam* had to be preceded by a verdict from the *thing* 'assembly'. In both ODan and OSw, it was regulated which parts of the owner's property could be legally entered when taking the *nam*, and the taker had to announce it to the neighbours. Contrasted to theft and robbery. Increasingly replaced by distraint and execution performed by someone impartial. The concept is often expressed with the corresponding verb *næma* (OSw).

deposit **OSw** *DL* Rb
personal surety **OSw** *UL* Äb, *VmL* Mb
security **OSw** *ÄVgL* Rlb
seizure **ODan** *ESjL* 3, *JyL* 2, *SkL* 85, **OSw** *ÖgL* Db
surety **OSw** *SdmL* Bb, *VmL* Kgb, Mb, *YVgL* Utgb

See also: *tak*, *væp*, *væpsætia*

Refs: KLNM s.v. *nam*

namfæ (OSw) noun

cattle taken as pledge **OSw** *YVgL* Utgb
cattle taken in custody **OSw** *ÄVgL* Föb

See also: *fæ*, *nam*

namn (OSw) **navn** (ODan) noun

Apart from name giving of children, also appearing on the one hand in punishable insults (such as *fult namn* 'foul name' OSw SdmL Mb), and on the other hand in legal identification of a wrongdoer, such as a thief (ODan VSjL 87), whore (OSw DL Kkb) or villain (OSw YvgL Urb).

name **ODan** *VSjL* 87, **OSw** *SdmL* Mb, *YVgL* Urb, Drb

namsdom (ODan) noun

judgement for seizure **ODan** *JyL* 3

nast (OGu) noun

buckle **OGu** *GL* A 23

See also: *nestli*

nauðahandsal (ON) noun

forced agreement **OIce** *Grg* Misc 244

nauðsynjalauss (ON) adj.

prevented by lawful impediment **ONorw** *EidsL* 10.3
unhindered **ONorw** *FrL* KrbB 12
unnecessarily **ONorw** *FrL* Var 46
without a lawful excuse **OIce** *Jó* Lbb 10 Fml 4, **ONorw** *FrL* KrbA 44
without compelling necessity **OIce** *Jó* Fml 19
without delay **OIce** *Jó* Llb 4
without due cause **ONorw** *FrL* Tfb 1
without good reason **ONorw** *FrL* KrbA 14
without legitimate excuse **OIce** *Grg* Lsþ 116 Lrþ 117 Lbþ 193 Hrs 234, *Js* Þfb 2 Lbb 7 Kab 3, *KRA* 1, 3 passim, **ONorw** *FrL* Leb 8 Rgb 5
without need **OIce** *Jó* Þfb 3, **ONorw** *BorgL* 5.13
without reason **OIce** *Jó* Llb 36, **ONorw** *FrL* Rgb 46

See also: *foráttalaust*, *ørendlauss*

nauðsynjalaust (ON) adv.

not prevented by necessity **ONorw** *GuL* Krb

nauðsynjaváttr (ON) noun

testimony of lawful absence **ONorw** *FrL* Rgb 3

nauðsynjavitni (ON) **nauðsynjarvitni** (ON) noun

testimony of necessity **OIce** *Js* Kab 2 Þjb 4
witness to legal excuses **ONorw** *GuL* Løb, Tjb
witness to necessity **OIce** *Jó* Þfb 4
witness to testify necessity **OIce** *Jó* Þjb 5

See also: *vitni*

nauðsynligr (ON) adj.

compulsory **OIce** *KRA* 12

naumdǿlir (pl.) (ON) noun

people from Namdalen **ONorw** *GuL* Leb

naumdǿll (ON) noun

person from Namdalen **ONorw** *FrL* Reb 3

naust (ON) noun

boathouse **OIce** *Grg* Feþ 165, **ONorw** *GuL* Llb, Leb

naustgerð (ON) noun

building of boat-houses **ONorw** *GuL* Leb

nautabo (OGu) noun

cattle **OGu** *GL* A 65

See also: *not*, *söþer*

nautamark (ON) noun

cattle mark **OIce** *Grg* Fjl 221

nautatröð (ON) noun

cattle trod **ONorw** *EidsL* 11.6

See also: *troth*

Refs: CV s.v. *tröð*; ONP *tröð*.

naþakona (OSw) noun

woman at the mercy of (someone) **OSw** *VmL* Äb

See also: *miskunnakona*

naþir (OSw) nathe (ODan) noun

The king could pardon an arsonist (ODan JyL) and execute an excommunicate who refused to ask for forgiveness (OSw HL), and parents could show mercy to a daughter who went against their choice of husband (OSw SdmL).

forgiveness **OSw** *HL* Kkb

mercy **ODan** *JyL* 3, **OSw** *SdmL* Gb

See also: *miskun*

náinn (ON) adj.

close **ONorw** *GuL* Krb, Løb, Olb

nálgask (ON) verb

be vague **OIce** *Grg* Þsþ 32

námágr (ON) noun

close kinsman by marriage **OIce** *Grg* Þsþ 25, 35 Vís 89 Bat 113 Fjl 223, *Js* Mah 13, 14 Kab 2, **ONorw** *FrL* Mhb 9 Rgb 14

near male relative related by marriage **ONorw** *GuL* Kpb, Løb, Tfb, Mhb, Olb, Sab

násessi (ON) noun

man sitting close to another **ONorw** *GuL* Mhb

náttin helga (ON) noun

Christmas Eve **ONorw** *GuL* Krb, Kpb, Løb, Arb, Olb, Leb

See also: *jólanátt, julaapton*

náttsetr (ON) náttsæting (ON) noun

nightwatch **ONorw** *BorgL* 12.9, *EidsL* 47.7

náttstaðarvitni (ON) noun

dwelling confirmation **ONorw** *FrL* Var 12

night-quarters testimony **OIce** *Js* Mah 21

See also: *vitni*

náttstaðr (ON) noun

dwelling **ONorw** *FrL* Mhb 7

night-quarters **OIce** *Js* Mah 14, **ONorw** *GuL* Arb, Tfb, Mhb

place where one spends nights **OIce** *Jó* Kge 26, 32

náungi (ON) náingi (ON) noun

close relative **ONorw** *BorgL* 9.14

near kinsman **ONorw** *GuL* Olb

návistarmaðr (ON) noun

eyewitness **OIce** *Jó* Mah 9, **ONorw** *GuL* Tjb

nearby person **OIce** *Js* Mah 10, 18 Þjb 7, **ONorw** *FrL* Mhb 35

neighbour witness **OIce** *Jó* Þjb 7

ne (OSw) nai (OGu) nei (OSw) næi (OSw) noun

denial **OGu** *GL* A 20a, **OSw** *UL* Kkb, Äb, Mb, Jb, Blb, *VmL* Kkb, Äb, Mb, Bb, Rb

See also: *dul, dylia, neka*

nef (ON) noun

nose **ONorw** *GuL* Tjb

person **ONorw** *GuL* Krb

person (in relation to enrolment) **ONorw** *GuL* Krb, Leb

See also: *félauss, þrot*

nefgildi (ON) noun

In OIce and ONorw referring to compensation for a killing, to be paid or received by kinsfolk on the mother's side.

cognate payment **OIce** *Grg* Bat 113, **ONorw** *FrL* Sab 7

compensation to be paid or received by kinsfolk on the mother's side **ONorw** *GuL* Olb

mother's side **ONorw** *FrL* ArbB 8, *GuL* Olb

See also: *bauggildi, manbot, nefgildismaðr*

Refs: Hertzberg s.v. *nefgildi*; KLNM s.v. *nefgildi*

nefgildingr (ON) noun

cognate kin **OIce** *Grg* Bat 113

nefgildismaðr (ON) noun

A *nefgildismaðr*, 'cognatic kinsman', was a near kinsman on the female side. In the GuL the circle of cognatic kinsmen extended up to and including first cousins.

cognate kinsfolk **ONorw** *FrL* Mhb 34 ArbB 20

cognate who has to pay or receive {nefgildi} **ONorw** *GuL* Krb, Løb, Tfb, Mhb, Olb

cognate-payment kinsman **OIce** *Grg* Bat 113, *Js* Mah 13, 34 Kab 2, **ONorw** *FrL* KrbB 1 Mhb 7, 9 Sab 15

kinsman on the mother's side **ONorw** *FrL* Var 9 ArbB 8

See also: *bogher, kvensvift, nefgildi*

Refs: Hertzberg s.v. *nefgildismaðr*; KLNM s.v.v. *nefgildi, straff; værge I*; RGA2 s.v. *ringgeld*; Robberstad 1981, 343

nefndarvitni (ON) noun

appointed witness **ONorw** *FrL* Mhb 8, 14 Var 9 Rgb 32

man appointed by the court **OIce** *Jó* Mah 10

testimony of nominated men **OIce** *Js* Mah 14, **ONorw** *FrL* Mhb 7

See also: *vitni*

neka (OSw) naikka (OGu) verb

deny **OSw** *UL* Kkb, Äb, Mb, Jb, Rb, *VmL* Kkb, Äb, Mb, Rb

reject **OGu** *GL* A 1

See also: *dul, dylia, ne*

neqvæþi (OSw) níkvæði (ON) nekuaþi (OSw) noun
  annullment **ONorw** *EidsL* 23.2
  denial **OSw** *ÄVgL* Rlb
  See also: *níkvæðr*

nerkumin (OGu) adj.
  closely related **OGu** *GL* A 14
  See also: *frændi, niþi, skylder (1)*

nes (ON) noun
  A spit or protrusion of land. Certain types of land, such
  as cutting woodland and nesting grounds, necessitated
  that walls be built around them rather than through
  them.
  intrusion **OIce** *Grg* Lbþ 181, *Jó* Llb 32
  Refs: CV s.v. *nes*; Fritzner s.v. *nes*;
  Hertzberg s.v. *nes*; ONP s.v. *nes*

nestli (OGu) noun
  clasp **OGu** *GL* A 23
  See also: *nast*

net (ON) noun
  fishing net **ONorw** *GuL* Llb

netlag (ON) noun
  net-laying line **OIce** *Grg* Lbþ 212, *Jó* Llb 58

niauta (OGu) verb
  Expressions:
  at niauta (OGu)
  benefit from **OGu** *GL* A 22

niðgjald (ON) noun
  kindred payments **OIce** *Grg* Vís 91 Bat 113
  See also: *mannsgjald*

nikulásmessa (ON) noun
  Feast of St Nicholas (6 December) **ONorw** *GuL* Krb
  St Nicholas's Day **OIce** *Grg* Klþ 13

niþ (OSw) noun
  family **OSw** *UL* Äb, *VmL* Äb
  kin **OSw** *SmL, UL* Äb, *VmL* Äb
  kinship **OSw** *DL* Gb
  See also: *kyn, skylder (1), æt*

niþararf (OSw) niþiar arf (OSw) noun
  kinsman's inheritance **OSw** *UL* Äb, *VmL* Äb
  relative's inheritance **OSw** *HL* Äb

niþi (OSw) nithe (ODan) niþi (OGu) niðr (ON) noun
  descendant **ODan** *JyL* 1
  family **ODan** *SkL* 129
  heir **ODan** *VSjL* 50
  kinsman **ODan** *ESjL* 2, 3, *JyL* 1, *SkL* 127,
  146, **OGu** *GL* A 7, 13, 14, 20, 28, **OIce**
  Grg Ómb 128, **ONorw** *GuL* Krb, Tfb

  relative **ODan** *SkL* 223, *VSjL* 41, 50, 53, 67
  See also: *frændi, kyn, skyldarman*

niþias (OSw) verb
  substantiate birthright by kinship **OSw** *VmL* Äb

niþiavitni (OGu) noun
  kin witness **OGu** *GL* A 25
  See also: *liksvitni, vitni*

niþinger (OSw) níðingr (ON) noun
  nithing **OSw** *YVgL* Urb
  villain **ONorw** *GuL* Leb
  See also: *níðingsherr, níðingsvíg*

niþingsværk (OSw) nithingsværk (ODan) níðingsverk
  (ON) noun
  A particularly shameful or ignominious act or deed
  which makes the perpetrator a *níðing* (see *niþinger*).
  An action classified as a *niþingsværk* was strongly
  condemned on moral grounds. Crimes which fell
  under the heading of *niþingsværk* varied according
  to time and place. Generally the term was reserved
  for the most egregious offenses, such as treason and
  breaking sworn truces, but it was applied to a variety
  of other offenses as well, such as destroying someone's
  household, piracy (both in ÄVgL) or killing someone
  on a king's ship (MLL IV 4).
  Penalties for committing a *niþingsværk* were
  usually severe. In the Danish laws the fine was
  forty marks for killing someone with whom one had
  previously made peace through compensation. In
  Norway and Iceland a *níðingsverk* was often marked
  as an unatonable crime (*óbótamál*, see *urbotamal*)
  and carried a penalty of property forfeiture and exile.
  There seem to have been some lesser offenses which
  were still considered *niþingsværk* but punished less
  severely, such as killing another man's domestic
  animals (JyL III.53) and slandering someone with
  defamatory language (*ókvæðisorð*, see *oqvæþinsorþ*;
  ÖgL Bb 38).
  In the Swedish laws such a crime required
  witnesses. It does not seem to figure in the laws of
  Svealand.
  It has been suggested, albeit without any concrete
  evidence, that in earlier eras someone who committed
  a *niþingsværk* could be sacrificed to the gods as
  punishment.
  act of outrage **OSw** *YVgL* Kkb, *ÄVgL* Kkb
  crime of outrage **OSw** *YVgL* Add
  deed of a villain **OIce** *Jó* Mah 1, 2, *Js*
  Mah 5, 29, **ONorw** *FrL* Mhb 4
  dishonourable crime **OIce** *Jó* Mah 2
  outrageous case **OSw** *YVgL* Urb, *ÄVgL* Urb

outrageous crime **OSw** *YVgL* Rlb, *ÄVgL* Rlb

outrageousness **OSw** *YVgL* Add

villain's act **ODan** *ESjL* 3

villainous act **ODan** *VSjL* 55

villainy **ONorw** *FrL* Mhb 1

See also: *níðingsvíg, niþinger, skemmðarvíg, svik, urbotamal*

Refs: Almqvist 1965; CV s.v. *níðingr*; F s.v. *níðingsverk*; KLNM s.v. *niddingsværk, sjörätt, straff*; LexMA s.v. *Strafe/Strafrecht*; Orning 2008, 120

niþra (OGu) **nidra** (OGu) verb

debase **OGu** *GL* Add. 1 (B 4)

níð (ON) noun

insult **OIce** *Js* Mah 25

shaming slander **OIce** *Grg* Misc 237, 238

slander **OIce** *Jó* Mah 26

See also: *bakmæli, fjölmæli, háðung, rógja, ýki*

níða (ON) verb

insult **ONorw** *GuL* Tfb

níðingsherr (ON) noun

band of traitors **ONorw** *GuL* Tfb

See also: *níðingsvíg, niþinger*

níðingsvíg (ON) noun

dishonourable killing **OIce** *Jó* Mah 2, 4

foul murder **ONorw** *GuL* Mhb

See also: *níðingsherr, niþinger, skemmðarvíg, vigh*

níðstöng (ON) noun

shame-pole **OIce** *Grg* Misc 237

See also: *níð*

níkvæðr (ON) adj.

which can be denied **ONorw** *GuL* Tjb

See also: *neqvæþi*

nokkadrumber (OSw) noun

A man or a woman who did not pay any tax and who refused employment.

sluggard **OSw** *YVgL* Utgb, Add

Refs: Hellquist s.v. *nucka*; Schlyter s.v. *nokkadrumber*

nokkefrue (ODan) noun

Synonymous with ODan *nokkekone* (q.v.).

single woman **ODan** *VSjL* 8, 10

See also: *nokkekone*

nokkekone (ODan) noun

A woman without a guardian or head of the household, which affected her right to inheritance. Synonymous with ODan *nokkefrue* (q.v.).

single woman **ODan** *VSjL* 9

See also: *nokkadrumber, nokkefrue*

Refs: Hellquist s.v. *nucka*; Lund s.v.v. *nokkæfrughæ, nokkækunæ*; Schlyter s.v. *nokka kona*; Tamm and Vogt, eds, 2016, 316

norðmórir (pl.) (ON) noun

people from Nordmøre **ONorw** *GuL* Leb

noregsmaðr (ON) noun

man from Norway **OIce** *Grg* Feþ 166

Norwegian **ONorw** *FrL* ArbB 5

noræn (OSw) **noren** (OSw) **norin** (OSw) adj.

Appears in regulations concerning the punishment for killing foreigners.

Norwegian **OSw** *YVgL* Drb, *ÄVgL* Md

not (OSw) **nøt** (ODan) **naut** (OGu) **naut** (ON) noun

bullock **OSw** *UL* Kgb, Blb, *VmL* Kgb, Mb, Bb

cattle **ODan** *ESjL* 3, **OGu** *GL* A 45a, Add. 2 (B 17), **OSw** *SdmL* Äb, *ÄVgL* Tb

horned cattle **ODan** *SkL* 169

livestock **ONorw** *GuL* Krb, Kpb, Leb

oxen **ODan** *JyL* 2, 3

seine-net **OSw** *UL* Blb, *VmL* Bb

See also: *nautabo, rus*

notadræt (OSw) noun

seine-net catches **OSw** *UL* Kkb

noyta (OGu) verb

enjoy **OGu** *GL* A 20, 28

noytga (OGu) **nauðga** (ON) **nauðiga** (ON) verb

compel **OGu** *GL* A 16

rape **OIce** *KRA* 36, **ONorw** *FrL* KrbB 3

See also: *noyþa, nöþogher*

noyþa (OGu) verb

compel **OGu** *GL* Add. 1 (B 4)

force **OGu** *GL* A 22, Add. 1 (B 4)

need arise **OGu** *GL* A 20

See also: *noytga, nöþogher*

nón (ON) noun

noon **ONorw** *GuL* Krb

nónheilagr (ON) adj.

holy after 3pm **ONorw** *FrL* Var 8

holy from nones onwards **OIce** *Grg* Klþ 9

holy from the preceding nones **ONorw** *GuL* Krb

nones-holy **OIce** *KRA* 28

nónhelgr (ON) noun

holiness from the preceding nones **ONorw** *GuL* Krb

vigil **ONorw** *EidsL* 9.3

nótari (ON) **notarius** (ON) noun

scribe **OFar** *Seyð* 0

nunna (ON) noun

> *nun* **OIce** *Grg* Feþ 158, **ONorw** *FrL* KrbB 3

> See also: *kloster, munk*

nunnuvígsla (ON) noun

> *consecration of a nun* **ONorw** *FrL* KrbB 14

ny (OSw) noun

> Expressions:

> **ny ok niþ, ny ok niþær** (OSw) **ny ok niþan** (OGu)

> *waxing and waning* **OGu** *GL* Add. 7
> (B 49) GS Ch. 1 **OSw** *UL* Blb

nykkia (OGu) verb

> *manhandle* **OGu** *GL* A 8

> *shake* **OGu** *GL* A 19

nykkr (OGu) noun

> *jerking* **OGu** *GL* A 19

> See also: *nykkia*

nytfall (ON) noun

> *loss of milk* **OIce** *Jó* Llb 39

nýlendi (ON) noun

> *new farm* **ONorw** *FrL* KrbA 23

> *recently cultivated land* **OIce** *Jó* Kge 33

nýmæli (ON) noun

> A new law issued by the Icelandic Law Council (ON *lögrétta*) or by the Norwegian king. Several provisions throughout Grg are marked as new laws, and there has been some speculation concerning whether these provisions were enforced or retained as law, in part due to the stipulation in Grg Klþ 19 that new laws become void if not recited every third summer. In Iceland new laws were announced at the General Assembly (ON *alþingi*; cf. Grg Vís 101) and at autumn meetings (ON *leið*) in each quarter of the country.

> *new information* **ONorw** *FrL* LlbB 6

> *new law* **OIce** *Grg* Klþ 18, 19 Þsþ 61
> Vís 101 Lrþ 117 Arþ 118 Lbþ 202

> *new ordinances* **ONorw** *GuL* Krb

> See also: *lagh, órskurðr, réttarbót*

> Refs: CV; Fritzner; GrgTr II:388; GAO s.v. *Grágás*; Hertzberg; Jochens 1993; KLNM s.v. *nýmæli*

nýtr (ON) adj.

> *useful* **ONorw** *GuL* Olb

næffer (OSw) **næfr** (ON) noun

> *birch bark* **ONorw** *GuL* Llb, Leb,
> **OSw** *UL* Blb, *VmL* Bb

> See also: *næfrabunki*

næfrabunki (OSw) noun

> *pile of birch bark* **OSw** *UL* Blb, *VmL* Bb

> See also: *næffer*

næfrakimbull (ON) noun

> *bundle of birch bark* **ONorw** *GuL* Leb

næfsa (OSw) **næpsa** (OSw) verb

> *punish* **OSw** *HL* För

næma (OSw) **nime** (ODan) **nema** (ON) verb

> *make a seizure* **ODan** *JyL* 2

> *seize* **ODan** *ESjL* 2, 3, *SkL* 85, 170

> *take a deposit* **OSw** *DL* Rb

> *take a pledge* **OSw** *SmL*

> *take as surety* **OSw** *DL* Rb, *SdmL* Till

> *take by pawn* **OSw** *YVgL* Drb, *ÄVgL* Md

> *take security* **OSw** *ÄVgL* Rlb

> *take seizure* **ODan** *ESjL* 3, *JyL* 2

> *take surety* **OSw** *VmL* Mb, *YVgL* Utgb

> Expressions:

> **nema af** (ON)

> *abolish* **ONorw** *GuL* Krb

> *declare oneself free of something* **ONorw** *GuL* Kpb

> **nöþa ok næma, nöþa ok næmia** (OSw)

> *demand a personal surety* **OSw** *VmL* Kgb

> See also: *nam*

næmd (OSw) **nævnd** (ODan) **næfnd** (OSw) **næmpd** (OSw) noun

> A group of men, often twelve (cf. *næmdarmaþer*), appointed to deal with and decide in legal matters. Its origin is debated, and may vary within the Nordic area. The Danish material suggests ecclesiastical incentive to replace formal evidence such as compurgators and ordeals with truth-seeking procedures. Certain variations may indicate a gradual change over time: they were appointed either for each case (ODan ESjL, SkL) or for a fixed period (ODan JyL), and they acquitted or convicted the accused either unanimously (OSw ÄVgL, YVgL) or by majority decision (OSw YVgL). There was a *næmd* for various judicial/administrative levels such as *hæraþ* (q.v.) and *land* (q.v.). Difficult to distinguish from *næmdarmaþer* (q.v.) and *næmd maþer* (cf. *næmna*), and frequently appearing alongside these as well as in mixed forms, such as *mæn af næmpþ* (YVgL Gb).

> *commission* **OSw** *DL* Rb

> *deputation* **OSw** *DL* Kkb

> *jury* **OSw** *DL* Rb, *ÖgL* Kkb, Eb, Db, Vm

> *nominated men* **ODan** *ESjL* 1–3, *SkKL* 7, *SkL* 66, 108, 146, 147, 177, 180, 217, 218, 221, 226, 230, *VSjL* passim, **OSw** *YVgL* Kkb, Frb, Gb, Rlb, Tb, Föb, Utgb, Add, *ÄVgL* Smb, Gb, Rlb

> *panel* **OSw** *DL* Eb, Rb, *SdmL* Kkb, Kgb, Jb, Bb, Kmb, Rb, Till, *SmL*, *UL* StfBM, Kkb, Kgb, Mb, Jb, Kmb, Rb, Add. 13, *VmL* Kkb, Kgb, Jb, Kmb, Bb, Rb

representatives **OSw** *UL* Kgb,
Kmb, *VmL* Kkb, Kgb, Kmb

{næmd} **OSw** *HL* Kgb, Äb

Expressions:

nævnd i kyn (ODan)

men of the kin **ODan** *JyL* 2, 3

Refs: Andersen 2014; KLNM s.v. *nämnd*; Lund
s.v. *næfnd*; Schlyter s.v. *næmd*, Schlyter (bihang)
s.v. *næmd*; SL ÄVgL, 69 note 33; Tamm and
Vogt, eds, 2016, 309; Åqvist 1989, 176–336

næmdarmaþer (OSw) nævndeman (ODan) nemda
maþr (OGu) nefndarmaðr (ON) næmdamæn
(OSw) næmningaman (OSw) noun

The first and the last four above are formally similar
and have the same etymology. Historically the
OSw *næmningaman* also belongs to this context.
Nevertheless, these words differ considerably in their
semantics over the Nordic area.

In ONorw this term refers to a delegate from the
fylki (q.v.) to the *lögþing* (see *laghþing*), whereas
in OIce (Jó) it refers to a delegate, appointed by
the *valdsmaðr* (see *valdsmaþer*) from the assembly
district (*þing*) to the General Assembly (*alþingi*). In
OSw, OGu and ODan it most often refers to a member
of a *næmd* (q.v.), and occasionally a man appointed to
another assignment (such as, in DL, making a request
to the bishop from the householders). In YVgL, it
refers to a local delegate dealing with certain legal
matters, possibly responsible for the *skiri* (i.e. part
of a *hæraþ* (q.v.)). The *næmningaman* in SdmL was
possibly a member of the *folklandsnæmd* 'provincial
panel' authorized to pass judgement besides the
lawman (*laghmaþer*) and the judge (*domari*).

chosen man **ODan** *ESjL* 1

commissioner **OGu** *GS* Ch. 4, **OSw** *DL* Kkb

delegate **ONorw** *FrL* Tfb 5, *GuL* Krb

man in a panel **OSw** *SdmL* Kmb, Rb, Till

man of a {næmd} **OSw** *HL* Äb

named man **OSw** *YVgL* Kkb, Frb, Drb,
Tb, Jb, Föb, Add, *ÄVgL* Md, Slb, Jb

nominated man **ODan** *ESjL* 1, **OIce** *Jó* Þfb 2

panel member **OSw** *UL* Rb, *VmL* Kgb, Rb

See also: *maþer*, *næmd*, *valdsmaþer*

Refs: CV s.v. *nefndarmaðr*; Einar Arnórsson 1945,
191–232; Fritzner s.v. *nefndarmaðr*; Hertzberg s.v.
nefndr (nemdr) maðr; KLNM s.v.v. *häradsdomare*,
nefndarmenn, *nämnd*, *nämningaman*, *rettergang*,
sexman, *syn*; Nilsson 2012, 148–59; Schlyter s.v.v.
næmdarmaþer, *næmningaman*; Åqvist 1989, 176–336

næmna (OSw) nævne (ODan) nemna (OGu) nefna
(ON) næfnæ (OSw) næmpna (OSw) verb

Literally 'to name'. Legally significant uses include
to baptize children, to nominate men for positions on
panels, guard duties, inspections etc., to call someone
to appear at a *þing* 'assembly', and to identify an
offender. When used of nomination, often appearing in
phrases such as *næmder maþer*, *næmde mæn* (OSw),
nævnd man, *nævnde mæn* (ODan), which are difficult
to distinguish from *næmd* (q.v.) and *næmdarmaþer*
(q.v.), and frequently appearing alongside these. When
used to lay blame at the start of legal proceedings,
occasionally translated as 'to charge', 'to prosecute'.

announce **OGu** *GS* Ch. 4, **OSw** *ÄVgL* Tb

appoint **ODan** *ESjL* 1, *JyL* 2, **OIce** *Jó* Mah 2, 24,
ONorw *FrL* Intr 16 KrbA 32 KrbB 1 Mhb 4 Var 46,
GuL Krb, Tfb, Leb, **OSw** *YVgL* Kvab, *ÄVgL* Jb, Kva

assemble **OSw** *YVgL* Rlb, *ÄVgL* Rlb

call **OSw** *DL* Tjdb, *HL* Kkb

charge (someone) with (something) **OSw** *VmL* Mb

choose **ODan** *ESjL* 1, **OSw** *DL* Bb, Rb

declare **OSw** *UL* Mb, *VmL* Mb, Rb

designate **OSw** *DL* Eb, Mb, *UL* Kkb,
Kgb, Jb, Rb, *VmL* Mb, Bb

fix **ODan** *JyL* 1

give name **OSw** *ÄVgL* Md

identify **OSw** *DL* Mb

make a declaration **OSw** *VmL* Rb

mention **ODan** *JyL* 1, 2, **OSw** *UL* StfBM

name **ODan** *ESjL* 2, 3, *JyL* 1, 2, *SkL* 139, 144,
145, **OIce** *Grg* Misc 251, **ONorw** *FrL* Mhb 7,
OSw *DL* Mb, Bb, Tjdb, *HL* Äb, Mb, Jb, Rb,
SdmL Kkb, Kgb, Jb, Bb, Kmb, Mb, Rb, *SmL*,
UL StfBM, Kgb, Äb, Mb, Jb, Kmb, *VmL* Kgb,
Mb, Kmb, *YVgL* Drb, Gb, *ÄVgL* Md, Gb

nominate **ODan** *ESjL* 2, 3, *JyL* 1–3, *SkKL* 3, 5–7,
SkL 4, 27, 28, 69, 70, 72, 80, 147, 231, *VSjL* 32, 72,
73, 75, 77, 82, 86, 87, **OGu** *GL* A 3, 37, Add. 1 (B 4),
OIce *Grg* passim, *Jó* passim, **OSw** *DL* Eb, Rb, *HL*
Äb, *UL* Kkb, Kgb, Äb, Mb, Jb, Kmb, Blb, Rb, *VmL*
Kkb, Kgb, Mb, Jb, Kmb, Bb, Rb, *YVgL* Add, *ÖgL* Db

prosecute **OSw** *DL* Tjdb

select **OGu** *GS* Ch. 4, **ONorw**
FrL Tfb 1, **OSw** *HL* Kgb

state **ODan** *JyL* 1

summon **OSw** *HL* Kkb

næmni (OSw) namni (OSw) næmne (OSw) noun

declaration **OSw** *VmL* Rb

name **OSw** *YVgL* Drb

næmpdarmal (OSw) noun
  case involving a {næmd} OSw *HL* Äb
næmpning (OSw) **nævning** (ODan) noun
  choosing representatives for commission
  or investigation OSw *DL* Rb
  nominated men ODan *JyL* 2, 3
næpnastulðr (ON) noun
  theft of turnips OIce *Jó* Þjb 11
næs (OSw) noun
  Appears once in the phrase *skiæra eller till næs fællæ*
  'acquit or sentence to defence by oath' (OSw *SmL*) of
  a *næmd* 'panel' making a decision.
  Refs: Schlyter s.v. *næs*
næsiavarþer (OSw) noun
  beach-guard OSw *HL* Kgb
næstabróðra (pl.) (ON) **næstabræðra** (ON)
  næstabróðri (ON) noun
  second cousins OIce *Grg* Þsþ 25, 35 Vís 89, 107
  Bat 113 Ómb 143 Feþ 157 Hrs 235 Misc 248
næstsystkenebarn (ODan) noun
  second cousin ODan *SkKL* 7
nætrgamall (ON) adj.
  one night old ONorw *GuL* Tjb
nævehog (ODan) **hnefahögg** (ON) noun
  fist blow ODan *JyL* 3, OIce *Grg* Vís 86
  strike with a fist ODan *SkL* 98, OIce *Jó* Mah 22
nöthus (OSw) **nöta hus** (OSw) **nötos** (OSw) noun
  cattle barn OSw *HL* Mb
  cattle house OSw *YVgL* Tb, *ÄVgL* Tb
  cow byre OSw *SmL*
  cow shed OSw *YVgL* Kkb
  See also: *not*
nöþogher (OSw) **nøthigh** (ODan) **nauþugr** (OGu) adj.
  against someone's wishes OSw *YVgL* Kkb
  by force ODan *SkL* 218, *VSjL* 61, 86,
  OSw *HL* Kkb, *UL* Jb, *VmL* Kkb
  forced OGu *GL* Add. 8 (B 55), OSw *UL* Kkb
  in need OGu *GL* Add. 8 (B 55)
  unwilling OGu *GL* Add. 1 (B 4)
  with force ODan *VSjL* 86
  See also: *noytga, noyþa*
nöþsyn (OSw) **nauþsyn** (OGu) **nauðsyn** (ON) noun
  Legitimate excuse given to avoid legal action, with
  varying emphasis on it being caused by necessity due
  to obligations or to misfortune. Mainly of failure to
  perform a duty, such as to appear at a *þing* 'assembly'.
  Certain excuses were stipulated in the laws, such as
  illness or injury, while others were assessed by prudent

men (such as the *lögmaðr* (see *laghmaþer*) and the
Law Council in Jó Þfb 2). In OSw SdmL, presumably
a pun interpreting *syn* (q.v.) as the homograph meaning
'inspection' etc.
  accident OSw *HL* Kmb
  circumstance OIce *Jó* Kab 22
  compelling reason ONorw *EidsL* 32.9
  48.10, *FrL* KrbB 19, *GuL* Krb
  difficulties OSw *HL* Kgb
  distress OIce *Jó* Fml 18
  emergency OGu *GL* A 6, ONorw *BorgL* 2
  excuse OIce *Jó* Fml 4
  genuine difficulty OFar *Seyð* 10
  great need ONorw *FrL* KrbA 14
  lawful extenuating circumstance ONorw *EidsL* 32.9
  lawful hindrance ONorw *FrL* KrbB 12
  legitimate necessity OIce *Jó* Þfb 8
  legitimate reason OIce *Js* Þfb 6 Mah 18
  necessity OIce *Grg* Þsþ 23, 34, *Jó* Þfb 2 Sg
  2 Mah 14, 17 Kge 12, 20 Lbb 1, 4 Llb 20,
  59 Þjb 12, 13 Fml 4, 13, *Js* Mah 30, 31 Lbb
  1, *KRA* 1, 11, ONorw *BorgL* 5.14, *EidsL*
  32.8, *FrL* Var 46 Leb 8, *GuL* Krb, Kpb
  necessity inspection OSw *SdmL* Bb
  need ONorw *EidsL* 47.7
  reason ONorw *FrL* Var 46
  time of need ONorw *BorgL* 12.11
  urgent need OIce *Jó* Mah 13
  valid excuse ONorw *GuL* Krb, Arb, Mhb
  Refs: Fritzner s.v. *nauðsyn*; Hertzberg s.v. *nauðsyn*;
  SAOB s.v. *nödsyn*; Schlyter s.v. *nöþsyn*
nøthtækt (ODan) noun
  rape ODan *ESjL* 2
  See also: *vald*
oborghaþer (OSw) adj.
  without security OSw *YVgL* Add
oborin (OSw) adj.
  unborn OSw *DL* Mb
  See also: *forlækisværk, oskabarn*
obrighþer (OSw) adj.
  undisputed OSw *UL* Kmb, *VmL* Kmb
ofdyri (ON) noun
  lintel ONorw *GuL* Tfb
  See also: *uppdyri*
ofdóma (ON) **ofdæma** (ON) verb
  judge too harshly OIce *Jó* Mah 17
  See also: *vandóma*

offerdagher (OSw) noun

day of offering **OSw** *YVgL* Kkb

sacrificial day **OSw** *SdmL* Kkb, Till

ofgangr (ON) noun

Expressions:

ganga ofgöngum yfir konu sinni (ON)

use violence toward one's wife **ONorw** *FrL* Mhb 35

ofhog (OSw) noun

excessive felling **OSw** *SdmL* Jb, Bb, Till

oflið (ON) noun

force of numbers **OIce** *Grg* Þsþ 58

ofmegri (ON) noun

starvation **ONorw** *GuL* Kpb

ofra (ON) verb

brandish **ONorw** *GuL* Mhb

ofrán (ON) noun

Ofrán was a robbery considered too bad to require the usual compensation.

overrobbery **ONorw** *GuL* Mhb

Refs: Helle 2001, 94; KLNM s.v. *rán*

ofrester (OGu) adj.

before being tortured **OGu** *GL* Add. 8 (B 55)

ofriþer (OSw) ufrith (ODan) noun

breaking of a man's peace **ODan** *ESjL* 2

distress **OSw** *UL* Kmb, *VmL* Kmb

something illegal **ODan** *ESjL* 2

unrest **OSw** *SdmL* Till

violence **OSw** *SdmL* Kmb, Till

See also: *friþer*

ofríki (ON) noun

force **OIce** *Grg* Þsþ 41, 77, *Js* Kab 1

force (illegally used) **ONorw** *GuL* Tfb

violence **ONorw** *FrL* KrbA 45

ofríkismaðr (ON) noun

A person who uses force or violence to coerce others. Used of men who attempt to influence or obstruct cases through intimidation. Transferring a case to such a person, presumably with the intention of strong-arming one's adversary, is explicitly forbidden in some laws (e.g. GuL Kpb [ch. 47] and Js Kab 8).

more powerful man **ONorw** *GuL* Kpb, Løb, Olb

powerful man **OIce** *Jó* Kab 10, *Js* Kab 8

tyrannous man **OIce** *Grg* Arþ 126

Refs: CV s.v. *ofríkismaðr*; Fritzner s.v. *ofríkismaðr*; Hertzberg s.v. *ofríkismaðr*; Schulman 2010, 311 note 196

ofræls (OSw) ofrels (OGu) ófrjáls (ON) adj.

Literally, 'unfree'. The word was used as an infrequent alternative to *þræl* (q.v.) and equivalent nouns, perhaps indicating a less permanent state of slavery (cf. *hemahion*). Such people had restricted rights and were subject to reduced compensation, but in certain circumstances they were treated as equals with free people. For instance in VmL, where a woman claims to have miscarried, the testimony of an unfree woman is as valid as that of a free woman. The same is true in the situation in which a woman claims that the child was born alive and this is challenged by relatives. In GL, the word is used in connection with assaults on unfree women, who received much lower compensation for rape and no compensation for assaults that did not result in injury.

slave **OGu** *GL* A 22

unfree **OGu** *GL* A 23, **ONorw** *EidsL* 48.5, **OSw** *SdmL* Äb, Bb, Kmb, Mb, *UL* Äb, Mb, Kmb, *VmL* Äb, Mb

See also: *ambat*, *fostre*, *fræls*, *hemahion*, *hemakona*, *þiþborin*, *þræl*

Refs: KLNM, s.v.v. *frälse*, *træl*; Nevéus 1974; Peel 2015, 149–50 note 23/8–9; Schlyter 1877, s.v. *ofræls*; SL UL, 85–86 note 60, 118 note 23, 157 note 7; SL VmL, 60 note 56, 63 note 91

ofse (OSw) ofpse (OSw) opse (OSw) noun

higher force **OSw** *VmL* Jb

ofsinnisarf (OSw) noun

inheritance after a disaster **OSw** *SdmL* Äb

inheritance after an accident **OSw** *HL* Äb, *UL* Äb, *VmL* Äb

ofsinnisvatn (OSw) offsinne (OSw) noun

accidental flooding **OSw** *UL* Blb, *VmL* Bb

See also: *vaþadrap*, *vaþaþer*, *vaþaværk*, *vaþi*, *viliaværk*

ofsokn (OSw) opsokn (OSw) upsokn (OSw) noun

harsh judgement **OSw** *VmL* Rb

ofsökia (OSw) offsökia (OSw) verb

over penalize **OSw** *UL* Rb, *VmL* Rb

See also: *mæta*

oftala (OSw) oftala (ON) noun

high estimate **ONorw** *FrL* Var 42

unreasonable action **OSw** *UL* Rb, Add. 16

ofværkaböter (OSw) noun

fines for violence **OSw** *HL* Kkb

ofylter (OSw) adj.

unsubstantiated **OSw** *UL* Rb, *VmL* Rb

ofæfli (OSw) **ofævle** (ODan) **oefli** (OSw) **ofvælli**
(OSw) **uræfle** (OSw) **uæfli** (OSw) noun
For details on usage, see *vanrökt*.

force **ODan** *SkL* 234

superior force **OSw** *YVgL* Rlb,
Utgb, Add, *ÄVgL* Rlb, Föb

See also: *vangöma*

ofæster (OSw) adj.
not promised **OSw** *YVgL* Add

ofödder (OSw) **ufød** (ODan) **uföder** (OSw) adj.
unborn **ODan** *VSjL* 6, **OSw** *DL* Mb, Gb

See also: *oskabarn*

oför (OSw) **óførr** (ON) **ófærr** (ON) **úførr** (ON) adj.
The latter part of the word (*-för*) is etymologically
connected to the verb (ON) *fara* 'go, travel'. The
meanings fall into two groups, one related to persons:
'unfit to work' (OSw, HL), 'disabled' (ONorw, GuL),
'not able bodied' (OIce, Jó); the other related to
ground, terrain: 'impassable' (ONorw, GuL), or ships:
'unseaworthy, not seaworthy' (ONorw, GuL). In the
sense 'impassable' *oför* is related to the noun *óføra*
(ON) 'impassable area'.

disabled **ONorw** *GuL* Tfb

impassable **ONorw** *GuL* Krb, Løb

not able bodied **OIce** *Jó* Kge 34

unfit to work **OSw** *HL* Mb

unseaworthy **ONorw** *GuL* Leb

ogilder (OSw) **ugild** (ODan) **ógildr** (ON) **ogilldær**
(OSw) **ogillt** (OSw) **ugilder** (OSw) adj.
Etymologically related to the verb *gælda* 'to pay
(for); to be worth'. As an antonym of *gilder* (q.v.),
used of that which does not meet legal standards,
translated as e.g. 'invalid', 'deficient', 'inadequate'.
Also applying to certain legal procedures — for which
the translations may overlap — such as the legal
denial of compensation, including that for a criminal
who is also victimized, reflected in translations such
as 'uncompensated', 'without compensation', 'not
repaid', of the dismissal of a plaintiff's request,
translated as e.g. 'dismissed', 'without a case',
'without voice in the matter', and of the dropping
of charges against a defendant, translated as 'with
impunity', making it partly synonymous with *saklös*
(q.v.).

deficient **OSw** *DL* Bb

dismissed **OSw** *HL* Kkb

entitled to no compensation **OSw** *DL* Eb

of forfeit immunity **OIce** *Jó* Llb 34

inadequate **OSw** *SdmL* Bb, *VmL* Kkb, Bb

ineligible for compensation **OSw** *HL* Kgb, Rb

invalid **OIce** *Js* Lbb 22, **OSw** *HL* Rb, *SdmL* Jb,
Bb, Rb, Till, *UL* Kkb, Jb, Blb, *VmL* Mb, Bb, Rb,
YVgL Tb, Jb, Add, *ÄVgL* Smb, Slb, Jb, Tb, Föb

no fine is to be paid out **OSw** *HL* Blb

no punishment is to be inferred **OSw** *DL* Kkb

not in accordance with the law **OIce** *Jó* Llb 33

not in order **OSw** *YVgL* Jb, Föb, Utgb

not liable to compensation or wergild
ONorw *GuL* Krb, Llb

not subject to compensation **OSw** *DL* Kkb, Tjdb, *UL*
Kkb, Mb, Jb, Kmb, Blb, *VmL* Kkb, Äb, Mb, Kmb

not to be compensated **OSw** *UL*
Blb, Rb, *VmL* Äb, Rb

not obliged to repay **OSw** *HL* Jb

not pay anything for somebody **ODan** *SkL* 215, 216

not repayed **OSw** *DL* Bb

uncompensated **OSw** *DL* Eb, Rb, *HL* Kgb, Äb,
Mb, Blb, *SdmL* Kkb, Kgb, Gb, Bb, Mb, *UL* Mb,
Blb, Add, 2, *VmL* Mb, Bb, *ÖgL* Kkb, Eb, Db

void **OSw** *YVgL* Frb, Drb, Tb

voided **OSw** *UL* Rb, *VmL* Rb

with impunity **OFar** *Seyð* 5

without a case **OSw** *YVgL* Rlb, *ÄVgL* Rlb, Lek

without cause **OSw** *YVgL* Tb

without compensation **OFar** *Seyð* 5, **OIce** *Jó*
Mah 2, *Js* Mah 6, 7, *KRA* 8, **ONorw** *FrL* Intr 1
KrbA 10 Var 14 Rgb 26 Kvb 14 LlbA 21, **OSw**
UL Kgb, Äb, Mb, Blb, Add. 2, *VmL* Kkb, Kgb,
Äb, Mb, Bb, *YVgL* Kkb, Drb, *ÄVgL* Kkb, Md

without voice in the matter **OSw** *HL* Kkb

See also: *aterbryta, atergangs, gilder*

Refs: Cleasby and Vigfússon s.v. *úgildr*; Hertzberg
s.v. *úgildr;* Schlyter s.v.v. *gilder, gælda, ogilder*

ogipter (OSw) **ugift** (ODan) **ogiptr** (OGu) **ógiftr** (ON)
ógipt (ON) adj.
unmarried **ODan** *JyL* 1, **OGu** *GL* A 20, 20a,
21, 28, **OIce** *Jó* Kge 2, *Js* Kvg 1, **ONorw**
FrL Kvb 2, *GuL* Arb, **OSw** *DL* Mb, Bb, *HL*
Kkb, *SdmL* Kkb, *YVgL* Kkb, Äb, *ÄVgL* Äb

See also: *gifter*

ogoymsla (OGu) noun
carelessness **OGu** *GL* Add. 2 (B 17)

See also: *vangöma*

ohailigr (OGu) **óheilagr** (ON) **úheilagr** (ON) adj.
This word, which does not occur in the Danish or
Swedish laws, is used in at least three distinct ways.
Firstly, it means 'unholy' in a general sense, the
opposite to *helagher* and cognates. Secondly (in GL
only), it refers to working or weekdays as opposed to
'holy' days: Sundays, saints' days, church festivals,

etc. Thirdly, it means unprotected in some way. In the senses 'of forfeit immunity' and 'unprotected', the word is related to the concepts of *manhælghþ*, the right to personal protection under the law, and *hemfriþer*, the protection that one had in one's own home against attack. This is the implication behind the majority of usages in OIce and ONorw law and occurs when a person is suspected of a crime, but perhaps not yet condemned by trial, in which case their right to compensation was removed. In GL it is used to refer to the loss of protection suffered if someone refused to admit a legally correct house-search for stolen goods. The search party could legally break down his door without fear of prosecution, even if no stolen goods were found. Similar rules, but without the use of the word *ohelagher*, are to be found in ÄVgL, YVgL and ÖgL.

condemned **ONorw** *FrL* Mhb 41

of forfeit immunity **OIce** *Grg* Þsþ 52, 55 Vís 87, 88 Bat 113 Feþ 159 Lbþ 181, 201 Rsþ 230 Misc 238, 242, *Js* Lbb 27 Kab 4

unholy **ONorw** *EidsL* 24.2 27.5

unprotected **OGu** *GL* A 14, 37

unprotected by the law **ONorw** *GuL* Krb, Kpb, Llb, Mhb

without legal redress **OIce** *Grg* Vís 90

without the protection of law **OIce** *Jó* Mah 4, 16 Llb 22, 30 Þjb 6

working **OGu** *GL* A 56

See also: *helagher*, *hemfriþer*, *manhælghi*

Refs: Heusler 1911, 6–68, 114–23; KLNM s.v.v. *hæmnd, rättlösa*; Miller 1984, 127 n. 126; Peel 2015, 172 note 37/7–9; Schlyter 1877, s.v. *ohailiger*

ohaiþverþr (OGu) adj.

indecent **OGu** *GL* A 23

ohemul (OSw) **óheimill** (ON) **óheimull** (ON) **úheimill** (ON) **ohemol** (OSw) **uhemol** (OSw) adj.

having no legal authentication of ownership **OSw** *UL* Jb, Kmb, *VmL* Kmb

having no warrantable rights **OIce** *Js* Lbb 10 Kab 9

illegal **ONorw** *GuL* Kpb, Llb, Olb

illegally **OIce** *Jó* Llb 1

illegitimate **ONorw** *FrL* Kvb 16

without authority **OSw** *YVgL* Add

ohemult (OSw) **uhemel** (ODan) **uhemleth** (ODan) **ohemolt** (OSw) **uhemolt** (OSw) adv.

without authority **OSw** *SdmL* Kmb

without giving a guarantee **OSw** *UL* Jb, *VmL* Jb

without title **ODan** *ESjL* 3, *JyL* 1, 3, **OSw** *SdmL* Jb

See also: *hemula*

oklandaþer (OSw) adj.

unchallenged **OSw** *UL* Jb, Kmb, *VmL* Kmb

without contention **OSw** *UL* Äb

Expressions:

oklandaþer ok oqvalder (OSw)

unchallenged and uncontested **OSw** *SdmL* Jb

oklutraþer ok oklandaþer (OSw)

unchallenged **OSw** *DL* Bb

oqviþat ok oklandat (OSw)

without blame and charge **OSw** *HL* Blb

See also: *oklutraþer*, *oqvalder*

oklutraþer (OSw) adj.

uncomplained **OSw** *SdmL* Jb

undisputed **OSw** *UL* Jb

without complaint **OSw** *UL* Äb

Expressions:

oklutraþer ok oklandaþer (OSw)

unchallenged **OSw** *DL* Bb

See also: *oklandaþer*

okr (ON) noun

usury **OIce** *KRA* 35

okrkarl (ON) noun

usurer **OIce** *KRA* 11, 35, **ONorw** *EidsL* 50.13

okærder (OSw) **ukærth** (ODan) adj.

unchallenged **ODan** *JyL* 1

undisputed **ODan** *JyL* 1

without dispute **OSw** *YVgL* Add

See also: *kæra*, *uilter*

olafsdagher (OSw) noun

Feast of St Olaf (29 July) **OSw** *UL* Rb, *VmL* Rb

See also: *olafsmæssa*

olafsmæssa (OSw) **olavsmisse** (ODan) **ólafsmessa** (ON) noun

Feast of St Olaf (29 July) **OSw** *UL* Kkb, Jb

Olaf's Mass **ODan** *SkKL* 9, **OSw** *SdmL* Bb, Rb, *ÖgL* Kkb

St Óláfr's Day **OIce** *Grg* Klþ 13

See also: *olafsdagher*

olagh (OSw) **ulogh** (ODan) **ólög** (ON) **úlög** (ON) noun

incorrect law **OSw** *SdmL* Till

injustice **ONorw** *FrL* Tfb 6

lawlessness **OFar** *Seyð* 4, **ONorw** *GuL* Llb

unlawful action **ODan** *ESjL* 2

unlawful ends **OIce** *Grg* Þsþ 46

unlawfully **ODan** *ESjL* 2, 3, *SkL* 66

unlawfulness **OSw** *YVgL* Add, *ÖgL* Kkb, Eb

olagha (OSw) adj.

    illegal **OSw** *SdmL* Kkb, Bb

    unlawful **OSw** *ÖgL* Eb, Db

olaghlika (OSw) uloghlik (ODan) olaglica (OGu) ulaghlika (OSw) adv.

    by unlawful means **ODan** *ESjL* 3

    unlawfully **OGu** *GS* Ch. 4, **OSw** *HL* Äb, *SdmL* Kmb, *ÖgL* Kkb, Eb, Vm

olerþr (OGu) ólærðr (ON) úlærðr (ON) adj.

    lay **OGu** *GL* A 5, 21, **ONorw** *GuL* Krb

    Expressions:

    ólærðr maðr (ON)

    layman **OIce** *Grg* Klþ 1, 2 *KRA* 15

olia (OSw) olea (ON) olía (ON) ola (OSw) olea (OSw) verb

    administer Extreme Unction **OSw** *YVgL* Kkb, *ÄVgL* Föb

    anoint **OSw** *ÖgL* Kkb

    give Extreme Unction **ONorw** *GuL* Krb, **OSw** *SmL*, *YVgL* Utgb, *ÄVgL* Kkb

oling (OSw) olean (ON) öleng (OSw) olning (OSw) noun

    anointment **OSw** *ÖgL* Kkb

    Extreme Unction **ONorw** *GuL* Krb, **OSw** *SmL*, *YVgL* Kkb, *ÄVgL* Kkb

    unction **OSw** *SmL*

    See also: *olia*

olof (OSw) ólof (ON) noun

    lack of permission **OIce** *Grg* Lrþ 117, *Jó* Llb 36

    without permission **OSw** *HL* Blb

olofliker (OSw) adj.

    non-permissible **OSw** *ÖgL* Kkb

olovandis (OSw) oloyfins (OGu) oloyfis (OGu) olovis (OSw) oluvis (OSw) ulovandis (OSw) adv.

    illegally **OGu** *GL* A 26, 63

    illicit **OSw** *DL* Bb

    without leave **OGu** *GL* A 35

    without permission **OGu** *GL* A 56, **OSw** *SdmL* Bb, *UL* Blb, *VmL* Mb, Bb, *YVgL* Jb, Föb, Utgb, *ÄVgL* Jb, Fös, Föb

    without promise **OSw** *HL* Blb

    See also: *lof*

omaghi (OSw) oformagi (OGu) ovormaghi (OGu) ómagi (ON) úmagi (ON) oformagi (OSw) oghormaghi (OSw) ovormaghi (OSw) owormaghi (OSw) ughurmaghi (OSw) noun

    According to the Svea laws (DL, HL, SdmL, VmL, UL), OGu GL and ONorw law a person was *omaghi* until he reached the age of 15, in OIce law until he was 16 years old. An *omaghi* was a person who could not maintain himself or manage his own affairs, either because he had no property and was unable to work for his living, or because he could not use his property in a sensible way. Old people, unable to work, were usually supported by their heirs. If they were freedmen and had no heirs, they were put in an open grave where they were left to die; their master had to support the one (of a couple) who lived longer (GuL Løb ch. 63). A person who became insane was also considered an *ómagi*. The *ómagi* had reduced personal rights and responsibility. According to the GuL (Mhb, ch. 190) a male was not legally responsible before he was 12 years old, then he was *halfréttismaðr* (q.v.) until he reached the age of 15 and became a *fullréttismaðr*. According to the FrL (Mhb ch. 36) he was *halfréttismaðr* between 8 and 15 years of age. If he damaged property, he paid only half compensation. He was not allowed to make deals, and if he killed someone, he had to leave the country within a fixed deadline; if exceeding that deadline he forfeited all his property. However, agnates and cognates might accompany him abroad and allow him to stay there with impunity (FrL ibid.). In ODan laws, the age of criminal responsibility was 15.

    With regard to maintenance, it was possible for people to donate their property to an ecclesiastical institution and receive maintenance in return. In general, however, the duty of maintenance was incumbent on the kin and distributed among the kinsfolk for certain fixed periods, in OIce law (Grg) for 2 to 4 years, depending on the degree (nearness) of kinship; failure to fulfil this duty implied penalty. Alternatively, the OIce commune (*hreppr*) or the quarter (*fjórðungr*, see *fiarþunger*) was responsible, in the last resort the entire country.

    OSw laws state that whoever was responsible for an *omaghi* and his property could not sell or trade in this property if it would be to the disfavour of the *omaghi*. The *omaghi* himself was not allowed to sell or trade in property unless his nearest kinsfolk consented. Only if he needed money for maintenance might his nearest kinsmen sell parts of his land. However, when he came of age (*maghandi alder*) he could reverse such bargains. As in the ONorw laws an *omaghi* was not considered to have full age and legal capacity. To kill him was a villainy (*níðingsverk*, see *niþingsværk*). He could not be outlawed and could not be sentenced to death if guilty of theft or murder. If guilty of theft and injury, he had to pay a smaller amount of compensation. He was not allowed to take an oath, neither could he marry, or pass on a message baton. The person responsible for an *omaghi* was his legal guardian.

ODan laws have no term corresponding exactly to *omaghi* in the sense of person under age. The nearest ones are *flatføring* (house-led person) and *oreght man* (a man who had no house or land and did not take part in military duty).

The condition of being an *ovormaghi* was termed (ON) *ómegð*.

dependent **OIce** *Grg* Klþ 18 Þsþ 22 passim, *Jó* Mah 2, 4 Kge 3, 7 Lbb 1 Kab 24 Þjb 16, *Js* Mah 8 Kab 18 Þjb 7, *KRA* 10, 14, **ONorw** *FrL* Mhb 32 Var 13 Leb 10

dependent child **OIce** *Grg* Feþ 148

disabled **OSw** *HL* Blb

incapable person **OIce** *Grg* Þsþ 49

infant **OSw** *YVgL* Jb, Add, *ÄVgL* Jb

legal minor **OSw** *YVgL* Tb, *ÄVgL* Tb

minor **OGu** *GL* A 14, 20, 28, 51, 59, **OIce** *Jó* Kge 16, 32 Þjb 8, **ONorw** *FrL* Mhb 34 ArbB 22, *GuL* Kvb, Løb, Llb, Arb, Mhb, Tjb, **OSw** *DL* Eb, Mb, Bb, Tjdb, Rb, *HL* Kkb, Kgb, Mb, Jb, *SdmL* Kkb, Kgb, Jb, Mb, Tjdb, *UL* Kkb, Kgb, Mb, Jb, *VmL* Kkb, Kgb, Äb, Mb, Jb, *YVgL* Kkb, Frb, Urb, Add, *ÄVgL* Slb, *ÖgL* Eb, Db, Vm

under-age **OSw** *HL* Äb, Mb

ward **OIce** *Grg* Arþ 122, *Jó* Llb 29 Þjb 1

See also: *alder*, *maghandi*, *ómegð*, *oraþamaþr*

Refs: Hertzberg s.v. *úmagi*; KLNM s.v.v. *alderdom*, *framfœrsla*, *tilregnelighed*, *úmagi*, *vitne*, *værge I*, *ægteskab*, *ætt*; Tamm and Vogt 2016, 20

omynd (OSw) noun

dowry **OSw** *ÖgL* Eb, Db, Vm

op (OSw) **op** (OGu) noun

cry **OGu** *GL* A 22

shout **OGu** *GL* A 22, 36, **OSw** *UL* Kgb, *VmL* Kgb

Expressions:

op ok (a) kallan (OSw)

cries and shouts **OSw** *ÖgL* Eb

cry or invocation **OSw** *YVgL* Add

scream or cry for help **OSw** *HL* Kgb

screams and shouts for help **OSw** *DL* Eb

shouting and calling for help **OSw** *SdmL* Kgb

openbar (OSw) **openbar** (ODan) adj.

Used of public, publicly known or otherwise apparent actions or states, often in phrases such as *openbart hor* 'evident adultery' (OSw YVgL Kkb), *openbær men* 'open perjury' (ODan JyL 2), *openbær uvin* 'open enemy' (ODan JyL 3), *yppinbar uitni* 'public/

clear witness' (OSw ÖgL Kkb/Eb), *yppinbar mal* 'clear case' (in OSw ÖgL Kkb contrasted to *humamal* 'suspected case') and *openbar skript* 'public penance' (in OSw YVgL Kkb).

apparent **ODan** *JyL* 2

clear **OSw** *ÖgL* Kkb, Eb

evident **OSw** *YVgL* Kkb, Rlb, Add

manifest **ODan** *JyL* 1

open **ODan** *JyL* 2, 3

public **OSw** *YVgL* Kkb, *ÖgL* kb

revealed **ODan** *JyL* 1

See also: *lönd*

Refs: Andersen 2011, 66

openbara (OSw) verb

announce **OSw** *YVgL* Add

publicly declare **OSw** *ÖgL* Eb

openbarlika (OSw) **openbarlik** (ODan) adv.

openly **ODan** *JyL* 2, 3, *SkKL* 11

publicly **OSw** *SdmL* Kkb, *YVgL* Kkb, Tb, *ÖgL* Kkb

See also: *lönlike*

oqueþinsvitr (OGu) noun

dumb animal **OGu** *GL* A 17

oqvalder (OSw) **oqvælder** (OSw) adj.

unchallenged **OSw** *UL* Jb, *VmL* Mb

uncontested **OSw** *SdmL* Kkb, Jb, Bb

See also: *oklandaþer*

oqvæþinsorþ (OSw) **oqueþinsorþ** (OGu) **ókvæðisorð** (ON) **ukvæþins orþ** (OSw) **uqvæþings orþ** (OSw) **uqvæþinsorþ** (OSw) noun

Unspeakable words. Certain words were considered so offensive, in particular to the recipient's honour, that they warranted harsh penalties. These included accusations of treason, allegations of infidelity against a man's wife or female relatives (Js Mah 24 andJó Mah 24), comparing a man to a female beast or accusing someone of being buggered (FrL Rgþ 35). SdmL stipulates further that location (e.g. assemblies, churches) be taken into account when assessing unspeakable words. The penalty for such insults was a fine up to full personal compensation (ON *fullrétti*). According to Gul Mhb 196 the injured party also had the right to avenge himself.

defamatory language **OIce** *Jó* Mah 24

insult **OGu** *GL* A 39, **OSw** *SdmL* Gb, Mb, *UL* Rb (E-text), *VmL* Äb

invective **OIce** *Js* Mah 24

opprobrious word **OSw** *YVgL* Rlb, *ÄVgL* Rlb

verbal abuse **ONorw** *FrL* Rgb 35

See also: *firnarorþ*, *fjölmæli*, *fullréttisorð*, *róg*, *ýki*

Refs: CV s.v. *úkvæðisorð*; Fritzner s.v.
úkvæðisorð; KLNM s.v. *ærekrænkelse*

ora (OSw) verb

seek revenge **OSw** *ÖgL* Db

oran (OSw) noun

feud **OSw** *ÖgL* Db

mortal enemy **OSw** *UL* Mb, *VmL* Mb

oranbot (OSw) noun

feuding compensation **OSw** *ÖgL* Db

See also: *bot, oran*

oraþamaþr (OGu) noun

unreasonable man **OGu** *GL* A 28

See also: *oraþlika*

oraþlika (OGu) adv.

ill advisedly **OGu** *GL* A 24d, 29

See also: *oraþamaþr*

ordela (OSw) verb

acquit **OSw** *YVgL* Föb

exonerate **OSw** *YVgL* Kkb

Expressions:

ordela sik (OSw)

acquit **OSw** *YVgL* Föb

exonerate **OSw** *YVgL* Kkb

orðfullr (ON) adj.

correctly worded **OIce** *Jó* Llb 17

oreghe (ODan) verb

despoil **ODan** *JyL* 2

oreghe (ODan) noun

outlying field **ODan** *ESjL* 3

oreghthman (ODan) noun

A man without property who did not pay military tax.

man without property **ODan** *JyL* 2

orf (OSw) **urf** (OSw) noun

The principal meaning is 'creature'. It frequently,
however, seems to have referred to an inheritance
in movables rather than in land. In this context, the
word was always coupled with a word meaning the
latter in the alliterative expression *arf ok orf*. Here
arf is a neuter form of the masculine noun *arver*
('land; inheritance, birthright'). It has also been
suggested that a different meaning of *orf* is involved
in this expression, and that it is just an example of
a parallelism, with *orf* containing its ON attested
meaning, 'scythe handle', just indicating insignificant
items of inheritance: an equivalent to the English
'goods and chattels'. Schlyter links the word to Anglo-
Saxon words referring to livestock, 'creatures', to
distinguish movables from real estate (the birthright

land). A similar meaning attaches to *fæ*, which can be
used to mean 'money' amongst other things. In UL
the expression is used in particular in connection with
situations in which inheritance might be disputed —
posthumous children or those born out of wedlock —
so the expression could well indicate that the child
concerned was to inherit both land and movables, and
not just the latter. The word occurs only in the laws of
Svealand.

inheritance in movables **OSw** *UL* Äb, *VmL* Äb

Expressions:

(taka) arf ok orf (OSw)

birthright and inheritance **OSw** *UL* Äb *VmL* Äb

inheritance **OSw** *HL* Äb

inheritance and birthright **OSw** *DL* Gb

inheritance in land and movables **OSw** *SdmL* Äb

right of inheritance and birthright **OSw** *DL* Kkb

See also: *arver, fæ*

Refs: KLNM, s.v. *arv*; Schlyter 1877,
s.v. *orf*; SL UL, 83–84 note 39

orka (OSw) **orka** (OGu) verb

be able to **OGu** *GL* A 14, **OSw** *UL* Kkb,
Kgb, Mb, Jb, Blb, *VmL* Mb, Jb, Kmb, Bb

afford to **OGu** *GL* A 13, 14, Add. 9 (B 81),
OSw *UL* Kkb, Kgb, Mb, Blb, *VmL* Kkb

orka (ON) noun

slave's work for his own benefit **ONorw** *GuL* Løb

orlof (OSw) **orlov** (ODan) **orlof** (ON) **orloff** (OSw)
noun

permission **ODan** *JyL* 2, 3, **OIce** *Jó* Llb 20, **OSw**
HL Kkb, Rb, *SdmL* Kkb, Kgb, Gb, *UL* Kkb

ormylia (OSw) noun

A pejorative term for a person breaking boundary
markers.

{ormylia} **OSw** *YVgL* Jb, *ÄVgL* Jb

Refs: Schlyter s.v. *ormylia*

ornume (ODan) noun

Privately owned cultivated land that was marked
off and exempt from land division between the
landowners of a village.

land apart **ODan** *JyL* 1, *SkL* 72

land outside the roping **ODan** *VSjL* 76

separate land **ODan** *JyL* 3

Refs: Hoff 1998, 150–53; KLNM s.v.
ornum; Lund s.v. *ornum*; Schlyter s.v.
ornum; Tamm and Vogt, eds, 2016, 307

ornumeskjal (ODan) noun

unroped boundary **ODan** *VSjL* 76

orosta (OSw) orreste (ODan) orista (OGu) noun
  battle **OGu** *GL* Add. 1 (B 4), **OSw** *YVgL* Äb
  war **ODan** *VSjL* 16

orsake (ODan) verb
  prove one's innocence **ODan** *JyL* 2

ortarvitni (OGu) noun
  evidence as to work **OGu** *GL* A 25
  See also: *vitni*

ortasoyþr (OGu) noun
  working beast **OGu** *GL* A 10

orudder (OSw) orydder (OSw) adj.
  uncultivated **OSw** *UL* Blb, *VmL* Bb

orunabot (OSw) noun
  unruly animal compensation **OSw** *UL* Mb
  See also: *bot*, *böta*

orvite (ODan) adj.
  witless **ODan** *ESjL* 2

orþ (OGu) orð (ON) noun
  pledge **OIce** *Jó* Kge 32, **ONorw** *FrL* Mhb 8
  promise **OIce** *Jó* Kab 17
  slander **OGu** *GL* A 2
  statement **OGu** *GL* Add. 8 (B 55)
  vote **OIce** *Grg* Lrþ 117
  word **OGu** *GL* A 20a, 39
  Expressions:
  jafnask orðum (ON)
  consider oneself somebody's equal **ONorw** *GuL* Løb
  orð ok eiðr (ON)
  pledge and promise **ONorw** *GuL* Krb, Kpb, Tfb
  See also: *eþer*

orþaskipti (OSw) noun
  squabble **OSw** *YVgL* Add

oræt (OSw) adv.
  wrongly **OSw** *YVgL* Add

orætlika (OSw) urættelik (ODan) adv.
  incorrectly **OSw** *SdmL* Bb
  unjustly **ODan** *SkL* 47, *VSjL* 82
  unlawfully **ODan** *ESjL* 2, **OSw** *UL* Blb, *VmL* Bb
  without justification **OSw** *UL* Kkb, Rb, *VmL* Kkb

orætter (OSw) uræt (ODan) uræt (ODan) noun
  injustice **ODan** *ESjL* 2, **OSw** *SdmL* För, Till

orætter (OSw) adj.
  illegal **OSw** *HL* Blb
  incorrect **OSw** *HL* Jb, *SdmL* Kkb
  unjust **ODan** *JyL* Fort, **OSw** *SdmL* För, Bb, Kgb
  unlawful **OSw** *HL* Kgb

osaker (OSw) orsak (ODan) ósekr (ON) ørsekr (ON) orsaker (OSw) ursaker (OSw) adj.
  Antonymous to *saker* (q.v.) and partly synonymous with *saklös* (q.v.), inasmuch as *osaker* also shows the ambiguity and translational overlap of the meanings 'innocent; not guilty', 'acquitted' and 'with impunity/without penalty'.
  blameless **ODan** *JyL* 2, *SkKL* 12
  free and innocent **ODan** *JyL* 2
  innocent **ODan** *JyL* 2, **OSw** *VmL* Rb
  not guilty **ONorw** *GuL* Mhb, Tjb, Leb, **OSw** *ÄVgL* Kkb, *ÖgL* Kkb
  with impunity **OFar** *Seyð* 3, **OIce** *Jó* Mah 8, 16 Kge 14, 34 Llb 6, 19 Kab 20 Þjb 12 Fml 3, 9
  without action taken against **ODan** *JyL* 2
  without guilt **ONorw** *FrL* KrbA 2, 37 Mhb 32, 41
  without penalty **OIce** *Grg* Ómb 132 Feþ 149 Fjl 225, *Jó* Þjb 3, *Js* Mah 8, 18 Þjb 6, *KRA* 26, **ONorw** *FrL* KrbB 1 Mhb 62 Leb 2 Rgb 3 LlbA 1
  without punishment **ONorw** *FrL* KrbB 1, *GuL* Løb, Llb, Tjb, Leb
  See also: *osander*, *saker*, *saklös*
  Refs: Fritzner s.v. *úsekr*; Hellquist s.v.v. *orsak*, *sak*, *saker*, *ursäkt*; de Vries s.v. *sekr*

osander (OSw) ósannr (ON) ósaðr (ON) osandær (OSw) usander (OSw) adj.
  innocent **OSw** *VmL* Kkb
  not guilty **OIce** *Grg* Feþ 157 Rsþ 227 Rsþ 230, *Jó* Þjb 6, **OSw** *YVgL* Tb
  See also: *osaker*, *saklös*, *sander*

osannind (OSw) noun
  deceit **OSw** *SdmL* Till
  untruth **OSw** *ÖgL* Kkb

osater (OSw) osatter (OSw) osætter (OSw) adj.
  as enemies **OSw** *HL* Kgb, *UL* Kkb, Kgb, Mb, *VmL* Kgb, *ÖgL* Eb
  as foes **OSw** *HL* Kgb, *YVgL* Add
  not settled **OSw** *HL* Kgb
  unreconciled **OSw** *SdmL* Kgb, Mb
  See also: *sater*

osiþer (OSw) ósiðr (ON) noun
  objectionable practice **OIce** *Jó* Kge 35
  sinful living **OSw** *ÖgL* Kkb

oskabarn (OSw) uskabarn (OSw) noun
  Appears in the context of compensation for children never conceived due to violence (e.g. castration or bride-robbery).
  anticipated children **OSw** *SdmL* Gb, Mb, *VmL* Äb

oskemdr (OGu) adj.

   without dishonour **OGu** *GL* A 13, 14

   without shame **OGu** *GL* Add. 1 (B4)

oskiel (OGu) **óskil** (ON) noun

   bad behaviour **ONorw** *FrL* KrbA 40

   dishonesty **OIce** *Jó* Kab 7

   injustice **OGu** *GL* A 37

   unfairness **ONorw** *FrL* Rgb 33

oskipter (OSw) **uskift** (ODan) **uskifteth** (ODan)
óskiftr (ON) **uskifter** (OSw) **uskipter** (OSw) adj.

   outlying **OSw** *YVgL* Kkb

   undistributed **ODan** *JyL* 1

   undivided **ODan** *ESjL* 2, *JyL* 1, *SkL* 65, 141,
   VSjL 70, **ONorw** *GuL* Llb, Arb, **OSw** *DL* Bb,
   SdmL Bb, Till, *YVgL* Tb, Föb, *ÖgL* Db

   without division **ODan** *SkL* 1

   See also: *skipta*

oskriptaþer (OSw) adj.

   unconfessed **OSw** *SdmL* Kkb

   unrepented **OSw** *ÖgL* Kkb

   unshriven **OSw** *UL* Kkb, *VmL* Kkb

oskylder (OSw) **uskyld** (ODan) **oskyldr** (OGu)
óskyldr (ON) **úskyldr** (ON) **uskylder** (OSw) adj.

   distantly related **OIce** *Jó* Kge 17

   having no duty **ONorw** *FrL* KrbA 12

   innocent **OGu** *GL* Add. 8 (B 55)

   not close in kin **OSw** *YVgL* Add

   not closely related **OIce** *Jó* Kge 23

   outside of kin **ONorw** *FrL* KrbB 3

   outside the kindred **ONorw** *GuL* Olb

   remotely related **OIce** *Grg* Arþ 122, *KRA* 36

   unkinned **OSw** *SmL*

   unrelated **OSw** *DL* Bb, Gb, *SdmL*
   Kkb, Jb, *VmL* Jb, *YVgL* Äb

   without guilt **ODan** *SkL* 111

   See also: *skylder (2)*

oskælika (OSw) **oskellika** (OGu) **uskælika** (OSw) adv.

   for no reason **OSw** *DL* Kkb

   illegally **OGu** *GL* A 25, **OSw** *YVgL* Add

   without reason **OSw** *SdmL* Conf, *YVgL* Kkb

oskær (OSw) **uskær** (ODan) **óskírðr** (ON) **oskir**
(OSw) **uskir** (OSw) adj.

   desecrated **OSw** *UL* Kkb

   impure **OSw** *YVgL* Kkb

   not cleansed **ODan** *SkL* 88, 121, 156, 217, 221

   unbaptized **OIce** *Grg* Klþ 2, *KRA* 1,
   11, **ONorw** *FrL* KrbA 3, 4

   unholy **OSw** *ÄVgL* Kkb

   See also: *skær*

osoyþr (OGu) **osoyþan** (OGu) noun

   unruly animal **OGu** *GL* A 17, 26, Add. 2 (B 17)

ospaker (OSw) adj.

   violent **OSw** *UL* För, *VmL* För

osvurin (OSw) **ósórr** (ON) adj.

   false **ONorw** *GuL* Krb, Arb

   perjured **OIce** *Jó* Þjb 22

   unsworn **OSw** *SdmL* Jb

   See also: *meneþer, sværia*

osökter (OSw) **usot** (ODan) **ósóttr** (ON) **osotter** (OSw)
usokter (OSw) **usoter** (OSw) adj.

   unchallenged **ODan** *SkKL* 11

   unclaimed **OIce** *Jó* Kge 20

   without being sued **OSw** *YVgL* Gb, Rlb, *ÄVgL* Rlb

   without legal proceedings **OSw** *VmL* Bb

   without prosecution **OSw** *DL* Bb, *SdmL* Mb

   See also: *sökia*

othelgarth (ODan) noun

   field fence **ODan** *ESjL* 2, *VSjL* 57, 58

ovanfal (OSw) noun

   *killing caused by somebody falling
   down by himself* **OSw** *DL* Mb

ovighþer (OSw) **uvighth** (ODan) **óvígðr** (ON) **úvígðr**
(ON) adj.

   desecrated **OSw** *ÖgL* Kkb

   unblessed **OSw** *DL* Kkb, *SdmL* Kkb

   unconsecrated **ODan** *SkKL* 1, **OIce** *KRA* 5, 15,
   ONorw *EidsL* 2.2, *GuL* Krb, **OSw** *ÖgL* Kkb

   without consecration **OSw** *HL* Kkb

   See also: *vighia*

ovili (OSw) **óvili** (ON) noun

   unwillingness **OSw** *DL* Bb

   Expressions:

   að óvilja (ON)

   against one's will **OIce** *Grg* Arþ 121

   unintentionally **OIce** *Js* Mah 30

   See also: *vili*

ovin (OSw) **uvin** (ODan) noun

   enemy **ODan** *JyL* 1, 3, *SkKL* 3, *SkL* 147,
   OSw *SdmL* Kgb, Till, *ÖgL* Eb

   fiend **OSw** *HL* Kgb

   foe **OSw** *YVgL* Add

   See also: *vin*

ovitagærning (OSw) noun

   senseless deed **OSw** *SdmL* Mb

ovæþiaþer (OSw) adj.

unpledged **OSw** *SdmL* Kkb, Rb, Till

without a pledge being laid down **OSw**
DL Tjdb, *UL* Mb, Rb, *VmL* Mb

without rebuking **OSw** *HL* Mb

See also: *væþ*

oxi (OSw) **uxi** (OGu) **oxi** (ON) noun

ox **OGu** *GL* A 6, 10, 17, 26, 33, **ONorw**
GuL Kpb, Løb, Tfb, Llb, Tjb, Leb, **OSw**
UL Mb, Kmb, Blb, *VmL* Mb, Kmb, Bb

oykvagn (OGu) noun

yoke (and) wagon **OGu** *GL* A 26

oþal (OSw) **óðal** (ON) **oþol** (OSw) noun

Inherited property, particularly land, which could not
be sold without restrictions, such as being offered to
relatives first, and which might be reclaimed within
a stipulated time. Originally, the specific type of
ownership and the rights pertaining to it; ONorw GuL
ch. 266 and FrL Jkb 4 state conditions of ownership
for a number of generations or years. Often, though,
used of any land regarding legal ownership.

allodial land **OIce** *Jó* MagBref, *Js* Kdb 3,
ONorw *FrL* Jkb 2, **OSw** *YVgL* Jb, *ÄVgL* Jb

ancestral land/birthright land **OSw** *DL* Bb

odal **ONorw** *GuL* Løb, Olb

odal land **OIce** *Jó* Kge 7, **ONorw** *GuL* Llb, Arb, Olb

odal right **ONorw** *GuL* Olb

Refs: Cleasby and Vigfusson s.v. *óðal*; Fritzner s.v.
óðal; Hertzberg s.v. *óðal*; KLNM s.v. *odelsrett*

oþalsmaþer (OSw) **óðalsmaðr** (ON) noun

allodial owner **ONorw** *FrL* Jkb 4

inheritor **ONorw** *EidsL* 39.4

landowner **OSw** *DL* Rb

man having a right to odal **ONorw** *GuL* Olb

oþolfastir (OSw) **oþals fastar** (pl.) (OSw) **oþilfastar**
(pl.) (OSw) **oþolfæstir** (OSw) **öþælfastir** (OSw)
noun

purchase witness **OSw** *DL* Bb

witness of allodial land **OSw** *YVgL* Jb

{*oþolfastir*} **OSw** *ÄVgL* Jb

See also: *styrifaster*

oþoliorþ (OSw) **óðaljörð** (ON) **óðalsjörð** (ON) noun

allodial estate **OIce** *Jó* Mah 4, *Js* Mah
2 Lbb 8, **ONorw** *FrL* ArbA 3

inherited land **ONorw** *FrL* Var 44

odal (allodial) land **OSw** *YVgL* Add

odal land **ONorw** *GuL* Krb, Llb, Mhb, Olb

See also: *aþal*

oþolskipti (OSw) **óðalskipti** (ON) **óðalsskifti** (ON)
óðalsskipti (ON) **othalskipte** (OSw) noun

division of allodial lands **ONorw** *FrL* LlbB 4

division of odal land **ONorw** *GuL* Llb

parcelling out of odal land **ONorw** *GuL* Olb

*regulation of possession between neighbours
of the village* **OSw** *ÄVgL* Jb

regulation of possessions **OSw** *YVgL* Jb

See also: *oþal*, *skipti*

oþolvatn (OSw) noun

odal (allodial) water **OSw** *YVgL* Add

oþolvatnværk (OSw) noun

odal (allodial) water works **OSw** *YVgL* Add

oþulbrut (OSw) noun

*fine for a crime concerning allodial
land* **OSw** *SdmL* Jb, Bb

óalinn (ON) **úalinn** (ON) adj.

unborn **ONorw** *GuL* Løb

óauðigr (ON) adj.

poor **OIce** *Grg* Ómb 142 Feþ 148 Hrs 234 Misc 249

óátun (ON) **óátan** (ON) **úátan** (ON) noun

forbidden food **ONorw** *GuL* Krb

See also: *átan*

óbótamaðr (ON) noun

An unatonable criminal; a person who has committed
a type of crime which deprives them of the opportunity
to pay compensation through legal settlements (cf.
urbotamal).

criminal **OIce** *Jó* Mah 2 Þjb 3,
ONorw *FrL* Intr 10, *GuL* Krb

unatonable criminal **OIce** *Js* Mah 6, 9,
KRA 6, 8, **ONorw** *FrL* Mhb 35 Var 44

See also: *udæthesman*, *urbotamal*

Refs: CV s.v. *úbótamaðr*; Fritzner s.v. *úbótamaðr*

óbótasök (ON) noun

unatonable crime **OIce** *Js* Mah 7

See also: *óbótaverk*, *urbotamal*

óbótaverk (ON) noun

unatonable crime **OIce** *Jó* Mah 4, **ONorw** *BorgL* 16

See also: *óbótasök*, *urbotamal*

óbyggð (ON) noun

uninhabited parts of the country **OIce**
Grg Feþ 164 Rsþ 231, *Jó* Þjb 13

óbyggðr (ON) adj.

not leased **OIce** *Jó* Llb 14

uninhabited **OIce** *Grg* Lbþ 183

óbǿttr (ON) adj.

unatoned **OIce** *Grg* Bat 113, *KRA* 35

without paying compensation **ONorw** *FrL* LlbA 21

See also: *bot*

óðáðaverk (ON) noun

crime **OIce** *Jó* Mah 20, **ONorw** *FrL*
Intr 12, *GuL* Krb, Løb, Tfb

See also: *urbotamal*

óðulðr (ON) adj.

knowingly **OIce** *Jó* Llb 45

óðalborinn (ON) adj.

born to odal right **ONorw** *GuL* Mhb, Olb

entitled to patrimony **OIce** *Js* Kdb 4

See also: *oþal*

óðalsbrigði (ON) noun

redemption of odal land **ONorw** *GuL* Olb

óðalskona (ON) noun

woman having a right to odal **ONorw** *GuL* Olb

óðalsnautar (pl.) (ON) noun

men sharing the same odal **ONorw** *GuL* Olb

óðalsvitni (ON) óðalvitni (ON) noun

ownership witness **ONorw** *FrL* LlbA 23

testimony of patrimonial rights **OIce** *Js* Lbb 1

witness to odal right **ONorw** *GuL* Olb

See also: *vitni*

óðinsnátt (ON) noun

night before Wednesday **ONorw** *GuL* Krb

óðr (ON) adj.

mad **ONorw** *GuL* Mhb

Expressions:

óðr maðr (ON)

madman **OIce** *Grg* Þsþ 80 *Jó* Mah 2, 8 *Js* Mah 8

óeinkynntr (ON) adj.

Lacking a mark of ownership; used particularly
concerning animals.

unmarked **OIce** *Grg* Fjl 225

Refs: CV s.v. *úeinkynntr*; Fritzner
(supp.) s.v. *úeinkynntr*

ófalsaðr (ON) adj.

without fraud **OIce** *Jó* Kab 24, *Js* Kab 18

óferjandi (ON) adj.

Untransportable. Refers to a full outlaw (ON
skógarmaðr) to whom no one is permitted to grant
passage out of the country.

to be denied passage **OIce** *Grg* Klþ 2 Þsþ 51

See also: *ferjandi, óóll, skógarmaðr*

Refs: CV s.v. *úferjandi*; Finsen III:672; Fritzner s.v.
ferja, úferjandi (suppl.); KLNM s.v. *fredløshed*

ófestr (ON) adj.

undecided **ONorw** *FrL* Kvb 11

ófolginn (ON) úfolginn (ON) adj.

unhidden **ONorw** *GuL* Kpb

ófrár (ON) adj.

weak **ONorw** *GuL* Krb

óför (ON) noun

accident **ONorw** *GuL* Mhb

ófóra (ON) noun

impassable area **ONorw** *GuL* Mhb

ógangsmaðr (ON) noun

miscreant **ONorw** *FrL* Mhb 43

ógildi (ON) noun

no compensation **OIce** *Jó* Llb 39

ógoldinn (ON) adj.

unpaid **OIce** *Grg* Lbþ 215 Tíg 256, *Js* Lbb 17

ógörr (ON) adj.

not contributed **ONorw** *GuL* Leb

óheimila (ON) verb

lose a right **ONorw** *GuL* Llb

lose title **OIce** *Jó* Llb 1

lose warranty **OIce** *Js* Lbb 10

óhelgi (ON) noun

forfeit immunity **OIce** *Grg* Vís 86, 90, *Js* Mah 1

óhlutr (ON) noun

injury **ONorw** *BorgL* 18.3

mistreatment **OIce** *Jó* Þfb 5, *Js* Þfb 4

óhygginn (ON) adj.

mentally incapable **OIce** *Grg* Vís 94

óhófuverk (ON) óhæfuverk (ON) noun

indecent act **OIce** *Jó* Mah 27

unseemly act **OIce** *Js* Mah 25

óknytti (ON) noun

bad trick **ONorw** *FrL* Intr 10

crime **OIce** *Jó* Mah 2 Fml 14

impropriety **OIce** *Js* Mah 7

ókostr (ON) noun

failing **OIce** *Grg* Ómb 140 Feþ 144

See also: *laster*

ólafsmessa hin fyrri (ON) noun

earlier Feast of St Olaf (29 July) **ONorw** *GuL* Krb

ólafsmessa hin øfri (ON) ólafsmessa hin síðarri (ON)
noun

later Feast of St Olaf (3 August) **ONorw** *GuL* Krb

ólafssáð (ON) noun

grain oblation **ONorw** *BorgL* 12.2

Olaf's measure **ONorw** *BorgL* 12.2

óleiddr (ON) adj.
not legitimated **ONorw** *GuL* Arb

óleigðr (ON) adj.
without borrowing **OIce** *Jó* Þjb 16

óleigis (ON) adv.
without interest **OIce** *Grg* Arþ 122
See also: *leigulauss, vaxtalauss*

óleyfa (ON) verb
deny permission **OIce** *Jó* Llb 19

óleyfi (ON) noun
without leave **OIce** *Grg* Lbþ 219
without permission **OIce** *Jó* Þjb 10, *Js* Þfb 3

óleyfiliga (ON) adv.
without permission **OIce** *KRA* 26

ólíkan (ON) noun
dead tissue **ONorw** *GuL* Mhb

ólofaðr (ON) adj.
without leave **OIce** *Grg* Feþ 164

ólýstr (ON) adj.
not announced **ONorw** *FrL* Mhb 14 Jkb 7 Bvb 4
not declared **ONorw** *FrL* Mhb 41
unpublished **OIce** *Grg* Lbþ 193

ólögligr (ON) adj.
illegitimate **OIce** *KRA* 16
unlawful **OIce** *Jó* Þfb 6

ómagabjörg (ON) noun
support of dependents **OIce** *Grg* Arþ 127 Ómb 143 Tíg 255, *Js* Lbb 4, *KRA* 15

ómagabölkr (ON) ómagabálkr (ON) noun
dependents section **OIce** *Grg* Ómb 128

ómagaeyrir (ON) noun
dependent's means **OIce** *Grg* Arþ 118, 120 Misc 249 Tíg 259, *Jó* Kge 13 Lbb 12, *Js* Ert 19, 24 Lbb 9, *KRA* 15
minor's property **ONorw** *FrL* ArbB 22

ómagafé (ON) noun
dependents' property **OIce** *Jó* Kge 14
minor's money **ONorw** *FrL* ArbB 28

ómagaframførsla (ON) ómagaframfærsla (ON) noun
maintenance of dependents **OIce** *Js* Lbb 9
maintenance of incapable people **OIce** *Grg* Þsþ 50

ómagakaup (ON) noun
purchase made by a minor **OIce** *Jó* Kab 24

ómagalandsbrigð (ON) noun
land claim where there is a dependent **OIce** *Jó* Lbb 12

ómagalauss (ON) adj.
free of dependents **OIce** *Jó* Sg 1
without dependents **OIce** *Grg* Feþ 148

ómagalýsing (ON) noun
publishing maintenance of dependents **OIce** *Grg* Ómb 130

ómagamál (ON) noun
dependent case **ONorw** *FrL* ArbB 27

ómagamót (ON) noun
A meeting of dependents. Refers to a situation in which a person responsible for providing for a dependent is themselves destitute and in need of support.
collision of the incapable **OIce** *Grg* Ómb 129
Refs: CV s.v. *ómagamót*

ómagaskifti (ON) noun
distribution of dependents **OIce** *Jó* Kge 25
distribution of wards **ONorw** *GuL* Arb

ómagasök (ON) noun
maintenance case **OIce** *Grg* Ómb 130, 143

ómagaverk (ON) noun
ward's actions **OIce** *Jó* Llb 29

ómarkaðr (ON) adj.
unmarked **OFar** *Seyð* 4, 5

ómegð (ON) noun
state of being a minor **ONorw** *GuL* Kvb, Løb, Arb, Llb, Olb
state of dependence **OIce** *Grg* Ómb 134 Lbþ 202, *Jó* Kge 14, *Js* Kvg 2, 4
See also: *omaghi*

ómennska (ON) ómenska (ON) noun
Expressions:
ómenska sakir (ON)
perversity **OIce** *Grg* Ómb 143

ómerkðr (ON) ómerktr (ON) úmerktr (ON) adj.
unmarked (of lots) **ONorw** *GuL* Llb

ómettinn (ON) adj.
unvalued **ONorw** *FrL* ArbB 22

ómætr (ON) adj.
invalid **OIce** *Grg* Þsþ 41, 47
See also: *ónýtr*

óneyttr (ON) úneyttr (ON) adj.
not eaten **ONorw** *GuL* Løb

ónýta (ON) verb
render invalid **ONorw** *GuL* Kpb
void **OIce** *Grg* Þsþ 27
See also: *ónýtr*

ónýtr (ON) **únýtr** (ON) adj.

   invalid **OIce** *Grg* Þsþ 23, 47, *Jó*
   Llb 52, **ONorw** *GuL* Kpb

   void **OIce** *Grg* Vís 89, 99 Bat 113
   Lbþ 172, 185 Misc 250

   See also: *ómœtr, ónýta*

óprófaðr (ON) adj.

   unproven **OIce** *KRA* 18

órannsakaðr (ON) adj.

   unsearched **ONorw** *FrL* Bvb 8

óraverk (ON) noun

   deeds of insanity **OIce** *Grg* Vís 93

óreiddr (ON) adj.

   not paid out **OIce** *Js* Lbb 21

órför (ON) noun

   withdrawal **ONorw** *GuL* Arb

órlausn (ON) noun

   solution **OIce** *Grg* Misc 244

órskurðr (ON) noun

   decision **OIce** *Jó* Þfb 9 Mah 7 Kge 26 Kab 14 Þjb
   4, *Js* Mah 13 Kab 3, *KRA* 34, **ONorw** *FrL* Intr 16

órǿkð (ON) **órækt** (ON) noun

   negligence **OIce** *Grg* Klþ 1 Feþ 158 Tíg
   261, *Jó* Llb 6, *Js* Lbb 13, *KRA* 1

órǿkðr (ON) adj.

   neglected **ONorw** *FrL* Kvb 17

ósáinn (ON) **úsáinn** (ON) adj.

   unsown **ONorw** *GuL* Llb

ósátt (ON) **ósætt** (ON) noun

   dissent **OIce** *Grg* Ómb 135 Feþ 148

óseldr (ON) **úseldr** (ON) adj.

   not sold **ONorw** *GuL* Olb

óskikkðr (ON) **óskiktr** (ON) adj.

   uncut (of cloth) **ONorw** *GuL* Mhb

   See also: *óskorinn*

óskjóti (ON) noun

   nuisance **ONorw** *FrL* Mhb 8

óskorinn (ON) **úskorinn** (ON) adj.

   uncut (of cloth) **ONorw** *GuL* Mhb

   See also: *óskikkðr*

óskuld (ON) noun

   liability **OIce** *Jó* Fml 22

ósóknardagr (ON) noun

   day on which prosecutions are not permitted
   OIce *KRA* 29, **ONorw** *FrL* KrbB 20

ósýnn (ON) adj.

   without justification **OIce** *Jó* Mah 20, *Js* Mah 23

ósöðlaðr (ON) adj.

   not saddled **ONorw** *GuL* Llb

ótalðr (ON) **ótaldr** (ON) adj.

   not enumerated **ONorw** *GuL* Arb

   not listed **ONorw** *GuL* Mhb

   untallied **OIce** *Js* Kab 1

   without having been inventoried **OIce** *Jó* Kab 1

ótekinn (ON) adj.

   unleased **OIce** *Jó* Llb 10

   unrented **ONorw** *FrL* LlbB 2

   unsecured **OIce** *Jó* Llb 26

ótíð (ON) noun

   improper time **ONorw** *BorgL* 6 13.3

óvarinn (ON) adj.

   not spent **OIce** *Jó* Kge 18

óvenja (ON) noun

   abuse **OIce** *Jó* Kge 29

   bad custom **OFar** *Seyð* 4

óvirðr (ON) **óvirt** (ON) adj.

   unappraised **OIce** *Jó* Kge 14 Llb 57

   unassessed **ONorw** *GuL* Arb

   unvalued **OIce** *Grg* Arþ 122, *Js* Kvg
   3 Ert 24, **ONorw** *FrL* Kvb 6

óviti (ON) adj.

   senseless **OIce** *Grg* Vís 101 Lrþ 117

óvitr (ON) adj.

   mentally deficient **OIce** *Grg* Klþ 16

óvizka (ON) noun

   insanity **ONorw** *GuL* Krb

óvísaelði (ON) adj.

   boarding (an outlaw) in ignorance **OIce** *Grg* Þsþ 77

óvísavargr (ON) **úvísavargr** (ON) noun

   outlaw not known to be such **ONorw** *GuL* Mhb

   unforeseen misfortune **ONorw** *FrL* Mhb 9, Var 9

óvæni (ON) noun

   bodily injury **OIce** *Js* Mah 16,
   ONorw *FrL* Mhb 56 Leb 24

   injury **ONorw** *GuL* Mhb

óvænishögg (ON) noun

   blemishing blow **OIce** *Grg* Vís 111

   injuring blow **ONorw** *FrL* Mhb 19

óværateigr (ON) noun

   irritant plot **OIce** *Grg* Lbþ 194

óæti (ON) noun

   forbidden food **OIce** *Grg* Klþ 16

óðll (ON) óæll (ON) adj.

not to be sustained **OIce** *Grg* Klþ 2 Þsþ 51,
53 Vís 86, 88, **ONorw** *FrL* KrbA 4

óðrr (ON) óærr (ON) adj.

sane **OIce** *Grg* Vís 93

panter (OSw) noun

A surety for failure to fulfil obligations or payments.
Such obligations included participation in church-
building (SdmL, UL, VmL) and wolf-hunting (SdmL).
The payments involved fines for accidental killing or
wounding (DL) and debts to the church (YVgL).

deposit **OSw** *DL* Mb

penalty **OSw** *UL* Kkb, *VmL* Kkb

pledge **OSw** *YVgL* Kkb

surety **OSw** *SdmL* Kkb, Bb

pantsætia (OSw) verb

pledge **OSw** *HL* Jb

paskadagher (OSw) páskadagr (ON) noun

Easter Day **OIce** *Grg* Klþ 4, **ONorw** *GuL* Krb,
OSw *DL* Kkb, *UL* Kkb, Mb, *VmL* Kkb

paskafriþer (OSw) noun

Between the Wednesday in Holy Week and Easter
Monday (YVgL) or the eighth day after (ÖgL).
Breaching it, in ÖgL explicitly with violence, was
punished with fines to the bishop.

peace at Easter **OSw** *ÖgL* Kkb

peace of Easter **OSw** *YVgL* Kkb

See also: *friþer, julafriþer, paskar,
þingizsdaghafriþer*

Refs: Schlyter s.v. *paska friþer*

paskapænningar (pl.) (OSw) noun

Easter money **OSw** *YVgL* Kkb

See also: *paskaskuld*

paskar (OSw) paske (ODan) páskar (ON) paschar
(OSw) noun

Easter **ODan** *JyL* 2, 3, **ONorw** *FrL* Bvb 5,
GuL Krb, **OSw** *DL* Bb, *SdmL* Kkb, *SmL*,
UL Kkb, Blb, Rb, *VmL* Kkb, Rb, *YVgL*
Kkb, Föb, Utgb, *ÄVgL* Föb, *ÖgL* Kkb

See also: *paskeuke*

paskaskuld (OSw) noun

Easter debt **OSw** *ÖgL* Kkb

See also: *paskapænningar (pl.)*

paskeuke (ODan) páskavika (ON) noun

Easter week **ODan** *SkKL* 9, **ONorw** *GuL* Krb, Olb

See also: *paskar*

patríarki (ON) noun

patriarch **OIce** *Grg* Bat 114

pavi (OSw) pave (ODan) páfi (ON) noun

pope **ODan** *JyL* Fort, 3, **OIce** *Grg* Bat
114, *Js* Kdb 4, *KRA* 6, 27, **ONorw** *FrL*
KrbA 26 KrbB 17, **OSw** *ÄVgL* Gb

páfabann (ON) noun

papal ban **OIce** *KRA* 11

pálsmessa (ON) noun

Feast of St Paul (25 January) **ONorw** *GuL* Krb

St Paul's Day **OIce** *Grg* Klþ 13

páskaaptann (ON) noun

Easter Eve **ONorw** *GuL* Krb

pell (OGu) noun

wedding canopy **OGu** *GL* A 65

petersmessa (OSw) pétrsmessa (ON) noun

Saint Peter's Mass **OSw** *HL* Rb, *SmL*, *ÖgL* Kkb

St Peter's Day (in the spring) **OIce** *Grg* Klþ 13

St Peter's Day (in the summer) **OIce** *Grg* Klþ 13, 17

St Peter's Mass (29 June) **ONorw** *GuL* Krb

See also: *apostlamæssudagher*

pétrsmessuaptann (ON) noun

St Peter's Eve (28 June) **ONorw** *GuL* Krb

philippus messa ok jakobus (ON) noun

Feast of SS Philip and James **OIce** *Grg* Klþ 12

pilegrim (ODan) noun

pilgrim **ODan** *JyL* Fort

pilægrimsfærþ (OSw) pilegrimsfærth (ODan) noun

pilgrimage **ODan** *JyL* 1, 2, **OSw** *DL* Rb

pine (ODan) pína (ON) verb

punish **ODan** *JyL* Fort

torture **OIce** *Grg* Vís 110, **ONorw**
FrL Rgb 40, *GuL* Mhb, Tjb

use force **OIce** *Grg* Feþ 161

pingetsuke (ODan) noun

Pentecost week **ODan** *SkKL* 9

pingizdagher (OSw) pingetsdagh (ODan)
pighizdagher (OSw) pikizdagher (OSw)
pinkizdagher (OSw) noun

Whitsunday **ODan** *JyL* 3, **OSw** *SdmL* Kkb,
Bb, Till, *SmL*, *YVgL* Föb, *ÖgL* Kkb

pingizsdaghafriþer (OSw) noun

Beginning on Whitsun eve and lasting eight days.
Breaching it with violence was punished with fines to
the bishop.

peace at Whitsun days **OSw** *ÖgL* Kkb

See also: *friþer, julafriþer, paskafriþer, pingizdagher*

Refs: Schlyter s.v. *pingizs dagha friþer*

ploghsærje (ODan) noun

Unit of taxation worth four *marker* of gold, corresponding to a third of a *havne* (see *hamna*).

ploughland **ODan** *JyL* 3

See also: *hamna, markland*

Refs: Tamm and Vogt, eds, 2016, 281

portkunumaþer (OSw) noun

man who visits harlots **OSw** *SmL*

See also: *putomaþer*

prestadómr (ON) noun

A court of priests; an ecclesiastical court. According to Grg Klþ 6 the bishop prosecuted cases against subordinates at a court of priests, and such cases were judged by twelve priests appointed by the bishop. The bishop and two other priests issued verdicts on cases. These courts were held during the annual General Assembly (*alþingi*). It is thought that the *prestadómr* was established in Iceland as a general court for ecclesiastical offenses from the introduction of Christianity until at least 1275 when KRA came into force.

court of priests **OIce** *Grg* Klþ 6

See also: *alþingi, domber*

Refs: CV; F; KLNM s.v. *alþingi, kyrkostraff*; MSE s.v. *alþingi*

prestamót (ON) noun

synod **ONorw** *BorgL* 12.20

prestastefna (ON) noun

synod **OIce** *KRA* 13

prestbarn (OGu) noun

priest's child **OGu** *GL* A 5

prester (OSw) **præst** (ODan) **prestr** (OGu) **prestr** (ON) **præster** (OSw) noun

clergyman **OSw** *HL* Kkb, Mb, Blb

priest **ODan** *ESjL* 2, *JyL* 1–3, *SkKL* 2, 5, 7, 11, 12, *SkL* 3, 156, *VSjL* 5, **OGu** *GS* Ch. 3, 4, **OIce** *KRA* 1, 4, **ONorw** *BorgL* 2.3 5.14, *EidsL* 2.1 4, *FrL* Tfb 3 KrbA 3 Mhb 8 LlbA 3, *GuL* Krb, Leb, **OSw** *DL* Kkb, Mb, *HL* Kkb, Äb, Mb, Jb, Blb, *SdmL* Kkb, Äb, Kmb, Mb, Till, *SmL*, *YVgL* Kkb, Drb, Äb, Rlb, Tb, Utgb, *ÄVgL* Kkb, Md, Äb, Rlb, Föb, *ÖgL* Kkb

See also: *biskuper, kennimaðr, lænspræster, soknaprester, ærchibiskuper*

prestgarþer (OSw) **prestgarþr** (OGu) **præsta garþer** (OSw) noun

priest's farm **OSw** *HL* Kkb

rectory land **OGu** *GL* A 8, 13

See also: *biskupsgarþer, kirkiubol, prester, præstastuva*

prestkuna (OGu) noun

priest's wife **OGu** *GL* A 5

prestlingr (ON) noun

priest's assistant **ONorw** *FrL* KrbA 17

priestling **OIce** *Grg* Klþ 4

prestreiða (ON) **prestareiða** (ON) noun

priest's dues **ONorw** *GuL* Krb

priests' pay **OIce** *Grg* Tíg 258

prestsfjórðungr (ON) noun

priest's quarter **OIce** *KRA* 15

prestskaup (ON) noun

priest's income **OIce** *KRA* 15

prestson (OGu) **prestssonr** (ON) noun

priest's son **OGu** *GL* Add. 1 (B 4)

son of a priest **ONorw** *GuL* Mhb

preststíund (ON) noun

priest tithe **OIce** *KRA* 15

primsigna (OSw) **prímsigna** (ON) verb

mark with a cross **ONorw** *FrL* KrbA 5

prime-sign **OIce** *Grg* Klþ 1, **ONorw** *BorgL* 1.3, **OSw** *SmL*, *YVgL* Kkb

See also: *skæra (1)*

privilege (ODan) noun

privilege **ODan** *JyL* 3

prímsigning (ON) noun

prime-signing **OIce** *Grg* Vís 89 Feþ 144

prímsignun (ON) **prímsignan** (ON) noun

prime-sign **ONorw** *BorgL* 15.10

prime-signing **OIce** *Grg* Þsþ 25

signing with the Christian cross **ONorw** *GuL* Krb

provastargift (OSw) noun

fee to a dean **OSw** *YVgL* Kkb

provaster (OSw) **proastr** (OGu) **proaster** (OSw) noun

dean **OSw** *HL* Kkb, Äb, *YVgL* Kkb

provost **OSw** *ÖgL* Kkb

rural dean **OGu** *GS* Ch. 3, **OSw** *UL* Add. 8, *VmL* Kkb

próf (ON) noun

legal examination of evidence **OIce** *Jó* Þjb 4

prófun (ON) **prófan** (ON) noun

proving **OIce** *KRA* 18, 34

præstastuva (OSw) noun

priest's house **OSw** *HL* Kkb

See also: *biskupsgarþer, kirkiubol, prester, prestgarþer*

pröva (OSw) **prøve** (ODan) **prófa** (ON) verb

prove **ODan** *JyL* 1, 2, **OIce** *Jó* Llb 62 Þjb 22

prove with evidence **OIce** *Js* Þfb 5, *KRA* 2, 11

try **OSw** *HL* Blb

pund (OSw) pund (OGu) pund (ON) noun

lispound **OGu** *GL* A 6, **OSw** *UL* Kgb, *VmL* Kkb, Kgb

pound **OIce** *Jó* Fml 7, 13, **OSw** *ÖgL* Kkb

unit of the weight system, c. 5 kg **ONorw** *GuL* Krb

{pund} **OSw** *SdmL* Kkb, Till

pundari (ON) noun

steelyard **OIce** *Grg* Lbþ 215, *Jó* Kab 26

puster (OSw) pústr (ON) noun

blow with the hand **OSw** *HL* Mb

box on the ear **OIce** *Jó* Mah 22

slap **OSw** *SdmL* Mb, *UL* Mb, *VmL* Mb

putomaþer (OSw) noun

man who visits whores **OSw** *SmL*

See also: *portkunumaþer*

pænningaböter (OSw) noun

compensation in money **OSw** *YVgL* Add

pænninger (OSw) pænning (ODan) penningr (OGu)
penningr (ON) panninger (OSw) penninger (OSw)
pæninger (OSw) pænunger (OSw) noun

coin **ODan** *JyL* 3, **OGu** *GL* A 2, 15, 16, 19–24,
63, Add. 3, 4 (B 19), *GS* Ch. 3, 4, **OSw** *SdmL*
Kkb, Add, *SmL*, *UL* Kkb, Kgb, Mb, Jb, Kmb, *VmL*
Kkb, Kgb, Kmb, Rb, *YVgL* Kkb, *ÄVgL* Kkb

fine **OSw** *DL* Rb, *HL*

funds **OSw** *UL* Kkb, Kmb, *VmL* Kkb

goods **OSw** *SdmL* Gb, *YVgL* Kkb, Äb, Add

monetary compensation **OSw** *DL* Mb

money **ODan** *ESjL* 3, *JyL* 1–3, **OGu** *GL* A 28,
OIce *Jó* Kge 2, 28 Kab 7 Fml 9, **OSw** *DL* Kkb,
Bb, Gb, Tjdb, Rb, *HL*, *SdmL* Kkb, Äb, Jb, Bb,
Kmb, Mb, Tjdb, Rb, Add, *SmL*, *UL* Kkb, Äb,
Mb, Jb, Kmb, *VmL* Kkb, Äb, Mb, Jb, Kmb, Rb,
YVgL Kkb, Urb, Äb, Tb, Add, *ÖgL* Kkb, Db

payment **OIce** *Jó* Þjb 12, **OSw** *SdmL* Kmb

penny **ODan** *ESjL* 1–3, *VSjL* 12, 14, 51, 60,
62, **OGu** *GL* A 45, 47, 49, 56a, **OIce** *Grg* Vís
112 Bat 113 Rsþ 227 Misc 245, *Jó* Llb 30 Fml
22, *KRA* 20, 30, **ONorw** *BorgL* 12.8, *EidsL*
24.2 27.5, *FrL* ArbB 28, **OSw** *ÖgL* Kkb

property **OSw** *DL* Tjdb, *YVgL* Kkb

recompense **OSw** *UL* Kmb, *VmL* Kmb

taxes **OSw** *HL*

*unit of the weight and monetary system, one
240th {mark}* **ONorw** *GuL* Krb, Mhb, Leb, Sab

{pænninger} **OSw** *DL* Kkb, Bb, *HL*, *SdmL* Kkb, Äb,
Bb, Kmb, Mb, Tjdb, Till, *SmL*, *UL* Kkb, Kgb, Mb,
Jb, Kmb, Blb, *VmL* Kkb, Kgb, Bb, *YVgL* Kkb, Drb

See also: *fæ, lösöre, mali, mark
(2), öre, örtogh, pænter*

pænningsöl (OSw) noun

alehouse **OSw** *ÖgL* Eb

drinking at the tavern **OSw** *YVgL* Add

drinking party **OSw** *UL* Kgb, *VmL* Kgb

drinking party at an inn **OSw** *DL* Eb

drinking-bout **OSw** *HL* Kgb

pænter (OSw) adj.

in coin **OSw** *UL* Mb

See also: *pænninger*

qui (OGu) kví (ON) noun

path between fences **OGu** *GL* A 24f (64)

pen **ONorw** *GuL* Llb, Mhb

quindi (OGu) noun

woman **OGu** *GL* A 20 (corrected in
translation from A 19), 28

quindi (OGu) adj.

female **OGu** *GL* A 20, Add. 1 (B 4)

quindismaþr (OGu) noun

female **OGu** *GL* A 14, 20, 28

quisl (OGu) kvísl (ON) noun

family line **ONorw** *GuL* Arb

generation **OGu** *GL* A 20

quislarmenn (pl.) (OGu) noun

*kinsmen from another branch of
the family* **OGu** *GL* A 28

quiþr (OGu) noun

womb **OGu** *GL* A 14, 18

qvalalös (OSw) adj.

unchallenged **OSw** *UL* Mb, *VmL* Rb

qvarstaþa (OSw) quærstaþa (OSw) noun

Literally 'remaining'. The handling of a legal case
awaiting further developments such as results of
appeals (HL, VmL), and confirmation of ownership of
disputed objects (SdmL, UL, VmL).

lien **OSw** *UL* Mb, *VmL* Mb

rest **OSw** *HL* Rb

suspension **OSw** *HL* Kkb, *SdmL* Jb, *VmL* Rb

qvarsæta (OSw) kværsæte (ODan) noun

In ODan JyL, land that was exempt, presumably from
military service (ODan *lething*, see *leþunger*), as well
as a fee paid for this. In OSw ÄVgL, synonymous
with *qvarsætutak* and *tak*, i.e. a surety for a disputed
object, but it is unclear who should hold it.

due for exempt land **ODan** *JyL* 3

exempt due **ODan** *JyL* 3

land where military dues are not paid **ODan** *JyL* 3

lien **OSw** *ÄVgL* Tb

non-military due **ODan** *JyL* 3

Refs: KLNM s.v. *leidang*; Lund s.v. *qvær*;
Ordbog over det danske sprog s.v. *kværsæde*;
Schlyter s.v.v. *qvarsæta, qvarsætu tak*;
Tamm and Vogt, eds, 2016, 307

qvarsætutak (OSw) **kyrrsetutak** (ON) **kuarsætu tak**
(OSw) noun

In OSw, deposition of disputed goods during the legal
handling of an accusation of theft; mentioned as a
legal *tak* (q.v.) alongside *brötartak* (q.v.) and *skælatak*
(q.v.). In ONorw, security for an obligation to attend
something.

lien **OSw** *ÄVgL* Tb

*security that a person be present at a
certain place* **ONorw** *GuL* Llb

sequestration security **OSw** *YVgL* Tb

Refs: CV s.v. *kyrrseta*; Fritzner s.v. *kyrrsetutak*;
Hertzberg s.v. *kyrrsetutak*; Schlyter s.v. *qvarsætu tak*

qviggrind (OSw) noun

fold's gate **OSw** *YVgL* Rlb, *ÄVgL* Rlb

qvikfæ (OSw) **kvikfæ** (ODan) **kvikfé** (ON) **kykfé** (ON)
noun

animal **OSw** *YVgL* Gb

livestock **ODan** *SkL* 142, **OIce** *Js* Ert 2

livestock quota **OIce** *Grg* Lbþ 180

living chattel **ODan** *JyL* 2

See also: *fæ*

qvikker (OSw) **quikr** (OGu) **kvikr** (ON) adj.

Legally significant contexts include tithes (paid in
livestock), capital punishment (see below), and rights
of inheritance, e.g. when a dying woman gave birth to
a living child, the child was assigned a number (13) in
the line of succession (ONorw GuL ch. 104).

alive **OGu** *GL* A 14, 18, **ONorw** *GuL* Løb, Arb, **OSw**
UL Kkb, Äb, Mb, Blb, Rb, *VmL* Kkb, Äb, Jb, Rb

cattle **OSw** *UL* Kkb, *VmL* Kkb

living **OSw** *UL* Kkb, Äb, Mb, Kmb,
Blb, *VmL* Äb, Mb, Kmb, Bb

quick **OSw** *UL* Kkb

Expressions:

qvikker i iorþ gravas (OSw)
Burying alive as a capital punishment for women
committing theft exceeding a certain value and
for men committing bestiality. In the latter case it
was specified that the plaintiff, i.e. the owner of
the abused animal, was to act as executioner.

to be buried (*in the earth*) *alive* **OSw** *DL* Kkb *HL* Mb

See also: *þyþilagh*

Refs: KLNM s.v. *dødsstraf*

qviktiundi (OSw) **qviktiund** (OSw) noun

cattle tithe **OSw** *HL* Kkb

livestock tithe **OSw** *HL* Kkb, *UL* Kkb, *VmL* Kkb

living tithe **OSw** *SdmL* Kkb, *YVgL* Kkb

See also: *tiund*

qvinnaarf (OSw) noun

maternal inheritance **OSw** *HL* Äb

qvinnabænker (OSw) noun

women's bench **OSw** *HL* Mb

qvinnafriþer (OSw) noun

Included among the peace declarations related to the
king and *eþsöre*, and breaching it (defined in HL as
rape and abduction) was considered a non-atoneable
crime.

peace of women **OSw** *YVgL* Add

women's inviolability **OSw** *HL* Kgb

women's peace **OSw** *SdmL* Kgb,Till

See also: *eþsöre, friþer, kona, urbotamal, vigher*

qvælia (OSw) verb

Literally 'to torment'. To complain about something
that could be handled at the *þing* 'assembly' (translated
as 'to complain', 'to challenge', 'to contest', 'to
criticize'), also to summon a formal meeting,
particularly a *þing*, and occasionally understood as
initiating legal proceedings (reflected in translations
such as 'to bring a case (against)', 'to prosecute', 'to
sue (for)', 'to appeal').

appeal **OSw** *DL* Bb

bring a case (against) **OSw** *DL* Gb, *UL* Mb, Rb

bring a case of inheritance against **OSw** *DL* Gb

challenge **OSw** *DL* Bb, *UL* Kkb, Blb,
Rb, *VmL* Kkb, Mb, Jb, Rb

complain **OSw** *HL* Kkb

complain (about something) **OSw** *UL* Mb, *VmL* Mb

contest **OSw** *SdmL* Äb, Jb, Mb

convene **OSw** *SdmL* Rb

criticize **OSw** *HL* Mb, Rb

make demands of **OSw** *UL* Kkb, Mb, *VmL* Mb

persecute **OSw** *UL* Mb, *VmL* Mb

prosecute **OSw** *DL* Kkb, Bb, *HL* Mb

raise a challenge **OSw** *UL* Kkb,
Kgb, *VmL* Kkb, Jb, Kmb

sue **OSw** *HL* Mb

sue for **OSw** *VmL* Mb

See also: *klanda, krævia, kæra, tiltala*

qværn (OSw) **kværn** (OSw) noun

mill **OSw** *DL* Bb, *HL* Blb, *SdmL* Bb

ra (OSw) rá (ON) noun

Literally, 'pole'. It is used to refer to a boundary or boundary line marked by a pole or poles. This word is frequently combined in an alliterative expression with *rör* 'pile of stones'. In that case, it could have signified a pile of stones topped by a stake or pole, used as a boundary marker. It is also combined with other nouns to indicate the function of the boundary referred to (frequently depending upon the context): village, highway, farmland, curtilage, enclave or plot. The word is widely used on its own to mean 'acceptable boundary marker' in general. In UL, for example, several arrangements are described that are counted as a ra, some of which include a pole, and some of which do not. A stake or pole was used as a boundary marker where stones would not be appropriate — at a shoreline, for instance.

sail-yard **ONorw** *GuL* Leb
boundary **OSw** *UL* Blb, *VmL* Bb
boundary line **OSw** *UL* Blb, *VmL* Bb
boundary marker **OSw** *DL* Bb, *SdmL* Bb, *UL* Blb, *VmL* Bb

Expressions:

ra ok rör (OSw)

boundary lines and markers **OSw** *UL* Jb, Blb *VmL* Bb

See also: *mærki, rör, skæl, tomptara*

Refs: KLNM s.v. *gränsläggning*; Schlyter s.v. *ra*; Tollin 1999 51–63

raförning (OSw) noun

shift of boundary markers **OSw** *SdmL* Bb

ragr (ON) adj.

womanish **OIce** *Grg* Misc 238

See also: *níð*

raiþkleþi (OGu) noun

saddlecloth **OGu** *GL* A 24c

raiþvengi (OGu) noun

riding cushion **OGu** *GL* A 24c

rakna (ON) verb

pay out **OIce** *Grg* Misc 249

ran (OSw) ran (ODan) ran (OGu) rán (ON) noun

There was a clear distinction between robbery (*ran*) and theft (*þiufi, styld* etc.). The thief operated in secret or under the cover of night, whereas the robber (*ransmaþer*) committed his depredations by daylight and often used violent methods, which were, however, regarded as less reprehensible than those of a sneak thief. In effect, *ran* sometimes took the form of a forced sale, it being not unusual for the 'robber' to leave behind a purchase price. Both material property

and immaterial rights could be robbed. *Ran* entailed compensation for the one who had suffered the robbery and the payment of a *ránbaugr* to the king.

abduction **OSw** *HL* Mb
bride kidnapping **OSw** *HL* Äb
case of rapine **ODan** *JyL* 3
force **OGu** *GL* A 21
open seizure **ODan** *SkL* 233
rapine **ODan** *ESjL* 2, 3, *JyL* 2, 3, *SkKL* 7, *SkL* 85, 106, 181, 231, *VSjL* 65, **OSw** *ÖgL* Vm
robbery **OIce** *Grg* Feþ 167, *Jó* Mah 3 Kge 19 Llb 15, 34 Kab 14 Fml 17, *Js* Lbb 15 Kab 10, *KRA* 34, **ONorw** *FrL* ArbB 23 Rgb 48 LlbA 17, *GuL* Krb, Kpb, Kvb, Llb, Arb, Mhb, Olb, **OSw** *DL* Bb, Tjdb, *HL* Mb, Rb, *SdmL* Kkb, Bb, Kmb, Mb, Rb, Till, *UL* För, Mb, Rb, *VmL* För, Kkb, Mb, *YVgL* Rlb, Tb, Utgb, *ÄVgL* Tb, Föb
seizure **OIce** *Grg* Fjl 224 Rsþ 228
violence **OSw** *YVgL* Tb, *ÄVgL* Tb

Expressions:

handraghit ran (OSw)

robbery from a man's hand **OSw** *HL* Mb *SdmL* Mb

See also: *ransbot, styld*

Refs: Helle 2001, 94; Hertzberg s.v. *rán*; KLNM s.v.v. *böter, dødsstraff, huvudsynd, krigsbytte, rannsakning, rån*

rangendi (ON) noun

injustice **OIce** *Jó* Mah 17, **ONorw** *FrL* Intr 21

rangfenginn (ON) adj.

wrongfully acquired **ONorw** *GuL* Leb

rangfluttr (ON) adj.

wrongly salvaged **OIce** *Jó* Llb 67

rangkvaddr (ON) adj.

wrongly called **OIce** *Grg* Þsþ 34, 35

ranglýstr (ON) adj.

wrongly published **OIce** *Grg* Lbþ 193

rannsóknaþáttr (ON) noun

searches section **OIce** *Grg* Rsþ 227, 230

ransak (OSw) ransak (ODan) ranzsak (OGu) rannsak (ON) ranzzak (OSw) noun

house search **OSw** *UL* Mb, *VmL* Mb
inquiry **OIce** *Jó* Mah 2
inspection **ONorw** *GuL* Mhb
investigation **OIce** *Jó* Þfb 9, **OSw** *YVgL* Add
legal investigation **OIce** *Jó* Þjb 4
right to search **ODan** *SkL* 140, **OGu** *GL* A 25
search **ODan** *SkL* 134, 140, 142, 159, **OIce** *Jó* Þjb 6, **ONorw** *FrL* Bvb 7

searching **ONorw** *GuL* Tjb

visitation **OSw** *ÖgL* Eb

ransaka (OSw) **ransake** (ODan) **ranzsaka** (OGu) **rannsaka** (ON) **ranzzakæ** (OSw) verb

conduct a house search **OSw** *UL* Mb, *VmL* Mb

examine **OIce** *Jó* Þfb 9

house search (permit a) **OGu** *GL* A 37, Add. 8 (B 55)

investigate **OGu** *GL* A 28, **ONorw** *FrL* Intr 21, **OSw** *UL* Kkb, Äb, Jb, *VmL* Kkb

make a house-search **OSw** *DL* Tjdb, *YVgL* Tb, *ÄVgL* Tb

perform visitation **OSw** *ÖgL* Vm

search **ODan** *ESjL* 3, *JyL* 2, *SkL* 134, 141, 159, **OGu** *GL* A 37, **OIce** *Grg* Rsþ 230, *Jó* Þjb 6, **OSw** *HL* Mb, *SdmL* Kkb, Jb, Mb, Tjdb, Rb

See also: *lösgiurþer*

ransakan (OSw) **ransaken** (ODan) **ranzsakan** (OGu) **rannsókn** (ON) noun

house search **OGu** *GL* A 37, **OSw** *UL* Mb, *VmL* Mb, *YVgL* Tb, *ÄVgL* Tb

house-searching **OSw** *HL* Mb

permission to search **ODan** *ESjL* 3

search **ODan** *ESjL* 3, **OIce** *Grg* Rsþ 229, 230, *Jó* Þjb 6, *Js* Þjb 5, **OSw** *HL* Mb, *SdmL* Bb, Tjdb

ransbot (OSw) noun

fine for enforcement **OSw** *UL* Rb

fine for robbery **OSw** *UL* Blb, Add. 6, *VmL* Bb

See also: *bot*, *böta*

ransdele (ODan) noun

action in a case of rapine **ODan** *JyL* 2

case of rapine **ODan** *JyL* 2

rapine **ODan** *JyL* 2

ranshævth (ODan) noun

possession by force **ODan** *SkL* 82

taking with force **ODan** *SkL* 80

ransmal (OSw) noun

rapine **OSw** *ÖgL* Kkb

ransmaþer (OSw) **ransman** (ODan) **ránsmaðr** (ON) noun

rapine man **ODan** *JyL* 2, 3

robber **OIce** *Jó* Mah 3 Þjb 3, *KRA* 11, **ONorw** *EidsL* 50.13, *GuL* Krb, Leb, **OSw** *HL* Mb, *SdmL* Kmb, Mb

ransnævning (ODan) noun

Eight householders from a district (ODan *hæreth*, see *hærap*) appointed for one year to deal with cases of rapine (ODan *ran*), accidents and theft.

men nominated for rapine cases **ODan** *JyL* 2

men of rapine cases **ODan** *JyL* 2

Refs: KLNM s.v. *nämnd*

ranssak (ODan) noun

action for rapine **ODan** *JyL* 2

case of rapine **ODan** *JyL* 2

ransvitne (ODan) noun

witness to rapine **ODan** *VSjL* 65

rantakin (OSw) **rantaken** (ODan) adj.

arrant seizure **ODan** *SkL* 142

kidnapped **OSw** *HL* Äb

raped **OSw** *HL* Äb

robbed **OSw** *YVgL* Tb, *ÄVgL* Tb

seized **ODan** *SkL* 157

taken by force **OSw** *UL* Äb, *VmL* Äb

taken by rapine **ODan** *SkL* 197

wrongfully taken **OSw** *SdmL* Äb

See also: *ran*

rassaklof (ON) noun

rectum **ONorw** *GuL* Mhb

rasshverfingr (ON) noun

horse having a protruded rectum **ONorw** *GuL* Mhb

rauðarán (ON) noun

'Red robbery'. The term is known only from Grg Rsþ 228 and is described as an extension of hand-seizure (ON *handrán*), where an item stolen out of someone's hands is then taken away. The penalty for *rauðarán* was full outlawry (ON *skóggangr*). The first element has been interpreted as an intensifier meaning 'outright, brazen, notorious'. This seems more likely than the alternative suggestion of 'petty' offered by Hoff. Saxo's colorful etymology associated the term with a pirate called Røtho.

arrant seizure **OIce** *Grg* Rsþ 228

See also: *handran*, *ran*

Refs: CV s.v. *rauðarán*; Fritzner s.v. *rauðarán*; GrgTr II:179; Hoff 2011, 223

rauferi (OGu) noun

violent robber **OGu** *GL* A 39

raukr (OGu) noun

stook **OGu** *GL* A 3

See also: *skyl*

raumdólir (pl.) (ON) noun

people from Romsdalen **ONorw** *GuL* Leb

raþ (OSw) **rath** (ODan) **raþ** (OGu) **ráð** (ON) noun

abetting **OSw** *HL* Mb

accord **OIce** *Grg* Tíg 268

advice **ODan** *ESjL* 1–3, *JyL* 1, *SkL* 48, 76, *VSjL* 80, 86, **OIce** *KRA* 2, **ONorw** *EidsL*

22.6, *FrL* Intr 1 Tfb 3 KrbA 2, *GuL* Krb,
Arb, **OSw** *DL* Gb, *HL* Äb, *UL* För, Äb

advisable (action) **OGu** *GL* A 8

agency **OGu** *GL* A 13

agreement **OSw** *UL* Jb, *VmL* Jb

approval **ONorw** *BorgL* 5.6

authority **OGu** *GL* A 21

cause of damage **OSw** *SmL*

collusion **OSw** *YVgL* Add

command **OIce** *Jó* Fml 17

conditions **ONorw** *GuL* Løb

consent **ODan** *JyL* 1–3, **OIce** *Grg* Klþ 2 Feþ
144, *Jó* Kge 1, 2 Fml 9, *Js* Mah 29 Kvg 3 Lbb 8,
ONorw *GuL* Krb, Kpb, Mhb, Løb, **OSw** *DL* Bb,
Gb, *HL* Jb, *SdmL* Kgb, Gb, Jb, Kmb, *YVgL* Kkb

council **OSw** *SdmL* Conf, Kgb, Kmb, Mb,
UL Mb, Kmb, *VmL* Mb, Kmb, *YVgL* Jb

counsel **ODan** *ESjL* 1, **ONorw** *FrL*
KrbB 17, **OSw** *UL* Kkb, *YVgL* Äb

counselling **OSw** *ÖgL* Db

deliberation **ODan** *JyL* Fort, 2

engagement **ONorw** *GuL* Kvb, Olb

intent **ODan** *JyL* 2

intrigue **ONorw** *FrL* Var 9

lot **OIce** *Jó* Kge 9

orders **ONorw** *FrL* KrbA 28

permission **OIce** *Jó* Kab 14, **ONorw**
GuL Løb, **OSw** *YVgL* Kkb

planning **ONorw** *GuL* Mhb

precedence **OSw** *HL* Blb

responsibility **OGu** *GL* A 24d,
OSw *UL* Kkb, *VmL* Kkb

social standing **OIce** *Js* Ert 16

solution **ODan** *SkL* 200

word **ODan** *ESjL* 3

plot (2)

See also: *samþykke*

raþa (OSw) **rathe** (ODan) **raþa** (OGu) **ráða** (ON) verb
Several legally significant uses exhibit considerable
overlap. Most commonly 'to take care of', with more
or less focus on control, reflected in translations such
as 'care for', 'be in charge', 'control', 'dispose over', 'be
responsible', 'manage', appearing, for instance, in the
context of guardianship over children, control over
keys, managing households and arranging marriages.
Sometimes with stronger emphasis on decision
making, as in 'decide (over)', 'determine', 'appoint',
'select', appearing, for instance, in the context of
determining dowries, bridal gifts and rents, choosing

law men or panels, and separating betrothed couples.
When the one exerting responsibility or control,
making decisions or giving advice is a leader, ranging
from God, king and bishop to local landowners, it
has sometimes been translated as 'carry authority',
'rule', 'prevail', 'have the say'. Often with ill-intent,
translated as 'conspire', 'contrive', 'instigate', 'plot',
'bring', appearing in contexts such as uprisings
against the king, hired killings of spouses or children,
assisting killings, and dealing with stolen goods. The
seemingly neutral meaning of considering, reflected
in translations such as 'advise', 'counsel', 'prepare', also
tends to appear in the context of crimes. Also, more
physically, as in 'attack', 'chasten', 'chastise', 'punish',
appearing in contexts such as unintentional killing of
spouses, and hurting somebody with weapons when
attacking them at their home.

advise **ODan** *ESjL* 2, *VSjL* 86, **OGu**
GL A 16, **OSw** *ÖgL* Eb

appoint **OSw** *UL* Kkb, *VmL* Kkb, Kgb

arrange **OIce** *Js* Kvg 1, **ONorw** *GuL* Løb

attack **ODan** *ESjL* 2

beat **OSw** *YVgL* Frb

bring **OSw** *YVgL* Tb, *ÄVgL* Tb

care for **OSw** *HL* Äb, *YVgL* Add

carry authority **OGu** *GS* Ch. 3, **OSw** *UL* Mb, Jb, Blb

chasten **OSw** *HL* Mb

chastise **OSw** *SdmL* Mb, *ÖgL* Eb

conspire **ONorw** *FrL* Mhb 35

contrive **OIce** *Grg* Misc 249

control **ONorw** *GuL* Kvb, **OSw** *ÄVgL* Äb

counsel **OSw** *ÖgL* Kkb

decide **OGu** *GL* A 14, 21, Add. 1 (B 4), **OIce**
Js Kvg 4, **ONorw** *FrL* KrbB 1, *GuL* Krb,
Kpb, Mhb, **OSw** *DL* Kkb, *HL* Kgb, Äb, Mb,
UL Kkb, Kgb, Blb, *VmL* Kkb, *YVgL* Rlb

decide over **OSw** *SdmL* Kgb, Gb,
Jb, Bb, Kmb, Tjdb, Rb, Till

determine **OIce** *Js* Kvg 1, **OSw** *UL* Äb, *VmL* Äb

direct **ONorw** *GuL* Llb

dispose over **ONorw** *GuL* Olb,
OSw *YVgL* Äb, *ÄVgL* Äb

be entitled to **ONorw** *GuL* Tfb

force **ONorw** *GuL* Løb

be forced **OSw** *VmL* Jb

govern **ONorw** *FrL* KrbA 11, *GuL* Krb

have control over **OSw** *UL* Blb,
Rb, *VmL* Bb, Rb, *YVgL* Äb

have the authority **OGu** *GL* A 28

have the say **OGu** *GL* A 47

help **OSw** *ÖgL* Eb

be in charge of **OSw** *HL* Mb

incite **OSw** *YVgL* Drb

instigate **ODan** *SkL* 112, **OIce** *Jó* Llb 30, **ONorw** *GuL* Llb, **OSw** *UL* Mb, *VmL* Mb, *ÄVgL* Md

interpret **OGu** *GS* Ch. 1

manage **OIce** *Js* Kvg 2, **ONorw** *GuL* Kvb, Arb

be one's own master **ONorw** *GuL* Kpb

plan **ONorw** *FrL* Bvb 14

plot **OIce** *Jó* Mah 24, *Js* Þjb 9, **OSw** *SdmL* Äb

prepare **OSw** *UL* Äb, *VmL* Äb

prevail **OIce** *Jó* Lbb 3, *KRA* 9

punish **ONorw** *GuL* Krb, Kvb, **OSw** *UL* Mb, *VmL* Mb

be responsible for something **OIce** *Grg* Ómb 131

be responsible for **OGu** *GL* Add. 1 (B 4), **OSw** *UL* Kkb, Äb, *VmL* Kkb, Äb, Mb

rule **OGu** *GS* Ch. 4, **OSw** *HL* Blb, *UL* Kgb, *YVgL* Kkb, Kvab

select **OSw** *UL* Jb, Kmb, Blb, Rb, *VmL* Jb, Kmb, Bb, Rb

steer **ONorw** *GuL* Mhb

supervise **OIce** *Jó* Kge 1

take care of **ODan** *VSjL* 6, **OSw** *DL* Bb

take charge of **OSw** *HL* Äb

take counsel **OGu** *GL* A 13

See also: *raþ*

raþasak (OSw) **rathesak** (ODan) noun

case of instigation **ODan** *SkL* 111, 112, 118

instigation **ODan** *SkL* 118, **OSw** *YVgL* Add

See also: *raþa*, *sak*

raþman (OSw) **raþmaþr** (OGu) **ráðsmaðr** (ON) **raþ maþer** (OSw) noun

A compound with the noun *raþ* (OGu, OSw)/*ráð* (ON), and thus referring to a man giving advice, being in charge, acting on somebody else's behalf etc. Specifically, a judge (OGu GL), one of several officials at a marketplace (OIce Jb), and a member of the king's council (OSw UL).

councillor **OSw** *UL* Mb

ealdorman **OIce** *Jó* Kge 28

magistrate **OGu** *GL* A 19, 31, 32, Add. 8 (B 55)

Refs: Cleasby and Vigfússon s.v. *ráð*; Fritzner s.v. *ráðsmaðr*; Hertzberg s.v. *ráðsmaðr*; Schlyter s.v. *raþman*

raþsbani (OSw) **raþbani** (OSw) noun

A person who assisted or instigated a killing.

instigator **OSw** *DL* Mb, *YVgL* Drb, *ÄVgL* Md

killer's advisor **OSw** *HL* Mb, *SdmL* Mb

See also: *atvistarmaþer*, *bani*, *forman*, *fylghi*, *haldbani*, *höfþingi*, *hovoþsmaþer*, *hærværk*, *raþ*, *raþa*, *raþsbænd*, *sanbani*

raþsbænd (OSw) **raþbænd** (OSw) noun

incitement to a killing **OSw** *VmL* Mb

instigation **OSw** *ÄVgL* Md

See also: *hovoþsmaþer*, *raþ*, *raþsbani*

raþstova (OSw) noun

council building **OSw** *VmL* Rb

ráðahagr (ON) noun

married state **OIce** *Grg* Feþ 151

ráðbót (ON) noun

private compensation **ONorw** *GuL* Mhb

ráðspell (ON) noun

fine paid for reduced marriage prospects **OIce** *Jó* Mah 30 Kge 5

spoiled prospects **OIce** *Js* Mah 36

ránbaugr (ON) noun

A 'robbery-ring'; a fine paid to the king for cases of *rán* ('robbery'). The amount of this fine is given as twelve *aurar* in GuL Krb 9 and half a mark in Jó Llb 62.

fine **ONorw** *FrL* Intr 23

fine for robbery **ONorw** *FrL* LlbA 11 LlbB 11

fine to the king for unlawful seizure or holding of property **ONorw** *FrL* Rgb 24, *GuL* Llb

robbery **OIce** *Jó* Llb 62

seizure fine **OIce** *Js* Lbb 15

See also: *bogher*

Refs: CV s.v. *ránbaugr*; Fritzner s.v. *ránbaugr*; Hertzberg s.v. *ránbaugr*

rás (ON) noun

pursuit **ONorw** *GuL* Mhb

running away **ONorw** *GuL* Mhb

refla (ON) verb

make enquiries **ONorw** *FrL* KrbA 22

refsa (ON) verb

punish **OIce** *Jó* Mah 7, 16, *Js* Mah 6, 34, **ONorw** *FrL* Intr 12 Var 45, *GuL* Krb

refsingarlauss (ON) adj.

unpunished **ONorw** *FrL* Intr 12

regluhald (ON) noun

discipline **OIce** *KRA* 16

reiða (ON) noun

contribution **ONorw** *GuL* Leb

dues **ONorw** *GuL* Krb

fee **ONorw** *FrL* KrbA 44

income **OIce** *Js* Þfb 2, **ONorw** *FrL* KrbA 14 Mhb 8

necessary item **OIce** *Grg* Þsþ

payment **ONorw** *EidsL* 32.8

reiðask (ON) verb

be offended **OIce** *Grg* Misc 237, 238

reiðaspell (ON) noun

damage to a ship's rigging **OIce** *Jó* Fml 16

reiðskjótaboð (ON) noun

request for riding horses **ONorw** *FrL* Intr 19

reiðskjótaskifti (ON) noun

meeting about providing horses **ONorw** *FrL* KrbA 44

reiðskjóti (ON) noun

The householders had a duty to provide saddle horses for the bishop and his men when he was coming to consecrate a church or provide other services to people. See, e.g., GuL ch. 33.

riding horse **OIce** *Grg* Klþ 5, *KRA* 3, **ONorw** *FrL* Intr 19

saddle horse **ONorw** *FrL* KrbA 44, *GuL* Krb

Refs: KLNM s.v. *skjutsväsen*

reifa (ON) verb

sum up **OIce** *Grg* Þsþ 40, 41

reifing (ON) noun

summing up **OIce** *Grg* Þsþ 40, 58

reifingarmaðr (ON) noun

man to sum up a case **OIce** *Grg* Þsþ 40

reisa (ON) verb

raise **ONorw** *GuL* Leb

rouse **ONorw** *GuL* Llb

set up **ONorw** *GuL* Mhb

reizla (ON) noun

weighing **OIce** *Grg* Rsþ 232

rek (ON) noun

things drifting ashore **ONorw** *GuL* Tfb

rekabölkr (ON) rekabálkr (ON) noun

section on drift rights **OIce** *Jó* Llb 60

rekafjara (ON) noun

drift-shore **OIce** *Grg* Lbþ 210, *Jó* Llb 61

rekahvalr (ON) rekhvalr (ON) noun

drift whale **OIce** *Grg* Lbþ 215, *Jó* Llb 66, 70, *KRA* 26

rekald (ON) noun

wreckage **OIce** *Grg* Arþ 126

rekamaðr (ON) noun

owner of drift rights **OIce** *Jó* Llb 61

rekamark (ON) noun

'Drift boundary'. Iceland is surrounded by ocean currents (Gulf stream, Polar stream) so the rights to gather driftwood and other things washed ashore was important and strictly regulated in the laws. The landowners had parts in the shore and had the right to collect anything that drifted ashore on his part of the shore and off of the coast out to an imaginative 'boundary' (*rekamark*) in the sea. He also had the right to all catch, with certain limitations, within another restricted area with a defined boundary (*netlag*).

drift boundary **OIce** *Jó* Llb 60, 61

See also: *reki*

Refs: CV s.v. *reki*; KLNM s.v. reki

rekaströnd (ON) noun

A 'wreck-strand'. A stretch of beach onto which something has drifted, usually a whale or flotsam and jetsam. Such beaches were considered to be significant amenities in medieval Iceland.

drift-strand **OIce** *Grg* Klþ 8, *Js* Mah 30

See also: *hvalreki*, *reki*, *vrak*

Refs: CV s.v. *reki*; F; NGL V s.v. *rekaströnd*

rekatré (ON) noun

driftwood **OIce** *Grg* Klþ 8, *Jó* Llb 6, *Js* Lbb 13

rekavarðveizla (ON) noun

taking care of drift **OIce** *Jó* Llb 62

rekendr (OGu) noun

chain **OGu** *GL* A 36

reki (ON) noun

Goods or items washed ashore. Also drift rights; ownership rights concerning flotsam, jetsam and other material floating offshore or washed ashore. Rights to drift generally belonged to the owner of the coastal land (cf. Grg Lbþ 209), though anything still at sea beyond a certain range (cf. ON *gildingr*) could be salvaged by anyone. Drift rights attached to land could be separately transferred to someone else by sale or gift. In some sagas *reki* appears in the phrase *gera ... reka* and refers to the pursuit of vengeance in killing cases.

drift rights **OIce** *Grg* Lbþ 174, 209, *Jó* Kge 14 Lbb 4, 6 Llb 28, 61, *Js* Lbb 2

drift-shore **OIce** *Jó* Llb 61 Fml 26

driftage **OIce** *Jó* Llb 26

driftwood **OIce** *Grg* Lbþ 172

item drifted ashore **OIce** *Grg* Arþ 122

See also: *gildingr*, *hvalreki*, *vágrek*, *veiðr*, *vrak*

Refs: CV; Fritzner; GAO s.v. *Rache*; Hertzberg s.v. *rek*, *reki*; KLNM s.v. *berging*, *reki*; ONP

rekstr (ON) noun

cattle-track **ONorw** *GuL* Llb

path used by animals **OIce** *Jó* Llb 44

reksþegn (ON) noun

A social class appearing solely in Norwegian wergild lists between the rank of freeborn man (ON *árborinn maðr*) and son of a freedman (ON *leysingjasonr*). Etymologies of the term are uncertain, but there have been suggestions connecting it to *rek* ('wreck, jetsam'), *reka* ('to drive' [e.g. cattle]) and *rekkr* ('warrior'). Since the wergild value of a *reksþegn* is given as half of a freeholder (ON *höldr*) in FrL, it has been suggested that it is the Trøndelag equivalent of a householder (ON *bóndi*, see *bonde*) elsewhere in Norway (e.g. GuL). It has also been put forth that *reksþegn* may refer to a class of hunters such as the Sámi who were more prevalent in the Trøndelag area than elsewhere (cf. KLNM).

{*reksþegn*} **ONorw** *FrL* Mhb 49 Rgb 35 LlbA 15

See also: *bonde, búþegn, þægn*

Refs: CV s.v. *rekkr*; F; Hertzberg 1890; KLNM s.v. *rekstegn*; LexMA s.v. *Bauer, Bauerntum*; Maurer 1890

rengja (ON) verb

reject **OIce** *Grg* Þsþ 25, 57

rennistaurr (ON) noun

pole **ONorw** *GuL* Kpb

rep (ODan) **reip** (ON) noun

measuring with rope **ODan** *ESjL* 2

rope **ODan** *JyL* 1, **ONorw** *GuL* Leb

roping **ODan** *ESjL* 2, *JyL* 1, 3, *SkKL* 3, *SkL* 56, 67, 73, 75, 76, *VSjL* 71, 78–80

See also: *fæst, mælistang, snóri, stangfall, vaþstang*

repa (OSw) **repe** (ODan) verb

To divide communal village land between landowners using a rope as measurement.

measure and divide land with ropes **OSw** *YVgL* Jb, *ÄVgL* Jb

rope **ODan** *ESjL* 2, *JyL* 1, 3, *SkKL* 3, *SkL* 67, 71, 73–76, *VSjL* 71, 78–80

Refs: KLNM s.v. *rebning*; Tamm and Vogt, eds, 2016, 307, 312

repdrøgh (ODan) adj.

roped **ODan** *JyL* 3, *SkKL* 3

See also: *rep*

rethsle (ODan) noun

due **ODan** *JyL* 3

reykmælir (ON) noun

measure of malt **ONorw** *FrL* Reb 1

reykr (ON) noun

smoke **ONorw** *GuL* Krb

reyna (ON) verb

confirm **OIce** *Grg* Misc 251

make a complaint **OIce** *Jó* Llb 5

test **OIce** *Grg* Lbþ 176, *Js* Þjb 3

reþa (OSw) **rethe** (ODan) **reiða** (ON) **ræþa** (OSw) verb

Literally 'to make ready'.

give **ODan** *SkL* 226

inquire **OSw** *SmL*

make even **ODan** *ESjL* 3

pay **ODan** *ESjL* 3, *SkL* 226, 239–241, *VSjL* 79, **ONorw** *GuL* Krb, Kpb, Mhb, Olb, Leb

pay out **OIce** *Grg* Feþ 166 Fjl 221, *Js* Þfb 2 Kvg 4 Kab 4

prepare **ODan** *SkL* 226

Refs: Hellquist s.v. *reda*; Fritzner s.v. *reiða*; OED s.v. *ready*; SAOB s.v. *reda* v1

reþe (OSw) **raiþi** (OGu) **reiði** (ON) noun

The word *reþe* on its own has the meanings 'driving equipment', 'tackle', 'tools', but in conjunction with the word *roþ* it takes on the meaning 'provisions'. In VmL this expression refers to the statutory duties of a free man. In this case, they are mentioned in a rather puzzling passage in connection with a homebred slave who, on his death, leaves property and possessions in the form of a house and its contents. It seems that his kin could maintain that he was, in fact, free and lay claim to those possessions rather than letting them revert to his master. In UL the phrase, *reþe ok roþ*, refers to the actual personnel and provisions for the levy.

driving equipment **OGu** *GL* A 26

provisions **OSw** *UL* Kgb

tackle **ONorw** *GuL* Leb

tools **OSw** *UL* Blb

Expressions:

reþe ok roþ (OSw)

oarsmen and provisions **OSw** *UL* Kgb

statutory levy duties **OSw** *VmL* Mb

See also: *leþunger, roþarætter*

Refs: Fritzner s.v. *reiða*; KLNM s.v. *roder*; ONP s.v. *reiða*; Schlyter 1877, s.v.v. *reþe, roþer*; SL UL, 55–56 note 30, 60–61 note 51; SL VmL, 99–100 notes 145–147

reþohion (OSw) noun

supporters of the bride **OSw** *UL* Äb

See also: *bruþmaþer, hion*

reþosven (OSw) **rethesven** (ODan) noun

A man who managed the property of another without co-ownership.

bailiff **OSw** *YVgL* Tb

farm-hand **ODan** *JyL* 2

Refs: Myrdal and Tollin 2003, 139; Nevéus 1974, 31

reþskaper (OSw) **raiþskepr** (OGu) **reþskepr** (OGu) **rezcaper** (OSw) **ræþskaper** (OSw) noun

Holy Communion **OSw** *ÖgL* Kkb

last rites **OSw** *UL* Kkb, *VmL* Kkb

sacrament **OSw** *UL* Kkb, *VmL* Kkb

support **OGu** *GS* Ch. 3, **OSw** *UL* Kmb, *VmL* Kmb

See also: *guþslikami*

reþuman (OSw) noun

Man with responsibility for organizing the wedding feast.

organizer **OSw** *DL* Gb

See also: *drozsieti, gerþamaþr*

rétt (ON) noun

An enclosure, particularly one for rounding up and separating livestock. Also this gathering of animals.

common fold **OFar** *Seyð* 5, **OIce** *Grg* Klþ 8 Fjl 225, *KRA* 26

gathering of sheep to folds **OIce** *Jó* Llb 49

See also: *samrétt*

Refs: Cleasby and Vigfusson s.v. *rétt*; Fritzner s.v. *rétt*; Hertzberg s.v. *rétt*; ONP s.v. *rétt*

rétta (ON) verb

frame **OIce** *Grg* Þsþ 36, 59 Lrþ 117 Misc 252

réttafarssök (ON) noun

case which requires personal compensation **OIce** *Grg* Þsþ 77 Vís 94, 95 Feþ 158

See also: *réttarsök*

réttarbót (ON) noun

A legal amendment, such as those issued by the king of Norway. Often these were used to grant privileges or dispensations, but any type of change to an earlier law could be given in a *réttarbót*. One such example is Seyðabræviðð, which grants special dispensation to Faroe Islanders in household and farming matters. These amendments were subject to approval of the assembly/-ies in which they were to take force. From the second half of the twelfth century, *réttarbætr* were increasingly used to issue new laws (ON *nýmælir*). Legislation of a similar nature was also passed under the names *bréf* ('letter') or *skipan* ('ordinance') during the thirteenth and fourteenth centuries. Both terms, along with *réttarbót*, could refer to royal ordinances or proclamations.

In several law codes (e.g. FrL and Jó) such amendments were transmitted in their own section as a kind of appendix to the law.

amendment **OIce** *Jó* MagBref, *Js* Mah 29, **ONorw** *FrL* Intr 22 KrbB 17 Reb 1, *GuL* Reb

See also: *bot, bref, nýmæli, skipan*

Refs: CV s.v. *réttarbót*; Fritzner s.v. *réttarbót*; Hertzberg s.v. *réttarbót*; KLNM s.v. *retterbot*; LexMA s.v. *Réttarbót*; *Seyð.* ed., 5

réttarfar (ON) **réttafar** (ON) noun

Compensation; the right to compensation for insults and other personal offenses. Thought to be identical to two other terms connoting personal compensation: *fullrétti* (q.v.) and *réttr* (see *rætter*).

compensation **OIce** *Grg* Vís 95 Arþ 122 Ómb 143 Feþ 158, *Jó* Mah 24 Kge 14, 27, **ONorw** *FrL* Kvb 11

compensation claim **OIce** *Js* Mah 24

personal compensation/right to personal compensation **ONorw** *GuL* Mhb

personal rights **ONorw** *FrL* Rgb 37

right to compensation **ONorw** *FrL* Rgb 34

See also: *bot, manbot, manhælghi, rætter*

Refs: CV s.v. *réttarfar*; Fritzner s.v. *réttafar, réttarfar*; Hertzberg s.v. *réttarfar*; KLNM s.v. *fullrétti, straff*; Lúðvík Ingvarsson 1970, 249; Vídalín 1854 s.v. *réttarfar*

réttarmál (ON) noun

right **ONorw** *FrL* Kvb 11

réttarstaðr (ON) noun

case **ONorw** *FrL* Mah 38

réttarsök (ON) noun

case involving personal compensation **OIce** *Grg* Þsþ 62

See also: *réttafarssök*

réttborinn (ON) adj.

correctly brought **OIce** *Grg* Þsþ 58

réttbundinn (ON) adj.

rightfully bound **ONorw** *GuL* Tjb

See also: *misbundinn*

réttendavald (ON) noun

right to enforce the law **OIce** *Jó* Mah 21

réttendi (ON) **réttindi** (ON) noun

justice **OIce** *Jó* Mah 2

legal competance **ONorw** *BorgL* 18.4

rights **OIce** *Jó* Þfb 9 HT 2, *Js* Þfb Mah 37

réttfluttr (ON) adj.

lawfully floated **OIce** *Jó* Llb 66

rétting (ON) noun

framing the wording (of testimony) **OIce** *Grg* Þsþ 32

réttkosinn (ON) adj.

correctly chosen **ONorw** *EidsL* 31.1

réttligr (ON) adj.

fitting **OIce** *KRA* 7

réttmæla (ON) verb

speak correctly **ONorw** *EidsL* 2.2

réttnæmr (ON) adj.

come of age **OIce** *Jó* Kge 14

eligible to take one's rights **OIce** *Js* Mah 27

entitled to demand compensation **OIce** *Jó* Mah 29

having personal rights **ONorw** *FrL* Mhb 7 LlbB 12

having reached full age **ONorw** *GuL* Arb

ri (OGu) noun

beam **OGu** *GL* A 19

riddarakona (ON) noun

wife of a knight **OIce** *Jó* Kab 24

riddari (OSw) **riddari** (ON) noun

In legal texts a *riddari* most often refers to a title or rank equivalent to the Latin *miles* or *eques*. It can refer both to a soldier and to someone holding a title of knight, though the feudal system, including the conferral of knighthoods, was much less pronounced in the medieval Nordic countries than elsewhere in Europe.

In Norway the term comes into use during the latter part of the twelfth century. Certain high-ranking positions such as squire (ON *skutilsveinn*) conferred the title of *riddari*. In Sweden the title of *riddari* may have eventually replaced the more general class of *hærrar* ('lords'), though both terms appear together at least as late as SdmL.

knight **OIce** *Jó* Llb 18, **OSw** *HL* Mb, *SdmL* Conf, Kmb, Till

See also: *hærra, lænder, skutilsveinn*

Refs: CV s.v. *riddari*; Fritzner s.v. *riddari*; Hertzberg s.v. *riddari*; KLNM s.v. *frälse, riddare*; ONP s.v. *riddari*

rifhrís (ON) noun

brush woodland **OIce** *Jó* Llb 24, 32

brushwood **OIce** *Jó* Llb 24

scrubland **OIce** *Grg* Lbþ 181

See also: *höggskógr*

rifta (ON) verb

cancel **OIce** *Grg* Arþ 127 Feþ 152, *Js* Lbb 2, 4

void **OIce** *Jó* Lbb 6

riki (OSw) **rike** (ODan) **riki** (OGu) **ríki** (ON) noun

Realm; domain; kingdom. Dominion or authority over such a region.

country **ODan** *ESjL* 2, 3

kingdom **OGu** *GS* Ch. 4, **ONorw** *FrL* Intr 20, **OSw** *DL* Eb, *UL* Mb

power **ONorw** *GuL* Krb

realm **ODan** *ESjL* 1, 3, *JyL* Fort, *VSjL* 19, **OIce** *Js* Mah 37, **OSw** *HL* Kgb, Mb, *SdmL* Kgb, Kmb, Mb, Tjdb, Till, *UL* Kgb, Mb, *VmL* Kgb, Mb, *YVgL* Add, *ÖgL* Eb

See also: *lagh, land, veldi*

Refs: CV s.v. *ríki*; Fritzner s.v. *ríki*; GAO s.v. *Reich*; Hertzberg s.v. *ríki*; LexMA s. v. Island > III. Der isl. Freistaat. Gerichtswesen, Verfassung, Kirchenorganisation > 3. Ausbildung von Territorialherrschaft; MSE s.v. *Iceland*; ONP s.v. *ríki*; von See 1964, 188; Wærdahl 2011, 55

rimnin (OGu) adj.

cracked **OGu** *GL* A 19

rinda (OSw) **rinda** (OGu) **hrinda** (ON) **rundit** (OSw) verb

deny **OSw** *ÄVgL* Tb

drive **ONorw** *GuL* Krb

exonerate oneself **OSw** *YVgL* Tb, *ÄVgL* Tb

nullify **ONorw** *GuL* Leb

oust **ONorw** *GuL* Krb

push **OGu** *GL* A 8, **ONorw** *GuL* Mhb

rindr (OGu) noun

pushing **OGu** *GL* A 19

ringer (OSw) noun

enclosure **OSw** *VmL* Mb

ringrör (OSw) noun

boundary marker ring **OSw** *SdmL* Bb

rinnare (OSw) noun

trotter **OSw** *VmL* Bb

risgarþer (OSw) noun

fence made by wood **OSw** *ÄVgL* Föb

fence of brush wood **OSw** *YVgL* Utgb

See also: *garþer*

rishofþe (OSw) noun

A derogatory term for a child conceived during outlawry, possibly alluding to a secret conception in the forest on a scrub heap. Such children were excluded from any inheritance. Appears to be a direct correspondence to ON *hrísungr* 'scrubling'.

brush-born **OSw** *UL* Äb, *VmL* Äb

scrub-child **OSw** *HL* Äb, *SdmL* Äb

Refs: Brink forthcoming; Ney 1998, 106–08, 115; Schlyter s.v. *rishofþe*

rit (ON) noun

Something written. As with modern English *writ*, ON *rit* can refer to an official letter or document, such as *rit biskups* (FrL KrbB 24) or *rit ok innsigli konungs* (Jb Mah 2).

document **ONorw** *FrL* KrbB 24

writ **OIce** *Jó* Mah 2, **ONorw** *FrL* Mhb 4 Bvb 1

See also: *bref*, *innsigli*, *máldagi*

Refs: CV; F; Hertzberg; KLNM s.v. *brev*; OED s.v. *writ*

ríkismaðr (ON) noun

man in authority **OIce** *Grg* Ómb 139

rof (ON) noun

breaking **ONorw** *FrL* KrbB 22

rofna (ON) verb

revoke **OIce** *Grg* Þsþ 53, 58 Arþ 127 Ómb 135 Feþ 150, *Js* Lbb 4

rofnaaker (OSw) rofu akr (OGu) noun

turnip field **OGu** *GL* A 48, **OSw** *UL* Rb

See also: *rova*

rofnaværk (OSw) noun

turnip clearing **OSw** *SdmL* Bb

rompnasviþiur (pl.) (OSw) noun

burn-beaten land for growing turnips **OSw** *DL* Bb

rotna (ON) verb

decay **ONorw** *GuL* Krb

rova (OSw) rown (OSw) noun

turnip **OSw** *UL* Kkb, Mb, Blb, *VmL* Kkb (D and E texts), Mb, Bb

See also: *rofnaaker*

royna (OGu) verb

test **OGu** *GL* A 33, 37, Add. 7 (B 49)

try **OGu** *GL* A 34

roþaretter (OSw) noun

This has two distinct meanings. Firstly, it refers to the law in force during the levy, or maritime law in general; secondly to the law of the Roden (that coastal part of Uppland not included in the *hundari* (q.v.) of *Tiundaland* and *Attundaland*) as opposed to the law of the whole province or of the nation.

The law in force at sea or during the levy was more stringent than that on land. During the levy, many crimes were punished as if they broke the King's Peace, even if similar crimes on land were not (UL

Kgb). While men were taking part in the levy, any crime against them or amongst them was seen as a crime against the king himself.

The local law applicable to the Roden differed in respect of the sequence of events applicable to the referral of cases for appeal (UL Rb).

There are suggestions (by Hjärne and others) that the meanings of *roþer* should not be linked and that two different words are involved.

law of Roden **OSw** *UL* För, Rb (table of contents only)

law of the {roþer} **OSw** *UL* För, Kgb, *VmL* För

sea regulation **OSw** *SdmL* Kgb

See also: *leþunger*, *reþe*, *skiplagh*

Refs: Hjärne 1947; KLNM s.v.v. *konge*, *leidang*, *roden*; Schlyter 1877, s.v. *roþaretter*; SL UL, 60–61 note 51

ró (ON) noun

rove **ONorw** *GuL* Leb

rófa (ON) noun

tail bone **ONorw** *GuL* Llb

róg (ON) noun

slander **OIce** *Jó* Mah 25, **ONorw** *GuL* Tfb

See also: *fjölmæli*

rógsmaðr (ON) noun

slanderer **OIce** *Jó* Mah 25, *Js* Mah 26

rómaskattr (ON) noun

Rome tax **OIce** *KRA* 13, 31

rótfastr (ON) adj.

rooted **ONorw** *GuL* Llb, Mhb

rugher (OSw) rug (OGu) rygr (OGu) noun

rye **OGu** *GL* A 20, 56a, **OSw** *UL* Kkb, *VmL* Kkb

runfempni (OGu) noun

ability to run **OGu** *GL* B 19

runþiuver (OSw) noun

absconding thief **OSw** *UL* Mb, *VmL* Mb

fugitive thief **OSw** *HL* Mb, *SdmL* Tjdb

rus (OGu) hross (ON) noun

draught horse **OGu** *GL* A 6, 26, 65, Add. 2 (B 17)

horse **OGu** *GL* A 45a, **ONorw** *GuL* Krb, Kpb, Llb

See also: *hófr*, *hrossakjöt*, *hæster*, *skiut*

ruþa (OSw) rjóðr (ON) noun

clearing **OIce** *Grg* Lbþ 199, *Jó* Llb 20, **OSw** *SdmL* Bb, *UL* Blb

cultivated land **OSw** *DL* Bb

cultivation **OSw** *UL* Blb, *VmL* Bb

See also: *hæfþ*, *ryþsl*

rúmheilagr (ON) adj.

Expressions:

rúmheilagr dagr (ON)

ordinary day OIce *Grg* Klþ 8 Þsþ 44 Feþ 144,
149 Lbþ 176, 198 Fjl 221 Hrs 234 KRA 24

weekday ONorw *FrL* LlbA 1

work day OIce *Jó* Llb 52 ONorw *FrL* LlbB 7

ryfte (ODan) verb

admit ODan *SkL* 161

rygir (pl.) (ON) noun

people from Rogaland ONorw *GuL* Leb

rykta (OGu) verb

enforce OGu *GL* A 48

prosecute OGu *GL* A 21

rypta (OGu) verb

invalidate an agreement OGu *GL* A 28

rysking (ON) noun

shaking OIce *Grg* Vís 87, *Jó* Mah 22

rystr (OGu) noun

shaking OGu *GL* A 19

ryva (OSw) **rifa** (OGu) **rjúfa** (ON) **rýfa** (ON) verb

break OIce *Jó* Fml 14, *Js* Ert 17, **ONorw**
EidsL 22.7, *FrL* KrbA 46 Mhb 4 Var 46

cancel OIce *Jó* Kab 24

disregard OIce *Jó* Þfb 5, 8 Kge 29 Lbb 3 Þjb 24

dissolve OSw *UL* Jb, *VmL* Jb

invalidate OIce *Jó* Kge 1, 3

nullify OIce *Js* Kvg 2, 3 Lbb 17 Kab 15, 18

pull down OGu *GL* A 63

re-distribute OSw *UL* Blb, *VmL* Bb

set aside ONorw *GuL* Olb

tear up OGu *GL* A 26, 63

violate OIce *Js* Þfb 3, 5 Mah 29, *KRA* 9

withdraw ONorw *FrL* ArbB 4

See also: *lösa, skilia*

ryve (ODan) verb

admit ODan *SkL* 148

ryþia (OSw) **ryðja** (ON) verb

annul ONorw *FrL* Rgb 15

challenge OIce *Grg* Þsþ 22, 24 Vís 89 [and
elsewhere possibly] Feþ 156 Lbþ 176, 202 Fjl 223
Hrs 234, *Js* Mah 20, *KRA* 29, **ONorw** *FrL* KrbB 20

clear OSw *SdmL* Bb, *UL* Blb, *VmL* Bb

See also: *frýja*

ryþning (OSw) **rudning** (OSw) noun

clearing OSw *DL* Bb, *SdmL* Bb

ryþsl (OSw) **ruzl** (OSw) **ryzl** (OSw) noun

burn-beaten land OSw *HL* Blb

clearing OSw *SdmL* Bb, *UL* Blb, *VmL* Bb

rýgjartó (ON) noun

linen tax ONorw *FrL* Reb 2

ræðismaðr (ON) noun

advisor ONorw *GuL* Mhb

ræfsing (OSw) **refsing** (ON) noun

punishment OFar *Seyð* 12, OIce *Jó* Mah 7, 14
Kge 1 Kab 7 Þjb 1, 2, *Js* Mah 31 Þjb 1, *KRA* 7,
ONorw *FrL* Var 43, OSw *YVgL* Add, *ÄVgL* Urb

See also: *ræfst, vite*

ræfsingaþing (OSw) noun

A *þing* 'assembly' held twice a year, where decisions
concerning criminal cases were made in the name
of the king. Originally, presumably referring to the
punishment (OSw *ræfsing*) to be implemented.

investigative assembly OSw *YVgL* Föb, Add

See also: *þing*

Refs: Schlyter s.v. *ræfsinga þing*

ræfst (OSw) noun

sentence OSw *YVgL* Urb

See also: *ræfsing*

rækkia (OSw) **rekkia** (OGu) verb

extend OSw *UL* Blb, *VmL* Bb

stretch OGu *GL* A 36

rækning (OSw) **rekning** (OGu) noun

drawing up of accounts OGu *GL*
A 28, OSw *UL* Äb, *VmL* Äb

ræna (OSw) **ræne** (ODan) **ræna** (ON) **rænna** (OSw)
verb

abduct OSw *HL* Mb

attack ONorw *GuL* Mhb

block ONorw *GuL* Llb

capture from another OSw *YVgL* Tb

commit rapine ODan *JyL* 2, *VSjL* 65

demand payment OSw *HL* Rb

deprive OSw *DL* Bb, Tjdb, *UL*
Äb, Mb, Add. 9, *VmL* Mb

plunder OIce *Js* Mah 6

do rapine ODan *JyL* 2

rob OIce *Jó* Mah 2, 3 Þjb 3, *KRA* 7, 9, **ONorw**
FrL Intr 23 Leb 25, *GuL* Krb, Tfb, Mhb, Leb,
OSw *DL* Tjdb, *HL* Mb, *SdmL* Kgb, Gb, Bb, Mb,
UL Kgb, Mb, Blb, *VmL* Mb, Bb, *YVgL* Urb, Äb,
Rlb, Tb, Utgb, Add, *ÄVgL* Md, Rlb, Tb, *ÖgL* Vm

steal OSw *UL* Kgb, Äb, *VmL* Äb, Mb

take (away) by rapine ODan *ESjL* 2,
3, *JyL* 2, *SkL* 192, OSw *ÖgL* Db

take something away from somebody **ONorw** *GuL* Leb

wrest away **OIce** *Grg* Vís 86, *Jó* Llb 44

See also: *ran, rantakin, stiæla*

ræt (OSw) **ræt** (ODan) **rétt** (ON) adv.

correctly **ONorw** *GuL* Mhb, Tfb, Olb

in the right place **ONorw** *GuL* Llb

rightly **ODan** *SkL* 27, **OSw** *DL* Rb

with reason **ONorw** *GuL* Leb

Expressions:

ræt göra (OSw)

do right **OSw** *UL* Kkb, Kgb, Mb, Kmb, Rb *VmL* Kkb, Äb, Jb, Kmb, Rb

rætlika (OSw) **rætlike** (ODan) **réttliga** (ON) adv.

according to the law **OSw** *UL* Kmb, *VmL* Kmb

by rights **OSw** *UL* Kgb, *VmL* Bb

correctly **OSw** *SdmL* Conf, Bb, Kmb, Rb

duly **OSw** *UL* Kkb, Blb, *VmL* Bb

lawfully **OIce** *Jó* Þjb 4, **OSw** *DL* Kkb, *HL* Rb, *UL* StfBM, Blb, *ÖgL* Eb

legally **OSw** *YVgL* Kkb, Add

legally stipulated **OSw** *HL* Rb

properly **ONorw** *GuL* Krb

rightfully **ODan** *ESjL* 1–3, *JyL* 1, *VSjL* 30, **OIce** *KRA* 10, **OSw** *SdmL* Gb

See also: *laghlika*

rætlosubolker (OSw) **rætlösubolker** (OSw) noun

book about lawlessness **OSw** *YVgL* Rlb, *ÄVgL* Rlb

rætlösa (OSw) **rætløse** (ODan) noun

incompliance with the law **ODan** *ESjL* 2, 3, *SkL* 19, 73, *VSjL* 66, 78

lawlessness **OSw** *YVgL* Föb

outside the law **OSw** *YVgL* Föb, Utgb, *ÄVgL* Fös, Föb

rætløs (ODan) **réttarlauss** (ON) **réttlauss** (ON) adj.

having no personal rights **ONorw** *FrL* Mhb 7 Bvb 6

lawless **ODan** *JyL* 2

without justice **ODan** *JyL* 2

without right to personal compensation **OIce** *Grg* Arþ 118, *Jó* Mah 29, *Js* Mah 14, **ONorw** *FrL* Leb 13 LlbA 25

rætmæli (OSw) noun

legal right **OSw** *YVgL* Rlb, *ÄVgL* Rlb

rætskyldigh (ODan) adj.

legal **ODan** *ESjL* 3

rætta (OSw) **rætte** (ODan) **retta** (OGu) **ræta** (OSw) verb

answer for **ODan** *JyL* 2

correct **ODan** *JyL* Fort, **OSw** *UL* StfBM

direct **OSw** *SdmL* Kmb

judge **OGu** *GL* A 31, *GS* Ch. 3

do justice **ODan** *JyL* Fort

let **OSw** *UL* Kkb, *VmL* Kkb

make amends **OSw** *ÖgL* Kkb

pay **ODan** *JyL* 2

raise **OSw** *UL* Mb

rectify **OSw** *SdmL* Conf

settle **ODan** *VSjL* 5

show someone to lodgings **OSw** *UL* Kmb, *VmL* Kmb

Expressions:

rætta ivir (OSw) **rætte yver** (ODan)

execute **ODan** *JyL* 3 **OSw** *SmL*

judge **ODan** *ESjL* 2

rætta sik, ræta sik (OSw)

clear oneself by oath **OSw** *SmL*

comply **OSw** *UL* Kkb *VmL* Kkb

do right **OSw** *SmL*

rættari (OSw) **rættere** (ODan) **réttari** (ON) noun

This was, in the Swedish laws SdmL, UL and VmL, the person in charge of providing lodgings in a town or village for travellers, particularly officials or others being billeted. He either had to provide lodgings himself, or direct travellers to a suitable host. Travellers in turn had to pay for what they received and not force themselves on people. Fines were extracted from those unwilling to provide hospitality and from the *rættari* if he did not himself then do so. There were stipulations concerning to whom a traveller might be directed and what had to be provided for him at cost. He in turn could be punished for abusing his position as houseguest. This meaning appears to have been the original one (von See). Although the translation 'bailiff' has been used by the translator of YVgL, it is clear from the context and from Schlyter's glossary that a facilitator of hospitality was intended in this case too.

In the Danish law, JyL, it seems that the *rættere* was an official carrying out judgements. This meaning is considered by von See to be a borrowing from MLG, rather than a development of the meaning of the OSw word. It is, however, possible that, as inns and lodging houses became more common, the person with the function of a *rættare* took over duties more associated with law enforcement. Even later in the middle ages, after the period of the provincial laws, the word referred to a functionary on a large estate or over several estates, who collected the rent and passed it to the stewards of the landowners.

In the Icelandic and Faroese laws, it is clear that this person is a justice or justiciary of some sort, which more closely equates with the meaning in JyL. The term also appears in later Norwegian legal texts that have not been excerpted. Here the person is defined as a 'court enforcer', a representative of the government (Hertzberg) or an 'appeal court judge' (Sunde).

bailiff **OSw** *YVgL* Add

justice **OIce** *Jó* Mah 1, 2 Kab 13 Þjb 7 Fml 25

justiciary **OFar** *Seyð* 12

official **ODan** *JyL* 2

provider of lodgings **OSw** *SdmL* Kmb, *UL* Kmb, *VmL* Kmb

See also: *bryti, gælkare, husabyman, længsmaþer, reþosven*

Refs: Hertzberg s.v. *réttari*; KLNM, s.v.v. *gästgiveri, gästning, rättare* (2); ODS s.v. retter; ONP s.v. *réttari*; SAOB s.v.v. *rättare* (2) and (3); Schlyter 1877, s.v. *rættari*; von See 1964, 44, 45; SL UL, 158 note 19; SL VmL, 128 note 47; SL YVgL, 397 note 1 to Add 6; Sunde 2014, 149–50

rætter (OSw) **ræt** (ODan) **retr** (OGu) **réttr** (ON) **ræt** (ODan) **retr** (OGu) **réttr** (ON) noun

This word has several different but associated meanings: 1) that which is considered proper, correct, or consonant with justice, 2) law, 3) the right to do something, 4) the privilege to do something, 5) punishment that a person deserves, 6) validity, 7) law-court.

belongings **OSw** *DL* Rb

compensation **ONorw** *FrL* Intr 23 KrbA 10

damages **OIce** *Jó* Mah 5

due **ODan** *ESjL* 2, *SkL* 156, *VSjL* 84, **OSw** *SdmL* Kkb, Mb, Tjdb

duty **ODan** *ESjL* 2, 3

free man's legal status **OIce** *Jó* Mah 2

justice **ODan** *ESjL* 2, 3, *JyL* Fort, 2, *VSjL* 78, 84, **OSw** *SdmL* För, Bb, *ÖgL* Kkb, Db, Vm

law **ODan** *ESjL* 1–3, *JyL* 1, *SkKL* Prol, 6, 12, *SkL* 22, 23, 25, 30, **OGu** *GL* A 38, 60, *GS* Ch. 4, **ONorw** *BorgL* 2.3, *FrL* KrbA 11, *GuL* Krb, **OSw** *HL* Äb, Rb, *UL* StfBM,, För, Kgb, Äb, *VmL* Äb, Mb, *YVgL* Rlb, Tb, *ÄVgL* Tb

legal rights **OIce** *Grg* Misc 247, 248

lot **OSw** *YVgL* Föb

part **OSw** *DL* Tjdb

personal compensation/right to personal compensation **OIce** *Grg* Þsþ 49, 56 Bat 113, 114 Feþ 144, 145 Misc 247, *Jó* Þfb 5 Sg 3 Kge 5 Llb 30 Kab 11 Þjb 8, 10, 16, *Js* Þfb 4 Mah 11, 16 Kvg 2, *KRA* 8, **ONorw** *FrL* KrbA 1

personal rights **ONorw** *GuL* Kvb, Løb, Arb, Tfb, Mhb

protection from the law **ONorw** *FrL* LlbB 13

punishment **OSw** *HL* Mb, *UL* Mb, Kmb, *VmL* Mb

regulation **OSw** *SdmL* Conf, För, Kmb, Till

right **ODan** *ESjL* 1–3, *JyL* 1, 2, *SkL* 14, 82, 83, 139, 140, *VSjL* 10, 62, 76, 87, **OGu** *GL* Add. 1 (B 4), **OIce** *Grg* Vís 111 Lbþ 220, *Jó* Þjb 8, *Js* Þjb 6, *KRA* 2, **ONorw** *FrL* Intr 23 KrbA 1 Mhb 18 ArbA 19 LlbB 12, **OSw** *DL* Kkb, Bb, Gb, Rb, *HL* För, Kkb, Äb, *SdmL* Conf, Kkb, Kgb, Bb, Kmb, Mb, Rb, Till, *SmL*, *UL* För, Jb, Kmb, Rb, *VmL* För, Kkb, Mb, Jb, Kmb, Rb, *YVgL* Kkb, Frb, Drb, Tb, Utgb, Add, *ÄVgL* Md, Smb, Vs, Slb, Lek, *ÖgL* Eb

rights **OGu** *GL* A 20, 65, Add. 1 (B 4), *GS* Ch. 2, **OSw** *UL* Kkb, Äb, Mb, *VmL* Äb, Mb

rites **OSw** *UL* Kkb, *VmL* Kkb

social standing **ONorw** *GuL* Tfb, Mhb

statute **OGu** *GS* Ch. 3

treaty **OGu** *GS* Ch. 2

trial **ODan** *ESjL* 2, *JyL* 2

what is rightful **OSw** *UL* Kgb

Expressions:

guþs rætter (OSw) **guths ræt** (ODan) **guðs réttr** (ON)

God's law **ODan** *SkKL* 1 *SkL* 9 *VSjL* 3 **OSw** *YVgL* Äb

law of God **ONorw** *GuL* Krb **OSw** *YVgL* Gb *ÄVgL* Gb

right of God **OSw** *ÄVgL* Gb

kirkiuna rætter (OSw)

right of the church **OSw** *YVgL* Kkb

mæþ rætæ (ODan)

lawfully **ODan** *VSjL* 13, 53

rightfully **ODan** *SkL* 82 *VSjL* 13, 16, 17, 20

ræt göra (OSw)

to do right **OSw** *UL* Kkb, Kgb, Mb, Kmb, Rb *VmL* Kkb, Äb, Jb, Kmb, Rb

til alz rætæ (ODan)

in all legal respects **ODan** *SkL* 20

See also: *bot, gæld, lagh, manhælghi, laghliker, lögfullr, rætter*

rætter (OSw) adj.

This word has several different but associated meanings: 1) right, 2) real, 3) true, straight, unfaltering, the way things should be, 4) equitable.

appropriate **OIce** *Jó* Kab 12

correct **ODan** *VSjL* 2, **OIce** *Jó* Mah 10 Fml 1, **ONorw** *GuL* Llb, Tfb, **OSw** *HL* Kkb, Äb, Jb, Blb, *UL* Kkb, Kgb, Äb, Blb, *VmL* Äb, Rb

expedient **OSw** *UL* Kkb, *VmL* Kkb

just **ODan** *JyL* Fort, 1, *SkL* 55, 231, *VSjL* 32,
60, 76, **OSw** *HL* Kkb, *YVgL* Rlb, Add

justified **OSw** *UL* Kkb, *VmL* Kkb

lawful **ODan** *ESjL* 2, 3, *JyL* 2, 3, *SkL* 67,
80, *VSjL* 27, **OIce** *Grg* Klþ 1, 2 passim, *Jó*
passim, **ONorw** *FrL* KrbA 46, **OSw** *DL* Rb

legal **OSw** *HL* Kgb, Rb, *YVgL* Urb, Add

ordinary **ODan** *JyL* 2

prescribed **OSw** *UL* Kgb, Blb

proper **ODan** *JyL* 2, **OGu** *GL* A 1, 61, *GS*
Ch. 4, **OIce** *KRA* 14, **ONorw** *BorgL* 7, *GuL*
Krb, Leb, **OSw** *HL* Kkb, *UL* Kkb, Kgb,
Mb, Blb, *VmL* Kkb, Kgb, *YVgL* Gb

qualified **OIce** *Grg* Þsþ 25, 58 Arþ 127

right **ODan** *ESjL* 1, 2, *JyL* 2, *SkL* 72, *VSjL* 3,
17, 71, **OSw** *DL* Kkb, Mb, Bb, Gb, Rb, *HL* Blb,
SdmL Äb, Jb, Bb, Tjdb, Rb, *YVgL* Kkb, Urb

righteous **ODan** *VSjL* 32, **OSw** *YVgL* Äb, *ÄVgL* Äb

rightful **ODan** *ESjL* 1–3, *JyL* 1–3, *SkL* 1, 7, 25,
29–31, 35, 80, 83, 144, 166, *VSjL* 2, 20. 82, **ONorw**
EidsL 22.1, *GuL* Krb, **OSw** *DL* Gb, Rb, *HL* Mb,
SdmL Kkb, Äb, Jb, Bb, Kmb, Mb, Tjdb, Rb, *UL*
Kkb, Kgb, Äb, Mb, Jb, Kmb, Blb, Rb, Add. 4, *VmL*
Kkb, Äb, Mb, Jb, Bb, Rb, *YVgL* Drb, *ÖgL* Kkb, Eb

straight **OSw** *UL* Blb, *VmL* Bb

true **ODan** *SkL* 72, **OIce** *Jó* Mah
10, **OSw** *YVgL* Tb, Föb

valid **OSw** *YVgL* Föb

rættindi (OSw) noun

right **OSw** *SmL*

rætvisa (OSw) **réttvísi** (ON) noun

justice **OIce** *Jó* Þjb 24, **OSw** *SdmL* För, Till

rævse (ODan) verb

chastise **ODan** *JyL* 2

rör (OSw) **hreys** (ON) **hreysi** (ON) noun
These words mean 'pile of stones'. Such piles seem
to have had two functions, to serve as: 1) boundary
markers, and 2) mounds.

In SdmL, VmL and UL a *rör* refers to a pile of
stones forming all or part of a boundary marker
plotting out the ownership of land in a village.

Norwegian law shows that burying a corpse under
a pile of stones was considered disgraceful in heathen
times and even more so after the introduction of
Christianity. See, e.g., GuL ch. 23. In OSw the word
for such a pile of stones was *rösar* n. pl.

boundary marker **OSw** *SdmL* Jb,
Bb, *UL* Blb, *VmL* Bb

heap of rocks or stones **ONorw** *GuL* Krb, Llb

Expressions:

ra ok rör (OSw)

boundary lines and markers **OSw**
UL Jb, Blb *VmL* Bb

See also: *ra*, *skæl*

Refs: KLNM s.v. *gränsläggning*; Schlyter s.v.v.
rör, *röra*; SL UL, 192 note 77; SL VmL, 161 notes
172–76; Söderwall s.v. *rös*; Tollin 1999, 51–63

röraruf (OSw) noun

stealing of boundary markers **OSw** *SdmL* Bb

rörtegher (OSw) noun

shoreline plot **OSw** *UL* Blb, *VmL* Bb

röst (OSw) noun

grounds **OSw** *VmL* Jb

vote **OSw** *SdmL* Till

röva (OSw) **røve** (ODan) verb

plunder **ODan** *JyL* 3

rob **ODan** *JyL* 2, 3

steal **OSw** *HL* Äb

rógja (ON) **rægja** (ON) verb

slander **OIce** *Jó* Mah 25, *Js* Mah 26

saga (OGu) **saga** (ON) noun

accusation **ONorw** *GuL* Løb, Mhb

admission **OGu** *GL* Add. 8 (B 55)

statement **OIce** *Jó* Mah 9, *Js* Mah 11,
14, **ONorw** *FrL* Mhb 5 LlbA 1

sak (OSw) **sak** (ODan) **sak** (OGu) **sök** (ON) noun
Primarily, '(legal) case', however often appearing in
alternative translations and used of related aspects
of the legal procedure, such as 'lawsuit', 'charge',
'claim' and 'indictment'. Sometimes used of the cause
for the legal case, occurring in translations such as
'crime', 'cause' or 'accusation'. Elsewhere used of the
result of legal proceedings, illustrated by translations
such as 'fines', 'compensation' and 'punishment'
but also 'guilt' and 'liability'. There is considerable
overlap between usages and it is not always possible
to determine which one is intended.

accusation **ODan** *SkL* 148, **ONorw** *GuL*
Krb, Mhb, Tjb, **OSw** *DL* Kkb, *YVgL* Tb

action **ODan** *JyL* 1, 2

case **ODan** *ESjL* 2, 3, *JyL* 1, 3, *SkKL* 11, *SkL* 85,
121, 145, 149, 156, *VSjL* 37, 41, 50, 87, **OGu** *GL*
A 4, 14, Add. 2 (B 17), **OIce** *Grg*, *Js* passim, *KRA*
15, 34, **ONorw** *BorgL* 16.7, *FrL* KrbA 32 Mhb
6, *GuL* Trm, **OSw** *DL* Kkb, *HL* Mb, Rb, *SdmL*
Kgb, Gb, Jb, Bb, Kmb, Mb, Tjdb, Rb, *UL* Kkb,
Kgb, Äb, Mb, Kmb, Blb, Rb, Add. 9, *VmL* Kkb,
Äb, Mb, Kmb, Bb, Rb, *YVgL* Kkb, Drb, Gb, Rlb,

Tb, Föb, Utgb, Add, *ÄVgL* Kkb, Md, Smb, Slb,
Gb, Rlb, Tb, Fös, Föb, *ÖgL* Kkb, Eb, Db, Vm

cause **ODan** *SkL* 112, **ONorw** *GuL* Mhb, **OSw** *SdmL*
Bb, Tjdb, *SmL*, *UL* Kkb, Blb, Rb, *VmL* Kkb, Mb, Rb

charge (1) **ONorw** *FrL* KrbA 46,
GuL Krb, **OSw** *YVgL* Gb

claim **ODan** *ESjL* 3, *JyL* 2, *SkKL*
11, **OGu** *GL* Add. 1 (B 4)

claim for compensation **OGu** *GL* A 14, Add. 1 (B 4)

compensation **ONorw** *GuL* Mhb, Sab, **OSw** *DL* Mb,
Gb, Tjdb, *YVgL* Kkb, Föb, Add, *ÄVgL* Kkb, Gb, Rlb

crime **OGu** *GL* A 5, 13, Add. 1 (B 4), **OSw**
DL Kkb, *UL* Mb, Rb, *VmL* Kkb, *YVgL* Kkb,
Drb, Rlb, Add, *ÄVgL* Rlb, Tb, *ÖgL* Eb, Db

errand **OSw** *HL* Kkb

fine **OGu** *GL* A 6–9, 25, 31, *GS* Ch. 3, **OIce** *Jó*
Fml 16, **OSw** *DL* Kkb, Mb, Bb, Tjdb, Rb, *HL*
Äb, Rb, *SdmL* Conf, Rb, *UL* Kkb, Kmb, Rb

guilt **ONorw** *GuL* Krb, Mhb, Tjb

indictment **OSw** *ÄVgL* Vs

lawsuit **OIce** *Grg* Þsþ 64

liability **OGu** *GL* A 17, **OSw** *UL* Mb

matter **ONorw** *FrL* Intr 10, **OSw** *DL* Tjdb, *UL*
StfBM, Mb, Rb, *VmL* Kkb, Rb, *YVgL* Föb

misdemeanour **OSw** *UL* Kkb, Äb, *VmL* Kkb, Äb

offence **OIce** *Grg* Þsþ 80, **ONorw** *GuL* Tfb,
OSw *HL* Äb, *UL* Mb, *ÖgL* Eb, Db, Vm

payment **ONorw** *GuL* Kpb

prosecution **ONorw** *GuL* Krb, Kpb, Mhb

punishment **OSw** *SdmL* Kkb, Bb, Rb

right to claim compensation **OGu** *GL* A 2

suit **OIce** *Grg* passim, **ONorw** *FrL* KrbB 20

Expressions:

kenna sak (OGu)

accuse **OGu** *GL* A 2

sak gifa, giva sak (OSw) **give sak**
(ODan) **gefa sök** (ON)

Literally 'to give (somebody) a case'. Used in the
early stages of legal proceedings, i.e. when the
victim of a crime wanted to start legal proceedings
or when a person who allegedly committed a crime
is informed of this, and has hence been translated
as 'to accuse', 'to summon', 'to charge', etc.

accuse **ODan** *JyL* 2 *SkL* 221 *VSjL* 41 **OSw** *SmL*
UL Kkb, Mb, Jb, Kmb, Blb, Rb *YVgL* Drb, Rlb,
Tb, Föb *ÄVgL* Md, Gb, Rlb, Tb, Föb *ÖgL* Eb, Vm

accuse of a crime **OSw** *HL* Rb

allege **OSw** *ÄVgL* Rlb

appeal **OSw** *ÄVgL* Tb

be a case against **ODan** *SkL* 203

blame for a crime **OSw** *HL* Äb

bring a case (against) **ODan** *JyL* 2 **OSw** *DL* Bb, Rb

bring an action against **ODan** *JyL* 2

bring a prosecution **OSw** *UL* Mb,
Rb *VmL* Kkb, Mb, Rb

challenge **OSw** *VmL* Mb, Bb

charge **ODan** *SkL* 89, 230 **OIce** *Jó* Llb
26 **OSw** *SdmL* Kkb, Kgb, Äb, Bb, Kmb,
Mb, Tjdb, Rb *YVgL* Kkb *ÄVgL* Gb

conduct prosecution **OSw** *DL* Rb

give indictment **OSw** *YVgL* Vs

give someone a case **ODan** *ESjL* 3 *SkL* 149, 219

give someone a case **OSw** *ÄVgL* Rlb

initiate a case **ODan** *SkL* 121

make a case **ODan** *SkL* 111, 140

make a suit **OSw** *YVgL* Drb *ÄVgL* Md

make suit against **OSw** *YVgL* Drb

prosecute **OSw** *UL* Kkb, Kgb, Mb, Blb, Rb
VmL Kkb, Kgb, Mb, Kmb, Bb, Rb *YVgL*
Kkb, Drb, Rlb, Tb, Föb, Add *ÖgL* Db

put in action (a case) **ODan** *SkL* 119

raise a case **ODan** *ESjL* 2 *SkL* 158 **OSw** *HL* Rb

raise a claim **ODan** *SkKL* 9, 12

raise an accusation **OSw** *YVgL* Frb, Tb *ÄVgL* Slb

state a claim **OSw** *HL* Rb

sue **ODan** *JyL* 2, 3 **OSw** *HL* Kkb, Mb
YVgL Frb, Gb, Add *ÄVgL* Slb

summon **ODan** *JyL* 2 *SkL* 145,
146, 200 *VSjL* 38, 41, 87

summon someone for a case **ODan** *SkL* 149

take action against **ODan** *ESjL*
2 *JyL* 2, 3 *SkL* 118, 120

sak sætia (OSw)

sue **OSw** *HL* Rb

sea sakum, sak sia (OGu)

demand compensation **OGu** *GL* Add 1 (B 4)

negotiate compensation **OGu** *GL* Add 1 (B 4)

sea viþer sakum, sakum viþr sia (OGu)

answer a demand for compensation
OGu *GL* Add 1 (B 4)

defend a claim **OGu** *GL* Add 1 (B 4)

sökia sak (OSw)

sue **OSw** *YVgL* Gb

accuse **ODan** *SkL* 147 *VSjL* 37

be the plaintiff **ODan** *SkL* 121

bring a case (against) **ODan** *SkL* 219

bring action **OSw** *ÄVgL* Md

complain **ODan** *SkL* 4

prosecute **OSw** *SdmL* Mb

pursue a case **ODan** *SkL* 147, 152

raise a case **ODan** *SkKL* 11 **OSw** *YVgL* Gb

raise a charge **ODan** *SkL* 86

raise a claim **ODan** *SkL* 14, 88

summon **ODan** *SkL* 147

take action **ODan** *ESjL* 1 *SkL* 121

viþer sak, viþr sak (OGu)

to the sum of **OGu** *GL* A 17

ægha sak (OSw)

be guilty **OSw** *HL* Mb

See also: *brut*, *fall*, *giva*, *gærning*, *kænna*, *kæra*, *mal (1)*, *sea*, *sökia*, *tiltala*, *tortryggð*

Refs: Bjorvand and Lindeman s.v. *sak*; Cleasby and Vigfússon s.v. *sök*; Fritzner s.v. *sök*; Hellquist s.v. *sak*; Hertzberg s.v. *sök*; SAOB s.v. *sak*; Schlyter s.v. *sak*

sakaaukabót (ON) noun

atonement extra compensation **ONorw** *FrL* Sab 14

sakaðr (ON) adj.

accused **OIce** *Jó* Þfb 3 Kab 2 Þjb 19, 21

charged **OIce** *KRA* 6, 11

sakaraðili (ON) noun

principal in the case **OIce** *Grg* Vís 87 Ómb 142, Feþ 156, 167 Misc 254

sakaráberi (ON) noun

case-bearer **ONorw** *EidsL* 44

plaintiff **OIce** *Jó* Þfb 5, 8 Mah 8, 22 Llb 27 Kab 13, *Js* Þfb 3, 5 Mah 8, 16, **ONorw** *FrL* Intr 16 KrbB 20 Mhb 8 Rgb 7, *GuL* Krb

prosecutor **ONorw** *FrL* Mhb 22 Var 12 Bvb 11

See also: *áberi*, *saksöki*, *sökiandi*

sakargift (ON) noun

accusation **ONorw** *FrL* Kvb 14

charge (1) **OIce** *Jó* Kge 5, *Js* Kvg 5

sakarspell (ON) noun

case-spoiler **OIce** *Grg* Þsþ 72 Vís 89

something which spoils a case **OIce** *Grg* Þsþ 35

sakarsökjandi (ON) **sakasókjandi** (ON) noun

prosecutor **OIce** *Grg* Þsþ 25, 58

sakarverjandi (ON) noun

defendant **OIce** *Grg* Þsþ 20

sakarvörn (ON) noun

defence in a case **OIce** *Grg* Vís 86

sakauki (ON) noun

This was an additional person (i.e. outside the circles of *baugamenn* (see *baugamaðr*) and *nefgildismenn*

(see *nefgildismaðr*), such as an illegitimate child, entitled to part of the wergild. See GuL chs 236 and 237.

atonement extras **OIce** *Grg* Bat 113, **ONorw** *FrL* Sab 5

increaser of the wergild **ONorw** *GuL* Mhb

Refs: Hertzberg s.v. *sakauki*; KLNM s.v. *mansbot*

sakbót (ON) **sakbætr** (ON) **sakbótr** (ON) noun

atonement **OIce** *Grg* Vís 102 Bat 113, *Js* Mah 15

compensation **ONorw** *GuL* Kpb

saker (OSw) **sakr** (OGu) **sekr** (ON) **sæker** (OSw) adj.

Derived from the noun *sak* 'case; cause; crime; fine'. Often translated as 'guilty' or occasionally 'sentenced'. Frequently appers with the amount to be paid in fines/compensation, which explains translations such as 'guilty/liable/obliged to pay', 'guilty/liable/responsible to compensate'. The specifically OIce usage (ON *sekr*) 'outlawed' (Grg) changed into 'liable to pay a fine' or 'under penalty' in the later Js and Jó, possibly related to a stronger emphasis on the expropriation of the convicted's possessions.

case **OSw** *YVgL* Föb

compensation **OSw** *YVgL* Jb

condemned **OIce** *Grg* Þsþ 48

fine **OSw** *YVgL* Jb

fined **OGu** *GL* A 4, **OIce** *Grg* Klþ 2, *Jó* Þfb 2, 3 Sg 1, *Js* Mah 12, *KRA* 1, 14, **ONorw** *FrL* KrbA 8 KrbB 4 Mhb 7, 9 Var 1 Bvb 6, **OSw** *ÖgL* Kkb

guilty **OIce** *Jó* Þjb 8, **OSw** *YVgL* Tb, *ÄVgL* Gb, Tb, Fös, *ÖgL* Kkb

guilty to compensate **OSw** *YVgL* Utgb, *ÖgL* Kkb, Db

guilty to pay **OSw** *ÖgL* Vm

liable **OSw** *DL* Bb, *UL* Rb

liable to (pay) **OGu** *GL* A 9, 10, 13, 25, 26, 31, 48, 55, 56a, 61, **OSw** *UL* Kkb, Mb, Kmb, Rb, *VmL* Kkb, Äb, Mb, Kmb, Bb

liable to compensate **OSw** *YVgL* Kkb, Föb, Utgb, *ÖgL* Kkb

liable to pay **OSw** *SdmL* Kkb, Äb, Bb, Kmb, Mb, Rb, Till

liable to pay compensation or a fine **ONorw** *GuL* Kpb, Løb, Llb, Leb

obliged to pay **OSw** *YVgL* Gb

obliged to pay a fine **OSw** *DL* Tjdb

outlawed **OIce** *Grg* Þsþ 48 Vís 102 Bat 113 Feþ 158

responsible to compensate **OSw** *YVgL* Tb

sentenced **OSw** *HL* Kkb

under penalty **OFar** *Seyð* 5, **OIce** *Grg* Klþ 1 Vís 90 Feþ 144 Lbþ 172 Misc 237

See also: *sækia*, *sókjask*

Refs: Breisch 1994, 162–63; Brink 2002; Cleasby and Vigfússon s.v. *sekr*; Fritzner s.v. *sekr*; Riisøy 2014; SAOB s.v. *sak*; Schlyter s.v. *saker*

sakfé (ON) noun

object paid in wergild **ONorw** *GuL* Mhb

sakgildr (ON) adj.

current **ONorw** *FrL* Rgb 46 LlbA 15

valid **OIce** *Grg* Bat 113

sakgivi (OSw) noun

person aggrieved **OSw** *YVgL* Add

saklös (OSw) **sakløs** (ODan) **saklaus** (OGu) **saklauss** (ON) adj.

Literally 'without a case' (cf. *sak*). Sometimes translated as 'innocent', 'not guilty', but often appearing in contexts that are ambiguous as to whether the defendant has been acquitted/declared not guilty, or whether the charges have been dropped. Potential translations of the former are 'exonerated', 'free from responsibility', 'blameless', 'without fault', while the latter might be reflected in translations such as 'discharged', 'with impunity', 'without a case', 'without cause', 'free of charge'. In addition, *saklös* might be used for cases where the victim/plaintiff does not receive any fines/compensation, or, possibly, is to be protected from loss, reflected in translations such as 'uncompensated', 'indemnified'.

blameless **OSw** *HL* Kkb, Mb, Jb, Blb, Rb, *UL* Kgb, Jb

clear of charge **OSw** *HL* Kgb

discharged **OSw** *DL* Kkb, Mb, Bb, Rb, *SdmL* Kkb, Kgb, Bb, Kmb, Mb, Tjdb, Rb, Till, *UL* Kkb, Mb, Kmb, Blb, Rb, *VmL* Kkb, Äb, Mb, Jb, Kmb, Bb, Rb

exempt **OSw** *UL* Kkb, Blb, *VmL* Kkb, Bb

exempt from having to pay a fine **OIce** *Jó* Mah 15

exempt from punishment **OIce** *Jó* Mah 21 Fml 15

exonerated **OSw** *UL* Blb, Add. 8

not to be forfeited **OSw** *DL* Eb

free from obligation **OGu** *GS* Ch. 4, **OSw** *UL* Kkb, Kgb, Mb, Blb, Rb

free from responsibility **OSw** *DL* Kkb, Bb, Rb, *HL* Äb, Mb, *SdmL* Kkb, Kgb, Jb, Bb, Kmb, Mb, Rb, *UL* Kkb, Kgb, Äb, Mb, Rb, *VmL* Kgb, Äb, Mb, Bb, Rb

free of any claim **ODan** *SkL* 241

free of charge **ODan** *ESjL* 2, 3, *JyL* 3, *SkL* 137, 147, 148, 163, 170, 233, 241, *VSjL* 87

free of guilt **OSw** *DL* Bb, Rb, *UL* Kkb, Kgb, Jb, *VmL* Kkb, Jb, Bb

freed **OSw** *DL* Kkb

guiltless **OSw** *DL* Bb

having no case to answer **OGu** *GL* A 2, **OSw** *UL* Kgb, Mb, Jb, Kmb, Blb, Rb, *VmL* Kgb, Mb, Jb, Kmb, Bb, Rb

illegal **OSw** *HL* Mb, *YVgL* Tb

indemnified **OSw** *SdmL* Bb

innocent **ODan** *ESjL* 2, **OIce** *Jó* Mah 14, 17, *Js* Mah 7, 36, *KRA* 18, **ONorw** *FrL* Intr 1, 6, *GuL* Mhb, **OSw** *HL* Kgb, Mb, Blb, *SdmL* Kgb, Kmb, Mb, Tjdb, *UL* Kkb, Kgb, Mb, Kmb, Blb, Rb, *VmL* Kgb, Mb, Kmb, Bb

inoffensive **OIce** *Grg* Misc 243

invalid **OSw** *YVgL* Jb, Add

lawful **OSw** *YVgL* Utgb

no fine in compensation is to be paid out **OSw** *HL* Blb

not guilty **OSw** *HL* Kgb, Mb

not implicated **OSw** *YVgL* Tb

not litigant **ODan** *JyL* Fort

not prosecuted **OSw** *YVgL* Tb

not responsible **OSw** *YVgL* Frb

not obliged **OSw** *DL* Bb, *HL* Kgb

uncompensated **OSw** *DL* Mb, Bb

with impunity **OGu** *GS* Ch. 4, **OSw** *SdmL* Kkb, Jb, Bb, Kmb, Tjdb, Rb, Till, *SmL*, *UL* Kkb, Blb, *VmL* Kkb, Bb

with right **OSw** *HL* Blb

without a case **ODan** *ESjL* 3, **OSw** *YVgL* Tb, Add, *ÄVgL* Tb, Föb

without a case to answer **OSw** *DL* Eb, Bb, Tjdb, *ÖgL* Kkb, Eb, Db

without cause **ODan** *JyL* 2, **OIce** *Jó* Mah 2 Kge 5, *Js* Mah 7 Kvg 5, **OSw** *HL* Kkb, *UL* Blb, *YVgL* Kkb, Frb, Urb, Drb, Tb, Föb, Utgb, Add, *ÄVgL* Md, Fös

without compensation **OSw** *HL* Jb, Blb

without consequences **OSw** *YVgL* Utgb, *ÄVgL* Tb

without fault **OSw** *UL* Kkb

without guilt **OSw** *HL* Kgb

without legal penalty **OSw** *UL* Kgb, *YVgL* Föb

without liability **OSw** *YVgL* Drb

without obligations **OSw** *DL* Eb, Mb, Bb, Gb

without reason **ONorw** *FrL* Intr 24 Kvb 14

Refs: Schlyter s.v. *saklös*; Fritzner s.v. *saklauss*; SAOB s.v. *saklös*

saklösa (OSw) noun

without a case to answer to **OSw** *ÖgL* Eb

saklöst (OSw) **sakløst** (ODan) **saklaust** (OGu) adv.

free of charge **ODan** *SkL* 133, 202

freely **OSw** *HL* Jb

with impunity **OSw** *SmL*, *UL* Kkb,
Blb, *VmL* Kkb, Jb, Bb, Rb

without a case **OSw** *DL* Rb, *YVgL* Add

without a case to answer **OSw** *ÖgL* Db

without compensation **OSw** *HL* Mb

without penalty **OGu** *GL* A 26, **OSw** *UL* Kgb

See also: *saklös*

saknæmr (ON) adj.

liable at law **OIce** *Grg* Feþ 155

sakráða (ON) verb

give advice on lawsuits **OIce** *Grg* Lrþ 117

sakrmaþr (OGu) noun

criminal **OGu** *GL* A 11

fugitive **OGu** *GL* A 8

saksætning (OSw) noun

suing **OSw** *HL* Rb

saksöki (OSw) **saksökjere** (ODan) **saksökiande** (OSw) noun

accuser **ODan** *SkL* 218

claimant **OSw** *YVgL* Kkb

person aggrieved **OSw** *YVgL* Add

plaintiff **ODan** *SkL* 147, **OSw** *YVgL* Kkb, Frb, Drb,
Äb, Gb, Rlb, *ÄVgL* Kkb, Md, Smb, Slb, Gb, Rlb, Fös

See also: *sak*, *sakaráberi*, *sökia*, *sökiandi*

saktal (ON) **saktala** (ON) **söktal** (ON) noun

atonement list **OIce** *Grg* Bat 113, *Js*
Mah 29, **ONorw** *FrL* Sab 1

fine **OIce** *Jó* Mah 1

scale of compensations **ONorw** *GuL* Sab

saköri (OSw) **sakeyrir** (ON) noun

fine **OIce** *Jó* Mah 21 Þjb 23

fines **OSw** *UL* Jb, *VmL* Kgb

monetary fines **OSw** *UL* Kgb, Mb, Rb, *VmL* Kgb

sakörisbrut (OSw) noun

fine **OSw** *SdmL* Till

sal (ODan) **sal** (ON) noun

hearing **ONorw** *FrL* Var 46

instalment **ODan** *ESjL* 1–3, *JyL*
2, 3, *SkL* 85, 92, 97, 109

part **ODan** *ESjL* 3

payment **OIce** *Js* Þfb 6, **ONorw** *GuL* Krb, Mhb

payment date (by instalments) **ONorw** *GuL* Krb

time fixed for payment **OIce** *Jó* Þfb 8

See also: *sali*, *sælia*, *værþ*

sala (OSw) **sal** (ODan) **sala** (ON) noun

sale **ODan** *ESjL* 1, **OIce** *Jó* Lbb
1, **OSw** *HL* Jb, *SdmL* Kmb

selling **ODan** *SkL* 12, 30

salastefna (ON) noun

instalment **OIce** *Jó* Mah 1, *Js*
Mah 4, **ONorw** *FrL* Intr 5

See also: *stæmna*

salhus (ODan) **salhús** (ON) noun

hall **ONorw** *GuL* Mhb

living house **ODan** *JyL* 2

sali (OSw) **sali** (OGu) **sali** (ON) **sæli** (OSw) noun

seller **ONorw** *GuL* Olb, **OSw** *SdmL*
Jb, *YVgL* Tb, *ÄVgL* Tb

vendor **OGu** *GL* A 34, Add. 7 (B 49)

See also: *sal*, *sælia*

salt (ON) noun

salt **ONorw** *GuL* Krb, Kpb, Llb

saltare (OSw) noun

psalter **OSw** *SmL*

saluman (OSw) **sölumaðr** (ON) noun

buyer **ONorw** *GuL* Olb

seller **ONorw** *FrL* Var 41

vendor **OSw** *DL* Bb

sambeit (ON) noun

joint grazing **OIce** *Grg* Lbþ 191

sambroþer (OSw) **sambrother** (ODan) noun

full brother **OSw** *ÖgL* Db

full sibling **ODan** *ESjL* 1

samburðaröl (ON) noun

This was a kind of social gathering. To finance,
arrange, and take part in such joint drinking (of beer)
was considered a duty and was mandatory according
to the Church Law. In the autumn, this ceremony took
on an explicit religious character, in so far as the ale
was to be blessed with thanks to Christ and Holy Mary
for good harvest and peace. See GuL ch. 6.

joint drinking **ONorw** *GuL* Krb

Refs: KLNM s.v.v. *drikkeoffer*, *drikkeseder*,
fagnaðaról, *gilde*, *jul*, *naboforhold*

sambúð (ON) noun

neighbour **ONorw** *FrL* LlbA 19

renting the same land **ONorw** *FrL* LlbA 17

samdóma (ON) adj.

agreed **ONorw** *FrL* Intr 16

of the same judgement **OIce** *Grg* Þsþ 58

unanimously decided **OIce** *Jó* Llb 27 Þjb 25

samdógris (ON) adv.

on the same day **ONorw** *GuL* Llb, Mhb

samfeddr (ON) **samfæddr** (ON) adj.

of the same father **OIce** *Jó* Kge
7-5, **ONorw** *FrL* KrbB 11

See also: *samfæthre*

samfjórðungs (ON) adv.

  within the same quarter **OIce** *Grg* Ómb
  130 Feþ 147 Lbþ 193 Misc 250

samfrænde (ODan) noun

  common kinsman **ODan** *ESjL* 3, *JyL* 1, *VSjL* 15, 20
  kinsmen **ODan** *ESjL* 1

samfund (OSw) **samfund** (ODan) noun

  company **ODan** *SkKL* 11
  gathering **ODan** *SkL* 97, **OSw** *SdmL* Kkb, Mb
  general gathering **OSw** *ÖgL* Kkb, Db

samfæthre (ODan) **samfeðra** (ON) **samfeðri** (ON) adj.

  of the same father **OIce** *Grg* Vís 94, 95 Bat 113
  Feþ 144, 156 Misc 253, *Jó* Kge 7-4, *Js* Ert 3
  with the same father **ODan** *SkL* 27

samför (ON) noun

  wedlock **OIce** *Grg* Feþ 144, 152

samgengr (ON) adj.

  Expressions:

  eiga samgengt (ON)

  to have joint right of access **OIce**
  Grg Fjl 225 *Jó* Llb 47

samheldi (ON) noun

  conspiracy **ONorw** *FrL* KrbA 46
  contract **OIce** *Jó* Sg 3

samheraðs (ON) **samsheraðs** (ON) adv.

  within the same district **OIce** *Grg* Ómb 128, 129

samkaupa (ON) adj.

  agreed to terms **OIce** *Jó* Fml 1

samkulla (OSw) **samkolli** (OSw) adj.

  of the same bed **OSw** *YVgL* Add
  full sibling **OSw** *HL* Äb, *UL* Äb, Add. 7
  of the same brood **OSw** *SdmL* Äb

  See also: *kolder*, *sunderkulla*

samkunda (ON) noun

  feast **ONorw** *GuL* Llb
  gathering **OIce** *Js* Ert 17, **ONorw** *FrL* Mhb 14
  party **ONorw** *FrL* Mhb 5

samkunduvitni (ON) noun

  wedding testimony **OIce** *Js* Kvg 3

  See also: *vitni*

samkvámulag (ON) noun

  agreement **OIce** *Jó* Kab 15

samkvámumaðr (ON) noun

  meeting member **OIce** *Grg* Tíg 255, 256, *KRA* 14, 15

samkvæði (ON) noun

  assent **OIce** *Grg* Þsþ 32, 38 Lrþ 117

samlendr (ON) adj.

  living in the same country **OIce** *Grg* Feþ 144

sammøthre (ODan) **sammǿddr** (ON) **sammǿðra** (ON)
sammǿðri (ON) adj.

  of the same mother **OIce** *Grg* Vís 94 Bat
  113 Feþ 144, 156 Misc 254, *Jó* Kge 7-4, *Js*
  Ert 5, **ONorw** *FrL* KrbB 11 ArbA 6
  with the same mother **ODan** *SkL* 27

samne (ODan) verb

  marry **ODan** *JyL* 1

samneth (ODan) noun

  gathering **ODan** *JyL* 3

samneyti (ON) noun

  company **OIce** *Grg* Þsþ 42

samqvæmd (OSw) **samkváma** (ON) noun

  commune meeting **OIce** *Grg* Feþ
  164 Lbþ 207 Fjl 225 Tíg 255
  gathering **OSw** *ÖgL* Kkb

  See also: *fynd*

samrétt (ON) **samrétti** (ON) noun

  common fold **OFar** *Seyð* 3, 5

  See also: *rétt*

samsyskine (OSw) **samsystken** (ODan) **samsizkini**
  (OSw) **samsyskane** (OSw) **samsyzkin** (OSw)
  samsyþini (OSw) **samsyþkini** (OSw) noun

  full siblings **ODan** *ESjL* 1, *JyL* 1, **OSw**
  SdmL Äb, *VmL* Äb, *ÖgL* Eb
  siblings of the same parents **ODan** *SkL* 28

  See also: *samkulla*

samsystir (OGu) noun

  full sister **OGu** *GL* A 20

samtýnis (ON) adv.

  in the same yard **ONorw** *GuL* Krb, Llb

samvigilse (OSw) noun

  wedding **OSw** *YVgL* Kkb

  See also: *vighia*

samvist (OSw) **samvist** (ON) noun

  In OSw appearing in the context of the offense of
  associating with criminals.
  association **OSw** *ÖgL* Eb, Db
  being together **OSw** *YVgL* Drb
  shared living quarters **OIce** *Grg* Klþ
  4, *KRA* 2, **ONorw** *FrL* KrbB 23

  Expressions:

  mot ok samvist (OSw)

  meet and be together with **OSw** *YVgL* Drb

  See also: *forvist*, *hema*, *husa*, *samværa*, *viþervist*

samvizka (ON) noun

conscience **OIce** *Jó* Þjb 24

samværa (OSw) noun

being together with **OSw** *HL* Kkb

See also: *forvist, hema, husa, samvist, viþervist*

samþinga (ON) **samþingi** (ON) adj.

belonging to the same assembly **OIce** *Grg*
Þsþ 49 Lbþ 185, 198 Fjl 222 Tíg 258

samþingendr (pl.) (ON) noun

*men belonging to the same law
district* **ONorw** *GuL* Kpb

samþingisgoði (ON) **samþingsgoði** (ON) noun

chieftain of the same assembly **OIce** *Grg* Þsþ
23, 36 Vís 96, 110 Lrþ 117 Misc 249

samþykkð (ON) **samþykt** (ON) noun

agreement **OIce** *Jó* Þfb 9

consent **OIce** *Jó* Kge 7 Þjb 24, *Js* Ert 14, *KRA* 9, 33

samþykke (OSw) **samþykki** (ON) noun

consent **OIce** *Js* Kdb 3, **OSw** *HL* För

See also: *raþ*

samþykkja (ON) verb

accept **OIce** *Jó* HT 1

agree **OIce** *Jó* Þfb 3, 4 Mah 20 Þjb 25

confirm **OIce** *Jó* Mah 4

consent to **OIce** *Jó* Þjb 25, *Js* Kdb 5

sanbani (OSw) **sandbani** (OSw) noun

An actual killer as opposed to one who restrained the victim or acted as an accessory in any other way.

perpetrator **OSw** *UL* Mb

true killer **OSw** *SdmL* Mb

See also: *bani, haldbani, raþsbani, sander*

sancta martens dagher (OSw) noun

St Martin's Day (11 November) **OSw** *UL* Jb

See also: *martinsmæssa*

sancta mikials dagher (OSw) noun

Michaelmas Day **OSw** *YVgL* Kkb

See also: *mikialsdagher*

sandblandaþer (OSw) adj.

adulterated with sand **OSw** *UL* Kmb, *VmL* Kmb

sander (OSw) **san** (ODan) **sandr** (OGu) **sannr** (ON)
saðr (ON) **san** (OSw) adj.

The literal meaning 'true, truthful' reflects that the legal proceedings also aimed at obtaining the truth, rather than mere formal criteria. In phrases such as *sander þiuver* 'real theif' (OSw ÄVgL, Tb; YVgL Tb), *sander bani* 'true killer' (OSw YVgL Drb; ODan SkL 121), *sander ok atakin* 'caught red handed' (OSw DL Kkb), *sander* has often been translated as 'true'

or 'guilty' and occasionally 'convicted' or 'proved', i.e. having had the truth of an accusation proven, reflecting that a criminal has been caught in the act and/or found guilty in a trial.

acknowledged **OSw** *VmL* Äb

appropriate **ONorw** *GuL* Llb

certain **OSw** *UL* Mb

convicted **OIce** *Jó* Þjb 1

found guilty **OSw** *SdmL* Kkb, Kgb, Bb, Mb, Tjdb

found guilty by witnesses **OSw**
DL Kkb, Mb, Bb, Tjdb

good **ONorw** *GuL* Llb

guilty **ODan** *SkL* 111, 149, 221, 222, **OGu** *GL* A 2, 4, 7, 22, 26, 35, 46, **OIce** *Grg* Feþ 158, *Jó* Mah 10 Þjb 6 Fml 8, *Js* Mah 14, **ONorw** *BorgL* 16.9, *EidsL* 29.4 45.2, *FrL* Intr 11 Rgb 32 Bvb 11, *GuL* Krb, Mhb, **OSw** *DL* Kkb, Mb, Bb, *UL* Kkb, Kgb, Mb, *VmL* Kkb, Äb, Mb, Bb, *YVgL* Kkb, Drb, Gb, Rlb, Tb, Föb, Utgb, Add, *ÄVgL* Md, Smb, Rlb, Fös, Föb, *ÖgL* Kkb, Db

legitimate **OSw** *SdmL* Kkb, Gb, Kmb

proved **OSw** *SmL*

real **OSw** *YVgL* Tb, *ÄVgL* Tb

reliable **OSw** *UL* Kkb, Mb, Blb

right **OSw** *DL* Kkb, Mb, Tjdb

rightful **OSw** *DL* Tjdb

true **ODan** *ESjL* 1–3, *JyL* 1, 2, *SkL* 121, *VSjL* 19, 37, **OGu** *GL* A 30, **OIce** *Grg* Þsþ 47, *KRA* 18, **ONorw** *EidsL* 3.2, *GuL* Llb, Olb, Leb, **OSw** *DL* Kkb, Eb, Rb, *HL* Kgb, Äb, Blb, Rb, *SdmL* Kgb, Mb, Tjdb, *SmL*, *UL* Kkb, Äb, Mb, Kmb, Blb, Rb, *VmL* Kkb, Kgb, Äb, Mb, Kmb, Bb, *YVgL* Drb, Rlb, Add, *ÄVgL* Md, Smb, Slb, *ÖgL* Kkb, Eb, Db

truthful **ODan** *ESjL* 1, 3, *JyL* 2, 3, **OSw** *SdmL* Kkb, Jb, *ÖgL* Db

Expressions:

kunnr ok sannr (ON)

identified and convicted **ONorw** *GuL* Krb, Løb, Llb

See also: *fulder, gilder, kunder, osander, rætter, saker, saklös, sanna, sannind, sannindaman, skylder (1)*

Refs: Andersen 2010; Andersen 2014; Bjorvand and Lindeman 2000 s.v.v. *sann, synd*; Hellquist, s.v.v. *sann, synd*; Hertzberg s.v. *sannr*; SAOB s.v. *sann*

sangbok (OSw) noun

song book **OSw** *SmL*

sanghus (OSw) noun

chancel **OSw** *HL* Kkb

sanghusdyr (OSw) noun

chapel door **OSw** *DL* Kkb

doorway to the chancel **OSw** *HL* Kkb

sankta eriks dagh (OSw) noun
St Erik's Day **OSw** *UL* Kkb

sankti petrs messa (OGu) noun
Saint Peter's Mass **OGu** *GS* Ch. 4

sanna (OSw) **sanne** (ODan) **sanna** (OGu) **sanna** (ON)
verb
acknowledge **ONorw** *GuL* Kpb, Mhb, Tjb
confirm **OIce** *Jó* Þfb 1 Llb 57 Fml 19, *Js*
Þfb 1 Mah 24 Kab 5, **ONorw** *FrL* KrbA
18, 29 KrbB 12 Var 22, *GuL* Olb
corroborate **OIce** *Jó* Mah 24 Þjb 19
prove the veracity (of something) **OGu** *GL* A 39
say that someone is guilty **ODan** *SkL* 89
substantiate **OSw** *SdmL* Mb, *UL* Kgb, *VmL* Mb
testify on being the truth **OSw** *DL* Tjdb
vouch for **OIce** *Grg* Þsþ 33 Arþ 124
Misc 248, *Jó* Kge 1 Kab 17, *Js* Mah
24, 37 Ert 24 Kab 12, *KRA* 1, 2
See also: *sander*

sannaðarvitni (ON) noun
witness for confirmation **ONorw** *GuL* Olb

sannendeeth (ODan) noun
man of truth **ODan** *JyL* 2
truth oath **ODan** *JyL* 2

sannind (OSw) **sannende** (ODan) **sannund** (OGu)
sannendi (ON) **sanind** (OSw) noun
man of truth **ODan** *JyL* 2
truth **ODan** *ESjL* 1–3, *JyL* Fort, 2, *SkL* 76,
VSjL 80, **OGu** *GS* Ch. 3, **OIce** *Jó* Þjb 24,
OSw *DL* Eb, *SdmL* För, Jb, Kmb, Till, *UL*
Jb, Blb, Rb, *VmL* Rb, *ÖgL* Kkb, Eb
truthfulness **OSw** *SdmL* Kkb
See also: *sander, sannindaman, syn*

sannindaman (OSw) **sannendeman** (ODan)
sannanarmaðr (ON) **sannaðarmaðr** (ON)
sanindaman (OSw) **sanundaman** (OSw) noun
Literally 'man of truth'. In ODan JyL, the king
appointed a permanent board of eight landowning
sannendemæn in each *hæreth* (see *hæraþ*), who, at
the *thing* (see *þing*), made decisions by oath in certain
serious cases such as killing, rape, church-theft and
disputed field boundaries. Their decision could,
however, be overruled by the bishop and 'the best men
of the area' (*bæste bygdemæn*). In OSw, the status and
function of *sannindamæn* seems more temporary; they
could replace members of a *næmd* (q.v.) when absent
(OSw SdmL), or be appointed in pairs by the priest
in matters of guardianship of orphans (OSw HL). In
OIce Grg, *sannaðarmenn* appear as two oath-helpers

who at the *þing* 'assembly' confirmed previous oaths,
specifically for verifying genealogies when appointing
a judge.
honest man **OSw** *HL* Äb
man of truth **ODan** *JyL* 1–3, **OSw** *SdmL* Till
man to vouch **OIce** *Grg* Þsþ 25, 35 Vís 110 Bat
113 Ómb 130 Feþ 147 Lbþ 215 Misc 248
righteous man **OSw** *HL* Äb
trustworthy man **OSw** *UL* Jb, *VmL* Rb
See also: *fastar (pl.), goþer, hæraþ,
hæsteleghe, maþer, minnungamæn (pl.),
mætsmæn (pl.), næmd, sander, sannaðarvitni,
sannendeeth, sannind, trygger, þing*
Refs: Andersen 2014; Cleasby and Vigfússon
s.v. *sannaðr, sannaðar-maðr*; Tamm 2002a,
93–94; Tamm and Vogt, eds, 2016, 309

sannleikr (ON) noun
truth **OIce** *Jó* Þjb 24

sannligr (ON) adj.
just **OIce** *Js* Þfb 6
lawful **OIce** *Jó* Þfb 9

sannprófa (ON) verb
prove **OIce** *Jó* Mah 2

sannsakaðr (ON) adj.
rightly accused **ONorw** *FrL* Intr 16

sannsorðinn (ON) adj.
*proven to have been engaged in unlawful
sexual intercourse* **ONorw** *GuL* Mhb
really been used as a woman **ONorw** *FrL* Rgb 35

sannspyrja (ON) verb
confirm **OIce** *Jó* Llb 28
find out about the truth **OIce** *Jó* Kge 18
prove **ONorw** *FrL* LlbB 5

sar (OSw) **sar** (ODan) **sar** (OGu) **sár** (ON) **sar** (ODan)
sárr (ON) noun
injury **ODan** *ESjL* 2, 3, **OGu** *GL* A 11,
12, **OSw** *HL* Kkb, Mb, *UL* Kkb, Äb,
Mb, Jb, *VmL* Kkb, Mb, *YVgL* Urb
injury case **OSw** *HL* Mb
wound **ODan** *ESjL* 1–3, *JyL* 2, 3, *SkL* passim,
VSjL 35–39, 54, 63, 86, **OGu** *GL* A 17, 19, Add.
2 (B 17), **OIce** *Grg* Vís 86, 87 Feþ 149 Misc 241,
Jó Mah 2, 13, *Js* Mah 6, 30, **ONorw** *FrL* KrbA 10
Mhb 12 Var 2-6, *GuL* Krb, Mhb, **OSw** *DL* Mb, Gb,
Tjdb, *HL* Mb, Rb, *SdmL* Kkb, Gb, Mb, *UL* För,
Kgb, Mb, Add. 2, *VmL* För, Kgb, Mb, *YVgL* Frb,
Add, *ÄVgL* Smb, Vs, Slb, Urb, *ÖgL* Kkb, Eb, Db

wounding **ODan** *JyL* 2, *VSjL* 30, 86, **OSw**
DL Eb, *HL* Mb, Rb, *SdmL* Kgb, Tjdb, Rb, *UL*
Kgb, Mb, Rb, *VmL* Kgb, Mb, *ÖgL* Vm

Expressions:

fulder sar (OSw)

wound subject to full compensation
OSw *UL* Kkb, Kgb, Mb *VmL* Mb

högst sar (OSw)

highest injury **OSw** *HL* Mb

highest wound **OSw** *HL* Mb *SdmL* Mb

See also: *skaþi, sære, bæn*

sar (OSw) adj.

injured **OSw** *HL* Mb

wounded **ODan** *ESjL* 3, *VSjL* 33, 36, **OIce** *Grg*
Þsþ 32 Vís 87 Misc 244, *Jó* Þfb 8 Mah 7, *Js*
Kab 19, **ONorw** *EidsL* 32.9 48.11, *FrL* Mhb
10, *GuL* Krb, Kvb, **OSw** *DL* Eb, *HL* Mb, *SdmL*
Kgb, Mb, *YVgL* Kkb, *ÄVgL* Smb, *ÖgL* Kkb

sarabot (OSw) sarbot (ODan) sárbót (ON) sárbætr
(ON) sárbǿtr (ON) noun

compensation for a wound **ODan** *ESjL*
2, *JyL* 3, *SkL* 116, *VSjL* 55, **ONorw** *GuL*
Mhb, **OSw** *DL* Mb, *HL* Mb, *UL* Mb

compensation for wounding **ODan** *ESjL* 2

compensation of wounds **OSw** *YVgL*
Äb, Add, *ÄVgL* Äb, *ÖgL* Eb

payment for wound **ODan** *SkL* 103

wound compensation **OIce** *Jó* Mah 8, 23 Llb
39, *Js* Mah 8, 15, **ONorw** *FrL* Mhb 11, 16

wound-fine **ODan** *VSjL* 30, 33,
34, 36, **OSw** *SdmL* Mb

See also: *bot, sar*

sarafar (OGu) noun

wound **OGu** *GL* A 19

saramal (OSw) saræmal (OSw) noun

case of wounds **OSw** *DL* Mb,
Tjdb, Rb, Vm, *ÄVgL* Smb

injury case **OSw** *HL* Kkb, *UL* Mb, *VmL* Mb

See also: *mal (1), sar*

saramaþer (OSw) noun

injurer **OSw** *ÄVgL* Smb

See also: *sar*

saremun (ODan) noun

worth of wounds **ODan** *ESjL* 2

saresak (ODan) noun

case of wound **ODan** *SkL* 118

sargha (OSw) sarga (OGu) særa (ON) verb

injure **OSw** *HL* Kkb, Kgb, Mb, Blb,
UL Kkb, Blb, *VmL* Mb, Bb

wound **OGu** *GL* A 8, 9, 19, **OIce** *Grg* Vís 86
Misc 242, *Jó* Þfb 5 Mah 3, 7, *Js* Þfb 4 Mah 8, 16,
KRA 6, 8, **ONorw** *FrL* Intr 6 KrbA 10 Mhb 5, 10,
OSw *DL* Eb, Mb, *HL* Mb, *SdmL* Kkb, Kgb, Gb,
Bb, Mb, *UL* Kkb, Kgb, Mb, Add. 2, *VmL* Kgb,
Mb, *YVgL* Kkb, Frb, Urb, Drb, Tb, Add, *ÄVgL*
Kkb, Smb, Vs, Slb, Lek, *ÖgL* Kkb, Eb, Vm

sarlyte (ODan) noun

maiming by wounding **ODan** *VSjL* 86

sarnaþer (OSw) noun

wounding **OSw** *SdmL* Mb

sarþuli (OSw) saradhule (OSw) saratoli (OSw)
sarþole (OSw) noun

wounded man **OSw** *VmL* Mb

sat (OSw) sát (ON) noun

ambush **OIce** *Grg* Vís 108, **OSw** *HL* Mb, *SdmL* Mb

hiding **OSw** *UL* Mb, *VmL* Mb

sater (OSw) sat (ODan) satr (OGu) sáttr (ON) satter
(OSw) adj.

agreed **ODan** *JyL* 2, 3, *SkL* 70, 108,
VSjL 32, **OIce** *Grg* Lbþ 181

agreeing **ONorw** *GuL* Kpb, Løb, Olb

as friends **OSw** *HL* Kgb, Mb, *UL* Kkb, Kgb,
Mb, *VmL* Kgb, *YVgL* Add, *ÖgL* Eb

in agreement **OGu** *GL* A 3

reconciled **ODan** *JyL* 2, **OSw** *SdmL*
Kgb, Mb, *YVgL* Vs, Jb

settled **ODan** *ESjL* 3, *SkL* 113

See also: *osater*

sauðagangr (ON) noun

sheep-walk **OIce** *Grg* Fjl 225

sauðamörk (ON) noun

sheep mark **OFar** *Seyð* 5

sauðbítr (ON) noun

A sheep biter; a dog which repeatedly bites sheep.
Used as an insult in manuscript variants of *Jóns saga
helga.*

sheep worrier **OFar** *Seyð* 6

Refs: CV s.v. *sauðbítr*; Fritzner s.v.
sauðbítr; Seyð. ed. p. 64

saumgjald (ON) noun

fine for sewn cloth **ONorw** *FrL* Leb 1

saurlífi (ON) noun

immoral life **OIce** *Jó* Kge 1

sauþr (OGu) noun

well **OGu** *GL* A 27

sax (ON) noun

> gunwales **ONorw** *GuL* Leb

saxbönd (pl.) (ON) noun

> crossbeams in the prow **ONorw** *GuL* Leb

sáðgerð (ON) noun

> corn **OFar** *Seyð* 2

sálarstefna (ON) noun

> time for payment **OIce** *Jó* Mah 21
>
> See also: *stæmna*

sáld (ON) noun

> cask **OIce** *Grg* Feþ 166
>
> {sáld} **ONorw** *GuL* Krb, Løb

sáldssáð (ON) noun

> sáld of seed corn **ONorw** *FrL* LlbA 1

sáluhús (ON) noun

> wayside shelter **ONorw** *GuL* Llb

sáluöl (ON) noun

> soul's ale **ONorw** *GuL* Krb
>
> See also: *sjaund*

sáraráð (ON) sárráð (ON) noun

> advice leading to injury **OIce** *Jó* Mah 11

sársauki (ON) noun

> added injury **OIce** *Js* Mah 11
>
> painful injury **OIce** *Jó* Mah 19

sáttaleyfi (ON) noun

> licence for settlement **OIce** *Grg* Lrþ 117

sáttargerð (ON) noun

> settlement (1) **OIce** *Grg* Misc 244

sáttargerðarváttr (ON) noun

> witness of settlement terms **OIce** *Grg* Þsþ 48

sáttarmaðr (ON) noun

> arbitrator **OIce** *Grg* Þsþ 60 Vís 102
>
> See also: *sættarmaðr*

sáttarstefna (ON) noun

> settlement meeting **OIce** *Grg* Bat 114

sáttarvætti (ON) noun

> testimony of settlement **OIce** *Grg* Þsþ 49

sáttmál (ON) noun

> agreement **ONorw** *FrL* Var 9 Sab 1

sea (OSw) se (ODan) asia (OGu) sia (OGu) ase (OSw) se (OSw) verb

> accept **OSw** *VmL* Mb, Rb
>
> appear **OSw** *UL* Mb, Rb, *VmL* Rb
>
> ascertain **OGu** *GL* A 6
>
> inspect **ODan** *ESjL* 2, **OSw** *SdmL* Bb, Mb, *UL* Äb, Kmb, *VmL* Mb, Kmb, *ÄVgL* Jb
>
> look **ODan** *ESjL* 1

> observe **OSw** *UL* Rb, *VmL* Bb
>
> see **OGu** *GL* A 19, 23, 26, 45a
>
> study **OGu** *GL* Add. 1 (B 4)
>
> be visible **OGu** *GL* A 19
>
> witness **OSw** *UL* Mb, Blb
>
> be an (eye) witness **OGu** *GL* A 22
>
> Expressions:
>
> **sia viþer** (OGu)
>
> negotiate compensation **OGu** *GL* A 13, 14, Add. 1 (B 4)
>
> **syna ok sea** (OSw)
>
> examine **OSw** *HL* Äb
>
> inspect and observe **OSw** *UL* Kkb, Äb, Mb, Blb, Rb *VmL* Kkb, Äb, Mb, Bb
>
> See also: *halda*, *sak*, *skuþa*

segja (ON) verb

> Expressions:
>
> **segja fyrir** (ON)
>
> give notice **ONorw** *GuL* Olb
>
> **segja í sundr** (ON)
>
> annul **ONorw** *GuL* Kvb
>
> **segja til** (ON)
>
> notify **ONorw** *GuL* Krb

segjandi (ON) noun

> someone who can tell what happened **ONorw** *FrL* Mhb 23

segl (ON) noun

> sail **ONorw** *GuL* Leb

sekðarfé (ON) sektarfé (ON) noun

> property under penalty **OIce** *Grg* Þsþ 49, 60

sekðarhandsal (ON) noun

> formal guarantee to accept outlawry **OIce** *Grg* Þsþ 60

sekðarlauss (ON) sektalauss (ON) sektarlauss (ON) sekðalauss (ON) adj.

> exempt from action **OIce** *Jó* Mah 13
>
> free of compensation **ONorw** *FrL* KrbB 12
>
> guiltlessly **ONorw** *EidsL* 16.3
>
> with impunity **ONorw** *BorgL* 14.7, *EidsL* 12.7 13.1
>
> without a fine **ONorw** *FrL* Mhb 39 Var 46
>
> without guilt **ONorw** *FrL* KrbA 23, 40
>
> without penalty **OIce** *Jó* Þfb 6 Þjb 18, 24 Fml 20, *Js* Þfb 5 Mah 10, 30 Ert 24, *KRA* 27, 33, **ONorw** *FrL* KrbA 37
>
> without punishment **ONorw** *FrL* Intr 7 KrbB 24 Mhb 18

sekðarsök (ON) sektarsök (ON) noun

> outlawry case **OIce** *Grg* Þsþ 77

sel (ON) noun

   shieling **OIce** *Grg* Klþ 8 Ómb 129 Lbþ 182, *KRA* 26

   See also: *sætr*

selastulðr (ON) noun

   theft of seals **OIce** *Jó* Þjb 9

seljamannamessa (ON) heilagra manna (messu) i Selju (ON) seljumannamessa (ON) noun

   day of the Saints of Selja **OIce** *Grg* Klþ 13, **ONorw** *FrL* KrbA 24, *GuL* Krb

seljandi (ON) noun

   seller **OIce** *Grg* Lbþ 174, *Js* Lbb 4

selr (ON) noun

   seal (2) **ONorw** *GuL* Llb

selver (ON) noun

   hunting grounds for seals **ONorw** *FrL* LlbB 11

senaþearf (OSw) noun

   late-month inheritance **OSw** *HL* Äb

sengakleþi (OGu) noun

   bedclothes **OGu** *GL* A 20

   See also: *klæþi*

serða (ON) streða (ON) verb

   bugger **OIce** *Grg* Misc 238

serkr (OGu) noun

   vest **OGu** *GL* A 19

sess (ON) noun

   oar bench **ONorw** *GuL* Llb, Olb, Leb

   seat **ONorw** *GuL* Løb

seta (ON) noun

   The *seta* was one of the two highest ranked bondwomen. It is assumed that her work was principally within the house.

   housemaid **ONorw** *GuL* Mhb

   See also: *deghia*

   Refs: Hertzberg s.v. *seta*; KLNM s.v.v. *bryde, tyende*; Schlyter s.v. *sæta*

seter (OGu) settir (OGu) noun

   mediator (i.e. one who makes good) **OGu** *GL* A 26

setjask (ON) verb

   Expressions:

   setjask fyrir (ON)

   ambush **ONorw** *GuL* Mhb

setning (ON) noun

   rite **OIce** *KRA* 16

setstokkr (ON) noun

   bench support **ONorw** *GuL* Llb

setuhús (ON) noun

   dwelling house **OIce** *Jó* Kge 32

setumaðr (ON) noun

   man with a fixed residence **OIce** *KRA* 30

   person staying at a farm **OIce** *Grg* Klþ 17

sexmannadómr (ON) noun

   assessment of six men **OIce** *Jó* Kge 18

sexmannaeiðr (ON) noun

   six-man oath **ONorw** *EidsL* 45.3

   See also: *eþer*, *séttareiðr*

seyma (ON) verb

   fasten **ONorw** *GuL* Leb

seþalaus (OGu) adj.

   having no arable land **OGu** *GL* A 48, 56a

séttareiðr (ON) noun

   oath of six **OIce** *Jó* Mah 5, 13 Llb 30 Kab 11 Þjb 6, 14 Fml 20, *Js* Kab 5, 9 Þjb 4, **ONorw** *EidsL* 46.2, *FrL* KrbB 20 Var 9 Rgb 32 Bvb 7

   six-man oath **ONorw** *GuL* Krb, Løb, Llb, Tfb, Mhb, Tjb

   See also: *eþer*, *sexmannaeiðr*

sialadagher (OSw) noun

   day of souls **OSw** *YVgL* Kkb

   See also: *sialamæssudagher*

sialagift (OSw) sjalegift (ODan) sálugjöf (ON) siælagift (OSw) siælagæf (OSw) noun

A gift for the soul, one's own or somebody else's, often to a religious institution and restricted as to the amount allowed to be given. In OIcc, also a mandatory gift as an addition to the *tiund* 'tithe' or as a contribution to the poor. Also a burial fee to the priest in OSw (as well as in ONorw, where it, however, only appears in later diplomas).

   gift for the soul **ODan** *ESjL* 1, *JyL* 1, 3

   gift for the soul's good **OIce** *Grg* Arþ 127

   soul gift **OIce** *KRA* 11, 13, **OSw** *HL* Kkb, *SdmL* Kkb, *SmL*

   spiritual gift **OSw** *YVgL* Add

   See also: *gæf*

   Refs: Fritzner s.v. *sálagipt*; Gerhold 2002, 206; Hertzberg s.v. *sálugjöf*; KLNM s.v. *sjelegave*

sialamæssa (OSw) siælamæssa (OSw) noun

   mass **OSw** *HL* Kkb

   mass for the dead **OSw** *HL* Kkb, *UL* Kkb, *VmL* Kkb, *ÖgL* Kkb

   soul mass **OSw** *SmL*, *UL* Kkb, *VmL* Kkb, *YVgL* Kkb

sialamæssudagher (OSw) noun

   Day of All Souls **OSw** *YVgL* Kkb

   See also: *sialadagher*

sialfræþi (OSw) noun

> *deliberation* **OSw** *YVgL* Föb
>
> See also: *raþa, vaþi, vili*

sialfskut (OSw) **siælffskot** (OSw) **siælfskot** (OSw) noun

> *arrow trap* **OSw** *DL* Bb, *UL* Mb, *VmL* Mb
>
> *spear* **OSw** *HL* Mb

sialfsviliande (OSw) adj.

> *of one's own free will* **OSw** *SdmL* Kkb

sialvasæt (OSw) **siælvasæt** (OSw) noun

> Literally, 'self agreement'. This was a system of mutual conciliation, whereby the injured party agreed with the person who had injured him on a compensation sum, as if it were an accidental injury. They did this before witnesses at the assembly. There was in this case no payment to the king, via his administrator as was usual in other cases of injury and it was thus considered to be an important concession, applicable in DL and VmL, that does not appear in UL. In DL it is made clear that the mutual conciliation must be in place before the king's administrator becomes involved. Once he has raised the case, mutual conciliation cannot be invoked, and any conciliation or agreement (*sæt*) must involve payment to the crown. In VmL further details of the system are given. The right is counterbalanced by an agreement to supply one ship each year to the levy. The fact that stress is laid on the arrangement in DL and VmL shows that it was an unusual concession. In Jó it is prohibited for cases to be settled between two parties privately, since it denies the fine to the king. Jó Mah 19 has the related adjective *sjalfsettr*, translated 'as a matter of course'.
>
> *conciliation* **OSw** *DL* Mb
>
> *mutual conciliation* **OSw** *DL* Mb, *VmL* Mb
>
> See also: *nam, sjalfsettr, sæt, sættargærþ*
>
> Refs: Schlyter 1877, s.v. *sjalvasæt*; SL DL, 44 note 53; SL VmL, 95–96 notes 93–95

siang (OSw) noun

> The marital bed where the woman became the responsibility of her husband (HL Äb, SdmL Gb) and where the rights of the spouses could be violated through adultery (HL Äb, SdmL Gb). The translation 'family' appears in expressions such as *innan siængæ drap* (HL Mb, SdmL Mb) and *iorþa köp innan siængar* (HL Jb) and refers to killing and land purchase within the family.
>
> *bed* **OSw** *HL* Äb, Jb, *SdmL* Gb, Mb
>
> *family* **OSw** *HL* Mb, *SdmL* Mb
>
> Refs: Schlyter s.v. *siang, siæng*

siangaran (OSw) **siænga ran** (OSw) noun

> The robbing of someone's marital rights through adultery, a crime specifically concerning the women involved, as the guilty woman was to compensate the offended wife directly.
>
> *bed-robbery* **OSw** *SdmL* Gb
>
> *violation of the marriage bed* **OSw** *UL* Kkb
>
> Refs: Carlsson 1942, 87; Schlyter s.v. *siangaran, siænga ran*

siðsemð (ON) noun

> *good conduct* **OIce** *Jó* Þfb 5, *Js* Þfb 4

sielfsvald (OGu) noun

> *freedom* **OGu** *GL* A 13
>
> *right* **OGu** *GL* A 24
>
> See also: *friþer*

siettungr (OGu) **séttungr** (ON) noun

> Literally 'a sixth' of something. An administrative judicial division at a low level.
>
> *sixth* **OGu** *GL* A 19, 31, Add. 8 (B55), **ONorw** *FrL* Mhb 8
>
> Refs: KLNM s.v. *settung*; Peel 2015, 14–16, 248–49, 286 note 1/18; Schlyter s.v. *siattunger*

sifjaðr (ON) adj.

> *related* **OIce** *Jó* Þfb 3
>
> *related by kinship* **ONorw** *FrL* Mhb 8
>
> *related by marriage* **OIce** *Jó* Þjb 19

sifjar (pl.) (ON) noun

> *affinity* **OIce** *Grg* Klþ 18 Feþ 144

sifjaspell (ON) noun

> *adultery with in-laws* **OIce** *Jó* Kge 7-6
>
> *incest with affines* **OIce** *Grg* Feþ 156

sifkona (ON) noun

> *woman related through spiritual kinship* **OIce** *KRA* 20
>
> See also: *kona, kyn, skylder (1), æt*

sifskaper (OSw) **sifskapr** (ON) noun

> *affinity by marriage* **OSw** *UL* Kkb, *VmL* Kkb
>
> *kinship by marriage* **OSw** *SdmL* Kkb
>
> *relation by marriage* **OSw** *ÄVgL* Gb
>
> *relationship by marriage* **OIce** *Jó* Kge 6, **ONorw** *EidsL* 22.5, *FrL* KrbB 1
>
> See also: *guþsivi, mansivi*

sifskapsspiæl (OSw) noun

> *incest in kinship by marriage* **OSw** *SdmL* Kkb

silafylli (OSw) noun

> *substitute for the harness* **OSw** *UL* Blb

silfrband (OGu) noun

> *silver band* **OGu** *GL* A 65

silfrgangr (ON) noun

Silver currency. Refers particularly to the purity or quality of silver in Grg Misc 245.

currency of silver **OIce** *Grg* Misc 245

See also: *konungssteði, kúgildi, lögsilfr, mark (2), vaþmal*

Refs: Arnljótr Ólafsson 1904; CV; Fritzner; Helgi Skúli Kjartansson 1988; Hertzberg; Jón Jóhannesson 2006, 330; KLNM s.v. *gangssylv*

silfrmetinn (ON) adj.

in measured silver **ONorw** *FrL* Mhb 45 Var 1 Kvb 25

measured in burnt silver **ONorw** *FrL* KrbA 18 KrbB 2

silfsmiþer (OSw) noun

silver smith **OSw** *HL* Kmb

silkisband (OGu) noun

satin ribbon **OGu** *GL* A 65

silver (OSw) silv (ODan) silfr (ON) noun

silver **ODan** *ESjL* 1–3, *JyL* 1–3, *SkL* 96, 98, 219, *VSjL* 1, 33, 36, 50, 86, 87, **ONorw** *GuL* Krb, Kpb, Mhb, Olb, **OSw** *HL* Kmb, *SdmL* Äb, Kmb, *YVgL* Jb, *ÄVgL* Jb

Expressions:

bleikt silfr (ON)

white silver **OIce** *Grg* Misc 245

brennt silfr (ON)

burnt silver **OIce** *Jó* Kab 5 **ONorw** *EidsL* 39.4

refined silver **OIce** *Grg* Klþ 4, 5 Arþ 125 Feþ 166 Fjl 221 Misc 246 Tíg 257 Js Ert 2 KRA 15

sinfallinn (ON) adj.

sexually impotent **OIce** *KRA* 17

See also: *hörundfall*

sior (OSw) siar (OGu) noun

lake **OSw** *UL* Mb, Blb, *VmL* Mb, Bb

sea **OGu** *GL* A 36, **OSw** *UL* Kgb

siskinaalder (OSw) noun

sibling brood **OSw** *UL* Jb

sitia (OSw) sitja (ON) verb

sit

Expressions:

sitia (a vægh) firi (OSw)

lie in wait for someone **OSw** *DL* Eb UL Kgb VmL Kgb

sit in ambush **OSw** *HL* Kgb *SdmL* Kgb *YVgL* Add *ÖgL* Eb

See also: *byggia, leghia*

siunættatak (OSw) noun

security in seven nights **OSw** *YVgL* Tb

siunættinger (OSw) noun

A legal time-limit of seven nights as well as a meeting held after it, where witnesses and compurgators were to handle a case. If a settlement was not reached, the case was passed on to the *þing* 'assembly'.

seven-night summons **OSw** *YVgL* Frb, Äb, Rlb, Tb, Jb, Föb, Utgb, Add, *ÄVgL* Slb, Äb, Rlb, Jb, Tb, Föb

See also: *endaghi, fimmnættingr, fœmt, sjaund, sægnarþing, þrenættinger*

Refs: Brink 2011b, 150; KLNM s.v. *sjunätting*

siunættingsdagher (OSw) noun

day of the seven-night summons **OSw** *YVgL* Jb, *ÄVgL* Jb

siunættingsgærþ (OSw) noun

seven-night meeting **OSw** *ÄVgL* Slb

seven-night summons **OSw** *YVgL* Jb

siviaslit (OSw) noun

incest with kin by marriage **OSw** *SmL*

See also: *sifskaper, ætskuspiæll*

siþer (OSw) siþr (OGu) noun

custom **OGu** *GS* Ch. 3, **OSw** *SdmL* Conf

tax **OGu** *GS* Ch. 3

siþvænia (OSw) siþvæne (OSw) noun

custom **OSw** *HL* Kkb, *SdmL* Till

siængaköp (OSw) sængarköp (OSw) sænghar köp (OSw) noun

A purchase made by married spouses. The man owned two thirds and the woman one third.

bed-purchase **OSw** *HL* Äb

items bought to a couple's common home **OSw** *DL* Gb

purchase into the marriage bed **OSw** *UL* Äb, Jb, *VmL* Äb, Jb

See also: *bolköp, væggiarköp*

siængalæghi (OSw) siænglæghe (OSw) sænglæghe (OSw) noun

conjugal rights **OSw** *UL* Kkb, *VmL* Kkb

marital bed **OSw** *SmL*

siængaralder (OSw) siængar alster (OSw) noun

brood **OSw** *UL* Äb, Jb

children of different batches **OSw** *HL* Äb

descendants **OSw** *DL* Äb

offspring **OSw** *HL* Kkb

offspring of a lawful bed **OSw** *HL* Äb

See also: *byrþaman, siængaralster, sængaslæt*

siængaralster (OSw) noun

offspring **OSw** *UL* Kkb, Äb

offspring of a man and wife **OSw**
VmL Äb (introduction)

spouses and parents and children **OSw** *HL* Äb

símonsmessudagr ok judas (ON) noun

SS Simon and Jude's Day **OIce** *Grg* Klþ 13

See also: *tveggjapostulamessa*

síþráðr (ON) noun

oakum **ONorw** *GuL* Leb

sjalfboðinn (ON) adj.

automatically called **OIce** *Js* Kdb
4, **ONorw** *FrL* Mhb 8

sjalfelðismaðr (ON) noun

self-supporting man **OIce** *Grg* Tíg 260

sjalfkvaddr (ON) adj.

automatically called **OIce** *Grg* Þsþ 58, 59

sjalfræði (ON) noun

one's own accord **OIce** *Grg* Arþ 121

sjalfsettr (ON) adj.

Self-set; self-appointed; automatically triggered by an event.

as a matter of course **OIce** *Jó* Mah 19

See also: *sialvasæt*

Refs: CV s.v. *sjálfsettr*; Fritzner s.v.
sjalfsettr; Hertzberg s.v. *sjálfsettr*

sjalfsfózlumaðr (ON) noun

man who sets up on his own **OFar** *Seyð* 7

sjalfskeytr (ON) adj.

automatically conveyed **ONorw** *FrL* Jkb 2

transferred automatically **ONorw** *FrL* LlbB 4

sjalfstefndr (ON) adj.

automatically summoned **OIce** *Jó*
Þfb 5, **ONorw** *FrL* Mhb 8

without a summons **ONorw** *FrL* LlbA 11

sjalftekinn (ON) adj.

automatically dissolved **OIce** *Jó* Kge 18

end automatically **ONorw** *FrL* LlbB 1

sjalfvili (ON) noun

one's own free-will **ONorw** *FrL* Var 45

sjaund (ON) noun

A legal meeting possibly synonymous with OSw *siunættinger* (q.v.), but in ONorw only used concerning the funeral, funeral feast and distribution of the estate seven days after a death.

period of seven days **OIce** *Js* Ert 18

seventh-day ale **ONorw** *GuL* Krb

See also: *endaghi, fimmnættinger, fœmt,
sáluöl, siunættinger, þrenættinger*

Refs: Cleasby and Vigfusson s.v.
sjaund; Fritzner s.v. *sjaund*

sjaundargerð (ON) noun

giving a seventh-day ale **ONorw** *GuL* Arb

See also: *sjaund*

sjauviknafasta (ON) noun

seven-week fast **ONorw** *FrL* Jkb 2

sjándi (ON) noun

eyewitness **ONorw** *FrL* Mhb 23

sjóðr (ON) noun

purse **ONorw** *GuL* Arb

sjónarváttr (ON) noun

eyewitness **OIce** *Js* Mah 18

sjúkr (ON) adj.

ill **ONorw** *GuL* Krb, Kvb, Løb

skaðabót (ON) **skaðabætr** (ON) noun

Compensation paid for damages, especially in cases of willful damage (ON *spellvirki*) (cf. Grg Þsþ 51 and 63). Use of the term appears to have been most common in Iceland, though it does appear later in the Faroes and in MLL. According to Grg Þsþ 63 the amount was determined by a panel of five neighbours. Failure to pay this compensation was grounds for outlawry. In one instance *skaðabót* refers specifically to losses incurred by sailors forced to jettison cargo (Grg Feþ 166).

The significance of a s*kaðabót* appears to have lessened in the later thirteenth century, when it refers to minor damages committed by grazing livestock (Js Lbb 13; Jó Llb 6; Seyð) and to driftwood (Jó Llb 61). In this sense it appears to resemble *skaþagæld* (q.v.), a term employed in Swedish (HL) and Danish (ESjL, JyL) laws.

compensation for damage **OFar** *Seyð* 5, **OIce**
Grg Þsþ 51, 63 Feþ 166, *Jó* Llb 6, 31, *Js* Lbb 13

See also: *bot, skaþagæld, spellvirki*

Refs: CV s.v. *skaðabætr*; Fritzner s.v.
skaðabót; Hertzberg s.v. *skaðabót*

skaf (ON) noun

scraped bark **ONorw** *GuL* Llb

skafl (OSw) **skafl** (OGu) noun

fruit crops **OSw** *UL* Mb (table of contents only)

tree fruit **OGu** *GL* A 59

skaflþiuver (OSw) noun

theft of fruit and vegetable **OSw** *HL* Mb

skaftøks (ODan) noun

axe with a handle **ODan** *ESjL* 3

skal (OGu) **skál** (ON) noun

A bowl (for drinking), and in the plural a pair of scales (for measuring coins and other small items).

bowl **OGu** *GL* A 19, 63, Add. 6 (B 33)

pair of scales **ONorw** *GuL* Løb, Mhb

scales **OGu** *GL* A 20

See also: *hiernskal*

skall (OSw) noun

battue **OSw** *SdmL* Bb

skam (OSw) skam (ODan) skam (OGu) skömm (ON) noun

dishonour **OIce** *Jó* Mah 16, 24

rape **OGu** *GL* A 22

shame **ODan** *JyL* 2, *VSjL* 41, 52, **OGu** *GL* A 22, Add. 1 (B 4), **OSw** *YVgL* Gb, *ÄVgL* Lek

skaning (ODan) noun

Scanian **ODan** *SkKL* Prol, *SkL* 79

skap (OGu) noun

genitals **OGu** *GL* A 19

See also: *skapt*

skapa (ON) verb

adjust **ONorw** *GuL* Løb

grant **ONorw** *GuL* Krb

make **ONorw** *GuL* Tjb

skaparfuni (ON) noun

natural heir **OIce** *Grg* Klþ 1

See also: *skaparvi*

skaparvi (OSw) skaparfi (ON) skæptarvi (OSw) noun

direct heir **OSw** *YVgL* Äb, *ÄVgL* Äb

heir of the body **OSw** *ÖgL* Eb

natural heir **OIce** *Grg* Arþ 118, 127 Ómb 134, *KRA* 1

See also: *skaparfuni*

skapbótandi (ON) skapbætandi (ON) noun

proper payer **OIce** *Grg* Bat 113

skapdróttinn (ON) noun

lawful master **ONorw** *EidsL* 28.2, *FrL* Mhb 56 ArbB 10 Kvb 23

master **ONorw** *GuL* Krb, Løb, Arb, Mhb, Leb

See also: *drotin*

skapker (ON) noun

ale cask **ONorw** *GuL* Løb

skapt (OSw) skapt (OGu) skaft (ON) noun

penis **OGu** *GL* A 19

shaft **ONorw** *GuL* Kvr, Mhb, **OSw** *UL* Mb

See also: *skap*

skapþiggjandi (ON) noun

proper receiver **OIce** *Grg* Bat 113

skapþing (ON) noun

established assembly **OIce** *Grg* Þsþ 82

See also: *þing*

skarlaþ (OGu) noun

fine woollen cloth **OGu** *GL* A 24b, 65

See also: *bladragning*

skatheløs (ODan) adj.

free of charge **ODan** *ESjL* 2

harmless **ODan** *ESjL* 2

without damage **ODan** *JyL* 3, *SkL* 203

skatheløst (ODan) adv.

without damage **ODan** *SkL* 179, 196, 198, 199, 201

skatskyldugher (OSw) adj.

liable to tax **OSw** *SdmL* Till

skattalaust (ON) adv.

free from dues **ONorw** *GuL* Løb

skatter (OSw) skattr (OGu) skattr (ON) noun

Etymologically 'livestock; valuables; coin; money' used of tributes/duties/taxes. In OIce Jó, paid to the king beside the *þingfararkaup* (q.v.). In OSw HL, explicitly linked to the king and *leþunger* (q.v.).

tax **OGu** *GS* Ch. 2, 4, **OSw** *HL* Kgb, *YVgL* Utgb

taxes **OIce** *Jó* Sg 1

Refs: Helgi Þorláksson 2011, 143–46; Jónsson and Boulhosa, 2011, 158–60; ONP s.v. *skattr*

skattgreizla (ON) noun

payment of tax **OIce** *Jó* Sg 1

skattman (OSw) noun

The *konungx rætter skatman* 'the king's legal tax-collector' in OSw HL Rb is presumed to be the *ari* (q.v.).

tax collector **OSw** *HL* Rb, *UL* Mb

See also: *ari*, *boghi*, *intækiuman*, *næmdarmaþer*, *skatter*, *tækiomaþer*

Refs: Förvaltningshistorisk ordbok s.v. *konungsåren*

skattsvarr (ON) adj.

acceptable as tax money **ONorw** *GuL* Llb, Mhb

skauðhvítr (ON) adj.

having a whitish sheath (of stallions) **ONorw** *GuL* Mhb

skauðmígr (ON) adj.

having weak urinating organs (of stallions) **ONorw** *GuL* Mhb

skaut (ON) noun

piece of cloth used for drawing lots **ONorw** *GuL* Llb

skaþa (OSw) skaða (ON) verb

cause damage **OSw** *DL* Bb

damage **OSw** *SdmL* Kkb

harm **OIce** *Jó* Lbb 3

skaþagæld (OSw) skathegjald (ODan) noun

compensation for damage **OSw** *HL* Blb

damages **OSw** *YVgL* Tb

indemnification **OSw** *HL* Blb

indemnity **OSw** *HL* Mb

payment for damage **ODan** *ESjL* 2, *JyL* 3

skaþamaþer (OSw) **skaðamaðr** (ON) **skaþaman** (OSw) noun

assailant **OSw** *UL* Mb (table of contents only), Rb, *VmL* Mb

attacker **OSw** *DL* Mb

culprit **OSw** *UL* Rb, *VmL* Mb, Rb

killer **OIce** *Js* Mah 12, **ONorw** *FrL* Mhb 15

offender **OSw** *HL* Mb, *SdmL* Mb, Tjdb, Rb

See also: *illgærningisman*

skaþi (OSw) **skathe** (ODan) **skaþi** (OGu) **skaði** (ON) noun

damage **ODan** *ESjL* 2, 3, *JyL* 1, 3, *SkL* passim, *VSjL* 56, 57, 64, **OFar** *Seyð* 1, 5, **OGu** *GL* A 17, 26, 50, Add. 2 (B 17), **OIce** *Grg* Feþ 164 Lbþ 175, 198 Fjl 224, 225 Misc 243, *Jó* Llb 4 Kab 20 Þjb 6, 11, *Js* Lbb 20 Kab 21, **ONorw** *EidsL* 35.4 37.2, *GuL* Llb, Tfb, **OSw** *DL* Kkb, Bb, *HL* Kgb, Mb, Kmb, Blb, *SdmL* Kkb, Bb, Mb, *UL* Kkb, Kgb, Mb, Blb, *VmL* Mb, Bb, *YVgL* Kkb, Rlb, Tb, Föb, Utgb, Add, *ÄVgL* Kkb, Rlb, Tb, Fös, Lek

deed (1) **OGu** *GL* A 16

detriment **ODan** *JyL* 1, **OSw** *UL* Blb

harm **ODan** *ESjL* 2, *JyL* 1, **OIce** *Grg* Vís 108, **OSw** *DL* Eb, *HL* Kgb, Blb, *SdmL* Kgb, *SmL*, *UL* Kgb, *VmL* Kgb, *ÄVgL* Fös, *ÖgL* Eb

injury **ODan** *JyL* 3, *VSjL* 86, **OGu** *GL* A 25, 50, 51, Add. 2 (B 17), **OIce** *Jó* Mah 11, 16, **ONorw** *FrL* Intr 1, *GuL* Mhb, **OSw** *DL* Mb, *HL* Kkb, Kgb, Blb, Rb, *SdmL* Kkb, Kgb, Bb, Kmb, Mb, *UL* Kkb, Kgb, Mb, Kmb, Blb, Rb, *VmL* Kkb, Kgb, Mb, Kmb, Bb, *YVgL* Add, *ÖgL* Eb

loss **OIce** *Jó* Fml 10, **OSw** *HL* Mb, *UL* Kmb

Expressions:

sla til skaþa (OSw)

injure **OSw** *VmL* Kkb

See also: *sar*, *spellvirki*, *spiæll*

skáldskaparmál (ON) noun

The speech used for creating poetic (skaldic) verse. Associated with defamatory poetry in the Icelandic laws.

language of poetry **OIce** *Grg* Misc 237

slander in verse form **OIce** *Jó* Mah 26

See also: *mansöngr*

Refs: CV s.v. *skáldskaparmál*; Fritzner s.v. *skáldskaparmál*; Hertzberg s.v. *skáldskaparmál*; LexMA s.v. *Skald, Skaldendichtung*

skáldskapr (ON) noun

poetry **OIce** *Grg* Misc 238, *Jó* Mah 26

skeðja (ON) verb

damage **OIce** *Grg* Lbþ 185, *Jó* Lbb 7, *Js* Lbb 3

skemma (OGu) verb

dishonour **OGu** *GL* A 22

harm **OFar** *Seyð* 12, **OIce** *Js* Mah 11

hurt **ONorw** *FrL* Intr 6

injure **ONorw** *FrL* Intr 7

shame **OIce** *Jó* Sg 3

skemmð (ON) noun

dishonour **OIce** *Js* Mah 33

injury **OIce** *Jó* Mah 19

skemmðarvíg (ON) noun

A shameful killing, similar or perhaps equivalent to a villainous killing (ON *níðingsvíg*) or villainous deed (ON *níðingsverk*, see *niþingsværk*). Three types of shameful killings are listed in Js Mah 5: killing someone after giving guarantees of peace (ON *tryggð*, see *trygth*), killing during a truce and committing murder (ON *myrða*, see *myrþa*). Other offenses called *níðingsvíg* are listed in Jó Mah 2, including bodily mutilation and taking vengeance for someone convicted of theft. Those convicted of committing a *skemmðarvíg* forfeit their lands and lost the right to atone for crimes through compensation (cf. ON *óbótamaðr*).

shameful killing **OIce** *Jó* Mah 1, 2, *Js* Mah 5, 29, **ONorw** *FrL* Mhb 1, 2

See also: *myrþa*, *níðingsvíg*, *niþingsværk*, *tryggrof*, *urbotamal*

Refs: CV s.v. *skemmdarvíg*; Fritzner s.v. *skemdarvíg*; Hertzberg s.v. *skemdarvíg*; KLNM s.v. *trygð*

skena (OSw) **skaina** (OGu) **skeina** (ON) **skene** (ODan) verb

hurt slightly **ONorw** *FrL* Rgb 41

scratch **OIce** *Grg* Vís 92

tear apart **OGu** *GL* A 19

wound **ONorw** *FrL* Mhb 17, **OSw** *YVgL* Add

skena (OSw) noun

external injury **ODan** *SkL* 96

flesh wound **OSw** *VmL* Mb, *ÖgL* Vm

open wound **OSw** *YVgL* Add, *ÖgL* Kkb, Eb, Vm

serious wound **OSw** *YVgL* Add

wound made with a weapon **OSw** *SdmL* Mb

skernár (ON) noun

skerry-corpse **OIce** *Grg* Bat 113

skeytingarvitni (ON) noun

witness of conveyance **ONorw** *FrL* Rgb 28

skila (OSw) noun

decision **OSw** *SdmL* Kkb, *UL* Kkb, Rb, Add. 18

skiladómr (ON) noun

This was a court of arbitration, a tribunal of twelve men. It had to decide on the facts of a case that was not entirely clear. The consequences were left to the negotiation of the parties involved. The *skiladómr* was opposed to the *sáttardómr*, which passed judgement on cases in which the circumstances were already clear.

court of arbitration **ONorw** *GuL* Kpb, Llb, Olb

decision **ONorw** *FrL* Jkb 6

decisive judgement **OIce** *Js* Ert 20 Lbb 16 Kab 10

lawful judgement **OIce** *Jó* Llb 5 Kab 14

private court for arbitration **ONorw** *FrL* Rgb 25 Jkb 6

See also: *laghedom*

Refs: Helle 2001, 91–97, 154; Hertzberg s.v. *skiladómr*; KLNM s.v.v. *dómr, ting, veddemål*; Robberstad 1981, 341, 343; Sunde 2014, 143

skilamaþer (OSw) noun

judge **OSw** *DL* Gb

skildagi (ON) noun

agreement **OIce** *Jó* Llb 45

terms **OIce** *Jó* Kab 12, *KRA* 16

skilfall (OSw) noun

fine for failing to take an oath with one's neighbours **OSw** *DL* Tjdb

See also: *grannaeþer*

skilfenginn (ON) adj.

lawfully wedded **OIce** *Jó* Kge 1, 7, *Js* Ert 4, 16, **ONorw** *FrL* KrbB 10

legitimate **ONorw** *FrL* ArbA 2

skilgetinn (ON) adj.

born in wedlock **ONorw** *FrL* Mhb 31, *GuL* Krb, Sab

legitimate **OIce** *Jó* Mah 17 Kge 7, 22, *Js* Kdb 4 Mah 8 Ert 2, 3, *KRA* 9, 10, **ONorw** *FrL* ArbA 3

See also: *skírgetinn*

skilia (OSw) **skilje** (ODan) **skilia** (OGu) **skilja** (ON) **skiljask** (ON) verb

Originally 'to split'. Legally significant uses include dissolving marriages ('divorce', 'part', 'separate'), partaking in other conflicts with legal consequences ('quarrel', '(have a) dispute', 'disagree'), evading legal duties ('withdraw', 'leave'). Also being separated from rights ('lose one's right') or obligations ('free'), analysing legal matters ('investigate', 'distinguish') and deciding legal matters ('decide', 'determine'), as well as stating the legally significant result of the analysis in more general terms ('say', 'declare', 'stipulate') or more specific terms ('take a stand', 'settle', 'prove', 'make an agreement').

annul **OIce** *Jó* Kge 6

bar **OSw** *HL* Äb

break an agreement **ODan** *SkL* 228

care for **OSw** *YVgL* Add

decide **ODan** *ESjL* 1, 3, *JyL* 1–3, *VSjL* 1, **OGu** *GL* A 26, **ONorw** *GuL* Kpb, Leb, **OSw** *UL* Kgb, Rb

detach **OSw** *ÄVgL* Jb

determine **OSw** *UL* StfBM, Blb, Rb, *VmL* Rb

differ **OSw** *UL* Kkb, Rb, *VmL* Kkb

disagree **ODan** *ESjL* 1–3, *JyL* 1, 2, *SkKL* 13, *SkL* 4, 27, 28, 67, 70, 72–74, 80, *VSjL* 2, 82, **OGu** *GL* A 3, **ONorw** *GuL* Krb, Llb, Tfb, Olb, Leb, **OSw** *DL* Eb, *HL* Jb, *UL* Kkb, Kgb, Kmb, *YVgL* Kkb, Äb, Rlb, Jb, Föb, Add, *ÄVgL* Kkb, Äb, Rlb, Jb, Föb

dispute **ODan** *JyL* 1, *VSjL* 15, 18, 71, 73, 76, 78, **OGu** *GL* Add. 7 (B 49), **OSw** *DL* Tjdb, *HL* Kgb, Rb, *YVgL* Kkb, Jb, Utgb

dissolve **OIce** *KRA* 17, **ONorw** *BorgL* 3.4 15.4, **OSw** *UL* Äb

distinguish **OSw** *UL* Äb, Blb, *VmL* Bb

divide **ONorw** *GuL* Llb, Arb, **OSw** *YVgL* Kkb

divorce **OIce** *Grg* Þsþ 81, **ONorw** *FrL* KrbB 10, **OSw** *YVgL* Kkb

be divorced **ONorw** *GuL* Kvb, Løb

exclude **ODan** *JyL* 2, **OSw** *UL* Äb, Jb, *VmL* Äb

free **ODan** *ESjL* 1

be free **ONorw** *GuL* Kvb

have a dispute **ODan** *ESjL* 2

investigate **OSw** *DL* Rb

leave **ODan** *SkKL* 2, *SkL* 19, 238, **OIce** *Jó* Kge 5

list **ONorw** *GuL* Mhb

lose one's right **ODan** *ESjL* 2

make an agreement **OSw** *YVgL* Gb, *ÄVgL* Gb

organize **OSw** *YVgL* Add

part **OGu** *GL* A 20, **ONorw** *EidsL* 4, **OSw** *UL* Kkb, Kgb, Mb, *VmL* Kkb, Kgb, *ÄVgL* Äb, Tb

prove **ONorw** *GuL* Mhb

quarrel **ODan** *JyL* 2, *VSjL* 75, 78

say **ONorw** *GuL* Tjb, **OSw** *ÄVgL* Gb

separate **ODan** *ESjL* 1, 3, *JyL* 1–3, *SkKL* 11, *SkL* 7, 9, 11, 17, 29, 221, 231, *VSjL* 2, 3, 8, **OGu** *GL* A 20, **OIce** *Grg* Feþ 149, *Js* Kvg 5, *KRA* 1, 16, **ONorw**

BorgL 15.4 17.1, *EidsL* 30.8 53.6, *GuL* Mhb, Olb,
OSw *HL* Äb, *SdmL* Gb, *UL* Äb, Blb, *YVgL* Kkb,
Frb, Äb, Gb, Jb, *ÄVgL* Slb, Äb, Gb, *ÖgL* Kkb

settle **OSw** *YVgL* Add, *ÄVgL* Kva

split up **ODan** *ESjL* 2, *JyL* 3, **OSw** *HL* Kkb, Äb

take a stand **ODan** *JyL* 2

withdraw **ODan** *SkKL* 7

See also: *askilia, dela, forskialamaþer,
raþa, skæl, vita*

skilnaðarsök (ON) noun

cause of divorce **OIce** *Jó* Kge 5

skilnaþer (OSw) **skilneth** (ODan) **skjalneth** (ODan)
skilnaðr (ON) **skilnuðr** (ON) **skialnaþer** (OSw)
skiælnaþer (OSw) noun

conflict **OSw** *SdmL* Kgb, Gb, *YVgL* Add

disagreement **ODan** *JyL* 1, 2, *SkL* 4, *VSjL* 1

dispute **ODan** *JyL* 1, 3, *VSjL* 6, 15, 16,
20, **OSw** *DL* Eb, *HL* Kgb, *UL* Kgb, Kmb,
VmL Kgb, *YVgL* Add, *ÖgL* Eb, Db

divorce **ONorw** *GuL* Kvb, Løb, Arb

separation **ONorw** *EidsL* 22.4, **OSw** *HL*
Kkb, *SdmL* Kkb, Gb, *UL* Kkb, Blb

skilorð (ON) noun

agreement **OIce** *Jó* Kab 12

condition **OIce** *Jó* Mah 4 Þjb 19,
Js Mah 31, 37, *KRA* 16, 32

provision **ONorw** *FrL* Intr 4

stipulation **OIce** *Jó* Kge 1

terms **OIce** *Jó* Kge 7-4 Llb 45

skilríkr (ON) adj.

discerning **OIce** *Jó* MagBref

responsible **OIce** *Jó* Þfb 2

trustworthy **OFar** *Seyð* 3

skilvangi (ON) noun

rule **ONorw** *FrL* KrbB 11

skin (OSw) noun

In the northernmost OSw laws, hunting for fur was
economically important and a basis for taxation. In
HL they appear as annual taxes paid in *twælyt skin*
'two-coloured pelt' and *blaskorin skin* 'blue-cut
pelt' permanently substituting the *leþunger* 'levy'.
For skin-taxes in DL see *bælskin, leþungsskin,
vighramannaskin.*

pelt **OSw** *HL* Kgb

skin-tax **OSw** *DL* Rb

Refs: KLNM s.v. skinnskatt

skiolder (OSw) **skjold** (ODan) **skjöldr** (ON) noun

sanctuary **ONorw** *BorgL* 18.3

shield **ODan** *ESjL* 2, *SkL* 87, **ONorw** *GuL* Leb,
OSw *HL* Mb, Rb, *SdmL* Mb, *UL* Mb, *VmL*
Mb, *YVgL* Urb, Add, *ÄVgL* Urb, *ÖgL* Eb

Expressions:

bæra skiold ivir þangbrekku (OSw)
Presumably refers to an attack from the
sea [as an act of military treason?].
bear shield over beach **OSw**
ÄVgL Urb *YVgL* Urb, Add

carry a shield across sea and sea shore **OSw** *ÖgL* Eb

See also: *avugher*

skip (OSw) **skip** (ODan) **skip** (OGu) **skip** (ON) noun

boat **OGu** *GL* A 49

ship **ODan** *ESjL* 2, 3, *JyL* 2, *SkL* 164, *VSjL* 64,
OGu *GL* A 13, 20, 36, Add. 8 (B 55), **ONorw**
GuL Krb, Kpb, Llb, Arb, Tfb, Reb, Kvr, Mhb,
Olb, Leb, **OSw** *HL* Kgb, Mb, Blb, *SdmL* Kgb, Bb,
Mb, *UL* Kgb, Äb, Mb, *YVgL* Äb, *ÄVgL* Äb, Fös

Expressions:

halfþrítugt skip (ON)
twenty-five bencher **ONorw** *GuL* Leb

þrítugt skip (ON)
thirty-bencher **ONorw** *GuL* Leb

See also: *bater, byrthing, farkoster, floti,
halfþrítugr, kaupskip, myndrikkia, skiplagh*

skipa (OSw) **skipa** (OGu) **skipa** (ON) verb

allocate **OSw** *UL* Blb, *VmL* Bb

allow **OSw** *UL* Blb, *VmL* Bb

arrange **ONorw** *GuL* Arb, Olb

decide **OSw** *YVgL* Kkb

design **OSw** *UL* StfBM

divide **OGu** *GL* A 40, 41, **OSw** *UL* Blb

draw up **ONorw** *GuL* Sab

enact **OSw** *UL* StfBM, För, *VmL* För

load **ONorw** *GuL* Tfb

man **ONorw** *GuL* Mhb, Olb, Leb

ordain **OSw** *UL* StfBM, Kkb

skipakaup (ON) noun

trading at ships **OIce** *Grg* Feþ 167

skipamaðr (ON) noun

shipman **OIce** *Grg* Hrs 234

skipan (OSw) **skipan** (ON) **skipun** (ON) noun

arrangement **OSw** *SdmL* Bb

contract **OIce** *Jó* Fml 8, **OSw** *HL* Jb

decree **OIce** *Jó* Kge 29

law **ONorw** *FrL* Intr 22

loading a ship **ONorw** *GuL* Tfb

new law **OFar** *Seyð* 0

order **OIce** *Js* Kdb 3 Mah 29, 37,
KRA 4, 6, **ONorw** *FrL* Intr 19

ordinance **OFar** *Seyð* 0, 4

provision **OIce** *Jó* MagBref

statute **ONorw** *FrL* Intr 7

skipari (OSw) **skipere** (ODan) **skipari** (ON) noun

crewman **OIce** *Jó* Fml 4, 8

man on a ship **OSw** *SdmL* Kgb, Mb

sailor **ODan** *ESjL* 3, **ONorw** *GuL* Llb

skipper **OSw** *HL* Mb, *UL* Äb, Mb

someone on a ship **ODan** *JyL* 2

skipasmíð (ON) noun

shipbuilding **ONorw** *GuL* Leb

skipbrotsmaðr (ON) noun

shipwrecked man **OIce** *Jó* Fml 12

skipbrut (ODan) noun

shipwreck **ODan** *JyL* 3

skipdráttr (ON) **skipsdráttr** (ON) noun

ship hauling **OIce** *Grg* Klþ 3, *Jó* Fml 3

skipdróttinn (ON) **skipsdróttinn** (ON) noun

ship's master **OIce** *Grg* Misc
249, **ONorw** *FrL* ArbB 5

See also: *styriman*

skipen (ODan) noun

ship-soke **ODan** *JyL* 3

See also: *skiplagh*

skiperfð (ON) noun

ship's inheritance **ONorw** *GuL* Arb

skipfarmr (ON) noun

boatload **OFar** *Seyð* 8

skiphlutr (ON) noun

boat share **OIce** *Jó* Llb 66

skiplagh (OSw) **skiplæghi** (OSw) noun

A naval sub-district (HL, SdmL, VmL, UL) which was
to equip, provision and man a ship for the *leþunger*, a
naval military defence organization.

ship-district **OSw** *SdmL* Kgb, Mb, Rb

{skiplagh} **OSw** *HL* Kgb, Äb, Mb, Blb,
Rb, *UL* Kgb, Mb, Rb, *VmL* Kgb

See also: *ar (1)*, *fiærþungsmaþer*, *hamna*, *har (1)*,
hundari, *leþunger*, *skip*, *skipreiða*, *manngerð*, *skipen*

Refs: Bagge 2010, 75; Hafström 1949, 18–20,
139–44 and passim; Helle 2001, 35, 77–78, 163–65,
168, 171, 174–75; Hertzberg 1895, s.v. *skipreiða*;
Hobæk 2013:5, 64–75; KLNM s.v.v. *leidang,
skipreide, skeppslag*; Robberstad 1981, 318–20,
390–92, 394, 399–401; Ødegaard 2013:5, 48

skipleiga (ON) noun

payment **OIce** *Jó* Fml 4

payment for cargo space **OIce** *Jó* Fml 22

rent for the ship **OIce** *Jó* Fml 6, 25

skipnöti (OSw) noun

{skipnöti} **OSw** *HL* Kgb, Mb

skipreiða (ON) noun

Originally a coastal district (within the *fylki*), which
had to provide a warship fully equipped with crew and
food for a period of two months. These obligations
were eventually transformed into yearly taxes.

warship district **ONorw** *GuL* Krb, Leb

See also: *skiplagh*, *skipen*, *ar (1)*,
har (1), *leþunger*, *hamna*

Refs: Bagge 2010, 75; Hafström 1949, 18–20,
139–44 and passim; Helle 2001, 35, 77–78, 163–65,
168, 171, 174–75; Hertzberg 1895, s.v. *skipreiða*;
Hobæk 2013:5, 64-75; KLNM s.v.v. *leidang,
skipreide, skeppslag*; Robberstad 1981, 318–20,
390–92, 394, 399–401; Ødegaard 2013:5, 48

skipreiðumenn (pl.) (ON) noun

*men belonging to the same levy
district* **ONorw** *GuL* Leb

See also: *skiplagh*

skipreiðuþing (ON) noun

levy district assembly **ONorw** *FrL* Intr 23

See also: *fylkisþing*, *þing*

skipslán (ON) noun

ship loan **OIce** *Jó* Fml 28

skipsnævning (ODan) noun

Men on board a ship appointed to deal with conflicts
between steersman (ODan *styreman*, see *styriman*)
and crew (ODan *skipere*, see *skipari*). Synonymous
with *farvitenævning* (q.v.).

men nominated from the ship **ODan** *JyL* 3

Refs: Lund s.v. *farvitnæfning*; Tamm
and Vogt, eds, 2016, 304

skipsstjórn (ON) noun

command of a ship **ONorw** *GuL* Leb

skipsverð (ON) noun

ship cost **ONorw** *FrL* Leb 2

skipsýsla (ON) noun

levy district **ONorw** *FrL* Leb 2

See also: *skiplagh*

skipta (OSw) **skifte** (ODan) **skipta** (OGu) **skifta** (ON)
skifta (OSw) verb

appoint **OSw** *ÄVgL* Rlb

apportion **ONorw** *GuL* Arb

bring **OSw** *ÄVgL* Gb

change **OSw** *DL* Bb

decide **ODan** *SkKL* 13, **OSw** *HL* Mb

detract **ONorw** *GuL* Krb

distribute **ODan** *JyL* 1, **OGu** *GL* A 25, **ONorw**
GuL Krb, Leb, **OSw** *HL* Kkb, Äb, Jb, *UL* StfBM,
Kgb, Äb, Mb, Blb, *VmL* Kgb, Äb, Mb, Jb, Bb

divide **ODan** *ESjL* 1–3, *JyL* 1, 2, *SkL* passim, *VSjL*
1–3, 6, 8, 18–21, 70, 87, **OGu** *GL* A 20, 24e, 28,
ONorw *GuL* Krb, Llb, Tfb, Leb, **OSw** *DL* Kkb,
Eb, Mb, Bb, Gb, Tjdb, *HL* Kkb, Kgb, Äb, Mb, Jb,
Blb, Rb, *SdmL* Kkb, Kgb, Gb, Äb, Jb, Bb, Mb,
Till, *SmL*, *UL* passim, *VmL* passim, *YVgL* passim,
ÄVgL Kkb, Md, Slb, Äb, Jb, *ÖgL* Eb, Db, Vm

divide inheritance **OGu** *GL* A 28

exchange **ODan** *ESjL* 1, 3, *JyL* 1, *SkL* 46,
OGu *GL* A 47, **ONorw** *GuL* Olb, **OSw** *DL*
Bb, *HL* Jb, *SdmL* Jb, Kmb, *UL* Äb, Jb, Kmb,
VmL Jb, Kmb, *YVgL* Kkb, *ÄVgL* Jb

judge **ONorw** *GuL* Arb

leave a household **ODan** *VSjL* 1

make a division **ODan** *ESjL* 1, *JyL* 1, *SkL* 27,
230, 231, *VSjL* 6, **OSw** *DL* Bb, *HL* Blb

make an exchange **ODan** *ESjL* 1, **OSw** *DL* Bb

partition **OSw** *YVgL* Föb, *ÖgL* Eb

reclaim **OSw** *DL* Bb

replace **ODan** *JyL* 2

separate **ODan** *ESjL* 1, **OSw** *DL* Eb, *HL*
Äb, *UL* Kgb, Äb, Rb, *VmL* Kgb, Äb, Rb

share **ODan** *JyL* 3

share out **OSw** *UL* Äb, Jb, *VmL* Äb

shift **OSw** *HL* Kgb

transfer **OGu** *GL* A 7

Expressions:

undan skipta (OSw)

separate out **OSw** *UL* Äb, Rb *VmL* Kgb, Äb, Rb

skipter (OSw) adj.

divided **OSw** *DL* Bb

divided concerning property **OSw** *DL* Mb

skipti (OSw) **skifte** (ODan) **skipti** (OGu) **skipti** (ON)
skift (OSw) **skipt** (OSw) noun

Derived from the verb *skipta* and referring to the
parting, sharing and distribution of property, mainly
land but also movables, through purchase, barter
and inheritance. Also the share of the property thus
obtained, often a specific piece of land.

barter **OSw** *UL* Mb, *VmL* Mb

distribution **OSw** *DL* Eb, *UL* Blb, *VmL* Bb

distribution of estate **ODan** *JyL* 1

division **ODan** *ESjL* 1, 2, *JyL* 1, *SkL* 21, 23, 27, 28,
55, 67, 71, 229, *VSjL* 17, 20, **OGu** *GL* A 28, **OSw** *DL*
Bb, *HL* Mb, Jb, *SdmL* Kgb, Gb, Bb, Mb, Till, *UL* Äb,
Jb, Blb, *VmL* Äb, Jb, Bb, *YVgL* Äb, Jb, Add, *ÖgL* Eb

division of land **ONorw** *GuL* Llb, Olb

division of odal land **ONorw** *GuL* Llb, Olb

division of property **OSw** *HL* Äb

exchange **ODan** *ESjL* 2, **OSw** *DL* Bb, *HL*
Jb, Kmb, Blb, *SdmL* Jb, Kmb, *UL* Jb, Kmb,
VmL Jb, Kmb, *YVgL* Jb, *ÄVgL* Jb

exchanged land **OSw** *ÄVgL* Jb

parcel of land **OSw** *YVgL* Jb, Add

partition **OSw** *YVgL* Äb, Föb, *ÄVgL* Äb

plot of land **OSw** *YVgL* Jb, *ÄVgL* Jb

property division **OSw** *UL* Äb,
Jb, Add. 5, *VmL* Äb, Jb

share **OSw** *HL* Mb

shift **OSw** *ÄVgL* Gb

See also: *bo, boskipti, egn, fæ, goþs, inviþi*

skiptisfastar (pl.) (OSw) noun

transaction witnesses for an exchange **OSw** *SdmL* Jb

See also: *fastar (pl.), skipti*

skipvist (OSw) **skipuist** (OSw) **skipwist** (OSw) noun

Provisions for the *leþunger* 'levy' supplied by all
landowning householders, and a tax that replaced it
during the thirteenth century.

provisions **OSw** *UL* För, Kgb, *VmL* För, Kgb, Mb

ship supplies **OSw** *SdmL* Kgb

See also: *husaby, leþunger, utgærþ, vist*

Refs: KLNM s.v. *skeppsvist*

skiri (OSw) noun

district **OSw** *YVgL* Add

skiut (OSw) noun

conveyance **OSw** *HL* Kgb

horse for conveyance **OSw** *HL* Kgb

mare **OSw** *HL* Blb, *UL* Mb, Kmb,
Blb, *VmL* Mb, Kmb, Bb

packhorse **OSw** *DL* Bb, Tjdb, Rb,
UL Kmb, Blb, *VmL* Kmb, Bb

See also: *faruskiaut*

skiuta (OSw) **skjute** (ODan) **skiauta** (OGu) **skjóta**
(ON) **skiuva** (OSw) verb

collect **OGu** *GL* A 53

convey **ONorw** *GuL* Olb

dismiss **ODan** *ESjL* 2, *VSjL* 39, 87

point **ONorw** *GuL* Llb

propel **OSw** *UL* Mb

push **OGu** *GL* A 8, 19, 23, **OSw** *UL* Mb

refer **ODan** *JyL* 2, **OGu** *GL* A 37,
OSw *DL* Bb, *VmL* Jb, Rb
refer to a higher court **ONorw** *GuL* Kpb, Mhb, Olb
repudiate **OSw** *ÄVgL* Äb
send **OSw** *VmL* Äb
shoot **OSw** *UL* Kgb, Mb, *VmL* Kgb, Mb, Bb
Expressions:
skjótast undan (ON)
escape **ONorw** *GuL* Leb
skjóta til (guðs) (ON)
appeal, swear to God **OIce** *Js* Þfb 1 Kdb 5
See also: *rinda, skut*
skiutabref (OSw) noun
letter requesting the provision of horses for transport **OSw** *VmL* Kmb
skiutafærþ (OSw) noun
conveyance **OSw** *HL* Kgb
skiutagærþ (OSw) skiuta giærþ (OSw) noun
conveyance **OSw** *HL* Kgb
conveyance duty **OSw** *HL* Kgb
payment for conveyance **OSw** *HL* Kgb
provision of horses for transport **OSw** *SdmL* Kmb, *UL* Kmb (table of contents only), *VmL* Kmb
skiuva (OSw) verb
push **OSw** *UL* Mb
skíð (ON) noun
ski **ONorw** *GuL* Mhb
skírborinn (ON) adj.
legitimate **OIce** *Grg* Vís 95
skírgetinn (ON) adj.
legitimate **OIce** *Grg* Arþ 118
See also: *skilgetinn*
skíring (ON) noun
baptism **ONorw** *EidsL* 2 8
skíringarvitni (ON) noun
compurgatory witness **ONorw** *FrL* ArbA 16
skírn (ON) noun
With some minor variations, all of the Norwegian Christian laws divide the year into several different baptismal terms, with Christmas day, Easter Eve, St John's Eve, and St Michael's Mass as the termins of each period (see Landro 2010, 77–81). This arrangement is quite unusual in a European context. In the year 385, Pope Siricius prescribed Easter and Pentecost as the only legitimate dates for baptism, with exceptions for emergency situations. Due to the spreading of the Augustinian notion of sin, it was later demanded (e.g. in Anglo-Saxon sources) that infants

should be baptized as soon as possible. This was emphasized in the provincial laws, except in Norway. The Norwegian baptismal terms do not correspond to any of these traditions, perhaps because the baptismal terms follow the *gagnfasta* (see *fasta*).

In baptism, a spiritual relationship (*cognatio spiritualis*) was established through godfathers and godmothers. Baptism was regarded as the child's second and spiritual birth, and created a spiritual kinship between the actors involved in the ceremony, with significant consequences: They were forbidden to marry one another in order to prevent sexual relations among spiritual kin, which were regarded as a kind of incest (see Lynch 1998, 17). The concept of spiritual kinship originated in the Eastern Church and was introduced to the western parts of Europe in the early Middle Ages.
baptism **OIce** *Grg* Klþ 1 Feþ 144 Tíg 261, *Jó* HT 1, *KRA* 11, **ONorw** *BorgL* 2.3, *FrL* KrbA 3, *GuL* Krb
Refs: Helle 2001, 184, 190–91; KLNM s.v.v. *dåp, fadder, katekes och katekisation, olja och oljeinvigning, primsigning, profetia, påsken*; Landro 2010, 77–81; Lynch 1998, 17; Robberstad 1981, 332, 338
skírslastefna (ON) noun
time limits for baptisms **ONorw** *BorgL* 4
skítr (ON) noun
dirt **ONorw** *GuL* Løb
skjal (ON) noun
document **OIce** *Jó* Kab 12
skjul (ODan) noun
hiding place **ODan** *JyL* 3
skoghabrænna (OSw) noun
fire in the wood **OSw** *YVgL* Föb, Add
skoghaganga (OSw) noun
dispute regarding forest **OSw** *HL* Blb
skoghamærki (OSw) skógarmark (ON) noun
boundary mark in woodland **OIce** *Grg* Lbþ 199
boundary marks between forests **OSw** *HL* Blb
woodland boundary **OIce** *Jó* Llb 21
skogharhug (OSw) skoghhog (ODan) noun
cutting **ODan** *SkL* 195
timber felling **OSw** *YVgL* Föb, *ÄVgL* Fös
wood cutting **ODan** *SkL* 194, *VSjL* 66
See also: *fang, hug, skogher*
skoghaskipti (OSw) skógarskifti (ON) skógaskifti (ON) noun
Woodland and forests may be divided between the farmers for different purposes. In UL and VmL *skogha*

skipan is a division of acorn forests with respect to the number of pigs each farmer is allowed.

In Grg Lbþ 199 and Jó Llb 20, it deals specifically with jointly owned land in which one party believes the other is using more resources.

division of forests **OSw** *HL* Blb

woodland division **OIce** *Grg* Lbþ 199, *Jó* Llb 20

See also: *skogher*

Refs: CV s.v. *skógarskipti*; Fritzner s.v. *skógarskipti*; Schlyter s.v.v. *skogha skipan, skogha skipti*

skoghaskæl (OSw) noun

woodland boundary **OSw** *SdmL* Bb, Till

skogher (OSw) **skogh** (ODan) **skogr** (OGu) **skógr** (ON) noun

The woods and forest were important economic assets yielding food for the animals, firewood and timber for building houses and joinery, iron and tar, hunting and fishing, birch-bark and bark for bast, and they were protected against misuse. Most important was also that the forest and woodlands offered next to unlimited land for expansion of cultivated land through slash and burn methods. These rights were also regulated. Mostly they were regarded as common resources.

forest **ODan** *JyL* 1, **ONorw** *GuL* Mhb, **OSw** *DL* Mb, *HL* Mb, Jb, Blb, Rb, *YVgL* Frb, Urb, Drb, Äb, Jb, Föb, Utgb, Add, *ÄVgL* Md, Slb, Urb, Äb, Jb, Fös, Föb

wood (1) **ODan** *ESjL* 3, *JyL* 1–3, *SkL* 69, 71, 192, 194, 196–98, 201–07, 210, *VSjL* 60, 66, 80, 87, **OGu** *GL* A 7, 13, 22, 25, 26, **OSw** *ÖgL* Db

woodland **ODan** *JyL* 3, **OGu** *GL* A 25, 26, 63, **OIce** *Grg* Klþ 8 Lbþ 174, 175, *Jó* Lbb 4, 6 Llb 6, 17, *Js* Mah 15, 30 Lbb 2, 13, **OSw** *DL* Bb, *SdmL* Jb, Mb, Till, *UL* Mb, Jb, Blb, *VmL* Kkb, Mb, Bb

woods **ONorw** *FrL* Mhb 22

Expressions:

hæghneth skogh (ODan)

enclosed wood(land) **ODan** *SkL* 191, 193, 195–98, 201, 203, 204, 206, 207, 210

See also: *almænninger, tré, viþer*

Refs: CV s.v. *skógr*; Fritzner s.v. *skógr*; Eliasson and Hamilton 1999, 47–54; Hoff 1997, 262–87; Kardell 2003, 54–105; KLNM s.v. *skog*; ONP s.v. *skógr*

skoghland (ODan) **skógland** (ON) noun

wood (1) **ODan** *ESjL* 2

woodland **OIce** *Grg* Lbþ 172

See also: *skogher*

skoghran (ODan) noun

wood rapine **ODan** *VSjL* 66

skoghvægh (ODan) noun

road in the wood **ODan** *ESjL* 3

wood road **ODan** *ESjL* 3

skoghæng (OSw) noun

woodland meadow **OSw** *SdmL* Bb

skor (ON) noun

notch **ONorw** *GuL* Tfb

skotbógr (ON) noun

shoulder of a deer **ONorw** *GuL* Llb

skotfé (ON) noun

'Shot-fee'. The portion of a whale due to the harpoonist.

harpoon-money **OIce** *Jó* Llb 64

See also: *skotmannshlutr*

Refs: CV s.v. *skotfé*; Fritzner s.v. *skotfé*; Hertzberg s.v. *skotfé*

skothlutr (ON) noun

harpoon-share **OIce** *Grg* Lbþ 217

harpooner's share **OIce** *Jó* Llb 67

See also: *skotmannshlutr*

skotmannshlutr (ON) noun

harpooner's share **OIce** *Grg* Lbþ 215, *Jó* Llb 61, 63

skógarkaup (ON) noun

payment for redemption from outlawry **ONorw** *GuL* Mhb

purchase of release from the woods **ONorw** *FrL* KrbB 24 Mhb 35

skógarmaðr (ON) noun

full outlaw **OIce** *Grg* Klþ 2, 4 Þsþ 44, 55 Vís 102 Arþ 118 Ómb 142 Feþ 156

skógarspell (ON) noun

damages done to the woodland **OIce** *Jó* Llb 19

See also: *markarspell*

skógarstaða (ON) noun

woodland floor **OIce** *Jó* Llb 21

skóggangr (ON) noun

'A going to the woods'; full outlawry. A sentence of outlawry which stripped the offender of all legal rights and protections. Several crimes warranted a penalty of full outlawry, including assault and homicide (Grg Víg 86), arson (Grg Vís 109) and horse theft (Grg Feþ 164). *Skóggangr* was a lifetime sentence, as opposed to 'lesser outlawry' (ON *fjörbaugsgarðr*), which was limited to three years.

full outlawry **OIce** *Grg* Vís 88 Feþ 166

See also: *sœkt, útlagi*

Refs: CV s.v. *skóggangr*; Fritzner s.v. *skóggangr*; GAO s.v. *Wargus*; Hertzberg s.v. *skóggangr*;

KLNM s.v.v. *fredløshed, straff*; LexMA s.v.
Strafe, Strafrecht; Lúðvík Ingvarsson 1970,
96–140; MSE s.v. *Outlawry*; Riisøy 2014

skra (ODan) noun

book OIce *Grg* Lrþ 117

deed (2) OIce *Grg* Klþ 4

ordeal of glowing ploughshares **ODan** *SkKL* 7

plough shares **ODan** *SkL* 121

skreiðartíund (ON) noun

tithe of cod **ONorw** *FrL* KrbA 19

skriftagangr (ON) noun

confession OIce *Grg* Klþ 5, *Js* Kdb 1, *KRA* 31

skriftrof (ON) noun

penance breaking OIce *KRA* 22

shrift-breaking **ONorw** *FrL* KrbB 16

skriftrofa (ON) adj.

breaking penance OIce *KRA* 22

shrift breaking **ONorw** *FrL* KrbB 16

skrin (ODan) noun

coffer **ODan** *ESjL* 3

skript (OSw) **skrift** (ODan) **skript** (OGu) **skrift** (ON)
skrifft (OSw) **skrift** (OSw) noun

Confession of one's sins, as well as the penance issued
in the form of, for instance, fasting and exclusion from
church services, that could be public (*openbar skript*)
or private (*löndaskript*). A punishment for, among
other things, adultery, murder, perjury, not observing
fast and working on holy days, Translations such as
'something written' refer to the written law itself.

atonement **ONorw** *FrL* KrbB 24

church fine **OSw** *HL* Mb

church penance **OSw** *DL* Kkb, *HL* Kkb,
SdmL Kkb, Mb, *SmL*, *YVgL* Kkb, Frb

confession **ODan** *SkKL* 12, **OIce** *Jó* Þjb 24, **ONorw**
BorgL 3.3 5.14, *EidsL* 27.3 29.3, *FrL* KrbA 2,
5 KrbB 9, *GuL* Krb, Mhb, **OSw** *ÖgL* Kkb

confession in church **OSw** *HL* Rb

confession or penance **OSw** *HL* Rb

fast **OSw** *HL* Kkb

penance **OGu** *GL* A 2, **OIce** *Jó* Mah 16, *Js* Mah 34,
KRA 16, 18, **ONorw** *BorgL* 10.5, **OSw** *SmL*, *UL*
Kkb, Mb, Rb, Add. 8, *VmL* Kkb, Mb, Rb, *ÖgL* Kkb

writ **OSw** *YVgL* Add

written document **ODan** *SkKL* 13

See also: *fasta*, *fasta*, *skæra (1)*

Refs: KLNM s.v. *botsakrament*

skripta (OSw) **skrifte** (ODan) **skripta** (OGu) **skrifta**
(ON) **skrifta** (OSw) verb

confess **ODan** *SkL* 216, **OGu** *GL* A 2, **OSw** *ÖgL* Kkb

give absolution **OSw** *UL* Kkb, *VmL* Kkb

give as penance **ONorw** *EidsL* 3.3

hear confession **OSw** *ÖgL* Kkb

listen to confessions **ODan** *JyL*
3, **OSw** *SdmL* Kkb, *SmL*

resolve through penance **OSw** *ÖgL* Kkb

shrive **OSw** *DL* Kkb, *UL* Kkb, *VmL* Kkb

See also: *skæra (1)*

skriptabrut (OSw) **skrifta brut** (OSw) noun

breach of a church penance **OSw** *SmL*

confessional offences **OSw** *ÄVgL* Gb

imposed church penance **OSw** *HL* Kkb

offence against penance **OSw** *YVgL* Kkb, *ÖgL* Kkb

See also: *skript*

skriptafaþer (OSw) noun

confessor **OSw** *DL* Mb, *SdmL* Mb, *VmL* Mb

skriptalös (OSw) **skrifta lös** (OSw) adj.

without having been shriven **OSw** *DL* Kkb

without having confessed one's sins **OSw** *HL* Kkb

skriptaman (OSw) **skriftaman** (OSw) **skriptaþæn**
man (OSw) noun

man subject to church penalty **OSw** *DL* Rb

*man who has had a church penance
imposed* **OSw** *UL* Kkb, *VmL* Kkb

skriptaþer (OSw) adj.

imposed with a church penance **OSw** *HL* Kkb

sentenced to church penance **OSw** *HL* Kkb

See also: *skriptaman*

skriptermal (OSw) **skriftamál** (ON) **skriftamal** (OSw)
skriftomal (OSw) noun

church penance **OSw** *SdmL* Kkb, *SmL*

confession OIce *KRA* 35, **ONorw** *EidsL* 31.4

See also: *mal (1)*, *skript*

skrive (ODan) verb

write **ODan** *JyL* Fort, 3

skroksak (OSw) noun

false prosecution **OSw** *ÄVgL* Smb

See also: *liugha*, *lygð*, *sak*

skroksokn (OSw) **skruk sokn** (OSw) noun

A judgement that was unsound because of false
witness or false presentation of the case.

unsafe judgement **OSw** *VmL* Rb

Refs: SAOB s.v. *skrocksocken*;
Schlyter s.v. *skroksokn*

skrokvitni (OSw) noun

Refers both to a person and to a testimony being false.
In OSw HL, explicitly defined as not supported by an
oath.

false witness **OSw** *HL* Rb, *SdmL* Kkb, Rb, *ÖgL* Kkb

See also: *skrökváttr*

Refs: Schlyter s.v. *skrokvitni*

skruk (OSw) **skrök** (ON) noun

A false, legally significant, statement, such as an accusation or a testimony. Not defined as being either a deliberate lie or an error.

false witness **ONorw** *GuL* Olb

falsehood **ONorw** *GuL* Krb, Mhb, **OSw** *YVgL* Äb

Refs: Hertzberg s.v. *skrök*; ONP s.v. *skrǫk*

skruþer (OSw) **skrúð** (ON) noun

finer cloth **ONorw** *GuL* Mhb

furnishings **OSw** *UL* Kkb

vessels and vestments **OSw** *VmL* Kkb

skrökváttr (ON) noun

false testimony **OIce** *Jó* Þjb 19, *Js* Þjb 9

false witness **ONorw** *FrL* LlbA 25, *GuL* Løb, Olb

See also: *skrokvitni*

skuldadómr (ON) **skuldardómr** (ON) noun

debt court **OIce** *Grg* Þsþ 49, 62 Fjl 223

See also: *domber*

skuldagildri (ON) noun

payment of debts **OIce** *Grg* Misc 254

skuldahjón (ON) **skuldarhjón** (ON) noun

dependent people **ONorw** *FrL* KrbA 27

household members who are a charge on the householder **OIce** *Grg* Víg 89

necessary member of a household **OIce** *Jó* Sg 1

skuldahjú (ON) noun

household members who are a charge on someone **OIce** *Grg* Vís 89

necessary member of a household **OIce** *Jó* Sg 1

skuldalauss (ON) **skuldarlauss** (ON) **skuldlauss** (ON) adj.

debt-free **OIce** *Grg* Vís 89, *KRA* 14

free **ONorw** *FrL* Intr 18

skuldalið (ON) noun

people one is required to maintain **OIce** *Grg* Ómb 143

skuldalykning (ON) **skuldalukðning** (ON) **skuldalykðing** (ON) noun

payment of debts **OIce** *Jó* Kge 12 Kab 1, 4

skuldamót (ON) noun

debt assembly **OIce** *Grg* Fjl 221

See also: *skuldaþing*

skuldarkona (ON) noun

A 'woman of debt'. The term is rare but would appear to be the female equivalent to the more common *skuldarmaðr* (q.v.).

woman in bondage for debt **ONorw** *GuL* Løb, Mhb

See also: *lögskuldarkona*, *skuldarmaðr*

Refs: F; Hertzberg

skuldarmaðr (ON) noun

A 'man of debt'. Can refer either to a creditor or a debtor. In the latter case the term seems to be synonymous with *lögskuldarmaðr* (q.v.). *Skuldarmenn* were required to repay their debts within a specified time or they could be summoned for robbery (ON *rán*, see ran). In a broader sense a *skuldarmaðr* is a person with obligations and can therefore refer to a kinsman (cf. OSw *skyldarman*).

bounden debtor **OIce** *Grg* Klþ 9, 14 Þsþ 44, *KRA* 13

creditor **OIce** *Jó* Kge 12, *Js* Ert 18, **ONorw** *GuL* Arb

debtor **ONorw** *GuL* Løb

See also: *lögskuldarkona*, *lögskuldarmaðr*, *skuldarkona*

Refs: CV s.v. *skuldarmaðr*; F s.v. *skuldarmaðr*; Hertzberg s.v. *skuldarmaðr*; KLNM s.v. *gæld*; RGA s.v. *Gesellschaft, Norwegen*

skuldarstaðr (ON) noun

place of debt **OIce** *Grg* Hrs 236, *Js* Kab 18

residence **OIce** *Jó* Kab 23

skuldaþing (ON) noun

debt assembly **OIce** *Grg* Þsþ 58 Fjl 221

See also: *þing*

skuldfastr (ON) adj.

bound by debt **OIce** *Grg* Vís 96

skuldfesta (ON) verb

make one a bounden debtor **OIce** *Grg* Ómb 128

skuldfesti (ON) noun

debt bondage **OIce** *Grg* Þsþ 44

skuldingi (ON) noun

relative **OIce** *Grg* Ómb 129

skuldlauss (ON) adj.

free from debt **ONorw** *GuL* Løb

free of debt **OIce** *Grg* Fjl 223 Hrs 234 Tíg 255, *Jó* Kge 34

skuldlaust (ON) adv.

free from debts **ONorw** *GuL* Løb

skuldleikr (ON) noun

relationship **OIce** *Grg* Vís 111 Ómb 129 Feþ 156

skuldskeyta (ON) verb

transfer a debt **OIce** *Jó* Kab 23, *Js*
Kab 18, **ONorw** *GuL* Kvb

skuldskeyting (ON) noun

transfer of debt **OIce** *Jó* Kab 23

skuldunautr (ON) **skuldanautr** (ON) noun

creditor **OIce** *Jó* Kge 13, *Js* Ert 19
Lbb 4, **ONorw** *GuL* Arb

debtor **OIce** *Jó* Kab 15

skuli (OSw) **skoli** (OSw) noun

assignor **OSw** *DL* Bb, *UL* Mb

guarantor **OSw** *VmL* Mb

See also: *borghanaman, fangaman,
fastar (pl.), hemulsman, taki*

skunkufalsmaþer (OSw) noun

A freed slave. Supposedly referring to a garment, and
possibly to be understood as derogatory, or to indicate
a ceremony accepting the former slave in an *æt* 'kin'
while wrapping him in a cloak.

{*skunkufalsmaþer*} **OSw** *YVgL* Drb

Refs: Nevéus 1974, 81; RGA s.v. *Geschlechtsleite*;
Schlyter s.v. *skunkufals maþer*

skurðr (ON) noun

cut **ONorw** *GuL* Mhb

skurtheman (ODan) noun

Usually plural. Men who kept track, possibly by notches
in a wooden stick, of landowners' responsibility to pay
military tax (ODan *havne*, see *hamna*) and fines for
not participating in the launching of a new ship for the
levy (ODan *lething*, see *leþunger*).

tally man **ODan** *JyL* 3

See also: *farvitenævning, hamna,
leþunger, skipsnævning*

Refs: Tamm and Vogt, eds, 2016, 314

skut (ODan) **skot** (ON) noun

appeal to a higher court **ONorw** *GuL* Kpb, Olb

reference **ODan** *JyL* 2

shot **ONorw** *GuL* Mhb

See also: *skiuta*

skutebot (ODan) noun

collective compensation **ODan** *SkL* 224

See also: *bot*

skutill (ON) noun

harpoon **ONorw** *GuL* Llb

skutilsveinn (ON) noun

The *skutilsveinn* was originally a waiter at the king's
table. This is evident from the etymology of ON *skutill*
(q.v.). The word is derived from Latin *scutella* 'plate,

small table'. Gradually, however, the service at the
king's table assumed a more ceremonial character,
which changed its function, transforming it into a kind
of chamberlain and an officer in the king's retinue and
bodyguard, where the *skutilsveinn* ranged next to the
lendr maðr ('landed man', see *lænder*). Together with
the *stallari* (the king's marshal), the *merkismaðr* (the
bearer of the royal standard) and the *lendir men* he was
counted among the *hirðstjórar* (officers of the king's
retinue, see *hirðstjóri*). In addition to their ceremonial
functions at the court, such as (e.g.) administering the
admission of new members of the king's retinue, the
skutilsveinar were obliged to organize and lead the
king's bodyguard (*fylgð*) and supervise its duties. The
skutilsveinn enjoyed the same personal rights as the
freeholder (*hauldsréttr*, see *hölðsréttr*, according to
GuL ch. 200 and FrL IV 60). However, by the middle
of the thirteenth century there was no longer any close
connection between the title of *skutilsveinn* and its
functions. The title itself disappeared 1277, when the
skutilsveinar were knighted and received the title of
herrar (lords, see *hærra*).

cup-bearer **ONorw** *FrL* Mhb 60

page serving at the royal table **ONorw** *GuL* Mhb

Refs: Hertzberg s.v. *skutilsveinn*; KLNM s.v.v.
befalingsmand, drikkekar, hird, skutilsveinn

skutsjarn (ODan) noun

carrying iron **ODan** *SkL* 121, 145

iron **ODan** *SkL* 55

See also: *jarn*

skutþilja (ON) noun

bottom board of the stern **ONorw** *GuL* Kvr, Mhb

skuþa (OSw) **skuþa** (OGu) **scutha** (OSw) **skoþa**
(OSw) verb

assess **OSw** *YVgL* Tb

declare to witnesses **OSw** *DL* Eb

examine **OSw** *SdmL* Conf, Kkb, Bb, Mb,
SmL, *UL* Kkb, Äb, Kmb, *VmL* Kkb, Kmb

inquire **OSw** *YVgL* Add

inspect **OSw** *HL* Blb

investigate **OGu** *GL* Add. 8. (B 55), **OSw**
DL Eb, *HL* Kkb, *UL* Kkb, *VmL* Rb

study **OSw** *UL* StfBM, Kkb, Mb, *VmL* Kkb

try a case **OSw** *HL* Äb, Jb

See also: *ransaka, sea, utröna*

skyfla (OSw) **skifla** (OSw) **sköfla** (OSw) verb

distribute **OSw** *VmL* Mb

skyl (OSw) **skuler** (OSw) **skyler** (OSw) noun

stook **OSw** *UL* Kkb, Mb, *VmL* Kkb

See also: *raukr*

skyld (OSw) **skyld** (ODan) **skyldir** (OGu) **skuld** (ON)
  skyld (ON) **skylda** (ON) **skuld** (OSw) noun
  debt OIce *Grg* Þsþ 53, 62 Arþ 118, 126 Ómb
  128 Feþ 158 Lbþ 172 Misc 254, *Jó* Þfb 8 Mah
  1, 4 Kge 12, 35 Lbb 1 Kab 2, 7, *Js* Þfb 6 Mah
  29;Ert 18 Lbb 4 Kab 2, ONorw *FrL* Intr 4 KrbB
  20, 23 Var 13, 42 ArbB 5 Kvb 7, *GuL* Krb, Kpb,
  Kvb, Løb, Arb, Mhb, Leb, OSw *YVgL* Kkb, Frb,
  Äb, Rlb, Jb, Föb, Add, *ÄVgL* Slb, Äb, Rlb, Jb
  debt-bondage OIce *Grg* Vís 110 Arþ
  127 Ómb 128, 134 Fjl 223 Hrs 234
  due ODan *JyL* 2, *SkL* 75, ONorw *EidsL* 48.8
  duty OIce *Jó* Llb 28, ONorw *BorgL* 10
  expense ODan *VSjL* 79, OGu *GL* A 54
  farm rent ODan *JyL* 3
  fault ODan *JyL* 2
  obligation OIce *Js* Mah 34, OSw *SdmL* Jb, *SmL*
  profit ODan *JyL* 1
  reason OSw *UL* StfBM, Kkb
  rent OSw *YVgL* Kkb, Utgb
  sake OSw *UL* Mb
  tax OSw *UL* Mb
skylda (OSw) verb
  indict OSw *SdmL* Till
skyldarf (OSw) noun
  inheritance by siblings OSw *UL* Äb
  inheritance from close relatives OSw *HL* Äb
skyldarman (OSw) **skyldr maþr** (OGu) **skyldaman**
  (OSw) **skyldar maþer** (OSw) **skylderman** (OSw)
  skyldman (OSw) noun
  close relative OSw *UL* Äb, Blb, *VmL* Äb, Jb
  close-related kin OGu *GL* A 28
  See also: *frændi, kyn, niþi*
skylder (1) (OSw) **skyldastr** (OGu) **skyldr** (OGu)
  skyldr (ON) **skildaster** (OSw) **skilder** (OSw) adj.
  close in kin OSw *YVgL* Kkb, Drb, Äb, Gb,
  Add, *ÄVgL* Mb, Äb, Gb, Lek, *ÖgL* Db
  closely related OGu *GL* A 28
  in kinship OSw *VmL* Kkb
  related OIce *Grg* Þsþ 84 Vís 101 Bat 113, *Jó*
  Mah 30 Kge 17, *KRA* 17, ONorw *BorgL* 15.3,
  FrL KrbB 6, OSw *DL* Kkb, Gb, Rb, *HL* Jb, *SdmL*
  Äb, Jb, Mb, *SmL*, *UL* Äb, *VmL* Kkb, Äb, Jb
  within kin ONorw *FrL* KrbB 3
  See also: *nerkumin*
skylder (2) (OSw) **skyld** (ODan) **skyldr** (OGu) **skilder**
  (OSw) adj.
  entitled ODan *JyL* 2, OSw *SmL*

guilty ODan *ESjL* 2, *SkL* 86, 121,
  156, OGu *GL* Add. 8 (B 55)
  obliged ODan *SkKL* 7, *SkL* 10, 85,
  ONorw *BorgL* 10.1, *EidsL* 15.2 47.2
  permitted OGu *GL* Add. 7 (B 49)
  required OIce *Grg* passim, *Jó* Mah 3, 6 Kab
  3 Fml 2, *Js* Mah 34 Kab 4 Þjb 2, *KRA* 1, 3
  See also: *skyldugher*
skyldskaper (OSw) noun
  kinship by lineage OSw *SdmL* Kkb
skyldugher (OSw) **skyldigh** (ODan) **skyldugr** (ON)
  skuldugher (OSw) adj.
  due ODan *ESjL* 1
  entitled OSw *SdmL* Kkb, Kgb, *UL* Kgb
  guilty ODan *ESjL* 2
  liable ODan *ESjL* 2
  obligated to OSw *UL* Kkb, Jb,
  Kmb, *VmL* Kkb, Jb, Kmb
  obliged ODan *JyL* Fort, 2, OIce *KRA* 1,
  7, OSw *SdmL* För, Äb, Jb, Kmb, *SmL*,
  YVgL Kkb, *ÄVgL* Kkb, *ÖgL* Kkb
  owing OSw *UL* Kkb, *VmL* Kkb
  responsible OSw *ÖgL* Db
  responsible for OSw *UL* Kkb, *VmL* Kkb
skyn (OGu) noun
  test OGu *GL* A 28
  See also: *skynian*
skynia (OGu) verb
  prove OGu *GL* A 28
  test OGu *GL* A 28
skyniakona (OSw) noun
  woman dependent on other person's
  discretion OSw *DL* Gb
skynian (OGu) noun
  discretion OGu *GL* A 28
  supervision OGu *GL* A 24d
  test OGu *GL* A 28
  See also: *skyn*
skyrta (OGu) **skyrta** (ON) noun
  shirt OGu *GL* A 19, ONorw *GuL* Tjb
skyvle (ODan) verb
  confiscate ODan *ESjL* 2, *VSjL* 55
  seize goods ODan *JyL* 2
skyþi (OGu) noun
  footwear OGu *GL* A 24a
skýlihögg (ON) noun
  A notch or cut made on wood which blemishes or
  defaces it. In the Icelandic laws these strikes are

mentioned as damage to ships (Grg Feþ 166) and standing woodland (Grg Lbþ 199). The penalty for hacking notches in another's timber was more severe in the case of ships (lesser outlawry) than for standing wood (a six-ounce fine). In addition to legal texts, the term appears in at least three sagas, including a verse in *Grettis saga*.

notch **OIce** *Grg* Feþ 166 Lbþ 199, *Jó* Llb 19 Fml 16

See also: *skor*

Refs: CV s.v. *skýlihögg*; Fritzner s.v. *skýlihögg*; GrgTr II:92 note 238; Hertzberg s.v. *skýlihögg*; Páll Vídalín 1854 s.v. *skýlihögg*

skýra (ON) verb

investigate **OIce** *Jó* Fml 2

skæl (OSw) **skjal** (ODan) **skiel** (OGu) **skil** (ON) **skial** (OSw) **skiel** (OSw) **skil** (OSw) **skiæl** (OSw) **skiæll** (OSw) noun

Etymologically related to a verb originally meaning 'to split' realized as *skilia* in OSw. Concretely, a border marker, appearing in various compounds (see Appendix C). Abstractly, frequently referring to something reasonable, or obliged, in general ('reason', 'plausibility', 'proper, right way'), and according to legal form in particular ('legal form', 'legal formality', 'justice', 'justification', 'law'), including legal analysis and its actual implementation ('legal proceeding', 'trial') as well as the grounds for and the result of the analysis ('condition', 'evidence', 'formal reason', 'proof', 'corroboration', 'decision').

arrangement **ODan** *VSjL* 1

border **OSw** *YVgL* Jb, *ÄVgL* Jb

boundary **ODan** *ESjL* 2, **OSw** *SdmL* Bb, *UL* Blb, *VmL* Bb

boundary marker **OSw** *UL* Blb, *VmL* Bb

condition **OSw** *UL* Kmb, Blb

corroboration **OGu** *GL* A 20, 37, **OSw** *VmL* Mb

decision **ODan** *ESjL* 2, 3, *VSjL* 15, 16

defence **OSw** *YVgL* Utgb

differentiation **OSw** *UL* För

duty **OIce** *Grg* Þsþ 25

evidence **OGu** *GL* A 13, 22, 37, **OSw** *UL* Mb, *VmL* Kkb, Jb

formal reason **OIce** *Grg* Ómb 128

justice **ODan** *VSjL* 60

justification **OSw** *SdmL* Conf

law **OSw** *DL* Tjdb, Rb

legal form **OSw** *SdmL* Jb, Bb, Kmb, Mb

legal formality **OSw** *DL* Bb, *HL* Äb, *UL* Mb, *VmL* Mb, Bb

legal proceeding **OSw** *HL* Äb

majority **OSw** *ÖgL* Eb

manner **OSw** *UL* Kkb

obligation **OIce** *Grg* Feþ 164, *Jó* Þjb 16

plausibility **ODan** *JyL* 2

proof **OSw** *DL* Kkb, Gb

proper way **ONorw** *GuL* Mhb, Olb

reason **ODan** *ESjL* 2

trial **ODan** *JyL* 2, **OSw** *SdmL* Jb

Expressions:

at skilum (ON)

properly, correctly **ONorw** passim

domber ok skæl (OSw)

excuse **OSw** *VmL* Mb

judgement and legal formality **OSw** *UL* Mb *VmL* Mb, Bb

legal grounds **OSw** *HL* Rb

legal procedures **OSw** *UL* Blb *VmL* Mb, Bb

høghre skjal (ODan)

higher court **ODan** *JyL* 1:50

meþ fullum skiællum (OSw)

fully proved **OSw** *DL* Kkb

mæþ skællum, med skiellum, miþ skiellum (OGu)

lawfully **OGu** *GL* A 39

legally **OGu** *GL* A 6, A 25

with the right of law **OGu** *GL* A 56a

mæth ræt skial (ODan)

plausibly **ODan** *JyL* 2

skæl skællum gin, skiel skielom gin (OGu)

counter-claim **OGu** *GL* Add 7 (B 49)

vara til skials kumin (OSw)

having reached majority **OSw** *ÖgL* Eb

See also: *bolstaþer, ra, rör*

Refs: Gammeldansk ordbog s.v. *skjal*; Guth 2002–03, 67; ONP s.v. *skil*; Schlyter s.v. *skæl*

skælalöst (OSw) **skiælælöst** (OSw) adv.

outside the law **OSw** *UL* Jb, Rb, *VmL* Rb

skælatak (OSw) noun

lawful lien **OSw** *YVgL* Tb, *ÄVgL* Tb

skælavæþ (OSw) **skiæla væþ** (OSw) noun

legal amount in redemption **OSw** *UL* Blb, *VmL* Bb

pledge in accordance with the legal form **OSw** *SdmL* Bb

skælika (OSw) adv.

lawfully **OSw** *DL* Tjdb

legally **OSw** *YVgL* Föb

skæliker (OSw) adj.

reasonable **OSw** *SdmL* Conf, *UL* StfBM

true **OSw** *YVgL* Utgb

trustworthy **OSw** *DL* Mb, *YVgL* Add

See also: *oskælika*

skæppa (OSw) **skæppe** (ODan) **skeppa** (ON) noun
 bushel **ODan** *SkL* 226, *VSjL* 87, **ONorw**
 FrL KrbA 18, **OSw** *YVgL* Kkb, Äb,
 Föb, Utgb, *ÄVgL* Kkb, Äb, Föb

skær (OSw) **skær** (ODan) **skir** (OGu) **skiær** (OSw)
 skiær (OSw) adj.
 clean **OGu** *GL* A 8, **OSw** *UL* Kmb, *VmL* Kmb
 cleansed **ODan** *SkL* 121, 145, 156, 221, *VSjL* 87
 innocent **OGu** *GL* A 2
 pure **OSw** *UL* Jb
 purified **OSw** *YVgL* Kkb
 See also: *osaker, osander, saklös*

skær (OSw) adv.
 clearly **OSw** *UL* Mb

skæra (1) (OSw) **skære** (ODan) **skira** (OGu) **skíra** (ON)
 skira (OSw) verb
 absolve **OSw** *UL* Mb, *VmL* Kgb, Mb
 acquit **OSw** *SmL*
 baptize **OIce** *Grg* Feþ 144 Tíg 261, *Jó*
 Kge 7, *KRA* 1, **ONorw** *BorgL* 2.2 4 10.6,
 EidsL 1, *FrL* KrbA 2, 3, *GuL* Krb
 clean **ODan** *SkKL* 3
 cleanse **ODan** *ESjL* 2, *SkL* 85, 86,
 88, 121, 145, 157, 177, 218
 clear **ODan** *SkKL* 7, 9, **OGu** *GL* A 2, **OIce** *Jó*
 Mah 9, *Js* Mah 11, **ONorw** *EidsL* 45.3, *FrL*
 Mhb 5 ArbB 10, **OSw** *SdmL* Kmb, Rb
 consecrate **OSw** *UL* Kkb
 excuse (of an oath or other obligation) **OSw** *UL* Mb
 free **ONorw** *FrL* KrbA 22
 make clear **ONorw** *GuL* Løb, **OSw** *SdmL* Jb
 note **OSw** *UL* Kgb
 purify **OSw** *ÖgL* Kkb
 say that someone is innocent **OSw** *HL* Äb
 See also: *buþ, fasta, fasta, kross, skript*

skæra (2) (OSw) **skære** (ODan) **skera** (ON) verb
 carve **OSw** *UL* Äb, Rb, *VmL* Mb, Rb
 carve and send forth message arrows or
 message batons **ONorw** *GuL* Krb, Mhb, Leb
 chop **ODan** *VSjL* 27, 28, 33
 cut **ODan** *ESjL* 2, *VSjL* 31, **OSw** *UL*
 Mb, Blb, *VmL* Mb, Bb, *ÄVgL* Urb
 dig **OSw** *UL* Blb
 gash **ODan** *VSjL* 33
 reap **OSw** *UL* Blb, *VmL* Bb

separate **OSw** *UL* Äb

slice **ODan** *VSjL* 27

be wanting **OSw** *UL* Kgb

Expressions:

skera krossa (ON)
 cut cross-tokens **OIce** *Grg* Þsþ 84
 Hrs 234 Misc 240 *Js* Rkb 2
 prepare a cross **ONorw** *FrL* KrbA 22

skera ör (ON)
 cut an arrow **OIce** *Jó* Mah 10 *Js* Mah
 10, 17 **ONorw** *FrL* Mhb 6, 23

See also: *arf, buþ, þingbuþ*

skærdagher (OSw) **skiærdagher** (OSw) noun
 Maundy Thursday **OSw** *YVgL* Kkb
 See also: *skærþorsdagher*

skærskuta (OSw) **skærskjute** (ODan) **skirskuta**
 (OGu) **skírskota** (ON) **skirskuta** (OSw) verb
 announce **OSw** *YVgL* Tb, Föb,
 ÄVgL Rlb, Tb, *ÖgL* Eb, Db
 announce to witnesses **OSw** *SdmL* Kgb,
 Bb, Mb, *YVgL* Frb, Rlb, Add
 appeal **ONorw** *FrL* KrbB 15, 22 Mhb 7
 appoint **ONorw** *FrL* KrbA 16 ArbB 23 Bvb 6
 call on one for testimony **OIce** *Js* Mah 14, 21
 Kab 7, *KRA* 18, **ONorw** *FrL* KrbB 5 Mhb 8
 call witnesses **ONorw** *GuL* Kpb, Tfb, Mhb, Olb, Leb
 confirm **ONorw** *BorgL* 14.5
 declare **ODan** *SkL* 192, **OGu** *GL* A
 18, 22, **OSw** *UL* Kgb, *VmL* Kgb
 make clear **ONorw** *FrL* Var 12
 make public **ODan** *SkL* 192
 prove **ONorw** *FrL* Mhb 14
 refer to judgement **OIce** *Js* Mah
 22, 25 Kab 10, *KRA* 11
 refer to witness **OSw** *ÄVgL* Rlb
 report **ONorw** *GuL* Mhb
 submit to witnesses **OSw** *YVgL* Rlb
 tell **ODan** *SkL* 181
 See also: *lysa, sværia, vita*

skærskutavitni (OSw) noun
 announcement of a case **OSw** *ÄVgL* Slb
 announcement with testimony **OSw** *ÄVgL* Rlb
 See also: *vitni*

skærsl (OSw) **skírsl** (ON) **skírsla** (ON) **skirsl** (OSw)
 noun
 Related to the verb *skíra* ('to cleanse, to purify, to
 baptise'). In the Norwegian laws *skírsla* is sometimes
 used as a synonym for *skírn* ('baptism'). Often used

to refer to an ordeal, carrying a hot iron (*jarnbyrþ*) for men or plucking stones from boiling water (*ketiltak*) for women. Since the ordeal was used as a means for determining guilt in certain cases, *skírsl* also bears the connotation of 'evidence' or 'proof of innocence'. Ordeals seem to have been brought into Scandinavia through Christian influence, though the turf ordeal (mentioned only in sagas) seems to have been native to Iceland, and some have argued that the concept of the ordeal was a native development (cf. Boyer 1990, 181).

In Grg ordeals are used specifically for paternity cases, adultery and incest. A few other infractions, such as theft and homicide, involve ordeals in Icelandic saga literature. Ordeals for legal procedures were prohibited by the Fourth Lateran Council in 1215, but they are thought to have remained in use in Iceland until sometime between 1248 and 1275 (cf. GrgTr II:49). It has been suggested that ordeals were less common in Iceland, where witness testimony was favoured, than in Norway, where compurgation was preferred.

baptism **ONorw** *BorgL* 2, *FrL* KrbA 3

defence **ONorw** *GuL* Mhb

evidence **OIce** *Js* Mah 18, *KRA* 33

ordeal **OIce** *Grg* Ómb 143 Feþ 156 Tíg 264, **ONorw** *FrL* KrbA 1

proof of innocence **OIce** *Jó* Þjb 24

purification **ONorw** *EidsL* 42.2, **OSw** *SdmL* Kkb, *YVgL* Kkb

trial by ordeal **ONorw** *GuL* Krb

Expressions:

guðs skírslir (ON)

ordeal **ONorw** *GuL* Krb

See also: *jarnbyrþ, skírn, skæra (1), vitni*

Refs: Boyer 1990; GrgTr; KLNM s.v. *gudsdom, dåp*; Miller 1988; NGL V s.v. *skírsl*; Nilsson 2001; von See 1964, 123−25

skærþa (OSw) skerða (ON) verb

reduce **ONorw** *GuL* Kpb

violate **OSw** *UL* Kkb

skærþorsdagher (OSw) skíriþórsdagr (ON) skæra þorsdagher (OSw) noun

Maundy Thursday **ONorw** *GuL* Krb, **OSw** *UL* Kkb, *VmL* Kkb

See also: *skærdagher*

sköghia (OSw) verb

hunt **OSw** *DL* Bb

sköghning (OSw) noun

hunting **OSw** *DL* Bb, *HL* Blb

skökia (OSw) noun

whore **OSw** *HL* Mb

sköta (OSw) sköte (ODan) skeyta (ON) verb

convey **ODan** *ESjL* 1−3, *JyL* 1, 3, *SkL* 37, 52, 59, 63, 64, 78−80, 84, *VSjL* 13, 68, 69, 82, 85, 87, **OIce** *Js* Ert 17, **ONorw** *FrL* ArbB 4, 19 Jkb 2, *GuL* Olb

give land with conveyance **OSw** *YVgL* Jb

transfer **ONorw** *FrL* LlbB 4

skötarf (OSw) noun

inheritance from a legitimate child **OSw** *HL* Äb

sköti (OSw) noun

arrow **OSw** *HL* Äb

skötning (OSw) skötning (ODan) skeyting (ON) skotning (OSw) noun

The transfer or conveyance of landed property. In all of the Nordic countries, as well as in England, this process is thought to have been accompanied by the symbolic placing of sod in the cloak (ON *skaut*) or lap of the person acquiring the property. The act is similar to an old Frankish legal custom of throwing a stick into the lap of the new owner and gives rise to the idea of a common Germanic custom of land transfer. Parts of this ceremonial process are described in various laws (e.g. GuL ch. 292 and Arne Sunesen's paraphrase of SkL 78–80), but it is nowhere described in its entirety.

In Norway *skeyting* required a fee to be paid by the buyer (*skeytingsaurar*) for the service of documenting the transaction (*bókarskeyting*). In MLL it is stipulated that all transfers worth more than ten marks had to bear a seal from the law-man (*lögmaðr*, see *laghmaþer*), sheriff (*sýslumaðr*, see *sysluman*) or other official, or, at the very least the two parties had to produce a chirograph.

The medieval Swedish *skaptfärdh* may be connected with the procedure of measuring the land that was to be handed over. We know that measuring the acreage was important and OSw *skapt* may refer to the measuring-stick that was used for this purpose.

In the Västgöta laws and in ÖgL *skötning* eventually took on the meaning of 'land given as a gift'.

conveyance **ODan** *ESjL* 1−3, *VSjL* 13, **OSw** *YVgL* Kkb, Jb, *ÄVgL* Jb

conveyance of land **ONorw** *GuL* Olb

donation **OSw** *ÖgL* Kkb

estate conveyance **OIce** *Js* Kvg 3, **ONorw** *FrL* ArbB 4 Kvb 8 Jkb 1

land (given to a church) **OSw** *SmL*

See also: *flatføring, sal, sköta, umfærþ*

Refs: CV s.v. *skeyting*; Du Cange 1883−87 s.v. *scotare*; F s.v. *skeyting*; KLNM s.v. *bréfalausn*, *fastebrev, rättssymbolik, skøyting*; Larsson 2009, 151–60; NGL V s.v. *skeyting*; Vinogradoff 1907

skötra (OSw) noun

corner boundary marker **OSw** *DL* Bb

See also: *ra*

Refs: Schlyter s.v. *skötra*.

skötsætubarn (OSw) noun

Literally, 'child set in the lap', translated as 'adopted or legitimized child'. This act was a sign of formal adoption, particularly of children born before the marriage of a couple, in acknowledgement that the husband accepted the wife's pre-existing child as his own. This was the case even if there had been an intervening marriage to other parties. In UL, a further situation is envisaged in which a couple were engaged and the man dies before a marriage takes place. With general acceptance or with appropriate witnesses to testify to the betrothal, the children would be accepted as the legitimate heirs to the dead man. In GL, a similar procedure is described but relating to the adoption by a grandfather of children whose own father had died.

legitimized child **OSw** *UL* Äb

See also: *arver*, *aþalkonubarn*, *frilla*, *fæsta*, *karl*, *löskalæghi*, *ættleiðing*

Refs: KLNM s.v. *ættleiing*; Peel 2015, 132 note 20/16; Schlyter 1877, s.v. *skötsætubarn*; SL GL, 266 note 5 to chapter 20; SL UL, 85 notes 57–59

skøt (ODan) noun

cloak tail **ODan** *SkL* 79, 80

See also: *sköta*

skøtevitne (ODan) noun

witness of a conveyance **ODan** *VSjL* 82

witness to a conveyance **ODan** *SkL* 78

sla (OSw) sla (ODan) sla (OGu) slá (ON) verb

beat **ODan** *ESjL* 2, *JyL* 2, *VSjL* 27, 31, 55, 86, **ONorw** *FrL* KrbA 10, **OSw** *HL* Kgb, *SdmL* Kgb, *YVgL* Drb, Add, *ÖgL* Kkb, Eb, Vm

cut **ODan** *JyL* 2, *VSjL* 33

cut down **OGu** *GL* A 25

gouge **ODan** *VSjL* 26

hit **OSw** *DL* Rb, *HL* Kkb, *SdmL* Mb, *YVgL* Föb

lift **OGu** *GL* A 8

punch **OGu** *GL* A 8, 11, 19

slay **OSw** *HL* Mb

sling **OSw** *VmL* Mb

strike **ODan** *ESjL* 1–3, *VSjL* 27, 28, 30, 33, 45, **OGu** *GL* A 8, 11, 12, 19, 23, Add. 4 (B 19), **OSw** *DL* Eb, Mb, Rb, *HL* Mb, *SdmL* Mb, *UL* Kkb, Kgb, Mb, Blb, *VmL* Kkb, Kgb, Mb, Bb, *ÖgL* Vm

throw **OGu** *GL* A 19

Expressions:

sla ihæl (OSw)

kill **OSw** *UL* Kkb, Äb *VmL* Kkb, Äb

slay **OSw** *VmL* Bb

sla til bloþs (OSw)

strike so that blood is spilt **OSw** *UL* Kgb, Mb

sla til skaþa (OSw)

injure **OSw** *VmL* Kkb

See also: *bæria*, *dræpa*, *vægha (1)*

slagh (OSw) slagh (ODan) noun

blow **ODan** *VSjL* 30

stroke **OSw** *SdmL* Mb

Expressions:

slagh ok bardaghi (OSw)

blows and battle **OSw** *UL* Kmb

slanbaugr (ON) noun

sloth-fine **ONorw** *GuL* Mhb

See also: *týja*

slátra (ON) verb

slaughter **OIce** *Grg* Þsþ 78

slegr (OGu) noun

assault **OGu** *GL* A 5

blow **OGu** *GL* A 19, 23, Add. 3 (B 19)

slenstrákr (ON) noun

vagabond **OIce** *Jó* Mah 29

slita (OSw) slita (OGu) slíta (ON) verb

decide **OGu** *GL* A 61

dissolve **OIce** *Jó* Þjb 14

settle **OSw** *DL* Rb, *ÖgL* Kkb, Eb

slitna (ON) verb

torn off **ONorw** *GuL* Kpb

slímuseta (ON) slímusetr (ON) noun

A 'slime-sitting'. Refers to someone who overstays the hospitality of another. Such unwanted guests could be forcibly removed without legal penalties for assault.

hangers on **OIce** *Jó* Mah 28

parasite **OIce** *Js* Mah 33

remaining as guest uninvited or longer than a certain time **ONorw** *GuL* Mhb

Expressions:

sitja slímusetri (ON)

to remain as a 'slime-sitter' **OIce** *Js* Mah 33

to stay afterward as a hanger on **OIce** *Jó* Mah 28

Refs: CV s.v. *slímusetr*; Fritzner s.v. *slímusetr*

slokifrilluson (OSw) sløkefrithesun (ODan) noun

concubine's son **OSw** *ÄVgL* Äb

son by/with a concubine **ODan** *ESjL* 1, 2, *JyL* 3

See also: *aþalkona*

slóðahrís (ON) noun

brushwood **OIce** *Jó* Llb 6

faggot-wood **OIce** *Grg* Lbþ 220

See also: *rifhrís*

slæppa (OSw) **sleppa** (OGu) verb

let go **OSw** *UL* Mb, *VmL* Mb

release **OGu** *GL* A 44

set free **OSw** *UL* Mb

See also: *lata*

slætringr (ON) noun

mown grass **ONorw** *GuL* Tjb

sløkefrithe (ODan) noun

A (free) woman living with a man without their being married. The woman could gain status of legal wife after three years (ODan *JyL*). Children were not called *horbarn* ('children born in adultery') and there could be varying rights to mutual paternal inheritance.

concubine **ODan** *JyL* 1, 2

See also: *amia, arinelia, aþalkona, deghia, frilla, horkona, husfrugha, kona, kæfsir, meinkona*

Refs: KLNM s.v. *slegfred*

sløkefrithebarn (ODan) noun

child by/with a concubine **ODan** *JyL* 1, *SkL* 59, 61, 63, 64, *VSjL* 68–70

concubine's child **ODan** *ESjL* 1, *JyL* 1

sløkefrithedotter (ODan) noun

concubine's daughter **ODan** *ESjL* 3, *JyL* 2

daughter by a concubine **ODan** *ESjL* 1, *SkL* 223

See also: *friðludóttir*

slóða (ON) **slæða** (ON) verb

dung **OIce** *Grg* Þsþ 78

smafileþi (OGu) noun

small farm animal **OGu** *GL* A 40

small livestock **OGu** *GL* A 40 (rubric)

smagris (OGu) noun

piglet **OGu** *GL* A 41

smali (ON) noun

cattle **ONorw** *GuL* Llb

smalænsker (OSw) adj.

from Småland **OSw** *ÄVgL* Md

smiþer (OSw) **smiðr** (ON) noun

shipwright **ONorw** *GuL* Leb

smith **OSw** *SdmL* Kmb, Mb

See also: *gullsmiþer, silfsmiþer*

smiþia (OSw) noun

smithy **OSw** *SdmL* Mb

smíðarkaup (ON) noun

work wages **ONorw** *FrL* Leb 2

smjör (ON) noun

butter **ONorw** *GuL* Krb, Kpb

smörmali (OSw) noun

butter tithe **OSw** *HL* Kkb

snattan (OSw) noun

pilferage **OSw** *DL* Tjdb

See also: *hvin, hvinska, þiuver*

snattarabot (OSw) **snattanbot** (OGu) noun

fine for petty larceny **OGu** *GL* A 38

fine for petty theft **OSw** *SdmL* Mb

See also: *bot, böta, snattan*

snápr (ON) noun

Commonly refers to a 'dolt', 'fool' or 'charlatan' and listed among the *heiti* synonymous with 'unwise man' in the *Poetic Edda*; cognate with ModE 'snob'. The term is also used to describe the tip of a gimlet or similar pointed object and can allude to male genitalia. In Medieval Icelandic law *snápr* refers specifically to someone who makes false boasts of having lain with a woman (Jó Mah 30). The penalty for this type of boast was the same as having actually committed the offense. *Snápr* also appears in a marginal gloss for *maðr at verri* ('a worse man') and elsewhere in MLL.

fool **OIce** *Jó* Mah 17

man who falsely boasts of having dishonoured a woman **OIce** *Jó* Mah 30

Refs: CV; F; Horstrup 1963; NGL V; ONP

snápsgjald (ON) noun

A 'snob-fine'. Compensation paid by someone convicted of being a *snápr*, someone who has falsely boasted of having lain with a woman.

fine of disgrace **OIce** *Jó* Mah 30

Refs: CV s.v. *snápr*; Fritzner s.v. *snápsgjöld*; Hertzberg s.v. *snápsgjöld*

sniðill (ON) noun

sickle **ONorw** *GuL* Tfb

sniðilsverp (ON) noun

throw of a pruning knife **ONorw** *FrL* LlbB 8

sniovægher (OSw) noun

road clear of snow **OSw** *HL* Kgb

snúðr (ON) noun

head-piece of a spindle **ONorw** *GuL* Olb

See also: *snælda*

snækkia (OSw) **snekkia** (OGu) noun

    longship **OGu** *GS* Ch. 4

    warship **OGu** *GS* Ch. 4, **OSw** *HL* Blb

    See also: *kaupskip*

snækkiufrither (OSw) noun

    Peace during the *leþunger* 'levy' including the journey to and from the ship. Breaching the peace was severely punished with fines to the king.

    ship peace **OSw** *HL* Mb

    See also: *friþer*, *leþunger*, *snækkia*

    Refs: Brink forthcoming

snælda (ON) noun

    distaff **ONorw** *GuL* Olb

    spindle **ONorw** *GuL* Olb

    See also: *gyrþlugyrt*, *snúðr*

snöpa (OSw) **sneypa** (ON) verb

    castrate **OSw** *SdmL* Mb

    disgrace **ONorw** *FrL* Kvb 11

    geld **OSw** *HL* Mb

snóri (ON) **snara** (ON) noun

    rope **ONorw** *GuL* Mhb

    See also: *fæst*, *rep*

sokn (OSw) **sokn** (ODan) **søkn** (ODan) **sokn** (OGu) **sókn** (ON) **sopn** (OSw) noun

    Derived from a verb realized in OSw as *sökia* 'to seek'. Translations related to 'parish' may refer to both a territory and a community, traditionally interpreted as the people who 'seek' together, not only applying to the church, as reflected in the translation 'jurisdiction'. For a description of the various translations related to the meaning of examination such as 'prosecution', 'suit', 'case' and 'accusation', see the verb *sökia*.

    accusation **ONorw** *FrL* Var 12, **OSw** *ÄVgL* Rlb

    case **ODan** *ESjL* 2, 3, **ONorw** *FrL* Mhb 7 Var 7 Kvb 11

    charge (1) **OSw** *YVgL* Rlb

    claim **ODan** *ESjL* 2, 3

    conduct of legal action **ONorw** *GuL* Olb

    demand **ODan** *ESjL* 2, **OSw** *YVgL* Jb

    exaction **OSw** *SdmL* Rb

    investigation **ONorw** *BorgL* 17.14

    lawful action **OIce** *Jó* Llb 39

    parish **ODan** *ESjL* 2, **OGu** *GL* A 2, 3, 14, 20a, 39, 48, 52, 55, 56a, 60, 61, *GS* Ch. 2, **OIce** *KRA* 35, **ONorw** *EidsL* 49.2, **OSw** *DL* Kkb, Bb, Gb, *HL* Kkb, Mb, Rb, *SdmL* Kkb, Bb, Kmb, Mb, Rb, Till, *SmL*, *UL* Kkb, Mb, Jb, *VmL* Kkb, Bb, *YVgL* Kkb, Jb, Utgb, Add, *ÄVgL* Kkb, Jb, Föb, *ÖgL* Kkb, Eb, Db

    parish men **OSw** *DL* Gb

    parishioners **OGu** *GL* A 40, **OSw** *UL* Kkb, Mb, Add. 1, *VmL* Kkb, Äb, Mb, Jb

    prosecution **OIce** *Grg* Þsþ 49 Vís 86, 104 Feþ 148, 156 Lbþ 192 Rsþ 230 Hrs 234, 235 Misc 250, 251 Tíg 256, *Jó* Þfb 6, *Js* Mah 13 Kab 5, 8, *KRA* 29, **ONorw** *FrL* KrbB 1 Mhb 8 Reb 2, *GuL* Kpb, Arb, Mhb, Olb, **OSw** *SdmL* Rb, *UL* Rb, *VmL* Mb, Rb

    prosecution for damages **OIce** *Jó* Lbb 7

    right of suit **OIce** *Jó* Kab 10

    right to prosecute **OIce** *Grg* Þsþ 80 Rsþ 227

    seeking of fines **OSw** *UL* Rb, *VmL* Mb

    suing **OSw** *HL* Rb

    suit **OIce** *Grg* Lbþ 206, *Js* Mah 20, 25, **ONorw** *FrL* KrbB 20 ArbB 10

    Expressions:

    innan sokna fulk (OGu)

    parishioners **OGu** *GL* A 24a

    See also: *asokn*, *mal (1)*, *soknamaþer*

    Refs: Brink 2016; Hellquist s.v. *socken*; Lindkvist forthcoming

soknaband (OSw) noun

    prosecution proof **OSw** *SdmL* Rb

    See also: *sokn*, *synaband*

soknamaþer (OSw) **sokneman** (ODan) **soknamenn** (pl.) (OGu) **sóknarmaðr** (ON) **soknamæn** (pl.) (OSw) noun

    Ultimately derived from the verb ODan *søkje*, ON *sókja*, OSw *sökia* 'to seek' in its various legal senses. In ODan, ONorw and OSw referring to parishioners (cf. *sokn*). In OIce referring to an official in the service of a local authority (*valdsmaðr*, see *valdsmaþer*, or *sýslumaðr*, see *sysluman*) prosecuting those who failed to meet their commune obligations (tithes, food gifts) and overseeing oaths. The *sóknarmenn* need not be landowners (Grg Hrs) and their numbers in each *hreppr* ('commune') or *fjórðungr* ('quarter', see *fiarþunger*) were specified.

    commission from the parish **OSw** *DL* Bb

    man of the parish **ODan** *SkL* 70, **OSw** *SdmL* Kkb, Bb, *YVgL* Kkb, Add, *ÄVgL* Kkb

    parish man **OSw** *ÖgL* Kkb

    parish men **ODan** *VSjL* 73, **OSw** *DL* Kkb, Mb, Bb

    parishioner **ONorw** *FrL* KrbA 14

    parishioners **OGu** *GL* A 3, 8, 16, 24d, 26, 28, 30, 39, 41, 44, 45a, Add. 2 (B 17), **OSw** *HL* Kkb, Mb, Rb, *SmL*, *UL* Kkb, Mb, Jb, Blb, *VmL* Kkb, Mb, Kmb, Bb

    prosecutor **OIce** *Grg* Hrs 234, *Jó* Þfb 2 Sg 2, *Js* Mah 13, 31 Lbb 15 Kab 1, 4 Þjb 2, 6

0

See also: *kirkiumæn (pl.)*, *lænsmaþer*, *maþer*, *sökia*, *sökiandi*, *sokn*, *soknar (pl.)*, *soknari*

Refs: Cleasby and Vigfusson s.v.v. *sókn, sóknar-maðr*; Fritzner s.v. *sóknarmaðr*; Hertzberg s.v. *sóknarmaðr*; Schlyter s.v. *soknamæn*

soknamærki (OSw) noun

border marker of the parish **OSw** *YVgL* Kkb

soknanæmd (OSw) noun

A *næmd* 'panel' dealing with violations of church penances (SmL), appeals (DL), disputed donations to the church and an entire parish's association with an outlaw (ÖgL).

parish commission **OSw** *DL* Rb

parish jury **OSw** *ÖgL* Kkb, Db

parish panel **OSw** *SmL*

See also: *næmd*, *sokn*

soknaprester (OSw) **sóknarprestr** (ON) **soknapræster** (OSw) noun

parish priest **OIce** *KRA* 13, 16, **OSw** *HL* Kkb

See also: *lænspræster*, *prester*

soknar (pl.) (OGu) noun

parishioners **OGu** *GL* A 40

soknari (OSw) **sóknari** (ON) **soknæri** (OSw) noun

A prosecutor. In OSw, a judicial official appearing in phrases such as *kunungs soknari, hæraþs soknari, biscups soknari*, i.e. a *soknari* of the king, a district and a bishop respectively.

administrator **OSw** *YVgL* Kkb

man bringing the case **OIce** *Grg* Hrs 234

official prosecutor **OSw** *UL* Kkb, *VmL* Kkb

prosecutor **OIce** *Jó* Mah 14, 22, *Js* Mah 13, **ONorw** *FrL* Mhb 24 Rgb 37, **OSw** *DL* Mb, Tjdb, *ÖgL* Kkb, Db, Vm

See also: *eftirsýnarmaðr*, *sakaráberi*, *sökiandi*, *soknamaþer*

Refs: KLNM s.v. *soknare*; ONP s.v. *sóknari*; Schlyter s.v. *soknari*

soknasyn (OSw) noun

parish inspection **OSw** *HL* Kkb

soknavitni (OSw) noun

witness of parishioners **OSw** *SdmL* Jb

See also: *sokn*, *vitni*

soknaþing (OSw) **sóknarþing** (ON) noun

In OSw HL, a *þing* 'assembly' of the men of the parish summoned by the *lænsmaþer* (q.v.) twice a year and held anywhere but at the church farm (OSw *kirkiubol*). In OIce, a part of an assembly, in Grg Þsþ 56 the *várþing* ('spring assembly'), dealing with

prosecutions and certain announcements. In ONorw, referring to procedures for dealing with multiple assemblies falling on the same day.

parish thing **OSw** *HL* Rb

prosecution assembly **OIce** *Grg* Þsþ 58, 59 Feþ 149 Fjl 225, **ONorw** *FrL* Rgb 3

thing (1) **OSw** *HL* Rb

See also: *kirkiubol*, *kirkjusóknarþing*, *lænsmaþer*, *sokn*, *þing*

Refs: Fritzner s.v. *sóknarþing*; Hertzberg s.v. *sóknarþing*

soldraghin (OSw) adj.

sun-divided **OSw** *DL* Bb

solskipt (OSw) **solskifte** (ODan) noun

Literally, 'sun division'. The 'sun' element refers to the position of each strip *field* (*aker, tegher*) in the field (*vang, gærþi*) and of the curtilage (*tompt*) in the village in a fixed order after the daily course of the sun through the sky, i.e. 'clockwise'. This division system ensured that all farms got their fair share of the common fields, meadows, grazing, fishing rights etc. in the village in accordance with the size and clockwise position of the curtilage around their dwellings (*tompt*), and that the strip fields were positioned accordingly.

sun division **ODan** *JyL* 1, **OSw** *SdmL* Bb, *UL* Blb, *VmL* Bb

See also: *attunger*, *bol*, *hamarskipt*, *markland*

Refs: Göransson 1961, 80–83; Göransson 1976, 22–37; Hafström 1951, 104–56; Hoff 1997, 197–209; KLNM, s.v.v. *bolskift, hammarskifte, solskifte, tegskifte*; Porsmose 1988, 270: Riddersporre 2001, 64–65; Schlyter s.v.v. *hamar, solskipt;* Sporrong 1992, 355

somi (OSw) **some** (ODan) noun

honour **OSw** *ÄVgL* Slb

will (2) **ODan** *VSjL* 60

sonarkona (ON) noun

son's wife **OIce** *KRA* 20, **ONorw** *EidsL* 52.1, *GuL* Krb, Kvb, Mhb

sóknaraðili (ON) noun

prosecution principal **OIce** *Grg* Þsþ 20, 35 Rsþ 227 Hrs 234

sóknardagr (ON) noun

A day on which prosecutions could lawfully be summoned.

prosecution day **OIce** *KRA* 29, **ONorw** *FrL* KrbB 20 Mhb 8

Refs: CV s.v. *sóknardagr*; Fritzner s.v. *sóknardagr*; Hertzberg s.v. *sóknardagr*

sóknargagn (ON) noun

prosecution means of proof **OIce** *Grg* Lbþ 176

sóknarkviðr (ON) noun

prosecution panel (verdict) **OIce**
Grg Vís 90 Ómb 143

sól (ON) noun

sun **ONorw** *GuL* Krb, Olb

spakmænni (pl.) (OSw) noun

peaceful men **OSw** *YVgL* Add

spander (OSw) **spann** (ON) **span** (OSw) noun

bucket **OSw** *HL* Kkb

bucket, a measure of volume **ONorw** *GuL* Leb

measure **OSw** *UL* Kkb, Kgb, Mb, *VmL* Kkb, Kgb, Bb

span **OSw** *DL* Bb, Rb

{spander} **OSw** *SdmL* Till

spann (ON) **spönn** (ON) noun

span, a measure of length **ONorw** *GuL* Llb

spannaland (OSw) noun

{spannaland} **OSw** *HL* Jb

spannamali (OSw) noun

grain **OSw** *UL* Kgb, *VmL* Kgb

See also: *korn, sæþ*

spannarlangr (ON) adj.

having the length of a span **ONorw** *GuL* Llb

See also: *spann*

sparka (OGu) verb

kick **OGu** *GL* A 19, 33a, 34

sparri (ON) noun

stick **ONorw** *GuL* Mhb

spá (ON) noun

soothsaying **ONorw** *GuL* Krb

spáför (ON) noun

prophecy **ONorw** *FrL* Var 45

soothsaying **OIce** *Jó* Mah 2, *Js* Mah 6

spásaga (ON) noun

prophecy **ONorw** *FrL* KrbB 15

spekð (ON) **spekt** (ON) noun

moderation **OIce** *Jó* Þfb 5

peace **OIce** *Js* Þfb 4

See also: *friþer, griþ*

spekðarmaðr (ON) noun

man of peace **ONorw** *FrL* KrbA 10

upstanding person **OIce** *KRA* 8

spellalauss (ON) adj.

unspoiled **OIce** *Js* Kvg 5, **ONorw** *FrL* Kvb 14

spellreið (ON) noun

damaging ride **OIce** *Grg* Feþ 164

spellvirki (ON) noun

damage **OIce** *Jó* Llb 20 Llb 56, **ONorw**
FrL LlbB 8, *GuL* Llb, Tfb

harm **OIce** *Jó* Llb 20

loss **OFar** *Seyð* 5

malicious damage **OIce** *Grg* Þsþ 51 Lbþ 203

property damage **OIce** *Jó* Fml 19

willful damage **OIce** *Grg* Þsþ 63

See also: *illvirki, skaþi*

spilla (OSw) **spiella** (OGu) **spilla** (ON) verb

damage **OGu** *GL* A 25, **OIce** *Grg* Þsþ 64 Fjl 226
Tíg 266, *Jó* Llb 4, *KRA* 26, **ONorw** *EidsL* 1.2,
GuL Llb, Tjb, **OSw** *UL* Kmb, Blb, *VmL* Kmb, Bb

destroy **OGu** *GL* A 9, **ONorw** *FrL* Intr 11 Mhb 36

disregard **OIce** *Jó* Llb 27

fall into disrepute **OGu** *GL* Add. 1 (B 4)

harm **OSw** *UL* Blb, *VmL* Bb

injure **ONorw** *FrL* Bvb 10, *GuL*
Llb, **OSw** *UL* Blb, *VmL* Bb

kill **OGu** *GL* A 2

let perish **ONorw** *GuL* Krb

lose **OSw** *ÄVgL* Smb

miscarry **OGu** *GL* A 18

spoil **OIce** *KRA* 5, **ONorw** *FrL*
KrbB 3, *GuL* Llb, Leb

See also: *firikomas, önd*

spini (OSw) **speni** (ON) noun

teat **ONorw** *GuL* Mhb, **OSw** *UL* Äb, *VmL* Kkb, Äb

spital (OSw) **spital** (ODan) noun

A beneficiary of tithes in OSw SdmL (obligations
of the *hamna* (q.v.)) and YVgL, and of soul gifts (or
possibly wills) in ODan JyL.

hospital **ODan** *JyL* 3, **OSw** *SdmL* Till, *YVgL* Kkb

spiut (OSw) **spjut** (ODan) **spjót** (ON) noun

spear **ODan** *ESjL* 3, *SkL* 87, 176, **ONorw** *GuL* Llb,
Kvr, Leb, **OSw** *DL* Bb, *SdmL* Bb, Mb, *ÄVgL* Rlb

spiæll (OSw) **spjal** (ODan) **spiell** (OGu) **spell** (ON)
spjall (ON) **spiall** (OSw) **spiæld** (OSw) noun

damage **ODan** *SkL* 174, 214, **OGu** *GL* A 25,
26, **OIce** *Jó* Lbb 7 Llb 19 Fml 16, *Js* Lbb 3,
ONorw *GuL* Arb, **OSw** *DL* Bb, *SdmL* Bb

flaw **OIce** *Grg* Tíg 259

harm **ONorw** *FrL* Rgb 24

injury **OGu** *GL* A 25, **OSw** *VmL* Bb

tear **OSw** *UL* Mb, *VmL* Mb

violation **OSw** *SdmL* Till, *UL* Kkb, Äb, *VmL* Kkb, Äb

wasting of property **ONorw** *GuL* Arb

spiællabot (OSw) spiæl bot (OSw) noun

    damage compensation **OSw** *DL* Bb

    See also: *bot*

spjótgarðr (ON) noun

    fence of spears **ONorw** *FrL* LlbB 9

spjótskaft (ON) noun

    spearshaft **ONorw** *GuL* Mhb

    See also: *geirskaft*

spjutsman (ODan) noun

    spear man **ODan** *ESjL* 1

sporðr (ON) noun

    tail **ONorw** *GuL* Kvr

sporgæld (OSw) noun

    Literally, 'discovery compensation'. It referred originally to compensation taken from a self-confessed killer, who confessed and offered compensation at the assembly. It later came to cover all cases in which single compensation was demanded from a known killer, as opposed to the higher compensation (*tvæböti*) taken in a case of *morþ* ('murder'), unacknowledged killing (*dulghadrap*), unsolved killing or killing aggravated by other circumstances. Examples of this last are a man killing a woman, someone being killed in their own home, someone being ambushed, someone being killed when undertaking a legal house-search.

    proof payment **OSw** *SdmL* Mb

    single compensation **OSw** *DL* Eb, Mb

    single compensation (from a known killer) **OSw** *UL* Mb, *VmL* Mb

    See also: *drap, dræpa, dulghadrap, mandrap, morþ, spyria, tvæböti*

    Refs: KLNM s.v. *spårgäld*; Schlyter 1877, s.v. *sporgæld*; SL DL40–41 note 12; SL UL119–20 notes 34–37; SL VmL, 91 note 41

sprængia (OSw) verb

    hurt **OSw** *UL* Blb, *VmL* Bb

spyria (OSw) spyrja (ON) verb

    follow **ONorw** *GuL* Tjb

    investigate **ONorw** *GuL* Mhb

    Expressions:

    spyria up (OSw)

    trace **OSw** *ÄVgL* Kkb

    See also: *sporgæld*

staddr (ON) adj.

    present **ONorw** *GuL* Mhb

staða (ON) noun

    summer solstice **ONorw** *GuL* Llb

staðarábúð (ON) noun

    householding on a church farm **OIce** *Grg* Tíg 266

staðfesta (ON) noun

    fixed place of residence **OIce** *Jó* Kge 30

staðfestulauss (ON) adj.

    without a fixed home **OIce** *Grg* Arþ 127

stafgarþr (OGu) noun

    Literally 'stake enclosure', but translated as 'ancient site' since the exact nature of these features is not clear. It has been proposed that they were the sites of abandoned Iron Age dwellings, which later became the subject of an ancestor cult, perhaps with the erection of stone pillars within the limits of the ruined foundations. Whilst there are several instances of a *stafr* 'stake' being forbidden by post-Christianization laws, with the assumption that these were objects of worship, whether or not they were actually engraved with heathen images, the *stafgarþr* seems to have been a uniquely Gotlandic phenomenon. A full study of *stafgarþr* has been made by Olsson (1976; 1992) and a short résumé of his conclusions and the suggestions of Måhl and Gösta Holm (in private correspondence) appears in Peel 2015.

    ancient site **OGu** *GS* Ch. 1

    See also: *höghabyr, hörgr, hult, høgh, høgheman, lunder, sten, vi*

    Refs: Cathey 1978; Måhl 1990; Olsson 1976; Olsson 1992; Peel 2015, 97–98, 261–62, 290–91 note 1/45; Schlyter 1877, s.v. *stafgarþer*

stafkarl (OSw) stavkarl (ODan) stafkarl (ON) stakkarl (OSw) noun

    A beggar, probably vagrant.

    beggar **ODan** *ESjL* 3, **ONorw** *FrL* KrbA 16, **OSw** *SdmL* Kkb, *UL* Kkb, *VmL* Kkb, *ÖgL* Kkb

    man with (beggar's) staff **OSw** *YVgL* Kkb, Tb, *ÄVgL* Kkb

    staff man **OSw** *HL* Mb

    Refs: Gerhold 2002, 85–86; KLNM s.v.v. *fattigvård, tiggar*

stafkarlaförsla (ON) noun

    Transportation of beggars between householders for support.

    housing homeless people **ONorw** *FrL* KrbA 23

    Refs: Hertzberg s.v. *stafkarlafœrsla*

staflægja (ON) noun

    cross-beam **ONorw** *GuL* Leb

stafnasmiðr (ON) noun

    prow builder **ONorw** *GuL* Leb

staka (ON) verb

stagger **ONorw** *GuL* Mhb

stakkgarðr (ON) noun

hay-yard **OIce** *Jó* Llb 9, 37

stackyard **OIce** *Grg* Lbþ 189

stallari (OSw) **stallari** (ON) noun

In Norway the king's marshal, the *stallari,* Medieval Lat. *comes stabuli* ('head of the horse-stable')*,* was originally in charge of the king's stables. He was the highest ranked officer of the royal bodyguard (*hirð*) and the king's spokesman there and at the assembly. According to Norwegian provincial laws (GuL ch. 185, FtL Mhb, ch. 60) he had the same rank and legal status as a *lendr maðr* (see *lænder*). In Sweden, the *stallari* was a prominent member of the retinue of other highly ranked persons, such as, e.g., bishops, with varying functions.

constable **OSw** *YVgL* Kkb

groom **OSw** *DL* Kkb

king's marshal **OIce** *Jó* Llb 18, **ONorw** *GuL* Mhb

marshal **OIce** *Js* Kdb 3 Mah 29, **ONorw** *FrL* Mhb 60, **OSw** *SdmL* Mb

staller **OSw** *ÖgL* Db

Refs: Hertzberg s.v. *stallari;* KLNM s.v.v. *befalingsmand, embedsindtægter, följe, lendmann, stallar;* ONP s.v. *stallari;* Schlyter s.v. *stallari*

staller (OSw) **stal** (ODan) noun

stable **ODan** *JyL* 2, **OSw** *YVgL* Tb

stamboi (OSw) noun

man in the stem of a ship **OSw** *UL* Mb, *VmL* Mb

See also: *stamn*

stamn (OSw) **stafn** (ON) noun

prow **ONorw** *GuL* Mhb, Leb

stem (2) **ONorw** *GuL* Leb, **OSw** *UL* Kgb, Mb

See also: *stamboi*

stampa (OSw) **stappa** (OSw) noun

log trap **OSw** *UL* Mb, *VmL* Mb

standa (OSw) **standa** (ON) verb

apply **ONorw** *GuL* Tfb

remain **ONorw** *GuL* Kpb

stop **ONorw** *GuL* Tfb

be valid **ONorw** *GuL* Løb, Mhb, Leb

Expressions:

eptir standa (ON)

remain to be paid **ONorw** *GuL* Løb

standa a (OGu, OSw)

last **OGu** *GL* A 9, 10

be a matter for (*someone*) to decide **OSw** *UL* Äb, Jb, Blb, Rb *VmL* Kkb, Mb, Jb, Bb, Rb

standa firi (OSw)

defend oneself **OSw** *DL* Gb

standa firi sik (OGu)

defend oneself **OGu** *GL* A 4, 37

standa fore (OSw)

cite in excuse **OSw** *UL* Blb

standa frammi (OGu, OSw)

be offered **OGu** *GL* A 28

present oneself **OSw** *UL* Jb

standa til ængs (OSw)

allow to go to seed **OSw** *VmL* Bb

See also: *ganga, væria*

stang (OSw) noun

post **OSw** *UL* Blb, *VmL* Bb

staff **OSw** *UL* Mb

upright **OSw** *UL* Blb, *VmL* Bb

stanga (ON) verb

butt **ONorw** *GuL* Tfb

stangehog (ODan) noun

blow with a staff **ODan** *ESjL* 2

staff-blow **ODan** *ESjL* 2, *SkL* 96, 109, *VSjL* 41, 47

stangehogsbardaghe (ODan) noun

staff-blow **ODan** *VSjL* 48

stangfall (OSw) noun

pole measuring **OSw** *SdmL* Bb

See also: *mælistang, rep, vaþstang*

starblindr (OGu) adj.

moonblind **OGu** *GL* A 34

starf (ON) noun

office **OIce** *Jó* Þfb 1

position **OIce** *Js* Þfb 1

staur (OGu) **staurr** (ON) noun

enclosure **OGu** *GL* A 25, 57, 63

farmstead **OGu** *GL* A 20

stake **ONorw** *GuL* Mhb

See also: *garþer*

staura (ON) verb

drive a stake down **ONorw** *GuL* Krb

staurgulf (OGu) noun

fence section **OGu** *GL* A 26

pair of fence supports **OGu** *GL* A 17

stava (OSw) verb

To dictate an oath; SdmL and YVgL state who had the right to do this, and HL states that the king's man was to dictate the verdict of acquittal or conviction of the *næmd* 'panel'.

> *dictate* **OSw** *HL* Kgb, *SdmL* Kkb, Bb, *YVgL* Föb

staver (OSw) **stav** (ODan) **stafr** (ON) noun
> *post* **ONorw** *GuL* Leb
> *staff* **OSw** *YVgL* Rlb, *ÄVgL* Rlb
> *stave* **ODan** *ESjL* 2
> *stick* **ODan** *JyL* 2

See also: *hyrnustokker*

stavre (ODan) verb
> *put staves* **ODan** *ESjL* 2
> *stave* **ODan** *ESjL* 2

stavring (ODan) noun
> *staving* **ODan** *ESjL* 2

See also: *staver*, *stavre*

stavshog (ODan) noun
> *blow with a rod* **ODan** *JyL* 3

staþfæsta (OSw) **staðfesta** (ON) verb
> *establish* **OSw** *SdmL* Conf
> *settle in a fixed home* **OIce** *Grg* Þsþ 62

staþga (OSw) verb
> *decree* **OSw** *SdmL* Conf, Kmb, Till
> *prescribe* **OSw** *YVgL* Kkb

staþgi (OSw) **staþgaþ** (OGu) **staþvi** (OSw) noun
> *agreement* **OSw** *HL* Jb, *ÄVgL* Föb
> *statute* **OGu** *GS* Ch. 2, **OSw** *SdmL* Conf

stefnandi (ON) noun
> *summoner* **OIce** *Jó* Þfb 9

stefnuboð (ON) noun
> *meeting-message* **ONorw** *EidsL* 33.1

stefnubýr (ON) noun
> *meeting-farm* **ONorw** *EidsL* 33.1

stefnugerð (ON) noun
> *setting of time limits* **ONorw** *BorgL* 16.1

stefnujörð (ON) noun

The *stefnujörð* ('land on lease') was land that had been sold for a term of years, and which was subject to redemption at the end of the term.
> *land on lease* **ONorw** *GuL* Olb

Refs: Helle 2001, 118; Hertzberg s.v. *stefnujörð*; Robberstad 1981, 385–87

stefnulag (ON) noun
> *appointment* **ONorw** *FrL* Intr 15

stefnulið (ON) noun
> *member of a meeting-party* **ONorw** *EidsL* 22.7

stefnustaðr (ON) noun
> *place for summoning* **OIce** *Grg* Feþ 144, 156 Lbþ 215 Tíg 256

stefnusök (ON) noun

A summoning case in which a summons was to be issued locally and neighbours were to be called at an assembly to serve on a panel. Summoning cases covered a variety of offenses, including refusal to vacate reserved seats for the Law Council (Grg Lrþ 117) and concealing a dead man's property from underage heirs (Grg Fjl 223).
> *summoning case* **OIce** *Grg* Þsþ 59 Vís 87 Lrþ 117 Arþ 118 Feþ 148, 155 Lbþ 172, 174 Fjl 223 Misc 238, 244

See also: *sak*

Refs: CV s.v. *stefnusök*; Fritzner s.v. *stefnusök*; GrgTr, I:259

stefnuváttr (ON) noun
> *summons witness* **OIce** *Grg* Þsþ 46

stefnuvitni (ON) noun
> *witness to a home summons* **OIce** *Jó* Lbb 1

See also: *heimstefnuvitni*, *vitni*

stefnuvætti (ON) noun
> *testimony of summoning* **OIce** *Grg* Þsþ 32, 33 Feþ 150 Lbþ 176, *Js* Lbb 1

steik (ON) noun
> *steak* **ONorw** *GuL* Tjb

stekarahus (OSw) noun
> *cook-house* **OSw** *DL* Kkb
> *kitchen* **OSw** *SdmL* Kkb

stekari (OSw) noun
> *cook* **OSw** *DL* Kkb, *SdmL* Mb

stelkr (OGu) noun
> *link* **OGu** *GL* A 36

See also: *rekendr*

sten (OSw) **steinn** (ON) noun

Stones appear as objects of pagan beliefs (OIce Klþ 7; OSw HL Kkb 1), border markers, impromptu weapons and tools of capital punishment.
> *rock* **ONorw** *GuL* Mhb
> *stone* **OSw** *HL* Kkb, *SdmL* Mb

Expressions:

döma under sten (OSw)

A capital punishment, presumably stoning, for women guilty of certain killings within the family. It was not specified who was to act as executioner.
> *sentence under stones* **OSw** *SdmL* Mb 28

**mærkia mæth sten æthe mæth stapel
æthe mæth gryft (ODan)**

*mark with stone or with stake or
with ditch* **ODan** *JyL* 1, 2

ren ok sten (OSw)

edges and stones **OSw** *YVgL* Jb *ÄVgL* Jb

stens mater ok strandar (OSw)

A capital punishment, often interpreted as
stoning, for women committing witchcraft
and for men stealing grain. It was not
specified who was to act as executioner.

food for stone and shore **OSw** *DL* Kkb, Tjdb

tyrfa meþ stenum (OSw)

stone **OSw** *UL* Mb

See also: *lunder*

Refs: Ambrius 1996, 48–49; KLNM
s.v. *dødsstraf*; Schlyter s.v. *strand*

stenaþer (OSw) adj.

Expressions:

rend ok stend (OSw)

have edges and stones **OSw** *YVgL* Jb *ÄVgL* Jb

stakat ok stenat (OSw)

marked with both stakes and stones **OSw** *DL* Bb

stenka (OSw) verb

stone **OSw** *ÖgL* Eb

stenmærki (OSw) noun

stone-mark **OSw** *HL* Blb

stenshog (ODan) noun

blow with a stone **ODan** *JyL* 3, *SkL* 98

strike with stone **ODan** *ESjL* 2

steypa (ON) verb

pour **ONorw** *GuL* Krb

stigheman (ODan) noun

highwayman **ODan** *JyL* 3

stighöre (OSw) noun

A fine for illegal use of another's boat.

stepping-{öre} **OSw** *SdmL* Bb

stika (ON) verb

block with stakes **ONorw** *GuL* Kvr

measure by rod **OIce** *Jó* Kab 5

See also: *stika*

stika (ON) noun

yard measuring rod **OIce** *Jó* Kab 26

stikæmæz (OSw) noun

sword **OSw** *YVgL* Föb

stilli (ON) noun

trap **ONorw** *GuL* Llb

See also: *gildri*

stinga (OSw) **stinga** (OGu) **stinga** (ON) verb

place **ONorw** *GuL* Mhb

poke **OGu** *GL* A 19, **OSw** *UL* Mb, *VmL* Mb

thrust **ONorw** *GuL* Mhb

Expressions:

stinga handum viþer (OSw)

lay claim to **OSw** *VmL* Mb

stingi (ON) noun

stitch **ONorw** *GuL* Løb

stionka (OSw) **stinqua** (OGu) verb

bounce **OSw** *UL* Mb, *VmL* Mb

fly **OGu** *GL* A 23

stiupbarn (OSw) **stjupbarn** (ODan) **stifbarn** (OSw)
stiufbarn (OSw) **stypbarn** (OSw) noun

stepchild **ODan** *ESjL* 1, *JyL* 1, *SkL* 21, *VSjL* 1, 2, 12,
13, 15, **OSw** *DL* Tjdb, *SdmL* Äb, *YVgL* Äb, *ÄVgL* Äb

See also: *barn*

stiupfaþer (OSw) **stjupfather** (ODan) noun

stepfather **ODan** *ESjL* 1, *JyL* 1, *VSjL* 2,
12, 13, 15, **OSw** *DL* Tjdb, *ÖgL* Eb

stiæla (OSw) **stjale** (ODan) **stolen** (ODan) **stiela** (OGu)
stela (ON) **stal** (OSw) **stolet** (OSw) **stolin** (OSw)
verb

grasp **OSw** *ÄVgL* Äb

rob **OIce** *Jó* Þjb 2, **OSw** *YVgL* Tb

steal **ODan** *ESjL* 2, 3, *JyL* 3, *SkL* 112, 130, 136,
141, 145, 151, 160, 162, 184, *VSjL* 86, 87, **OGu** *GL*
A 38, Add. 8 (B 55), **OIce** *Grg* Feþ 170 Rsþ 227,
Jó Þfb 7 Þjb 1, *Js* Mah 7 Þjb 1, *KRA* 7, **ONorw** *FrL*
Intr 9, 22 Rgb 38 Bvb 7, *GuL* Llb, Tjb, **OSw** *DL* Bb,
Tjdb, *HL* Kkb, Mb, Jb, Blb, *SdmL* Kkb, Kgb, Jb,
Bb, Kmb, Tjdb, Rb, *UL* Kkb, Kgb, Mb, Jb, Kmb,
Blb, *VmL* Kkb, Mb, Kmb, Bb, *YVgL* Kkb, Drb, Äb,
Rlb, Tb, *ÄVgL* Kkb, Md, Äb, Rlb, Tb, *ÖgL* Eb, Vm

take by stealth **OSw** *HL* Kkb

See also: *ræna*, *þiuver*

stífla (ON) noun

dam **OIce** *Jó* Llb 22, 24

stjarfi (ON) noun

epilepsy **ONorw** *GuL* Løb

stjórn (ON) noun

administration **OIce** *Jó* Kge 31

starboard side **ONorw** *GuL* Leb

stjupdotter (ODan) **stjúpdóttir** (ON) noun

stepdaughter **ODan** *ESjL* 1, *VSjL* 12,
ONorw *FrL* Mhb 39, *GuL* Krb

stjupmother (ODan) stjúpmóðir (ON) stýfmóðir (ON) noun

stepmother **ODan** *ESjL* 1, *JyL* 1, **ONorw** *EidsL* 52.1, *GuL* Krb, Mhb

stjupsun (ODan) stjúpsonr (ON) noun

stepson **ODan** *JyL* 1, *VSjL* 9, 12, **OIce** *Grg* Bat 113

stjupsystken (ODan) noun

stepsiblings **ODan** *JyL* 1

stofuhurð (ON) noun

door of a living-room **ONorw** *GuL* Llb

stokka (OSw) verb

put in the stocks **OSw** *SdmL* Mb, *UL* Mb, *VmL* Mb, *YVgL* Tb, Add, *ÖgL* Eb, Db, Vm

stokker (OSw) stok (ODan) stukkr (OGu) stokkr (ON) noun

Literally 'log' appearing in contexts such as legal and illegal felling of trees, including risk of injury or death in the process; the right to claim bees, described in particular detail in some Danish laws; as a boundary marker; and as an implement of detention or penalty through public humiliation or corporal punishment (i.e. a pillory). The construction and use of the latter was not specified, but it may have been vertical or horizontal with or without holes or irons for neck, hands or feet, and it is unclear if the *stokker* referring to a chopping block for mutilations (ODan JyL, OSw HL, UL, VmL) also denoted such a device. Temporary detention in a *stokker* of certain criminals was allowed (ODan JyL, OSw YVgL, SdmL, ÖgL), but illegal use was severely punished. It was used for punishment in cases of adultery (OGu GL), theft (OSw YVgL) and murder (OSw ÖgL) and in ODan SkL it appeared in conjunction with certain ordeals. It is generally not specified where the *stokker* was placed or who was to perform the punishments assumed to be associated with it, such as flogging or locking into it.

bee-hive **ODan** *ESjL* 3

bollard **OGu** *GL* A 36

pillar **OSw** *UL* Blb

stake **ODan** *JyL* 2

stock (1) **ODan** *JyL* 2, **ONorw** *GuL* Mhb, **OSw** *HL* Mb, *YVgL* Add, *ÖgL* Eb

stocks **OGu** *GL* A 20a

stump **OSw** *UL* Kgb, Mb, Blb, *VmL* Kgb, Mb

trunk **OSw** *UL* Blb

Expressions:

band ok stok (ODan)

ropes and iron **ODan** *SkL* 138

Refs: Fritzner s.v. *stokkr*; KLNM s.v.v. *kåk, skamstraff, straffredskap, stupa*; ONP s.v. *stokkr*

stokkland (ON) noun

isolated land **ONorw** *EidsL* 15

storþahug (OSw) noun

The crime of illegally felling a certain number of trees or amount of wood.

big wood-pile of young trees **OSw** *YVgL* Föb

felling in brushwood **OSw** *YVgL* Add

See also: *vithstorth*

stoth (ODan) noun

Defined as twelve horses. JyL considered intentional illegal grazing by a *stoth* a gang crime (ODan *hærværk*), which was severely punished. Contrasted to damage made by stray or single animals.

horse troop **ODan** *JyL* 3

troop **ODan** *JyL* 3, *SkL* 169

troop of horses **ODan** *SkL* 169

See also: *hiorþ, vrath*

stoþhors (OSw) stothhors (ODan) noun

breeding mare **OSw** *ÄVgL* Äb

troop horse **ODan** *JyL* 3, *SkL* 179, 180

troop of horses **ODan** *JyL* 3

stórglópr (ON) noun

serious crime **ONorw** *FrL* KrbA 46

stórmál (ON) noun

weighty case **OIce** *Jó* Mah 17

stórnauðsyn (ON) noun

compelling reasons **ONorw** *GuL* Krb

serious trouble **OIce** *Jó* Þfb 8

urgent need **OIce** *KRA* 17

See also: *nöþsyn*

stórskrift (ON) noun

serious penance **OIce** *KRA* 31

stórskuld (ON) noun

major debt **OIce** *Grg* Misc 245

strandsetr (ON) noun

someone left on a shore **OIce** *Grg* Ómb 132

strithe (ODan) verb

contest **ODan** *ESjL* 2

striþ (OSw) striþ (OGu) noun

battle **OSw** *UL* Äb, *VmL* Äb

quarrel **OGu** *GL* A 39

stryka (OSw) verb

abort **OSw** *ÄVgL* Rlb

strænger (OSw) noun

snare **OSw** *UL* Mb, *VmL* Mb

stubbi (OSw) stumbil (OGu) noun

stump **OGu** *GL* A 25, **OSw** *UL* Blb, *VmL* Bb

stumn (OSw) **stuvn** (ODan) noun

    separate part **ODan** *JyL* 1, 3

    stub **OSw** *ÄVgL* Fös

    stump **ODan** *JyL* 2, *SkL* 192, *VSjL* 66

stumnsyn (OSw) noun

    stump inspection **OSw** *SdmL* Bb

stungafóli (ON) noun

    Stolen goods which have been planted in order to implicate an innocent person. Thought to be synonymous with *borafóli* (q.v.).

    sting-felony **ONorw** *EidsL* 24.5

    See also: *borafóli*

    Refs: CV s.v. *stungafóli*; Frtizner s.v. *stungafoli*; Hertzberg s.v. *stungafoli*

stuva (OSw) **stova** (OSw) **stuga** (OSw) noun

    cottage **OSw** *DL* Kkb, *YVgL* Äb, *ÄVgL* Äb

    dwelling house **OSw** *SdmL* Kkb, Mb, *SmL*, *YVgL* Kkb

    dwelling quarters **OSw** *DL* Bb

stuver (OSw) **stúfr** (ON) noun

    stump of wood **ONorw** *GuL* Mhb

stuvkøp (ODan) noun

    bought land **ODan** *JyL* 2

    See also: *köp*, *stumn*

stuþ (OSw) **stuth** (ODan) noun

    Literally 'support'. In JyL, the relatives' contribution to compensation for murder. In ESjL, SkL and VSjL, an annual tax, presumably paid in grain by all landowning householders, replacing earlier contributions of food for the king's travels (cf. *gengærþ*) or for his horses.

    contribution **ODan** *JyL* 2

    other dues **ODan** *SkL* 75, *VSjL* 79

    pillar **OSw** *UL* Mb, *VmL* Mb

    prop **OSw** *UL* Jb, Blb, *VmL* Bb

    support **ODan** *JyL* 2

    tax **ODan** *ESjL* 3

    Refs: KLNM s.v. *stud*, Schlyter s.v. *stuþ*; Venge 2002, 16–21, 116

stúfa (ON) noun

    female thief whose nose has been cut off **ONorw** *GuL* Tjb

    See also: *hnúfa*

styggr (ON) adj.

    wild **OFar** *Seyð* 10

styld (OSw) **styld** (ODan) **stuldr** (ON) **stulðr** (ON) noun

    Derived from the verb *stiæla* 'to steal' referring to the act of stealing rather than the stolen object. Sometimes contrasted to *ran* 'robbery' and *köp* 'purchase'. For more on stealing, see *þiufnaþer*.

    stealing **OIce** *Grg* Rsþ 229, **OSw** *SdmL* Bb, Tjdb

    theft **ODan** *JyL* 2, *VSjL* 86, **OIce** *Jó* Þjb 1, 5, *Js* Þjb 1, 4, *KRA* 28, 34, **ONorw** *GuL* Tjb, **OSw** *HL* Mb, *YVgL* Rlb, Tb, *ÄVgL* Rlb, Tb, *ÖgL* Vm

    Refs: Ekholst 2014, 57–62; KLNM s.v. *tyveri*; SAOB s.v.v. *stjäla*, *stöld*; Schlyter s.v.v. *styld*, *þiufnaþer*, *þiuft*

styltingsrast (OSw) noun

    A *rast* was the distance travelled between breaks, while the meaning of *stylting* is unclear. Appears in the context of a settler claiming new land.

    {styltingsrast} **OSw** *HL* Blb

    Refs: Brink forthcoming; Schlyter s.v. *styltingsrast*

styra (OSw) **styre** (ODan) verb

    govern **ODan** *JyL* Fort, **OSw** *SdmL* Till

    rule **ODan** *JyL* Fort

styremanspænningar (pl.) (OSw) noun

    An annual fee to the ship's master paid by 'all those who eat their own bread, no matter whom they belong to'.

    payment to a shipmaster **OSw** *SdmL* Till

    Refs: Schlyter s.v. *styremans pænningar*

styreshavne (ODan) noun

    Possibly the office of *styreman* (ODan, see *styriman*) 'steersman' in the *lething* (ODan, see *leþunger*) 'military duty', or some landed property belonging to this office. Alternatively, the position on the rowing team. The laws deal with the right to inherit this.

    steering land **ODan** *JyL* 3

    steering office **ODan** *JyL* 3

    See also: *hamna*, *styriman*

    Refs: Gammeldansk ordbog s.v. *styreshavne*; Tamm and Vogt, eds, 2016, 314

styrifaster (OSw) noun

    first among witnesses **OSw** *YVgL* Jb

    {styrifaster} **OSw** *ÄVgL* Jb

    See also: *fastar (pl.)*, *oþolfastir*

styriman (OSw) **styreman** (ODan) **stýrimaðr** (ON) **styre maþer** (OSw) **styrimaþer** (OSw) noun

    A ship's master on a ship in the *leþunger* (naval defence organization, Denmark, Norway, Sweden) with duties also when the ship was in the harbour. In Iceland a ship's master.

    captain **OIce** *Js* Kab 20

    ship captain **ONorw** *FrL* Leb 7

    ship's master **OIce** *Grg* Klþ 10 Þsþ 53 Vís 97 Arþ 120 Ómb 132, 139 Feþ 156, 166 Misc 243,

250, *Jó* Sg 3 Kge 17 Fml 1, 2, **ONorw** *FrL* Intr
20 KrbA 27, *GuL* Llb, Arb, Leb, **OSw** *SdmL*
Kgb, Till, *UL* Kgb, Mb, *VmL* Kgb, Mb

steersman **ODan** *ESjL* 3, *JyL* 2, **OSw** *HL* Kgb

See also: *hamna, leþunger, styreshavne*

Refs: KLNM s.v. *styresmann*; Tamm
and Vogt, eds, 2016, 314

styva (OSw) verb

maim **OSw** *DL* Bb, *VmL* Bb

mutilate **OSw** *YVgL* Tb

stýri (ON) noun

rudder **ONorw** *GuL* Kvr, Mhb, Leb

See also: *stýrihamla*

stýrihamla (ON) noun

rudder strap **ONorw** *GuL* Leb

See also: *stýri*

stýrisdrengr (ON) noun

tiller **ONorw** *GuL* Leb

stæghl (OSw) noun

Literally 'stake, pole' referring to an implement for capital punishment of disputed construction and usage. Presumably, a wheel placed on top of a pole used for breaking a criminal's limbs or joints and/or for attaching and displaying the dead or dying body. Used for certain male murderers, whereas the corresponding female offender was to be stoned. It was not specified who was to act as executioner, but OSw ÖgL Eb suggests the plaintiff.

wheel **OSw** *HL* Mb, *SdmL* Mb

Refs: Ambrius 1996, 63; Kjus 2011, 100–01; KLNM s.v.v. *dödsstraf, straffredskap*; Schlyter s.v. *stæghla*

stæghla (OSw) steghla (OSw) verb

bind to the stake **OSw** *UL* Mb, *VmL* Mb

break on a wheel **OSw** *HL* Mb, *ÖgL* Eb

See also: *döma*

stækkia (OSw) stakka (OSw) verb

mutilate **OSw** *DL* Bb, *VmL* Bb

stæmma (OSw) verb

dam up **OSw** *UL* Blb

stæmna (OSw) stævne (ODan) stefna (OGu) stemma (OGu) stefna (ON) stefna (OSw) stæmpna (OSw) stæfnæ (ODan) stævne (ODan) stefna (OGu) stemna (OGu) stefna (ON) stæmpna (OSw) verb

Etymologically 'to fix'. Frequently used for setting a formal meeting, particularly a *þing* 'assembly', and specifically a *þing* for handling one's case, usually translated as 'to summon' or 'to call'. With stronger emphasis on the legal proceedings thus started, occasionally translated as 'to sue'. Andersen (2010)

contrasts summoning an accused with witnesses ahead of the *þing* to a law suit initiated by *lysning* 'announcement' at the *þing* in that it was quicker, allowed the plaintiff compensation if the accused failed to appear, allowed the accused to prepare his defence and allowed them both to settle the case outside of court before the *þing*.

assemble **ONorw** *BorgL* 17.5

call **ODan** *JyL* 2, **ONorw** *BorgL* 14.5

challenge **ONorw** *GuL* Mhb

direct **ONorw** *GuL* Leb

go **ONorw** *GuL* Leb

raise a case **OSw** *ÖgL* Kkb

sue **OSw** *HL* Rb, *YVgL* Föb, Add, *ÖgL* Kkb, Db

summon **ODan** *ESjL* 2, 3, *JyL* 1, 2, *SkKL* 11, *SkL* 14, 67, 73, 83, 121, 145, 146, 173, 233, 241, *VSjL* 78, 84, 87, **OFar** *Seyð* 1, **OGu** *GL* A 30, 39, **OIce** *Grg* passim, *Jó* passim, *Js* passim, *KRA* 29, 36, **ONorw** *EidsL* 33.3, *FrL* Intr 15 Tfb 1 KrbA 1, 22 KrbB 1 Mhb 7, *GuL* Kpb, Løb, Llb, Tfb, Mhb, Tjb, Olb, Leb, **OSw** *DL* Eb, *HL* Rb, *SdmL* Kkb, Rb, Till, *SmL*, *UL* Kkb, Rb, Add. 18, *VmL* Rb, *YVgL* Add, *ÖgL* Kkb, Eb, Db

See also: *biuþa, buþ*

Refs: Andersen 2010, 81–83; Hellquist s.v. *stämma*; Hertzberg s.v. *stefna*; Schlyter s.v. *stæmna*

stæmna (OSw) noun

appointed day **ONorw** *GuL* Kpb, Llb, Olb

appointed muster **ONorw** *GuL* Leb

appointment **ONorw** *FrL* Leb 2

assembly **OSw** *YVgL* Urb

case **OGu** *GL* A 31

certain number **OSw** *UL* Äb, *VmL* Äb

lawful time **OSw** *HL* Mb

lease **ONorw** *GuL* Olb

meeting **ODan** *ESjL* 1, **ONorw** *EidsL* 22.7, *GuL* Llb, Leb, **OSw** *HL* Mb, *UL* Blb, *YVgL* Tb, Add, *ÄVgL* Tb, *ÖgL* Kkb, Eb

plaint **OSw** *YVgL* Add

suit **OSw** *YVgL* Add

summoning **ODan** *ESjL* 2, *SkKL* 11

summons **ODan** *ESjL* 3, *SkKL* 7, 11, **OGu** *GL* A 32, 39, **OIce** *Grg* Þsþ 72, *Jó* Þfb 9, *Js* Kvg 2, *KRA* 16, **ONorw** *FrL* Intr 16 Mhb 7, *GuL* Krb, Kvb, Arb, Leb

term **ODan** *SkL* 146, **ONorw** *GuL* Krb, Olb

stæmning (OSw) stævning (ODan) stæmpnung (OSw) noun

suing at the Thing **OSw** *HL* Rb

summons **ODan** *SkKL* 11, **OSw** *SdmL* Jb, Till

stæmnudagher (OSw) **stævnedagh** (ODan)
   stefnudagr (ON) **stæmnodagher** (OSw) noun
   appointed day **ONorw** *GuL* Krb, Olb
   contract day **OSw** *YVgL* Utgb, *ÄVgL* Föb
   day agreed upon **OSw** *SmL*
   day of summoning **OSw** *YVgL* Add
   day summoned **ODan** *SkL* 241
   deadline **OSw** *HL* Jb, Rb
   determined day/time **OSw** *DL* Bb, *YVgL* Föb
   due time **OSw** *HL* Kmb, Blb
   end of contract time **OSw** *HL* Blb
   expiry date **OSw** *UL* Jb, Blb, Rb, *VmL* Bb, Rb
   meeting date **OSw** *SdmL* Kkb, *UL* Kkb, *VmL* Kkb
   period of possible redemption **OSw** *HL* Rb
   prescribed time **OSw** *HL* Rb
   set day **OSw** *UL* Kkb, Kgb, *VmL* Kkb, *YVgL* Kkb, Äb
   settled respite **OSw** *YVgL* Föb
   specified date **OSw** *DL* Bb
   summoning day **ODan** *SkL* 240, **OIce** *Grg* Þsþ 57, 58, *KRA* 16
   time limit **OSw** *DL* Gb, *SdmL* Kkb, Jb, Bb, Kmb, Tjdb, *UL* Kkb, Äb, Jb, Kmb, Blb, *VmL* Kkb, Äb, Jb, Kmb
   See also: *stæmna*

stæmnufriþer (OSw) noun
   Peace of legal gatherings, presumably including the participants' journey to and from it. Breaching this peace was an unatonable crime.
   peace of assembly **OSw** *YVgL* Add
   See also: *friþer, stæmna*
   Refs: Schlyter s.v. *stæmnufriþer*

stæmnumæn (pl.) (OSw) noun
   meeting men **OSw** *SdmL* Gb

stæniza (OSw) noun
   chemise **OSw** *UL* Äb, *VmL* Äb

stæþia (OSw) **stæthje** (ODan) verb
   agree **OSw** *YVgL* Kkb
   marry **ODan** *JyL* 1

suarþsprangr (OGu) noun
   split scalp **OGu** *GL* A 19

subdjakn (ODan) **subdjákn** (ON) noun
   subdeacon **ODan** *JyL* 1, **OIce** *KRA* 17

suigin (OGu) adj.
   indented **OGu** *GL* A 19

sumar (ON) noun
   summer **ONorw** *GuL* Llb, Kvr

sumarhagi (ON) noun
   summer pasture **OIce** *Jó* Llb 51

   See also: *haghi*
   Refs: CV s.v. *sumarhagi*

sumarhlass (ON) noun
   summer load **ONorw** *FrL* LlbA 1

sumarmál (ON) noun
   beginning of summer **ONorw** *FrL* LlbA 1

sumarnat (OSw) noun
   The first day, literally night, of summer. In OSw, not specified as to the date, but in OIce and ONorw, 14 April, indicating certain legally significant time limits.
   beginning of summertime **OSw** *DL* Bb
   Refs: KLNM s.v.v. *første vinterdag, sommerdag*; Schlyter s.v. *vinternat*

sumarsetr (ON) noun
   summer stay **ONorw** *FrL* LlbB 8

sumartenlunger (OSw) **sumarten unger** (OSw) noun
   beast born the same summer **OSw** *UL* Blb, *VmL* Mb, Bb

sumermylne (ODan) noun
   summer mill **ODan** *ESjL* 3
   See also: *mylna, vintermylne*

sunararver (OSw) noun
   inheritance after a son **OSw** *YVgL* Äb

sunderkulla (OSw) adj.
   of another bed **OSw** *YVgL* Add
   half-siblings **OSw** *DL* Gb, *HL* Äb
   of separate broods **OSw** *SdmL* Äb
   See also: *kolder, samkulla*

sundersla (OGu) verb
   break **OGu** *GL* Add. 3, 4 (B 19)

sundr (OGu) adv.
   broken **OGu** *GL* A 19

sundrisker (OSw) adj.
   Possibly German. Appears in the context of the punishment for violence against foreigners.
   southern (man) **OSw** *ÄVgL* Slb
   See also: *supermaþer*

sunnudagahald (ON) noun
   observance of Sundays **ONorw** *GuL* Krb

sunnudagr (ON) noun
   Sunday **ONorw** *GuL* Krb, Kpb, Leb

sunnudagshelgr (ON) noun
   Sunday holy period **ONorw** *EidsL* 12

sunnudagsverk (ON) noun
   work on Sundays **ONorw** *GuL* Krb

sunnuhátíðisdagr (ON) noun
   Sunday Holiday **OIce** *KRA* 29

sunnunátt (ON) noun

night before Sunday **ONorw** *GuL* Krb

suþermaþer (OSw) noun

Appears in the context of punishment for violence against foreigners. Also, however not included here, the people to which OSw SdmL applied.

Southerner **OSw** *YVgL* Frb, Drb, *ÄVgL* Md, Smb

sútari (ON) noun

shoemaker **OIce** *Grg* Vís 101

svar (OSw) **svar** (ON) noun

answer **ONorw** *GuL* Kpb, Olb, **OSw** *YVgL* Add

defence **OSw** *HL* Rb, *YVgL* Add

svara (OSw) **svare** (ODan) **svara** (ON) verb

answer **ODan** *JyL* 2, *SkKL* 11, *SkL* 73, 152, **ONorw** *GuL* Olb, **OSw** *DL* Mb, *SdmL* Kkb, Jb

answer for **OSw** *UL* Kkb, Kgb, Äb, Mb, *VmL* Kkb, Mb

defend **OSw** *DL* Rb, *UL* Jb, *VmL* Jb

respond **OSw** *HL* Äb, *UL* Jb, Rb, *VmL* Kkb, Jb, *YVgL* Föb

svaralösa (OSw) noun

defiance **OSw** *HL* Rb

fine for refusal **OSw** *DL* Rb

freedom from responsibility **OSw** *DL* Rb

svarandi (OSw) noun

defendant **OSw** *DL* Rb, *HL* Kgb, Äb, Rb, *SdmL* Jb, Bb, Kmb, Rb, *YVgL* Add

respondent **OSw** *UL* Jb, Kmb, Blb, Rb, Add. 15, *VmL* Jb, Kmb, Bb, Rb

See also: *kærande*

svartaslagh (OSw) **svartaslag** (ON) **svartslagh** (OSw) noun

black blow **ONorw** *GuL* Mhb

black wound **OSw** *YVgL* Frb

blow that makes a bruise **OSw** *ÖgL* Vm

svartmunk (ODan) noun

black monk **ODan** *JyL* 3

svear (pl.) (OSw) noun

Men from Svealand had the right to choose a new king.

{*svear*} **OSw** *YVgL* Rlb, *ÄVgL* Rlb

sveit (ON) noun

In Iceland a *sveit* was a type of geographical division akin to a smaller district (ON *herað*, see *hæraþ*), though it has also been suggested that it corresponded to an area overseen by a chieftain (ON *góði*). The term persists into modern Icelandic as a type of administrative district. In the Norwegian GuL a *sveit* refers to a division of the military, a squad. A *svet* in early Danish law appears to have been a division of a quarter (ODan *fjarthing*, see *fjarþunger*), though it is first attested in the fifteenth century. A *sveit* may also refer to a retinue, as of soldiers or of people accompanying someone performing sorcery (ON *seiðr*).

district **ONorw** *FrL* Mhb 14

group **OIce** *Grg* Lrþ 117

part of the country **OIce** *Grg* Lrþ 117

region **OIce** *KRA* 15

squad **ONorw** *GuL* Leb

See also: *fylki, hreppr, hæraþ*

Refs: CV s.v. *sveit*; Fritzner s.v. *sveit*; GDO s.v. *II. svet*; Hertzberg s.v. sveit; Hollander 1916; Jón Viðar Sigurðsson 1993; KLNM s.v. *hird, militære enheder, sejd*; Svavar Sigmundsson 2003

svelta (ON) verb

underfeed **ONorw** *GuL* Kpb

sven (OSw) **sven** (ODan) **sveinn** (ON) noun

A young man, particularly a free, young man in someone's service, sometimes specifically one performing military service in the retinue of a high-ranking man. In ONorw GuL, also a male, otherwise unspecified, unfree servant or a slave.

boy **ODan** *ESjL* 1, **OSw** *VmL* Äb

farm-hand **ODan** *JyL* 2

man **ODan** *JyL* 3

servant **ODan** *JyL* 2, *VSjL* 42, **ONorw** *GuL* Løb, Mhb, Leb, **OSw** *DL* Tjdb, Rb, *SdmL* Kkb, Kmb, Mb, *UL* Kkb, Kmb, Mb, *VmL* Kkb, Kmb, *YVgL* Äb, Rlb, Jb

squire **OSw** *HL* Mb, *SdmL* Kmb, Till, *VmL* Rb

young boy **ODan** *ESjL* 1

See also: *verkasveinn*

Refs: Brink 2012, 151–54; Hellquist s.v. *sven*; Hertzberg s.v. *sveinn*

svensker (OSw) **svænsker** (OSw) adj.

Used of a man from Svealand. Appears in the context of varying punishments for killing someone from different parts of the realm.

Swedish **OSw** *ÄVgL* Md

sverðskriði (ON) noun

sword cutler **OIce** *Grg* Vís 101

svidda (ON) adj.

dead from unknown causes **OIce** *Grg* Klþ 16, *KRA* 32

sviða (ON) noun

burned spot **ONorw** *GuL* Mhb

svik (ON) noun

deceit **OIce** *Jó* Kge 6

fraud **OIce** *Jó* Fml 2, **ONorw** *GuL* Kpb

treachery **OIce** *KRA* 6

trickery **ONorw** *GuL* Olb

svin (OSw) **svin** (ODan) **suin** (OGu) noun

pig **ODan** *JyL* 3, *SkL* 169, 206, **OSw** *UL* Kkb, Blb, *VmL* Bb

swine **OGu** *GL* A 26, 41, Add. 2 (B 17), **OSw** *UL* Blb, *VmL* Bb

See also: *gris, smagris*

svinavalder (OSw) **swinawaller** (OSw) noun

swine grazing common **OSw** *UL* Blb, *VmL* Bb

See also: *almænninger, hiorþvalder*

svinesti (ODan) noun

pig sty **ODan** *VSjL* 57, 58

svinevrath (ODan) noun

drove of pigs **ODan** *SkL* 168, 206

svintæppa (OSw) verb

swine-proof the fencing **OSw** *UL* Blb, *VmL* Bb

See also: *atertæppa, tæppa*

svitunsmessa (ON) noun

St Swithun's Day (2 July) **ONorw** *GuL* Krb

sviþ (OSw) noun

clearing in the forest **OSw** *HL* Blb

svídauðr (ON) adj.

dead from unknown causes **ONorw** *BorgL* 5.9

svídái (ON) adj.

dead from accident or disease **ONorw** *BorgL* 5.1, *EidsL* 26.2, *GuL* Krb

svívirðing (ON) noun

disgrace **ONorw** *FrL* KrbB 13

svær (OSw) noun

male in-law **OSw** *SdmL* Äb

sværa (OSw) noun

female in-law **OSw** *SdmL* Äb

sværia (OSw) **sværje** (ODan) **sueria** (OGu) **sverja** (ON) **svoret** (OSw) **svorin** (OSw) verb

declare **OSw** *UL* Jb, *VmL* Jb

defend by oath **OSw** *DL* Tjdb

free by oath **OSw** *DL* Bb

invigorate **OSw** *HL* Äb

make an oath **OSw** *YVgL* Add

produce an oath **ODan** *SkL* 114

prove with oaths **OSw** *HL* Kkb, Mb

substantiate an accusation **OGu** *GL* A 20a

swear **ODan** *ESjL* 1–3, *JyL* 1–3, *SkKL* 6, 7, 11, *SkL* passim, *VSjL* passim, **OGu** *GL* A 19, 20a, 39, 61, **OIce** *Jó* Þfb 1, 3 Mah 24 Kge 2 Llb 26, 52 Kab 18, *Js* Þfb 1 Kdb 4 Mah 14, *KRA* 15, **ONorw** *EidsL*

11.1 39.4, *FrL* KrbA 2, 29 Mhb 7, **OSw** *DL* Eb, Mb, Bb, Rb, *HL* Äb, Jb, Rb, *SdmL* Kkb, Kgb, Äb, Jb, Bb, Kmb, Mb, Tjdb, Rb, Till, *UL* passim, *VmL* Kkb, Äb, Mb, Jb, Kmb, Bb, Rb, *YVgL* passim, *ÄVgL* Kkb, Md, Smb, Vs, Rlb, Jb, Tb, Föb, *ÖgL* Kkb, Db

take an oath **ONorw** *GuL* Krb, Llb, Arb, Tfb, Mhb, Olb, Leb, **OSw** *HL* Rb, *ÄVgL* Kkb

testify **OIce** *Jó* Llb 26, **OSw** *ÖgL* Eb

try with oaths **OSw** *HL* Blb

utter an oath **OSw** *HL* Kkb

See also: *lysa*

sværþ (OSw) **sværth** (ODan) **sverð** (ON) noun

In OSw, execution by sword was considered more honourable than other methods and could be used for robbery (HL, SdmL) and rape (SdmL). It seems generally assumed that capital punishments were carried out by the plaintiffs, but the king is given responsibility for the execution by sword in cases of excommunication over a year (DL, HL, SdmL). Swords were included among the common weapons of defence known as *folkvapn* (q.v.). The buying and selling of swords could be subject to regulations, in ÄVgL Tb concerning trade in bulk, *diker sværþ* 'tens of swords' and in ESjL 3 concerning the trade of swords with or without belts attached.

sword **ODan** *ESjL* 3, *JyL* 3, *SkL* 143, 144, **ONorw** *GuL* Mhb, Leb, **OSw** *DL* Kkb, Eb, *HL* Kkb, Kgb, Mb, Rb, *SdmL* Kkb, Kgb, Mb, *YVgL* Tb, *ÄVgL* Tb

Expressions:

(döma) undir sværþ (OSw)

(to sentence) to the sword **OSw** *DL* Kkb, Eb *SdmL* Kgb

put to the sword **OSw** *UL* Kkb, Kgb, Mb *VmL* Kkb, Kgb, Mb

sentence to be decapitated **OSw** *HL* Kkb

sentence to decapitation **OSw** *HL* Kgb

sentence under the sword **OSw** *HL* Mb

ivir meþ sværþ rætta (OSw)

execute by sword **OSw** *HL* Kkb

konungs sverð (ON)

the king's sword (for execution) **OIce** *Js* Mah 3 **ONorw** *FrL* Intr 3

See also: *hals*

Refs: Ambrius 1996, 45–47; Kjus 2011, 94–96; KLNM s.v. *dødsstraf, sverd*; Schlyter s.v. *diker*

sygnir (pl.) (ON) noun

people from Sogn **ONorw** *GuL* Leb

sykn (OSw) **sykn** (ON) adj.

Etymologically unclear.

blameless **ONorw** *FrL* KrbA 28

free **OIce** *Jó* Þjb 16

free of guilt **ONorw** *FrL* KrbA 2

free of the charge **ONorw** *BorgL* 5.7 16.7

innocent **ONorw** *FrL* LlbB 2

not under legal penalty **OIce** *Grg* Þsþ 42, 53 Vís 107 Arþ 125 Feþ 156, **ONorw** *FrL* KrbA 32

ordinary **ONorw** *BorgL* 14.10

public **OSw** *HL* Kkb, *SdmL* Kkb, Tjdb

reprieved **OIce** *Grg* Lbþ 201

Expressions:

sykn dagher, suknan dagher, söknan dagher (OSw) **sýkn dagr, sóknardagr** (ON)

A non-holy day when legal procedures were allowed.

case-day **ONorw** *EidsL* 30.7

litigation day **ONorw** *GuL* Llb, Olb

public-day **OSw** *HL* Kkb *SdmL* Kkb, Tjdb

work day **ONorw** *GuL* Krb, Leb

See also: *virkr*

Refs: Cleasby and Vigfusson s.v. *sykn*; Hellquist s.v. *söcken*; SAOB s.v. *söcken*; de Vries s.v.v. *sykn; sýkn, sœkn*

sykna (ON) noun

reprieve **OIce** *Grg* Vís 110

terms of mitigation **OIce** *Grg* Þsþ 54, 55 Bat 113 Feþ 162

syknuleyfi (ON) noun

licence for mitigation of penalty **OIce** *Grg* Lsþ 116

sylftal (OSw) noun

value in silver **OSw** *HL* Äb

See also: *silver*

syma (OGu) verb

confirm the honour **OGu** *GL* A 2

restore the honour **OGu** *GL* A 39

symnhus (OSw) söminhus (OSw) sympnhus (OSw) noun

bedchamber **OSw** *UL* Kkb, *VmL* Kkb

sleeping house **OSw** *SdmL* Kkb

See also: *symnskæmma*

symni (OGu) svefni (ON) noun

rape **ONorw** *GuL* Mhb

sexual intercourse **OGu** *GL* A 22

symnskæmma (OSw) noun

sleeping house **OSw** *ÄVgL* Tb

See also: *kornskæmma, matskamma, symnhus*

syn (OSw) noun

Derived from a verb meaning 'to see'. In OSw, both an inspection and a group of inspectors. Inspections were performed by a varying number of men, typically nominated by the disputing parties in specific matters dealing with disputed property: land, grazing, fences, crops, boundaries, timber felling, fire, injured or killed game, fishing waters, mills etc. A *syn* could be accompanied by valuations or assessments, but the majority decision by the *syn* generally settled the matter. A *syn* could also be more permanent, mainly when the object was to inspect communal obligations such as fences and roads. In ODan ESjL, used in the context of finds that should be brought for inspection to avoid accusation of theft, a procedure that also entailed *virthning* (ODan) 'valuation' and to *ljuse* (ODan) 'make public' (see *lysa*) the find at church and at three *thing* (ODan) 'assemblies' (see *þing*). In JyL, used in the context of theft where the stolen property could not be brought to inspection, rendering it a *vanesak* (ODan) 'case of suspicion'. The concept also appears in OIce and ONorw laws albeit without this word.

commission **OSw** *DL* Bb, Rb

inspection **OSw** *SdmL* Jb, Bb, Mb, Till, *UL* Blb, Add. 13, *VmL* Bb

investigation **OSw** *DL* Bb, *UL* Blb, *VmL* Bb

investigators **OSw** *DL* Rb

panel of inspectors **OSw** *UL* Kkb, Blb, *VmL* Bb

panel of investigators **OSw** *UL* Blb, Rb, *VmL* Jb, Bb

Expressions:

syn ok sannind (OSw)

decision of an investigation panel **OSw** *UL* Blb, Rb

væþia undi sanna syn (OSw)

appeal for an investigation **OSw** *DL* Bb

See also: *næmd, sannind, syna*

Refs: KLNM s.v. *syn*

syna (OSw) sjune (ODan) sýna (ON) sýnask (ON) synas (OSw) verb

can be seen **OSw** *UL* Kgb, Äb, Mb, Blb, *VmL* Kkb, Mb

be considered **ONorw** *GuL* Leb

inspect **OSw** *DL* Gb, *SdmL* Bb, Mb, Tjdb, *YVgL* Föb, *ÄVgL* Smb

look (intransitive) **ONorw** *GuL* Mhb

notice **OSw** *UL* Blb

see **ODan** *JyL* 2, **OSw** *YVgL* Tb, Add

show **ONorw** *GuL* Kpb, Mhb, Olb, Leb

be visible **OSw** *YVgL* Add

Expressions:

syna ok sea (OSw)

examine **OSw** *HL* Äb

have sight and inspection **OSw** *UL* Mb

inspect and observe **OSw** *UL* Kkb, Äb,
Mb, Blb, Rb *VmL* Kkb, Äb, Mb, Bb

synaband (OSw) noun

inspection proof **OSw** *SdmL* Rb

synamal (OSw) noun

case of inspection **OSw** *SdmL* Bb, Rb

synaman (OSw) sjuneman (ODan) asynarmæn (OSw)
noun

examiner **OSw** *YVgL* Jb, *ÄVgL* Jb

inspector **OSw** *HL* Kkb, *SdmL*
Jb, Bb, Rb, *UL* Kkb, Blb

investigator **OSw** *DL* Bb, *UL* Blb, *VmL* Mb, Jb, Bb

surveyor **ODan** *JyL* 1, **OSw** *YVgL* Kvab

See also: *syn*

synarvitni (OSw) asjunevitne (ODan) sjónarvitni
(ON) asynarvitni (OSw) noun

eyewitness **ONorw** *FrL* KrbB 5, **OSw**
DL Mb, *YVgL* Rlb, *ÄVgL* Slb, Rlb

eyewitness testimony **OIce** *Jó* Mah 10, *Js*
Mah 14, *KRA* 18, **ONorw** *FrL* Mhb 7

obvious to witnesses **ODan** *SkKL* 7

ocular witness **OSw** *ÄVgL* Rlb

See also: *asyn*, *vitni*

synd (OSw) synd (ODan) noun

sin **ODan** *SkKL* 12, **OSw** *SmL*, *YVgL*
Kkb, Urb, Add, *ÖgL* Kkb

synda (OSw) synde (ODan) verb

sin **ODan** *JyL* 2, **OSw** *YVgL* Kkb

syndamal (OSw) noun

sin **OSw** *YVgL* Rlb, *ÄVgL* Rlb

See also: *mal (1)*, *synd*

synðalauss (ON) syndalauss (ON) adj.

without punishment **OIce** *Jó* Mah 16

without sin **OIce** *Js* Mah 34

synia (OSw) synje (ODan) synia (OGu) synja (ON)
verb

decline (to do something) **OGu** *GL* A 25

deny **ODan** *JyL* 3, *SkL* 140, 192, **OFar** *Seyð* 1, **OGu**
GL A 37, **OIce** *Jó* Mah 5 Þjb 6 Fml 15, *Js* Mah 7, 19
Þjb 4, *KRA* 2, 20, **ONorw** *EidsL* 3.2, *FrL* KrbA 15,
32, *GuL* Krb, Kpb, Tfb, Leb, **OSw** *HL* Äb, Blb, *SmL*,
UL Kkb, Mb, Blb, *YVgL* Rlb, Tb, *ÄVgL* Rlb, Tb

forbid **OGu** *GL* A 37

hinder **ODan** *SkL* 134

refuse **ODan** *ESjL* 3, *SkL* 140, **OIce** *Js* Mah 13,
ONorw *FrL* Intr 15 Mhb 6, *GuL* Krb, Kpb, Llb, Arb,
Olb, Leb, **OSw** *HL* Kmb, *SdmL* Kkb, *UL* Kkb, Äb,
VmL Kkb, Äb, *YVgL* Drb, Gb, Tb, Föb, *ÄVgL* Fös

synjar (pl.) (ON) noun

ways to deny or repel an allegation **ONorw** *GuL* Krb

synjarspönn (ON) noun

pail of butter **ONorw** *FrL* Reb 3

See also: *vinjarspann*

sysel (ODan) sýsla (ON) noun

The highest administrative/judicial district beneath
land (q.v.) in JyL and in the east and north of Norway.
Following Icelandic submission to Norway in 1262/4,
Norwegian authorities sent sheriffs (*sýslumenn*,
see *sysluman*) to govern regions of Iceland. Their
jurisdiction was called a *sýsla* (see *sysel*). During
the Middle Ages a *sýsla* had no fixed geographic
boundaries, and their number and size changed over
time.

activity **OIce** *Grg* Lbþ 206

business **OIce** *Jó* Sg 2

district **OIce** *Jó* Þfb 2, 5 Sg 2 Kab 26, *KRA* 3

region **ODan** *JyL* 1, 2

sheriff's district **ONorw** *GuL* Krb

See also: *syselthing*, *sýsla*, *sysluman*

Refs: Andersen 2011, 32–33; KLNM s.v. *syssel*

syselthing (ODan) noun

A *þing* 'assembly' of a *sysel* (q.v.), the judicial district
between *land* (q.v.) and *hæreth* (see *hærap*) in ODan
JyL, where it appears as one of the assemblies for
conveying land sales.

regional assembly **ODan** *JyL* 1

See also: *þing*

Refs: Andersen 2011, 29, 32–33,
225; KLNM s.v. *ting*

sysluman (OSw) sýslumaðr (ON) noun

Usually refers to a royal official responsible for local
affairs in a given district; a sheriff. In Norway the
sýslumaðr conducted the king's business within a *fylki*
(q.v.); in Iceland within a *sýsla* (see *sysel*) or *fjórðungr*
('quarter'). He was among the highest-ranking royal
officials and was responsible for collecting royal
incomes (esp. taxes, fines and, in Norway, levy dues),
overseeing legal proceedings and nominating judges.
When necessary he also prosecuted cases on behalf
of the Crown (cf. FrL Mhb 41). The *sýslumaðr* (see
sysluman) was also involved in organizing military
operations and overseeing trade. Some of these duties
appear to have been taken over from the *ármaðr* (q.v.),
whom the *sýslumaðr* replaced over the course of the

twelfth and thirteenth centuries. Icelandic *sýslumenn* were subordinate to the *hirðstjóri* (q.v.) from the end of the thirteenth century. It has been suggested that certain other officials worked under the *sýslumaðr*, such as the *sóknari* (see *soknari*), *sóknarmaðr* (see *soknamaþer*), *réttari* (see *rættari*) and *lénsmaðr* (see *lænsmaþer*) (KLNM s.v. *sysselmann*).

The Swedish *sysluman* often refers to an administrator of ecclesiastical goods at a church. In Iceland and the Faroes the *sýslumaðr* has been viewed as an early form of police officer.

representative **OSw** *HL* Rb

sheriff **OIce** *Jó* Þfb 2, 5 Sg 2 Mah 3, 6 Kge 28 Kab 11, 26 Þjb 2, 3 Fml 14, **ONorw** *FrL* Intr 12 Mhb 41 Var 46, *GuL* Krb, Kpb

steward **OSw** *UL* Jb

See also: *ari, ármaðr, hirðstjóri, lænsmaþer, rættari, soknari, valdsmaþer*

Refs: CV s.v. *sýslumaðr*; Einar Arnórsson 1945, 248–57; F s.v. *sýslumaðr*; KLNM s.v. *embedsindtægter, kyrkliga räkenskaper, sysselmann*; NF s.v. *sysselmand*

systkin (ON) noun

brother and sister **OIce** *Grg* Ómb 128, Feþ 147, *Jó* Sg 1 Kge 23, **ONorw** *FrL* KrbB 1

siblings **OIce** *KRA* 20, **ONorw** *FrL* KrbB 1

systkinadóttir (pl.) (ON) noun

daughters of siblings **ONorw** *FrL* ArbA 12

female first cousins **OIce** *Jó* Kge 7-6

systkinasynir (pl.) (ON) noun

male first cousins **OIce** *Grg* Bat 113, *Jó* Kge 7-6, **ONorw** *FrL* Sab 7, 10

sons of siblings **ONorw** *FrL* ArbA 12

systrabarn (ON) noun

children of sisters **OIce** *Jó* Kge 7-10

systradóttir (pl.) (ON) noun

female first cousins **OIce** *Jó* Kge 7-6

systrasynir (pl.) (ON) noun

male first cousins **OIce** *Jó* Kge 7-6

systrunger (OSw) **systling** (ODan) **systrungr** (ON) **syslingi** (OSw) **syslungi** (OSw) **systlungi** (OSw) **systrunga** (OSw) **systrungi** (OSw) **syzllungi** (OSw) noun

Derived from a word meaning 'sister', referring to maternal relatives, originally possibly descendants of a maternal aunt. The masculine form *systrunger* (OSw) would be expected to refer to male relatives, possibly cousins, the feminine form *systrunga* (OSw) to females, and the male collective form *systrungi* (OSw) to both males and females, but the usage in the laws is often unclear. This and other kinship notations in the Nordic laws are often misleading to modern interpreters, as they do not necessarily refer to *ego*.

children of one's sister and brother **OSw** *HL* Äb

closer relatives **ODan** *VSjL* 87

daughter of mother's sister **OSw** *YVgL* Urb

first cousin **OIce** *Grg* Bat 113 Ómb 143, **ONorw** *FrL* KrbB 1, 8

kin **ODan** *ESjL* 3

maternal cousin **OSw** *SdmL* Äb, *UL* Äb, Jb

nephew **ODan** *ESjL* 2

niece **OSw** *DL* Gb, *HL* Mb

sister's daughters **OSw** *ÄVgL* Gb

sister's sons **OSw** *YVgL* Gb, *ÄVgL* Gb

See also: *bröþrungi*

Refs: Hellquist s.v. *syssling*

sytning (OSw) noun

Support of the old and disabled, primarily by relatives, in return for their property.

support **OSw** *HL* Jb

See also: *flatföring*

Refs: KLNM s.v.v. *fattigvård, flatföring*

sýsla (ON) verb

look after **ONorw** *GuL* Løb

provide **ONorw** *GuL* Løb

See also: *sysel*

sægnarþing (OSw) noun

A *þing* 'assembly' where the verdict was given in a case that had been handled at a preceding legal meeting, an *endaghi* (q.v.) 'one-day'.

assembly of the one-day **OSw** *YVgL* Drb, Äb, Jb, *ÄVgL* Md, Smb, Slb, Äb, Jb

See also: *endaghi, þing*

Refs: Brink 2011b, 151; Lindkvist forthcoming; Schlyter s.v. *sægnarþing*

sækia (OSw) **sekja** (ON) **sækja** (ON) **sókja** (ON) verb

Related to the adjective *saker* (OSw) 'guilty', 'liable', and meaning 'to make oneself or somebody else guilty' generally understood as liable to pay a fine or compensation, often of a stipulated sum, and frequently appearing in the reflexive and the passive *sekia sik* (OGu), *sækia sik* (OSw), *sekjask* (ON), *sækias* (OSw).

attack **OIce** *Jó* Kab 3

bring a claim or case **OIce** *Jó* Þfb 6, **ONorw** *FrL* Intr 23

bring a suit **ONorw** *FrL* KrbB 20

charge **ONorw** *FrL* Tfb 4

compensate **OSw** *ÄVgL* Jb, Föb

compensation **OSw** *YVgL* Utgb

get (someone) condemned **OIce** *Grg* Þsþ 48

be guilty to compensate **OSw** *YVgL* Utgb

be guilty to compensation **OSw** *ÄVgL* Tb

be guilty to/of **OSw** *ÄVgL* Föb

be guilty **ONorw** *FrL* Tfb 1

make oneself guilty **OSw** *ÄVgL* Rlb

make oneself liable to compensation
OSw *YVgL* Rlb, Tb

*make someone liable to pay a
compensation* **ONorw** *GuL* Olb

owe **ONorw** *EidsL* 8.2

pay a fine **OFar** *Seyð* 3, **OIce** *Jó* Þfb 9, *Js* Þfb
4, *KRA* 14, 29, **ONorw** *FrL* Tfb 2 KrbB 1

prosecute **OIce** *Grg* passim, *Jó* passim, *Js* passim,
KRA 2, 18, **ONorw** *FrL* KrbA 1 KrbB 3, 5 Mhb 4

pursue **OIce** *Jó* Mah 16, **ONorw** *BorgL* 17.8

sue **ONorw** *FrL* KrbA 29

Expressions:

sækia sik, sekia sik (OGu)

to be liable for **OGu** *GL* A 3

See also: *saker*

sækt (OSw) **sekt** (ON) **sekð** (ON) noun

compensation **ONorw** *FrL* Intr 21, **OSw** *YVgL* Kkb

fine **OFar** *Seyð* 3, **OIce** *Grg* Lbþ 215, *Jó* Þfb
5, 8 Mah 19 Kab 10 Þjb 1, 5 Fml 3, 14, *Js* Þfb
6, **ONorw** *BorgL* 16.1, *FrL* Intr 16 Tfb 1 KrbA
28 Var 9 Leb 2 Rgb 24, *GuL* Krb, Tjb, Leb

outlawry **OIce** *Grg* Þsþ 49 Feþ 156 Misc 244

owed money **ONorw** *EidsL* 32.6

penalty **OIce** *Js* Ert 24, **ONorw**
EidsL 27.3 29.3, *FrL* KrbB 20

sækta (OSw) **sækte** (ODan) verb

Related to the adj. *saker* (OSw) 'guilty'; basically
'to lay blame on'. The various translations focus
on several aspects of legal proceedings that can
be difficult to distinguish between, ranging from
making a claim about something (such as a crime or a
condition), over an accusation ('to accuse') to a legal
prosecution ('to sue'). There is considerable overlap
between usages and translations. Participles may be
construed as adjectives (for instance ODan SkL 67
'liable').

accuse **ODan** *ESjL* 2, 3, *JyL* 2, 3, *SkKL* 7, 11, 12,
SkL 86, 121, 161, 217, 230, *VSjL* 65, 76, 86, 87

charge **ODan** *JyL* 1, 2, *SkKL* 7, 11, *SkL* 106, 229

claim **ODan** *ESjL* 3

make a claim **ODan** *ESjL* 2

prosecute **ODan** *ESjL* 2

raise a claim **ODan** *SkKL* 9

sue **ODan** *ESjL* 3, *JyL* 2, **OSw** *YVgL* Add, *ÖgL* Eb

summon **ODan** *SkL* 72, 85, 146–148, 180, 182

take action **ODan** *JyL* 1, 2

take action against **ODan** *ESjL* 2, 3, *JyL*
2, 3, *SkL* 67, 121, 127, *VSjL* 76

sælia (OSw) **sælje** (ODan) **selja** (ON) **salt** (OSw) verb

convey **ONorw** *GuL* Llb

hand over **ONorw** *GuL* Kpb, Tfb, Olb

lend **ONorw** *GuL* Kpb

prove **ODan** *ESjL* 1, 3

relinquish **ONorw** *GuL* Kpb

rent out **ONorw** *GuL* Llb

sell **ODan** *ESjL* 1, 3, *JyL* 1, *SkL* passim, *VSjL*
79, 80, 82, 83, **OIce** *Grg* Lbþ 172, *Jó* Lbb 7 Kab
11, **ONorw** *GuL* Krb, Kpb, Løb, Tjb, **OSw** *DL*
Bb, *HL* Kgb, Jb, Kmb, *SdmL* Jb, Kmb, *YVgL*
Kkb, Äb, Tb, Jb, Föb, Add, *ÄVgL* Äb, Jb

transfer **OIce** *Grg* passim, *Jó* Kge
16 Kab 10, **ONorw** *GuL* Arb

See also: *köpa, sal, sali*

sæljen (ODan) noun

selling **ODan** *ESjL* 1

sællaboþ (OSw) noun

shieling **OSw** *DL* Bb

sæluskip (ON) noun

A 'bliss ship' or 'soul ship'. These ferries were funded
by benefactors [although the KLNM says they (as part
of *kristfé* 'Christ's properties', i.e. property especially
used to pay for the maintanance of paupers) were
administered by the *hreppr* 'commune'?] and intended
for public use. Several versions of 'The Old Tithe
Law of the Icelanders' (ON *Tíundarlög íslendínga hin
fornu*) state that property given to establish a *sæluskip*
is exempt from inclusion in the tithe (e.g. DI I:22a
item 2). Often mentioned with charity bridges (ON
sálubrú) and other charitable establishments.

charity boat **OIce** *Grg* Tíg 255

Refs: CV s.v. *brú sæla*; Fritzner s.v.
sæluskip; KLNM s.v. *kristfé*

sæmia (OSw) verb

Expressions:

sæmia sik (OSw) **semia sik** (OGu)

agree **OGu** *GL* A 31, 52, 53, 59, 61, 65
OSw *UL* Kkb, Mb, Jb, Blb, Rb

stipulate **OGu** *GL* A 24d

sændimaþer (OSw) **sændumaþr** (OSw) noun

envoy **OSw** *YVgL* Rlb, *ÄVgL* Rlb

sængarferð (ON) noun

childbed **OIce** *KRA* 2

See also: *sængför*

sængaslæt (OSw) noun

descendant **OSw** *DL* Gb

direct descendant **OSw** *VmL* Äb

See also: *byrþaman, siængaralder*

sængför (ON) noun

labour **ONorw** *BorgL* 3, *EidsL* 1.3 3.1

sære (ODan) **særa** (ON) verb

inflict a wound **ODan** *JyL* 3

wound **ODan** *ESjL* 1–3, *JyL* 1, 2, *SkL* 91, 104, 124, *VSjL* 30, 35, 40, 56, 63, 86, **OIce** *Jó* Mah 3, *Js* Mah 16, **ONorw** *EidsL* 50.13, *FrL* passim, *GuL* Mhb, Tfb

See also: *sar*

særkul (ODan) noun

group of siblings **ODan** *JyL* 1

See also: *kolder*

særkøp (ODan) noun

Cultivated land that was sold and thus added to the property share of the buyer and reduced from the property share of the seller when roping, i.e. measuring and allocating (see *repa* (OSw)), the land of the village.

land bought specially **ODan** *JyL* 1

See also: *enkøp*

Refs: Tamm and Vogt, eds, 2016, 301

særnævnd (ODan) noun

nominated men **ODan** *VSjL* 39

proof against wound by nominated men **ODan** *VSjL* 39

See also: *næmd*

særsystken (ODan) noun

particular sibling **ODan** *JyL* 1

sæssi (OSw) **sessi** (ON) noun

benchmate **ONorw** *GuL* Mhb

rower **OSw** *ÖgL* Db

sæt (OSw) **sátt** (ON) **sætt** (ON) **sætti** (ON) noun

Literally 'something set'. Mostly appearing in the context of breaching a *sæt* (OSw) concerning a serious crime such as murder, where it is often related to concepts of truce (OSw *grið*), paid fines/ compensations, unjust revenge, dishonourable killings (ON *misvígi*), unatonable crimes (OSw *urbotamal*), acts of villainy/outrage (OSw *niþingsværk*) or breaching the king's (sworn) peace (OSw *eþsöre*), and is as such severely punished. Also appearing in the context of requirements for proving a *sæt* with oaths and witnesses. Occasionally appearing in the context of the initial agreement of a *sæt*, which seems to have been announced at the *þing* 'assembly', whether reached privately outside of court or as a result of legal proceedings at the *þing*.

agreement **OIce** *Jó* Mah 2

arrangement **ONorw** *GuL* Mhb

compromise **ONorw** *GuL* Mhb, Tjb

conciliation **OSw** *DL* Eb, Mb, *UL* Kgb, *VmL* Kgb, Mb, *YVgL* Rlb, *ÄVgL* Urb, Rlb

private settlement **OIce** *Grg* Þsþ 60 Misc 244

reconciliation **ONorw** *FrL* Sab 21, **OSw** *HL* Mb, *YVgL* Urb, Add

settlement (1) **OIce** *Grg* Vís 95 Bat 113 Feþ 156, *Jó* Þjb 3, **OSw** *HL* Kgb, *SdmL* Kgb

See also: *grið, sætta, sættarkaup*

Refs: Hertzberg s.v. *sætt*; ONP s.v. *sǽtt*; Schlyter s.v. *sæt*

sætesambut (ODan) noun

house slave **ODan** *VSjL* 86

See also: *ambat*

sætia (OSw) **setja** (ON) **utsætia** (OSw) verb

appoint **ONorw** *GuL* Krb, Kpb

inspect **OSw** *YVgL* Jb

lay down **ONorw** *GuL* Krb

settle **ONorw** *GuL* Mhb

sue **OSw** *HL* Rb

sætiseþer (OSw) noun

oath of attendance **OSw** *ÖgL* Kkb

sætr (ON) noun

shieling **OIce** *Jó* Kge 31 Llb 42, *Js* Lbb 25, **ONorw** *GuL* Llb

See also: *sel*

sætraferð (ON) noun

travel to shielings **OIce** *Jó* Llb 42, *Js* Lbb 19

sætralaþa (OSw) noun

barn on summer pasture **OSw** *DL* Tjdb, *VmL* Bb

sætrgata (ON) noun

path to the shielings **OIce** *Jó* Llb 44

sætta (OSw) **sætte** (ODan) **sætta** (ON) **sættask** (ON) **sattir** (OSw) verb

come to terms with **ONorw** *GuL* Krb, Mhb, Leb

comply **ODan** *JyL* 2

conclude **ONorw** *GuL* Trm

pay **ODan** *JyL* 2

reconcile **OSw** *YVgL* Tb, Add, *ÄVgL* Jb, Tb, *ÖgL* Eb

become reconciled **OIce** *Jó* Mah 27, **OSw** *HL* Kgb

settle **OIce** *Grg* Vís 94 Bat 113, *Jó* Sg 3 Mah 21, *Js* Kvg 5, **OSw** *HL* Mb, *SdmL* Kgb, Mb, *ÖgL* Db

See also: *sæt, sættarkaup*

sættara (OSw) noun

oarsmen **OSw** *HL* Kgb

sættargærþ (OSw) **sættargerð** (ON) noun

arbitration **OIce** *Grg* Misc 244

conciliation **OSw** *ÄVgL* Vs

settlement (1) **OIce** *Js* Mah 37, *KRA* 29

sættarkaup (ON) noun

price for settlement **ONorw** *GuL* Mhb

See also: *sæt, sætta*

sættarmaðr (ON) noun

arbitrator **OIce** *Grg* Bat 113

See also: *sáttarmaðr*

sættarstefna (ON) noun

peace-meeting **ONorw** *FrL* Var 9

sætugarþer (OSw) noun

residence **OSw** *SdmL* Rb, Till

sæþ (OSw) **seþ** (OGu) **sæþi** (OSw) noun

arable land **OGu** *GL* A 48, **OSw** *UL* Kkb

grain **OSw** *UL* Kkb, *VmL* Kkb, Jb, Bb

seed **OGu** *GL* A 56a, **OSw** *UL* Jb, Blb

sowing time **OGu** *GL* A 10

See also: *korn, spannamali*

sæþaspander (OSw) noun

bushel basket **OSw** *UL* Blb

söðla (ON) verb

saddle **ONorw** *GuL* Llb

sögn (ON) noun

indictment **ONorw** *GuL* Mhb

testimony **OIce** *Jó* Mah 9

sökia (OSw) **søkje** (ODan) **sykia** (OGu) **sǿkja** (ON) verb

Literally 'to seek' and etymologically derived from the noun *sak* '(legal) case'. Refers to the initiation of a legal procedure, typically by the injured party although for instance OSw UL Rb discusses the rights of a (public) prosecutor (*lænsmaþer*) to *sökia*, which can be translated as e.g. 'to have a case', 'to prosecute', 'to pursue (a case)', 'to take action (against)'. It might also refer to preceding or complementary actions and be translated as 'to accuse', 'to call', 'to summon'. It has been suggested that a characteristic trait in relation to *kæra* (another verb for initiating and pursuing a legal procedure) is that *sökia* centres on the injured party's request for justice. This might be reflected in translations such as 'to demand', with a stronger focus on the outcome of the procedure, e.g. 'to distrain', 'to

exact', 'to extract', 'to recover', often in constructions with a preposition or an adverb (particle).

accuse **ODan** *ESjL* 3, *SkKL* 9, **OSw** *ÄVgL* Rlb, *ÖgL* Eb

appear before **ODan** *SkL* 14

attack **ODan** *ESjL* 2

attend **OSw** *UL* Rb

bring **ODan** *ESjL* 2

bring a claim **ODan** *ESjL* 2

bring a prosecution **OSw** *UL* Äb, Mb, Jb, Rb, *VmL* Äb, Mb

bring an action **OGu** *GL* A 8, 59, **OSw** *UL* Rb

call **OSw** *ÄVgL* Föb

carry forward actions of law **ONorw** *GuL* Krb

charge **ONorw** *GuL* Leb, **OSw** *VmL* Rb

claim **ODan** *ESjL* 3, *SkL* 121, 145, **ONorw** *GuL* Krb, Kpb, **OSw** *YVgL* Drb

collect **ONorw** *GuL* Løb

come **ONorw** *GuL* Krb

complain **ONorw** *GuL* Llb

deem **OSw** *ÄVgL* Smb

demand **ODan** *JyL* 2, **OGu** *GL* A 2, **OSw** *DL* Bb, *UL* Mb, Rb, *YVgL* Jb, Add, *ÄVgL* Jb

demand one's right **ONorw** *GuL* Krb

distrain **OSw** *HL* Rb

exact **OSw** *SdmL* Kmb

have a case **ODan** *ESjL* 2

impose **OGu** *GL* A 31

prosecute **OGu** *GL* A 3, 4, 11, 39, 61, **ONorw** *GuL* Kpb, **OSw** *DL* Tjdb, *SdmL* Kkb, Jb, Bb, Mb, Tjdb, Rb, *UL* Kkb, Mb, Jb, Rb, *VmL* Kkb, Äb, Mb, Jb, Kmb, Bb, Rb, *YVgL* Gb, Rlb, Föb, Utgb, *ÄVgL* Md, Rlb, Fös, *ÖgL* Kkb

prosecute an action (for something) **OGu** *GL* A 11

pursue **ODan** *ESjL* 2, 3, *JyL* 3, *SkKL* 12

pursue a case **ODan** *ESjL* 3

raise a claim **ODan** *SkKL* 7

recover **OSw** *DL* Tjdb

seek **ODan** *ESjL* 2, **OSw** *HL* Äb, *UL* Kkb, Kgb, *VmL* Kkb, Mb, *YVgL* Add, *ÄVgL* Jb

sue **ODan** *ESjL* 3, *JyL* 1–3, **ONorw** *GuL* Kpb, Olb, **OSw** *HL* Kkb, *YVgL* Kkb, Drb, Gb, Fö, Add, *ÄVgL* Gb, Rlb, *ÖgL* Kkb, Eb, Db, Vm

summon **ODan** *ESjL* 2, *SkL* 14, 121, 145, **OSw** *YVgL* Rlb

take action **ODan** *ESjL* 2

take action against **ODan** *ESjL* 3, *JyL* 2, *SkKL* 7

take refuge **OGu** *GL* A 13

visit **OGu** *GL* A 3, 13

Expressions:

sökia sak (OSw) **søkje sak** (ODan)

accuse **ODan** *SkL* 147 *VSjL* 37

be the plaintiff **ODan** *SkL* 121

bring a case (*against*) **ODan** *SkL* 219

bring action **OSw** *ÄVgL* Md

complain **ODan** *SkL* 4

prosecute **OSw** *SdmL* Mb

pursue a case **ODan** *SkL* 147, 152

raise a case **ODan** *SkKL* 11 **OSw** *YVgL* Gb

raise a charge **ODan** *SkL* 86

raise a claim **ODan** *SkL* 14, 88

summon **ODan** *SkL* 147

take action **ODan** *ESjL* 1 *SkL* 121

sökia ut/æptir (OSw)

exact **OSw** *SdmL* Äb, Bb, Rb, Till

See also: *giva, kæra, næmna, sak, tiltala, viþerbinda*

Refs: Hellquist s.v. *söka*; Schlyter s.v.v. *kæra, sökia*

sökiandi (OSw) **sækjandi** (ON) **søkjandi** (ON) noun

man bringing the suit **OIce** *Grg* Ómb 143
Feþ 144 Fjl 221 Hrs 234 Misc 250

plaintiff **OIce** *Jó* Lbb 1 Kab 3, **ONorw** *FrL* Rgb
11 Jkb 8, *GuL* Kpb, Løb, Llb, Olb, **OSw** *DL* Rb

prosecutor **OIce** *Grg* Vís 89, 102 Bat 113 Feþ 158
Tíg 257, *Jó* Kab 8, *Js* Kab 4, 6, **ONorw** *FrL* Mhb 8

See also: *sakaráberi, saksöki, soknamaþer, soknari*

sökning (OSw) noun

prosecution **OSw** *SdmL* Mb

See also: *sykn*

sökunautr (ON) noun

opponent in a lawsuit **ONorw** *GuL* Kpb, Løb

sörgata (OSw) noun

An illegal road that was the result of repeatedly driving
across someone else's growing field or meadow.

dirty road **OSw** *YVgL* Föb, *ÄVgL* Fös

See also: *gata*

Refs: Schlyter s.v.v. *sör*; *sörgap*; *sörgata*

söþer (OSw) **soyþr** (OGu) noun

beast **OGu** *GL* A 6, 17, 26, 27

cattle **OGu** *GL* A 10, **OSw** *DL* Bb

creature **OGu** *GL* A 26, Add. 2 (B 17), **OSw** *UL* Blb

farm animal **OGu** *GL* A 26

søkkr (ON) noun

lying in water **ONorw** *GuL* Leb

sófask (ON) verb

be killed **ONorw** *GuL* Kvr

sókjask (OSw) **sekjask** (ON) verb

be liable to a fine **ONorw** *GuL* Krb

be prosecuted **ONorw** *GuL* Kpb

See also: *saker*

sórr (ON) **særr** (ON) adj.

Derived from a verb realized in ON as *sverja* 'to
swear'. Appearing in ONorw GuL in the phrase *sórr
dagr* (ON) 'oath day' of a day when swearing an oath
was allowed or possibly even prescribed.

oath-taking **OIce** *Jó* Þfb 1 Llb 30, 39, *Js*
Þfb 1, *KRA* 29, **ONorw** *FrL* KrbB 20

Expressions:

sórr dagr (ON)

oath day **ONorw** *GuL* Krb, Løb, Llb, Tfb, Leb

ta (OSw) **tæ** (OSw) noun

village lane **OSw** *DL* Mb, Bb

Expressions:

ta ok tomtara, ta ok tompta ra (OSw)

*village highway and property
boundaries* **OSw** *VmL* Bb

See also: *gata, vægher*

taða (ON) noun

A fertilized meadow, or hay from one.

hayfield **OIce** *Grg* Lbþ 180, *Jó*
Lbb 3, 4 Llb 17, *Js* Lbb 26

See also: *töðuvöllr*

Refs: CV s.v. *taða*; ONP s.v. *taða*; Zoega s.v. *taða*

taðfall (ON) noun

manure **OIce** *Jó* Llb 14

taðfórsla (ON) **taðfærsla** (ON) noun

removal of manure **OIce** *Jó* Llb 8

tafastr (OGu) adj.

bordering a right of way **OGu** *GL* A 24f (64)

bounding a road **OGu** *GL* A 25

tagarþr (OGu) noun

fence along a road **OGu** *GL* A 25

tagbænda (OSw) noun

A type of sewn boat.

{tagbænda} **OSw** *ÄVgL* Fös

Refs: Steen 1933b, 284

tak (OSw) **tak** (ODan) **tak** (ON) noun

(The state of) a person or an object functioning as a
surety for a person not to evade justice, to pay a debt
or to fulfil an obligation, sometimes involving an
impartial *taki* (q.v.) to hold goods deposited during a
dispute. Often appearing in the context of accusations
of theft.

bail **ONorw** *FrL* KrbB 20, **OSw** *HL* Rb

custody **OSw** *YVgL* Äb

hands of a surety man **OSw** *DL* Bb

lien **OSw** *ÄVgL* Tb

pledge **OSw** *ÄVgL* Tb

responsibility **ODan** *JyL* 2

*right to submit goods in the hands of
a surety man* **OSw** *DL* Bb, Tjdb

security **ODan** *JyL* 2, *SkL* 137, 139, 142,
159, **ONorw** *FrL* KrbB 23 ArbB 28,
GuL Llb, Tjb, Leb, **OSw** *YVgL* Tb

surety **ODan** *ESjL* 3, *JyL* 2, *SkL* 159, *VSjL* 60,
87, **OIce** *Grg* Misc 248, *Js* Þjb 3, **ONorw** *FrL*
Mhb 12 Reb 2, **OSw** *UL* Mb, Blb, Rb, *VmL* Rb

taking **OSw** *HL* Blb

Expressions:

ganga í tak (ON)

give security **ONorw** *GuL* Llb

ræna taks ok leþsnar, ræna taks ok leznar (OSw)

*deprive of the right to put matters into
the hands of a surety man and permit
proof of provenance* **OSw** *VmL* Mb

æsta taks (ON)

give security **ONorw** *GuL* Llb, Tjb

to demand surety **OIce** *Grg* Misc 248

See also: *nam*, *taka*, *taki*, *væþ*

Refs: Hertzberg s.v. *tak*; KLNM
s.v. *borgen*; Schlyter s.v. *tak*

taka (OSw) **taka** (ON) verb

There are mainly two legally significant uses: 1) to seize goods in pursuance of a judicial order (often *taka in* (OSw) or *take til* (ODan)), and 2) to apprehend criminals, particularly thieves, but also certain sex criminals and killers, in circumstances that made their guilt evident, typically with the stolen goods on their person or locked in their home. Provided that the apprehension and its circumstances were properly announced, a criminal caught in this way could be more severely punished, and sometimes even killed, without legal consequences. Expressions include *bar ok/æller* (*a*)*takin* (*viþer/mæþ*), *innitakin*, *take i hænde*, *takin mæþ*, *takin* (*ok gripin*) *a færsko gærning*, *takin viþ*.

apprehend **OSw** *UL* Mb, Blb, Rb, *VmL* Mb, Bb

capture **OIce** *Jó* Þjb 2, **OSw** *UL* Kgb,
Äb, Kmb, *VmL* Kgb, Kmb

seize **OIce** *Jó* Kab 1

Expressions:

bar ok ataka (OSw)

catch in the act **OSw** *UL* Kkb, Äb,
Mb, Blb *VmL* Kkb, Äb, Mb, Bb

caught in action **OSw** *HL* Blb

bar ok/ællæ a takin viþer/mæþ (OSw)

caught in action **OSw** *HL* Blb

caught in the (very) act **OSw** *DL* Kkb, Tjdb

caught red-handed **OSw** *DL* Bb *SdmL* Kkb, Bb, Mb

i handum taka (OSw) **take i hænde** (ODan)

be found in someone's hands **OSw** *YVgL* Rlb, Tb

*take someone with something in
his possession* **ODan** *JyL* 2

*take someone with something in
their hands* **ODan** *JyL* 2

inni takin (OSw)

caught in the act **OSw** *YVgL* Kkb

taka af (ON)

abolish **ONorw** *GuL* Krb

kill **ONorw** *GuL* Sab

taka in (OSw) **in take** (ODan)

fence **OSw** *YVgL* Jb, Kvab *ÄVgL* Kva

seize **OSw** *SdmL* Bb **ODan** *SkL*
170, 179, 181, 189, 206

take out **ODan** *JyL* 3

taka mæþ (OSw)

take in flagrante delicto **OSw** *VmL* Äb

taka nauðga (ON)

rape **OIce** *Jó* Mah 2

taka upp (ON)

confiscate **ONorw** *GuL* Mhb

have **ONorw** *GuL* Krb

seize **ONorw** *GuL* Tfb

taka við (ON)

receive **ONorw** *GuL* Løb, Tjb

take i hænde (ODan)

*take someone with something in
his possession* **ODan** *JyL* 2

*take someone with something in
their hands* **ODan** *JyL* 2

take til (ODan)

seize **ODan** *ESjL* 3 *SkL* 226

take seizure **ODan** *JyL* 2

take viþer (ODan)

admit **ODan** *SkL* 118

takin a uærkium (ODan)

caught in the act **ODan** *SkL* 190

takin mæþ (OSw, ODan)

caught with (*it*) **OSw** *SdmL* Bb, Mb, Tjdb

taken with it **ODan** *SkL* 162, 184

takin ok gripin a færsko gærning (OSw)

apprehended redhanded **OSw** *HL* Kgb

*caught and apprehended in the very
act* **OSw** *SdmL* Kgb, Kmb

takin viþ (OSw) taken vither (ODan)

caught **ODan** *JyL* 2

caught at (it) **OSw** *SdmL* Gb, Bb, Mb, Tjdb, Rb

caught in the (very) act **OSw** *YVgL* Rlb *ÖgL* Kkb, Eb

caught there **ODan** *JyL* 3

taken in the act **ODan** *SkL* 85

taken with **ODan** *JyL* 2

takin ælla fangin a samu gærning (OSw)

caught or captured in the act **OSw** *DL* Eb

telja ok taka (ON)

list and seize **ONorw** *GuL* Mhb

See also: *atakin*, *fanga*, *gærning*, *innitakin*

Refs: KLNM s.v. *frihedsberøvelse*

takføre (ODan) verb

give security **ODan** *SkL* 136, 137, 142

have a pledge **ODan** *SkL* 197

have as security **ODan** *SkL* 159

See also: *tak*

taki (OSw) taki (OGu) noun

Person with whom pledges or challenged goods were placed pending resolution of a dispute. Often appearing in expressions such as *i taka hænder* 'in the hands of a *taki*' Also one who guarantees something abstract, particularly an oath, without sequestration.

bailsman **OSw** *YVgL* Tb

capture **OSw** *HL* Blb

guarantor **OSw** *UL* Mb, Rb, *VmL* Rb

pledge man **OSw** *HL* Rb

surety **OSw** *VmL* Mb, *YVgL* Tb, *ÄVgL* Tb, *ÖgL* Db

surety man **OGu** *GL* Add. 1 (B 4),
OSw *UL* Kkb, Mb, Jb, Kmb, Blb, Rb,
VmL Kkb, Mb, Jb, Kmb, Bb, Rb,

taker **OSw** *ÖgL* Kkb

trustee **OSw** *SdmL* Jb, Bb, Kmb, Mb, Tjdb, Rb, Till

See also: *borghanaman*, *fangaman*, *fastar (pl.)*, *hemulsman*, *skuli*, *tak*, *taksmaþer*, *tækiomaþer*

Refs: Schlyter s.v. *taki*

takmark (ON) noun

Boundary marker, border, frontier.

limit **OIce** *Grg* Feþ 167, *KRA* 6, 8

Refs: CV s.v. *takmark*; Fritzner s.v. *takmark*; Schlyter s.v. *takmark*.

taksmaþer (OSw) taks man (OSw) noun

surety man **OSw** *DL* Bb, *VmL* Mb

See also: *taki*

taksæsting (ON) noun

demand for security **ONorw** *GuL* Llb

demand for surety **OIce** *Grg* Misc 248

taksæstingarváttr (ON) noun

witnesses of the demand for surety
OIce *Grg* Misc 248

taksætia (OSw) taksætje (ODan) taksetja (ON) i tak sætia (OSw) verb

put in security **OSw** *YVgL* Tb, *ÄVgL* Tb

put to bail **OIce** *KRA* 29

demand a surety **ODan** *VSjL* 87

get surety **ODan** *JyL* 2

give surety **ODan** *ESjL* 3

have surety **ODan** *ESjL* 3

See also: *tak*

takuskæl (OSw) noun

agreement **OSw** *UL* Jb

tenant's contract **OSw** *HL* Jb

tal (ON) noun

count of men **ONorw** *GuL* Leb

See also: *hafþatal*, *mantal*, *vighramannatal*

tala (1) (OSw) tale (ODan) noun

appeal **OSw** *DL* Rb

case **ODan** *JyL* 2, **OSw** *DL* Mb, Rb, *HL* Rb

grounds **OSw** *UL* Rb, *VmL* Rb

suit **OSw** *YVgL* Jb

See also: *talan*

tala (2) (ON) noun

calculation **ONorw** *GuL* Kpb, Arb, Mhb, Leb, Sab

talan (OSw) noun

accusation **OSw** *SmL*

talaut (OGu) noun

land by a road **OGu** *GL* A 24f (64)

taluman (OSw) noun

man knowledgeable in genealogies **OSw** *HL* Äb

tassal (OGu) noun

buckle **OGu** *GL* A 65

taumburðr (ON) noun

measurement (with a line) **ONorw** *FrL* LlbA 9

tegher (OSw) teigr (ON) noun

A strip field (parcel) in a *gærþi* (OSw), *vang* (ODan) or *teiglag* (ONorw, not in the laws) or, sometimes, an enclosed strip of land for grazing or hay harvest as in Iceland. *Tegher* also has a more general meaning 'particular piece of land'. The corresponding ODan term was *aker* (q.v.).

arable land **OSw** *DL* Bb

grazing plot **OIce** *Grg* Lbþ 194

piece of grassland **OIce** *Jó* Llb 14 Kab 20

plot (1) **OSw** *UL* Blb, *VmL* Bb

strip **OSw** *SdmL* Bb, *YVgL* Jb, *ÄVgL* Jb

See also: *aker, deld, gærþi, tompt, vang*

Refs: Hoff 1997, 142–49; KLNM
s.v. *teig,*; Schlyter s.v. *tegher*

telgia (OGu) noun

cutting off or splitting a smaller bone
OGu *GL* A 19, Add. 3 (B 19)

telja (ON) verb

calculate **OIce** *Grg* Lbþ 201, *Jó* Lbb 4 Llb 51

claim **OIce** *Grg* Klþ 4

count **OIce** *Jó* Llb 47, **ONorw** *GuL* Krb, Arb

enumerate **OIce** *Grg* Ómb 130, *Jó* Kab 22,
ONorw *GuL* Krb, Arb, Mhb, Olb, Leb

list **ONorw** *GuL* Mhb

See also: *heimta*

teljandi (ON) noun

enumerator **OIce** *Grg* Þsþ 35

tengð (ON) noun

connection **OIce** *Grg* Þsþ 36 Vís 89
Arþ 122, 127 Fjl 221, 225

testament (OSw) **testament** (ODan) **testamentum**
(ON) noun

The laws deal mainly with wills that favour religious
institutions, in OIce KRA and OSw SdmL also others,
and focus on potential disputes, which are to be settled
by the bishop according to OIce KRA and OSw YVgL.
Only in ODan JyL explicitly a written document.

testament **OIce** *KRA* 9, 10

will (2) **ODan** *JyL* 3, **OSw** *HL* Kkb,
SdmL Conf, Kkb, Äb, *YVgL* Kkb

thinghøring (ODan) noun

A person appointed to observe a case being handled at
the *thing* (ODan) 'assembly' (see *þing*).

assembly hearers **ODan** *ESjL* 3, *JyL* 2

nominated assembly men **ODan** *JyL* 1

people of an assembly **ODan** *JyL* 1

See also: *þing*

Refs: Tamm and Vogt, eds, 2016, 301

thingljuse (ODan) verb

make public **ODan** *SkL* 223

make public at the assembly **ODan** *ESjL* 1, 3,
JyL 1, 2, *SkL* 60–62, 64, *VSjL* 21, 68, 69

See also: *lysa, þing*

thingrath (ODan) noun

advice of the assembly **ODan** *ESjL* 3

See also: *þing*

thingstævne (ODan) verb

summon to the assembly **ODan** *ESjL* 3

See also: *stæmna, þing*

thjuvgilde (ODan) noun

*double value as compensation
for theft* **ODan** *VSjL* 87

thjuvnethsak (ODan) noun

theft **ODan** *VSjL* 87

thjuvsmærke (ODan) noun

A thief could be marked by losing the nose or an ear
or being branded or flogged, which also allowed the
identification of repeat offenders. The concept, albeit
not the word, also appears in other ODan as well as in
OIce, ONorw and OSw laws.

thief's mark **ODan** *JyL* 2

Refs: KLNM s.v.v. *kroppsstraff, skamstraff*;
Tamm and Vogt, eds, 2016, 36, 315

thjuvsnavn (ODan) noun

being called a thief **ODan** *JyL* 2

thjuvsvite (ODan) noun

accomplice of a thief **ODan** *JyL* 2

thokkeland (ODan) noun

separate land **ODan** *SkKL* 3

thomasmessa (ON) noun

St Thomas' Day (21 December) **OIce**
Grg Klþ 13, **ONorw** *GuL* Krb

St Thomas's Mass (21 December) **ONorw** *GuL* Krb

thorpemark (ODan) noun

thorp field **ODan** *SkL* 185

thrylmærke (ODan) noun

three half marks **ODan** *VSjL* 86

thrælbarth (ODan) adj.

beaten as a slave **ODan** *JyL* 3

thrælsmark (ODan) noun

Giving a free man the mark of a slave by cutting up
both nostrils was punishable by half a *manbot* (ODan)
'man's compensation'.

mark of a slave **ODan** *VSjL* 28

tigla (ON) verb

recompense **OIce** *Grg* Feþ 164

tilbiuþa (OSw) verb

make an offer **OSw** *UL* Mb, Jb, Rb, *VmL* Bb

tilbuþ (OSw) noun

oath **OSw** *UL* Mb

offer **OSw** *SdmL* Kkb

offer proceedings **OSw** *UL* Mb, Blb

tilfelli (ON) noun

circumstance **OIce** *Jó* Kab 7

tilför (ON) noun

legal seizure of a debtor's property **ONorw** *GuL* Arb

tilgæf (OSw) tilgjöf (ON) noun

A gift from the bridegroom given directly after the betrothal. In OIce and ONorw, the property of the bride to be inherited by the couple's mutual children. In OSw, given to the relatives of the bride other than her *giftarmaþer* (q.v.), i.e. the man authorized to marry her off.

betrothal gift **OIce** *Js* Kvg 1, 2 Ert 19, *KRA* 4

bridal gift **OIce** *Jó* Kge 1, 2, **ONorw** *GuL* Arb

gift **OSw** *YVgL* Gb

husband's gift **ONorw** *GuL* Arb

{tilgæf} **OSw** *ÄVgL* Gb

See also: *fæst, gagngjald, giftarmaþer, gæf, hemfylghþ, morghongæf, munder, vingæf*

Refs: Fritzner s.v. *tilgjöf*; KLNM s.v. *festermål*; Schlyter s.v. *tilgæf*

tilgærth (ODan) noun

additional land **ODan** *SkL* 56

tilhlaup (ON) noun

assault **ONorw** *FrL* Var 7

tillag (ON) tilllaga (ON) noun

contribution **OIce** *Jó* Kge 23, *KRA* 4

obligation **OIce** *Grg* Þsþ 81

tillagha (OSw) tillægha (OSw) noun

additional charges **OSw** *SmL*

payment in coin **OSw** *UL* Kkb, *VmL* Kkb

See also: *mali*

tilmæla (OSw) verb

prosecute **OSw** *YVgL* Tb

tilmæli (OSw) noun

Related to the noun *mal* 'speech; case' etc., referring to various types of formal address at the assembly.

accusation **OSw** *DL* Rb

gathering **OSw** *ÖgL* Eb

indictment **OSw** *HL* Kgb

prosecution **OSw** *DL* Mb

pursuit **OSw** *SdmL* Kgb, Bb, Mb, Till

summons **OSw** *DL* Rb

Refs: Schlyter s.v. *tilmæli*

tilræði (ON) noun

assault **OIce** *KRA* 7

tiltala (OSw) verb

Literally 'to speak to', specifically of starting legal proceedings.

arraign **OSw** *SdmL* Äb, Mb, Rb

bring a case (against) **OSw** *DL* Mb, Bb, Rb, *UL* Kkb, Äb, *VmL* Bb, Rb

See also: *atala, giva, kæra, sak, sökia*

tiltalandi (OSw) noun

plaintiff **OSw** *HL* Äb, Rb, *UL* Rb, *VmL* Rb

tilæsteskip (ODan) noun

ten-load ship **ODan** *ESjL* 3

timber (OSw) timbr (OGu) timbr (ON) tymber (OSw) noun

timber **OGu** *GL* A 26, **ONorw** *GuL* Krb, **OSw** *UL* Blb, *VmL* Bb

See also: *garþsvirki, langviðr, verkviðr, viþer*

tiund (OSw) tiende (ODan) tiunt (OGu) tíund (ON) tiundi (OSw) tyund (OSw) noun

Tithes, generally consisting of a tenth of the annual income, were paid by householders for the maintenance of the priest, the bishop, the poor and the church building, though the number of beneficiaries and the distribution between them varied.

arable tithe **OSw** *HL* Kkb

tenth **OSw** *ÖgL* Kkb

tithe **ODan** *SkKL* 12, **OGu** *GL* A 3, 13, **OIce** *Grg* Klþ 4, 5 Ómb 143 Feþ 163 Hrs 234 Tíg 255, 259, *Jó* Kge 31, 34 Llb 69, *KRA* 4, 13, **ONorw** *BorgL* 11.1, *EidsL* 31.3, *FrL* KrbA 18 KrbB 17, *GuL* Krb, Arb, **OSw** *DL* Kkb, Rb, *HL* Kkb, *SdmL* Kkb, Till, *SmL*, *UL* Kkb, Rb, *VmL* Kkb, Rb, *YVgL* Kkb, Gb, Add, *ÄVgL* Kkb, Gb

Expressions:

tíund hin meiri (ON)

capital tithe **OIce** *Grg* Klþ 18 Arþ 127 Feþ 144, 163

Refs: Cleasby and Vigfússon s.v. *tíund*; Fritzner s.v. *tíund*; Gerhold 2002, 207–08; Hertzberg s.v. *tíund*; KLNM s.v.v. *fattigvård, tiend*; Lindkvist 1998

tiunda (OSw) tíunda (ON) verb

give a tenth **ONorw** *FrL* ArbB 18

make a tenth **OSw** *ÖgL* Kkb

pay tithes **OSw** *DL* Kkb, *SdmL* Kkb, *SmL*

tithe **OIce** *Grg* Arþ 127 Tíg 255, 259, *Js* Ert 17, *KRA* 14, 15

See also: *tiund*

tiþafall (OSw) noun

neglect of services **OSw** *SmL*

See also: *tiþir (pl.)*

tiþaköp (OSw) tíðakaup (ON) noun

annual fee **OSw** *DL* Kkb

annuity **OSw** *YVgL* Kkb

fee for church services **OIce** *Grg* Tíg 265

mass for the dead **OSw** *HL* Kkb

remuneration for services **OIce** *KRA* 15

tiþir (pl.) (OSw) **tiþir (pl.)** (OGu) **tíð** (ON) **tíðir (pl.)** (ON) **tyþir (pl.)** (OSw) noun

church services **OIce** *Grg* Tíg 258, 263, **ONorw** *GuL* Krb, **OSw** *HL* Kkb, *SdmL* Kkb

feasts **OSw** *SmL*

holy office **OGu** *GL* A 6, 8

hours **OSw** *SmL*

liturgical service **ONorw** *EidsL* 10.2

mass **ONorw** *EidsL* 32.7

religious service **ONorw** *EidsL* 31.2

services **OGu** *GL* A 3, 13, **OSw** *UL* Kkb, *VmL* Kkb, *ÄVgL* Kkb

Expressions:

sætia aff tyþum (OSw)

set in prohibition **OSw** *HL* Kkb

tiældra (OSw) noun

Boundary marker; *tiældrubrut* (q.v.) is to break up the stones of a boundary marker; *tiældrusten* (q.v.) stone used to form a boundary marker. In YVgL Jb 22 it says that two stones should be dug into the ground with a third on top to form a boundary marker.

boundary marker **OSw** *YVgL* Jb, Föb, Utgb, Add, *ÄVgL* Jb

See also: *ra*, *rör*, *tiældrubrut*, *tiældrusten*

Refs: Schlyter 1877 *s.v. tiældra*

tiældrubrut (OSw) noun

breaking of a boundary marker **OSw** *YVgL* Kkb, Add

See also: *tiældra*

tiældrusten (OSw) noun

Stone used as a boundary marker.

boundary stone **OSw** *YVgL* Jb, *ÄVgL* Jb

See also: *tiældra*

Refs: Schlyter *s.v. tiældra*

tína (ON) verb

rehearse **OIce** *Grg* Þsþ 41

tíundargerð (ON) **tíundagerð** (ON) noun

remission of tithes **OIce** *KRA* 14

tithe payment **ONorw** *BorgL* 11, *FrL* KrbA 18

tíundargjald (ON) noun

tithe payment **OIce** *Grg* Tíg 255

tíundargjöf (ON) noun

A gift of a tenth; a type of legal gift (ON *löggjöf*). In Jó Kge 22 it is specified that a person may give away up to a tenth of inherited goods to whomever he wishes, whereas a person may dispense up to a

quarter of one's possessions acquired elsewhere (ON *fjórðungsgjöf*). References to tenth gifts and quarter gifts appear in several late medieval Norwegian and Icelandic diplomas.

gift of a tenth **ONorw** *FrL* ArbB 4

tenth-gift **OIce** *Jó* Kge 22

See also: *fjórðungsgjöf, gæf, löggjöf, vingæf*

Refs: Agnes Arnórsdóttir 2005; CV *s.v. tíund*; Fritzner; Hertzberg; KLNM *s.v. donasjon, tiend*; Páll Vídalín 1854 *s.v. tíund, tíundargjöf*

tíundargreizla (ON) noun

discharge of tithes **OIce** *KRA* 15

tíundarhald (ON) noun

withholding of tithe **OIce** *Grg* Tíg 256, *KRA* 15

tíundarmál (ON) **tíundamál** (ON) noun

tithe case **OIce** *Grg* Tíg 258, 259

tithe matters **OIce** *Grg* Tíg 260

tíundarsekð (ON) noun

fine for failing to pay tithes **ONorw** *FrL* KrbB 2

tíundarskifti (ON) noun

allocation of tithes **OIce** *Grg* Hrs 234, *Jó* Kge 34

tjald (ON) noun

tent cover **ONorw** *GuL* Leb

tjaldbúð (ON) noun

tentbooth **ONorw** *GuL* Arb

tjara (ON) noun

tar **ONorw** *GuL* Llb, Leb

tjóðr (ON) noun

tether **ONorw** *GuL* Llb

tjun (ODan) noun

something stolen **ODan** *JyL* 2

tolfeyringr (ON) noun

twelve ounce ring **OIce** *Grg* Bat 113, **ONorw** *FrL* Mhb 18

tolfmannadómr (ON) noun

judgment of twelve men **OIce** *Jó* Mah 3

twelve man judgment **ONorw** *FrL* Rgb 13

twelve-man court **OIce** *Grg* Feþ 167

tolftakyrkia (OSw) **tolfptæ kirkia** (OSw) noun

parish church **OSw** *UL* Kkb, Kgb

tolftarkviðr (ON) noun

panel of twelve **OIce** *Grg* Klþ 7, 17 Þsþ 22, 26 Vís 86, 89 Arþ 118 Ómb 136 Lbþ 176

See also: *búakviðr, kviðr*

tolftidagher (OSw) **tolftedagh** (ODan) noun

Twelfth Day **ODan** *JyL* 2, *SkKL* 9

Twelfth Night **OSw** *YVgL* Kkb

tompt (OSw) **toft** (ODan) **tóft** (ON) **tuft** (ON) **toft**
(OSw) **tomt** (OSw) **topt** (OSw) noun

Tompt (OSw) and *toft* (ODan) refer to the enclosed area
immediately surrounding the farm houses (curtilage,
plot), the size and use of which varied considerably
throughout the North. The words have a number of
related meanings in the East Norse laws, all of which
seem to carry some legal significance. The ON *tóft*,
might also refer to the foundation and walls before
a roof was put on, and later it was used to describe
ruined buildings. A corresponding word in Norwegian
is (not in the laws) *tún* and in Icelandic *bær* (q.v. *byr*).

building plot **OSw** *DL* Gb

building site **OIce** *Jó* Fml 27, **ONorw**
FrL KrbA 12, *GuL* Krb, Leb

curtilage **OSw** *DL* Bb, Rb, *UL* Jb, Blb, *VmL* Bb

ground **ONorw** *FrL* LlbA 2

ground plot **OSw** *YVgL* Urb, Jb,
Kvab, Föb, Add, *ÄVgL* Jb, Kva

land **OSw** *DL* Bb, *ÖgL* Eb

land allocated (to someone) **OSw** *UL* Blb, *VmL* Bb

plot (1) **OSw** *HL* Blb, *SdmL* Äb, Bb,
Till, *UL* Jb, Blb, *VmL* Mb, Jb, Bb

property **OSw** *VmL* Bb

toft **ODan** *ESjL* 2, 3, *JyL* 1, 3

Expressions:

lagha tompt (OSw)

A *tompt* of a specified size.

lawful ground plot **OSw** *YVgL* Jb

rightful ground **OSw** *YVgL* Jb

svoren toft (ODan)

A *toft* converted from common land (ODan
almænning, see *almænninger*) by all men of the
village, and contrasted to old *toft*. Cp. *vægher*.

sworn toft **ODan** *JyL* 1:51

ta ok tomta ra, **ta ok tompta ra** (OSw)

*village highway and property
boundaries* **OSw** *VmL* Bb

See also: *brut, burtomt, byamal, byr, deld, jorþ,
tegher, tomptagarþer, tomptara, tomptaskipti,
tomptaskæl, tomptastæmna, tomtamal, tún*

Refs: CV s.v. *topt*; Hoff 1997, 84–121; Holmberg
1946; Jón Hnefill Aðalsteinsson 1986–89,
38; KLNM s.v. *tomt*; Schlyter s.v. *tompt*

tomptagarþer (OSw) **toftegarth** (ODan) **toftegærthe**
(ODan) noun

fence of a ground **OSw** *YVgL* Äb, Jb, *ÄVgL* Äb, Jb

fence to a house **ODan** *SkL* 187

toft garden **ODan** *JyL* 3

See also: *garþer, tompt*

tomptara (OSw) noun

boundary markers of plots **OSw** *SdmL* Mb

building plot boundary marker **OSw**
DL Mb, Bb, *UL* Mb, Blb

Expressions:

ta ok tomtara, **ta ok tompta ra** (OSw)

*village highway and property
boundaries* **OSw** *VmL* Bb

tomptaskipti (OSw) noun

division of plots **OSw** *SdmL* Bb

tomptaskæl (OSw) noun

plot boundary **OSw** *SdmL* Bb, Till

tomptastæmna (OSw) noun

A meeting for dividing the plots in a village.

plot meeting **OSw** *SdmL* Bb

tomtamal (OSw) noun

part in the village measurements **OSw** *DL* Bb

Expressions:

brut ok tomtamal, **brot ok tomtamal** (OSw)

part of the village measurement **OSw** *VmL* Jb

See also: *brut, byamal*

torf (OSw) **torf** (ON) **torv** (OSw) noun

sod **ONorw** *GuL* Krb, Kvr

turf **ONorw** *GuL* Løb, **OSw** *UL* Mb, Blb, *VmL* Bb

See also: *mold, suarþsprangr, torfa*

torfa (OGu) **torfa** (ON) noun

piece of scalp and hair **OGu** *GL* A 19

scalp **OGu** *GL* Add. 5 (B 20), **ONorw** *GuL* Mhb

sod **ONorw** *GuL* Krb, Kvr

turf **ONorw** *GuL* Leb

See also: *torf*

torfsmaðr (ON) noun

man of the turf **ONorw** *FrL* LlbB 12

torfvölr (ON) noun

turf lath **ONorw** *GuL* Leb

torgh (OSw) **torgh** (ODan) **torg** (OGu) noun

Presumed originally to have referred to the function
of a market for trade, later also to its location and as
such occasionally (ODan *ESjL* 2:22, 23) appearing
alongside, for example, church and 'beer bench' (OSw
YVgL Frb) as places where acts of violence were
more severely punished. Also appearing in the context
of correct procedure for transactions, not least with
high status objects such as weapons, horses and cattle,
cut and uncut cloth, silver and gold (cf. *torghköp*).
The time and place for these is not specified, but was
probably not restricted to towns.

market **ODan** *ESjL* 2, **OSw** *DL* Bb, *HL* Mb, *SdmL* Kmb, Mb, Tjdb, *UL* Mb, Kmb, *VmL* Kmb

market square **OGu** *GL* A 6, **OSw** *UL* Mb, *VmL* Mb

marketplace **ODan** *ESjL* 2, *VSjL* 63, **OSw** *YVgL* Frb, Tb, *ÄVgL* Tb

Refs: Andrén 1985, 90–91; KLNM s.v.v. *torgfrid, torvevæsen, marked, handelsplass*

torghfrith (ODan) noun

Appears once, where violence in breach of the *torghfrith* resulted in heavy fines to the king in addition to the victim. The concept, however, of a market peace appears elsewhere as well (ODan JyL 3, the sections dealing with *manhælghi* (q.v.) in OSw DL, SdmL, UL, VmL, and YVgL Fb).

breach of the peace in the market place **ODan** *VSjL* 63

See also: *byarfriþer, friþer, köpþingafriþer, torgh*

Refs: KLNM s.v.v. *torgfrid, torvevæsen*

torghköp (OSw) **torghkøp** (ODan) noun

Transactions made at the market were restricted in certain ways, including requirements of specific witnesses and oaths in order to avoid accusation of theft and forgery. Conversely, general restrictions concerning purchases might not apply to *torghköp*, such as the purchase sum that women and children were allowed to handle and time limits for cancelling purchases (OSw SdmL). Appearing as *torghköp ræt* (ODan), *torghköp rætta* (OSw) of lawful transactions, particularly concerning high status objects such as weapons and cloth.

purchase at a market **ODan** *SkL* 143, **OSw** *SdmL* Kmb, *YVgL* Tb, *ÄVgL* Tb

Refs: Andrén 1985, 91; Tamm and Vogt, eds, 2016, 28–29

torghkøpe (ODan) verb

buy at the market **ODan** *JyL* 2

torghskipti (OSw) noun

exchange at the market **OSw** *SdmL* Kmb

tortryggð (ON) noun

charge (2) **OFar** *Seyð* 10

doubt **OIce** *Js* Mah 8

question **OIce** *Jó* Fml 23

See also: *sak*

tortryggva (ON) **tortryggja** (ON) verb

doubt **ONorw** *GuL* Olb

question **OIce** *Jó* Kge 18

be unsure **ONorw** *FrL* KrbA 3

torvogæld (OSw) noun

The payment for burying somebody alive (between stone and turf) who is found and rescued.

turf payment **OSw** *SdmL* Mb

See also: *grafnár, qvikker*

traðargarðr (ON) noun

fence between pasture and cultivated land **ONorw** *FrL* LlbA 2

See also: *troth, træþi*

Refs: Fritzner s.v. *traðargarðr*

traðgjöf (ON) noun

fodder **OIce** *Jó* Llb 12

tré (ON) noun

mast **ONorw** *GuL* Leb

piece of timber **ONorw** *GuL* Krb, Leb

tree **ONorw** *GuL* Mhb

See also: *borð, skogher, viþer*

tréníð (ON) noun

This form of insult was primarily carving a person's likeness in an obscene position on an upraised post or pole. It was often accompanied by a libellous poem and qualified as a crime subject to outlawry. See GuL ch. 138.

libel by carving on a tree **ONorw** *GuL* Tfb

wood-shame **OIce** *Grg* Misc 237

See also: *fjölmæli, níð, róg, tunguníð*

Refs: KLNM s.v.v. *nid, offer, tunge ond, ærekrenkelse*

tréör (ON) noun

wooden arrow **ONorw** *GuL* Leb

tro (OSw) noun

fealty **OSw** *YVgL* Urb

{trö} **OSw** *DL* Kkb

trogivin (OSw) adj.

Appears in the phrase *trogivin man* 'man of allegiance', i.e. a man bound to a master by honour, presumably reflecting a feudal system.

of allegiance **OSw** *YVgL* Add

Refs: Lindkvist forthcoming

troldomber (OSw) **truldom** (ODan) **trulldomber** (OSw) noun

sorcery **ODan** *SkKL* 7

witchcraft **OSw** *DL* Kkb, *SmL*, *YVgL* Add, *ÖgL* Kkb, Vm

See also: *fìrigæra, gærning, viþskipli*

troll (ON) noun

troll **OIce** *Jó* Mah 2, *Js* Mah 6, **ONorw** *GuL* Krb, Mhb

witch **ONorw** *BorgL* 16.8

See also: *trollkona*

trollkona (ON) noun

>   witch **ONorw** *GuL* Krb

>   See also: *troll*

trolshamber (OSw) noun

>   An insult to a woman.

>   guise of a hobgoblin **OSw** *YVgL* Rlb, *ÄVgL* Rlb

trolskaper (OSw) noun

>   witchcraft **OSw** *YVgL* Tb, *ÄVgL* Tb

>   See also: *troldomber*

troth (ODan) **tröð** (ON) noun

>   1. 'enclosure', 2. (pl. *traðir*) 'a trodden path, passage', 3. 'a plot of land allotted for cultivation, a fallow field'.

>   enclosed fallow land where cattle are kept grazing **ONorw** *FrL* LlbA 1, 22

>   pasture **ODan** *ESjL* 2

>   See also: *nautatröð*, *traðargarðr*, *træþi*

>   Refs: CV s.v. *tröð*; Lund 1967 s.v. *troth*, ONP s.v. *tröð*; Schlyter s.v. *troþ*

troþr (OGu) **tróða** (ON) noun

>   fencing wood **OGu** *GL* A 25

>   roof board **ONorw** *GuL* Leb

>   See also: *garþsvirki*, *timber*

trughsjarn (ODan) noun

>   A type of *jarnbyrþ* (OSw) 'ordeal' where the accused was to throw a piece of hot iron into a trough twelve steps away.

>   trough-iron **ODan** *SkL* 156

>   See also: *jarn*

>   Refs: Nilsson 2001

trulkarl (OSw) noun

>   sorcerer **OSw** *HL* Mb

trulkærling (OSw) noun

>   troll bitch **OSw** *HL* Mb

trúnaðarváttr (ON) noun

>   reliance witness **OIce** *Grg* Þsþ 32

>   See also: *kviðr*

trúnuðr (ON) **trúnaðr** (ON) noun

>   trust **OIce** *Grg* Fjl 221, *Jó* Þjb 15

trygdareþer (OSw) **trygthereth** (ODan) noun

>   In ODan SkL, an oath sworn when receiving compensation for a killing, otherwise known as *trygth* (q.v.). In OSw SdmL, an oath sworn by the new king directly after being chosen by the lawman and twelve representatives from each jurisdiction; its six articles are given in SdmL Till 1, together with the corresponding oath sworn by the voters.

>   oath of security **ODan** *ESjL* 2, 3, *SkL* 114

>   protection oath **OSw** *SdmL* Till

>   Refs: Tamm and Vogt, eds, 2016, 310

tryggðamaðr (ON) **trygðamaðr** (ON) noun

>   man who has been pledged security **ONorw** *GuL* Mhb

>   person with whom one has exchanged pledges of peace **OIce** *Jó* Mah 2

tryggðamál (ON) **trygðamál** (ON) noun

>   Defined by F as 'the formula given for completing settlements in a killing case'.

>   peace guarantee speech **OIce** *Grg* Bat 115

>   peace pledge **ONorw** *GuL* Trm

>   See also: *eiðstafr*, *mal (1)*, *munhaf*, *trygth*

trygger (OSw) adj.

>   trustworthy **OSw** *ÄVgL* Smb

>   upright **OSw** *UL* Mb, *VmL* Mb

>   See also: *sannindaman*

tryggrof (ON) noun

>   truce-breaking **ONorw** *FrL* ArbB 19

>   violation of a peace pledge **ONorw** *GuL* Tfb

>   See also: *trygth*

tryggrofamaðr (ON) noun

>   truce-breaker **OIce** *Js* Kvg 5

tryggrofi (ON) **tryggðrofi** (ON) noun

>   pledge-breaker **OIce** *KRA* 11

>   truce-breaker **OIce** *Jó* Þfb 8 Mah 27, *Js* Þfb 6 Kvg 5, **ONorw** *FrL* Mhb 38 Var 9, 10 ArbB 19 Kvb 14 Jkb 4 LlbB 4

>   violator of a peace pledge **ONorw** *GuL* Krb, Sab

>   See also: *tryggrof*

tryggvakaup (ON) noun

>   payment for peace pledge **ONorw** *GuL* Mhb

>   See also: *trygth*

tryggvaváttr (ON) noun

>   security witness **ONorw** *FrL* Jkb 1

trygth (ODan) **tryggð** (ON) **trygð** (ON) noun

>   oath of security **ODan** *SkL* 85, 97

>   peace **ONorw** *FrL* Intr 3 Mhb 4

>   peace guarantee **OIce** *Grg* Bat 113, *Js* Mah 3, 5 Kvg 5 Ert 17, **ONorw** *FrL* Sab 21

>   peace pledge **OIce** *Jó* Mah 2, **ONorw** *GuL* Krb, Mhb, Trm

>   security **ONorw** *FrL* Mhb 2, 22 Var 9 ArbB 4 Bvb 3

>   truce **OIce** *Jó* Mah 27

>   See also: *friþer*, *griþ*, *tryggrof*, *tryggvakaup*

tryllska (ON) noun

>   witchcraft **ONorw** *BorgL* 16.8

trægarþer (OSw) noun

    garden **OSw** *SdmL* Bb

træmærki (OSw) noun

    Boundary marker of wood.

    tree-mark **OSw** *HL* Blb

    See also: *merkibjörk*

træþi (OSw) noun

    fallow **OSw** *HL* Jb, *SdmL* Bb, *ÖgL* Kkb

    fallow land **OSw** *UL* Jb, Blb, *VmL* Bb

    ploughing **OSw** *UL* Jb, *VmL* Jb

    uncultivated field **OSw** *YVgL* Jb, *ÄVgL* Jb

    See also: *aterlæggia, aterlægha, lata, liggia, traðargarðr, troth*

træþislön (OSw) noun

    payment for ploughing **OSw** *HL* Jb, *SdmL* Jb

tug (OGu) noun

    train **OGu** *GL* A 6

tuldr (OGu) **tollr** (ON) noun

    toll **OGu** *GS* Ch. 2, **OIce** *Grg* Misc 248, *Jó* Fml 5

tulkr (ON) **túlkr** (ON) noun

    interpreter **OIce** *Jó* Fml 7

tunga (ON) noun

    Men who did not speak Norse were exempted from fines to the bishop related to the eating of horse flesh (GuL ch. 20). It seems to have been required that oaths were to be taken in the Norse language (GuL ch. 24).

    language **ONorw** *GuL* Krb

    Refs: KLNM s.v. *dansk tunge*

tungarþer (OSw) **túngarðr** (ON) noun

    courtyard **OSw** *HL* Blb

    home field wall **OIce** *Grg* Þsþ 78 Lbþ 181, *KRA* 11

tunguníð (ON) noun

    libel by word of mouth **ONorw** *GuL* Tfb

    See also: *fjölmæli, róg, tréníð*

tungupundari (ON) noun

    tongue steelyard **OIce** *Jó* Kab 26

    See also: *pundari*

tuppr (OGu) noun

    headdress **OGu** *GL* A 23

    See also: *huifr*

tutte (ODan) verb

    push **ODan** *JyL* 2, *VSjL* 45, 56

tutten (ODan) **tuttan** (ON) noun

    hair pulling **ONorw** *GuL* Mhb

    pushing **ODan** *VSjL* 54

    See also: *har (1)*

tún (ON) noun

    Tún is related to words meaning 'fence', 'barrier'. In Norwegian (not in the laws) it refers to the area around which the farmhouses were grouped. In Icelandic laws it refers to the cultivated land surrounding the farm, which might be enclosed by a *túngarðr* (see *tungarþer*) or *túnvöllr* (q.v.).

    home field **OIce** *Grg* Klþ 2, 4 Ómb 129 Misc 238 Tíg 256, 257, *KRA* 15, 24

    See also: *tompt*

    Refs: CV s.v. *tún*; Hastrup 1992, 108; Helle 2001, 106–16; Holmberg, KA 1969, 247–61; KLNM s.v. *tún*, ONP s.v. *tún*

túnvöllr (ON) noun

    home field **OIce** *Jó* Lbb 3 Þjb 6

    See also: *garþer*

tveggjamannaeiðr (ON) noun

    oath of two **OIce** *Jó* Þjb 21, *Js* Þjb 11

    See also: *eþer*

tveggjapostulamessa (ON) **tveggjapostulamessudagr** (ON) noun

    Two Apostles' Mass (28 October) **ONorw** *FrL* KrbA 25 Kvb 15, *GuL* Krb

    See also: *símonsmessudagr ok judas*

tvímánuðr (ON) **tvímánaðr** (ON) noun

    'Double-month'. The fifth month of summer, which normally began on Tuesday, 12–18 August. It may have been used as a synonym for the summer month called *heyannir*.

    double month **OIce** *Grg* Þsþ 80, **ONorw** *GuL* Llb

    See also: *einmánuðr*

    Refs: CV s.v. *tvímánuðr*; Fritzner s.v. *tvímánaðr*; GAO s.v. *Misseristal*; GrgTr I:129; Hertzberg s.v. *tvímánaðr*; KLNM s.v. *mánadsnamn*

tvítugsessa (ON) noun

    A ship with twenty pairs of oars. The size of a ship was indicated by the number of thwarts (benches); a twenty-bencher would thus have seats for twenty pairs of oarsmen.

    twenty-bencher **ONorw** *GuL* Leb

    See also: *skip*

tvæböti (OSw) **tuibyt** (OGu) **tveböte** (OSw) noun

    double compensation **OSw** *DL* Eb, *UL* Äb, Mb, *VmL* Äb, Mb

    double fine **OGu** *GL* A 63, Add. 6 (B 33), **OSw** *DL* Mb, Rb, *SdmL* Gb, Mb, Tjdb

    See also: *bot, böta, sporgæld*

tvæbötisdrap (OSw) noun

   killing for double fines **OSw** *SdmL* Mb

  See also: *bot*, *drap*

tvæbötismal (OSw) noun

   case of double fines **OSw** *SdmL* Mb

tvægilda (OSw) tvígilda (ON) verb

   pay double **OIce** *Jó* Llb 8, 30 Kab 15 Þjb 11

   recompense with the double value **OSw** *YVgL* Rlb

tvægilder (OSw) adj.

   paid with double penalty **OSw** *YVgL* Add

   two-fold compensated **OSw** *ÖgL* Eb, Vm

tvægildi (OSw) tvigilde (ODan) noun

   compensation of twice the value **OSw** *ÄVgL* Rlb

   double value **ODan** *JyL* 2, *SkL* 145, *VSjL* 87

   twice the value **ODan** *SkL* 141, 144, 177

  Expressions:

   igjald ok tvigjald (ODan)

   what was stolen and the double of it **ODan** *JyL* 2

  See also: *halfgildi*

tvægipter (OSw) adj.

   twice married **OSw** *HL* Äb

tvæskipti (OSw) noun

   division in two **OSw** *DL* Mb

   division in two parts **OSw** *DL* Rb

tvæskylder (OSw) adj.

   liable to pay double **OSw** *YVgL* Föb

tvæsværi (OSw) noun

   contradictory oath **OSw** *ÖgL* Kkb

tvætala (OSw) noun

  If one party changed his plea or evidence during legal proceedings, he was fined. OSw DL, UL and VmL specify it as changing one's plea from one *þing* 'assembly' to another.

   altered case **OSw** *UL* Rb, *VmL* Rb

   case-changing **OSw** *HL* Rb

   self-contradiction **OSw** *DL* Rb, *SdmL* Rb

  Refs: Schlyter s.v. *tvætala*

tyghende (ODan) noun

  Appears in the phrase *hæræthz tyundæ* 'statement from the district' which could help the *kunings umbuzman* 'king's official' to prosecute in certain cases of wounding.

   statement **ODan** *ESjL* 3

tykr (OGu) adj.

   able to be seized **OGu** *GL* A 6

   able to be taken **OGu** *GL* A 25

tylft (OSw) tylft (ODan) noun

   oath of twelve **ODan** *ESjL* 1–3, *SkL* 32, 86, 89, 142, 144, 218, *VSjL* 2, 12, 38, 52, 56, 57, 59, 60, 82, 86

   twelfth **OSw** *YVgL* passim, *ÄVgL* Md, Smb, Slb, Äb, Gb, Rlb, Jb, Kva

   twelve **ODan** *ESjL* 1, *SkL* 109, 111, 120

  See also: *eþer*, *tylftareþer*

tylftareþer (OSw) tylftareiðr (ON) noun

   oath of twelve **OIce** *Jó* Mah 9, 27 Llb 30 Þjb 19, Js Mah 7, 8 Þjb 9, *KRA* 20, **ONorw** *FrL* Mhb 7, 8 Var 9 Bvb 1, **OSw** *YVgL* passim, *ÄVgL* passim

   twelve-man oath **ONorw** *GuL* Tfb, Mhb, Leb

  See also: *eþer*, *tylft*

tyrfa (ON) verb

   pelt with turf **ONorw** *GuL* Tjb

  Expressions:

   tyrfa meþ stenum (OSw)

   stone **OSw** *UL* Mb

týja (ON) verb

   help **ONorw** *GuL* Mhb

  See also: *slanbaugr*

tæbundin (OSw) tæbyndin (OSw) adj.

   bound by a village highway **OSw** *UL* Blb, *VmL* Bb

  See also: *ta*

tækiomaþer (OSw) takuman (OSw) tekiuman (OSw) tækiuman (OSw) tækkiumaþer (OSw) noun

  A man receiving something on behalf of somebody else, as a synonym for *intækiuman* 'tax collector' or for *taki* lit. 'taker'.

   man to receive **OSw** *ÄVgL* Smb

   tax-collector **OSw** *UL* Kgb, Add. 4, *VmL* Kgb

  See also: *ari*, *intækiuman*, *næmdarmaþer*, *skattman*, *tak*, *taki*

  Refs: Schlyter s.v. *tækio maþer*

tækiufæ (OSw) tækkiu fæ (OSw) noun

   cattle taken as lien **OSw** *YVgL* Utgb, *ÄVgL* Föb

  See also: *tak*

tækt (OSw) noun

   claimed item **OSw** *HL* Blb

   reclaimed land **OSw** *DL* Bb

tæktatak (OSw) noun

   taken land **OSw** *HL* Blb

tælghekniver (OSw) noun

   carving knife **OSw** *SdmL* Mb

  See also: *kniver*, *morþvapn*

tæppa (OSw) verb

  Expressions:

   tæppa vatn (OSw)

   hinder the flow of water **OSw** *UL* Blb *VmL* Bb

  See also: *atertæppa*, *svintæppa*

töðuvöllr (ON) noun

    A manured infield.

    hayfield **OIce** *Grg* Lbþ 181, *Jó* Mah 2 Lbb 4 Llb 31

    See also: *taða*

    Refs: CV s.v. *töðuvöllr*

tökuvætti (ON) noun

    witness of taking **OIce** *Grg* Þsþ 58

tölueyrir (ON) noun

    current coin **ONorw** *FrL* LlbA 17

tölumaðr (ON) noun

    counting-man **ONorw** *EidsL* 30.5

    kin-counter **ONorw** *BorgL* 15.8

    man who has been counted or enumerated **ONorw** *GuL* Arb

ubrutliker (OSw) adj.

    not culpable **OSw** *YVgL* Add

    not guilty **OSw** *YVgL* Urb

uböti (OSw) noun

    not subject to compensation **OSw** *DL* Mb

udræpen (ODan) **ódrepinn** (ON) adj.

    not killed **ODan** *SkL* 124, **ONorw** *FrL* Mhb 15

udæthesman (ODan) **ódáðamaðr** (ON) noun

    criminal **OIce** *Jó* Þfb 5, **ONorw** *FrL* Intr 12 Kvb 20

    evildoer **ODan** *JyL* Fort, **ONorw** *GuL* Krb

    iniquitous criminal **OIce** *KRA* 11

    See also: *óbótamaðr*, *ódáðaverk*, *urbotamal*

udømd (ODan) **ódæmðr** (ON) **ódǿmdr** (ON) **ódómðr** (ON) adj.

    not condemned **ODan** *ESjL* 2

    undecided **ONorw** *FrL* Var 7

    unjudged **OIce** *Js* Mah 20 Kab 1

    unsentenced **ONorw** *GuL* Tjb

ufortheth (ODan) adj.

    Expressions:

    ufortheth ok uspilt (ODan)

    undamaged and unspoiled **ODan** *ESjL* 3

ufritheman (ODan) noun

    disturber of the peace **ODan** *SkL* 165

    See also: *friþer*

ufyrmd (ODan) noun

    harm **ODan** *JyL* 2

ufyrme (ODan) verb

    harm **ODan** *JyL* 2

ufælder (OSw) **ufæld** (ODan) adj.

    not condemned **OSw** *YVgL* Rlb

    unconvicted **ODan** *SkKL* 7

    without conviction **OSw** *ÄVgL* Rlb

    without resolution **OSw** *YVgL* Urb

    See also: *fælla*

ugga (ON) verb

    suspect **ONorw** *GuL* Løb

uhæghth (ODan) noun

    neglect **ODan** *JyL* 1

uhæghthe (ODan) verb

    squander **ODan** *SkL* 58

uiafliker (OSw) adj.

    undisputable **OSw** *YVgL* Add

uilsketh (ODan) adj.

    unchallenged **ODan** *ESjL* 3, *VSjL* 80, 82

    undisputed **ODan** *JyL* 2

    See also: *illa*, *uilter*

uilter (OSw) adj.

    without complaint **OSw** *YVgL* Jb

    Expressions:

    u ilter ok oklandat (OSw)

    without dispute and protest **OSw** *YVgL* Add

    uilt ok uspilt (ODan)

    unclaimed and unharmed **ODan** *SkL* 53

    uncontested and unchallenged **ODan** *SkL* 80

    without charge and challenge **ODan** *SkL* 76

    See also: *illa*, *klanda*, *okærder*, *uilsketh*

ukesjo (ODan) noun

    nautical mile **ODan** *ESjL* 3

    See also: *vika*

ukristin (OSw) adj.

    pagan **OSw** *SmL*

    without being christened **OSw** *DL* Kkb

    See also: *heþin*

ulovlika (ODan) adv.

    illegally **ODan** *SkL* 47

    unlawfully **ODan** *ESjL* 2

ulv (ODan) **ulfr** (ON) noun

    Wolves appear in the laws as a threat to domestic animals and people, and in ONorw GuL they were always hunted with impunity. In ODan laws, predators — wolves, bears and hawks — only appear as domestic animals, for which the owner was responsible if they attacked somebody.

    wolf **ODan** *SkL* 104, **ONorw** *GuL* Llb, Mhb

    See also: *biorn*, *kasnavargher*, *morðvargr*, *vargher*

ulykke (ODan) noun

    accident **ODan** *JyL* 2

    See also: *vaþi*

umanneth (ODan) adj.

  unmarried **ODan** *JyL* 1

  See also: *manlos*, *ogipter*

umbót (ON) noun

  improvement **OIce** *Jó* MagBref

  reparation **OIce** *KRA* 11

umbuþ (OSw) umbuþ (OGu) umboð (ON) ombuþ (OSw) noun

  acting on behalf of another **ONorw** *FrL* Rgb 29

  agent **OSw** *SdmL* Kkb, Kgb, Till

  appointment **ONorw** *FrL* LlbB 1

  authority **OGu** *GL* A 28

  authorization **OIce** *Jó* Llb 28 Kab 10, 23

  charge (1) **OSw** *YVgL* Tb

  permission **OIce** *Jó* Llb 26

  representative **OSw** *UL* Kgb, *VmL* Kgb, Äb, Mb

  responsibility **OIce** *Jó* Mah 2, **ONorw** *FrL* LlbB 2

  stewardship **OIce** *Jó* Kge 18

umbuþsman (OSw) umbuthsman (ODan) umboðsmaðr (ON) noun

  A person endowed with legal authority on behalf of another. Variously given the title of 'trusty manager', 'commissary' and 'steward' in CV/Z. F adds that an *umbuþsman* has full power, suggesting something akin to the modern concept of full power of attorney.

  agent **OIce** *Jó* Þfb 1, 2 HT 2 Sg 1 Mah 2, 4 Kge 17, 33 Lbb 10 Llb 10 Kab 1, 22 Þjb 2 Fml 1, 17, *Js* Þfb 1, 2 Mah 5, 13 Kab 3, *KRA* 2, 11, **ONorw** *FrL* Var 9, 46 Rgb 3

  deputy **ONorw** *FrL* Rgb 29, **OSw** *YVgL* Föb

  king's official **ODan** *ESjL* 2, 3

  official **ODan** *ESjL* 1–3, *JyL* 2, 3, *SkKL* 11, *SkL* 108, 130, 153, 163, 165, 166, *VSjL* 32, 50, 60, 86, 87

  representative **ONorw** *FrL* Intr 12 KrbA 23 Kvb 15 LlbA 14 LlbB 1, *GuL* Krb, **OSw** *YVgL* Kkb

  See also: *buþ*, *halzmaþer*, *ørendreki*

  Refs: CV; F; Z

umdómi (ON) umdæmi (ON) noun

  decision **OIce** *Js* Mah 20

  opinion **ONorw** *FrL* Var 2-6

  thinking **ONorw** *FrL* Var 2-6

umeghn (OSw) om eghn (OSw) omæghn (OSw) noun

  outlying land **OSw** *HL* Rb, *SdmL* Äb, *UL* Äb, Rb, *VmL* Äb, Rb

umfærþ (OSw) noun

  A procedure confirming a purchase, where the buyer (or other recipient), the seller (or donor etc.), witnesses and landowners of the village inspected a piece of land when it was transferred.

  circumambulation **OSw** *YVgL* Gb, Jb, Kvab, Add, *ÄVgL* Jb, Kva

  Refs: Ejdestam 1946, 86–114; Larsson 2009, 156–57; Lindkvist forthcoming

umhvarf (ON) noun

  area within which one is permitted to move around **ONorw** *GuL* Løb

umiorþ (OSw) noun

  outlying land **OSw** *HL* Äb

ummerki (ON) noun

  boundary mark **OIce** *Jó* Lbb 6

  surrounding boundary **OIce** *Js* Lbb 2

umstaþumæn (pl.) (OSw) noun

  men present at the deed **OSw** *YVgL* Drb

  present men **OSw** *ÄVgL* Mb, Slb

  See also: *atvistarmaþer*, *fylghi*, *haldbani*, *laghsman*

umælende (ODan) adj.

  under-age **ODan** *JyL* 1

una (ON) verb

  be satisfied **ONorw** *GuL* Llb, Olb

unda (OSw) verb

  wound **OSw** *UL* Mb, *VmL* Mb

undanfórsla (ON) undanfærsla (ON) noun

  defence **OIce** *Jó* Þjb 22

  defence by oath **ONorw** *GuL* Kpb

  means for acquittal **OIce** *Js* Mah 25, *KRA* 33

  vindication of a charge **OIce** *Jó* Mah 27

underrættere (ODan) noun

  one who act on another's order **ODan** *JyL* Fort

undersoknere (ODan) noun

  subordinate **ODan** *JyL* 2

undirgift (OSw) undi gæf (OSw) undigipt (OSw) noun

  encroachment on tenancy **OSw** *SdmL* Jb

  illegal deposit **OSw** *UL* Jb, *VmL* Jb

undirmál (ON) noun

  private conditions **OIce** *Grg* Arþ 127

undirviþer (OSw) noun

  Mostly appearing in expressions such as *löf oc loc oc vnðir viþu* 'leaves and grass and plants under the trees' (OSw YVgL Jb) concerning rights to natural resources in relation to one's property. Occasionally contrasted to fruit bearing trees.

  brush wood **OSw** *YVgL* Add

  plants of the forest **OSw** *YVgL* Jb, *ÄVgL* Jb

  small tree **OSw** *YVgL* Utgb, *ÄVgL* Föb

young tree **OSw** *YVgL* Föb, *ÄVgL* Fös

See also: *aldin, gisningaskogher*

Refs: Schlyter s.v. *undirviþer*

ungimaþr (OGu) noun

bridegroom **OGu** *GL* A 24

ungr maðr (ON) noun

ward **OIce** *Grg* Misc 249

unna (OSw) **unna** (OGu) verb

grant **OGu** *GL* A 1, **OSw** *UL* Kkb, Mb

See also: *lufa*

unningjalausn (ON) noun

Refers to a reward for a runaway slave.

finder's reward **ONorw** *GuL* Løb

See also: *vinningælogh*

upbyrþer (OSw) noun

case **OSw** *DL* Rb

updöma (OSw) **updøme** (ODan) verb

condemn **ODan** *ESjL* 2, *VSjL* 58

judge invalid **OSw** *YVgL* Add

upgiva (OSw) **op giva** (OSw) verb

excuse (of an oath or other obligation)
OSw *UL* Rb, *VmL* Mb, Rb

See also: *forfall*

upgærþ (OSw) **op gærþ** (OSw) noun

cleared plot of land **OSw** *HL* Blb

cultivation **OSw** *UL* Blb, *VmL* Bb

See also: *ruþa*

upgöra (OSw) verb

present **OSw** *VmL* Mb

repair **OSw** *UL* Blb

uphald (OSw) noun

delay **OSw** *HL* Rb

fine for delay **OSw** *HL* Rb

uphalde (ODan) verb

detain **ODan** *JyL* 2

uphaldsman (ODan) **upphaldsmaðr** (ON) noun

In ODan, in the phrase *laghe uphaldsmæn* of the men of legal age in charge of their own property, who were to pay and receive specified instalments of a man's compensation. In ONorw FrL, someone in charge of a church, presumably when the priest was absent. In OIce KrbB 16, the priest or the *upphaldsmaðr* was responsible for accepting the bodies of the dead when they were delivered to the church, and in LlbB 3 the *upphaldsmaðr* appears to be the person appointed by the archbishop to manage church lands in a given area.

law-paying man **ODan** *JyL* 2

person responsible **ONorw** *FrL* KrbA 16

warden **ONorw** *FrL* LlbB 3

Refs: Tamm and Vogt, eds, 2016, 262, 309

uphov (ODan) noun

boundary **ODan** *JyL* 1

uplata (OSw) verb

open **OSw** *UL* Blb

uppdrykkia (OGu) noun

drunkenness **OGu** *GL* A 39

uppdyri (ON) noun

lintel **ONorw** *GuL* Llb

See also: *ofdyri*

upphaita (OGu) verb

declare **OGu** *GL* A 42, 45, 45a

See also: *heta, upphaizlusoyþr*

upphaizlusoyþr (OGu) noun

animal to be declared **OGu** *GL* A 45a

See also: *upphaita*

uppheldi (OGu) noun

provisions **OGu** *GL* A 20

See also: *föþa*

uppihalda (OSw) **op halda** (OSw) **oppehalda** (OSw)
uppehalda (OSw) verb

default **OSw** *VmL* Rb

provide for **OSw** *UL* Kkb, Jb, Kmb, *VmL* Kkb, Jb

be responsible for **OSw** *UL* Mb,
Blb, *VmL* Mb, Jb, Bb

withhold **OSw** *UL* Kkb, *VmL* Kkb

See also: *halda*

uppnám (ON) noun

The taking of a fine/compensation for killings, as well as the group of relatives, more distant than the *baugr* (see *bogher*), receiving it.

group of receivers **ONorw** *GuL* Mhb

See also: *bogher, gæld, nam, uppnámamenn (pl.)*

Refs: Hertzberg s.v. *uppnám*

uppnámamenn (pl.) (ON) noun

*men in the groups ('rings') of
receivers* **ONorw** *GuL* Mhb

See also: *uppnám*

uppnæmr (ON) adj.

seizable **OIce** *Js* Þjb 3, **ONorw** *GuL* Mhb, Tjb, Leb

which can be kept **ONorw** *GuL* Tjb

uppreist (ON) noun

hearing **OIce** *Jó* Þfb 3

renewing a claim **ONorw** *GuL* Kpb, Kvb, Arb, Olb

uppsaga (ON) noun

announcement **OIce** *Grg* Þsþ 55

law recital **OIce** *Grg* Bat 117

uppsát (ON) noun

  place to set up a ship **ONorw** *GuL* Leb

  See also: *uppsetning*

uppsátseyrir (ON) noun

  laying-up dues **OIce** *Grg* Feþ 166

uppsetning (ON) noun

  drawing a ship ashore **ONorw** *GuL* Leb

  See also: *uppsát*

uppstigningardagr (ON) noun

  Ascension Day **OIce** *Grg* Klþ 12

  See also: *hælghiþorsdagher*

upptekð (ON) **upptekt** (ON) noun

  confiscation **ONorw** *GuL* Mhb

upptókr (ON) **upptækr** (ON) adj.

  confiscable **OIce** *KRA* 35

  confiscated **ONorw** *FrL* Tfb 3

  forfeit **OIce** *Jó* Þfb 3

uprættareþer (OSw) noun

  oath of redress **OSw** *ÖgL* Kkb

uptaka (OSw) **upptaka** (OGu) **op taka** (OSw) verb

  collect **OGu** *GL* A 20, **OSw** *UL* Kkb,
  Jb, Kmb, *VmL* Kkb, Kgb, Bb, Rb

  demolish **OSw** *UL* Blb

  withdraw **OSw** *UL* Kkb, Äb

urbotamal (OSw) **orbotemal** (ODan) **óbótamál** (ON) **úbótamál** (ON) noun

'A non-compensation case'. A case involving a crime that, due to its severity and perceived disruption to the general peace, could not be expiated with a fine as was the custom for most legal infractions in the medieval Nordic areas. Such crimes included rape, killing a man at his home, in the churchyard or at an assembly (*þing*) or the violation of a settlement or truce. Sorcery and witchcraft are also cited as grounds for an *urbotamal*. It has been suggested that punishment of loss of personal rights incurred by committing an *urbotamal* was a result of influence from the Christian church.

The number of crimes that constituted an *óbótamál* in Norway increased over the course of the twelfth century during the legal reforms of King Magnus Erlingsson. Forging a letter or seal of the king, for instance, became an *óbótamál* in MLL (IV.4). At the same time, it seems that many suits dubbed *óbótamál* in Norway were nevertheless resolved by means of compensation, especially in cases where the king granted clemency.

After the institution of Jb in Iceland, the property of a person convicted of an *óbótamál* was seized and divided between the bishop and the king. This probably replaced the earlier practice of holding a confiscation court (ON *féránsdómr*) for outlaws.

Similarly, according to the medieval Danish laws, those convicted of an *orbotemal* had their property confiscated and transferred to the outlaw's heirs or the king, depending on the circumstances of the offence.

In certain Swedish laws (e.g. UL and ÖgL), an *urbotamal* was listed among breaches of the king's peace (OSw *eþsöre*). Crimes classified as *urbotamal*, in particular murder (OSw *morþ*), were later punishable by the death penalty in the late medieval and early modern periods.

  crime **ONorw** *GuL* Krb

  crime that cannot be expiated by fine **OSw** *DL* Mb

  non-compensable crime **ODan**
  ESjL 2, *VSjL* 50, 53, 54

  outlaw cases **OSw** *YVgL* Urb, Add, *ÄVgL* Urb

  unatonable crime **OIce** *Jó* Mah 2, 4
  Llb 30, 63 Þjb 3, 19, *Js* Þjb 9

  See also: *bot*, *mal (1)*, *niþingsværk*,
  óbótasök, *óbótaverk*, *ódáðaverk*

  Refs: CV s.v. *úbótamál*; Fritzner s.v. *úbótamál*;
  Hertzberg s.v. *úbótamál*; Imsen 2009; KLNM
  s.v.v. *böter*, *drab*, *edgärdsman*, *fredløshed*;
  konfiskation, *landsvist*, *niddingsværk*, *orbodemål*,
  spådom, *straff* [suppl.], *torvevæsen*, *trolldom*,
  trygð, *tyveri*, *urkundsförfalskning*, *voldtægt*;
  LexMA s.v.v. *Buße*, *Eid*, *Landfrieden*, *Strafe*;
  Lund 1967 s.v. *orbotæmal*; Orning 2014; Schlyter
  1877 s.v. *urbota*; SL YVgL, 249–50; SL ÄVgL,
  71–72; Tamm and Vogt 2016; Tveito 2005

urfiælder (OSw) noun

A piece of land, usually without buildings, separated and marked off from the owner's other land, and often located in another village. This land was excluded from the division/distribution of the village.

  enclave **OSw** *SdmL* Jb, *UL* Blb, *VmL* Bb

  See also: *fiælder*, *flutfiælder*, *lutfal*,
  ornume, *óværateigr*, *repa*

  Refs: Hellquist s.v. *urfjäll*; Hoff 1997, 150–53;
  KLNM s.v.v. *urfjäll*, *utjord*; Nordisk familjebok
  1892, s.v. *utjord*; Schlyter s.v. *urfiælder*

urþinga (OSw) **orthinge** (ODan) **orþinga** (OSw) adj.

  assembly is over **ODan** *SkL* 156

  too late for thing assembly proceedings **OSw** *VmL* Rb
  {*urþinga*} **OSw** *ÖgL* Kkb

  See also: *afkænnuþing*, *laghþing*, *þing*,
  þingariþ, *þingfastar (pl.)*, *þinglami*

urþiuva (OSw) **orþiufva** (OSw) **orþiuva** (OSw)
oþiufva (OSw) adj.
exonerated of theft **OSw** *DL* Bb, *SdmL* Kmb,
Tjdb, *UL* Mb, Kmb, *VmL* Mb, Kmb
not a thief **OSw** *HL* Mb, *YVgL* Tb, *ÄVgL* Tb
See also: *þiuver*

uskabarnabot (OSw) noun
fine for anticipated children **OSw** *SdmL* Gb
See also: *bot*, *oskabarn*

uskylt (ODan) adv.
without due cause **ODan** *SkL* 112

uskærilse (OSw) **uskirlse** (OSw) noun
desecration **OSw** *SmL*

uspilt (ODan) **úspilltr** (ON) **óspilltr** (ON) adj.
inviolate **OIce** *Jó* Mah 27, *Js* Kvg
5, **ONorw** *FrL* Kvb 14
unimpaired **ONorw** *GuL* Llb, Tjb
unspoiled **OIce** *Grg* Þsþ 34
Expressions:
ufortheth ok uspilt (ODan)
undamaged and unspoiled **ODan** *ESjL* 3
uilt ok uspilt (ODan)
unclaimed and unharmed **ODan** *SkL* 53
uncontested and unchallenged **ODan** *SkL* 80
without charge and challenge **ODan** *SkL* 76

usækteth (ODan) adj.
unaccused **ODan** *JyL* 2

utanlands (OSw) **utenlands** (ODan) **utanlanz** (OSw)
adv.
abroad **ODan** *JyL* 1, *SkL* 83, **OGu** *GL* Add. 1 (B 4)
foreign (land) **OSw** *YVgL* Kkb
outside the province **ODan** *ESjL* 1–3,
JyL 1, *SkL* 133, 146, *VSjL* 16, 86, **OSw**
VmL Kgb, *YVgL* Urb, Tb, Utgb
See also: *innanlands*, *land*

utanmenn (pl.) (OGu) noun
men outside the family **OGu** *GL* A 28

utanrikes (OSw) **utenrikes** (ODan) adv.
foreign **OSw** *YVgL* Drb
outside the kingdom **OSw** *YVgL* Gb
outside the realm **ODan** *ESjL* 1, *VSjL*
19, 20, 50, 87, **OSw** *YVgL* Add

utarve (ODan) **utarving** (ODan) **útarfi** (ON) noun
Literally an 'out-heir'. Defined in CV as distant heirs
not in the direct line of inheritance.
distant heirs **OIce** *KRA* 9
heir outside (a partnership) **ODan** *ESjL*
1, *JyL* 1, *SkL* 21, *VSjL* 1, 3, 7, 8

heir who has left (the household) **ODan** *VSjL* 3
heirs other than children **OIce** *Jó* Kge 4
See also: *fælagh*, *utarve*
Refs: CV

utdele (ODan) verb
claim **ODan** *ESjL* 2

utdöma (OSw) verb
deem compensation from **OSw** *ÄVgL* Smb
demand compensation **OSw** *VmL* Mb
impose **OSw** *VmL* Kgb, Jb

utenmarkesman (ODan) noun
Man who was not a co-owner of a specific piece of
land.
other men **ODan** *JyL* 3
Refs: Ordbog over det danske
Sprog s.v. *udenmarkmand*

utgarþer (OSw) noun
fence around fields **OSw** *YVgL* Utgb
fence around fields and meadows **OSw** *ÄVgL* Föb
outer fence (around fields and meadows)
OSw *SdmL* Jb, *ÄVgL* Föb

utgærthe (ODan) noun
fence **ODan** *SkL* 187
field **ODan** *SkL* 75
outland **ODan** *SkL* 75

utgærthsman (ODan) noun
one who shall pay **ODan** *JyL* 3

utgærþ (OSw) **utgærth** (ODan) **útgerð** (ON) **útgerðir**
(ON) **útgörð** (ON) noun
In ON, an obligation to perform military naval service
and to contribute to it with provisions or money. In
OSw, also a tax that replaced it during the thirteenth
century, and occassionally similar obligations to the
church.
debt **OSw** *HL* Rb
defence duties **ONorw** *GuL* Leb
dues **OSw** *DL* Rb, *UL* Kgb, Mb, *VmL* Mb
military service **OIce** *Grg* Misc 248
payment **ODan** *JyL* 3
provisions **OSw** *VmL* Kgb
tax **OSw** *SdmL* Kgb, Bb, Rb, *UL* Kkb
See also: *leþunger*, *matgærþ*, *skipvist*

utgærþa (OSw) **utgærthe** (ODan) verb
fence out **ODan** *ESjL* 2
Expressions:
utgærþa sik (OSw)
fence oneself **OSw** *ÄVgL* Jb

utgærþabolker (OSw) noun

book about fences **OSw** *YVgL* Utgb

See also: *utgarþer*

utgærþis (OSw) **utgierþis** (OSw) adv.

Refers to land 'outside the enclosure'. The use of this land was characterized by versatile use and expansion of farmland.

outside enclosures **OSw** *SdmL* Bb

without the enclosure **OSw** *VmL* Kkb

See also: *almænninger, ingærþis, utjorth*

Refs: KLNM s.v. *utmark*; Myrdal 1999a, 125–30; 2011, 77–97

uthus (OSw) **úthús** (ON) noun

In ONorw and OSw, houses detached from the main building and not lived in, such as barns, cattle houses and stables (OSw YVgL). In OIce, the functions are unspecified.

outhouse **ONorw** *GuL* Krb, **OSw** *YVgL* Tb, *ÄVgL* Tb

outlying house **OIce** *Jó* Þjb 6, *KRA* 11

See also: *hus, invistarhus, utvistarhus*

Refs: CV s.v. *úthús*; Fritzner s.v. *úthús*

utiunda (OSw) adj.

unpaid tithes **OSw** *SmL*

utjorth (ODan) **útjörð** (ON) noun

Refers to 'land outside the enclosure'. In ON it is used of tenant estates and is equated with ON *leiguból* (cf. Sveinbjörn Rafnsson 1985, 153). *Útjarðir* were also the parcels of land that were not covered by odal in the kin. They could be inherited by women, whereas sons received the 'primary estate' (*höfuðból*) according to Jó Kge 7.

fields outside the village **ODan** *SkL* 56

outlying land **OIce** *Jó* Kge 7

See also: *almænninger, höfuðból*

Refs: KLNM s.v. *utmark*; Myrdal 1999a, 125–30; 2011, 77–97; Rafnsson 1985, 153

utlænde (ODan) **ollandæ** (ODan) noun

land **ODan** *SkL* 75

landholding **ODan** *SkL* 76

outland **ODan** *VSjL* 79

outlands **ODan** *ESjL* 2

outlying field **ODan** *VSjL* 80

utlændinger (OSw) **utlænding** (ODan) **utlendingr** (OGu) noun

foreigner **OGu** *GL* A 28, **OSw** *ÖgL* Db

man from outside the province **OSw** *SdmL* Till, *ÖgL* Db

someone from another province **ODan** *ESjL* 3

utlændis (OSw) **utlendis** (OGu) **uttlændis** (OSw) adv.

abroad **OGu** *GL* A 13, **OSw** *HL* Äb, *UL* Kkb, Äb, Mb, Jb, *VmL* Mb

out of the land **OSw** *HL* Blb

out of the province **OSw** *UL* Kkb, *VmL* Kkb

outside the province **OSw** *SdmL* Kkb, Äb, Jb, Mb, *UL* Äb, Mb, *VmL* Äb, Mb

utlændsker (OSw) **utlændsk** (ODan) **útlendr** (ON) **útlenzkr** (ON) **utlensker** (OSw) adj.

foreign **ODan** *JyL* Fort, **OIce** *Grg* Vís 94, 97 Arþ 120 Ómb 138 Misc 248 Tíg 259, *Jó* Kge 17, 28 Fml 14, **ONorw** *GuL* Krb, **OSw** *DL* Gb, *HL* Mb, *VmL* Mb, *YVgL* Kkb, Drb, Tb, *ÄVgL* Md, Tb, *ÖgL* Eb

foreigners **ONorw** *GuL* Mhb, Tjb

from outside the province **OSw** *SdmL* Mb

utmæta (OSw) verb

deliver **OSw** *UL* Rb, *VmL* Rb

utretta (OGu) **ut raiþa** (OGu) **ut reyda** (OGu) verb

discharge **OGu** *GL* A 13, 20 (B-text only)

utrikis (OSw) **utenrikes** (ODan) adj.

foreign **ODan** *ESjL* 2, **OSw** *YVgL* Drb

utrikis (OSw) adv.

abroad **OSw** *UL* Kgb, Mb, Jb, *VmL* Kgb, Jb

utroþer (OSw) noun

outward sea expedition **OSw** *HL* Kgb

utröna (OSw) verb

investigate **OSw** *UL* Kkb, Rb, *VmL* Kkb, Rb

try **OSw** *HL* Rb

try and settle **OSw** *HL* Rb

utskipt (OSw) noun

outlying field **OSw** *YVgL* Jb

part in outlying land **OSw** *YVgL* Kkb, *ÄVgL* Jb

See also: *skipti*

utskutstola (OSw) **utskuts stol** (OSw) noun

bride-seat-eviction **OSw** *HL* Äb

utskyld (OSw) noun

A general term for duties or taxes, mostly appearing in the context of the church's tax exemption.

dues **OSw** *UL* Kgb

obligation **OSw** *SdmL* Bb, Till

tax **OSw** *HL* Kkb, *UL* Kkb, *VmL* Kkb

utsökia (OSw) verb

extract **OSw** *UL* Kgb, *VmL* Äb, Mb, Jb, Bb

See also: *sökia*

utvarþer (OSw) noun

outer guard **OSw** *SdmL* Kgb

utvistarhus (OSw) noun

outhouse **OSw** *YVgL* Tb

utængi (OSw) noun

    outlying meadow **OSw** *HL* Blb

uvildigh (ODan) adj.

    impartial **ODan** *ESjL* 2, *JyL* 3

    See also: *vildigh*

útanfjórðungsmaðr (ON) noun

    someone from a different quarter
    OIce *Grg* Vís 104 Feþ 147

útanhreppsmaðr (ON) noun

    person from outside the commune **OIce**
    Grg Hrs 234, 235 Tíg 256, *KRA* 15

útanlandsmaðr (ON) noun

    foreigner **OIce** *Grg* Feþ 167

útansveitarmaðr (ON) noun

    man from outside the district **OIce** *Jó* Þfb 7

útanváði (ON) noun

    external injury **ONorw** *GuL* Mhb

útanþingsmaðr (ON) noun

    man of a different assembly **OIce**
    Grg Þsþ 49, 58 Misc 239

útbeizla (ON) noun

    claiming **ONorw** *FrL* ArbB 30 Rgb 24

útborði (ON) noun

    outer side of a moored ship **ONorw** *GuL* Mhb

úteynaþing (ON) noun

    A *þing* 'assembly' at a specified location for the
    inhabitants of the outer islands, (*Eyin ýtri*, now
    Ytterøya, in Trøndelag), explicitly equivalent to the
    right of other inhabitants of the ON *fylki* 'county'.

    assembly in the outer islands **ONorw** *FrL* ArbA 19

úteynn (ON) noun

    person from the outer islands **ONorw** *FrL* Bvb 16

útför (ON) noun

    Carries a spectrum of meanings relating to 'travelling
    out'. In GuL Leb and Grg Misc 248 it refers specifically
    to the performance of naval military service.

    duty in the naval service **ONorw** *GuL* Leb

    military service **OIce** *Grg* Misc 248

    right to leave **OIce** *Grg* Misc 248

    See also: *leþunger*

    Refs: CV s.v.v. *útferð*, *útför*; Fritzner s.v.v.
    útferð, *útför*; Hertzberg s.v. *útför*

útganga (ON) noun

    payment **OIce** *Grg* Vís 110

    release **OIce** *Grg* Fjl 221 Misc 249 Tíg 256

útgerðarbölkr (ON) noun

    book on the naval levy **ONorw** *GuL* Leb

útgrunnr (ON) adj.

    shoaling gradually from the shore **ONorw** *GuL* Kvr

úthagi (ON) noun

    outer-pastures **OIce** *Jó* Llb 20

    See also: *haghi*

    Refs: CV s.v. *úthagi*; Fritzner s.v. *úthagi*

útheraðsmenn (pl.) (ON) noun

    men from outside the district **ONorw** *GuL* Olb

úthurð (ON) noun

    outer door **ONorw** *GuL* Llb

úthýsi (ON) noun

    outlying building **OIce** *Grg* Klþ 2

útilega (ON) noun

    'Outlying', highway robbery; lying in wait to rob
    passersby.

    robbery **OIce** *Jó* Mah 2, *Js* Mah
    6, **ONorw** *FrL* Var 45

    sitting out at night **ONorw** *GuL* Krb

    See also: *útiseta*

    Refs: CV s.v. *útilega*; Fritzner s.v.
    útilega; Hertzberg s.v. *útilega*

útiseta (ON) noun

    Sitting outside with the intention of performing
    sorcery. It has been classified as a type of divination
    or necromancy and was considered an unatoneable
    crime (*óbótamál*, see *urbotamal*) in the Icelandic and
    Norwegian laws. *Útiseta* appears to have been known
    in Norway and Iceland, and there may have been some
    connection to similar practices found in Scotland and
    on the Continent.

    sitting out at night **ONorw** *GuL* Krb

    sitting outside **OIce** *Jó* Mah 2, *Js* Mah 6

    staying outside **ONorw** *FrL* Var 45

    Expressions:

    útiseta at vekja tröll upp (ON)

    sitting outside to wake up trolls **OIce**
    Js Mah 6 **ONorw** *GuL* Krb

    *spending the night outside to practice
    witchcraft* **OIce** *Jó* Mah 2

    staying outside to wake up ghosts **ONorw** *FrL* Var 45

    See also: *fordeþskepr*, *gærning*, *troldomber*, *útilega*

    Refs: CV; F; GAO s.v. *Ekstase*, *Orakel*,
    Seherinnen; KLNM s.v. *spådom*

útlagaverk (ON) noun

    act of an outlaw **OIce** *KRA* 20

útlagi (ON) noun

    outlaw **OIce** *Jó* Mah 6, **ONorw** *FrL* Intr 4, 5

    See also: *skógarmaðr*, *útlagr*, *útlegð*, *útlægja*, *útlægr*

útlagr (ON) adj.

> *belonging to an outlaw* **ONorw** *FrL* Var 13
>
> *fined* **OIce** *Grg* Klþ 1, 2 Vís 89 Lsþ 116
>
> *forfeit* **OIce** *Grg* Þsþ 61
>
> *outlawed* **OIce** *Grg* Bat 114, **ONorw** *FrL* Intr 1
> Mhb 1, 19 LlbA 1 LlbB 12 Reb 1, *GuL* Krb, Kpb,
> Kvb, Llb, Arb, Tfb, Reb, Mhb, Tjb, Olb, Leb

See also: *útlagi, útlegð, útlægja, útlægr*

útlegð (ON) **útlægð** (ON) noun

Outlawry (*útlegð*) was a common form of punishment in the Middle Ages. The most important crimes qualifying to such punishment were treachery, murder, breach of truces and pledges, and theft (see the survey in Riisøy 2015, 76). The person who was sentenced to *útlegð* was called *útlagi* (q.v.), *utlægher*, *útlægr* (q.v.) or *útlagr* (q.v.); OSw *biltugher* (q.v.), *friþlös* (q.v.). (The same word was also used to denote the property of an outlawed person: *útlagt/útlægt fé, útlægr eyrir; útlegðarfé*.) This meant that he or she was outside the law and excluded from society. Those who had committed even worse crimes, such as treason towards a lord or a master, aggravated arson, and murder by night, were considered to be *níðingar* (see *niþinger*) or *vargar* (see *vargher*) (the latter word esp. in compounds like *brennuvargr, morðvargr*, etc.). The corresponding verb was *útlægja* 'to outlaw'. A deed leading to outlawry was said to be *níðingsverk* (OSw *niþingsværk*) or *útlegðarverk* (q.v.) .

The punishment was of two kinds:

(1) Common outlawry, which meant the same as expatriation, from which the outlaw could be released by making certain payments (so-called *skógarkaup* (q.v.) or *friðkaup*) to the king — in which case he was allowed to stay in the country or the district (within a restricted area, usually in the woods, hence the OIce terms *skóggangr* (q.v.), *fjörbaugsgarðr* (q.v.)) — and to the family of the aggrieved party. In more serious cases, he might even forfeit his property, which was then called *útlegðarfé* (q.v.). According to Grágás, the person who was sentenced to *fjörbaugsgarðr* was granted three sanctuaries (*heimili*, q.v.) within which he was safe during three years in Iceland. After that, he had to go abroad for three years. A resemblance to these three sanctuaries in Grágás is found in ch. 13 of the GL: If a man killed another, he could flee to one of three churches, which had status as sanctuary churches. These churches were situated in each third of the island and were therefore convenient places of asylum. After forty days had expired the killer must ride to the place where he wanted to draw up his peace circle, and someone else might negotiate compensation on his behalf (see Peel 2015, 113). The stipulation relating to a peace circle bears resemblance to an older parallel in Sweden. The ninth-century Oklunda runic inscription from Õstergötland is an early pre-Christian example of (legal) sanctuary: *Gunnarr faði runaR þessaR. En sa flau sakiR, sotti vi þetta* 'Gunnar cut these runes. And he fled *sakiR* ("under penalty", "guilty" or "outlawed") and sought this sanctuary' (see Peel 2015, 44–45). This means that before he reached the sanctuary, Gunnar was subject to pursuit and killing, with impunity of the pursuers. — In mainland Scandinavia the outlaw was excluded from the law province, alternatively (in the Göta laws) from the local court district.

(2) A more severe punishment was permanent or irredeemable outlawry, from which there was no escape. One who was sent into permanent outlawry was an *óbótamaðr* (q.v.), one from whom, or for whom, no fine could be received. It has been suggested (by Imsen 2014, 64) that being labelled *útlægr* signified execution: '… the perpetrator [of manslaughter] [was] ipso facto an outlaw, … . The latter probably implied that he was executed, even though some killers may have escaped to the forest and joined crowds of criminal vagabonds.' The outlaw was usually denied Christian burial. According to the GuL (ch. 23) he or she had to be buried on the foreshore (*í flóðarmáli*), where 'the tide and the green sod meet', perhaps in order to avoid corpses being placed back in the heathen burial mounds. Outlaws who were executed were often buried at the place of their execution.

> *exile* **ONorw** *FrL* Intr 4
>
> *fining case* **OIce** *Grg* Lrþ 117 Tíg 259
>
> *outlawry* **OIce** *Jó* Mah 1 Llb 30, *Js* Mah 4, 24 Þjb
> 4, **ONorw** *EidsL* 7, *FrL* Intr 3, 5 Mhb 7, 62 Var
> 9 Bvb 11, *GuL* Krb, Llb, Tfb, Mhb, Tjb, Leb

See also: *bandavereldi, útlagi, útlagr, útlægja, útlægr*

Refs: Breisch 1994, 130–33; Helle 2001, 99–101, 153; Hertzberg s.v.v. *útlagi, útlagr, útlegð; vargr*; Imsen 2014, 64; Iversen 1997, 57–58; Jones 1940; KLNM s.v.v. *asyl, benådning, böter, drab, excommunicatio og interdikt, exekution, fredlöshed, förbrytelse, hämnd, incest, konfiskation, kviðr, landsvist, mansbot, niddingsværk, orbodemål, stigmenn, straff, styresmann, svangerskab, trolldom, tyveri, véfang, vindikasjon, ægteskab, ægteskabsbrud, ærekrenkelse*; Nilsson 1989, 270–83; Peel 2015, 46, 115; RGA2 s.v. *friedlosigkeit*; Riisøy 2010; 2014, 102, 106–23; 2015; 2016; Strauch 2016, 24, 50, 158, 228, 231; Wennström 1933

útlegðareiðr (ON) noun

> *oath involving outlawry* **ONorw** *FrL* Mhb 8

útlegðarfé (ON) noun

Property forfeiture in serious outlawry cases which could reduce the degree of outlawry.

outlaw-property **OIce** *Jó* Mah 7, *Js*
Mah 13, **ONorw** *FrL* Mhb 10

outlawry-wealth **ONorw** *EidsL* 25 44

See also: *fæ*, *útlagi*

útlegðarmaðr (ON) noun

outlaw **ONorw** *FrL* Intr 12

útlegðarmál (ON) noun

cases involving outlawry **OIce** *KRA*
39, **ONorw** *FrL* Mhb 8

útlegðarsök (ON) noun

fining case **OIce** *Grg* Þsþ 57

útlegðarverk (ON) noun

act of an outlaw **OIce** *Jó* Mah 3, 6

deed leading to outlawry **ONorw** *GuL* Tfb

deed punishable by outlawry **OIce** *Js* Kab 1

útlægja (ON) verb

outlaw **ONorw** *FrL* KrbB 3, *GuL* Mhb

See also: *útlagi*, *útlagr*, *útlegð*, *útlægr*

útlægr (ON) adj.

belonging to an outlaw **ONorw** *EidsL* 30.11
44, *FrL* KrbB 23 Var 13, *GuL* Tjb

outlawed **OIce** *Jó* Þfb 8 Mah 1, 6 Kge 1 Llb
30, 63 Kab 14 Þjb 1, *Js* Þfb 6, Mah 5 Lbb 21
Kab 1, 4 Þjb 1, *KRA* 1, 22, **ONorw** *BorgL* 8.13,
EidsL 3.3 30.10, *FrL* KrbA 40 KrbB 3 Bvb 4

See also: *saker*, *útlagi*, *útlagr*, *útlegð*, *útlægja*

útmerki (ON) noun

A rare term within Nordic law. CV defines it as 'a locality; the place of a summons for launching a ship'. A note from the translators of Grg (II:90) state: 'A compound *útmerki* is not otherwise known. It might mean "external marks" and conceivably refer to means of identifying the vessel and/or its location. The reading may also possibly be an error for *um merki*, with the whole clause then meaning "and make a statement about the marks" or "about the boundaries". This might then refer to the limits of the territory from which men were expected to come for the ship-hauling.'

boundary **OIce** *Jó* Llb 17

external marks **OIce** *Grg* Feþ 166

Refs: Grg trans. II:90

útslátta (ON) noun

exposure **ONorw** *FrL* KrbA 2

útþróndr (ON) noun

someone from outer Trondelag **ONorw** *FrL* Mhb 56

útþrónzkr (ON) adj.

of outer Trondelag **ONorw** *FrL* Mhb 54

vaðr (ON) noun

fishing line **ONorw** *GuL* Krb, Mhb

vaflanarför (ON) noun

pointless journey **OIce** *Grg* Þsþ 82

vaggubarn (OSw) noun

infant **OSw** *DL* Mb

See also: *kroklokarl*

vaghli (OSw) **vagli** (OGu) noun

perch **OGu** *GL* A 19

roost **OSw** *VmL* Mb

vaghrakki (OSw) noun

willow tie **OSw** *UL* Blb

vagn (OGu) noun

wagon **OGu** *GL* A 6, 24, 26

See also: *kerra*

vagniklaferþ (OGu) noun

wagon-riders' procession **OGu** *GL* A 24

See also: *magaraiþ*, *vagniklar (pl.)*

vagniklar (pl.) (OGu) noun

wagon-riders **OGu** *GL* A 63, Add. 6 (B 33)

vaizlurol (OGu) noun

feast **OGu** *GL* A 24

See also: *mungat*, *öl*, *væzla*

vaka (OSw) noun

Appears in expressions such as *vtan warþ oc wacu* (SdmL) 'outside the guard and watch' concerning the naval defence.

watch **OSw** *SdmL* Kgb, Mb, *UL* Kgb

See also: *leþunger*, *roþarætter*, *varþer*

vaksen (ODan) adj.

adult **ODan** *ESjL* 1

grown-up **ODan** *SkL* 141

See also: *laghvaksen*, *omaghi*

vakta (OSw) verb

observe **OSw** *UL* Kkb, Add. 15, *VmL* Kkb

val (OSw) noun

election **OSw** *SdmL* Till, *ÖgL* Kkb

valborghamæssa (OSw) **valborgamessa** (OGu) noun

Walpurgis' Day **OSw** *VmL* Bb

Walpurgis' Mass **OSw** *SdmL* Kkb, Bb

Walpurgis' Night **OGu** *GS* Ch. 3

vald (OSw) **vald** (ODan) **vald** (OGu) **vald** (ON) **val** (OSw) **vold** (OSw) noun

Frequently appearing in various translations related to a central meaning of 'power', often rather abstract and translated as 'power (to choose)', 'right (to choose)' but also 'precedence' or 'choice'. From this usage an associated meaning of domination can be discerned, referring both to a privilege and to a territory, and reflected in translations such as 'control', 'authority', 'reign' and 'dominion'. Another line of usage centres on aspects of brutality, which is reflected in translations such as 'force', 'violence' and 'fear'. When referring to a person, these two lines of usage have been translated as 'proxy' and 'rapist' respectively.

action **OIce** *Grg* Þsþ 54, *Jó* Þjb 16

authority **OIce** *Js* Þfb 2, 5, *KRA* 4, 6, **OSw** *SdmL* Conf, Kkb, Gb, Äb, Jb, Bb, Kmb, Mb, Tjdb, Rb, Till, *UL* StfBM, Kgb

choice **OSw** *UL* Mb

control **OGu** *GL* A 6

decision **OSw** *YVgL* Gb

dominion **OIce** *Jó* HT 2

fear **ODan** *JyL* 3

force **ODan** *JyL* 2, 3, *VSjL* 60, **OSw** *SdmL* Kmb, *UL* Kmb, *ÖgL* Eb, Db

power **ODan** *ESjL* 1–3, *JyL* Fort, 2, 3, *SkL* 42, 81, 130, 140, 151, 153, *VSjL* 13, 15, 20, 22, 43, 58, 82, 86, 87, **OSw** *DL* Tjdb, *UL* Jb, Kmb, Blb, *VmL* Jb, Bb, *YVgL* Kkb, Rlb, *ÄVgL* Rlb, Tb, *ÖgL* Eb

power to choose **ODan** *ESjL* 3, *SkL* 123

precedence **OSw** *DL* Bb, *SmL*

proxy **OSw** *HL* Rb

rapist **ODan** *JyL* 2

reign **OIce** *Jó* HT 1

right **ODan** *JyL* 1, 2, *SkL* 180, **OSw** *DL* Kkb, Bb, Gb, Tjdb, Rb, *HL* Kgb, Äb, Mb, Jb, Rb, *UL* Kkb, Äb, Mb, Jb, Kmb, Blb, Rb, *VmL* passim, *YVgL* Drb, Äb, Tb, Jb, Kvab, Föb, Add, *ÄVgL* Mb, Äb, Jb, Kva, Tb

right to choose **ODan** *SkL* 234, **OSw** *SmL*

violence **ODan** *JyL* Fort, 2, 3, **OGu** *GL* A 19, 21, **OIce** *Jó* Þfb 5, *KRA* 6

Expressions:

taka mæþ vald (OSw) **mæth wald takæ** (ODan) Much debated expressions without any clear consensus. Most notable are the questions whether they refer to rape or abduction, if the victim's lack of consent was a prerequisite for the crime, whether it was considered a violation of the guardian or the victim him- or herself, if completed sexual intercourse was a prerequisite, and the importance of a resultant deprivation of virginity, or if the real issue was whether the offender married the victim or not. The laws make it clear that it was a serious crime which was severely punished with high fines/

compensation, or even outlawry or death. The victim was not penalized (cf. *hor*, *lægher*). Legal requirements concerning proof stipulated proper announcement (*lysning*), and emphasized signs of the victim's dissent, such as calls for help (*op ok akallan*), torn clothes or scratch marks or bruises.

rape **OSw** *HL* Kgb, Äb *YVgL* Add

take away with violence **ODan** *VSjL* 56

take by force **OSw** *HL* Kgb

take by violence **OSw** *HL* Äb *YVgL* Urb

take forcefully **ODan** *VSjL* 25

See also: *kvinnetakt*, *raþ*

Refs: Carlsson 1965, 32; Dübeck 2003a, 56–58; Ekholst 2014, 190–208; KLNM s.v.v. *kvinnerov*, *voldtægt*; Ljungqvist 2005; Riisøy 2009, 45

valda (OSw) valde (ODan) valda (OGu) valda (ON) verb

cause **OGu** *GL* A 16, **ONorw** *GuL* Llb, Mhb, **OSw** *UL* Kkb, Blb, *VmL* Kkb, Kgb, Bb, *ÄVgL* Tb

choose **ODan** *JyL* 2

decide **ODan** *JyL* 3, *SkL* 46, 219, **OSw** *ÄVgL* Rlb

dispose of **ODan** *JyL* 2, *SkL* 29, **OSw** *YVgL* Jb

dispose over **ODan** *SkL* 29

do (i.e. commit) **OGu** *GL* Add. 8 (B 55)

force **OSw** *VmL* Bb

be guilty **OSw** *YVgL* Tb, *ÄVgL* Tb

have a right **OSw** *ÄVgL* Jb

have command over **OGu** *GL* A 7

get power **ODan** *JyL* 1

be responsible **OIce** *Grg* Þsþ 58

retain authority over **OGu** *GL* A 7

rule **OSw** *ÄVgL* Kkb

take care of **ODan** *SkL* 58

See also: *abyrghia*, *lata*, *vald*

valder (OSw) völlr (ON) noun

field **OIce** *Grg* Lbþ 181, *Jó* Llb 8, 14

ground **OIce** *Grg* Vís 86

pasture ground **OSw** *SdmL* Till

See also: *hiorþvalder*

Refs: CV s.v. *völlr*; ONP s.v. *völlr*; Schlyter s.v. *valder*.

valdeygðr (ON) adj.

wall-eyed (of a horse) **ONorw** *GuL* Mhb

valdföra (OSw) verb

forcefully abduct **OSw** *SdmL* Tjdb

take by force **OSw** *UL* Mb

take with violence **OSw** *YVgL* Add

See also: *band*, *binda*

valdsgærning (OSw) **valzgiærning** (OSw) **walz gærning** (OSw) noun

   act of violence **OSw** *HL* Kgb, *UL*
Kgb, Kmb, *VmL* Kgb, Kmb

   violent deed **OSw** *SdmL* Kgb, Kmb, Rb, Till

   See also: *valdsværk, vigh, værn*

valdsmaþer (OSw) **valdsmaðr** (ON) noun

A 'man of power' or 'man of authority'. In Norwegian-ruled Iceland a *valdsmaðr* appears to have been synonymous with a royal official (ON *konungs umboðsmaðr*, see *umbuþsman*) or sheriff (ON *sýslumaðr*, see *sysluman*). As such the Icelandic *valdsmaðr* had a variety of administrative responsibilities, such as convening assemblies and appearing on behalf of the king. After the position of *jarl* (q.v.) was abolished in Iceland in 1268, governance of the country was said to be in the hands of *valdsmenn*.

   man of authority **OSw** *SdmL* Jb, Kmb

   official **OIce** *Jó* Kab 9

   sheriff **OIce** *Jó* Þfb 1, 2 Kab 9, *Js* Þfb 1, 2 Mah 26, 34 Kab 1 Þjb 6

   Expressions:

   valdsmanna by (OSw)

   village of a man of authority **OSw** *SdmL* Jb

   See also: *hirðstjóri, jarl, næmdarmaþer, sysluman, umbuþsman*

   Refs: Bagge 2013; CV; F; Hertzberg; KLNM s.v. *sysselmann*; MSE s.v. Iceland; Strauch 2011, 260; Wærdahl 2011, 147–48

valdsværk (OSw) noun

   act of violence **OSw** *SdmL* Bb, Kmb, *YVgL* Rlb, Föb, Add

   crime **OSw** *YVgL* Drb

   force of arms **OSw** *UL* Blb, *VmL* För

   violence **OSw** *HL* Blb, *YVgL* Drb, Utgb, Add

   See also: *valdsgærning, vigh, værn*

valdtaka (OSw) **valdtake** (ODan) **valltaka** (OSw) verb

   rape **ODan** *JyL* 2, **OSw** *UL* Kgb, Äb, *VmL* Kgb, Äb

   rob **OSw** *DL* Bb, *HL* Jb

   take by force **OSw** *UL* Kgb, Äb, Jb, Kmb, *VmL* Kgb, Äb, Kmb

   take forcefully **OSw** *SdmL* Gb, Jb, Kmb

   See also: *ræna*

valdtækt (ODan) noun

   rape **ODan** *JyL* 2

valinkunnr (ON) adj.

   impartial **OIce** *Jó* Kge 26 Lbb 5 Kab 14 Þjb 19, **ONorw** *GuL* Krb, Kpb, Løb, Llb, Arb, Olb

   respectable **ONorw** *FrL* Mhb 45

vallaskifti (ON) noun

   division of fields **OIce** *Jó* Llb 14

valrof (OSw) **valrov** (ODan) **valrof** (ON) noun

   corpse-robbery **ODan** *JyL* 3, *SkL* 110, **OSw** *ÖgL* Db

   plundering of the slain **ONorw** *GuL* Mhb

   robbing the corpse of a dead man **ODan** *ESjL* 2

vamm (ON) noun

   blemish **ONorw** *GuL* Mhb

   See also: *laster*

van (OSw) noun

   right to inherit from a home-born thrall **OSw** *ÖgL* Db

vana (ON) verb

   damage **ONorw** *FrL* Rgb 46

vanda (ON) verb

   select **OIce** *Grg* Þsþ 77

vandhǿfr (ON) **vandhæfi** (ON) adj.

   safeguarded **OIce** *Grg* Þsþ 52

vandreþi (OGu) **vandræði** (ON) noun

   danger **OGu** *GL* A 13

   difficulties **ONorw** *GuL* Sab

   ill intent **ONorw** *FrL* Var 7

   poverty **ONorw** *GuL* Løb

vandóma (ON) **vandæma** (ON) verb

   judge too mildly **OIce** *Jó* Mah 17

   See also: *ofdóma, vanrefsa*

vanefni (ON) noun

   inadequate means **OIce** *Grg* Ómb 130, 137

vanerfð (ON) noun

   incomplete inheritance rights **ONorw** *FrL* ArbB 14

vanesak (ODan) noun

A case without witnesses or proof, where a suspect was to be summoned to a *thing* (ODan) 'assembly' (see *þing*), accused at a second, and have the case settled by nominated men at a third.

   case of suspicion **ODan** *JyL* 2

   See also: *grun, humamal, jæva, næmd, væna, þing*

   Refs: Tamm and Vogt, eds, 2016, 302

vanför (OSw) **vanfør** (ODan) adj.

   debilitated **ODan** *VSjL* 21, 22

   disabled **ODan** *SkL* 41, 42, **OSw** *HL* Kmb, *SdmL* Kmb, *UL* Kmb, *VmL* Kmb

vang (ODan) noun

The large individual cultivated field in a field rotation system was called *gærþi* (OSw), *vang* (ODan) or (to the extent that field rotation systems existed in Norway) *teiglag* (ONorw, not in the laws).

   arable field **ODan** *SkL* 75, 168, 169, 189, *VSjL* 79

   cultivated field **ODan** *ESjL* 2, *JyL* 1, 3

field **ODan** *ESjL* 3, *JyL* 3, *SkL* 185, *VSjL* 79

land **ODan** *JyL* 3

See also: *gærþi*, *staur*

vangrov (ODan) noun

violent seizure **ODan** *ESjL* 2

vangsgarth (ODan) noun

fence around cultivated field **ODan** *JyL* 3

vangæzla (ON) noun

carelessness **OIce** *Jó* Þjb 16, **ONorw** *FrL* LlbB 3

See also: *vangöma*

vangöma (OSw) vangøme (ODan) vangömsla (OSw) noun

For details on usage, see *vanrökt*.

awkwardness **ODan** *JyL* 3

carelessness **OSw** *DL* Bb, *UL* Kkb, *VmL* Kkb

neglect **OSw** *SmL*, *YVgL* Rlb, Utgb, *ÄVgL* Rlb, Föb

want of proper care **OSw** *DL* Kkb

See also: *ofæfli*, *vanrökt*

vanhafôr (ON) adj.

badly done **OIce** *Grg* Ómb 133

vanheill (ON) adj.

in poor health **OIce** *Grg* Ómb 141

infirm **OIce** *Grg* Þsþ 35, 77

vanheilsa (ON) noun

poor health **ONorw** *GuL* Leb

vanhluti (ON) adj.

suffered **OIce** *Grg* Þsþ 80

vanlokinn (ON) adj.

not fully paid **OIce** *Grg* Þsþ 53

vanlykð (ON) noun

failure **OIce** *Grg* Þsþ 54, 60

vanr (ON) adj.

wanting **ONorw** *GuL* Krb

vanrefsa (ON) verb

punish mildly **OIce** *Jó* Mah 17

vanrökt (OSw) vanrøkt (ODan) vanrækt (ON) vanrókð (ON) vanrykt (OSw) noun

Domestic animals and other items borrowed, hired, taken as security or otherwise kept by someone other than the owner were to be cared for and returned unharmed or be compensated to their value. In OSw ÄVgL and YVgL, neglect of this caring duty included drowning, injuries from shackles and starvation, but they also allowed exceptions to this duty in cases of *ofæfli* 'superior force' which included natural disasters (thunder and fire), disease (boils and epilepsy) and bears. Thieves and wolves were alternately treated as *vanrökt* and *ofæfli*. ODan SkL also mentions *ofævle*,

albeit undefined, but includes it in the caring duty. Other mentions of *vanrökt*, *vangöma* (q.v.), *vangömsla* are not defined and often deal with fire or delapidation of houses.

neglect **OSw** *HL* Kkb, *UL* Kkb, Äb, *VmL* Kkb, Äb

negligence **ODan** *ESjL* 3, *SkL* 226, 235, **OIce** *Jó* Llb 71, **ONorw** *FrL* ArbB 24

See also: *vangöma*

vantala (ON) noun

low estimate **ONorw** *FrL* Var 42

vanvirða (ON) noun

dishonour **OIce** *Jó* Sg 3 Mah 11, 20

insult **OIce** *Jó* Mah 21

vanvirðing (ON) noun

Lasting, disabling wound caused by assault.

dishonour **OIce** *Jó* Mah 21

insult **OIce** *Jó* Sg 3

vanviti (OSw) noun

crazy person **OSw** *DL* Bb

vapn (OSw) vapn (ODan) vápn (ON) vakn (OSw) vapin (OSw) noun

arms **OSw** *DL* Eb

weapon **ODan** *ESjL* 3, *JyL* 2, 3, *SkL* 106, 107, 176, **ONorw** *GuL* Kpb, Llb, Tfb, Mhb, Leb, **OSw** *HL* Kgb, *SdmL* Kgb, Mb, *YVgL* Drb, Tb, Add, *ÄVgL* Md, *ÖgL* Eb

vapnaskipti (OSw) vaknaskipte (OSw) vapn skipte (OSw) noun

armed combat **OSw** *SdmL* Kgb

armed conflict **OSw** *DL* Eb, *HL* Mb, *UL* Kgb, *VmL* Kgb

assault at arms **OSw** *YVgL* Add

clash of weapons **OSw** *ÖgL* Eb

combat with arms **OSw** *HL* Kgb

See also: *vapn*

vapntak (ODan) vápnatak (ON) noun

The closing proceedings of an assembly; synonymous with *þinglausnir* (see *þinglausn*). In earlier times this was signified by a brandishing or clashing of weapons as a sign of assent to the proceedings. As a means of assent the *vápnatak* might a very old institution, some parallels of which have been seen in Tacitus' *Germania*. It is believed that it was the custom at assemblies (*þing*) to make noise with weapons to express agreement, e.g. with a judgment. In MLL (I.5) it is stated that judgments passed by the Law Council (*lögrétta*) were not valid until those seated outside of its boundaries (*vébönd*) clashed their weapons in assent (*vápnatak* or *þingtak*). The term was borrowed into Old English and became *wapentake*, which was used to indicate a lower-level administrative district in areas under the former Danelaw. In Norway a *vápnatak* may also refer to an assembly of weapons (*vápnaþing*) which was convened in order to ensure that those who were required to furnish arms for a levy were able to do so (cf. Gul ch. 309; LandsL). The *vápnatak* seems to have lost its connotation of 'validation' in Iceland already by the time *Grágás* was compiled, in which it stands for the end of an assembly, possibly heralded by the clashing of weapons. However the older sense of the word was reintroduced in Iceland during the later medieval period through influence from Norway. In Denmark the *vapntak* went out of use comparatively early. It is mentioned only in SkL as part of the process of removing someone's personal rights (*fredlöshetsförklaring*). *Våbentag* is also the term used by Anders Sunesen (par. 90) to refer to an oath of fealty to one's lord in Denmark. There is no form of *vapntak* extant in the medieval Swedish laws.

close of assembly **OIce** *Grg* Klþ 2, 3 Þsþ 47, 48 Arþ 122 Ómb 128 Feþ 166 Lbþ 177 Fjl 222 Hrs 234 Tíg 259, *Jó* Þfb 5, *Js* Þfb 5

raising of weapons **ONorw** *FrL* Var 46 Jkb 2 LlbB 4, *GuL* Olb

sound of weapons **ODan** *SkL* 145

weapon-taking **OIce** *Grg* Misc 248

See also: *þinglausn, þingtak*

Refs: Brink 2008a; CV s.v. *vápnatak*; F s.v. *vápnatak, vápnaþing*; KLNM s.v. *ceremonivåben, lagting, ting*; Larsson 2009, 151–60; LexMA s.v. *Danelaw, Wapentake*; NF s.v. *vapentag*; NGL V s.v. *vápnatak*

vara (ON) noun

cargo **ONorw** *GuL* Tfb

trade goods **OIce** *Grg* Þsþ 32 Arþ 125 Feþ 166, *Jó* Llb 71 Fml 7, *Js* Ert 2 Kab 20

wares **OIce** *Jó* Fml 2

See also: *varningr*

varafrudagher (OSw) noun

Three major feasts of the Blessed Virgin Mary
Expressions:

varafrudagher i fastu (OSw)

Lady Day (Annunciation, March 25th) **OSw** *VmL* Bb

varafrudagher þæn fyrre (OSw)

Day of Our Lady (Assumption, August 15th) **OSw** *SdmL* Kkb *YVgL* Kkb

varafrudagher þæn öfri (OSw)

Feast of the Nativity of Our Lady (September 8th) **OSw** *UL* Kkb

See also: *mariumæssa*

vararfeldr (ON) noun

cloak of fur **ONorw** *GuL* Mhb

trade cloak **OIce** *Grg* Klþ 4, 5 Fjl 221 Misc 246, *KRA* 15

varðveizla (ON) noun

care **OIce** *Grg* Þsþ 39, 49 Arþ 122 Misc 249, *Jó* Llb 62, *Js* Lbb 1

charge (2) **OIce** *Grg* Tíg 267

custody **OIce** *Jó* Lbb 1

keeping **OIce** *Jó* Mah 1

protection **OIce** *Jó* Sg 1 Fml 29

varðveizlumaðr (ON) noun

caretaker **OIce** *KRA* 30

varfriþer (OSw) **varfriþr** (OGu) noun

The spring peace lasted during the time of sowing (OGu GL), in OSw HL defined as between Rogation Day (*gangdagher litli*, 25 April) and St Botulf's Mass (17 June), during which time lawsuits were prohibited (OSw HL, UL, VmL) and certain rules applied concerning taking and reclaiming draft animals (GL, HL).

spring peace **OSw** *DL* Rb, *SdmL* Rb

spring sanctity **OSw** *HL* Rb

springtime immunity **OSw** *UL* Rb, *VmL* Rb

springtime sanctity **OGu** *GL* A 10

See also: *akerfrith, anfriþer, friþer, høsthælgh, önn (pl. annir)*

Refs: Schlyter s.v. *varfriþer*

vargdropi (ON) noun

Literally 'wolf droppings', a derogatory term for a child conceived during the father's outlawry. Such children were excluded from any inheritance.

outcast's brat **OIce** *Grg* Arþ 118

See also: *biltugher, bæsingr, friþlös, horbarn, hrísungr, rishofþe*

Refs: KLNM s.v. *oäkta barn*; Ney 2012, 484–85; Schlyter s.v. *rishofþe*

varghagarþer (OSw) noun

fenced-in space for trapping wolves **OSw** *YVgL* Föb

wolf trap **OSw** *SdmL* Kkb, Jb

varghanæt (OSw) noun

net for wolves **OSw** *SdmL* Bb, *YVgL* Föb

vargher (OSw) **vargr** (ON) noun

Etymologically presumably 'strangler'. In OSw, used of both wolves and humans, and in OIce, specifically of outlawed criminals. The animal appears as a threat to domestic animals and people, and the hunting of wolves was either an obligation, always done with impunity, or entitled the hunter to a reward from others in the district (SdmL, UL, VmL, YVgL) (cp. *ulv*). In OSw ÄVgL and YVgL, if wolves killed domestic animals in one's care it was occasionally considered neglect, in contrast to bears, which were always seen as superior force.

outcast **OIce** *Grg* Bat 115

wolf **ONorw** *GuL* Krb, Kpb, **OSw** *HL* Blb, *SdmL* Bb, *YVgL* Rlb, Utgb, *ÄVgL* Rlb, Föb

See also: *biorn, brennuvargr, gorvargher, kasnavargher, morðvargr, ulv, vangöma*

Refs: Hellquist s.v. *varg*

varna (ON) verb

abstain from **ONorw** *GuL* Krb

varnaraðili (ON) noun

defence principal **OIce** *Grg* Þsþ 20, 25

varnargagn (ON) **varnargögn** (ON) noun

formal means of proof for the defence **OIce** *Grg* Þsþ 38 Lbþ 176

varnarkviðr (ON) noun

defence panel **OIce** *Grg* Ómb 143

varnarmaðr (ON) noun

defender **ONorw** *FrL* Jkb 8, *GuL* Olb

guardian **ONorw** *FrL* Rgb 36, *GuL* Olb

varningr (ON) noun

trade goods **OIce** *Grg* Klþ 8, *Jó* Fml 8, *KRA* 26

wares **OIce** *Jó* Þjb 23

See also: *vara*

varp (OSw) noun

catch **OSw** *UL* Blb, *VmL* Bb

varskogher (OSw) noun

private woodland **OSw** *UL* Blb

varzla (ON) noun

compensation **ONorw** *FrL* Intr 6

pledge **OIce** *Jó* Llb 50

security **ONorw** *FrL* Intr 6

surety **OIce** *Jó* Kge 15, 17 Llb 64 Þjb 4, *Js* Ert 24

value **ONorw** *FrL* Intr 15

See also: *veðmáli, væþ*

varþa (OSw) **varthe** (ODan) **varþa** (OGu) **varða** (ON) verb

answer for **ODan** *JyL* 2, *SkL* 103, 106, 126, **OGu** *GL* Add. 7 (B 49), **OSw** *HL* Blb, *UL* Jb, Blb, *VmL* Mb, Jb, Bb

be answerable for **OGu** *GL* A 17, 19, 28, Add. 2 (B 17), **OSw** *DL* Mb, *UL* Mb, Jb, *VmL* Kkb, Mb

attend **ONorw** *GuL* Tjb

care for **OSw** *HL* Blb, *ÄVgL* Jb

cause **OGu** *GL* A 18, 19

compensate **ODan** *SkL* 78, *VSjL* 82

concern **OSw** *UL* StfBM, För, Kkb

be in control over **OSw** *ÄVgL* Äb

defend **ODan** *SkL* 17, 179, *VSjL* 82

be forced **OGu** *GL* A 20

guard **OSw** *HL* Blb

hand over **OSw** *UL* Kmb

be liable for **ODan** *SkL* 43, 203, 205, **OGu** *GL* Add. 2 (B 17), **OSw** *UL* Jb, Kmb

pay **ONorw** *GuL* Leb

pay for **OGu** *GL* A 26

protect **ODan** *JyL* 3, **OSw** *UL* Kkb

be punishable by **OIce** *Grg* passim, *KRA* 1, 26, **ONorw** *FrL* KrbA 7 Mhb 10 Var 12

respond for **OSw** *ÄVgL* Jb

be responsible (for) **ODan** *ESjL* 2, *SkL* 235, *VSjL* 41, **OGu** *GL* A 16, 17, 24f (64), 25–27, 36, Add. 7 (B 49), **ONorw** *GuL* Krb, **OSw** *HL* Mb, Blb, *SdmL* Kkb, *UL* Blb, *VmL* Bb, *YVgL* Kkb, Äb, Gb, Rlb, Tb, Jb, Utgb, Add, *ÄVgL* Kkb, Äb, Gb, Rlb, Jb, Tb, Föb

serve **ONorw** *GuL* Llb

take (care of) **OGu** *GL* A 14, 36, **OSw** *UL* Kkb

take care of **ODan** *ESjL* 2

take responsibility for **ODan** *ESjL* 2

vouch for **ODan** *JyL* 1, *VSjL* 23

See also: *atergælda, raþa, uppihalda*

varþalaus (OGu) **varþarlaus** (OGu) adj.

unattended **OGu** *GL* A 36

unprotected **OGu** *GL* Add. 8 (B 55)

unsupervised **OGu** *GL* A 18

varþer (OSw) **varþr** (OGu) **vörðr** (ON) **værþer** (OSw) noun

care **ONorw** *GuL* Kpb, Løb, Arb, Mhb, Olb

guard **OSw** *HL* Kgb, *SdmL* Kgb, Mb

guard duty **OSw** *HL* Kgb

guardianship **OIce** *Jó* Kge 16

protection **OSw** *VmL* Bb

watch **OGu** *GL* A 54, **ONorw** *GuL* Leb, **OSw** *UL* Kgb

See also: *varþhald*

varþhald (OSw) **varðhald** (ON) noun

guard duty **OSw** *HL* Kgb, *SdmL* Kgb

guard posting **OIce** *Jó* Fml 24

watch **ONorw** *GuL* Leb

See also: *leþunger, varþer*

varþing (OSw) **várþing** (ON) noun

A *þing* 'assembly' held in spring. In OIce Grg, the venue for *sóknarþing* (see *soknaþing*) and *skuldaþing* (q.v.), dealing with verdicts and payments respectively, and presumably held in each quarter (ON *fjórðung*, see *fiarþunger*). In OSw YVgL, appearing, along with *höstþing* (q.v.) 'assembly held in autumn', in the context of refusal to fence, suggesting that this *þing* dealt with local village matters, but also appearing in reference to *ræfsingaþing* (q.v.), literally 'punishment assembly'.

spring assembly **OIce** *Grg* Klþ 4, 10 Þsþ 49, 54 Vís 100 Lrþ 117 Arþ 122 Ómb 128 Feþ 147, **OSw** *YVgL* Utgb, Add

See also: *þing*

Refs: KLNM s.v. *várþing*

varþmaþer (OSw) **varðmaðr** (ON) noun

A general term for watchman or guard. The context of Grg Misc 248 suggests that there was some form of organized watch in Norwegian trading centres (ON *kaupangar*, see *köpunger*). In HL IX it is specified that guardsmen had to be householders and residents, not vagrants (OSw *löskæ mæn*, see *löska*). HL IX also makes mention of where guards could be posted, including the hills (OSw *bærgvarþer*), headlands (OSw *næsiavarþer*) and at harbours. Concerning the last, SdmL XII stipulates that a *varþmaþer* watching over a ship was liable to pay a fine if something were stolen from it.

guard **OSw** *HL* Kgb, *SdmL* Kgb

warden **OIce** *Grg* Misc 248

See also: *byavarþer, bærgvarþer, köpunger*

Refs: CV; Fritzner; GrgTr II:211; Hertzberg

varþnaþahion (OSw) noun

servant **OSw** *HL* Blb

varþnaþer (OSw) **varthneth** (ODan) **varnaþer** (OGu) **vardnaþ** (OSw) **varnaþer** (OSw) **varþnæþ** (OSw) noun

custody **OSw** *ÄVgL* Rlb

defender **ODan** *SkL* 146

dependent **OSw** *UL* Kkb, Kgb, Mb, Jb, *VmL* Kkb, Mb

person someone answers for **ODan** *ESjL* 3

protection **OSw** *DL* Gb, *UL* Äb, Blb, *VmL* Äb

responsibility **ODan** *JyL* 2, **OSw** *SdmL* Kkb

someone to vouch **ODan** *SkL* 192

supervision **OGu** *GL* A 36

surety **ODan** *ESjL* 1–3

ward **OGu** *GL* A 21

Expressions:

høghre varthneth (ODan)

higher answering **ODan** *JyL* 1

See also: *hegnan, varþa, vitni*

varþþenningar (pl.) (OGu) noun

This is defined in Schlyter as an annual tax paid in Easter Week by each man on Gotland of age to bear arms and take part in military service. Comparison with other medieval Nordic laws, however, suggests that it might be the penalty for failing to keep watch properly, particularly since in the same chapter mention is made of those keeping watch paying their own expenses.

watch-money **OGu** *GL* A 54

See also: *vaka, varþer, varþhald, varþmaþer, vitavörðr*

Refs: KLNM s.v. *vård och vaka*; Peel 2015, 184–85 note 54/2–4; Schlyter 1877, s.v. *varþþenningar*; SL GL, 287 note 1 to chapter 54

varþveta (OSw) **varðveita** (ON) verb

administer **OIce** *Jó* Kge 5

be in charge of **OIce** *Grg* passim, *Js* Mah 8 Kvg 5 Ert 22, *KRA* 7

keep **OIce** *Jó* Mah 7

look after **OIce** *Jó* Mah 8 Llb 62

manage **OIce** *Jó* Mah 1

preserve **ONorw** *EidsL* 31.4

protect **ONorw** *EidsL* 2.2

provide for **ONorw** *GuL* Arb

be responsible (for) **OSw** *ÄVgL* Jb

take care of **OIce** *Grg* Feþ 156, *Jó* Kge 17 Þjb 15, *Js* Rkb 2 Kab 11, *KRA* 15, **ONorw** *EidsL* 32.2, *FrL* Intr 5 ArbB 20, *GuL* Llb, **OSw** *YVgL* Kkb, *ÄVgL* Kkb

See also: *varþa*

vathegærning (ODan) noun

accident **ODan** *JyL* 2

accidental deed **ODan** *JyL* 2, 3

See also: *vaþi*

vatheløs (ODan) adj.

without harm **ODan** *ESjL* 3

See also: *vaþi*

vathvesar (ODan) **vöðvasár** (ON) noun

case over flesh wounds **ODan** *SkL* 89

flesh wound **ODan** *SkL* 89, 96, **OIce** *Grg* Vís 86

muscle wound **ONorw** *FrL* Mhb 47

vatn (ON) noun

Everyone was to have the same right to use lakes as he had from the past. See GuL ch. 85.

lake **ONorw** *GuL* Llb, Mhb

stream **ONorw** *GuL* Llb

water **ONorw** *GuL* Krb, Llb, Tfb, Mhb, Tjb, Olb

Expressions:

halda undir vatn (ON)

baptise **OIce** *Grg* Þsþ 25

See also: *á*

vatnfynd (OSw) noun

find in water **OSw** *HL* Mb, *SdmL* Tjdb

vatnqværn (OSw) noun

water-mill **OSw** *SdmL* Bb

vatter (OSw) **váttr** (ON) noun

In ON, various types of witnesses, such as eyewitnesses (ONorw FrL, GuL), compurgators at denials (ONorw FrL) and those giving testimony concerning legal proceedings at the *þing* 'assembly' (ONorw Eids, FrL, GuL). In OSw, a witness in a *tylft* (oath of twelve) and only appearing in an oath formula.

man of oath **OSw** *YVgL* Tb

witness **OIce** *Grg* passim, *Jó* Þfb 4, 8 Mah 2, 24, *Js* Þfb 6 Kvg 1 Lbb 1 Kab 2, *KRA* 3, 11, **ONorw** *BorgL* 14.5, *EidsL* 7, *FrL* Intr 15, 16 Tfb 2 KrbA 16, 22 KrbB 5 Mhb 8, **OSw** *YVgL* Kkb, Add, *ÄVgL* Kkb, Md, Smb, Vs, Gb, Rlb, Jb, Tb

witness (i.e. person giving testimony) **ONorw** *GuL* Arb, Kpb, Llb, Mhb, Tjb, Krb, Løb, Olb, Tfb, Kvr, Leb

See also: *lögváttr, vætti*

Refs: Cleasby and Vigfusson s.v. *váttr*; Fritzner s.v. *váttr*; Hertzberg s.v. *váttr*; Schlyter s.v. *vatter*

vatubanda (OGu) noun

The *vatubanda* was a provisional 'legally witnessed or testified safety circle', later replaced by a more permanent one drawn up during the general period of peace following Easter. Of the medieval Nordic provincial laws, this word occurs only in GL. Kock suggests a relationship with Norwegian *vátta*, 'take notice of; suffice', giving *vatubanda* as 'a circle of safety that one took notice of', or which 'sufficed for the time being'. Wessén thinks that a more likely root is a Gutnish *vatta* or *vata* f. with a meaning related to Old Swedish *vat, vatt* f., 'the twelve men collectively swearing an oath; the oath itself' or *vatter, vætti* m., 'one of the twelve witness; the witness statement itself'. This may be compared to the expressions *vattum minum* and *vattum sinum* in ÄVgL (Md 1 and 3, Gb 7) and YVgL (Kkb 3 and Tb 1). The concept would thus be one of a 'witnessed safety circle'. Comparison may be made with provisions related to the Icelandic *fjörbaugsgarðr*, 'lesser outlawry'.

testified safety circle **OGu** *GL* A 13

See also: *banda, bandavereldi, fjörbaugsgarðr, grið, vatter, værgæld*

Refs: KLNM s.v. *drab*; Kock 1918, 364–68; SL GL, 256–57 note 9; Peel 2015, 111–13 notes 13/7–13/23–24; Schlyter 1877, s.v. *vatubanda*

vax (ON) noun

wax **ONorw** *GuL* Krb

vaxtalauss (ON) adj.

without interest **OIce** *Grg* Vís 97 Ómb 143 Misc 249

See also: *leigulauss, óleigis, vöxtr*

vaþ (OSw) noun

boundary path **OSw** *SdmL* Bb

path **OSw** *DL* Bb

vaþablod (OSw) noun

blood spilled by accident **OSw** *YVgL* Kkb, *ÄVgL* Kkb

See also: *vaþi*

vaþabot (OSw) **waþæ bot** (OSw) noun

accident compensation **OSw** *UL* Kkb, Äb, Mb, Kmb, *VmL* Kkb, Äb, Mb, Kmb

accident fine **OSw** *SdmL* Kkb, Bb, Kmb, Mb

accidental damage compensation **OSw** *DL* Mb, Bb, *UL* Blb, Add. 14, *VmL* Bb

book of accidental cases **OSw** *ÖgL* Eb

compensation for accidental injury **OSw** *UL* Mb, Blb, *VmL* Mb

compensation for an accidental act **OSw** *HL* Blb, *UL* Mb, *VmL* Mb

misadventure compensation **OSw** *HL* Mb

misadventure fine **OSw** *HL* Mb

See also: *bot, böta, fulder, gælda (1), vaþagæld, vaþi*

vaþabrænna (OSw) noun

burning by accident **OSw** *YVgL* Utgb

See also: *brandvaþa*

vaþadrap (OSw) noun

accidental killing **OSw** *SdmL* Mb, *VmL* Mb (rubric only)

See also: *drap, ofsinnisvatn, vaþaeþer, vaþaværk, vaþi, viliaværk*

vaþaelder (OSw) **váðaeldr** (ON) noun

accidental fire **OIce** *Jó* Llb 29, **OSw** *SdmL* Bb

fire by accident **OSw** *HL* Blb

See also: *brandvaþa, vaþi*

vaþaeþer (OSw) noun

accident oath **OSw** *SdmL* Kkb, Bb, Mb

misadventure oath **OSw** *HL* Mb

oath about/concerning misadventure **OSw** *HL* Mb, *YVgL* Add

oath as to accidental damage **OSw** *DL* Mb, Bb, *UL* Kkb, Mb, Blb, Add. 14, *VmL* Kkb, Mb, Bb *oath as to accidental injury* **OSw** *UL* Mb, *VmL* Mb

oath as to an accident **OSw** *UL* Mb, *VmL* Mb, Bb

oath concerning accidental injury
case **OSw** *YVgL* Vs

oath of accidental deed **OSw** *ÖgL* Db, Vm

See also: *eþer, ofsinnisvatn, vaþadrap, vaþaværk, vaþi, viliaværk*

vaþagæld (OSw) **waþagælld** (OSw) noun

accidental damage compensation **OSw** *DL* Mb, Bb

accidental injury compensation **OSw** *UL* Kkb, Mb, Blb, *VmL* Kkb, Mb, Bb

compensation for an accidental act **OSw** *HL* Blb

compensation for misadventure **OSw** *HL* Mb

misadventure payment **OSw** *HL* Mb

See also: *vaþabot, vaþi*

vaþahug (OSw) noun

accidental wound **OSw** *YVgL* Frb, *ÄVgL* Slb

See also: *vaþi*

vaþakast (OSw) noun

wagering **OSw** *DL* Bb

See also: *væþ*

vaþalæst (OSw) noun

defect by accident **OSw** *ÄVgL* Smb

See also: *vaþi*

vaþamal (OSw) noun

accidental case **OSw** *ÖgL* Vm

case of accidents **OSw** *ÖgL* Vm

See also: *mal (1), vaþi*

vaþasar (OSw) **vathesar** (ODan) noun

accidental wound **ODan** *ESjL* 3, *SkL* 108

wound by accident **OSw** *ÄVgL* Vs

See also: *sar, vaþi*

vaþaskena (OSw) noun

accidental scratch **OSw** *YVgL* Vs, *ÄVgL* Vs

See also: *skena, vaþi*

vaþaskuver (OSw) noun

accidental pushing **OSw** *SdmL* Mb

See also: *vaþi*

vaþaværk (OSw) **vatheværk** (ODan) **váðaverk** (ON) noun

accident **ODan** *JyL* 2, **OIce** *Grg* Vís 92, *Jó* Mah 13 Fml 19, *Js* Mah 8, 30, *KRA* 11, **ONorw** *EidsL* 37.5, **OSw** *YVgL* Äb, Add, *ÄVgL* Äb

accidental act **OSw** *UL* Mb, *VmL* Mb

something done unwillingly **ONorw** *FrL* LlbB 8

unintentional harm **ONorw** *GuL* Mhb

unwitting injury **ONorw** *FrL* Var 21

See also: *ofsinnisvatn, vaþabot, vaþadrap, vaþaeþer, vaþi, viliagærning, viliaværk*

vaþi (OSw) **vathe** (ODan) **vaþi** (OGu) **váði** (ON) noun

Literally 'danger; accident; harm'. In the laws primarily contrasted to *vili* 'will', a distinction presumed to be influenced by canon law. Definitions and examples of deeds characterized as committed by *vaþi* differ, but generally, harm done by animals, inanimate objects, particularly those under no direct control of their owner, as well as by dependent people — women, minors, the insane — were seen as done by *vaþi*. Whether a deed was done by *vaþi* or by *vili* had legal consequences; a deed done by *vaþi* was less severely punished — if punished at all — and was seen as a breach only against the victim, not against society.

accident **ODan** *ESjL* 2, 3, *JyL* 2, 3, *SkKL* 9, *SkL* 96, 102, 108, 168, 172, *VSjL* 26, **OGu** *GL* A 23, **ONorw** *EidsL* 37.4, **OSw** *DL* Mb, Bb, *HL* Mb, *SdmL* Kkb, KgbBb, Mb, *UL* Kkb, Äb, Mb, *VmL* Kkb, Äb, Mb, *YVgL* Utgb, Add, *ÄVgL* Vs, *ÖgL* Eb, Db, Vm

accidental act **OSw** *DL* Mb, *UL* Mb, Blb

danger **OIce** *Grg* Vís 108

injury **OGu** *GL* A 27, **ONorw** *GuL* Mhb

misadventure **OGu** *GL* A 18, **OSw** *HL* Äb, Mb

Expressions:

handlös vaþi (OSw) **handløs vathe** (ODan)

handless accident **ODan** *ESjL* 2 *SkL* 102, 205

misadventure **OSw** *HL* Mb

misadventure without interference by someone **OSw** *HL* Mb

mæþ vaþa (OSw) **mæþ uaþæ** (ODan)

accidentally, by accident **ODan** *SkL* 172 **OSw** *UL* Kgb, Äb, Mb, Blb *VmL* Äb, Mb, Bb

by accident **OSw** *HL* Mb

by misadventure **OSw** *HL* Äb

See also: *avund, brandvaþa, handaværk, ofsinnisvatn, vaþadrap, vaþaeþer, vaþaværk, vili, viliagærning, viliandis, viliaværk, vreþe*

Refs: Descheemaeker 2009, 70–73; KLNM s.v.v. *förbrytelse, vådaverk*; Tamm and Vogt, eds, 2016, 300

vaþmal (OSw) **vaðmál** (ON) noun

Woven woollen cloth, occasionally appearing as currency or payment. Appears in a list of currencies in Jb Þjb 23, and its value is discussed in Grg Misc 246.

homespun **OIce** *Grg* Klþ 2, 4 Þsþ 78 Ómb 143, *Jó* Sg 1 Llb 34 Þjb 23, *KRA* 14, 15 *homespun wool* **OSw** *ÖgL* Db

payment cloth **ONorw** *BorgL* 12.18

wadmal **ONorw** *GuL* Løb, Mhb

woollen cloth **ONorw** *FrL* KrbA 8

See also: *alin*, *læript*

Refs: KLNM s.v. *vadmål*

vaþstang (OSw) noun

OSw *vaþ* refers to a boundary between meadows (SdmL Jb 4). To mark it, you walk (*vaþa* v.) or ride in a straight line between stakes (*vaþ stang*) set at the boundary markers.

pole for marking a boundary path **OSw** *SdmL* Bb

See also: *mælistang*, *rep*, *stangfall*

Refs: Schlyter s.v. *vaþ*

váglati (ON) noun

accident **OIce** *Grg* Fjl 224

vágr (ON) noun

cove **ONorw** *GuL* Kvr

vágrek (ON) noun

wave drift **OIce** *Grg* Lbþ 218, *Jó* Llb 61, 71, *Js* Rkb 1

vánarmaðr (ON) noun

man expecting an inheritance **ONorw** *FrL* ArbB 10

vápnaburðr (ON) noun

bearing of arms **OIce** *Grg* Tíg 263

vápnaspell (ON) noun

damage to weapons **ONorw** *GuL* Tfb

vápnaþing (ON) noun

A *þing* 'assembly' for inspecting the weapons of those obliged to participate in the ON *leiðangr* 'levy' (see *leþunger*).

assembly to muster weapons **ONorw** *FrL* Rgb 3

inspection of weapons **ONorw** *GuL* Leb

See also: *þing*

Refs: Fritzner s.v. *vápnaþing*; Hertzberg s.v. *vápnaþing*

várfóðr (ON) noun

spring fodder **ONorw** *GuL* Llb

várkunn (ON) noun

extenuating circumstance **OIce** *Jó* Mah 18

vártíund (ON) noun

spring tithe **OIce** *Grg* Tíg 260

vátta (ON) verb

attest **OIce** *Js* Mah 36

indicate **OIce** *Jó* Sg 1 Llb 20

prescribe **OFar** *Seyð* 10

say **OIce** *Jó* Þfb 1

set **OIce** *Jó* HT 2

testify **OFar** *Seyð* 0

witness **OFar** *Seyð* 11

váttakvöð (ON) noun

calling witnesses **OIce** *Grg* Misc 252

váttasaga (ON) noun

deposition **OIce** *Jó* Kge 12

testimony **OIce** *Js* Ert 18

testimony of witnesses **ONorw** *GuL* Kpb, Arb

váttbærr (ON) adj.

able to testify **ONorw** *FrL* Rgb 7

admissible as a witness **OIce** *Jó* Llb 40, *Js* Mah 12

allowed to testify **ONorw** *FrL* Mhb 15 LlbA 25

váttlauss (ON) **váttalauss** (ON) adj.

without witnesses **OIce** *Grg* Feþ 169 Fjl 221, *Jó* Lbb 6

váttorð (ON) noun

testimony **OIce** *Grg* Klþ 5 Þsþ 26, 32 Vís 99 Fjl 221 Rsþ 227 Misc 237 Tíg 263

witness **OIce** *Grg* Misc 251

veðflærð (ON) noun

pledge fraud **OIce** *Js* Kab 17

See also: *veðfox*

veðfox (ON) noun

fraudulent pledge **OIce** *Jó* Kab 22

veðjaðardómr (ON) **veðjanardómr** (ON) noun

court of appeal **ONorw** *FrL* Rgb 15 Jkb 8

See also: *domber*, *væþ*, *væþia*

veðjun (ON) **veðjan** (ON) noun

decision made by bet **ONorw** *GuL* Olb

veðmáli (ON) noun

pledge **OIce** *Grg* Þsþ 49, 62

See also: *varzla*, *væþ*

veðmæla (ON) verb

pledge **OIce** *Grg* Fjl 223

vegabót (ON) noun

improvement of highways **ONorw** *FrL* KrbB 19

vegarán (ON) noun

unlawful prevention of someone using a path **OIce** *Jó* Llb 44

vegarfall (ON) noun

hindering of travel **OIce** *Jó* Llb 45

veggjarhlaza (ON) noun

building of walls **OIce** *Jó* Llb 2

See also: *garðlag*

veginn (ON) adj.

killed **OIce** *Grg* Þsþ 25 Vís 86, 87 Bat 113, *Jó* Mah 10, **ONorw** *FrL* Mhb 14

vegsl (OGu) noun

> *having to flee* **OGu** *GL* A 14

vegþueri (OGu) noun

> *blocking of the way* **OGu** *GL* A 19

veiðiá (ON) noun

> *fishing stream* **OIce** *Jó* Llb 56

veiðibúð (ON) noun

> *hunting shed* **OIce** *Jó* Llb 59, **ONorw** *FrL* LlbB 8

veiðispell (ON) noun

> *spoiled catching rights* **OIce** *Js* Lbb 24

veiðistígr (ON) noun

> *course of a hunted animal* **ONorw** *GuL* Llb

veiðistöð (ON) veiðistaðr (ON) noun

> *catching place* **OIce** *Grg* Lbþ 208, *Js* Lbb 24
> *fishing place* **OIce** *Jó* Llb 17, **ONorw** *GuL* Llb
> *fishing waters* **OIce** *Jó* Llb 56
> *hunting grounds* **ONorw** *FrL* LlbA 9

veiðivatn (ON) noun

> *fishing waters* **OIce** *Jó* Llb 56, **ONorw** *GuL* Llb

veiðivél (ON) noun

> *fishing gear* **ONorw** *GuL* Llb

veiðr (ON) noun

> *catch* **ONorw** *GuL* Llb
> *catching* **OIce** *Jó* Llb 61
> *catching rights* **OIce** *Grg* Lbþ 174, 208, *Jó* Lbb 4, 6 Llb 6, *Js* Lbb 2
> *hunting* **ONorw** *GuL* Llb

veilendi (ON) vélindi (ON) noun

> *ailment* **OIce** *Grg* Þsþ 32 Feþ 144

veita (ON) noun

> *irrigation* **OIce** *Jó* Llb 22, 56
> *irrigation channels* **OIce** *Grg* Lbþ 187

veizlujörð (ON) noun

> Land given by the king to his officials, esp. landed men, on certain conditions: Such land was not to be used by others (GuL ch. 101) and could not be sold (GuL ch. 264).
> *land held as a grant* **ONorw** *GuL* Llb, Mhb, Tjb
> See also: *væzla*
> Refs: KLNM s.v.v. *embedsindtægter, gästning, kungsgård, veitsle*

vekja (ON) verb

> *begin* **ONorw** *GuL* Mhb
> *call forth* **ONorw** *GuL* Krb

vela (OGu) verb

> *conspire* **OGu** *GL* A 14

veldi (ON) noun

> *authority* **OIce** *Grg* Tíg 255

vengi (OGu) noun

> *pillow* **OGu** *GL* A 20
> See also: *raiþvengi*

vensl (OGu) venzl (OGu) noun

> *suspicion* **OGu** *GL* A 4, Add. 8 (B 55)

verðgangr (ON) noun

> Vagrancy, particularly — but not exclusively — of beggars.
> *vagrancy* **OIce** *Grg* Arþ 118
> Refs: Cleasby and Vigfusson s.v. *verð-gangr*; Fritzner s.v. *verðgangr*

verðlauss (ON) adj.

> *without payment* **ONorw** *GuL* Olb

verðr (ON) adj.

> *entitled to* **ONorw** *GuL* Kpb, Tfb, Olb
> *worth* **ONorw** *GuL* Løb

verðslykðing (ON) noun

> *price* **OIce** *Jó* Llb 11

verelzmaþr (OGu) noun

> *layman* **OGu** *GL* A 7

verkafall (ON) noun

> *loss of use* **OIce** *Jó* Llb 39

verkakaup (ON) noun

> *work wages* **OIce** *Grg* Þsþ 78
> See also: *köp, legha*

verkasveinn (ON) noun

> *workman* **ONorw** *GuL* Løb
> See also: *sven, verkmaðr*

verkatjón (ON) noun

> *loss of work* **OIce** *Jó* Kab 25, *Js* Kab 19, **ONorw** *GuL* Løb

verkfórr (ON) adj.

> *able to work* **ONorw** *GuL* Løb
> *capable of working* **OIce** *Jó* Mah 29

verkhailigr (OGu) adj.

> *designated holy* **OGu** *GL* A 8
> Expressions:
> **verkhailigr dagr** (OGu)
> *holy day* **OGu** *GL* A 8
> See also: *dagher, hælghidagher*

verkkaupamaðr (ON) noun

> *piece-worker* **OIce** *Jó* Kab 25
> See also: *verkakaup, vinnumaðr*

verklaun (ON) noun

> *compensation for loss of work* **ONorw** *GuL* Mhb

verkmaðr (ON) noun

> *workman* **OIce** *Grg* Klþ 17 Vís 89, *Jó* Sg 1, *KRA* 30, **ONorw** *FrL* KrbB 19 Rgb 10, *GuL* Løb

See also: *verkasveinn*

verkviðr (ON) noun

> *timber* **ONorw** *GuL* Llb

See also: *langviðr*, *timber*

veta (OSw) vaita (OGu) veita (OGu) veita (ON) vaita (OSw) veita (OSw) væitta (OSw) væta (OSw) verb

> *cause* **OGu** *GL* A 11, 12, 17
>
> *commit* **OSw** *ÄVgL* Rlb
>
> *give* **ONorw** *GuL* Kpb
>
> *grant* **OSw** *YVgL* Kvab
>
> *happen* **ONorw** *GuL* Krb
>
> *impose* **OSw** *SmL*
>
> *lead water* **ONorw** *GuL* Llb
>
> *serve* **ONorw** *GuL* Mhb
>
> *take off* **ONorw** *GuL* Llb
>
> *testify* **OSw** *ÄVgL* Slb

vetrarstefna (ON) noun

> *term which expires at the end of the winter* **ONorw** *GuL* Olb

vetrhagi (ON) noun

> *winter pasture* **OIce** *Jó* Llb 51

vetrhús (ON) noun

> *winter dwelling* **ONorw** *GuL* Krb, Tfb
>
> *winter residence* **OIce** *Jó* Kge 31

vetrrugr (ON) noun

> *winter rye* **ONorw** *GuL* Llb

vetrvist (ON) noun

> *winter board and lodging* **OIce** *Grg* Þsþ 80

veþa (OSw) veiða (ON) verb

> Fishing and hunting were subject to a number of restrictions. See, e.g., GuL chs 85, 91, 94, and 149.
>
> *catch* **OIce** *Grg* Lbþ 208
>
> *fish* **ONorw** *GuL* Llb
>
> *have the right to fish* **OIce** *Jó* Llb 56
>
> *hunt* **OIce** *KRA* 26, **ONorw** *GuL* Llb, Kvr
>
> *kill* **OSw** *HL* Blb
>
> Refs: KLNM s.v.v. *fiskeret, jakt, laxfiske, skalljakt, säljakt, älgjakt*

veþur (OGu) noun

> *ram* **OGu** *GL* A 43, 44, *GS* Ch. 2

vébönd (pl.) (ON) noun

> A rope or cord attached to stakes, which surrounded certain courts, such as the *lögrétta* 'Law Council' at an assembly. A description of the *vébönd* using ropes and hazel poles is given in *Egils saga*. Most likely considered a hallowed area, as the first element (ON *vé*, see *vi*) was used throughout the North to indicate pre-Christian holy grounds. The tradition is thought to be very old, as a similar practice is known from the eighth-century *Lex Ribuaria*.
>
> It was the duty of the *ármaðr* (q.v.) (FrL Tfb 2) or the *lögmaðr* (see *laghmaþer*) (Js Þfb 3) to set up the *vébönd* at assemblies. The term also appears in Magnus Lagabætr's *Bylov*, where it is used in Norwegian guild houses, and in the Faroese *Hundabrævið*. In *Hirðskrá* 38 it is stated that the king's banner was to be placed within a *vébönd* at musters.
>
> *boundary ropes* **OIce** *Jó* Þfb 3, *Js* Þfb 3
>
> *enclosure* **ONorw** *FrL* Tfb 2
>
> *holiness of the assembly* **ONorw** *FrL* Tfb 2
>
> See also: *banda*, *vatubanda*, *vi*
>
> Refs: Brink 2004b; CV s.v. *vébönd*; Fritzner s.v. *vébönd*; KLNM s.v.v. *dómhringr, krigsbytte, tingsted, vi*; LexMA s.v. *Ding > II. Skandinavien*; Riisøy 2013; von See 1964, 129–30

véfang (ON) noun

> *divided judgement* **OIce** *Grg* Þsþ 40, 42 Lbþ 176

véfangseiðr (ON) noun

> *divided judgement oath* **OIce** *Grg* Þsþ 42 Lrþ 117
>
> See also: *eþer*

véfangsmál (ON) noun

> *divided judgement speech* **OIce** *Grg* Þsþ 42

véfengja (ON) verb

> *give divided judgements* **OIce** *Grg* Þsþ 58 Lbþ 176

vélaboð (ON) noun

> *fraud* **ONorw** *GuL* Olb

vélakaup (ON) noun

> *fraudulent agreement* **OIce** *Jó* Kge 12
>
> *fraudulent contract* **OIce** *Jó* Kge 30, **ONorw** *GuL* Løb

vélasókn (ON) noun

> *fraudulent prosecution* **ONorw** *GuL* Kpb
>
> *fraudulent suit* **OIce** *Jó* Kab 10

vélaverk (ON) noun

> *fraud* **ONorw** *GuL* Olb

véllauss (ON) vélalauss (ON) adj.

> *without deceit* **ONorw** *FrL* Jkb 1
>
> *without guile* **OIce** *Grg* Þsþ 22, 44 Arþ 123 Lbþ 172

vi (OGu) noun

> The context in which *vi*, ON *vé*, is used in GL is as one of five objects of the verb *heta* (OGu *haita*), 'pray to' and in GS as one of the five objects of the verb *troþa*, 'believe in'. The other objects of these verbs

are 'groves and grave howes, ancient sites and heathen idols'. This suggests that, at least in Gotland, it might have meant something more concrete and specific than simply a 'holy place', but no assumptions can be made from any archaeological finds yet made. It seems to have referred to a place in which pagan sacrifices were conducted, sometimes specifically to one god, although not all place-names containing the element *vi*, either as a prefix or suffix, can be associated with that meaning. Many seem to derive from *viþer*, 'wood'. The etymological relationship between *vi* and the town name Visby is debatable and references in Peel 2015 discuss this. It appears that there was a place-name *Vi* at the time that GS was written, since it is referred to in one of the story elements, but there are arguments for the name referring to a natural feature of the land, rather than its being a 'holy place'.

holy place **OGu** *GL* A 4, *GS* Ch. 1

See also: *guþ*, *heta*, *hörgr*, *hult*, *høgh*, *lunder*, *stafgarþr*, *sten*, *vébönd (pl.)*

Refs: Brink 2004a, 291–316; KLNM s.v. *vi*; Peel 2015, 97 note 4/4, 261–62, 290 note 1/44–46, 302–03 note 3/8; Schlyter 1877, s.v. *vi*; SL GL, 248–49 note 2, 304 note 13, 312 note 33

vidve (ODan) noun

widow **ODan** *ESjL* 3, *JyL* Fort

viða (ON) verb

build a barricade in a stream **ONorw** *GuL* Llb

See also: *viða*, *viða*

viða (ON) noun

barricade **ONorw** *GuL* Llb

viðarflutning (ON) noun

timber salvaging **OIce** *Grg* Lbþ 211

viðarhlass (ON) noun

cart-load of wood **ONorw** *GuL* Llb

viðarmark (ON) noun

timber-mark **OIce** *Grg* Lbþ 209, *Jó* Llb 60

viðarspell (ON) noun

wood damage **ONorw** *FrL* LlbA 11

viðarverð (ON) noun

value of timber **OIce** *Grg* Arþ 122

value of wood **ONorw** *FrL* LlbA 10

viðrbjóðandi (ON) noun

counter-bidder **OIce** *Grg* Lbþ 192

viðrelði (ON) **viðreldi** (ON) noun

livestock **ONorw** *GuL* Krb

viðrelðistíund (ON) noun

tithe of stock **ONorw** *FrL* KrbA 18

viðrmæli (ON) noun

defence **OIce** *Jó* Þfb 9, *Js* Kab 3

See also: *værn*

viðrtaka (ON) noun

reception of stolen property **ONorw** *GuL* Tjb

See also: *viþertaka*

viðtaka (ON) noun

payment received **OIce** *Grg* Þsþ 49, 62

reception **OIce** *Jó* Fml 26

viðtökumaðr (ON) noun

rightful receiver **OIce** *Grg* Fjl 221, *Jó* Kge 17

vigh (OSw) **vigh** (ODan) **vig** (OGu) **víg** (ON) noun

A common term for combat or killing/homicide, especially in the Icelandic in Norwegian laws. Equivalent to ODan and OSw *drap* (q.v.). Used in contrast to *morþ/morð* 'murder'.

battle **OGu** *GL* A 20, **OSw** *UL* Äb, Add. 2

fight **ODan** *JyL* 2, **OIce** *Jó* Mah 7, **OSw** *ÄVgL* Urb

fighting **OSw** *HL* Äb

force **OSw** *HL* Rb

killing **OIce** *Grg* Þsþ 25 Vís 86, 87 Ómb 143 Misc 238, *Jó* Mah 8, 9, *Js* Mah 11, 14, **ONorw** *FrL* KrbA 10 Mhb 5, *GuL* Mhb, **OSw** *YVgL* Drb

manslaughter/homicide **OSw** *ÄVgL* Md

Expressions:

vigh ok værn (OSw)

force of arms **OSw** *UL* Mb *VmL* Mb, Rb

See also: *dræpa*, *orosta*, *striþ*, *valdsgærning*, *valdsværk*, *víglýsing*

Refs: CV s.v. *víg*; Fritzner s.v. *víg*; GAO s.v. *Totschlag*; Hertzberg s.v. *víg*; Maček 2009; Riisøy 2014; von See 1964, 21–22

vighanzvakn (OSw) noun

drawn weapon **OSw** *HL* Kgb

vigharf (OSw) **vighærfþ** (OSw) noun

May refer to an inheritance of weapons and/or to an obligation to avenge a killing.

combat inheritance **OSw** *HL* Äb

See also: *arf*, *vigh*

Refs: Brink forthcoming

vigharvi (OSw) noun

combat heir **OSw** *HL* Äb

vigher (OSw) **vígr** (ON) adj.

fit for combat **OSw** *HL* Jb, Rb

Expressions:

eiga vígt um (ON)

entitled to defend and revenge **ONorw** *GuL* Krb

vigher ok vælför (OSw)

sturdy and secure **OSw** *UL* Jb, Blb *VmL* Bb

vighia (OSw) **vighje** (ODan) **vigia** (OGu) **vígja** (ON) **via** (OSw) verb

anoint **OSw** *UL* Kgb

bless **ONorw** *EidsL* 2.1, *FrL* KrbA 32, *GuL* Krb, **OSw** *DL* Kkb, Mb, *HL* Kkb, *SdmL* Kkb, *UL* Kkb, *VmL* Kkb

consecrate **ODan** *SkKL* 1, 3, **OGu** *GL* A 3, *GS* Ch. 3, **OIce** *KRA* 3, 4, **ONorw** *EidsL* 40.2, *FrL* KrbA 8, **OSw** *DL* Kkb, *HL* Kkb, *SdmL* Kkb, Kgb, *SmL*, *UL* Kkb, *VmL* Kkb, *YVgL* Kkb, *ÄVgL* Kkb, *ÖgL* Kkb

inaugurate **OSw** *SdmL* Till

marry **ODan** *ESjL* 1, 3, *JyL* 1, *VSjL* 86, **OSw** *DL* Kkb, *HL* Kkb, *UL* Kkb, Äb, *VmL* Kkb, Äb, *ÖgL* Kkb

ordain **OGu** *GL* Add. 1 (B 4)

wed **OSw** *HL* Kkb, Äb

See also: *vighthman*

vighning (OSw) **víging** (ON) noun

consecration **ONorw** *BorgL* 18.2, **OSw** *UL* Kkb (table of contents only), *VmL* Kkb

wedding **OSw** *UL* Kkb

See also: *hionavighning, vigsl*

vighramannaskin (OSw) noun

Literally 'skin (supplied) by men fit for combat'. A tax paid in animal skin replacing the *leþungsskin* (q.v.) when the *leþunger* 'levy' was cancelled. Contrasted to the other skin-taxes, *bælskin* (q.v.) and *leþungsskin* (q.v.).

{vighramannaskin}-tax **OSw** *DL* Rb

Refs: KLNM s.v. *skinnskatt*; Schlyter s.v. *skin*

vighramannatal (OSw) noun

number of men allowed to bear arms **OSw** *HL* Kkb

See also: *hafþatal, mantal, tal*

vighthman (ODan) noun

consecrated man **ODan** *SkKL* 8

ordained man **ODan** *JyL* 2

vighvalder (OSw) **vighisvalder** (OSw) **vighvaller** (OSw) noun

place of a crime **OSw** *YVgL* Drb, *ÄVgL* Smb

scene of the killing **OSw** *DL* Mb, *UL* Mb, *VmL* Mb, *ÖgL* Db

site of a killing **OSw** *HL* Kkb

See also: *vigh*

vigniauri (OGu) noun

testicle **OGu** *GL* A 19

vigsl (OSw) **vigsl** (OGu) **vígsla** (ON) **vighilsi** (OSw) **vixl** (OSw) noun

consecration **OGu** *GL* A 3, 8, **ONorw** *BorgL* 18.1, **OSw** *DL* Kkb, *SdmL* Kkb, Kgb, Till, *SmL*, *YVgL* Kkb, Rlb, *ÄVgL* Kkb, Rlb, *ÖgL* Kkb

marriage **OSw** *DL* Kkb

ordination **OIce** *Grg* Klþ 6

wedding **OSw** *VmL* Kkb, *YVgL* Kkb

See also: *brullöp, gifta, giftarmal, vighia, vighning*

vigslafæ (OSw) noun

consecration fee **OSw** *DL* Kkb, *VmL* Kkb

vika (OSw) noun

nautical mile **OSw** *HL* Rb

See also: *ukesjo*

vild (OSw) **vild** (ODan) **vild** (ON) **vilð** (ON) **villir** (OSw) noun

favourable gift **OSw** *SdmL* Jb

prejudice **ODan** *JyL* 2

Expressions:

með vilð (ON)

on purpose **OIce** *Jó* Fml 19

vildigh (ODan) adj.

partial **ODan** *JyL* Fort

See also: *uvildigh*

vilðr (ON) **vildr** (ON) adj.

good **ONorw** *GuL* Mhb

vili (OSw) **vilje** (ODan) **vilia** (OGu) **vili** (ON) noun

Literally, 'will'. Mainly contrasted to *vaþi* 'accident', a distinction presumed to be influenced by canon law. Definitions and examples of deeds characterized as committed by *vili* differ greatly. Whether a deed was done by *vili* or by *vaþi* had legal consequences; a deed done by *vili* was more severely punished and was seen as a breach not only against the victim but also against society.

acceptance **OSw** *HL* Mb

accord **OIce** *KRA* 12

agreement **OGu** *GL* A 32, **OSw** *UL* Kkb, Jb, Add. 1, *VmL* Kkb, Jb

consent **ODan** *ESjL* 2, 3, *JyL* Fort, 1, 3, *SkKL* 2, *SkL* 167, 219, *VSjL* 14, 53, 87, **OGu** *GL* A 28, **OSw** *DL* Bb, Gb, *HL* Kkb, Äb, Mb, Blb, *SmL*, *UL* Äb, Mb, Jb, Blb, Add. 6, *VmL* Äb, Bb, *YVgL* Add

desire **OGu** *GL* A 1, **OSw** *UL* Rb

inclination **OGu** *GL* A 24

intent **ODan** *ESjL* 2, 3, *SkKL* 9, *SkL* 168, *VSjL* 26, 57, 58, **OSw** *HL* Mb, *SdmL* Kgb, Bb, Mb, Rb, Till, *ÖgL* Db, Vm

intent (to damage) **OSw** *YVgL* Add

intention **OIce** *Jó* Þfb 5 Mah 2, **OSw** *SdmL* Bb, *UL* Blb, *VmL* Bb, *ÖgL* Eb

permission **ODan** *ESjL* 2, *SkL* 201, **OSw** *VmL* Jb

purpose **OSw** *HL* Äb

will (1) **ODan** *JyL* 1–3, *SkL* 108, 172, 226, **OGu**
GL Add. 1 (B 4), **OIce** *KRA* 13, **OSw** *DL* Gb,
Tjdb, *HL* Äb, Mb, *UL* Mb, *YVgL* Utgb, Add
wish **ODan** *ESjL* 1, *SkL* 50, 131, **ONorw**
GuL Krb, Kvb, Leb, **OSw** *HL* Kkb
Expressions:
avund ok ilder vili (OSw) **avend ok ilvilje** (ODan)
malignancy and wrath **OSw** *YVgL* Rlb
hate or ill will **ODan** *SkL* 149
at vili (ODan) **at vilja** (ON)
deliberately **ONorw** *GuL* Leb
wilfully **ODan** *JyL* 3
mæþ vilia (OSw) **mæth vilje** (ODan)
according to the wishes **ODan** *SkL* 131
by will **OSw** *HL* Mb
intentionally **OSw** *UL* Mb *VmL* Mb
ODan *ESjL* 3 *SkL* 168 *VSjL* 57, 58
on purpose **OSw** *HL* Äb
wilfully **ODan** *SkL* 108, 172, 226
with consent **ODan** *SkL* 219
with intent **ODan** *ESjL* 2 *VSjL* 26 **OSw**
SdmL Kgb *UL* Mb, Blb *VmL* Mb
with intention **ODan** *SkKL* 9
See also: *avund, goþvili, handaværk, ilvilje, vaþi,*
vilia, viliagærning, viliandis, viliaværk, vreþe
Refs: Descheemaeker 2009, 70–73;
KLNM s.v.v. *förbrytelse, vådaverk*
vilia (OSw) **vilia** (OGu) verb
intend **OSw** *UL* Mb, Blb, Rb, *VmL* Mb, Bb, Rb
mean **OGu** *GL* A 37
want **OGu** *GL* A 3, 6, 13, 20, 22–24,
28, Add. 1, 7 (B 4, 49)
will **OGu** *GL* A 2, 13
be willing **OGu** *GL* A 3, 20a, 28
wish **OGu** *GL* A 3, 7, 13, 14, 19, 20, 20a. 24a, 24d,
24f (64), 25, 26, 28, 32, 34, 36, 37, 44, 47, 61, Add.
1, 9 (B 4, 81), **OSw** *UL* passim, *VmL* passim
See also: *vaþi, vili*
viliabrænna (OSw) noun
arson **OSw** *YVgL* Utgb
viliagærning (OSw) noun
intent **OSw** *SdmL* Äb
intentional act **OSw** *VmL* Mb
See also: *handaværk, vaþi, vili, viliandis, viliaværk*
vilialæst (OSw) noun
defect by intent **OSw** *ÄVgL* Smb
See also: *læst, vili*

viliandis (OSw) adv.
with the intention **OSw** *UL* Kgb, *VmL* Kgb
See also: *handaværk, vaþi, vili,*
viliagærning, viliaværk
viliaværk (OSw) noun
deliberate act **OSw** *UL* Kgb, Mb, Blb, *VmL* Mb, Bb
intent **OSw** *DL* Bb, *HL* Blb, *YVgL* Urb, Add
intentional deed **OSw** *SdmL* Kkb, Mb
intentional killing **OSw** *HL* Mb
intentional killing fine **OSw** *HL* Mb
wilful act **OSw** *DL* Mb, Bb
will (1) **OSw** *YVgL* Utgb
See also: *handaværk, vaþaværk, vaþi,*
vili, viliagærning, viliandis
viliaværksbot (OSw) noun
fine for an intentional deed **OSw** *SdmL* Bb, Mb
See also: *bot*
viliaværksdrap (OSw) noun
intentional killing **OSw** *HL* Mb
See also: *drap, vili*
viljaligr (ON) adj.
voluntary **OIce** *KRA* 12
villa (ON) verb
counterfeit **OIce** *Jó* Llb 71 Þjb 16
falsify **OIce** *Grg* Lbþ 175 Rsþ 227,
Js Rkb 1, **ONorw** *FrL* Rgb 26
lose track **OIce** *Grg* Lbþ 172
mislead **OIce** *Grg* Lbþ 172
villinger (OSw) noun
madman **OSw** *HL* Jb
villuþoka (ON) noun
fog of error **OIce** *Js* Kdb 3
vin (OSw) **vin** (ODan) noun
Literally 'friend', who, in addition to other witnesses,
was present at certain purchases and who was obliged
to testify or produce the seller in case of a later dispute.
aide **ODan** *ESjL* 2, 3, *JyL* 2, *SkL* 144
friend **ODan** *ESjL* 2, 3, *SkL* 113, *VSjL* 32,
OSw *YVgL* Vs, Tb, Add, *ÄVgL* Tb
See also: *fastar (pl.), vitni*
Refs: Schlyter s.v. *vin*
vinga (OSw) verb
act as a purchase agent **OSw** *SdmL* Kmb
buy with a friend **OSw** *ÄVgL* Tb
sell with a friend **OSw** *YVgL* Tb
See also: *vin*

vinganaman (OSw) noun

  purchase agent **OSw** *SdmL* Kmb, Tjdb

  See also: *vin*

vinghan (OSw) noun

  agency **OSw** *SdmL* Kmb

vingretta (ON) noun

  squabble between friends **ONorw** *GuL* Mhb

  See also: *barsmíð*, *dela*

vingæf (OSw) **vingjöf** (ON) noun

  Literally, 'friend gift'. This word is used in three
  different ways. In Grg, it seems to have an entirely
  literal sense, with the ruling being that one might give
  such gifts as one wished to one's friends during one's
  lifetime. The heir could only object if it seemed that
  the gift-giver was trying to dispossess him. In the
  Swedish provincial laws, it seems most often to have
  a similar significance to *fæstnaþafæ* (q.v.), which is
  the expression used in HL, UL and VmL in similar
  circumstances. In this second meaning, it was the
  consideration given by the prospective husband to
  the *giftarmaþer* (q.v.), either at the meeting agreeing
  the betrothal, shortly after or on completion of the
  marriage. In ÄVgL and YVgL it is laid down as three
  marks, one mark for a freed male slave, but elsewhere
  no sum is mentioned. According to ÖgL, considerations
  were given to more than one member of the bride's
  family. Unlike the *munder* (q.v.), mentioned in ÄVgL
  as an important element of the marriage process, and
  which was passed to the bride by the *giftarmaþer*, it
  seems that the *vingæf* was retained by the *giftarmaþer*.
  There appears to be little doubt that this reflects the
  history of the transaction as bride purchase. In ÖgL, in
  addition, a *vingæf* is given as an extra sum (six *örar*)
  to a landowner to seal lease of land. If the arrangement
  failed, both the advance rental and the *vingæf* were
  returned.

  amity gift **OSw** *DL* Gb

  friendship gift **OIce** *Grg* Arþ 127, *Jó* Kge 22

  gift in return **OSw** *ÄVgL* Äb

  gift of friendship **OSw** *YVgL* Drb,
  Äb, Gb, Add, *ÄVgL* Gb

  See also: *fæstnaþafæ*, *giftarmaþer*, *gæf*, *munder*, *vin*

  Refs: KLNM s.v. *vängåva*; Korpiola 2004; Schlyter
  1877, s.v. *vingæf*; SL DL, 90 notes 44–46; SL
  YVgL, 289 note 9; SL ÄVgL, 85–86 note 20,
  103 note 6; SL ÖgL, 119 note 32; Vogt 2010

vinjarspann (ON) noun

  Possible scribal error for *vinjar toddi oc smiörspann*, a
  tax paid in butter by every household.

  butter tax **ONorw** *FrL* Reb 2

  Refs: Cleasby and Vigfusson s.v.
  vinjarspann; NGL I, 257, note

vinna (OSw) **vinna** (OGu) **vinna** (ON) **vinnask** (ON)
  vinnas (OSw) verb

  afford to **OGu** *GL* A 20a, Add. 8 (B 55)

  convict **OSw** *HL* Mb, *SdmL* Bb, *UL* Kgb, *ÖgL* Vm

  be enough **ONorw** *GuL* Krb, Arb

  find guilty **OSw** *HL* Mb

  harvest **ONorw** *GuL* Llb

  hunt **ONorw** *GuL* Krb

  manage **ONorw** *GuL* Llb

  prove **OSw** *SdmL* Kgb, *YVgL* Tb, *ÄVgL* Tb

  be sufficient **OSw** *UL* Äb, Mb, Blb,
  Rb, *VmL* Äb, Mb, Bb, Rb

  swear **OGu** *GL* A 16

  testify **OSw** *YVgL* Jb, Add

  win **OSw** *YVgL* Add

  witness against **OSw** *YVgL* Add

  work **ONorw** *GuL* Krb, Løb, Llb

  Expressions:

  til vinna, til wnnæ, vinna til (OSw)

  convict **OSw** *UL* Äb, Mb, Blb, Add 12 *VmL* Mb

  prove **OSw** *UL* Äb *VmL* Äb

  laghlika til vinna, laghlica til vinna (OSw)

  lawfully convict **OSw** *UL* Kkb, Äb,
  Mb, Blb *VmL* Kgb, Äb, Mb

  See also: *binda*, *döma*, *fælla*,
  laghbinda, *laghvinna*, *vita*

vinningælogh (OSw) **unningelogh** (ODan) noun

  In ODan and OSw, an oath that a person was the
  owner of an object that somebody else had found.
  Also a reward that the finder should receive.

  finder's reward **ONorw** *FrL* Rgb 40

  legal reward **OSw** *ÄVgL* Tb

  oath of acquisition **ODan** *ESjL* 3, *SkL* 166, *VSjL* 87

  recompense **OSw** *YVgL* Tb

  reward **OSw** *YVgL* Tb, *ÄVgL* Tb

  See also: *unningjalausn*

  Refs: CV s.v. *unningi*; F s.v. *undingi*; KLNM
  s.v. *hittegods*; Schlyter s.v. *vinningælogh*;
  Tamm and Vogt, eds, 2016, 310

vinnumaðr (ON) noun

  hired man **OIce** *Jó* Kab 25 Fml 3

  servant **OFar** *Seyð* 7

  worker **ONorw** *FrL* Intr 20

vinorþ (OSw) **vinsorþ** (OSw) noun

  acting as a friend **OSw** *YVgL* Tb

  witness at a purchase **OSw** *ÄVgL* Tb

  See also: *vin*

vinsked (OSw) **vindskeið** (ON) noun

A board nailed to the slanting gable side of a roof protecting it against the wind. In ONorw GuL (ch. 307), the person commissioned to provide a *vindskeið* to a boathouse for a warship was fined if he failed to do this. In OSw, appearing as one of several boundaries delimiting the borders of a house or farm, and as such deciding who was responsible for finding the killer of a guest killed on either side of it.

bargeboard **ONorw** *GuL* Leb, **OSw** *DL* Mb

Refs: CV s.v. *vindskeið*; KLNM s.v. *vindski*

vinterdagher (OSw) noun

winter day **OSw** *SdmL* Bb

See also: *vinternat*

vintermylne (ODan) noun

winter mill **ODan** *ESjL* 3

See also: *mylna, sumermylne*

vinternat (OSw) **vetrnætr (pl.)** (ON) noun

The first day, literally night, of winter. In OSw, not specified as to the date, but in OIce and ONorw, 14 October, indicating certain legally significant time limits. In the plural, at least in OIce Grg, referring to the preceding Thursday and Friday night before the beginning of winter (on a Saturday).

beginning of winter **ONorw** *GuL* Llb, Olb

first day of winter **OSw** *DL* Bb

first night of winter **OSw** *SdmL* Bb

first winter's night **OSw** *HL* Blb

Winter Nights **OIce** *Grg* Klþ 3 Lbþ 174, *Jó* Llb 9, 21

See also: *sumarnat*

Refs: KLNM s.v.v. *første vinterdag, sommerdag*; Schlyter s.v. *vinternat*

virðingarfé (ON) noun

item whose value is open to assessment **OIce** *Grg* Misc 246

virðingarváttr (ON) noun

witness to a stipulation **ONorw** *GuL* Arb

virkr (ON) noun

Expressions:

virkr dagr (ON)

weekday **ONorw** *GuL* Olb

See also: *sykn*

virthepænning (ODan) noun

something valued in money **ODan** *JyL* 2

virthning (ODan) **virðing** (ON) noun

appraisal **OIce** *Jó* Lbb 4 Llb 38

assessment **OIce** *Jó* Kge 7 Llb 18 Kab 22 Þjb 23

estimate **ODan** *SkL* 176, 207, 210, 234, 235

estimated value **ODan** *SkL* 150

estimation **ODan** *ESjL* 2

stipulation **ONorw** *GuL* Arb

valuation **ODan** *ESjL* 1–3, *VSjL* 17, 32, **OIce** *Grg* Lbþ 178, *Jó* Kge 16, **ONorw** *GuL* Mhb

value **ODan** *SkL* 145, 170, 200, 203

valuing **OIce** *Grg* Arþ 122, 125 Lbþ 215, *Js* Ert 25

worth **ODan** *JyL* 3

virþa (OSw) **virthe** (ODan) **virþa** (OGu) **virða** (ON) verb

appraise **OIce** *Jó* Kge 14 Fml 22, **ONorw** *GuL* Arb

assess **ODan** *VSjL* 32, **ONorw** *FrL* Intr 10, *GuL* Arb

claim **OGu** *GL* A 10

decide **OGu** *GL* A 32

estimate **ODan** *ESjL* 2, **ONorw** *GuL* Trm

evaluate **ODan** *ESjL* 3

give (someone) the value (of something) **OGu** *GL* Add. 9. (B 81)

make a valuation **OGu** *GL* A 30, **OSw** *UL* Blb, *VmL* Kmb

seize **OGu** *GL* A 10

set a value upon **OGu** *GL* A 40, 41, 45a, **OSw** *UL* Blb, *VmL* Mb

take in payment of a debt **OGu** *GL* A 63

value **ODan** *ESjL* 2, *VSjL* 32, 87, **OFar** *Seyð* 5, **OIce** *Grg* Arþ 122, *Jó* Llb 50, 64, *Js* Kvg 1 Kab 4, 17, *KRA* 1, 14

See also: *bregþa, lata, raþa, skilia, vita*

visa (OSw) **vise** (ODan) **visa** (OGu) verb

appoint **ODan** *SkL* 44

send **OGu** *GL* A 51

summon **OSw** *YVgL* Drb, Jb, Utgb, *ÄVgL* Md, Slb, Rlb

visse (ODan) noun

security **ODan** *JyL* 1

vist (OSw) **vist** (OGu) **vist** (ON) noun

board **OSw** *YVgL* Utgb, *ÄVgL* Föb

food **ONorw** *GuL* Mhb

hospitality **ONorw** *EidsL* 32.11

keep **OIce** *Jó* Kab 25

lodging **OIce** *Grg* Klþ 1, 2 Þsþ 22, 53 Vís 97 Bat 113 Arþ 120 Ómb 143 Feþ 144 Misc 237, 249, *Jó* Kge 17, *Js* Kab 19, *KRA* 1, 26, **ONorw** *FrL* Rgb 10

position **OFar** *Seyð* 3

provisions **OGu** *GS* Ch. 4

residence **ONorw** *GuL* Kpb

work **OIce** *Jó* Mah 29, **ONorw** *GuL* Løb

See also: *ala, gæstning, skipvist*

vistafar (ON) noun

domicile **OIce** *Grg* Arþ 118 Feþ 158

vistahus (OSw) noun

pantry **OSw** *SdmL* Kkb

storehouse **OSw** *DL* Kkb, *UL*
Kkb, Kgb, *VmL* Kkb, Kgb

vistavitni (OSw) noun

oath of defence **OSw** *ÖgL* Db

See also: *vitni*

vistfastr (ON) vistfestr (ON) adj.

having a fixed abode **OIce** *Jó* Kge 24, 31

in settled lodging **OIce** *Grg* Þsþ
35, 78 Hrs 235 Tíg 260

vit (OSw) noun

knowledge **OSw** *UL* Mb

majority **OSw** *HL* Äb, *UL* Kkb,
Äb, *VmL* Kkb, Äb, *ÖgL* Eb

See also: *maghandi, omaghi*

vita (OSw) vite (ODan) vita (OGu) vita (ON) vitas
(OSw) vite (ODan) vita (OGu) verb

Etymologically related to the homonym *vita* 'to know'
and many of its different usages might be subsumed
under a general meaning 'to make known', which is
reflected in translations such as 'to declare'. Used in
various stages of the legal procedure with more specific
translations; when focusing on the announcement of a
case to be handled at the *þing*, it might be translated
as 'to accuse', 'to charge', 'to sue', 'to prosecute'.
When implying an investigation leading to an ensuing
declaration, it might be translated as 'to try', 'to
examine', 'to investigate', 'to value'. When referring
to corresponding oaths and/or testimonies, it might be
translated as 'to confirm', 'to witness', 'to strengthen',
'to substantiate', 'to defend'. When focusing on the
result of such preceding procedures it might be
translated as 'to prove', 'to convict', 'to determine',
'to ascribe'.

accuse **ODan** *JyL* 2, 3, **OSw** *DL* Kkb, Mb, Bb,
Gb, *HL* Mb, *SdmL* Kkb, Kgb, Bb, Kmb, Mb,
Tjdb, *SmL*, *UL* Mb, Kmb, Rb, Add. 8, *VmL* Kkb,
Mb, Kmb, *YVgL* Rlb, Tb, Föb, *ÖgL* Kkb

be accused **OSw** *UL* Kkb, Äb, Mb,
Kmb, *VmL* Kkb, Mb, Kmb

acknowledge **OSw** *UL* Äb

act as witness **OSw** *HL* Mb

allege **OSw** *YVgL* Tb

be appraised **OSw** *UL* StfBM

ascribe **OSw** *YVgL* Add

bear witness **ODan** *JyL* 1, 2, **OGu** *GL*
A 14, 18, **OSw** *ÖgL* Eb, Db

blame **ODan** *JyL* 3, **OSw** *HL* Mb

charge **ODan** *JyL* 2, 3, **OGu** *GL* A 2, **OSw** *HL* Mb,
UL Mb, Blb, *VmL* Rb, *YVgL* Tb, Utgb, *ÄVgL* Tb

be charged **OSw** *UL* Blb

claim **OSw** *UL* Äb, *VmL* Äb

confirm **OGu** *GL* A 13, 23, 26, **OSw** *DL*
Mb, Bb, *HL* Kkb, Äb, Jb, Rb, *UL* Kgb, Äb,
Mb, Kmb, Blb, *VmL* Äb, Jb, Kmb, *YVgL*
passim, *ÄVgL* Äb, Jb, Tb, *ÖgL* Db

confirm by oath **OSw** *SmL*, *ÄVgL*
Md, Smb, Vs, Slb, Äb

convict **ODan** *JyL* 3

corroborate **OSw** *HL* Äb

declare **OGu** *GL* A 3, **OSw** *HL* Äb, *SdmL* Kkb, Kgb,
Gb, Äb, Jb, Bb, Kmb, Mb, Tjdb, Rb, *UL* Rb, *VmL* Rb

defend **OSw** *YVgL* Drb, Rlb

determine **ODan** *ESjL* 2

examine **OSw** *DL* Eb, *HL* Kkb, Blb

excuse by oath **OSw** *SmL*

fine **OIce** *Jó* Þfb 5

give evidence **OSw** *HL* Kkb

give proof **ODan** *ESjL* 3

give witness **ODan** *ESjL* 1

inquest **OSw** *YVgL* Add

inquire **OSw** *YVgL* Add, *ÖgL* Eb, Db

investigate **OSw** *DL* Eb, Gb, *UL* Kkb, Äb,
Mb, Jb, Rb, *VmL* Kkb, Kgb, Äb, Mb

know **OGu** *GL* A 2, 37, **ONorw**
GuL Krb, Kpb, Tfb, Mhb

probe **OSw** *YVgL* Add

prosecute **OSw** *YVgL* Föb

prove **ODan** *ESjL* 3, *JyL* 1, *SkKL* 3–7, 12,
SkL passim, *VSjL* 1, 2, 16–18, 24, 71, 72,
OGu *GL* A 19, **OSw** *DL* Mb, Bb, Gb, Tjdb,
HL Mb, Jb, Rb, *UL* Kkb, *VmL* Kkb, *YVgL* Jb,
Kvab, *ÄVgL* Rlb, Jb, Kva, Tb, *ÖgL* Kkb

prove lawful acquisition **OSw** *DL* Bb

prove one's right **OSw** *HL* Äb

put responsibility on **OSw** *VmL* Äb

state **OSw** *YVgL* Rlb

strengthen one's case **OSw** *HL* Blb

substantiate **OSw** *DL* Bb, *UL* Kkb, Äb, Mb, Jb, Blb,
Rb, Add. 13, *VmL* Kkb, Äb, Mb, Jb, Kmb, Bb, Rb

sue **OSw** *YVgL* Add

swear **ODan** *ESjL* 3, *JyL* 1, 3, *SkL* 13,
14, 18, 32, 72, 75, *VSjL* 73, 79

swear to (something) **OGu** *GL* A 14

testify **OGu** *GL* Add. 8 (B 55), **OSw** *UL*
Äb, Mb, Jb, Blb, Add. 1, *ÖgL* Db

try **OSw** *DL* Mb, Bb, *HL* Kgb, Äb, Mb, Jb, Blb, Rb,
UL Kmb, Rb, *VmL* Kkb, Äb, Mb, Jb, Kmb, Rb
value **OSw** *DL* Tjdb
verify **OGu** *GL* A 19, **OSw** *UL* Mb
witness **ODan** *ESjL* 3, *JyL* 1, 2,
SkL 4, 67, 109, *VSjL* 6
See also: *dylia, sanna, skynia, skærskuta, sökia,*
vinna, vita, vitna, vitni, vita, vitni, vitsorþ
Refs: Hertzberg s.v. *vita* 4

vita (OSw) noun
case of defence **OSw** *YVgL* Tb
confirmation **OSw** *YVgL* Äb
defence **OSw** *YVgL* Tb
judgement **OSw** *YVgL* Tb, Jb, *ÄVgL* Jb, Tb, Föb, Lek
knowledge **OSw** *VmL* Kmb
precedence **OSw** *DL* Bb, *VmL* Kkb, Jb
proof **ODan** *SkL* 26, *VSjL* 1, 71
right **OGu** *GL* A 24f (64), **OSw** *DL* Eb,
Mb, Gb, *VmL* Kkb, Mb, Jb, *YVgL* Äb,
Tb, Jb, Utgb, Add, *ÄVgL* Äb, Föb
right of defence **OSw** *DL* Tjdb
right to clear oneself by oath **OSw** *SmL*
right to confirm **OSw** *YVgL* Utgb
right to defend oneself **OSw** *DL* Kkb
right to prove **ODan** *SkL* 84
testimony **OSw** *UL* Äb, *YVgL* Jb, *ÄVgL* Jb, Föb
verdict **OSw** *YVgL* Jb
witness **ODan** *SkL* 37, **OSw** *YVgL* Tb

vitafé (ON) noun
Literally 'known property'. The term is used for cases
involving debts for which there is evidence (e.g.
witness testimony). Such cases cannot be contested
by the defendant, thus the definition of 'secure
money' given by CV. *Vitafé* is defined in Js Kab 16
as 'everything that witnesses know of' (*það er allt*
vitafé er váttar vitu) and in FrL Rgb 19 as 'that which
is secured before witnesses' (*Þat er vita fé er fest er*
fyrir váttum). This definition was expanded in Jó (Kab
21) to include property adjudged by a court or by the
lögmaðr. By the fourteenth century this debt may have
been documented in written form.
goods secured by verdict **ONorw** *FrL* Rgb 19
known debt **OIce** *Js* Kab 16, 21
notorious debt **OIce** *Jó* Þfb 2 Llb
4, 13 Kab 4, 16 Fml 15
notorious property **ONorw** *GuL* Kpb, Llb, Tfb
Refs: CV; Dyrhaug 2012; F; NGL V

vitavörðr (ON) noun
watch at the beacons **ONorw** *FrL* Var 1, *GuL* Leb

vite (ODan) **víti** (ON) noun
compensation **ODan** *JyL* 3, *SkL* 189
financial penalty **ONorw** *EidsL* 11.1
fine **ODan** *ESjL* 2, **OIce** *Grg* Feþ 147, **ONorw**
FrL KrbA 22, 29 Rgb 33, *GuL* Krb, Mhb
offence **OIce** *Grg* Hrs 234
penalty payment **OIce** *Grg* Feþ 147 Hrs 234
security **ODan** *ESjL* 2
See also: *ræfsing*

vitende (ODan) **vitandi** (ON) adv.
knowingly **ODan** *JyL* 2, **OIce** *Jó* Kab 14, *Js* Mah 7

viter (OSw) **vitr** (ON) adj.
wise **ONorw** *GuL* Krb
Expressions:
viter maþer (OSw)
knowledgeable man **OSw** *HL* Kkb
wise man **OSw** *YVgL* Add

vitfirring (ON) noun
insanity **OIce** *Grg* Þsþ 80, **ONorw** *GuL* Krb

vitherlogh (ODan) **viþrlag** (OGu) **viðlaga** (ON)
viðrlag (ON) **viðrlög** (ON) noun
additional fine **OIce** *Jó* Sg 3
compensation **OGu** *GL* Add. 8 (B 55)
deposit **OGu** *GL* Add. 8 (B 55)
fine **ONorw** *GuL* Krb
penal law **ODan** *JyL* Fort
penalty **OIce** *Grg* Tíg 268

vitherlæghisbrut (OSw) **vidherlaghabrut** (OSw)
vitherlagha brut (OSw) noun
breach of agreement **OSw** *SmL*

vithermalsthing (ODan) noun
A *thing* 'assembly' (see *þing*) where an accused
responded to the charges against him.
answering assembly **ODan** *JyL* 2
assembly of reply **ODan** *JyL* 2
assembly where one should answer **ODan** *JyL* 1
Refs: Tamm and Vogt, eds, 2016, 301

vithersake (ODan) noun
counterpart **ODan** *JyL* 2

vithstorth (ODan) noun
Illegal felling and chopping of a specified, large
quantity of wood.
{vithstorth} **ODan** *VSjL* 66
See also: *storþahug*
Refs: Tamm and Vogt, eds, 2016, 316

viti (ON) noun

beacon **ONorw** *GuL* Leb

beacon fire **ONorw** *FrL* Var 1

vitna (OSw) **vitne** (ODan) **vitna** (OGu) **vitna** (ON) verb

attest **ONorw** *GuL* Kpb

bear witness **OGu** *GL* A 25, **OSw** *DL* Kkb, Tjdb, *UL* Kkb, Jb, *ÖgL* Eb, Db, Vm

bring testimony against **OSw** *ÖgL* Kkb

bring witness **OSw** *ÖgL* Eb

confirm **OSw** *YVgL* Tb

consider (something) substantiated **OSw** *DL* Eb

decide **OSw** *HL* Jb

give precedence **OSw** *HL* Blb

prove **ODan** *VSjL* 72, **OGu** *GL* A 25, **OSw** *DL* Bb, *HL* Kgb, Blb

prove with witness **OSw** *HL* Mb

substantiate **OSw** *UL* Kgb, Mb, Jb, Kmb, Blb, Rb, *VmL* Kgb, Äb, Jb, Kmb, Bb

swear **OGu** *GL* A 25, **OSw** *HL* Äb

testify **ODan** *ESjL* 1, 3, **OSw** *HL* Rb, *SmL*, *UL* Kkb, Mb, Jb, Blb, Rb, Add. 17, *VmL* Mb, Jb, Bb, Rb, *YVgL* Tb, Kvab, *ÄVgL* Jb, Tb, *ÖgL* Eb

tie to a crime using witnesses **OSw** *HL* Mb

try **OSw** *HL* Kgb

witness **ODan** *JyL* 1, 2, *SkL* 146, 155, 230, *VSjL* 51, 77, **OGu** *GL* A 25, Add. 8 (B 55), **OIce** *Jó* Kab 13, **OSw** *DL* Kkb, *HL* Rb, *SdmL* Kgb, Jb, Bb, Rb, *UL* Mb, *YVgL* Rlb, Add

Expressions:

til vitna (OSw)

substantiate **OSw** *UL* Mb

See also: *uppihalda, vita, vitni*

vitnalös (OSw) adj.

without witnesses **OSw** *YVgL* Add

vitnesbyrth (ODan) **vitnisburðr** (ON) noun

confirmation **OFar** *Seyð* 0

testifying **OIce** *Grg* Þsþ 31, *Jó* Kab 13, *KRA* 9

testimony **ODan** *JyL* 3, **ONorw** *FrL* ArbB 10 Jkb 1, *GuL* Løb

witness **ODan** *JyL* 1–3

witness statement **ODan** *VSjL* 20

witness-bearing **ONorw** *EidsL* 3.2

See also: *vitni, vættisburðr*

vitni (OSw) **vitne** (ODan) **vitni** (OGu) **vitni** (ON) noun

Originally 'knowledge', used for declaration of knowledge in a legal case, reflected in translations such as 'testimony', 'statement', 'oath', and hence for the facts in a case that such a declaration provided, which is reflected in translations such as 'evidence', 'proof'. Also a person testifying or being present at the scene of e.g. a crime or agreement, or at an announcement of such matters, as well as for one who resides in the area or for some other reason is presumed to have the knowledge required in a case, reflected in the translation 'witness', and hence for the act of witnessing e.g. a transaction, negotiation or agreement, which is reflected in the translation 'supervision'. It is not always possible to determine which of the different usages is intended. Appearing in many compounds specifying type, function or circumstance. A *vitni* could thus be an actual eyewitness of a crime, transaction etc., or a witness of an announcement of a crime etc., or a type of character or local witness. A woman could act as a *vitni* in certain cases, particularly those involving childbirth.

confirmation **OSw** *HL* Äb

evidence **OGu** *GL* A 18, 19, 20a, 25, **OIce** *Js* Mah 10, **ONorw** *BorgL* 17.13, *EidsL* 12.5, **OSw** *UL* Kkb, *VmL* Kkb

judgement **OSw** *DL* Bb

oath **OSw** *HL* Rb

proof **ODan** *ESjL* 3, *JyL* 2, **ONorw** *FrL* LlbB 10, **OSw** *HL* Mb

statement **ONorw** *FrL* Intr 13

supervision **OSw** *UL* Äb, *VmL* Äb

testimony **ODan** *JyL* 2, 3, **OFar** *Seyð* 12, **OIce** *Grg* Klþ 6, *Jó* Þfb 4, *Js* Þfb 6 Mah 11 Lbb 25 Kab 2, *KRA* 2, 11, **ONorw** *FrL* KrbB 22 Var 7, *GuL* Krb, Kpb, Løb, Llb, Kvr, Mhb, Olb, **OSw** *DL* Kkb, Mb, Gb, Rb, *HL* Mb, Rb, *UL* Kkb, Kgb, Äb, Mb, Jb, Kmb, Blb, Rb, *VmL* Kkb, Äb, Mb, Kmb, Bb, Rb, *YVgL* Drb, Rlb, Tb, Jb, Föb, Add, *ÄVgL* Md, Smb, Slb, Rlb, Jb, Föb, *ÖgL* Eb, Db

verification **OSw** *DL* Bb, Tjdb

witness **ODan** *ESjL* 1–3, *JyL* 1–3, *SkKL* 5, 12, *SkL* passim, *VSjL* passim, **OFar** *Seyð* 1, **OGu** *GL* A 2–4, 16, 18–20 (B-text), 22, 23, 25, 26, 28, 44, **OIce** *Jó* Mah 7 Kge 18, **ONorw** *BorgL* 12.1 16.8, *EidsL* 30.7, *FrL* Intr 15 KrbA 2, **OSw** *DL* Kkb, Mb, Bb, Gb, Tjdb, *HL* Kkb, Äb, Mb, Jb, Kmb, Blb, Rb, *SdmL* Kkb, Kgb, Gb, Äb, Jb, Bb, Kmb, Mb, Tjdb, Rb, *SmL*, *UL* Kkb, Kgb, Äb, Mb, Jb, Kmb, Blb, Rb, *VmL* Kkb, Äb, Mb, Jb, Kmb, Bb, Rb, *YVgL* passim, *ÄVgL* Md, Gb, Rlb, Jb, Kva, Tb, *ÖgL* Kkb, Eb, Db

witness (i.e. person giving testimony) **ONorw** *GuL* Kpb, Løb, Llb, Arb, Kvr, Mhb, Tjb, Olb, Leb

witness (i.e. testimony) **ONorw** *GuL* Løb, Llb, Mhb, Olb

Expressions:

biskops vitne (ODan)

bishop witness **ODan** *JyL* 2

bæra vitni (OSw)

testify **OSw** *UL* Äb, Rb *VmL* Äb, Rb

gothe mæns vitne (ODan)

testimony of good men **ODan** *JyL* 2

granna vitne (OSw)

witness of neighbours **OSw** *SdmL* Jb

jæflik vitni (OSw)

uncertain testimony **OSw** *YVgL* Add

unsure testimony **OSw** *YVgL* Add

mæþ lagha witnum ok lagha domum (OSw)

with lawful witness and lawful judgment **OSw** *ÖgL* Kkb

mæþ vin ok vitni (OSw)

with a friend and witness **OSw** *YVgL* Tb, Add *ÄVgL* Tb

uiaflik vitni (OSw)

undisputable testimony **OSw** *YVgL* Add

ymyslik vitni (OSw)

disputable testimony **OSw** *YVgL* Add

contradictory testimony **OSw** *YVgL* Add

vitnit mikla (ON)

ordeal **ONorw** *GuL* Mhb

See also: *andvitni, jarnbyrþ, skæl, skærsl, vita, vitna, vitnesbyrth, vitsorþ, vætti*

Refs: Cleasby and Vigfússon s.v. *vitni*; Fritzner s.v. *vitni*; Hellquist s.v. *vittne*; Hertzberg s.v. *vitni*; KLNM s.v. *vitne*; Lund s.v. *vitni*; Schlyter s.v. *vitni*

vitnisfastr (ON) adj.

proven **OIce** *Jó* Sg 3 Mah 26 Kge 29 Llb 35, 48

vitnisgilder (OSw) adj.

allowed to witness **OSw** *DL* Rb

See also: *gilder, vitni*

vitniskuna (OGu) noun

woman witness **OGu** *GL* A 2

See also: *vitni*

vitnismal (OSw) noun

prosecution substantiated by testimony **OSw** *UL* Blb, Rb

testimony **OSw** *HL* Rb, *SdmL* Rb, *UL* Rb

See also: *mal (1), vitni*

vitnismaþer (OSw) **vitnismaðr** (ON) noun

witness **OIce** *Jó* Fml 23, **ONorw** *FrL* Jkb 8, **OSw** *DL* Bb, Rb, *HL* Rb, *SdmL* Kmb, *YVgL* Rlb, Tb, Add, *ÄVgL* Rlb, Tb, *ÖgL* Db

See also: *maþer, vitni*

vitnissannr (ON) adj.

proven guilty **OIce** *Jó* Fml 8

witnessed **ONorw** *EidsL* 50.12

vitra (OGu) verb

confirm **OGu** *GL* A 20

See also: *uppihalda, vita*

vitskustir (pl.) (OSw) noun

precedence **OSw** *SmL*

vitsorþ (OSw) **vitorþ** (OGu) **vituorþ** (OSw) **vizorþ** (OSw) noun

The right, granted to one party in a conflict, to provide evidence (such as testimony, witnesses, compurgators); if successful the counterpart was not allowed to reply. Generally granted to the defendant if there was some concealment involved, otherwise to the plaintiff. The translations reflect different aspects of this central meaning; focusing on the evidence: 'evidence', 'testimony' and 'oath', on the right: 'right to prove', 'right to defend (oneself)', 'right to substantiate', 'right', 'precedence (to prosecute)', 'advantage', 'preference', or on the evidence being the final word in the matter: 'final verdict', 'judgement', 'deciding word', 'winning a case'. Corresponding to ON *vitorð* 'knowledge', appearing in other sources.

admissible evidence **OSw** *SdmL* Kkb, Kgb, Gb, Äb, Jb, Bb, Kmb, Mb, Tjdb, Rb, Till

advantage **OSw** *HL* Äb

deciding word **OSw** *ÖgL* Kkb, Eb, Db

evidence **OSw** *DL* Kkb, *UL* Mb, Kmb, Blb, Rb, *VmL* Rb

final verdict **OSw** *HL* Kkb

judgement **OSw** *YVgL* Tb, Jb, Add, *ÄVgL* Jb

oath **OSw** *HL* Rb, *YVgL* Add

precedence **OSw** *DL* Bb, Gb, *HL* Mb, Kmb, Blb, Rb, *UL* Kkb, Äb, Mb, Jb, Kmb, Blb, Rb, *VmL* Kkb, Äb, Mb, Jb, Kmb, Bb, Rb

precedence to prosecute **OSw** *DL* Mb

preference **OSw** *HL* Mb

right **OGu** *GL* A 28, **OSw** *DL* Bb, Gb, Tjdb, Rb, *SmL*, *UL* Kgb, Äb, Mb, *VmL* Äb, Rb, *ÖgL* Db

right of proof **OSw** *DL* Tjdb

right to be compensated **OSw** *DL* Mb

right to defend **OSw** *DL* Bb

right to defend oneself **OSw** *DL* Kkb, Mb, *HL* Mb

right to prove **OSw** *HL* Rb

right to substantiate **OGu** *GL* A 13, 19, 20, 20a, 22, 23, 25, Add. 7 (B 49), **OSw** *VmL* Mb, Kmb

testimony **OSw** *YVgL* Add, *ÖgL* Kkb

winning a case **OSw** *HL* Kkb

See also: *váttorð*, *vita*

Refs: Hellquist s.v. *vitsord*; Hertzberg s.v. *vitorð*; KLNM s.v. *rettergang*; Schlyter s.v. *vitsorþ*; Strauch 2008a; Åqvist 1989, 182

vittia (OSw) verb

inspect **OSw** *ÄVgL* Äb

vitulös (OSw) adj.

without judgement **OSw** *YVgL* Tb, Jb

without legal defence **OSw** *YVgL* Tb

without rights **OSw** *YVgL* Jb, *ÄVgL* Jb

vitulösa (OSw) noun

case without a defence **OSw** *YVgL* Tb, *ÄVgL* Tb

See also: *vita*

vitvillinger (OSw) **wituillingær** (OSw) **witwilling** (OSw) noun

defective **OSw** *UL* Kkb, Kgb, Jb, *VmL* Kkb, Jb

madman **OSw** *SdmL* Jb

See also: *afvita*

vixlaspiæll (OSw) noun

violation of the church sanctity **OSw** *HL* Kkb

viþakaster (OSw) **viðköstr** (ON) noun

pile of wood **ONorw** *GuL* Llb, Tjb

woodpile **OSw** *UL* Mb, *VmL* Mb

viþer (OSw) **viþr** (OGu) **viðr** (ON) noun

firewood **OGu** *GL* A 25, 26

forest **ONorw** *GuL* Llb

timber **ONorw** *GuL* Kpb, Llb, Tfb, Olb, **OSw** *VmL* Kkb

wood (2) **OSw** *SdmL* Kkb

See also: *döfviþer*, *garþsvirki*, *skogher*, *timber*, *tré*

Refs: CV s.v *viðr*; Schlyter s.v. *viþer*

viþerband (OSw) noun

case in which a plaintiff is to prove his case against the defendant **OSw** *VmL* Rb

evidence **OSw** *UL* Rb

viþerbinda (OSw) **viþbinda** (OSw) verb

charge (someone) with (something) **OSw** *UL* Mb, Rb, *VmL* Äb, Mb (table of contents only), Rb

convict **OSw** *UL* Mb, Kmb, Blb, Rb, *VmL* Kmb, Bb, Rb

find guilty **OSw** *UL* Mb, Rb, *VmL* Mb, Rb

See also: *binda*, *fælla*, *laghvinna*

viþerbo (OSw) noun

community **OSw** *UL* Blb

viþerbobalker (OSw) noun

book concerning building or community **OSw** *HL* För, Blb

See also: *balker*

viþerdelas (OSw) verb

disagree **OSw** *UL* Kkb, *VmL* Kkb

dispute **OSw** *UL* Äb, Rb

See also: *dela*

viþerdelumaþer (OSw) noun

adversary **OSw** *SdmL* Rb

disputing man **OSw** *ÖgL* Kkb

viþerganga (OSw) **viþganga** (OSw) verb

acknowledge **OSw** *HL* Mb

admit **OSw** *DL* Kkb, Bb, *HL* Rb, *SdmL* Bb, Mb, Tjdb, *UL* Kkb, Äb, *VmL* Kkb, Äb, Rb, *YVgL* Kkb, Drb, Gb, Rlb, Tb, Föb, Add, *ÄVgL* Md, Tb, Fös, *ÖgL* Eb, Db

avow **OSw** *ÄVgL* Md

confess **OSw** *DL* Mb

recognize **OSw** *ÄVgL* Äb

viþerganga (OSw) noun

admission **OSw** *ÖgL* Db

viþergæld (OSw) **viðgjald** (ON) **viðgjöld** (ON) noun

counter-payment **OIce** *Grg* Arþ 118

payment **OSw** *SdmL* Bb

viþerhætta (OSw) **viþr heta** (OGu) **viþhæta** (OSw) verb

compensate **OSw** *YVgL* Utgb, Add

be fined **OSw** *DL* Kkb, Bb

be guilty to compensate **OSw** *YVgL* Tb

be liable for **OSw** *UL* Blb

be liable to a fine of **OSw** *UL* Kkb, Rb, *VmL* Kkb, Kgb, Äb, Mb, Jb, Kmb, Bb, Rb

be liable to compensate **OSw** *YVgL* Föb

lose **OSw** *YVgL* Utgb

pay a fine **OSw** *DL* Bb, Tjdb, Rb, *UL* Rb, *VmL* Rb

pay compensation **OSw** *DL* Bb

risk **OSw** *YVgL* Kkb

risk (a fine of) **OGu** *GL* A 6, 58

viþerkænnas (OSw) **viþerkænna** (OSw) **viþkennas** (OSw) **viþkiænnas** (OSw) verb

acknowledge **OSw** *SdmL* Kmb, *UL* Äb, Rb, *VmL* Äb, Rb

admit **OSw** *HL* Mb

admit to **OSw** *UL* Mb, Rb, *VmL* Mb, Rb

claim **OSw** *UL* Jb

make an admission **OSw** *UL* Mb

See also: *kænna*

viþertaka (OSw) **vithertake** (ODan) **viþr taka** (OGu) **viþtaka** (OSw) verb

accept **OGu** *GL* A 6, **OSw** *UL* Jb, Kmb, Blb, Rb, *VmL* Jb *acknowledge* **ODan** *ESjL* 2

admit **ODan** *SkL* 118

admit to **OGu** *GL* A 14, **OSw** *UL* Kmb, *VmL* Kmb

adopt **OGu** *GL* A 20a

catch **ODan** *ESjL* 3

receive **OSw** *UL* Kgb, Äb, *VmL* Kkb, Äb

take **OGu** *GL* A 20

take back **OGu** *GL* A 34

take responsibility **OGu** *GL* A 20a, 37

See also: *liuta, lypta*

viþertakuþiufnaþer (OSw) noun

receiving stolen goods **OSw** *SdmL* Tjdb

viþertakuþiuver (OSw) noun

hider of theft **OSw** *YVgL* Tb

receiver **OSw** *ÄVgL* Tb

receiver of stolen goods **OSw** *SdmL* Tjdb

someone who hides stolen goods **OSw** *HL* Mb

See also: *þiuver*

viþervaruman (OSw) **viþer væra man** (OSw) noun

Literally 'present man', who, in addition to other witnesses, was present at for instance a land transaction or at the payment of a debt.

eyewitness **OSw** *SdmL* Kgb, Jb, Kmb, Mb, *UL* Äb, *VmL* Mb

Refs: Schlyter s.v. *viþervaru man, viþer væra man*

viþervist (OSw) **viðrvist** (ON) noun

abetting **OSw** *ÖgL* Db

presence **OIce** *Jó* Kab 13

See also: *atvist, forvist, hema, husa, samvist, samværa*

viþratta (OGu) noun

dispute **OGu** *GS* Ch. 1

viþskipli (OSw) noun

superstition **OSw** *YVgL* Rlb, Add

See also: *troldomber*

vígaferði (ON) **vígaferli** (ON) **vígaferð** (ON) noun

battle **OIce** *Jó* Kab 2

case of killing **ONorw** *GuL* Krb

homicide **OIce** *Jó* MagBref Þfb 8

killing **ONorw** *FrL* Intr 2

killing case **OIce** *Js* Þfb 6, **ONorw** *FrL* Var 44

víglýsing (ON) noun

The *víglýsing* ('killer's report') was the announcement given by a killer that he had committed a killing for which he assumed full responsibility.

announcement of killing **ONorw** *GuL* Mhb

declaration of a killing **OIce** *Jó* Mah 10

killing announcement **OIce** *Js* Mah 14, **ONorw** *FrL* Mhb 7 Var 12

Refs: Helle 2001, 90; Jurasinski 2002; KLNM s.v. *drab, lysing, provsbrev, vitne, landsvist*

víglýsingarvitni (ON) noun

testimony of a killing announcement **OIce** *Js* Mah 14, **ONorw** *FrL* Mhb 7

testimony to the declaration of a killing **OIce** *Jó* Mah 10

witness to the report of a killing **ONorw** *GuL* Mhb

See also: *vitni*

vígsakabót (ON) **vígsakarbætr** (ON) noun

compensation in killing cases **OIce** *Grg* Misc 249

See also: *rœtter, vígsbót*

vígsbót (ON) **vígsbætr** (ON) noun

compensation for killing **OIce** *Grg* Vís 95 Bat 113, *Jó* Kge 17

See also: *rœtter, vigsakabót*

vígslóði (ON) noun

treatment of homicide **OIce** *Grg* Vís 86

vígsvættvangsbúi (ON) **vígsvettvangsbúi** (ON) noun

neighbour of a killing place **OIce** *Grg* Vís 90

vígsök (ON) noun

killing case **OIce** *Grg* Þsþ 57, 80 Vís 86, 87 Bat 113 Arþ 120 Feþ 167 Misc 238, 254

vígvölr (ON) noun

A 'battle-stick'; a cudgel.

whatever does duty for a weapon **OIce** *Grg* Vís 86

Refs: CV s.v. *vígvölr*; Fritzner s.v. *vígvölr*

víkingr (ON) noun

viking **ONorw** *GuL* Leb

víkverir (pl.) (ON) noun

people from Vika **ONorw** *GuL* Leb

vísendr (pl.) (ON) noun

family members who act as guarantors **ONorw** *FrL* Sab 2

vísvitandi (ON) adj.

knowing **OIce** *Jó* Llb 57 Kab 25 Þjb 1, *KRA* 10

witting **OIce** *Grg* Feþ 158 Lbþ 194 Fjl 224 Rsþ 227

See also: *vitende*

vítigjald (ON) noun

penalty payment **OIce** *Grg* Hrs 234

vítislauss (ON) **vítilauss** (ON) adj.

unpenalized **OIce** *Grg* Þsþ 78 Lrþ 117 Lbþ 201 Fjl 225

víttr (ON) adj.

liable to a fine **ONorw** *GuL* Krb, Tfb, Mhb, Leb

vrak (ODan) noun

   wreck **ODan** *ESjL* 3, *JyL* 3, *SkL* 164, 165

vrakelot (ODan) noun

   casting of lot **ODan** *ESjL* 1

vranger (OSw) rangr (ON) adj.

   false **OSw** *YVgL* Frb, *ÄVgL* Slb

   wrong **ONorw** *GuL* Leb

vranglika (ODan) adv.

   wrongfully **ODan** *SkL* 78

vrangt (ODan) rangt (ON) adv.

   falsely **ODan** *JyL* 2

   without good reason **ONorw** *GuL* Leb

   wrongly **ONorw** *GuL* Tfb

vrangvisa (OSw) noun

   wrong **OSw** *SdmL* Till

vrath (ODan) noun

   Defined as twelve pigs. JyL considered intentional illegal grazing by a *vrath* a gang crime (ODan *hærværk*), which was severely punished. Contrasted to damage made by stray or single animals.

   drove **ODan** *JyL* 3, *SkL* 169

   pig drove **ODan** *JyL* 3

   See also: *hiorþ*, *hærværk*, *stoth*

vretagarþer (OSw) noun

   fence around a clearing strip **OSw** *SdmL* Bb

vreter (OSw) noun

   clearing strip **OSw** *SdmL* Bb

vreþe (OSw) vrethe (ODan) raiþi (OGu) noun

   Literally 'wrath, anger, rage'. Used of unpremeditated deeds and accusations, such as a husband accusing his wife of adultery which he later retracts (OSw SmL), as well as of violent deeds, such as attacking a man at his home when he has laid down his spear (ODan SkL). Appearing in expressions such as *mæþ vreþe* (ODan) 'in anger'; *vreþe ok bræþe* (OSw) 'anger and haste'.

   anger **ODan** *ESjL* 2, *SkL* 87, **OGu** *GL* A 8, **OSw** *SmL*

vreþer (OSw) adj.

   angry **OSw** *ÖgL* Eb

   in wrath **OSw** *YVgL* Rlb, Add

vreþshand (OSw) noun

   anger **OSw** *ÖgL* Vm

   rage **OSw** *DL* Eb

vreþsvili (OSw) vræsvili (OSw) noun

   anger **OSw** *ÄVgL* Md

   wrath **OSw** *ÄVgL* Smb, Rlb

   See also: *vaþi*

vreþsværk (OSw) noun

   fit of rage **OSw** *ÖgL* Kkb

vræka (OSw) vræke (ODan) rvaka (OSw) rvæka (OSw) vraka (OSw) verb

   drive away **OSw** *UL* Äb, Jb, Kmb, Blb, *VmL* Äb, Jb, Kmb, Bb, Rb

   evict **OSw** *VmL* Jb

   exclude **OSw** *UL* Rb, *VmL* Kkb

   expel **OSw** *SmL*

   pursue **ODan** *ESjL* 3

   refuse **OSw** *SmL*

   reject **OSw** *ÄVgL* Rlb

   release **OSw** *UL* Blb

   send away **OSw** *UL* Blb

   See also: *invræka*

væggiarköp (OSw) noun

   Literally a 'purchase (within the) walls', i.e. between spouses. These were not made public at the *þing* 'assembly'.

   wall purchase **OSw** *YVgL* Jb, *ÄVgL* Jb

   Refs: Schlyter s.v. *væggiar köp*, *væggia köp*

vægha (1) (OSw) væghe (ODan) vega (OGu) vega (ON) viga (ON) verb

   commit manslaughter **OGu** *GL* Add. 1 (B 4)

   kill **ODan** *ESjL* 3, *SkKL* 7, **OGu** *GL* A 8, 14, Add. 1 (B 4), **OIce** *Grg* Vís 86, 87 Misc 249, *Jó* Þfb 5 Mah 1, 16, *Js* Mah 1, **ONorw** *FrL* Mhb 1, *GuL* Krb, Tfb, Mhb

   slay **OSw** *UL* Mb, *VmL* Mb

   See also: *dræpa*, *sla*, *spilla*

vægha (2) (OSw) verb

   waver **OSw** *VmL* Bb

   weigh **OSw** *VmL* Kkb

væghafynd (OSw) noun

   find on a road **OSw** *HL* Mb, *SdmL* Tjdb

væghandi (OSw) vegandi (ON) noun

   killer **OIce** *Grg* Þsþ 25, 80 Bat 113, *Jó* Mah 1, 9, *Js* Mah 2, 11, **ONorw** *FrL* Intr 3 Mhb 7 Sab 2, *GuL* Mhb, Sab, **OSw** *DL* Mb, *YVgL* Drb, *ÄVgL* Md

vægher (OSw) vægh (ODan) vegr (OGu) vegr (ON) vægh (OSw) noun

   Roads appear, among other things, concerning the responsibility for their building and maintenance to varying width according to place and function (cf. *þjóðvegr*). They also appear regarding, the protection enjoyed by travellers particularly to and from church, assembly etc., the risk of encountering crime, which was less severely punished on the road than in for instance one's home, and the procedure for dealing with lost and found objects on the road (cf. *fynd* and *lysning*). There are numerous compounds for various types of roads referring to their function, such as OSw *likvægher* and *græsvægher*, i.e. roads for transportation of corpses and hay respectively. There are also several compounds for various public roads, possibly suggesting a difference in status or standard, e.g. ODan *athelvægh* (q.v.), *hærethsvægh* (q.v.), ON *þjóðvegr* and OSw *almænningsvægher* (q.v.), *farvægher* (q.v.).

common highway **OSw** *DL* Bb

highway **OIce** *Jó* Þjb 12, **ONorw** *FrL* KrbB 19, **OSw** *DL* Bb, *UL* Blb, *VmL* Bb

journey **OSw** *UL* Äb, *VmL* Äb

path **ODan** *ESjL* 3, *SkL* 186

pathway **OSw** *UL* Kkb, *VmL* Kkb

right of way **OGu** *GL* A 24f (64)

road **ODan** *ESjL* 2, 3, *JyL* 1, *SkL* 68–70, 97, 137, *VSjL* 72, **OGu** *GL* A 22 (B-text only), **OSw** *DL* Eb, Bb, *HL* Kgb, Mb, Blb, *SdmL* Kkb, Kgb, Gb, Bb, Mb, *UL* Kgb, Mb, Blb, *VmL* Kgb, Mb, Bb, *YVgL* Kkb, Rlb, Tb, Jb, Kvab, Föb, Add, *ÄVgL* Kkb, Jb, Kva, Tb

route **OSw** *UL* Blb, *VmL* Bb

side **OSw** *UL* Blb, Rb, *VmL* Bb, Rb

way **OSw** *HL* Blb, *UL* Kgb, *VmL* Kgb

Expressions:

sitia a vægh (OSw)

wait in ambush **OSw** *HL* Kgb

farin vægher (OSw) **faren vægh** (ODan)

common road **ODan** *JyL* 2, 3

highway **ODan** *JyL* 3

road **OSw** *YVgL* Tb *ÄVgL* Tb

svoren vægh (ODan)

Not defined, but possibly analogous to *svoren toft* (cf. *tompt*) and hence a road converted from common land (ODan *almænning*) by all men of the village. Seems to have entailed some special status and protection for its travellers.

sworn road **ODan** *JyL* 1:56

See also: *farvægher*, *gata*, *ta*

Refs: Lundbye 1933a; Schück 1933; Steen 1933a

væghfarandi (OSw) **væghfarende** (ODan) adj.

itinerant **ODan** *JyL* 2, 3

travelling **OSw** *UL* Kkb, Mb, Kmb, *VmL* Kmb

wayfaring **OSw** *HL* Mb, *SdmL* Kkb, Bb, Tjdb, *SmL*, *YVgL* Add, *ÖgL* Kkb

See also: *vægher*

væghin (OSw) adj.

Appears in the phrase *mark væghin* translated as 'silver in weight' etc., contrasted to the current value of coins.

in weight **OSw** *YVgL* Äb, *ÄVgL* Äb

weighed **OSw** *HL* Mb

Refs: Steinnes 1936, 130

væghsel (ODan) noun

bribe **ODan** *ESjL* 2

See also: *muta*

væna (OSw) **vænask** (ON) verb

In ONorw, to charge/sue/accuse in a regular manner, but only appearing concerning adultery. In OSw, specifically concerning cases without witnesses or proof, such as certain cases of adultery (UL, VmL), killing of unbaptized children (ÖgL) and complicity in crime. Some regulations reveal special handling of cases based on suspicion: ÖgL problematizes that ordeals were no longer allowed and states that these cases should not lead to a death sentence, and in HL the accused was to appoint part of the *næmd* 'panel' settling the case.

accuse **ONorw** *GuL* Mhb

claim **ONorw** *GuL* Tjb

suspect **OSw** *HL* Äb, *SdmL* Tjdb, Rb, *UL* Äb, *VmL* Äb, Bb, *ÖgL* Kkb, Eb

See also: *grun*, *humamal*, *jæva*, *vanesak*

vænslabot (OSw) noun

fine for a crime based on suspicion **OSw** *SdmL* Tjdb

See also: *bot*, *væna*

vænslamal (OSw) **vænslomal** (OSw) noun

case where there is mere suspicion **OSw** *UL* Äb, Mb, *VmL* Mb

vænslasak (OSw) **vænslosak** (OSw) noun

case based on circumstances **OSw** *SdmL* Rb

case where there is mere suspicion **OSw** *UL* Mb, Blb, *VmL* Bb

vænta (OSw) **vænte** (ODan) verb

believe **OSw** *UL* Äb, *VmL* Äb

expect **OSw** *UL* Kgb

suspect **ODan** *JyL* 2

væreldshøvthing (ODan) **veraldarhöfðingi** (ON) noun

secular chieftain **OIce** *KRA* 7

secular lord **ODan** *JyL* Fort

See also: *höfþingi*

væreldsskøte (ODan) verb

convey forever **ODan** *SkL* 84

convey to eternal possession **ODan** *VSjL* 85

convey to ownership as long as the world may last **ODan** *VSjL* 85

værgæld (OSw) **vereldi** (OGu) **værold** (OSw) noun

The wergild ('man price', 'worth of a man') payable for a killing. There are equivalents in other West Germanic languages and the first element of the word is related to ON *verr*, 'man'. The second element is related to ON *giald*, OSw *gæld* (q.v.), 'payment'. Schlyter in his glossary points out that the only OSw instance of the word, as found in HL (*værold*), should be *værgæld*. He records the OGu form under a separate entry. Wessén suggests that both *vereldi* and *værold* were loan words from a West Germanic language, but this has been rejected by Brink (2010b, 127). He instead suggests that the forms found came into OGu and OSw (where it occurs only in HL), via ON legal texts, and ultimately from OE *wergild*, but that the form was altered by confusion with OSw *verold*, 'world'. In the context in which it occurs in HL, it refers only to the king's portion of the man-price. The usual word in Swedish provincial laws is *manbot* (q.v.) (ÄVgL) and cognates, whereas ON has *vígsbót* (q.v.) and *vígsbœtr*.

It was the sum of money that a killer owed to the kindred of the victim to compensate them for the death. It was the means by which a wronged family could obtain satisfaction from wrongdoers, without resorting to a blood feud. Swedish provincial laws demonstrate how the latter was gradually replaced by a system of compensation. In HL, the family is given the choice of revenge or payment (seven *marker* in silver, or 9 1/3 *marker* in coin, to the family and four, or 5 1/3 in coin, to the king). Levels of wergild are defined in GL chapters 14 and 15. These varied with the status of the person killed and sometimes with the status of the killer. The sums varied from six *örar* in coin for a slave in his *banda* (q.v.) to three *marker* in gold, 96 *marker* in coin, for a Gotlander, the coinage being considerably less valuable in Gotland than in Hälsingland, for example. The level of wergild seems in GL to have been used as a basis for calculating fines to be paid in general. It was sometimes demanded of a thief of between two *örar* and a *mark* of silver, equating theft with a killing (GU 38), but leaving an ambiguity over whether the amount depended on the status of the thief or the person from whom he had stolen. It could also be the punishment for the abduction of a woman and rape (GL 21, 22) and for taking stolen goods into another's house to incriminate him (GL 37). It was also demanded of a person causing injury by carrying fire to another's house (GL 51). A third of a wergild was even payable if an animal caused someone's death (GL 17).

In ONorw laws, a wergild ring (see *bogher*) was the compensation to be paid by a member of the killer's family to the corresponding member of the family of the killed man. Outside the circle of the closest relatives (the 'ring men' mentioned in the GuL 218–22), the GuL distinguishes three circles, groups of receivers and corresponding groups of payers. Each group of receivers or payers was called an *uppnám* (q.v.). The amount to be paid was differentiated between the values of the lives of individuals of various social classes. GuL contains different systems of assessing the wergild (cf. Robberstad).

compensation **OGu** *GL* A 15

fine for manslaughter **OSw** *HL* Mb

wergild **OGu** *GL* A 9, 12–18, 20–22, 28, 37, 38, 51, Add. 1, 2 (B 4, 17), *GS* Ch. 2

wergild compensation **OGu** *GL* A 15

See also: *bandavereldi, bogher, bot, griþ, gæld, krafarvereldi, lögbaugr, manbot, mangæld, vígsakabót, vígsbót*

Refs: Brink 2010b; Helle 2001, 14, 110, 117, 144; Hertzberg, s.v. *þversök*; KLNM, s.v. *mansbot*; Peel 2015, 106–07 note 9/10–11, 118–19 notes 15/2–6–15/6–12, 119–20 notes 16/2–4–16/9–13, 121–22 notes 17/17–19–17/19–21; Radding 1989, 617; Robberstad 1981, 370–75, 380; Schlyter 1877, s.v.v. *vereldi, værold*; SL GL, 250 note 20; Vogt 2010, 121, 133, 143–51

væria (OSw) **værje** (ODan) **veria** (OGu) **verja** (ON) **værþia** (OSw) verb

Refers to defence and acquittal in a legal case. Although displaying some overlap, the defence is represented in translations such as 'defend', 'deny', 'excuse', 'give defence', 'respond', 'substantiate', and the acquittal is reflected in translations such as 'acquit', 'exonerate', 'free', 'clear', 'free from fines'. Both defence and acquittal could be performed by the defendant alone as well as by oath-helpers, witnesses, occasionally other men involved in the dealings at hand, sometimes other actual eye-witnesses or other local men assumed to have knowledge of the facts of the case, or a group of nominated men, sometimes referred to as a *nœmd* (q.v.). Both defence and acquittal could be reached through an *eþer* 'oath'. Appearing in numerous phrases and expressions, such as: *döma warþæn* 'deem innocent' (OSw UL Kkb 19), *gitær han æy swa wart* 'if he cannot defend it like this' (ODan SkL 80), *með fastum wæriæ* 'to defend with transaction witnesses' (OSw SdmL Jb 9), *wæri sik medh landzlaghum* 'defend oneself according to the law of the land' (OSw HL Mb 8), *wæri mæþ fiughurtan manna eþe* 'defend with an oath of fourteen men' (OSw ÖgL Kkb 24), *verjask at lögum* 'defend himself according to the law' (OIce Js Mah 13). Also 'to fend for', 'to fend off', 'to defend' referring to the care, protection and defence of children, houses, land etc., for example *værje ok æj hærje* 'defend and not destroy' (ODan SkL 57).

acquit **OSw** *SdmL* Kkb, Kgb, Jb, Kmb, Tjdb, Rb, *UL* Kkb, Kgb, Mb, Kmb, Blb, Rb, *VmL* Kgb, Äb, Mb, Jb, Kmb, Bb, Rb, *YVgL* Äb, Gb, Tb, Add, *ÖgL* Kkb, Eb

clear **OSw** *HL* Kgb, Äb, Mb, Blb, Rb, *YVgL* Add

confirm **OSw** *ÄVgL* Äb

declare innocent **OSw** *HL* Kkb

defend **ODan** *ESjL* 2, *JyL* Fort, 1–3, *SkL* passim, *VSjL* 5, 12, 65, 82, 83, 86, 87, **OIce** *Grg* Þsþ 35 Vís 90, *Jó* Mah 7, 16 Kab 2 Þjb 2, *Js* Mah 13 Þjb 2, **ONorw** *FrL* Mhb 10, 30 LlbB 12, *GuL* Kpb, Løb, Arb, Mhb, Olb, **OSw** *DL* Kkb, Eb, Mb, Bb, Tjdb, *HL* Kkb, Kgb, Mb, Blb, Rb, *SdmL* Kkb, Kgb, Gb, Äb, Jb, Bb, Kmb, Mb, Tjdb, Rb, Till, *SmL*, *UL* passim, *VmL* passim, *YVgL* passim, *ÄVgL* Kkb, Md, Slb, Äb, Gb, Rlb, Jb, Tb, Fös, Föb, *ÖgL* Kkb, Eb, Db

deny **OSw** *UL* Mb

excuse **OSw** *YVgL* Jb, *ÄVgL* Jb

exonerate **OSw** *UL* Äb, Mb, Rb

free **ODan** *ESjL* 3, **OSw** *DL* Kkb, Bb, Rb, *HL* Äb, Mb, *YVgL* Add, *ÄVgL* Fös

free from fines **OSw** *UL* Kkb, *VmL* Kkb

give defence **ODan** *SkL* 142

guard **OSw** *ÄVgL* Jb

be innocent **OGu** *GL* A 37, **OSw** *UL* Kkb

invest **OIce** *Jó* Kge 18

keep back **OGu** *GL* A 19

make defence **ODan** *VSjL* 37

manage **ONorw** *GuL* Leb

pay (someone's) penalty **OGu** *GL* A 22

possess **OGu** *GL* A 28

protect **ONorw** *GuL* Krb

prove **ODan** *ESjL* 2, 3, *VSjL* 1, 16, 76, **OSw** *HL* Jb, *ÄVgL* Tb

prove someone right **OSw** *HL* Rb

purge **OSw** *HL* Kkb, Kgb

respond **OSw** *ÄVgL* Rlb

substantiate **OSw** *UL* Mb, *VmL* Mb, Kmb

swear **ODan** *VSjL* 76

vindicate **OSw** *HL* Mb

Expressions:

verja lýritti (ON)

to forbid by veto **OIce** *Grg* Þsþ 58

væria sik (OSw) **verias** (OGu)

defend oneself **OSw** *UL* Kkb, Kgb, Mb, Kmb, Blb, Rb *VmL* passim OGu *GL* A 4, 20a, 22

to be the defendant **OGu** *GL* A 19, 22

substantiate a denial **OSw** *UL* Kkb, Äb

See also: *standa*

Refs: Andersen 2010; Bjorvand and Lindeman 2000, s.v. *værje*; Hellquist s.v. *värja*; Hertzberg s.v. *verja*; Schlyter s.v. *væria*

væriandi (OSw) **værjende** (ODan) **verjandi** (ON) noun

advocate **OSw** *UL* Rb, *VmL* Rb

defence **ODan** *ESjL* 1, **OSw** *SdmL* Add

defendant **OIce** *Jó* Llb 26 Kab 4, **ONorw** *FrL* Mhb 8 Rgb 7 Jkb 8 Bvb 11, *GuL* Kpb, Arb, Olb, **OSw** *DL* Mb, *HL* Rb, *SdmL* Mb, *UL* Mb, *VmL* Mb, *ÄVgL* Lek

defender **OIce** *Grg* Þsþ 25 Feþ 158 Hrs 234, *Js* Kab 5

guarantor **ODan** *VSjL* 87

guardian **ODan** *ESjL* 1–3, *JyL* 1, 2, *SkL* 1, 2, 9, 10, 57, *VSjL* 1, 2, 10, 13, 61, 62, **OSw** *SdmL* Mb, *UL* Mb

the one who wants to defend himself **OSw** *DL* Kkb

parent **OSw** *HL* Mb

protector **ODan** *VSjL* 1

værje (ODan) noun

guardian **ODan** *ESjL* 2, 3, *JyL* 1, 2

guardianship **ODan** *JyL* 1

værjeløs (ODan) adj.

child without protection **ODan** *ESjL* 3

defenceless **ODan** *JyL* Fort

værk (OSw) **værk** (ODan) **verk** (OGu) **verk** (ON) noun

act **OSw** *VmL* Kmb

action **ODan** *JyL* 1, **OGu** *GL* A 28, **OSw** *SdmL* Kgb, Gb, Bb

case **ONorw** *GuL* Kpb

deed (1) **ONorw** *EidsL* 12.4, *GuL* Mhb, **OSw** *DL* Gb, Tjdb, *HL* Mb, *SmL*, *YVgL* Drb, Äb, Tb, *ÄVgL* Md, Äb

device **OSw** *SdmL* Bb

labour **OIce** *Jó* Kab 25

mischievious deed **ONorw** *FrL* KrbA 10

misdeed **ONorw** *GuL* Tjb

violence **OSw** *ÄVgL* Smb

work **OGu** *GL* A 6, 56, **ONorw** *GuL* Krb, Løb, Llb, Arb, Tfb

See also: *gærning, tala (1), viliaværk*

værka (OSw) **verkia** (OGu) **værkia** (OSw) verb

commit a crime/offence **OSw** *UL* Rb, *VmL* Rb

hurt **OGu** *GL* Add. 7 (B 49)

værki (OSw) noun

fishery **OSw** *UL* Blb, *VmL* Bb

værkiande (OSw) **værkandi** (OSw) noun

offender **OSw** *DL* Mb

perpetrator **OSw** *DL* Mb, *VmL* Mb

værknaþer (OSw) noun

labour **OSw** *UL* Kkb, *VmL* Kkb

See also: *aþal*

værn (OSw) **værn** (ODan) **vörn** (ON) noun

collective **OSw** *UL* Blb, *VmL* Bb

defence **ODan** *SkL* 78, 79, 82, 84, **OIce** *Grg* Þsþ 30, 32 Lbþ 199 Misc 251, *Jó* Kab 10, *Js* Kab 8, **ONorw** *FrL* KrbA 45 ArbB 10, *GuL* Kpb, Olb, **OSw** *YVgL* Tb

enclosure **OSw** *DL* Bb, *UL* Kkb, Blb

fence **OSw** *VmL* Bb

fencing **OSw** *SdmL* Kkb, Bb

guardian **ODan** *ESjL* 1, *SkL* 57, 58, 224

proof **ODan** *VSjL* 83

protection **ODan** *SkL* 219, **OSw** *UL* För, *VmL* För, *YVgL* Tb, *ÖgL* Eb

right of defence **ODan** *SkL* 76

right to defend **ODan** *VSjL* 80, 82

safeguard **OSw** *ÄVgL* Tb

Expressions:

vigh ok værn (OSw)

force of arms **OSw** *UL* Mb *VmL* Mb, Rb

wæræ wiþær wærn (ODan)

defend **ODan** *SkL* 79, 82

with wærn wæræ (ODan)

have the right to defend **ODan** *VSjL* 80, 82

bring proof **ODan** *VSjL* 83

See also: *garþer, gærþi, valdsgærning, valdsværk, vigh*

værna (OSw) verb

defend **OSw** *ÄVgL* Jb

protect **OSw** *SdmL* Conf

See also: *væria*

værnalagh (OSw) noun

This referred to all the householders, in this case farmers in particular, collectively who owned land in the same enclosure (*værn*, q.v.). For administrative purposes, it was all the farmers in one collective. It also referred to the collective itself. Each member of the collective individually was a *værnalaghi*. They had a responsibility for each other and an obligation to help with harvesting if a member was let down by his workers and not to damage his crop by harvesting too early, for instance.

The word *værn* alone had a multiple of meanings apart from simply a physical enclosure, usually bounded by fencing. It meant, amongst other things, 'defence', 'guardian', 'proof' and 'protection'.

all the farmers in a collective **OSw** *UL* Blb, *VmL* Bb

See also: *staur, værn, værnalaghi, værnareþer, værnarord, værnaruf, værnkallaþer*

Refs: KLNM s.v.v. hegn, trøghbolagh; Schlyter s.v. værnalagh

værnalaghi (OSw) **wærnalage** (OSw) noun

farmer in a collective **OSw** *UL* Kkb, Blb, *VmL* Bb

See also: *bolfaster, bolstaþsmaþer, bonde, jorþeghandi, karl*

værnareþer (OSw) **varnareiðr** (ON) noun

defence oath **OIce** *Grg* Þsþ 47

oath in cases of defence **OSw** *DL* Rb

See also: *eþer*

værnarord (OSw) noun

right to defend oneself **OSw** *DL* Mb

værnaruf (OSw) noun

destruction of fences **OSw** *HL* Blb

værnkallaþer (OSw) adj.

protected **OSw** *UL* Blb, *VmL* Bb

See also: *friþkallaþer*

værsla (OSw) noun

custody **OSw** *YVgL* Rlb

værþ (OSw) **værth** (ODan) **verð** (ON) **værdhe** (OSw) noun

amount paid **OSw** *HL* Jb

cost **OIce** *Js* Rkb 1 Kab 13

goods **OSw** *UL* Jb

money **ODan** *ESjL* 3

payment **ODan** *SkL* 12, 78, **OFar** *Seyð* 10, **ONorw** *GuL* Krb, Løb, Leb

price **OIce** *Jó* Lbb 6 Kab 20 Þjb 16 Fml 25

purchase sum **OSw** *DL* Bb, *HL* Kmb, *YVgL* Jb, Add, *ÄVgL* Jb

value **ODan** *JyL* 1, *SkL* 47, **OIce** *Jó* Kab 18, **OSw** *HL* Kkb, Blb, *UL* Jb, *ÄVgL* Jb

worth **ONorw** *GuL* Kpb, Olb, **OSw** *UL* Jb

See also: *sal*

værþörar (pl.) (OSw) **verðaurar** (pl.) (ON) **verðeyrir** (ON) noun

money **OSw** *YVgL* Add

purchase sum **OIce** *Grg* Ómb 137

ransom fee **ONorw** *GuL* Løb

valuables **OSw** *SdmL* Äb

value **OIce** *Jó* Llb 39

worth **OIce** *Jó* Llb 35

See also: *leysingsaurar (pl.)*

væslirmæn (pl.) (OSw) noun

poor **OSw** *ÄVgL* Kkb

væstgötar (pl.) (OSw) noun

{*væstgötar*} **OSw** *ÄVgL* Kkb

Expressions:

allir væstgötar (pl.) (OSw)

all Västgötar **OSw** *YVgL* Gb

væstgötsker (OSw) adj.

from Västergötland **OSw** *YVgL* Drb, *ÄVgL* Md

væta (ON) verb

wet **ONorw** *GuL* Mhb

væta (ON) noun

liquid **ONorw** *GuL* Krb

væthskøte (ODan) verb

convey as pledge **ODan** *VSjL* 85

væthskøtning (ODan) noun

conveying as pledge **ODan** *SkL* 84

See also: *sköta, væþ*

vætt (ON) noun

Expressions:

hálf vætt (ON)

forty pounds **OIce** *Grg* Klþ 8

vætti (OSw) **vætti** (ON) noun

In ON (neuter), a testimony, particularly one given by a witness known as *váttr* (see *vatter*). In OSw (masc.), a testimony as well as a witness or a group of witnesses.

oath **OSw** *YVgL* Föb

oath-making **OSw** *YVgL* Rlb

oath-taking **OSw** *ÄVgL* Rlb

testimony **OIce** *Grg* Þsþ 22, 31 Feþ 144

witness **OSw** *YVgL* Tb, Add

See also: *andvitni, vatter, vitni*

Refs: Cleasby and Vigfusson s.v. *vætti*; Fritzner s.v. *vætti*; Hertzberg s.v. *vætti*; Schlyter s.v.v. *vat, vatter, vætti*

vættisburðr (ON) noun

testifying **OIce** *Grg* Þsþ 31, 58

See also: *vitnesbyrth*

vættisvætti (ON) noun

men to witness testimony produced **OIce** *Grg* Þsþ 53, 62

vættvangr (ON) **vettvangr** (ON) noun

place of action **OIce** *Grg* Þsþ 38 Vís 86 Feþ 155

vættvangsbúi (ON) **vettvangsbúi** (ON) noun

neighbour of the place of action **OIce** *Grg* Vís 90, 105 Misc 238

vævildræt (OSw) adv.

Appears in the context of division of common ground between two *hundari* ('districts').

following a tight string **OSw** *UL* Blb

Refs: Schlyter s.v. *vævildræt*

væzla (OSw) **veizla** (ON) noun

This is derived from the verb *veta* (OSw)/*veita* (ON) in the sense 'give, grant, provide'. It was an old tradition to provide travellers with board and lodging, and, as indicated by the more specialized meaning of the verb ('serve, treat'), *væzla* came also to signify a feast. In addition *væzla* was the board and lodging provided by the tenant when the landowner (or his representative) came to visit his lands.

With the development of a royal and ecclesiastical administration the *væzla* became closely tied to the concept of billeting, i.e. the provision of board and lodging to the king, the bishop and royal officials on their journeys through the country. Negligence in providing such hospitality was called *væzlufal* (q.v.) (OSw HL Kgb). The duty of billeting was later replaced by a regular tax.

Esp. in ONorw sources *veizla* was also a feudal concept, understood as 'land given as a grant', namely by the king to some of his highly trusted men, who became *ármenn* (see *ármaðr*) or *lendir menn* (see *lænder*). In return these men were obliged to serve the king as officers in the bodyguard and in the army, and to act on his behalf in their local community, e.g. as prosecutors. Such granted land was also called *veizlujörð* (q.v.).

billeting **ONorw** *FrL* KrbA 8, **OSw** *HL* Kgb

help **OIce** *Grg* Vís 86

hospitality **ONorw** *EidsL* 34.3 40.1

land held as a grant **ONorw** *GuL* Mhb, Leb

See also: *gengærþ, gæstning, liþ (2), veizlujörð*

Refs: Brink 2013a, 441; KLNM s.v.v. *bygsel, embedsindtægter, gästning, kungsgård, veitsle*

væzlufal (OSw) noun

negligence to provide hospitality **OSw** *HL* Kgb

væþ (OSw) **væth** (ODan) **veþ** (OGu) **veð** (ON) **vaþ** (OSw) noun

The most common word for 'pledge', i.e. something deposited as security for a payment or the fulfilment of an obligation. A *væþ* could consist of movables or fixed property and be worth more or less than the claim. If it consisted of fixed property, primarily land, the creditor could use it until the maturity of the obligation, and keep the yield, which can be seen as a means of negotiating the church's prohibition against interest. The *væþ* became the property of the creditor if the debtor did not fulfil the obligation, and thus allowed the circumvention of restrictions concerning land sales, although often with the prospect of a repurchase within a stipulated time. The *væþ* was presumably made public, and, in OSw, should be witnessed by *fastar* (q.v.) or at the *þing* 'assembly' or church, and could be subject to certain procedures otherwise used at sales (*umfærþ*, q.v.). Also specifically a stake ventured by disputing parties, and sometimes handed over to an impartial *taki* (q.v.) before or after a search, seizure, trial etc. The latter case, when for instance a judgement or a statement by a *syn* (q.v.) or *næmd* (q.v.) was challenged, can be seen as an appeal, that is the *væþ* could refer both to the appeal itself in a legal case, as well as to the deposit put down to pursue the appeal. When the dispute had been settled, the winner received the *væþ* of both parties.

appeal **OSw** *DL* Rb, *HL* Rb, *UL* Blb, *VmL* Bb

bond **OSw** *VmL* Kkb

lien **OIce** *Jó* Kge 13

mortgage **OSw** *YVgL* Gb, *ÄVgL* Gb

pawn **ODan** *JyL* 2, **OSw** *ÄVgL* Jb

pledge **ODan** *ESjL* 2, *JyL* 2, 3, *SkL* 84, 179, 182, 183, 192, *VSjL* 85, **OGu** *GL* A 26, **OIce** *Grg* Lbþ 192, 193, *Jó* Lbb 8, 11 Llb 34 Kab 16, *Js* Mah 13, 20 Ert 19 Lbb 6, 8 Kab 11, 17, **ONorw** *BorgL* 12.15, *GuL* Kpb, Arb, **OSw** *DL* Bb, Tjdb, *HL* Jb, *SdmL* Bb, Kmb, Tjdb, Till, *UL* Mb, *VmL* Rb, *YVgL* Jb

redemption **OSw** *UL* Blb

security **ODan** *SkL* 168, **ONorw** *FrL* ArbB 28

surety **OGu** *GL* A 30, **OSw** *UL* Kmb, *VmL* Kmb

wager **OSw** *HL* Mb

See also: *fastar (pl.)*, *jæmnaþahænder*, *nam*, *næmd*, *panter*, *skælavæþ*, *syn*, *tak*, *taki*, *umfærþ*, *varzla*, *veðmáli*, *væþning*

Refs: KLNM s.v.v. *dómr*, *pant*, *rettergang*, *veddemål*; Peel 2015, 167 note to 30/2–4; Schlyter s.v. *væþ*

væþerquærn (OSw) noun

wind-mill **OSw** *SdmL* Bb

væþfæ (OSw) **veðfé** (ON) noun

pledge **OSw** *HL* Äb

pledged money **OSw** *SdmL* Tjdb, Rb, Till

stake in a bet **ONorw** *GuL* Tfb, Olb

wager **OIce** *Js* Kab 21, **OSw** *HL* Äb

væþia (OSw) **væthje** (ODan) **veðja** (ON) verb

appeal **OSw** *DL* Bb, Rb, *HL* Kkb, Rb, *UL* Kkb, Jb, Blb, Rb, *VmL* Jb, Bb, Rb

bet **ONorw** *GuL* Tfb, Olb, **OSw** *HL* Jb

lay down a pledge **OSw** *UL* Blb, *VmL* Bb

lodge an appeal **OSw** *UL* Blb, Rb, *VmL* Bb, Rb

make an appeal **OSw** *DL* Rb

oppose **OSw** *HL* Rb

pledge **ODan** *ESjL* 2, **OSw** *HL* Äb, *SdmL* Jb, Bb, Rb, Till

wager **OIce** *Jó* Þjb 18, *Js* Kab 21, **ONorw** *FrL* Rbg 15, **OSw** *HL* Mb

Expressions:

væþia bort (OSw)

free oneself for responsibility **OSw** *DL* Bb

See also: *veðjaðardómr*

væþiafastar (pl.) (OSw) noun

pawn witnesses **OSw** *DL* Bb

transaction witnesses for pledges **OSw** *SdmL* Jb

væþiataki (OSw) noun

pledge trustee **OSw** *SdmL* Rb

taking of appeals **OSw** *HL* Rb

væþning (OSw) noun

appeal **OSw** *HL* Kkb, Rb, *UL* Blb, Rb, *VmL* Rb

case concerning appeal **OSw** *DL* Rb

pledge **OSw** *SdmL* Bb, Rb, *UL* Mb, Blb, Rb, *VmL* Mb, Bb

setting in surety **OSw** *UL* Rb

væþsætia (OSw) verb

pawn **OSw** *DL* Bb

pledge **OSw** *SdmL* Jb, *SmL*, *YVgL* Jb

set in surety **OSw** *UL* Kkb, Mb, Jb, Kmb, *VmL* Kkb, Jb, Kmb

See also: *nam*

væþsætning (OSw) noun

pledge **OSw** *HL* Kmb, *VmL* Mb

pledging **OSw** *SdmL* Jb, Kmb, Tjdb

vöðvi (ON) noun

flesh **ONorw** *GuL* Mhb

vögnhögg (ON) **vagnhögg** (ON) noun

killer cuts **OFar** *Seyð* 11

vörzlumaðr (ON) noun

guarantor **OIce** *Jó* Kge 14 Llb 34, *Js* Ert 25

one who gives security **ONorw** *GuL* Arb

warranter **ONorw** *BorgL* 12.15

vöxtr (ON) noun

income **OIce** *Jó* Kge 15, 17

interest **OIce** *Grg* Ómb 136, *KRA* 15

yield **OIce** *Grg* Arþ 118 Feþ 150 Misc 249 Tíg 259

See also: *vaxtalauss*

vözt (ON) noun

fishing ground **ONorw** *GuL* Kvr, Mhb

yfirboð (ON) noun

authority **OIce** *Jó* HT 2

command **OIce** *Js* Kdb 2

yfirbót (ON) noun

atonement **OIce** *Jó* Kge 5, *Js* Kvg 5, *KRA* 35, **ONorw** *FrL* KrbB 24 Mhb 62

repentance **ONorw** *FrL* Kvb 14

See also: *bot*

yfirferð (ON) noun

visitation **OIce** *KRA* 3, **ONorw** *BorgL* 10

yfirhor (OGu) noun

Double adultery, that is, where both participants were married. This word occurs only in GL. The wronged party (*malsaigandi*, see *malsæghandi*) was considered to be the husband of the woman in the case, and he received twelve *marker* as did the 'authorities'. The wife of the man not receiving any compensation. This is comparable to the situation where a married man commits adultery with an unmarried woman, in which case he pays her, but his wife receives nothing. The penalty was far higher (wergild equivalent or death) if the pair were discovered *in flagrante* as was the case if only the woman were married. It is worth noting that the expression *lerdir ella olerdir* 'ordained or not ordained' in the B-text of GL, implies that married priests were still a feature of Gotlandic society in the thirteenth century.

double adultery **OGu** *GL* A 21

See also: *hor, hordomber, værgæld*

Refs: KLNM s.v. *ægteskabsbrud*; Peel 2015, 145 note 21/4; Schlyter 1877, s.v. *yfir hor;* SL GL, 271 note 2

yfirsókn (ON) noun

jurisdiction **OIce** *Grg* Klþ 4

right to govern and to prosecute **ONorw** *GuL* Olb, Leb

yfirsóknarmaðr (ON) **yfirsóknarmenn** (ON) noun

These were men acting as public prosecutors.

official **ONorw** *GuL* Krb

surveyor **ONorw** *FrL* Var 13

Refs: Hertzberg s.v. *yfirsóknarmaðr*; KLNM s.v.v. *lejde, sysselmann*; RGA2 s.v. *lender menn*

ykia (OSw) verb

dispute **OSw** SmL

ylfa (ON) verb

bully **ONorw** *FrL* Var 46

yliansmæssa (OSw) noun

Saint Ilian's Mass **OSw** DL Bb

ymil (OGu) noun

rumour **OGu** *GL* A 20a

ymsir (OSw) **ymis** (OGu) adj.

on each side **OSw** *VmL* Bb

several (of them) **OGu** *GL* A 28

yrkia (OSw) **yrkia** (OGu) verb

extend their slavery **OGu** *GL* A 6

work **OGu** *GL* A 16, 25, **OSw** *UL* Mb, *VmL* Mb

yrknaþafæ (OSw) **öknaþa fæ** (OSw) **værknaþa fæ** (OSw) noun

working animal **OSw** *UL* Blb, *YVgL* Bb

ýki (ON) noun

exaggeration **OIce** *Grg* Misc 237

impossible tale **ONorw** *GuL* Tfb

þarnask (ON) verb

accept loss or reduction **ONorw** *GuL* Krb, Arb

þarseta (ON) noun

loitering **OIce** *Js* Lbb 19

remaining there **OIce** *Jó* Llb 42, **ONorw** *GuL* Llb

þáttr (ON) noun

section **OIce** *Grg* Lsþ 116 Lrþ 117

þegnskaparlagning (ON) noun

giving one's word of honour **OIce** *Grg* Þsþ 25 Ómb 130

þegnskaparlagningareiðr (ON) noun

An oath given one's word of honour. Thought to be a sort of preliminary oath given by anyone taking part in law at an assembly and served as a prerequisite for submitting one's word of honour (ON *leggja undir þegnskap sinn*).

word-of-honour oath **OIce** *Grg* Feþ 147

See also: *eþer, læggia*

Refs: CV s.v. *þegnskapr*; Finsen III:698–99; Fritzner; GrgTr II:61

þegnskapr (ON) noun

word of honour **OIce** *Grg* Þsþ 25 Feþ 144

þegnskylda (ON) noun

allegiance **OIce** *Jó* HT 2, *Js* Kdb 7, **ONorw** *FrL* Intr 19

duty of a subject **OIce** *Jó* MagBref HT 1 Sg 1

See also: *lýðskylda*

þengsbani (OSw) **þegnsbani** (OSw) noun

killer of a free man **OSw** *YVgL* Drb

See also: *bani, þægn*

þiaufgildi (OGu) noun

fine for theft **OGu** *GL* A 28

þiauþ (OGu) noun

person **OGu** *GL* A 18

þigia (OSw) **thigje** (ODan) **þegja** (ON) verb

Keeping silent mainly appears in contexts where it was interpreted as consent or where it had implications for the legal proceedings. Failing to challenge a land transaction and thus making it legal after a stipulated time (ODan JyL 1:51, 2:71; SkL 49). Failing to claim an inheritance and thus losing one's right to it (ONorw GuL ch. 122). A woman's failure to answer a proposal was interpreted as consent (ONorw EidsL 22.7, FrL KrbB 22). Failing to prosecute in cases of illicit sexual relations, and thus making rape seem less credible or allowing the woman's male relatives to prosecute for her (ODan 2:17, 18). Failing to prosecute in cases of physical violence, and thus allowing an official to prosecute instead of the victim (ODan JyL 2:81, OSw DL Mb). Prohibiting nominated men from failing to reach a decision and risk a person's life or property by keeping quiet (ODan JyL 2:80; 3:10).

fail to claim **ONorw** *GuL* Arb

keep quiet **ODan** *JyL* 3

keep silent **ODan** *JyL* 2, **OSw** *DL* Mb

not decide **ODan** *JyL* 2

remain silent **ODan** *SkL* 49, **ONorw** *EidsL* 22.7, *FrL* KrbB 22

stay silent **ODan** *JyL* 2

Expressions:

þigiande mæssa (OSw)

secret of the Mass **OSw** *UL* Kkb *VmL* Kkb

silent mass **OSw** *YVgL* Kkb *ÄVgL* Kkb

þing (OSw) **thing** (ODan) **þing** (OGu) **þing** (ON) **thing** (OSw) noun

A meeting/assembly, its congregation and district area and location as well as the activities — judicial, administrative, economic and fiscal matters — publicly and communally dealt with there. To be legal, meetings with the *þing* were held at predetermined times and locations that vary between the laws and have a stipulated minimum of participating free men, but extraordinary meetings would be summoned when need be.

Many usages are reflected in the numerous compounds containing *þing*, giving the terminology an impression of far-reaching complexity. For instance, a *þing* could be held with a specific function (1) for a specific judicial district (2) at a specific time (3). The assemblies of the various judicial districts were not strictly hierarchical, but rather served separate purposes reflecting the opinion and power of the different sets of inhabitants that they included, which in turn affected the compliance with the decisions of the assembly.

1. a *þing* with a specific function or an extraordinary *þing*: *afkænnuþing, ennætþing, konungsþing, malþing, manndrápsþing, manntalsþing, ræfsingaþing, skuldaþing, soknaþing, sægnarþing, vápnaþing, vithermælesthing, örvarþing.*

2. a *þing* with a specific judicial area mentioned in the name: *aldragöta þing, alþingi, almænningsþing, fiærþungsþing, fylkisþing, hálfuþing, hreppstjórnarþing, hærapsþing, hundarisþing, kirkjusóknarþing, landsþing, skapþing, skipreiðuþing, syselthing, thrithiungsthing.*

3. a *þing* with reference to the time of the meeting in the name: *höstþing, jamlangaþing, leiðarþing, varþing.*

4. a *þing* held within five days or with five days' notice: *fimmtarþing.*

5. a *þing* with the name of the meeting place in its name: *Eidhsifathing, Frostuthing, Gulaþing, Lionga þing, Øxarárþing.*

6. a *þing* held at the right place at the right time: *laghþing*

7. a *þing* with the term for the official in charge of the meeting: *laghmans þing*

In the OIce Grg *þing* also could refer to a church parish, and in the OGu GL to a local judicial district, possibly synonymous with OGu *hundari* (q.v.).

assembly **ODan** *ESjL* 1–3, *JyL* 1–3, *SkL* passim, *VSjL* passim, **OGu** *GL* A 2, 4, 7, 11, 13, 14, 21, 28, 30, 31, 37–42, 45, 45a, 48, 52, 61, Add. 8 (B 55), *GS* Ch. 4, **OIce** *Grg* passim, *Jó* passim, *Js* passim, *KRA* 29, 36, **ONorw** *FrL* Intr 15 Tfb 1 KrbA 1, 22 KrbB 1 Mhb 5, 6 passim, *GuL* Krb, Kpb, Kvb, Løb, Llb, Arb, Tfb, Mhb, Tjb, Olb, Leb, **OSw** *SdmL* Kkb, Kgb, Jb, Bb, Kmb, Mb, Tjdb, Rb, Till, *YVgL* passim, *ÄVgL* Md, Smb, Slb, Urb, Äb, Gb, Rlb, Jb, Tb, *ÖgL* Kkb, Eb, Db

assembly area **OGu** *GL* A 28

district **OIce** *Grg* Tíg 265, *Jó* Þfb 1 Kge 33

judgement from the assembly **OSw** *SdmL* Mb

legal thing assembly **OSw** *DL* Eb

meeting **OSw** *DL* Mb

place of assembly **OGu** *GL* A 13

property **OIce** *Jó* Kge 6, *Js* Kvg 5

thing (1) **ONorw** *EidsL* 15.2 30.7, *FrL* Tfb 5, **OSw** *HL* Kkb, Kgb, Äb, Mb, Jb, Blb, Rb

thing assembly **ONorw** *BorgL* 8.12 17.5,
OSw *DL* Eb, Mb, Bb, Gb, Tjdb, Rb, *HL* Kgb,
Äb, Mb, *SmL*, *UL* passim, *VmL* passim
Thing assembly meeting **OSw** *DL* Rb
Expressions:
þing fyri alla lyþi, þing firi alla lyþi (OGu)
all the people at the general assembly
OGu *GL* Add 1 (B 4)
general assembly **OGu** *GL* Add 1 (B 4)
þing gengt (ON)
free passage to the assembly **OIce** *Js* Mah 19

See also: *afkænnuþing, alþingi, disaþing,*
Eiðsifaþing, ennætþing, fimmtarþing,
fiærþungsþing, folklandsþing, Frostuþing,
fylkisþing, Gulaþing, gutnalþing, hölfuþing,
höstþing, hreppstjórnarþing, hundarisþing,
hærapsþing, jamlangaþing, kirkjusóknarþing,
konungsþing, laghþing, land, landsþing,
leiðarþing, lekmannething, lyþir (pl.), malþing,
manndrápsþing, manntalsþing, Mostrarþing,
örvarþing, ræfsingaþing, skapþing, skipreiðuþing,
skuldaþing, soknaþing, syselthing, sægnarþing,
urþinga, úteynaþing, varþing, vithermalsthing,
Øxarárþing, þingariþ, þingfastar (pl.), þinglami

Refs: Andersen 2011, 29–36; Brink 2004b; Cleasby
and Vigfússon s.v. *þing*; Foote 1984, 74–83; Fritzner,
s.v. *þing*; KLNM s.v. *ting*; Schlyter s.v. *þing*; Sunde
2005, 83–85; Tamm and Vogt, eds, 2016, 22–24, 300.

þinga (OSw) **þingta** (OSw) **þinkta** (OSw) verb
hold an assembly **OSw** *SdmL* Kmb
hold thing **OSw** *HL* Kgb
inform **OSw** *DL* Eb
See also: *þing*

þingadómr (ON) noun
assembly court **OIce** *Grg* Lbþ
172, 176 Fjl 223 Hrs 234

þingakvöð (ON) noun
calling to serve on an assembly
panel **OIce** *Grg* Þsþ 77

þingariþ (OSw) **þinghriþ** (OSw) noun
meeting of the Thing assembly
OSw *DL* Rb, *VmL* Mb, Bb
See also: *afkænnuþing, laghþing, urþinga,*
þing, þingfastar (pl.), þinglami

þingbalker (OSw) noun
book concerning the legal process **OSw** *DL* Rb
See also: *balker, þing*

þingborinn (ON) adj.
announced at the assembly **OIce** *Jó* Llb 63

assembly-displayed **OIce** *Grg* Lbþ 217
þingbrekka (ON) noun
assembly slope **OIce** *Grg* Þsþ 57, 58 Vís 100,
110 Arþ 122 Feþ 147 Lbþ 201 Fjl 222, 223
þingbuþ (OSw) **þingboð** (ON) **þingsboð** (ON) noun
assembly summons **OIce** *Jó* Llb 52, *Js* Mah
21, **ONorw** *FrL* Tfb 4 KrbA 23 LlbB 7
message baton to summon an
assembly **ONorw** *GuL* Mhb
order concerning an assembly **OSw** *SdmL* Rb
summons to an assembly **ONorw** *GuL* Tfb
See also: *buþ, þing*

þingfall (OSw) **þings fall** (OSw) noun
absence from a Thing **OSw** *HL* Rb
failure of thing assembly (to make
a quorum) **OSw** *UL* Rb
failure to come to a Thing **OSw** *HL* Rb
neglect of assemblies **OSw** *SdmL* Rb
See also: *þing, þinglami*

þingfararbölkr (ON) **þingfararbálkr** (ON) noun
chapter on traveling to the
assembly **OIce** *Jó* MagBref

þingfararfé (ON) noun
fee for travelling to parliament **ONorw** *FrL* Tfb 1
See also: *þingfararkaup*

þingfararkaup (ON) noun
Fee paid by householders with specified minimum
assets that entitled them to certain rights at the *þing*
'assembly'. Also a compensation paid annually by
householders failing to attend the *alþingi* 'general
assembly', and conversely a compensation paid
to those attending it. In Jó, travel expenses for a
lögréttumaðr 'man of the Law Council'.
assembly attendance dues **OIce** *Grg* Klþ 1, 8 Þsþ
23, 35 Vís 89, 110 Arþ 127 Feþ 166 Hrs 234, 235
Misc 251 Tíg 255, *Jó* Þfb 2 Sg 1, *KRA* 1, 14
See also: *farareyrir*

Refs: Gerhold 2002, 60; Helgi Þorláksson
2011, 143–46; Jónsson and Boulhosa, 2011,
158–60; KLNM s.v. *þingfararkaup*

þingfastar (pl.) (OSw) noun
thing assembly witnesses **OSw** *VmL* Jb
See also: *afkænnuþing, fasta, laghþing,*
urþinga, þing, þingariþ, þinglami

þingfastr (ON) adj.
attached to an assembly **OIce** *Grg* Þsþ 79

þingfat (ON) noun
assembly baggage **OIce** *Grg* Klþ 8
assembly gear **OIce** *KRA* 26

þingfestr (ON) þingfesti (ON) noun
    assembly attachment **OIce** *Grg* Þsþ 22, 48 Ómb 136

þingfiæll (OSw) noun
    home assembly **OSw** *SdmL* Kkb

    See also: *þing*

þingför (ON) noun
    assembly attendance **OIce** *Grg* Vís 87, 99 Misc 251
    assembly journey **OIce** *Grg* Feþ 164, *Jó* Þjb 13
    travel to an assembly **ONorw**
    FrL Tfb 5 Mhb 62 Leb 6

þingförr (ON) þingfærr (ON) noun
    assembly-fit **OIce** *Grg* Þsþ 32 Vís 89

þinggilder (OSw) adj.
    {*þingilder*} **OSw** *DL* Rb

    See also: *gilder*, *þing*

þinghá (ON) þingá (ON) noun
    assembly district **OIce** *Jó* Llb 52, **ONorw** *FrL* LlbB 7
    community **OIce** *Js* Mah 14

þinghámaðr (ON) noun
    assembly participant **OIce** *Grg* Þsþ 35

þinghelgi (ON) þinghelgr (ON) noun
    formal inauguration of an assembly
    OIce *Grg* Klþ 10 Þsþ 56

þinghestr (ON) noun
    assembly horse **OIce** *Grg* Feþ 164, *Jó* Llb 36

þingheyjandi (ON) noun
    assembly participant **OIce** *Grg* Klþ 10 Þsþ 23, 27
    Vís 89, 97 Feþ 147, 149 Lbþ 205 Fjl 223, 225

þingkænun (OSw) noun
    word from the Thing assembly **OSw** *DL* Rb

    See also: *þing*

þinglami (OSw) noun
    Literally 'hindrance to the assembly'. This word is used in two different ways. On the one hand, in VmL and DL, it refers to the similar situation covered by *þingfall* (q.v.), which is to be found in HL, SdmL and UL, and is translated in a number of different ways. Reference here is to the failure of a prescribed assembly to take place, as a quorum of its members is not present. This failure was the subject of a fine and the word *þinglami* came to refer to the fine (or tax) itself (as in the Roden, the historical region along the coast of Uppland) A similar transfer of meaning applied to *leþungslami* (q.v.). Thus in UL *þinglami* refers to a tax payable by those inhabitants of the Roden area, who would normally be obliged to attend the local assembly (e.g. adult male householders). Wessén considers that Schlyter's interpretation of this as an amount payable as a fine when the levy was raised because the assembly was then not held is unlikely, since those called up to the levy are elsewhere stated to be free of obligation to attend the assembly. He thinks that it is more likely that it was a tax payable on an annual basis by the inhabitants of the Roden district, where an assembly was not held at all, in addition to other taxes mentioned in the same passage of UL.
    *failure of thing assembly (to make
    a quorum)* **OSw** *VmL* Rb
    failure to make a quorum **OSw** *DL* Rb
    thing assembly tax **OSw** *UL* Kgb

    See also: *afkænnuþing*, *laghþing*, *leþungslami*, *roþarætter*, *urþinga*, *þing*, *þingariþ*, *þingfall*, *þingfastar (pl.)*, *þingviti*

    Refs: KLNM s.v.v. *skatter, smörskatt, ting*; Lexikon des Mittelalters, s.v. *ding*; Schlyter 1877, s.v.v. *leþungslami, þingfall, þinglami*; SL DL, 108 note 4; SL UL, 60–61 notes 51, 52

þinglaun (OGu) þinglausn (OGu) þingslaun (OGu)
    þingslausn (OGu) noun
    assembly fee **OGu** *GL* A 40, 41

    See also: *lön*, *þing*

þinglausn (ON) noun
    end of the assembly **OIce** *Grg* Klþ 2 Þsþ 23, 76 Vís 104 Lsþ 116 Rsþ 233 Hrs 235 Misc 250, *Jó* Llb 37

    See also: *vapntak*

þinglausnadagr (ON) noun
    closing day of an assembly **OIce** *Grg* Lrþ 117

þingmalabalker (OSw) noun
    book concerning legal process **OSw** *HL* För, Rb
    legal procedure section **OSw** *SdmL* För, Rb

    See also: *balker*, *mal (1)*, *þing*

þingmannadómr (ON) noun
    assemblymen's judgment **OIce** *Jó* Kge 26

þingmark (ON) noun
    assembly boundary **OIce** *Grg* Þsþ 23, 56

þingmál (ON) noun
    lawsuit presented at the assembly **ONorw** *GuL* Olb

þingreið (ON) noun
    assembly attendance **OIce** *Grg* Vís 99
    riding to the assembly **OIce** *Grg* Feþ 164, *Jó* Þfb 2

    See also: *þingför*

þingreiðr (ON) adj.
    *having the right to attend an
    assembly* **OIce** *Grg* Vís 86, 99

þingrof (ON) noun
    assembly disruption **ONorw** *FrL* Rgb 30

þingsafglöpun (ON) noun

   assembly balking **OIce** *Grg* Þsþ 23, 25 Lrþ 117

þingsdagher (OSw) noun

   assembly day **OSw** *SdmL* Jb, Tjdb, Rb

   Thing day **OSw** *DL* Rb

   See also: *þing*

þingsdomi (OSw) **thingsdom** (ODan) noun

   decision by the assembly **ODan** *JyL* 1, 2

   judgement of the assembly **ODan**
   ESjL 2, *JyL* 2, **OSw** *ÄVgL* Jb

   See also: *domber*, *þing*

þingsfriþer (OSw) **thingfrith** (ODan) þingfriþr (OGu)
þingfriþer (OSw) noun

   Peace for the participants of a *þing* 'assembly',
   including their direct journey between it and home.
   In ODan ESjL and OGu GL, criminals were excluded
   from this peace. Violence — however mild, such as
   hair-pulling — in breach of *þingsfriþer* was fined. In
   OSw, this peace was guaranteed by the king as part of
   the *eþsöre* 'king's (sworn) peace'.

   assembly peace **ODan** *ESjL* 2,
   OSw *SdmL* Kgb, Mb, Till

   assembly sanctity **OGu** *GL* A 11

   peace of thing **OSw** *YVgL* Add

   thing assembly inviolability **OSw** *HL* Kgb

   Thing assembly peace **OSw** *DL* Eb

   thing inviolability **OSw** *HL* Kgb

   thing peace **OSw** *HL* Mb

   See also: *friþer*, *þing*

þingsganga (OSw) þingganga (ON) þinganga (OSw)
noun

   access to an assembly **OIce** *Js* Mah 19,
   ONorw *FrL* Mhb 30, *GuL* Mhb

   appearance at the assembly **OSw** *ÄVgL* Md

   coming to the assembly **OSw** *YVgL* Drb

   See also: *þing*

þingskapaþáttr (ON) noun

   assembly procedures section **OIce** *Grg* Þsþ 20

þingskot (ON) noun

   appeal to an assembly **ONorw** *FrL* Tfb 2

þingsköp (pl.) (ON) noun

   assembly procedures **OIce** *Grg* Þsþ
   21, 57 Lsþ 116 Lrþ 117

þingsmannavitni (OSw) **thingmannevitne** (ODan)
þingsmannavita (OSw) noun

   testimony of the men of the assembly **OSw** *YVgL* Add

   witness of assembly men **ODan** *ESjL* 1

   witness of the men of the assembly **OSw**
   YVgL Drb, Jb, *ÄVgL* Smb, Slb, Jb

   See also: *maþer*, *vitni*, *þing*

þingsmæn (pl.) (OSw) **thingman** (ODan) þingsmenn
(pl.) (OGu) þingmaðr (ON) þingmenn (pl.) (ON)
þinxmæn (pl.) (OSw) noun

   assembly members **OGu** *GL* A 2, 4

   assembly men **ODan** *ESjL* 1–3, *VSjL* 24, **OGu**
   GL A 11, 28, **OIce** *Grg* Vís 110 Lbþ 205 Misc
   251, *Jó* Þfb 1 Kge 19, 26 Llb 37 Kab 7 Þjb 25,
   Js Þfb 2 Mah 18 Lbb 15 Kab 3, **ONorw** *FrL*
   Jkb 2 Bvb 4, **OSw** *UL* Mb, Rb, *ÖgL* Kkb

   members of the assembly **ONorw**
   FrL Tfb 3 KrbB 24 Rgb 30

   men of the assembly **ODan** *ESjL* 2, 3, *SkL* passim,
   VSjL 22, 60, 68, 71, 84–87, **OGu** *GL* A 30, **OSw**
   YVgL Drb, Add, *ÄVgL* Md, Smb, Slb, Jb

   men present at an assembly **ONorw** *GuL*
   Krb, Kpb, Llb, Arb, Tfb, Mhb, Olb

   thingmen **OSw** *HL* Kkb

   See also: *maþer*, *þing*

þingsókn (ON) noun

   assembly district **OIce** *Grg* Ómb 143,
   Jó Kge 34, **ONorw** *GuL* Mhb, Olb

þingsóknarmaðr (ON) noun

   man belonging to the assembly
   district **ONorw** *GuL* Olb

þingsstaþer (OSw) þingstaðr (ON) þingstöð (ON)
noun

   In order to be legal, assemblies had to be held at
   specific locations, of which not much else is specified
   in the laws. The assembly site was only named in
   the OIce Jó and Js (*øxaráþing*). ONorw *Gulaþing*
   (q.v.) etc. presumably referred to districts rather
   than specific locations. There was to be one in each
   hundari (q.v.) according to OSw SdmL and UL, and
   according to HL the *þingsstaþer* of the *sokn* 'parish'
   was to be located anywhere but at the vicarage (OSw
   kirkiubol, q.v.) reflecting a division between secular
   and ecclesiastical matters. Although the word does not
   appear in ODan laws, the assembly site, according to
   ESjL, was decided by the king and approved by the
   men of the *hæreth* (see *hærap*), suggesting one in each
   such district.

   assembly place **OIce** *Grg* Þsþ 61

   assembly site **OIce** *Jó* Þfb 1, *Js* Þfb 1 Mah 18, **OSw**
   SdmL Mb, Tjdb, Rb, Till, *UL* Mb, Rb, *VmL* Rb

   place where an assembly is held **ONorw** *FrL* Var 12

   thing site **OSw** *DL* Rb, *HL* Rb

See also: *þing*

Refs: Brink forthcoming; KLNM s.v. *tingsted*

þingstefnuvitni (ON) noun

testimony of an assembly summons **OIce** *Js* Kab 2

witness that lawful summons to the assembly has taken place **ONorw** *GuL* Kpb, Løb

witness to an assembly summons **OIce** *Jó* Þfb 4, **ONorw** *FrL* Rgb 7

See also: *vitni*

þingstæmna (OSw) **thingstævne** (ODan) **þingstefna** (ON) **þings stæmna** (OSw) **þingstæmpning** (OSw) noun

assembly meeting **OSw** *YVgL* Add, *ÖgL* Eb

assembly summons **ODan** *ESjL* 3, **OSw** *SdmL* Mb, Rb, *ÖgL* Db

summons to an assembly **OIce** *Jó* Þfb 6, *Js* Mah 22, **ONorw** *FrL* KrbB 4, 20 Mhb 18 ArbB 23 LlbB 1, *GuL* Kpb, Løb, **OSw** *ÖgL* Db

See also: *stæmna*, *þing*

þingstöð (ON) noun

place where the assembly was held **ONorw** *GuL* Mhb

þingsvægher (OSw) **thingvægh** (ODan) noun

assembly road **OSw** *SdmL* Kgb

road to the assembly **ODan** *JyL* 2, 3, **OSw** *YVgL* Add

road to the Thing assembly **OSw** *DL* Eb, Bb

thing road **OSw** *HL* Kgb

way to the assembly **OSw** *ÖgL* Eb, Db

See also: *þing*, *þingsfriþer*

þingtak (ON) noun

Acceptance (of legislation) at an assembly.

assembly legislation **OIce** *Js* Kdb 3

Refs: CV s.v. *þingtak*; Fritzner s.v. *þingtak*; Hertzberg s.v. *þingtak*

þingunöti (OSw) **þingunautr** (ON) noun

jurisdiction of the assembly **OSw** *ÖgL* Db

man of the district **OIce** *Grg* Tíg 265

man of the same assembly **OIce** *Grg* Þsþ 49, 56 Misc 239

member of the Thing assembly **OSw** *DL* Rb

See also: *innanþingsmaðr*, *þing*

þingvist (ON) noun

assembly membership **OIce** *Grg* Þsþ 22, 59

þingviti (OSw) **þingvíti** (ON) noun

fine for not appearing at the assembly when summoned **ONorw** *GuL* Tfb, Mhb

fine for not appearing when summoned **OIce** *Jó* Þfb 5 Kge 34

fine for not attending an assembly **ONorw** *FrL* Leb 8

thing penalty **OSw** *HL* Rb

See also: *þing*

þingvitni (OSw) **thingsvitne** (ODan) **þings vitni** (OSw) noun

Defined in ODan JyL 1:38 as the men, at least seven, present at a *thing* (ODan) 'assembly' (see *þing*) who witnessed cases being handled there. These could be called on to testify later, and ODan laws repeatedly state that no oaths could be sworn against their testimony. In OSw DL Rb:9, three men from each *broafiol* (OSw) 'quarter of a Thing assembly area' were to be called to swear as *þingvitni*, and in ODan SkL 18 they were two. One of their main functions seems to have been to ensure and confirm proper public announcements, not least concerning land transactions, but they also appear in matters of inheritance, wounds, killings, etc.

assembly witness **ODan** *ESjL* 1–3, *JyL* 1, 2, *SkL* 18, 59, 121, 140, 170, 233, **OSw** *SdmL* Jb, Mb, Rb

Thing assembly witness **OSw** *DL* Bb, Gb, Rb

witness of the assembly **OSw** *YVgL* Jb, *ÄVgL* Jb

See also: *vitni*, *þing*

Refs: Andersen 2010, 84, 96; Schlyter s.v. *þingvitni*, Tamm and Vogt, eds, 2016, 301

þingværr (ON) adj.

having the right to be present at an assembly **OIce** *Grg* Vís 105

þingvöllr (ON) noun

assembly ground **OIce** *Grg* Þsþ 50 Vís 101

spring assembly place **OIce** *Grg* Klþ 2

þiufbogher (OSw) noun

A fine paid for theft.

thief-{bogher} **OSw** *HL* Mb

Refs: Brink forthcoming

þiufbot (OSw) **þiufsböter** (OSw) noun

compensation for theft **OSw** *YVgL* Tb, Föb, *ÄVgL* Tb

thief-fine **OSw** *HL* Mb

See also: *bot*, *þiuver*

þiufhol (OSw) noun

thief lair **OSw** *HL* Mb

þiufnaþabalker (OSw) noun

theft section **OSw** *SdmL* Tjdb

See also: *balker*, *þiufnaþer*

þiufnaþer (OSw) **thjuvneth** (ODan) **þiaufnaþr** (OGu) **þjófnaðr** (ON) **þjófnuðr** (ON) noun

The taking or withholding of somebody else's belongings, as well as the actual stolen goods. With an element of concealment, in contrast to the act of openly — but still illegally — taking something (OSw *ræna* 'to rob'). Occasionally delimited against legally conducted purchases (OSw *köp*, q.v.). The stealthy nature of the deed made it dishonourable and could entail harsh punishments, including mutilation, hanging and outlawry (in Iceland) under certain conditions, such as being caught in the act and relapsing, or depending on the value of the stolen goods or the gender and status of the thief.

case of theft **ODan** *ESjL* 2, **OSw** *DL* Tjdb, *VmL* Rb, *ÖgL* Eb

stealing **OSw** *HL* Mb

stolen goods **ODan** *ESjL* 3, *JyL* 2, *SkL* 141, *VSjL* 86, 87, **OGu** *GL* Add. 8 (B 55), **OSw** *DL* Tjdb, *HL* Mb, *SdmL* Tjdb, *UL* Mb, *VmL* Mb, *YVgL* Rlb, Add, *ÄVgL* Rlb, *ÖgL* Eb

theft **ODan** *ESjL* 2, 3, *JyL* 2, 3, *SkL* 85, 146, 161, 201, *VSjL* 41, 87, **OIce** *Jó* Þjb 20, 25, **OSw** *DL* Tjdb, *HL* Mb, *SdmL* Kkb, Bb, Kmb, Tjdb, Rb, *UL* För, Kkb, Mb, Rb, *VmL* För, Mb, *YVgL* Gb, Rlb, Föb, Add, *ÄVgL* Gb, Tb, Fös, *ÖgL* Eb, Vm

theft case **OSw** *HL* Mb

Expressions:

fulder þiufnaþer, full þyft (OSw)
Usually a theft of half a *mark* or more.

full theft **OSw** *UL* Mb *VmL* Mb *YVgL* Tb

See also: *bodræt, bospænd, fulder, fyli, urþiuva, þiufska, þiuft, þiuver*

Refs: Ekholst 2009, 107–12; KLNM s.v. *tyveri*; SAOB s.v.v. *stjäla, stöld*; Schlyter s.v.v. *styld, þiufnaþer, þiuft*

þiufsak (OSw) **thjuvsak** (ODan) **þjófsök** (ON) **þiufs sak** (OSw) noun

case of theft **ODan** *ESjL* 2, *SkL* 152, 157, 158, **OIce** *Jó* Llb 48, 71 Þjb 9, 13 Fml 21, **OSw** *ÄVgL* Tb

stealing **OSw** *ÄVgL* Tb

theft **ODan** *JyL* 2, *SkL* 145, 230, *VSjL* 87, **OSw** *YVgL* Tb, Add

thieving case **OIce** *Grg* Þsþ 49, 62 Vís 110

See also: *sak, þiuver*

þiufseþer (OSw) **þýfieiðr** (ON) noun

oath concerning theft **OSw** *YVgL* Add

oath of denial in cases of theft **ONorw** *GuL* Tfb

þiufska (OSw) **þýfska** (ON) noun

theft **ONorw** *FrL* Var 45, *GuL* Krb, Tjb, **OSw** *YVgL* Tb, *ÄVgL* Tb

thievery **OIce** *Jó* Mah 2, *Js* Mah 6 Þjb 1, 7, **ONorw** *FrL* Intr 22

See also: *styld, þiuft, þiuver*

þiufsrætter (OSw) **þiaufa retr** (OGu) noun

law of theft/thieves **OGu** *GL* A 38

thief's due **OSw** *SdmL* Kmb

thief's punishment **OSw** *HL* Mb

þiufstolin (OSw) **thjuvstolen** (ODan) **þjófstolinn** (ON) adj.

something thieved **OIce** *Grg* Rsþ 227

stolen **ODan** *SkL* 141, 142, **OIce** *Grg* Klþ 5 Ómb 131, *Jó* Þjb 1, 3, *Js* Þjb 3, **ONorw** *GuL* Tjb, **OSw** *HL* Mb, *YVgL* Tb, *ÄVgL* Tb

stolen goods **ODan** *SkL* 197

taken by theft **ODan** *SkL* 157

þiuft (OSw) **þypt** (OGu) **þypti** (OGu) **þýfi** (ON) **þýft** (ON) **þýfð** (ON) **þiufti** (OSw) **þiupti** (OSw) **þyfft** (OSw) **þyfpt** (OSw) **þyft** (OSw) **þypt** (OSw) noun

stolen goods **OGu** *GL* Add. 8 (B 55), **OIce** *Jó* Þjb 6, **OSw** *HL* Mb, *UL* Mb, *VmL* Mb, *YVgL* Drb, Tb, *ÄVgL* Md, Tb

theft **OGu** *GL* Add. 8 (B 55), **OIce** *Grg* Lbþ 186, 199 Fjl 221, *Jó* Þjb 5, 8, *KRA* 29, **ONorw** *FrL* KrbB 20, *GuL* Tfb, Tjb, **OSw** *DL* Tjdb, *HL* Mb, *UL* Mb, Kmb, *VmL* Kkb, Mb, Kmb, *YVgL* Drb, Tb

See also: *agriper, fyli, styld, þiufnaþer, þiufska*

þiuftamal (OSw) noun

theft **OSw** *ÖgL* Kkb

þiuftas (OSw) **thjuvtes** (ODan) **þyftas** (OSw) verb

act like a thief **ODan** *SkL* 177

make oneself a thief **OSw** *YVgL* Tb, *ÄVgL* Tb

take in a thief's way **ODan** *SkL* 85

See also: *þiuver*

þiufvalabot (OSw) noun

fine for harbouring a thief **OSw** *VmL* Mb

See also: *bot, böta*

þiuvabalker (OSw) **þjófabálkr** (ON) **þjófabölkr** (ON) **þiufna bolker** (OSw) **þiufnaþa balker** (OSw) noun

book on theft **ONorw** *GuL* Tjb, **OSw** *YVgL* Tb, *ÄVgL* Tb

chapter on theft **OIce** *Jó* MagBref Þjb 1, 20

theft section **OSw** *SdmL* För

See also: *balker, þiuver*

þiuver (OSw) **thjuv** (ODan) **þiaufr** (OGu) **þjófr** (ON) noun

thief **ODan** *ESjL* 2, 3, *JyL* 2, 3, *SkL* passim, *VSjL* 87, **OFar** Seyð 5, **OGu** *GL* A 38, 39, Add. 8 (B 55), **OIce** *Jó* Mah 2, 20 Llb 19, 45 Kab 2 Þjb 1, 2, *Js* Lbb 24 Rkb 1 Þjb 1, *KRA* 11, **ONorw** *EidsL* 50.13, *FrL* Intr 21, 22 Mhb 30 LlbB 11, *GuL* Krb, Llb, Tfb, Kvr, Mhb, Tjb, **OSw** *DL* Tjdb, Rb, *HL* Kkb, Äb, Mb, *SdmL* Kkb, Bb, Kmb, Mb, Tjdb, Rb, *UL* Kkb, Mb, Kmb, Blb, Add. 9, *VmL* Kkb, Mb, Kmb,

Bb, *YVgL* Kkb, Urb, Drb, Äb, Tb, Utgb, Add, *ÄVgL* Md, Urb, Äb, Rlb, Tb, Föb, *ÖgL* Kkb, Eb, Vm

See also: *hvin, hvinska, snattan*

þiþborin (OSw) **þýborinn** (ON) adj.

born of a bondwoman **OIce** *Grg* Bat 113, **ONorw** *FrL* Sab 5 ArbA 8 ArbB 1 Rgb 47, *GuL* Løb, Arb, Mhb

son of a slave-woman **OSw** *VmL* Kmb

See also: *þræl, þybarn, þydotir*

þiælasyn (OSw) **þiala syn** (OSw) noun

frost-bound investigations **OSw** *VmL* Bb

ground frost inspection **OSw** *SdmL* Bb

þiæna (OSw) **þiana** (OSw) verb

perform armed service **OSw** *UL* Kmb, Rb, *VmL* Kmb, Rb

þiængsgæld (OSw) **thæghngjald** (ODan) **þegngildi** (ON) **þingsgæld** (OSw) **þiægnsgæld** (OSw) noun

A 'subject payment' ; a fine paid to the king when one of his subjects was killed. The fine appears in several provincial laws throughout the North. Þegngildi was set quite high at 12 marks (JyL II.13), 13 marks (Jó Mah 1) or 40 marks (VmL Mb 11). In Icelandic texts the term is occasionally abbreviated as *þegn*. The payment of the þegngildi was one part of the process of obtaining amnesty from the king in Norway (see *landsvist*).

compensation for a free man **ONorw** *FrL* Intr 2

thane's compensation **OSw** *DL* Mb, *VmL* Mb

thanegeld **ONorw** *EidsL* 28.2

tribute for a subject **OIce** *Js* Mah 2, 29

wergild for a subject **OIce** *Jó* Þfb 5 Mah 1, 4 Fml 17

{thæghn} money **ODan** *JyL* 2

See also: *bot, frælsmansbot, landsvist, mannsgildi, saköri, þokkabot*

Refs: CV s.v. *þegngildi*; F s.v. *þegngildi*; Jørgensen 2014; KLNM s.v. *þegngildi, straff*; NGL V s.v. *þegngildi*

þiænista (OSw) **thjaneste** (ODan) **þianista** (OGu) **þianista** (OSw) **þiænist** (OSw) noun

divine service **OSw** *SdmL* Kkb

God's service **OGu** *GL* A 6

mass **ODan** *SkKL* 11

sacrament **OSw** *YVgL* Kkb

service **ODan** *ESjL* 1, 3, **OGu** *GL* Add. 1 (B 4), **OSw** *SdmL* Kkb, Tjdb, Till, *UL* Kkb, Mb, Jb, *VmL* Kkb, Mb, *YVgL* Kkb, Rlb, Jb, *ÖgL* Kkb

Expressions:

guþs þiænist (OSw)

church service **OSw** *SdmL* Till

þiænistulös (OSw) adj.

unemployed **OSw** *DL* Tjdb

þiænistumaþer (OSw) noun

liegeman **OSw** *UL* StfBM, Kgb, Rb

man in service **OSw** *YVgL* Föb

office holder **OSw** *YVgL* Add

servant **OSw** *SdmL* Conf, Till, *UL* Mb

serving man **OSw** *SdmL* Kgb

þjóðbraut (ON) noun

This word, together with ON *þjóðgata* (q.v.) and *þjóðvegr* (q.v.), all meaning 'highway', referred to public roads (as opposed to farm roads and private roads). Highways had to meet certain standards with respect to breadth. A passage in Grg (Lbþ 181) states that if a fence crossed a *þjóðbraut* there should be a gateway in it with a breadth of 4 1/2 ells. The *þjóðgata* was required to have a breadth roughly equal to the length of a spear (specified in detail in GuL ch. 90). The *þjóðvegir* had to be at least 8 ells broad.

It is not always clear who were responsible for the supervision of these roads, but FrL held the bishops responsible, since it was vital to the interests of the church that the roads were in good condition. The duties of building and maintenance were imposed on the peasants.

highway **OIce** *Grg* Lbþ 181, *Jó* Llb 21, 32

See also: *þjóðgata, þjóðleið, þjóðvegr*

Refs: Hertzberg s.v.v. *þjóðbraut, þjóðgata, þjóðvegr*; KLNM s.v.v. *ferjemann, kongevej, veg*

þjóðgata (ON) noun

highway **OIce** *Jó* Llb 44, **ONorw** *GuL* Llb

See also: *þjóðbraut, þjóðleið, þjóðvegr*

þjóðleið (ON) noun

fairway **ONorw** *GuL* Leb

highway **OIce** *Grg* Lbþ 206

þjóðstefna (ON) noun

array **OIce** *Grg* Bat 115

þjóðvegr (ON) noun

highway **OIce** *Jó* Llb 32

See also: *gata, þjóðbraut, þjóðgata, þjóðleið*

þjóflaun (ON) noun

thief concealment **OIce** *Grg* Fjl 225 Rsþ 227

þjófnaðarmál (ON) noun

case of theft **OIce** *Jó* Þjb 20

þjófráð (ON) noun

advising to steal **OIce** *Jó* Þjb 1

theft plot **OIce** *Grg* Rsþ 227

þjófskapr (ON) noun

case of theft **OIce** *Grg* Rsþ 227

theft **OIce** *Grg* Rsþ 227, 230

þjófsnautr (ON) noun

thief's accomplice **OIce** *Grg* Rsþ 227, *Jó* Llb 45 Þjb 1

þjónn (ON) noun

Both free and unfree servants, particularly ones entrusted with certain responsibilities.

personal servant **ONorw** *GuL* Mhb

servant **ONorw** *EidsL* 46.1, *FrL* Kvb 21

slave **ONorw** *EidsL* 28.2

Refs: Brink 2012, 127–32; Fritzner s.v. *þjónn*; Hertzberg s.v. *þjónn*

þofta (ON) **þopta** (ON) noun

thwart **ONorw** *GuL* Llb, Leb

þoftugjöld (pl.) (ON) noun

thwart fines **ONorw** *GuL* Leb

þokkabot (OSw) **thokkebot** (ODan) **þokkabót** (ON) **þukka bot** (OSw) noun

A fine for breaches of honour; a supplementary fine. A *þokkabót* has been equated with 'punitive damages' or 'exemplary damages' in modern US and UK court systems (Jó trans. p. 243). As a payment to satisfy a breach of honour the fine is thought to be a practice older than written provincial laws. The amount due for a *þokkabot* varied by rank according to some of the Swedish provincial laws. There it is predominantly specified as a fine paid to one's superior, such as when a slave is injured. A special instance of *þokkabot* features as part of the king's *roðarætter* (see *roþarætter*), whereby he is entitled to a fine when someone is killed aboard a ship he is on (cf. KLNM s.v. *konge*). In Denmark the term appears only in SkL as a two-*øre* fine. The same amount is specified in Iceland (Jó Llb 45, Þjb 11). In Iceland it might have been used synonymously with *öfundarbót* (q.v.). In Norway this was primarily a common fine for theft and defamation.

compensation for unfriendly conduct **ONorw** *GuL* Llb

fine for shaming **ODan** *SkL* 103

honorary fine **OSw** *HL* Mb

honour fine **OSw** *HL* Mb, *SdmL* Mb, *UL* Mb, *VmL* Mb

payment for shaming **ODan** *SkL* 175

redress **OIce** *Jó* Llb 45 Þjb 11

See also: *bot, böta, öfundarbót, þiængsgæld, þokki*

Refs: CV s.v. *þokkabót*; F s.v. *þokkabót*; GAO s.v. *Mannheiligkeit*; KLNM s.v. *böter, konge, straff, tyveri, ærekrenkelse*; LexMA s.v. *Buße*; NGL V s.v. *þokkabót*

þokkaorþ (OSw) noun

insulting words **OSw** *HL* Mb

þokki (OSw) **thokke** (ODan) **þunki** (OGu) noun

dishonour **OSw** *SdmL* Äb

honorary fine **OSw** *HL* Mb

honour fine **OSw** *UL* Mb

honour payment **OSw** *ÖgL* Db, Vm

insult **OGu** *GL* A 19

offence **OSw** *HL* Äb

shaming **ODan** *SkL* 122, 172, 175, 217, 228

See also: *þokkabot*

þola (ON) verb

accept **ONorw** *GuL* Olb

þorláksmessa (ON) noun

St Þorlákr's Day **OIce** *Grg* Klþ 13

þorp (OSw) **thorp** (ODan) noun

In Danish laws *thorp* refers to a new settlement ('outlying village') created from the main (old) village (*athelby*, q.v.), and the laws regulate the relationship between the old and the new village, boundaries, size and the use of deserted settlements. In the Swedish laws, *þorp* seems to refer to a single (often small) farm, possibly moved out from a village.

croft **OSw** *YVgL* Jb, *ÄVgL* Jb

new settlement **OSw** *YVgL* Jb

smallholding **OSw** *UL* Kkb, *VmL* Kkb

thorp **ODan** *ESjL* 3, *JyL* 1, *SkL* 72, 185

See also: *þorpakarl*

Refs: Berg 2013, 22–23; Hoff 1998, 122–41; KLNM s.v. *torp*; Porsmose 1988, 240–48; Schlyter s.v. *þorp*

þorpakarl (OSw) noun

crofter **OSw** *HL* Rb, *UL* Rb, *VmL* Rb

þorva (OSw) **þorfa** (OGu) verb

benefit **OGu** *GL* A 1

be forced **OGu** *GL* A 28

be liable **OGu** *GL* Add. 8 (B55)

must (i.e. have to) **OGu** *GL* A 53, 37, **OSw** *UL* Blb

need **OGu** *GL* A 2, 10, **OSw** *UL* För, Kkb, Kgb, Jb, Kmb, Blb, Rb, *VmL* För, Kkb, Jb, Kmb, Bb

ought **OSw** *UL* Kgb, Mb, Jb, Blb, *VmL* Mb, Bb

require **OSw** *UL* Kkb, Blb, *VmL* Kkb

Expressions:

við þorva, viþer þorva (OSw) **viþr þorfa** (OGu)

demand **OGu** *GL* A 3

need **OGu** *GL* A 10, 14, 19, 49 **OSw** *UL* StfBM, För, Kkb, Jb, Kmb, Blb *VmL* För

See also: *varþa*

þrang (OSw) **þrang** (OGu) **þröng** (ON) noun

extremity **OSw** *VmL* Jb

necessity **OSw** *VmL* Bb

need **OGu** *GL* A 28, **OSw** *VmL* Kkb

pressing need **OGu** *GL* A 28, **OSw** *UL* Kgb

throng **OGu** *GL* A 18, **ONorw** *GuL* Llb

þrangaköp (OSw) noun

hardship sale **OSw** *SdmL* Jb

þrangalös (OSw) þranglaus (OGu) adj.

without coercion **OGu** *GL* A 63

without necessary cause **OSw** *VmL* Bb

þrásk (ON) verb

be stubborn **ONorw** *GuL* Mhb

þrenættinger (OSw) noun

A legal meeting summoned three days in advance, only appearing in the context of a stolen animal found in another province by the owner.

three night summons **OSw** *YVgL* Tb

See also: *endaghi, fæmt, siunættinger*

þrettándi dagr jóla (ON) noun

Thirteenth Day of Christmas (6 January) **ONorw** *GuL* Krb

See also: *prættandidagher*

þrettánsessa (ON) noun

thirteen-bencher **ONorw** *GuL* Leb

þriðjabróðra (pl.) (ON) þriðjabræðri (ON) noun

fourth cousins **OIce** *Grg* Þsþ 80 Vís 94, 97 Bat 113 Ómb 143

þriðjungsmaðr (ON) noun

man of an assembly third **OIce** *Grg* Þsþ 22, 25

man of the riding **ONorw** *EidsL* 38.5

man of the Third **ONorw** *EidsL* 34.2, *FrL* KrbA 7

þriggjamannaeiðr (ON) noun

three-man oath **ONorw** *GuL* Krb, Kpb, Løb, Llb, Arb, Tfb, Mhb, Tjb, Leb

See also: *eþer, lýrittareiðr*

þriggjamarkamál (ON) noun

three {marka} case **ONorw** *GuL* Krb

þriggjamarkasekð (ON) noun

fine of three marks **OIce** *Grg* Þsþ 59, **ONorw** *FrL* Intr 16

þriggjaþingamál (ON) noun

A three-assembly case. Appears only once in Grg Feþ 156, where it refers to cases of illicit sexual unions. The term has been interpreted to mean that such cases had to be prosecuted before the end of the third assembly after the incident took place (or after the principal learned of it). Otherwise the case expired.

three-assembly case **OIce** *Grg* Feþ 156

See also: *fall, fyrna, mal (1)*

Refs: CV s.v. *þingmál*; Fritzner s.v. *þingmál*; GrgTr II:73

þrigildi (OGu) noun

threefold fine **OGu** *GL* Add. 8 (B 55)

triple fine **OGu** *GL* Add. 8 (B 55)

þriskuldi (OSw) thærskeld (ODan) þresköldr (ON) noun

Appears in several legally significant contexts as a boundary, for instance concerning certain deals (OSw YVgL Jb), violent crimes (OSw HL Mb) or ownership in cases of theft (ODan JyL 2).

threshold **ODan** *ESjL* 3, *JyL* 2, *VSjL* 87, **ONorw** *GuL* Krb, Llb, **OSw** *HL* Mb, *YVgL* Gb, Jb

þriþiobyrþ (OSw) noun

kinship of the third degree **OSw** *VmL* Kkb, Äb

See also: *attunger*

þriþiunger (OSw) þriþiungr (OGu) þriðjungr (ON) noun

Literally a 'third' of something. An administrative/judicial division on different levels in the administrative hierarchy. The division into *þriþiungar* in Uppland was limited to very few districts (Hafström 1949, 142–43), and might not have existed in Västmanland as Schlyter indicates that the manuscript might have been corrupt in the actual passage (Schlyter s.v. *þriþiunger*). In GL, DL and HL it is the highest administrative district below *land* (q.v.). In Norwegian laws it was a district on the highest level in FrL and a district below *fylki* (q.v.) in BorgL, EidsL, GuL. In Iceland (Grg) a *þriðjungr* corresponds to the group of men attached to a particular *goði* (q.v.) at a spring assembly. There were three goðar per spring assembly, thus they were responsible for an 'assembly third' [cf. Grg tr. I:240].

assembly third **OIce** *Grg* Þsþ 23, 45

riding **OGu** *GL* A 31, 41, 42, 45a

third **OGu** *GS* Ch. 1, 3, **ONorw** *EidsL* 32.7, *GuL* Krb, Kvb, Løb, Mhb, Sab, **OSw** *HL* Äb, Mb, Jb, Kmb, Blb, Rb, *UL* passim, *VmL* passim

three lots **OSw** *HL* Kkb, Kgb, Mb, Blb

{þriþiunger} **OSw** *DL* Eb, Bb, Rb, *HL* Mb

See also: *attunger, fiarþunger, goði, hundari, land, þing, þriðjungsmaðr, varþing*

Refs: KLNM, s.v. *treding*; Lundberg 1972, 91–92; Peel 2015, 14–15, 248–49, 286 note 1/18; Schlyter s.v. *þriþiunger*; SL DL, xxi; SL GL, lxxxiv–lxxxvii

þriþiungsskipti (OSw) noun

division into thirds **OSw** *YVgL* Gb

þrítíðungr (ON) adj.

three years old **ONorw** *GuL* Løb

þrítugsmorginn (ON) noun

   morning of the thirtieth day **ONorw** *GuL* Krb, Arb

þrjóta (ON) verb

   be destitute **OIce** *Grg* Ómb 128, 129

   be wanting **ONorw** *GuL* Leb

þrot (ON) noun

   poverty **OIce** *Jó* Kge 24, **ONorw**

   GuL Løb, Arb, Olb, Leb

   state of destitution **OIce** *Grg* Ómb 135

þrotamaðr (ON) þrotsmenn (ON) noun

   pauper **ONorw** *FrL* ArbB 13, *GuL* Arb

þrotráði (ON) adj.

   destitute **OIce** *Grg* Ómb 128, 138 Hrs 234

þrútr (ON) noun

   mouth **ONorw** *GuL* Llb

þryska (OSw) noun

   contumacy **OSw** *YVgL* Kkb, Add

   defiance **OSw** *SdmL* Kkb, Till

   stubbornness **OSw** *YVgL* Utgb

   See also: *þryskas*, *þryter*

þryskas (OSw) þryska (OSw) þryta (OSw) þryzkas (OSw) verb

   be contumacious **OSw** *HL* Kgb

   be defiant **OSw** *UL* Kkb, *VmL* Kkb

   defy **OSw** *SdmL* Kkb, Bb, Till

   evade **OSw** *HL* Kkb

   be refractory **OSw** *HL* Rb

   be stubborn **OSw** *YVgL* Utgb

   See also: *þryska*, *þryter*

þryter (OSw) þrjótr (ON) þryt (OSw) noun

   contumacy **OSw** *YVgL* Add

   defiance **OSw** *VmL* Rb

   obstinacy **OSw** *YVgL* Rlb, *ÄVgL* Rlb

   one too stubborn to pay **OIce** *Jó* Kab 3

   reluctant or stubborn person

   ONorw *GuL* Løb, Llb, Olb

   stubbornness **OSw** *YVgL* Utgb

   villain **OIce** *Jó* Llb 12

   See also: *þryskas*

þræböti (OSw) noun

   triple compensation **OSw** *VmL* Mb

   triple fine **OSw** *SdmL* Mb

   See also: *bot*, *böta*

þræbötisdrap (OSw) noun

   killing for triple fines **OSw** *SdmL* Mb

   See also: *bot*, *drap*

þræl (OSw) thræl (ODan) þrel (OGu) þrell (OGu) þræll (ON) noun

   slave **ODan** *ESjL* 2, 3, *JyL* 1, 3, *SkKL* 10, *SkL* 115, 119, 122–125, 130, 151, 160–162, *VSjL* 43, 86, **OGu** *GL* A 6, 8, 15, 16, 19, 22, Add. 8 (B 55), **OIce** *Grg* Klþ 9, 14 Þsþ 44 Vís 102, 111 Arþ 118 Ómb 128 Rsþ 229 Misc 237, *KRA* 10, **ONorw** *FrL* KrbA 1, 2 Mhb 5, 55 Var 20 ArbB 12 Rgb 40 Kvb 20 LlbA 21 LlbB 10, *GuL* Kvb, Løb, Llb, Mhb, Tjb, Leb, **OSw** *SdmL* Kmb, Mb, Tjdb, *UL* Äb (table of contents only), Mb, Kmb, *VmL* Kkb, Äb (rubric only), Mb, Kmb

   thrall **OSw** *DL* Kkb, Gb, *YVgL* Vs, Frb, Drb, Äb, Gb, Rlb, Tb, Föb, Add, *ÄVgL* Md, Smb, Vs, Slb, Äb, Gb, Rlb, Tb, Fös, *ÖgL* Eb, Db, Vm

   See also: *ambat*, *annöþogher*, *deghia*, *fostra*, *fostre*, *frælsgiva*, *frælsgivi*, *gæfþræl*, *hemahion*, *hemakona*, *hion*, *huskona*, *leysingi*, *man*, *mansmaðr*, *ofræls*, *skuldarmaðr*, *þiþborin*, *þjónn*

þræla (ON) verb

   call a person a slave **ONorw** *GuL* Mhb

þrælaarf (OSw) noun

   inheritance from a thrall **OSw** *HL* Äb

þrælbaugr (ON) noun

   Compensation rings, wergild paid by slaves or for slaves.

   slave ring **OIce** *Grg* Bat 113

   Refs: CV s.v. *þrælbaugr*; Fritzner *þrælbaugr*

þrælbot (OSw) noun

   compensation for a thrall **OSw** *YVgL* Frb

   See also: *bot*, *þræl*

þrældómr (ON) noun

   slavery **OIce** *Grg* Rsþ 229

þræmænninger (OSw) þrímenningr (ON) noun

   person related in the third degree

   OIce *Jó* Kge 23, *KRA* 20

   second cousin **OIce** *Jó* Kge 17, 31,

   OSw *DL* Kkb, Mb, *HL* Mb

þræskipta (OSw) verb

   divide in three **OSw** *DL* Gb, *SdmL* Mb

   divide in three lots **OSw** *HL* Mb

   divide in three parts **OSw** *DL* Mb

þræskipti (OSw) noun

   Mostly used of fines divided and distributed between three parties, occasionally explicit, such as the leader (the king, the shipmaster, etc.), the collective (the district, the oarsmen, etc.) and the plaintiff. Also of, for instance, tithes divided and distributed between the church, the priest and the poor.

division in three **OSw** *DL* Kkb, Mb, Bb, Tjdb, Rb, *SdmL* Kgb, Jb, Bb, Kmb, Mb, Tjdb, Rb, Till

division in three lots **OSw** *HL* Kkb, Äb, Mb, Jb, Blb, Rb

fine divided in three **OSw** *DL* Tjdb

three instalments **OSw** *HL* Kgb

þræstene (OSw) noun

boundary marker consisting of three stones **OSw** *SdmL* Bb

See also: *lýrittr*, *mark (3)*, *marksteinn*, *mærki*, *rör*, *tiældrusten*

Refs: Schlyter s.v. *þræstene*

þræta (OSw) **þrætte** (ODan) noun

disagreement **OSw** *ÖgL* Kkb

dispute **ODan** *ESjL* 1, 2, *JyL* 1, **OSw** *ÖgL* Eb

quarrel **ODan** *ESjL* 2, **OSw** *DL* Mb

þrættandidagher (OSw) noun

Epiphany **OSw** *UL* Rb, *VmL* Rb

Twelfth Day **OSw** *SdmL* Rb, Till

See also: *þrettándi dagr jóla*

þróndir (pl.) (ON) **þróndr** (ON) noun

people from Trøndelag **ONorw** *GuL* Leb

person from Trøndelag **ONorw** *FrL* Reb 3

þumalfingr (ON) noun

thumb **ONorw** *GuL* Llb, Mhb

þumalöln (ON) **þumalalin** (ON) noun

thumb-ell **OIce** *Grg* Misc 246, **ONorw** *FrL* LlbA 21

þumlungr (ON) noun

thumb-width **OIce** *Grg* Misc 246, *Jó* Kab 5

þurfamaðr (ON) noun

needy person **OIce** *Grg* Tíg 255

þveiti (ON) noun

bit **OIce** *Grg* Bat 113

small coin **ONorw** *FrL* LlbB 12

þvergarðr (ON) noun

dam **OIce** *Jó* Llb 56

þverra (ON) verb

decrease **ONorw** *GuL* Arb, Mhb

þversök (ON) noun

The *þversök* ('cross payment') was a part of the *værgæld* that was paid by a certain group (*uppnám*, q.v.) in the killer's kindred to two others but not exactly correspondent groups (*uppnám*) in the kindred of the killed man.

cross payment **ONorw** *GuL* Mhb

Refs: Hertzberg s.v. *þversök*

þverþili (ON) noun

wainscot **ONorw** *GuL* Llb

þværfoter (OSw) noun

breadth of a foot **OSw** *SdmL* Bb

þybarn (OGu) noun

illegitimate child **OGu** *GL* A 20

See also: *frillubarn*

þydisker (OSw) adj.

German **OSw** *YVgL* Äb, *ÄVgL* Äb

þydotir (OGu) noun

illegitimate daughter **OGu** *GL* A 20

þyn (OSw) noun

barrel **OSw** *DL* Kkb, *VmL* Kkb, *ÖgL* Kkb

{þyn} **OSw** *SdmL* Kkb, Jb

þyrma (ON) verb

observe **ONorw** *GuL* Krb

remain in dependence **ONorw** *GuL* Løb

See also: *þyrmsl*

þyrmsl (ON) noun

loyalty of slave to master **ONorw** *GuL* Løb

obligation **OIce** *KRA* 6, 7, **ONorw** *FrL* ArbB 10

See also: *leysingi*, *þyrma*

þyrmslamaðr (ON) noun

dependent man **ONorw** *FrL* Rgb 14 Bvb 1

þysun (OGu) noun

illegitimate son **OGu** *GL* A 20

þyþilagh (OSw) noun

bestiality **OSw** *SdmL* Kkb, *UL* Kkb, *VmL* Kkb

sexual intercourse with an animal **OSw** *DL* Kkb

þægn (OSw) **þegn** (ON) **þiængn** (OSw) noun

A type of free man, possibly one who had the right to attend assemblies. Later someone who was subject to a king or prince; a liegeman. *Þegn*, along with *drengr* (see *drænger*), is thought to have held the connotation of an honourable or upright man. It has also been assumed that a *þegn* earlier referred to a type of warrior or a general type of free person, but an alternative etymology suggests that a *þegn* was a type of servant or slave. At least one MS variant of *þegn* reads *þjónar* (servants, see *þjónn*), and *þegn* has been used to gloss Lat. *servus*. The Nordic *þegn* bears some similarity to the OE *þegn*, but it is unclear how the two are connected, particularly since both terms are often used in poetic contexts. In Scandinavian-controlled areas of England, a *þegn* ranked under a *hölðr* (q.v.). In later Anglo-Saxon England a *þegn* eventually came to be mean magnates (i.e. owners of large landholdings) who received their lands as a reward for war service, but this does not seem to have been the case in the Nordic areas. Much of the research on the term *þegn* to date focuses on evidence found on runestones, where the term has been interpreted as something akin to 'member of a royal retinue'. Both *þegn* and *drengr* have at times been viewed as a type of military or social rank, but this hypothesis seems to be losing favour. It has been postulated that a Danish *þegn* referred to someone who had given an oath of fealty to the king and perhaps served as some sort of royal official. In some instances (e.g. Jb Kge 26) *þegn* is used as a synonym for *þegngildi*, a type of fine paid to the king.

> *dues to be paid for a subject of the crown* **OIce** *Jó* Kge 26, 29
>
> *free man* **ONorw** *GuL* Llb, Mhb, Olb, Leb, **OSw** *YVgL* Drb, *ÄVgL* Md
>
> *good man and true* **OIce** *Grg* Þsþ 20, 45
>
> *man* **ONorw** *FrL* Intr 8 Bvb 1
>
> *subject* **OIce** *Jó* MagBref Mah 2 Fml 14, *Js* Kdb 4, 5 Mah 5, 7 Þjb 9
>
> *thane* **ONorw** *FrL* Mhb 5

See also: *búþegn*, *drænger*, *höldr*, *rekspegn*, *þiængsgæld*

Refs: CV s.v. *þegn*; F s.v. *þegn*; GAO s.v. *Untertan*; Goetting 2006; KLNM s.v. *þegn*; NF s.v. *thegn*; NGL V s.v. *þegn*; ONP s.v. *þegn*; Orning 2008, 73, 80; Sundkvist 2008; Syrett 2000

þörf (ON) noun

> *benefit* **ONorw** *GuL* Kvb
>
> *need* **ONorw** *GuL* Krb, Leb
>
> *relieving oneself* **ONorw** *GuL* Mhb

æftermal (ODan) noun

> *action* **ODan** *JyL* 2
>
> *suit* **ODan** *JyL* 2

ægha (OSw) **aiga** (OGu) **eyga** (OGu) **eiga** (ON) noun

> *land* **OGu** *GL* A 63, Add. 9 (B 81), **OSw** *DL* Bb, Gb, *UL* Jb
>
> *ownership* **OSw** *UL* Blb
>
> *ownership of land* **OSw** *DL* Bb
>
> *possession* **OIce** *KRA* 10
>
> *property* **OGu** *GL* A 7, 24d, 25, Add. 9 (B 81), **OSw** *UL* Kkb
>
> *real property* **OSw** *DL* Gb

See also: *egn*

æghandasyn (OSw) noun

> *inspection by owners* **OSw** *SdmL* Till

æghandi (OSw) **eghende** (ODan) **eigandi** (ON) **eghandi** (OSw) noun

> *assignor* **OSw** *UL* Äb, Jb
>
> *landowner* **OSw** *UL* Jb, Blb, *VmL* Bb
>
> *owner* **ODan** *ESjL* 3, *SkL* 80, 83, *VSjL* 82, **OIce** *Grg* Feþ 164, 170 Fjl 225 Misc 239, *Jó* Þfb 2 Mah 23 Kge 17 Lbb 6 Llb 17 Kab 22 Þjb 13, 16 Fml 21, *Js* Mah 5, 29 Lbb 7 Rkb 1, **ONorw** *BorgL* 5.6, *FrL* Intr 17 Mhb 4 Var 16 Rgb 42 LlbA 13, **OSw** *SdmL* Kmb, *UL* Äb, Mb, Jb, Kmb, Blb, *VmL* Äb, Mb, Jb, Kmb, Bb
>
> *possessor* **ODan** *SkL* 166

See also: *jorþeghandi*, *malsæghandi*

æghas (OSw) verb

> *fight* **OSw** *HL* Mb, *YVgL* Add

ægholuter (OSw) noun

> *property plot* **OSw** *YVgL* Jb

See also: *luter*

ældari (OSw) noun

> *vagrant* **OSw** *YVgL* Utgb

ælgher (OSw) noun

The hunting of elks was regulated in OSw laws (HL, YVgL, ÄVgL), and in HL it was such an important economic resource that a shoulder from each kill was to be paid as tithes.

> *elk* **OSw** *HL* Blb, *ÄVgL* Föb

See also: *qviktiundi*

ælgstokker (OSw) noun

> *elk block* **OSw** *YVgL* Drb

æmbæte (ODan) **embætti** (ON) noun

> *duty* **ODan** *JyL* Fort
>
> *mass* **ONorw** *EidsL* 10.4
>
> *office* **ONorw** *EidsL* 31.2 35.1
>
> *service* **ONorw** *EidsL* 31.4

ændakarl (OSw) noun

> *householder furthest away in the village* **OSw** *UL* Blb, *VmL* Bb

æng (OSw) **æng** (ODan) **engi** (OGu) **eng** (ON) **engi** (ON) **ængi** (OSw) noun

Refers to enclosed open land, which was not cultivated but, most often, cleared of trees and stone, and where hay was harvested. After the harvest, the meadow as well as any cultivated field lying fallow were used for grazing, and thus became fertilized to some extent. In Norway, a farm might lack arable land (ON *akr*, see *aker*) but never *eng*. The *æng* was an asset not included in the common village land, but was treated as private property.

Both cultivated fields and meadows would be enclosed with stone walls or wooden fences as shown by the many rules about enclosures in the laws (ODan SkL, JyL 3; OSw DL Bb, HL Blb; SdmL Jb; YVgL Utgb; ÄVgL Föb). These rules may also reveal information about the different farming systems — one-field system, two-field system, and three-field system (Dan *envangs- tovangs-* and *trevangsbrug*) — that were used in different areas. See Appendix B.

hay **OSw** *ÄVgL* Jb

meadow **ODan** *JyL* 2, 3, *SkKL* 3, *SkL* 75, 76, 168, 169, 174, 179, 186, 187, 213, 214, *VSjL* 79, 80, **OGu** *GL* A 3, 27, **ONorw** *GuL* Krb, Llb, Tfb, Olb, Leb, **OSw** *DL* Kkb, Bb, Rb, *HL* Mb, Blb, *SdmL* Kkb, Jb, Bb, *SmL* Kkb, *UL* Jb, Blb, *VmL* Kkb, Jb, Bb, *YVgL* Kkb, Äb, Jb, Kvab, Föb, Utgb, *ÄVgL* Äb, Jb, Kva, Fös, Föb, *ÖgL* Kkb, Eb, Vm

meadowland **ODan** *JyL* 1, **OIce** *Grg* Klþ 2 Þsþ 48, 62 Feþ 164, 166 Lbþ 174, 175 Fjl 222 Hrs 234, *Jó* Mah 2 Lbb 4, 6 Llb 2, 3 Fml 27, *Js* Mah 11 Lbb 2, 11, *KRA* 11, **ONorw** *BorgL* 14.5, *EidsL* 11.5, *FrL* Intr 18 Leb 26 LlbA 2 Bvb 5

Expressions:

enka æng (OSw)

separate meadow **OSw** *YVgL* Äb

See also: *aker*, *garþer*, *hiorþlöt*, *hiorþvalder*, *deld*, *skoghæng*

Refs: CV s.v. *eng*; KLNM s.v.v. *eng*, *odlingssystem* (with further refs); *ängsskötsel*; ONP s.v.v. *eng*, *engi*; Schlyter s.v. *æng*

ængialaghi (OSw) noun

fellow meadow owners **OSw** *DL* Bb

See also: *æng*

ængialaþa (OSw) noun

meadow barn **OSw** *DL* Bb

See also: *æng*

ænkia (OSw) **ænkje** (ODan) **ekkja** (ON) noun

widow **ODan** *JyL* 1, 2, *SkL* 46, *VSjL* 13, **OIce** *Grg* Vís 94 Feþ 144, *Jó* Kge 1, 34 Llb 19, *Js* Kvg 1, 2, **ONorw** *BorgL* 5.3, *FrL* Rgb 37 Kvb 4, *GuL* Kvb, Tfb, Olb, Leb, **OSw** *DL* Gb, Rb, *SdmL* Gb, *YVgL* Äb, Gb, Add, *ÄVgL* Gb

See also: *vidve*

ænkjebo (ODan) noun

household of a widow **ODan** *JyL* 1

See also: *bo*, *konubú*, *ænkia*

ænsker (OSw) adj.

English **OSw** *YVgL* Frb, Drb, Äb, *ÄVgL* Md, Smb, Slb, Äb

æplesbarn (pl.) (ODan) noun

Literally 'apple children', supposedly referring to children who were so small that they played with apples.

apple-children **ODan** *SkL* 50

Refs: Lund s.v. *æplisbarn*; Tamm and Vogt, eds, 2016, 300

æptirganga (OSw) verb

make an oath **OSw** *ÄVgL* Slb

æptirmæla (OSw) **æftermæle** (ODan) verb

claim **ODan** *SkL* 233

prosecute **OSw** *YVgL* Drb

raise a suit **OSw** *ÄVgL* Smb

speak for **OSw** *ÄVgL* Smb

sue **OSw** *ÄVgL* Mb

take action **ODan** *JyL* 2, *SkL* 127

take action against **ODan** *ESjL* 3

æptirmælandi (OSw) **eftirmælandi** (ON) noun

An 'after speaker'. Refers to a person who takes up a legal case on behalf of someone who is not able to do so. The *eftirmælandi* can be a kinsman, usually the next of kin, or an agent (ON *umboðsmaðr*, see *umbuþsman*). An *eftirmælandi* usually appears on behalf of someone who has been killed, but he might also represent someone who is injured and unable to travel to the assembly (cf. Js Mah 20).

later claimant **OSw** *YVgL* Frb, Drb, Tb, *ÄVgL* Md, Slb, Tb

slaying prosecutor **OIce** *Js* Mah 20, **ONorw** *FrL* Mhb 54

someone intending to prosecute **ONorw** *FrL* Var 2-6

See also: *soknari*

Refs: CV s.v. *eptirmælandi*; Hertzberg s.v. *eptirmælandi*; ONP s.v. *eftirmǽlandi*

æptirmæli (OSw) noun

prosecution **OSw** *YVgL* Drb

ær (ON) noun

ewe **ONorw** *GuL* Kvr

ærchibiskuper (OSw) **ærkebiskop** (ODan) **erkibiskup** (ON) **erkibyskup** (ON) noun

archbishop **ODan** *JyL* Fort, *SkL* 43, 57, 67, 69, 70, 82, 102, 108, 121, 133, 137, 172, **OIce** *Jó* Llb 18, *Js* Kdb 3 Mah 7, 29, *KRA* 36, **ONorw** *EidsL* 32.9, *FrL* Intr 1 Tfb 3 KrbA 21, 44 KrbB 17 Mhb 24 Var 44 Rgb 29 LlbA 15 LlbB 3, *GuL* Krb, **OSw** *SdmL* Kgb, Till, *YVgL* Kkb

See also: *biskuper*, *prester*

ærfdakona (OSw) noun

woman taking inheritance **OSw** *DL* Gb

See also: *kona*, *ærfþ*

ærfþ (OSw) **ærvth** (ODan) **erfð** (ON) **ærfd** (OSw) noun

birthright **OSw** *UL* Äb, *VmL* Äb

class of inheritance **ONorw** *GuL* Krb, Arb, Løb

inheritance **ODan** *ESjL* 1, **OIce** *Grg* Vís 94 Arþ 118 Ómb 128, 129 Feþ 150, 154 Lbþ 172, *Jó*

MagBref Mah 4 Kge 1, 4 Lbb 1, *Js* Kdb 3 Kvg 3,
5 Ert 2 Lbb 1, *KRA* 10, **ONorw** *FrL* KrbB 11, 17
ArbA 2 Kvb 5, *GuL* Arb, **OSw** *UL* För, *YVgL* Add

Expressions:

litla erfð (ON)

lesser inheritance **ONorw** *GuL* Arb

See also: *arver*, *ærva*

ærfþaiorþ (OSw) noun

Inherited land appearing in the context of the evidence
required to prove ownership in land disputes.

inherited land **OSw** *YVgL* Äb

See also: *afling*, *byrþ*, *fang*, *förning*, *fæþerni*,
hæfþ, *jorþ*, *köpoiorþ*, *möþerni*, *oþal*, *ærfþ*

ærfþaloter (OSw) noun

inheritance **OSw** *HL* Äb

part of inheritance **OSw** *YVgL* Add

share of inheritance **OSw** *YVgL* Add

See also: *luter*, *ærfþ*

ærfþarbalker (OSw) **erfðabölkr** (ON) **arvabolke**
(OSw) **arvabolker** (OSw) noun

book concerning inheritance **ONorw** *GuL*
Arb, **OSw** *HL* Äb, *YVgL* Äb, *ÄVgL* Äb

inheritance section **OSw** *SdmL* För, Äb

See also: *balker*, *ærfþ*

ærfþarvitni (OSw) noun

witness of inheritance **OSw** *YVgL* Jb, *ÄVgL* Jb

See also: *vitni*, *ærfþ*

ærfþavita (OSw) noun

testimony of inheritance **OSw** *YVgL* Add

See also: *vita*, *ærfþ*

ærmaband (OSw) noun

Literally, 'armband'. Outside the legal texts, this
referred to an item of jewellery, a bracelet or arm-ring.
From the contexts in which it is used in VmL, it seems
that it could also refer to a minor form of restraint,
handcuffs held in front of the body, rather than a
humiliating form of capture, *bastaþer ok bundin* (see
basta), where the hands were behind the back. In
VmL the penalty for allowing a thief to escape from
ærmaband was only three marks, but if he had been
bastaþer ok bundin and escaped, the penalty was 40
marks. This implies that the latter was considerably
more restrictive than the former.

handcuffs **OSw** *VmL* Mb

See also: *basta*, *baugband*, *binda*

Refs: Schlyter 1877, s.v. *ærmaband*;
SL VmL, 101 note 164a

ærraþer (OSw) adj.

scarred **OSw** *UL* Mb, *VmL* Mb

ærva (OSw) **ærve** (ODan) verb

inherit **ODan** *ESjL* 1, 2, *JyL* 1, 3, *SkL* 3, 64,
VSjL 1–3, 6–8, 10, 14, 20, 86, **OSw** *DL* Gb,
HL Äb, Jb, Rb, *SdmL* Kkb, Äb, Jb, Till, *YVgL*
Kkb, Jb, Add, *ÄVgL* Jb, *ÖgL* Eb, Db

take inheritance **OSw** *HL* Äb, Jb

See also: *arver*

ærve (OSw) noun

funeral feast **OSw** *SdmL* Äb

See also: *ærvisöl*

ærvisöl (OSw) noun

inheritance beer **OSw** *YVgL* Drb, *ÄVgL* Md

See also: *öl*

æsta (ON) verb

call upon **ONorw** *GuL* Llb, Tjb, Mhb, Olb

demand **OSw** *VmL* Äb

æt (OSw) **æt** (ODan) **ett** (OGu) **ætt** (ON) **ett** (OSw)
ætt (OSw) **átt** (ON) noun

Etymologically related to the verb *ægha* 'to own',
and referring to a group of people belonging together.
The nature of this relationship has been debated,
and kinship, whether originating in an ancestor or
an individual in the present, seems central but not
necessary. The laws do not define the term. Certain
inheritance and paternity rules suggest a unilineal,
primarily patrilineal, *ætt* (OIce Grg, KRA), *æt* (OSw
SdmL, VmL); in OIce Js it refers to a royal dynasty.
Also appearing in the context of compensation for
killings, where it seems to refer both to paternal and
maternal relatives of the killer or the victim (ONorw
FrL, OSw DL, YVgL, ÄVgL, ÖgL, cf. OSw *ættarbot*
and OSw *ættarstuþi*). Often appearing in the context
of a person — related or not — becoming part of an
æt, which thereby accepts legal responsibility for them
(the only usage in ODan, but also appearing in OIce
Grg, Js; ONorw FrL, GuL; OSw ÄVgL, YVgL, cf.
ON *ættleiðing*), and of dependents being cared for by
members of the *æt* (OIce Grg, Jó, Js; ONorw GuL,
cf. OSw *omaghi*). OGu GL states that land must not
be sold outside the OGu *ett*, a notion that appears
elsewhere in expressions with OSw *byrþ* (q.v.), ODan
byrd, and which in older research was interpreted as a
remnant of an old, collective form of ownership and
organization of society.

family **OGu** *GL* A 28, **OIce** *Grg* Vís 94 Ómb
138 Rsþ 229, *Js* Mah 7 Ert 16, *KRA* 2, **ONorw**
FrL Intr 1, **OSw** *SdmL* Äb, *UL* Äb, *VmL* Äb

kin **ODan** *SkL* 126, 127, **ONorw** *FrL* KrbB
1, *GuL* Løb, Arb, Mhb, Tjb, Olb, **OSw**
YVgL Drb, Add, *ÄVgL* Md, *ÖgL* Db

kindred **OIce** *Jó* Kge 24

lineage **OIce** *Js* Kdb 4

relatives **OSw** *DL* Mb

Expressions:

ater i æt, attær i ætt (OSw)

by descendent inheritance **OSw** *VmL* Äb

fram i æt (OSw)

Used of inheritance from a later
generation by an earlier.

by reversion **OSw** *VmL* Äb

leiða í ætt (ON)

adopt **OIce** *Jó* Kge 9 *Js* Ert 16

See also: *kyn, niþi, ættleiðing*

Refs: Bjorvand and Lindeman 2000 s.v.
ætt; Hellquist s.v. *ätt*; KLNM s.v. *ætt*;
Lindkvist 2010; Winberg 1985, 10–30

ætahögher (OSw) noun

Appears in the context of grave desecration.

family burial mound **OSw** *SmL*

See also: *æt, høgh*

ætborin (OSw) **ættborinn** (ON) adj.

born in kin **OSw** *YVgL* Vs, Gb,
ÄVgL Smb, Vs, Gb, Rlb

freeborn **ONorw** *FrL* KrbA 1 Var 13

legitimate **OIce** *Js* Ert 1, **ONorw** *FrL* ArbA 1 ArbB 1

well-born **ONorw** *GuL* Løb, Mhb, Tjb

See also: *frælsgivi, æt*

ætiubot (OSw) noun

fine for damage by grazing animals **OSw** *VmL* Bb

grazing compensation **OSw** *DL* Bb

See also: *bot, bóta*

ætleder (OSw) adj.

led into a kin **OSw** *YVgL* Drb, Rlb, *ÄVgL* Md, Äb

See also: *æt*

ætleþa (OSw) **ættleiða** (ON) verb

adopt **OIce** *Jó* Kge 30, *Js* Ert 16

lead into a kin **OSw** *YVgL* Äb, Rlb, *ÄVgL* Äb, Rlb

See also: *frælsgivi, æt*

ætskuspiæll (OSw) noun

consanguinity **OSw** *ÖgL* Kkb

incest with kin by blood **OSw** *SmL*

{*ætskuspiæll*} **OSw** *ÖgL* Kkb

See also: *moþnahæfþ, siviaslit, æt*

ættalægger (OSw) noun

kin **OSw** *ÖgL* Eb

See also: *æt*

ættarbot (OSw) **ættebot** (ODan) noun

Fine/compensation from the relatives of the killer to
the relatives of the killed.

compensation of the kin **OSw** *YVgL* Add

compensation to the kin **OSw** *DL*
Gb, *YVgL* Drb, *ÄVgL* Md

fine to kin **OSw** *ÄVgL* Md

kin's compensation **ODan** *JyL* 2

kinship fine **OSw** *HL* Mb

kinsman's share **ODan** *SkL* 92

kinsmen's compensation **ODan** *JyL* 3, *SkL* 92

*kinsmen's compensation of a man's
compensation* **ODan** *SkL* 85

See also: *baugatal, bot, manbot, æt, ættarstuþi*

Refs: Schlyter s.v. *ættarbot*

ættarskarð (ON) noun

family loss **OIce** *Js* Mah 7, **ONorw** *FrL* Intr 8

ættarstuþi (OSw) noun

Contribution from a killer's relatives to pay the fine/
compensation.

collection of the kin **OSw** *YVgL* Drb

See also: *bauggildi, manbot, nefgildi, æt, ættarbot*

Refs: Schlyter s.v. *ættarstuþi*

ættaþer (OSw) adj.

born in kin **OSw** *YVgL* Gb, Rlb, *ÄVgL* Md, Gb

of kin **OSw** *YVgL* Drb, Add

See also: *æt, ætleder*

ættkvísl (ON) noun

branch of a family **OIce** *Jó* Kge 7-2

ættleiðing (ON) noun

Adoption, in the sense of taking a freeborn person
into another *ætt* (see *æt*), is not mentioned in medieval
Nordic law. (A possible exception is Jó V 9, which
contains a provision for adoption of brothers or
nephews, though it is unclear whether they are
illegitimate.) The *ættleiðing* was the act of officially
recognizing an illegitimate child and including it in
the kin, thus giving it the right to inherit and partake
of odal right. To begin with, this arrangement seems to
have been used to adopt illegitimate children of unfree
women into their father's kin. In addition, however,
other children born out of wedlock could be adopted
in this way (e.g. slaves), and this became the only way
of legitimization after the disappearance of slavery.

The act had to be performed in a special ceremony,
described at length in the GuL (Løb, ch. 58). The

legitimizer (the father) was obliged to give an ale feast with ale brewed from 3 *sáld* (ca. 290 l) of malt according to the measure used in Hordaland (Western Norway) and slaughter a 3-year-old bull. He had to flay the skin off the right foreleg, make a shoe of it and place it beside the ale cask. He who was to legitimize must be the first to put on the shoe, then the one who was to be legitimized, then the one who was to grant him inheritance, then the one who was to grant him the odal right, then the other kinsmen. The father had to state that 'I conduct this man to the property that I give him, and to wergild and gift, to seat and to settle, to fines and to [payment of] wergild, and to all personal rights, as if his mother had been bought with bride price'. A brother and a sister might legitimize a brother with themselves, and a father's brother a brother's son. A nookling and a scrubling (ON *hornungr* (q.v.) and *hrísungr* (q.v.)) might be legitimized in the same way as the son of a bondwoman. Other kinsmen might be legitimized and granted inheritance in the same way, if the nearest heir consented. He whom the father gave his freedom before he was 15 years old might also be legitimized, but all those who were in the same class as him with respect to inheritance had to give their consent.

The procedure described in the FrL (ArbB, ch.1) is less detailed and somewhat different. An important addition is the sentence that allows for the legitimization of a slave who had been given his freedom. (Whether this means that the slave in question was only partly or completely free, i.e. having given his freedom ale, is not clear.)

The ONorw provincial laws require the ceremony to take place at an ale feast, probably in order to make the act publicly known. It also had to be announced in public every 20 years until the adoptee had received his inheritance; from then on his inheritance testified for him the rest of his life and ever after.

The OSw verb for legitimization was *ætleþa* (q.v.); ODan used the phrase *takæ i æt mæþ sæ* 'take into one's æt'. In OSw and ODan law legitimization was a necessary element in the manumission of a slave, because only a free person could be adopted into a free kin. The ÄVgL (Äb 21) also mentions legitimization of children born out of wedlock. Legitimization had to take place in the assembly. In Scania a freed slave was adopted into a kin in the assembly (SkL 126). As in Norway the *ættleiðing* had to be performed by a special ritual, e.g. a previous notice of 7 nights (OSw *siunættinger*, q.v.) before the act could take place, the acceptance of the owner (to give his slave freedom), the payment of ransom, and the presentation of

oath-bound men. The details are somewhat different in the various OSw laws.

adoption **OIce** *Jó* Kge 9, *Js* Ert 16, **ONorw** *FrL* ArbB 1

legitimation **ONorw** *GuL* Løb

See also: *leysingi*, *skötsætubarn*, *æt*

Refs: Bagge 2010, 218; Helle 2001, 15, 127, 138; Hertzberg s.v. *ættleiðing*; Iversen 1997, 229, 231, 264, 267; KLNM s.v.v. *adoption, træl, ætt, ættleiing*; Nevéus 1974, 48, 80–82, 103–04, 128–29, 150–51; RGA2 s.v. *geschlechtsleite*; Robberstad 1981, 349; Schlyter s.v.v. *ætleþa, ætleþer*; Strauch 2016, 53, 94–96; Tamm and Vogt 2016, 20

ættleiðingr (ON) noun

adopted child **OIce** *Js* Ert 1

adopted son **ONorw** *FrL* ArbA 1

adoptee **OIce** *Jó* Kge 7-2

ættmaðr (ON) noun

kinsman **ONorw** *FrL* ArbB 5

ættærgæld (OSw) **attærgæld** (OSw) **ættar gæld** (OSw) noun

The derivation of this word is obscure, made even more so by the fact that there is no consensus in the manuscripts over the spelling. It can hardly be related to *æt*, 'family' but might be derived from *ater*, 'return' or even *atta*, 'eight'. It appears to refer to the tribute paid by the crew of each levy ship according to two of the levy laws of Svealand, UL and VmL. There are records of its payment throughout the fourteenth century and through to the beginning of the seventeenth. The amount for each *hundari* (q.v.) was set in UL at 30 *marker*, ten per ship's crew, but the amount is not specified in VmL. In the Roden (the historical region along the coast of Uppland), the tax was 10 *marker* per *skiplagh* (q.v.). It is considered to be one of the oldest fixed taxes, but its history is obscure and attempts to state how much it was per person have been unsuccessful. Although recorded in the laws in the context of the levy, it was probably more likely to have been an unrelated general communal tax, linked to the same divisions as the levy.

This word is not to be confused with *ættarbot* (q.v.), which is the compensation payable to the family of the victim of a killing by the family of the killer.

tribute **OSw** *UL* Kgb, *VmL* Kgb

See also: *hamna*, *leþunger*, *leþungslami*, *leþungsskin*, *matgærþ*, *roþarætter*, *skiplagh*, *skipvist*, *utgærþ*, *vighramannaskin*

Refs: KLNM s.v. *ättargäld*; Lindkvist 1993, 21–23; Schlyter 1877, s.v. *ættærgæld*; SL UL, 60 note 45, 61 note 52; SL VmL, 42 note 27

ödmark (OSw) **øthemark** (ODan) **odmark** (OSw)
   öthæ mark (OSw) noun
   uncultivated land **ODan** *SkL* 71
   wasteland **OSw** *YVgL* Kkb, *ÄVgL* Kkb
   See also: *eyðijörð*, *mark (3)*

öðlask (ON) verb
   be entitled to **ONorw** *GuL* Olb
   gain **ONorw** *GuL* Krb
   reward **ONorw** *GuL* Krb

öfunda (ON) verb
   mistreat **ONorw** *GuL* Mhb

öfundarblóð (ON) noun
   blood of conflict **ONorw** *EidsL* 37.3
   malicious blood **OIce** *KRA* 5

öfundarbót (ON) noun
   compensation for intent **ONorw** *FrL* Mhb 17 Rgb 41
   compensation for malice **OFar** *Seyð* 5,
   10, **ONorw** *FrL* Mhb 12 Bvb 6
   damages for the outrage **OIce** *Jó*
   Llb 16, 19 Þjb 7, 16 Fml 16
   fee for malicious intent **ONorw** *FrL* Kvb 25
   See also: *bot*

öfundardrep (ON) noun
   premeditated blow **ONorw** *GuL* Mhb

öfundarhögg (ON) noun
   blow with evil intent **ONorw** *GuL* Mhb

öfundarréttr (ON) noun
   case resulting in damages for outrage **OIce** *Jó* Llb 39

öfundlauss (ON) **öfundarlauss** (ON) adj.
   free of spiteful intent **OIce** *Grg* Hrs 234
   without ill will **ONorw** *FrL* KrbA 10
   without malice **OIce** *KRA* 5

öghlysa (OSw) verb
   show **OSw** *YVgL* Tb

öiadrap (OSw) noun
   killing on islands **OSw** *HL* Mb
   See also: *drap*

öker (OSw) **øk** (ODan) **oykr** (OGu) **eykr** (ON) noun
   draught animal **ODan** *JyL* 2, **OIce**
   Grg Klþ 11, **OSw** *SdmL* Jb
   pair **OGu** *GL* A 6
   yoke **OGu** *GL* A 26, 48

ökiaafl (OSw) noun
   The basis for deciding the householders' obligation to
   provide transport in conjunction with church building.
   Appearing as a parallel to *mantal* (q.v.) and *fearnyt*
   (q.v.) which concerned the corresponding obligation
   to provide labour and food respectively.

   force of beasts of draught **OSw** *SmL*
   Refs: SL SmL, 436, note 4

ökn (OSw) noun
   uncultivated land **OSw** *UL* Mb, Blb, *VmL* Mb

öl (OSw) **ol** (OGu) **öl** (ON) **öldr** (ON) noun
   Literally 'ale' or 'beer'. As a necessary provision
   in festivities, the word took on a legal significance
   referring to social gatherings where legally important
   actions took place, such as ON *ölgerð* 'The Ale
   feast', OSw *(lagha) ölstæmna* 'legal feast', *giftaröl*
   'marriage beer' and *ærvisöl* 'commemorative feast'.
   In connection with funerals, this feast was generally
   given on the seventh or 30th day after the funeral.
   Instructions to give ale feasts are mentioned in several
   kings' sagas. *Öl*, including its various compounds, also
   appears as a public place where violence or accusations
   of adultery had specific legal consequences (DL Kb,
   HL Mb, YVgL Urb, ÄVgL Urb). Cf. *ölfriþer* 'banquet
   peace' and other *öl-* compounds.
   ale **OGu** *GL* A 24, **ONorw** *GuL* Krb, Løb
   ale feast **ONorw** *GuL* Kvb, Løb, Arb
   beer **OSw** *DL* Mb, *YVgL* Gb, Add, *ÄVgL* Gb
   feast **OSw** *YVgL* Drb, *ÄVgL* Md
   Refs: GuL, ch. 115; Helle 2001, 170, 191;
   KLNM s.v.v. *arbeidsfest, bryggestol, drikkeoffer,*
   einer, handelsafgifter, humle, jord, pors,
   øl, ølhandel; Robberstad 1981, 322, 334;
   Schlyter s.v. *öl*; Thunaeus 1968, 52–56

ölbuþin (OSw) adj.
   invited to a wedding **OSw** *HL* Äb

ölbuþsman (OSw) noun
   Participant at a wedding.
   man at a feast **OSw** *HL* Äb

ölbænker (OSw) noun
   beer bench **OSw** *YVgL* Frb, Urb, *ÄVgL* Slb, Urb
   See also: *öl*

öldrykker (OSw) noun
   ale banquet **OSw** *HL* Mb, *UL* Mb
   festivity **OSw** *SdmL* Kkb, Mb

öldrykkjar (pl.) (ON) noun
   drinking-mates **ONorw** *GuL* Mhb
   See also: *ölhúsmenn (pl.)*

öldrhús (ON) **öldrhús** (ON) noun
   alehouse **ONorw** *FrL* Mhb 14,
   15, *GuL* Løb, Mhb, Olb
   tavern **ONorw** *FrL* Mhb 15

öldrhúsvitni (ON) **öldrhúsvitni** (ON) noun
   banqueting house witness **ONorw** *FrL* ArbA 16
   funeral witness **ONorw** *FrL* Kvb 8

ölfriþer (OSw) noun

Peace at a banquet appears in the context of regulations concerning wedding celebrations.

banquet peace **OSw** *HL* Äb

See also: *brullöp, friþer, öl*

Refs: Thunaeus 1968, 52–56

ölförr (ON) ölfærr (ON) adj.

able to drink **OIce** *Jó* Kge 21

able to take part in ale feasts **ONorw** *GuL* Arb

ölgerð (ON) noun

ale feast **ONorw** *GuL* Krb, Llb

ölhúsmenn (pl.) (ON) noun

men in an ale house **ONorw** *GuL* Mhb

See also: *öldrykkjar (pl.)*

ölmusugerð (ON) noun

giving of alms **OIce** *Js* Kdb 1, *KRA* 12, 13, **ONorw** *FrL* KrbA 33

ölmusugjöf (ON) noun

charity **OIce** *Grg* Þsþ 82

ölmusumaðr (ON) noun

One who receives alms.

almsman **OIce** *KRA* 13

Refs: CV s.v. *ölmusumaðr*; Fritzner s.v. *ölmusumaðr*; Hertzberg s.v. *ölmusumaðr*

ölstuva (OSw) noun

beer cottage **OSw** *YVgL* Drb, *ÄVgL* Md

beer-house **OSw** *DL* Kkb

See also: *öl, stuva*

ölstæmna (OSw) noun

feast **OSw** *ÄVgL* Gb

legal feast **OSw** *YVgL* Gb

See also: *mungatstiþir (pl.), öl, stæmna*

önd (ON) noun

life **ONorw** *GuL* Krb, Kpb

See also: *spilla*

öndvegi (ON) andvegi (ON) noun

The *öndvegi* was the most honoured seat in the hall, where the master of the house was to sit on certain formal occasions. See GuL chs 35, 62, 115, 266, 299.

high seat **ONorw** *GuL* Kpb, Løb, Arb, Olb

Refs: KLNM s.v.v. *högsäte, rättssymbolik*

önn (pl. annir) (ON) noun

working season **OIce** *Grg* Þsþ 80 Lbþ 181, *Jó* Llb 54

See also: *anfriþer, anværkdagher, høsthælgh, varfriþer*

önnungsverk (ON) noun

labouring work **OIce** *Grg* Klþ 17

öpa (OSw) ypa (OGu) verb

shout **OGu** *GL* A 36, **OSw** *UL* Kgb

öra (OSw) øre (ODan) eyra (ON) noun

Appears in the context of cutting off ears as a punishment for theft.

ear **ODan** *SkL* 153, 184, **ONorw** *GuL* Tjb, **OSw** *SdmL* Tjdb, *YVgL* Tb

See also: *afhug, hnífa, huþ, huþstryka, limber, stúfa, thjuvsmærke*

ördrag (ON) noun

bowshot **OIce** *Grg* Vís 87 Lbþ 213

See also: *örskot, örskotshelgr*

örð (ON) noun

crop **ONorw** *GuL* Llb

one year's crop **ONorw** *FrL* Kvb 15 LlbB 2

öre (OSw) øre (ODan) oyri (OGu) aurar (pl.) (ON) eyrir (ON) örar (pl.) (OSw) noun

asset **OIce** *Grg* Feþ 166, *Js* Mah 29

debt **ONorw** *GuL* Løb

fine **ONorw** *FrL* KrbB 2

money **OGu** *GL* A 28, 53, Add. 9 (B 81), **OIce** *Jó* Lbb 9, **ONorw** *GuL* Kvb, Olb, Trm, **OSw** *YVgL* Add

movables **OGu** *GL* A 20, **ONorw** *GuL* Kvb, Arb, Mhb, Olb

ounce **ODan** *ESjL* 1–3, *JyL* 3, *SkKL* 1, 4, 7, 11, *VSjL* 40, 66, 78, 81, 84, 86, 87, **OFar** *Seyð* 2, 5, **OIce** *Grg* passim, **ONorw** *BorgL* 11.3

payment **OIce** *Jó* Llb 24, *Js* Mah 16

property **OIce** *Jó* Kge 14, **ONorw** *FrL* Kvb 6

sum **OIce** *Grg* Þsþ 62

unit of the weight and monetary system, 1/8 {mark} **ONorw** *GuL* Krb, Sab, Løb, Kvb, Mhb, Leb, Arb, Olb, Llb, Tfb, Kpb

{öre} **ODan** *SkL* passim, **OGu** *GL* A 2, 6, 8, 16, 17, 19, 22–24, 26, 31, 38, 39, 48, 55, 56a, 59, 60, 61, 63, Add. 2, 8 (B 17, 55), *GS* Ch. 3, **OSw** *DL* Kkb, Mb, Bb, Gb, Tjdb, Rb, *HL* passim, *SdmL* passim, *SmL*, *UL* Kkb, Kkb, Äb, Mb, Jb, Blb, Rb, *VmL* Kkb, Kgb, Äb, Mb, Jb, Kmb, Bb, *YVgL* passim, *ÄVgL* passim, *ÖgL* Kkb, Db

Expressions:

lauss eyrir (ON)

chattels **OIce** *Grg* Klþ 4 Arþ 122 Tíg 255 *Jó* MagBref Þfb 5 Mah 1 Kge 22 Þjb 1 *Js* Mah 2, 9 Kvg 3 Þjb 1 *KRA* 14, 15 **ONorw** *BorgL* 3.2 4.2 *FrL* Mhb 2, 12 *GuL* Mhb

movable property **ONorw** *GuL* Krb

movables **ONorw** *FrL* Tfb 5 LlbB 12 *GuL* Llb

See also: *lösöre, mark (2), örtogh, pænninger*

öresland (OSw) øreland (ODan) örisland (OSw) noun

    land for an ounce **ODan** *VSjL* 80

    land one ounce of worth **ODan** *SkL* 76

    {*öresland*} **OSw** *UL* Blb, *VmL* Bb, *ÄVgL* Jb

    {*öre*} *field* **OSw** *YVgL* Jb

örkostr (ON) noun

    means to pay **OIce** *Grg* Bat 113

örnavingi (OSw) noun

    Probably a foreign coin worth 18 *pænningar*.

    {*örnavingi*} **OSw** *YVgL* Drb

    See also: *pænninger*

    Refs: Lindkvist forthcoming; Schlyter s.v. *örnavingi*

örs (OSw) noun

    war-horse **OSw** *SdmL* Kmb, Rb,
    UL Kmb, *VmL* Kmb, Bb

örskot (ON) noun

    bowshot **OIce** *Grg* Lbþ 181

    See also: *ördrag*, *örskotshelgr*

örskotshelgr (ON) örvarskotshelgr (ON) noun

    An area of sanctuary or legal immunity determined by the range of a bowshot.

    bowshot **OIce** *Grg* Klþ 2 Þsþ 52, 62 Lbþ 191, 215 Fjl 222 Hrs 234, *Jó* Llb 31, *Js* Lbb 27, *KRA* 11

    See also: *ördrag*, *örskot*

    Refs: CV s.v. *örskotshelgr*; Fritzner s.v. *örskotshelgr*; Hertzberg s.v. *örskotshelgi*

örtogh (OSw) ørtogh (ODan) ertaug (OGu) ertog (ON) ørtog (ON) örtugh (OSw) noun

    ertog **OIce** *Jó* Fml 8, **ONorw** *FrL* Rgb 1 LlbB 12

    shilling **ODan** *ESjL* 1–3, *JyL* 3, *VSjL* 40, 86, 87

    unit of the weight and monetary system, 1/24 {mark} **ONorw** *GuL* Kvb, Mhb, Sab

    {*örtogh*} **OGu** *GL* A 19, 23, 26, 35, 41, 43, 45, 45a, 56, **OSw** *DL* Kkb, Tjdb, *HL* Mb, Kmb, Rb, *SdmL* passim, *SmL*, *UL* Kkb, Kgb, Mb, Jb, Blb, *VmL* Mb, Jb, Kmb, Bb, Rb, *YVgL* passim, *ÄVgL* passim, *ÖgL* Kkb, Eb, Db

    See also: *mark (2)*, *öre*, *pænninger*

örtoghaland (OSw) örtoghland (OSw) örtughsland (OSw) ortugsland (OSw) yrtugh land (OSw) noun

    {*örtoghaland*} **OSw** *SmL*, *UL* Jb, *VmL* Mb, Jb, Bb, Rb

örvarhúnn (ON) noun

    shaft of an arrow **ONorw** *GuL* Kvr

örvarþing (ON) örvaþing (ON) noun

    An assembly convened as soon as possible (i.e. on the same day or the following morning) after certain serious crimes, including killings, grave injuries, plundering (*hervirki*, see *hærværk*) and abuse of office.

To convene the assembly the prosecutor, usually the slaying prosecutor (*eftirmælandi*, see *æptirmælandi*) or nearest kinsman (or widow?), sent summons betokened by an arrow (*boð* (see *buþ*), *örvarskurðr*) to neighbours, who were legally obligated to pass it on to further neighbours. In lieu of a regular prosecutor, an arrow-assembly could be initiated by the king's representative (*ármaðr*).

The arrow-assembly seems to have been primarily used to establish evidence. It took place at the scene of the crime and required 27 assembly-men in attendance to be considered valid. The suit was subsequently prosecuted five days later at another assembly (ON *fimmtarþing*).

Arrow-assemblies appear almost exclusively in the Norwegian laws, through which the practice entered Icelandic laws (Js and Jb) somewhat later.

    arrow assembly **OIce** *Jó* Mah 10, *Js* Mah 14, 17, **ONorw** *FrL* Mhb 7, 29 Var 7 Rgb 3

    arrow thing **ONorw** *GuL* Mhb

    See also: *buþ*, *fimmtarþing*, *kafli*, *skæra (2)*, *þing*

    Refs: KLNM s.v. *frostatingsloven*, *rettergang*, *våpensyn*, *ǫrvarþing*; NGL V s.v. *örvarþing*; Z s.v. *ör*, *örvarþing*

öthe (OSw) noun

    folly **OSw** *SmL*

öxabyrþ (OSw) noun

    right to bring an axe **OSw** *YVgL* Jb

    right to bring an axe to the forest **OSw** *ÄVgL* Jb

öxaol (OSw) noun

    axe handle binding **OSw** *UL* Mb, *VmL* Mb

öxe (OSw) øx (ON) öx (OSw) yxi (OSw) noun

    axe **ONorw** *GuL* Mhb, Leb, **OSw** *HL* Rb, *ÄVgL* Fös

öþebol (OSw) noun

    deserted farm **OSw** *YVgL* Föb, Add

öþer (OSw) auðr (ON) noun

    'Wealth, abundance'. In OSw, in the phrase *upsala öþer* 'wealth of Uppsala' referring to farms of the Swedish crown. Its origin, function and relation to *husaby* (q.v.) and *kononggsarþer* (q.v.), which it presumably included, has long been debated. HL and YVgL list *upsala öþer* farms, stating that they may not be sold or disposed of in any way. SdmL declares it the property of the king, being one of the sources of income for the crown, and prohibits its depletion.

    wealth **OIce** *Grg* Klþ 3, **OSw** *SdmL* Kgb, Till, *YVgL* Kvab

    {*öþer*} **OSw** *HL* Kkb, Kgb

    See also: *bo*, *fjáreign*, *husaby*, *kononggsarþer*

    Refs: Brink 2000a; Brink 2000b; Brink forthcoming; KLNM s.v. *kronogods*; Pettersson 2000

öþi (OSw) øthe (ODan) adj.
  deserted **ODan** *ESjL* 3, **OSw** *YVgL*
  Kvab, Föb, *ÄVgL* Kva
öþisbyr (OSw) öþisby (OSw) noun
  uncultivated village **OSw** *UL* Blb, *VmL* Bb
  See also: *eyðijörð*
ølfylle (ODan) noun
  beer drinking **ODan** *ESjL* 3
øreigð (ON) noun
  state of poverty **OIce** *Grg* Feþ 153
øreigi (ON) óreigi (ON) noun
  dependent **OIce** *Jó* Kge 4
  indigent man **OIce** *Jó* Kab 7
  pauper **ONorw** *FrL* Kvb 8
  poor person **OIce** *Js* Kvg 3
øreigi (ON) adj.
  destitute **OIce** *Grg* Fjl 223
  poor **ONorw** *GuL* Kvb, Arb
  without property **ONorw** *FrL* KrbB 20
ørendlauss (ON) adj.
  for no good reason **OFar** *Seyð* 3
  See also: *foráttalaust, forfallalöst, nauðsynjalauss*
ørendreki (ON) noun
  An official, mainly of the bishop (ONorw GuL Krb) or
  the king (ONorw GuL Krb, Ulb, ONorw FrL LlbB 7),
  possibly synonymous with *ármaðr* (q.v.).
  king's messenger **ONorw** *FrL* LlbB 7
  representative **ONorw** *GuL* Krb, Olb
  Expressions:
  biskups erendreki (ON)
  bishop's representative **ONorw** *GuL* Krb
  konungs erendreki (ON)
  king's representative **ONorw** *GuL* Krb, Olb

  See also: *biskuper, kununger*
  Refs: Hertzberg s.v. *erendreki*
ørhófi (ON) ørhæfi (ON) noun
  open, harbourless coastline **OIce** *Jó* Fml 3
ørkuml (ON) ørkyml (ON) ørkymli (ON) noun
  deformity **ONorw** *EidsL* 1.2
  ill mark **ONorw** *BorgL* 1.2, *EidsL* 5
  lasting injury **OIce** *Grg* Klþ 4 Vís 88, 91
  Ómb 131 Feþ 161 Misc 241, 254
  physical deformity **ONorw** *GuL* Krb
ørlendis (ON) adv.
  abroad **OIce** *Grg* Lbþ 173, *Js* Mah 8
  in foreign countries **OIce** *Grg* Þsþ 55
ørvasi (ON) noun
  old person **ONorw** *FrL* Var 13
øthe (ODan) eyða (ON) verb
  destroy **ODan** *ESjL* 2
  leave vacant **ONorw** *GuL* Krb, Leb
Øxarárþing (ON) noun
  general assembly **OIce** *Jó* Þjb 13
  See also: *alþingi, þing*
øxarskaft (ON) noun
  axe handle **ONorw** *GuL* Mhb
óði (ON) noun
  madness **ONorw** *FrL* Mhb 31
óll (ON) æll (ON) adj.
  sustainable **OIce** *Grg* Vís 86 Feþ 144
órr (ON) adj.
  insane **OIce** *Grg* Vís 93, **ONorw** *FrL* Mhb 31
  See also: *afvita, galin*
óxla (ON) verb
  earn **ONorw** *GuL* Løb
  make a profit **OIce** *Grg* Þsþ 54

English to Nordic

https://doi.org/10.11647/OBP.0188.03

abandon (verb) *aflæggia* (OSw)

abandoned field (noun) *aterlægha* (OSw)

abbess (noun) *abbadís* (ON)

abbey (noun) *kloster* (OSw)

abbot (noun) *abbet* (ODan)

abduct (verb) *hærtaka* (OSw), *ræna* (OSw)

abduction (noun) *ran* (OSw)

abduction of a woman (noun) *konunám* (ON)

abetting (noun) *raþ* (OSw), *viþervist* (OSw)

abide by (verb) *halda* (OSw)

ability to run (noun) *runfempni* (OGu)

ability to walk (noun) *gangfempni* (OGu)

able to be seized (adj.) *tykr* (OGu)

able to be taken (adj.) *tykr* (OGu)

able to drink (adj.) *ölførr* (ON)

able to ride a horse (adj.) *hestførr* (ON)

able to take part in ale feasts (adj.) *ölførr* (ON)

able to testify (adj.) *váttbærr* (ON)

able to work (adj.) *verkførr* (ON)

abolished (adj.) *aftakin* (OGu)

abort (verb) *stryka* (OSw)

abortion (noun) *bælgmord* (OSw)

abroad (adv.) *utanlands* (OSw), *utlændis* (OSw), *utrikis* (OSw), *ørlendis* (ON)

absconding thief (noun) *runþiuver* (OSw)

absence (noun) *forfall* (OSw)

absence from a Thing (noun) *þingfall* (OSw)

absolution (noun) *banslætter* (OSw), *formal* (ODan)

absolve (verb) *friþa* (OSw), *lösa* (OSw), *skæra (1)* (OSw)

abstain from (verb) *varna* (ON)

abstention from spiritual kinswomen (noun) *guðsifjavörnun* (ON)

abuse (verb) *bregþa* (OGu), *misfara* (ON), *misfyrma* (OSw)

abuse (noun) *óvenja* (ON)

accept (verb) *fæsta* (OSw), *samþykkja* (ON), *sea* (OSw), *viþertaka* (OSw), *þola* (ON)

accept a conviction (verb) *fæsta* (OSw)

accept fines (verb) *fæsta* (OSw)

accept loss or reduction (verb) *þarnask* (ON)

acceptable as tax money (adj.) *skattsvarr* (ON)

acceptance (noun) *fæsta* (OSw), *vili* (OSw)

acceptance of a bribe (noun) *fétaka* (ON)

access to an assembly (noun) *þingsganga* (OSw)

accident (noun) *nöþsyn* (OSw), *óför* (ON), *ulykke* (ODan), *váglati* (ON), *vathegærning* (ODan), *vaþaværk* (OSw), *vaþi* (OSw)

accident compensation (noun) *vaþabot* (OSw)

accident fine (noun) *vaþabot* (OSw)

accident oath (noun) *vaþaeþer* (OSw)

accidental act (noun) *vaþaværk* (OSw), *vaþi* (OSw)

accidental case (noun) *vaþamal* (OSw)

accidental damage compensation (noun) *vaþabot* (OSw), *vaþagæld* (OSw)

accidental deed (noun) *vathegærning* (ODan)

accidental fire (noun) *brandvaþa* (OSw), *vaþaelder* (OSw)

accidental flooding (noun) *ofsinnisvatn* (OSw)

accidental injury compensation (noun) *vaþagæld* (OSw)

accidental killing (noun) *vaþadrap* (OSw)

accidental killing through a backwards blow (noun) *bakvaþi* (OSw)

accidental pushing (noun) *vaþaskuver* (OSw)

accidental scratch (noun) *vaþaskena* (OSw)

accidental wound (noun) *vaþahug* (OSw), *vaþasar* (OSw)

accommodate (verb) *husa* (OSw)

accomplice (noun) *atvistarmaþer* (OSw), *haldbani* (OSw)

accomplice of a thief (noun) *thjuvsvite* (ODan)

accord (noun) *raþ* (OSw), *vili* (OSw)

according to how much a person is to inherit (adj.) *arvstathe* (ODan)

according to the law (adj.) *lagha* (OSw), *laghtakin* (OSw)

according to the law (adv.) *laghlika* (OSw), *rætlika* (OSw)

accusation (noun) *kennsl* (ON), *saga* (OGu), *sak* (OSw), *sakargift* (ON), *sokn* (OSw), *talan* (OSw), *tilmæli* (OSw)

accusation of homicide (noun) *banasak* (OSw)

accusation of killing (noun) *banasak* (OSw)

accuse (verb) *fælla* (OSw), *krævia* (OSw), *kænna* (OSw), *kæra* (OSw), *sökia* (OSw), *sækta* (OSw), *vita* (OSw), *væna* (OSw)

accused (adj.) *sakaðr* (ON)

accuser (noun) *saksöki* (OSw)

acknowledge (verb) *sanna* (OSw), *vita* (OSw), *viþerganga* (OSw), *viþerkænnas* (OSw), *viþertaka* (OSw)

acknowledged (adj.) *sander* (OSw)

acorn (noun) *akern* (ODan), *aldin* (OSw)

acorn bearer (noun) *alda* (OSw)

acorn lease (noun) *aldinlegha* (OSw)

acorn oak (noun) *gisningaek* (OSw)

acorn tree (noun) *aldinviþer* (OSw)

acorn woodland (noun) *gisningaskogher* (OSw)

acquired land (noun) *aflingaiorþ* (OSw), *fang* (OSw), *fangejorth* (ODan), *jorthefang* (ODan)

acquired property (noun) *afling* (OSw)

acquisition (noun) *fang* (OSw), *hæfþ* (OSw)

acquit (verb) *ordela* (OSw), *skæra (1)* (OSw), *væria* (OSw)

acquittal (noun) *dul* (OSw)

act (noun) *brut* (OSw), *gærning* (OSw), *værk* (OSw)

act as a purchase agent (verb) *vinga* (OSw)

act as guarantor (verb) *hemula* (OSw)

act as witness (verb) *vita* (OSw)

act like a thief (verb) *þiuftas* (OSw)

act of abomination (noun) *firnarværk* (OSw)

act of an outlaw (noun) *útlagaverk* (ON), *útlegðarverk* (ON)

act of outrage (noun) *niþingsværk* (OSw)

act of violence (noun) *gærning* (OSw), *gærþ* (OSw), *valdsgærning* (OSw), *valdsværk* (OSw)

act requiring full compensation (noun) *fullréttisverk* (ON)

act wrongly (verb) *misgøre* (ODan)

acting as a friend (noun) *vinorþ* (OSw)

acting on behalf of another (noun) *umbuþ* (OSw)

action (noun) *gærning* (OSw), *handgærning* (ODan), *kæra* (OSw), *sak* (OSw), *vald* (OSw), *værk* (OSw), *æftermal* (ODan)

action for rapine (noun) *ranssak* (ODan)

action in a case of rapine (noun) *ransdele* (ODan)

activity (noun) *sysel* (ODan)

actual possession (noun) *ábúð* (ON)

added injury (noun) *sársauki* (ON)

additional charges (noun) *tillagha* (OSw)

additional compensation (noun) *gærsemi* (OSw)

additional fine (noun) *vitherlogh* (ODan)

additional land (noun) *tilgærth* (ODan)

adequate (adj.) *gilder* (OSw)

adjudge (verb) *döma* (OSw)

adjudicate (verb) *döma* (OSw)

adjure (verb) *biuþa* (OSw)

adjust (verb) *skapa* (ON)

administer (verb) *varþveta* (OSw)

administer Extreme Unction (verb) *olia* (OSw)

administer Holy Communion (verb) *husla* (OSw)

administration (noun) *stjórn* (ON)

administration of money (noun) *fjárhald* (ON)

administrator (noun) *forráðandi* (ON), *lænsmaþer* (OSw), *soknari* (OSw)

admissible as a witness (adj.) *váttbærr* (ON)

admissible evidence (noun) *vitsorþ* (OSw)

admission (noun) *saga* (OGu), *viþerganga* (OSw)

admit (verb) *ryfte* (ODan), *ryve* (ODan), *viþerganga* (OSw), *viþerkænnas* (OSw), *viþertaka* (OSw)

admit to (verb) *viþerkænnas* (OSw), *viþertaka* (OSw)

adopt (verb) *viþertaka* (OSw), *ætleþa* (OSw)

adopted child (noun) *ættleiðingr* (ON)

adopted son (noun) *ættleiðingr* (ON)

adoptee (noun) *ættleiðingr* (ON)

adoption (noun) *ættleiðing* (ON)

adult (adj.) *fultiþa* (OSw), *fulvaksen* (ODan), *maghandi* (OSw), *vaksen* (ODan)

adult man (noun) *bonde* (OSw)

adulterated with sand (adj.) *sandblandaþer* (OSw)

adulterer (noun) *horkarl* (ODan)

adulteress (noun) *horkona* (OSw)

adulterous bed (noun) *horsiang* (OSw)

adultery (noun) *giolsæmi* (OSw), *hor* (OSw), *hordomber* (OSw), *hordomssak* (ODan), *hormal* (OSw), *horsak* (OSw), *horsiang* (OSw), *legorð* (ON)

adultery bed (noun) *horsiang* (OSw)

adultery case (noun) *hormal* (OSw)

adultery with in-laws (noun) *sifjaspell* (ON)

advance of inheritance (noun) *hemfylghþ* (OSw)

advantage (noun) *vitsorþ* (OSw)

Advent (noun) *advent* (OSw)

adversary (noun) *viþerdelumaþer* (OSw)

advice (noun) *raþ* (OSw)

advice leading to death (noun) *banaráð* (ON)

advice leading to injury (noun) *sáraráð* (ON)

advice of the assembly (noun) *thingrath* (ODan)

advisable (action) (noun) *raþ* (OSw)

advise (verb) *raþa* (OSw)

advising to steal (noun) *þjófráð* (ON)

advisor (noun) *ræðismaðr* (ON)

advocate (noun) *mælandi* (ON), *væriandi* (OSw)

affair (noun) *ensak* (OSw), *mal (1)* (OSw)

affinity (noun) *sifjar (pl.)* (ON)

affinity by marriage (noun) *sifskaper* (OSw)

afford to (verb) *orka* (OSw), *vinna* (OSw)

after one year (noun) *jamlangi* (OSw)

aftermath (noun) *há* (ON)

against someone's wishes (adj.) *nöþogher* (OSw)

agency (noun) *raþ* (OSw), *vinghan* (OSw)

agent (noun) *halzmaþer* (OSw), *umbuþ* (OSw),
  umbuþsman (OSw)

agents (noun) *jamkyrnismæn (pl.)* (OSw)

aggregated property (noun) *bolagh* (OSw)

agnate (noun) *bauggildismaðr* (ON)

agnate kinsman (noun) *bauggildismaðr* (ON)

agnate who has to pay or receive {bauggildi} (noun)
  bauggildismaðr (ON)

agree (verb) *fæsta* (OSw), *játa* (ON), *mæla (1)* (OSw),
  samþykkja (ON), *stæþia* (OSw)

agree on with a handshake (verb) *handsala* (ON)

agreed (adj.) *samdóma* (ON), *sater* (OSw)

agreed day (noun) *laghastæmna* (OSw)

agreed partnership (noun) *fælaghlagh* (ODan)

agreed to terms (adj.) *samkaupa* (ON)

agreeing (adj.) *sater* (OSw)

agreement (noun) *formali* (OGu), *goþvili* (OSw), *köp*
  (OSw), *lagh* (OSw), *mal (1)* (OSw), *málamundi*
  (ON), *máldagi* (ON), *mali* (OSw), *raþ* (OSw),
  samkvámulag (ON), *samþykkð* (ON), *sáttmál* (ON),
  skildagi (ON), *skilorð* (ON), *staþgi* (OSw), *sæt*
  (OSw), *takuskæl* (OSw), *vili* (OSw)

agreement of compensation (noun) *botefæstning*
  (ODan)

agreement of heirs (noun) *erfingjasátt* (ON)

agreement of payment (noun) *botefæstning* (ODan)

agreement on keep (noun) *fulgumáli* (ON)

agreement over partnership (noun) *fælaghlagh*
  (ODan)

agreement to pay a compensation (noun) *botefæstning*
  (ODan)

agreements on church endowment (noun)
  kirkjumáldagi (ON)

agricultural law (noun) *búnaðarbölkr* (ON)

aide (noun) *vin* (OSw)

aiding (noun) *forvist* (OSw)

ailment (noun) *veilendi* (ON)

alarm (noun) *hærop* (OSw)

ale (noun) *mungat* (OGu), *öl* (OSw)

ale banquet (noun) *öldrykker* (OSw)

ale cask (noun) *skapker* (ON)

ale feast (noun) *öl* (OSw), *ölgerð* (ON)

alehouse (noun) *ölðrhús* (ON), *pænningsöl* (OSw)

alienate (verb) *afhænda* (OSw), *firigæra* (OSw)

alive (adj.) *qvikker* (OSw)

All Men's Fast (noun) *allramannafasta* (ON)

All Saints' Day (noun) *aldra hælghuna dagher* (OSw),
  allraheilagramessa (ON), *hælghunamæssudagher*
  (OSw)

all the farmers in a collective (noun) *værnalagh* (OSw)

allege (verb) *klanda* (OSw), *vita* (OSw)

allegiance (noun) *þegnskylda* (ON)

allocate (verb) *skipa* (OSw)

allocation of tithes (noun) *tíundarskifti* (ON)

allodial estate (noun) *oþoliorþ* (OSw)

allodial land (noun) *oþal* (OSw)

allodial owner (noun) *brigðarmaðr* (ON), *oþalsmaþer*
  (OSw)

allotment (noun) *deld* (OSw), *luter* (OSw)

allow (verb) *lata* (OSw), *skipa* (OSw)

allow to lie fallow (verb) *aterlæggia* (OSw)

allowed to swear an oath (adj.) *eþsört* (OSw)

allowed to testify (adj.) *váttbærr* (ON)

allowed to witness (adj.) *vitnisgilder* (OSw)

alms (noun) *almosa* (OSw)

almsman (noun) *ölmusumaðr* (ON)

altar cloth (noun) *altaraklæþi* (OSw)

altar donations (noun) *altaralæghi* (OSw),
  altaraværning (OSw)

altar gift (noun) *altarabyrþ* (OSw), *altaralæghi* (OSw)

altered case (noun) *tvætala* (OSw)

altogether holy (adj.) *alheilagr* (ON)

ambler (noun) *gangare* (OSw)

ambush (noun) *arath* (ODan), *forsat* (OSw), *sat* (OSw)

amendment (noun) *réttarbót* (ON)

amity gift (noun) *vingæf* (OSw)

amount (noun) *fæ* (OSw)

amount of property (noun) *fjármegin* (ON)

amount paid (noun) *værþ* (OSw)

amount paid in rent (noun) *leiguburðr* (ON)

amusement (noun) *kæti* (OSw)

ancestor (noun) *langfeðgar (pl.)* (ON)

ancestors (noun) *forældre* (ODan)

ancestors on the father's side (noun) *langfeðgar (pl.)*
  (ON)

ancestral home (noun) *fæþerni* (OSw)

ancestral land (noun) *byrþ* (OSw), *fæþernisiorþ* (OSw)

ancestral land from time immemorial (noun) *aldaoþal*
  (OSw)

ancestral land/birthright land (noun) *oþal* (OSw)

ancestral rights (noun) *fyrning* (OSw)

anchor (noun) *akkeri* (ON)

anchorage (noun) *akkerissát* (ON)

ancient (adj.) *forn* (OSw)

ancient possession (noun) *fornhæfþ* (OSw)

ancient site (noun) *stafgarþr* (OGu)

angelica garden (noun) *hvanngarðr* (ON)

anger (noun) *bræþe* (OSw), *harmber* (OSw), *vreþe* (OSw), *vreþshand* (OSw), *vreþsvili* (OSw)

angry (adj.) *vreþer* (OSw)

animal (noun) *diur* (OSw), *fæ* (OSw), *fælaþi* (OSw), *fænaþer* (OSw), *griper* (OSw), *qvikfæ* (OSw)

animal equivalent to one milk cow (noun) *málnytukúgildi* (ON)

animal fence (noun) *dýrgarðr* (ON)

animal that is home bred (noun) *hemföþa* (OSw)

animal to be declared (noun) *upphaizlusoyþr* (OGu)

animals (noun) *bofæ* (ODan), *fulgufé* (ON), *fæ* (OSw)

animals in communal pasture (noun) *afréttarfé* (ON)

anniversary (noun) *jamlangadagher* (OSw)

announce (verb) *biuþa* (OSw), *fæsta* (OSw), *kalla* (OSw), *lysa* (OSw), *næmna* (OSw), *openbara* (OSw), *skærskuta* (OSw)

announce lawfully (verb) *laghlysa* (OSw), *lysa* (OSw)

announce to witnesses (verb) *skærskuta* (OSw)

announced at the assembly (adj.) *þingborinn* (ON)

announced/promised (adj.) *fæster* (OSw)

announcement (noun) *lysning* (OSw), *uppsaga* (ON)

announcement of a case (noun) *skærskutavitni* (OSw)

announcement of killing (noun) *víglýsing* (ON)

announcement with testimony (noun) *skærskutavitni* (OSw)

announcement witness (noun) *lysningavitni* (OSw)

announcing (noun) *lysning* (OSw)

annual fee (noun) *tiþaköp* (OSw)

annual rent (noun) *afraþ* (OSw)

annual sacrifice (noun) *jamlangaoffer* (OSw)

annuity (noun) *tiþaköp* (OSw)

annul (verb) *brigþa* (OGu), *ryþia* (OSw), *skilia* (OSw)

annullment (noun) *neqvæþi* (OSw)

anoint (verb) *olia* (OSw), *vighia* (OSw)

anointment (noun) *oling* (OSw)

answer (verb) *svara* (OSw)

answer (noun) *svar* (OSw)

answer for (verb) *andverþa* (OGu), *rætta* (OSw), *svara* (OSw), *varþa* (OSw)

answering assembly (noun) *vithermalsthing* (ODan)

antagonist (noun) *delobroþir* (OSw)

anticipated children (noun) *oskabarn* (OSw)

apparent (adj.) *openbar* (OSw)

appeal (verb) *dela* (OSw), *qvælia* (OSw), *skærskuta* (OSw), *væpia* (OSw)

appeal (noun) *mal (1)* (OSw), *tala (1)* (OSw), *væþ* (OSw), *væþning* (OSw)

appeal to a court (noun) *dómfesta* (ON)

appeal to a higher court (noun) *skut* (ODan)

appeal to an assembly (noun) *þingskot* (ON)

appear (verb) *sea* (OSw)

appear at the Thing and defend oneself (verb) *firiganga* (OSw)

appear before (verb) *sökia* (OSw)

appearance at the assembly (noun) *þingsganga* (OSw)

appellant (noun) *malsæghandi* (OSw)

apple garden (noun) *apeldgarth* (ODan)

apple-children (noun) *æplesbarn (pl.)* (ODan)

apply (verb) *standa* (OSw)

appoint (verb) *eindaga* (ON), *fylla* (OSw), *næmna* (OSw), *raþa* (OSw), *skipta* (OSw), *skærskuta* (OSw), *sætia* (OSw), *visa* (OSw)

appointed day (noun) *endaghi* (OSw), *stæmna* (OSw), *stæmnudagher* (OSw)

appointed muster (noun) *stæmna* (OSw)

appointed times for walling work (noun) *garðlagsstefna* (ON)

appointed witness (noun) *kvöðuváttr* (ON), *nefndarvitni* (ON)

appointment (noun) *stefnulag* (ON), *stæmna* (OSw), *umbuþ* (OSw)

apportion (verb) *skipta* (OSw)

appraisal (noun) *virthning* (ODan)

appraise (verb) *virþa* (OSw)

apprehend (verb) *taka* (OSw)

appropriate (adj.) *rætter* (OSw), *sander* (OSw)

appropriation (noun) *görtóki* (ON)

appropriation case (noun) *görtókissök* (ON)

appropriation mulct (noun) *görtóki* (ON)

approval (noun) *goþvili* (OSw), *raþ* (OSw)

arable field (noun) *aker* (OSw), *vang* (ODan)

arable field plot (noun) *akermal* (OSw)

arable land (noun) *aker* (OSw), *akerland* (ODan), *jorþ* (OSw), *sæþ* (OSw), *tegher* (OSw)

arable tithe (noun) *tiund* (OSw)

arbiters (noun) *jamkyrnismæn (pl.)* (OSw)

arbitration (noun) *gærþ* (OSw), *sættargærþ* (OSw)

arbitrator (noun) *gerþamaþr* (OGu), *sáttarmaðr* (ON), *sættarmaðr* (ON)

archbishop (noun) *biskuper* (OSw), *ærchibiskuper* (OSw)

area (noun) *bygd* (OSw)

area of an office (noun) *læn* (OSw)

area where common rights exist (noun) *almænninger* (OSw) area which pays due for military tax (noun) *hamna* (OSw)

area within which one is permitted to move around (noun) *umhvarf* (ON)

argue (verb) *dela* (OSw)

armed attendants (noun) *hælmninger* (OSw)

armed combat (noun) *vapnaskipti* (OSw)

armed conflict (noun) *vapnaskipti* (OSw)

armed escort (noun) *föruneyti* (ON)

armed gang (noun) *hærskjold* (ODan)

armour (noun) *musa* (OSw)

arms (noun) *vapn* (OSw)

army (noun) *hær* (OSw)

arraign (verb) *tiltala* (OSw)

arrange (verb) *raþa* (OSw), *skipa* (OSw)

arrangement (noun) *köp* (OSw), *mal (1)* (OSw), *máldagi* (ON), *skipan* (OSw), *skæl* (OSw), *sæt* (OSw)

arrant seizure (noun) *rantakin* (OSw), *rauðarán* (ON)

array (noun) *þjóðstefna* (ON)

arrest (noun) *hæfta* (OSw)

arrow (noun) *arf* (OSw), *sköti* (OSw)

arrow assembly (noun) *örvarþing* (ON)

arrow thing (noun) *örvarþing* (ON)

arrow trap (noun) *sialfskut* (OSw)

arson (noun) *bruni* (ON), *brænna* (OSw), *elder* (ON), *viliabrænna* (OSw)

arson-murder (noun) *morthbrand* (ODan)

arson-wolf (noun) *brennuvargr* (ON)

arsonist (noun) *brennuvargr* (ON)

article (noun) *griper* (OSw)

article of law (noun) *mal (1)* (OSw)

article of the law (noun) *laghmal* (OSw)

artisan (noun) *gærningisman* (OSw)

as a finder entitled to the whole (adj.) *einfyndr* (ON)

as a matter of course (adj.) *sjalfsettr* (ON)

as enemies (adj.) *osater* (OSw)

as foes (adj.) *osater* (OSw)

as friends (adj.) *sater* (OSw)

as good as (adj.) *gilder* (OSw)

as holy (adj.) *jafndýrr* (ON), *jafnheilagr* (ON)

as much (adj.) *jafnmikill* (ON)

as rightful (adj.) *jafnréttr* (ON)

ascendant inheritance (noun) *bakarf* (OSw)

Ascension Day (noun) *uppstigningardagr* (ON)

ascertain (verb) *sea* (OSw)

ascribe (verb) *vita* (OSw)

Ash Wednesday (noun) *askuoþensdagher* (OSw)

ask (verb) *biuþa* (OSw), *biþia* (OSw), *krævia* (OSw)

ask for (verb) *biþia* (OSw), *krævia* (OSw)

assailant (noun) *frumhlaupsmaðr* (ON), *skaþamaþer* (OSw)

assassin (noun) *bani* (OSw), *drapari* (OSw), *flugumaðr* (ON)

assault (verb) *misfyrma* (OSw)

assault (noun) *atlöp* (OSw), *bardaghi* (OSw), *frumhlaup* (ON), *gripr* (OGu), *hlaup* (ON), *laghe* (ODan), *misfyrmilse* (OSw), *slegr* (OGu), *tilhlaup* (ON), *tilræði* (ON)

assault at arms (noun) *vapnaskipti* (OSw)

assault on someone in his home (noun) *hemsokn* (OSw)

assemble (verb) *næmna* (OSw), *stæmna* (OSw)

assembled men (noun) *fjölði* (ON)

assembling for war (noun) *herhlaup* (ON)

assembly (noun) *laghþing* (OSw), *mot* (OSw), *stæmna* (OSw), *þing* (OSw)

assembly area (noun) *þing* (OSw)

assembly attachment (noun) *þingfestr* (ON)

assembly attendance (noun) *þingför* (ON), *þingreið* (ON)

assembly attendance dues (noun) *þingfararkaup* (ON)

assembly baggage (noun) *þingfat* (ON)

assembly balking (noun) *þingsafglöpun* (ON)

assembly boundary (noun) *þingmark* (ON)

assembly court (noun) *þingadómr* (ON)

assembly day (noun) *þingsdagher* (OSw)

assembly disruption (noun) *þingrof* (ON)

assembly district (noun) *þinghá* (ON), *þingsókn* (ON)

assembly fee (noun) *þinglaun* (OGu)

assembly gear (noun) *þingfat* (ON)

assembly ground (noun) *þingvöllr* (ON)

assembly hearers (noun) *thinghøring* (ODan)

assembly held on account of a murder (noun) *manndrápsþing* (ON)

assembly horse (noun) *þinghestr* (ON)

assembly in the district (noun) *hærapsþing* (OSw)

assembly in the outer islands (noun) *úteynaþing* (ON)

assembly is over (adj.) *urþinga* (OSw)

assembly journey (noun) *þingför* (ON)

assembly legislation (noun) *þingtak* (ON)

assembly meeting (noun) *þingstæmna* (OSw)

assembly members (noun) *þingsmæn (pl.)* (OSw)

assembly membership (noun) *þingvist* (ON)

assembly men (noun) *þingsmæn (pl.)* (OSw)

assembly of a province (noun) *landsrætter* (OSw)

assembly of reply (noun) *vithermalsthing* (ODan)

assembly of the district (noun) *hærapsþing* (OSw)

assembly of the fourth (noun) *fiærþungsþing* (OSw)

assembly of the hundari (noun) *hundarisþing* (OSw)

assembly of the one-day (noun) *sægnarþing* (OSw)

assembly of the province (noun) *landsþing* (OSw)

assembly participant (noun) *þinghámaðr* (ON), *þingheyjandi* (ON)

assembly peace (noun) *þingsfriþer* (OSw)

assembly place (noun) *þingsstaþer* (OSw)

assembly procedures (noun) *þingsköp (pl.)* (ON)

assembly procedures section (noun) *þingskapaþáttr* (ON)

assembly road (noun) *þingsvægher* (OSw)

assembly sanctity (noun) *þingsfriþer* (OSw)

assembly site (noun) *þingsstaþer* (OSw)

assembly slope (noun) *þingbrekka* (ON)

assembly summons (noun) *þingbuþ* (OSw), *þingstæmna* (OSw)

assembly third (noun) *þriþiunger* (OSw)

assembly to muster weapons (noun) *vápnaþing* (ON)

assembly where one should answer (noun) *vithermalsthing* (ODan)

assembly with a five-day notice (noun) *fimmtarstefna* (ON), *fimmtarþing* (ON)

assembly with five days' notice (noun) *fimmnættingr* (ON)

assembly witness (noun) *þingvitni* (OSw)

assembly-displayed (adj.) *þingborinn* (ON)

assembly-fit (noun) *þingfőrr* (ON)

assembly-site pole (noun) *motstukkr* (OGu)

assemblymen's judgment (noun) *þingmannadómr* (ON)

assent (noun) *samkvæði* (ON)

assert (verb) *kalla* (OSw)

assert a claim (verb) *brigþa* (OGu)

assess (verb) *mæla (2)* (OSw), *mæta* (OSw), *skuþa* (OSw), *virþa* (OSw)

assessment (noun) *mæt* (OSw), *mætansorþ* (OSw), *virthning* (ODan)

assessment of six men (noun) *sexmannadómr* (ON)

assessor (noun) *metandi* (ON)

assessors (noun) *mætsmæn (pl.)* (OSw)

asset (noun) *öre* (OSw)

assets (noun) *bo* (OSw)

assign by lots (verb) *luta* (OSw)

assignor (noun) *fang* (OSw), *fangaman* (OSw), *skuli* (OSw), *æghandi* (OSw)

assistance (noun) *björg* (ON), *liðskostr* (ON), *lið (2)* (OSw)

association (noun) *samvist* (OSw)

asylum (noun) *friþer* (OSw), *griþ* (OSw)

at home (adv.) *innanlands* (OSw)

at one's free disposal (adj.) *hemul* (OSw)

atone (verb) *böta* (OSw), *gælda (1)* (OSw)

atonement (noun) *bot* (OSw), *sakbót* (ON), *skript* (OSw), *yfirbót* (ON)

atonement extra compensation (noun) *sakaaukabót* (ON)

atonement extras (noun) *sakauki* (ON)

atonement list (noun) *saktal* (ON)

atonement of one ounce-unit (noun) *eyrisbót* (ON)

atonement payment (noun) *fæbot* (OSw)

attached to an assembly (adj.) *þingfastr* (ON)

attack (verb) *fælla* (OSw), *raþa* (OSw), *ræna* (OSw), *sökia* (OSw), *sækia* (OSw)

attack (noun) *arath* (ODan), *atlöp* (OSw), *atvígi* (ON), *gærþ* (OSw)

attack at/in one's home (noun) *hemsokn* (OSw)

attack of a crowd (noun) *flokkaatvígi* (ON)

attacker (noun) *skaþamaþer* (OSw)

attend (verb) *sökia* (OSw), *varþa* (OSw)

attendance at the General Assembly (noun) *alþingisreið* (ON)

attendant (noun) *knapi* (ON)

attest (verb) *dylia* (OSw), *vátta* (ON), *vitna* (OSw)

attestation that formal means of proof have been produced (noun) *gagnagagn* (ON)

auditory man (noun) *hörængi* (OSw)

authenticated in legal ownership (adj.) *hemul* (OSw)

authentication (noun) *hemuld* (OSw)

authorities (noun) *land* (OSw)

authority (noun) *forráð* (ON), *forræðismaðr* (ON), *raþ* (OSw), *umbuþ* (OSw), *vald* (OSw), *veldi* (ON), *yfirboð* (ON)

authorization (noun) *umbuþ* (OSw)

authorize (verb) *biuþa* (OSw)

authorized (adj.) *fulder* (OSw)

automatically called (adj.) *sjalfboðinn* (ON), *sjalfkvaddr* (ON)

automatically conveyed (adj.) *sjalfskeytr* (ON)

automatically dissolved (adj.) *sjalftekinn* (ON)

automatically summoned (adj.) *sjalfstefndr* (ON)

autumn assembly (noun) *höstþing* (OSw), *leiðarþing* (ON)

autumn meeting (noun) *leið* (ON)

autumn meeting matters (noun) *leiðarmál* (ON)

autumn meeting place (noun) *leiðarvöllr* (ON)

autumn tithe (noun) *hausttíund* (ON)

available (adj.) *fræls* (OSw)

avenge (verb) *hæmna* (OSw)

avoid (verb) *firrask* (ON), *flya* (OSw)

avow (verb) *viþerganga* (OSw)

award (verb) *döma* (OSw)

awkwardness (noun) *vangöma* (OSw)

axe (noun) *öxe* (OSw)

axe handle (noun) *øxarskaft* (ON)

axe handle binding (noun) *öxaol* (OSw)

axe with a handle (noun) *skaftøks* (ODan)

back (noun) *hryggr* (ON)

backbiting (noun) *bakmæli* (ON)

backwards (adj.) *avugher* (OSw)

bad behaviour (noun) *oskiel* (OGu)

bad custom (noun) *óvenja* (ON)

bad trick (noun) *óknytti* (ON)

badly done (adj.) *vanhafðr* (ON)

bail (noun) *borghan* (OSw), *fæsta* (OSw), *tak* (OSw)

bailiff (noun) *bryti* (OSw), *lænsmaþer* (OSw), *reþosven* (OSw), *rættari* (OSw)

bailiff in partnership (noun) *fælaghsbryte* (ODan)

bailiffs (noun) *mætsmæn (pl.)* (OSw)

bailing water out of a boat (noun) *austr* (ON)

bailsman (noun) *taki* (OSw)

baiting verdict (noun) *egningarkviðr* (ON)

bake-house (noun) *bakhærbærghi* (OSw)

bald patch (noun) *loyski* (OGu)

balk (verb) *afglapa* (ON), *glepja* (ON)

balking (noun) *glöp* (ON)

balking an affair (noun) *málsafglöpun* (ON)

ban (verb) *banna* (ON), *forbuþa* (OSw), *forlægje* (ODan)

ban (noun) *ban* (OSw), *forbuþ* (OSw), *lagh* (OSw), *lögfesta* (ON)

ban against trade in corn (noun) *kornband* (OGu)

band (of withy) (noun) *bandi* (OGu)

band of men (noun) *flokker* (OSw)

band of traitors (noun) *níðingsherr* (ON)

banquet peace (noun) *ölfriþer* (OSw)

banqueting house witness (noun) *ölðrhúsvitni* (ON)

baptism (noun) *döpilse* (OSw), *hafning* (ON), *kristindomber* (OSw), *kristna* (OSw), *skíring* (ON), *skírn* (ON), *skærsl* (OSw)

baptism by a couple (noun) *hjónaskírn* (ON)

baptism of a child (noun) *barnskírn* (ON)

baptize (verb) *döpa* (OSw), *kristna* (OSw), *skæra (1)* (OSw)

bar (verb) *mena* (OSw), *skilia* (OSw)

bar (noun) *hun* (OSw)

barbed spear (noun) *krókspjót* (ON)

bareheaded (adj.) *ivinaxlaþer* (OSw)

bargain (noun) *köp* (OSw), *mal (1)* (OSw)

bargeboard (noun) *vinsked* (OSw)

barley (noun) *korn* (OSw)

barn (noun) *hjalm* (ODan), *lathegarth* (ODan), *laþa* (OSw)

barn on summer pasture (noun) *sætralaþa* (OSw)

barn with barley or hay (noun) *anlaþi* (OSw)

baron (noun) *barún* (ON)

barrel (noun) *þyn* (OSw)

barricade (noun) *viða* (ON)

barrow man (noun) *høgheman* (ODan)

barter (noun) *skipti* (OSw)

bast (noun) *bast* (ON)

bastard (noun) *horbarn* (OSw)

batch (noun) *kolder* (OSw)

bath house (noun) *baþstova* (OSw)

battle (noun) *orosta* (OSw), *striþ* (OSw), *vígaferði* (ON), *vigh* (OSw)

battle weapon (noun) *folkvapn* (OSw)

battue (noun) *skall* (OSw)

be a case for (verb) *høghe* (ODan)

be a dispute (verb) *ilviljes* (ODan)

be a householder (verb) *búa* (ON)

be able to (verb) *orka* (OSw)

be accused (verb) *vita* (OSw)

be an (eye) witness (verb) *sea* (OSw)

be annulled (verb) *fælla* (OSw)

be answerable for (verb) *andverþa* (OGu), *varþa* (OSw)

be appraised (verb) *vita* (OSw)

be binding (verb) *halda* (OSw)

be burned (verb) *brænna* (OSw)

be called (verb) *heta* (OSw)

be captive (verb) *hæfta* (OSw)

be charged (verb) *vita* (OSw)

be compensated (verb) *böta* (OSw), *gilda* (OSw)

be considered (verb) *syna* (OSw)

be considered to be (verb) *heta* (OSw)

be contumacious (verb) *dylkas* (OSw), *þryskas* (OSw)

be convicted (verb) *brista* (OSw), *fælla* (OSw)

be damaged (verb) *misfara* (ON)

be declared (verb) *heta* (OSw)

be defiant (verb) *þryskas* (OSw)

be destitute (verb) *þrjóta* (ON)

be dismissed (verb) *aterganga* (OSw)

be divorced (verb) *skilia* (OSw)

be enough (verb) *vinna* (OSw)

be entitled to (verb) *öðlask* (ON), *raþa* (OSw)

be entitled to a man's lot (verb) *mynde* (ODan)

be fined (verb) *böta* (OSw), *gælda (1)* (OSw), *viþerhætta* (OSw)

be forced (verb) *raþa* (OSw), *varþa* (OSw), *þorva* (OSw)

be found guilty (verb) *fælla* (OSw), *kænna* (OSw)

be free (verb) *skilia* (OSw)

be guilty (verb) *sækia* (OSw), *valda* (OSw)

be guilty and fined (verb) *fælla* (OSw)

be guilty to compensate (verb) *sækia* (OSw), *viþerhætta* (OSw)

be guilty to compensation (verb) *sækia* (OSw)

be guilty to/of (verb) *sækia* (OSw)

be held to be (verb) *heta* (OSw)

be in charge of (verb) *raþa* (OSw), *varþveta* (OSw)

be in control over (verb) *varþa* (OSw)

be innocent (verb) *væria* (OSw)

be itinerant (verb) *fara* (ON)

be joined (verb) *hanga* (ON)

be judged as invalid (verb) *aterganga* (OSw)

be killed (verb) *söfask* (ON)

be known as (verb) *heta* (OSw)

be lawfully convicted (verb) *fælla* (OSw)

be liable (verb) *þorva* (OSw)

be liable for (verb) *varþa* (OSw), *viþerhætta* (OSw)

be liable to (pay) a fine (verb) *böta* (OSw)

be liable to a fine (verb) *sökjask* (OSw)

be liable to a fine of (verb) *viþerhætta* (OSw)

be liable to compensate (verb) *viþerhætta* (OSw)

be looked upon (verb) *heta* (OSw)

be named (verb) *heta* (OSw)

be offended (verb) *reiðask* (ON)

be one's own master (verb) *raþa* (OSw)

be place for (verb) *lata* (OSw)

be prosecuted (verb) *sökjask* (OSw)

be punishable by (verb) *varþa* (OSw)

be reduced (verb) *fælla* (OSw)

be refractory (verb) *þryskas* (OSw)

be responsible (verb) *abyrghia* (OSw), *valda* (OSw)

be responsible (for) (verb) *varþa* (OSw), *varþveta* (OSw)

be responsible for (verb) *raþa* (OSw), *uppihalda* (OSw)

be responsible for something (verb) *raþa* (OSw)

be responsible for upkeep (verb) *gilda* (OSw)

be satisfied (verb) *una* (ON)

be secret (verb) *løne* (ODan)

be slain (verb) *fælla* (OSw)

be stubborn (verb) *þrásk* (ON), *þryskas* (OSw)

be subject to compensation (verb) *gilda* (OSw)

be sufficient (verb) *vinna* (OSw)

be taken (verb) *ganga* (OSw)

be unfaithful (verb) *hóra* (ON)

be unsure (verb) *tortryggva* (ON)

be vacant (verb) *fljóta* (ON)

be vague (verb) *nálgask* (ON)

be valid (verb) *abyrghia* (OSw), *gælda (1)* (OSw), *standa* (OSw)

be visible (verb) *sea* (OSw), *syna* (OSw)

be void (verb) *fælla* (OSw)

be wanting (verb) *brista* (OSw), *skæra (2)* (OSw), *þrjóta* (ON)

be willing (verb) *vilia* (OSw)

be without sons (verb) *ganga* (OSw)

be worth (verb) *gælda (1)* (OSw)

beach-guard (noun) *næsiavarþer* (OSw)

beacon (noun) *viti* (ON)

beacon fire (noun) *viti* (ON)

beacon guard (noun) *bötavarþer* (OSw)

beam (noun) *bjalki* (ON), *ri* (OGu)

bear (verb) *föþa* (OSw)

bear (noun) *biorn* (OSw)

bear witness (verb) *vita* (OSw), *vitna* (OSw)

beard (noun) *kampr* (ON)

bearing of arms (noun) *vápnaburðr* (ON)

beast (noun) *fæ* (OSw), *fænaþer* (OSw), *griper* (OSw), *söþer* (OSw)

beast born the same summer (noun) *sumartenlunger* (OSw)

beat (verb) *bæria* (OSw), *diunga* (OSw), *dræpa* (OSw), *lysta (1)* (OSw), *raþa* (OSw), *sla* (OSw)

beat (noun) *bardaghi* (OSw)

beat someone to the ground (verb) *jorthhog* (ODan)

beaten as a slave (adj.) *þrælbarth* (ODan)

beating (noun) *bardaghi* (OSw), *barsmíð* (ON), *drep* (ON), *hug* (OSw)

become a vagrant (verb) *ganga* (OSw)

become invalid (verb) *fyrirskjóta* (ON)

become reconciled (verb) *sætta* (OSw)

become time-barred (verb) *fyrna* (OSw)

become useless with age (verb) *fyrna* (OSw)

bed (noun) *siang* (OSw)

bed of adultery (noun) *horsiang* (OSw)

bed-purchase (noun) *siængaköp* (OSw)

bed-robbery (noun) *siangaran* (OSw)

bed-wetting (noun) *beþroyta* (OGu)

bedchamber (noun) *symnhus* (OSw)

bedclothes (noun) *klæþi* (OSw), *sengaklepi* (OGu)

bedcover (noun) *falda* (OGu)

bedfellow (noun) *karnaðr* (ON)

bedspread (noun) *aklæþi* (OSw)

bee (noun) *bi* (OSw)

bee garden (noun) *bigarth* (ODan)

bee-hive (noun) *bistokker* (OSw), *stokker* (OSw)

bee-swarm (noun) *koppofunder* (OSw)

beech nut (noun) *bok (2)* (ODan)

beer (noun) *öl* (OSw)

beer bench (noun) *ölbænker* (OSw)

beer cottage (noun) *ölstuva* (OSw)

beer drinking (noun) *ølfylle* (ODan)

beer-house (noun) *ölstuva* (OSw)

before being tortured (adj.) *ofrester* (OGu)

beggar (noun) *húsgangsmaðr* (ON), *lurker* (OSw), *stafkarl* (OSw)

begging (noun) *húsgangr* (ON)

begin (verb) *vekja* (ON)

begin an oath (verb) *hofþa* (OSw)

beginning of summer (noun) *sumarmál* (ON)

beginning of summertime (noun) *sumarnat* (OSw)

beginning of the fast (noun) *fastuganger* (OSw)

beginning of winter (noun) *vinternat* (OSw)

behead (verb) *halshugga* (OSw)

behest (noun) *buþ* (OSw)

being allowed to stay in the country (adj.) *inlænder* (OSw)

being called a thief (noun) *thjuvsnavn* (ODan)

being entitled to inheritance (noun) *erfðatal* (ON)

being entitled to make decisions about marriage (noun) *forráð* (ON)

being killed (noun) *bani* (OSw)

being killed under a ship (noun) *hlunnroð* (ON)

being outside the peace (noun) *friþlösa* (OSw)

being together (noun) *fylghi* (OSw), *samvist* (OSw)

being together with (noun) *samværa* (OSw)

being without peace (noun) *friþlösa* (OSw)

believe (verb) *vænta* (OSw)

bell ringer (noun) *klokkari* (OSw)

Bell Wednesday (noun) *kloknaoþensdagher* (OSw)

belong to (verb) *eigna* (ON)

belong to an assembly (verb) *heyja* (ON)

belonging to an outlaw (adj.) *útlagr* (ON), *útlægr* (ON)

belonging to the same assembly (adj.) *samþinga* (ON)

belongings (noun) *egn* (OSw), *fæ* (OSw), *koster* (OSw), *rætter* (OSw)

belt-fine (noun) *lindebot* (ODan)

bench (noun) *flat* (OSw)

bench boards (noun) *brík* (ON)

bench support (noun) *setstokkr* (ON)

benchmate (noun) *sæssi* (OSw)

benefit (verb) *þorva* (OSw)

benefit (noun) *mak* (OGu), *þörf* (ON)

berth theft (noun) *hafnarrán* (ON)

bestiality (noun) *þyþilagh* (OSw)

bet (verb) *væþia* (OSw)

betray (verb) *forraþa* (OSw), *hóra* (ON)

betrayal against one's land (noun) *landráð* (ON)

betroth (verb) *fastna* (ON), *fæsta* (OSw)

betrothal (noun) *festarmál* (ON), *fæst* (OSw), *fæsta* (OSw), *fæstning* (OSw), *fæstningamal* (OSw)

betrothal agreement (noun) *fæstningamal* (OSw)

betrothal case (noun) *fæstningamal* (OSw)

betrothal gift (noun) *förning* (OSw), *tilgæf* (OSw)

betrothal man (noun) *giftarmaþer* (OSw)

betrothal meeting (noun) *fæstningastæmpna* (OSw), *malaþing* (OGu)

betrothal payment (noun) *fæstningafæ* (OSw)

betrothal price (noun) *fæstnaþafæ* (OSw), *fæstningafæ* (OSw)

betrothal witness (noun) *festaváttorð* (ON), *festaváttr* (ON), *festavætti* (ON)

betrothed (noun) *fæstamaþer* (OSw)

betrothed couple (noun) *hion* (OSw)

betrothed man (noun) *fæstamaþer* (OSw)

betrothed woman (noun) *fæstakona* (OSw)

betrother (noun) *fastnandi* (ON)

bewitch (verb) *firigæra* (OSw)

bible/lawbook/book (noun) *bok (1)* (OSw)

bid for (verb) *biuþa* (OSw)

bidder (noun) *bjóðandi* (ON)

big wood-pile of young trees (noun) *storþahug* (OSw)

billeting (noun) *gengærþ* (OSw), *væzla* (OSw)

billy-goat (noun) *bukker* (OSw)

bind (verb) *binda* (OSw), *fæsta* (OSw)

bind by gold (verb) *gulfæste* (ODan)

bind to the stake (verb) *stæghla* (OSw)

binding (noun) *band* (OSw)

binding (adj.) *fulder* (OSw), *gilder* (OSw)

binding relationship (noun) *band* (OSw)

birch bark (noun) *næffer* (OSw)

birth (noun) *byrþ* (OSw)

birthright (noun) *arver* (OSw), *byrþ* (OSw), *ærfþ* (OSw)

birthright inheritance (noun) *byrþ* (OSw)

birthright land (noun) *byrþ* (OSw)

bishop (noun) *biskuper* (OSw), *lyþbiskuper* (OSw)

bishopric (noun) *biskupsdöme* (OSw), *byskupsríki* (ON)

bishop's administrator (noun) *lænsmaþer* (OSw)

bishop's case (noun) *biskupssak* (OSw)

bishop's cause (noun) *biskupssak* (OSw)

bishop's due (noun) *biskupsrætter* (OSw)

bishop's farm (noun) *biskupsgarþer* (OSw)

bishop's fine (noun) *biskupsrætter* (OSw)

bishop's jury (noun) *biskupsnæmd* (OSw)

bishop's man (noun) *biskupsmaþer* (OSw)

bishop's manor (noun) *biskupsgarþer* (OSw)

bishop's panel (noun) *biskupsnæmd* (OSw)

bishop's representative (noun) *biskuper* (OSw)

bishop's right (noun) *biskupsrætter* (OSw)

bishop's seat (noun) *byskupsstóll* (ON)

bishop's son (noun) *byskupssonr* (ON)

bishop's tithe (noun) *byskupstíund* (ON)

bit (noun) *þveiti* (ON)

bit of land (noun) *jorthebit* (ODan)

bitch (noun) *grey* (ON)

bite (verb) *bita* (OGu)

biting inheritance (noun) *arvbit* (ODan)

Bjarkey law (noun) *bjarkeyjarréttr* (ON)

black blow (noun) *svartaslagh* (OSw)

black monk (noun) *svartmunk* (ODan)

black sorcery (noun) *fordeþskepr* (OGu)

black wound (noun) *svartaslagh* (OSw)

blame (verb) *klanda* (OSw), *kænna* (OSw), *vita* (OSw)

blameless (adj.) *angerløs* (ODan), *osaker* (OSw), *saklös* (OSw), *sykn* (OSw)

bleeding wound (noun) *bloþsar* (OSw)

blemish (noun) *lyti* (OSw), *vamm* (ON)

blemishing blow (noun) *óvænishögg* (ON)

bless (verb) *vighia* (OSw)

block (verb) *ræna* (OSw)

block with stakes (verb) *stika* (ON)

blocking of the way (noun) *vegþueri* (OGu)

blood (noun) *bloþ* (OSw)

blood fine (noun) *bloþviti* (OSw)

blood injury (noun) *bloþviti* (OSw)

blood of conflict (noun) *öfundarblóð* (ON)

blood payment (noun) *bloþviti* (OSw)

blood relative (noun) *bloþ* (OSw)

blood spilled by accident (noun) *vaþablod* (OSw)

blood wound (noun) *bloþsar* (OSw)

bloodletting (noun) *bloþviti* (OSw)

bloodshed (noun) *bloþ* (OSw), *bloþlæti* (OSw), *bloþviti* (OSw), *mannskaði* (ON)

blow (noun) *bardaghi* (OSw), *drep* (ON), *dynter* (OSw), *hug* (OSw), *slagh* (OSw), *slegr* (OGu)

blow classed among injuries (noun) *áverkadrep* (ON)

blow that does not cause blood to be spilt (noun) *lukahagg* (OGu)

blow that makes a bruise (noun) *svartaslagh* (OSw)

blow with a rod (noun) *stavshog* (ODan)

blow with a staff (noun) *stangehog* (ODan)

blow with a stone (noun) *stenshog* (ODan)

blow with evil intent (noun) *öfundarhögg* (ON)

blow with the hand (noun) *puster* (OSw)

blunt, heavy arrow (noun) *kolfr* (ON)

boar (noun) *galter* (OSw)

board (noun) *borð* (ON), *koster* (OSw), *vist* (OSw)

board and lodging (noun) *hærbærghi* (OSw)

board-bridge (noun) *fjölbrú* (ON)

boarding (noun) *elði* (ON)

boarding (an outlaw) in ignorance (noun) *óvísaelði* (ON)

boarding a ship (noun) *bunkebrut* (ODan)

boat (noun) *bater* (OSw), *skip* (OSw)

boat (i.e. afloat) (noun) *flut* (OGu)

boat share (noun) *skiphlutr* (ON)

boat tackle (noun) *farkoster* (OSw)

boathouse (noun) *naust* (ON)

boatload (noun) *batsfarmber* (OSw), *skipfarmr* (ON)

bodily injury (noun) *akoma* (OSw), *fjörskaði* (ON), *óvæni* (ON)

bodyguard (noun) *hirð* (ON)

bodyguard's horse (noun) *hirðhestr* (ON)

bodyguard's ship (noun) *hirðskip* (ON)

bollard (noun) *stokker* (OSw)

bolt (noun) *hæl (1)* (OSw)

bolt-rope (noun) *líksíma* (ON)

bond (noun) *band* (OSw), *væþ* (OSw)

bondmaid (noun) *ambat* (OSw)

bonds (noun) *band* (OSw)

bondsman (noun) *gæfþræl* (OSw), *mansmaðr* (ON)

bondwoman (noun) *ambat* (OSw)

bone (noun) *ben (1)* (ODan)

bone extraction (noun) *benlösning* (OSw)

bone payment (noun) *beingjald* (ON)

book (noun) *balker* (OSw), *bok (1)* (OSw), *skra* (ODan)

book about fences (noun) *utgærþabolker* (OSw)

book about illegal appropriation (noun) *fornæmisbalker* (OSw)

book about killing (noun) *draparibalker* (OSw)

book about lawlessness (noun) *rætlosubolker* (OSw)

book about marriage (noun) *giptarbalker* (OSw)

book about mills (noun) *mylnobolker* (OSw)

book about peace (noun) *friþbalker* (OSw)

book concerning building and community (noun) *bygningabalker* (OSw)

book concerning building or community (noun) *viþerbobalker* (OSw)

book concerning Christian law (noun) *kristnubalker* (OSw)

book concerning Church or Christian law (noun) *kirkiubalker* (OSw)

book concerning inheritance (noun) *ærfþarbalker* (OSw)

book concerning land (noun) *jorþarbalker* (OSw)

book concerning legal process (noun) *þingmalabalker* (OSw)

book concerning matrimony (noun) *giptarbalker* (OSw)

book concerning personal and property rights (noun) *manhælghisbalker* (OSw)

book concerning the legal process (noun) *þingbalker* (OSw)

book concerning trade (noun) *köpmalabalker* (OSw)

book of accidental cases (noun) *vaþabot* (OSw)

book of killings (noun) *drapabalker* (OSw)

book of manslaughter (noun) *drapamal* (OSw)

book of personal rights (noun) *manhælghi* (OSw)

book of the law of the land (noun) *landslagabók* (ON)

book on tenancy (noun) *landsleigubölkr* (ON)

book on the naval levy (noun) *útgerðarbölkr* (ON)

book on theft (noun) *þiuvabalker* (OSw)

book on trade (noun) *kaupabölkr* (ON)

book-learned (adj.) *boklærder* (OSw)

booth (noun) *boþ* (OSw)

booth-mate (noun) *búðunautr* (ON)

booth-panel (noun) *búðakviðr* (ON)

booth-resident (adj.) *búðfastr* (ON)

booth-space (noun) *búðarrúm* (ON)

booty (noun) *féfang* (ON), *herfang* (ON)

border (noun) *endimark* (ON), *landamæri* (OSw), *skæl* (OSw)

border marker (noun) *landamæri* (OSw)

border marker of the parish (noun) *soknamærki* (OSw)

border marker of the province (noun) *landamærki* (OSw)

border of a farm (noun) *garþsliþ* (OSw)

bordering a right of way (adj.) *tafastr* (OGu)

born a lawful heir (adj.) *arfgænger* (OSw)

born at home (adj.) *hemaföder* (OSw)

born free (adj.) *frælsboren* (ODan)

born in kin (adj.) *ætborin* (OSw), *ættaþer* (OSw)

born in wedlock (adj.) *skilgetinn* (ON)

born of a bondwoman (adj.) *þiþborin* (OSw)

born to odal right (adj.) *óðalborinn* (ON)

borrow (verb) *lana* (OSw), *leghia* (OSw)

borrowed chattels (noun) *lánfé* (ON)

borrowed thing (noun) *lánfé* (ON)

bottom board of the stern (noun) *skutþilja* (ON)

bought goods (noun) *köpskatter* (OSw)

bought land (noun) *köpoiorþ* (OSw), *stuvkøp* (ODan)

bought mark (noun) *kaupamark* (ON)

bounce (verb) *stionka* (OSw)

bound by a village highway (adj.) *tæbundin* (OSw)

bound by debt (adj.) *faster* (ON), *skuldfastr* (ON)

boundary (noun) *landamærki* (OSw), *markarskæl* (OSw), *mærki* (OSw), *ra* (OSw), *skæl* (OSw), *uphov* (ODan), *útmerki* (ON)

boundary between communes (noun) *hreppamót* (ON)

boundary between districts (noun) *hærethsskjal* (ODan)

boundary between fields (noun) *markarskæl* (OSw)

boundary birch (noun) *merkibjörk* (ON)

boundary fence (noun) *merkigarðr* (ON)

boundary land (noun) *mærki* (OSw)

boundary line (noun) *markreina* (ON), *ra* (OSw)

boundary mark (noun) *landamærki* (OSw), *mark (1)* (ON), *mærki* (OSw), *ummerki* (ON)

boundary mark in woodland (noun) *skoghamærki* (OSw)

boundary marker (noun) *mærki* (OSw), *ra* (OSw), *rör* (OSw), *skæl* (OSw), *tiældra* (OSw)

boundary marker consisting of three stones (noun) *þræstene* (OSw)

boundary marker ring (noun) *ringrör* (OSw)

boundary markers of plots (noun) *tomptara* (OSw)

boundary marks between forests (noun) *skoghamærki* (OSw)

boundary marks between lands (noun) *landamæri* (OSw)

boundary of the province (noun) *landamæri* (OSw)

boundary path (noun) *vaþ* (OSw)

boundary river (noun) *merkiá* (ON)

boundary rivermouth (noun) *merkióss* (ON)

boundary ropes (noun) *vébönd (pl.)* (ON)

boundary showing (noun) *merkjasýning* (ON)

boundary stone (noun) *lýritti* (ON), *marksteinn* (ON), *tiældrusten* (OSw)

boundary stream (noun) *merkivatn* (ON)

boundary walk (noun) *merkjaganga* (ON)

boundary wall (noun) *merkigarðr* (ON)

bounden debtor (noun) *lögskuldarmaðr* (ON), *skuldarmaðr* (ON)

bounding a road (adj.) *tafastr* (OGu)

bow (noun) *boghi* (OSw)

bowl (noun) *skal* (OGu)

bowshot (noun) *ördrag* (ON), *örskot* (ON), *örskotshelgr* (ON)

box on the ear (noun) *puster* (OSw)

box trap (noun) *bas* (OSw)

boy (noun) *sven* (OSw)

brain wound (noun) *heilund* (ON)

branch of a family (noun) *knérunnr* (ON), *ættkvísl* (ON)

brand (verb) *merkia* (OGu)

brand (noun) *bolsmærki* (OSw), *mærki* (OSw)

brandish (verb) *ofra* (ON)

breach (verb) *bryta* (OSw)

breach in the transference of title (noun) *handsalsslit* (ON)

breach of a church penance (noun) *skriptabrut* (OSw)

breach of a judgement (noun) *dombrut* (OSw)

breach of agreement (noun) *malaruf* (OSw), *vitherlæghisbrut* (OSw)

breach of bargain (noun) *köpruf* (OSw)

breach of contract (noun) *handsalsslit* (ON)

breach of employment (noun) *leghuruf* (OSw)

breach of law (noun) *lögbrot* (ON)

breach of personal peace (noun) *manhælghismal* (OSw)

breach of purchase (noun) *köpruf* (OSw)

breach of safe conduct (noun) *gruþspiæl* (OSw)

breach of the king's sworn peace (noun) *eþsöre* (OSw), *eþsörisbrut* (OSw)

breach of the law (noun) *laghslit* (OSw)

breach of the peace (noun) *friþbrut* (OSw)

breach of the peace in the market place (noun) *torghfrith* (ODan)

breach-of-agreement payment (noun) *handsalsslit* (ON)

breaching of a work contract (noun) *leghuruf* (OSw)

breadth of a foot (noun) *þværfoter* (OSw)

break (verb) *brista* (OSw), *bryta* (OSw), *ryva* (OSw), *sundersla* (OGu)

break an agreement (verb) *skilia* (OSw)

break on a wheel (verb) *stæghla* (OSw)

break out (verb) *bryta* (OSw)

breaker of a truce (noun) *gruthnithing* (ODan)

breaking (noun) *rof* (ON)

breaking (a bone) (noun) *brut* (OSw)

breaking into a ship (noun) *bunkebrut* (ODan)

breaking of a boundary marker (noun) *tiældrubrut* (OSw)

breaking of a man's peace (noun) *ofriþer* (OSw)

breaking of an employment contract (noun) *leghuruf* (OSw)

breaking penance (adj.) *skriftrofa* (ON)

breaking the peace (noun) *friþbrut* (OSw), *hælghebrut* (ODan)

breeding mare (noun) *stoþhors* (OSw)

bribe (noun) *muta* (OSw), *væghsel* (ODan)

bridal bench (noun) *bruþbænker* (OSw)

bridal chair (noun) *brúðstóll* (ON)

bridal cloths (noun) *bruþvaþir (pl.)* (OSw)

bridal gift (noun) *gagngjald* (ON), *munder* (OSw), *tilgæf* (OSw)

bridal journey (noun) *bruþfærd* (OSw)

bridal men (noun) *bruþmaþer* (OSw)

bridal pages (noun) *bruþmaþer* (OSw)

bridal seat (noun) *bruþasæti* (OSw)

bride (noun) *bruþ* (OSw), *kona* (OSw)

bride kidnapping (noun) *ran* (OSw)

bride price (noun) *hindradagsgæf* (OSw), *kvánarmundr* (ON), *morghongæf* (OSw), *munder* (OSw)

bride-seat-eviction (noun) *utskutstola* (OSw)

bridegroom (noun) *bruþgome* (OSw), *ungimaþr* (OGu)

bridesmaid (noun) *brúðkona* (ON), *bruþframma* (OSw)

bridesman (noun) *bruþmaþer* (OSw)

bride's dresser (noun) *brudsæta* (OSw)

bride's journey (noun) *bruþfærd* (OSw)

bride's swains (noun) *bruþkalla* (OSw)

bridge (noun) *bro* (OSw), *markabro* (OSw)

bridge fine (noun) *broabot* (OSw)

bridge inspection (noun) *broasyn* (OSw)

bridge of a quarter (noun) *fiarþungsbro* (OSw)

bridge of a {hundari} (noun) *hundarisbro* (OSw)

bridge of an eighth (noun) *attungsbro* (OSw)

bridge of half a {hundari} (noun) *halfhundarisbro* (OSw)

bridge or causeway (noun) *bro* (OSw)

bridge-plank (noun) *broafiol* (OSw)

bring (verb) *lata* (OSw), *raþa* (OSw), *skipta* (OSw), *sökia* (OSw)

bring a case (against) (verb) *atala* (OSw), *kæra* (OSw), *qvælia* (OSw), *tiltala* (OSw)

bring a case before the Thing assembly (verb) *kæra* (OSw)

bring a case lawfully (verb) *laghfylghia* (OSw)

bring a case of inheritance against (verb) *qvælia* (OSw)

bring a claim (verb) *sökia* (OSw)

bring a claim or case (verb) *sækia* (OSw)

bring a complaint (verb) *kæra* (OSw)

bring a complaint against (verb) *kænna* (OSw)

bring a prosecution (verb) *kæra* (OSw), *sökia* (OSw)

bring a suit (verb) *sækia* (OSw)

bring an action (verb) *sökia* (OSw)

bring an action against (verb) *atala* (OSw)

bring testimony against (verb) *vitna* (OSw)

bring up (verb) *föþa* (OSw)

bring witness (verb) *vitna* (OSw)

broad-axe (noun) *brethøks* (ODan)

broadcloth (noun) *klæþi* (OSw)

broken (adv.) *sundr* (OGu)

broken betrothal (noun) *fæstaruf* (OSw)

broken ends of bone (noun) *brut* (OSw)

broken peace (noun) *friþbrut* (OSw)

brood (noun) *kolder* (OSw), *siængaralder* (OSw)

brood of children (noun) *kolder* (OSw)

brother and sister (noun) *systkin* (ON)

brother-in-law (noun) *magher* (OSw)

brothers' daughters (noun) *bröþrungi* (OSw), *bróðradótr (pl.)* (ON)

brothers' sons (noun) *bröþrungi* (OSw), *bróðrasynir (pl.)* (ON)

brother's lot (noun) *broþursluter* (OSw)

brother's ring (noun) *bróðurbaugr* (ON)

brother's wife (noun) *bróðurkván* (ON)

brought to church (adj.) *kirkiuleþer* (OSw)

bruise (noun) *asyn* (OSw), *bardaghi* (OSw), *blami* (OSw)

bruising (noun) *blami* (OSw)

brush wood (noun) *undirviþer* (OSw)

brush woodland (noun) *rifhrís* (ON)

brush-born (noun) *rishofþe* (OSw)

brushwood (noun) *rifhrís* (ON), *slóðahrís* (ON)

bucket (noun) *spander* (OSw)

bucket, a measure of volume (noun) *spander* (OSw)

buckle (noun) *nast* (OGu), *tassal* (OGu)

bugger (verb) *serða* (ON)

build a barricade in a stream (verb) *viða* (ON)

build a fence (verb) *fælla* (OSw), *gærþa* (OSw)

building (noun) *bygning* (OSw), *hus* (OSw)

building berth (noun) *bakkastokkar (pl.)* (ON)

building material (noun) *anbol* (OGu)

building of boat-houses (noun) *naustgerð* (ON)

building of churches (noun) *kirkiugærþ* (OSw)

building of walls (noun) *veggjarhlaza* (ON)

building plot (noun) *burtomt* (OSw), *tompt* (OSw)

building plot boundary marker (noun) *tomptara* (OSw)

building site (noun) *jorþ* (OSw), *tompt* (OSw)

bullock (noun) *not* (OSw)

bully (verb) *ylfa* (ON)

bundle (noun) *fang* (OSw)

bundle of birch bark (noun) *næfrakimbull* (ON)

burden (noun) *áþyngð* (ON), *byrþi* (OSw)

burglary (noun) *bosran* (OSw), *lokurán* (ON)

burial (noun) *gröftr* (ON), *líkagröftr* (ON)

burial church (noun) *graftarkirkja* (ON)

burial fee (noun) *legkaup* (ON)

burial ground (noun) *gravarbakki* (OSw)

burial mound (noun) *høgh* (ODan)

burial place (noun) *lægherstaþer* (OSw)

burial service (noun) *líksöngr* (ON)

burial service fee (noun) *líksöngskaup* (ON)

burial-place for farmers (noun) *bóndalega* (ON)

buried property (noun) *jarðfé* (ON)

burn (verb) *brænna* (OSw)

burn down (verb) *brænna* (OSw)

burn-beaten land (noun) *rybsl* (OSw)

burn-beaten land for growing turnips (noun) *rompnasviþiur (pl.)* (OSw)

burned spot (noun) *sviða* (ON)

burning (noun) *brænna* (OSw)

burning by accident (noun) *vaþabrænna* (OSw)
burnt place (noun) *brennustaðr* (ON)
bushel (noun) *laupr* (OGu), *skæppa* (OSw)
bushel basket (noun) *sæþaspander* (OSw)
bushel-land (noun) *laupsland* (OGu)
business (noun) *enfæ* (OSw), *mal (1)* (OSw), *sysel* (ODan)
business travel (noun) *köpfærþ* (OSw)
butt (verb) *stanga* (ON)
butt of an axe (noun) *hamarr* (ON)
butter (noun) *smjör* (ON)
butter tax (noun) *vinjarspann* (ON)
butter tithe (noun) *smörmali* (OSw)
buy (verb) *gælda (1)* (OSw), *köpa* (OSw), *lösa* (OSw)
buy at the market (verb) *torghköpe* (ODan)
buy with a friend (verb) *vinga* (OSw)
buyer (noun) *kaupandi* (ON), *köpi* (OSw), *saluman* (OSw)
buying (noun) *köp* (OSw)
buying and selling (noun) *köp* (OSw)
by force (adv.) *nöþogher* (OSw)
by law (adv.) *hemul* (OSw)
by rights (adv.) *rætlika* (OSw)
by unlawful means (adv.) *olaghlika* (OSw)
byre (noun) *bas* (OSw), *fjós* (ON), *fæhus* (OSw)
cabbage garden (noun) *kalgarth* (ODan)
cabin (noun) *kotsæte* (ODan)
calculate (verb) *telja* (ON)
calculation (noun) *tala (2)* (ON)
calculation of quotas (noun) *ítala* (ON)
calendar (noun) *misseristal* (ON)
calf (noun) *kalfr* (ON)
call (verb) *döma* (OSw), *kalla* (OSw), *kveðja* (ON), *næmna* (OSw), *sökia* (OSw), *stæmna* (OSw)
call (noun) *buþ* (OSw)
call a person a slave (verb) *þræla* (ON)
call by a nickname (verb) *kalla* (OSw)
call forth (verb) *vekja* (ON)
call on one for testimony (verb) *skærskuta* (OSw)
call out (verb) *biuþa* (OSw)
call someone at his farm (verb) *hemstæmpna* (OSw)
call upon (verb) *kalla* (OSw), *æsta* (ON)
call witnesses (verb) *skærskuta* (OSw)
calling to serve on an assembly panel (noun) *þingakvöð* (ON)
calling witness (noun) *kvaðarváttr* (ON)
calling witnesses (noun) *váttakvöð* (ON)
calve (verb) *kelfa* (ON)

campaign (noun) *hærfærþ* (OSw)
can be seen (verb) *syna* (OSw)
cancel (verb) *fælla* (OSw), *rifta* (ON), *ryva* (OSw)
cancelled mass (noun) *mæssufall* (OSw)
Candlemas (noun) *kyndilmæssa* (OSw)
canon (noun) *kórsbróðir* (ON)
canon law (noun) *kirkiurætter* (OSw)
capable of bearing children (adj.) *barnbærr* (ON)
capable of riding a horse (adj.) *hestfœrr* (ON)
capable of working (adj.) *verkfœrr* (ON)
capital (noun) *innstóða* (ON)
capital for maintenance (noun) *innstóðueyrir* (ON)
capital in a household (noun) *bo* (OSw)
capital lot (noun) *bosloter* (OSw), *hovoþloter* (OSw)
capital ring (noun) *höfuðbaugr* (ON)
capital sin (noun) *hovoþsynd* (OSw)
capital tithe (noun) *hovoþtiundi* (OSw)
capital toft (noun) *hovethtoft* (ODan)
captain (noun) *hirðstjóri* (ON), *styriman* (OSw)
captive (noun) *band* (OSw)
captives crime (noun) *gislingabrut* (OSw)
capture (verb) *fanga* (OSw), *handla* (ON), *taka* (OSw)
capture (noun) *taki* (OSw)
capture from another (verb) *ræna* (OSw)
captured (adj.) *fanginfæst* (OSw)
carcass (noun) *bráð* (ON)
cardinal (noun) *kardinali* (ON)
care (noun) *foster* (OSw), *gætsla* (OSw), *varðveizla* (ON), *varþer* (OSw)
care for (verb) *raþa* (OSw), *skilia* (OSw), *varþa* (OSw)
care for a fence (verb) *gærþa* (OSw)
care of property (noun) *fjárhald* (ON), *fjárvarðveizla* (ON)
carelessness (noun) *handvömm (pl.)* (ON), *ogoymsla* (OGu), *vangöma* (OSw), *vangæzla* (ON)
caretaker (noun) *varðveizlumaðr* (ON)
cargo (noun) *áhöfn* (ON), *bulki* (ON), *farmr* (ON), *lest* (ON), *vara* (ON)
cargo vessel (of the smaller type) (noun) *byrthing* (ODan)
carry authority (verb) *raþa* (OSw)
carry forward actions of law (verb) *sökia* (OSw)
carrying a loss for oneself (noun) *hemegjald* (ODan)
carrying iron (noun) *jarn* (OSw), *skutsjarn* (ODan)
carrying off (noun) *brauthöfn* (ON)
cart (verb) *aka* (OSw)
cart (noun) *kerra* (OGu)
cart-load (noun) *lass* (OSw)

cart-load of wood (noun) *viðarhlass* (ON)

carting (noun) *aka* (OSw)

carting-job (noun) *aka* (OSw)

carve (verb) *skæra (2)* (OSw)

carve and send forth message arrows or message batons (verb) *skæra (2)* (OSw)

carving knife (noun) *tælghekniver* (OSw)

case (noun) *dela* (OSw), *ensak* (OSw), *fall* (OSw), *kæra* (OSw), *laghmal* (OSw), *luter* (OSw), *mal (1)* (OSw), *réttarstaðr* (ON), *sak* (OSw), *saker* (OSw), *sokn* (OSw), *stæmna* (OSw), *tala (1)* (OSw), *upbyrþer* (OSw), *værk* (OSw)

case based on circumstances (noun) *vænslasak* (OSw)

case concering the king's sworn oath (noun) *eþsörismal* (OSw)

case concerning adultery (noun) *hor* (OSw)

case concerning appeal (noun) *væþning* (OSw)

case concerning intercourse with women (noun) *kvennalegorð* (ON)

case concerning personal and property right (noun) *manhælghismal* (OSw)

case concerning property (noun) *fésök* (ON), *fjársókn* (ON)

case concerning the seduction of women (noun) *kvennalegorð* (ON)

case for a man's personal peace (noun) *manhælghismal* (OSw)

case for taking property (noun) *fjártaka* (ON)

case for the Fifth Court (noun) *fimmtardómssök* (ON)

case having been brought to trial (noun) *asokn* (OSw)

case in which a defendant defends himself with an oath (noun) *laghmal* (OSw)

case in which a plaintiff is to prove his case against the defendant (noun) *viþerband* (OSw)

case involving a {næmd} (noun) *næmpdarmal* (OSw)

case involving all property (noun) *aleigumál* (ON)

case involving personal compensation (noun) *réttarsök* (ON)

case of (breach of) mass (peace) (noun) *mæssufall* (OSw)

case of abomination (noun) *firnarværk* (OSw)

case of accidents (noun) *vaþamal* (OSw)

case of adultery (noun) *hormal* (OSw), *horsak* (OSw)

case of ban (noun) *banzmal* (OSw)

case of being in company (noun) *fylghessak* (ODan)

case of defence (noun) *vita* (OSw)

case of double fines (noun) *tvæbötismal* (OSw)

case of excommunication (noun) *banzmal* (OSw)

case of gang crime (noun) *hærværksak* (ODan)

case of homicide (noun) *mandrap* (OSw)

case of illegal appropriation (noun) *fornæmissak* (OSw)

case of inspection (noun) *synamal* (OSw)

case of instigation (noun) *raþasak* (OSw)

case of killing (noun) *banaorþ* (OSw), *banasak* (OSw), *drap* (OSw), *mandrap* (OSw), *mandrapsmal* (ODan), *vígaferði* (ON)

case of loss of peace (noun) *frithløsmal* (ODan)

case of manslaughter (noun) *drapamal* (OSw)

case of rapine (noun) *ran* (OSw), *ransdele* (ODan), *ranssak* (ODan)

case of restraining (noun) *haldbænd* (OSw)

case of sacrilege (noun) *hælghebrutsak* (ODan)

case of seduction (noun) *legorðssök* (ON)

case of suspicion (noun) *vanesak* (ODan)

case of the disposal of property (noun) *fjárlag* (ON)

case of the test of the red iron (noun) *jarnbyrþamal* (OSw)

case of theft (noun) *þiufnaþer* (OSw), *þiufsak* (OSw), *þjófnaðarmál* (ON), *þjófskapr* (ON)

case of wound (noun) *saresak* (ODan)

case of wounds (noun) *saramal* (OSw)

case of {atvist} accomplice (noun) *atvist* (OSw)

case of {haldbænd} accomplice (noun) *haldbænd* (OSw)

case over flesh wounds (noun) *vathvesar* (ODan)

case resulting in damages for outrage (noun) *öfundarréttr* (ON)

case where there is mere suspicion (noun) *vænslamal* (OSw), *vænslasak* (OSw)

case which requires personal compensation (noun) *réttafarssök* (ON)

case with compensation to the bishop (noun) *biskupssak* (OSw)

case without a defence (noun) *vitulösa* (OSw)

case-bearer (noun) *sakarábeti* (ON)

case-changing (noun) *tvætala* (OSw)

case-spoiler (noun) *sakarspell* (ON)

cases involving outlawry (noun) *útlegðarmál* (ON)

cash (noun) *fæ* (OSw)

cash compensation (noun) *fæbot* (OSw)

cash penalty (noun) *févíti* (ON)

cask (noun) *sáld* (ON)

cast lots (verb) *luta* (OSw)

castigation (noun) *hegning* (ON)

casting of lot (noun) *vrakelot* (ODan)

castle (noun) *hus* (OSw)

castrate (verb) *gælda (2)* (OSw), *snöpa* (OSw)

catch (verb) *handleggja* (ON), *veþa* (OSw), *viþertaka* (OSw)

catch (noun) *varp* (OSw), *veiðr* (ON)

catching (noun) *veiðr* (ON)

catching place (noun) *veiðistöð* (ON)

catching rights (noun) *veiðr* (ON)

catering (noun) *brytjun* (ON)

cathedral establishment (noun) *byskupsstóll* (ON)

cattle (noun) *bo* (OSw), *bofæ* (ODan), *fæ* (OSw), *fælaþi* (OSw), *fænaþer* (OSw), *fæshoveth* (ODan), *nautabo* (OGu), *not* (OSw), *qvikker* (OSw), *smali* (ON), *söþer* (OSw)

cattle and household goods (noun) *boskaper* (OSw)

cattle barn (noun) *nöthus* (OSw)

cattle foddered by contract (noun) *fulgunaut* (ON)

cattle herd (noun) *hiorþ* (OSw)

cattle house (noun) *nöthus* (OSw)

cattle land (noun) *fælath* (ODan)

cattle mark (noun) *nautamark* (ON)

cattle path (noun) *klöftroþ* (OSw)

cattle pen (noun) *fægarþer* (OSw)

cattle shed (noun) *fæhus* (OSw)

cattle slaughter (noun) *búhögg* (ON)

cattle taken as lien (noun) *tækiufæ* (OSw)

cattle taken as pledge (noun) *namfæ* (OSw)

cattle taken for foddering (noun) *foþerfæ* (OSw)

cattle taken in custody (noun) *akernam* (OSw), *namfæ* (OSw)

cattle taken to keep (noun) *fulgunaut* (ON)

cattle thief (noun) *gorþiuver* (OSw)

cattle tithe (noun) *qviktiundi* (OSw)

cattle trod (noun) *nautatröð* (ON)

cattle-track (noun) *rekstr* (ON)

cattle-yard (noun) *fægarþer* (OSw)

caught (adj.) *handnuminn* (ON)

caught in the (very) act (adj.) *innitakin* (OSw)

caught in the act (adj.) *atakin* (OSw)

caught red-handed (adj.) *innitakin* (OSw)

cause (verb) *lata* (OSw), *valda* (OSw), *varþa* (OSw), *veta* (OSw)

cause (noun) *mal (1)* (OSw), *sak* (OSw)

cause damage (verb) *skaþa* (OSw)

cause of damage (noun) *raþ* (OSw)

cause of death (noun) *bani* (OSw)

cause of divorce (noun) *skilnaðarsök* (ON)

cause of fine (noun) *fæsak* (OSw)

cause where one shall defend oneself by oath (noun) *dulsak* (OSw)

census oath (noun) *manntalseiðr* (ON)

certain (adj.) *sander* (OSw)

certain number (noun) *stæmna* (OSw)

chain (noun) *rekendr* (OGu)

challenge (verb) *frýja* (ON), *illa* (OSw), *klanda* (OSw), *kæra* (OSw), *qvælia* (OSw), *ryþia* (OSw), *stæmna* (OSw)

challenge (noun) *hruðning* (ON), *klandan* (OSw)

challenge to landholding (noun) *brigþ* (OSw)

challenging a court (noun) *dómruðning* (ON)

chancel (noun) *sanghus* (OSw)

chancellor (noun) *kanceler* (ON)

change (verb) *skipta* (OSw)

changed position (noun) *lighrisvilla* (OSw)

chapel door (noun) *sanghusdyr* (OSw)

chaplain (noun) *kapellan* (OSw)

chapter (noun) *flokker* (OSw)

chapter on bridges (noun) *broaflokker* (OSw)

chapter on land claims (noun) *landsbrigðabölkr* (ON)

chapter on tenancy (noun) *landsleigubölkr* (ON)

chapter on theft (noun) *þiuvabalker* (OSw)

chapter on trade (noun) *kaupabölkr* (ON)

chapter on traveling to the assembly (noun) *þingfararbölkr* (ON)

characteristics (noun) *jartighni (pl.)* (OSw)

charge (verb) *illa* (OSw), *kænna* (OSw), *kæra* (OSw), *sökia* (OSw), *sækia* (OSw), *sækta* (OSw), *vita* (OSw)

charge (1) (noun) *mal (1)* (OSw), *sak* (OSw), *sakargift* (ON), *sokn* (OSw), *umbuþ* (OSw)

charge (2) (noun) *forráð* (ON), *tortryggð* (ON), *varðveizla* (ON)

charge (someone) with (something) (verb) *fælla* (OSw), *næmna* (OSw), *viþerbinda* (OSw)

charge for keep (noun) *fulga* (ON), *fulgumáli* (ON)

charge of a district (noun) *læn* (OSw)

charged (adj.) *kenndr* (ON), *sakaðr* (ON)

charity (noun) *almosa* (OSw), *ölmusugjöf* (ON)

charity boat (noun) *sæluskip* (ON)

charter (noun) *bref* (OSw)

chasten (verb) *raþa* (OSw)

chastise (verb) *raþa* (OSw), *rævse* (ODan)

chattels (noun) *boskaper* (OSw), *fæ* (OSw), *invistar (pl.)* (OSw), *lausafé* (ON), *lauss eyrir* (ON), *lösöre* (OSw)

cheek (noun) *kinn* (ON)

chemise (noun) *stæniza* (OSw)

chest (noun) *kiste* (ODan)

chief bridal attendant (noun) *bruþtugha* (OSw)

chieftain (noun) *goði* (ON), *höfþingi* (OSw)

chieftain of the same assembly (noun) *samþingisgoði* (ON)

chieftaincy (noun) *goðorð* (ON)

chieftain's panel (noun) *goðakviðr* (ON)

chieftain's veto (noun) *goðalýrittr* (ON)

child (noun) *barn* (OSw)

child (born) of a legitimate wife (noun) *aþalkonubarn* (OSw)

child born in adultery (noun) *horbarn* (OSw)

child by/with a concubine (noun) *sløkefrithebarn* (ODan)

child by/with a lawful wife (noun) *aþalkonubarn* (OSw)

child of a bondswoman (noun) *ambáttarbarn* (ON)

child of a husband (noun) *athelbondebarn* (ODan)

child of a lawfully wedded wife/woman (noun) *aþalkonubarn* (OSw)

child of a married woman (noun) *aþalkonubarn* (OSw)

child of adultery (noun) *horbarn* (OSw)

child of fornication (noun) *lægherbarn* (OSw)

child without protection (noun) *værjeløs* (ODan)

childbed (noun) *sængarferð* (ON)

childbirth (noun) *barn* (OSw), *barnsot* (OSw)

childless (adj.) *barnlauss* (ON)

children of a father's half-brother (noun) *halfbróðrungr* (ON)

children of different batches (noun) *siængaralder* (OSw)

children of fully freed slaves (noun) *leysingjabarn* (ON)

children of one's sister and brother (noun) *systrunger* (OSw)

children of sisters (noun) *systrabarn* (ON)

children's inheritance (noun) *barnagoþs* (OSw)

children's property (noun) *barnagoþs* (OSw)

chirograph (noun) *chirographum* (ON)

choice (noun) *vald* (OSw)

choke (verb) *kvæfa* (ON)

choose (verb) *næmna* (OSw), *valda* (OSw)

choosing representatives for commission or investigation (noun) *næmpning* (OSw)

chop (verb) *hugga* (OSw), *skæra (2)* (OSw)

chopping off (noun) *afhug* (OSw)

chopping off hand or foot (noun) *afhug* (OSw)

chosen man (noun) *næmdarmaþer* (OSw)

christen (verb) *kristna* (OSw)

Christendom (noun) *kristindomber* (OSw)

christened (adj.) *kristin* (OSw)

christening (noun) *kristindomber* (OSw), *kristna* (OSw), *kristning* (OSw)

Christian (adj.) *kristin* (OSw)

Christian faith (noun) *kristna* (OSw)

Christian God (noun) *guþ* (OSw)

Christian law (noun) *kristindómsbölkr* (ON), *kristinréttr* (ON)

Christian laws chapter (noun) *kristindómsbölkr* (ON)

Christian times (noun) *kristna* (OSw)

Christianity (noun) *kristindomber* (OSw), *kristna* (OSw)

Christianity book (noun) *kristnubalker* (OSw)

Christianity/cases concerning Christianity (noun) *kristindomber* (OSw)

christianize (verb) *kristna* (OSw)

Christmas (noun) *jólahelgr* (ON), *jul* (OSw)

Christmas Day (and the days following) (noun) *jóladagr* (ON)

Christmas Eve (noun) *jólanátt* (ON), *julaapton* (OSw), *náttin helga* (ON)

Christmas gifts (noun) *jólagjafir (pl.)* (ON)

Christmas peace (noun) *julafriþer* (OSw), *julehælgh* (ODan)

church (verb) *inleþa* (OSw)

church (noun) *guthshus* (ODan), *kirkia* (OSw)

church assembly (noun) *kirkjestævne* (ODan)

church attendance (noun) *kirkiusokn* (OSw)

church book (noun) *kristnubalker* (OSw)

church bridge (noun) *kirkiubro* (OSw)

church clerk (noun) *klokkari* (OSw)

church clothes (noun) *kirkiuklæþi* (OSw)

church congregation (noun) *kirkiusokn* (OSw)

church consecration day (noun) *kirkjudagr* (ON)

Church Dedication Mass (noun) *kirkmæssa* (OSw)

Church Dedication Mass Day (noun) *kirkmæssa* (OSw), *kirkmæssudagher* (OSw)

church door (noun) *kirkiudyr* (OSw)

church enclosure (noun) *kirkiugarþer* (OSw)

church farm (noun) *kirkiubol* (OSw)

church fence (noun) *kirkiugarþer* (OSw)

church fine (noun) *skript* (OSw)

church gathering (noun) *kirkiusokn* (OSw)

church goods (noun) *kirkiugoþs* (OSw)

church ground (noun) *kirkiuiorþ* (OSw)

church land (noun) *kirkiuiorþ* (OSw)

church law (noun) *kristindomber* (OSw), *kristinréttr* (ON)

Church Mass Day (noun) *kirkmæssa* (OSw)

church meeting (noun) *kirkjestævne* (ODan)

church parish (noun) *kirkiusokn* (OSw)

church peace (noun) *kirkiufriþer* (OSw)

church penalty (noun) *fasta* (OSw)

church penance (noun) *skript* (OSw), *skriptermal* (OSw)

church privilege (noun) *kirkjufrelsi* (ON)

church property (noun) *kirkiufæ* (OSw), *kirkiugoþs* (OSw), *kirkjueign* (ON)

church rapine (noun) *kirkiuran* (OSw)

church regulation (noun) *kirkiurætter* (OSw)

church road (noun) *kirkiuvægher* (OSw)

church sanctity (noun) *kirkiufriþer* (OSw)

church section (noun) *kirkiubalker* (OSw)

church services (noun) *tiþir (pl.)* (OSw)

church theft (noun) *kirkiuþiuver* (OSw)

church thief (noun) *kirkiubrytare* (OSw), *kirkiuþiuver* (OSw)

church village (noun) *kirkiubyr* (OSw)

church warden (noun) *kirkiudroten* (OSw), *kirkiugömari* (OSw), *kirkiuværiandi* (OSw)

church-building (noun) *kirkiugærþ* (OSw)

church-farm (noun) *kirkiubol* (OSw), *kirkiubyr* (OSw)

church-farm where burial is permitted (noun) *graftarkirkjubór* (ON)

church-goers (noun) *kirkiusokn* (OSw)

church-priest (noun) *kirkiupræster* (OSw)

churchgoing clothes (noun) *kirkiuklæþi* (OSw)

churching (noun) *inleþning* (OSw), *kirkiuganga* (OSw)

churchman (noun) *kirkjeman* (ODan)

churchyard (noun) *gravarbakki* (OSw), *kirkiugarþer* (OSw)

churchyard fence (noun) *kirkiugarþer* (OSw)

church's wood (noun) *kirkjeskogh* (ODan)

circle of judges (noun) *dómhringr* (ON)

circulating silver (noun) *gangsilfr* (ON)

circumambulation (noun) *umfærþ* (OSw)

circumstance (noun) *atvik* (ON), *nöþsyn* (OSw), *tilfelli* (ON)

circumstances of a case (noun) *málaefni* (ON), *málavöxtr* (ON)

civil law (noun) *bondalagh* (OSw)

claim (verb) *beiðask* (ON), *brigþa* (OGu), *dela* (OSw), *heimta* (ON), *illa* (OSw), *kalla* (OSw), *klanda* (OSw), *krævia* (OSw), *kveðja* (ON), *kænna* (OSw), *kæra* (OSw), *laghklanda* (OSw), *lata* (OSw), *lögfesta* (ON), *sökia* (OSw), *sækta* (OSw), *telja* (ON), *utdele* (ODan), *virþa* (OSw), *vita* (OSw), *viþerkænnas* (OSw), *væna* (OSw), *æptirmæla* (OSw)

claim (noun) *fjárheimting* (ON), *fjármegin* (ON), *heimilðartaka* (ON), *heimta* (ON), *heimting* (ON), *krafa* (ON), *kvöð* (ON), *kæra* (OSw), *laghmæli* (OSw), *mali* (OSw), *sak* (OSw), *sokn* (OSw)

claim a birthright portion (verb) *byrþa* (OSw)

claim for compensation (noun) *sak* (OSw)

claim for money (noun) *fearkraf* (OGu)

claim for payment (noun) *fjárheimta* (ON)

claim size (noun) *fjármegin* (ON)

claimant (noun) *malsæghandi* (OSw), *saksöki* (OSw)

claimed item (noun) *tækt* (OSw)

claiming (noun) *útbeizla* (ON)

clash of weapons (noun) *vapnaskipti* (OSw)

clasp (noun) *nestli* (OGu)

class of inheritance (noun) *ærfþ* (OSw)

clay-sacrifice (noun) *leirblót* (ON)

clean (verb) *skæra (1)* (OSw)

clean (adj.) *skær* (OSw)

cleanse (verb) *skæra (1)* (OSw)

cleansed (adj.) *skær* (OSw)

cleansing of the country (noun) *landhreinsun* (ON)

cleansing of the land (noun) *landhreinsun* (ON)

clear (verb) *ryþia* (OSw), *skæra (1)* (OSw), *væria* (OSw)

clear (adj.) *openbar* (OSw)

clear of charge (adj.) *saklös* (OSw)

cleared plot of land (noun) *upgærþ* (OSw)

clearing (noun) *ruþa* (OSw), *ryþning* (OSw), *ryþsl* (OSw)

clearing in the forest (noun) *sviþ* (OSw)

clearing strip (noun) *vreter* (OSw)

clearing verdict (noun) *bjargkviðr* (ON)

clearly (adv.) *skær* (OSw)

cleat (noun) *kló* (ON)

clergyman (noun) *klerker* (OSw), *prester* (OSw)

cleric (noun) *kennimaðr* (ON), *klerker* (OSw), *lærder* (OSw)

cliff (noun) *berg* (ON)

cloak (noun) *mantul* (OSw)

cloak of fur (noun) *bláfeldr* (ON), *vararfeldr* (ON)

cloak tail (noun) *skøt* (ODan)

close (adj.) *náinn* (ON)

close in kin (adj.) *skylder (1)* (OSw)

close kinsman by marriage (noun) *námágr* (ON)

close neighbour (noun) *nagranni* (OSw)

close of assembly (noun) *vapntak* (ODan)

close relative (noun) *náungi* (ON), *skyldarman* (OSw)

close-related kin (noun) *skyldarman* (OSw)

closely related (adj.) *nerkumin* (OGu), *skylder (1)* (OSw)

closer relatives (noun) *systrunger* (OSw)

closing day of an assembly (noun) *þinglausnadagr* (ON)

cloth (noun) *klæþi* (OSw)

clothes (noun) *klæþi* (OSw)

clothing (noun) *klæþi* (OSw)

coat of mail (noun) *brynia* (OSw)

cockcrow (noun) *hanaótta* (ON)

coffer (noun) *skrin* (ODan)

coffin (noun) *kiste* (ODan)

cognate kin (noun) *nefgildingr* (ON)

cognate kinsfolk (noun) *nefgildismaðr* (ON)

cognate payment (noun) *nefgildi* (ON)

cognate who has to pay or receive {nefgildi} (noun) *nefgildismaðr* (ON)

cognate-payment kinsman (noun) *nefgildismaðr* (ON)

cohort (noun) *flokker* (OSw)

coif (noun) *hovuþduker* (OSw)

coin (noun) *pænninger* (OSw)

collect (verb) *heimta* (ON), *skiuta* (OSw), *sökia* (OSw), *uptaka* (OSw)

collection (noun) *flokker* (OSw)

collection of the kin (noun) *ættarstuþi* (OSw)

collective (noun) *værn* (OSw)

collective compensation (noun) *skutebot* (ODan)

collision of the incapable (noun) *ómagamót* (ON)

collusion (noun) *raþ* (OSw)

combat heir (noun) *vigharvi* (OSw)

combat inheritance (noun) *vigharf* (OSw)

combat with arms (noun) *vapnaskipti* (OSw)

come (verb) *sökia* (OSw)

come of age (adj.) *réttnæmr* (ON)

come to terms with (verb) *sætta* (OSw)

comfort-church (noun) *hógendiskirkja* (ON)

coming to the assembly (noun) *þingsganga* (OSw)

command (noun) *buþ* (OSw), *raþ* (OSw), *yfirboð* (ON)

command of a ship (noun) *skipsstjórn* (ON)

commandment (noun) *boðorð* (ON), *buþ* (OSw), *laghmal* (OSw)

commemoration day (noun) *högtiþisdagher* (OSw)

commission (noun) *næmd* (OSw), *syn* (OSw)

commission from the parish (noun) *soknamaþer* (OSw)

commissioner (noun) *næmdarmaþer* (OSw)

commit (verb) *döma* (OSw), *veta* (OSw)

commit a crime/offence (verb) *bryta* (OSw), *værka* (OSw)

commit adultery (verb) *forligje* (ODan)

commit manslaughter (verb) *vægha (1)* (OSw)

commit rapine (verb) *ræna* (OSw)

common (noun) *almænninger* (OSw)

common (adj.) *almenniligr* (ON)

common area (noun) *almænninger* (OSw)

common bridge (noun) *almænningsbro* (OSw)

common fold (noun) *rétt* (ON), *samrétt* (ON)

common grazing land (noun) *hiorþvalder* (OSw)

common highway (noun) *almenningsgata* (ON), *vægher* (OSw)

common household (noun) *bolagh* (OSw)

common householder (noun) *almænnigsbonde* (OSw)

common inheritance (noun) *gangearv* (ODan)

common kinsman (noun) *samfrænde* (ODan)

common land (noun) *almænninger* (OSw), *almænningsiorþ* (OSw), *fælath* (ODan)

common money (noun) *bopænningar (pl.)* (OSw)

common pasture (noun) *almænninger* (OSw)

common people (noun) *alþýða* (ON)

common property (noun) *bo* (OSw), *egn* (OSw)

common road (noun) *almænningsvægher* (OSw)

common strip (noun) *akerskifte* (ODan)

common water (noun) *almænningsvatn* (OSw)

common weal (noun) *landsbú* (ON)

common well (noun) *almænningsbrun* (ODan)

common wood (noun) *almænninger* (OSw), *almænningsskogh* (ODan)

commons (noun) *fælath* (ODan)

communal pasture (noun) *afréttr* (ON)

communal pasture court (noun) *afréttardómr* (ON)

communal pasture owner (noun) *afréttarmaðr* (ON)

commune (noun) *hreppr* (ON), *hæraþ* (OSw)

commune assembly (noun) *hreppstjórnarþing* (ON)

commune business (noun) *hreppaskil* (ON)

commune council (noun) *hreppstjórn* (ON)

commune councilman (noun) *hreppstjóri* (ON), *hreppstjórnarmaðr* (ON)

commune court (noun) *hreppadómr* (ON)

commune leader (noun) *hreppstjóri* (ON)

commune list (noun) *hreppatal* (ON)

commune meeting (noun) *samqvæmd* (OSw)

commune meeting in the last month of winter (noun) *einmánaðarsamkváma* (ON)

commune obligations (noun) *hreppaskil* (ON)

commune prosecution (noun) *hreppsókn* (ON)

commune prosecutor (noun) *hreppsóknarmaðr* (ON)

commune rules (noun) *hreppamál* (ON)

commune-meeting message (noun) *hreppsfundarboð* (ON)

community (noun) *bygd* (OSw), *mogi* (OGu), *viþerbo* (OSw), *þinghá* (ON)

community of the householders (noun) *bondalagh* (OSw)

community property (noun) *hionafælagh* (OSw)

companion (noun) *lagsmaðr* (ON)

companion in the fishing colony (noun) *boþakarl* (OSw)

companions (noun) *fylghi* (OSw)

company (noun) *flokker* (OSw), *samfund* (OSw), *samneyti* (ON)

compel (verb) *noytga* (OGu), *noyþa* (OGu)

compelling reason (noun) *nöþsyn* (OSw)

compelling reasons (noun) *stórnauðsyn* (ON)

compensate (verb) *böta* (OSw), *fulla* (OSw), *gælda (1)* (OSw), *leiðrétta* (ON), *luka* (OSw), *sækia* (OSw), *varþa* (OSw), *viþerhætta* (OSw)

compensate according to the law (verb) *laghböta* (OSw)

compensated (adj.) *gilder* (OSw)

compensation (noun) *atergildi* (OSw), *bot* (OSw), *botebuth* (ODan), *botefæ* (ODan), *bætring* (ODan), *frændbót* (ON), *fylling* (ODan), *gildi* (OSw), *göþsl* (OSw), *gæld* (OSw), *lösn* (OSw), *réttarfar* (ON), *rætter* (OSw), *sak* (OSw), *sakbót* (ON), *saker* (OSw), *sækia* (OSw), *sækt* (OSw), *varzla* (ON), *vite* (ODan), *vitherlogh* (ODan), *værgæld* (OSw)

compensation case (noun) *botemal* (ODan)

compensation claim (noun) *réttarfar* (ON)

compensation for a free man (noun) *þiængsgæld* (OSw)

compensation for a thrall (noun) *þrælbot* (OSw)

compensation for a wound (noun) *sarabot* (OSw)

compensation for accidental injury (noun) *vaþabot* (OSw)

compensation for adultery (noun) *horbot* (ODan)

compensation for an accidental act (noun) *vaþabot* (OSw), *vaþagæld* (OSw)

compensation for an assault (noun) *aværkan* (OSw)

compensation for clothes (noun) *klæðaspell* (ON)

compensation for cutting (noun) *hogsbot* (ODan)

compensation for damage (noun) *áverkabót* (ON), *skaðabót* (ON), *skaþagæld* (OSw)

compensation for damages (noun) *auvislabót* (ON), *auvislagjald* (ON), *auvisli* (ON), *aværkan* (OSw)

compensation for defect (noun) *læstisbot* (OSw)

compensation for fire (noun) *brandstuþ* (OSw)

compensation for fornication (noun) *læghersbot* (OSw)

compensation for intent (noun) *öfundarbót* (ON)

compensation for killing (noun) *vígsbót* (ON)

compensation for loss of work (noun) *verklaun* (ON)

compensation for maiming (noun) *lytisbot* (OSw)

compensation for malice (noun) *öfundarbót* (ON)

compensation for misadventure (noun) *vaþagæld* (OSw)

compensation for murder (noun) *morþgæld* (OSw)

compensation for seduction (noun) *lighrisbot* (OSw)

compensation for stealing grass (noun) *grasránsbaugr* (ON)

compensation for theft (noun) *þiufbot* (OSw)

compensation for unfriendly conduct (noun) *þokkabot* (OSw)

compensation for wergild (noun) *manhæliæsbot* (OSw)

compensation for wounding (noun) *sarabot* (OSw)

compensation in killing cases (noun) *vígsakabót* (ON)

compensation in money (noun) *pænningaböter* (OSw)

compensation of a freeholder (noun) *hölðmannsréttr* (ON)

compensation of blows (noun) *bardaghaböter* (OSw)

compensation of the kin (noun) *ættarbot* (OSw)

compensation of twice the value (noun) *tvægildi* (OSw)

compensation of wounds (noun) *sarabot* (OSw)

compensation to be paid or received by kinsfolk on the father's side (noun) *bauggildi* (ON)

compensation to be paid or received by kinsfolk on the mother's side (noun) *nefgildi* (ON)

compensation to the captor (noun) *lösn* (OSw)

compensation to the heirs (noun) *arvabot* (OSw)

compensation to the kin (noun) *ættarbot* (OSw)

compensations for fences (noun) *garþaviti* (OSw)

compenser (noun) *bótamaðr* (ON)

complain (verb) *frýja* (ON), *illa* (OSw), *kalla* (OSw), *klanda* (OSw), *klutra* (OSw), *kæra* (OSw), *qvælia* (OSw), *sökia* (OSw)

complain (about something) (verb) *klutra* (OSw), *qvælia* (OSw)

complainant (noun) *malsæghandi* (OSw)

complaint (noun) *kæra* (OSw), *kæromal* (OSw)

complete a lawful case (verb) *laghdele* (ODan)

complete satisfaction (noun) *alsætti* (ON)

completely holy (adj.) *allhelagher* (OSw)

completely reprieved (adj.) *alsýkn* (ON)

comply (verb) *sætta* (OSw)

compromise (noun) *sæt* (OSw)

compulsory (adj.) *nauðsynligr* (ON)

compurgatory witness (noun) *skíringarvitni* (ON)

conceal (verb) *løne* (ODan)

concern (verb) *varþa* (OSw)

conciliation (noun) *sialvasæt* (OSw), *sæt* (OSw), *sættargærþ* (OSw)

conclude (verb) *sætta* (OSw)

conclusive testimony (noun) *lyktarvitni* (OSw)

concord (noun) *griþ* (OSw)

concubinage (noun) *friðlulífi* (ON)

concubinal man of a slave woman (noun) *kæfsir* (OSw)

concubine (noun) *arinelja* (ON), *frilla* (OSw), *meinkona* (ON), *sløkefrithe* (ODan)

concubine's child (noun) *frillubarn* (OSw), *sløkefrithebarn* (ODan)

concubine's daughter (noun) *friðludóttir* (ON), *sløkefrithedotter* (ODan)

concubine's son (noun) *frillusun* (OSw), *slokifrilluson* (OSw)

condemn (verb) *bita* (OGu), *döma* (OSw), *fordøme* (ODan), *fælla* (OSw), *updöma* (OSw)

condemned (adj.) *ful* (OSw), *ohailigr* (OGu), *saker* (OSw)

condemned to death (adj.) *fegher* (OSw)

condition (noun) *skilorð* (ON), *skæl* (OSw)

conditions (noun) *forskæl* (OSw), *mali* (OSw), *raþ* (OSw)

conditions and means of payment (noun) *fjárskilorð* (ON)

condone (verb) *firilata* (OSw)

conduct a house search (verb) *ransaka* (OSw)

conduct a prosecution (verb) *klanda* (OSw), *kæra* (OSw)

conduct of legal action (noun) *sokn* (OSw)

confess (verb) *skripta* (OSw), *viþerganga* (OSw)

confession (noun) *skriftagangr* (ON), *skript* (OSw), *skriptermal* (OSw)

confession in church (noun) *skript* (OSw)

confession or penance (noun) *skript* (OSw)

confessional offences (noun) *skriptabrut* (OSw)

confessor (noun) *skriptafaþer* (OSw)

confine (verb) *hæfta* (OSw)

confinement (noun) *hæfta* (OSw)

confirm (verb) *binda* (OSw), *dylia* (OSw), *ferma* (OSw), *fulla* (OSw), *fylla* (OSw), *fæsta* (OSw), *leþa* (OSw), *reyna* (ON), *samþykkja* (ON), *sanna* (OSw), *sannspyrja* (ON), *skærskuta* (OSw), *vita* (OSw), *vitna* (OSw), *vitra* (OGu), *væria* (OSw)

confirm by handshaking (verb) *handsala* (ON), *handselja* (ON)

confirm by oath (verb) *vita* (OSw)

confirm not guilty (verb) *dylia* (OSw)

confirm the baptism (verb) *ferma* (OSw)

confirm the honour (verb) *syma* (OGu)

confirmation (noun) *byskupan* (ON), *ferming* (ON), *fæst* (OSw), *lof* (OSw), *vita* (OSw), *vitnesbyrth* (ODan), *vitni* (OSw)

confirmation of purchase (noun) *köpfæst* (OSw)

confirmed (ownership of goods) (adj.) *hemul* (OSw)

confiscable (adj.) *upptókr* (ON)

confiscate (verb) *firigæra* (OSw), *halda* (OSw), *mæta* (OSw), *skyvle* (ODan)

confiscated (adj.) *upptókr* (ON)

confiscated item(s) (noun) *aftækt* (OSw), *agriper* (OSw)

confiscation (noun) *aftækt* (OSw), *agriper* (OSw), *gæld* (OSw), *mæt* (OSw), *upptekð* (ON)

confiscation court (noun) *féránsdómr* (ON)

confiscation of all property (noun) *aleigumál* (ON)

conflict (noun) *skilnaþer* (OSw)

confusion in the state of land ownership (noun) *lighrisvilla* (OSw)

conjugal rights (noun) *siængalæghi* (OSw)

conjugality (noun) *hionalagh* (OSw)

connection (noun) *tengð* (ON)

connubial union (noun) *hionalagh* (OSw)

consanguinity (noun) *frændsimi* (OSw), *ætskuspiæll* (OSw)

conscience (noun) *samvizka* (ON)

consecrate (verb) *hælghe* (ODan), *skæra (1)* (OSw), *vighia* (OSw)

consecrated man (noun) *vighthman* (ODan)

consecration (noun) *vighning* (OSw), *vigsl* (OSw)

consecration fee (noun) *vigslafæ* (OSw)

consecration of a church (noun) *kirkjuvígsla* (ON)

consecration of a nun (noun) *nunnuvígsla* (ON)

consent (verb) *játa* (ON)

consent (noun) *goþvili* (OSw), *hemuld* (OSw), *jáyrði* (ON), *lof* (OSw), *raþ* (OSw), *samþykke* (OSw), *samþykkð* (ON), *vili* (OSw)

consent to (verb) *samþykkja* (ON)

consider (verb) *halda* (OSw), *mæta* (OSw)

consider (something) substantiated (verb) *vitna* (OSw)

consolation (noun) *hogsl* (OGu)

conspiracy (noun) *samheldi* (ON)

conspire (verb) *raþa* (OSw), *vela* (OGu)

constable (noun) *stallari* (OSw)

construction of houses (noun) *húsgerð* (ON)

consuetude (noun) *hæfþ* (OSw)

contempt of law (noun) *lögleysa* (ON)

contempt of the law (noun) *laghslit* (OSw)

content of an oath (noun) *eþsorþ* (OSw)

contest (verb) *qvælia* (OSw), *strithe* (ODan)

contest (noun) *dela* (OSw)

contract (verb) *binda* (OSw)

contract (noun) *kaupmáli* (ON), *köp* (OSw), *legha* (OSw), *leghemal* (ODan), *mal (1)* (OSw), *samheldi* (ON), *skipan* (OSw)

contract about foddering (noun) *fulgumáli* (ON)

contract day (noun) *stæmnudagher* (OSw)

contract money (noun) *fæstipæninger* (OSw)

contract of affreightment (noun) *fartekja* (ON)

contract payment (noun) *fæstipæninger* (OSw)

contract to pay (verb) *köpa* (OSw)

contradictory evidence (noun) *andvitni* (ON)

contradictory oath (noun) *tvæsværi* (OSw)

contrary testimony (noun) *andvitni* (ON)

contribution (noun) *gærþ* (OSw), *reiða* (ON), *stuþ* (OSw), *tillag* (ON)

contribution of fish (noun) *fiskigjöf* (ON)

contrive (verb) *raþa* (OSw)

contrive deceitfully (verb) *gildra* (OSw)

control (verb) *raþa* (OSw)

control (noun) *vald* (OSw)

contumacy (noun) *þryska* (OSw), *þryter* (OSw)

convene (verb) *qvælia* (OSw)

convenience (noun) *mak* (OGu)

conversion (noun) *fornæmi* (OSw)

convey (verb) *skiuta* (OSw), *sköta* (OSw), *sælia* (OSw)

convey as pledge (verb) *væthsköte* (ODan)

convey forever (verb) *væreldssköte* (ODan)

convey to eternal possession (verb) *væreldssköte* (ODan)

convey to ownership as long as the world may last (verb) *væreldssköte* (ODan)

conveyance (noun) *skiut* (OSw), *skiutafærþ* (OSw), *skiutagærþ* (OSw), *skötning* (OSw)

conveyance duty (noun) *skiutagærþ* (OSw)

conveyance of land (noun) *jarðarskeyting* (ON), *skötning* (OSw)

conveyance repair (noun) *farargreiðabót* (ON)

conveying as pledge (noun) *væthskötning* (ODan)

convict (verb) *döma* (OSw), *forvinna* (OSw), *fælla* (OSw), *fæsta* (OSw), *vinna* (OSw), *vita* (OSw), *viþerbinda* (OSw)

convicted (adj.) *ful* (OSw), *fulder* (OSw), *sander* (OSw)

conviction (noun) *domber* (OSw), *fall* (OSw)

cook (noun) *matgerðarmaðr* (ON), *stekari* (OSw)

cook-house (noun) *stekarahus* (OSw)

cord (noun) *bændil* (OSw), *famn* (OSw)

corn (noun) *korn* (OSw), *sáðgerð* (ON)

corn barn (noun) *kornlaþa* (OSw)

corn damage (noun) *kornspell* (ON)

corn theft (noun) *agnabaker* (OSw)

corn thief (noun) *agnabaker* (OSw)

corn tithe (noun) *korntiund* (OSw)

corner boundary marker (noun) *skötra* (OSw)

corner of a house (noun) *hyrnustokker* (OSw)

corner post (noun) *hornstafr* (ON)

cornfield (noun) *aker* (OSw)

corpse (noun) *lík* (ON)

corpse-robbery (noun) *valrof* (OSw)

correct (verb) *rætta* (OSw)

correct (adj.) *rætter* (OSw)

correctly (adv.) *ræt* (OSw), *rætlika* (OSw)

correctly brought (adj.) *réttborinn* (ON)

correctly chosen (adj.) *réttkosinn* (ON)

correctly worded (adj.) *orðfullr* (ON)

corroborate (verb) *sanna* (OSw), *vita* (OSw)

corroboration (noun) *skæl* (OSw)

cost (noun) *koster* (OSw), *værþ* (OSw)

cost of a house (noun) *húsverð* (ON)

costing the same (adj.) *jafndýrr* (ON)

cottage (noun) *stuva* (OSw)

cottager (noun) *hussætumaþer* (OSw)

council (noun) *raþ* (OSw)

council building (noun) *raþstova* (OSw)

councillor (noun) *raþman* (OSw)

counsel (verb) *raþa* (OSw)

counsel (noun) *raþ* (OSw)

counselling (noun) *raþ* (OSw)

count (verb) *telja* (ON)

count (noun) *mantal* (OSw)

count of men (noun) *tal* (ON)

counter-bidder (noun) *viðrbjóðandi* (ON)

counter-calling (noun) *gagnkvöð* (ON)

counter-payment (noun) *viþergæld* (OSw)

counter-suit (noun) *gagnsök* (ON)

counter-witness (noun) *andvitni* (ON)

counter-witnessing (noun) *andvitni* (ON)

counterfeit (verb) *villa* (ON)

counterfeit (noun) *fals* (OSw), *flærþ* (OSw)

counterfeit goods (noun) *fox* (ON)

counteroath (noun) *geneþer* (OSw)

counterpart (noun) *deleman* (ODan), *vithersake* (ODan)

counting-man (noun) *tölumaðr* (ON)

country (noun) *land* (OSw), *riki* (OSw)

country-dweller (noun) *landsmaþer* (OSw)

countryman (noun) *landsmaþer* (OSw)

countryside (noun) *hæraþ* (OSw), *land* (OSw)

country's law (noun) *landslagh* (OSw)

county (noun) *fylki* (ON), *grevadöme* (OSw), *læn* (OSw)

county assembly (noun) *fylkisþing* (ON)

county church (noun) *fylkiskirkja* (ON)

county priest (noun) *fylkisprestr* (ON)

couple (noun) *hion* (OSw), *hionalagh* (OSw)

couplet (noun) *fiarþunger* (OSw)

course of a hunted animal (noun) *veiðistígr* (ON)

course of a year (noun) *jamlangi* (OSw)

court (1) (noun) *domber* (OSw)

court (2) (noun) *bo* (OSw)

court bar (noun) *dómstaurr* (ON)

court for settling a claim (noun) *kvöðudómr* (ON)

court guarding (noun) *dómvarzla* (ON)

court meeting (noun) *domber* (OSw)

court nomination (noun) *dómnefna* (ON)

court of appeal (noun) *veðjaðardómr* (ON)

court of arbitration (noun) *skiladómr* (ON)

court of priests (noun) *prestadómr* (ON)

court-guard (noun) *dómvörzlumaðr* (ON)

court-meeting (noun) *dómstefna* (ON)

court-place (noun) *dómstaðr* (ON)

court-sitting (noun) *domber* (OSw)

courtyard (noun) *tungarþer* (OSw)

cove (noun) *vágr* (ON)

cover (noun) *lok* (ON)

cover up (verb) *løne* (ODan)

cow (noun) *kýr* (ON)

cow byre (noun) *nöthus* (OSw)

cow equivalent (noun) *kúgildi* (ON)

cow shed (noun) *nöthus* (OSw)

cow value (noun) *kúgildi* (ON)

cowardly assault (noun) *argafas* (ON)

cowardly attack (noun) *argafas* (ON)

cow's worth (noun) *kúgildi* (ON)

crack (verb) *brista* (OSw)

cracked (adj.) *rimnin* (OGu)

crawling through fences (adj.) *garðsmögull* (ON)

crazy person (noun) *vanviti* (OSw)

create grazing enclosure (verb) *gærþa* (OSw)

creature (noun) *fæ* (OSw), *fælaþi* (OSw), *söþer* (OSw)

credit (noun) *borghan* (OSw)

creditor (noun) *skuldarmaðr* (ON), *skuldunautr* (ON)

crew (noun) *liþ (2)* (OSw)

crewman (noun) *hasæti* (OSw), *skipari* (OSw)

cribling (noun) *bæsingr* (ON)

crime (noun) *afgærþ* (OSw), *banaorþ* (OSw), *brut* (OSw), *glópr* (ON), *gærning* (OSw), *gærþ* (OSw), *mal (1)* (OSw), *misgerning* (ON), *ódáðaverk* (ON), *óknytti* (ON), *sak* (OSw), *urbotamal* (OSw), *valdsværk* (OSw)

crime against the personal peace (noun) *manhælghi* (OSw)

crime in kinship (noun) *frændsimisspiæl* (OSw)

crime of abomination (noun) *firnarværk* (OSw)

crime of hiding a dead animal (noun) *fæarföling* (OSw)

crime of outrage (noun) *niþingsværk* (OSw)

crime on a ship (noun) *bunkebrut* (ODan)

crime that cannot be expiated by fine (noun) *urbotamal* (OSw)

criminal (noun) *óbótamaðr* (ON), *sakrmaþr* (OGu), *udæthesman* (ODan)

criminal (adj.) *brutliker* (OSw)

crippling beating (noun) *lamabarning* (ON)

criticize (verb) *qvælia* (OSw)

croft (noun) *kot* (ON), *þorp* (OSw)

croft household (noun) *bodsæti* (OSw)

crofter (noun) *þorpakarl* (OSw)

crop (noun) *korn* (OSw), *lóð* (ON), *örð* (ON)

crop tithe (noun) *ávaxtartíund* (ON)

crop-eared sheep (noun) *alstýfingr* (ON)

crop-fields (noun) *aker* (OSw)

cropland (noun) *aker* (OSw), *akerland* (ODan)

crops (noun) *andvirki* (ON)

cross (noun) *kross* (ON)

cross cutting (noun) *krossskurðr* (ON)

cross fine (noun) *krossvíti* (ON)

Cross Mass (noun) *crucismisse* (ODan)

cross payment (noun) *þversök* (ON)

Cross week (noun) *crucisuke* (ODan)

cross-beam (noun) *staflægja* (ON)

crossbeams in the prow (noun) *saxbönd (pl.)* (ON)

crossing (noun) *flutning* (ON)

crossroads (noun) *gatnamót* (ON)

crown (verb) *krona* (OSw)

crown prince (noun) *konungsefni* (ON)

crush someone's legs (verb) *benbæria* (OSw)

cry (noun) *op* (OSw)

culprit (noun) *skaþamaþer* (OSw)

culprit/headman (noun) *hovoþsmaþer* (OSw)

cultivate (verb) *bröta* (OSw), *bryta* (OSw)

cultivated (adj.) *aþal* (OSw)

cultivated field (noun) *deld* (OSw), *vang* (ODan)

cultivated land (noun) *bol* (OSw), *bygning* (OSw), *ruþa* (OSw)

cultivation (noun) *hæfþ* (OSw), *ruþa* (OSw), *upgærþ* (OSw)

culvert (verb) *bylia* (OSw)

cup-bearer (noun) *skutilsveinn* (ON)

currency of silver (noun) *silfrgangr* (ON)

current (adj.) *sakgildr* (ON)

current coin (noun) *tölueyrir* (ON)

curtilage (noun) *burtomt* (OSw), *tompt* (OSw)

custodian (noun) *halzmaþer* (OSw)

custody (noun) *forráð* (ON), *göma* (OSw), *gætsla* (OSw), *tak* (OSw), *varðveizla* (ON), *varþnaþer* (OSw), *værsla* (OSw)

custom (noun) *siþer* (OSw), *siþvænia* (OSw)

custom of the province (noun) *landsrætter* (OSw)

customary (adj.) *gamal* (OSw)

cut (verb) *hugga* (OSw), *kliaufa* (OGu), *lysta (1)* (OSw), *skæra (2)* (OSw), *sla* (OSw)

cut (noun) *afhug* (OSw), *hug* (OSw), *skurðr* (ON)

cut (down) wood (verb) *hugga* (OSw)

cut down (verb) *hugga* (OSw), *sla* (OSw)

cut off (verb) *hugga* (OSw), *klappa* (OGu)

cut someone's head off (verb) *halshugga* (OSw)

cutting (noun) *skogharhug* (OSw)

cutting off limbs (noun) *afhug* (OSw)

cutting off or splitting a smaller bone (noun) *telgia* (OGu)

cutting weapon (noun) *hugvakn* (OSw)

cutting woodland (noun) *höggskógr* (ON)

daily clothes (noun) *hvardagsklæþi* (OSw)

dairy produce (noun) *mielkmatr* (OGu)

dairy stock (noun) *málnyta* (ON)

dam (noun) *garþer* (OSw), *stífla* (ON), *þvergarðr* (ON)

dam up (verb) *stæmma* (OSw)

damage (verb) *bryta* (OSw), *granda* (ON), *læsta* (OSw), *meiða* (ON), *skaþa* (OSw), *skeðja* (ON), *spilla* (OSw), *vana* (ON)

damage (noun) *afrækt* (OSw), *aftækt* (OSw), *afærþ* (OSw), *andmarki* (OSw), *aværkan* (OSw), *brut* (OSw), *laster* (OSw), *lyti* (OSw), *men* (OSw), *skaþi* (OSw), *spellvirki* (ON), *spiæll* (OSw)

damage compensation (noun) *spiællabot* (OSw)

damage equivalent to the price of a cow (noun) *kúgildisskaði* (ON)

damage for crop (noun) *korngjald* (ODan)

damage for which full compensation is to be paid (noun) *fullréttisskaði* (ON)

damage of livestock (noun) *fæarlæstir (pl.)* (OSw)

damage to a building (noun) *husbrut* (OSw)

damage to a field (noun) *akerspjal* (ODan)

damage to a ship's rigging (noun) *reiðaspell* (ON)

damage to weapons (noun) *vápnaspell* (ON)

damaged (adj.) *lytter* (OSw)

damages (noun) *auvisli* (ON), *fullrétti* (ON), *haildir (pl.)* (OGu), *mangæld* (OSw), *rætter* (OSw), *skaþagæld* (OSw)

damages done to the woodland (noun) *markarspell* (ON), *skógarspell* (ON)

damages for the outrage (noun) *öfundarbót* (ON)

damages to the land (noun) *jarðarspell* (ON)

damaging ride (noun) *spellreið* (ON)

danger (noun) *vandreþi* (OGu), *vaþi* (OSw)

dangerous disease (noun) *fársótt* (ON)

dangerous place (noun) *forað* (ON)

Danish (adj.) *dansker* (OSw)

daughter by a concubine (noun) *sløkefrithedotter* (ODan)

daughter of father's brother (noun) *bröþrungi* (OSw)

daughter of mother's sister (noun) *systrunger* (OSw)

daughters of a father's brothers (noun) *bróðradótr (pl.)* (ON)

daughters of siblings (noun) *systkinadóttir (pl.)* (ON)

dawn (verb) *lysa* (OSw)

day after the wedding (noun) *hindradagher* (OSw)

day agreed upon (noun) *stæmnudagher* (OSw)

day decided (noun) *laghastæmna* (OSw), *laghdagh* (ODan)

day for a hearing (noun) *endaghi* (OSw)

day for the annual rent to be paid (noun) *afrapsdagher* (OSw)

Day of All Souls (noun) *sialamæssudagher* (OSw)

day of church mass (noun) *kirkmæssa* (OSw)

day of division (noun) *lutadagr* (OGu)

day of offering (noun) *offerdagher* (OSw)

day of preparation for a feast day (noun) *forhælgþ* (OSw)

day of souls (noun) *sialadagher* (OSw)

day of summoning (noun) *stæmnudagher* (OSw)

Day of the Apostles (noun) *apostlamæssudagher* (OSw)

day of the Saints of Selja (noun) *seljamannamessa* (ON)

day of the seven-night summons (noun) *siunættingsdagher* (OSw)

day on which prosecutions are not permitted (noun) *ósóknardagr* (ON)

day set by the assembly (noun) *laghdagh* (ODan)

day specified for payment (noun) *endaghi* (OSw)

day summoned (noun) *stæmnudagher* (OSw)

day wages (noun) *dagakaup* (ON)

day's work (noun) *dagsværki* (OSw)

deacon (noun) *djakn* (ODan)

dead from accident or disease (adj.) *svídái* (ON)

dead from unknown causes (adj.) *svídauðr* (ON), *svidda* (ON)

dead man's lot (noun) *døthelot* (ODan)

dead man's property (noun) *danefæ* (ODan)

dead tissue (noun) *ólikan* (ON)

deadline (noun) *stæmnudagher* (OSw)

deadline for oaths (noun) *eiðastefna* (ON)

deal (verb) *köpa* (OSw), *liuta* (OSw)

deal (noun) *köp* (OSw)

deal hewer (noun) *filungr* (ON)

deal with (verb) *dela* (OSw)

dealing (noun) *kaupskil* (ON)

dean (noun) *provaster* (OSw)

death (noun) *bani* (OSw), *hælraþ* (OSw)

death at different times (noun) *misdauði* (ON)

death by accident (noun) *afallsdrap* (OSw)

death by chastening (noun) *morþraþ* (OSw)

death plot (noun) *fjörráð* (ON)

death wound (noun) *banesar* (ODan)

debase (verb) *niþra* (OGu)

debilitated (adj.) *vanför* (OSw)

debt (noun) *gieldeti* (OGu), *gæld* (OSw), *öre* (OSw), *skyld* (OSw), *utgærþ* (OSw)

debt assembly (noun) *skuldamót* (ON), *skuldaþing* (ON)

debt bondage (noun) *skuldfesti* (ON)

debt court (noun) *skuldadómr* (ON)

debt of the church (noun) *kirkiuskuld* (OSw)

debt-bondage (noun) *skyld* (OSw)

debt-free (adj.) *skuldalauss* (ON)

debtor (noun) *gjaldandi* (ON), *heimtandi* (ON), *skuldarmaðr* (ON), *skuldunautr* (ON)

decay (verb) *rotna* (ON)

decay (noun) *fall* (OSw), *fyrnska* (OGu)

deceit (noun) *brek* (ON), *flærþ* (OSw), *osannind* (OSw), *svik* (ON)

deceitful bid (noun) *brekboð* (ON)

deception at law (noun) *lögvilla* (ON)

deception encountered when buying (noun) *flærþaköp* (OSw)

deceptive outlawry (noun) *breksekð* (ON)

decide (verb) *dela* (OSw), *döma* (OSw), *mæta* (OSw), *raþa* (OSw), *skilia* (OSw), *skipa* (OSw), *skipta* (OSw), *slita* (OSw), *valda* (OSw), *virþa* (OSw), *vitna* (OSw)

decide over (verb) *raþa* (OSw)

deciding word (noun) *vitsorþ* (OSw)

decision (noun) *álykð* (ON), *domber* (OSw), *órskurðr* (ON), *skila* (OSw), *skiladómr* (ON), *skæl* (OSw), *umdómi* (ON), *vald* (OSw)

decision by the assembly (noun) *þingsdomi* (OSw)

decision made by bet (noun) *veðjun* (ON)

decision-making (noun) *forráð* (ON)

decisive judgement (noun) *skiladómr* (ON)

deck (noun) *fiti* (OSw)

declaration (noun) *lysning* (OSw), *næmni* (OSw)

declaration of a killing (noun) *víglýsing* (ON)

declare (verb) *biuþa* (OSw), *döma* (OSw), *hætte* (ODan), *lysa* (OSw), *læggia* (OSw), *næmna* (OSw), *skærskuta* (OSw), *sværia* (OSw), *upphaita* (OGu), *vita* (OSw)

declare innocent (verb) *væria* (OSw)

declare oneself free of something (verb) *brigþa* (OGu)

declare to witnesses (verb) *skuþa* (OSw)

declared in peace (adj.) *friþhelagher* (OSw)

decline (to do something) (verb) *fælla* (OSw), *synia* (OSw)

decrease (verb) *firrask* (ON), *þverra* (ON)

decree (verb) *læggia* (OSw), *staþga* (OSw)

decree (noun) *atkvæði* (ON), *grein* (ON), *skipan* (OSw)

deed (1) (noun) *gærning* (OSw), *gærþ* (OSw), *handaværk* (OSw), *skaþi* (OSw), *værk* (OSw)

deed (2) (noun) *skra* (ODan)

deed leading to outlawry (noun) *útlegðarverk* (ON)

deed of a villain (noun) *niþingsværk* (OSw)

deed punishable by outlawry (noun) *útlegðarverk* (ON)

deeds of insanity (noun) *óraverk* (ON)

deem (verb) *döma* (OSw), *kalla* (OSw), *mæta* (OSw), *sökia* (OSw)

deem appropriate (verb) *döma* (OSw)

deem compensation from (verb) *utdöma* (OSw)

deem invalid (verb) *aterganga* (OSw)

deem right (verb) *laghdöma* (OSw)

deemed by law (adj.) *lögmætr* (ON)

deer hunting (noun) *dýrveiðr* (ON)

defamation (noun) *fjölmæli* (ON), *háðung* (ON), *laster* (OSw), *lastmæli* (ON)

defamatory language (noun) *oqvæþinsorþ* (OSw)

defamatory word (noun) *fullréttisorð* (ON)

default (verb) *uppihalda* (OSw)

defaulter (noun) *dómflogi* (ON)

defect (noun) *andmarki* (OSw), *laster* (OSw), *læst* (OSw)

defect by accident (noun) *vaþalæst* (OSw)

defect by intent (noun) *vilialæst* (OSw)

defective (noun) *vitvillinger* (OSw)

defective (adj.) *afvita* (OSw), *lytter* (OSw)

defence (noun) *aftersaghn* (ODan), *skæl* (OSw), *skærsl* (OSw), *svar* (OSw), *undanförsla* (ON), *vita* (OSw), *viðrmæli* (ON), *væriandi* (OSw), *værn* (OSw)

defence by oath (noun) *undanförsla* (ON)

defence duties (noun) *utgærþ* (OSw)

defence in a case (noun) *sakarvörn* (ON)

defence oath (noun) *værnareþer* (OSw)

defence of land (noun) *jortheværn* (ODan)

defence of the country (noun) *landværn* (OSw)

defence of the land (noun) *landværn* (OSw)

defence panel (noun) *varnarkviðr* (ON)

defence principal (noun) *varnaraðili* (ON)

defenceless (adj.) *værjeløs* (ODan)

defend (verb) *dylia* (OSw), *firiganga* (OSw), *hemula* (OSw), *hæghna* (OSw), *svara* (OSw), *varþa* (OSw), *vita* (OSw), *væria* (OSw), *værna* (OSw)

defend by oath (verb) *sværia* (OSw)

defend one's position (verb) *dylia* (OSw)

defend the claim of ownership (verb) *hemula* (OSw)

defendant (noun) *sakarverjandi* (ON), *svarandi* (OSw), *væriandi* (OSw)

defender (noun) *varnarmaðr* (ON), *varþnaþer* (OSw), *væriandi* (OSw)

defiance (noun) *svaralösa* (OSw), *þryska* (OSw), *þryter* (OSw)

deficient (adj.) *ogilder* (OSw)

deformed (adj.) *avugher* (OSw)

deformity (noun) *lyti* (OSw), *ørkuml* (ON)

deformity fine (noun) *læstisbot* (OSw)

deformity in the hand (noun) *handalestr* (OGu)

defy (verb) *þryskas* (OSw)

degree (of kinship) (noun) *byrþ* (OSw)

degree in relationship or lineage (noun) *kné* (ON), *liþer* (OSw)

delay (noun) *uphald* (OSw)

delegate (noun) *næmdarmaþer* (OSw)

delegates to the Gulathing (noun) *gulaþingsmenn (pl.)* (ON)

deliberate act (noun) *viliaværk* (OSw)

deliberation (noun) *raþ* (OSw), *sialfræþi* (OSw)

deliberation at a meeting (noun) *malstævne* (ODan)

deliver (verb) *utmæta* (OSw)

deliver by oath (verb) *eiðföra* (ON)

deliver capital tithe (verb) *hovoþtiunda* (OSw)

delivering by oath (noun) *eiðförsla* (ON)

delivery (noun) *framburðr* (ON)

demand (verb) *biuþa* (OSw), *biþia* (OSw), *heimta* (ON), *illa* (OSw), *kalla* (OSw), *krævia* (OSw), *kæra* (OSw), *laghkrævje* (ODan), *sökia* (OSw), *æsta* (ON)

demand (noun) *kvöð* (ON), *sokn* (OSw)

demand a surety (verb) *taksætia* (OSw)

demand compensation (verb) *utdöma* (OSw)

demand for security (noun) *taksæsting* (ON)

demand for surety (noun) *taksæsting* (ON)

demand one's right (verb) *sökia* (OSw)

demand payment (verb) *ræna* (OSw)

demolish (verb) *firigæra* (OSw), *uptaka* (OSw)

denial (noun) *dul* (OSw), *genmæli* (OSw), *ne* (OSw), *neqvæþi* (OSw)

denial by oath (noun) *dul* (OSw)

denial of legal right (noun) *lögrán* (ON)

denounce (verb) *döma* (OSw)

deny (verb) *banna* (ON), *dylia* (OSw), *neka* (OSw), *rinda* (OSw), *synia* (OSw), *væria* (OSw)

deny by/on oath (verb) *dylia* (OSw)

deny permission (verb) *óleyfa* (ON)

deny responsibility (verb) *dylia* (OSw)

dependent (noun) *omaghi* (OSw), *varþnaþer* (OSw), *øreigi* (ON)

dependent case (noun) *ómagamál* (ON)

dependent child (noun) *omaghi* (OSw)

dependent from whom one stands to inherit (noun) *erfðarómagi* (ON)

dependent man (noun) *þyrmslamaðr* (ON)

dependent people (noun) *skuldahjón* (ON)

dependents (noun) *husfolk* (OSw)

dependents section (noun) *ómagabölkr* (ON)

dependents' property (noun) *ómagafé* (ON)

dependent's means (noun) *ómagaeyrir* (ON)

deposit (verb)

deposit (noun) *nam* (OSw), *panter* (OSw), *vitherlogh* (ODan)

deposited property (noun) *inlaghsfæ* (OSw)

deposition (noun) *váttasaga* (ON)

depository (noun) *lægarth* (ODan)

deprive (verb) *ræna* (OSw)

deprive by court judgement (verb) *döma* (OSw)

deprived of something (adj.) *lös* (OSw)

deputation (noun) *næmd* (OSw)

deputy (noun) *lænsmaþer* (OSw), *umbuþsman* (OSw)

deputy priest (noun) *lænspræster* (OSw)

descendant (noun) *bloþ* (OSw), *byrþaman* (OSw), *framarve* (ODan), *niþi* (OSw), *sængaslæt* (OSw)

descendant within the third degree (noun) *attunger* (OSw)

descendants (noun) *siængaralder* (OSw)

desecrate (verb) *bryta* (OSw)

desecrated (adj.) *oskær* (OSw), *ovighþer* (OSw)

desecration (noun) *uskærilse* (OSw)

deserted (adj.) *öþi* (OSw)

deserted farm (noun) *eyðijörð* (ON), *öþebol* (OSw)

desertion (noun) *einlát* (ON)

desertion of a farm (noun) *kaldakol* (ON)

deserving of death (adj.) *deyddr* (ON), *deyðandi* (ON)

design (verb) *skipa* (OSw)

design against one's life (noun) *fjörvél* (ON)

designate (verb) *næmna* (OSw)

designated holy (adj.) *verkhailigr* (OGu)

desire (noun) *vili* (OSw)

despoil (verb) *oreghe* (ODan)

destitute (adj.) *øreigi* (ON), *þrotráði* (ON)

destitution (noun) *auðn* (ON)

destroy (verb) *firigæra* (OSw), *hæria* (OSw), *spilla* (OSw), *øthe* (ODan)

destroy/damn (verb) *firigæra* (OSw)

destroyer (noun) *hærjende* (ODan)

destruction of fences (noun) *værnaruf* (OSw)

detach (verb) *skilia* (OSw)

detain (verb) *hæfta* (OSw), *uphalde* (ODan)

determine (verb) *mæta* (OSw), *raþa* (OSw), *skilia* (OSw), *vita* (OSw)

determined day/time (noun) *stæmnudagher* (OSw)

detract (verb) *skipta* (OSw)

detriment (noun) *auvirði* (ON), *skaþi* (OSw)

detrimental purchase (noun) *forköp* (OSw)

devastate (verb) *hæria* (OSw)

deviation (noun) *afbrigð* (ON)

deviation from the law (noun) *lagaafbrigði* (ON)

device (noun) *værk* (OSw)

device against one's property (noun) *févél* (ON)

devil (noun) *fiandi* (OGu)

dictate (verb) *stava* (OSw)

dictate an oath (verb) *hofþa* (OSw)

differ (verb) *skilia* (OSw)

difference (noun) *agærþ* (OSw)

differentiation (noun) *skæl* (OSw)

difficulties (noun) *nöþsyn* (OSw), *vandreþi* (OGu)

dig (verb) *skæra (2)* (OSw)

diocese (noun) *biskupsdöme* (OSw), *byskupsríki* (ON), *byskupsstóll* (ON)

direct (verb) *raþa* (OSw), *rætta* (OSw), *stæmna* (OSw)

direct descendant (noun) *byrþaman* (OSw), *sængaslæt* (OSw)

direct heir (noun) *skaparvi* (OSw)

direct inheritance (noun) *brystarf* (OSw)

dirt (noun) *skítr* (ON)

dirty road (noun) *sörgata* (OSw)

disability (noun) *laster* (OSw), *limalastr* (OGu), *lom* (OSw)

disable (verb) *lemja* (ON)

disabled (adj.) *oför* (OSw), *omaghi* (OSw), *vanför* (OSw)

disabling wound (noun) *lemstrarsár* (ON)

disadvantage (noun) *lyti* (OSw)

disagree (verb) *askilia* (OGu), *dela* (OSw), *skilia* (OSw), *viþerdelas* (OSw)

disagreement (noun) *dela* (OSw), *skilnaþer* (OSw), *þræta* (OSw)

disagreement over inheritance (noun) *arvedele* (ODan)

disallow (verb) *aterdöma* (OSw)

disbelieve (verb) *mistroa* (OGu)

disburse (verb) *luka* (OSw)

discerning (adj.) *skilríkr* (ON)

discharge (verb) *lösa* (OSw), *luka* (OSw), *utretta* (OGu)

discharge of tithes (noun) *tíundargreizla* (ON)

discharged (adj.) *saklös* (OSw)

discipline (noun) *regluhald* (ON)

discovered in the act (adj.) *innitakin* (OSw)

discovery of illicit intercourse (noun) *intækt* (OSw)

discretion (noun) *skynian* (OGu)

discuss (verb) *dela* (OSw)

disfigurement (noun) *lyti* (OSw), *læst* (OSw), *læstisbot* (OSw), *misleti* (OGu)

disfigurement compensation (noun) *læstisbot* (OSw)

disfigurement fine (noun) *lytisbot* (OSw)

disgrace (verb) *snöpa* (OSw)

disgrace (noun) *háðung* (ON), *svívirðing* (ON)

dishonesty (noun) *oskiel* (OGu)

dishonour (verb) *skemma* (OGu)

dishonour (noun) *hneyksli* (ON), *skam* (OSw), *skemmð* (ON), *vanvirða* (ON), *vanvirðing* (ON), *þokki* (OSw)

dishonourable crime (noun) *niþingsværk* (OSw)

dishonourable killing (noun) *misvígi* (ON), *níðingsvíg* (ON)

dismember (verb) *aflima* (ON)

dismemberment (noun) *afhug* (OSw), *hug* (OSw)

dismiss (verb) *fælla* (OSw), *skiuta* (OSw)

dismissed (adj.) *ogilder* (OSw)

dismissed oath (noun) *atergangseþer* (OSw)

dispense with (verb) *afhænda* (OSw)

disposable funds (noun) *eyzlueyrir* (ON)

disposal (noun) *forráð* (ON)

dispose away (verb) *afhænda* (OSw)

dispose of (verb) *afhænda* (OSw), *valda* (OSw)

dispose of a lot after the wife (verb) *mynde* (ODan)

dispose over (verb) *raþa* (OSw), *valda* (OSw)

dispossession of heirs (noun) *arfskot* (ON)

dispute (verb) *askilia* (OGu), *brigþa* (OGu), *dela* (OSw), *illa* (OSw), *jæva* (OSw), *klanda* (OSw), *lasta* (OGu), *skilia* (OSw), *viþerdelas* (OSw), *ykia* (OSw)

dispute (noun) *aganga* (OSw), *brigsl* (OGu), *dela* (OSw), *mal (1)* (OSw), *skilnaþer* (OSw), *viþratta* (OGu), *þræta* (OSw)

dispute about (verb) *brigþa* (OGu)

dispute over land (noun) *jorþadela* (OSw)

dispute regarding arable land (noun) *jorþadela* (OSw)

dispute regarding forest (noun) *skoghaganga* (OSw)

disputed land (noun) *delejorth* (ODan)

disputed property (noun) *brigþ* (OSw)

disputing man (noun) *viþerdelumaþer* (OSw)

disregard (verb) *brigþa* (OGu), *ryva* (OSw), *spilla* (OSw)

disregard of judgement (noun) *dómrof* (ON)

disregard of the judgement (noun) *dombrut* (OSw)

disrepair of a church enclosure (noun) *kirkjugarðsniðrfall* (ON)

dissemble (verb) *dylia* (OSw)

dissent (noun) *genmæli* (OSw), *ósátt* (ON)

dissolution of marriage (noun) *hjónskapsslit* (ON)

dissolve (verb) *lösa* (OSw), *ryva* (OSw), *skilia* (OSw), *slita* (OSw)

distaff (noun) *snælda* (ON)

distance as far away the peace (for a man) goes (noun) *hemsokn* (OSw)

distance from land where the caught fish belongs to the owner of the shore (noun) *fiskhelgr* (ON)

distant heirs (noun) *utarve* (ODan)

distantly related (adj.) *oskylder* (OSw)

disthing (noun) *disaþing* (OSw)

distinguish (verb) *skilia* (OSw)

distrain (verb) *sökia* (OSw)

distraint (noun) *atför* (ON), *harðafang* (ON)

distress (noun) *nöþsyn* (OSw), *ofriþer* (OSw)

distribute (verb) *bryta* (OSw), *skipta* (OSw), *skyfla* (OSw)

distribution (noun) *brut* (OSw), *skipti* (OSw)

distribution of dependents (noun) *ómagaskifti* (ON)

distribution of estate (noun) *skipti* (OSw)

distribution of wards (noun) *ómagaskifti* (ON)

district (noun) *bygd* (OSw), *hæraþ* (OSw), *skiri* (OSw), *sveit* (ON), *sysel* (ODan), *þing* (OSw)

district assembly (noun) *hæraþsþing* (OSw)

district beggar (noun) *hæraþspiækker* (OSw)

district church (noun) *heraðskirkja* (ON)

district court (noun) *heraðsdómr* (ON), *hreppadómr* (ON)

district judge (noun) *landsdomari* (OGu)

district jury (noun) *hæraþsnæmd* (OSw)

district law (noun) *hæraþsrætter* (OSw)

district limit (noun) *heraðstakmark* (ON)

district men (noun) *hæraþsmaþer* (OSw)

district priest (noun) *heraðsprestr* (ON)

district principal (noun) *hæraþshöfþingi* (OSw)

district prosecution (noun) *heraðssókn* (ON)

district witness (noun) *hærethsvitne* (ODan)

district-sent (adj.) *heraðsfleyttr* (ON)

disturber of the peace (noun) *ufritheman* (ODan)

divide (verb) *bryta* (OSw), *dela* (OSw), *skilia* (OSw), *skipa* (OSw), *skipta* (OSw)

divide according to law (verb) *laghskipta* (OSw)

divide equally (verb) *jamna* (OSw)

divide in an unfair way (verb) *misskifta* (ON)

divide in three (verb) *þræskipta* (OSw)

divide in three lots (verb) *þræskipta* (OSw)

divide in three parts (verb) *þræskipta* (OSw)

divide incorrectly (verb) *misskifta* (ON)

divide inheritance (verb) *skipta* (OSw)

divided (adj.) *skipter* (OSw)

divided concerning property (adj.) *skipter* (OSw)

divided into lots (adj.) *lutskipter* (OSw)

divided judgement (noun) *véfang* (ON)

divided judgement oath (noun) *véfangseiðr* (ON)

divided judgement speech (noun) *véfangsmál* (ON)

dividing mark (noun) *mærki* (OSw)

divine service (noun) *þiænista* (OSw)

division (noun) *boskipti* (OSw), *skipti* (OSw)

division between broods (noun) *kollaskipti* (OSw)

division in three (noun) *þræskipti* (OSw)

division in three lots (noun) *þræskipti* (OSw)

division in two (noun) *tvæskipti* (OSw)

division in two parts (noun) *tvæskipti* (OSw)

division into thirds (noun) *þriþiungsskipti* (OSw)

division made by tenants (noun) *leiguliðaskifti* (ON)

division of allodial lands (noun) *oþolskipti* (OSw)

division of arable land (noun) *akrlandadeild* (ON), *akrlandaskifti* (ON)

division of fields (noun) *vallaskifti* (ON)

division of forests (noun) *skoghaskipti* (OSw)

division of hay (noun) *heysdeild* (ON)

division of home (noun) *boskipti* (OSw)

division of houses (noun) *húsaskifti* (ON)

division of inheritance (noun) *arfskifti* (ON), *arvedele* (ODan)

division of land (noun) *jorþadela* (OSw), *jorþaskifti* (OSw), *landsdeild* (ON), *skipti* (OSw)

division of meadowlands (noun) *engjaskifti* (ON)

division of odal land (noun) *oþolskipti* (OSw), *skipti* (OSw)

division of plots (noun) *tomptaskipti* (OSw)

division of property (noun) *féskifti* (ON), *skipti* (OSw)

divorce (verb) *skilia* (OSw)

divorce (noun) *skilnaþer* (OSw)

do (i.e. commit) (verb) *valda* (OSw)

do damage (verb) *firigæra* (OSw)

do harm (verb) *misgøre* (ODan)

do justice (verb) *rætta* (OSw)

do penance (verb) *böta* (OSw), *fasta* (OSw)

do rapine (verb) *ræna* (OSw)

do something inappropriate (verb) *misgøre* (ODan)

doctor (noun) *lækir* (OSw)

doctor's fee (noun) *lækersbot* (OSw), *lækærisfæ* (OSw)

doctor's payment (noun) *lækærisfæ* (OSw)

document (noun) *bref* (OSw), *rit* (ON), *skjal* (ON)

dog (noun) *hund* (ODan)

doings of one's hands (noun) *handaværk* (OSw)

domestic animal (noun) *fæ* (OSw), *fælaþi* (OSw), *griper* (OSw), *kvikvendi* (ON)

domestic animals taken up (noun) *intæktefæ* (ODan)

domestic servant (noun) *hion* (OSw)

domestic servants with immunity (noun) *hælghhion* (OSw)

domesticated (adj.) *hemaföder* (OSw)

domicile (noun) *vistafar* (ON)

dominion (noun) *vald* (OSw)

donation (noun) *skötning* (OSw)

doom (verb) *döma* (OSw)

doomed (adj.) *fegher* (OSw)

door (noun) *dyrr* (ON)

door leaf (noun) *hurð* (ON)

door of a living-room (noun) *stofuhurð* (ON)

door to storehouse (noun) *búrshurð* (ON)

door-frame (noun) *gættitré* (ON)

doorway to the chancel (noun) *sanghusdyr* (OSw)

doorway to the church (noun) *kirkiudyr* (OSw)

double adultery (noun) *yfirhor* (OGu)

double compensation (noun) *tvæböti* (OSw)

double fine (noun) *tvæböti* (OSw)

double month (noun) *tvímánuðr* (ON)

double value (noun) *tvægildi* (OSw)

double value as compensation for theft (noun) *thjuvgilde* (ODan)

doubt (verb) *jæva* (OSw), *tortryggva* (ON)

doubt (noun) *tortryggð* (ON)

doubt-free (adj.) *ifalauss* (ON)

doubtful case (noun) *ifasök* (ON)

down payment (noun) *fæstipæninger* (OSw)

dowry (noun) *fylghia* (OSw), *gift* (OSw), *heimanferð* (ON), *heimangerð* (ON), *hemfylghþ* (OSw), *hemfærth* (ODan), *hemgæf* (OSw), *omynd* (OSw)

draught animal (noun) *faruskiaut* (OGu), *öker* (OSw)

draught horse (noun) *rus* (OGu)

draw lots (verb) *luta* (OSw)

draw up (verb) *skipa* (OSw)

drawing a ship ashore (noun) *uppsetning* (ON)

drawing lots (noun) *hlutfall* (ON)

drawing of blood (noun) *bloþlæti* (OSw), *bloþviti* (OSw)

drawing up of accounts (noun) *rækning* (OSw)

drawn weapon (noun) *vighanzvakn* (OSw)

drift boundary (noun) *rekamark* (ON)

drift rights (noun) *reki* (ON)

drift whale (noun) *rekahvalr* (ON)

drift-shore (noun) *rekafjara* (ON), *reki* (ON)

drift-strand (noun) *rekaströnd* (ON)

driftage (noun) *reki* (ON)

driftwood (noun) *rekatré* (ON), *reki* (ON)

drink away (verb) *fordrikke* (ODan)

drinker (noun) *drinkare* (OSw)

drinking at the tavern (noun) *pænningsöl* (OSw)

drinking party (noun) *pænningsöl* (OSw)

drinking party at an inn (noun) *pænningsöl* (OSw)

drinking-bout (noun) *pænningsöl* (OSw)

drinking-mates (noun) *öldrykkjar (pl.)* (ON)

drive (verb) *rinda* (OSw)

drive a stake down (verb) *staura* (ON)

drive away (verb) *hnekkja* (ON), *vræka* (OSw)

drive in (verb) *invræka* (OSw)

driving equipment (noun) *reþe* (OSw)

driving passage (noun) *farliþ* (OSw)

dropping the summons (noun) *boðfall* (ON)

drove (noun) *vrath* (ODan)

drove of pigs (noun) *svinevrath* (ODan)

drunkenness (noun) *uppdrykkia* (OGu)

dry stock (noun) *geldfé* (ON)

due (noun) *rethsle* (ODan), *rætter* (OSw), *skyld* (OSw)

due (adj.) *skyldugher* (OSw)

due for exempt land (noun) *qvarsæta* (OSw)

due time (noun) *stæmnudagher* (OSw)

dues (noun) *afraþ* (OSw), *reiða* (ON), *utgærþ* (OSw), *utskyld* (OSw)

dues to be paid for a subject of the crown (noun) *þægn* (OSw)

duke (noun) *hærtughi* (OSw)

dukedom (noun) *hertogadómr* (ON)

duly (adv.) *rætlika* (OSw)

dumb animal (noun) *oqueþinsvitr* (OGu)

dung (verb) *slóða* (ON)

during a year (noun) *jamlangi* (OSw)

duty (noun) *alagh* (OSw), *rætter* (OSw), *skyld* (OSw), *skæl* (OSw), *æmbæte* (ODan)

duty in the naval service (noun) *útför* (ON)

duty of a subject (noun) *þegnskylda* (ON)

duty of forwarding the summons (noun) *boðgreizla* (ON)

dwelling (noun) *náttstaðr* (ON)

dwelling confirmation (noun) *náttstaðarvitni* (ON)

dwelling house (noun) *bol* (OSw), *eldhus* (ODan), *innihús* (ON), *setuhús* (ON), *stuva* (OSw)

dwelling quarters (noun) *stuva* (OSw)

dwelling-place (noun) *búðarstaðr* (ON), *heimsvist* (ON)

dying at different times (noun) *misdauði* (ON)

ealdorman (noun) *raþman* (OSw)

ear (noun) *öra* (OSw)

Earl (noun) *jarl* (OSw)

earlier Feast of St Olaf (29 July) (noun) *ólafsmessa hin fyrri* (ON)

earl's farm (noun) *jarlsjörð* (ON)

earl's son (noun) *jarlssonr* (ON)

earn (verb) *óxla* (ON)

ears of grain (noun) *ax* (OSw)

earth (noun) *jorþ* (OSw)

ease-church (noun) *hógendiskirkja* (ON)

Easter (noun) *paskar* (OSw)

Easter Day (noun) *paskadagher* (OSw)

Easter debt (noun) *paskaskuld* (OSw)

Easter Eve (noun) *páskaaptann* (ON)

Easter money (noun) *paskapænningar (pl.)* (OSw)

Easter week (noun) *paskeuke* (ODan)

eat improperly (verb) *miseta* (ON)

eatables (noun) *átan* (ON)

eating in common (noun) *mötuneyti* (ON)

ecclesiastical law (noun) *kristindómsbölkr* (ON)

edge of the shore (noun) *marreinsbakki* (ON)

edict (noun) *boðorð* (ON), *buþ* (OSw)

effort (noun) *arvuþi* (OSw), *fjölskyldi* (ON)

eighth (noun) *attunger* (OSw)

eighth church (noun) *áttungskirkja* (ON)

Eighth Day of Christmas (noun) *áttandi dagr jóla* (ON), *attundidagher* (OSw)

eighth of a village (noun) *attunger* (OSw)

eighth of a {fylki} (noun) *attunger* (OSw)

eighth of a {hundari} (noun) *attunger* (OSw)

eighth of the inhabitants of an area (noun) *attunger* (OSw)

Eiðsiva assembly (noun) *Eiðsifaþing* (ON)

election (noun) *val* (OSw)

eligible to inherit (adj.) *arfgænger* (OSw)

eligible to sit in court (adj.) *dómsætr* (ON)

eligible to take one's rights (adj.) *réttnæmr* (ON)

elk (noun) *ælgher* (OSw)

elk block (noun) *ælgstokker* (OSw)

ell (noun) *alin* (OSw)

Ember Days (noun) *imbrudagr* (ON)

embezzle (verb) *firigæra* (OSw)

emergency (noun) *nöþsyn* (OSw)

emissary (noun) *ari* (OSw)

emolument (noun) *hlunnendi* (ON)

emperor (noun) *keisari* (ON)

employ (verb) *leghia* (OSw)

employer (noun) *husbonde* (OSw)

employment (noun) *legha* (OSw)

employment period (noun) *leghustæmpna* (OSw)

enact (verb) *skipa* (OSw)

enclave (noun) *fiælder* (OSw), *lutfal* (OSw), *urfiælder* (OSw)

enclose (verb) *gærþa* (OSw)

enclose in strip (verb) *invængje* (ODan)

enclosed fallow land where cattle are kept grazing (noun) *troth* (ODan)

enclosed field (noun) *akergærþi* (OSw)

enclosed land (noun) *intaka* (OSw)

enclosed wood(land) (noun) *gærþi* (OSw), *hæghnaskogher* (OSw)

enclosing (noun) *hæghnaþer* (OSw)

enclosure (noun) *garþer* (OSw), *gærþi* (OSw), *haghi* (OSw), *hæghnaþer* (OSw), *ringer* (OSw), *staur* (OGu), *vébönd (pl.)* (ON), *værn* (OSw)

encroachment on another persons fishing rights (noun) *forfiski* (OSw)

encroachment on tenancy (noun) *undirgift* (OSw)

end automatically (verb) *sjalftekinn* (ON)

end of a half-year (noun) *misseramót* (ON)

end of contract time (noun) *stæmnudagher* (OSw)

end of the assembly (noun) *þinglausn* (ON)

endowment (noun) *hemfylghþ* (OSw)

endowment agreement (noun) *máldagi* (ON)

enemy (noun) *ovin* (OSw)

enemy force (noun) *hær* (OSw)

enfeoffment (noun) *læn* (OSw)

enforce (verb) *biuþa* (OSw), *halda* (OSw), *rykta* (OGu)

engaged couple (noun) *hion* (OSw)

engagement (noun) *festarmál* (ON), *fæstningamal* (OSw), *raþ* (OSw)

English (adj.) *ænsker* (OSw)

enjoy (verb) *noyta* (OGu)

enmity (noun) *avund* (OSw), *fegþ* (OSw), *heift* (ON)

enquiry (noun) *asyn* (OSw)

enslave (verb) *ánauðga* (ON)

enslaved (adj.) *annöþogher* (OSw)

enter into marriage relations (verb) *mægjask* (ON)

entered into a land (adj.) *inlænder* (OSw)

enticing servants to steal (noun) *hionaspan* (OSw)

entitle (verb) *hemula* (OSw)

entitled (adj.) *skylder (2)* (OSw), *skyldugher* (OSw)

entitled by birth (adj.) *byrþaþer* (OSw)

entitled to (adj.) *verðr* (ON)

entitled to compensation (adj.) *gilder* (OSw)

entitled to demand compensation (adj.) *réttnæmr* (ON)

entitled to equally big compensation (adj.) *jafndýrr* (ON)

entitled to inherit (adj.) *arfgænger* (OSw)

entitled to no compensation (adj.) *ogilder* (OSw)

entitled to patrimony (adj.) *óðalborinn* (ON)

entitled to payment (adj.) *gilder* (OSw)

entitlement by the birth of a child (noun) *barnmynd* (ODan)

entrance into co-ownership (noun) *félagsgerð* (ON)

entrance pillar (noun) *liþstukkr* (OGu)

entrusted goods (noun) *handsalufæ* (OSw)

entrusted with (adv.) *handamællum* (OSw)

entry fee for one year (noun) *arsfæsta* (OSw)

enumerate (verb) *telja* (ON)

enumeration of kinship (noun) *frændsemistala* (ON)

enumerator (noun) *teljandi* (ON)

envoy (noun) *sændimaþer* (OSw)

epilepsy (noun) *stjarfi* (ON)

Epiphany (noun) *þrættandidagher* (OSw)

episcopal fine (noun) *byskupssekð* (ON)

equable inheritance (noun) *jæmpnaþaarf* (OSw)

equal division (noun) *jamföri* (OSw), *javneth* (ODan)

equal in inheritance (adj.) *jamnarva* (OSw)

equal match (noun) *jafnræði* (ON)

equal share (noun) *javneth* (ODan)

equal share or proportions (noun) *javneth* (ODan)

equalisation (noun) *javneth* (ODan)

equality of rights and social standing (noun) *jafnrétti* (ON)

equally available (adj.) *jafnheimill* (ON)

equally close in kin (adj.) *jamkunder* (OSw), *jamnskylder* (OSw)

equally close to inheritance (adj.) *jafnnáinn* (ON)

equally closely related (adj.) *jamnskylder* (OSw)

equally guilty (adj.) *jafnsekr* (ON)

equally holy (adj.) *jafnheilagr* (ON)

equally justified (adj.) *jamskiala* (OSw)

equally near as heirs (adj.) *jamnarva* (OSw)

equally obliged (adj.) *jamnskylder* (OSw)

equally outlawed (adj.) *jafnútlagr* (ON)

equally related (adj.) *jamnskylder* (OSw)

equally required (adj.) *jamnskylder* (OSw)

equally strong in evidence (adj.) *jamskiala* (OSw)

equally warrantable (adj.) *jafnheimill* (ON)

equipment (noun) *búsbúhlutr* (ON)

equitable allocation (noun) *jamföri* (OSw)

equivalent to the rest (noun) *fulnaþer* (OSw)

erect a fence (verb) *gærþa* (OSw)

Erik's street (noun) *eriksgata* (OSw)

errand (noun) *sak* (OSw)

ertog (noun) *örtogh* (OSw)

escort (noun) *fylghi* (OSw), *liþ (2)* (OSw)

espouse (verb) *fæsta* (OSw)

establish (verb) *staþfæsta* (OSw)

establish immunity (verb) *hælghe* (ODan)

established assembly (noun) *skapþing* (ON)

established autumnal meeting (noun) *lögleið* (ON)

established commune (noun) *löghreppr* (ON)

established fast (noun) *lögfasta* (ON)

established gateway (noun) *löghlið* (ON)

established services (noun) *lögtiðir (pl.)* (ON)

estate (noun) *bo* (OSw), *egn* (OSw), *fjárhlutr* (ON), *garþer* (OSw), *hæskaper* (OSw), *jorþ* (OSw), *land* (OSw)

estate conveyance (noun) *skötning* (OSw)

estimate (verb) *mæta* (OSw), *virþa* (OSw)

estimate (noun) *asyn* (OSw), *virthning* (ODan)

estimated value (noun) *virthning* (ODan)

estimation (noun) *virthning* (ODan)

evade (verb) *þryskas* (OSw)

evaluate (verb) *virþa* (OSw)

evaluators (noun) *mætsmæn (pl.)* (OSw)

eve of a holy day (noun) *forhælgþ* (OSw)

even out (verb) *jamna* (OSw)

evened out (adj.) *javneth* (ODan)

everything one owns (noun) *aleiga* (ON)

evict (verb) *afsighia* (OSw), *forbiuþa* (OSw), *vræka* (OSw)

eviction (noun) *forbuþ* (OSw)

evidence (noun) *gagn* (ON), *kennsl* (ON), *skæl* (OSw), *skærsl* (OSw), *vitni* (OSw), *vitsorþ* (OSw), *viþerband* (OSw)

evidence as to work (noun) *ortarvitni* (OGu)

evidence case (noun) *kennslumál* (ON)

evidence from a verdict given by homestead neighbours (noun) *heimiliskviðarvitni* (ON)

evidence of long-standing possession (noun) *minnung* (OSw)

evidence of neighbours (noun) *liksvitni* (OGu)

evident (adj.) *openbar* (OSw)

evil deed (noun) *gærning* (OSw)

evil intent (noun) *avund* (OSw)

evildoer (noun) *udæthesman* (ODan)

ewe (noun) *ær* (ON)

exact (verb) *sökia* (OSw)

exaction (noun) *sokn* (OSw)

exaggeration (noun) *ýki* (ON)

Exaltation of the Cross (noun) *crucismisse* (ODan), *krossmessa hin øfri* (ON), *krossmessa um haustit* (ON)

examination (noun) *asyn* (OSw)

examine (verb) *mæta* (OSw), *ransaka* (OSw), *skuþa* (OSw), *vita* (OSw)

examiner (noun) *synaman* (OSw)

exception (noun) *afnæmning* (OSw)

exception to a purchase (noun) *afnæmning* (OSw)

excessive felling (noun) *ofhog* (OSw)

exchange (verb) *giefa* (OGu), *gælda (1)* (OSw), *köpa* (OSw), *skipta* (OSw)

exchange (noun) *skipti* (OSw)

exchange at the market (noun) *torghskipti* (OSw)

exchange of land (noun) *jorþaskifti* (OSw), *makeskifte* (ODan)

exchange of legal title (noun) *heimilðartaka* (ON)

exchange of real property (noun) *makeskifte* (ODan)

exchanged land (noun) *skipti* (OSw)

exclude (verb) *afnæma* (OSw), *forbiuþa* (OSw), *skilia* (OSw), *vræka* (OSw)

exclusion (noun) *afnæmning* (OSw), *aftökisfæ* (OSw)

exclusive property (noun) *enfæ* (OSw)

exclusive right (noun) *ensak* (OSw)

excommunicate (verb) *banliusa* (OSw), *bannføra* (ON), *bansætia* (OSw), *forbuþa* (OSw)

excommunicated (adj.) *bansatter* (OSw)

excommunication (noun) *ban* (OSw), *bannsetning* (ON), *banzmal* (OSw)

excommunication case (noun) *banzmal* (OSw)

excusal (noun) *forfall* (OSw)

excuse (verb) *væria* (OSw)

excuse (noun) *forfall* (OSw), *genmæli* (OSw), *nöþsyn* (OSw) excuse (of an oath or other obligation) (verb) *skæra (1)* (OSw), *upgiva* (OSw)

excuse by oath (verb) *vita* (OSw)

excuse witness (noun) *forfallsvitni* (OSw)

excuses concerning tracing (noun) *leþsnaforfall* (OSw)

execute (verb) *fylla* (OSw)

execute (e.g. an oath) (verb) *ganga* (OSw)

execution (noun) *aftaka* (ON), *atferð* (ON), *bani* (OSw), *drap* (OSw)

executioner (noun) *bani* (OSw)

exempt (adj.) *fræls* (OSw), *saklös* (OSw)

exempt due (noun) *qvarsæta* (OSw)

exempt from action (adj.) *sekðarlauss* (ON)

exempt from having to pay a fine (adj.) *saklös* (OSw)

exempt from punishment (adj.) *saklös* (OSw)

exile (noun) *útlegð* (ON)

exonerate (verb) *ordela* (OSw), *væria* (OSw)

exonerate oneself (verb) *rinda* (OSw)

exonerated (adj.) *saklös* (OSw)

exonerated of theft (adj.) *urþiuva* (OSw)

expect (verb) *vænta* (OSw)

expected to die (adj.) *helvænn* (ON)

expedient (adj.) *rætter* (OSw)

expel (verb) *vræka* (OSw)

expend (verb) *firigæra* (OSw)

expense (noun) *afneyzla* (ON), *andvirði* (ON), *fjárlát* (ON), *koster* (OSw), *kostnuðr* (ON), *skyld* (OSw)

expiry date (noun) *stæmnudagher* (OSw)

expiry period (noun) *lyktrygguar (pl.)* (OGu)

exposure (noun) *útslátta* (ON)

expulsion in order to purify the land (noun) *landhreinsun* (ON)

extend (verb) *rækkia* (OSw)

extend their slavery (verb) *yrkia* (OSw)

extenuating circumstance (noun) *várkunn* (ON)

external injury (noun) *skena* (OSw), *útanváði* (ON)

external marks (noun) *útmerki* (ON)

extra payment (noun) *gærsemi* (OSw)

extract (verb) *böta* (OSw), *mæta* (OSw), *utsökia* (OSw)

extraordinary thing assembly (noun) *afkænnuþing* (OSw)

Extreme Unction (noun) *oling* (OSw)

extremity (noun) *þrang* (OSw)

eye (noun) *auga* (OGu)

eyelet (noun) *kló* (ON)

eyewitness (noun) *asyn* (OSw), *návistarmaðr* (ON), *sjándi* (ON), *sjónaváttr* (ON), *synarvitni* (OSw), *viþervaruman* (OSw)

eyewitness testimony (noun) *synarvitni* (OSw)

facial defect (noun) *litvan* (OGu)

faggot-wood (noun) *slóðahrís* (ON)

fail (verb) *brista* (OSw), *fælla* (OSw), *lata* (OSw)

fail (to observe or fulfil something) (verb) *bryta* (OSw), *fælla* (OSw)

fail an oath (verb) *fælla* (OSw)

fail one's case of defending (verb) *fælla* (OSw)

fail to claim (verb) *þigia* (OSw)

fail to defend successfully (verb) *misverja* (ON)

failing (noun) *lyti* (OSw), *ókostr* (ON)

failing in one's oath (noun) *eiðfall* (ON)

failure (noun) *vanlykð* (ON)

failure of thing assembly (to make a quorum) (noun) *þingfall* (OSw), *þinglami* (OSw)

failure to come to a Thing (noun) *þingfall* (OSw)

failure to make a quorum (noun) *þinglami* (OSw)

failure to say mass (noun) *mæssufall* (OSw)

failure to trace proof of provenance (noun) *leþsnafall* (OSw)

fair agreement (noun) *jafnmæli* (ON)

fairway (noun) *þjóðleið* (ON)

fall (verb) *fælla* (OSw)

fall into disrepute (verb) *spilla* (OSw)

fall over a cliff (verb) *fljúga* (ON)

fallow (noun) *træþi* (OSw)

fallow land (noun) *aterlægha* (OSw), *træþi* (OSw)

false (adj.) *osvurin* (OSw), *vranger* (OSw)

false identification (noun) *mannvilla* (ON)

false oath (noun) *meneþer* (OSw)

false prosecution (noun) *skroksak* (OSw)

false testimony (noun) *skrökváttr* (ON)

false thing (noun) *fox* (ON)

false verdict (noun) *ljúgkviðr* (ON)

false witness (noun) *falsvitni* (OSw), *ljúgvitni* (ON), *ljúgvætti* (ON), *skrökváttr* (ON), *skrokvitni* (OSw), *skruk* (OSw)

falsehood (noun) *fals* (OSw), *skruk* (OSw)

falsely (adv.) *vrangt* (ODan)

falsify (verb) *villa* (ON)

family (noun) *átt* (ON), *hus* (OSw), *kyn* (OSw), *niþ* (OSw), *niþi* (OSw), *siang* (OSw), *æt* (OSw)

family burial mound (noun) *ætahögher* (OSw)

family line (noun) *quisl* (OGu)

family link (noun) *áttarmót* (ON)

family loss (noun) *ættarskarð* (ON)

family members (noun) *etarmen (pl.)* (OGu)

family members who act as guarantors (noun) *vísendr (pl.)* (ON)

family of a freedman (noun) *leysingskyn* (ON)

family of freedmen (noun) *leysingjaætt* (ON)

fare (noun) *koster* (OSw)

farm (verb) *hæfþa* (OSw)

farm (noun) *bo* (OSw), *bol* (OSw), *bolstaþer* (OSw), *boskaper* (OSw), *bygd* (OSw), *byr* (OSw), *garþer* (OSw), *garþsliþ* (OSw), *haimþorp* (OGu), *jather* (ODan), *kirkiubol* (OSw)

farm administrator (noun) *bryti* (OSw)

farm animal (noun) *söþer* (OSw)

farm brand (noun) *bolsmærki* (OSw)

farm equipment (noun) *ankostir (pl.)* (OSw)

farm estate (noun) *garþer* (OSw)

farm hand (noun) *drænger* (OSw)

farm land (noun) *boland* (OGu)

farm of a lord's retinue (noun) *hirþgarþer* (OSw)

farm rent (noun) *fæsta* (OSw), *skyld* (OSw)

farm unit (noun) *garþer* (OSw)

farm-hand (noun) *drænger* (OSw), *leghodrænger* (OSw), *reþosven* (OSw), *sven* (OSw)

farm-maid (noun) *leghokona* (OSw)

farm-trespassing (noun) *garthgang* (ODan)

farmer (noun) *bonde* (OSw), *maþer* (OSw)

farmer in a collective (noun) *værnalaghi* (OSw)

farmer who has no help (noun) *einvirki* (ON)

farmers' law (noun) *bondalagh* (OSw), *bóndaréttr* (ON)

farmer's son (noun) *bondasun* (OSw)

farmgate (noun) *garþsliþ* (OSw)

farmhouse (noun) *bygning* (OSw)

farmland (noun) *bol* (OSw), *bolstaþer* (OSw), *bygning* (OSw)

farmland boundary (noun) *bolstaþaskæl* (OSw)

farmland bridge (noun) *bolstaþabro* (OSw)

farmland of a village (noun) *byabolstaþer* (OSw)

farmstead (noun) *bo* (OSw), *bol* (OSw), *bolstaþer* (OSw), *byr* (OSw), *garþer* (OSw), *garþsliþ* (OSw), *jather* (ODan), *staur* (OGu)

farmstead or village (noun) *bolstaþer* (OSw)

farmyard (noun) *garþer* (OSw)

fast (verb) *fasta* (OSw)

fast (noun) *fasta* (OSw), *skript* (OSw)

fast day (noun) *fastehælgh* (ODan)

fast holiday (noun) *fastehælgh* (ODan)

fast infraction (noun) *föstuafbrot* (ON)

fast-day (noun) *fastudagher* (OSw)

fasten (verb) *fæsta* (OSw), *seyma* (ON)

fastened with a nail (adj.) *naglfastr* (ON)

fasting (noun) *fasta* (OSw)

father and daughter (noun) *feðgin* (ON)

father and son (noun) *faþghar (pl.)* (OSw)

father-line (noun) *fæþerni* (OSw)

fathering (noun) *fæþerni* (OSw)

fatherland (noun) *fosterland* (OSw)

father's (noun) *fæþerni* (OSw)

father's family (noun) *fæþerni* (OSw)

father's home (noun) *föðurgarðr* (ON)

father's house (noun) *föðurgarðr* (ON)

father's part (noun) *fæþerni* (OSw)

father's side (noun) *bauggildi* (ON), *fæþerni* (OSw)

fathom (noun) *famn* (OSw)

fault (noun) *laster* (OSw), *skyld* (OSw)

faulty goods (noun) *fals* (OSw)

favourable gift (noun) *vild* (OSw)

fealty (noun) *tro* (OSw)

fear (noun) *vald* (OSw)

feast (noun) *mungat* (OGu), *öl* (OSw), *ölstæmna* (OSw), *samkunda* (ON), *vaizlurol* (OGu)

feast day (noun) *hælghidagher* (OSw), *messudagr* (ON)

Feast of SS Philip and James (noun) *philippus messa ok jakobus* (ON)

Feast of St Brictiva (11 January) (noun) *brettifumessa* (ON)

Feast of St Clement (23 November) (noun) *klementsmessa* (ON)

Feast of St Hallvard (15 May) (noun) *hallvarðarmessa* (ON)

Feast of St John the Baptist (noun) *jónsmessa* (ON), *jónsvaka* (ON)

Feast of St Knut (10 July) (noun) *knútsmessa* (ON)

Feast of St Lawrence (noun) *lafrinzmæssa* (OSw)

Feast of St Magnus (noun) *magnúsmessa* (ON)

Feast of St Matthias (24 February) (noun) *mattíasmessa* (ON)

Feast of St Nicholas (6 December) (noun) *nikulásmessa* (ON)

Feast of St Olaf (29 July) (noun) *olafsdagher* (OSw), *olafsmæssa* (OSw)

Feast of St Paul (25 January) (noun) *pálsmessa* (ON)

feasts (noun) *mungatstiþir (pl.)* (OSw), *tiþir (pl.)* (OSw)

fee (noun) *legha* (OSw), *lön* (OSw), *lösn* (OSw), *reiða* (ON)

fee for church services (noun) *tiþaköp* (OSw)

fee for malicious intent (noun) *öfundarbót* (ON)

fee for travelling to parliament (noun) *þingfararfé* (ON)

fee to a dean (noun) *provastargift* (OSw)

feed (verb) *föþa* (OSw)

fell (verb) *fælla* (OSw), *hugga* (OSw)

felling in brushwood (noun) *storþahug* (OSw)

felling of trees (noun) *hug* (OSw)

fellow field owners (noun) *akralaghi* (OSw)

fellow meadow owners (noun) *ængialaghi* (OSw)

fellow traveller (noun) *farunöti* (OSw)

fellowship (noun) *flokker* (OSw)

felonious (adj.) *brutliker* (OSw)

female (noun) *quindismaþr* (OGu)

female (adj.) *gyrþlugyrt* (OGu), *quindi* (OGu)

female animal (noun) *berendi* (ON)

female first cousins (noun) *systkinadóttir (pl.)* (ON), *systradóttir (pl.)* (ON)

female in-law (noun) *sværa* (OSw)

female neighbour (noun) *grannekone* (ODan)

female nookling (noun) *horna* (ON)

female scrubling (noun) *hrísa* (ON)

female servant (noun) *huskona* (OSw)

female slave (noun) *ambat* (OSw), *hemakona* (OSw), *huskona* (OSw)

female steward (noun) *deghia* (OSw)

female thief whose nose has been cut off (noun) *hnúfa* (ON), *stúfa* (ON)

female thrall (noun) *ambat* (OSw)

feminine side (noun) *kvensvift* (ON)

fen sedge (noun) *agr* (OGu)

fence (verb) *gærþa* (OSw), *hæghna* (OSw)

fence (noun) *bolsbrygþi* (OSw), *garþer* (OSw), *gærthsle* (ODan), *gærþi* (OSw), *gærþning* (OSw), *hagh* (OSw), *hæghnaþer* (OSw), *utgærthe* (ODan), *værn* (OSw)

fence allotment (noun) *garþadeld* (OSw)

fence along a road (noun) *tagarþr* (OGu)

fence around a clearing strip (noun) *vretagarþer* (OSw)

fence around a village plot (noun) *bolgarþer* (OSw)

fence around cultivated field (noun) *vangsgarth* (ODan)

fence around fields (noun) *ekrugerði* (ON), *utgarþer* (OSw)

fence around fields and meadows (noun) *utgarþer* (OSw)

fence around the churchyard (noun) *kirkiugarþer* (OSw)

fence between pasture and cultivated land (noun) *traðargarðr* (ON)

fence between tofts (noun) *akergærþi* (OSw)

fence in (verb) *gærþa* (OSw)

fence inspection (noun) *garþasyn* (OSw)

fence made by wood (noun) *risgarþer* (OSw)

fence of a churchyard (noun) *kirkiugarþer* (OSw)

fence of a farm (noun) *garþsliþ* (OSw)

fence of a ground (noun) *tomptagarþer* (OSw)

fence of brush wood (noun) *risgarþer* (OSw)

fence of spears (noun) *spjótgarðr* (ON)

fence out (verb) *utgærþa* (OSw)

fence post (noun) *garðstaurr* (ON)

fence section (noun) *staurgulf* (OGu)

fence to a house (noun) *tomptagarþer* (OSw)

fence-breaker (noun) *garðbrjótr* (ON)

fenced area (noun) *grasgarðr* (ON)

fenced-in space for trapping wolves (noun) *varghagarþer* (OSw)

fencing (noun) *garðafar* (ON), *gærþning* (OSw), *værn* (OSw)

fencing of strips (noun) *akergærþi* (OSw)

fencing wood (noun) *garþsvirki* (OGu), *troþr* (OGu)

ferry (verb) *ferja* (ON)

ferryman (noun) *farhirðir* (ON)

fertilize (verb) *göþa* (OSw)

festival (noun) *kirkmæssuhælgþ* (OSw)

festivity (noun) *öldrykker* (OSw)

fetch (verb) *heimta* (ON)

fetter (verb) *binda* (OSw), *fiætra* (OSw)

fetter (noun) *haft* (ON), *hæfta* (OSw)

fetterlock (noun) *hæfta* (OSw)

fetters (noun) *fiætur* (OSw)

feud (noun) *oran* (OSw)

feuding compensation (noun) *oranbot* (OSw)

fiancé (noun) *fæstamaþer* (OSw)

fiancée (noun) *fæstakona* (OSw)

fief (noun) *læn* (OSw)

field (noun) *aker* (OSw), *akergærþi* (OSw), *akerland* (ODan), *gærþi* (OSw), *jorþ* (OSw), *mark (3)* (OSw), *utgærthe* (ODan), *valder* (OSw), *vang* (ODan)

field allotment (noun) *akerdeld* (OSw)

field boundary (noun) *markarskæl* (OSw)

field fence (noun) *othelgarth* (ODan)

field margin (noun) *fuglaren* (OSw)

field of a church (noun) *kirkjeaker* (ODan)

field of a village (noun) *byamark* (OSw)

field plot (noun) *deld* (OSw)

field rapine (noun) *akerran* (ODan), *markeran* (ODan)

field-tithe (noun) *akrtíund* (ON)

fields outside the village (noun) *utjorth* (ODan)

fiend (noun) *ovin* (OSw)

fifth (noun) *fimmtungr* (ON), *fæmt* (OSw)

fifth assembly (noun) *fimmtarþing* (ON)

Fifth Court (noun) *fimmtardómr* (ON)

Fifth Court oath (noun) *fimmtardómseiðr* (ON)

fifth Sunday in Lent — Passion Sunday (noun)
kærasunnudagher (OSw)

fight (verb) *bæria* (OSw), *fljúga* (ON), *hittas* (OSw),
æghas (OSw)

fight (noun) *arath* (ODan), *bardaghi* (OSw), *barsmíð*
(ON), *deld* (OSw), *vigh* (OSw)

fighting (noun) *bardaghi* (OSw), *vigh* (OSw)

fighting force (noun) *lið (2)* (OSw)

final verdict (noun) *vitsorþ* (OSw)

final witness (noun) *lyktarvitni* (OSw)

financial ability (noun) *fjármegin* (ON)

financial penalty (noun) *vite* (ODan)

find (verb) *kænna* (OSw)

find (noun) *fynd* (OSw)

find guilty (verb) *fælla* (OSw), *laghvinna* (OSw), *leþa*
(OSw), *vinna* (OSw), *viþerbinda* (OSw)

find in water (noun) *vatnfynd* (OSw)

find on a road (noun) *væghafynd* (OSw)

find out about the truth (verb) *sannspyrja* (ON)

finder's blubber (noun) *finnandaspik* (ON)

finder's lot (noun) *fyndarluter* (OSw)

finder's reward (noun) *unningjalausn* (ON),
vinningælogh (OSw)

finding a guarantor (noun) *leþsn* (OSw)

Finding of the Holy Cross (3 May) (noun) *krossmessa
um várit* (ON)

fine (verb) *böta* (OSw), *vita* (OSw)

fine (noun) *áfang* (ON), *alagh* (OSw), *bot* (OSw), *brut*
(OSw), *fésekð* (ON), *fæ* (OSw), *fæbot* (OSw), *fægæld*
(OSw), *gæld* (OSw), *laghslit* (OSw), *öre* (OSw),
pænninger (OSw), *ránbaugr* (ON), *sak* (OSw), *saker*
(OSw), *saköri* (OSw), *saköris brut* (OSw), *saktal*
(ON), *sækt* (OSw), *vite* (ODan), *vitherlogh* (ODan)

fine belonging to one party (noun) *ensak* (OSw)

fine divided in three (noun) *præskipti* (OSw)

fine for a blow (noun) *hogsbot* (ODan)

fine for a crime based on suspicion (noun) *vænslabot*
(OSw)

fine for a crime concerning allodial land (noun)
oþulbrut (OSw)

fine for adultery (noun) *læghersbot* (OSw)

fine for an adultery case (noun) *hormalsbot* (OSw)

fine for an attack in the home (noun) *hemsokn* (OSw)

fine for an intentional deed (noun) *viliaværksbot*
(OSw)

fine for anticipated children (noun) *uskabarnabot*
(OSw)

fine for damage by grazing animals (noun) *ætiubot*
(OSw)

fine for delay (noun) *uphald* (OSw)

fine for enforcement (noun) *ransbot* (OSw)

fine for failing to pay tithes (noun) *tíundarsekð* (ON)

fine for failing to take an oath with one's neighbours
(noun) *skilfall* (OSw)

fine for harbouring a thief (noun) *þiufvalabot* (OSw)

fine for hiding (noun) *dylsbot* (OSw)

fine for hiding a crime (noun) *dylsbot* (OSw)

fine for maiming (noun) *lytisbot* (OSw)

fine for manslaughter (noun) *mangæld* (OSw),
værgæld (OSw)

fine for neglecting the levy (noun) *leiðangrsvíti* (ON)

fine for not appearing at the assembly when
summoned (noun) *þingviti* (OSw)

fine for not appearing when summoned (noun)
þingviti (OSw)

fine for not attending an assembly (noun) *þingviti*
(OSw)

fine for petty larceny (noun) *snattarabot* (OSw)

fine for petty theft (noun) *snattarabot* (OSw)

fine for refusal (noun) *svaralösa* (OSw)

fine for robbery (noun) *ránbaugr* (ON), *ransbot* (OSw)

fine for Sabbath-breaking (noun) *hælghebrut* (ODan)

fine for serious bodily injury (noun) *áljótseyrir* (ON)

fine for sewn cloth (noun) *saumgjald* (ON)

fine for shaming (noun) *þokkabot* (OSw)

fine for the wrong oath (noun) *eiðasekð* (ON)

fine for theft (noun) *þiaufgildi* (OGu)

fine for trespass (noun) *landnám* (ON)

fine of a free man (noun) *frælsmansbot* (OSw)

fine of disgrace (noun) *snápsgjald* (ON)

fine of three marks (noun) *þriggjamarkasekð* (ON)

fine paid for reduced marriage prospects (noun)
ráðspell (ON)

fine to an heir (noun) *arvabot* (OSw)

fine to kin (noun) *ættarbot* (OSw)

fine to the bishop (noun) *biskupssak* (OSw)

fine to the general assembly (noun) *landasak* (OGu)

fine to the king (noun) *konungsrætter* (OSw)

fine to the king for unlawful seizure or holding of property (noun) *ránbaugr* (ON)

fine woollen cloth (noun) *skarlaþ* (OGu)

fine-mark (noun) *botmark* (OSw)

fined (adj.) *saker* (OSw), *útlagr* (ON)

finer cloth (noun) *skruþer* (OSw)

fines (noun) *aviti* (OSw), *fæbot* (OSw), *saköri* (OSw)

fines for breaching the king's peace (noun) *eþsörisböter* (OSw)

fines for breaking the king's sworn peace (noun) *eþsörisböter* (OSw)

fines for injury to animals (noun) *gorbötir (pl.)* (OSw)

fines for violence (noun) *ofværkaböter* (OSw)

finger (noun) *fingr* (ON)

fining case (noun) *útlegð* (ON), *útlegðarsök* (ON)

fire (noun) *brander* (OSw), *brænna* (OSw), *elder* (ON)

fire by accident (noun) *vaþaelder* (OSw)

fire compensation (noun) *brandstuþ* (OSw)

fire in the wood (noun) *skoghabrænna* (OSw)

fire-wolf (noun) *brennuvargr* (ON), *kasnavargher* (OSw)

firewood (noun) *döfviþer* (OSw), *viþer* (OSw)

first among witnesses (noun) *styrifaster* (OSw)

first church attendance of a newly-married couple (noun) *inleþning* (OSw)

first cousin (noun) *bröþrungi* (OSw), *systrunger* (OSw)

first cousin's ring (noun) *bróðrungsbaugr* (ON)

first day of winter (noun) *vinternat* (OSw)

first night of winter (noun) *vinternat* (OSw)

first Sunday in Lent (noun) *hvitisunnudagher* (OSw)

first winter's night (noun) *vinternat* (OSw)

fish (verb) *fiskja* (ON), *veþa* (OSw)

fish (noun) *fiskr* (ON)

fish garth (noun) *fiskigarþer* (OSw)

fish trap (noun) *fiskigarþer* (OSw)

fishery (noun) *fiskigarþer* (OSw), *fiskiværk* (OSw), *værki* (OSw)

fishing (noun) *fiski* (ON)

fishing construction (noun) *fiskiahus* (OSw)

fishing gear (noun) *veiðivél* (ON)

fishing ground (noun) *vözt* (ON)

fishing hut (noun) *fiskiskáli* (ON)

fishing line (noun) *vaðr* (ON)

fishing net (noun) *net* (ON)

fishing place (noun) *fiskigarþer* (OSw), *veiðistöð* (ON)

fishing rights (noun) *fiskveiðr* (ON)

fishing stream (noun) *veiðiá* (ON)

fishing tackle (noun) *fisketol* (OSw)

fishing tool (noun) *fisketol* (OSw)

fishing waters (noun) *veiðistöð* (ON), *veiðivatn* (ON)

fist blow (noun) *nævehog* (ODan)

fit (adj.) *helbryghþu* (OSw)

fit for combat (adj.) *vigher* (OSw)

fit of rage (noun) *vreþsværk* (OSw)

fitting (adj.) *réttligr* (ON)

five day term (noun) *fæmt* (OSw)

five days (noun) *fæmt* (OSw)

five day's notice summons (noun) *fæmt* (OSw)

five nights' summons (noun) *fimmtarstefna* (ON)

five-day assembly (noun) *fimmtarþing* (ON)

five-day deadline (noun) *fæmt* (OSw)

five-day grace period (noun) *fæmt* (OSw)

five-day interval (noun) *fæmt* (OSw)

five-day moot (noun) *fimmtarstefna* (ON)

five-day notice (noun) *fimmtarnafn* (ON)

five-day time limit (noun) *fæmt* (OSw)

five-days-notice summons (noun) *fimmtarstefna* (ON)

five-days' grace (noun) *fimmtargrið* (ON)

fix (verb) *næmna* (OSw)

fixed day (noun) *laghastæmna* (OSw), *laghestævnedagh* (ODan)

fixed day/date (noun) *laghdagh* (ODan)

fixed place of residence (noun) *staðfesta* (ON)

flat (adj.) *flatr* (ON)

flat of the hand (noun) *lofi* (OGu)

flaw (noun) *spiæll* (OSw)

flaw in a bargain (noun) *kauplöstr* (ON)

fled (adj.) *löpstigher* (OSw)

flee (verb) *flya* (OSw)

flesh (noun) *kjöt* (ON), *vöðvi* (ON)

flesh wound (noun) *skena* (OSw), *vathvesar* (ODan)

floating options (noun) *lausakør* (ON)

flock (noun) *flokker* (OSw)

flog (verb) *huþstryka* (OSw), *hýða* (ON)

flogging (noun) *hýðing* (ON)

floor planks running lengthwise (noun) *langþili* (ON)

flotsam at sea (noun) *flut* (OGu)

fly (verb) *stionka* (OSw)

fly out (verb) *hrjóta* (ON)

fly-man (noun) *flugumaðr* (ON)

fodder (noun) *fóðr* (ON), *föþa* (OSw), *traðgjöf* (ON)

fodder from the farm (noun) *garðfóðr* (ON)

foddering by contract (noun) *fulga* (ON)

foe (noun) *ovin* (OSw)

foetus (noun) *afling* (OSw)

fog of error (noun) *villuþoka* (ON)

fold (noun) *fald* (ODan)

fold's gate (noun) *qviggrind* (OSw)

folk (noun) *hion* (OSw)

folk weapon (noun) *folkvapn* (OSw)

folk-law-oath (noun) *lýrittareiðr* (ON)

follow (verb) *spyria* (OSw)

follow the law (verb) *laghbiuþa* (OSw)

followers (noun) *laghsman* (ODan)

following (noun) *fylghi* (OSw)

following a tight string (adv.) *vævildræt* (OSw)

folly (noun) *öthe* (OSw)

food (noun) *föþa* (OSw), *koster* (OSw), *matnaþr* (OGu), *matr* (OGu), *vist* (OSw)

food contribution (noun) *matskut* (OSw)

food gift (noun) *matgjöf* (ON)

food house (noun) *matskamma* (OSw)

food payment (noun) *matgjald* (ON)

food provision (noun) *matgærþ* (OSw)

food to eat with a loaf of bread (noun) *lefssufl* (OSw)

food-ban (noun) *matban* (ODan)

food-ban decision (noun) *matban* (ODan)

food-sacrifice (noun) *matblót* (ON)

fool (noun) *snápr* (ON)

foolish (adj.) *heimskr* (ON)

foot (noun) *fiæt* (OSw), *foter* (OSw)

footprints (noun) *forvegr* (ON)

footwear (noun) *skyþi* (OGu)

for himself (adv.) *ensak* (OSw)

for no good reason (adj.) *ørendlauss* (ON)

for no reason (adv.) *oskælika* (OSw)

for sale (adj.) *falr* (ON)

forbid (verb) *banna* (ON), *forbiuþa* (OSw), *forbuþa* (OSw), *kviðja* (ON), *mena* (OSw), *synia* (OSw)

forbidden food (noun) *óátun* (ON), *óæti* (ON)

force (verb) *kuska* (OSw), *lata* (OSw), *noyþa* (OGu), *raþa* (OSw), *valda* (OSw)

force (noun) *kuskan* (OSw), *ofríki* (ON), *ofæfli* (OSw), *ran* (OSw), *vald* (OSw), *vigh* (OSw)

force (illegally used) (noun) *ofríki* (ON)

force of arms (noun) *valdsværk* (OSw)

force of beasts of draught (noun) *ökiaafl* (OSw)

force of numbers (noun) *oflið* (ON)

forced (adj.) *nöþogher* (OSw)

forced agreement (noun) *nauðahandsal* (ON)

forcefully abduct (verb) *valdföra* (OSw)

forcible seizure from someone's grasp (noun) *handran* (OSw)

forefathers (noun) *langfeðgar (pl.)* (ON)

foreign (adj.) *utanrikes* (OSw), *utlændsker* (OSw), *utrikis* (OSw)

foreign (land) (adj.) *utanlands* (OSw)

foreigner (noun) *útanlandsmaðr* (ON), *utlændinger* (OSw)

foreigners (noun) *utlændsker* (OSw)

foreman (noun) *forman* (OSw)

foreshore (noun) *fjara* (ON), *flothemal* (ODan)

forest (noun) *mark (3)* (OSw), *skogher* (OSw), *viþer* (OSw)

forest lot (noun) *markteigr* (ON)

forfeit (verb) *bryta* (OSw), *firifara* (OSw), *firigiva* (OSw), *firigæra* (OSw), *firiköpa* (OSw), *firistiæla* (OSw), *foreföra* (OSw), *forestanda* (OSw), *forlöpa* (OSw), *forsighia* (OSw), *fortaka* (OSw), *forværka* (OSw), *fyrirskjóta* (ON), *gælda (1)* (OSw)

forfeit (adj.) *forveði* (ON), *forvæþia* (OSw), *upptókr* (ON), *útlagr* (ON)

forfeit (by carrying) (verb) *firibiera* (OGu)

forfeit by abandoning (verb) *firiganga* (OSw)

forfeit by killing (verb) *fyrirvega* (ON)

forfeit by stealing (verb) *firistiæla* (OSw)

forfeit by wandering (verb) *firiganga* (OSw)

forfeit immunity (noun) *óhelgi* (ON)

forfeit through theft (verb) *firistiæla* (OSw)

forfeited (adj.) *forvæþia* (OSw)

forge (verb) *falsa* (ON)

forger (noun) *falsere* (ODan)

forgery (noun) *fals* (OSw), *flærþ* (OSw)

forgive (verb) *firigiva* (OSw), *firilata* (OSw)

forgiveness (noun) *naþir* (OSw)

formal agreement (noun) *fæstning* (OSw)

formal guarantee (noun) *handsal* (ON)

formal guarantee to accept outlawry (noun) *sekðarhandsal* (ON)

formal inauguration of an assembly (noun) *þinghelgi* (ON)

formal means of proof (noun) *gagn* (ON)

formal means of proof for the defence (noun) *varnargagn* (ON)

formal means of proof in an original suit (noun) *frumgagn* (ON)

formal reason (noun) *skæl* (OSw)

formalities of the General Assembly (noun) *alþingismál* (ON)

formally agree (verb) *fæsta* (OSw), *handsala* (ON)

formally guarantee (verb) *handsala* (ON), *handselja* (ON)

formally transfer (verb) *handsala* (ON)

formula (noun) *munhaf* (OSw)

fornication (noun) *horsiang* (OSw), *löskalæghi* (OSw), *lægher* (OSw)

forsake (verb) *firigæra* (OSw)

forswear (verb) *forsværje* (ODan)

fortune (noun) *fjármegin* (ON)

forty years old (adj.) *fertugr* (ON)

forwarding summons (noun) *boðburðr* (ON)

forwarding the message baton (noun) *boðburðr* (ON)

foster inheritance (noun) *branderfð* (ON)

foster-brother (noun) *fóstbróðir* (ON)

foster-daughter (noun) *fostra* (OSw)

foster-father (noun) *barnfóstri* (ON), *fostre* (OSw)

foster-home (noun) *foster* (OSw)

foster-kin (noun) *foster* (OSw)

foster-mother (noun) *fostra* (OSw)

foster-son (noun) *fostre* (OSw)

fostering (noun) *foster* (OSw), *fosterløn* (ODan)

fostering a child (noun) *barnfóstr* (ON)

fostering payment (noun) *fosterløn* (ODan)

foul (adj.) *ful* (OSw)

foul murder (noun) *morþ* (OSw), *níðingsvíg* (ON)

found guilty (adj.) *sander* (OSw)

found guilty (in trial by ordeal) (adj.) *ful* (OSw)

found guilty by witnesses (adj.) *sander* (OSw)

found in flagrante delicto (adj.) *innitakin* (OSw)

found in someone's hands (adj.) *handnuminn* (ON)

four-footed (adj.) *ferfóttr* (ON)

fourth (noun) *fiarþunger* (OSw)

fourth cousins (noun) *þriðjabróðra (pl.)* (ON)

fowling rights (noun) *fuglveiðr* (ON)

frame (verb) *rétta* (ON)

framing the wording (of testimony) (noun) *rétting* (ON)

fraud (noun) *fals* (OSw), *fár* (ON), *kaupfox* (ON), *svik* (ON), *vélaboð* (ON), *vélaverk* (ON)

fraud in matters of inheritance (noun) *arfsvik* (ON)

fraud in purchase (noun) *flærþaköp* (OSw)

fraud in trading (noun) *flærþaköp* (OSw)

fraudulent agreement (noun) *vélakaup* (ON)

fraudulent contract (noun) *vélakaup* (ON)

fraudulent goods (noun) *flærþ* (OSw)

fraudulent pledge (noun) *veðfox* (ON)

fraudulent prosecution (noun) *vélasókn* (ON)

fraudulent suit (noun) *vélasókn* (ON)

fraudulent thing (noun) *flærþ* (OSw)

fraudulently adulterated (adj.) *blekoblandaþer* (OSw)

free (verb) *afreþa* (OSw), *frælsa* (OSw), *hælghe* (ODan), *lösa* (OSw), *skilia* (OSw), *skæra (1)* (OSw), *væria* (OSw)

free (adj.) *fræls* (OSw), *kauplauss* (ON), *liþugher* (OSw), *lös* (OSw), *skuldalauss* (ON), *sykn* (OSw)

free and innocent (adj.) *osaker* (OSw)

free by oath (verb) *sværia* (OSw)

free female servant (noun) *griþkuna* (OGu)

free from debt (adj.) *skuldlauss* (ON)

free from debts (adv.) *skuldlaust* (ON)

free from dues (adv.) *skattalaust* (ON)

free from fines (verb) *væria* (OSw)

free from obligation (adj.) *saklös* (OSw)

free from responsibility (adj.) *saklös* (OSw)

free male servant (noun) *griðmaðr* (ON)

free man (noun) *frelsingr* (ON), *þegn* (OSw)

free man's compensation (noun) *frælsmansbot* (OSw)

free man's legal status (noun) *rætter* (OSw)

free of any claim (adj.) *saklös* (OSw)

free of charge (adj.) *saklös* (OSw), *saklöst* (OSw), *skatheløs* (ODan)

free of compensation (adj.) *sekðarlauss* (ON)

free of debt (adj.) *skuldlauss* (ON)

free of defects (adj.) *lastalaus* (OGu)

free of dependents (adj.) *ómagalauss* (ON)

free of guilt (adj.) *saklös* (OSw), *sykn* (OSw)

free of pre-emption right (adj.) *málalauss* (ON)

free of spiteful intent (adj.) *öfundlauss* (ON)

free of the charge (adj.) *sykn* (OSw)

free-folk (adj.) *folkfræls* (OSw)

freeborn (adj.) *árborinn* (ON), *friþviter* (OSw), *friþætta* (OSw), *fræls* (OSw), *frælsboren* (ODan), *fullkyniaþer* (OSw), *ætborin* (OSw)

freed (adj.) *liþugher* (OSw), *saklös* (OSw)

freed from proof (adj.) *laghalös* (OSw)

freed slave (noun) *frælsgivi* (OSw), *leysingi* (ON)

freedman (noun) *frælsgivi* (OSw), *leysingi* (ON)

freedman's child (noun) *leysingjabarn* (ON)

freedman's inheritance (noun) *leysingserfð* (ON)

Freedman's Law (noun) *leysingslög* (ON)

freedman's purchase money (noun) *leysingsaurar (pl.)* (ON)

freedman's wife (noun) *leysingskona* (ON)

freedom (noun) *friþer* (OSw), *frælsi* (OSw), *sielfsvald* (OGu)

freedom ale (noun) *frelsisöl* (ON)

freedom from responsibility (noun) *svaralösa* (OSw)

freedom-giver (noun) *frælsgivi* (OSw)

freedwoman (noun) *frælsgiva* (OSw), *leysingja* (ON)

freeholder (noun) *bonde* (OSw), *hölðmaðr* (ON), *hölðr* (ON)

freeholder-born (adj.) *hölðborinn* (ON)

freeholder's right (noun) *hölðmannsréttr* (ON)

freeholder's rights to compensation (noun) *hölðsréttr* (ON)

freeing of slaves (noun) *mannfrelsi* (ON)

freely (adv.) *frælst* (OSw), *saklöst* (OSw)

freely selected witness (noun) *fangaváttr* (ON)

Friday (noun) *frjádagr* (ON)

Friday of providing food (noun) *matskutsfredagher* (OSw)

friend (noun) *vin* (OSw)

friend at purchases (noun) *köpavin* (OSw)

friendship gift (noun) *vingæf* (OSw)

from Hordaland (adj.) *hörzkr* (ON)

from outside the province (adj.) *utlændsker* (OSw)

from Småland (adj.) *smalænsker* (OSw)

from the province (adj.) *hærlænsker* (OSw), *inlændsker* (OSw)

from Västergötland (adj.) *væstgötsker* (OSw)

frost-bound investigations (noun) *þiælasyn* (OSw)

Frostathing book (noun) *Frostuþingsbók* (ON)

Frostathing law (noun) *frostuþingslög* (ON)

Frostaþing (noun) *Frostuþing* (ON)

fruit crops (noun) *skafl* (OSw)

fuel and timber (noun) *fang* (OSw)

fugitive (noun) *muslegumaþr* (OGu), *sakrmaþr* (OGu)

fugitive thief (noun) *runþiuver* (OSw)

fulfil (verb) *fylla* (OSw)

full (adj.) *fulder* (OSw)

full agreement (noun) *alsætti* (ON)

full brother (noun) *sambroþer* (OSw)

full compensation (noun) *algildi* (ON), *fullrétti* (ON), *fylling* (ODan)

full day's journey (noun) *dagleið* (ON)

full farm (noun) *mannsverk* (ON)

full outlaw (noun) *skógarmaðr* (ON)

full outlawry (noun) *skóggangr* (ON)

full payment (noun) *fylling* (ODan)

full personal compensation (noun) *fullrétti* (ON)

full sibling (noun) *sambroþer* (OSw)

full sibling (adj.) *samkulla* (OSw)

full siblings (noun) *samsyskine* (OSw)

full sister (noun) *samsystir* (OGu)

full use of one's senses (noun) *forskæl* (OSw)

full value (noun) *fullvirði* (ON)

full village (noun) *fullbyr* (OSw)

full wound (noun) *fullsæri* (OSw)

full-grown (adj.) *fultiþa* (OSw)

fully competent (adj.) *fulder* (OSw)

fully freed slave (noun) *leysingi* (ON)

fully grown (adj.) *fulvaksen* (ODan)

fully holy (adj.) *allhelagher* (OSw)

fully make public (verb) *fulljuse* (ODan)

fully manned (adj.) *fullliða* (ON)

fully of age (adj.) *fulaldre* (ODan)

fully taxable man (noun) *fulgærþabondi* (OSw)

fully tied (adj.) *bandhail* (OGu)

funds (noun) *fæ* (OSw), *pænninger* (OSw)

funeral feast (noun) *erfisgierþ* (OGu), *ærve* (OSw)

funeral fee (noun) *kirkiugif* (OSw), *líksöngskaup* (ON)

funeral service (noun) *líksöngr* (ON)

funeral witness (noun) *ölðrhúsvitni* (ON)

fungible loan (noun) *haldsfæ* (ODan)

furnishings (noun) *skruþer* (OSw)

furrow (noun) *for* (OSw)

gain (verb) *köpa* (OSw), *öðlask* (ON)

gain (noun) *fæ* (OSw)

gallows (noun) *gren* (OSw)

gallows-corpse (noun) *galgnár* (ON)

gamble (verb) *fordoble* (ODan)

gamble away (verb) *fordoble* (ODan)

gambler (noun) *dobblare* (OSw)

gambling (noun) *dufl* (OGu)

game (noun) *diur* (OSw)

gang (noun) *fylghi* (OSw)

gang crime (noun) *hærværk* (ODan)

gang crime case (noun) *hærvirkesmal* (ODan)

gap (noun) *liþ (1)* (OSw)

gap to drive through (noun) *liþsmeli* (OGu)

garden (noun) *trægarþer* (OSw)

garden of hops (noun) *humblagarþer* (OSw)

garment (noun) *klæþi* (OSw)

gash (verb) *skæra (2)* (OSw)

gate (noun) *farliþ* (OSw), *garþsliþ* (OSw), *grind* (OSw), *liþ (1)* (OSw)

gate of a farmstead (noun) *garþsliþ* (OSw)

gate of a farm's fence (noun) *garþsliþ* (OSw)

gate to a house (noun) *garþsliþ* (OSw)

gatepost (noun) *grindastolpi* (OSw)

gathering (noun) *fæmt* (OSw), *mannsöfnuðr* (ON), *samfund* (OSw), *samkunda* (ON), *samneth* (ODan), *samqvæmd* (OSw), *tilmæli* (OSw)

gathering at church (noun) *kirkiusokn* (OSw)

gathering of sheep to folds (noun) *rétt* (ON)

gauntlet (noun) *gata* (OSw), *geil* (ON)

geld (verb) *gælda (2)* (OSw), *snöpa* (OSw)

genealogical table (noun) *etarmannaskra* (OGu)

general assembly (noun) *alþingi* (ON), *Øxarárþing* (ON)

General Assembly court (noun) *alþingisdómr* (ON)

General Assembly regulation (noun) *alþingismál* (ON)

general duty (noun) *almænningsgæld* (OSw)

general gathering (noun) *samfund* (OSw)

general levy (noun) *almænninger* (OSw)

general public (noun) *alþýða* (ON)

general/common purchase (noun) *almænningsköp* (OSw)

generation (noun) *byrþ* (OSw), *maþer* (OSw), *quisl* (OGu)

genitals (noun) *skap* (OGu)

genuine difficulty (noun) *nöþsyn* (OSw)

German (adj.) *þydisker* (OSw)

get (verb) *liuta* (OSw)

get (someone) condemned (verb) *sækia* (OSw)

get a man (verb) *manne* (ODan)

get back (verb) *lösa* (OSw)

get back against payment (verb) *lösa* (OSw)

get or be assigned by lot (verb) *liuta* (OSw)

get power (verb) *valda* (OSw)

get surety (verb) *taksætia* (OSw)

gibbet (noun) *galghi* (OSw)

gift (noun) *förning* (OSw), *gift* (OSw), *gjavstuth* (ODan), *gæf* (OSw), *hæzla* (OSw), *muta* (OSw), *tilgæf* (OSw)

gift allowed by law (noun) *löggjöf* (ON)

gift for the soul (noun) *sialagift* (OSw)

gift for the soul's good (noun) *sialagift* (OSw)

gift in return (noun) *vingæf* (OSw)

gift in reward for hospitality (noun) *drekkulaun* (ON)

gift of a tenth (noun) *tíundargjöf* (ON)

gift of friendship (noun) *vingæf* (OSw)

gift of property (noun) *fjárgjöf* (ON)

gift on the altar (noun) *altaralæghi* (OSw)

gift thrall (noun) *gæfþræl* (OSw)

gifts to women (noun) *kvengjafir (pl.)* (ON)

gilding (noun) *gylning* (OGu)

gin (trap) (noun) *gildri* (OSw)

girder (noun) *biti* (ON)

girl (noun) *mö* (OSw)

give (verb) *afsifja* (ON), *biuþa* (OSw), *böta* (OSw), *gifta* (OSw), *lata* (OSw), *reþa* (OSw), *veta* (OSw)

give (someone) the value (of something) (verb) *virþa* (OSw)

give a right (verb) *hemula* (OSw)

give a tenth (verb) *tiunda* (OSw)

give a verdict (verb) *döma* (OSw)

give absolution (verb) *lösa* (OSw), *skripta* (OSw)

give advice on lawsuits (verb) *sakráða* (ON)

give an oath (verb) *ethe* (ODan), *framflytja* (ON), *hofþa* (OSw)

give an opinion (verb) *döma* (OSw)

give as a marriage gift (verb) *hemfylghia* (OSw), *hemgiva* (OSw)

give as penance (verb) *skripta* (OSw)

give as wife (verb) *gifta* (OSw)

give back (verb) *lösa* (OSw)

give billeting (verb) *gengöra* (OSw)

give birth to (verb) *föþa* (OSw)

give board (verb) *ala* (ON)

give communion (verb) *husla* (OSw)

give defence (verb) *væria* (OSw)

give divided judgements (verb) *véfengja* (ON)

give evidence (verb) *vita* (OSw)

give Extreme Unction (verb) *olia* (OSw)

give freedom (verb) *frælsa* (OSw)

give in marriage (verb) *gifta* (OSw)

give judgement (verb) *döma* (OSw)

give land with conveyance (verb) *sköta* (OSw)

give leave (verb) *lufa* (OGu)

give name (verb) *næmna* (OSw)

give permission (verb) *leyfa* (ON), *lufa* (OGu)

give precedence (verb) *vitna* (OSw)

give proof (verb) *vita* (OSw)

give security (verb) *takføre* (ODan)

give surety (verb) *fæsta* (OSw), *hætte* (ODan), *taksætia* (OSw)

give testimony (verb) *flytja* (ON)

give title (verb) *hemula* (OSw)

give warrantable title (verb) *hemula* (OSw)

give witness (verb) *vita* (OSw)

give/pay consolation (verb) *hogsla* (OGu)

given mark (noun) *gjafamark* (ON)

giving a seventh-day ale (noun) *sjaundargerð* (ON)

giving of alms (noun) *ölmusugerð* (ON)

giving one's word of honour (noun) *þegnskaparlagning* (ON)

glebe (noun) *kirkiubol* (OSw)

glebe land (noun) *kirkiubol* (OSw)

glove (noun) *glófi* (ON)

go (verb) *ganga* (OSw), *stæmna* (OSw)

go against (verb) *fælla* (OSw)

go from someone's hand (verb) *afhænda* (OSw)

go on raids (verb) *hæria* (OSw)

go out of date (verb) *fyrna* (OSw)

goat (noun) *get* (OSw)

godfather (noun) *guþfaþir* (OSw)

godmother (noun) *guþmoþir* (OSw)

godparent (noun) *guþsivi* (OSw)

God's gift (noun) *guðsgæfi* (ON)

God's house (noun) *guthshus* (ODan)

God's service (noun) *þiænista* (OSw)

going up to the mountain to gather sheep (noun) *fjallganga* (ON)

gold (noun) *gull* (OSw)

golden headdress (noun) *gullaþ* (OGu)

goldsmith (noun) *gullsmiþer* (OSw)

good (adj.) *sander* (OSw), *vilðr* (ON)

good conduct (noun) *siðsemð* (ON)

Good Friday (noun) *langafredagher* (OSw)

good man and true (noun) *þægn* (OSw)

good will (noun) *goþvili* (OSw)

goods (noun) *auðhófi* (ON), *bo* (OSw), *farkoster* (OSw), *fjárhlutr* (ON), *fæ* (OSw), *goþs* (OSw), *koster* (OSw), *lausafé* (ON), *lösöre* (OSw), *mun* (ODan), *pænninger* (OSw), *værþ* (OSw)

goods and chattels (noun) *koster* (OSw)

goods in common (noun) *bolaghsfæ* (OSw)

goods in custody (noun) *halzörar (pl.)* (OSw)

goods in partnership (noun) *fælagh* (OSw)

goods in storage (noun) *geymslufé* (ON)

goods of the church (noun) *kirkiufæ* (OSw)

goods secured by verdict (noun) *vitafé* (ON)

goose (noun) *gas* (OSw)

goose's crime (noun) *gassaglópr* (ON)

gore thief (noun) *gorþiuver* (OSw)

gore villain (noun) *gornithing* (ODan)

gossip oath (noun) *glafseþer* (OSw)

Gotlanders' general assembly (noun) *gutnalþing* (OGu)

gouge (verb) *sla* (OSw)

govern (verb) *raþa* (OSw), *styra* (OSw)

governor (noun) *landstjórnarmaðr* (ON)

gown (noun) *ivirklæþi* (OSw), *mantul* (OSw)

grace (noun) *fræst* (OSw), *fæmt* (OSw), *miskun* (OSw)

grain (noun) *korn* (OSw), *spannamali* (OSw), *sæþ* (OSw)

grain house (noun) *kornhærbærghi* (OSw), *kornskæmma* (OSw)

grain oblation (noun) *ólafssáð* (ON)

grain store (noun) *kornhærbærghi* (OSw)

grain thief (noun) *agnabaker* (OSw)

granary (noun) *kornhærbærghi* (OSw)

grandfather (noun) *karl* (OSw)

grant (verb) *döma* (OSw), *játa* (ON), *lata* (OSw), *lösa* (OSw), *lufa* (OGu), *skapa* (ON), *unna* (OSw), *veta* (OSw)

grant tenancy (verb) *byggia* (OSw)

grant truce (verb) *gruthe* (ODan)

granting of security (noun) *griðsala* (ON)

grasp (verb) *stiæla* (OSw)

grass (noun) *gras* (ON)

grass road (noun) *græsvægher* (OSw)

grass robbery (noun) *grasrán* (ON)

grass robbery ring (noun) *grasránsbaugr* (ON)

grass snatcher (noun) *græsspæri* (OSw)

grave (noun) *gript* (OSw), *lægherstaþer* (OSw)

grave fee (noun) *legkaup* (ON)

grave robbery (noun) *greftarrán* (ON)

grave-corpse (noun) *grafnár* (ON)

gravegoer (noun) *grafgangsmaðr* (ON)

graze (verb) *beita* (ON)

graze off (verb) *etja* (ON)

grazing (within the enclosed part of the village) (noun) *gærþi* (OSw)

grazing compensation (noun) *ætiubot* (OSw)

grazing constantly (adj.) *hagfastr* (ON)

grazing ground (noun) *hafnbit* (ON)

grazing land (noun) *hiorþvalder* (OSw)

grazing plot (noun) *beititeigr* (ON), *tegher* (OSw)

great need (noun) *nöþsyn* (OSw)

greater tithe (noun) *hovoþtiundi* (OSw)

grey monk (noun) *gramunk* (ODan)

grimacing fine (noun) *granbragðseyrir* (ON)

groom (noun) *stallari* (OSw)

ground (noun) *jorþ* (OSw), *tompt* (OSw), *valder* (OSw)

ground consecration (noun) *jarðarvígsla* (ON)

ground frost inspection (noun) *þiælasyn* (OSw)

ground plot (noun) *tompt* (OSw)

ground rent (noun) *jarðarleiga* (ON)

grounds (noun) *röst* (OSw), *tala (1)* (OSw)

group (noun) *flokker* (OSw), *sveit* (ON)

group of armed men (noun) *hær* (OSw)

group of full siblings (noun) *kolder* (OSw)

group of receivers (noun) *uppnám* (ON)

group of siblings (noun) *kolder* (OSw), *særkul* (ODan)

grove (noun) *hult* (OGu), *lunder* (OSw)

grown (adj.) *maghandi* (OSw)

grown-up (adj.) *fulvaksen* (ODan), *vaksen* (ODan)

guarantee (verb) *borgha* (OSw)

guarantee (noun) *borghan* (OSw)

guarantee a sale (verb) *hemula* (OSw)

guarantor (noun) *borghanaman* (OSw), *borghare* (OSw), *fangaman* (OSw), *hemulsman* (OSw), *skuli* (OSw), *taki* (OSw), *vörzlumaðr* (ON), *væriandi* (OSw)

guarantor for an oath (noun) *eþataki* (OSw)

guarantor of ownership (noun) *hemulsman* (OSw)

guard (verb) *varþa* (OSw), *væria* (OSw)

guard (noun) *varþer* (OSw), *varþmaþer* (OSw)

guard duty (noun) *varþer* (OSw), *varþhald* (OSw)

guard posting (noun) *varþhald* (OSw)

guardian (noun) *fjárhaldsmaðr* (ON), *forræðismaðr* (ON), *halzmaþer* (OSw), *malsmaþer* (OSw), *varnarmaðr* (ON), *væriandi* (OSw), *værje* (ODan), *værn* (OSw)

guardian of the estate (noun) *fjárvarðveizlumaðr* (ON)

guardianship (noun) *fjárhald* (ON), *forráð* (ON), *varþer* (OSw), *værje* (ODan)

guest (noun) *gæster* (OSw)

guest's contribution to a meal (noun) *förning* (OSw)

guest's inheritance (noun) *gesterfð* (ON)

guide (noun) *leiðsögumaðr* (ON)

guild (noun) *lagh* (OSw)

guilt (noun) *sak* (OSw)

guiltless (adj.) *saklös* (OSw)

guilty (adj.) *brutliker* (OSw), *ful* (OSw), *saker* (OSw), *sander* (OSw), *skylder (2)* (OSw), *skyldugher* (OSw)

guilty man (noun) *gælmaþer* (OSw)

guilty to compensate (adj.) *saker* (OSw)

guilty to pay (verb) *saker* (OSw)

guise of a hobgoblin (noun) *trolshamber* (OSw)

guiltlessly (adj.) *sekðarlauss* (ON)

Gulathing Law (noun) *Gulaþingsbók* (ON)

Gulathing assembly (noun) *Gulaþing* (ON)

Gulathing law district (noun) *Gulaþingslög* (ON)

gunwales (noun) *sax* (ON)

habit (noun) *klæþi* (OSw)

habitation (noun) *bygd* (OSw), *byr* (OSw)

hair (noun) *har (1)* (OSw)

hair pulling (noun) *tutten* (ODan)

half compensation (noun) *halfgildi* (OSw)

half fence (noun) *halfgarþer* (OSw)

half holy (adj.) *halvhelagh* (ODan)

half of a year (noun) *misseri* (ON)

half personal compensation (noun) *halfrétti* (ON)

half recompense (noun) *halfgildi* (OSw)

half room (noun) *halfrými* (ON)

half share (noun) *helmingr* (ON)

half sibling (noun) *halvsystken* (ODan)

half value (noun) *halfvirði* (ON)

half wergild (noun) *halfgildi* (OSw)

half-brother (noun) *halvbrother* (ODan)

half-compensated (adj.) *halfgildr* (ON)

half-district assembly (noun) *hölfuþing* (ON)

half-siblings (noun) *sunderkulla* (OSw)

half-year (noun) *misseri* (ON)

hall (noun) *salhus* (ODan)

hallow (verb) *blota* (OSw)

hallowed (adj.) *helagher* (OSw)

halter (noun) *klafi* (ON)

hamlet (noun) *byr* (OSw)

hammer division (noun) *hamarskipt* (OSw)

hand (noun) *hand* (OSw), *handaværk* (OSw)

hand giving (noun) *handlagh* (ODan)

hand off (verb) *afhænda* (OSw)

hand over (verb) *sælia* (OSw), *varþa* (OSw)

hand rapine (noun) *handran* (OSw)

hand-oath (noun) *handlagh* (ODan)

hand-robbery (noun) *handran* (OSw)

hand-seizure (noun) *handran* (OSw)

handcuffs (noun) *ærmaband* (OSw)

handheld steelyard (noun) *handpundari* (ON)

handiwork (noun) *handaværk* (OSw)

handle of a shield (noun) *mundriði* (ON)

handmark (noun) *handaværk* (OSw)

hands of a surety man (noun) *tak* (OSw)

hands of an enemy (noun) *hershendr (pl.)* (OGu)

handshake (noun) *handlagh* (ODan), *handsal* (ON)

hang (verb) *hængia* (OSw)

hangers on (noun) *slímuseta* (ON)

hanging (noun) *hang* (ODan)

hank (noun) *hespa* (ON)

happen (verb) *veta* (OSw)

harbouring (noun) *innihafnir (pl.)* (ON)

hardship sale (noun) *þrangaköp* (OSw)

harm (verb) *skaþa* (OSw), *skemma* (OGu), *spilla* (OSw), *ufyrme* (ODan)

harm (noun) *akoma* (OSw), *men* (OSw), *skaþi* (OSw), *spellvirki* (ON), *spiæll* (OSw), *ufyrmd* (ODan)

harm with words (verb) *fyrirmæla* (ON)

harmless (adj.) *skatheløs* (ODan)

harpoon (verb) *lysta (1)* (OSw)

harpoon (noun) *skutill* (ON)

harpoon-money (noun) *skotfé* (ON)

harpoon-share (noun) *skothlutr* (ON)

harpooner's share (noun) *skothlutr* (ON), *skotmannshlutr* (ON)

harrassment (noun) *bølesak* (ODan)

harry (verb) *hæria* (OSw)

harsh judgement (noun) *ofsokn* (OSw)

harsh terms (noun) *afarkostr* (ON)

harvest (verb) *læsa* (OSw), *vinna* (OSw)

harvest (noun) *avaxter* (OSw)

harvest holiday (noun) *høsthælgh* (ODan)

harvest immunity (noun) *anfriþer* (OSw)

harvest peace (noun) *akerfrith* (ODan), *anfriþer* (OSw), *høsthælgh* (ODan)

harvest sanctity (noun) *anfriþer* (OSw)

harvesting of hay or corn in another man's land (noun) *aslata* (OSw)

hate (noun) *heift* (ON)

hatred (noun) *avund* (OSw)

have a case (verb) *sökia* (OSw)

have a decision (verb) *döma* (OSw)

have a dispute (verb) *skilia* (OSw)

have a liability (verb) *böta* (OSw)

have a pledge (verb) *takføre* (ODan)

have a right (verb) *valda* (OSw)

have a right by a child (verb) *mynde* (ODan)

have a right to take something by the birth of a child (verb) *mynde* (ODan)

have a suspicion about (verb) *jæva* (OSw)

have as security (verb) *takføre* (ODan)

have as surety (verb) *hætte* (ODan)

have command over (verb) *valda* (OSw)

have control over (verb) *raþa* (OSw)

have legal possession of something (verb) *laghhæfþa* (OSw)

have sexual intercourse with (verb) *blandask* (ON)

have surety (verb) *taksætia* (OSw)

have the authority (verb) *raþa* (OSw)

have the right to fish (verb) *veþa* (OSw)

have the say (verb) *raþa* (OSw)

have title (verb) *hemula* (OSw)

have warrantable rights (verb) *hemula* (OSw)

having a fixed abode (adj.) *vistfastr* (ON)

having a healthy mind (adj.) *heilvita* (ON)

having a seat in court (adj.) *dómsætr* (ON)

having a settled home (adj.) *heimilisfastr* (ON)

having a warrantable right (adj.) *hemul* (OSw)

having a whitish sheath (of stallions) (adj.) *skauðhvítr* (ON)

having cash value (adj.) *fémætr* (ON)

having lost one's peace (adj.) *friþlös* (OSw)

having men enough (adj.) *fulllíða* (ON)

having no arable land (adj.) *seþalaus* (OGu)

having no case to answer (adj.) *saklös* (OSw)

having no duty (adj.) *oskylder* (OSw)

having no legal authentication of ownership (adj.) *ohemul* (OSw)

having no means of maintenance (adj.) *framfœrslulauss* (ON)

having no personal rights (adj.) *rætløs* (ODan)

having no warrantable rights (adj.) *ohemul* (OSw)

having personal rights (adj.) *réttnæmr* (ON)

having reached full age (adj.) *réttnæmr* (ON)

having the length of a span (adj.) *spannarlangr* (ON)

having the right to a church burial (adj.) *kirkjugrófr* (ON), *kirkjulægr* (ON)

having the right to attend an assembly (adj.) *þingreiðr* (ON)

having the right to be in the country (adj.) *landværr* (ON)

having the right to be present at an assembly (adj.) *þingværr* (ON)

having the same immunity (adj.) *jafnheilagr* (ON)

having the same validity (adj.) *jafnréttr* (ON)

having the value of a cow (adj.) *kúgildr* (ON)

having to flee (noun) *vegsl* (OGu)

having weak urinating organs (of stallions) (adj.) *skauðmígr* (ON)

hawk (noun) *haukr* (ON)

hay (noun) *andvirki* (ON), *hö* (OSw), *æng* (OSw)

hay barn (noun) *halmlaþa* (OSw), *hölaþa* (OSw)

hay price (noun) *heygjald* (ON), *heyverð* (ON)

hay-yard (noun) *garþer* (OSw), *stakkgarðr* (ON)

hayfield (noun) *taða* (ON), *töðuvöllr* (ON)

haymaking (noun) *hoysletr* (OGu)

haystores (noun) *andvirki* (ON)

head of animals (noun) *höfuð* (ON)

head of human beings (noun) *höfuð* (ON)

head of the family (noun) *karl* (OSw)

head of the household (noun) *bonde* (OSw), *bursven* (ODan)

head ring (noun) *höfuðbaugr* (ON)

head share (noun) *hovoþloter* (OSw)

head wound (noun) *huvuþsar* (OSw)

head-piece of a spindle (noun) *snúðr* (ON)

headcount (noun) *mantal* (OSw)

headdress (noun) *tuppr* (OGu)

heap of rocks or stones (noun) *rör* (OSw)

hear confession (verb) *skripta* (OSw)

hearing (noun) *liuþ* (OSw), *sal* (ODan), *uppreist* (ON)

heath (noun) *heiðr* (ON)

heathen (adj.) *heþin* (OSw)

heathen cursing (noun) *bölvun* (ON)

heathen practice (noun) *blot* (OGu), *blótskapr* (ON)

heathendom (noun) *heþna* (OSw)

hedge (noun) *haghi* (OSw)

heir (noun) *arftaki* (OSw), *arftökumaðr* (ON), *arvi* (OSw), *arvingi* (OSw), *erðarmaðr* (ON), *niþi* (OSw)

heir of the body (noun) *skaparvi* (OSw)

heir outside (a partnership) (noun) *utarve* (ODan)

heir to a son (noun) *magararfi* (ON)

heir who has left (the household) (noun) *utarve* (ODan)

heiress (noun) *arfa* (ON), *erfilytia* (OGu)

heirless man (noun) *gestfeðri* (ON)

heirs other than children (noun) *utarve* (ODan)

help (verb) *raþa* (OSw), *týja* (ON)

help (noun) *beini* (ON), *liþ (2)* (OSw), *væzla* (OSw)

herb (noun) *lyf* (ON)

herd (noun) *hiorþ* (OSw)

herdsman (noun) *féhirðir* (ON), *gætsleman* (ODan), *halzmaþer* (OSw)

hereditary farm (noun) *arvibol* (OSw)

heritage (noun) *arver* (OSw)

heritor (noun) *arftaki* (OSw)

hew (verb) *hugga* (OSw)

hidden goods (noun) *abyrþ* (OSw)

hidden homicide (noun) *dulghadrap* (OSw)

hidden killing (noun) *dulghadrap* (OSw)

hidden stolen goods (noun) *borafóli* (ON)

hidden-homicide fine (noun) *dulghadrap* (OSw)

hide (verb) *hirða* (ON), *løne* (ODan)

hide (noun) *huþ* (OSw)

hide whipping (noun) *huþ* (OSw)

hide-ransom (noun) *húðarlausn* (ON)

hider of theft (noun) *viþertakuþiuver* (OSw)

hiding (noun) *dul* (OSw), *sat* (OSw)

hiding of cattle (noun) *fæarföling* (OSw)

hiding of killed animal (noun) *fæarföling* (OSw)

hiding place (noun) *skjul* (ODan)

high church (noun) *höfuðkirkja* (ON)

high estimate (noun) *oftala* (OSw)

high seat (noun) *öndvegi* (ON)

high treason (noun) *dróttinssvik* (ON), *landráð* (ON)

high water mark (noun) *flothemal* (ODan)

high-water line (noun) *flothemal* (ODan)

higher force (noun) *ofse* (OSw)

highest ranked (adj.) *goþer* (OSw)

highroad (noun) *hærstræte* (ODan)

highway (noun) *farvægher* (OSw), *gata* (OSw), *landsvægher* (OSw), *vægher* (OSw), *þjóðbraut* (ON), *þjóðgata* (ON), *þjóðleið* (ON), *þjóðvegr* (ON)

highwayman (noun) *stigheman* (ODan)

hill (noun) *høgh* (ODan)

hill-guard (noun) *bærgvarþer* (OSw)

hinder (verb) *fortaka* (OSw), *fælla* (OSw), *synia* (OSw)

hinder by letting lie fallow (verb) *fyrna* (OSw)

hindering of travel (noun) *vegarfall* (ON)

hindrance (noun) *forfall* (OSw), *forstaða* (ON), *hinder* (OSw), *men* (OSw), *menföre* (OSw)

hire (verb) *fæsta* (OSw), *leghia* (OSw)

hire (noun) *legha* (OSw)

hire agreement (noun) *leghemal* (ODan)

hire charge (noun) *legha* (OSw)

hire of property (noun) *fjárleiga* (ON)

hired (adj.) *annöþogher* (OSw)

hired bandit (noun) *flugumaðr* (ON)

hired cattle (noun) *leghofæ* (OSw)

hired cow (noun) *leigukýr* (ON)

hired livestock (noun) *leghofæ* (OSw)

hired man (noun) *húskarl* (ON), *leghodrænger* (OSw), *leghomaþer* (OSw), *vinnumaðr* (ON)

hired servant (noun) *leghodrænger* (OSw), *leghohion* (OSw), *leghosven* (OSw)

hired stock (noun) *leghofæ* (OSw)

hired woman (noun) *leghokona* (OSw)

hired worker (noun) *leghomaþer* (OSw)

hireling (noun) *leghohion* (OSw), *malakarl* (OSw)

hiring slaves (noun) *mansleiga* (ON)

hiring stock (noun) *fjárleiga* (ON)

hit (verb) *hugga* (OSw), *sla* (OSw)

hold (verb) *halda* (OSw)

hold an assembly (verb) *heyja* (ON), *þinga* (OSw)

hold thing (verb) *þinga* (OSw)

holding a wedding (noun) *bruþlöpsgærþ* (OSw)

holiday (noun) *hátíð* (ON), *hælgh* (OSw), *hælghidagher* (OSw)

holiness from the preceding nones (noun) *nónhelgr* (ON)

holiness of the assembly (noun) *vébönd (pl.)* (ON)

holiness of the day (noun) *dagríki* (ON)

holy (adj.) *helagher* (OSw)

holy after 3pm (adj.) *nónheilagr* (ON)

Holy Communion (noun) *guþslikami* (OSw), *husl* (OSw), *reþskaper* (OSw)

holy day (noun) *hælgh* (OSw), *hælghidagher* (OSw)

holy from nones onwards (adj.) *nónheilagr* (ON)

holy from the preceding nones (adj.) *nónheilagr* (ON)

holy object (noun) *hælghidomber* (OSw)

holy office (noun) *tiþir (pl.)* (OSw)

holy peace (noun) *hælgh* (OSw)

holy period (noun) *hælgh* (OSw)

holy place (noun) *hælghidomber* (OSw), *vi* (OGu)

holy relic (noun) *hælghidomber* (OSw)

Holy Thursday (Ascension Day) (noun) *hælghiþorsdagher* (OSw)

holy time (noun) *hælgh* (OSw)

Holy week (noun) *dymbilvika* (OSw)

homage (noun) *lýðskylda* (ON)

home (noun) *bo* (OSw), *fæ* (OSw), *garþer* (OSw), *heimili* (ON), *hýbýli* (ON)

home assembly (noun) *þingfiæll* (OSw)

home attack (noun) *hemsokn* (OSw)

home attack testimony (noun) *heimsóknarvitni* (ON)

home born (adj.) *hemaföder* (OSw)

home born female thrall (noun) *fostra* (OSw)

home born slave (noun) *fostre* (OSw)

home born slave woman (noun) *fostra* (OSw)

home born thrall woman (noun) *fostra* (OSw)

home bred (adj.) *hemaföder* (OSw)

home district (noun) *bygd* (OSw), *hæraþ* (OSw)

home farm (noun) *höfuðból* (ON)

home field (noun) *garþer* (OSw), *heimaland* (ON), *tún* (ON), *túnvöllr* (ON)

home field wall (noun) *tungarþer* (OSw)

home made (adj.) *hemagiorþer* (OSw)

home pasture (noun) *húshagi* (ON)

home peace (noun) *hemfriþer* (OSw)

home province (noun) *fosterland* (OSw)

home summons (noun) *hemstæmpnung* (OSw)

home surety (noun) *brötartak* (OSw)

home-born thrall (noun) *fostre* (OSw)

home-bred slave (noun) *fostre* (OSw)

home-man (noun) *heimamaðr* (ON), *heimilismaðr* (ON)

homeless person (noun) *búslitsmaðr* (ON)

homemade (noun) *hemgærþ* (OSw)

homespun (noun) *vaþmal* (OSw)

homespun wool (noun) *vaþmal* (OSw)

homestead (noun) *bol* (OSw), *byr* (OSw), *garþer* (OSw), *haimþorp* (OGu), *heimili* (ON)

homestead sanctity (noun) *hemfriþer* (OSw)

homicidal arsonist (noun) *kasnavargher* (OSw)

homicide (noun) *banaorþ* (OSw), *bani* (OSw), *drap* (OSw), *mandrap* (OSw), *manvæt* (ODan), *vígaferði* (ON)

homicide case (noun) *banasak* (OSw)

honest man (noun) *sannindaman* (OSw)

honorary fine (noun) *þokkabot* (OSw), *þokki* (OSw)

honour (noun) *somi* (OSw)

honour fine (noun) *þokkabot* (OSw), *þokki* (OSw)

honour payment (noun) *þokki* (OSw)

hooding ends (noun) *hals* (OSw)

hoof (noun) *hófr* (ON)

hop (noun) *humbli* (OSw)

hop-garden (noun) *humblagarþer* (OSw)

horn hobble (noun) *hornband* (OGu)

horn on a cow (noun) *horn* (ON)

horned cattle (noun) *not* (OSw)

horse (noun) *griper* (OSw), *hæster* (OSw), *rus* (OGu)

horse flesh (noun) *hrossakjöt* (ON)

horse fodder (noun) *eykjafóðr* (ON)

horse for conveyance (noun) *skiut* (OSw)

horse having a protruded rectum (noun) *rasshverfingr* (ON)

horse loan (noun) *hrosslán* (ON)

horse rent (noun) *hæsteleghe* (ODan)

horse troop (noun) *stoth* (ODan)

hospital (noun) *spital* (OSw)

hospitality (noun) *beini* (ON), *gengærþ* (OSw), *gæster* (OSw), *gæstning* (OSw), *koster* (OSw), *vist* (OSw), *væzla* (OSw)

Host of the sacrament (noun) *guþslikami* (OSw)

hostage (noun) *gisli* (OSw)

hostile (adj.) *avugher* (OSw), *heiftugr* (ON)

hostile act (noun) *aganga* (OSw)

hostile fleet (noun) *herfloti* (ON)

hot iron (noun) *jarn* (OSw)

hours (noun) *tiþir (pl.)* (OSw)

house (verb) *ala* (ON), *herbergja* (ON), *husa* (OSw)

house (noun) *bo* (OSw), *byr* (OSw), *flat* (OSw), *garþer* (OSw), *heimili* (ON), *hus* (OSw), *hýbýli* (ON), *hærbærghi* (OSw), *hæskaper* (OSw), *jather* (ODan)

house of a landed man (noun) *lendsmannsgarðr* (ON)

house of God (noun) *guthshus* (ODan)

house owner (noun) *húseigandi* (ON)

house rapine (noun) *bosran* (OSw)

house search (noun) *ransak* (OSw), *ransakan* (OSw)

house search (permit a) (verb) *ransaka* (OSw)

house site (noun) *húsbeða* (ON)

house slave (noun) *sætesambut* (ODan)

house theft (noun) *bodræt* (OSw)

house toft (noun) *husetoft* (ODan)

house-lead (verb) *flatføre* (ODan)

house-leading (noun) *flatføring* (ODan)

house-led (noun) *flat* (OSw), *flatføring* (ODan)

house-room (noun) *húsrúm* (ON)

house-searching (noun) *ransakan* (OSw)

house-to-house vagrancy (noun) *húsgangr* (ON)

housebreaking (noun) *husbrut* (OSw)

housecarl's inheritance (noun) *húskarlserfð* (ON)

household (noun) *bo* (OSw), *boskaper* (OSw), *brytstokker* (OSw), *búferill* (ON), *búnuðr* (ON), *fælagh* (OSw), *hion* (OSw), *hus* (OSw), *hæskaper* (OSw)

household attachment (noun) *griþ* (OSw)

household community (noun) *fælagh* (OSw)

household effects (noun) *boskaper* (OSw), *inviþi* (OSw)

household helpers (noun) *hjónalið* (ON)

household implements (noun) *búsbúhlutr* (ON)

household led by a woman (noun) *konubú* (ON)

household man (noun) *griðmaðr* (ON), *heimamaðr* (ON)

household member (noun) *hion* (OSw)

household members (noun) *hion* (OSw)

household members (as a group) (noun) *man* (OSw)

household members who are a charge on someone (noun) *skuldahjú* (ON)

household members who are a charge on the householder (noun) *skuldahjón* (ON)

household movables (noun) *bofæ* (ODan)

household of a widow (noun) *ænkjebo* (ODan)

household people (noun) *hjú* (ON)

household serf (noun) *hemahion* (OSw)

household servant (noun) *hion* (OSw)

household servants (noun) *hion* (OSw), *husþiauþ* (OGu)

household stock (noun) *bo* (OSw)

household theft (noun) *bospænd* (OSw)

household-joining (noun) *griðtaka* (ON)

householder (noun) *bonde* (OSw), *búþegn* (ON), *husbonde* (OSw), *húsbúandi* (ON), *karl* (OSw), *maþer* (OSw)

householder furthest away in the village (noun) *ændakarl* (OSw)

householder in a recruiting area (noun) *havnebonde* (ODan)

householder's churchyard (noun) *búandakirkjugarðr* (ON)

householder's right (noun) *bóndaréttr* (ON)

householder's son (noun) *bondasun* (OSw)

householder's village (noun) *bondaby* (OSw)

householder's wife (noun) *bondakona* (OSw)

householding on a church farm (noun) *staðarábúð* (ON)

householding period (noun) *ábúð* (ON)

housekeeper (noun) *deghia* (OSw)

housel (verb) *husla* (OSw)

housemaid (noun) *seta* (ON)

housewife (noun) *husfrugha* (OSw)

housing homeless people (noun) *stafkarlafőrsla* (ON)

howe (noun) *høgh* (ODan)

hundred (noun) *hundari* (OSw), *hundrað* (ON)

hunt (verb) *sköghia* (OSw), *veþa* (OSw), *vinna* (OSw)

hunt birds (verb) *fygla* (ON)

hunting (noun) *sköghning* (OSw), *veiðr* (ON)

hunting ground (noun) *haghi* (OSw)

hunting grounds (noun) *veiðistöð* (ON)

hunting grounds for seals (noun) *selver* (ON)

hunting of bears (noun) *bjarnveiðr* (ON)

hunting shed (noun) *veiðibúð* (ON)

hurt (verb) *lysta (1)* (OSw), *meiða* (ON), *skemma* (OGu), *sprængia* (OSw), *værka* (OSw)

hurt slightly (verb) *skena* (OSw)

husband (noun) *aþalman* (OSw), *bonde* (OSw), *husbonde* (OSw), *karl* (OSw), *maþer* (OSw)

husband's gift (noun) *gagngjald* (ON), *tilgæf* (OSw)

husband's son (noun) *bondasun* (OSw)

hut (noun) *boþ* (OSw)

hut-mate (noun) *búðunautr* (ON)

hut-utensil hire (noun) *búðargagnaleiga* (ON)

Icelander (noun) *íslendingr* (ON)

identification (noun) *mærki* (OSw)

identified (adj.) *kenndr* (ON)

identifier (noun) *kennandi* (ON)

identify (verb) *kænna* (OSw), *næmna* (OSw)

identifying features (noun) *jartighni (pl.)* (OSw)

ill (adj.) *sjúkr* (ON)

ill advisedly (adv.) *oraþlika* (OGu)

ill intent (noun) *vandreþi* (OGu)

ill mark (noun) *ørkuml* (ON)

ill will (noun) *illska* (ON)

illegal (adj.) *aflagha* (OSw), *laghalös* (OSw), *ohemul* (OSw), *olagha* (OSw), *orætter* (OSw), *saklös* (OSw)

illegal activity (noun) *afærþ* (OSw)

illegal appropriation (noun) *fornæmi* (OSw)

illegal breaking (noun) *hömlufall* (ON)

illegal deposit (noun) *undirgift* (OSw)

illegal intercourse (noun) *læghervite* (ODan)

illegal land use (noun) *fornæmi* (OSw)

illegal products (noun) *aværkan* (OSw)

illegal sale (noun) *gærsala* (OSw)

illegal use of another man's property (noun) *áfang* (ON)

illegal work (noun) *aværkan* (OSw)

illegally (adv.) *ohemul* (OSw), *olovandis* (OSw), *oskælika* (OSw), *ulovlika* (ODan)

illegitimate (adj.) *frillusun* (OSw), *friðluborinn* (ON), *laungetinn* (ON), *ohemul* (OSw), *ólögligr* (ON)

illegitimate brother (a concubine's) (noun) *frillubroþir* (OSw)

illegitimate child (noun) *frillubarn* (OSw), *horbarn* (OSw), *launbarn* (ON), *þybarn* (OGu)

illegitimate daughter (noun) *friðludóttir* (ON), *þydotir* (OGu)

illegitimate sister (noun) *frillusystir* (OSw)

illegitimate son (noun) *þysun* (OGu)

illicit (adj.) *olovandis* (OSw)

illicit relations (noun) *gælskaper* (OSw)

illicit relationship (noun) *löskalæghi* (OSw)

illicit sexual intercourse (noun) *kvennamál* (ON)

illicit use (noun) *aværkan* (OSw)

immoral life (noun) *saurlifi* (ON)

immune (adj.) *helagher* (OSw)

immune by the law (adj.) *helagher* (OSw)

immunity (noun) *friþer* (OSw), *hælgh* (OSw)

impartial (adj.) *lutlös* (OSw), *uvildigh* (ODan), *valinkunnr* (ON)

impartial hands (noun) *jæmnaþahænder* (OSw)

impassable (adj.) *oför* (OSw)

impassable area (noun) *ófœra* (ON)

impediment (noun) *forfall* (OSw), *meinbugr* (ON), *meinleiki* (ON)

impose (verb) *döma* (OSw), *sökia* (OSw), *utdöma* (OSw), *veta* (OSw)

imposed church penance (noun) *skriptabrut* (OSw)

imposed with a church penance (adj.) *skriptaþer* (OSw)

impossible tale (noun) *ýki* (ON)

impotence (noun) *hörundfall* (ON)

improper time (noun) *ótíð* (ON)

impropriety (noun) *óknytti* (ON)

improve (verb) *böta* (OSw)

improvement (noun) *umbót* (ON)

improvement of highways (noun) *vegabót* (ON)

impure (adj.) *oskær* (OSw)

in a good state (adj.) *gilder* (OSw)

in a year (adv.) *jamlangi* (OSw)

in accordance with law (prep.) *gilder* (OSw)

in agreement (adj.) *sater* (OSw)

in coin (adj.) *pænter* (OSw)

in foreign countries (prep.) *ørlendis* (ON)

in full (e.g. of compensation) (adv.) *fullt* (OSw)

in good repair (adj.) *gilder* (OSw)

in kinship (adj.) *skylder (1)* (OSw)

in law (adv.) *laghlika* (OSw)

in livestock (prep.) *fríðr* (ON)

in measured silver (prep.) *silfrmetinn* (ON)

in need (adj.) *nöþogher* (OSw)

in order (adj.) *gilder* (OSw)

in poor health (adj.) *vanheill* (ON)

in possession of (adv.) *handamællum* (OSw)

in settled lodging (prep.) *vistfastr* (ON)

in the absence of material evidence (adj.) *agripslaus* (OGu)

in the land (adv.) *inlændis* (OSw)

in the province (adv.) *hærlænsker* (OSw), *inlændis* (OSw)

in the realm (adv.) *inrikis* (OSw)

in the right place (adv.) *ræt* (OSw)

in the same yard (adv.) *samtýnis* (ON)

in weight (adj.) *væghin* (OSw)

in wrath (adv.) *vreþer* (OSw)

in-dweller (noun) *innismaþer* (OSw)

in-dwellers (noun) *innisfolk* (OSw)

in-law (noun) *magher* (OSw)

inadequate (adj.) *ogilder* (OSw)

inadequate means (noun) *vanefni* (ON)

inappropriate quarrel (noun) *misdeild* (ON)

inaugurate (verb) *vighia* (OSw)

inaugurate formally (verb) *hælghe* (ODan)

incapable person (noun) *omaghi* (OSw)

incapacitate (verb) *læsta* (OSw)

incest (noun) *frændsimisspiæl* (OSw)

incest in kinship by marriage (noun) *sifskapsspiæl* (OSw)

incest with affines (noun) *sifjaspell* (ON)

incest with kin by blood (noun) *ætskuspiæll* (OSw)

incest with kin by marriage (noun) *siviaslit* (OSw)

incitation to a fight (noun) *bjarneggjun* (ON)

incite (verb) *raþa* (OSw)

incited killing (noun) *hælraþ* (OSw)

incitement to a killing (noun) *raþsbænd* (OSw)

inclination (noun) *vili* (OSw)

included in the law (adj.) *laghtakin* (OSw)

income (noun) *afli* (ON), *avaxter* (OSw), *gift* (OSw), *ingæld* (OSw), *reiða* (ON), *vöxtr* (ON)

incomplete inheritance rights (noun) *vanerfð* (ON)

incompliance with the law (noun) *rætlösa* (OSw)

inconvenience (noun) *men* (OSw)

incorrect (adj.) *orætter* (OSw)

incorrect law (noun) *olagh* (OSw)

incorrectly (adv.) *orætlika* (OSw)

incorrectly mark (verb) *mismarka* (ON)

increase (noun) *avaxter* (OSw)

increaser of the wergild (noun) *sakauki* (ON)

indecent (adj.) *ohaiþverþr* (OGu)

indecent act (noun) *óhófuverk* (ON)

indemnification (noun) *skaþagæld* (OSw)

indemnified (adj.) *saklös* (OSw)

indemnity (noun) *gæld* (OSw), *skaþagæld* (OSw)

indented (adj.) *suigin* (OGu)

indicate (verb) *vátta* (ON)

indication (noun) *mærki* (OSw)

indict (verb) *skylda* (OSw)

indictment (noun) *sak* (OSw), *sögn* (ON), *tilmæli* (OSw)

indigent (adj.) *fatöker* (OSw)

indigent man (noun) *øreigi* (ON)

indigent person (noun) *förumannaförsla* (ON)

individual's right to peace and security (noun) *manhælghi* (OSw)

individual's right to protection (noun) *manhælghi* (OSw)

ineligible for compensation (adj.) *ogilder* (OSw)

infant (noun) *omaghi* (OSw), *vaggubarn* (OSw)

infanticide (noun) *barnamorþ* (OSw)

infertile land (noun) *daufiorþ* (OGu)

infirm (adj.) *vanheill* (ON)

inflict a wound (verb) *sære* (ODan)

inform (verb) *þinga* (OSw)

infringe against (verb) *bryta* (OSw)

inhabitant (noun) *landsmaþer* (OSw)

inhabitants (noun) *almoghe* (OSw)

inhabited area (noun) *bygd* (OSw)

inhabited land (noun) *boland* (OGu)

inhabited place (noun) *bygd* (OSw)

inherit (verb) *liuta* (OSw), *ærva* (OSw)

inheritance (noun) *arftak* (ON), *arver* (OSw), *byrþ* (OSw), *föðurleifð* (ON), *luter* (OSw), *ærfþ* (OSw), *ærfþaloter* (OSw)

inheritance after a disaster (noun) *ofsinnisarf* (OSw)

inheritance after a son (noun) *sunararver* (OSw)

inheritance after an accident (noun) *ofsinnisarf* (OSw)

inheritance ale (noun) *erfðaölðr* (ON)

inheritance among kinsmen (noun) *frænderfð* (ON)

inheritance beer (noun) *ærvisöl* (OSw)

inheritance between broods (noun) *kollararf* (OSw)

inheritance between kin (noun) *kynsarv* (ODan)

inheritance by direct heirs (noun) *brystarf* (OSw)

inheritance by gift (noun) *gjaferfð* (ON)

inheritance by right of occupancy (noun) *ísetuarfr* (ON)

inheritance by siblings (noun) *skyldarf* (OSw)

inheritance case (noun) *arvemal* (ODan)

inheritance chapter (noun) *erfðatal* (ON)

inheritance chase (noun) *arvbet* (ODan)

inheritance chased on both sides (noun) *arvbet* (ODan)

inheritance claim (noun) *arfsókn* (ON)

inheritance division (noun) *arfskifti* (ON)

inheritance fraud (noun) *arfsvik* (ON)

inheritance from a father (noun) *föðurarfr* (ON)

inheritance from a legitimate child (noun) *skötarf* (OSw)

inheritance from a mother (noun) *móðurarfr* (ON)

inheritance from a thrall (noun) *þrælaarf* (OSw)

inheritance from close relatives (noun) *skyldarf* (OSw)

inheritance from descendants (noun) *bakarf* (OSw)

inheritance from siblings and half-siblings (noun) *kollararf* (OSw)

inheritance had together (noun) *arvfælagh* (ODan)

inheritance in movables (noun) *orf* (OSw)

inheritance list (noun) *erfðatal* (ON)

inheritance on both sides (noun) *arvbet* (ODan)

inheritance on the male side (noun) *karlerfðir (pl.)* (ON)

inheritance prospect (noun) *arfván* (ON)

inheritance sale (noun) *arfsal* (ON)

inheritance section (noun) *erðatal* (ON), *ærfþarbalker* (OSw)

inheritance taking (noun) *arftaka* (ON)

inheritance trade (noun) *arfsal* (ON)

inheritance-trade dependent (noun) *arftaksómagi* (ON)

inherited (adj.) *arftakin* (OSw)

inherited land (noun) *byrþ* (OSw), *oþoliorþ* (OSw), *ærfþaiorþ* (OSw)

inherited ownership mark (noun) *erðamark* (ON)

inherited property (noun) *erðafé* (ON)

inheritence that bites inheritance (noun) *arvebitning* (ODan)

inheritor (noun) *arftaki* (OSw), *arvingi* (OSw), *oþalsmaþer* (OSw)

iniquitous criminal (noun) *udæthesman* (ODan)

injure (verb) *bryta* (OSw), *granda* (ON), *læsta* (OSw), *misfyrma* (OSw), *sargha* (OSw), *skemma* (OGu), *spilla* (OSw)

injured (adj.) *sar* (OSw)

injured party (noun) *malsæghandi* (OSw)

injurer (noun) *saramaþer* (OSw)

injuring blow (noun) *óvænishögg* (ON)

injury (noun) *akoma* (OSw), *aværkan* (OSw), *bardaghi* (OSw), *laster* (OSw), *lemð* (ON), *lyti* (OSw), *men* (OSw), *óhlutr* (ON), *óvæni* (ON), *sar* (OSw), *skaþi* (OSw), *skemmð* (ON), *spiæll* (OSw), *vaþi* (OSw)

injury case (noun) *sar* (OSw), *saramal* (OSw)

injury caused by a human hand (noun) *handaværk* (OSw)

injury that draws blood (noun) *bloþlæti* (OSw), *bloþsar* (OSw), *bloþviti* (OSw)

injustice (noun) *olagh* (OSw), *orætter* (OSw), *oskiel* (OGu), *rangendi* (ON)

inland guard (noun) *invarþer* (OSw)

innocent (adj.) *osaker* (OSw), *osander* (OSw), *oskylder* (OSw), *saklös* (OSw), *skær* (OSw), *sykn* (OSw)

inoffensive (adj.) *saklös* (OSw)

inquest (verb) *vita* (OSw)

inquire (verb) *reþa* (OSw), *skuþa* (OSw), *vita* (OSw)

inquire into (verb) *leta* (OSw)

inquiry (noun) *frétt* (ON), *ransak* (OSw)

insane (adj.) *galin* (OSw), *órr* (ON)

insanity (noun) *óvizka* (ON), *vitfirring* (ON)

inside the country (adv.) *inrikis* (OSw)

inside the realm (adv.) *inrikis* (OSw)

inspect (verb) *sea* (OSw), *skuþa* (OSw), *syna* (OSw), *sætia* (OSw), *vittia* (OSw)

inspection (noun) *asyn* (OSw), *ransak* (OSw), *syn* (OSw)

inspection by a {hundari} (noun) *hundarissyn* (OSw)

inspection by owners (noun) *æghandasyn* (OSw)

inspection of weapons (noun) *vápnaþing* (ON)

inspection proof (noun) *synaband* (OSw)

inspector (noun) *synaman* (OSw)

instalment (noun) *luter* (OSw), *sal* (ODan), *salastefna* (ON)

instigate (verb) *biuþa* (OSw), *raþa* (OSw)

instigation (noun) *raþasak* (OSw), *raþsbænd* (OSw)

instigator (noun) *hovoþsmaþer* (OSw), *raþsbani* (OSw)

insult (verb) *misfyrma* (OSw), *níða* (ON)

insult (noun) *níð* (ON), *oqvæþinsorþ* (OSw), *vanvirða* (ON), *vanvirðing* (ON), *þokki* (OSw)

insulting words (noun) *þokkaorþ* (OSw)

insulting words for which one should be compensated (noun) *fullréttisorð* (ON)

intend (verb) *vilia* (OSw)

intended action (noun) *handaværk* (OSw)

intent (noun) *raþ* (OSw), *vili* (OSw), *viliagærning* (OSw), *viliaværk* (OSw)

intent (to damage) (noun) *vili* (OSw)

intention (noun) *forhugsun* (ON), *vili* (OSw)

intentional act (noun) *viliagærning* (OSw)

intentional crime (noun) *eþsörisbrut* (OSw)

intentional deed (noun) *viliaværk* (OSw)

intentional killing (noun) *viliaværk* (OSw), *viliaværksdrap* (OSw)

intentional killing fine (noun) *viliaværk* (OSw)

intercourse (noun) *hionalagh* (OSw), *legorð* (ON)

intercourse case (noun) *legorðssök* (ON)

intercourse in secrecy (noun) *lønlæghe* (ODan)

intercourse with mother or daughter (noun) *moþnahæfþ* (OSw)

interdict (verb) *forbuþa* (OSw)

interdict (noun) *forbuþ* (OSw)

interdiction (noun) *forbuþ* (OSw)

interest (noun) *afli* (ON), *avaxter* (OSw), *fjárleiga* (ON), *legha* (OSw), *völxtr* (ON)

interest at a legal rate (noun) *lögleiga* (ON)

internal wound (noun) *holund* (ON), *holundarsár* (ON), *hulsar* (OSw)

interpret (verb) *raþa* (OSw)

interpreter (noun) *tulkr* (ON)

intrigue (noun) *raþ* (OSw)

intrusion (noun) *nes* (ON)

invalid (adj.) *atergangs* (OSw), *ogilder* (OSw), *ómætr* (ON), *ónýtr* (ON), *saklös* (OSw)

invalid oath (noun) *falzeþer* (OSw)

invalidate (verb) *ryva* (OSw)

invalidate an agreement (verb) *rypta* (OGu)

invective (noun) *oqvæþinsorþ* (OSw)

Invention of the Cross (noun) *crucismisse* (ODan)

invest (verb) *væria* (OSw)

investigate (verb) *ransaka* (OSw), *skilia* (OSw), *skuþa* (OSw), *skýra* (ON), *spyria* (OSw), *utröna* (OSw), *vita* (OSw)

investigation (noun) *ransak* (OSw), *sokn* (OSw), *syn* (OSw)

investigative assembly (noun) *ræfsingaþing* (OSw)

investigator (noun) *synaman* (OSw)

investigators (noun) *syn* (OSw)

investigators' decision (noun) *mætansorþ* (OSw)

invigorate (verb) *sværia* (OSw)

inviolability (noun) *friþer* (OSw)

inviolability of the person (noun) *manhælghi* (OSw)

inviolate (adj.) *friþhelagher* (OSw), *helagher* (OSw), *uspilt* (ODan)

invite (verb) *biuþa* (OSw)

invited to a wedding (adj.) *ölbuþin* (OSw)

invocation (noun) *haizl* (OGu)

iron (noun) *jarn* (OSw), *skutsjarn* (ODan)

iron arrow (noun) *járnör* (ON)

iron clasp (noun) *járnspöng* (ON)

iron hat (noun) *jarnhatter* (OSw)

iron nail (noun) *járnsaumr* (ON)

iron-bearing (noun) *jarnbyrþ* (OSw)

irons (noun) *jarn* (OSw)

irreparable harm (noun) *forlækisværk* (OSw)

irrigation (noun) *veita* (ON)

irrigation channels (noun) *veita* (ON)

irritant plot (noun) *óværateigr* (ON)

island (noun) *land* (OSw)

islanders (noun) *land* (OSw)

isolated land (noun) *stokkland* (ON)

item (noun) *griper* (OSw)

item drifted ashore (noun) *reki* (ON)

item of full value (noun) *gildingr* (ON)

item whose value is open to assessment (noun) *virðingarfé* (ON)

items bought to a couple's common home (noun) *siængaköp* (OSw)

itinerant (adj.) *væghfarandi* (OSw)

jail (noun) *hæfta* (OSw)

jarl (noun) *jarl* (OSw)

jerk (verb) *hnykkja* (ON)

jerking (noun) *nykkr* (OGu)

jester (noun) *lekari* (OSw)

joining of hands (noun) *handtak* (ODan)

joint (noun) *liþer* (OSw)

joint drinking (noun) *samburðaröl* (ON)

joint grazing (noun) *sambeit* (ON)

journey (noun) *vægher* (OSw)

journey companion (noun) *farunöti* (OSw)

journey that is incumbent on the bishop (noun) *biskupsfærþ* (OSw)

journey to the General Assembly (noun) *alþingisför* (ON)

judge (verb) *döma* (OSw), *fælla* (OSw), *rætta* (OSw), *skipta* (OSw)

judge (noun) *dómandi* (ON), *domari* (OSw), *domber* (OSw), *dómsmaðr* (ON), *skilamaþer* (OSw)

judge invalid (verb) *aterbryta* (OSw), *updöma* (OSw)

judge too harshly (verb) *ofdóma* (ON)

judge too mildly (verb) *vandóma* (ON)

judgement (noun) *domber* (OSw), *laghskila* (OSw), *vita* (OSw), *vitni* (OSw), *vitsorþ* (OSw)

judgement breaking (noun) *dómrof* (ON)

judgement for seizure (noun) *namsdom* (ODan)

judgement from the assembly (noun) *þing* (OSw)

judgement in a payment suit (noun) *fjárdóming* (ON)

judgement of distraint (noun) *atfarardómr* (ON)

judgement of the assembly (noun) *þingsdomi* (OSw)

judgment of twelve men (noun) *tolfmannadómr* (ON)

judicial power (noun) *domber* (OSw)

jurisdiction (noun) *lagh* (OSw), *laghsagha* (OSw), *yfirsókn* (ON)

jurisdiction of the assembly (noun) *þingunöti* (OSw)

jury (noun) *næmd* (OSw)

just (adj.) *rætter* (OSw), *sannligr* (ON)

just as valid (adj.) *jafnfullr* (ON)

justice (noun) *réttendi* (ON), *rættari* (OSw), *rætter* (OSw), *rætvisa* (OSw), *skæl* (OSw)

justiciary (noun) *rættari* (OSw)

justification (noun) *skæl* (OSw)

justified (adj.) *rætter* (OSw)

keel (noun) *kjölr* (ON)

keep (verb) *föþa* (OSw), *halda* (OSw), *hirða* (ON), *varþveta* (OSw)

keep (noun) *vist* (OSw)

keep back (verb) *væria* (OSw)

keep quiet (verb) *þigia* (OSw)

keep silent (verb) *þigia* (OSw)

keep to (verb) *halda* (OSw)

keeping (noun) *gætsla* (OSw), *varðveizla* (ON)

keeping a General Assembly settlement (noun) *alþingissáttarhald* (ON)

keeping of holy days (noun) *helgihald* (ON)

kept stock (noun) *fulgufé* (ON)

key (noun) *lykil* (OSw)

key of the church (noun) *kirkiunykil* (OSw)

kick (verb) *sparka* (OGu)

kick with a leg (noun) *benhog* (ODan)

kick with the heel (verb) *hæla* (ON)

kicking with a leg (noun) *benhog* (ODan)

kidnapped (adj.) *rantakin* (OSw)

kill (verb) *dræpa* (OSw), *myrþa* (OSw), *spilla* (OSw), *veþa* (OSw), *vægha (1)* (OSw)

killed (noun) *veginn* (ON)

killer (noun) *bani* (OSw), *drapari* (OSw), *mansbani* (OSw), *morþari* (OSw), *skaþamaþer* (OSw), *væghandi* (OSw)

killer cuts (noun) *vögnhögg* (ON)

killer of a free man (noun) *þengsbani* (OSw)

killer's accomplice (noun) *haldbani* (OSw)

killer's advisor (noun) *raþsbani* (OSw)

killer's aide (noun) *haldbani* (OSw)

killing (noun) *aftaka* (ON), *banaorþ* (OSw), *bani* (OSw), *döþsdrap* (OSw), *drap* (OSw), *mandrap* (OSw), *mannskaði* (ON), *vígaferði* (ON), *vigh* (OSw)

killing announcement (noun) *víglýsing* (ON)

killing by witchcraft (noun) *forgærning* (OSw)

killing case (noun) *vígaferði* (ON), *vígsök* (ON)

killing caused by somebody falling down by himself (noun) *ovanfal* (OSw)

killing caused by something falling down (noun) *afald* (OSw)

killing for double fines (noun) *tvæbötisdrap* (OSw)

killing for triple fines (noun) *þræbötisdrap* (OSw)

killing in a group fight (noun) *flokksvíg* (ON)

killing of a man (noun) *mandrap* (OSw)

killing on islands (noun) *öiadrap* (OSw)

killing-weapon (noun) *banavapn* (OSw)

kin (noun) *bloþ* (OSw), *byrþ* (OSw), *frændi* (OSw), *frændsimi* (OSw), *kolder* (OSw), *kyn* (OSw), *niþ* (OSw), *systrunger* (OSw), *æt* (OSw), *ættalægger* (OSw)

kin in blood (noun) *mansivi* (OSw)

kin in God (noun) *guþsivi* (OSw)

kin on mother's side (noun) *móðurætt* (ON)

kin witness (noun) *niþiavitni* (OGu)

kin-compensation (noun) *frændbót* (ON)

kin-counter (noun) *tölumaðr* (ON)

kindred (noun) *átt* (ON), *æt* (OSw)

kindred payments (noun) *niðgjald* (ON)

kinfolk (noun) *frændi* (OSw)

king (noun) *kununger* (OSw), *kunungsdömi* (OSw)

kingdom (noun) *konongsriki* (OSw), *konungsveldi* (ON), *kunungsdömi* (OSw), *land* (OSw), *riki* (OSw)

king's administrator (noun) *lænsmaþer* (OSw)

king's assembly (noun) *konungsþing* (ON)

king's authority (noun) *konungsvald* (ON)

king's bodyguard (noun) *hirð* (ON)

king's book (noun) *kunungsbalker* (OSw)

king's business (noun) *konungsørendi* (ON)

king's coin (noun) *konungssteði* (ON)

king's commission (noun) *kunungsnæmd* (OSw)

king's court (noun) *hirð* (ON), *konongsgarþer* (OSw)

king's due (noun) *konungsrætter* (OSw)

king's estate (noun) *konongsgarþer* (OSw)

king's farm (noun) *husaby* (OSw), *konongsgarþer* (OSw), *konungsjörð* (ON)

king's fine (noun) *konungsrætter* (OSw)

king's forest (noun) *konungsmörk* (ON)

king's household (noun) *konongsgarþer* (OSw)

king's inquest (noun) *kunungsræfst* (OSw)

king's jury (noun) *kunungsnæmd* (OSw)

king's land (noun) *konungsjörð* (ON)

king's letter (noun) *konungsbréf* (ON)

king's local administrator (noun) *lænsmaþer* (OSw)

king's man (noun) *hirþman* (OSw), *konungsman* (OSw)

king's manor (noun) *konongsgarþer* (OSw)

king's marshal (noun) *stallari* (OSw)

king's messenger (noun) *ørendreki* (ON)

king's mint (noun) *konungssteði* (ON)

King's Oath (noun) *eþsöre* (OSw)

king's official (noun) *ármaðr* (ON), *konungsman* (OSw), *umbuþsman* (OSw)

King's Peace (noun) *eþsöre* (OSw), *friþer* (OSw)

king's realm (noun) *konongsriki* (OSw)

king's representative (noun) *ármaðr* (ON)

king's rights (noun) *konungsrætter* (OSw)

king's route (noun) *eriksgata* (OSw)

king's section (noun) *kunungsbalker* (OSw)

king's sworn peace (noun) *eþsöre* (OSw)

kinsfolk (noun) *frændi* (OSw)

kinship (noun) *byrþ* (OSw), *frændsimi* (OSw), *kyn* (OSw), *kynsæme* (ODan), *niþ* (OSw)

kinship by lineage (noun) *skyldskaper* (OSw)

kinship by marriage (noun) *mægð* (ON), *sifskaper* (OSw)

kinship fine (noun) *ættarbot* (OSw)

kinship of the third degree (noun) *þriþiobyrþ* (OSw)

kinship traced through men (noun) *karlsvift* (ON)

kinship traced through women (noun) *kvensift* (ON)

kinsman (noun) *byrþ* (OSw), *byrþaman* (OSw), *frændi* (OSw), *frændsimi* (OSw), *kyn* (OSw), *magher* (OSw), *niþi* (OSw), *ættmaðr* (ON)

kinsman by marriage (noun) *magher* (OSw)

kinsman on the father's side (noun) *bauggildismaðr* (ON), *föðurfrændi* (ON)

kinsman on the male side (noun) *karlsviftarmaðr* (ON)

kinsman on the mother's side (noun) *móðurfrændi* (ON), *nefgildismaðr* (ON)

kinsman's inheritance (noun) *niþararf* (OSw)

kinsman's portion (noun) *afraþr* (OGu)

kinsman's share (noun) *ættarbot* (OSw)

kinsman's widow (noun) *frændleif* (ON)

kinsmen (noun) *samfrænde* (ODan)

kinsmen from another branch of the family (noun) *quislarmenn (pl.)* (OGu)

kinsmen's compensation (noun) *ættarbot* (OSw)

kinsmen's compensation of a man's compensation (noun) *ættarbot* (OSw)

kinswoman (noun) *frændkona* (OSw)

kin's compensation (noun) *ættarbot* (OSw)

kin's lot (noun) *byrþaluter* (OSw)

kirtle (noun) *kiurtil* (OSw)

kitchen (noun) *eldhus* (ODan), *stekarahus* (OSw)

kitchen door (noun) *eldhúshurð* (ON)

knee (body part) (noun) *kné* (ON)

knee timber on a ship (noun) *krapti* (ON)

knife (noun) *kniver* (OSw)

knife wound (noun) *knifslagh* (OSw)

knight (noun) *riddari* (OSw)

knocking down (noun) *felling* (ON)

know (verb) *vita* (OSw)

knowing (adj.) *vísvitandi* (ON)

knowingly (adv.) *ódulðr* (ON), *vitende* (ODan)

knowledge (noun) *vit* (OSw), *vita* (OSw)

known debt (noun) *vitafé* (ON)

known to be free (adj.) *friþviter* (OSw)

labour (noun) *arvuþi* (OSw), *barnfar* (OGu), *inne* (ODan), *sængför* (ON), *værk* (OSw), *værknaþer* (OSw)

labour lost (noun) *daghsværksspjal* (ODan)

labourer (noun) *forverksmaðr* (ON), *leghomaþer* (OSw)

labouring work (noun) *önnungsverk* (ON)

lack of care (noun) *bjargleysi* (ON)

lack of permission (noun) *olof* (OSw)

lacking in milk (adj.) *mielkstulin* (OGu)

lady of the house (noun) *husfrugha* (OSw)

lair (noun) *híð* (ON)

lake (noun) *sior* (OSw), *vatn* (ON)

lamb (noun) *lamb* (OSw)

land (noun) *aker* (OSw), *bo* (OSw), *bol* (OSw), *bolstaþer* (OSw), *egn* (OSw), *fang* (OSw), *gærþi* (OSw), *haghi* (OSw), *jorþ* (OSw), *land* (OSw), *landeign* (ON), *leigujörð* (ON), *luter* (OSw), *mark (3)* (OSw), *tompt* (OSw), *utlænde* (ODan), *vang* (ODan), *ægha* (OSw)

land (given to a church) (noun) *skötning* (OSw)

land allocated (to someone) (noun) *tompt* (OSw)

land apart (noun) *ornume* (ODan)

land around the house (noun) *husetoft* (ODan)

land benefit (noun) *landsnyt* (ON)

land bought specially (noun) *særkøp* (ODan)

land boundary (noun) *landamærki* (OSw)

land bringing/valued at/worth (a specified amount) in rent (noun) *laigi* (OGu)

land by a road (noun) *talaut* (OGu)

land challenge (noun) *jorþaklandan* (OSw)

land claim where there is a dependent (noun) *ómagalandsbrigð* (ON)

land claim where there is a right of pre-emption (noun) *málalandsbrigð* (ON)

land deal (noun) *landkaup* (ON)

land dispute (noun) *jorþadela* (OSw)

land dues (noun) *landaurar (pl.)* (ON)

land exchange (noun) *jorþaskifti* (OSw)

land for an ounce (noun) *öresland* (OSw)

land for sale (noun) *jorþaköp* (OSw)

land given in mortgage (noun) *málajörð* (ON)

land given to the church (noun) *kirkjestuv* (ODan)

land held as a grant (noun) *veizlujörð* (ON), *væzla* (OSw)

land held in pledge (noun) *festuaiga* (OGu)

land inheritance (noun) *landerfð* (ON)

land marked separately (noun) *kænneland* (ODan)

land of a man (noun) *eniorþ* (OSw)

land of a village (noun) *byamark* (OSw)

land of the church (noun) *kirkiuiorþ* (OSw)

land of the farm (noun) *aboliiorþ* (OSw)

land on lease (noun) *stefnujörð* (ON)

land on which the main house is (noun) *höfuðból* (ON)

land one ounce of worth (noun) *öresland* (OSw)

land outside the roping (noun) *ornume* (ODan)

land pledge (noun) *jorþapanter* (OSw)

land price (noun) *landsverð* (ON)

land purchase (noun) *jorþaköp* (OSw)

land ransom (noun) *jorþalösn* (OSw)

land rapine (noun) *jorþaran* (OSw)

land rent (noun) *jarðarleiga* (ON), *landgilde* (ODan), *landskyld* (OSw), *landslaigha* (OGu)

land section (noun) *jorþarbalker* (OSw)

land share (noun) *landshlutr* (ON)

land subject to a right of lawful pre-emption (noun) *lögmálaland* (ON)

land subject to pre-emption right (noun) *málajörð* (ON), *málaland* (ON)

land that has been offered (noun) *buþsiorþ* (OSw)

land theft (noun) *moldran* (OSw)

land thief (noun) *jarðarþjófr* (ON)

land value (noun) *jorþaværþ* (OSw), *landsverð* (ON)

land where military dues are not paid (noun) *qvarsæta* (OSw)

land which one buys (noun) *köpoiorþ* (OSw)

land-claim (noun) *landsbrigð* (ON)

land-claims section (noun) *landbrigðaþáttr* (ON)

land-division (noun) *jorthemal* (ODan)

land-sale (noun) *landsala* (ON)

land-valuing (noun) *landsvirðing* (ON)

landed property (noun) *egn* (OSw), *jorþ* (OSw), *jorþægha* (OSw), *land* (OSw)

landholding (noun) *jarðarhöfn* (ON), *utlænde* (ODan)

landing place (noun) *höfn* (ON)

landing-place toll (noun) *hafnartollr* (ON)

landlord (noun) *garðsbóndi* (ON), *landsdróttin* (ON)

landowner (noun) *athelbonde* (ODan), *bolstaþsmaþer* (OSw), *eghere* (ODan), *jorthdrotten* (ODan), *jorþeghandi* (OSw), *lanardroten* (OSw), *landeigandi* (ON), *oþalsmaþer* (OSw), *æghandi* (OSw)

landowning (adj.) *bolfaster* (OSw), *jorþeghandi* (OSw)

landowning man (noun) *athelbonde* (ODan), *bondeman* (ODan), *jorþeghandi* (OSw)

Land's End (noun) *landsendi* (ON)

language (noun) *mal (1)* (OSw), *tunga* (ON)

language of poetry (noun) *skáldskaparmál* (ON)

larger bone splinter (noun) *huaifibain* (OGu)

last rites (noun) *reþskaper* (OSw)

lasting injury (noun) *ørkuml* (ON)

late-month inheritance (noun) *senaþearf* (OSw)

later claimant (noun) *æptirmælandi* (OSw)

later Feast of St Olaf (3 August) (noun) *ólafsmessa hin øfri* (ON)

law (noun) *lagasetning* (ON), *lagh* (OSw), *laghbok* (OSw), *laghmæli* (OSw), *lýrittr* (ON), *rætter* (OSw), *skipan* (OSw), *skæl* (OSw)

law code (noun) *laghbok* (OSw)

Law Council (noun) *lögrétta* (ON)

Law Council money (noun) *lögréttufé* (ON)

law council section (noun) *lögréttuþáttr* (ON)

Law Council's funds (noun) *lögréttufé* (ON)

law district (noun) *lagh* (OSw)

law of captives (noun) *gislingalagh* (OSw)

law of householders (noun) *bondalagh* (OSw)

law of Roden (noun) *roþarætter* (OSw)

law of the country (noun) *landslagh* (OSw)

law of the king's peace (noun) *eþsörisrætter* (OSw)

law of the land (noun) *lagh* (OSw), *landslagh* (OSw)

law of the province (noun) *landslagh* (OSw)

law of the {roþer} (noun) *roþarætter* (OSw)

law of theft/thieves (noun) *þiufsrætter* (OSw)

law on whaling (noun) *hvalrétti* (ON)

law recital (noun) *uppsaga* (ON)

Law Rock (noun) *Lögberg* (ON)

law section (noun) *laghabalker* (OSw)

law-book (noun) *bok (1)* (OSw), *laghbok* (OSw)

law-paying man (noun) *uphaldsman* (ODan)

law-speaking (noun) *laghsagha* (OSw), *lögsögn* (ON)

law-stick (noun) *lagakefli* (ON)

lawbreaking (noun) *lagalöstr* (ON)

lawful (adj.) *lagha* (OSw), *laghliker* (OSw), *lögfullr* (ON), *rætter* (OSw), *saklös* (OSw), *sannligr* (ON)

lawful absence (noun) *forfall* (OSw)

lawful action (noun) *lagasókn* (ON), *sokn* (OSw)

lawful announcement (noun) *laghlysning* (OSw)

lawful case (noun) *laghmal* (OSw)

lawful claim (noun) *lagabeizla* (ON)

lawful compensation (noun) *lagabót* (ON)

lawful court (noun) *laghedom* (ODan)

lawful day (noun) *laghdagh* (ODan)

lawful day set by the assembly (noun) *laghdagh* (ODan)

lawful excuse (noun) *forfall* (OSw)

lawful extenuating circumstance (noun) *nöþsyn* (OSw)

lawful eyewitness (noun) *lögsjándi* (ON)

lawful fence (noun) *laghegarth* (ODan)

lawful fines (noun) *laghabötir (pl.)* (OSw)

lawful fold (noun) *lögrétt* (ON)

lawful for swearing oaths (adj.) *eþsört* (OSw)

lawful hindrance (noun) *nöþsyn* (OSw)

lawful husband (noun) *eiginmaðr* (ON)

lawful judgement (noun) *laghedom* (ODan), *skiladómr* (ON)

lawful length (noun) *löglengð* (ON)

lawful lien (noun) *skælatak* (OSw)

lawful mark (noun) *lögmark* (ON)

lawful master (noun) *skapdróttinn* (ON)

lawful money (noun) *lögeyrir* (ON)

lawful oath (noun) *lögeiðr* (ON)

lawful offer of compensation (noun) *lagaboð* (ON)

lawful owner (noun) *lagheeghere* (ODan)

lawful pledge (noun) *laghevæth* (ODan)

lawful possession (noun) *hæfþ* (OSw)

lawful prohibition (noun) *lögfesta* (ON)

lawful proof (noun) *lagh* (OSw)

lawful pursuit (noun) *laghdeling* (ODan)

lawful reporter (noun) *lögsegjandi* (ON)

lawful reward (noun) *laghegift* (ODan)

lawful roping (noun) *lagherep* (ODan)

lawful spouse (noun) *aþalman* (OSw)

lawful steelyard (noun) *lögpundari* (ON)

lawful summons (noun) *laghastæmna* (OSw)

lawful time (noun) *fræst* (OSw), *stæmna* (OSw)

lawful valuer (noun) *lögmetandi* (ON)

lawful viewer (noun) *lögsjándi* (ON)

lawful wife (noun) *aþalkona* (OSw), *eiginkona* (ON)

lawful witness (noun) *lögváttr* (ON)

lawful-married woman's child (noun) *aþalkonubarn* (OSw)

lawfully (adv.) *laghlika* (OSw), *rætlika* (OSw), *skælika* (OSw)

lawfully acceptable (adj.) *laggiertr* (OGu)

lawfully announced (adj.) *laghkallaþer* (OSw)

lawfully caught (adj.) *laghbundin* (OSw)

lawfully claim (verb) *laghvara* (OSw)

lawfully claimed (adj.) *laghtakin* (OSw)

lawfully convict (verb) *laghbinda* (OSw), *laghfylla* (OSw), *laghvinna* (OSw)

lawfully convicted (adj.) *laghfælder* (OSw)

lawfully defend (verb) *laghværje* (ODan)

lawfully dismissed (adj.) *laghfælder* (OSw)

lawfully divided (adj.) *laghskipter* (OSw)

lawfully entitled (adj.) *lögkominn* (ON)

lawfully floated (adj.) *réttfluttr* (ON)

lawfully married (adj.) *laghgifter* (OSw)

lawfully marry (verb) *laghgive* (ODan)

lawfully offer (verb) *laghbiuþa* (OSw)

lawfully proclaim (verb) *laghlysa* (OSw)

lawfully pronounced (adj.) *lögsamðr* (ON)

lawfully pursue (verb) *laghdele* (ODan)

lawfully relinquish (verb) *laghsighia* (OSw)

lawfully secure (verb) *lagreka* (OGu)

lawfully sue (verb) *dela* (OSw), *laghsökia* (OSw), *laghstæmna* (OSw)

lawfully summoned (adj.) *laghkallaþer* (OSw)

lawfully taken (adj.) *laghtakin* (OSw)

lawfully tell (verb) *laghvara* (OSw)

lawfully wedded (adj.) *laghgifter* (OSw), *skilfenginn* (ON)

lawfully wedded woman's child (noun) *aþalkonubarn* (OSw)

lawless (adj.) *rætløs* (ODan)

lawlessness (noun) *olagh* (OSw), *rætlösa* (OSw)

lawman (noun) *laghmaþer* (OSw)

lawmanship (noun) *laghmansdöme* (OSw)

lawman's jurisdiction (noun) *laghmansdöme* (OSw)

laws of land (noun) *jorþalagh* (OSw)

laws of the people (noun) *lýrittr* (ON)

laws of trading (noun) *köplagh* (OSw)

Lawspeaker (noun) *lögsögumaðr* (ON)

Lawspeakership (noun) *laghsagha* (OSw)

lawspeaker's section (noun) *lögsögumannsþáttr* (ON)

lawsuit (noun) *mal (1)* (OSw), *sak* (OSw)

lawsuit presented at the assembly (noun) *þingmál* (ON)

lay (adj.) *olerþr* (OGu)

lay a complaint (verb) *kæra* (OSw)

lay a legal claim (verb) *lagryþia* (OGu)

lay a trap (verb) *gildra* (OSw)

lay claim (verb) *illa* (OSw)

lay down (verb) *sætia* (OSw)

lay down a pledge (verb) *væþia* (OSw)

laying-up dues (noun) *uppsátseyrir* (ON)

layman (noun) *lekman* (OSw), *verelzmaþr* (OGu)

layperson's assembly (noun) *lekmannething* (ODan)

lead (verb) *leþa* (OSw)

lead into a kin (verb) *ætleþa* (OSw)

lead water (verb) *veta* (OSw)

leader (noun) *forman* (OSw), *höfþingi* (OSw), *hovoþsmaþer* (OSw)

learned (adj.) *lærder* (OSw)

lease (verb) *byggia* (OSw), *leghia* (OSw)

lease (noun) *legha* (OSw), *leghemal* (ODan), *mal (1)* (OSw), *stæmna* (OSw)

leased land (noun) *leigujörð* (ON)

leased thing (noun) *leghofæ* (OSw)

leash (noun) *band* (OSw)

leave (verb) *giefa* (OGu), *lata* (OSw), *loyfa* (OGu), *skilia* (OSw)

leave (noun) *lof* (OSw)

leave a household (verb) *skipta* (OSw)

leave blocked (verb) *aterlæggia* (OSw)

leave in custody (verb) *abyrghia* (OSw)

leave of the General Assembly (noun) *alþingislof* (ON)

leave to remain in the country (noun) *landsvist* (OSw)

leave to remain in the kingdom (noun) *landsvist* (OSw)

leave vacant (verb) *øthe* (ODan)

leaving too early (noun) *kaldakol* (ON)

led into a kin (adj.) *ætleder* (OSw)

leech money (noun) *lækærisfæ* (OSw)

leech's fee (noun) *lækirsgæf* (OSw)

left-over household stores (noun) *búsafleif* (ON)

legal (adj.) *gilder* (OSw), *lagha* (OSw), *laghliker* (OSw), *lögsamðr* (ON), *rætskyldigh* (ODan), *rætter* (OSw)

legal acquirement (noun) *fangaman* (OSw)

legal acquisition (noun) *fang* (OSw)

legal action (noun) *fjársókn* (ON)

legal administrator (noun) *lögráðandi* (ON)

legal age (noun) *laghealder* (ODan)

legal agreement (noun) *leghemal* (ODan)

legal amount in redemption (noun) *skælavæþ* (OSw)

legal amount of rent (noun) *lagaleiga* (ON)

legal asking (noun) *lögspurning* (ON)

legal assembly (noun) *laghþing* (OSw)

legal ban (noun) *lögfesta* (ON)

legal bargain (noun) *lagakaup* (ON)

legal betrothal (noun) *lögföstnun* (ON)

legal business (noun) *lögskil* (ON)

legal calling (noun) *lögkvöð* (ON)

legal case (noun) *laghmal* (OSw)

legal claim (noun) *laghakland* (OSw)

legal commune (noun) *löghreppr* (ON)

legal compensation (noun) *lagaréttr* (ON)

legal competance (noun) *réttendi* (ON)

legal debt-bondage (noun) *lögskuld* (ON)

legal decision (noun) *lagaórskurðr* (ON), *laghedom* (ODan), *lögsögn* (ON)

legal defence (noun) *dul* (OSw), *lögvörn* (ON)

legal deferral (noun) *lagafrest* (ON)

legal district (noun) *lagh* (OSw), *laghsagha* (OSw), *laghskila* (OSw)

legal division (noun) *lögskifti* (ON)

legal domicile (noun) *griðfang* (ON), *löggrið* (ON)

legal duties (noun) *lögskil* (ON)

legal examination of evidence (noun) *próf* (ON)

legal excuse (noun) *forfall* (OSw)

legal expert (noun) *laghmaþer* (OSw)

legal fast (noun) *lögfasta* (ON)

legal feast (noun) *ölstæmna* (OSw)

legal fee (noun) *lögkaup* (ON)

legal fencing (noun) *laghværn* (OSw)

legal fine (noun) *lagasekð* (ON)

legal form (noun) *skæl* (OSw)

legal form for building (noun) *bygþaskæl* (OSw)

legal formalities (noun) *fullskæl* (OSw), *lögskil* (ON)

legal formality (noun) *skæl* (OSw)

legal foster-son (noun) *lögfóstri* (ON)

legal fostering (noun) *lögfóstr* (ON)

legal gate (noun) *löggrind* (ON)

legal gateway (noun) *löghlið* (ON)

legal heir (noun) *lögarfi* (ON)

legal home (noun) *lögheimili* (ON)

legal information (noun) *lögfrétt* (ON)

legal investigation (noun) *ransak* (OSw)

legal judgement (noun) *laghedom* (ODan)

legal marriage day (noun) *bryllöpsdagher* (OSw)

legal meeting (noun) *laghastæmna* (OSw)

legal minor (noun) *omaghi* (OSw)

legal moving days (noun) *lögfardagar (pl.)* (ON)

legal oblation (noun) *lagagift* (ON)

legal offer (noun) *lögboð* (ON)

legal part (noun) *laghaloter* (OSw)

legal pay (noun) *lögkaup* (ON)

legal payment (noun) *lögfé* (ON)

legal pledge (noun) *laghevæth* (ODan)

legal procedure section (noun) *þingmalabalker* (OSw)

legal proceeding (noun) *skæl* (OSw)

legal proceedings (noun) *fjársókn* (ON)

legal proceedings before a district court (noun) *heraðssókn* (ON)

legal proceedings on holy days (noun) *heilagradagasókn* (ON) legal prosecution (noun) *laghasökning* (OSw)

legal protection (noun) *griþ* (OSw)

legal protection for five days (noun) *fimmtargrið* (ON)

legal provision (noun) *lagaskilorð* (ON)

legal publishing (noun) *löglýsing* (ON)

legal rate (noun) *laghgæld* (OSw)

legal rent (noun) *lögleiga* (ON)

legal request (noun) *lögbeiðing* (ON)

legal restitution (noun) *laghgæld* (OSw)

legal reward (noun) *vinningælogh* (OSw)

legal right (noun) *koster* (OSw), *rætmæli* (OSw)

legal right to something (noun) *hemuld* (OSw)

legal rights (noun) *rætter* (OSw)

legal sale of land (noun) *lagakaup* (ON)

legal seizure of a debtor's property (noun) *tilför* (ON)

legal separation (noun) *lögskilnuðr* (ON)

legal settling day (noun) *lögeindagi* (ON)

legal shutting in (noun) *lagainnsetning* (ON)

legal silver (noun) *lögsilfr* (ON)

legal stackyard (noun) *lögstakkgarðr* (ON)

legal sum (noun) *laghaskillinger* (OSw)

legal summons (noun) *laghastæmna* (OSw)

legal tender (noun) *lögeyrir* (ON)

legal thing assembly (noun) *laghþing* (OSw), *þing* (OSw)

legal time (noun) *fræst* (OSw)

legal time limit (noun) *laghastæmna* (OSw)

legal tithe (noun) *lögtíund* (ON)

legal title (noun) *hemuld* (OSw)

legal to provide an oath (adj.) *eþsört* (OSw)

legal trade (noun) *lagakaup* (ON)

legal valuation (noun) *lögmet* (ON)

legal veto (noun) *löglýrittr* (ON)

legal wall (noun) *laghegarth* (ODan)

legally (adv.) *laghlika* (OSw), *rætlika* (OSw), *skælika* (OSw)

legally acceptable reason (noun) *meinleiki* (ON)

legally acquired (land) (adj.) *laghfangen* (OSw)

legally address (verb) *laghmæla* (OSw)

legally announce (verb) *laghlysa* (OSw)

legally bid (verb) *laghbiuþa* (OSw)

legally convict (verb) *laghvinna* (OSw)

legally convicted (adj.) *laghfælder* (OSw)

legally decide (verb) *laghvinna* (OSw)

legally divide (verb) *laghskipta* (OSw)

legally inform (verb) *laghvara* (OSw)

legally judge (verb) *laghdöma* (OSw)

legally married (adj.) *laghgifter* (OSw), *mundgipt* (OSw)

legally married wife's child (noun) *aþalkonubarn* (OSw)

legally offer (verb) *laghbiuþa* (OSw)

legally offer to the kin (verb) *laghbiuþa* (OSw)

legally prosecute (verb) *laghsökia* (OSw)

legally purchased (adj.) *lagkauptr* (OGu)

legally qualified (adj.) *gilder* (OSw)

legally recognize (verb) *laghvinna* (OSw)

legally required (adj.) *lögskyldr* (ON)

legally resident (adj.) *lögfastr* (ON)

legally set (adj.) *laghstandin* (OSw), *lögsamðr* (ON)

legally stipulated (adv.) *rætlika* (OSw)

legally summon (verb) *laghstæmna* (OSw)

legally summoned (adj.) *laghkallaþer* (OSw)

legally valid (adj.) *laghstandin* (OSw)

legislation (noun) *lagh* (OSw), *laghsagha* (OSw)

legitimate (adj.) *aþal* (OSw), *hemul* (OSw), *laghliker* (OSw), *sander* (OSw), *skilfenginn* (ON), *skilgetinn* (ON), *skírborinn* (ON), *skírgetinn* (ON), *ætborin* (OSw)

legitimate child (noun) *athelbarn* (ODan), *aþalkonubarn* (OSw)

legitimate necessity (noun) *nöþsyn* (OSw)

legitimate offspring (noun) *aþalkonubarn* (OSw)

legitimate reason (noun) *nöþsyn* (OSw)

legitimate son (noun) *aþalkonusun* (OSw)

legitimation (noun) *ættleiðing* (ON)

legitimized child (noun) *skötsætubarn* (OSw)

lend (verb) *lana* (OSw), *læa* (OSw), *sælia* (OSw)

lender (noun) *læande* (OSw)

Lent (noun) *fasta* (OSw), *fastudagher* (OSw), *langafasta* (ON)

lent property (noun) *lánfé* (ON)

leprous (adj.) *líkþrár* (ON)

lesser ban (noun) *forbuþ* (OSw)

lesser outlaw (noun) *fjörbaugsmaðr* (ON)

lesser outlawry (noun) *fjörbaugsgarðr* (ON), *fjörbaugssekð* (ON)

lesser outlawry case (noun) *fjörbaugssök* (ON)

lesser outlawry offence (noun) *fjörbaugssök* (ON)

let (verb) *lata* (OSw), *rætta* (OSw)

let go (verb) *slæppa* (OSw)

let in peace (verb) *friþa* (OSw)

let out (verb) *byggia* (OSw)

let perish (verb) *spilla* (OSw)

lethal wound (noun) *bani* (OSw), *bæn* (OSw), *fiorlæsting* (OSw)

letter (noun) *bref* (OSw)

letter fee (noun) *brevafæ* (OSw)

letter requesting the provision of horses for transport (noun) *skiutabref* (OSw)

letter-writing (noun) *bréfagerð* (ON)

letting the hearth fire go out (noun) *kaldakol* (ON)

levelling oath (noun) *jamnaþareþer* (OSw)

levy (noun) *leþunger* (OSw)

levy census assembly (noun) *manntalsþing* (ON)

levy district (noun) *manngerð* (ON), *skipsýsla* (ON)

levy district assembly (noun) *skipreiðuþing* (ON)

levy duty (noun) *leþunger* (OSw)

levy expedition duty (noun) *leiðangrsferð* (ON)

levy fine (noun) *leiðangrsvíti* (ON)

levy journey (noun) *leiðangrsfar* (ON)

levy preparation duty (noun) *leiðangrsgerð* (ON)

levy provisions (noun) *leiðangrsfé* (ON), *leiðangrsvist* (ON)

levy ship (noun) *leiðangrsskip* (ON)

levy tax (noun) *leþungslami* (OSw)

liability (noun) *óskuld* (ON), *sak* (OSw)

liable (adj.) *saker* (OSw), *skyldugher* (OSw)

liable at law (adj.) *saknæmr* (ON)

liable to (pay) (adj.) *saker* (OSw)

liable to a fine (adj.) *víttr* (ON)

liable to compensate (adj.) *saker* (OSw)

liable to pay (adj.) *saker* (OSw)

liable to pay compensation or a fine (adj.) *saker* (OSw)

liable to pay double (adj.) *tvæskylder* (OSw)

liable to tax (adj.) *skatskyldugher* (OSw)

liar (noun) *liughari* (OSw)

libel by carving on a tree (noun) *tréníð* (ON)

libel by word of mouth (noun) *tunguníð* (ON)

liberty (noun) *frælsi* (OSw)

licence (noun) *lof* (OSw), *loyfi* (OGu)

licence for mitigation of penalty (noun) *syknuleyfi* (ON)

licence for settlement (noun) *sáttaleyfi* (ON)

lie (noun) *lygð* (ON)

lie (1) (verb) *liggia* (OSw)

lie (2) (verb) *forligje* (ODan)

lie (3) (verb) *liugha* (OSw)

lie with (verb) *hæfþa* (OSw)

liege lord (noun) *lanardroten* (OSw)

liegeman (noun) *þiænistumaþer* (OSw)

lien (noun) *qvarstaþa* (OSw), *qvarsæta* (OSw), *qvarsætutak* (OSw), *tak* (OSw), *væþ* (OSw)

life (noun) *hals* (OSw), *lif* (OSw), *önd* (ON)

life ring (noun) *fjörbaugr* (ON)

life-threatening wound (noun) *liflat* (OSw)

lift (verb) *halda* (OSw), *sla* (OSw)

light toll (noun) *lýsistollr* (ON)

limb (noun) *limber* (OSw)

limit (noun) *takmark* (ON)

line (of inheritance) (noun) *luter* (OSw)

lineage (noun) *byrþ* (OSw), *æt* (OSw)

linen (noun) *læript* (OSw)

linen cloth (noun) *læript* (OSw)

linen tax (noun) *rýgjartó* (ON)

link (verb) *binda* (OSw)

link (noun) *stelkr* (OGu)

lintel (noun) *ofdyri* (ON), *uppdyri* (ON)

lips twitching (in pain) (noun) *granbragð* (ON)

liquid (noun) *væta* (ON)

lispound (noun) *lifspund* (OSw), *pund* (OSw)

list (verb) *skilia* (OSw), *telja* (ON)

listen to confessions (verb) *skripta* (OSw)

listening guard (noun) *lyznuvarþer* (OSw)

liturgical service (noun) *tiþir (pl.)* (OSw)

live (verb) *búa* (ON)

livestock (noun) *bofæ* (ODan), *fæ* (OSw), *fælaþi* (OSw), *fænaþer* (OSw), *ganganzfoter* (OSw), *ganganzfæ* (OSw), *not* (OSw), *qvikfæ* (OSw), *viðrelði* (ON)

livestock born at home (noun) *hemföþa* (OSw)

livestock brand (noun) *bokumbel* (OSw)

livestock quota (noun) *qvikfæ* (OSw)

livestock rustling (noun) *bosran* (OSw)

livestock taking (noun) *bosbrigþ* (OSw)

livestock tithe (noun) *qviktiundi* (OSw)

living (adj.) *qvikker* (OSw)

living chattel (noun) *qvikfæ* (OSw)

living house (noun) *salhus* (ODan)

living in the same country (adj.) *samlendr* (ON)

living tithe (noun) *qviktiundi* (OSw)

load (verb) *skipa* (OSw)

load (noun) *lass* (OSw)

load from a field (noun) *akerlas* (OSw)

loading a ship (noun) *skipan* (OSw)

loan (verb) *læa* (OSw)

loan (noun) *lan* (OSw)

loan of valuables (noun) *gripalán* (ON)

loan witness (noun) *lansvitni* (OSw)

local administrator (noun) *husabyman* (OSw), *lænsmaþer* (OSw)

local assembly (noun) *malþing* (OSw)

local calling (noun) *heimankvöð* (ON)

local man (noun) *hæraþsmaþer* (OSw)

location where a deal was concluded (noun) *kaupreina* (ON)

lock (noun) *las* (OSw)

locking-up (noun) *hæfta* (OSw)

lodge (verb) *gæsta* (OSw)

lodge an appeal (verb) *væþia* (OSw)

lodger (noun) *hussætumaþer* (OSw)

lodgers (noun) *hussætisfolk* (ÓSw)

lodging (noun) *griþ* (OSw), *gæstning* (OSw), *vist* (OSw)

lodging in a commune (noun) *hreppsvist* (ON)

log trap (noun) *stampa* (OSw)

loin (noun) *lend* (OGu)

loitering (noun) *þarseta* (ON)

lone farmer (noun) *einvirki* (ON)

long log (noun) *langviðr* (ON)

long-standing possession (noun) *minnung* (OSw)

longship (noun) *langskip* (ON), *snækkia* (OSw)

look (verb) *sea* (OSw)

look (intransitive) (verb) *syna* (OSw)

look after (verb) *göma* (OSw), *gæta* (ON), *sýsla* (ON), *varþveta* (OSw)

loose (adj.) *lös* (OSw)

loose boards in the stable (noun) *flórfili* (ON)

loose talk (noun) *hægume* (ODan)

loosely girded (adj.) *lösgiurþer* (OSw)

lord (noun) *drotin* (OGu), *höfþingi* (OSw), *hærra* (OSw), *junkhærre* (ODan), *lanardroten* (OSw), *lavarþer* (OSw)

lord of the land/province (noun) *landshærra* (OSw)

lord or master (noun) *hærra* (OSw)

lord-cheater (noun) *dróttinssvikari* (ON)

lordsman (noun) *hærraman* (OSw), *konungsman* (OSw)

lose (verb) *forhæghthe* (ODan), *fyrirskjóta* (ON), *lata* (OSw), *spilla* (OSw), *viþerhætta* (OSw)

lose (e.g. a case) (verb) *fyrirtaka* (ON)

lose a right (verb) *óheimila* (ON)

lose one's peace (adj.) *friþlösa* (OSw)

lose one's right (verb) *skilia* (OSw)

lose title (verb) *óheimila* (ON)

lose track (verb) *villa* (ON)

lose warranty (verb) *óheimila* (ON)

loss (noun) *afvöxtr* (ON), *fjárskaði* (ON), *lat* (OSw), *skaþi* (OSw), *spellvirki* (ON)

loss of kinsmen (noun) *frændatjón* (ON)

loss of life (noun) *liflat* (OSw), *liftapilse* (OSw)

loss of milk (noun) *nytfall* (ON)

loss of money (noun) *fjárskaði* (ON)

loss of use (noun) *verkafall* (ON)

loss of work (noun) *verkatjón* (ON)

lost labour (noun) *daghsværksspjal* (ODan)

lost one's senses (adj.) *afvita* (OSw)

lost property (noun) *affarefæ* (ODan), *fynd* (OSw)

lot (noun) *lotfal* (ODan), *luter* (OSw), *raþ* (OSw), *rætter* (OSw)

lot baton (noun) *lotkafli* (OSw)

lot in a household (noun) *bosloter* (OSw)

lot in property through the birth of a child (noun) *barnmynd* (ODan)

love-verse (noun) *mansöngr* (ON)

low estimate (noun) *vantala* (ON)

loyalty of slave to master (noun) *þyrmsl* (ON)

lying in water (noun) *søkkr* (ON)

lying with a woman (noun) *læghervite* (ODan)

mad (adj.) *galin* (OSw), *óðr* (ON)

made-up mark (noun) *gerðarmark* (ON)

madman (noun) *villinger* (OSw), *vitvillinger* (OSw)

madness (noun) *óði* (ON)

magic (noun) *fjölkynngi* (ON)

magistrate (noun) *laghmaþer* (OSw), *raþman* (OSw)

maid (noun) *mö* (OSw)

maiden (noun) *frændmø* (ODan), *mö* (OSw)

maim (verb) *lyte* (ODan), *læsta* (OSw), *meiða* (ON), *styva* (OSw)

maimed (adj.) *lytter* (OSw)

maiming (noun) *afhug* (OSw), *laster* (OSw), *limalyti* (OGu), *lyti* (OSw), *meiðing* (ON)

maiming by wounding (noun) *sarlyte* (ODan)

maiming compensation (noun) *lytisbot* (OSw)

maiming wound (noun) *lytessar* (ODan)

maiming-fine (noun) *lytisbot* (OSw)

main case (noun) *hovethsak* (ODan)

main church (noun) *höfuðkirkja* (ON)

main claim (noun) *hovethsak* (ODan)

main doorway (noun) *karldyrr* (ON)

main estate (noun) *aðalból* (ON)

main priest (noun) *höfuðprestr* (ON)

main ring (noun) *höfuðbaugr* (ON)

main road (noun) *athelvægh* (ODan), *landsvægher* (OSw)

main sum (noun) *innstóða* (ON)

main village (noun) *athelby* (ODan)

main-tithe (noun) *hovoþtiundi* (OSw)

maintain (verb) *gæta* (ON), *halda* (OSw)

maintenance (noun) *forlag* (ON), *forlagseyrir* (ON), *foster* (OSw), *föþa* (OSw), *framförsla* (ON), *fulga* (ON), *koster* (OSw)

maintenance case (noun) *ómagasök* (ON)

maintenance for the poor (noun) *elði* (ON)

maintenance money (noun) *forlagseyrir* (ON)

maintenance of bridges (noun) *brúarhald* (ON)

maintenance of dependents (noun) *ómagaframförsla* (ON)

maintenance of ferries (noun) *ferjuhald* (ON)

maintenance of incapable people (noun) *ómagaframförsla* (ON)

major debt (noun) *stórskuld* (ON)

majority (noun) *afl* (ON), *skæl* (OSw), *vit* (OSw)

make (verb) *skapa* (ON)

make a claim (verb) *ámálga* (ON), *kalla* (OSw), *kæra* (OSw), *mæla (1)* (OSw), *sækta* (OSw)

make a complaint (verb) *illa* (OSw), *kæra* (OSw), *reyna* (ON)

make a deal (verb) *köpa* (OSw)

make a declaration (verb) *lysa* (OSw), *næmna* (OSw)

make a demand (verb) *klanda* (OSw)

make a division (verb) *skipta* (OSw)

make a fence (verb) *gærþa* (OSw)

make a guarantee (verb) *borgha* (OSw)

make a house-search (verb) *ransaka* (OSw)

make a judgement (verb) *döma* (OSw)

make a partnership (verb) *bolæggia* (OSw)

make a profit (verb) *öxla* (ON)

make a public declaration (verb) *lysa* (OSw)

make a purchase (verb) *köpa* (OSw)

make a return (verb) *löna* (OSw)

make a security (verb) *borgha* (OSw)

make a seizure (verb) *næma* (OSw)

make a tenth (verb) *tiunda* (OSw)

make a valuation (verb) *virþa* (OSw)

make amends (verb) *aflæggia* (OSw), *rætta* (OSw)

make an accusation (verb) *kæra* (OSw)

make an admission (verb) *viþerkænnas* (OSw)

make an agreement (verb) *skilia* (OSw)

make an agreement on partnership (verb) *bolæggia* (OSw)

make an appeal (verb) *væþia* (OSw)

make an exchange (verb) *skipta* (OSw)

make an oath (verb) *sværia* (OSw), *æptirganga* (OSw)

make an offer (verb) *tilbiuþa* (OSw)

make at fault (verb) *fælla* (OSw)

make charges (verb) *kæra* (OSw)

make clear (verb) *skæra (1)* (OSw), *skærskuta* (OSw)

make defence (verb) *væria* (OSw)

make demands (verb) *abeþas* (OSw)

make demands of (verb) *qvælia* (OSw)

make enquiries (verb) *refla* (ON)

make equal (verb) *jamna* (OSw)

make even (verb) *jamna* (OSw), *reþa* (OSw)

make good (verb) *aterfylla* (OSw), *böta* (OSw), *fylla* (OSw), *gælda (1)* (OSw)

make invalid (verb) *fælla* (OSw)

make known (verb) *lysa* (OSw)

make one a bounden debtor (verb) *skuldfesta* (ON)

make one legally immune (verb) *friðhelga* (ON)

make oneself a thief (verb) *þiuftas* (OSw)

make oneself guilty (verb) *sækia* (OSw)

make oneself liable to compensation (verb) *sækia* (OSw)

make public (verb) *lysa* (OSw), *skærskuta* (OSw), *thingljuse* (ODan)

make public at church (verb) *kirkjelyse* (ODan)

make public at the assembly (verb) *lysa* (OSw), *thingljuse* (ODan)

make redress (verb) *leiðrétta* (ON)

make reparation (verb) *gælda (1)* (OSw)

make repayment (verb) *aterlösa* (OSw)

make restitution (verb) *atergælda* (OSw)

make roads good (verb) *broa* (OSw)

make someone liable to pay a compensation (verb) *sækia* (OSw)

make up the difference (verb) *böta* (OSw)

make use of (verb) *fénýta* (ON)

making even between children (verb) *børnevirthning* (ODan)

male (noun) *kerldi* (OGu)

male (adj.) *lindagyrt* (OGu)

male first cousin (noun) *bröþrungi* (OSw)

male first cousins (noun) *bróðrabarn (pl.)* (ON), *bróðrasynir (pl.)* (ON), *systkinasynir (pl.)* (ON), *systrasynir (pl.)* (ON)

male in-law (noun) *svær* (OSw)

male side (noun) *höfuðbarmr* (ON), *karlsvift* (ON)

malefactor (noun) *illgærningisman* (OSw)

malice (noun) *avund* (OSw), *illgirni* (ON), *ilvilje* (ODan) malicious (adj.) *illaviliaþer* (OSw)

malicious blood (noun) *öfundarblóð* (ON)

malicious damage (noun) *illvirki* (ON), *spellvirki* (ON)

malicious speech (noun) *illmæli* (ON)

malt (noun) *malt* (ON)

maltreat (verb) *fyrma (2)* (OSw)

maltreatment (noun) *mishælde* (ODan)

man (verb) *skipa* (OSw)

man (noun) *bonde* (OSw), *husbonde* (OSw), *karl* (OSw), *kerldi* (OGu), *landsmaþer* (OSw), *maþer* (OSw), *sven* (OSw), *þægn* (OSw)

man and wife (noun) *hion* (OSw), *hjú* (ON)

man appointed by the court (noun) *nefndarvitni* (ON)

man asserting a claim (noun) *brigðandi* (ON)

man at a feast (noun) *ölbuþsman* (OSw)

man authorized to give away a woman (noun) *giftarmaþer* (OSw)

man belonging to a {fylki} (noun) *fylkismaðr* (ON)

man belonging to the assembly district (noun) *þingsóknarmaðr* (ON)

man belonging to the same law district (noun) *lögunautr* (ON)

man better than his father (noun) *betrfeðrungr* (ON)

man bringing the case (noun) *soknari* (OSw)

man bringing the suit (noun) *sökiandi* (OSw)

man enjoying the same rights as anybody else (noun) *jafnréttismaðr* (ON)

man entitled to a quarter (noun) *fiærþungsmaþer* (OSw)

man entitled to half compensation (noun) *halfréttismaðr* (ON)

man expecting an inheritance (noun) *vánarmaðr* (ON)

man from inside the commune (noun) *innanhreppsmaðr* (ON)

man from Norway (noun) *noregsmaðr* (ON)

man from outside the district (noun) *útansveitarmaðr* (ON)

man from outside the province (noun) *utlændinger* (OSw)

man from overseas (noun) *austmaðr* (ON)

man from the province (noun) *landsmaþer* (OSw)

man from the provinces (noun) *inlændinger* (OSw)

man from the realm (noun) *innankonungsrikismaþer* (OSw)

man having a right to odal (noun) *oþalsmaþer* (OSw)

man holding the victim (noun) *haldbani* (OSw)

man in a panel (noun) *næmdarmaþer* (OSw)

man in an oath (noun) *istaþamaþer* (OSw)

man in authority (noun) *ríkismaðr* (ON)

man in charge (noun) *forræðismaðr* (ON)

man in disguise (noun) *grimumaþer* (OSw)

man in possession (noun) *haldandi* (ON)

man in service (noun) *þiænistumaþer* (OSw)

man in state of mercy towards another (noun) *miskunnarmaþer* (OSw)

man in the stem of a ship (noun) *stamboi* (OSw)

man knowledgeable in genealogies (noun) *taluman* (OSw)

man of a different assembly (noun) *útanþingsmaðr* (ON)

man of a parish (noun) *kirkjeman* (ODan)

man of a province (noun) *landi* (OSw)

man of a quarter (noun) *fiærþungsmaþer* (OSw)

man of a village (noun) *byaman* (OSw)

man of a {næmd} (noun) *næmdarmaþer* (OSw)

man of alms (noun) *almosomaþer* (OSw)

man of an assembly third (noun) *þriðjungsmaðr* (ON)

man of authority (noun) *valdsmaþer* (OSw)

man of half personal right (noun) *halfréttismaðr* (ON)

man of oath (noun) *vatter* (OSw)

man of peace (noun) *spekðarmaðr* (ON)

man of the area (noun) *nagranni* (OSw)

man of the commune (noun) *hreppsmaðr* (ON)

man of the country (noun) *landsmaþer* (OSw)

man of the county (noun) *fylkismaðr* (ON)

man of the district (noun) *hreppsmaðr* (ON), *hæraþsmaþer* (OSw), *innanheraðsmaðr* (ON), *þingunöti* (OSw)

man of the king's guard (noun) *hirþman* (OSw)

man of the land (noun) *landsmaþer* (OSw)

man of the Law Council (noun) *lögréttumaðr* (ON)

man of the levy (noun) *leiðangrsmaðr* (ON)

man of the parish (noun) *soknamaþer* (OSw)

man of the province (noun) *inlændinger* (OSw)

man of the quarter (noun) *fiærþungsmaþer* (OSw)

man of the riding (noun) *þriðjungsmaðr* (ON)

man of the same assembly (noun) *innanþingsmaðr* (ON), *þingunöti* (OSw)

man of the Third (noun) *þriðjungsmaðr* (ON)

man of the turf (noun) *torfsmaðr* (ON)

man of the village (noun) *granni* (OSw)

man of truth (noun) *sannendeeth* (ODan), *sannind* (OSw), *sannindaman* (OSw)

man on a ship (noun) *skipari* (OSw)

man preceding or following across generations (noun) *afi* (ON)

man present at the deed (noun) *atvistarmaþer* (OSw)

man sitting close to another (noun) *násessi* (ON)

man subject to church penalty (noun) *skriptaman* (OSw)

man to receive (noun) *tækiomaþer* (OSw)

man to sum up a case (noun) *reifingarmaðr* (ON)

man to vouch (noun) *sannindaman* (OSw)

man who falsely boasts of having dishonoured a woman (noun) *snápr* (ON)

man who formally agreed to accept a settlement (noun) *handsalsmaðr* (ON)

man who has been counted or enumerated (noun) *tölumaðr* (ON)

man who has been pledged security (noun) *tryggðamaðr* (ON)

man who has broken into the church (noun) *kirkiubrytare* (OSw)

man who has care of others' property (noun) *fjárvarðveizlumaðr* (ON)

man who has care of the property (noun) *fjárhaldsmaðr* (ON)

man who has had a church penance imposed (noun) *skriptaman* (OSw)

man who holds the title (noun) *hemulsman* (OSw)

man who owns grazing (noun) *beitarmaðr* (ON)

man who sets up on his own (noun) *sjalfsfózlumaðr* (ON)

man who shares the ring payment (noun) *baugamaðr* (ON)

man who swears first (noun) *foreþismaþer* (OSw)

man who visits harlots (noun) *portkunumaþer* (OSw)

man who visits whores (noun) *putomaþer* (OSw)

man who works for his living (noun) *matlaunarmaðr* (ON)

man who works for his meals (noun) *matlaunarmaðr* (ON)

man with (beggar's) staff (noun) *stafkarl* (OSw)

man with a fixed residence (noun) *setumaðr* (ON)

man with a legal right to atone by paying compensation (noun) *bótamaðr* (ON)

man within the quarter (noun) *innanfjórðungsmaðr* (ON)

man without property (noun) *oreghthman* (ODan)

man-made harm (noun) *handaværk* (OSw)

man-servant (noun) *húskarl* (ON)

manage (verb) *raþa* (OSw), *varþveta* (OSw), *vinna* (OSw), *væria* (OSw)

management (noun) *forráð* (ON)

manager (noun) *fjárhaldsmaðr* (ON)

managing a farm (noun) *búrekstr* (ON)

managing pasture for dry stock (noun) *geldfjárrekstr* (ON)

maneater (noun) *mannæta* (ON)

manhandle (verb) *nykkia* (OGu)

manifest (adj.) *openbar* (OSw)

manipulation (noun) *handaværk* (OSw)

manner (noun) *koster* (OSw), *skæl* (OSw)

manor (noun) *bo* (OSw), *garþer* (OSw)

manslaughter (noun) *döþsdrap* (OSw), *drap* (OSw), *mandrap* (OSw)

manslaughter assembly (noun) *manndrápsþing* (ON)

manslaughter/homicide (noun) *vigh* (OSw)

manslayer (noun) *mandrapare* (OSw)

manumission of a slave (noun) *frelsisgjöf* (ON)

manure (noun) *taðfall* (ON)

man's compensation (noun) *manbot* (OSw)

man's fine (noun) *manbot* (OSw)

man's measure (noun) *karlaskr* (ON)

man's personal peace (noun) *manhælghi* (OSw)

man's work (noun) *mannsverk* (ON)

mare (noun) *merr* (ON), *skiut* (OSw)

marital bed (noun) *siængalæghi* (OSw)

marital co-ownership (noun) *fælagh* (OSw)

marital intercourse (noun) *hionalagh* (OSw)

maritime law (noun) *farlög* (ON), *farmannalög* (ON)

mark (verb) *einkynna* (ON), *marka* (ON), *merkia* (OGu)

mark (noun) *akoma* (OSw), *asyn* (OSw), *mærki* (OSw)

mark (a unit of the weight and monetary system) (noun) *mark (2)* (OSw)

mark (of ownership) (noun) *mark (1)* (ON)

mark of a slave (noun) *þrælsmark* (ODan)

mark of repentance (noun) *iðranarmark* (ON)

mark of violence (noun) *handaværk* (OSw)

mark with a cross (verb) *primsigna* (OSw)

markbrand (noun) *mærki* (OSw)

marked boundary (noun) *markrá* (ON)

market (noun) *kaupstefna* (ON), *torgh* (OSw)

market peace (noun) *köpþingafriþer* (OSw)

market square (noun) *torgh* (OSw)

market town (noun) *köpstaþer* (OSw), *köpunger* (OSw)

market town-dweller (noun) *köpstaþsman* (OSw)

marketplace (noun) *köpunger* (OSw), *torgh* (OSw)

marks of violence (noun) *handaværk* (OSw)

marriage (noun) *eiginorð* (ON), *gift* (OSw), *gifta* (OSw), *giftarmal* (OSw), *giftarorþ* (OSw), *giftasæng* (OSw), *giptning* (OSw), *hionafælagh*

(OSw), *hionalagh* (OSw), *hionavighning* (OSw), *hjúskaparráð* (ON), *hjúskapr* (ON), *hæskaper* (OSw), *kvánfang* (ON), *vigsl* (OSw)

marriage agent (noun) *giftarmaþer* (OSw)

marriage bed (noun) *giftasæng* (OSw)

marriage beer (noun) *giftaröl* (OSw)

marriage ceremony (noun) *giftarmal* (OSw)

marriage contract (noun) *hionalagh* (OSw)

marriage gift (noun) *hemfylghþ* (OSw), *hemgæf* (OSw)

marriage guardian (noun) *giftarmaþer* (OSw)

marriage man (noun) *giftarmaþer* (OSw)

marriage oath (noun) *giptareþer* (OSw)

marriage of women (noun) *kvennagifting* (ON)

marriage portion (noun) *fylghia* (OSw), *hemfylghþ* (OSw), *mæþfylghþ* (OSw)

marriage relations (noun) *mægð* (ON)

marriage section (noun) *giptarbalker* (OSw)

marriage union (noun) *hionalagh* (OSw)

married (adj.) *frangipter* (OSw), *gifter* (OSw)

married couple (noun) *hion* (OSw), *hionalagh* (OSw), *hjú* (ON)

married state (noun) *ráðahagr* (ON)

marrow wound (noun) *mergund* (ON)

marry (verb) *fæsta* (OSw), *gifta* (OSw), *hjones* (ODan), *kvánga* (ON), *kvænes* (ODan), *manne* (ODan), *samne* (ODan), *stæþia* (OSw), *vighia* (OSw)

marry away (verb) *gifta* (OSw)

marry off (verb) *gifta* (OSw)

marshal (noun) *stallari* (OSw)

marshland (noun) *kelda* (ON), *myr* (OGu)

Martinmas (11 November) (noun) *martinsmæssa* (OSw)

mask oath (noun) *grímueiðr* (ON)

mass (noun) *sialamæssa* (OSw), *tiþir (pl.)* (OSw), *æmbæte* (ODan), *þiænista* (OSw)

mass chant (noun) *messusöngr* (ON)

mass for the dead (noun) *sialamæssa* (OSw), *tiþaköp* (OSw)

mass vessels and vestments (noun) *mæssuskruþer* (OSw)

mass vestments (noun) *mæssuklæþi* (OSw)

mass-day (noun) *messudagr* (ON)

mass-priest (noun) *messuprestr* (ON)

mast (noun) *tré* (ON)

master (noun) *bonde* (OSw), *drotin* (OGu), *husbonde* (OSw), *hærra* (OSw), *lanardroten* (OSw), *skapdróttinn* (ON)

master of a house (noun) *husbonde* (OSw)

master of the feast (noun) *gerþamaþr* (OGu)

maternal (adj.) *möþerni* (OSw)

maternal cousin (noun) *systrunger* (OSw)

maternal goods (noun) *möþerni* (OSw)

maternal inheritance (noun) *möþerni* (OSw), *qvinnaarf* (OSw)

maternal kin (noun) *móðurætt* (ON), *möþerni* (OSw)

maternal kinsmen (noun) *móðurfrændi* (ON)

maternal land (noun) *möþerni* (OSw)

maternal part (noun) *möþerni* (OSw)

maternal side (noun) *möþerni* (OSw)

matrimony (noun) *giftarmal* (OSw), *hionalagh* (OSw), *hjúskapr* (ON)

matron of honour (noun) *brudsæta* (OSw), *bruþframma* (OSw), *bruþtugha* (OSw)

matter (noun) *ensak* (OSw), *mal (1)* (OSw), *sak* (OSw)

matter of conflict (noun) *dailumal* (OGu)

mature (adj.) *maghandi* (OSw)

Maundy Thursday (noun) *skærdagher* (OSw), *skærþorsdagher* (OSw)

meadow (noun) *æng* (OSw)

meadow barn (noun) *ængialaþa* (OSw)

meadow boundaries (noun) *engimark* (ON)

meadow bounds (noun) *engimark* (ON)

meadow plot (noun) *deld* (OSw)

meadowland (noun) *engiteigr* (ON), *æng* (OSw)

meadowland boundary mark (noun) *engjamerki* (ON)

meadowland claim (noun) *engjabrigð* (ON)

meadowland court (noun) *engidómr* (ON)

meadowland division (noun) *engiskiftisbúi* (ON)

meal (noun) *málsmatr* (ON), *mjöl* (ON)

mean (verb) *vilia* (OSw)

means (noun) *fang* (OSw), *fjárhlutr* (ON), *fæ* (OSw), *föri* (ON), *mun* (ODan)

means for acquittal (noun) *undanförsla* (ON)

means of livelihood (noun) *atvinna* (ON)

means of subsistence (noun) *forlagseyrir* (ON)

means to pay (noun) *örkostr* (ON)

means to pay fines (noun) *bot* (OSw)

means to support (noun) *björg* (ON)

measure (verb) *mæla (2)* (OSw), *mæta* (OSw)

measure (noun) *mælir* (ON), *spander* (OSw)

measure and divide land with ropes (verb) *repa* (OSw)

measure by rod (verb) *stika* (ON)

measure men (noun) *mætsmæn (pl.)* (OSw)

measure of capacity, ca. 1/2 bushel (noun) *mælir* (ON)

measure of malt (noun) *reykmælir* (ON)

measured in burnt silver (adj.) *silfrmetinn* (ON)

measurement (noun) *mal (2)* (OSw)

measurement (with a line) (noun) *taumburðr* (ON)

measurers (noun) *mætsmæn (pl.)* (OSw)

measuring (noun) *mal (2)* (OSw)

measuring men (noun) *mætsmæn (pl.)* (OSw)

measuring of land with a rope (noun) *álburðr* (ON)

measuring pole (noun) *mælistang* (OSw)

measuring vessel (noun) *mælikerald* (ON)

measuring with rope (noun) *rep* (ODan)

measuring with the eye (noun) *augnaskot* (ON)

mediator (i.e. one who makes good) (noun) *seter* (OGu)

medical expenses (noun) *lækirsgæf* (OSw)

medical treatment (noun) *lekisskepr* (OGu)

meeting (noun) *fynd* (OSw), *stæmna* (OSw), *þing* (OSw)

meeting about providing horses (noun) *reiðskjótaskifti* (ON)

meeting date (noun) *stæmnudagher* (OSw)

meeting for payment (noun) *aurastefna* (ON)

meeting for the kinsmen (noun) *frændstævne* (ODan)

meeting member (noun) *samkvámumaðr* (ON)

meeting men (noun) *stæmnumæn (pl.)* (OSw)

meeting of betrothal (noun) *fæstnaþarstæmna* (OSw)

meeting of neighbours (noun) *grannestævne* (ODan)

meeting of the Thing assembly (noun) *þingariþ* (OSw)

meeting on the autumn assembly site (noun) *leið* (ON)

meeting with a bishop (noun) *byskupsfundr* (ON)

meeting-farm (noun) *stefnubýr* (ON)

meeting-message (noun) *stefnuboð* (ON)

member of a church (noun) *kirkjusóknarmaðr* (ON)

member of a court (noun) *dómandi* (ON)

member of a household (noun) *hion* (OSw)

member of a jurisdiction (noun) *lögunautr* (ON)

member of a meeting-party (noun) *stefnulið* (ON)

member of the General Assembly (noun) *alþingismaðr* (ON)

member of the ship's company (noun) *hasæti* (OSw)

member of the Thing assembly (noun) *þingunöti* (OSw)

members of the assembly (noun) *þingsmæn (pl.)* (OSw)

membrane (noun) *hinna* (OGu)

men at peace (noun) *friðmenn (pl.)* (ON)

men belonging to the same law district (noun) *samþingendr (pl.)* (ON)

men belonging to the same levy district (noun) *manngerðarmenn (pl.)* (ON), *skipreiðumenn (pl.)* (ON)

men from outside the district (noun) *útheraðsmenn (pl.)* (ON)

men holding the victim (noun) *haldbænd* (OSw)

men in an ale house (noun) *ölhúsmenn (pl.)* (ON)

men in the groups ('rings') of receivers (noun) *uppnámamenn (pl.)* (ON)

men named from the kin (noun) *kynsnævnd* (ODan)

men nominated by the bishop (noun) *biskopsnævning* (ODan)

men nominated for rapine cases (noun) *ransnævning* (ODan)

men nominated from the ship (noun) *skipsnævning* (ODan)

men of a district (noun) *hæraþsnæmd* (OSw)

men of a sea warrior district (noun) *hamnumæn (pl.)* (OSw)

men of one's kin (noun) *frændeth* (ODan), *kynsnævnd* (ODan)

men of rapine cases (noun) *ransnævning* (ODan)

men of the area (noun) *bygdamæn (pl.)* (OSw)

men of the assembly (noun) *þingsmæn (pl.)* (OSw)

men of the community (noun) *bygdamæn (pl.)* (OSw)

men of the hundred (noun) *hunderismenn (pl.)* (OGu)

men of the kin (noun) *kynseth* (ODan), *kynsnævnd* (ODan)

men outside the family (noun) *utanmenn (pl.)* (OGu)

men present at an assembly (noun) *þingsmæn (pl.)* (OSw)

men present at the deed (noun) *umstaþumæn (pl.)* (OSw)

men sharing the same odal (noun) *óðalsnautar (pl.)* (ON)

men to witness testimony produced (noun) *vættisvætti* (ON)

men with good memory (noun) *minnungamæn (pl.)* (OSw)

men with memory (noun) *minnungamæn (pl.)* (OSw)

mend (verb) *böta* (OSw)

mentally deficient (adj.) *óvitr* (ON)

mentally incapable (adj.) *óhygginn* (ON)

mention (verb) *næmna* (OSw)

men's clothes (noun) *karlklæði* (ON)

merchant (noun) *köpman* (OSw)

merchant journey (noun) *köpfærþ* (OSw)

merchant ship (noun) *kaupskip* (OGu)

merchant vessel (noun) *byrthing* (ODan)

merchants' duties (noun) *kaupmannaskylda* (ON)

mercy (noun) *naþir* (OSw)

message (noun) *buþ* (OSw)

message baton (noun) *arf* (OSw), *boðburðr* (ON), *buþ* (OSw)

message baton to summon an assembly (noun) *þingbuþ* (OSw)

message scroll (noun) *buþkafli* (OSw)

messenger (noun) *buþ* (OSw)

messmate (noun) *mötunautr* (ON)

Michaelmas (noun) *mikialsmæssa* (OSw)

Michaelmas Day (noun) *mikialsmæssodagher* (OSw), *sancta mikials dagher* (OSw)

mid-Lent (noun) *miþfasta* (OSw)

middle group of payers or receivers of wergild (noun) *miðuppnám* (ON)

midship oar (noun) *miðskipsár* (ON)

midsummer (noun) *miþsumar* (OSw)

midwife (noun) *griþkuna* (OGu)

military due (noun) *landværn* (OSw), *leþunger* (OSw)

military duty (noun) *leþunger* (OSw)

military expedition (noun) *hærfærþ* (OSw)

military service (noun) *útför* (ON), *utgærþ* (OSw)

military service due (noun) *leþunger* (OSw)

military tax (noun) *hamna* (OSw), *landværn* (OSw), *leþunger* (OSw)

milk (verb) *molka* (OSw)

mill (noun) *mylna* (OSw), *qværn* (OSw)

miller (noun) *myllari* (OSw)

millrace (noun) *mylnustaþer* (OSw)

minor (noun) *omaghi* (OSw)

minor excommunication (noun) *forbuþ* (OSw)

minor walking day (noun)

minor's money (noun) *ómagafé* (ON)

minor's property (noun) *ómagaeyrir* (ON)

mint-master (noun) *myntere* (ODan)

mis-eating (noun) *misæti* (ON)

misadventure (noun) *vaþi* (OSw)

misadventure compensation (noun) *vaþabot* (OSw)

misadventure fine (noun) *vaþabot* (OSw)

misadventure oath (noun) *vaþaeþer* (OSw)

misadventure payment (noun) *vaþagæld* (OSw)

misappropriate (verb) *firigæra* (OSw)

misburied (adj.) *misgrafinn* (ON)

miscarriage of justice (noun) *domvilla* (OSw)

miscarry (verb) *firikomas* (OSw), *spilla* (OSw)

mischief (noun) *fár* (ON)

mischievious deed (noun) *værk* (OSw)

misconduct (noun) *misganga* (ON)

miscreant (noun) *illgærningisman* (OSw), *ógangsmaðr* (ON)

misdeed (noun) *gærning* (OSw), *misverki* (ON), *værk* (OSw)

misdemeanour (noun) *brut* (OSw), *misfall* (OSw), *sak* (OSw)

mishandling (noun) *handvömm (pl.)* (ON)

misjudgement (noun) *misdómi* (ON)

mislead (verb) *villa* (ON)

mismanage (verb) *mishægha* (OSw)

misproclaim (verb) *misbjóða* (ON)

mission (noun) *buþ* (OSw)

mistake (noun) *misfangi* (ON)

mistreat (verb) *misfyrma* (OSw), *misþyrma* (ON), *öfunda* (ON)

mistreatment (noun) *óhlutr* (ON)

mistress (1) (noun) *dróttning* (ON), *husfrugha* (OSw)

mistress (2) (noun) *amia* (OSw), *frilla* (OSw)

mistress of the house (noun) *husfrugha* (OSw)

misuse (noun) *aværkan* (OSw)

mobilization (noun) *almænninger* (OSw), *liþstæmpna* (OSw)

mockery (noun) *háðung* (ON)

moderation (noun) *spekð* (ON)

molar (noun) *jaxl* (ON)

monastery (noun) *kloster* (OSw)

monastery escaper (noun) *klosterlöpare* (OSw)

monetary compensation (noun) *pænninger* (OSw)

monetary debt (noun) *fægæld* (OSw)

monetary fine (noun) *fæbot* (OSw)

monetary fines (noun) *saköri* (OSw)

monetary value (noun) *luter* (OSw)

money (noun) *andvirði* (ON), *fæ* (OSw), *öre* (OSw), *pænninger* (OSw), *værþ* (OSw), *værþörar (pl.)* (OSw)

money affairs (noun) *fjárfar* (ON)

money as compensation (noun) *fæbot* (OSw)

money claim (noun) *fjársókn* (ON)

money debt (noun) *fjárskuld* (ON)

money fine (noun) *fægæld* (OSw)

money for expenses (noun) *kostningsgjald* (ODan)

money matters (noun) *fjárreiða* (ON)

money of the church (noun) *kirkiupænningar (pl.)* (OSw)

money penalty (noun) *févíti* (ON)

money trustee (noun) *feartaki* (OSw)

money value (noun) *auralag* (ON)

money-trick (noun) *féprettr* (ON)

monk (noun) *klosterman* (ODan), *munk* (ODan)

month's food (noun) *mánaðarmatr* (ON)

moonblind (adj.) *starblindr* (OGu)

mooring (noun) *fæst* (OSw)

mooring stakes (noun) *festarhæll* (ON)

moorland (noun) *heiðr* (ON)

more powerful man (noun) *ofríkismaðr* (ON)

morning gift (noun) *hemgæf* (OSw), *hindradagsgæf* (OSw), *morghongæf* (OSw)

morning of the thirtieth day (noun) *þrítugsmorginn* (ON)

mortal enemy (noun) *oran* (OSw)

mortal wound (noun) *banesar* (ODan), *bæn* (OSw)

mortal-wound witness (noun) *benjaváttr* (ON)

mortgage (noun) *mali* (OSw), *væþ* (OSw)

mortgage agreement (noun) *forsölumáli* (ON)

mortgaged estate (noun) *forsölujörð* (ON)

mortgaged land (noun) *forsölujörð* (ON)

mortise joint (noun) *greyping* (ON)

Moster assembly (noun) *Mostrarþing* (ON)

mother and daughter (noun) *moþghur (pl.)* (OSw)

mother's (adj.) *möþerni* (OSw)

mother's family (noun) *móðurætt* (ON)

mother's side (noun) *möþerni* (OSw), *möþringar (pl.)* (OSw), *nefgildi* (ON)

mound (noun) *høgh* (ODan)

mountain pasture (noun) *fjallhagi* (ON)

mountain-corpse (noun) *fjallnár* (ON)

mouth (noun) *þrútr* (ON)

movable goods (noun) *bofæ* (ODan), *boskaper* (OSw), *fæ* (OSw), *fæmune* (ODan), *koster* (OSw), *lösöre* (OSw)

movable property (noun) *lauss eyrir* (ON), *lösöre* (OSw)

movables (noun) *bo* (OSw), *bofæ* (ODan), *bolfæ* (ODan), *boskaper* (OSw), *fang* (OSw), *fæ* (OSw), *fæmune* (ODan), *hus* (OSw), *inviþi* (OSw), *lausafé* (ON), *lauss eyrir* (ON), *lösöre* (OSw), *mun* (ODan), *öre* (OSw)

movables in a partnership (noun) *fælaghsfæ* (ODan)

move to another's house (verb) *flatfara* (OSw)

moving day (noun) *fardagher* (OSw)

moving days (noun) *fardagher* (OSw)

moving out courts (noun) *dómaútförsla* (ON)

mown grass (noun) *slætringr* (ON)

murder (verb) *myrþa* (OSw)

murder (noun) *morþ* (OSw)

murder fine (noun) *morþgæld* (OSw)

murder oath (noun) *morðseiðr* (ON)

murder weapon (noun) *morþvapn* (OSw)

murder-wolf (noun) *morðvargr* (ON)

murderer (noun) *banaorþ* (OSw), *drapari* (OSw), *mandrapare* (OSw), *morðvargr* (ON), *morþari* (OSw), *morþingi* (OGu)

murdering arsonist (noun) *kasnavargher* (OSw)

murderous arson (noun) *morthbrand* (ODan)

muscle wound (noun) *vathvesar* (ODan)

must (i.e. have to) (verb) *þorva* (OSw)

muster (noun) *mantal* (OSw)

mustering thing (noun) *manntalsþing* (ON)

mutilate (verb) *hamle* (ODan), *læsta* (OSw), *meiða* (ON), *styva* (OSw), *stækkia* (OSw)

mutilated whore (noun) *horstakka* (OSw)

mutilation (noun) *afhug* (OSw), *hamblan* (OSw), *læst* (OSw)

mutilation case (noun) *læstemal* (ODan)

mutual conciliation (noun) *sialvasæt* (OSw)

nail (of tree or metal) (noun) *nagli* (ON)

name (verb) *kalla* (OSw), *næmna* (OSw)

name (noun) *namn* (OSw), *næmni* (OSw)

named man (noun) *næmdarmaþer* (OSw)

nanny-goat (noun) *get* (OSw)

National Law (noun) *bok (1)* (OSw), *laghbok* (OSw), *landsbók* (ON)

native (adj.) *hærlænsker* (OSw)

nativity (noun) *byrþ* (OSw)

natural child (noun) *launbarn* (ON)

natural heir (noun) *skaparfuni* (ON), *skaparvi* (OSw)

natural resource (noun) *góði* (ON)

nature (noun) *fall* (OSw)

nautical mile (noun) *ukesjo* (ODan), *vika* (OSw)

naval levy (noun) *leþunger* (OSw)

navigable sound (noun) *leþsund* (OSw)

near kinsman (noun) *náungi* (ON)

near male relative related by marriage (noun) *námágr* (ON)

near neighbour (noun) *nagranni* (OSw)

nearby person (noun) *návistarmaðr* (ON)

necessary item (noun) *reiða* (ON)

necessary member of a household (noun) *skuldahjón* (ON), *skuldahjú* (ON)

necessity (noun) *forfall* (OSw), *nöþsyn* (OSw), *þrang* (OSw)

necessity inspection (noun) *nöþsyn* (OSw)

neck (noun) *hals* (OSw)

neck-payment (noun) *halslausn* (ON)

need (verb) *þorva* (OSw)

need (noun) *nöþsyn* (OSw), *þörf* (ON), *þrang* (OSw)

need arise (verb) *noyþa* (OGu)

needy person (noun) *þurfamaðr* (ON)

neglect (verb) *afrökja* (ON), *fyrirnemask* (ON), *fælla* (OSw)

neglect (noun) *fall* (OSw), *forfall* (OSw), *uhæghth* (ODan), *vangöma* (OSw), *vanrökt* (OSw)

neglect concerning tracing (noun) *leþsnafall* (OSw)

neglect of assemblies (noun) *þingfall* (OSw)

neglect of bridges (noun) *broafall* (OSw)

neglect of farm(stead) (noun) *bolöþsla* (OSw)

neglect of fences (noun) *garþafall* (OSw)

neglect of services (noun) *tiþafall* (OSw)

neglect of the mass (noun) *mæssufall* (OSw)

neglected (adj.) *órókðr* (ON)

neglected maintenance of fences (noun) *garþafall* (OSw)

neglecting a fast (noun) *föstuafbrigð* (ON)

negligence (noun) *glömska* (OSw), *handvömm (pl.)* (ON), *órókð* (ON), *vanrökt* (OSw)

negligence to provide hospitality (noun) *væzlufal* (OSw)

negotiable (i.e. in coin) (adj.) *köpgilder* (OSw)

neighbour (noun) *bonde* (OSw), *búi* (ON), *granni* (OSw), *heimilisbúi* (ON), *nagranni* (OSw), *sambúð* (ON)

neighbour oath (noun) *grannaeþer* (OSw)

neighbour of a killing place (noun) *vígsvættvangsbúi* (ON)

neighbour of the court-place (noun) *dómstaðarbúi* (ON)

neighbour of the land (noun) *landboe* (OSw)

neighbour of the place of action (noun) *vættvangsbúi* (ON)

neighbour witness (noun) *návistarmaðr* (ON)

neighbour woman (noun) *grannekone* (ODan)

neighbour-calling (noun) *búakvöð* (ON)

neighbourhood (noun) *grennd* (ON)

neighbouring (adj.) *afastr* (OGu)

nephew (noun) *bröþrungi* (OSw), *systrunger* (OSw)

nest (noun) *hreiðr* (ON)

nesting grounds (noun) *eggver* (ON)

net for wolves (noun) *varghanæt* (OSw)

net-laying line (noun) *netlag* (ON)

new farm (noun) *nýlendi* (ON)

new information (noun) *nýmæli* (ON)

new law (noun) *nýmæli* (ON), *skipan* (OSw)

new ordinances (noun) *nýmæli* (ON)

new settlement (noun) *þorp* (OSw)

niece (noun) *systrunger* (OSw)

night before Friday (noun) *frjánátt* (ON)

night before Sunday (noun) *sunnunátt* (ON)

night before Wednesday (noun) *óðinsnátt* (ON)

night-quarters (noun) *náttstaðr* (ON)

night-quarters testimony (noun) *náttstaðarvitni* (ON)

nightwatch (noun) *náttsetr* (ON)

nithing (noun) *niþinger* (OSw)

no compensation (noun) *hemegjald* (ODan), *ógildi* (ON)

no fine in compensation is to be paid out (adj.) *saklös* (OSw)

no fine is to be paid out (adj.) *ogilder* (OSw)

no punishment is to be inferred (adj.) *ogilder* (OSw)

nobleman (noun) *hærra* (OSw), *hærraman* (OSw)

nominate (verb) *næmna* (OSw)

nominated assembly men (noun) *thinghøring* (ODan)

nominated man (noun) *næmdarmaþer* (OSw)

nominated men (noun) *næmd* (OSw), *næmpning* (OSw), *særnævnd* (ODan)

nominated men of the district (noun) *hæraþsnæmd* (OSw)

nominated men of the fourth (noun) *fiarþungsnæmd* (OSw)

nominated penalty men (noun) *farvitenævning* (ODan)

nomination at the General Assembly (noun) *alþingisnefna* (ON)

nomination of judges (noun) *dómnefna* (ON)

non-compensable crime (noun) *urbotamal* (OSw)

non-domestic animal (noun) *diur* (OSw)

non-fruit bearing tree (noun) *döfviþer* (OSw)

non-living movables (noun) *jorthebit* (ODan)

non-military due (noun) *qvarsæta* (OSw)

non-milking stock (noun) *geldfé* (ON)

non-permissible (adj.) *olofliker* (OSw)

nones-holy (adj.) *nónheilagr* (ON)

nookling (noun) *hornungr* (ON)

noon (noun) *nón* (ON)

Norwegian (noun) *noregsmaðr* (ON)

Norwegian (adj.) *noræn* (OSw)

nose (noun) *nef* (ON)

not a thief (adj.) *urþiuva* (OSw)

not able bodied (adj.) *oför* (OSw)

not announced (adj.) *ólýstr* (ON)

not castrated (adj.) *graðr* (ON)

not cleansed (adj.) *oskær* (OSw)

not close in kin (adj.) *oskylder* (OSw)

not closely related (adj.) *oskylder* (OSw)

not condemned (adj.) *udømd* (ODan), *ufælder* (OSw)

not contributed (adj.) *ógörr* (ON)

not culpable (adj.) *ubrutliker* (OSw)

not decide (verb) *þigia* (OSw)

not declared (adj.) *ólýstr* (ON)

not eaten (adj.) *óneyttr* (ON)

not enumerated (adj.) *ótalðr* (ON)

not fully paid (adj.) *vanlokinn* (ON)

not guilty (adj.) *osaker* (OSw), *osander* (OSw), *saklös* (OSw), *ubrutliker* (OSw)

not hindered (adv.) *forfallalöst* (OSw)

not implicated (adj.) *saklös* (OSw)

not in accordance with the law (adj.) *ogilder* (OSw)

not in order (adj.) *ogilder* (OSw)

not involved (adj.) *lutlös* (OSw)

not killed (adj.) *udræpen* (ODan)

not leased (adj.) *óbyggðr* (ON)

not legitimated (adj.) *óleiddr* (ON)

not liable to compensation or wergild (adj.) *ogilder* (OSw)

not listed (adj.) *ótalðr* (ON)

not litigant (adj.) *saklös* (OSw)

not obliged (adj.) *saklös* (OSw)

not obliged to repay (adj.) *ogilder* (OSw)

not paid out (adj.) *óreiddr* (ON)

not pay anything for somebody (adj.) *ogilder* (OSw)

not prevented (adj.) *meinlauss* (ON)

not prevented by necessity (adv.) *nauðsynjalaust* (ON)

not promised (adj.) *ofæster* (OSw)

not prosecuted (adj.) *saklös* (OSw)

not recognize (verb) *dylia* (OSw)

not repayed (adj.) *ogilder* (OSw)

not respecting the peace of the church (noun) *kirkjufriðbrot* (ON)

not responsible (adj.) *saklös* (OSw)

not saddled (adj.) *ósöðlaðr* (ON)

not settled (adj.) *osater* (OSw)

not sold (adj.) *óseldr* (ON)

not spent (adj.) *óvarinn* (ON)

not subject to compensation (adj.) *ogilder* (OSw), *ubóti* (OSw)

not to be compensated (adj.) *ogilder* (OSw)

not to be forfeited (adj.) *saklös* (OSw)

not to be sustained (adj.) *óóll* (ON)

not under legal penalty (adj.) *sykn* (OSw)

notch (noun) *skor* (ON), *skýlihögg* (ON)

note (verb) *skæra (1)* (OSw)

notice (verb) *syna* (OSw)

notice (noun) *buþ* (OSw), *fæmt* (OSw), *mél* (ON)

notice of redemption (noun) *forsögn* (ON)

notification (noun) *buþ* (OSw)

notify (verb) *laghbiuþa* (OSw)

notorious debt (noun) *vitafé* (ON)

notorious property (noun) *vitafé* (ON)

nuisance (noun) *óskjóti* (ON)

null and void (adj.) *lös* (OSw)

nullify (verb) *rinda* (OSw), *ryva* (OSw)

number (noun) *hafþatal* (OGu), *mantal* (OSw)

number of hides (noun) *húðafang* (ON)

number of men (noun) *mantal* (OSw)

number of men allowed to bear arms (noun) *vighramannatal* (OSw)

number of people (noun) *mannmergð* (ON), *mantal* (OSw)

number of persons (noun) *mantal* (OSw)

nun (noun) *nunna* (ON)

nunnery (noun) *kloster* (OSw)

nunnery and monastery (noun) *kloster* (OSw)

nuptial mass (noun) *bruþmessa* (OGu)

oak (noun) *ek* (OSw)

oak wood where pannage is permitted (noun) *aldin* (OSw)

oakum (noun) *síþráðr* (ON)

oar (noun) *ar (1)* (OSw)

oar bench (noun) *hamla* (ON), *sess* (ON)

oar-grummet (noun) *hamla* (ON)

oarsman (noun) *ar (1)* (OSw), *hamla* (ON), *hasæti* (OSw), *hömlumaðr* (ON)

oarsmen (noun) *sættara* (OSw)

oath (noun) *asöreseþer* (OSw), *ethelagh* (ODan), *eþer* (OSw), *eþsorþ* (OSw), *foreþer* (OSw), *lagh* (OSw), *tilbuþ* (OSw), *vitni* (OSw), *vitsorþ* (OSw), *vætti* (OSw)

oath about a foal (noun) *fylsvat* (OSw)

oath about birth at home (noun) *hemföþoeþer* (OSw)

oath about inherited land (noun) *fyrning* (OSw)

oath about/concerning misadventure (noun) *vaþaeþer* (OSw)

oath as to accidental damage (noun) *vaþaeþer* (OSw)

oath as to accidental injury (noun) *vaþaeþer* (OSw)

oath as to an accident (noun) *vaþaeþer* (OSw)

oath by {fastar} (noun) *fastaeþer* (OSw)

oath concerning accidental injury case (noun) *vaþaeþer* (OSw)

oath concerning theft (noun) *þiufseþer* (OSw)

oath for half personal compensation (noun) *halfréttiseiðr* (ON)

oath for homicide (noun) *mandraplogh* (ODan)

oath helper (noun) *fangaváttr* (ON)

oath helpers (noun) *eiðalið* (ON)

oath in cases of defence (noun) *værnareþer* (OSw)

oath involving outlawry (noun) *útlegðareiðr* (ON)

oath of accidental deed (noun) *vaþaeþer* (OSw)

oath of acquisition (noun) *vinningælogh* (OSw)

oath of attendance (noun) *sætiseþer* (OSw)

oath of confirmation (noun) *göþslueþer* (OSw)

oath of defence (noun) *vistavitni* (OSw)

oath of denial (noun) *duleiðr* (ON)

oath of denial in cases of theft (noun) *þiufseþer* (OSw)

oath of equality (noun) *jamnaþareþer* (OSw)

oath of equity (noun) *jamnaþareþer* (OSw)

oath of five (noun) *fimmtareiðr* (ON)

oath of guilt (noun) *asöreseþer* (OSw)

oath of inheritance from ancient times (noun) *minnung* (OSw)

oath of kinsmen (noun) *frændeth* (ODan)

oath of one (noun) *eneþer* (OSw)

oath of paternal inheritance (noun) *forhæfþiseþer* (OSw), *fæþerniseþer* (OSw)

oath of redress (noun) *uprættareþer* (OSw)

oath of security (noun) *trygdareþer* (OSw), *trygth* (ODan)

oath of six (noun) *séttareiðr* (ON)

oath of substantiation (noun) *asöreseþer* (OSw)

oath of three (noun) *lýrittareiðr* (ON)

oath of transaction witnesses (noun) *fastaeþer* (OSw)

oath of transactions witnesses for repurchases (noun) *aterköpsfastaeþer* (OSw)

oath of twelve (noun) *tylft* (OSw), *tylftareþer* (OSw)

oath of two (noun) *tveggjamannaeiðr* (ON)

oath of validity (noun) *forfallseþer* (OSw)

oath of/to a person's guilt (noun) *asöreseþer* (OSw)

oath that someone bred a foal (noun) *fylsvat* (OSw)

oath together with all neighbours (noun) *grannaeþer* (OSw)

oath trustee (noun) *eþataki* (OSw)

oath-breaking (noun) *eiðrof* (ON)

oath-breaking (adj.) *eiðrofi* (ON)

oath-formula (noun) *eiðstafr* (ON)

oath-lapse (noun) *eiðfall* (ON)

oath-making (noun) *vætti* (OSw)

oath-receiver (noun) *eþataki* (OSw)

oath-spellers (noun) *forskialamaþer* (OSw)

oath-summons day (noun) *eiðstefnudagr* (ON)

oath-swearing (noun) *eiðunning* (ON)

oath-taker (noun) *eþafylli* (OSw), *eþataki* (OSw)

oath-takers (noun) *eþamæn (pl.)* (OSw), *eþviti* (OSw)

oath-taking (noun) *eiðspjall* (ON), *eþataki* (OSw), *laghagærþ* (OSw), *vætti* (OSw)

oath-taking (adj.) *sórr* (ON)

oath-witness (noun) *eþviti* (OSw)

oathsman (noun) *eþviti* (OSw)

oathsmen (noun) *eþamæn (pl.)* (OSw)

oats (noun) *hagri* (OGu)

object (verb) *mena* (OSw)

object of bargaining (noun) *fékaup* (ON)

object of value (noun) *griper* (OSw)

object paid in wergild (noun) *sakfé* (ON)

objection (noun) *forbuþ* (OSw), *klandan* (OSw)

objectionable practice (noun) *osiþer* (OSw)

oblation (noun) *gift* (OSw)

obligated to (adj.) *skyldugher* (OSw)

obligation (noun) *fulnaþer* (OSw), *skyld* (OSw), *skæl* (OSw), *tillag* (ON), *utskyld* (OSw), *þyrmsl* (ON)

obligation to build a house (noun) *húsgerð* (ON)

obliged (adj.) *skylder (2)* (OSw), *skyldugher* (OSw)

obliged to pay (adj.) *saker* (OSw)

obliged to pay a fine (adj.) *saker* (OSw)

obliged to pay compensation (adj.) *gilder* (OSw)

observance (noun) *hælgh* (OSw)

observance of Christianity (noun) *kristinsdómshald* (ON)

observance of festivals (noun) *hátíðahald* (ON)

observance of marriage (noun) *hjúskaparhald* (ON)

observance of Sundays (noun) *sunnudagahald* (ON)

observation (noun) *asyn* (OSw)

observe (verb) *gæta* (ON), *halda* (OSw), *sea* (OSw), *vakta* (OSw), *þyrma* (ON)

observe the fast (verb) *fasta* (OSw)

observe the {fyrma} (verb) *fyrma (1)* (OSw)

obstacle (noun) *forfall* (OSw)

obstinacy (noun) *þryter* (OSw)

obstruct (verb) *atertæppa* (OSw)

obtain the right (verb) *göþa* (OSw)

obvious to witnesses (adj.) *synarvitni* (OSw)

occupy (verb) *byggia* (OSw)

ocular witness (noun) *synarvitni* (OSw)

odal (noun) *oþal* (OSw)

odal (allodial) land (noun) *oþoliorþ* (OSw)

odal (allodial) water (noun) *oþolvatn* (OSw)

odal (allodial) water works (noun) *oþolvatnværk* (OSw)

odal land (noun) *oþal* (OSw), *oþoliorþ* (OSw)

odal plot (noun) *aðaltóft* (ON)

odal right (noun) *oþal* (OSw)

of age (adj.) *fultiþa* (OSw), *laghvaksen* (ODan), *maghandi* (OSw)

of allegiance (adj.) *trogivin* (OSw)

of another bed (adj.) *sunderkulla* (OSw)

of equal birth (adj.) *jafnborinn* (ON)

of equal rank (adj.) *jafnborinn* (ON)

of forfeit immunity (adj.) *ogilder* (OSw), *ohailigr* (OGu)

of full age (adj.) *fulaldre* (ODan), *fultiþa* (OSw), *maghandi* (OSw)

of higher social standing (adj.) *goþer* (OSw)

of inner Trondelag (adj.) *innþrónzkr* (ON)

of kin (adj.) *ættaþer* (OSw)

of lawful length (adj.) *löglangr* (ON)

of native birth (adj.) *héralinn* (ON)

of one's own free will (adj.) *sialfsviliande* (OSw)

of outer Trondelag (adj.) *útþrónzkr* (ON)

of separate broods (adj.) *sunderkulla* (OSw)

of silver (adj.) *karlgilder* (OSw)

of the butt side of a weapon (adj.) *avugher* (OSw)

of the highest social standing (adj.) *goþer* (OSw)

of the same bed (adj.) *samkulla* (OSw)

of the same brood (adj.) *samkulla* (OSw)

of the same father (adj.) *samfeddr* (ON), *samfæthre* (ODan)

of the same judgement (adj.) *samdóma* (ON)

of the same kinship (adj.) *jamnskylder* (OSw)

of the same mother (adj.) *sammøthre* (ODan)

of the same social class (adj.) *jafnborinn* (ON)

of the same social standing (adj.) *jafnborinn* (ON)

of the same social status (adj.) *jafnborinn* (ON)

offence (noun) *afbrot* (ON), *brut* (OSw), *gærning* (OSw), *gærþ* (OSw), *mal (1)* (OSw), *mishælde* (ODan), *sak* (OSw), *vite* (ODan), *þokki* (OSw)

offence against penance (noun) *skriptabrut* (OSw)

offence against the peace of the home (noun) *hemfriþer* (OSw)

offence on a holy day (noun) *hælghudaghabrut* (OSw)

offences as to kinship relations (noun) *kynsæmesbrut* (ODan)

offend (verb) *bryta* (OSw), *misgøre* (ODan)

offender (noun) *skaþamaþer* (OSw), *værkiande* (OSw)

offer (verb) *biuþa* (OSw), *fæsta* (OSw)

offer (noun) *buþ* (OSw), *tilbuþ* (OSw)

offer a legal option (verb) *laghbiuþa* (OSw)

offer according to the law (verb) *laghbiuþa* (OSw)

offer legally (verb) *laghbiuþa* (OSw)

offer of a bribe (noun) *féboð* (ON)

offer of payment (noun) *botebuth* (ODan)

offer of payment to get the peace back (noun) *frithkøp* (ODan)

offer one's land (verb) *biuþa* (OSw)

offer proceedings (noun) *tilbuþ* (OSw)

offer with a purchase option to one's kin/offer legal option on ownership (verb) *laghbiuþa* (OSw)

offering of oaths (noun) *eþabuþ* (OSw)

office (noun) *ármenning* (ON), *læn* (OSw), *starf* (ON), *æmbæte* (ODan)

office as district principal (noun) *hærapsmannamal* (OSw)

office holder (noun) *þiænistumaþer* (OSw)

officer of the King's bodyguard (noun) *hirðstjóri* (ON)

official (noun) *ármaðr* (ON), *bryti* (OSw), *lænsmaþer* (OSw), *rættari* (OSw), *umbuþsman* (OSw), *valdsmaþer* (OSw), *yfirsóknarmaðr* (ON)

official prosecutor (noun) *soknari* (OSw)

offspring (noun) *afkome* (ODan), *siængaralder* (OSw), *siængaralster* (OSw)

offspring of a lawful bed (noun) *siængaralder* (OSw)

offspring of a man and wife (noun) *siængaralster* (OSw)

Olaf's Mass (noun) *olafsmæssa* (OSw)

Olaf's measure (noun) *ólafssáð* (ON)

old (adj.) *forn* (OSw)

old customs (noun) *fyrnska* (OGu)

old man on crutches (noun) *kroklokarl* (OSw)

old person (noun) *ørvasi* (ON)

omnipotent (adj.) *envaldugher* (OSw)

on each side (adj.) *ymsir* (OSw)

on fair terms (prep.) *afarkostalauss* (ON)

on the following day (adv.) *hindardags* (ON)

on the same day (adv.) *samdógris* (ON)

one (noun) *maþer* (OSw)

one mark worth of damage (noun) *merkrskaði* (ON)

one night old (adj.) *nætrgamall* (ON)

one oath alone (noun) *eneþer* (OSw)

one single oath (noun) *eneþer* (OSw)

one too stubborn to pay (noun) *þryter* (OSw)

one who act on another's order (noun) *underrættere* (ODan)

one who can earn his food (noun) *matlauni* (ON)

one who gives security (noun) *vörzlumaðr* (ON)

one who intends to prosecute (noun) *eftirætlandi* (ON)

one who lives on purchased land (noun) *kauplendingr* (ON)

one who says he has acquired something (noun) *fangaman* (OSw)

one who shall pay (noun) *utgærthsman* (ODan)

one who shall take the inheritance (noun) *arftaki* (OSw)

one year (noun) *jamlangi* (OSw)

one year's crop (noun) *örð* (ON)

one-day (noun) *endaghi* (OSw)

one-month time limit (noun) *mánaðarstefna* (ON)

one-night assembly (noun) *ennætþing* (OSw)

one's own accord (noun) *sjalfræði* (ON)

one's own free-will (noun) *sjalfvili* (ON)

one's own oath (noun) *eneþer* (OSw)

only one's own oath (noun) *eneþer* (OSw)

open (verb) *uplata* (OSw)

open (adj.) *openbar* (OSw)

open passage (noun) *barliþ* (OSw)

open seizure (noun) *ran* (OSw)

open wound (noun) *skena* (OSw)

open, harbourless coastline (noun) *ørhófi* (ON)

opening of a court meeting (noun) *dómsetning* (ON)

openly (adv.) *barlike* (ODan), *openbarlika* (OSw)

opinion (noun) *asyn* (OSw), *umdómi* (ON)

opponent (noun) *deleman* (ODan)

opponent in a lawsuit (noun) *sökunautr* (ON)

oppose (verb) *væþia* (OSw)

opprobrious word (noun) *oqvæþinsorþ* (OSw)

oratory (noun) *bónhús* (ON)

orchard (noun) *apeldgarth* (ODan)

ordain (verb) *skipa* (OSw), *vighia* (OSw)

ordained (adj.) *lærder* (OSw)

ordained man (noun) *vighthman* (ODan)

ordeal (noun) *guðskírsl* (ON), *jarnbyrþ* (OSw), *skærsl* (OSw)

ordeal of glowing ploughshares (noun) *skra* (ODan)

ordeal of hot iron (noun) *jarnbyrþ* (OSw)

order (verb) *döma* (OSw), *mæla (1)* (OSw)

order (noun) *buþ* (OSw), *buþskaper* (OSw), *skipan* (OSw)

order concerning an assembly (noun) *þingbuþ* (OSw)

order of inheritance (noun) *erfðaskipun* (ON)

orders (noun) *raþ* (OSw)

ordinance (noun) *skipan* (OSw)

ordinary (adj.) *rætter* (OSw), *sykn* (OSw)

ordinary assembly (noun) *almænningsthing* (ODan)

ordinary householder (noun) *innebonde* (ODan)

ordination (noun) *vigsl* (OSw)

organize (verb) *skilia* (OSw)

organizer (noun) *reþuman* (OSw)

original suit (noun) *frumsök* (ON)

original witness (noun) *frumváttr* (ON)

osier fish basket (noun) *miærþi* (OSw)

other dues (noun) *stuþ* (OSw)

other men (noun) *utenmarkesman* (ODan)

ought (verb) *þorva* (OSw)

ounce (noun) *öre* (OSw)

Our Lord (noun) *hærra* (OSw)

oust (verb) *rinda* (OSw)

out of the land (adv.) *utlændis* (OSw)

out of the province (adv.) *utlændis* (OSw)

outcast (noun) *vargher* (OSw)

outcast's brat (noun) *vargdropi* (ON)

outer door (noun) *úthurð* (ON)

outer fence (around fields and meadows) (noun) *utgarþer* (OSw)

outer garments (noun) *ivirklæþi* (OSw)

outer guard (noun) *utvarþer* (OSw)

outer side of a moored ship (noun) *útborði* (ON)

outer toft (noun) *høretoft* (ODan)

outer-pastures (noun) *úthagi* (ON)

outfield haymaking (noun) *engiverk* (ON)

outhouse (noun) *uthus* (OSw), *utvistarhus* (OSw)

outland (noun) *utgærthe* (ODan), *utlænde* (ODan)

outlands (noun) *utlænde* (ODan)

outlaw (verb) *útlægja* (ON)

outlaw (noun) *biltugher* (OSw), *útlagi* (ON), *útlegðarmaðr* (ON)

outlaw cases (noun) *urbotamal* (OSw)

outlaw not known to be such (noun) *óvísavargr* (ON)

outlaw-property (noun) *útlegðarfé* (ON)

outlawed (adj.) *biltugher* (OSw), *friþlös* (OSw), *saker* (OSw), *útlagr* (ON), *útlægr* (ON)

outlawry (noun) *sækt* (OSw), *útlegð* (ON)

outlawry case (noun) *sekðarsök* (ON)

outlawry-wealth (noun) *útlegðarfé* (ON)

outlying (adj.) *oskipter* (OSw)

outlying building (noun) *úthýsi* (ON)

outlying field (noun) *oreghe* (ODan), *utlænde* (ODan), *utskipt* (OSw) outlying house (noun) *uthus* (OSw)

outlying land (noun) *umeghn* (OSw), *umiorþ* (OSw), *utjorth* (ODan)

outlying meadow (noun) *utængi* (OSw)

outrageous case (noun) *niþingsværk* (OSw)

outrageous crime (noun) *niþingsværk* (OSw)

outrageousness (noun) *niþingsværk* (OSw)

outside enclosures (adv.) *utgærþis* (OSw)

outside of kin (prep.) *oskylder* (OSw)

outside the kindred (adj.) *oskylder* (OSw)

outside the kingdom (adv.) *utanrikes* (OSw)

outside the law (adv.) *rætlösa* (OSw), *skælalöst* (OSw)

outside the province (adv.) *utanlands* (OSw), *utlændis* (OSw)

outside the realm (adv.) *utanrikes* (OSw)

outward sea expedition (noun) *utroþer* (OSw)

over penalize (verb) *ofsökia* (OSw)

over-branding (noun) *amerki* (OGu)

overrobbery (noun) *ofrán* (ON)

overseas (adv.) *austr* (ON)

overseer (noun) *bryti* (OSw), *forman* (OSw), *forseaman* (OSw), *forstjóri* (ON)

oversight (noun) *forsjá* (ON)

overthrow (verb) *fælla* (OSw)

owe (verb) *gælda (1)* (OSw), *sækia* (OSw)

owed money (noun) *sækt* (OSw)

owing (adj.) *skyldugher* (OSw)

own business (noun) *enfæ* (OSw), *ensak* (OSw)

own case (noun) *ensak* (OSw)

own decision (noun) *einrædi* (ON)

own matter (noun) *ensak* (OSw)

owner (noun) *eghere* (ODan), *eghereman* (ODan), *eignarmaðr* (ON), *husbonde* (OSw), *æghandi* (OSw)

owner of a pre-emption right (noun) *málamaðr* (ON)

owner of drift rights (noun) *fjörumaðr* (ON), *rekamaðr* (ON)

owner of the land (noun) *jorþeghandi* (OSw), *landsdróttin* (ON)

owner of the oak wood where pannage is permitted (noun) *aldinkarl* (OSw)

ownership (noun) *egn* (OSw), *eiginorð* (ON), *einkunn* (ON), *ægha* (OSw)

ownership claim (noun) *brigsl* (OGu)

ownership mark (noun) *einkunn* (ON)

ownership of land (noun) *egn* (OSw), *ægha* (OSw)

ownership witness (noun) *óðalsvitni* (ON)

owner's lot (noun) *athelbit* (ODan)

owner's mark (noun) *bolsmærki* (OSw)

owning alone (adj.) *einfyndr* (ON)

owning or renting (adj.) *húsfastr* (ON)

ox (noun) *oxi* (OSw)

oxen (noun) *not* (OSw)

packhorse (noun) *klyf* (OSw), *skiut* (OSw)

pagan (adj.) *heþin* (OSw), *ukristin* (OSw)

pagan god (noun) *afguþ* (OSw), *guþ* (OSw)

pagan times (noun) *heþna* (OSw)

paganism (noun) *heþna* (OSw)

page serving at the royal table (noun) *skutilsveinn* (ON)

paid with double penalty (adj.) *tvægilder* (OSw)

pail of butter (noun) *synjarspönn* (ON)

painful injury (noun) *sársauki* (ON)

painstaking in oath-taking (adj.) *eiðavandr* (ON)

pair (noun) *band* (OSw), *öker* (OSw)

pair of fence supports (noun) *staurgulf* (OGu)

pair of scales (noun) *skal* (OGu)

panel (noun) *næmd* (OSw)

panel (verdict) for an original suit (noun) *frumkviðr* (ON)

panel from the {hæraþ} (noun) *hæraþsnæmd* (OSw)

panel from/of the {hundari} (noun) *hundarisnæmd* (OSw)

panel member (noun) *kviðmaðr* (ON), *næmdarmaþer* (OSw)

panel of inspectors (noun) *syn* (OSw)

panel of investigators (noun) *syn* (OSw)

panel of neighbours (noun) *búakviðr* (ON)

panel of twelve (noun) *tolftarkviðr* (ON)

pantry (noun) *vistahus* (OSw)

papal ban (noun) *páfabann* (ON)

parasite (noun) *slímuseta* (ON)

parcel legally (verb) *laghskipta* (OSw)

parcel of land (noun) *skipti* (OSw)

parcelled land (noun) *bolbyr* (OSw)

parcelling out of odal land (noun) *oþolskipti* (OSw)

parcelling out pastureland (noun) *hagaskipti* (ON)

pardon (noun) *friþer* (OSw)

parent (noun) *væriandi* (OSw)

parents (noun) *feðgin* (ON), *forældre* (ODan)

parish (noun) *fjársókn* (ON), *kirkiusokn* (OSw), *sokn* (OSw)

parish assembly (noun) *kirkjusóknarþing* (ON)

parish church (noun) *heraðskirkja* (ON), *tolftakyrkia* (OSw)

parish clerk (noun) *klokkari* (OSw)

parish commission (noun) *soknanæmd* (OSw)

parish inspection (noun) *soknasyn* (OSw)

parish jury (noun) *soknanæmd* (OSw)

parish man (noun) *kirkjeman* (ODan), *soknamaþer* (OSw)

parish men (noun) *sokn* (OSw), *soknamaþer* (OSw)

parish panel (noun) *soknanæmd* (OSw)

parish priest (noun) *soknaprester* (OSw)

parish thing (noun) *soknaþing* (OSw)

parishioner (noun) *bonde* (OSw), *kirkjusóknarmaðr* (ON), *soknamaþer* (OSw)

parishioners (noun) *innansoknafulk* (OGu), *kirkiumæn (pl.)* (OGu), *sokn* (OSw), *soknamaþer* (OSw), *soknar (pl.)* (OGu)

part (verb) *skilia* (OSw)

part (noun) *bosloter* (OSw), *luter* (OSw), *rætter* (OSw), *sal* (ODan)

part in outlying land (noun) *utskipt* (OSw)

part in the village measurements (noun) *tomtamal* (OSw)

part of an inheritance (noun) *aþalbogher* (OSw)

part of inheritance (noun) *ærfþaloter* (OSw)

part of the country (noun) *sveit* (ON)

part of the home (noun) *bosloter* (OSw)

part of the village land (noun) *deld* (OSw)

part with (verb) *afhænda* (OSw), *firihægþa* (OSw)

part-freed slave (noun) *frælsgivi* (OSw)

partial (adj.) *vildigh* (ODan)

participant (noun) *lottakari* (OSw)

participate in an assembly (verb) *heyja* (ON)

participate in an oath (verb) *hofþa* (OSw)

particular sibling (noun) *særsystken* (ODan)

particular to (adj.) *ensak* (OSw)

partition (verb) *skipta* (OSw)

partition (noun) *skipti* (OSw)

partition by a fence (noun) *garðskifti* (ON)

partition of home (noun) *boskipti* (OSw)

partition of property (noun) *boskipti* (OSw)

partner (noun) *bolaghsmaþer* (OSw), *félagi* (ON)

partnership (noun) *bolagh* (OSw), *félagsskapr* (ON), *flat* (OSw), *fælagh* (OSw), *lagh* (OSw)

partnership fastar (noun) *bolaghsfastar (pl.)* (OSw)

partnership making (noun) *félagslagning* (ON)

partnership man (noun) *bolaghsmaþer* (OSw)

partnership with a bailiff (noun) *brytefælagh* (ODan)

partnership witness (noun) *félagsvætti* (ON)

partner's inheritance (noun) *félagaerfð* (ON)

party (noun) *flokker* (OSw), *liþ (2)* (OSw), *samkunda* (ON)

pass away (verb) *fælla* (OSw)

pass judgement (verb) *döma* (OSw)

passage (noun) *far* (ON), *fæarganger* (OSw), *liþ (1)* (OSw)

passage from the country (noun) *farning* (ON)

passage money (noun) *legha* (OSw)

pasture (noun) *bait* (OGu), *fæarganger* (OSw), *haghi* (OSw), *haglendi* (ON), *hiorþvalder* (OSw), *löt* (OSw), *troth* (ODan)

pasture boundary line (noun) *hagamark* (ON)

pasture ground (noun) *fælöt* (OSw), *valder* (OSw)

pastureland (noun) *fæmark* (OSw), *haghi* (OSw), *hiorþlöt* (OSw), *löt* (OSw)

pastureland grazing (noun) *hagabeit* (ON)

paternal (adj.) *fæþerni* (OSw)

paternal belongings (noun) *fæþerni* (OSw)

paternal cousin (noun) *bröþrungi* (OSw)

paternal goods (noun) *fæþerni* (OSw)

paternal inheritance (noun) *forhæfþi* (OSw), *föðurarfr* (ON), *fæthrenærvth* (ODan), *fæþerni* (OSw)

paternal kin (noun) *föðurætt* (ON), *fæþerni* (OSw)

paternal kinsman (noun) *höfuðbarmsmaðr* (ON)

paternal kinsmen (noun) *föðurfrændi* (ON)

paternal land (noun) *fæþerni* (OSw), *fæþernisiorþ* (OSw)

paternal lot (noun) *fæthrenelot* (ODan)

paternal property (noun) *fæþerni* (OSw)

paternal relative (noun) *höfuðbarmsmaðr* (ON)

paternal side (noun) *fæþerni* (OSw)

paternity (noun) *fæþerni* (OSw)

path (noun) *gangr* (OGu), *gata* (OSw), *liþ (1)* (OSw), *vaþ* (OSw), *vægher* (OSw)

path between fences (noun) *qui* (OGu)

path to the shielings (noun) *sætrgata* (ON)

path used by animals (noun) *rekstr* (ON)

pathway (noun) *vægher* (OSw)

patriarch (noun) *patríarki* (ON)

patrimony (noun) *byrþ* (OSw), *fæþerni* (OSw)

patron (noun) *husbonde* (OSw)

pauper (noun) *øreigi* (ON), *þrotamaðr* (ON)

pauper freedman (noun) *grafgangsmaðr* (ON)

pauper-burden (noun) *afrapalas* (OSw)

pawn (verb) *væþsætia* (OSw)

pawn (noun) *væþ* (OSw)

pawn witnesses (noun) *væþiafastar (pl.)* (OSw)

pawning of land (noun) *jorþavæþsætning* (OSw)

pay (verb) *böta* (OSw), *firigielda* (OGu), *fylla* (OSw), *fæsta* (OSw), *giefa* (OGu), *greiða* (ON), *gælda (1)* (OSw), *hofþa* (OSw), *inna* (ON), *koste* (ODan), *löna* (OSw), *lösa* (OSw), *luka* (OSw), *reþa* (OSw), *rætta* (OSw), *sætta* (OSw), *varþa* (OSw)

pay (noun) *köp* (OSw), *lön* (OSw)

pay (someone's) penalty (verb) *væria* (OSw)

pay a dowry (verb) *mynde* (ODan)

pay a fee (verb) *lösa* (OSw)

pay a fine (verb) *böta* (OSw), *fæsta* (OSw), *gælda (1)* (OSw), *sækia* (OSw), *viþerhætta* (OSw)

pay attention to (verb) *hlýða* (ON)

pay back (verb) *aterfylla* (OSw), *atergælda* (OSw), *greiða* (ON), *lösa* (OSw), *loyfa* (OGu)

pay bail (verb) *borgha* (OSw)

pay compensation (verb) *atergælda* (OSw), *böta* (OSw), *gælda (1)* (OSw), *viþerhætta* (OSw)

pay damages (verb) *böta* (OSw)

pay double (verb) *tvægilda* (OSw)

pay for (verb) *forehalda* (OSw), *varþa* (OSw)

pay for one's life (verb) *lösa* (OSw)

pay interest (verb) *leghia* (OSw)

pay out (verb) *gælda (1)* (OSw), *rakna* (ON), *reþa* (OSw)

pay rental (verb) *leghia* (OSw)

pay the bride price ({munder}) (verb) *mynde* (ODan)

pay tithes (verb) *tiunda* (OSw)

payer (noun) *gjaldandi* (ON)

payer of the ring (noun) *baugbótandi* (ON)

paying for the peace (noun) *frithkøp* (ODan)

paying rent (noun) *landskyldarlykð* (ON)

paying the bride price ({munder}) (noun) *mynding* (ODan)

paymaster (noun) *gælkare* (OSw)

payment (noun) *andvirði* (ON), *bot* (OSw), *fulnaþer* (OSw), *fæ* (OSw), *fægæld* (OSw), *gæld* (OSw), *legha* (OSw), *lösn* (OSw), *öre* (OSw), *pænninger* (OSw), *reiða* (ON), *sak* (OSw), *sal* (ODan), *skipleiga* (ON), *útganga* (ON), *utgærþ* (OSw), *viþergæld* (OSw), *værþ* (OSw)

payment cloth (noun) *vaþmal* (OSw)

payment date (by instalments) (noun) *sal* (ODan)

payment day (noun) *gjalddagi* (ON)

payment for a summons (noun) *botestævne* (ODan)

payment for cargo space (noun) *skipleiga* (ON)

payment for churching (noun) *inleþning* (OSw)

payment for conveyance (noun) *skiutagærþ* (OSw)

payment for crop (noun) *korngjald* (ODan)

payment for damage (noun) *skaþagæld* (OSw)

payment for damage to a field (noun) *akergjald* (ODan)

payment for damaged crop (noun) *korngjald* (ODan)

payment for freedom (noun) *lösn* (OSw)

payment for grass (noun) *græsgjald* (ODan)

payment for keep (noun) *forgift* (ON)

payment for loss of stock (noun) *búmissa* (ON)

payment for maiming (noun) *lytisbot* (OSw)

payment for maintenance of a child (noun) *barnfulga* (ON), *fosterløn* (ODan)

payment for peace pledge (noun) *tryggvakaup* (ON)

payment for ploughing (noun) *træpislön* (OSw)

payment for redemption from outlawry (noun) *skógarkaup* (ON)

payment for seed (noun) *frölön* (OSw)

payment for shaming (noun) *þokkabot* (OSw)

payment for wound (noun) *sarabot* (OSw)

payment in coin (noun) *mali* (OSw), *tillagha* (OSw)

payment in kind (noun) *gengærþ* (OSw)

payment of debts (noun) *skuldagildri* (ON), *skuldalykning* (ON)

payment of financial compensation (noun) *fæbot* (OSw)

payment of money (noun) *fægæld* (OSw)

payment of servants (noun) *hjoneleghe* (ODan)

payment of tax (noun) *skattgreizla* (ON)

payment or reward for fostering children (noun) *barnfóstrlaun* (ON)

payment received (noun) *viðtaka* (ON)

payment to a judge (noun) *domarapænningar (pl.)* (OSw)

payment to a lawman (noun) *laghmanspænningar (pl.)* (OSw)

payment to a shipmaster (noun) *styremanspænningar (pl.)* (OSw)

payment to get the peace back (noun) *frithkøp* (ODan)

payment to keep the peace (noun) *frithløsen* (ODan)

payment to the king (noun) *konungsrætter* (OSw)

peace (noun) *friþer* (OSw), *griþ* (OSw), *hælgh* (OSw), *spekð* (ON), *trygth* (ODan)

peace (or rule of law) (noun) *friþer* (OSw)

peace at Christmas (noun) *julafriþer* (OSw)

peace at Easter (noun) *paskafriþer* (OSw)

peace at Whitsun days (noun) *pingizsdaghafriþer* (OSw)

peace circle (noun) *banda* (OGu)

peace crime (noun) *friþbrut* (OSw)

peace during the military duty (noun) *lethingshælgh* (ODan)

peace fine (noun) *friþbot* (OSw), *friþbrut* (OSw)

peace for the outlawed (noun) *friþer* (OSw)

peace guarantee (noun) *trygth* (ODan)

peace guarantee speech (noun) *tryggðamál* (ON)

peace in the field (noun) *akerfrith* (ODan)

peace of a village (noun) *byarfriþer* (OSw)

peace of assembly (noun) *stæmnufriþer* (OSw)

peace of Christmas (noun) *julafriþer* (OSw)

peace of church mass (noun) *kirkmæssufriþer* (OSw)

peace of Easter (noun) *paskafriþer* (OSw)

peace of home (noun) *hemfriþer* (OSw)

peace of the church (noun) *kirkiufriþer* (OSw), *kirkjugrið* (ON)

peace of the land (noun) *landfrith* (ODan)

peace of thing (noun) *þingsfriþer* (OSw)

peace of women (noun) *qvinnafriþer* (OSw)

peace pledge (noun) *tryggðamál* (ON), *trygth* (ODan)

peace weapon (noun) *friþvakn* (OSw)

peace-breaker (noun) *gruthnithing* (ODan)

peace-meeting (noun) *sættarstefna* (ON)

peaceful men (noun) *spakmænni (pl.)* (OSw)

peasant (noun) *bonde* (OSw)

peasantry (noun) *almoghe* (OSw)

pecuniary claim (noun) *fearkraf* (OGu)

pelt (noun) *skin* (OSw)

pelt with turf (verb) *tyrfa* (ON)

pen (noun) *qui* (OGu)

penal law (noun) *vitherlogh* (ODan)

penalty (noun) *fésekð* (ON), *laghslit* (OSw), *panter* (OSw), *sækt* (OSw), *vitherlogh* (ODan)

penalty payment (noun) *alagh* (OSw), *vite* (ODan), *vítigjald* (ON)

penance (noun) *skript* (OSw)

penance breaking (noun) *skriftrof* (ON)

penance by fasting (noun) *karina* (OSw)

penis (noun) *skapt* (OSw)

penniless (adj.) *félauss* (ON)

penny (noun) *pænninger* (OSw)

Pentecost week (noun) *pingetsuke* (ODan)

penury (noun) *auðn* (ON)

people (noun) *almoghe* (OSw), *folk* (OSw), *lyþir (pl.)* (OSw)

people belonging to the household (noun) *hion* (OSw)

people for boarding (noun) *mannelði* (ON)

people from Agder (noun) *egðir (pl.)* (ON)

people from Fjordane (noun) *firðir (pl.)* (ON)

people from Grenland (Lower Telemark) (noun) *grónir (pl.)* (ON)

people from Hordaland (noun) *hörðar (pl.)* (ON)

people from Hålogaland (noun) *háleygir (pl.)* (ON)

people from Namdalen (noun) *naumdólir (pl.)* (ON)

people from Nordmøre (noun) *norðmórir (pl.)* (ON)

people from Rogaland (noun) *rygir (pl.)* (ON)

people from Romsdalen (noun) *raumdólir (pl.)* (ON)

people from Sogn (noun) *sygnir (pl.)* (ON)

people from Sunnmøre (noun) *mórir (pl.)* (ON)

people from Trøndelag (noun) *þróndir (pl.)* (ON)

people from Vika (noun) *víkverir (pl.)* (ON)

people of an assembly (noun) *thinghøring* (ODan)

people of the household (noun) *hion* (OSw)

people of the island (noun) *land* (OSw)

people of the land (noun) *land* (OSw), *landsfolk* (ON)

people one is required to maintain (noun) *skuldalið* (ON)

people related to the fourth degree (noun) *fiurmænninger* (OSw)

people's bishop (noun) *lyþbiskuper* (OSw)

per capita share (noun) *hovoþloter* (OSw)

perch (noun) *vaghli* (OSw)

perforation (noun) *hulsar* (OSw)

perform armed service (verb) *þiæna* (OSw)

perform visitation (verb) *ransaka* (OSw)

perilous place (noun) *forað* (ON)

period (noun) *fræst* (OSw), *fræstning* (OSw)

period of employment (noun) *leghustæmpna* (OSw)

period of five days (noun) *fæmt* (OSw)

period of grace (noun) *fræstmark* (OSw), *griþ* (OSw)

period of lease (noun) *bolaghsstæmpna* (OSw)

period of partnership (noun) *bolaghsstæmpna* (OSw)

period of peace (noun) *hælgh* (OSw)

period of peace and protection (noun) *friþer* (OSw)

period of peace and security (noun) *friþer* (OSw)

period of possible redemption (noun) *stæmnudagher* (OSw)

period of sanctity (noun) *friþer* (OSw)

period of seven days (noun) *sjaund* (ON)

perjure oneself (verb) *missverja* (ON)

perjured (adj.) *osvurin* (OSw)

perjurer (noun) *meinsórismaðr* (ON)

perjury (noun) *meinsóri* (ON), *men* (OSw), *meneþer* (OSw)

permissible (adj.) *lofliker* (OSw)

permission (noun) *domber* (OSw), *lof* (OSw), *loyfi* (OGu), *orlof* (OSw), *raþ* (OSw), *umbuþ* (OSw), *vili* (OSw)

permission to search (noun) *ransakan* (OSw)

permission witness (noun) *lofsvitni* (OSw)

permit (verb) *döma* (OSw), *lata* (OSw), *lufa* (OGu)

permitted (adj.) *skylder (2)* (OSw)

permitted to be revenged (adj.) *gilder* (OSw)

permitted to take an oath (adj.) *eþsört* (OSw)

perpetrate a crime (verb) *misgøre* (ODan)

perpetrator (noun) *sanbani* (OSw), *værkiande* (OSw)

persecute (verb) *qvælia* (OSw)

person (noun) *nef* (ON), *þiauþ* (OGu)

person (in relation to enrolment) (noun) *nef* (ON)

person aggrieved (noun) *malsæghandi* (OSw), *sakgivi* (OSw), *saksöki* (OSw)

person from Namdalen (noun) *naumdóll* (ON)

person from outside the commune (noun) *útanhreppsmaðr* (ON)

person from the outer islands (noun) *úteynn* (ON)

person from Trøndelag (noun) *þróndir (pl.)* (ON)

person in charge of property (noun) *fjárhaldsmaðr* (ON)

person of the parish (noun) *kirkjusóknarmaðr* (ON)

person related in the third degree (noun) *þræmænninger* (OSw)

person responsible (noun) *uphaldsman* (ODan)

person someone answers for (noun) *varþnaþer* (OSw)

person staying at a farm (noun) *setumaðr* (ON)

person who has the right to give the bride away (noun) *hömtaman* (OSw)

person who keeps property (noun) *fjárhaldsmaðr* (ON)

person who maintains a dependant (noun) *framførslumaðr* (ON)

person who promised or leased out (noun) *hemulsman* (OSw)

person who reclaims (noun) *brigðandi* (ON)

person with no heirs (noun) *gestfeðri* (ON)

person with whom one has exchanged pledges of peace (noun) *tryggðamaðr* (ON)

personal and property rights (noun) *manhælghi* (OSw)

personal atonement (noun) *fullrétti* (ON)

personal compensation fixed by law (noun) *lögréttr* (ON)

personal compensation/right to personal compensation (noun) *réttarfar* (ON), *rætter* (OSw)

personal goods (noun) *lösöre* (OSw)

personal liberty (noun) *manhælghi* (OSw)

personal oath (noun) *eneþer* (OSw)

personal peace (noun) *manhælghi* (OSw)

personal rights (noun) *hælgh* (OSw), *manhælghi* (OSw), *réttarfar* (ON), *rætter* (OSw)

personal rights section (noun) *manhælghisbalker* (OSw)

personal security or liberty (noun) *manhælghi* (OSw)

personal servant (noun) *þjónn* (ON)

personal share (noun) *hovoþloter* (OSw)

personal surety (noun) *nam* (OSw)

person's share (noun) *lagh* (OSw)

petition (verb) *kæra* (OSw)

petty larcener (noun) *hvin* (OSw)

petty larceny (noun) *hvinska* (OSw)

petty theft (noun) *hvinska* (OSw)

physical deformity (noun) *ørkuml* (ON)

physical injury (noun) *akoma* (OSw)

physician (noun) *lækir* (OSw)

physician's fee (noun) *lækirsgæf* (OSw), *lækningarkaup* (ON)

piece of cloth used for drawing lots (noun) *skaut* (ON)

piece of grassland (noun) *tegher* (OSw)

piece of land (noun) *egn* (OSw), *jorthebit* (ODan)

piece of scalp and hair (noun) *torfa* (OGu)

piece of timber (noun) *tré* (ON)

piece-worker (noun) *verkkaupamaðr* (ON)

pieces of whale (noun) *hvalflystri* (ON)

piecework (noun) *ákvæðisverk* (ON)

pig (noun) *gris* (OSw), *svin* (OSw)

pig drove (noun) *vrath* (ODan)

pig sty (noun) *svinesti* (ODan)

piglet (noun) *gris* (OSw), *smagris* (OGu)

pile of birch bark (noun) *næfrabunki* (OSw)

pile of wood (noun) *viþakaster* (OSw)

pilferage (noun) *snattan* (OSw)

pilferer (noun) *hvin* (OSw)

pilfering (noun) *hvinska* (OSw)

pilgrim (noun) *pilegrim* (ODan)

pilgrimage (noun) *pilægrimsfærþ* (OSw)

pillar (noun) *stokker* (OSw), *stuþ* (OSw)

pillow (noun) *vengi* (OGu)

pinch (verb) *klýpa* (ON)

pirate (noun) *bunkabrytari* (OSw)

place (verb) *fela* (ON), *stinga* (OSw)

place (noun) *bygd* (OSw), *garþer* (OSw), *hærbærghi* (OSw), *lagh* (OSw)

place a ban on (verb) *lögfesta* (ON)

place for summoning (noun) *stefnustaðr* (ON)

place in church (noun) *kirkiurum* (OGu)

place of a crime (noun) *vighvalder* (OSw)

place of action (noun) *vættvangr* (ON)

place of assembly (noun) *þing* (OSw)

place of asylum (noun) *griðastaðr* (ON)

place of debt (noun) *skuldarstaðr* (ON)

place of residence (noun) *heimili* (ON)

place of truce (noun) *griðastaðr* (ON)

place to set up a ship (noun) *uppsát* (ON)

place where a bargain or contract was made (noun) *kaupreina* (ON)

place where a contract was made (noun) *kaupreina* (ON)

place where an assembly is held (noun) *þingsstaþer* (OSw)

place where business is transacted (noun) *kaupreina* (ON)

place where one spends nights (noun) *náttstaðr* (ON)

place where people live (noun) *hýbýli* (ON)

place where the assembly was held (noun) *þingstöð* (ON)

plaint (noun) *stæmna* (OSw)

plaintiff (noun) *áberi* (ON), *kærande* (OSw), *malsæghandi* (OSw), *sakaráberi* (ON), *saksöki* (OSw), *sökiandi* (OSw), *tiltalandi* (OSw)

plan (verb) *raþa* (OSw)

plan with security (verb) *máltryggva* (ON)

plank (noun) *borð* (ON)

plank one ell long (noun) *alnarborð* (ON)

plank over (verb) *bylia* (OSw)

planning (noun) *raþ* (OSw)

plantation (noun) *garþer* (OSw)

plants of the forest (noun) *undirviþer* (OSw)

plausibility (noun) *skæl* (OSw)

plead (verb) *biþia* (OSw), *flytja* (ON), *kæra* (OSw), *mæla (1)* (OSw)

pledge (verb) *fæsta* (OSw), *hætte* (ODan), *pantsætia* (OSw), *veðmæla* (ON), *væþia* (OSw), *væþsætia* (OSw)

pledge (noun) *orþ* (OGu), *panter* (OSw), *tak* (OSw), *varzla* (ON), *veðmáli* (ON), *væþ* (OSw), *væþfæ* (OSw), *væþning* (OSw), *væþsætning* (OSw)

pledge concerning movable property (noun) *lösörapanter* (OSw)

pledge fraud (noun) *veðflærð* (ON)

pledge in accordance with the legal form (noun) *skælavæþ* (OSw)

pledge man (noun) *taki* (OSw)

pledge man for an oath (noun) *eþataki* (OSw)

pledge man for money (noun) *feartaki* (OSw)

pledge to swear (verb) *fæsta* (OSw)

pledge trustee (noun) *væþiataki* (OSw)

pledge-breaker (noun) *tryggrofi* (ON)

pledged money (noun) *væþfæ* (OSw)

pledging (noun) *væþsætning* (OSw)

plot (verb) *raþa* (OSw)

plot (1) (noun) *deld* (OSw), *tegher* (OSw), *tompt* (OSw)

plot (2) (noun) *raþ* (OSw)

plot boundary (noun) *tomptaskæl* (OSw)

plot meeting (noun) *tomptastæmna* (OSw)

plot of land (noun) *skipti* (OSw)

plot size (noun) *jarðarmegin* (ON)

plot to disfigure (noun) *áljótsráð* (ON)

plot to strike (noun) *drepráð* (ON)

plough (noun) *arþer* (OSw), *jorþ* (OSw), *krok* (ODan)

plough share (noun) *arþer* (OSw)

plough shares (noun) *skra* (ODan)

ploughing (noun) *træpi* (OSw)

ploughing in another man's land (noun) *aplöghia* (OSw)

ploughland (noun) *ploghsærje* (ODan)

plunder (verb) *röva* (OSw), *ræna* (OSw)

plunder (noun) *hernuðr* (ON)

plundering (noun) *fornæmi* (OSw)

plundering of the slain (noun) *valrof* (OSw)

poetry (noun) *skáldskapr* (ON)

point (verb) *skiuta* (OSw)

pointless journey (noun) *vaflanarför* (ON)

poison (noun) *gærning* (OSw)

poisoning (noun) *forgærning* (OSw)

poke (verb) *stinga* (OSw)

pole (noun) *rennistaurr* (ON)

pole for marking a boundary path (noun) *vaþstang* (OSw)

pole measuring (noun) *stangfall* (OSw)

poop deck (noun) *lyptinger* (OSw)

poor (noun) *væslirmæn (pl.)* (OSw)

poor (adj.) *fatöker* (OSw), *félauss* (ON), *óauðigr* (ON), *øreigi* (ON)

poor creature (noun) *boldiur* (OSw)

poor health (noun) *vanheilsa* (ON)

poor person (noun) *förumannaflutningr* (ON), *øreigi* (ON)

pope (noun) *pavi* (OSw)

population (noun) *folk* (OSw)

portion (noun) *kafli* (OSw), *luter* (OSw), *mali* (OSw)

portion of a property (noun) *boskipti* (OSw)

position (noun) *starf* (ON), *vist* (OSw)

possess (verb) *hæfþa* (OSw), *væria* (OSw)

possessing a legal right (adj.) *hemul* (OSw)

possessing the same legal right (adj.) *jafnheimill* (ON)

possession (noun) *hald* (ON), *hæfþ* (OSw), *ægha* (OSw)

possession by force (noun) *ranshævth* (ODan)

possession mark (noun) *fylsmærke* (ODan)

possessions (noun) *fjárhlutr* (ON), *fæ* (OSw), *koster* (OSw)

possessor (noun) *æghandi* (OSw)

post (noun) *stang* (OSw), *staver* (OSw)

postmortem rites (noun) *líksöngr* (ON)

pound (noun) *pund* (OSw)

pour (verb) *steypa* (ON)

poverty (noun) *fatökt* (OSw), *féleysi* (ON), *vandreþi* (OGu), *þrot* (ON)

power (noun) *makt* (OSw), *mæghen* (ODan), *riki* (OSw), *vald* (OSw)

power to choose (noun) *vald* (OSw)

powerful man (noun) *ofríkismaðr* (ON)

pray to (verb) *heta* (OSw)

prayer (noun) *bön* (OSw)

prayer book (noun) *halsbók* (ON)

pre-emption right (noun) *mali* (OSw)

pre-emption rights on land (noun) *landsmáli* (ON)

pre-fast day (noun) *genfasta* (OSw)

pre-oath (noun) *foreþer* (OSw)

precedence (noun) *raþ* (OSw), *vald* (OSw), *vita* (OSw), *vitskustir (pl.)* (OSw), *vitsorþ* (OSw)

precedence to prosecute (noun) *vitsorþ* (OSw)

precious object (noun) *gærsemi* (OSw)

precipitate oath (noun) *löpiseþer* (OSw)

preference (noun) *vitsorþ* (OSw)

pregnant (adj.) *havandi* (OSw)

prejudice (noun) *vild* (OSw)

premeditated blow (noun) *öfundardrep* (ON)

premeditated harm (noun) *avund* (OSw)

premises (noun) *garþer* (OSw)

preparatory fast (beginning at Septuagesima) (noun) *genfasta* (OSw)

prepare (verb) *raþa* (OSw), *reþa* (OSw)

prescribe (verb) *biuþa* (OSw), *lysa* (OSw), *staþga* (OSw), *vátta* (ON)

prescribe an oath (verb) *hofþa* (OSw)

prescribed (adj.) *lagha* (OSw), *rætter* (OSw)

prescribed holy (adj.) *buthhelagh* (ODan)

prescribed time (noun) *stæmnudagher* (OSw)

presence (noun) *viþervist* (OSw)

present (verb) *ganga* (OSw), *leþa* (OSw), *löna* (OSw), *upgöra* (OSw)

present (adj.) *staddr* (ON)

present a claim (verb) *kveðja* (ON), *kæra* (OSw)

present men (noun) *umstaþumæn (pl.)* (OSw)

presentation (noun) *framsaga* (ON)

presentation procedure (noun) *framsæld* (OSw)

preserve (verb) *varþveta* (OSw)

presiding judge (noun) *laghmaþer* (OSw)

press charges (verb) *dela* (OSw)

pressing need (noun) *þrang* (OSw)

presume (verb) *dirfas* (OGu)

prevail (verb) *raþa* (OSw)

prevent (verb) *forbiuþa* (OSw), *lemja* (ON), *mena* (OSw)

prevent from being seen (verb) *fela* (ON)

prevented by lawful impediment (adj.) *nauðsynjalauss* (ON)

prevention (noun) *forfall* (OSw)

price (noun) *fæ* (OSw), *verðslykðing* (ON), *værþ* (OSw)

price for food (noun) *matarverð* (ON)

price for settlement (noun) *sættarkaup* (ON)

price of a cow (noun) *kúgildi* (ON)

price paid for an inheritance (noun) *arfkaup* (ON)

priest (noun) *kennimaðr* (ON), *lerþrmaþr* (OGu), *prester* (OSw)

priest tithe (noun) *preststíund* (ON)

priestling (noun) *prestlingr* (ON)

priests' pay (noun) *prestreiða* (ON)

priest's assistant (noun) *prestlingr* (ON)

priest's child (noun) *prestbarn* (OGu)

priest's dues (noun) *prestreiða* (ON)

priest's farm (noun) *prestgarþer* (OSw)

priest's house (noun) *præstastuva* (OSw)

priest's income (noun) *prestskaup* (ON)

priest's quarter (noun) *prestsfjórðungr* (ON)

priest's son (noun) *prestson* (OGu)

priest's wife (noun) *prestkuna* (OGu)

prime-sign (verb) *primsigna* (OSw)

prime-sign (noun) *prímsignun* (ON)

prime-signing (noun) *prímsigning* (ON), *prímsignun* (ON)

principal (noun) *aðili* (ON), *hovoþsmaþer* (OSw), *innstóða* (ON)

principal capital (noun) *innstóðueyrir* (ON)

principal door (noun) *karldyrr* (ON)

principal in the case (noun) *sakaraðili* (ON)

principal limbs (noun) *hovethlim* (ODan)

principal parcel (noun) *hovoþloter* (OSw)

principal part (noun) *hovoþloter* (OSw)

private chapel (noun) *hógendiskirkja* (ON)

private chaplain (noun) *hógendisprestr* (ON)

private church (noun) *hógendiskirkja* (ON)

private church penalty (noun) *löndaskript* (OSw)

private church penance (noun) *löndaskript* (OSw)

private compensation (noun) *ráðbót* (ON)

private conditions (noun) *undirmál* (ON)

private court for arbitration (noun) *skiladómr* (ON)

private judgement (noun) *festardómr* (ON)

private part (noun) *lönd* (OSw)

private property (noun) *egn* (OSw)

private settlement (noun) *sæt* (OSw)

private woodland (noun) *varskogher* (OSw)

privilege (noun) *loyfi* (OGu), *privilege* (ODan)

probation (noun) *fræst* (OSw), *fræstning* (OSw)

probe (verb) *vita* (OSw)

procedure (noun) *atferli* (ON), *mal (1)* (OSw)

proceed (verb) *laghvinna* (OSw)

proclaim (verb) *kalla* (OSw), *lysa* (OSw)

proclaim wrongly (verb) *misbjóða* (ON)

proclamation of ember days (noun) *imbrudagaboð* (ON)

proclamation of feast days (noun) *messudagaboð* (ON)

proclamation route (noun) *boðleið* (ON)

procuration (noun) *gæstning* (OSw)

produce an oath (verb) *sværia* (OSw)

produce from the land (noun) *lóð* (ON)

produce of the land (noun) *aværkan* (OSw)

proffer (verb) *gælda (1)* (OSw)

profit (verb) *fénýta* (ON)

profit (noun) *áauki* (ON), *afskyld* (OSw), *skyld* (OSw)

prohibited (adj.) *aftakin* (OGu)

prohibition (noun) *ban* (OSw), *forbuþ* (OSw)

promise (verb) *fæsta* (OSw), *játa* (ON), *lufa* (OGu), *mæla (1)* (OSw)

promise (noun) *eþer* (OSw), *fæsta* (OSw), *heit* (ON), *lof* (OSw), *orþ* (OGu)

promise of an oath (noun) *fæsta* (OSw)

promise of compensation (noun) *botefæstning* (ODan)

promise of immunity (noun) *griþ* (OSw)

promise of oaths (noun) *laghfæstning* (ODan)

pronounce (verb) *döma* (OSw)

pronouncing excommunication (noun) *banzmal* (OSw)

proof (noun) *jartighni (pl.)* (OSw), *lagh* (OSw), *skæl* (OSw), *vita* (OSw), *vitni* (OSw), *værn* (OSw)

proof against wound by nominated men (noun) *særnævnd* (ODan)

proof of home birth (noun) *hemefødvitne* (ODan)

proof of innocence (noun) *skærsl* (OSw)

proof of provenance (noun) *leþsn* (OSw)

proof payment (noun) *sporgæld* (OSw)

prop (noun) *stuþ* (OSw)

propel (verb) *skiuta* (OSw)

proper (adj.) *aþal* (OSw), *rætter* (OSw)

proper payer (noun) *skapbótandi* (ON)

proper receiver (noun) *skapþiggjandi* (ON)

proper ring payer (noun) *baugsskapbótandi* (ON)

proper way (noun) *skæl* (OSw)

properly (adv.) *rætlika* (OSw)

property (noun) *bo* (OSw), *egn* (OSw), *fjárhlutr* (ON), *fæ* (OSw), *goþs* (OSw), *griper* (OSw), *hæfþ* (OSw), *hæskaper* (OSw), *jorþ* (OSw), *koster* (OSw), *lausafé* (ON), *lunnendi* (OSw), *öre* (OSw), *pænninger* (OSw), *tompt* (OSw), *ægha* (OSw), *þing* (OSw)

property caretaker (noun) *halzmaþer* (OSw)

property claim (noun) *fjárheimting* (ON)

property damage (noun) *spellvirki* (ON)

property division (noun) *boskipti* (OSw), *skipti* (OSw)

property in common (noun) *bolaghsfæ* (OSw)

property in the form of land (noun) *egn* (OSw), *iorþaign* (OGu)

property in trust (noun) *inlaghsfæ* (OSw)

property loss (noun) *fjártöpun* (ON)

property of the church (noun) *kirkiufæ* (OSw)

property owned in partnership (noun) *bolaghsfæ* (OSw)

property ownership (noun) *fjáreign* (ON)

property placed in safe keeping (noun) *inlaghsfæ* (OSw)

property plot (noun) *ægholuter* (OSw)

property rapine (noun) *bosran* (OSw)

property seizure (noun) *fjáruptekð* (ON)

property share (noun) *fjárhlutr* (ON)

property under penalty (noun) *sekðarfé* (ON)

prophecy (noun) *spáför* (ON), *spásaga* (ON)

proprietary church (noun) *hógendiskirkja* (ON)

prosecute (verb) *asaka* (OSw), *atala* (OSw), *kæra* (OSw), *mæla (1)* (OSw), *næmna* (OSw), *qvælia* (OSw), *rykta* (OGu), *sökia* (OSw), *sækia* (OSw), *sækta* (OSw), *tilmæla* (OSw), *vita* (OSw), *æptirmæla* (OSw)

prosecute an action (for something) (verb) *sökia* (OSw)

prosecute at a legal thing (verb) *laghþinga* (OSw)

prosecuting the case (noun) *asokn* (OSw)

prosecution (noun) *asokn* (OSw), *atala* (OSw), *sak* (OSw), *sokn* (OSw), *sökning* (OSw), *tilmæli* (OSw), *æptirmæli* (OSw)

prosecution assembly (noun) *soknaþing* (OSw)

prosecution at law (noun) *lögsókn* (ON)

prosecution day (noun) *sóknardagr* (ON)

prosecution for damages (noun) *sokn* (OSw)

prosecution for property (noun) *fjársókn* (ON)

prosecution means of proof (noun) *sóknargagn* (ON)

prosecution panel (verdict) (noun) *sóknarkviðr* (ON)

prosecution principal (noun) *sóknaraðili* (ON)

prosecution proof (noun) *soknaband* (OSw)

prosecution substantiated by testimony (noun) *vitnismal* (OSw)

prosecutor (noun) *eftirsýnarmaðr* (ON), *sakaráberi* (ON), *sakarsókjandi* (ON), *sökiandi* (OSw), *soknamaþer* (OSw), *soknari* (OSw)

protect (verb) *friþa* (OSw), *gæta* (ON), *halda* (OSw), *hæghna* (OSw), *hælghe* (ODan), *varþa* (OSw), *varþveta* (OSw), *væria* (OSw), *værna* (OSw)

protected (adj.) *friþkallaþer* (OSw), *helagher* (OSw), *værnkallaþer* (OSw)

protected by law (adj.) *friþhelagher* (OSw), *helagher* (OSw)

protected field (noun) *friþgærþi* (OSw)

protection (noun) *friþer* (OSw), *hegnan* (OGu), *hælgh* (OSw), *varðveizla* (ON), *varþer* (OSw), *varþnaþer* (OSw), *værn* (OSw)

protection from the law (noun) *rætter* (OSw)

protection oath (noun) *trygdareþer* (OSw)

protection of a ring (noun) *baugshelgi* (ON)

protection of the district (noun) *hæraþsræfst* (OSw)

protective weapon (noun) *lifvakn* (OSw)

protector (noun) *gætsla* (OSw), *gætsleman* (ODan), *væriandi* (OSw)

prove (verb) *binda* (OSw), *dryghe* (ODan), *dylia* (OSw), *fylla* (OSw), *leþa* (OSw), *pröva* (OSw), *sannprófa* (ON), *sannspyrja* (ON), *skilia* (OSw), *skynia* (OGu), *skærskuta* (OSw), *sælia* (OSw), *vinna* (OSw), *vita* (OSw), *vitna* (OSw), *væria* (OSw)

prove in law (verb) *laghvinna* (OSw)

prove lawful acquisition (verb) *vita* (OSw)

prove one's innocence (verb) *dylia* (OSw), *orsake* (ODan)

prove one's right (verb) *vita* (OSw)

prove someone right (verb) *væria* (OSw)

prove the veracity (of something) (verb) *sanna* (OSw)

prove with evidence (verb) *pröva* (OSw)

prove with oaths (verb) *sværia* (OSw)

prove with witness (verb) *vitna* (OSw)

proved (adj.) *sander* (OSw)

proven (adj.) *vitnisfastr* (ON)

proven guilty (adj.) *vitnissannr* (ON)

proven to have been engaged in unlawful sexual intercourse (adj.) *sannsorðinn* (ON)

provenance (noun) *leþsn* (OSw)

provide (verb) *fylla* (OSw), *sýsla* (ON)

provide for (verb) *föþa* (OSw), *uppihalda* (OSw), *varþveta* (OSw)

provide home (verb) *hema* (OSw)

provide hospitality (verb) *gengöra* (OSw)

provide house (verb) *husa* (OSw)

provide surety (verb) *hætte* (ODan)

provide with land (verb) *lenda* (ON)

provided day (noun) *laghastæmna* (OSw)

provider of lodgings (noun) *rættari* (OSw)

province (noun) *folkland* (OSw), *fylki* (ON), *land* (OSw), *landskap* (OSw)

province rights (noun) *landsrætter* (OSw)

province's commission (noun) *landsnæmd* (OSw)

provincial assembly (noun) *land* (OSw), *landsþing* (OSw)

provincial law (noun) *landslagh* (OSw)

provincial panel (noun) *folklandsnæmd* (OSw)

provincial tax (noun) *inlænding* (OSw)

provincial thing assembly (noun) *folklandsþing* (OSw)

proving (noun) *lagh* (OSw), *prófun* (ON)

provision (noun) *afli* (ON), *björg* (ON), *einkamál* (ON), *iþ* (OGu), *skilorð* (ON), *skipan* (OSw)

provision house (noun) *invistarhus* (OSw)

provision of food (noun) *gengærþ* (OSw)

provision of horses for transport (noun) *skiutagærþ* (OSw)

provision of the law (noun) *lagaskilorð* (ON)

provisions (noun) *koster* (OSw), *reþe* (OSw), *skipvist* (OSw), *uppheldi* (OGu), *utgærþ* (OSw), *vist* (OSw)

provost (noun) *provaster* (OSw)

prow (noun) *stamn* (OSw)

prow builder (noun) *stafnasmiðr* (ON)

proxy (noun) *vald* (OSw)

prudent (adj.) *lagha* (OSw), *laghfast* (ODan)

psalter (noun) *saltare* (OSw)

public (noun) *almænni* (OSw)

public (adj.) *openbar* (OSw), *sykn* (OSw)

public ferry (noun) *almenningsfar* (ON)

public labour (noun) *inne* (ODan)

public law (noun) *landslagh* (OSw)

public road (noun) *almænningsvægher* (OSw)

public square (noun) *almænningstorgh* (OSw)

public waterway (noun) *almannaleþ* (OSw)

publication (noun) *lysning* (OSw)

publicly (adv.) *openbarlika* (OSw)

publicly declare (verb) *lysa* (OSw), *openbara* (OSw)

publicly offer (verb) *laghbiuþa* (OSw)

publish (verb) *lysa* (OSw)

publishing (noun) *lysning* (OSw)

publishing maintenance of dependents (noun) *ómagalýsing* (ON)

pull down (verb) *ryva* (OSw)

pulley-payment (noun) *hankagjald* (ON)

pulling of hair (noun) *hardræt* (ODan), *hargrip* (ODan)

punch (verb) *hugga* (OSw), *sla* (OSw)

punish (verb) *næfsa* (OSw), *pine* (ODan), *raþa* (OSw), *refsa* (ON)

punish mildly (verb) *vanrefsa* (ON)

punishment (noun) *brut* (OSw), *hegning* (ON), *ræfsing* (OSw), *rætter* (OSw), *sak* (OSw)

punishment for sexual intercourse (noun) *legorðssekð* (ON)

punishment in accordance with the law (noun) *lagarefsing* (ON)

purchase (verb) *gælda (1)* (OSw), *köpa* (OSw)

purchase (noun) *köp* (OSw), *köpfæst* (OSw)

purchase agent (noun) *vinganaman* (OSw)

purchase agreement (noun) *köp* (OSw)

purchase at a market (noun) *torghköp* (OSw)

purchase by a freedman (noun) *leysingjakaup* (ON)

purchase into the household (noun) *bolköp* (OSw)

purchase into the marriage bed (noun) *siængaköp* (OSw)

purchase made by a minor (noun) *ómagakaup* (ON)

purchase of hay (noun) *heykaup* (ON)

purchase of land (noun) *landkaup* (ON)

purchase of peace (noun) *frithkøp* (ODan)

purchase of release from the woods (noun) *skógarkaup* (ON)

purchase sum (noun) *jorþaværþ* (OSw), *værþ* (OSw), *værþörar (pl.)* (OSw)

purchase to the home (noun) *bolköp* (OSw)

purchase witness (noun) *kaupváttr* (ON), *köpvitni* (OSw), *oþolfastir* (OSw)

purchase witness testimony (noun) *kaupsvætti* (ON)

purchase witnesses (noun) *fastar (pl.)* (OSw)

purchased land (noun) *köpoiorþ* (OSw)

purchaser (noun) *köpi* (OSw), *köpuman* (OSw)

pure (adj.) *skær* (OSw)

purge (verb) *væria* (OSw)

purification (noun) *skærsl* (OSw)

Purification of the Blessed Virgin Mary (noun) *mariumæssa* (OSw)

purified (adj.) *skær* (OSw)

purify (verb) *skæra (1)* (OSw)

purpose (noun) *vili* (OSw)

purse (noun) *sjóðr* (ON)

pursue (verb) *fulkome* (ODan), *fulla* (OSw), *fylla* (OSw), *kæra* (OSw), *sökia* (OSw), *sækia* (OSw), *vræka* (OSw)

pursue a case (verb) *sökia* (OSw)

pursuit (noun) *eftirför* (ON), *rás* (ON), *tilmæli* (OSw)

push (verb) *fælla* (OSw), *rinda* (OSw), *skiuta* (OSw), *skiuva* (OSw), *tutte* (ODan)

pushing (noun) *rindr* (OGu), *tutten* (ODan)

pushing to the ground (noun) *jorthskuv* (ODan)

put a case (verb) *krævia* (OSw)

put a fetter on (verb) *hæfta* (OSw)

put down (verb) *gælda (1)* (OSw)

put in ban (verb) *forbuþa* (OSw)

put in prohibition (verb) *forbiuþa* (OSw)

put in security (verb) *taksætia* (OSw)

put in the stocks (verb) *stokka* (OSw)

put into care (verb) *fela* (ON)

put out to tenancy (verb) *gifta* (OSw)

put responsibility on (verb) *vita* (OSw)

put staves (verb) *stavre* (ODan)

put to (cultivation) (verb) *lata* (OSw)

put to bail (verb) *taksætia* (OSw)

put under interdict (verb) *forbuþa* (OSw)

put up fence (verb) *gærþa* (OSw)

pylon on the pier (noun) *festarhæll* (ON)

pyre (noun) *bal* (OSw)

qualified (adj.) *rætter* (OSw)

quarrel (verb) *dela* (OSw), *skilia* (OSw)

quarrel (noun) *dela* (OSw), *deld* (OSw), *striþ* (OSw), *þræta* (OSw)

quarrel inappropriately (verb) *misdeila* (ON)

quarter (noun) *fiarþunger* (OSw)

quarter boundary (noun) *fjórðungamót* (ON)

quarter church (noun) *fjórðungskirkja* (ON)

Quarter Court (noun) *fjórðungsdómr* (ON)

quarter dependent (noun) *fjórðungsómagi* (ON)

quarter of a Thing assembly area (noun) *broafiol* (OSw)

quarter of a {fylki} (noun) *fiarþunger* (OSw)

quarter payment (noun) *fjórðungsgjald* (ON)

quarter stanza (noun) *fiarþunger* (OSw)

quarter thing assembly (noun) *fiærþungsþing* (OSw)

quarter weight (noun) *fjórðungavætt* (ON)

quarter-district jury (noun) *fiarþungsnæmd* (OSw)

quarter-gift (noun) *fjórðungsgjöf* (ON)

quarter-share (noun) *fiarþunger* (OSw)

question (verb) *frýja* (ON), *tortryggva* (ON)

question (noun) *tortryggð* (ON)

quick (adj.) *qvikker* (OSw)

quick witness (noun) *bræþavitni* (OSw)

quiet (adj.) *kyrr* (ON)

raft (noun) *floti* (OSw)

rafter (noun) *fleyðr* (ON)

rage (noun) *vreþshand* (OSw)

raid (verb) *for* (OSw), *hæria* (OSw)

raid (noun) *hernuðr* (ON)

raiding (noun) *hernuðr* (ON)

raise (verb) *föþa* (OSw), *reisa* (ON), *rætta* (OSw)

raise a case (verb) *krævia* (OSw), *stæmna* (OSw)

raise a challenge (verb) *klanda* (OSw), *qvælia* (OSw)

raise a claim (verb) *dela* (OSw), *kalla* (OSw), *kæra* (OSw), *sökia* (OSw), *sækta* (OSw)

raise a complaint (verb) *dela* (OSw), *kalla* (OSw), *kæra* (OSw)

raise a demand (verb) *kalla* (OSw)

raise a suit (verb) *æptirmæla* (OSw)

raising of weapons (noun) *vapntak* (ODan)

ram (noun) *veþur* (OGu)

ramming (noun) *asighling* (OSw)

range grazed by livestock (noun) *búfjárgangr* (ON)

rank (noun) *nafnbót* (ON)

ransom (verb) *aterlösa* (OSw), *lösa* (OSw)

ransom (noun) *fæ* (OSw), *lösn* (OSw)

ransom fee (noun) *leysingsaurar (pl.)* (ON), *værþörar (pl.)* (OSw)

rape (verb) *noytga* (OGu), *valdtaka* (OSw)

rape (noun) *kvinnetakt* (ODan), *nøthtækt* (ODan), *skam* (OSw), *symni* (OGu), *valdtækt* (ODan)

rape of women (noun) *kvinnetakt* (ODan)

raped (adj.) *rantakin* (OSw)

rapine (noun) *ran* (OSw), *ransdele* (ODan), *ransmal* (OSw)

rapine from churches (noun) *kirkiuran* (OSw)

rapine man (noun) *ransmaþer* (OSw)

rapist (noun) *vald* (OSw)

ravage (verb) *hæria* (OSw)

re-distribute (verb) *ryva* (OSw)

read (verb) *læsa* (OSw)

read the banns (verb) *lysa* (OSw)

real (adj.) *fulder* (OSw), *sander* (OSw)

real estate (noun) *jorþ* (OSw)

real householder (noun) *athelbonde* (ODan)

real property (noun) *ægha* (OSw)

really been used as a woman (adj.) *sannsorðinn* (ON)

realm (noun) *konongsriki* (OSw), *landeign* (ON), *riki* (OSw)

realms belonging to the king (noun) *konongsriki* (OSw)

realms of the king (noun) *konungsveldi* (ON)

reap (verb) *skæra (2)* (OSw)

reason (noun) *lagh* (OSw), *mal (1)* (OSw), *nöþsyn* (OSw), *skyld* (OSw), *skæl* (OSw)

reasonable (adj.) *skæliker* (OSw)

reasonable excuse (noun) *forfall* (OSw)

reasons (noun) *forfall* (OSw)

receipt of money (noun) *aurataka* (ON), *fétaka* (ON)

receive (verb) *viþertaka* (OSw)

receiver (noun) *viþertakuþiuver* (OSw)

receiver of stolen goods (noun) *viþertakuþiuver* (OSw)

receiver of the ring (noun) *baugþiggjandi* (ON)

receiving of the fine for trespass (noun) *landnámstaka* (ON)

receiving stolen goods (noun) *viþertakuþiufnaþer* (OSw)

recently cultivated land (noun) *nýlendi* (ON)

reception (noun) *viðtaka* (ON)

reception of stolen property (noun) *viðrtaka* (ON)

recitation of prayers (noun) *bónahald* (ON)

recitation of the law (noun) *laghsagha* (OSw)

reclaim (verb) *skipta* (OSw)

reclaimed land (noun) *tækt* (OSw)

reclaiming of sold goods (noun) *gældruf* (OSw)

recognize (verb) *kænna* (OSw), *viþerganga* (OSw)

recognized (adj.) *kenndr* (ON)

recompense (verb) *gælda (1)* (OSw), *tigla* (ON)

recompense (noun) *atergildi* (OSw), *bot* (OSw), *gæld* (OSw), *pænninger* (OSw), *vinningælogh* (OSw)

recompense with the double value (verb) *tvægilda* (OSw)

reconcile (verb) *sætta* (OSw)

reconciled (adj.) *sater* (OSw)

reconciliation (noun) *alsætti* (ON), *sæt* (OSw)

recover (verb) *sökia* (OSw)

recovered property (noun) *aterfang* (OSw)

recovery mulct (noun) *harðafang* (ON)

recruiting unit brother (noun) *havnebrother* (ODan)

rectify (verb) *rætta* (OSw)

rectory land (noun) *prestgarþer* (OSw)

rectum (noun) *rassaklof* (ON)

redeem (verb) *aterlösa* (OSw), *brigþa* (OGu), *köpa* (OSw), *lösa* (OSw), *luka* (OSw)

redemption (noun) *lösn* (OSw), *væþ* (OSw)

redemption fine (noun) *heptalaun* (OGu)

redemption land (noun) *aftrlausnarjörð* (ON)

redemption of land (noun) *brigþ* (OSw), *jarðabrigð* (ON)

redemption of livestock (noun) *búsútlausn* (ON)

redemption of odal land (noun) *óðalsbrigði* (ON)

redemption process (noun) *brigþ* (OSw)

redemption witness (noun) *árofi* (ON)

redress (verb) *böta* (OSw), *gælda (1)* (OSw)

redress (noun) *þokkabot* (OSw)

reduce (verb) *skærþa* (OSw)

reduction by a fifth (noun) *fimmtungsfall* (ON)

refer (verb) *skiuta* (OSw)

refer to a higher court (verb) *skiuta* (OSw)

refer to judgement (verb) *skærskuta* (OSw)

refer to witness (verb) *skærskuta* (OSw)

reference (noun) *skut* (ODan)

referral (noun) *avisning* (OSw)

refuse (verb) *dylia* (OSw), *ginmela* (OGu), *synia* (OSw), *vræka* (OSw)

refute (verb) *dylia* (OSw)

region (noun) *fylki* (ON), *sveit* (ON), *sysel* (ODan)

regional assembly (noun) *syselthing* (ODan)

register (noun) *máldagi* (ON)

regular (adj.) *lagha* (OSw)

regular ship (noun) *lagheskip* (ODan)

regulation (noun) *javneth* (ODan), *rætter* (OSw)

regulation of possession between neighbours of the village (noun) *oþolskipti* (OSw)

regulation of possessions (noun) *oþolskipti* (OSw)

rehearse (verb) *tína* (ON)

reign (noun) *vald* (OSw)

reject (verb) *fælla* (OSw), *neka* (OSw), *rengja* (ON), *vræka* (OSw)

rejection at law (noun) *lögrengð* (ON)

related (adj.) *byrþ* (OSw), *frankumin* (OGu), *kunder* (OSw), *sifjaðr* (ON), *skylder (1)* (OSw)

related by kinship (adj.) *sifjaðr* (ON)

related by marriage (adj.) *sifjaðr* (ON)

related woman (noun) *frændkona* (OSw)

relation by marriage (noun) *sifskaper* (OSw)

relations (noun) *hjúskapr* (ON)

relationship (noun) *hionalagh* (OSw), *kyn* (OSw), *skuldleikr* (ON)

relationship by marriage (noun) *sifskaper* (OSw)

relative (noun) *arvi* (OSw), *arvingi* (OSw), *byrþaman* (OSw), *frændi* (OSw), *magher* (OSw), *niþi* (OSw), *skuldingi* (ON)

relatives (noun) *frændsimi* (OSw), *æt* (OSw)

relatives on the maternal side (noun) *möþringar (pl.)* (OSw)

relatives on the paternal side (noun) *fæþringar (pl.)* (OSw)

relative's inheritance (noun) *niþararf* (OSw)

release (verb) *aterlösa* (OSw), *köpa* (OSw), *lata* (OSw), *lösa* (OSw), *slæppa* (OSw), *vræka* (OSw)

release (noun) *útganga* (ON)

released (adj.) *lös* (OSw)

reliable (adj.) *sander* (OSw)

reliance witness (noun) *trúnaðarváttr* (ON)

relieving oneself (noun) *þörf* (ON)

religious kinswoman (noun) *guþsivia* (OSw)

religious service (noun) *tiþir (pl.)* (OSw)

relinquish (verb) *atersighia* (OSw), *sælia* (OSw)

reluctant or stubborn person (noun) *þryter* (OSw)

remain (verb) *standa* (OSw)

remain in dependence (verb) *þyrma* (ON)

remain silent (verb) *þigia* (OSw)

remaining as guest uninvited or longer than a certain time (noun) *slímuseta* (ON)

remaining there (noun) *þarseta* (ON)

remedy (noun) *bot* (OSw)

remission of tithes (noun) *tíundargerð* (ON)

remit (verb) *gælda (1)* (OSw)

remotely related (adj.) *oskylder* (OSw)

removal of found corpse (noun) *abyrþ* (OSw)

removal of manure (noun) *taðförsla* (ON)

remuneration for services (noun) *tiþaköp* (OSw)

render invalid (verb) *ónýta* (ON)

renewing a claim (noun) *uppreist* (ON)

renounce (verb) *hafna* (ON)

rent (verb) *fæsta* (OSw), *leghia* (OSw), *læa* (OSw)

rent (noun) *afgildi* (OSw), *afraþ* (OSw), *landgilde* (ODan), *landskyld* (OSw), *legha* (OSw), *skyld* (OSw)

rent for the ship (noun) *skipleiga* (ON)

rent free (adj.) *leigulauss* (ON)

rent of livestock (noun) *búfjárleiga* (ON)

rent out (verb) *byggia* (OSw), *sælia* (OSw)

rental (noun) *legha* (OSw)

rental farm (noun) *leigujörð* (ON)

rented land (noun) *bólfesta* (ON)

rented livestock (noun) *leigufénuðr* (ON)

renting the same land (noun) *sambúð* (ON)

repair (verb) *böta* (OSw), *upgöra* (OSw)

repair (noun) *bonaþer* (OSw), *bot* (OSw)

reparation (noun) *umbót* (ON)

reparation mulct (noun) *aværkan* (OSw)

repay (verb) *gælda (1)* (OSw)

repayment {fastar} (noun) *aterköpsfastar (pl.)* (OSw)

repent (verb) *iðra* (ON)

repentance (noun) *iðrun* (ON), *yfirbót* (ON)

replace (verb) *gælda (1)* (OSw), *skipta* (OSw)

replacement (noun) *atergildi* (OSw)

report (verb) *lysa* (OSw), *skærskuta* (OSw)

report of an impending attack (noun) *hersaga* (ON)

reports of war (noun) *hersaga* (ON)

representation (noun) *koster* (OSw)

representative (noun) *ármaðr* (ON), *buþ* (OSw), *halzmaþer* (OSw), *lænsmaþer* (OSw), *sysluman* (OSw), *umbuþ* (OSw), *umbuþsman* (OSw), *ørendreki* (ON)

representative of the hundari (noun) *karl* (OSw)

representatives (noun) *næmd* (OSw)

reprieve (noun) *sykna* (ON)

reprieved (adj.) *sykn* (OSw)

reprimand (noun) *hembuþ* (OSw)

reprobation (noun) *klandan* (OSw)

repudiate (verb) *skiuta* (OSw)

request (noun) *buþ* (OSw)

request for judicial decision (noun) *dómstefna* (ON)

request for riding horses (noun) *reiðskjótaboð* (ON)

require (verb) *þorva* (OSw)

required (adj.) *skylder (2)* (OSw)

required in the same way (adj.) *jamnskylder* (OSw)

requiring no compensation (adj.) *bótalauss* (ON)

requite (verb) *gælda (1)* (OSw), *löna* (OSw)

residence (noun) *bo* (OSw), *garþer* (OSw), *heimilisfang* (ON), *skuldarstaðr* (ON), *sætugarþer* (OSw), *vist* (OSw)

resident (noun) *bokarl* (OSw), *byaman* (OSw), *byfaster* (OSw), *bygdfaster* (OSw)

resident (adj.) *bofaster* (OSw), *bolfaster* (OSw)

resident farmer (noun) *bolfaster* (OSw)

resident since the previous year (noun) *fjorðingi* (ON)

resolve (verb) *lösa* (OSw)

resolve through penance (verb) *skripta* (OSw)

resources (noun) *auðhófi* (ON)

respect (noun) *luter* (OSw)

respectable (adj.) *valinkunnr* (ON)

respite (noun) *fræst* (OSw)

respite of five days (noun) *fimmtarstefna* (ON)

respond (verb) *svara* (OSw), *væria* (OSw)

respond for (verb) *varþa* (OSw)

respondent (noun) *svarandi* (OSw)

responsibility (noun) *ábyrgð* (ON), *forráð* (ON), *raþ* (OSw), *tak* (OSw), *umbuþ* (OSw), *varþnaþer* (OSw)

responsible (adj.) *hemul* (OSw), *skilríkr* (ON), *skyldugher* (OSw)

responsible (man) (noun) *hovoþsmaþer* (OSw)

responsible for (adj.) *skyldugher* (OSw)

responsible to compensate (adj.) *saker* (OSw)

rest (noun) *qvarstaþa* (OSw)

restitution (noun) *aftrførsla* (ON)

restore (verb) *böta* (OSw)

restore the honour (verb) *syma* (OGu)

restored to its former condition (adj.) *jafnheimill* (ON)

restrain (verb) *hæfta* (OSw)

restrainer (noun) *haldbani* (OSw)

restrainer's compensation (noun) *haldsböter* (OSw)

restraint (noun) *hæfta* (OSw)

retain (verb) *göma* (OSw), *halda* (OSw)

retain authority over (verb) *valda* (OSw)

retainer (noun) *hirþman* (OSw), *húskarl* (ON)

retaining legal immunity (adj.) *friþhelagher* (OSw)

retinue (noun) *hirð* (ON)

retrieve from (verb) *ahænda* (OSw)

return (verb) *aterganga* (OSw), *aterlösa* (OSw), *gælda (1)* (OSw)

return (noun) *atergildi* (OSw), *lön* (OSw)

revealed (adj.) *openbar* (OSw)

revenge (verb) *hæmna* (OSw)

revenge (noun) *hæmd* (OSw)

reversionary inheritance (noun) *bakarf* (OSw)

revert (verb) *aterganga* (OSw)

revoke (verb) *rofna* (ON)

reward (verb) *öðlask* (ON)

reward (noun) *fyndalön* (OSw), *fæ* (OSw), *lösn* (OSw), *vinningælogh* (OSw)

reward for finding (noun) *fyndarluter* (OSw)

rib (in a ship) (noun) *innviðartré* (ON)

ride of the relatives (noun) *magaraiþ* (OGu)

ridiculous bid (noun) *fjándboð* (ON)

riding (noun) *þriþiunger* (OSw)

riding cushion (noun) *raiþvengi* (OGu)

riding horse (noun) *reiðskjóti* (ON)

riding to the assembly (noun) *þingreið* (ON)

right (noun) *hemuld* (OSw), *lagh* (OSw), *réttarmál* (ON), *rætter* (OSw), *rættindi* (OSw), *sielfsvald* (OGu), *vald* (OSw), *vita* (OSw), *vitsorþ* (OSw)

right (adj.) *lagha* (OSw), *rætter* (OSw), *sander* (OSw)

right by a child (noun) *mynding* (ODan)

right of a bishop (noun) *biskupsrætter* (OSw)

right of being principal (noun) *aðilð* (ON)

right of claim (noun) *heimting* (ON)

right of defence (noun) *vita* (OSw), *værn* (OSw)

right of land tenancy (noun) *lægþorætter* (OSw)

right of lawful pre-emption (noun) *lögmáli* (ON)

right of proof (noun) *vitsorþ* (OSw)

right of redemption (noun) *lösn* (OSw)

right of suit (noun) *sokn* (OSw)

right of the district (noun) *hærapsrætter* (OSw)

right of the king (noun) *konungsrætter* (OSw)

right of the king's representative (noun) *ármannsréttr* (ON)

right of way (noun) *farliþ* (OSw), *farvægher* (OSw), *vægher* (OSw)

right person to give the bride away (noun) *giftarmaþer* (OSw)

right to be compensated (noun) *vitsorþ* (OSw)

right to bring an axe (noun) *öxabyrþ* (OSw)

right to bring an axe to the forest (noun) *öxabyrþ* (OSw)

right to choose (noun) *vald* (OSw)

right to claim (noun) *brigþ* (OSw)

right to claim compensation (noun) *sak* (OSw)

right to claim recompense (noun) *heimta* (ON)

right to clear oneself by oath (noun) *vita* (OSw)

right to command (noun) *buþ* (OSw)

right to compensation (noun) *réttarfar* (ON)

right to confirm (noun) *vita* (OSw)

right to defend (noun) *vitsorþ* (OSw), *værn* (OSw)

right to defend land (noun) *jortheværn* (ODan)

right to defend oneself (noun) *vita* (OSw), *vitsorþ* (OSw), *værnarord* (OSw)

right to defend with an oath (noun) *dul* (OSw)

right to enforce the law (noun) *réttendavald* (ON)

right to gather eggs (noun) *eggver* (ON)

right to govern and to prosecute (noun) *yfirsókn* (ON)

right to inherit from a home-born thrall (noun) *van* (OSw)

right to inviolability (noun) *friþer* (OSw)

right to judge (noun) *domber* (OSw)

right to leave (noun) *útför* (ON)

right to live in the land (noun) *landsvist* (OSw)

right to live in the province (noun) *landsvist* (OSw)

right to ownership (noun) *egn* (OSw), *eignarskifti* (ON)

right to place a ban (noun) *laghfæstning* (ODan)

right to plead (noun) *bön* (OSw)

right to prosecute (noun) *sokn* (OSw)

right to prove (noun) *lagh* (OSw), *vita* (OSw), *vitsorþ* (OSw)

right to reclaim (noun) *brigþ* (OSw)

right to redeem land (noun) *buþ* (OSw)

right to remain in the land (noun) *landsvist* (OSw)

right to search (noun) *ransak* (OSw)

right to seize (noun) *innam* (ODan)

right to submit goods in the hands of a surety man (noun) *tak* (OSw)

right to substantiate (noun) *vitsorþ* (OSw)

right to use grass (noun) *grasnautn* (ON)

righteous (adj.) *rætter* (OSw)

righteous man (noun) *sannindaman* (OSw)

rightful (adj.) *lagha* (OSw), *rætter* (OSw), *sander* (OSw)

rightful (ownership) (adj.) *hemul* (OSw)

rightful absence (noun) *forfall* (OSw)

rightful receiver (noun) *viðtökumaðr* (ON)

rightfully (adv.) *rætlika* (OSw)

rightfully bound (adj.) *réttbundinn* (ON)

rightly (adv.) *ræt* (OSw)

rightly accused (adj.) *sannsakaðr* (ON)

rights (noun) *friþer* (OSw), *ítak* (ON), *réttendi* (ON), *rætter* (OSw)

ring (noun) *bogher* (OSw)

ring (wergild) fixed by law (noun) *lögbaugr* (ON)

ring payment (noun) *bauggildi* (ON)

ring-atonement (noun) *baugbót* (ON)

ring-lady (noun) *baugrýgr* (ON)

ring-man (noun) *baugamaðr* (ON)

rise to half a hundred (i.e. sixty) (verb) *hyndask* (ON)

risk (verb) *viþerhætta* (OSw)

risk (a fine of) (verb) *viþerhætta* (OSw)

rite (noun) *setning* (ON)

rites (noun) *rætter* (OSw)

river boat (noun) *ekia* (OSw)

road (noun) *farvægher* (OSw), *gata* (OSw), *markavægher* (OSw), *vægher* (OSw) road clear of snow (noun) *sniovægher* (OSw)

road for dead bodies (noun) *likvægher* (OSw)

road in the wood (noun) *skoghvægh* (ODan)

road of a district (noun) *hærethsvægh* (ODan)

road of escape (noun) *löpstigher* (OSw)

road over land (noun) *landsvægher* (OSw)

road to the assembly (noun) *þingsvægher* (OSw)

road to the church (noun) *kirkiuvægher* (OSw)

road to the Thing assembly (noun) *þingsvægher* (OSw)

rob (verb) *röva* (OSw), *ræna* (OSw), *stiæla* (OSw), *valdtaka* (OSw)

robbed (adj.) *rantakin* (OSw)

robber (noun) *ransmaþer* (OSw)

robber in the forest (noun) *grimumaþer* (OSw)

robbery (noun) *bosran* (OSw), *férán* (ON), *gripdeild* (ON), *ran* (OSw), *ránbaugr* (ON), *útilega* (ON)

robbery at home (noun) *bosran* (OSw)

robbery from a corpse (noun) *likran* (OSw)

robbery from a person's hands (noun) *handran* (OSw)

robbery of betrothal (noun) *fæstningaran* (OSw)

robbery of confiscated goods (noun) *lyktaran* (OSw)

robbery of goods which shall be divided by lots (noun) *lotran* (OSw)

robbing the corpse of a dead man (noun) *valrof* (OSw)

rock (noun) *sten* (OSw)

rocky ground (noun) *hölkn* (ON)

Rogation Day (noun) *gangdagher* (OSw)

Rogation Days (noun) *gangdagahelgr* (ON), *gangdagher* (OSw)

Rogation Week (noun) *helgavika* (ON)

rollers (noun) *hlunnar (pl.)* (ON)

rolling pin (noun) *kafli* (OSw)

Rome tax (noun) *rómaskattr* (ON)

roof board (noun) *troþr* (OGu)

rookery (noun) *látr* (ON)

room (noun) *hærbærghi* (OSw)

roost (noun) *vaghli* (OSw)

rooted (adj.) *rótfastr* (ON)

rope (verb) *repa* (OSw)

rope (noun) *band* (OSw), *fæst* (OSw), *rep* (ODan), *snóri* (ON)

roped (adj.) *repdrøgh* (ODan)

roping (noun) *rep* (ODan)

rouse (verb) *reisa* (ON)

route (noun) *vægher* (OSw)

route for forwarding messages (noun) *boðburðr* (ON)

rove (noun) *ró* (ON)

rower (noun) *sæssi* (OSw)

rowing bench (noun) *hasæti* (OSw)

royal authority (noun) *konungsvald* (ON)

royal progress (noun) *eriksgata* (OSw)

royal property (noun) *konungsfé* (ON)

rudder (noun) *stýri* (ON)

rudder strap (noun) *stýrihamla* (ON)

ruin with slander (verb) *fyrirrógja* (ON)

rule (verb) *raþa* (OSw), *styra* (OSw), *valda* (OSw)

rule (noun) *endimark* (ON), *lagh* (OSw), *skilvangi* (ON)

rule of law (noun) *friþer* (OSw)

rumour (noun) *ymil* (OGu)

rumoured in the district (adj.) *heraðsfleyttr* (ON)

run (noun) *löpstigher* (OSw)

run away (verb) *löpstigher* (OSw), *løpe* (ODan)

run off (verb) *løpe* (ODan)

runaway from court (noun) *dómflogi* (ON)

runaway from her betrothed man (noun) *flannfluga* (ON)

runaway from his betrothed woman (noun) *fuðflogi* (ON)

running away (noun) *löpstigher* (OSw), *rás* (ON)

running out of food (adj.) *matþrota* (ON)

rural dean (noun) *provaster* (OSw)

rural men (noun) *landsmaþer* (OSw)

rush (noun) *hlaup* (ON)

rye (noun) *rugher* (OSw)

Sabbath-breaking (noun) *hælghebrut* (ODan), *hælghudaghabrut* (OSw)

sacrament (noun) *repskaper* (OSw), *þiænista* (OSw)

sacred (adj.) *helagher* (OSw)

sacrifice (verb) *blota* (OSw)

sacrifice (noun) *blot* (OGu), *blotan* (OGu)

sacrificial day (noun) *offerdagher* (OSw)

sacrilege (noun) *hælghebrut* (ODan)

saddle (verb) *söðla* (ON)

saddle horse (noun) *reiðskjóti* (ON)

saddlecloth (noun) *raiþklepi* (OGu)

safe conduct (noun) *griþ* (OSw)

safeguard (noun) *laghvardnaþer* (OSw), *værn* (OSw)

safeguarded (adj.) *vandhófr* (ON)

safekeeping (noun) *hirzla* (ON)

safety (noun) *hælgh* (OSw)

sail (noun) *segl* (ON)

sail-yard (noun) *ra* (OSw)

sailing upon someone (noun) *asighling* (OSw)

sailor (noun) *skipari* (OSw)

Saint Botulf's Mass (17 June) (noun) *botulfsmæssa* (OSw)

Saint Ilian's Mass (noun) *yliansmæssa* (OSw)

Saint Katrin's Mass (noun) *katrinamæssa* (OSw)

Saint Lawrence's Day (noun) *lafrinzsmæssa* (OSw)

Saint Michael's Day (noun) *mikialsdagher* (OSw)

Saint Peter's Mass (noun) *petersmessa* (OSw), *sankti petrs messa* (OGu)

Saints' Mass of Selja (8 July) (noun) *heilagra manna messa í Selju* (ON)

sake (noun) *skyld* (OSw)

salaried work (noun) *legheværk* (ODan)

salary (noun) *legha* (OSw)

salary reduction (noun) *leigufall* (ON)

sale (noun) *köp* (OSw), *sala* (OSw)

sale of a slave (noun) *mansal* (ON)

sale of hay (noun) *heysala* (ON)

saleable without being subject to a kinsman's portion (adj.) *afraþalaus* (OGu)

salesman (noun) *köpi* (OSw), *köpman* (OSw)

salmon stream (noun) *laxá* (ON)

salt (noun) *salt* (ON)

salvage (noun) *flutning* (ON)

salvaged whale (noun) *flutningshvalr* (ON)

same time the following year (noun) *jamlangi* (OSw)

sanctified (adj.) *helagher* (OSw)

sanctity (noun) *friþer* (OSw), *hælgh* (OSw)

sanctuary (noun) *friþer* (OSw), *heli* (OGu), *hælgh* (OSw), *skiolder* (OSw)

sandbank (noun) *eyrr* (ON)

sane (adj.) *óórr* (ON)

satin ribbon (noun) *silkisband* (OGu)

satisfactory (adj.) *gilder* (OSw)

satisfy (verb) *fylla* (OSw), *ganga* (OSw)

saving advice (noun) *bjargráð* (ON)

say (verb) *skilia* (OSw), *vátta* (ON)

say that someone is guilty (verb) *sanna* (OSw)

say that someone is innocent (verb) *skæra (1)* (OSw)

scab (noun) *hrufa* (ON)

scale of compensations (noun) *saktal* (ON)

scale of measurement (noun) *mæt* (OSw)

scales (noun) *skal* (OGu)

scalp (noun) *torfa* (OGu)

Scanian (noun) *skaning* (ODan)

scar (noun) *ílit* (ON)

scar on the head (noun) *kambstaðr* (ON)

scarred (adj.) *ærraþer* (OSw)

scene of the killing (noun) *vighvalder* (OSw)

scheming (noun) *fjörráð* (ON)

scoop (noun) *austker* (ON)

scoundrel (noun) *illgærningisman* (OSw)

scraped bark (noun) *skaf* (ON)

scratch (verb) *hrífa* (ON), *skena* (OSw)

scribe (noun) *nótari* (ON)

scrub-child (noun) *rishofþe* (OSw)

scrubland (noun) *rifhrís* (ON)

scrubling (noun) *hrísungr* (ON)

scrubling's inheritance (noun) *hrísungserfð* (ON)

sea (noun) *sior* (OSw)

sea bank (noun) *marbakki* (ON)

sea regulation (noun) *roþarætter* (OSw)

sea warrior district (noun) *hamna* (OSw)

seal (verb) *lykkia* (OGu)

seal (1) (noun) *innsigli* (ON)

seal (2) (noun) *selr* (ON)

seal a bargain (verb) *köpa* (OSw)

seal of the presiding judge (noun) *lögmannsinnsigli* (ON)

sealing ground (noun) *látr* (ON)

search (verb) *leta* (OSw), *ransaka* (OSw)

search (noun) *ransak* (OSw), *ransakan* (OSw)

searches section (noun) *rannsóknaþáttr* (ON)

searching (noun) *ransak* (OSw)

season (noun) *misseri* (ON)

seat (noun) *hamna* (OSw), *sess* (ON)

seat on the Law Council (noun) *lögréttuseta* (ON)

seaworthy (adj.) *fœrr* (ON)

second cousin (noun) *bróðrungsbarn* (ON), *næstsystkenebarn* (ODan), *þræmænninger* (OSw)

second cousins (noun) *næstabróðra (pl.)* (ON)

second cousins in the agnatic line (noun) *eftirbróðrasynir (pl.)* (ON)

secret hiding of a corpse (noun) *abyrþ* (OSw)

secret of the Mass (noun)

secretly (adv.) *lønlike* (ODan)

section (noun) *balker* (OSw), *luter* (OSw), *þáttr* (ON)

section of a fence (noun) *balker* (OSw)

section of the law (noun) *lögþáttr* (ON), *mal (1)* (OSw)

section on drift rights (noun) *rekabölkr* (ON)

section on the maintenance of dependents and indigent people (noun) *framfœrslubölkr* (ON)

secular chieftain (noun) *væreldshøvthing* (ODan)

secular lord (noun) *væreldshøvthing* (ODan)

secure by law (verb) *lögfesta* (ON)

security (noun) *borghan* (OSw), *brötartak* (OSw), *gilzl* (OSw), *griþ* (OSw), *nam* (OSw), *tak* (OSw), *trygth*

(ODan), *varzla* (ON), *visse* (ODan), *vite* (ODan), *væþ* (OSw)

security in seven nights (noun) *siunættatak* (OSw)

security of stolen goods given on the road (noun) *brötartak* (OSw)

security that a person be present at a certain place (noun) *qvarsætutak* (OSw)

security witness (noun) *tryggvaváttr* (ON)

seduce (verb) *gilia* (OSw), *glópa* (ON), *lighra* (OSw), *lukka* (OGu)

seduction (noun) *lighri* (OSw)

seduction of women (noun) *kvennalegorð* (ON)

see (verb) *sea* (OSw), *syna* (OSw)

seed (noun) *sæþ* (OSw)

seek (verb) *leta* (OSw), *sökia* (OSw)

seek a person's peace (verb) *friþsökia* (OSw)

seek revenge (verb) *ora* (OSw)

seeking of fines (noun) *sokn* (OSw)

seine-net (noun) *not* (OSw)

seine-net catches (noun) *notadræt* (OSw)

seizable (adj.) *uppnæmr* (ON)

seize (verb) *mæta* (OSw), *næma* (OSw), *taka* (OSw), *virþa* (OSw)

seize goods (verb) *skyvle* (ODan)

seized (adj.) *rantakin* (OSw)

seized cattle (noun) *innam* (ODan)

seized property (noun) *intækt* (OSw)

seizing of hair (noun) *hargrip* (ODan)

seizure (noun) *atför* (ON), *innam* (ODan), *intækt* (OSw), *mæt* (OSw), *nam* (OSw), *ran* (OSw)

seizure fine (noun) *ránbaugr* (ON)

seizure mulct (noun) *áfang* (ON)

seizure of animals (noun) *innam* (ODan)

seizure of goods (noun) *fjárrán* (ON)

seizure process (noun) *mæt* (OSw)

select (verb) *næmna* (OSw), *raþa* (OSw), *vanda* (ON)

self-contradiction (noun) *tvætala* (OSw)

self-supporting man (noun) *sjalfelðismaðr* (ON)

self-witness (noun) *ainsyri* (OGu)

sell (verb) *afhænda* (OSw), *köpa* (OSw), *sælia* (OSw)

sell away (verb) *forhæghthe* (ODan)

sell with a friend (verb) *vinga* (OSw)

seller (noun) *köpi* (OSw), *sali* (OSw), *saluman* (OSw), *seljandi* (ON)

selling (noun) *köp* (OSw), *sala* (OSw), *sæljen* (ODan)

selling of forgeries (noun) *flærþsala* (OSw)

send (verb) *skiuta* (OSw), *visa* (OSw)

send away (noun) *vræka* (OSw)

send bailiffs (to someone) (verb) *mæta* (OSw)

senseless (adj.) *óviti* (ON)

senseless deed (noun) *ovitagærning* (OSw)

sentence (verb) *döma* (OSw), *fælla* (OSw)

sentence (noun) *áfall* (ON), *domber* (OSw), *ræfst* (OSw)

sentence to greater excommunication (verb) *bansætia* (OSw)

sentenced (adj.) *laghfælder* (OSw), *saker* (OSw)

sentenced to church penance (adj.) *skriptaþer* (OSw)

separate (verb) *skilia* (OSw), *skipta* (OSw), *skæra (2)* (OSw)

separate land (noun) *ornume* (ODan), *thokkeland* (ODan)

separate part (noun) *stumn* (OSw)

separation (noun) *skilnaþer* (OSw)

separation of man and wife (noun) *hjónaskilnuðr* (ON)

sequestration security (noun) *qvarsætutak* (OSw)

serious (adj.) *fulder* (OSw)

serious crime (noun) *stórglópr* (ON)

serious penance (noun) *stórskrift* (ON)

serious trespassing (in someone's home) (noun) *hemsokn* (OSw)

serious trouble (noun) *stórnauðsyn* (ON)

serious wound (noun) *skena* (OSw)

servant (noun) *annöþogher* (OSw), *hion* (OSw), *húskarl* (ON), *leghohion* (OSw), *sven* (OSw), *varþnaþahion* (OSw), *vinnumaðr* (ON), *þiænistumaþer* (OSw), *þjónn* (ON)

servant killing (noun) *hývíg* (ON)

servant of god (noun) *guthsthjanesteman* (ODan)

servant-woman (noun) *griþkuna* (OGu), *huskona* (OSw)

servant's payment (noun) *hionamali* (OSw)

serve (verb) *varþa* (OSw), *veta* (OSw)

service (noun) *liþ (2)* (OSw), *æmbæte* (ODan), *þiænista* (OSw)

serviceable (adj.) *gilder* (OSw)

services (noun) *tiþir (pl.)* (OSw)

serving man (noun) *húskarl* (ON), *þiænistumaþer* (OSw)

servitude (noun) *annöþogherdomber* (OSw)

set (verb) *fæsta* (OSw), *vátta* (ON)

set a date (verb) *eindaga* (ON)

set a trap (verb) *gildra* (OSw)

set a value upon (verb) *virþa* (OSw)

set aside (verb) *afsætia* (OSw), *ryva* (OSw)

set day (noun) *laghdagh* (ODan), *stæmnudagher* (OSw)

set free (verb) *slæppa* (OSw)

set in surety (verb) *væþsætia* (OSw)

set off (verb) *jamka* (OSw)

set on fire (verb) *brænna* (OSw)

set up (verb) *reisa* (ON)

set up fence (verb) *gærþa* (OSw)

set value (noun) *mæt* (OSw)

set-aside (noun) *göþning* (OSw)

set-aside area (noun) *göþning* (OSw)

setting in surety (noun) *væpning* (OSw)

setting of time limits (noun) *stefnugerð* (ON)

settle (verb) *aflæggia* (OSw), *döma* (OSw), *lösa* (OSw), *luka* (OSw), *rætta* (OSw), *skilia* (OSw), *slita* (OSw), *sætia* (OSw), *sætta* (OSw)

settle in a fixed home (verb) *staþfæsta* (OSw)

settled (adj.) *boandi* (OSw), *bofaster* (OSw), *sater* (OSw)

settled respite (noun) *stæmnudagher* (OSw)

settlement (1) (noun) *gærþ* (OSw), *sáttargerð* (ON), *sæt* (OSw), *sættargærþ* (OSw)

settlement (2) (noun) *bygd* (OSw), *bygning* (OSw)

settlement meeting (noun) *sáttarstefna* (ON)

settlement-sent (adj.) *byggðfleyttr* (ON)

settling day (noun) *endaghi* (OSw)

seven-night meeting (noun) *siunættingsgærþ* (OSw)

seven-night summons (noun) *siunættinger* (OSw), *siunættingsgærþ* (OSw)

seven-week fast (noun) *sjauviknafasta* (ON)

seventh-day ale (noun) *sjaund* (ON)

several (of them) (adj.) *ymsir* (OSw)

severe blow with a blunt object (noun) *blokhogg* (OSw)

sex organs (noun) *hreðjar (pl.)* (ON)

sexton (noun) *klokkari* (OSw)

sexton's remuneration (noun) *klokkaragiald* (OSw)

sexual intercourse (noun) *hæfþ* (OSw), *lighri* (OSw), *líkamslosti* (ON), *symni* (OGu)

sexual intercourse with an animal (noun) *þyþilagh* (OSw)

sexually impotent (adj.) *sinfallinn* (ON)

shackle (noun) *fiætur* (OSw)

shaft (noun) *skapt* (OSw)

shaft of an arrow (noun) *örvarhúnn* (ON)

shake (verb) *nykkia* (OGu)

shaking (noun) *rysking* (ON), *rystr* (OGu)

shame (verb) *skemma* (OGu)

shame (noun) *hneyksli* (ON), *skam* (OSw)

shame-pole (noun) *níðstöng* (ON)

shame-stroke (noun) *klámhögg* (ON)

shameful killing (noun) *skemmðarvíg* (ON)

shameful word (noun) *firnarorþ* (OSw)

shaming (noun) *þokki* (OSw)

shaming slander (noun) *níð* (ON)

share (verb) *jamna* (OSw), *skipta* (OSw)

share (noun) *luter* (OSw), *skipti* (OSw)

share of inheritance (noun) *ærfþaloter* (OSw)

share out (verb) *skipta* (OSw)

shared fences (noun) *halfgierþi* (OGu)

shared living quarters (noun) *samvist* (OSw)

shear (verb) *klippa* (OGu)

shed (noun) *boþ* (OSw)

sheep (noun) *færsauðr* (ON), *lamb* (OSw)

sheep gathering (noun) *lögrétt* (ON)

sheep mark (noun) *sauðamörk* (ON)

sheep worrier (noun) *sauðbítr* (ON)

sheep-walk (noun) *færganger* (OSw), *sauðagangr* (ON)

shelter (verb) *halda* (OSw), *husa* (OSw)

shelter (noun) *boþ* (OSw), *hærbærghi* (OSw)

shepherd (noun) *akerhirthe* (ODan), *hirþe* (OSw)

sheriff (noun) *foghati* (OSw), *lænsmaþer* (OSw), *sysluman* (OSw), *valdsmaþer* (OSw)

sheriff's district (noun) *sysel* (ODan)

shield (verb) *göma* (OSw)

shield (noun) *skiolder* (OSw)

shieling (noun) *sel* (ON), *sællaboþ* (OSw), *sætr* (ON)

shift (verb) *skipta* (OSw)

shift (noun) *skipti* (OSw)

shift in the order of inheritance (noun) *knéskot* (ON)

shift of boundary markers (noun) *raförning* (OSw)

shilling (noun) *örtogh* (OSw)

ship (noun) *skip* (OSw)

ship captain (noun) *styriman* (OSw)

ship cost (noun) *skipsverð* (ON)

ship hauling (noun) *skipdráttr* (ON)

ship loan (noun) *skipslán* (ON)

ship peace (noun) *snækkiufrither* (OSw)

ship supplies (noun) *skipvist* (OSw)

ship-district (noun) *skiplagh* (OSw)

ship-soke (noun) *skipen* (ODan)

shipbuilding (noun) *skipasmíð* (ON)

shipman (noun) *skipamaðr* (ON)

shipping lane (noun) *bataleþ* (OSw)

shipwreck (noun) *hafrek* (OGu), *skipbrut* (ODan)

shipwrecked man (noun) *skipbrotsmaðr* (ON)

shipwright (noun) *smiþer* (OSw)

ship's inheritance (noun) *skiperfð* (ON)

ship's master (noun) *skipdróttinn* (ON), *styriman* (OSw)

shirt (noun) *skyrta* (OGu)

shoal of herring (noun) *áta* (ON)

shoaling gradually from the shore (adj.) *útgrunnr* (ON)

shoemaker (noun) *sútari* (ON)

shoot (verb) *skiuta* (OSw)

shore (noun) *fjara* (ON), *land* (OSw)

shore of tenant land (noun) *leigulandsfjara* (ON)

shore-bounds (noun) *fjörumark* (ON)

shoreline plot (noun) *rörtegher* (OSw)

shortfall (noun) *aterstaþa* (OSw)

shot (noun) *skut* (ODan)

shoulder of a deer (noun) *skotbógr* (ON)

shout (verb) *öpa* (OSw)

shout (noun) *op* (OSw)

show (verb) *öghlysa* (OSw), *syna* (OSw)

show someone to lodgings (verb) *rætta* (OSw)

shrift breaking (adj.) *skriftrofa* (ON)

shrift-breaking (noun) *skriftrof* (ON)

shrive (verb) *skripta* (OSw)

Shrove Sunday (meat Sunday) (noun) *kötsunnudagher* (OSw)

sibling brood (noun) *siskinaalder* (OSw)

siblings (noun) *systkin* (ON)

siblings of the same parents (noun) *samsyskine* (OSw)

sickle (noun) *sniðill* (ON)

side (noun) *flokker* (OSw), *hand* (OSw), *vægher* (OSw)

side of the family (noun) *kolder* (OSw)

sight of land (noun) *landssyn* (OGu)

sign (noun) *jartighni (pl.)* (OSw)

sign of the cross (noun) *kross* (ON)

signing with the Christian cross (noun) *prímsignun* (ON)

silver (noun) *silver* (OSw)

silver band (noun) *silfrband* (OGu)

silver smith (noun) *silfsmiþer* (OSw)

sin (verb) *synda* (OSw)

sin (noun) *glópr* (ON), *synd* (OSw), *syndamal* (OSw)

sinful living (noun) *osiþer* (OSw)

single (adj.) *ainloypr* (OGu)

single assembly (noun) *ennætþing* (OSw)

single buy (noun) *enkøp* (ODan)

single compensation (noun) *enböte* (OSw), *sporgæld* (OSw)

single compensation (from a known killer) (noun) *sporgæld* (OSw)

single fine (noun) *enböte* (OSw)

single man (noun) *enløpman* (ODan)

single month (noun) *einmánuðr* (ON)

single woman (noun) *enlöpkona* (OSw), *nokkefrue* (ODan), *nokkekone* (ODan)

single worker (noun) *einvirki* (ON)

single-handed farmer (noun) *einvirki* (ON)

Sir (noun) *hærra* (OSw)

sister's daughters (noun) *systrunger* (OSw)

sister's sons (noun) *systrunger* (OSw)

sit (verb) *sitia* (OSw)

site of a killing (noun) *vighvalder* (OSw)

sitting out at night (noun) *útilega* (ON), *útiseta* (ON)

sitting outside (noun) *útiseta* (ON)

situation (noun) *fall* (OSw), *mal (1)* (OSw)

six months (noun) *misseri* (ON)

six-man oath (noun) *séttareiðr* (ON), *sexmannaeiðr* (ON)

sixth (noun) *siettungr* (OGu)

size of land (noun) *jarðarmegin* (ON)

size of the share (noun) *jarðarmegin* (ON)

skerry-corpse (noun) *skernár* (ON)

ski (noun) *skíð* (ON)

skiff (noun) *ekia* (OSw)

skin (noun) *harund* (OGu), *huþ* (OSw)

skin of animals (noun) *huþ* (OSw)

skin of human beings (noun) *huþ* (OSw)

skin of the feet of animals (noun) *fit* (ON)

skin-scratch (noun) *huþsverf* (OSw)

skin-tax (noun) *skin* (OSw)

skipper (noun) *skipari* (OSw)

skull (noun) *hiernskal* (OGu)

slander (verb) *rógja* (ON)

slander (noun) *fjölmæli* (ON), *illmæli* (ON), *níð* (ON), *orþ* (OGu), *róg* (ON)

slander in verse form (noun) *skáldskaparmál* (ON)

slanderer (noun) *fjölmælismaðr* (ON), *rógsmaðr* (ON)

slap (noun) *blak* (ON), *puster* (OSw)

slaughter (verb) *dræpa* (OSw), *slátra* (ON)

slave (noun) *ambat* (OSw), *annöþogher* (OSw), *hion* (OSw), *man* (OSw), *mansmaðr* (ON), *maþer* (OSw), *þjónn* (ON), *þræl* (OSw)

slave (adj.) *ofrœls* (OSw)

slave in payment of a debt (noun) *gæfþræl* (OSw)

slave ring (noun) *þrælbaugr* (ON)

slave-woman (noun) *ambat* (OSw), *huskona* (OSw)

slavery (noun) *ánauð* (ON), *annöþogher* (OSw), *annöþogherdomber* (OSw), *þrældómr* (ON)

slave's work for his own benefit (noun) *orka* (ON)

slay (verb) *dræpa* (OSw), *hugga* (OSw), *sla* (OSw), *vægha (1)* (OSw)

slayer (noun) *banaman* (OSw), *bani* (OSw), *drapari* (OSw)

slaying (noun) *aftaka* (ON)

slaying prosecutor (noun) *æptirmælandi* (OSw)

sledge dragging rights (noun) *kælkadræt* (OSw)

sleep with (verb) *liggia* (OSw), *lighra* (OSw)

sleeping house (noun) *symnhus* (OSw), *symnskæmma* (OSw)

sleeping quarters (noun) *hærbærghi* (OSw)

sleeping with (noun) *lægher* (OSw)

slice (verb) *skæra (2)* (OSw)

sling (verb) *sla* (OSw)

slip rail (noun) *liþ (1)* (OSw)

sliver (noun) *flís* (ON)

sloth-fine (noun) *slanbaugr* (ON)

sluggard (noun) *nokkadrumber* (OSw)

small boat (noun) *ekia* (OSw), *floti* (OSw)

small coin (noun) *þveiti* (ON)

small farm animal (noun) *smafileþi* (OGu)

small livestock (noun) *smafileþi* (OGu)

small tree (noun) *undirviþer* (OSw)

small vessel (noun) *myndrikkia* (OGu)

smallholding (noun) *þorp* (OSw)

smash (verb) *hugga* (OSw)

smith (noun) *smiþer* (OSw)

smithy (noun) *smiþia* (OSw)

smoke (noun) *reykr* (ON)

smuggled stolen goods (noun) *abyrþ* (OSw)

snare (noun) *strænger* (OSw)

social standing (noun) *raþ* (OSw), *rætter* (OSw)

socket (of a spear) (noun) *falr* (ON)

sod (noun) *mold* (ON), *torf* (OSw), *torfa* (OGu)

soil (noun) *jorþ* (OSw)

soldier (noun) *drengmaðr* (ON)

sole heiress (noun) *baugrýgr* (ON)

solution (noun) *órlausn* (ON), *raþ* (OSw)

solve (verb) *lösa* (OSw)

somebody (noun) *maþer* (OSw)

someone (noun) *maþer* (OSw)

someone from a different quarter (noun) *útanfjórðungsmaðr* (ON)

someone from another province (noun) *utlændinger* (OSw)

someone from inner Trondelag (noun) *innþróndr* (ON)

someone from outer Trondelag (noun) *útþróndr* (ON)

someone intending to prosecute (noun) *æptirmælandi* (OSw)

someone left on a shore (noun) *strandsetr* (ON)

someone on a ship (noun) *skipari* (ON)

someone to vouch (noun) *varþnaþer* (OSw)

someone who can tell what happened (noun) *segjandi* (ON)

someone who hides stolen goods (noun) *viþertakuþiuver* (OSw)

something brought in secret (noun) *abyrþ* (OSw)

something done unwillingly (noun) *vaþaværk* (OSw)

something faulty (noun) *fals* (OSw)

something illegal (noun) *ofriþer* (OSw)

something stolen (noun) *tjun* (ODan)

something taken (noun) *griper* (OSw)

something thieved (noun) *þiufstolin* (OSw)

something valued in money (noun) *virthepænning* (ODan)

something which spoils a case (noun) *sakarspell* (ON)

son (noun) *mögr* (ON)

son by/with a concubine (noun) *frillusun* (OSw), *slokifrilluson* (OSw)

son of a father's brother (noun) *bróðrasynir (pl.)* (ON)

son of a freedman (noun) *leysingssonr* (ON)

son of a fully freed slave (noun) *leysingssonr* (ON)

son of a lawfully married woman (noun) *aþalkonusun* (OSw)

son of a legitimate wife (noun) *aþalkonusun* (OSw)

son of a mistress (noun) *frillusun* (OSw)

son of a paternal uncle (noun) *bröþrungi* (OSw)

son of a priest (noun) *prestson* (OGu)

son of a slave-woman (adj.) *þiþborin* (OSw)

son of a wife (noun) *aþalkonusun* (OSw)

son-in-law (noun) *magher* (OSw)

song book (noun) *sangbok* (OSw)

sons of father's brothers (noun) *bröþrungi* (OSw)

sons of siblings (noun) *systkinasynir (pl.)* (ON)

son's inheritance (noun) *maghararf* (OSw)

son's wife (noun) *sonarkona* (ON)

soothsaying (noun) *spá* (ON), *spáför* (ON)

sorcerer (noun) *fordæða* (ON), *gærningisman* (OSw), *trulkarl* (OSw)

sorcery (noun) *fordeþskepr* (OGu), *galdr* (ON), *gærning* (OSw), *troldomber* (OSw)

soul gift (noun) *sialagift* (OSw)

soul mass (noun) *sialamæssa* (OSw)

soul's ale (noun) *sáluöl* (ON)

sound in limb (adj.) *limheill* (ON)

sound of weapons (noun) *vapntak* (ODan)

southern (man) (adj.) *sundrisker* (OSw)

Southerner (noun) *suþermaþer* (OSw)

sowing time (noun) *sæþ* (OSw)

spade-freedman (noun) *grefleysingr* (ON)

span (noun) *spander* (OSw)

span, a measure of length (noun) *spann* (ON)

spawning ground (for fish) (noun) *fiskeleker* (OSw)

spawning season (for fish) (noun) *fiskeleker* (OSw)

spay (verb) *gælda (2)* (OSw)

speak correctly (verb) *réttmæla* (ON)

speak for (verb) *æptirmæla* (OSw)

spear (noun) *asker* (OSw), *sialfskut* (OSw), *spiut* (OSw)

spear man (noun) *spjutsman* (ODan)

spearshaft (noun) *geirskaft* (ON), *spjótskaft* (ON)

special commune meeting (noun) *hreppsfundr* (ON)

special leave (noun) *einkaleyfi* (ON), *einkalof* (ON)

special right (noun) *einkamál* (ON)

specifications (noun) *forskæl* (OSw)

specified date (noun) *stæmnudagher* (OSw)

specified time (noun) *fræst* (OSw)

speech (noun) *mal (1)* (OSw)

spell (noun) *fordath* (ODan), *forgærning* (OSw), *galdr* (ON)

spindle (noun) *snælda* (ON)

spinster (noun) *mö* (OSw)

spiritual affinity (noun) *guþsivalagh* (OSw), *guþsivi* (OSw)

spiritual gift (noun) *sialagift* (OSw)

spiritual incest (noun) *guþsivalaghspiæl* (OSw)

spiritual kinship (noun) *guþsivalagh* (OSw), *guþsivi* (OSw)

spiritual kinswoman (noun) *guþsivia* (OSw)

spit (verb) *hrækja* (ON)

split scalp (noun) *suarþsprangr* (OGu)

split up (verb) *skilia* (OSw)

spoil (verb) *firigæra* (OSw), *forhæghthe* (ODan), *spilla* (OSw)

spoil by slander (verb) *fyrirrógja* (ON)

spoil by word (verb) *fyrirmæla* (ON)

spoiled catching rights (noun) *veiðispell* (ON)

spoiled prospects (noun) *ráðspell* (ON)

spokesman (noun) *malsmaþer* (OSw), *mælandi* (ON)

spouse (noun) *hion* (OSw), *husfrugha* (OSw), *kona* (OSw)

spouses and parents and children (noun) *siængaralster* (OSw)

spring assembly (noun) *varþing* (OSw)

spring assembly place (noun) *þingvöllr* (ON)

spring county meeting (noun) *manntalsþing* (ON)

spring fodder (noun) *várfóðr* (ON)

spring peace (noun) *varfriþer* (OSw)

spring sanctity (noun) *varfriþer* (OSw)

spring tithe (noun) *vártíund* (ON)

springtime immunity (noun) *varfriþer* (OSw)

springtime sanctity (noun) *varfriþer* (OSw)

squabble (noun) *orþaskipti* (OSw)

squabble between friends (noun) *vingretta* (ON)

squad (noun) *sveit* (ON)

squander (verb) *firihæghþa* (OSw), *forhæghthe* (ODan), *uhæghthe* (ODan)

square piece of a whale's blubber (noun) *húnn* (ON)

squire (noun) *sven* (OSw)

squirrel (noun) *ikorni* (OSw)

squirrel pelt (noun) *graskin* (OSw)

SS Simon and Jude's Day (noun) *símonsmessudagr ok judas* (ON)

St Agnes's Day (noun) *agnesmessa* (ON)

St Ambrose's Day (noun) *ambrósiusmessa* (ON)

St Andrew's Day (noun) *andreasmessa* (ON)

St Andrew's Mass (30 November) (noun) *andreasmessa* (ON)

St Bartholomew's Day (24 August) (noun) *bartholomeusmessa* (ON)

St Bartholomew's Mass (24 August) (noun) *bartholomeusmessa* (ON)

St Benedict's Day (21 March) (noun) *benedictusmessa* (ON)

St Brigid's Day (noun) *brigíðarmessa* (ON)

St Cecilia's Day (noun) *ceciliomessa* (ON)

St Clement's Day (noun) *klementsmessa* (ON)

St Columba's Day (noun) *kolumbamessa* (ON)

St Erik's Day (noun) *sankta eriks dagh* (OSw)

St Gregory's Day (noun) *gregoriusmessa* (ON)

St James's Day (noun) *jakobsmessa* (ON)

St James's Mass (25 July) (noun) *jakobsmessa* (ON)

St Jón's Day (Ögmundarson) (noun) *jóhannesmessa* (ON)

St Lawrence's Mass (10 August) (noun) *lafrinzsmæssa* (OSw)

St Magnus's Day (noun) *magnúsmessa* (ON)

St Martin's Day (11 November) (noun) *sancta martens dagher* (OSw)

St Matthew's Day (noun) *mattéimessa* (ON)

St Matthew's Mass (21 September) (noun) *mattéimessa* (ON)

St Matthias's Day (noun) *mattíasmessa* (ON)

St Michael's Mass (29 September) (noun) *mikialsmæssa* (OSw)

St Nicholas's Day (noun) *nikulásmessa* (ON)

St Paul's Day (noun) *pálsmessa* (ON)

St Peter's Day (in the spring) (noun) *petersmessa* (OSw)

St Peter's Day (in the summer) (noun) *petersmessa* (OSw)

St Peter's Eve (28 June) (noun) *pétrsmessuaptann* (ON)

St Peter's Mass (29 June) (noun) *petersmessa* (OSw)

St Swithun's Day (2 July) (noun) *svitunsmessa* (ON)

St Thomas' Day (21 December) (noun) *thomasmessa* (ON)

St Thomas's Mass (21 December) (noun) *thomasmessa* (ON)

St Óláfr's Day (noun) *olafsmæssa* (OSw)

St Þorlákr's Day (noun) *þorláksmessa* (ON)

stab (verb) *hugga* (OSw)

stabbing (noun) *hug* (OSw)

stable (noun) *fægarþer* (OSw), *fæhus* (OSw), *hæsthus* (OSw), *staller* (OSw)

stack (noun) *hjalm* (ODan)

stack supports (noun) *hjalmróður (pl.)* (ON)

stackyard (noun) *stakkgarðr* (ON)

staff (noun) *stang* (OSw), *staver* (OSw)

staff man (noun) *stafkarl* (OSw)

staff-blow (noun) *bardaghi* (OSw), *stangehog* (ODan), *stangehogsbardaghe* (ODan)

stagger (verb) *staka* (ON)

stake (noun) *bal* (OSw), *staur* (OGu), *stokker* (OSw)

stake in a bet (noun) *væþfæ* (OSw)

staller (noun) *stallari* (OSw)

stand surety (verb) *borgha* (OSw)

standard bearer (noun) *merkismaðr* (ON)

standard value (noun) *fjárlag* (ON), *lagh* (OSw)

starboard side (noun) *stjórn* (ON)

start accusation (verb) *kæra* (OSw)

starvation (noun) *ofmegri* (ON)

state (verb) *kveða* (ON), *næmna* (OSw), *vita* (OSw)

state of being a minor (noun) *ómegð* (ON)

state of dependence (noun) *ómegð* (ON)

state of destitution (noun) *þrot* (ON)

state of engagement (noun) *fæst* (OSw)

state of means (noun) *fjárfar* (ON)

state of ownership (in a village) (noun) *lighri* (OSw)

state of poverty (noun) *øreigð* (ON)

statement (noun) *atkvæði* (ON), *munhaf* (OSw), *orþ* (OGu), *saga* (OGu), *tyghende* (ODan), *vitni* (OSw)

statement of the law (noun) *laghsagha* (OSw)

statute (noun) *rætter* (OSw), *skipan* (OSw), *staþgi* (OSw)

stave (verb) *stavre* (ODan)

stave (noun) *staver* (OSw)

staving (noun) *stavring* (ODan)

stay (noun) *ívist* (ON)

stay silent (verb) *þigia* (OSw)

staying at home (noun) *heimaseta* (ON)

staying outside (noun) *útiseta* (ON)

steak (noun) *steik* (ON)

steal (verb) *röva* (OSw), *ræna* (OSw), *stiæla* (OSw)

stealing (noun) *styld* (OSw), *þiufnaþer* (OSw), *þiufsak* (OSw)

stealing grass (noun) *grasrán* (ON)

stealing of boundary markers (noun) *röraruf* (OSw)

steelyard (noun) *bismari* (OSw), *pundari* (ON)

steer (verb) *raþa* (OSw)

steering land (noun) *styreshavne* (ODan)

steering office (noun) *styreshavne* (ODan)

steersman (noun) *styriman* (OSw)

stem (1) (noun) *barð* (ON)

stem (2) (noun) *stamn* (OSw)

stemming up water (noun) *flothemal* (ODan)

stepchild (noun) *stiupbarn* (OSw)

stepdaughter (noun) *stjupdotter* (ODan)

stepfather (noun) *stiupfaþer* (OSw)

stepmother (noun) *stjupmother* (ODan)

stepping-{öre} (noun) *stighöre* (OSw)

stepsiblings (noun) *stjupsystken* (ODan)

stepson (noun) *stjupsun* (ODan)

steward (noun) *ármaðr* (ON), *bryti* (OSw), *sysluman* (OSw)

stewardship (noun) *umbuþ* (OSw)

stick (noun) *sparri* (ON), *staver* (OSw)

stiffened (adj.) *liþstarkr* (OGu)

sting-felony (noun) *stungafóli* (ON)

stipulate (verb) *handtaka* (ON)

stipulated (adj.) *lagha* (OSw)

stipulated fine (noun) *lagh* (OSw)

stipulation (noun) *skilorð* (ON), *virthning* (ODan)

stitch (noun) *stingi* (ON)

stock (1) (noun) *stokker* (OSw)

stock (2) (noun) *fæ* (OSw)

stock animals (noun) *bo* (OSw)

stock shed (noun) *fæhus* (OSw)

stock whose value is open to assessment (noun) *metfé* (ON)

stocks (noun) *stokker* (OSw)

stolen (adj.) *þiufstolin* (OSw)

stolen goods (noun) *agriper* (OSw), *borafóli* (ON), *fyli* (OGu), *þiufnaþer* (OSw), *þiufstolin* (OSw), *þiuft* (OSw)

stolen goods (secretly carried into someone's house) (noun) *abyrþ* (OSw)

stolen property (noun) *agriper* (OSw)

stone (verb) *stenka* (OSw)

stone (noun) *sten* (OSw)

stone altar (noun) *hörgr* (ON)

stone-mark (noun) *stenmærki* (OSw)

stony ground (noun) *hölkn* (ON), *hrjóstr* (ON)

stony place (noun) *hreysi* (ON)

stood for a lawful period (adj.) *laghstandin* (OSw)

stook (noun) *raukr* (OGu), *skyl* (OSw)

stop (verb) *standa* (OSw)

storage shed (noun) *hirzla* (ON)

storehouse (noun) *boþ* (OSw), *búr* (ON), *hærbærghi* (OSw), *lægarth* (ODan), *vistahus* (OSw)

stores (noun) *andvirki* (ON)

straight (adj.) *rætter* (OSw)

strakes (noun) *húfr* (ON)

strangle (verb) *kyrkja* (ON)

strap (noun) *band* (OSw), *hanki* (ON)

straw (noun) *halmr* (ON)

stream (noun) *á* (ON), *vatn* (ON)

street (noun) *gata* (OSw)

street gate (noun) *gatelith* (ODan)

strength of numbers (noun) *afl* (ON)

strengthen (verb) *dylia* (OSw)

strengthen one's case (verb) *dylia* (OSw), *vita* (OSw)

strengthen with an oath (verb) *fylla* (OSw)

stretch (verb) *rækkia* (OSw)

strike (verb) *bæria* (OSw), *dræpa* (OSw), *hugga* (OSw), *lysta (1)* (OSw), *sla* (OSw)

strike with a fist (noun) *nævehog* (ODan)

strike with bone (noun) *benhog* (ODan)

strike with stone (noun) *stenshog* (ODan)

strip (noun) *aker* (OSw), *akerland* (ODan), *tegher* (OSw)

strip bark from trees (verb) *barka* (OSw)

stroke (noun) *hug* (OSw), *slagh* (OSw)

stronghold (noun) *borgh* (OSw)

stub (noun) *stumn* (OSw)

stubbornness (noun) *þryska* (OSw), *þryter* (OSw)

study (verb) *sea* (OSw), *skuþa* (OSw)

stump (noun) *stokker* (OSw), *stubbi* (OSw), *stumn* (OSw)

stump inspection (noun) *stumnsyn* (OSw)

stump of wood (noun) *stuver* (OSw)

subdeacon (noun) *subdjakn* (ODan)

subject (noun) *þægn* (OSw)

submit (verb) *döma* (OSw)

submit to something (verb) *fæsta* (OSw)

submit to witnesses (verb) *skærskuta* (OSw)

subordinate (noun) *undersoknere* (ODan)

subsistence (noun) *atvinna* (ON)

substance of a case (noun) *málaefni* (ON)

substantiate (verb) *bæra* (OSw), *fulla* (OSw), *fylla* (OSw), *göþa* (OSw), *sanna* (OSw), *vita* (OSw), *vitna* (OSw), *væria* (OSw)

substantiate a denial (verb) *dylia* (OSw)

substantiate an accusation (verb) *sværia* (OSw)

substantiate birthright by kinship (verb) *niþias* (OSw)

substantiate one's denial (verb) *dylia* (OSw)

substitute for the harness (noun) *silafylli* (OSw)

succeed (verb) *fylla* (OSw)

successor (noun) *eftirkomandi* (ON)

sue (verb) *dela* (OSw), *fæmta* (OSw), *kalla* (OSw), *kæra* (OSw), *laghsökia* (OSw), *qvælia* (OSw), *sökia* (OSw), *stæmna* (OSw), *sækia* (OSw), *sækta* (OSw), *sætia* (OSw), *vita* (OSw), *æptirmæla* (OSw)

sue a person at his home (verb) *hemstæmpna* (OSw)

sue for (verb) *qvælia* (OSw)

suffer (verb) *halda* (OSw), *liuta* (OSw)

suffered (adj.) *vanhluti* (ON)

sufficiently manned (adj.) *liðførr* (ON)

suffragan bishop (noun) *lypbiskuper* (OSw)

suing (noun) *atala* (OSw), *saksætning* (OSw), *sokn* (OSw)

suing at the Thing (noun) *stæmning* (OSw)

suit (noun) *akallan* (OSw), *kæra* (OSw), *kæromal* (OSw), *mal (1)* (OSw), *sak* (OSw), *sokn* (OSw), *stæmna* (OSw), *tala (1)* (OSw), *æftermal* (ODan)

suit concerning money (noun) *fémál* (ON)

suit concerning property (noun) *fjársókn* (ON)

suit for inheritance (noun) *arfsókn* (ON)

suitor (noun) *kærande* (OSw)

sum (noun) *fjártala* (ON), *fæ* (OSw), *gæld* (OSw), *öre* (OSw)

sum up (verb) *reifa* (ON)

summer (noun) *sumar* (ON)

summer load (noun) *sumarhlass* (ON)

summer mill (noun) *sumermylne* (ODan)

summer pasture (noun) *sumarhagi* (ON)

summer solstice (noun) *staða* (ON)

summer stay (noun) *sumarsetr* (ON)

summing up (noun) *reifing* (ON)

summon (verb) *biuþa* (OSw), *biþia* (OSw), *buþa* (OSw), *göma* (OSw), *kalla* (OSw), *næmna* (OSw), *sökia* (OSw), *stæmna* (OSw), *sækta* (OSw), *visa* (OSw)

summon somebody home (verb) *hemstæmpna* (OSw)

summon to be at home (verb) *hemstæmpna* (OSw)

summon to legal assemblies (verb) *laghþinga* (OSw)

summon to the assembly (verb) *thingstævne* (ODan)

summoner (noun) *stefnandi* (ON)

summoning (noun) *stæmna* (OSw)

summoning a person at his home (noun) *hemstæmpnung* (OSw)

summoning baton (noun) *boðskurðr* (ON), *buþkafli* (OSw)

summoning case (noun) *stefnusök* (ON)

summoning day (noun) *stæmnudagher* (OSw)

summons (noun) *buþ* (OSw), *buþskaper* (OSw), *stæmna* (OSw), *stæmning* (OSw), *tilmæli* (OSw)

summons at the assembly (noun) *laghastæmna* (OSw)

summons baton (noun) *buþ* (OSw), *buþkafli* (OSw)

summons for military service (noun) *hærbuþ* (OSw)

summons for truce (noun) *griðastefna* (ON)

summons route (noun) *boðleið* (ON)

summons to a deserted farm (noun) *eyðijarðarboðburðr* (ON)

summons to an assembly (noun) *þingbuþ* (OSw), *þingstæmna* (OSw)

summons to appear within half a month (noun) *halfsmánaðarstefna* (ON)

summons to be at home (noun) *hemstæmpnung* (OSw)

summons to the assembly (noun) *laghastæmna* (OSw)

summons with one month notice (noun) *mánaðarstefna* (ON)

summons witness (noun) *stefnuváttr* (ON)

sun (noun) *sól* (ON)

sun division (noun) *solskipt* (OSw)

sun-divided (adj.) *soldraghin* (OSw)

Sunday (noun) *sunnudagr* (ON)

Sunday Holiday (noun) *sunnuhátíðisdagr* (ON)

Sunday holy period (noun) *sunnudagshelgr* (ON)

superior force (noun) *ofæfli* (OSw)

superstition (noun) *hindrvitni* (ON), *viþskipli* (OSw)

supervise (verb) *raþa* (OSw)

supervision (noun) *forsjá* (ON), *skynian* (OGu), *varþnaþer* (OSw), *vitni* (OSw)

supervisor (noun) *forman* (OSw)

supplement (noun) *baugþak* (ON)

supply (verb) *halda* (OSw)

support (verb) *föþa* (OSw), *halda* (OSw)

support (noun) *foster* (OSw), *fulga* (ON), *fylgja* (ON), *liþ (2)* (OSw), *reþskaper* (OSw), *stuþ* (OSw), *sytning* (OSw)

support of dependents (noun) *ómagabjörg* (ON)

supporter (of the bride) (noun) *bruþmaþer* (OSw)

supporters of the bride (noun) *reþohion* (OSw)

surety (noun) *borghan* (OSw), *borghare* (OSw), *fæsta* (OSw), *nam* (OSw), *panter* (OSw), *tak* (OSw), *taki* (OSw), *varzla* (ON), *varþnaþer* (OSw), *væþ* (OSw)

surety man (noun) *taki* (OSw), *taksmaþer* (OSw)

surrender (verb) *lata* (OSw)

surrounding boundary (noun) *ummerki* (ON)

survey (noun) *asyn* (OSw)

surveyor (noun) *synaman* (OSw), *yfirsóknarmaðr* (ON)

suspect (verb) *mistroa* (OGu), *ugga* (ON), *væna* (OSw), *vænta* (OSw)

suspected case (noun) *humamal* (OSw)

suspension (noun) *qvarstaþa* (OSw)

suspension of purchase (noun) *köpruf* (OSw)

suspicion (noun) *grun* (OSw), *vensl* (OGu)

sustain (verb) *ala* (ON)

sustainable (adj.) *óll* (ON)

sustenance (noun) *elði* (ON)

sustenance pledge (noun) *alaðsfestr* (ON)

swarm of bees (noun) *bisvarm* (ODan)

swear (verb) *ethe* (ODan), *framflytja* (ON), *fæsta* (OSw), *hofþa* (OSw), *sværia* (OSw), *vinna* (OSw), *vita* (OSw), *vitna* (OSw), *væria* (OSw)

swear on a book (verb) *bóka* (ON)

swear to (something) (verb) *vita* (OSw)

swearing by taking hands (noun) *handlagh* (ODan)

Swedish (adj.) *svensker* (OSw)

swine (noun) *svin* (OSw)

swine grazing common (noun) *svinavalder* (OSw)

swine-proof the fencing (verb) *svintæppa* (OSw)

swivel (noun) *hes* (ON)

sword (noun) *stikæmæz* (OSw), *sværþ* (OSw)

sword cutler (noun) *sverðskriði* (ON)

sworn brother (noun) *eiðbróðir* (ON)

sworn peace (noun) *eþsöre* (OSw)

sworn peace day (noun) *eþsöre* (OSw), *eþsört* (OSw)

sworn testimony concerning final judgement (noun) *lyktarvitni* (OSw)

synod (noun) *prestamót* (ON), *prestastefna* (ON)

sáld of seed corn (noun) *sáldssáð* (ON)

Sámi-seeking (noun) *finnför* (ON)

table knife (noun) *matkniver* (OSw)

tackle (noun) *reþe* (OSw)

tail (noun) *hali* (ON), *sporðr* (ON)

tail bone (noun) *rófa* (ON)

take (verb) *lata* (OSw), *leþa* (OSw), *lögræna* (ON), *lypta* (OGu), *viþertaka* (OSw)

take (away) by rapine (verb) *ræna* (OSw)

take (care of) (verb) *göma* (OSw), *gæta* (ON), *varþa* (OSw)

take (e.g. an oath) (verb) *ganga* (OSw)

take a deposit (verb) *næma* (OSw)

take a lot after the wife (verb) *mynde* (ODan)

take a pledge (verb) *næma* (OSw)

take a share (verb) *liuta* (OSw)

take a stand (verb) *skilia* (OSw)

take action (verb) *dela* (OSw), *kalla* (OSw), *kæra* (OSw), *laghsökia* (OSw), *sökia* (OSw), *sækta* (OSw), *æptirmæla* (OSw)

take action against (verb) *sökia* (OSw), *sækta* (OSw), *æptirmæla* (OSw)

take against rent (verb) *leghia* (OSw)

take an oath (verb) *ethe* (ODan), *sværia* (OSw)

take as surety (verb) *næma* (OSw)

take away (verb) *afhænda* (OSw)

take away a house after five days (verb) *fæmta* (OSw)

take back (verb) *lösa* (OSw), *viþertaka* (OSw)

take by force (verb) *valdföra* (OSw), *valdtaka* (OSw)

take by mistake (verb) *mistaka* (ON)

take by pawn (verb) *næma* (OSw)

take by stealth (verb) *stiæla* (OSw)

take care of (verb) *abyrghia* (OSw), *raþa* (OSw), *valda* (OSw), *varþa* (OSw), *varþveta* (OSw)

take charge of (verb) *raþa* (OSw)

take counsel (verb) *raþa* (OSw)

take forcefully (verb) *valdtaka* (OSw)

take in a thief's way (verb) *þiuftas* (OSw)

take in battle (verb) *hærtaka* (OSw)

take in custody (verb) *göma* (OSw)

take in payment of a debt (verb) *virþa* (OSw)

take in pledge (verb) *fæsta* (OSw)

take inheritance (verb) *ærva* (OSw)

take into one's service (verb) *fæsta* (OSw)

take into possession (verb) *hæfþa* (OSw)

take off (verb) *veta* (OSw)

take or give as hostages (verb) *gísla* (ON)

take refuge (verb) *sökia* (OSw)

take responsibility (verb) *hætte* (ODan), *viþertaka* (OSw)

take responsibility for (verb) *varþa* (OSw)

take revenge (verb) *hæmna* (OSw)

take security (verb) *næma* (OSw)

take seizure (verb) *næma* (OSw)

take something away from somebody (verb) *ræna* (OSw)

take surety (verb) *næma* (OSw)

take tenancy (verb) *gifta* (OSw)

take vengeance (verb) *hæmna* (OSw)

take with violence (verb) *valdföra* (OSw)

taken by force (adj.) *rantakin* (OSw)

taken by rapine (adj.) *rantakin* (OSw)

taken by theft (adj.) *þiufstolin* (OSw)

taken captive (adj.) *hernuminn* (ON)

taken hostage (adj.) *hershendr (pl.)* (OGu)

taken in flagrante delicto (adj.) *innitakin* (OSw)

taken land (noun) *tæktatak* (OSw)

taker (noun) *taki* (OSw)

taking (noun) *fornæmi* (OSw), *tak* (OSw)

taking another man's animals to his field (noun) *akernam* (OSw)

taking articles (noun) *gripatak* (ON)

taking care of drift (noun) *rekavarðveizla* (ON)

taking hands (noun) *handtak* (ODan)

taking in to cultivated fields (noun) *invænge* (ODan)

taking of appeals (noun) *væþiataki* (OSw)

taking of bones (out of a wound) (noun) *benlösning* (OSw)

taking of money (noun) *feartaki* (OSw)

taking on by inheritance trade (noun) *arftak* (ON)

taking out domestic animals (noun) *intæktefæ* (ODan)

taking passage in a ship (noun) *fartekja* (ON)

taking property (noun) *fétaka* (ON)

taking the law into one's own hands (noun) *gripdeild* (ON)

taking with force (noun) *ranshævth* (ODan)

taking-time (noun) *fangtíð* (ON)

tale (noun) *mal (1)* (OSw)

talk (noun) *mal (1)* (OSw)

tally man (noun) *skurtheman* (ODan)

tame (verb) *kyrra* (ON)

tame sheep (noun) *bolamb* (OGu)

tar (noun) *tjara* (ON)

taunt (noun) *brigsl* (OGu)

tavern (noun) *ölðrhús* (ON)

tax (noun) *landskyld* (OSw), *leþunger* (OSw), *siþer* (OSw), *skatter* (OSw), *skyld* (OSw), *stuþ* (OSw), *utgærþ* (OSw), *utskyld* (OSw)

tax collector (noun) *intækiuman* (OSw), *skattman* (OSw)

tax free (adj.) *fræls* (OSw)

tax-collector (noun) *tækiomaþer* (OSw)

taxation (noun) *bondatal* (OSw)

taxes (noun) *pænninger* (OSw), *skatter* (OSw)

tear (noun) *spiæll* (OSw)

tear apart (verb) *skena* (OSw)

tear up (verb) *ryva* (OSw)

teat (noun) *spini* (OSw)

tell (verb) *skærskuta* (OSw)

tell according to the law (verb) *laghvara* (OSw)

ten-load ship (noun) *tilæsteskip* (ODan)

tenancy (noun) *ábúð* (ON), *bygning* (OSw), *gift* (OSw)

tenancy agreement (noun) *ábúð* (ON), *leghemal* (ODan)

tenancy payment (noun) *afgipt* (OSw), *gift* (OSw)

tenancy period (noun) *bolatækkia* (OSw), *giftastæmna* (OSw)

tenancy witness (noun) *bygningavitni* (OSw)

tenant (noun) *aboi* (OSw), *afradskarl* (OSw), *garthsæte* (ODan), *innismaþer* (OSw), *laigulenningr* (OGu), *landboe* (OSw), *leghomaþer* (OSw), *leiguliði* (ON)

tenant farm (noun) *leiguból* (ON)

tenant farmer (noun) *landboe* (OSw)

tenant farmer on common land (noun) *almænnigslandboe* (OSw)

tenant land (noun) *leiguland* (ON)

tenantry (noun) *landsbyggð* (ON)

tenants' section (noun) *leiglendingaþáttr* (ON)

tenant's contract (noun) *takuskæl* (OSw)

tenant's wife (noun) *innestkone* (ODan)

tend to (verb) *göma* (OSw)

tender in payment (verb) *gælda (1)* (OSw)

tending (noun) *gætsla* (OSw)

tent cover (noun) *tjald* (ON)

tentbooth (noun) *tjaldbúð* (ON)

tenth (noun) *tiund* (OSw)

tenth-gift (noun) *tíundargjöf* (ON)

term (noun) *endaghi* (OSw), *fæsta* (OSw), *stæmna* (OSw)

term of five days (noun) *fæmt* (OSw)

term which expires at the end of the winter (noun) *vetrarstefna* (ON)

terminate an agreement (verb) *afsighia* (OSw)

terms (noun) *máldagi* (ON), *skildagi* (ON), *skilorð* (ON)

terms of mitigation (noun) *sykna* (ON)

test (verb) *reyna* (ON), *royna* (OGu), *skynia* (OGu)

test (noun) *skyn* (OGu), *skynian* (OGu)

test of the red iron (noun) *jarnbyrþ* (OSw)

testament (noun) *testament* (OSw)

testicle (noun) *vigniauri* (OGu)

testified safety circle (noun) *vatubanda* (OGu)

testify (verb) *fylla* (OSw), *sværia* (OSw), *vátta* (ON), *veta* (OSw), *vinna* (OSw), *vita* (OSw), *vitna* (OSw)

testify on being the truth (verb) *sanna* (OSw)

testifying (noun) *vitnesbyrth* (ODan), *vættisburðr* (ON)

testimony (noun) *byrþ* (OSw), *eþer* (OSw), *fæst* (OSw), *sögn* (ON), *váttasaga* (ON), *váttorð* (ON), *vita* (OSw), *vitnesbyrth* (ODan), *vitni* (OSw), *vitnismal* (OSw), *vitsorþ* (OSw), *vætti* (OSw)

testimony about purchase (noun) *köpvitni* (OSw)

testimony of a claim (noun) *kvöðuvitni* (ON)

testimony of a declaration (noun) *forsagnarvitni* (ON)

testimony of a home summons (noun) *heimstefnuvitni* (ON)

testimony of a killing announcement (noun) *víglýsingarvitni* (ON)

testimony of a verdict from homestead neighbours (noun) *heimiliskviðarvitni* (ON)

testimony of an assembly summons (noun) *þingstefnuvitni* (ON)

testimony of inheritance (noun) *ærfþavita* (OSw)

testimony of lawful absence (noun) *nauðsynjaváttr* (ON)

testimony of necessity (noun) *nauðsynjavitni* (ON)

testimony of nominated men (noun) *nefndarvitni* (ON)

testimony of old holding (noun) *minnung* (OSw)

testimony of old possession (noun) *minnung* (OSw)

testimony of patrimonial rights (noun) *óðalsvitni* (ON)

testimony of purchase (noun) *köpvitni* (OSw)

testimony of settlement (noun) *sáttarvætti* (ON)

testimony of summoning (noun) *stefnuvætti* (ON)

testimony of the announcement of judgement (noun) *dómsuppsöguvætti* (ON) testimony of the men of the assembly (noun) *þingsmannavitni* (OSw)

testimony of witnesses (noun) *váttasaga* (ON)

testimony to the declaration of a killing (noun) *víglýsingarvitni* (ON)

testimony with an oath sworn on the holy book (noun) *bókarvitni* (ON)

tether (verb) *hæfta* (OSw)

tether (noun) *hæfta* (OSw), *tjóðr* (ON)

thane (noun) *þægn* (OSw)

thanegeld (noun) *þiængsgæld* (OSw)

thane's compensation (noun) *þiængsgæld* (OSw)

the Crown (noun) *krona* (OSw), *kunungsdömi* (OSw)

the Lawspeaker's seat (noun) *lögsögumannsrúm* (ON)

the old way (noun) *fyrning* (OSw)

the one who has the land (noun) *jorþeghandi* (OSw)

the one who wants to defend himself (noun) *væriandi* (OSw)

the past (noun) *fyrnska* (OGu)

the yearly day (noun) *jamlangadagher* (OSw)

theft (noun) *bosran* (OSw), *gripdeild* (ON), *styld* (OSw), *thjuvnethsak* (ODan), *þiufnaþer* (OSw), *þiufsak* (OSw), *þiufska* (OSw), *þiuft* (OSw), *þiuftamal* (OSw), *þjófskapr* (ON)

theft by incitement within the household (noun) *bodræt* (OSw)

theft case (noun) *þiufnaþer* (OSw)

theft in someone's home (noun) *hemsokn* (OSw)

theft of angelica (noun) *hvannastulðr* (ON)

theft of falcons (noun) *haukastulðr* (ON)

theft of food (noun) *átuþýfi* (ON)

theft of fruit and vegetable (noun) *skaflþiuver* (OSw)

theft of hay (noun) *heytaka* (ON)

theft of land (noun) *moldran* (OSw)

theft of livestock (noun) *bosran* (OSw)

theft of seals (noun) *selastulðr* (ON)

theft of turnips (noun) *næpnastulðr* (ON)

theft payment (noun) *fólagjald* (ON)

theft plot (noun) *þjófráð* (ON)

theft section (noun) *þiufnaþabalker* (OSw), *þiuvabalker* (OSw)

thief (noun) *þiuver* (OSw)

thief concealment (noun) *þjóflaun* (ON)

thief lair (noun) *þiufhol* (OSw)

thief-fine (noun) *þiufbot* (OSw)

thief-{bogher} (noun) *þiufbogher* (OSw)

thief's accomplice (noun) *þjófsnautr* (ON)

thief's due (noun) *þiufsrætter* (OSw)

thief's mark (noun) *thjuvsmærke* (ODan)

thief's punishment (noun) *þiufsrætter* (OSw)

thievery (noun) *þiufska* (OSw)

thieving case (noun) *þiufsak* (OSw)

thin board (noun) *fíla* (ON)

thing (1) (noun) *soknaþing* (OSw), *þing* (OSw)

thing (2) (noun) *luter* (OSw)

thing assembly (noun) *þing* (OSw)

Thing assembly held within one year (noun) *jamlangaþing* (OSw)

thing assembly inviolability (noun) *þingsfriþer* (OSw)

Thing assembly meeting (noun) *þing* (OSw)

thing assembly of the folkland (noun) *folklandsþing* (OSw)

Thing assembly peace (noun) *þingsfriþer* (OSw)

thing assembly tax (noun) *þinglami* (OSw)

Thing assembly witness (noun) *þingvitni* (OSw)

thing assembly witnesses (noun) *þingfastar (pl.)* (OSw)

Thing day (noun) *þingsdagher* (OSw)

thing inviolability (noun) *þingsfriþer* (OSw)

thing of the land (noun) *landsþing* (OSw)

thing peace (noun) *þingsfriþer* (OSw)

thing penalty (noun) *þingviti* (OSw)

thing road (noun) *þingsvægher* (OSw)

thing site (noun) *þingsstaþer* (OSw)

thingmen (noun) *þingsmæn (pl.)* (OSw)

things drifting ashore (noun) *hafrek* (OGu), *rek* (ON)

thinking (noun) *umdómi* (ON)

third (noun) *luter* (OSw), *þriþiunger* (OSw)

third cousin (noun) *fiurmænninger* (OSw)

third cousins (noun) *annarrabróðra (pl.)* (ON)

thirteen-bencher (noun) *þrettánsessa* (ON)

Thirteenth Day of Christmas (6 January) (noun) *þrettándi dagr jóla* (ON)

thorp (noun) *þorp* (OSw)

thorp field (noun) *thorpemark* (ODan)

thrall (noun) *annöþogher* (OSw), *man* (OSw), *þræl* (OSw)

thrall woman (noun) *ambat* (OSw), *huskona* (OSw)

thrall woman's concubinal man (noun) *kæfsir* (OSw)

thralldom (noun) *annöþogherdomber* (OSw)

threat (noun) *fryghtheorth* (ODan), *hötsl* (OSw)

threaten (verb) *höta* (OSw)

threatening (noun) *hötning* (OSw)

threatening behaviour (noun) *atlöp* (OSw)

three half marks (noun) *thrylmærke* (ODan)

three instalments (noun) *þræskipti* (OSw)

three lots (noun) *þriþiunger* (OSw)

Three major feasts of the Blessed Virgin Mary (noun) *varafrudagher* (OSw)

three night summons (noun) *þrenættinger* (OSw)

three years old (adj.) *þrítíðungr* (ON)

three {marka} case (noun) *þriggjamarkamál* (ON)

three-assembly case (noun) *þriggjaþingamál* (ON)

three-man oath (noun) *lýrittareiðr* (ON), *þriggjamannaeiðr* (ON)

threefold fine (noun) *þrigildi* (OGu)

thresh (verb) *bæria* (OSw)

threshold (noun) *broafiol* (OSw), *þriskuldi* (OSw)

throng (noun) *þrang* (OSw)

throttle (verb) *kyrkja* (ON)

throttling (noun) *kyrking* (ON)

throw (verb) *sla* (OSw)

throw (noun) *kast* (ON)

throw of a pruning knife (noun) *sniðilsverp* (ON)

throwing to the earth (noun) *jorthhog* (ODan)

throwing to the ground (noun) *jorthskuv* (ODan)

thrust (verb) *stinga* (OSw)

thumb (noun) *þumalfingr* (ON)

thumb-ell (noun) *þumalöln* (ON)

thumb-nail's breadth (noun) *mundr* (OGu)

thumb-width (noun) *þumlungr* (ON)

thwart (noun) *þofta* (ON)

thwart fines (noun) *þoftugjöld (pl.)* (ON)

tie to a crime using witnesses (verb) *vitna* (OSw)

tie up (verb) *binda* (OSw)

tiller (noun) *stýrisdrengr* (ON)

timber (noun) *fang* (OSw), *timber* (OSw), *verkviðr* (ON), *viþer* (OSw)

timber felling (noun) *skogharhug* (OSw)

timber salvaging (noun) *viðarflutning* (ON)

timber-mark (noun) *viðarmark* (ON)

time (point) (noun) *mal (2)* (OSw)

time fixed for payment (noun) *sal* (ODan)

time for payment (noun) *sálarstefna* (ON)

time limit (noun) *stæmnudagher* (OSw)

time limit for repurchase (noun) *fræstmark* (OSw)

time limit of a partnership (noun) *bolaghsstæmpna* (OSw)

time limits for baptisms (noun) *skírslastefna* (ON)

time of marriage (noun) *bruþlöpstimi* (OSw)

time of need (noun) *nöþsyn* (OSw)

time of peace (noun) *friþer* (OSw)

time of slavery (noun) *mali* (OSw)

time of truce (noun) *griðatími* (ON)

times for feasts (noun) *mungatstiþir (pl.)* (OSw)

tinder-wolf (noun) *kasnavargher* (OSw)

tithe (verb) *tiunda* (OSw)

tithe (noun) *mali* (OSw), *tiund* (OSw)

tithe case (noun) *tíundarmál* (ON)

tithe for churches (noun) *kirkjutíund* (ON)

tithe matters (noun) *tíundarmál* (ON)

tithe of cod (noun) *skreiðartíund* (ON)

tithe of stock (noun) *viðrelðistíund* (ON)

tithe payment (noun) *tíundargerð* (ON), *tíundargjald* (ON)

title (noun) *egn* (OSw), *hemuld* (OSw)

to be denied passage (adj.) *óferjandi* (ON)

to be killed (adj.) *dræpr* (ON)

toast (noun) *minni* (OGu)

toft (noun) *tompt* (OSw)

toft garden (noun) *tomptagarþer* (OSw)

token (noun) *jartighni (pl.)* (OSw)

token duty (noun) *boðburðr* (ON)

token of seizure (noun) *kross* (ON)

token-path (noun) *boðleið* (ON)

token-route (noun) *boðleið* (ON)

tokens (noun) *buþ* (OSw)

toll (noun) *tuldr* (OGu)

tongue steelyard (noun) *tungupundari* (ON)

tonsure (noun) *krona* (OSw)

too late for thing assembly proceedings (adj.) *urþinga* (OSw)

tools (noun) *reþe* (OSw)

tools or fruits of unauthorized labour (noun) *aværkan* (OSw)

torn off (verb) *slitna* (ON)

torture (verb) *fresta* (OGu), *pine* (ODan)

town (noun) *byr* (OSw), *köpunger* (OSw)

town dweller (noun) *byaman* (OSw)

town law (noun) *kaupangrslög* (ON), *kaupangrsréttr* (ON)

town sheriff (noun) *gælkare* (OSw)

town-meeting (noun) *mot* (OSw)

township (noun) *köpunger* (OSw)

townsman (noun) *byaman* (OSw), *køpingsman* (ODan)

trace (verb) *leþa* (OSw)

tracing (noun) *leþsn* (OSw)

tracing to an assignor (noun) *leþsn* (OSw)

tracing witness (noun) *leþsnavitni* (OSw)

track (noun) *gata* (OSw), *liþ (1)* (OSw)

trade (verb) *köpa* (OSw)

trade (noun) *köp* (OSw)

trade cloak (noun) *vararfeldr* (ON)

trade goods (noun) *vara* (ON), *varningr* (ON)

trade partner (noun) *félagi* (ON)

trade partnership (noun) *fjárfélag* (ON), *fælagh* (OSw), *hjáfélag* (ON)

trade section (noun) *köpmalabalker* (OSw)

trade voyage (noun) *köpfærþ* (OSw)

trader (noun) *fangaman* (OSw), *farmaðr* (ON)

traders' hut (noun) *farmannabúð* (ON)

trading at ships (noun) *skipakaup* (ON)

trading journey (noun) *kaupför* (ON), *köpfærþ* (OSw)

trail (noun) *fiæt* (OSw)

train (noun) *tug* (OGu)

traitor (noun) *dróttinssvikari* (ON), *landráðamaðr* (ON)

traitor to the king (noun) *dróttinssvikari* (ON)

tramp (noun) *húsgangsmaðr* (ON)

transaction (noun) *köp* (OSw)

transaction with shaking hands (noun) *handsalsband* (ON)

transaction witnesses (noun) *fastar (pl.)* (OSw)

transaction witnesses for a purchase (noun) *köpfastar (pl.)* (OSw)

transaction witnesses for a repurchase (noun) *aterköpsfastar (pl.)* (OSw)

transaction witnesses for an exchange (noun) *skiptisfastar (pl.)* (OSw)

transaction witnesses for pledges (noun) *væþiafastar (pl.)* (OSw)

transaction witnesses of a partnership (noun) *bolaghsfastar (pl.)* (OSw)

transfer (verb) *halda* (OSw), *skipta* (OSw), *sköta* (OSw), *sælia* (OSw)

transfer a debt (verb) *skuldskeyta* (ON)

transfer enclave (noun) *flutfiælder* (OSw)

transfer of debt (noun) *skuldskeyting* (ON)

transfer of warranty (noun) *heimilðartaka* (ON)

transferred automatically (adj.) *sjalfskeytr* (ON)

transgression (noun) *afbrigð* (ON)

transport (noun) *aka* (OSw), *flutning* (ON)

transportation of poor people (noun) *fátókramannaflutningr* (ON)

trap (verb) *gildra* (OSw)

trap (noun) *forsat* (OSw), *garþer* (OSw), *gildri* (OSw), *stilli* (ON)

trapping pit (noun) *graf* (OSw)

travel companion (noun) *farunöti* (OSw)

travel delay (noun) *farartalmi* (ON)

travel expenses (noun) *farareyrir* (ON)

travel to an assembly (noun) *þingför* (ON)

travel to shielings (noun) *sætraferð* (ON)

travellers' pathway (noun) *farvægher* (OSw)

travelling (adj.) *væghfarandi* (OSw)

travelling boar (noun) *fargalter* (OSw)

treachery (noun) *svik* (ON)

treason (noun) *landráð* (ON), *landráðasök* (ON)

treasure trove (noun) *danefæ* (ODan)

treasurer (noun) *gælkare* (OSw)

treat in the same way (verb) *jamna* (OSw)

treated unfairly (adj.) *mishaldinn* (ON)

treatment of homicide (noun) *vígslóði* (ON)

treaty (noun) *rætter* (OSw)

tree (noun) *tré* (ON)

tree fruit (noun) *aldin* (OSw), *skafl* (OSw)

tree with acorn (noun) *aldinviþer* (OSw)

tree-mark (noun) *træmærki* (OSw)

trespass (noun) *aganga* (OSw), *garthgang* (ODan)

trespass and compensation for this (noun) *landnám* (ON)

trespassing (noun) *bothegang* (ODan)

trespassing in someone's home (noun) *hemsokn* (OSw)

trial (noun) *rætter* (OSw), *skæl* (OSw)

trial by iron (noun) *jarnbyrþ* (OSw)

trial by ordeal (noun) *skærsl* (OSw)

tribute (noun) *ættærgæld* (OSw)

tribute for a subject (noun) *þiængsgæld* (OSw)

trickery (noun) *svik* (ON)

triple compensation (noun) *þræböti* (OSw)

triple fine (noun) *þrigildi* (OGu), *þræböti* (OSw)

troll (noun) *troll* (ON)

troll bitch (noun) *trulkærling* (OSw)

troop (noun) *liþ (2)* (OSw), *stoth* (ODan)

troop horse (noun) *stoþhors* (OSw)

troop of horses (noun) *stoth* (ODan), *stoþhors* (OSw)

trotter (noun) *rinnare* (OSw)

trouble (noun) *arvuþi* (OSw)

trough-iron (noun) *trughsjarn* (ODan)

trousers (noun) *brok* (OGu)

truce (noun) *friþer* (OSw), *griþ* (OSw), *trygth* (ODan)

truce speech (noun) *griðamál* (ON)

truce-breaker (noun) *gruthnithing* (ODan), *tryggrofamaðr* (ON), *tryggrofi* (ON)

truce-breaking (noun) *griðarof* (ON), *tryggrof* (ON)

truce-guarantee (noun) *griðsala* (ON)

truce-ravener (noun) *griðbítr* (ON)

true (adj.) *rætter* (OSw), *sander* (OSw), *skæliker* (OSw) true killer (noun) *sanbani* (OSw)

trueborn (adj.) *aþal* (OSw)

trunk (noun) *stokker* (OSw)

trust (noun) *trúnuðr* (ON)

trustee (noun) *taki* (OSw)

trustworthy (adj.) *skilríkr* (ON), *skæliker* (OSw), *trygger* (OSw)

trustworthy man (noun) *sannindaman* (OSw)

truth (noun) *sannind* (OSw), *sannleikr* (ON)

truth oath (noun) *sannendeeth* (ODan)

truthful (adj.) *sander* (OSw)

truthfulness (noun) *sannind* (OSw)

try (verb) *pröva* (OSw), *royna* (OGu), *utröna* (OSw), *vita* (OSw), *vitna* (OSw)

try a case (verb) *skuþa* (OSw)

try and lawfully convict (verb) *laghvinna* (OSw)

try and settle (verb) *utröna* (OSw)

try with oaths (verb) *sværia* (OSw)

turf (noun) *torf* (OSw), *torfa* (OGu)

turf lath (noun) *torfvölr* (ON)

turf payment (noun) *torvogæld* (OSw)

turnip (noun) *rova* (OSw)

turnip clearing (noun) *rofnaværk* (OSw)

turnip field (noun) *rofnaaker* (OSw)

twelfth (noun) *tylft* (OSw)

Twelfth Day (noun) *tolftidagher* (OSw), *þrættandidagher* (OSw)

Twelfth Night (noun) *tolftidagher* (OSw)

twelve (noun) *tylft* (OSw)

twelve man judgment (noun) *tolfmannadómr* (ON)

twelve ounce ring (noun) *tolfeyringr* (ON)

twelve-man court (noun) *tolfmannadómr* (ON)

twelve-man oath (noun) *tylftareþer* (OSw)

twenty-bencher (noun) *tvítugsessa* (ON)

twenty-five (adj.) *halfþrítugr* (ON)

twice married (adj.) *tvægipter* (OSw)

twice the value (noun) *tvægildi* (OSw)

Two Apostles' Mass (28 October) (noun) *tveggjapostulamessa* (ON)

two-fold compensated (adj.) *tvægilder* (OSw)

type of legal outlawry (noun) *lögsekð* (ON)

tyrannous man (noun) *ofríkismaðr* (ON)

ultimate court of law (noun) *lögrétta* (ON)

unaccused (adj.) *usækteth* (ODan)

unanimously decided (adj.) *samdóma* (ON)

unappraised (adj.) *óvirðr* (ON)

unassessed (adj.) *óvirðr* (ON)

unatonable crime (noun) *óbótasök* (ON), *óbótaverk* (ON), *urbotamal* (OSw)

unatonable criminal (noun) *óbótamaðr* (ON)

unatoned (adj.) *óbóttr* (ON)

unattended (adj.) *varþalaus* (OGu)

unbaptized (adj.) *heþin* (OSw), *oskær* (OSw)

unbind (verb) *lösa* (OSw)

unblessed (adj.) *ovighþer* (OSw)

unborn (adj.) *óalinn* (ON), *oborin* (OSw), *ofödder* (OSw)

unbound (adj.) *lös* (OSw)

uncastrated (adj.) *fastr* (OGu)

unchain (verb) *lösa* (OSw)

unchallenged (adj.) *oklandaþer* (OSw), *okærder* (OSw), *oqvalder* (OSw), *osökter* (OSw), *qvalalös* (OSw), *uilsketh* (ODan)

unchristian (adj.) *heþin* (OSw)

unclaimed (adj.) *osökter* (OSw)

unclaimed inheritance (noun) *danaarver* (OSw)

unclean (adj.) *ful* (OSw)

uncompensated (adj.) *ogilder* (OSw), *saklös* (OSw)

uncomplained (adj.) *oklutraþer* (OSw)

unconditional sale or purchase (noun) *aþalköp* (OSw)

unconfessed (adj.) *oskriptaþer* (OSw)

unconsecrated (adj.) *ovighþer* (OSw)

uncontested (adj.) *oqvalder* (OSw)

unconvicted (adj.) *ufælder* (OSw)

unction (noun) *oling* (OSw)

uncultivated (adj.) *orudder* (OSw)

uncultivated field (noun) *træþi* (OSw)

uncultivated land (noun) *aterlægha* (OSw), *auðn* (ON), *ödmark* (OSw), *ökn* (OSw)

uncultivated village (noun) *öþisbyr* (OSw)

uncut (of cloth) (adj.) *óskikkðr* (ON), *óskorinn* (ON)

undecided (adj.) *ófestr* (ON), *udømd* (ODan)

undeclared killing (noun) *dulghadrap* (OSw)

undeed (noun) *fordeþskepr* (OGu)

under legal penalty (prep.) *lögsekr* (ON)

under money penalty (prep.) *fésekr* (ON)

under penalty (prep.) *saker* (OSw)

under the same penalty (adj.) *jafnsekr* (ON)

under-age (adj.) *omaghi* (OSw), *umælende* (ODan)

under-blanket (noun) *legvita* (OGu)

underfeed (verb) *svelta* (ON)

undergarments (noun) *likvari* (OGu)

underskirt decorations (noun) *kurtilbonaþr* (OGu)

undetected murder (noun) *dulghadrap* (OSw)

undisputable (adj.) *uiafliker* (OSw)

undisputed (adj.) *obrighþer* (OSw), *oklutraþer* (OSw), *okærder* (OSw), *uilsketh* (ODan)

undistributed (adj.) *oskipter* (OSw)

undivided (adj.) *oskipter* (OSw)

unemployed (adj.) *þiænistulös* (OSw)

unfairness (noun) *oskiel* (OGu)

unfettered (adj.) *fræls* (OSw)

unfit to work (adj.) *oför* (OSw)

unforeseen misfortune (noun) *óvísavargr* (ON)

unfree (adj.) *annöþogher* (OSw), *ofræls* (OSw)

unfree servant (noun) *ambat* (OSw), *annöþogher* (OSw), *annöþogherdomber* (OSw), *hion* (OSw)

unhallowed ground (noun) *forvé* (ON)

unhidden (adj.) *ófolginn* (ON)

unhindered (adj.) *fræls* (OSw), *nauðsynjalauss* (ON)

unholy (adj.) *ohailigr* (OGu), *oskær* (OSw)

unhurt (adj.) *heill* (ON)

unimpaired (adj.) *uspilt* (ODan)

uninhabited (adj.) *óbyggðr* (ON)

uninhabited farm (noun) *auðn* (ON)

uninhabited land (noun) *auðn* (ON)

uninhabited parts of the country (noun) *óbyggð* (ON)

uninhabited place (noun) *hölkn* (ON)

unintentional harm (noun) *vaþaværk* (OSw)

uninvited guest (noun) *boðslöttr* (ON)

union (noun) *hionalagh* (OSw)

unit of the weight and monetary system, 1/24 {mark} (noun) *örtogh* (OSw)

unit of the weight and monetary system, 1/8 {mark} (noun) *öre* (OSw)

unit of the weight and monetary system, one 240th {mark} (noun) *pænninger* (OSw)

unit of the weight system, c. 5 kg (noun) *pund* (OSw)

unjudged (adj.) *udømd* (ODan)

unjust (adj.) *orætter* (OSw)

unjust verdict (noun) *domvilla* (OSw)

unjustly (adv.) *orætlika* (OSw)

unkinned (adj.) *oskylder* (OSw)

unlanded man (noun) *innismaþer* (OSw)

unlanded servant (noun) *græssæti* (OSw)

unlawful (adj.) *olagha* (OSw), *ólögligr* (ON), *orætter* (OSw)

unlawful action (noun) *olagh* (OSw)

unlawful ends (noun) *olagh* (OSw)

unlawful grazing (noun) *grasrán* (ON)

unlawful prevention of someone using a path (noun) *vegarán* (ON)

unlawful sale (noun) *gærsala* (OSw)

unlawful seizure (noun) *mistekja* (ON)

unlawful usage of arable land (noun) *aværkan* (OSw), *jorþaaværkan* (OSw)

unlawful use (noun) *aværkan* (OSw)

unlawfully (adv.) *aflag* (ON), *olagh* (OSw), *olaghlika* (OSw), *orætlika* (OSw), *ulovlika* (ODan)

unlawfully bound (adj.) *misbundinn* (ON)

unlawfulness (noun) *olagh* (OSw)

unleased (adj.) *ótekinn* (ON)

unmarked (adj.) *óeinkynntr* (ON), *ómarkaðr* (ON)

unmarked (of lots) (adj.) *ómerkðr* (ON)

unmarried (adj.) *ainloypr* (OGu), *manløs* (ODan), *ogipter* (OSw), *umanneth* (ODan)

unmarried and without a fixed household (adj.) *einhleypr* (ON)

unmarried man (noun) *drengmaðr* (ON), *enløpman* (ODan)

unmarried sister (noun) *mö* (OSw)

unmarried woman (noun) *enlöpkona* (OSw), *mö* (OSw)

unnecessarily (adv.) *nauðsynjalauss* (ON)

unpaid (adj.) *ógoldinn* (ON)

unpaid tithes (adj.) *utiunda* (OSw)

unpenalized (adj.) *vítislauss* (ON)

unpledged (adj.) *forveði* (ON), *ovæþiaþer* (OSw)

unprotected (adj.) *ohailigr* (OGu), *varþalaus* (OGu)

unprotected by the law (adj.) *ohailigr* (OGu)

unprotected opening (noun) *barliþ* (OSw)

unproven (adj.) *óprófaðr* (ON)

unpublished (adj.) *ólýstr* (ON)

unpunished (adj.) *refsingarlauss* (ON)

unreasonable action (noun) *oftala* (OSw)

unreasonable man (noun) *oraþamaþr* (OGu)

unreconciled (adj.) *osater* (OSw)

unrelated (adj.) *oskylder* (OSw)

unreliable report (noun) *lausungarorð* (ON)

unrented (adj.) *ótekinn* (ON)

unrepented (adj.) *oskriptaþer* (OSw)

unrest (noun) *ofriþer* (OSw)

unroped boundary (noun) *ornumeskjal* (ODan)

unruly animal (noun) *osoyþr* (OGu)

unruly animal compensation (noun) *orunabot* (OSw)

unsafe judgement (noun) *skroksokn* (OSw)

unsearched (adj.) *órannsakaðr* (ON)

unseaworthy (adj.) *oför* (OSw)

unsecured (adj.) *ótekinn* (ON)

unseemly act (noun) *óhófuverk* (ON)

unsentenced (adj.) *udømd* (ODan)

unshriven (adj.) *oskriptaþer* (OSw)

unsown (adj.) *ósáinn* (ON)

unspoiled (adj.) *uspilt* (ODan), *spellalauss* (ON)

unsubstantiated (adj.) *ofylter* (OSw)

unsupervised (adj.) *varþalaus* (OGu)

unsworn (adj.) *osvurin* (OSw)

untallied (adj.) *ótalðr* (ON)

untenanted (adj.) *leigulauss* (ON)

untruth (noun) *osannind* (OSw)

unvalued (adj.) *ómettinn* (ON), *óvirðr* (ON)

unwilling (adj.) *nöþogher* (OSw)

unwillingness (noun) *ovili* (OSw)

unwitting injury (noun) *vaþaværk* (OSw)

uphold (verb) *göma* (OSw), *halda* (OSw)

upkeep (noun) *föþa* (OSw)

upkeep of buildings (noun) *húsaupphald* (ON)

upright (noun) *stang* (OSw)

upright (adj.) *trygger* (OSw)

upstanding person (noun) *spekðarmaðr* (ON)

urgent need (noun) *nöþsyn* (OSw), *stórnauðsyn* (ON)

urine (noun) *hland* (ON)

usable (adj.) *gilder* (OSw)

usable by all (adj.) *jafnheimill* (ON)

use (verb) *fikia* (OSw), *firigæra* (OSw), *hæfþa* (OSw)

use force (verb) *pine* (ODan)

useful (adj.) *nýtr* (ON)

usurer (noun) *okrkarl* (ON)

usury (noun) *okr* (ON)

utter an oath (verb) *sværia* (OSw)

vacant (adj.) *lös* (OSw)

vagabond (noun) *landsofringi* (ON), *slenstrákr* (ON)

vagrancy (noun) *verðgangr* (ON)

vagrant (noun) *drivari* (OSw), *göngumaðr* (ON), *löfvirkinger* (OSw), *lösvittinger* (OSw), *ældari* (OSw)

vagrant woman (noun) *göngukona* (ON)

vagrant's baggage (noun) *göngumannafat* (ON)

valid (adj.) *fulder* (OSw), *gilder* (OSw), *lagha* (OSw), *mætr* (ON), *rætter* (OSw), *sakgildr* (ON)

valid as a form of payment (adj.) *gjaldgengr* (ON)

valid excuse (noun) *nöþsyn* (OSw)

valid testimony (noun) *algildisvitni* (ON)

valuable (noun) *griper* (OSw), *gærsemi* (OSw)

valuable fish (noun) *gørsæmefisk* (ODan)

valuable property (noun) *koster* (OSw)

valuables (noun) *mun* (ODan), *værþörar (pl.)* (OSw)

valuation (noun) *virthning* (ODan)

valuation in gold (noun) *gulvirthning* (ODan)

valuation of maiming (noun) *lytesvirthning* (ODan)

value (verb) *mæta* (OSw), *virþa* (OSw), *vita* (OSw)

value (noun) *gildi* (OSw), *varzla* (ON), *virthning* (ODan), *værþ* (OSw), *værþörar (pl.)* (OSw)

value for fines (verb) *gilda* (OSw)

value for the grass (noun) *grasverð* (ON)

value in silver (noun) *sylftal* (OSw)

value in {marker} (noun) *markatal* (OSw)

value of a bird (noun) *fuglverð* (ON)

value of a compensation (noun) *botevirthning* (ODan)

value of a cow (noun) *kýrverð* (ON)

value of a house (noun) *húsverð* (ON)

value of food (noun) *matarverð* (ON)

value of grass (noun) *grasverð* (ON)

value of the property (noun) *aterfang* (OSw)

value of timber (noun) *viðarverð* (ON)

value of wares (noun) *fjármegin* (ON)

value of wood (noun) *viðarverð* (ON)

valued (adj.) *gilder* (OSw)

valued at (adj.) *gilder* (OSw)

valued for fines (adj.) *gilder* (OSw)

valuer (noun) *metandi* (ON)

valuing (noun) *virthning* (ODan)

Various feasts of the Blessed Virgin Mary (noun) *mariumæssa* (OSw)

vegetable garden (noun) *kalgarth* (ODan)

vendor (noun) *sali* (OSw), *saluman* (OSw)

vengeance (noun) *hæmd* (OSw)

verbal abuse (noun) *oqvæþinsorþ* (OSw)

verdict (noun) *domber* (OSw), *kviðr* (ON), *laghedom* (ODan), *vita* (OSw)

verdict-giving (noun) *kviðburðr* (ON)

verification (noun) *vitni* (OSw)

verify (verb) *vita* (OSw)

vessel (noun) *farkoster* (OSw)

vessels and vestments (noun) *skruþer* (OSw)

vest (noun) *serkr* (OGu)

veto (noun) *lýrittr* (ON)

veto-ban (noun) *lýrittarvörn* (ON)

vicarage (noun) *kirkiubol* (OSw)

vicarage building (noun) *kirkiubolsgarþer* (OSw)

vicinity (noun) *grennd* (ON)

vigil (noun) *nónhelgr* (ON)

vigils (noun) *forhælgþ* (OSw)

viking (noun) *víkingr* (ON)

village (noun) *bolstaþer* (OSw), *bygd* (OSw), *byr* (OSw)

village assembly (noun) *gatestævne* (ODan)

village assessment (noun) *byvirthning* (ODan)

village boundary (noun) *byaskæl* (OSw)

village bridge (noun) *byabro* (OSw)

village community regulation (noun) *bygningarætter* (OSw)

village community section (noun) *bygningabalker* (OSw)

village distribution (noun) *byabrut* (OSw)

village field (noun) *byamark* (OSw)

village guard (noun) *byavarþer* (OSw)

village land (noun) *byaland* (OSw)

village lane (noun) *ta* (OSw)

village measurement (noun) *byabrut* (OSw), *byamal* (OSw)

village meeting (noun) *gatestævne* (ODan), *grannestævne* (ODan)

village passage (noun) *forta* (OSw)

village property (noun) *bolstaþer* (OSw)

village space (noun) *forta* (OSw)

village surroundings (noun) *bygd* (OSw)

village unit (noun) *bol* (OSw)

village where the plague is present (noun) *falbyr* (OSw)

village with a mound (noun) *höghabyr* (OSw)

village woodland (noun) *byarskogher* (OSw)

villager (noun) *bolstaþer* (OSw), *byaman* (OSw), *granni* (OSw)

villain (noun) *niþinger* (OSw), *þryter* (OSw)

villainous act (noun) *niþingsværk* (OSw)

villainy (noun) *niþingsværk* (OSw)

villainy goring (noun) *gornithingsværk* (ODan)

villain's act (noun) *niþingsværk* (OSw)

vindicate (verb) *væria* (OSw)

vindication of a charge (noun) *undanförsla* (ON)

violate (verb) *bryta* (OSw), *hæria* (OSw), *ryva* (OSw), *skærþa* (OSw)

violation (noun) *brut* (OSw), *friþbrut* (OSw), *misþyrmsl* (ON), *spiæll* (OSw)

violation of a holy day (noun) *hælghudaghabrut* (OSw)

violation of a peace pledge (noun) *tryggrof* (ON)

violation of Christian law (noun) *kristinsdómsbrot* (ON)

violation of kinship rules (incest) (noun) *frændsimisspiæl* (OSw)

violation of someone's personal liberty (noun) *manhælghi* (OSw)

violation of someone's personal rights (noun) *manhælghi* (OSw)

violation of spiritual kinship rules (noun) *guþsivalaghspiæl* (OSw)

violation of the church sanctity (noun) *vixlaspiæll* (OSw)

violation of the marriage bed (noun) *siangaran* (OSw)

violation of the sanctity (noun) *friþbrut* (OSw)

violator of a peace pledge (noun) *tryggrofi* (ON)

violence (noun) *bardaghi* (OSw), *gærning* (OSw), *ofríki* (ON), *ofriþer* (OSw), *ran* (OSw), *vald* (OSw), *valdsværk* (OSw), *værk* (OSw)

violent (adj.) *ospaker* (OSw)

violent act (noun) *gærning* (OSw)

violent deed (noun) *gærning* (OSw), *valdsgærning* (OSw)

violent robber (noun) *rauferi* (OGu)

violent seizure (noun) *vangrov* (ODan)

virgin (noun) *mö* (OSw)

virginity (noun) *möiaralder* (OSw)

visible indication (noun) *mærki* (OSw)

visible mark (noun) *asyn* (OSw), *ílit* (ON)

visible score (noun) *asyn* (OSw)

visible wound (noun) *handaværk* (OSw)

visit (verb) *sökia* (OSw)

visitation (noun) *ransak* (OSw), *yfirferð* (ON)

void (verb) *ónýta* (ON), *rifta* (ON)

void (adj.) *ogilder* (OSw), *ónýtr* (ON)

voided (adj.) *ogilder* (OSw)

voluntary (adj.) *viljaligr* (ON)

voluntary oath (noun) *kostebuthseth* (ODan)

vote (noun) *orþ* (OGu), *röst* (OSw)

vouch (verb) *borgha* (OSw)

vouch for (verb) *sanna* (OSw), *varþa* (OSw)

vow (verb) *hætte* (ODan)

vow (noun) *heit* (ON)

voyage (noun) *flutning* (ON)

wadmal (noun) *vaþmal* (OSw)

wage reduction (noun) *leigufall* (ON)

wager (verb) *væþia* (OSw)

wager (noun) *væþ* (OSw), *væþfæ* (OSw)

wagering (noun) *vaþakast* (OSw)

wages (noun) *köp* (OSw), *legha* (OSw), *lön* (OSw), *mal (1)* (OSw), *mali* (OSw)

wages for sailors (noun) *fararkaup* (ON)

wagon (noun) *vagn* (OGu)

wagon-load (noun) *lass* (OSw)

wagon-riders (noun) *vagniklar (pl.)* (OGu)

wagon-riders' procession (noun) *vagniklaferþ* (OGu)

wainscot (noun) *þverþili* (ON)

waive a claim (verb) *hafna* (ON)

wake (noun) *erfi* (ON)

walking alone (in a pasture) (noun) *einganga* (ON)

walking-clothes (noun) *gangkleþi* (OGu)

wall (noun) *garþer* (OSw)

wall building (noun) *gærþning* (OSw)

wall coverings of black or blue cloth (noun) *bladragning* (OGu)

wall division (noun) *garðskifti* (ON)

wall purchase (noun) *væggiarköp* (OSw)

wall-eyed (of a horse) (adj.) *valdeygðr* (ON)

walling work (noun) *garðlag* (ON)

walling work-season (noun) *garðönn* (ON)

Walpurgis' Day (noun) *valborghamæssa* (OSw)

Walpurgis' Mass (noun) *valborghamæssa* (OSw)

Walpurgis' Night (noun) *valborghamæssa* (OSw)

wandering minstrel (noun) *lekari* (OSw)

want (verb) *játa* (ON), *vilia* (OSw)

want of proper care (noun) *vangöma* (OSw)

wanting (adj.) *vanr* (ON)

war (noun) *orosta* (OSw)

war captive (adj.) *hærfangin* (OSw)

war expedition (noun) *hærfærþ* (OSw)

war-horse (noun) *örs* (OSw)

ward (noun) *omaghi* (OSw), *ungr maðr* (ON), *varþnaþer* (OSw)

warden (noun) *uphaldsman* (ODan), *varþmaþer* (OSw)

ward's actions (noun) *ómagaverk* (ON)

wares (noun) *köpskatter* (OSw), *vara* (ON), *varningr* (ON)

warfare (noun) *hærfærþ* (OSw), *leþunger* (OSw)

warning (noun) *hembuþ* (OSw)

warrant (verb) *hemula* (OSw)

warrant (noun) *hemuld* (OSw)

warrant a title (verb) *hemula* (OSw)

warrant for ownership (noun) *leþsn* (OSw)

warrant one's ownership (verb) *hemula* (OSw)

warrantable (adj.) *hemul* (OSw)

warranter (noun) *vörzlumaðr* (ON)

warranty (noun) *hemuld* (OSw)

warranty man (noun) *hemulsman* (OSw)

warranty witness (noun) *heimilðarváttr* (ON)

warrior (noun) *hærman* (OSw)

warship (noun) *hærskip* (OSw), *snækkia* (OSw)

warship district (noun) *skipreiða* (ON)

wasteland (noun) *auðn* (ON), *ödmark* (OSw)

wasting of property (noun) *spiæll* (OSw)

watch (noun) *vaka* (OSw), *varþer* (OSw), *varþhald* (OSw)

watch at the beacons (noun) *vitavörðr* (ON)

watch-money (noun) *varþpenningar (pl.)* (OGu)

water (noun) *vatn* (ON)

water-mill (noun) *vatnqværn* (OSw)

waters where common rights exist (noun) *almænninger* (OSw)

waterway sound (noun) *leþsund* (OSw)

wave drift (noun) *vágrek* (ON)

waver (verb) *vægha (2)* (OSw)

wax (noun) *vax* (ON)

way (noun) *vægher* (OSw)

way to church (noun) *kirkiuvægher* (OSw)

way to the assembly (noun) *þingsvægher* (OSw)

wayfaring (adj.) *væghfarandi* (OSw)

ways to deny or repel an allegation (noun) *synjar (pl.)* (ON)

wayside shelter (noun) *sáluhús* (ON)

weak (adj.) *ófrár* (ON)

wealth (noun) *auðhófi* (ON), *fjáreign* (ON), *fjármegin* (ON), *fæ* (OSw), *öþer* (OSw)

wealth of farmers (noun) *bóndafé* (ON)

weapon (noun) *vapn* (OSw)

weapon-taking (noun) *vapntak* (ODan)

weapons of the sea warrior district (noun) *hamnuvapn* (OSw)

wed (verb) *vighia* (OSw)

wedded wife (noun) *eiginkona* (ON)

wedding (noun) *brullöp* (OSw), *bruþlöpsgærþ* (OSw), *gift* (OSw), *gifta* (OSw), *hionavighning* (OSw), *samvigilse* (OSw), *vighning* (OSw), *vigsl* (OSw)

wedding canopy (noun) *pell* (OGu)

wedding celebration (noun) *brúðkaup* (ON), *bruþlöpsgærþ* (OSw)

wedding day (noun) *giftingardagr* (ON)

wedding feast (noun) *brullöp* (OSw)

wedding gift (noun) *hindradagsgæf* (OSw), *morghongæf* (OSw)

wedding host (noun) *drozsieti* (OGu)

wedding journey (noun) *bruþfærd* (OSw)

wedding provisions (noun) *bruþlöpsgærþ* (OSw)

wedding testimony (noun) *samkunduvitni* (ON)

wedding-time (noun) *bruþlöpstimi* (OSw)

wedlock (noun) *hjúskapr* (ON), *samför* (ON)

weigh (verb) *vægha (2)* (OSw)

weigh a decision (verb) *akta* (ON)

weighed (adj.) *væghin* (OSw)

weighing (noun) *reizla* (ON)

weight of cargo (noun) *lestatal* (ON)

weighty case (noun) *stórmál* (ON)

well (noun) *sauþr* (OGu)

well disposed (adj.) *goþvili* (OSw)

well-born (adj.) *ætborin* (OSw)

werewolf (noun) *gylfin* (ON)

wergild (noun) *bogher* (OSw), *gæld* (OSw), *lögbaugr* (ON), *manbot* (OSw), *mangæld* (OSw), *mannsgildi* (ON), *mannsgjald* (ON), *værgæld* (OSw)

wergild compensation (noun) *hælghisbot* (OSw), *værgæld* (OSw)

wergild for a subject (noun) *þiængsgæld* (OSw)

wergild ring (noun) *bogher* (OSw)

wergild ring list (noun) *baugatal* (ON)

wergild subject to claim (noun) *krafarvereldi* (OGu)

wergild to the kinsmen (noun) *frændbót* (ON)

wergild within the peace circle (noun) *bandavereldi* (OGu)

wet (verb) *væta* (ON)

wet-nurse (noun) *fostermoþer* (OSw)

whale (noun) *hval* (ODan)

whale drift rights (noun) *hvalreki* (ON)

whale finding (noun) *hvalfundr* (ON)

whale in waters where common rights exist (noun) *almenningshvalr* (ON)

whale rights (noun) *hvalréttr* (ON)

whale salvaging (noun) *hvalflutningr* (ON)

whale-price (noun) *hvalsverð* (ON)

what grows on meadowland (noun) *engivöxtr* (ON)

what is from the father (noun) *fæþerni* (OSw)

what is from the mother (noun) *möþerni* (OSw)

what is rightful (noun) *rætter* (OSw)

whatever does duty for a weapon (noun) *vígvölr* (ON)

wheel (noun) *hjul* (ODan), *stæghl* (OSw)

which can be denied (adj.) *níkvæðr* (ON)

which can be kept (adj.) *uppnæmr* (ON)

which everyone has a right to carve (adj.) *lýðskærr* (ON)

whip (verb) *huþ* (OSw), *huþstryka* (OSw)

whipping (noun) *huþ* (OSw)

white ribbon worn at confirmation (noun) *fermidregill* (ON)

white robes (noun) *hvítaváðir (pl.)* (ON)

Whitsunday (noun) *pingizdagher* (OSw)

who can be buried at a church (adj.) *kirkjugrófr* (ON)

who may be given passage (adj.) *ferjandi* (ON)

who may be killed with impunity (adj.) *dræpr* (ON)

whole in bone (adj.) *bainheil* (OGu)

whole in breathing (adj.) *brustheil* (OGu)

whore (verb) *hóra* (ON)

whore (noun) *hóra* (ON), *horkona* (OSw), *hortuta* (OSw), *skökia* (OSw)

whoring (noun) *hóran* (ON)

wicket-gate (noun) *liþ (1)* (OSw)

widow (noun) *vidve* (ODan), *ænkia* (OSw)

widow of a kinsman (noun) *frændleif* (ON)

widow of a relative (noun) *frændleif* (ON)

wife (noun) *aþalkona* (OSw), *eiginkona* (ON), *frue* (ODan), *husfrugha* (OSw), *kona* (OSw), *kærling* (OSw), *málakona* (ON)

wife of a baron (noun) *lendsmannskona* (ON)

wife of a householder (noun) *bondakona* (OSw), *husfrugha* (OSw)

wife of a knight (noun) *riddarakona* (ON)

wife/woman (noun) *kona* (OSw)

wife's daughter (noun) *athelkonedotter* (ODan)

wild (adj.) *styggr* (ON)

wild animal (noun) *diur* (OSw)

wilful act (noun) *viliaværk* (OSw)

will (verb) *vilia* (OSw)

will (1) (noun) *vili* (OSw), *viliaværk* (OSw)

will (2) (noun) *somi* (OSw), *testament* (OSw)

willful damage (noun) *spellvirki* (ON)

willow tie (noun) *vaghrakki* (OSw)

wimple (noun) *huifr* (OGu)

win (verb) *vinna* (OSw)

win by lot (verb) *liuta* (OSw)

wind-mill (noun) *væþerquærn* (OSw)

winning a case (noun) *vitsorþ* (OSw)

winter board and lodging (noun) *vetrvist* (ON)

winter day (noun) *vinterdagher* (OSw)

winter dwelling (noun) *vetrhús* (ON)

winter mill (noun) *vintermylne* (ODan)

Winter Nights (noun) *vinternat* (OSw)

winter pasture (noun) *vetrhagi* (ON)

winter residence (noun) *vetrhús* (ON)

winter rye (noun) *vetrrugr* (ON)

wise (adj.) *viter* (OSw)

wish (verb) *lysta (2)* (OSw), *vilia* (OSw)

wish (noun) *vili* (OSw)

witch (noun) *fordæða* (ON), *troll* (ON), *trollkona* (ON)

witchcraft (noun) *fordeþskepr* (OGu), *forgærning* (OSw), *gærning* (OSw), *troldomber* (OSw), *trolskaper* (OSw), *tryllska* (ON)

witchcraft-paraphernalia (noun) *fordeþskepr* (OGu)

with a fixed abode (adj.) *bolfaster* (OSw)

with a right to inherit (prep.) *arfgænger* (OSw)

with acorns (adj.) *aldinbær* (OSw)

with belts undone (adj.) *lösgiurþer* (OSw)

with evil intent (adj.) *heiftugr* (ON)

with force (adj.) *nöþogher* (OSw)

with full security (prep.) *fullveðja* (ON)

with impunity (adj.) *ogilder* (OSw), *osaker* (OSw), *saklös* (OSw), *sekðarlauss* (ON)

with impunity (adv.) *saklöst* (OSw)

with loose girdle (adj.) *lösgiurþer* (OSw)

with reason (adv.) *ræt* (OSw)

with right (adj.) *saklös* (OSw)

with the intention (adv.) *viliandis* (OSw)

with the right to equal portions of inheritance (adj.) *jamnarva* (OSw)

with the right to inherit (adj.) *arfgænger* (OSw)

with the right to swear an oath (adj.) *edgilder* (OSw)

with the same father (adj.) *samfæthre* (ODan)

with the same mother (adj.) *sammøthre* (ODan)

with unhurt teats (adj.) *heilspenaðr* (ON)

with warranty (prep.) *heimiliga* (ON)

withdraw (verb) *afsighia* (OSw), *ryva* (OSw), *skilia* (OSw), *uptaka* (OSw)

withdrawal (noun) *órför* (ON)

withhold (verb) *halda* (OSw), *løne* (ODan), *uppihalda* (OSw)

withholding of tithe (noun) *tíundarhald* (ON)

within a year (adv.) *jamlangadagher* (OSw)

within enclosures (adv.) *ingærþis* (OSw)

within five days (adv.) *fæmt* (OSw)

within kin (prep.) *skylder (1)* (OSw)

within the country (adv.) *inrikis* (OSw)

within the enclosure (adv.) *ingærþis* (OSw)

within the province (adv.) *innanlands* (OSw)

within the realm (adv.) *inrikis* (OSw)

within the same district (prep.) *samheraðs* (ON)

within the same quarter (prep.) *samfjórðungs* (ON)

without a belt (adj.) *lösgiurþer* (OSw)

without a case (adj.) *ogilder* (OSw), *saklös* (OSw)

without a case (adv.) *saklöst* (OSw)

without a case to answer (adj.) *saklös* (OSw), *saklöst* (OSw)

without a case to answer to (adj.) *saklösa* (OSw)

without a fence (adj.) *garðlauss* (ON)

without a fine (prep.) *sekðarlauss* (ON)

without a fixed home (prep.) *staðfestulauss* (ON)

without a fixed household (prep.) *búlauss* (ON)

without a husband (adj.) *manløs* (ODan)

without a lawful excuse (prep.) *nauðsynjalauss* (ON)

without a pledge being laid down (adj.) *ovæþiaþer* (OSw)

without a summons (prep.) *sjalfstefndr* (ON)

without action taken against (adj.) *osaker* (OSw)

without authority (adj.) *ohemul* (OSw), *ohemult* (OSw)

without being christened (adj.) *ukristin* (OSw)

without being sued (adj.) *osökter* (OSw)

without borrowing (prep.) *óleigðr* (ON)

without cause (adj.) *ogilder* (OSw), *saklös* (OSw)

without cause (adv.) *foryftalaust* (ON)

without coercion (adj.) *þrangalös* (OSw)

without compelling necessity (prep.) *nauðsynjalauss* (ON)

without compensation (adj.) *ogilder* (OSw), *saklös* (OSw), *saklöst* (OSw)

without complaint (adj.) *oklutraþer* (OSw), *uilter* (OSw)

without consecration (adj.) *ovighþer* (OSw)

without consequences (adj.) *saklös* (OSw)

without contention (adj.) *oklandaþer* (OSw)

without conviction (adj.) *ufælder* (OSw)

without damage (adj.) *skatheløs* (ODan)

without damage (adv.) *skatheløst* (ODan)

without deceit (prep.) *breklauss* (ON), *véllauss* (ON)

without defect (adj.) *lastalaus* (OGu)

without delay (prep.) *nauðsynjalauss* (ON)

without dependents (adj.) *ómagalauss* (ON)

without dishonour (adj.) *oskemdr* (OGu)

without dispute (adj.) *átölulauss* (ON), *okærder* (OSw)

without division (adj.) *oskipter* (OSw)

without due cause (adj.) *nauðsynjalauss* (ON)

without due cause (adv.) *uskylt* (ODan)

without excuse (adv.) *forfallalöst* (OSw)

without fault (adj.) *saklös* (OSw)

without fine for trespass (prep.) *landnámlaust* (ON)

without fraud (prep.) *ófalsaðr* (ON)

without giving a guarantee (adv.) *ohemult* (OSw)

without good cause (adv.) *foráttalaust* (ON)

without good reason (adj.) *nauðsynjalauss* (ON)

without good reason (adv.) *vrangt* (ODan)

without guile (prep.) *véllauss* (ON)

without guilt (adj.) *helagher* (OSw), *osaker* (OSw), *oskylder* (OSw), *saklös* (OSw), *sekðarlauss* (ON)

without harm (adj.) *vatheløs* (ODan)

without having been inventoried (prep.) *ótalðr* (ON)

without having been shriven (adj.) *skriptalös* (OSw)

without having confessed one's sins (adj.) *skriptalös* (OSw)

without hope (adj.) *fegher* (OSw)

without ill will (prep.) *öfundlauss* (ON)

without impediment (prep.) *meinbugalaust* (ON)

without interest (prep.) *ávaxtalauss* (ON), *leigulauss* (ON), *óleigis* (ON), *vaxtalauss* (ON)

without judgement (adj.) *vitulös* (OSw)

without judgement (adv.) *domalöst* (OSw)

without justice (adj.) *rætløs* (ODan)

without justification (prep.) *orætlika* (OSw), *ósýnn* (ON)

without kin (prep.) *frændlauss* (ON)

without leave (adv.) *óleyfi* (ON), *ólofaðr* (ON), *olovandis* (OSw)

without legal cause (prep.) *forfallalöst* (OSw)

without legal defence (adj.) *vitulös* (OSw)

without legal penalty (adj.) *saklös* (OSw)

without legal proceedings (adj.) *osökter* (OSw)

without legal redress (prep.) *ohailigr* (OGu)

without legitimate excuse (prep.) *nauðsynjalauss* (ON)

without legitimate hindrance (prep.) *forfallalöst* (OSw)

without liability (adj.) *saklös* (OSw)

without maintenance (prep.) *framførslulauss* (ON)

without malice (prep.) *öfundlauss* (ON)

without means (prep.) *félauss* (ON)

without necessary cause (adj.) *þrangalös* (OSw)

without need (prep.) *nauðsynjalauss* (ON)

without oaths (prep.) *eiðlauss* (ON)

without obligations (adj.) *saklös* (OSw)

without paying compensation (prep.) *óbóttr* (ON)

without payment (adj.) *kauplauss* (ON), *kauplaust* (ON), *verðlauss* (ON)

without peace (adj.) *friþlös* (OSw)

without penalty (adj.) *osaker* (OSw), *sekðarlauss* (ON)

without penalty (adv.) *saklöst* (OSw)

without permission (adv.) *leyfislaust* (ON), *óleyfi* (ON), *óleyfiliga* (ON), *olof* (OSw), *olovandis* (OSw)

without promise (adj.) *olovandis* (OSw)

without property (adj.) *øreigi* (ON)

without prosecution (adj.) *osökter* (OSw)

without punishment (prep.) *osaker* (OSw), *sekðarlauss* (ON), *synðalauss* (ON)

without reason (adj.) *nauðsynjalauss* (ON), *saklös* (OSw)

without reason (adv.) *oskælika* (OSw)

without rebuking (adj.) *ovæþiaþer* (OSw)

without resolution (adj.) *ufælder* (OSw)

without right to personal compensation (adj.) *rætløs* (ODan)

without rights (adj.) *vitulös* (OSw)

without security (adj.) *oborghaþer* (OSw)

without shame (adj.) *oskemdr* (OGu)

without share (adj.) *lutlös* (OSw)

without sin (prep.) *synðalauss* (ON)

without the enclosure (adv.) *utgærþis* (OSw)

without the protection of law (prep.) *ohailigr* (OGu)

without title (adv.) *ohemult* (OSw)

without valid excuse (prep.) *forfallalöst* (OSw)

without voice in the matter (adj.) *ogilder* (OSw)

without witnesses (prep.) *váttlauss* (ON), *vitnalös* (OSw)

witless (adj.) *orvite* (ODan)

witness (verb) *sea* (OSw), *vátta* (ON), *vita* (OSw), *vitna* (OSw)

witness (noun) *fæst* (OSw), *vatter* (OSw), *váttorð* (ON), *vita* (OSw), *vitnesbyrth* (ODan), *vitni* (OSw), *vitnismaþer* (OSw), *vætti* (OSw)

witness (i.e. person giving testimony) (noun) *vatter* (OSw), *vitni* (OSw)

witness (i.e. testimony) (noun) *vitni* (OSw)

witness against (verb) *vinna* (OSw)

witness as to permission (noun) *lofsvitni* (OSw)

witness at a purchase (noun) *vinorþ* (OSw)

witness at someone's home (noun) *heimstefnuváttr* (ON)

witness concerning confiscated items (noun) *aftæktavitne* (OSw)

witness for confirmation (noun) *sannaðarvitni* (ON)

witness from the district (noun) *hærethsvitne* (ODan)

witness from the district assembly (noun) *hærethsthingsvitne* (ODan)

witness of a conveyance (noun) *skøtevitne* (ODan)

witness of a sudden act (noun) *bræþavitni* (OSw)

witness of allodial land (noun) *oþolfastir* (OSw)

witness of assembly men (noun) *þingsmannavitni* (OSw)

witness of conveyance (noun) *skeytingarvitni* (ON)

witness of inheritance (noun) *ærfþarvitni* (OSw)

witness of parishioners (noun) *soknavitni* (OSw)

witness of purchase (noun) *köpfæst* (OSw)

witness of settlement terms (noun) *sáttargerðarváttr* (ON)

witness of taking (noun) *tökuvætti* (ON)

witness of the anouncement of judgement (noun) *dómsuppsöguváttr* (ON)

witness of the assembly (noun) *þingvitni* (OSw)

witness of the men of the assembly (noun) *þingsmannavitni* (OSw)

witness selected at random (noun) *fangaváttr* (ON)

witness statement (noun) *vitnesbyrth* (ODan)

witness that lawful summons to the assembly has taken place (noun) *þingstefnuvitni* (ON)

witness that one has permission (noun) *lofsvitni* (OSw)

witness that something was announced (noun) *lysningavitni* (OSw)

witness to a bid (noun) *boðsváttr* (ON)

witness to a claim (noun) *kvöðuváttr* (ON), *kvöðuvitni* (ON)

witness to a conveyance (noun) *skøtevitne* (ODan)

witness to a demand for the surrender of odal land (noun) *forsagnarvitni* (ON)

witness to a formal claim (noun) *kvöðuvitni* (ON)

witness to a home summons (noun) *heimstefnuvitni* (ON), *stefnuvitni* (ON)

witness to a sale (noun) *köpvitni* (OSw)

witness to a stipulation (noun) *virðingarváttr* (ON)

witness to a wedding (noun) *brúðkaupsvitni* (ON)

witness to an announcement of a crime (noun) *lysningavitni* (OSw)

witness to an assembly summons (noun) *þingstefnuvitni* (ON)

witness to an attack (noun) *heimsóknarvitni* (ON)

witness to an oath (noun) *eþarvitni* (OSw)

witness to legal excuses (noun) *nauðsynjavitni* (ON)

witness to necessity (noun) *nauðsynjavitni* (ON)

witness to odal right (noun) *óðalsvitni* (ON)

witness to rapine (noun) *ransvitne* (ODan)

witness to testify necessity (noun) *nauðsynjavitni* (ON)

witness to the freeing process (noun) *leysingjavitni* (ON)

witness to the report of a killing (noun) *víglýsingarvitni* (ON)

witness to the right of ownership (noun) *eignarvitni* (ON)

witness to the right to live on the land (noun) *hafnarvitni* (ON)

witness-bearing (noun) *vitnesbyrth* (ODan)

witnessed (adj.) *vitnissannr* (ON)

witnesses (noun) *fastar (pl.)* (OSw)

witnesses of the demand for surety (noun) *taksæstingarváttr* (ON)

witnesses outside the court (noun) *heyrendr (pl.)* (ON), *hörængi* (OSw)

witting (adj.) *vísvitandi* (ON)

wolf (noun) *ulv* (ODan), *vargher* (OSw)

wolf trap (noun) *varghagarþer* (OSw)

woman (noun) *frue* (ODan), *husfrugha* (OSw), *kona* (OSw), *quindi* (OGu)

woman at the mercy of (someone) (noun) *miskunnakona* (OSw), *naþakona* (OSw)

woman dependent on compassion (noun) *miskunnakona* (OSw)

woman dependent on other person's discretion (noun) *skyniakona* (OSw)

woman from the district (noun) *heraðskona* (ON)

woman having a right to odal (noun) *óðalskona* (ON)

woman in bondage for debt (noun) *skuldarkona* (ON)

woman in legal debt-bondage (noun) *lögskuldarkona* (ON)

woman in shame (noun) *hathkone* (ODan)

woman in spiritual affinity (noun) *guþsivia* (OSw)

woman related through spiritual kinship (noun) *sifkona* (ON)

woman taking inheritance (noun) *ærfdakona* (OSw)

woman witness (noun) *vitniskuna* (OGu)

womanish (adj.) *ragr* (ON)

woman's clothes (noun) *kvenklæði* (ON)

woman's measure (noun) *kvenaskr* (ON)

womb (noun) *quiþr* (OGu)

women's bench (noun) *qvinnabænker* (OSw)

women's inviolability (noun) *qvinnafriþer* (OSw)

women's marriage (noun) *kvennagifting* (ON)

women's peace (noun) *qvinnafriþer* (OSw)

wood (1) (noun) *skogher* (OSw), *skoghland* (ODan)

wood (2) (noun) *fang* (OSw), *viþer* (OSw)

wood cutting (noun) *skogharhug* (OSw)

wood damage (noun) *viðarspell* (ON)

wood load (noun) *fløghelas* (ODan)

wood rapine (noun) *skoghran* (ODan)

wood road (noun) *skoghvægh* (ODan)

wood-shame (noun) *tréníð* (ON)

wooded lot (noun) *hult* (OGu)

wooden arrow (noun) *tréör* (ON)

woodland (noun) *skogher* (OSw), *skoghland* (ODan)

woodland boundary (noun) *skoghamærki* (OSw), *skoghaskæl* (OSw)

woodland division (noun) *skoghaskipti* (OSw)

woodland floor (noun) *skógarstaða* (ON)

woodland meadow (noun) *skoghæng* (OSw)

woodpile (noun) *viþakaster* (OSw)

woods (noun) *hult* (OGu), *skogher* (OSw)

woollen cloth (noun) *klæþi* (OSw), *vaþmal* (OSw)

word (noun) *buþ* (OSw), *orþ* (OGu), *raþ* (OSw)

word from the Thing assembly (noun) *þingkænun* (OSw)

word of honour (noun) *þegnskapr* (ON)

word-of-honour oath (noun) *þegnskaparlagningareiðr* (ON)

wording (noun) *munhaf* (OSw)

wording of an oath (noun) *munhaf* (OSw)

words of challenge (noun) *hruðningarmál* (ON)

words of investigators (noun) *mætansorþ* (OSw)

words requiring full personal compensation (noun) *fullréttisorð* (ON)

words to swear an oath (noun) *eiðstafr* (ON)

work (verb) *vinna* (OSw), *yrkia* (OSw)

work (noun) *arvuþi* (OSw), *inne* (ODan), *vist* (OSw), *værk* (OSw)

work by an artisan (noun) *gærning* (OSw)

work in another man's land (noun) *ayrkia* (OSw)

work of a man (noun) *handaværk* (OSw)

work of labourers (noun) *forverk* (ON)

work on Sundays (noun) *sunnudagsverk* (ON)

work wages (noun) *smíðarkaup* (ON), *verkakaup* (ON)

work wrongfully (verb) *misvinna* (ON)

worker (noun) *drænger* (OSw), *leghodrænger* (OSw), *vinnumaðr* (ON)

working (adj.) *alyrkr* (ON), *ohailigr* (OGu)

working animal (noun) *yrknaþafæ* (OSw)

working beast (noun) *ortasoyþr* (OGu)

working day (noun) *anværkdagher* (OSw)

working season (noun) *önn (pl. annir)* (ON)

workman (noun) *leghomaþer* (OSw), *verkasveinn* (ON), *verkmaðr* (ON)

worship (verb) *blota* (OSw)

worth (noun) *virthning* (ODan), *værþ* (OSw), *værþorar (pl.)* (OSw)

worth (adj.) *verðr* (ON)

worth a certain payment in fine (adj.) *gilder* (OSw)

worth as much (adj.) *jafndýrr* (ON)

worth of one's seed (noun) *frøsgjald* (ODan)

worth of the land (noun) *jorþaværþ* (OSw)

worth of wounds (noun) *saremun* (ODan)

worth the least (adj.) *félítill* (ON)

worthless goods (noun) *flærþ* (OSw)

worthless trade (noun) *kaupfox* (ON)

worthy (adj.) *goþer* (OSw)

wound (verb) *bæria* (OSw), *hugga* (OSw), *sargha* (OSw), *skena* (OSw), *sære* (ODan), *unda* (OSw)

wound (noun) *akoma* (OSw), *atvígi* (ON), *banesar* (ODan), *bæn* (OSw), *gærþ* (OSw), *hulsar* (OSw), *men* (OSw), *sar* (OSw), *sarafar* (OGu)

wound by accident (verb) *mishöggva* (ON)

wound by accident (noun) *vaþasar* (OSw)

wound compensation (noun) *sarabot* (OSw)

wound covered by the law (noun) *laghesar* (ODan)

wound in the cavities (noun) *hulsar* (OSw)

wound in the head (noun) *huvuþsar* (OSw)

wound in the trunk (noun) *hulsar* (OSw)

wound made with a weapon (noun) *skena* (OSw)

wound subject to full compensation (noun) *fullsæri* (OSw)

wound that has penetrated the abdominal or breast cavity (noun) *hulsar* (OSw)

wound-fine (noun) *sarabot* (OSw)

wounded (adj.) *sar* (OSw)

wounded internally (adj.) *holunda* (ON)

wounded man (noun) *sarþuli* (OSw)

wounded to the marrow (adj.) *mergundaðr* (ON)

wounding (noun) *aværkan* (OSw), *hug* (OSw), *sar* (OSw), *sarnaþer* (OSw)

wrath (noun) *vreþsvili* (OSw)

wreck (noun) *vrak* (ODan)

wreckage (noun) *rekald* (ON)

wrest away (verb) *ræna* (OSw)

wrist (noun) *baugliþr* (OGu)

wristband (noun) *baugband* (OGu)

writ (noun) *bref* (OSw), *rit* (ON), *skript* (OSw)

write (verb) *skrive* (ODan)

write off (verb) *afgiva* (OSw), *fælla* (OSw)

written document (noun) *skript* (OSw)

wrong (verb) *misgøre* (ODan)

wrong (noun) *vrangvisa* (OSw)

wrong (adj.) *vranger* (OSw)

wrongdoing (noun) *brut* (OSw)

wrongful (sexual) intercourse (noun) *misróða* (ON)

wrongfully (adv.) *vranglika* (ODan)

wrongfully acquired (adj.) *rangfenginn* (ON)

wrongfully conducted (adj.) *misgörr* (ON)

wrongfully taken (adj.) *rantakin* (OSw)

wrongly (adv.) *oræt* (OSw), *vrangt* (ODan)

wrongly called (adj.) *rangkvaddr* (ON)

wrongly published (adv.) *ranglýstr* (ON)

wrongly salvaged (adv.) *rangfluttr* (ON)

yard (noun) *garþer* (OSw)

yard measuring rod (noun) *stika* (ON)

year (noun) *atmeli* (OGu), *jamlangi* (OSw)

year and a day (noun) *jamlangadagher* (OSw),
  jamlangi (OSw)

year and a day from (adv.) *jamlangadagher* (OSw)

yeoman (noun) *hölðmaðr* (ON)

yield (noun) *avaxter* (OSw), *legha* (OSw), *vöxtr* (ON)

yield at the legal rate (noun) *lögvöxtr* (ON)

yield of cattle (noun) *fearnyt* (OSw)

yoke (noun) *öker* (OSw)

yoke (and) wagon (noun) *oykvagn* (OGu)

you (noun) *maþer* (OSw)

young boy (noun) *sven* (OSw)

young man (noun) *drænger* (OSw)

young tree (noun) *undirviþer* (OSw)

youngstock (noun) *foster* (OSw)

Yule (noun) *jul* (OSw)

Yule sanctity (noun) *julafriþer* (OSw)

Yule time (noun) *jul* (OSw)

Untranslated terms

agnabaker (OSw)
alin (OSw)
almænningsöre (OSw)
ambat (OSw)
attunger (OSw)
balker (OSw)
bogha fines (OSw)
bogher (OSw)
broafiol (OSw)
bryti (OSw)
bälg-tax (OSw)
danaarver (OSw)
eþsöre (OSw)
fastar (OSw)
fastar at land purchase (OSw)
fastar at repayment (OSw)
fiæt (OSw)
folkland (OSw)
forta (OSw)
fylkis assembly (ON)
fylkis church (ON)
fæstingafæ (OSw)
gorvargher (OSw)
hamarskipt (OSw)
hamna (OSw)
har (OSw)
holmsköp (OSw)
holmstompt (OSw)
hundari (OSw)
hærapshöfþingi (OSw)
kirkmæssufriþer (OSw)
lekararætter (OSw)
leþunger (OSw)
leþungslami (OSw)
leþungs-tax (OSw)
löndaskript (OSw)

markland (OSw)
næmd (OSw)
ormylia (OSw)
oþolfastir (OSw)
pund (OSw)
pænninger (OSw)
reksþegn (ON)
skiplagh (OSw)
skipnöti (OSw)
skunkufalsmaþer (OSw)
spander (OSw)
spannaland (OSw)
styltingsrast (OSw)
styrifaster (OSw)
svear (OSw)
sáld (ON)
tagbænda (OSw)
thæghn money (OSw)
tilgæf (OSw)
trö (OSw)
urþinga (OSw)
vighramannaskin-tax (OSw)
vithstorth (ODan)
væstgötar (OSw)
ætskuspiæll (OSw)
öresland (OSw)
öre (OSw)
öre field (OSw)
örnavingi (OSw)
örtoghaland (OSw)
örtogh (OSw)
öþer (OSw)
þingilder (OSw)
þriþiunger (OSw)
þyn (OSw)

Appendix A:
Administrative, Judicial and Fiscal Subdivisions

This appendix outlines the administrative, judicial and fiscal subdivisions, according to Danish laws, Swedish provincial laws, Guta law, Norwegian laws before the Norwegian law of the realm (1274) and Icelandic laws. This is an attempt to show the relevant hierarchies within each law as expressed in that particular law, and supplemented by old and recent research as noted in the encyclopedic articles.

This type of presentation might lead to the conclusion that the medieval borders as well as the administrative, judicial and fiscal divisions are well known and well researched.

However, the degree to which the medieval borders and the administrative, judicial and fiscal divisions are known and researched varies substantially, from established facts to mere assumptions on behalf of an individual researcher. It must also be remembered that any law may reflect different chronological layers of divisions, and that the divisions may have various origins and have been made for different purposes. You may, therefore, also find two different terms in the same 'box', thus indicating that their relationship is not fully investigated or that there were parallel systems. The ecclesiastical divisions are not included here as they do not appear in the translated versions of the laws used for the lexicon.

Headwords in the lexicon: ar (1), attunger, bol, broafiol, fiarþunger, folkland, fylki, hamna, har, hundari, hæraþ, land, leþunger, leþungslami, manngerð, roþin (see roþarætter in the lexicon) siettungr skipen, skiplagh, skipreiða, sysel, þriþiunger.

Danish laws

JyL. The Law of Jutland (*Jyske lov*).
VSjL. Valdemar's Law for Zealand (*Valdemars sjællandske lov*).
ESjL. Erik's Law for Zealand (*Eriks sjællandske lov*).
SkL. The Law of Scania (*Skånske Lov, Skånelagen*).
SkKL. The Church Law of Scania (*Skånske kirkelov*).

JyL	VSjL, ESjL	SkL
land	land	land
sysel	-	-
hæreth	hæreth	hæreth
fiarthing	-	-
bol / skipen	bol / atting	bol / atting
havne	havne	havne

Fiarthing used as an administrative unit is found only in JyL.

The use and meaning of the low-level divisions (*atting, bol, havne* and *skipen*) may vary depending on time and geographical area. By the 1250s the ecclesiastical divisions into *sokn* were gradually gaining importance and so was *landsby*. This, however, is not reflected in the translated versions of the laws, and therefore not shown here.

 https://doi.org/10.11647/OBP.0188.04

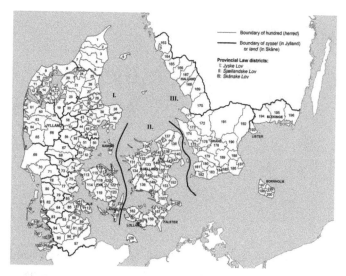

Figure 1. *Sysel- hæreth-* and
land- borders. Map drawn for this
publication by Johnny G. G. Jakobsen.

Figure 2. Division into *hundari* (grey)
and *hærap* in Sweden and Denmark
in the Middle Ages. Map from
Thorsten Andersson 1982a: p. 53. By
permission from the author.

Swedish legislative regions

Svea Laws

Hälsingland: The Law of the Hälsingar (HL). Finland was then part of Sweden and Hälsingelagen was their law too.

Uppland: (including Tiundaland, Attundaland, and Fjädrundaland): The Law of Uppland (UL).

Västmanland and Dala: The (Younger) Law of Västmanland (VmL) and The Law of Dalarna or The (Older) law of Västmanland (DL).

Södermanland: The Law of the Södermän (SdmL).

Närke: The Law of Närke (now lost) (NL).

Värmland: The Law of Värmland (now lost) (VrmL).

Göta Laws

Västergötland: The Older Law of the Västgötar (ÄVgL) and The Younger Law of the Västgötar (YVgL).

Östergötland: The Law of Östergötland (ÖgL).

Tiohärad (Småland): The Law of Tiohärad or The Law of Småland (only the book concerning Church law) (SmL).

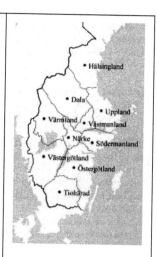

Figure 3. Swedish
legislative regions. Map
drawn by Inger Larsson.

Göta laws

ÄVgL. The Older Law of the Västgötar (*Äldre Västgötalagen*).
YVgL. The Younger Law of the Västgötar (*Yngre Västgötalagen*).
ÖgL. The Law of the Östgötar (*Östgötalagen*).
SmL. The Law of Småland (*Smålandslagen* or *Tiohäradslagen*).

SmL	ÄVgL, YVgL	ÖgL
land	land	land
hæraþ	hæraþ	hæraþ
-	fiarþunger	fiarþunger
-	-	hamna*
-	-	attunger, har*

The military naval defence organization, *leþunger*, is mentioned in Danish, Norwegian and Swedish laws. Originally, men, equipment and ships were to be provided, but already at the time when the Swedish laws were written down in the form we know them today these obligations had been transformed into yearly taxes in times of peace.

Whether *hamna** and *har** existed in Östergötland has been debated (Ericsson 2007, 113 and passim). Ericsson suggests that a *hamna* might have consisted of eight *attungar*, but its very existence in Östergötland has also been questioned (Söderlind 1989, 16–17).

bo (OSw) n.

In ÖgL a *bo* could denote a farm with an administrative function under the control of a king, bishop or *jarl*, or their *bryti*. In the Swedish province of Västergötland, albeit not mentioned in the versions of the law translated into English but present in a recent edition of the law (Wiktorsson 2011:II, 160–65), a *bo* was an administrative district of an unknown function comprising one or several *hæraþ*, that was probably named after, and associated with, the local royal estates of *upsala öþer*.

Svea laws

DL. The Law of Dalarna (*Dalalagen*).

HL. The Law of the Hälsingar (*Hälsingelagen*).

SdmL. The Law of the Södermän (*Södermannalagen*).

UL. The Law of Uppland (*Upplandslagen*).

VmL. The Law of Västmanland (*Västmannalagen*).

The Law of Närke and the Law of Värmland are mentioned in other sources, but no manuscripts of these laws have been found.

UL	VmL	DL	SdmL	HL
folkland (3) / roþin (1)***	land	land	land	land
hundari (25) / skiplagh	hundari (8)	þriþiunger	hundari (12)	þriþiunger
—	broafiol	broafiol-	skiplagh	skiplagh
fiarþunger / ar*	fiarþunger / skiplagh		fiarþunger	fiarþunger
hamna / attunger**	hamna		hamna / attunger	har

Key to the table:

Numbers in brackets indicate the number of districts known of the particular kind. / between two terms indicate parallel systems in different areas.

In UL a division into þriþiunger was limited to very few districts (Hafström 1949a, 142–43, Lundberg 1972, 92) and might not have existed in VmL, as Schlyter indicates that the manuscript might have been corrupt in the actual passage (Schlyter s.v. þriþiunger).

* Whether an administrative division into *ar* did exist or not is debated. Andersson 2014, 15; Hjärne 1980, I: 96–102; Schlyter s.v. *ar*; SL UL 61 not 52.

** *Hamna* and *attunger* seem to be parallel systems in UL never occurring in the same areas (Lindkvist 1995, 20–21). According to Lundberg (1972, 76–77) *hamna* was an administrative unit connected to *leþunger*, taxation and *buþkafli* but not necessarily a subdivision of the *hundari*.

*** The coastal area along the Baltic was called *Roden* and it was divided into *skiplagh*. The size of *Roden* has been debated. Refs: Hafström 1949, 19–20; KLNM s.v. *roden*; Lundberg 1972, 82–83.

The relationships between *fiarþunger* and *skiplagh* (VmL), *hamna* and *attunger* (SdmL) or *fiarþunger* and *har* (HL) have not been fully investigated.

Guta lag and Guta saga

GL. The Law of the Gotlanders (*Guta lag*)
GS. *Guta saga.*

GL
Gotland, land
þriþiunger
siettungr
hundari / þing

The relationship between *hundari* and *thing* has not been fully investigated.

Norwegian laws

BorgL. The Borgarting Law (*Borgartingsloven*).
EidsL. The Eidsivathing Law (*Eidsivatingsloven*).
GuL. The Gulathing Law (*Gulatingsloven*).
FrL. The Frostathing Law (*Frostatingsloven*).

BorgL	EidsL	GuL	FrL
fylki	fylki	fylki, sýsla	fylki, sýsla[1]
–	þriðjungr	fjórðungr	Þriðjungr[2] / fjórðungr
herað	herað	áttungr	séttungr / áttungr
skipreiða		skipreiða	
		manngerð	

Key to the table: The relationship between *fylki* and *sýsla* has not been fully investigated.
/ between two terms indicates parallel systems.
1) presupposed by the term *sýslumaðr*. 2) presupposed by the term *þriðjungsmaðr*.

Figure 4. Norwegian legislative regions. Map from Mykland 1989, map 28. © Cappelen Damm, with permission from the publisher.

Icelandic laws

The Laws of Iceland during the Free State period:
Grg. *Grágás*.
Jó. *Jónsbók* (1281).
Js. *Járnsíða*.

Icelandic laws
Island, land
fjórðungr
herað
hreppr

Sýsla: Following Icelandic submission to Norway in 1262/4, Norwegian authorities sent sheriffs (*sýslumenn*) to govern regions of Iceland. Their jurisdiction was called a *sýsla*. During the Middle Ages a *sýsla* had no fixed geographic boundaries, and their number and size changed over time.

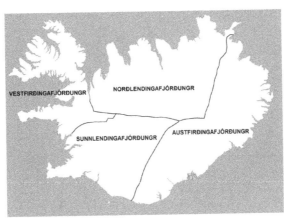

Figure 5. Map of division into fjórðungr drawn for this publication by Johnny G. G. Jakobsen.

Appendix B: Agriculture and Forestry

Diagram 1. A landowner's assets in different types of land and common resources.
Diagram produced by Inger Larsson.

A landowner during the time of the Nordic provincial laws (c. 1240–1350) would have his share in the cultivated land, the non-cultivated land used for hay harvest and grazing, the woods and forests, which constituted an important economic asset, as well as in other common resources such as fishing waters, hunting and wells. His rights and commitments were regulated by the provincial laws. The details might differ with each law and likewise the terminology. The Middle Ages in the Nordic countries lasted from c. 1000 to 1500–30.

The diagram above shows roughly how all these assets were interdependent and intertwined.

The *cultivated land* was the most valuable asset. In all Nordic countries there was a vast expansion in the Early Middle Ages of arable land through cultivating part of the meadow-land or through slash and burn clearance of moors, woodlands and forests.

The *non-cultivated land used for hay harvest and grazing* was almost equally important, as the area available for hay harvesting and grazing determined the number of cattle a farmer was able to feed during the winter-stalling, and thus how much fertilizer he had access to for use on the cultivated land.

The *woods and forests* were important for providing grazing, timber and firewood and not least, land for future cultivation. In the south of Scandinavia they also provided food for pigs, i.e. acorns, beechnuts and hazelnuts.

Common resources were assets for the common use of all landowners or tenants such as fishing-waters, streams, pastures, woodlands or forests. The right of use to these assets was regulated and differed between laws, and misuse was punished.

Ingierþis (OSw) and *utgierþis* (OSw), literally 'within enclosure', i.e. within the village arable land, and 'outside the enclosure', is a contemporary dichotomy of land of crucial importance in the laws and in society.

The following is an effort to give an overview of the most frequent terms/words used in the laws and their meaning and relations to each other.

https://doi.org/10.11647/OBP.0188.05

General

jorþ (OSw), **jorth** (ODan), **jörð** (ON) n.

1) earth, 2) ground, soil, land for a specific purpose, 3) cultivated land and 4) immovables, property

Refs: CV s.v. *jörþ*; Herzberg s.v. *jörþ*; Lund s.v. *iorþ*; Schlyter s.v. *jorþ*.

land (OSw, ODan, ON) n.

1) arable land, 2) province, kingdom, 3) ground, 4) shore, 5) property, 6) countryside as opposed to town and 7) parcel of land. As a place-name element it means large island or peninsula i.e. Öland, Langeland, Lolland.

Refs: Brink 2008b, 99, 106; CV *land*; Herzberg s.v. *land*; KLNM s.v. *-land*; Lund s.v. *land*; Ruthström 2002, 118–28; Schlyter s.v. *land*.

mark (OSw, ODan), **mörk** (ON) n.

The word form *mark* n. represents three homonyms: 1) *mark* 'mark, sign; border mark, boundary line'; 2) *mark* 'unit of weight and coinage', 3) *mark* 'forest, wood; outlying field, outland'. For homonyms 2 and 3 the ON standard form is *mörk*. The oldest sense of the neuter *mark* and the feminine variant *mark* (the latter originally collective plural) was 'border/boundary mark'. Since forests often functioned as borderland the word *mark* (both neuter and feminine) also came to mean 'forest, wood', and (by extension) 'land, field'.

Refs: Bjorvand 1994, 79–80, 158–59; 2007, 722; Brink 2008b, passim; CV s.v. *mörk*; Fritzner s.v.v. *mörk*, *mǫrk*; KLNM s.v.v. *-mark*, *mark*, *rågång*, *utmark*; Schlyter s.v. *mark*. See also Appendix C.

ingærþis, **ingierþis** (OSw) adv.

Refers to land 'within enclosure'. Cultivated fields, meadows and some areas used for grazing would be fenced in. The use of this land in Sweden was characterized by annual cropping and intensive use. The main part of the food supply originated in the land 'within enclosure'.

See also *garþer*, *gærþi*.

Refs: KLNM s.v. *ager* sp. 37–38; Myrdal 1999, 125–30.

utgærþis (OSw) adv., **utjorth** (ODan) n., **útjörð** (OIce) n.

Refer to land 'outside the enclosure'. Outside the enclosure were moorland, woodland and forest land. The use of this land in Sweden was characterized by versatile use and expansion of farmland. See also *ollandæ* (ODan), *utlænde* (ODan) commented below under *aker*.

In ON it is used of tenant estates and is equated with ON *leiguból* (cf. Rafnsson 1985, 153). Útjarðir were also the parcels of land which could be inherited by women, whereas sons received the 'primary estate' (*höfuðból*) according to Jó Kge 7.

Refs: KLNM s.v. *utmark*; Myrdal 1999, 125–30; 2011, 77–97; Rafnsson 1985, 153. See also *almænninger*.

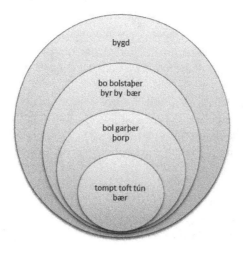

Diagram 2. Illustration of the sematic scope of words in the laws denoting inhabited areas. Diagram produced by Inger Larsson.

Cultivated land: village, farmstead and farmyard

There are a large number of different words denoting a specific area or district, a village or a single farm. Some words include the buildings, others do not. Some include all the land and rights belonging to a farm, others do not. The diagram below roughly illustrates the relations between the different words and their semantic scope although the extension of a single word may vary between laws and/or provinces.

district (not administrative)	*bygd* (OSw, ODan), *byggð* (ON) n.
a village, a single or a group of farms, belongings, district	*bo* (ODan, OGu, OSw), *bú* (ON) n.
village, farm and/or land surrounding the farmstead	*bolstaþer* (OSw), *bólstaðr* (ON) n.
	by, byr (OSw), *býr* (ON), *bær* (ON) n.
the farm as an economic asset or unclear reference	*bol* (OSw, ODan, OGu), *ból* (ON) n.
the farmstead, sometimes including land as an economic asset	*garþer* (OSw), *garth* (ODan), *garþr* (OGu), *garðr* (ON) n.
the farmyard or the farm as an economic asset	*tompt* (OSw), *toft* (ODan), *tóft* (ON) *tún* (ON), *bær* (ON) n.
new settlement from an old village/farm	*þorp* (OSw), *thorp* (ODan) n.

bygd (OSw, ODan), **byggð** (ON) n.

Inhabited area or district sometimes including the inhabitants and the cultivated land.

Refs: CV s.v. *bygð*; Hertzberg s.v. *bygð*; KLNM s.v. *-bygd*; ONP s.v. *byggð*; Schlyter s.v. *bygd*; Zoega s.v. *bygð*.

bo (ODan, OGu, OSw), **bú** (ON) n.

Literally 'dwelling' with many separate meanings in the laws: 1) a farm or a group of farms, a village, 2) the houses themselves and the function of the dwelling as an economic unit sometimes including the people living and working there, 3) the belongings representing a substantial part of its value including livestock. In Iceland a *bú* might be a farm unity of which two, three or more combined on the land of a larger farm. When two people had a *bú* at the same *bær*, they were said to have a *bú* together (*eiga bú saman*).

In SkL and ÖgL a *bo* could also denote a farm with an administrative function under the control of a king, bishop or *jarl*, or their *bryti*. In the Swedish province of Västergötland, albeit not explicitly mentioned in the version of the laws translated into English, but present in a recent edition of ÄVgL (Wiktorsson 2011:II, 160–65), a *bo* was an administrative district of an unknown function comprising one or several *hærap*, that was probably associated with the royal estates (*bona regalia*) of *upsala öper*.

See also Appendix A.

Refs: Árni Júlíusson 2010, 8; CV s.v. *bú*; KLNM, s.v.v. *bo, kronogods*; Miller 1990, 115; Schlyter s.v. *bo*; Wiktorsson 2011:II, 160–65.

bol (OSw, ODan, OGu), **ból** (ON) n.

Literally 'dwelling' and by extension referring to a farm including its farmland.

In Danish laws (except in Halland and Blekinge) *bol* refers to a certain part of the village land and the rights and obligations that followed, but may also be used as a land assessment unit. The details concerning the origin and varying size or value of a *bol* are unclear, but the number of *bol* in a specific village seems to have been static and a farm could consist of a whole *bol* or part(s) of a *bol*.

A specifically judicial use of *bol* in Norwegian laws was as a farming unit of a certain size, which was originally the basis for calculating the lease and later the taxation, and usually specified as to the unit measure, i.e. *marker* or *mánaðarmatr*.

There are several, sometimes conflicting, ideas of the nature of the *bol* in the Swedish laws and it is unclear whether it also was a unit of a specified size or value, a farm where the owner resided or – possibly later – a new settlement.

bolskift (ODan) n. is a land division system in Denmark supposed to have preceded the *solskift*. It is not mentioned in the laws. See *Land-division systems* below.

Refs: Andersson 2014, 24; Ericsson 2012, 22, 24, 28, 270; Hoff 1997, 197; KLNM s.v.v. *bol, bolskift, hammarskifte, solskifte, tegskifte*; Porsmose 1988, 234–36, 270; Rahmqvist 1996, 29; Schlyter s.v. *bol*; Tamm and Vogt 2016, 25; Venge 2002, 8, 173, 283; Åström 1897, 193–98.

bolstaþer (OSw), **bólstaðr** (ON) n.

Village or farmstead in a village or the area around the dwelling on a farm. Also used of farming land delineated by boundary markers as being part of a specific village. As a place-name element it is found in Iceland, Shetland, Orkney, The Hebrides, Norway, Södermanland, Uppland, Åland and the very south of Finland.

by ok bolstaþer (OSw) is an alliterative expression for a village and the related farmland, which might be translated alternatively as 'village and environs'.

Refs: CV s.v. *bólstaðr*; Gammeltoft 2001, 15; KLNM s.v. *bolstadh*; ONP s.v. *bólstaðr*; Schlyter s.v. *bolstaþer*; Zoega s.v. *bólstaðr*.

byr, by (OSw), **býr, bær** (ON) n.

This word has several different but associated meanings: 1) the farm and its buildings, i.e. the farmstead, 2) 'village' (comprising a number of farmsteads forming a community) or habitation in general and 3) 'town' (as opposed to the countryside). The first two meanings are the most common.

-by/bær has been a very productive place-name suffix for a long time in all the Nordic countries as well as in the Nordic areas in Britain.

Used in the expression *by ok bolstaþer* or the compound *byabolstaþer* to mean 'village and the related farmland'.

Refs: CV s.v. *bær*; KLNM, s.v.v. *landsby, stad*; Miller 1990, 115; Schlyter s.v. *byr*.

garþer (OSw), **garth** (ODan), **garþr** (OGu), **garðr** (ON) n.

The main meanings of *garþer* are 'fence, barrier' and 'enclosed land', but *garþer* also may refer to the houses themselves and/or to the open space enclosed by those houses. In some areas in Sweden and Norway a *garþer* was regarded as an economic unit corresponding to the Danish *bol*. In the Norwegian GuL it was then referred to as *bær*, also including resources such as woodland, fishing waters etc. The concepts expressed by *garþer* also correspond to *bær* (see *byr*) and *jörð* (see *jorþ*) in Icelandic laws, but in Iceland the word *garðr* later came to refer to a high-status dwelling.

The layout of a *garþer*, referring to the different farm-buildings, varied greatly both regionally and over time. VgL and UL (e.g. YVgL Kkb 2, Tb 30; ÄVgL Tb 5; UL Kkb 2) mention some of the various types of buildings to be found on a *garþer*.

Garþer meaning 'fence' is quite common as the maintenance of fencing was an obligation connected to the holding of land of a particular kind, the period for the maintenance of the fencing, and who was legally responsible for the fencing. Neglect of this obligation carried legal penalties.

Garþer is also found in compounds referring to a small enclosed area, i.e. some kind of garden: *kalgarþer* (OSw, kailyard), *yrtagarþer* (OSw, herb garden), *apæld garth* (ODan, apple or fruit garden), *hvannagarðr* (ON, angelica garden).

Refs: Adams 1976 s.v. *settlement*; CV s.v. *garðr*; Helle 2001, 106–16; Hellquist [1948] 1964, s.v. *gård*; KLNM, s.v. *gård*; Pelijeff 1967, passim; Schlyter s.v. *garþer*.

tompt, toft (OSw), **toft** (ODan), **tóft, tópt** (ON) n.

Tompt (OSw) and *toft* (ODan) refer to the enclosed area immediately surrounding the farm buildings (curtilage, plot), the size and use of which varied considerably throughout the North.

Tompt is mentioned in all Swedish laws, it was enclosed, and the ownership of a *tompt* entitled to certain legal rights and obligations. It was the responsibility of the person to whom each plot was allocated to keep fencing around it in good order. In UL and VmL the word is occasionally used as a synonym for *burtomt* in the sense of 'curtilage', that is the land immediately surrounding a dwelling that was subject of special protection.

The often quoted wording *Tompt ær teghs/akærs moþir*; 'the *tompt* is the mother of the strip fields/ cultivated fields' (SdmL; DL; UL; VmL) has been taken as a proof that not only the arrangement of the individual strips in the *gærþi* (see *gærþi*) but also their size was determined by the situation and size of the *tompt* in the village when *solskipt* was carried through (see *solskipt* under *Land-division systems* below). VgL states that ownership of a *tompt* and fields and meadows of a certain size entitled one to part in the common resources (ÄVgL Jb 7; YVgL Jb 19). According to YVgL the size of a legal *tompt* was 20x10 alnar (YVgL Jb 18). In ÖgL and UL it was stated that the size of all ownership: field, meadow, fencing, forests and fishing was to be related to the size of the *tompt* (ÖgL Bb 2; UL Jb 4, Blb 2). Fencing between neighbouring plots was regulated (ÖgL Bb 13) as well as the fines for destroying the fencing around the *tompt* (ÖgL Bb 23). In UL it is described in detail how to divide a village legally whether it is a new or an old village, how to calculate the size of each individual *tompt* and how to arrange the roads, the buildings and fencing (UL Blb 1–2).

In Denmark the *toft* was comparatively large and contained cultivated fields. In these fields the land was held in severalty. In the *toft* are mentioned enclosed *apæld garth* (apple or fruit garden), *kalgarth* (kailyard), *hialm garth* (hay shed) as well as *toftæ garth* (JyL 3 60). The size of the *toft* determined the size of the taxes paid to the king and the physical arrangement of the order in which the different strip fields (*aker*) were laid out if the village land was shifted (JyL 1 55, ESjL 2 55; (see *solskipt* under *Land-division systems* below). The size of the *toft* is still not fully investigated, but in the late middle ages the large *toft* was eventually divided into smaller more garden-like areas (Hoff 1997, 84–121).

The ON *tóft,* might refer to the foundation and walls before a roof was put on, and later it was used to describe ruined buildings.

Refs: Aðalsteinsson 1986–89, 38; CV s.v. *topt*; Hoff 1997, 84–121; Holmberg 1946, passim; KLNM s.v.v. *tomt, tún.*

tún (ON) n.

Tún is related to words meaning 'fence, barrier'. In Norwegian [not in the laws] it refers to the area around which the farmhouses were grouped. In Icelandic laws it refers to the cultivated land surrounding the farm, which might be enclosed by a *túngarðr* or *túnvöllr.*

See also *tompt.*

Refs: CV s.v. *tún*; Hastrup 1992, 108; Helle 2001, 106–16; Holmberg 1969, 247–61; KLNM s.v. *tún.*

þorp (OSw), **thorp** (ODan) n.

The word þorp, *thorp* is only found in Danish and Swedish laws. It has been very productive as a place-name suffix since the late Viking Age, with around 10,000 names ending in þorp, *thorp*, whereas in Norway only a handful of names of this kind is found.

In Danish laws *thorp* refers to a new settlement ('outlying village') created from the main (old) village (*athelby*), and the laws regulate terms between the old and the new village, boundaries, size and the use of deserted settlements.

In the Swedish laws þorp seems to refer to a single (often small) farm, possibly moved out from a village.

See also þorpakarl in the lexicon.

Refs: Berg 2013, 22–23; Hoff 1997, 122–141; KLNM s.v. *torp*; Porsmose 1988, 240–48; Schlyter s.v. *þorp*

Cultivated land: arable land

The property rights, distribution, use and individual size of arable land, land used for hay harvest, grazing and as a common resource available to a single landowner or user varied a great deal between the Nordic provinces and between individuals. Climate, soil fertility, landscape as well as social, economic and cultural differences determined the practical forms for utilizing these assets.

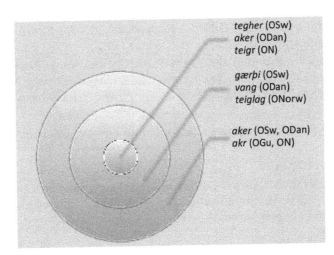

Diagram 3. Illustration of the sematic scope of words in the laws denoting cultivated land. Diagram produced by Inger Larsson.

aker (OSw, ODan), akr (OG, ON) n.

Aker, akr, which is found in all laws, refers to arable open land, field, often as opposed to meadow (OSw æng) and wood or forest (OSw *skogher*). An *aker,* was cultivated (permanent, tilled, manured), a lot of work had been invested in it, and it was the most valuable land for growing food plants. What crops would be cultivated of course differed between provinces and climate. In the Swedish laws stealing barley, oats, rye, beans, peas, turnips or brassicas was regarded as a crime.

Where a system of single farms existed the farmer was free to use his cultivated land at his own will, but when the population grew and farms became grouped in village-like structures the cultivated land became an economic asset that needed to be divided between the different farms. At the time when the laws were written down in Denmark and southern Sweden, the cultivated land belonging to a certain village would be divided into one-, two- or three- permanent fields depending on the rotation system practiced, and terms for land measurement and evaluation appear in the laws.

In the Danish laws an *aker* was also a strip field in the *vang* (see below) whereas the following words, which all appear in the laws, *akærland* (ODan), *akerskifte* (ODan), *ollandæ* (ODan), *utlænde* (ODan) refer to cultivated land and/or meadows, sometimes, as opposed to land within the enclosure of the *toft.* According to Hoff they all, except *akærland* are remnants from cultivating systems possibly preceding the rotation systems described above (Hoff 1997, 142–49).

Refs: Hertzberg 1895, s.v. *akr*; GDO s.v. *aker;* Hoff 1997, 142–49; KLNM, s.v.v. *ager, envangs-brug, gödsling, odlingssystem, svedjebruk, teig, tovangsbrug, trevangsbrug;* Myrdal 1999, 19–109; 2011, 49–52, 77–81; Schlyter s.v. *aker.*

akerland (ODan), akrland (OIce) n.

In Danish laws it refers to strip fields. In Icelandic laws to arable land or cropland in general.

Refs: CV s.v. *akrland*; Hoff 1997, 142–49.

akerskifte (ODan) n.

Common strip field.

Ref: Hoff 1997, 142–49.

gærþi (OSw), vang (ODan), teiglag (ONorw) n.

The large individual cultivated field in a field rotation system was called *gærþi* (OSw), *vang* (ODan) or *teiglag* (ONorw, not in the laws). Each farm had at least one strip field (*tegher* (OSw), *teigr* (ON), *aker* (ODan)) in each field (*gærþi* (OSw), *vang* (ODan)). The distribution and size of these strip fields was regulated in most laws, and a number of shift systems were practiced to divide and distribute the land (see below). The size and situation in the village of the *tompt, toft,* i.e. the land on which the farm-buildings were situated, were important as they determined the size and situation in the *gærþi* (OSw) and the *vang* (ODan) of the strip fields. The use of the strip fields was regulated in the laws as to fencing, what crops to grow, harvesting and grazing. The original meaning of *gærþi* (OSw), *gærthe* (ODan, OGu) was 'fence' or 'fenced in land'.

In the Norwegian system we find *teiglag* (ONorw) corresponding to (OSw) *gærþi,* with a number of strip fields, *teigr* (ON) forming a *teiglag* (not in the laws).

Refs: Hellquist [1948] 1964, s.v. *gärda*; Hoff 1997, 142–49; KLNM, s.v.v. *gärde, hegn, odlingssystem, envangsbrug, teig, teigkast, teiglag, tovangsbrug, trevangsbrug, vang*; Myrdal 1999, 19–109, 2011, 77–95; SAOB, s.v. *gärde*; Schlyter s.v. *gærþi*; Widgren 1997, passim.

gerði (ON) n.

Refers to fenced in land that was used for grazing after harvesting in Norwegian laws.

Ref: Herzberg s.v. *gerði.*

tegher (OSw), teigr (ON), aker (ODan)

A strip field (parcel) in a *gærþi* (OSw), *vang* (ODan*)* or *teiglag* (ONorw, not in the laws) or, sometimes, an enclosed piece of land for grazing or hay harvest as in Iceland. *Tegher* also had a more general meaning 'particular piece of land', i.e. *ængtegher* meadow-, *skoghtegher* forest-, *rörtegher* a piece of land along a shore where reed was growing, *markteigr* (ONorw) forest lot.

The corresponding Danish term was *aker.*

Refs: Hoff 1997, 142–49; KLNM, s.v. *teig*; Schlyter s.v. *tegher*

deld (OSw, ODan) n.

In the Danish laws and the Svea laws (except HL) it refers to a part of the village land, sometimes a strip field in a *gærþi* (OSw) or *vang* (ODan).

Refs: Hoff 1997, 204; Schlyter s.v. *deld.*

akerdeld (OSw) n.

A strip field in a *gærþi* (OSw) or in arable land generally.

Ref: Schlyter s.v. *aker deld.*

See also *delda ra* in Appendix C.

valder (OSw), **völlr** (ON) n.

Field, ground.

Refs: CV s.v. *völlr*; Schlyter s.v. *valder.*

vreter (OSw) n.

A clearing, possibly fenced in.

Refs: KLNM s.v. *vret*; Schlyter s.v. *vreter*

værn (OSw) n.

A word for an enclosed field used in DL, SdmL, UL and VmL.

Ref: Schlyter s.v. *værn.*

fiælder (Osw), **urfiælder** (OSw), **lutfal** (OSw), **humper** (OSw), **ornume** (ODan) n.

All these words seem to refer to approximately the same type of land regarding situation and obligations.

In SdmL *fiælder* (Osw) and SdmL, UL and VmL, *urfiælder* (OSw) refer to a piece of land separated and (often) marked off from the village land, and often located in another village than the owner's own. This land was treated as private property and thus exempt from communal rights and obligations and from division of land between the landowners in a village. In DL this kind of land is called *lutfal*, in ÖgL *humper*. Corresponding word in Danish laws is *ornume.*

Refs: Hoff 1997, 150–53; KLNM s.v.v. *hump, ornum, urfjäll*; Lund 1967, s.v. *ornum*; Schlyter s.v.v. *fiælder, urfiælder, lutfal, humper*; Tamm and Vogt, eds 2016, 307.

Land-division systems

There are three known different land-division systems practised before and at the time when the laws were written down. Not all of them are mentioned in the laws, but known from other sources. In addition there are a few words for land division that are not land-division systems.

solskipt/e (OSw), **solskift** (ODan) n.

Literally 'sun division'. The 'sun' element refers to the position of each *aker/tegher* in the *vang/gærde* and of the *toft/tompt* in the village in a fixed order after the daily course of the sun through the sky, i.e. 'clockwise'. This division system ensured that all farms got their fair share of the common fields, meadows, grazing, fishing rights etc. in the village in accordance with the size and clockwise position of the curtilage around their dwellings (*tompt*), and that the strip fields were positioned accordingly.

Solskipt is supposed to have replaced older land division systems and is mentioned in SmL, ÖgL, DL, SdmL, UL and VmL. It is also mentioned in JyL and ESjL, but there it is assumed to have had more in common with the older land-division and assessment system called *bolskift* (not mentioned in the laws), although the size of the *toft* determined the size and often the position of the cultivated fields belonging to a certain farm.

It is unknown in Norway and Iceland.

bolskift (ODan) n.

A land division system in Denmark supposed to have preceded the *solskift*. It is not mentioned in the translated laws. See also *bol* (above).

hammarskipt (OSw) n.

An older land division system than *solskipt*. It is mentioned in SdmL, UL and VmL only. The exact meaning is still obscure. According to an older explanation, the term might refer to uncultivated and stony land available for reclamation and cultivation on the village common land. Another explanation suggests that it was an individually based cultivation and reclamation of land in common meadows and pastures.

hagaskipti (ONorw) n.

Parcelling out pastureland.

teghskipt (OSw) n.

The distribution of strip fields in the village land.

engjaskifti (OIce) n.

Division of meadowlands.

Refs: Brink 1991, 2, http://www.norna.org/?q=nonelex s.v. *–hammare*; CV s.v. *engjaskipti*; Göransson 1961, 80–83; Göransson 1976, 22–37; Hafström 1951, 104–56; Hoff 1997, 197–209; Hertzberg s.v. *engjaskipti*; KLNM, s.v.v. *bolskift, hammarskifte, solskifte, tegskifte*; Porsmose 1988, 270; Riddersporre 2001, 64–65; Sporrong 1992, 355; Schlyter s.v.v. *hamar, solskipt*.

See also the different land assessment units *attunger, bol* and *markland* in the lexicon.

repa (OSw), **repe** (ODan) v.

To divide communal village land between landowners using a rope as measurement.

See also *álburðr, byamal, jorthemal, mal, mælistang, ornume, rep, repdrøgh, skipt, stangfall, stika, taumburðr, urfiælder, vaþstang*

Refs: KLNM s.v. *rebning*; Tamm and Vogt, eds, 2016, 307, 312.

Non-cultivated land: meadow, pasture

Meadow

æng (OSw, ODan), **eng**(i) (ON) n.

Æng, eng refer to enclosed open land which was not cultivated but, most often, cleared from trees and stone, and where hay was harvested. After the harvest the meadow as well as any cultivated fields lying fallow were used for grazing, and thus became fertilized to some extent. In Norway a farm might lack *aker* but never *eng*.

Both cultivated fields and meadows would be enclosed with stone walls or wooden fences as the many rules about enclosures in the laws bear witness about. These rules may also reveal information about the different farming systems that were used in different areas. Damage to a meadow had to be compensated. See GuL chs 82, 83, 90.

skoghæng (SdmL) woodland meadow.

Refs: CV s.v. *eng*; KLNM, s.v.v. *eng, ängsskötsel*; Schlyter s.v. *æng*.

boland (OG), **búland** (OIce) n.

Inhabited land, agricultural land on a farm including grazing area.

Refs: CV s.v. *búland*; ONP s.v. *búland*; Schlyter s.v. *bo land*; Zoega s.v. *búland*.

taða (OIce) n.

A fertilized meadow, or hay from one.

See also *töðuvöllr* (below).

Refs: CV s.v. *taða*; ONP s.v. *taða*; Zoega s.v. *taða*.

traðargarðr (ONorw) n.

Fence between pasture and cultivated land.

Ref: Fritzner s.v. *traðargarðr*.

töðuvöllr (OIce) n.

A manured infield.

See also *taða*.

Ref: CV s.v. *töðuvöllr*.

Pasture

Grazing and land for grazing was important all over the North, and non-cultivated land and forest land were important assets. The number of cattle a single farmer could keep depended on the amount of food available during the winter stalling. There are a number of words for land used for grazing reflecting its importance. Grazing took place in the *toft*, in the cultivated fields after harvest, in the fallow, in the meadow after the hay harvest and in the forests or in the Norwegian, Faroese and Icelandic grass plains and mountains. Some of the more frequent words are listed here.

bait (OGu), beit (ON) n.

    Pasture.

    Refs: CV s.v. *beit*; KLNM s.v. *beite*; Schlyter s.v. *bet*.

haghi (OSw), haghe (ODan), hagi (OGu), hagi (ON) n.

    Enclosed area, in particular a fenced in pasture. Often in compounds for example *hagabeit* pastureland grazing (OIce), *húshagi*, home pasture (OIce); *hema haghi*, home pasture (OSw); *hagamark* pasture boundary (OFar); *hagfastr* grazing constantly (OFar); *haglendi* pasture (OFar); *fjellhagi* mountain pasture (OIce).

    Refs: CV s.v. *hagi*; KLNM s.v. *beite*, Schlyter s.v. *haghi*.

fælöt (OSw) n.

    Pasture.

    See also *löt* below.

    Ref: Schlyter s.v. *fæ löt*.

fæmark (OSw) n.

    Common pasture land of a village.

    Ref: Schlyter s.v. *fæ mark*.

fæarganger (OSw), fægang (ODan), fjárgangr (OIce) n.

    The grazing of cattle or a passage or path used by the cattle (ODan, OIce).

    Refs: CV s.v. *fé*; Lund s.v. *fægang*; Schlyter s.v. *fæar ganger*.

hiorþlöt (OSw) n.

    Pasture land.

    See also *löt*.

    Ref: Schlyter s.v. *hiorþlöt*.

hiorþvalder (OSw) n.

    Pasture.

    Ref: Schlyter s.v. *hiorþvalder*

löt (OSw), laut (OGu) n.

    Pasture, green grass-ground, level field and a direct synonym of ON *vall/völlr* (pl. *vellir*).

    Ref: Brink 2004, 210.

nautatröð (ON) n.

    Pasture.

    Refs: CV s.v. *tröð*; ONP s.v. *tröð*.

sumarhagi (OIce) n.

    Summer pasture.

    Ref: CV s.v. *sumarhagi*.

troth (ODan), tröð (ON) n.

    1) 'enclosure', 2) (pl. *traðir*) 'a trodden path, passage' and 3) 'a plot of land allotted for cultivation, a fallow field'.

    Refs: CV s.v. *tröð*; Lund 1967 s.v. *troth*; ONP s.v. *tröð*; Schlyter s.v. *troþ*.

úthági (OIce) n.

    Outer pasture.

    Ref: CV s.v. *úthagi*.

valder (OSw), völlr (ON) n.

> Pasture, field, a particular place. In compounds i.e. *hviorþvalder* (OSw, pasture), *svina valder* (OSw grazing for pigs) *vighvalder* (OSw a place of crime).
>
> Refs: Brink 2004; CV s.v. *völlr*; ONP s.v. *völlr*; Schlyter s.v. *valder*.

Common resources and public property

Common resources were resources 'outside the enclosure', i.e. pastures (see above), fishing waters, woodland, forests or wells. Originally, these were for the common use of all men, but eventually these rights were often restricted to various extents in the different provinces.

skogher (OSw), skogh (ODan), skógr (ON) n.

> Translated as woods, woodland or forest depending on where they were. In Denmark and the very south of Sweden it would mainly be leaf trees such as birch, oak and hazel, while further north birch and conifers and in Iceland birch or willows or a single conifer. The woods and forest were important assets yielding food for the animals, firewood, timber for building houses and joinery, iron and tar, hunting and fishing, birch-bark and bark for bast, and they were protected against misuse. Especially SdmL, UL, VgL VmL and ÖgL are very detailed on the rights and use of these assets for example the use of the acorn forests for pigs or the oak as the most valuable species. Most important was also that the forest and woodlands offered next to unlimited land for expansion of cultivated land through slash and burn methods. According to the laws, the forest would also provide shelter for criminals and robbers, for vagrants and outlaws.
>
> In compounds: *almænningsskogh* (ODan) common wood, *byarskogher* (OSw) village woodland, *gisningaskogher* (OSw) acorn woodland, *hæghnaskogher* (OSw) enclosed wood(land), *kirkjeskogh* (ODan) church's wood, *varskogher* (OSw) private woodland.
>
> Woodland and forests were land 'outside the enclosure', i.e. common resources, *almænninger*, and the use of most assets was regulated in the laws. See *almænninger* below.
>
> Refs: CV s.v. *skógr*; Fritzner s.v. *skógr*; Eliasson and Hamilton 1999 47–54; Hoff 1997, 262–87; Kardell 2003, 54–105; KLNM s.v. *skog*; ONP s.v. *skógr*.

almænninger (OSw), almænning (ODan), almenningr (ON) n.

> Literally 'all men'. The village land included the cultivated land and the land used for hay harvest and (partly) grazing, i.e. 'land within enclosure'. The land 'outside the enclosure', the *almænninger* was regarded as a common resource and the rights to reclaim land for cultivating on the *almænninger*, thus intruding on the common resource, is regulated in all Swedish laws. It is only in ÖgL (Jb 1) that the king and his rights are mentioned. ÖgL regulates the procedure to be undertaken if the king wishes to sell an *almænninger*. Contemporary material shows that the king most probably had rights to a third of the common land in Västergötland, Östergötland and Småland (Rosén 1949, 36 f.).
>
> It is important to distinguish between ownership and the right of usufruct. According to the Danish laws the king owned the *almænning* but the farmers had the right to use assets from the woods, with or without royal permission. The village common, *byalmænninger*, was owned jointly by the villagers both according to Danish and Swedish law.
>
> There are many compounds with *almænninger* indicating its importance: *almænningsiorþ* OSw ('-property'), *almænningsskogh* OSw ('-forest'), *almænningsvatn* OSw ('-water'), *hæræþs almænninger* OSw ('common land of the härad'), *landsalmænninger* OSw ('common land of the province').
>
> There were also a number of man-made assets regarded as public property: *almænningsbro* OSw ('-bridge'), *almænningsbrun* OSw ('-well'), *almenningsfar* OIce ('public ferry'), *almænningstorgh* OSw ('-square', '-market'), *almænningsvægher* OSw ('-road').
>
> Refs: Helle 2001, 111–14; Hertzberg 1895, s.v. *almenningr*; Hoff 1997, 255–62; Holmbäck 1920; KLNM, s.v.v. *alminding, beite, bergsregale, envangsbrug, hvalfangst, häradsallmänning, jordejendom, landnåm II, regale*; Rosén 1949, 36 f.; Porsmose 1988, 298–301; Schlyter s.v. *almænninger*.

skoghaskipti (OSw), skógarskifti (OIce) n.

> Woodland and forests might be divided between the farmers for different purposes. In UL and VmL *skogha skipan* is a division of acorn forests with respect to the number of pigs each farmer is allowed.

In Grg 199 and Jó VII.20 it deals specifically with jointly owned land in which one party believes the other is using more resources and the process of woodland division is described in some detail.

See also *skogher.*

Refs: CV s.v. *skógarskipti*; Fritzner s.v. *skógarskipti*; Schlyter s.v.v. *skogha skipan, skogha skipti.*

afréttr (OIce) n.

Communal pasture owned by two or more men, sometimes by a whole commune. Lýður Björnsson (1972–79, I:44–45) briefly discusses *afréttir* (along with *fjallskil*). The discussion is framed as problems involving grazing for farmers, and he summarizes material from Grg.

Refs: Björnsson 1972–79. CV s.v. *afréttr.*

viþer (OGu, OSw), **viðr** (ON) n.

Firewood, timber, wood or forest.

Refs: CV s.v. *viðr* Schlyter s.v. *viþer.*

Appendix C:
Borders, Boundaries and Boundary Markers

Strict borders with boundary markers can be found as early as in the Viking Age or the Scandinavian early Middle Ages (after c. 1050; Brink 2008b, 95). Apart from certain rune-stones, the oldest written documentation of borders concerns the borders between Denmark and the Continent and Denmark and Norway. The border between Denmark and Sweden is first documented in 1343. Before that this border was referred to as a *landamaeri* (border area) marked by stones or using physical land elements, such as streams, roads, mountains or wetlands. Border markers between Sweden and Norway are mentioned in manuscripts of the Norwegian law of the realm (thirteenth century) and other late medieval sources.

The Nordic provincial laws contain a wealth of different words and expressions for borders, boundaries and boundary markers. These may regulate borders between administrative units, provinces, districts or villages, but most rules in the provincial laws regulate boundaries between different landowners, and there seems to be no strict definition for any of the different words. These borders and boundaries may follow streams, roads, significant cliffs or hills, or be marked with stakes, stones, or sometimes even fences, a significant tree or an imaginative boundary off the shore. The form of the boundary marker may be described. The stones may number three to five, one in the middle and the others around it. If the boundary marker contains fewer stones something (for example a bone) would be placed under the stone. What was important was that you should be able to distinguish a boundary marker from an ordinary heap of stones. Boundary markers between strip fields may even be a furrow (*for*, SdmL Jb4). To move or destroy a boundary marker was heavily punished.

Refs: Brink 2008b, 95; Holm 2003, 135–237; KLNM s.v.v. *gränsläggning, rigsgrænse, rågång*; Tollin 1999, 11–26, 51–63.

Borders between provinces, districts or villages or with the type of border as part of the name

fjórðungamót (ON) n.

'Quarter boundary', i.e. the border between quarters in Iceland (Grg ch. 99).

Refs: CV s.v. *fjórðungr*.

landamæri, landamäre (OSw), **landamæri** (OIce) n.

Boundary or border/border area between provinces. In OIce it refers to border land or border marker.

Refs: CV s.v. *land-*; KLNM s.v.v. *gränsläggning, rigsgrænse*; Schlyter s.v. *landamæri*.

landamærki (OSw), **landamerki, landsmerki** (OIce) n.

Border marker between provinces in VgL. In OIce sometimes between estates.

Refs: CV s.v. *land-*; Schlyter s.v. *landamaerki*.

mark (OSw, ODan), **mark, mörk** (ON) n.

The word form *mark* n. represents three homonyms: 1) *mark* 'mark, sign; border mark, boundary line', 2) *mark* 'unit of weight and coinage', 3) *mark* 'forest, wood; outlying field, outland'. For homonyms 2 and 3 the ON standard form is *mörk*.

The oldest sense of the neuter *mark* and the feminine variant *mark* (the latter originally collective plural) was 'border/boundary mark'. Since forests often functioned as borderland the word *mark* also came to mean 'forest, wood', and (by extension) 'land, field'.

https://doi.org/10.11647/OBP.0188.06

The sense 'forest, wood' seems to be the usual one in ON, whereas the sense 'cultivated field' seems to be peculiar to ODan. The sense 'land' is also known from OSw and ONorw.

The name of the nation, Denmark (*Danmark*), contains the word *mark* 'dividing forest'.

See also Appendix B.

Refs: Bjorvand 1994, 79–80, 158–59; 2007, 722; Brink 2008b, passim.; CV s.v. *mörk*; Fritzner s.v. *mörk, mǫrk*; KLNM s.v.v. *-mark, mark, utmark, rågång*. Schlyter s.v. *mark*.

markrá (ONorw) n.

Boundary line.

Refs: CV s.v. *markrá*

markreina (OFar, ONorw) n.

Boundary line.

Refs: CV s.v. *markreina.*

markarskæl (OSw), **markeskjal** (ODan) n.

Boundary between villages or provinces or, in Denmark, between fields.

Refs: KLNM s.v.v. *rågång, gränsläggning*; Schlyter s.v. *markar skael*; Tamm and Vogt 2016 s.v. *markeskjal*, 332.

skoghaskæl (OSw) n.

Woodland boundary.

Ref: Schlyter s.v. *skogha skæl.*

takmark (OIce) n.

Border, frontier.

Refs: CV s.v. *takmark*; Fritzner s.v. *takmark*; Schlyter s.v. *takmark.*

Boundaries between fields or meadows

engimark (OIce) n.

Boundary of a meadow.

Refs: CV s.v. *eng.*

for (OSw) n.

A furrow and also a boundary line between strip fields.

Refs: Schlyter s.v. *for.*

hagamark (OFar) n.

Pasture boundary/border area, possibly referring to 'where different pasture lands meet'.

See also Appendix B.

Refs: Hertzberg s.v. *hagamark.*

vaþ (OSw) n., **vaþ stang** (OSw) n.

(OSw) *vaþ* refers to a boundary between strip fields or meadows (SdmL Jb 4). To mark it you walk (*vaþa* v.) or ride (*riþa vaþa*) in a straight line between stakes (*vaþ stang*) set at the boundary markers (VmL Jb 12:1, DL Jb 22:2).

Refs: Andersson 2010, 16–19, 49–50; Schlyter s.v. *vaþ.*

Boundary markers

engjamerki (OIce) n.

Meadowland boundary marker.

Refs: CV s.v. *eng.*

lýritti (ON) n.

Three boundary stones marking divisions between properties. According to Jó Lbb 3 (and MLL VI.3) these are also called *marksteinar*. Associated with the power of 'veto' (ON *lýrittr*). It has been suggested that these stones serve as a type of witness and derive their name from the legal term for a three-man oath (ON *lýrittareiðr*), though at least one scholar has argued that the stones predate the oath (cf. Páll Vídalín 1854 s.v. *lýrittar*).

See also *lýrittr, mark, marksteinn, mærki, tiældrusten*.

Refs: Fritzner s.v. *lýrittarstein, lýritti*; Hertzberg s.v. *lýriti, lýrittarstein*; KLNM s.v.v. *jordejendom, lýrittr*; Páll Vídalín 1854 s.v. *lýrittar*.

marksteinn (OIce) n.

Boundary stone.

Refs: CV s.v. *marksteinn*.

mærki (OSw), **merki** (ON) n.

A mark of any kind. When meaning boundary marker, it is often preceded by a qualification: *ra-* 'stake' (VgL), *rör-* 'cairn of stones'(MELL), *skóga-* 'forest' (ON), *skogs-* 'forest' (HL),
sokna- 'parish' (YVgL), *sten-* 'stone'(HL), *træ-* 'wooden'(HL).

Refs: CV s.v. *merki*; Schlyter s.v. *mærki*.

merkibjörk (ON) n.

A birch tree which served as a boundary marker between land plots in Iceland.

Refs: CV s.v. *merkibjörk*: KLNM s.v. *gränsläggning*; NGL V s.v. *merkibjörk*.

merkióss (ON) n.

The outlet of a river or lake serving as a boundary marker.

Refs: CV. s.v. *merkióss*.

ra (OSw) n.

A stake used as a boundary marker and, when preceded by a qualification, the boundary itself: (*bolstaþa*), 'village' (UL, VmL), (*delda*), 'strip field' (UL, VmL), (*farvægs* UL), 'highway', (*tompta* UL, SdmL, VmL), 'plot' or 'village'. *Tompta ra* is supposed to have been a boundary marker in a corner of the boundary enclosing all village plots. Another word for this is *skötra* ('corner' + 'boundary marker', DL). The marker as a whole was a stake (*ra*) thrust into a small cairn of stones (*rör*).

Refs: KLNM s.v. *gränsläggning*; Schlyter s.v.v. *tompta ra, ra*; Tollin 1999, 51–63.

rör (OSw), **hreysar** ON) n.

Boundary marker consisting of a small cairn of stones. According to UL (Blb 18) the *rör* should consist of five stones, one in the middle and four around it. The text continues describing when a *rör* may contain fewer stones. The important idea was that you should be able to distinguish a *rör* from an ordinary heap of stones. The alliterative expression *ra oc rör* is generally used where an attribute to *ra* is not specified. The marker as a whole was a stake thrust into a small cairn of stones, the *rör*.

Refs: KLNM s.v. *gränsläggning*; Tollin 1999, 51–63.

skæl (OSw), **skial** (ODan) n.

Boundary or boundary marker. Often preceded by a qualification, *bolstaþaskæl* 'farmland-' (SdmL UL), *byaskæl* 'village-' (SdmL), *skoghaskæl* 'forest-' (SdmL), *tomptaskæl* 'plot-' (SdmL). Etymologically related to a verb originally meaning 'to split' realized as *skilia* in OSw. See *skæl* in the lexicon.

Refs: Gammeldansk ordbog (beta online) s.v. *skjal*; ONP (online) s.v. *skil*; Schlyter s.v. *skæl*.

sten ok ren (OSw) n.

'Stones and edges' i.e. boundary markers standing on the edges of a field (VgL).

tiældra (OSw) n.

Boundary marker. *Tiældrubrut*: to break up the stones of a boundary marker; *tiældru sten*: stone used to form a boundary marker. In YVgL Jb 22 it says that two stones should be dug into the ground with a third on top to form a boundary marker; *tiældrubyrd*: to move a boundary stone to another place.

Refs: Schlyter s.v. *tiældra*.

þræstene (OSw) n.

A boundary marker consisting of only three stones.

Refs: Schlyter s.v. *þræstene*.

Boundaries at sea

marbakki (ON) n.

Translated in Jó Llb 68 as 'sea bank'. A note in the translation says that this is 'the border between the shoal and deep water along the coast' (cf. CV) and was relevant to ownership rights of fish, seals and porpoises on the shore. Hertzberg mentions it as well and equates the term with both ON *mararbakki* and *marreinsbakki*.

Refs: CV s.v. *marbakki*.

netlag (OIce) n.

'Net-laying line'. See *rekamark* below.

Refs: CV s.v. *reki*. KLNM s.v. *reki*.

rekamark (OIce) n.

'Drift boundary'. Iceland is surrounded by ocean currents (Gulf Stream, Polar Stream) so the rights to gather driftwood and other things washed ashore was important and strictly regulated in the laws. A landowner had parts in the shore and had the right to collect anything that drifted ashore on his part, but also between the shore and an imaginative 'boundary' (*rekamark*) out in the sea. He also had the right to all catch, with certain limitations, within another restricted area with a defined boundary (*netlög*).

Appendix D1: The Monetary System

The central unit of the weight and monetary system was the (OSw and ODan) *mark*, (ON) *mörk*.

1 *mark* = 8 øre (ON *aurar*, pl. of *eyrir*) = 24 *örtugar* (ON *ertogar*) = 240 *pænningar* (ON *penningar*). The number of *pænningar* per *mark* varied considerably over time and area.

In the eleventh century the value of 1 *mörk* in Norway was c. 214 g *brent* (pure) silver, the value of 1 *eyrir* c. 1 ounce. In Iceland the value of 1 *eyrir* was stipulated to be 6 ells of wadmal; 3 1/3 *aurar* equalled 120 *alnar*, which was the value of one cow (1 *kúgildi*), the equivalent of 1 *hundrað*. Gotlanders also operated with a gold mark, equivalent to 8 silver *marker*.

A distinction was made between a weighed *mark* (*mörk vegin*) and a current or counted *mark* (*mörk töld*). Although they probably had the same value initially − containing the same percentage of silver (90−95%) − the value of the counted *mark* was gradually reduced.

In the twelfth century, 1 weighed *mark* was equivalent to 2 counted *merkr*. OSw law (*Upplandslagen*) made a similar distinction between *karlgild* (i.e. weighed) and *köpgild* (i.e. current) *mark*. A *karlgild mark* was worth 50% more than a *köpgild mark*.

In the thirteenth century Norway the ratio between the weighed *mark* and the current *mark* was 1:3, during the fourteenth century 1:4, latter even 1:5. The ration 1:3 was also common in ODan law.

Mark, øre, and *örtug* were units of calculation rather than coins, only *pænningar* were used as such. Fines were usually stated in terms of *merkr, aurar* or *ertogar*.

Refs: Helle 2001, 157; Hertzberg 1895 s.v. *mörk*; KLNM s.v.v. *mark øre*; NK 29, 201−12 and passim; NK 30, 129−30, 152 and passim; Peel 2015, 207; Pettersen 2013, 2−5, 76−84; Robberstad 1981, 306−14; Schlyter 1877 s.v. *karlgilder*; Tamm and Vogt 2016, 309.

https://doi.org/10.11647/OBP.0188.07

Appendix D2: Weights and Measures

The medieval Nordic systems of weights and measures varied considerably over space and time, and with respect to the object(s) being measured. One must distinguish between

A) measures of capacity and volume ('rummål'),

B) measures of 1) length and 2) surface/area ('jordmål') and

C) measures of weight.

Some terms occurred in more than one category, for example *tunna* and *fjärding*, which might denote volume as well as area or length, depending on context. The units were generally parts of larger, hierarchically structured terminological systems. As examples of such connections, some terms have been included that are not found in the provincial laws (e.g. *tunna*, *skippund* and *skålpund*). On the other hand, it is virtually impossible, for reasons of space, to accommodate all local variations in a general survey. For this reason, only the more important regional differences are considered.

A) With respect to capacity and volume, dry and liquid goods were measured differently.

OSw measures of grain were *sal(d)/soldh* (145.8 litres in WSweden), usually divided into 6 *skæppor*, each containing c. 24.6 litres. Of the same size as the *soldh* was the *tunna*. Much used was the unit *spander* (ODan *spand*, ON *spann*) (c. 73 litres), divided into *fiærþungar* ('fourths') of 18.3 litres.

In Denmark the main unit was *tunna* (ODan *tønde*), varying in size from 139 to 194 litres. *Spand* was 1/8 *tønde*, i.e. c. 17 litres as a measure of oats; usually *spand* was a measure of butter (1/16 *tønde*, i.e. 8.7 litres).

In Norway and Iceland the *sáld* was the largest unit (in Iceland also a measure of liquids), varying in size between 97.2 and 132.4 litres, divided into 6 *mælar* of 22 litres (Iceland) or 16.2 litres (Norway). The *sáld* could also be divided into 4 *skeppur* of 24.3 (SNorway) or 32.4 litres (NNorway). Alternatively, in ENorway (including Bohuslän) the *sáld* was divided into 12 *séttungar* (OSw *siattungar*, known from Norrland); in *Magnus lagabœtrs landslög*, 'King Magnus the Law-Mender's Law of the Realm' (1274) 1 *séttungr* equalled 1/4 *mælir*, varying in size between 5. 4 and 12.1 litres.

Towards the end of the Middle Ages, the *sáld* was replaced by the *tunna*, varying in size between 97 and 145 litres, in WNorway even 162 litres. The *tunna* was usually divided into 4 *mælar* or 6 *spæn* (pl. of *spander*); in WSweden 6 *skæppor* of 24.8 litres; in DL 1/6 *tunna* was called a *trö*.

As a measure of butter, *spander* and *tunna* were used in all the Nordic countries. The *spann* varied in Norway from c. 4 to c. 16 litres. The Icelandic *skjóla* (= *spann*) contained c. 4 litres.

A third frequent unit was the (OSw) *löper* (ODan *løp*, ON *laupr*), varying in size between 10 and 21 litres (i.e. from 2 up to 4 steelyard pounds, 'bismerpund', or from 48 to 96 *merkr*); in WSweden 1/9 *tunna*, in Denmark usually 1/6 *tønde*, in Gotland 1/4 *tunna*.

As far as shiploads and cargo of salted goods, e.g. fish (but also grain), are concerned, the largest unit was the *læst* (ON *lest*) (c. 1,600–2,000 kg), divided into 10 or 12 *skippund* of 170 kg (in Denmark 126 kg, in ENorway 185, in WNorway 148 kg); 1 *skippund* equalled 24 *li(f)spund* (lispound) of 8 kg (Sweden and Denmark) or 9 kg (Norway). The *li(f)spund* was divided into 16 *skålpund* of 415 g (Sweden) or 496 g (Denmark) or 428 g (Norway).

An important ON grain measure was the *vétt/vætt*, ranging from 6 to 46 kg. In weighing fish the *vág* (18 kg) was a unit in WNorway.

https://doi.org/10.11647/OBP.0188.08

B) 1) Measures of length were the (OSw) *alin* (ODan *alæn*, ON *öln*); (OSw) *foter/fiæt* (ODan *fiat*, ON *fet/fótr*); (OSw) *spann*, (ON) *spönn*; (ON) *stik(k)a*; *hundrað*; and (OSw) *famn* (ODan *fafn*, ON *faðmr*).

The *alin* ('ell') varied between 47 and 64 cm, in Zealand and Scania 63.26 cm, in Jutland c. 57 cm.

Sweden had at least two types of *alin*. In addition to the old *alin* of 55.5 cm and the old Stockholm *alin* of 52.3 cm, there was (since the middle of the fifteenth century) a newer *alin* of 60–61 cm.

Norway had also two types of *alin*, a shorter one (called *alin* or *öln*) and a longer one (called *stik(k)a*); but these three terms were often used interchangeably. The shorter *alin*, also (in the FrL) called þumalöln, was 47.4 cm, the longer one 55.3 cm.

The OIce *öln* has been calculated to 49.2 cm, a younger one, the so-called 'Hamborgaralen', was usually 57.3 cm in all the Nordic countries. The length of the OIce *stika* is uncertain, but it may have been identical to the ONorw *stik(k)a*.

The *foter* ('foot') usually measured 26–34 cm; in Sweden 25.9 cm ('the Tychonic foot'), 33–35 cm ('den nordliga foten'), or 26.8 cm (the so-called 'östsvensk aln'). In addition, a Guthnic foot of 27.5–27.7 cm was used in Gotland and parts of Sweden, and a Zealandic foot of c. 31.4 cm in large parts of Southern and Central Sweden. Due to lack of sources, the length of the Norwegian foot cannot be ascertained. The OIce foot was probably 23–24 cm.

The *spann* varied from 6 to 8 or 9 inches ('tummar').

The OIce *hundrað* was equivalent to 120 ells of wadmal. It was the measure for the value of a cow or six sheep, and also for a certain quantity (weight) of fish (see below).

The *famn* ('fathom') was usually 3 ells (in Hälsingland and Iceland 3 1/2), i.e. c. 1.5 m. This was the square measure for the height and breadth of a woodpile. In Iceland, the fathom was also a cubic measure of hay (*málfaðmr*), 42.875 ells^3.

A *fiærþunger* ('quarter', namely of a mile) varied between 1,500 and 3,750 m, dependent on the size of an old Nordic mile. This term (*fiærþunger*) was also used as a measure of volume (see above).

Much used were also the *stång* ('stick, pole', OSw, ODan *stang*, ON *stöng*) and the *rep* ('rope', ON *reip*), both usually of 4.5–9 (in Norway 6 or 8) *alnar*. In Norway, the *stöng* equalled 2 *faðmar*, in Denmark 10–18 feet.

B) 2) The area of a surface was measured in different ways. Arable land was often measured in terms of i) the amount of seed sown, ii) the size of the crop or harvest, or iii) worth (land rent).

i) The amount of seed sown. *Sædesland* (from *sæde* 'seed') is used as a general term for land sowed with a certain amount of grain, specified in the first part of the compound in question. Under this term may be subsumed, e.g., *mælisland* and *sáldsáð*. A *mælisland* (Norway) was sown with 1 *mælir*, its size equalled 4.7 are; a *sáldsáð* (Norway) with 1 *sáld*, possibly c. 4 decare (c. 1/4 acre); a *pundssáð* (Norway) with 1 *skippund*. The same pattern is shown by OSw *spannaland* and *tunnland* (c. 4,000 m^2). A special OSw term is *seland* (Ångermanl.), for which the quantity of sowed grain is not known; its size has been estimated to 800 square fathoms.

ii) The size of the crop or harvest. OSw *snesland* (from *snes*, 'score, set of twenty', 1 *snesland* = 9 *bandland*) (measured according to the size of the harvest), and the OFar *tunnulendi* (64 square fathoms).

iii) Worth (land rent). Much more frequent are measurements based on rent ('landskyld', the tax or fee paid by the tenant to the landowner), where the first part of the compound denotes the size of the rent. Examples are (OSw) *löpsbol*, (ONorw) *laupsból, laupsleiga*, (OSw) *markland*, (OGu) *laupsland, marklaigi*, (OSw, ODan) *öre(s)land*, (ODan) *ørebol*, (ONorw) *ørtuga(r)ból*, (OSw) *örtoghaland*, (OSw) *pænningsland*, (ONorw) *mánaðarmatarból, merkrból, markaból, øyrisból, auraból*.

The OSw *öresland* equalled 3 *örtoghaland*, each comprising 3,000–4,000 m^2 (= 1 *tunnland* or 1 *dagsværk* ('day's work') or 36 *snesland*). The ONorw *merkrból* equalled 8 *auraból* (= 24 ørtogaból or 480 *penningaból*). 1 *mánaðarmatarból* equalled 1 *laupsból* (= 1/3 *merkrból*).

The central ODan unit was *bol*, the value of which was normally (in Zealand) 1 *mark* 'skyldjord', in Zealand it corresponded to c. 110 *tønder* (sown) grain. But the size of the *bol* varied considerably. Those valued less than 1 *mark* 'skyldjord' were divided into *fjerdinger* (fourths) or *ottinger* (eighths).

The OSw *attunger* was originally 1/8 of a village (*by*) or of the smallest conscription unit of the levy (the *hamna*). It was primarily not an area measure, but a measure of wealth, a unit used in the taxation of farms as a base for the military levy. As an area measure, it expressed the size of fields. In the Early Middle Ages a normal *attunger* was equal to the size of a field sown with 2 *tunnor* each year, when half of the field lay fallow, and the crop was 12 *tunnor*. In the High Middle Ages it became a norm for the rent (OSw *avrad*), in Sweden and Denmark normally 24 *spand*. It was equal to 1/2 *markland* in Svealand, 1/8 *bol* in Denmark.

The OIce *kristfé* ('Christ's properties') constituted a special case. These were freeholding foundations *ad pios usus*, properties or parts thereof encumbered with servitudes implying that the rent should be used to pay for the maintenance of paupers in the local district. Dependant on the size of this rent the property in question was called *karlgildr* (196 ells) or *kvengildr* (144 ells), irrespective of the gender of the recipient.

C) **Measures of weight** were partly the same as the units mentioned in the Appendix D1 (q.v.). This especially applies to the *mark, öre* and *örtogh*. The *mark* had the weight of c. 210 g, varying somewhat over time and regions (in Sweden 213.3 g (Skara), 207.2 g (Stockholm); in Denmark 217.5 g (1282), 210.47 g (1332–33) and c. 230 g ('the Cologne mark'); in Norway c. 214.3 g (1287) and 214.5 g (1329)). The *öre* was 1/8 *mark*, the *örtogh* 1/24 *mark*. Larger measures were the *skálpund, li(f)spund, skeppund, vétt/vætt* and *vág* (see above). In Iceland, larger quantities of fish were weighed in *hundruð* (pl. of *hundrað*). 1 *hundrað* equalled 120 *gildir fiskar* (40 of 4 *merkr* and 80 of 5 *merkr*).

Refs: Ericsson 2007; 2008a, 8–10; 2008b, 39–63; KLNM s.v.v. *bol, byamål, fiskhandel, hundrað, hömått, jordmått, kornmål, kristfé, mil, sædesland, tegskifte, ytmått*; all with further references; NK 29, passim; NK 30, passim; Pettersen 2013, 142, 224–25; Riddersporre 2008, 23–38; Siltberg 2008, 85–117; Sporrong 2008, 242–47; Tollin 2008, 139–48.

Appendix E: Kinship

The concept and institution of kin (OSw, ODan, OGu, ON *kyn*, OSw, ODan *æt*, ON *ætt*), the (extended) family, was of fundamental importance in the medieval Nordic society; socially, economically and legally. Kinship (ON *frændsemi, skyldskapr*), the state of belonging to a kin, was constituted by birth. Children born in lawful wedlock belonged equally to the father's and the mother's kin, although the agnatic kinship seems to have been considered more important. Children born out of wedlock and other illegitimate children had an inferior legal status, especially with regard to inheritance.

Kinship was measured in two ways. In the inherited ON system persons equally distant from a common ancestor, numbered in generations, belonged to the same *kné* (knee). First cousins belonged to the 1st knee, sixth cousins belonged to the 6th knee. According to the canonical system, which was introduced in Norway by bishop Grimkjell, the counting started with brothers and sisters: They were related in the 1st degree, sixth cousins in the 7th degree. The rule in GuL, chapter 24, allows for marriage between sixth cousins, but prohibits marriage between persons more closely related. This corresponds to the rules of the other Norwegian Church Laws (*Frostuþing, Eiðsifaþing* and *Borgarþing*). We should have expected a wording 'sixth knee and seventh degree', but here 'knee' and 'degree' are used synonymously, either erroneously or deliberately, see Hertzberg 1895, 350.

The legal implications of kinship were manifest in three respects: 1) the duty of mutual help, protection and responsibility in case of assault or violation from outside; 2) guardianship for minors and persons without legal capacity; and 3) obligations to support family members who could not take care of themselves, i.e. children, old, sick and disabled persons (ON *ómagar*). In all three respects the kin was collectively responsible. It follows from (1) that this also applies to violations committed: the kin of the guilty person had to pay compensation to the kin of the aggrieved person.

In social and economic respects kinship was the basis for rights of inheritance. The positions of members of the kin varied according to distance/proximity (to the deceased). Closer relatives usually took precedence over more distant ones with respect to rights and duties. Gender played a role: men (sons) inherited twice as much as women (daughters), and only men were allowed to give women in marriage (ON *festa konu*). In Sweden women's and men's land brought to the marriage was kept apart during marriage. If no children were produced the land went back to where it came from. Odal right was involved in purchase and sale of land. If inherited land should be sold, members of the seller's kin had a right of pre-emption. To keep inherited land within the kin was an overriding concern, and usually men had precedence over women although they belonged to the same knee.

On the function of kinship in general, see also Vogt 2010, 9–25 with further references. On the function of kinship in practice, see also Larsson 2010, 95–108, 115–17, 140–50, 176–202, 234–37; 2012.

Refs: Helle 2001, 182; Hertzberg 1895 s.v. *kné*; KLNM s.v. *ætt*; Larsson 2010; 2012; Robberstad 1981, 334–36; Vogt 2010, 9–25.

https://doi.org/10.11647/OBP.0188.09

Appendix F:
Calendar of Church Feast and Fast Days

The ecclesiastical calendar below combines the information given in the OSw, ODan, OGu, OFar, OIce and ONorw laws. The language of the last three of these is throughout recorded as ON. The dates given are those known from the medieval Catholic calendar, supplemented by information from current practice. Where a saint was celebrated on a number of days in the year, the date(s) given derive either from a specific statement in the law, or from the context. Some of the dates given differ from those now current in England and these have been noted. The English equivalents given here are those that are most often used currently, whereas the actual translations employed by the individual editors of the laws are not consistent. The latter can be found in the body of the lexicon.

Ref: Lithberg and Wessén 1939, 75–113.

Date or extent of feast where more than one day; range of dates for the feast, where it is movable	Feast name in the Old Norse Laws	Language	(Standard) English translation and explanatory notes
movable: 27th November–3rd December	advent	ODan, OSw	Advent
6th December	nikulásmessa	ON	Feast of St Nicholas
7th December	ambrósiusmessa	ON	Feast of St Ambrose
13th December	magnúsmessa	ON	Feast of the Translation of St Magnus (Erlendsson of Orkney)
21st December	thomasmessa	ON	Feast of St Thomas
23rd December	þorláksmessa	ON	Feast of St Þorlákr
24th December	helga náttin	ON	Christmas Eve
	jólanátt	ON	
25th December	jóladagr	ON	Christmas Day/Season
	jólahelgr	ON	
	jul	OSw, ODan	
	jól	ON	
5th January	tolftidagher	OSw	Twelfth Night
	tolftidagher	ODan	
6th January	þrættandidagher	OSw	Feast of the Epiphany
	þrettándi dagr jóla	ON	Not Twelfth Day, but Epiphany. Twelfth Night is 5 Jan, the vigil of this Feast.
11th January	brettifumessa	ON	Feast of St Brictiva
21st January	agnesmessa	ON	Feast of St Agnes
25th January	pálsmessa	ON	Feast of St Paul (not to be confused with the Feast of SS Peter and Paul, 29th June)

https://doi.org/10.11647/OBP.0188.10

1st February	*brigíðarmessa*	ON	Feast of St Brigid
movable: the Sunday before Ash Wednesday: 1st February–7th March	*kötsunnudagher*	OSw	Sunday before Lent, Quinquagesima
2nd February	*maríumessa* recorded as *kyndilmessa* in a manuscript variant	ON	Purification of the Blessed Virgin Mary
	kyndilmæssa	OSw	Candlemas
movable: 4th February–10th March	*askuoþensdagher*	OSw	Ash Wednesday
movable: from Ash Wednesday to Holy Saturday (the day before Easter Sunday): 4th February until 21st March–10th March until 24th April	*langafasta*	ON	Lent
movable: 8th February–14th March	*hvitisunnudagher* (*drottins dags i hvita dogum* in Grg)	OSw	First Sunday in Lent
22nd February	*pétrsmessa*	ON	Feast of St Peter (not to be confused with the Feast of SS Peter and Paul, 29th June)
24th February	*matthiasmessa*	ON	Feast of St Matthias
	mattíasmessa	ON	An alternative date is 14th May
movable: the Sunday before Palm Sunday: 8th March–11th April	*kæra sunnudagher*	OSw	Fifth Sunday in Lent, otherwise called Passion Sunday
12th March	*gregoriusmessa*	ON	Feast of St Gregory
movable, starting with Palm Sunday: 15th March–18th April	*dymbilvika*	OSw	Holy Week (the week before Easter)
movable: 18th March–21st April	*kloknaoþensdagher*	OSw	Wednesday in Holy Week, Wednesday next before Easter
movable: 19th March–22nd April	*skærþorsdagher*	OSw	Maundy Thursday
	skíriþórsdagr	ON	
movable: 20th March–23rd April	*langafre(a)dagher*	OSw	Good Friday
	langafrjádagr	ON	
21st March	*benedictusmessa*	ON	Feast of St Benedict
movable: 22nd March–25th April	*paskadagher*	OSw	Easter Day
	páskadagr	ON	Easter Day
movable: 22nd March–25th April	*paskar*	OSw	Easter season
	paske	ODan	
	páskar	ON	
25th March	*mariumessa i fastu*	OGu	Feast of the Annunciation, also called Lady Day
	maríumessa í föstu	ON	
	maríumessa um várit	ON	
	varafrudagher (i fastu)	OSw	
16th April	*magnúsmessa*	ON	Feast of St Magnus (Erlendsson of Orkney)
23rd April	*jóhannesmessa* (variant of: *jóansmessa*)	ON	Feast of St Jón Ögmundarson, bishop of Hólar 1106–21 (celebrated from 1200; cf. note in the translation of *Grágás*)

25th April	*(litli) gangdagher*	OSw	Rogation Day; despite its Nordic designation, the original and principal Rogation Day in the Catholic Calendar, possibly the successor to the Roman *ambarvalia*, a ceremony designed to guard against blight in the seed
	gangdagr	ON	
26th April–2nd May	*crucisuke*	ODan	The week following the Feast of St Mark on 25th April and thus followed by *krossmessa*, the Invention of the Cross, on 3rd May (see below)
movable: the 3 days preceding Ascension Day: 27th to 29th April–31st May to 2nd June	*gangdagahelgr*	ON	Rogation Days (sometimes coinciding with *crucisuke*, q.v., if Easter were at its earliest date)
	gangdaghar	OGu	
	gangdagar	ON	
	helgavika	ON	Rogation Week
movable: 30th April–3rd June	*hælghiþorsdagher*	OSw	Ascension Day
	uppstigningardagr	ON	
1st May	*philippus messa ok jakobus*	ON	Feast of SS Philip and James (the lesser)
1st May	*valborghamæssa*	OSw	This is usually called Walpurgis' Day, rather than the Feast of St Walpurga, as it had and has secular overtones. It is not clear in the texts if it is the Eve, 30th April that is referred to, or to the feast day itself.
3rd May	*crucismisse*	ODan	Invention of the Cross (3rd May according to glossary in Routledge edition. That is, the Sunday following *crucisuke*, q.v. The word 'invention' in this context = 'finding')
	krossmessa	ON	The same word is used for both this feast and for that of the Exaltation of the Cross, 14th September
	krossmessa um várit	ON	
movable: 10th May–13th June	*pingizdagher*	ODan, OSw	Whitsunday
15th May	*hallvarðarmessa*	ON	Feast of St Hallvard
18th May	*sankta eriks dagh*	OSw	Feast of St Erik
9th June	*kolumbamessa*	ON	Feast of St Columba
17th June	*botulfsmæssa*	OSw	Feast of St Botulf
	bótolfsmessa	ON	
24th June	*jónsmessa*	ON	Feast of St John the Baptist
	jóansmessa	ON	
	jónsvaka	ONorw	
28th June	*pétrsmessuaptann*	ON	Vigil of the Feast of St Peter

29th June	apostlamœssudagher	OSw	Feast of SS Peter and Paul
	petersmessa	OSw	Feast of St Peter (specifically this June date, shared with St Paul, not the February date, which is only mentioned in Grg)
	sankti petrs messa	OGu	
	pétrsmessa	ON	
2nd July	svitunsmessa	ON	St Swithun's Day (note that in the English calendar St Swithun's Day is 15 July)
8th July	seljamannamessa	ON	Feast of the Saints of Selja (i.e. St Sunniva and her companions; St Sunniva's shrine was moved to Bergen in 1170)
	seljumannamessa	ON	
	heilagra manna (messa) í Selju	ON	
10th July	knútsmessa	ON	Feast of St Canute (celebrated on 19th January in England)
25th July	jakobsmessa	ON	Feast of St James (the Great)
29th July	olafsdagher	OSw	(Earlier) Feast of St Olaf
	olafsmœssa	OSw, ODan	
	ólafsmessa	ON	
	ólafsmessa hin fyrri	ON	
3rd August	ólafsmessa hin øfri	ON	Later Feast of St Olaf
10th August	laurinzardagher	OSw	Feast of St Lawrence
	laurinzardagher	OSw	
	lafrinzsmœssa	OSw	
	laurentiusmessa	ON	
	laurentiusmessa	ON	
15th August	mariumœssa (fyrra)	OSw	Feast of the Assumption of the Blessed Virgin Mary
	mariemisse fyrre	ODan	
	maríumessa fyrri	ON	
	maríumessa fyrri	ON	
24th August	bartholomeusmessa	ON	Feast of St Bartholomew
	bartholomeusmessa	ON	
1st September	yliansmœssa	OSw	Feast of St Giles
8th September	mariumœssa (öfra)	OSw	Feast of the Nativity of Our Lady (or the Blessed Virgin Mary)
	maríumessa øfri	ON	
	maríumessa síðari	ON	
14th September	krossmessa	ON	Feast of the Exaltation of the Cross. (The same name is used for both this and the Invention of the Cross, 3rd May)
	krossmessa um haustit	ON	
	krossmessa hin øfri	ON	
21st September	mattéimessa; mattéusmessa	ON	Feast of St Matthew
	matthaeusmessa	ON	

29th September	*mikialsmæssa*	OSw	Michaelmas
	mikjalsmisse	ODan	
	mikjálsmessa	ON	
	mikialsmæssodagher	OSw	Michaelmas Day
	mikialsdagher	OSw	
30th September–6th October	*sialadagher*	OSw	Monday after Michaelmas
28th October	*símonsmessudagr ok judas*	ON	Feast of SS Simon and Jude
	tveggjapostulamessa/- messudagr	ON	Feast of the Two Apostles
1st November	*hælghunamæssudagher; aldra hælghuna dagher*	OSw	All Saints' Day
	helgunamessa	OGu	
	allraheilagramessa	ON	
2nd November	*sialamæssudagher*	OSw	All Souls' Day
11th November	*martinsmæssa*	OSw	Martinmas
	marteinsmessa	ON	
	sancta martens dagher	OSw	St Martin's Day
22nd November	*ceciliomessa*	ON	Feast of St Cecilia
23rd November	*klementsmessa*	ON	Feast of St Clement
	clemensmessa	ON	Feast of St Clement
25th November	*katrinamæssa*	OSw	Feast of St Catherine of Alexandria
30th November	*andreasmessa*	ON	Feast of St Andrew
Various: Wednesday, Friday, and Saturday following St Lucy's Day (13 December), the first Sunday in Lent, Pentecost (Whitsun), and Holy Cross Day (14 September)	*imbrudagr*	ON	Ember Days (i.e. the days of fasting at the turn of the seasons: winter, spring, summer and autumn respectively)

Bibliography

Primary

Brøndum-Nielsen, Johs. and Poul Johannes Jørgensen, eds. 1933–61. *Danmarks gamle landskabslove, med kirkelovene.* 8 vols. København: Gyldendalske boghandel.

Clunies Ross, Margaret, et al. eds. 2007–. *Skaldic Poetry of the Scandinavian Middle Ages.* 9 vols. Turnhout: Brepols, http://www.abdn.ac.uk/skaldic/db.php

Collin, Hans Samuel and Carl Johan Schlyter, eds. 1980. *Östgöta-lagen: Facsimile Edition with Addendum by the Main part of Emil Olson, Östgötalagens 1300-talsfragment and Carl Ivar Ståhle, De Liedgrenska fragmenten av Östgötalagens C-text.* Lund: Ekstrand.

DGL = Brøndum-Nielsen and Jørgensen 1933–1961.

DI = Jón Þorkelsson and Jón Sigurðsson, eds. 1857–1972. *Diplomatarium Islandicum. Íslenzkt fornbréfasafn.* 16 vols. Reykjavík: Hið íslenzka bókmenntafjelag.

DN = Storm, Gustav, et al., eds. 1847–. *Diplomatarium Norvegicum.* 23 vols. Oslo: Riksarkivet.

Eithun, Bjørn, Magnus Rindal and Tor Ulset, eds. 1994. *Den eldre Gulatingslova.* Norrøne tekster 6. Oslo: Riksarkivet.

GDO = *Gammeldansk Ordbog.* Det Danske Sprog- og Litteraturselskab, https://gammeldanskordbog.dk/.

GrgTr = Dennis, Andrew, Peter Foote and Richard Perkins, trans. 1980–2000. *Laws of Early Iceland. Grágás.* 2 vols. Winnipeg: University of Manitoba Press.

Gunnar Karlsson, Kristján Sveinsson, Mörður Árnason, eds. 1992. *Grágás: Lagasafn íslenska þjóðveldisins.* Reykjavík: Mál og menning.

Hagland, Jan Ragnar and Jørn Sandnes, trans. 1994. *Frostatingslova.* Oslo: Det Norske Samlaget.

Hagland, Jan Ragnar and Jørn Sandnes, trans. 1997. *Bjarkøyretten. Nidaros eldste bylov.* Oslo: Det Norske Samlaget.

Halvorsen, Eyvind Fjeld and Magnus Rindal, eds. 2008. *De eldste østlandske kristenrettene* [Borgartings og Eidsivatings eldre kristenretter]. Norrøne tekster 7. Oslo: Riksarkivet.

Haraldur Bernharðsson, Magnús Lyngdal Magnússon and Már Jónsson, eds. 2005. *Járnsíða og kristinréttur Árna Þorlákssonar.* Reykjavík: Sögufélag.

Hertzberg = Hertzberg, Ebbe and Gustav Storm. 1895. *Norges gamle love indtil 1387.* Vol. 5. Christiania: Grøndahl.

Heusler, Andreas, trans. 1937. *Isländisches Recht: Die Graugans.* Germanenrechte 9. Weimar: Böhlau.

Hødnebø, Finn and Magnus Rindal, eds. 1995. *Den eldre Gulatingsloven.* Corpus codicum Norvegicorum medii aevi, Quarto series, vol. IX (facs. ed.). Oslo: Selskapet til utgivelse av gamle norske håndskrifter.

Imsen, Steinar, ed. and trans. 2000. *Hirdskråe: Hirdloven til Norges konge og hans håndgangne menn.* Oslo: Riksarkivet.

Kroman, Erik and Stig Juul, trans. 1945–48. *Danmarks gamle love paa nutidsdansk.* 3 vols. København: G. E. C. Gad.

Larson, Lawrence M., trans. 1935. *The Earliest Norwegian laws: Being the Gulathing Law and the Frostathing Law.* Records of Civilization 20. New York: Morningside Heights.

Már Jónsson, ed. 2004. *Jónsbók: Lögbók Íslendinga hver samþykkt var á alþingi árið 1281 og endurnýjuð um miðja 14. öld en fyrst prentuð árið 1578*. Sýnisbók íslenskrar alþýðumenningar 8. Reykjavík: Háskólaútgafan.

Meissner, Rudolf, trans. 1935. *Das Rechtsbuch des Gulathings*. Germanenrechte 6, Norwegisches Recht. Weimar: Verlag Herm. Böhlaus Nachf.

NGL = Keyser, Rudolf, et al., eds. 1846–95. *Norges gamle love indtil 1387*. 5 vols. Christiania: C. Gröndahl.

Ólafur Halldórsson, ed. 1904 [repr. 1970]. *Jónsbók: Kong Magnus Hakonssons lovbog for Island vedtaget paa Altinget 1281; Réttarbœtr: de for Island givne Retterbøder af 1294, 1305 og 1314*. Odense: Universitetsforlag.

Ólafur Lárusson, ed. 1923. *Grágás og Lögbœkurnar*. Arbók Háskóla Islands 1921–22. Fylgirit. Reykjavik: Gutenberg.

Ólafur Lárusson, ed. 1936. *Staðarhóltsbók: The Ancient Lawbooks Grágás and Járnsida. Ms. No 334 fol. in the Arna-Magnaean Coll. in the Univ. Libr. of Copenhagen*. Corpus codicum Islandicorum medii aevi 9. Copenhagen: Levin & Munksgaard.

Peel, Christine, ed. 1999. *Guta saga: The History of the Gotlanders*. Viking Society for Northern Research, Text series 12. London: Viking Society for Northern Research.

Peel, Christine, ed. and trans. 2009. *Guta lag: The Law of the Gotlanders*. Viking Society for Northern Research, Text series 18. London: Viking Society for Northern Research.

Peel, Christine, ed. and trans. 2015. *Guta lag and Guta saga: The Law and History of the Gotlanders*. London and New York: Routledge.

Pipping, Hugo. 1905–07. *Guta lag och Guta saga jämte ordbok*. Samfund til Udgivelse af gammel nordisk Litteratur 33. Copenhagen: Møller.

Poulsen, Jóhan Hendrik W., et al., ed. and trans. 1971. *Seyðabrævið*. Tórshavn: Føroya fróðskaparfelag.

Rindal, Magnus and Knut Berg, eds. 1983. *King Magnus Håkonsson's Laws of Norway and Other Legal Texts*. Corpus codicum Norvegicorum medii aevi, Quarto series, vol. 7 (facs. ed.). Oslo: Selskapet til utgivelse av gamle norske håndskrifter.

Robberstad, Knut, trans. 1923. *Magnus Lagabøters bylov*. Kristiania: Cammermeyers Boghandel.

Robberstad, Knut, trans. 1981. *Gulatingslovi*. 4th ed. Norrøne bokverk 33. Oslo: Det Norske Samlaget.

Schlyter, C. J. and Hans Samuel Collin, eds. 1827–77. *Corpus iuris Sueo-Gotorum antiqui : Samling af Sweriges gamla lagar*. 13 vols. Stockholm: Z. Haeggström.

Schulman, Jana K., trans. 2010. *Jónsbók: The Laws of Later Iceland; The Icelandic text according to MS AM 351 fol. Skálholtsbók eldri*. Bibliotheca Germanica. Series nova 4. Saarbrücken: AQ-Verlag.

Seip, Didrik A., ed. 1950. *Oslo Bylov etter middelalderlige håndskrifter*. Corpus codicum Norvegicorum medii aevi, Folio series, vol. 1 (facs. ed.). Oslo: Selskapet til utgivelse av gamle norske håndskrifter.

Seip, Jens A. and Gudmund Sandvik, eds. and trans. 1956. *Gammelnorske lovtekster med oversettelse*. Bergen and Oslo: Universitetsforlaget.

Sjöros, Bruno, ed. 1919. *Äldre västgötalagen i diplomatariskt avtryck och normaliserad text jämte inledning och kommentar*. Svenska litteratursällskapet i Finland 144. Helsingfors: Tidnings- och tryckeri-aktiebolaget.

Sjöros, Bruno, ed. 1923. *Äldre västgötalagen, i nysvensk översättning*. Helsingfors: Schildt.

SL = Holmbäck, Åke and Elias Wessén. 1933–46 [repr. 1979]. *Svenska landskapslagar: Tolkade och förklarade för nutidens svenskar*. 5 vols. Stockholm: AWE/Geber.

Tamm, Ditlev and Helle Vogt, trans. 2016. *The Danish Medieval Laws: The Laws of Scania, Zealand and Jutland*. New York: Routledge.

Taranger, Absalon, trans. 1915. *Magnus Lagabøters landslov*. Kristiania: Cammermeyers boghandel.

Taranger, Absalon, et al., eds. 1904–95. *Norges gamle love, anden række, 1388–1604*. 4 vols. Christiania: Grøndahl & son.

Vilhjálmur Finsen, ed. and trans. 1852–70. *Grágás: Islændernes Lovbog i Fristatens Tíd*. 4 vols. Kjøbenhavn: Berlings.

Vilhjálmur Finsen, ed. 1879 [repr. 1974]. *Grágás, Staðarhólsbók*. Odense: Universitetsforlag.

Vilhjálmur Finsen, ed. 1883 [repr. 1974]. *Grágás, Skálhóltsbók m.m*. Odense: Universitetsforlag.

Wiktorsson, Per-Axel, ed. 2011. *Äldre Västgötalagen och dess bilagor i Cod. Holm. B 59. 1–2*. Skara stiftshistoriska sällskaps skriftserie. Skara: Föreningen för Västgötalitteratur.

Secondary

Aakjær, Svend. ed. 1936. *Mønt*. Nordisk kultur 29. Stockholm: Bonnier.

Aakjær, Svend. ed. 1936. *Maal og vægt*. Nordisk kultur 30. Stockholm: Bonnier.

Adams, Ian H. 1976. *Agrarian Landscape Terms: A Glossary for Historical Geography*. Institute of British Geographers Special Publication 9. London: Institute of British Geographers.

Agnes S. Arnórsdóttir. 2005. "Death and Donation: Different Channels of Property Transfer in Late Medieval Iceland." In *The Marital Economy in Scandinavia and Britain 1400–1900*, ed. Maria Ågren and Amy Louise Erickson, pp. 207–19. Aldershot: Ashgate.

Agnes S. Arnórsdóttir. 2006. "Þróun eignarréttar á miðöldum. Þankar í tengslum við rannsókn á málsögulegri og réttarsögulegri þróun í fornum lögum." *Saga* 44.1: 205–13.

Agnes S. Arnórsdóttir. 2010. *Property and Virginity: The Christianization of Marriage in Medieval Iceland 1200–1600*. Aarhus: Aarhus University Press.

Agnes S. Arnórsdóttir and Thyra Nors. 1999. "Ægteskabet i Norden og det europæiske perspektiv – overvejelser om især danske og islandske normer for ægteskab i 12.–14. århundrede." In *Ægteskab i Norden fra Saxo til i dag*, ed. Kari Melby, Ana Pylkkänen and Bente Rosenbeck, pp. 25–54. København: Nordgraf.

Almqvist, Bo. 1965. *Norrön niddiktning: Traditionshistoriska studier i versmagi. 1. Nid mot furstar*. Nordiska texter och undersökningar 21. 2 vols. Uppsala: Almqvist & Wiksell.

Almquist, Jan Eric. 1955. *Lagsagor och domsagor i Sverige med särskild hänsyn till den judiciella indelningen I–II*. Skrifter utgivna av Rättsgenetiska Institutet vid Stockholms Högskola 2:1–2. Stockholm: Norstedt.

Ambrius, Jonny. 1996. *Att dömas till döden: Tortyr, kroppsstraff och avrättningar genom historien*. Vällingby: Strömberg.

Andersen, Per. 2006. *Lærd ret og verdslig lovgivning: Retlig kommunikation og udvikling i middelalderens Danmark*. Copenhagen: Jurist- og Økonomforbundet.

Andersen, Per. 2010. *Studier i dansk proceshistorie: Tiden indtil Danske Lov 1683*. Bibliotek for ret og kultur 2. Copenhagen: Jurist- og Økonomforbundet.

Andersen, Per. 2011. *Legal Procedure and Practice in Medieval Denmark*. Medieval Law and Its Practice 11. Boston: Brill.

Andersen, Per. 2014. "'The Truth Must Always Be Stronger': The Introduction and Development of *Næfnd* in the Danish Provincial Laws". In *New Approaches to Early Law in Scandinavia*, ed. Stefan Brink and Lisa Collinson, pp. 7–36. Turnhout: Brepols.

Andersen, Per and Mia Münster-Swendsen, eds. 2009. *Custom: The Development and Use of a Legal Concept in the Middle Ages; Proceedings of the Fifth Carlsberg Academy Conference on Medieval Legal History 2008*. Copenhagen: DJØF.

Andersen, Per, ed. 2013. *Law and Disputing in the Middle Ages: Proceedings of the Ninth Carlsberg Academy Conference on Medieval Legal History 2012*. Copenhagen: DJØF.

Andersen, Per Mia Münster-Swendsen, and Helle Vogt, eds. 2007. *Law before Gratian: Law in Western Europe c. 500–1100: Proceedings of the Third Carlsberg Academy Conference on Medieval Legal History 2006*. Copenhagen: DJØF.

Andersen, Per Mia Münster-Swendsen, and Helle Vogt, eds. 2012. *Law and Power in the Middle Ages: Proceedings of the Fourth Carlsberg Academy Conference on Medieval Legal History 2007*. 2nd ed. Copenhagen: DJØF.

Andersen, Per Mia Münster-Swendsen, and Helle Vogt, eds. 2011. *Law and Private Life in the Middle Ages: Proceedings of the Sixth Carlsberg Academy Conference on Medieval Legal History 2009*. Copenhagen: DJØF.

Andersen, Per et al., eds. 2011. *Liber amicorum Ditlev Tamm: Law, History and Culture*. Copenhagen: DJØF.

Andersen, Per et al., eds. 2012. *Law and Marriage in Medieval and Early Modern Times: Proceedings of the Eighth Carlsberg Academy Conference on Medieval Legal History 2011*. Copenhagen: DJØF.

Andersen, Per Sveaas. 1977. *Samlingen av Norge og kristningen av landet 800–1130*. Handbok i Norges historie 2. Bergen, Oslo and Tromsø: Universitetsforlaget.

Andersson, Thorsten. 1979. "Die schwedischen Bezirksbezeichnungen *hund* und *hundare*: Ein Beitrag zur Diskussion einer germanischen Wortfamilie". *Frühmittelalterliche Studien* 13: 88–124.

Andersson, Thorsten. 1982. "*Hund, hundare* och *härad* från språklig synpunkt." *Bebyggelsehistorisk tidskrift* 4: 52–66.

Andersson, Thorsten. 1982a. "Äldre territoriell indelning i Sverige." *Bebyggelsehistorisk tidskrift* 4.

Andersson, Thorsten. 1984. "Danska bygde- och häradsnamn." *Namn och Bygd*: 90.

Andersson, Thorsten. 1999. "*Hundare* och det germanska hundratalet." *Namn och Bygd*: 5–12.

Andersson, Thorsten. 2010. Vad *och* vade. *Svensk slåtter-, rågångs- och arealterminologi*. Acta Academiae Regiae Gustavi Adolphi 110. Uppsala: Kungl. Gustav Adolfs Akademien för svensk folkkultur.

Andersson, Thorsten. 2014. "Nordiska distriktsbeteckningar i gammal tid." *Namn och Bygd* 102: 5–40.

Andrae, Carl Göran. 1960. *Kyrka och frälse i Sverige under äldre medeltid*. Studia historica Upsaliensia 4. Uppsala: Almqvist and Wiksell.

Andrén, Anders. 1985. *Den urbana scenen. Städer och samhälle i det medeltida Danmark. = The Urban Scene. Towns and Society in Mediaeval Denmark*. Acta archaeologica Lundensia. Series in 8o 13. Malmö: LiberFörlag.

Ankarloo, Bengt. 1971. *Trolldomsprocesserna i Sverige*. Skrifter utgivna av Institutet för rättshistorisk forskning, grundat av Gustav och Carin Olin. Serien 1: Rättshistoriskt bibliotek 17. Stockholm: Nord. bokh. (distr.).

Arnljótr Ólafsson. 1904. "Um lögaura og silfrgang fyrrum á Íslandi." *Tímarit hins íslenzka bókmentafélags* 25: 1–26.

Árni Björnsson. 1995. *High Days and Holidays in Iceland*. Trans. Anna H. Yates. Reykjavík: Mál og menning.

Árni Daníel Júlíusson. 2010. "Signs of Power: Manorial Demesnes in Medieval Iceland." *Viking and Medieval Scandinavia* 6: 1–29.

Auður Magnúsdóttir. 2011. "Islänningarna och arvsrätten 1264–1281." In *Arverettens handlingsrom: Strategier, relasjoner og historisk utvikling, 1100–2000*, ed. Per Andersen, 27–39. Stamsund: Orkana akademisk.

Axboe, Morten and Magnus Källström. 2013. "Guldbrakteater fra Trollhättan – 1844 og 2009." *Fornvännen* 108: 153–71.

Bagge, Sverre. 1991. *Society and Politics in Snorri Sturluson's Heimskringla*. Berkeley: University of California Press.

Bagge, Sverre. 2010. *From Viking Stronghold to Christian Kingdom: State Formation in Norway c. 900–1350*. Copenhagen: Tusculanum.

Bagge, Sverre. 2013. "From Fist to Scepter: Authority in Norway in the Middle Ages." In *Fundamentals of Medieval and Early Modern Culture, Volume 12: Authorities in the Middle Ages; Influence, Legitimacy, and Power in Medieval Society*, ed. Sini Kangas, Mia Korpiola and Tuija Ainonen, pp. 161–81. Berlin: De Gruyter.

Bandlien, Björn. 2005. *Strategies of Passion: Love and Marriage in Old Norse Society*. Turnhout: Brepols.

Baum, Bärbel. 1986. *Der Stabreim im Recht*. Rechtshistorische Reihe 46. Frankfurt am Main: Lang.

Bayley, David H. 1990. *Patterns of Policing: A Comparative International Analysis*. New Brunswick, NJ: Rutgers University Press.

Beal, Peter. 2008. *A Dictionary of English Manuscript Terminology 1450–2000*. Oxford: Oxford University Press.

Beck, Heinrich. 1975. "Philologische Bemerkungen zu 'Bauer' im Germanischen." In *Wort und Begriff 'Bauer'*, ed. Reinhard Wenskus, Herbert Jankuhn and Klaus Grinda, pp. 58–72. Göttingen: Vandenhoeck & Ruprecht.

Beck, Heinrich. 1983. *Verbwörterbuch zur altisländischen Grágás (Konungsbók)*. 2 vols. Frankfurt am Main: Peter Lang.

Beck, Sigríður. 2011. "I kungens frånvaro. Formeringen av en isländsk aristokrati 1271–1387." PhD Diss. University of Gothenburg.

Berend, Nora. 2007. *Christianization and the Rise of Christian Monarchy: Scandinavia, Central Europe and Rus' c. 900–1200*. Cambridge: Cambridge University Press.

Beresford, Maurice Warwick and John Kenneth Sinclair St Joseph. 1979. *Medieval England: An Aerial Survey*. Cambridge: Cambridge University Press.

Berg, Johan. 2013. "Skänninge i landskapet." In *Borgare, bröder och bönder. Arkeologiska perspektiv på Skänninges äldre historia*, ed. Rikard Hedvall et al., pp. 19–42. Stockholm: Riksantikvarieämbetet.

Bertell, Erik. 1993. *Medeltida skattesystem på Åland*. Skrifter utgivna av Ålands kulturstiftelse 15. Mariehamn: Ålands kulturstiftelse.

Bjarni Einarsson. 2003. "'Mansǫngr' Revisited." In *Opuscula 11*, ed. Britta Olrik Frederiksen, pp. 307–15. Bibliotheca Arnamagnaeana 42. Hafniae: C. A. Reitzel.

Bjorvand, Harald. 1994. *Holt og holtar. Utviklingen av det indoeuropeiske kollektivum i norrønt*. Oslo: Solum.

Bjorvand, Harald and Fredrik Otto Lindeman. 2007. *Våre arveord: Etymologisk ordbok*. Instituttet for sammenlignende kulturforskning, Serie B Skrifter 105. 2nd ed. Oslo: Novus.

Bjørk, Erik Arne. 1959. "Strandarrætturin í Føroyum." *Fróðskaparrit* 8: 66–102.

Bjørk, Erik Arne. 1963. "Nevtollur og nýggjari føroysk løggáva um oyðing av skaðafugli." *Fróðskaparrit* 12: 7–52.

Blomkvist, Nils. 2011. "The skattland – a Concept Suitable for Export? The Role of Loosely Integrated Territories in the Emergence of the Medieval State." In *Taxes, Tributes and Tributary Lands in the Making of the Scandinavian Kingdoms in the Middle Ages*, ed. Steinar Imsen, pp. 167–188. Trondheim: Tapir Academic Press.

Blöndal, Sigfús. 1920–24. *Íslensk-dönsk orðabók*. Reykjavík: Gutenberg.

Bolton, Timothy. 2009. *The Empire of Cnut the Great: Conquest and the Consolidation of Power in Northern Europe in the Early Eleventh Century*. Leiden: Brill.

Bosworth, Joseph and Thomas Northcote Toller. 1898. *An Anglo-Saxon Dictionary*. Oxford: Clarendon.

Boyer, Régis. 1990. "Einige Überlegungen über das Gottesurteil im mittelalterlichen Skandinavien." In *Das Mittelalter – Unsere fremde Vergangenheit: Beiträge der Stuttgarter Tagung vom 17. bis 19. September 1987*, ed. Joachim Kuolt, Harald Kleinschmidt and Peter Dinzelbacher, pp. 173–93. Stuttgart: Helfant Ed.

Brandt, Frederik. 1880. *Forelæsninger over den norske retshistorie*. 2 vols. Kristiania: Damm.

Bredberg, Anette. 1996. *Vikingatida rättssystem: Om rätten i Birka och Adelsö/Birka-tinget*. Stockholm: Arkeologiska institutionen, Stockholms Universitet.

Breisch, Agneta. 1994. *Frid och fredlöshet. Sociala band och utanförskap på Island under äldre medeltid*. Studia historica Upsaliensia 174. Uppsala: Uppsala University.

Brink, Stefan. 1990. *Sockenbildning och sockennamn: Studier i äldre territoriell indelning i Norden = Parish-Formation and Parish-names: Studies in Early Territorial Division in Scandinavia*. Acta Academiae Regiae Gustavi Adolphi 57. Studier till en svensk ortnamnsatlas 14. Uppsala: Gustav Adolfs akad.

Brink, Stefan. 1991. "-*hammare*". In *NORNA, NONELex*, https://www.norna.org/content/%E2%80%90hammare

Brink, Stefan. 1994. *Hälsinglands äldsta skattelängd. Hjälpskattelängden "Gärder och hjälper" från år 1535*. Skrifter utgivna genom Ortnamnsarkivet i Uppsala. Serie C. Källskrifter 2. Uppsala: Ortnamnsarkivet.

Brink, Stefan. 1996. "Forsaringen – Nordens äldsta lagbud." In *Beretning fra femtende tværfaglige vikingesymposium*, ed. Else Roesdahl, Preben Meulengracht Sørensen, pp. 27–55. Højbjerg: Hikuin.

Brink, Stefan. 1998. "Land, bygd, distrikt och centralort i Sydskandinavien. Några bebyggelsehistoriska nedslag." In *Centrala platser centrala frågor. Samhällsstrukturen under järnåldern. En Vänbok till Berta Stjernquist*, ed. Lars Larsson & Birgitta Hårdh, pp. 297–326. Acta Archaeologica Lundensia Ser. in 8°, No. 28. Stockholm: Almqvist and Wiksell.

Brink, Stefan. 2000a. "Husby." In *Reallexikon der Germanischen Altertumskunde* 15, ed. Heinrich Beck, Dieter Geuenich, Heiko Steuer, pp. 275–78. Berlin, New York: De Gruyter.

Brink, Stefan. 2000b. "Nordens Husabyar – unga eller gamla?" In *En bok om husbyar*, ed. Michael Olausson, pp. 65–74. Riksantikvarieämbetet. Avdelningen för arkeologiska undersökningar. Skrifter 33. Stockholm: Riksantikvarieämbetet.

Brink, Stefan. 2002. "Law and Legal Customs in Viking Age Scandinavia." In *Scandinavians from the Vendel Period to the Tenth Century*, ed. Judith Jesch, pp. 87–117. Studies in Historical Archaeoethnology 5. Woodbridge: Boydell.

Brink, Stefan. 2003. "Legal Assemblies and Judicial Structure in Early Scandinavia." In *Political Assemblies in the Earlier Middle Ages*, ed. Paul Barnwell and Marco Mostert, pp. 61–72. Studies in the Early Middle Ages 7. Turnhout: Brepols.

Brink, Stefan. 2004a. "Mytologiska rum och eskatologiska föreställningar i det vikingatida Norden." In *Ordning mot kaos: Studier av nordisk förkristen kosmologi*, ed. Anders Andrén, Kristina Jennbert and Catharina Raudvere, pp. 291–316. Lund: Nordic Academic Press.

Brink, Stefan. 2004b. "Legal Assembly Sites in Early Scandinavia." In *Assembly Places and Practices in Medieval Europe*, ed. Aliki Pantos and Sarah Semple, pp. 205–16. Dublin: Four Courts.

Brink, Stefan. 2008a. "Law and Society: Polities and Legal Customs in Viking Scandinavia." In *The Viking World*, ed. Stefan Brink and Neil Price, pp. 23–31. London: Routledge.

Brink, Stefan. 2008b. "People and Land in early Scandinavia." In *Franks, Northmen, and Slavs : Identities and State Formation in Early Medieval Europe*, ed. Ildar H. Garipzanov, Patrick J. Geary and Przemysław Urbańczyk, pp. 87–112. Turnhout: Brepols.

Brink, Stefan. 2008c. *Lord and Lady – bryti and deigja*. The Dorothea Coke Memorial Lecture in Northern Studies delivered at University College London 17 March 2005. London: The Viking Society for Northern Research.

Brink, Stefan. 2010a. "Är Forsaringen medeltida?" *Hälsingerunor* 2010: 109–17.

Brink, Stefan. 2010b. "Hälsingelagens ställning mellan väst och syd, och mellan kung, kyrka och lokala traditioner." *Kungl. Vitterhets Historie och Antikvitetsakademiens årsbok* 2010: 119–35.

Brink, Stefan. 2011a. "Mediality and Usage of Medieval Laws: The Case of the Hälsinge Law." In *Liber Amicorum Ditlev Tamm: Law, History and Culture*, ed. Per Andersen et al., pp. 71–74. Copenhagen: Djøf.

Brink, Stefan. 2011b. "Oral Fragments in The Earliest Old-Swedish Laws?" In *Medieval Legal Process: Physical, Spoken and Written Performance in the Middle Ages*, ed. Marco Mostert and Paul S. Barnwell, pp. 147–56. Utrecht Studies in Medieval Literacy 22. Turnhout: Brepols.

Brink, Stefan. 2012. *Vikingarnas slavar: Den nordiska träldomen under yngre järnålder och äldsta medeltid*. Stockhom: Atlantis.

Brink, Stefan. 2013a. "The Creation of a Scandinavian Provincial Law: How Was It Done?" *Historical Research* 86/233: 432–42.

Brink, Stefan. 2013b. "Early Ecclesiastical Organization of Scandinavia, Especially Sweden." In *Medieval Christianity in the North*, ed. Kirsi Salonen, Kurt Villads Jensen and Torstein Jørgensen, pp. 23–39. Turnhout: Brepols.

Brink, Stefan. 2014a. "*Minnunga mæn*: The Usage of Old Knowledgeable Men in Legal Cases." In Minni *and* Muninn: *Memory in Medieval Nordic Culture*, ed. Pernille Hermann, Stephen A. Mitchell and Agnes S. Arnórsdóttir, pp. 197–210. Acta Scandinavica. Aberdeen Studies in the Scandinavian World 4. Turnhout: Brepols.

Brink, Stefan. 2014b. "Bryten." In *Medeltida storgårdar: 15 uppsatser om ett tvärvetenskapligt forskningsproblem*, ed. Olof Karsvall and Kristofer Jupiter, pp. 73–82. Acta Academiae Regiae Gustavi Adolphi 131. Uppsala: Kungl. Gustav Adolfs akademien för svensk folkkultur.

Brink, Stefan and Lisa Collinson, eds. 2014. *New Approaches to Early Law in Scandinavia*. Turnhout: Brepols.

Brink, Stefan. 2016. "Sockenbildningen i Sverige. Forskningsläget 25 år senare." In *Den svenska socknen*, ed. Carl Henrik Carlsson, pp. 23–35. Riksarkivets årsbok 2016. Stockholm: Riksarkivet.

Brink, Stefan. Forthcoming. *The Law of the Hälsingar:* Hälsingelagen: *A translation from Old Swedish with an Introduction and Commentary*. Medieval Nordic Laws.

Brink, Stefan, Oliver Grimm, Frode Iversen, Halldis Hobæk, Marie Ødegaard, Ulf Näsman, Alexandra Sanmark, Przemyslaw Urbanczyk, Orri Vésteinsson and Inger Storli. 2011. "Court Sites of Arctic Norway: Remains of Thing Sites and Representations of Political Consolidation Processes in the Northern Germanic World during the First Millennium AD?" *Norwegian Archaeological Review* 44.1: 89–117.

Baetke, Walter. 1942. *Das Heilige im Germanischen*. Tübingen: Mohr.

Calissendorff, Karin. 1964. "Helgö." *Namn och Bygd* 52: 105–51.

Calissendorff, Karin. 1995. "Ortnamn och rättshistoria: Två praktiska exempel." *Saga och sed* 1995: 49–60.

Carlsson, Lizzie. 1934. "De medeltida skamstraffen. Ett stycke svensk kulturhistoria." *Rig* 17: 121–50.

Carlsson, Lizzie. 1942. "Nyckeln som rättslig symbol." *Rig* 25: 81–99.

Carlsson, Lizzie. 1965. *"Jag giver dig min dotter": Trolovning och äktenskap i den svenska kvinnans äldre historia*. Skrifter utgivna av Institutet för rättshistorisk forskning. Serien 1: Rättshistoriskt bibliotek 8. Stockholm: Nordiska Bokhandeln.

Cathey, James E. 1978. Review of "Gotlands stavgardar: En ortnamnsstudie" by Ingemar Olsson. *Scandinavian Studies* 50.2: 218–20.

Cederschiöld, Gustaf. 1887. "Studier öfver isländska Kyrkomåldagar från Fristatstiden." *Aarbøger for nordisk oldkyndighed og historie* 2: 1–72.

Christensen, Carl Andreas. 1983. "*Begrebet bol*. Et vidnesbyrd om vikingetidens storbondesamfund." *Historisk tidsskrift* (Copenhagen) 83: 1–34.

Clover, Carol. 1986. "Maiden Warriors and Other Sons." *Journal of English and Germanic Philology* 85: 35–49.

Clover, Carol. 1993. "Regardless of Sex: Men, Women and Power." *Speculum* 68.2: 363–87.

Clunies Ross, Margaret. 1985. "Concubinage in Anglo-Saxon England." *Past & Present* 108: 3–34.

Collin, Peter Hodgson. 1989. *English Law Dictionary: Engelsk-svensk-engelsk*. Stockholm: Esselte ordbok.

Crawford, Barbara E. 2013. *The Northern Earldoms: Orkney and Caithness form AD 870 to 1470*. Edinburgh: John Donald.

CV = Cleasby, Richard, Guðbrandur Vigfússon and William A. Craigie. 1975. *An Icelandic-English Dictionary*. 2nd ed. Oxford: Clarendon.

Dalberg, Vibeke and John Kousgård Sørensen, 1984. "Bygd og herred og bygdeherred." *Namn och Bygd* 1984: 76–89.

Debes, Hans Jacob. 1995. *Føroya søga. 2, Skattland og len*. Tórshavn: Føroya Skúlabókagrunnur.

Debes Joensen, Høgni and Jens Peder Hart Hansen. 1973. "Dráp og frásagnir um dráp í Føroyum." *Fróðskaparrit* 21: 72–85.

Descheemaeker, Eric. 2009. *The Division of Wrongs: A Historical Comparative Study.* Oxford: Oxford University Press.

DMA = Strayer, Joseph R., ed. 1982–89. *Dictionary of the Middle Ages.* 13 vols. New York: Scribner.

Dovring, Folke. 1947a. "'Gilzla oc grutha' i Smålandslagen." *Arkiv för nordisk filologi* 62: 258–60.

Dovring, Folke, 1947b. "Attungen och marklandet: studier över agrara förhållanden i medeltidens Sverige." PhD Diss. Lund University.

Dybdahl, Audun and Jørn Sandnes, eds. 1996. *Nordiske middelalderlover: Tekst og kontekst; Rapport fra seminar ved Senter for middelalderstudier 29.–30. nov. 1996.* Skrifter - Senter for middelalderstudier 5. Trondheim: Tapir.

Dübeck, Inger. 2003a. "Voldtægtsforbrydelsen i retshistorisk belysning." *Historisk Tidsskrift* (Copenhagen) 2003: 53–81.

Dübeck, Inger. 2003b. *Kvinder, familie og formue: Studier i dansk og europæisk retshistorie.* Copenhagen: Museum Tusculanum.

Dübeck, Inger. 2012. "Concubinage and Marriage in Denmark between the Viking Age and the Reformation. A Comparison between Danish and European Medieval Law." In *Law and Marriage in Medieval and Early Modern Times: Proceedings of the Eighth Carlsberg Academy Conference on Medieval Legal History 2011,* ed. Per Andersen et al., pp. 111–25. Copenhagen: DJØF.

Du Cange et al. 1883–87. *Glossarium mediae et infimae latinitatis.* Niort: L. Favre.

Dufeu, Val. (forthcoming). "Researching the Emergence of Commercial Fishing in Iceland & the Faroes: Sagas & Archives."

Dyrhaug, Sverre. 2012. "Kjøp, kreditt og kontanter i utenrikshandel på 1300-tallet." *Collegium Medievale* 25: 41–66.

Düwel, Klaus. 1975. "Runische Zeugnisse zu 'Bauer'." In *Wort und Begriff 'Bauer',* ed. Reinhard Wenskus, Herbert Jankuhn and Klaus Grinda, pp. 180–206. Göttingen: Vandenhoeck & Ruprecht.

Ebel, Else. 1993. *Der Konkubinat nach altwestnordischen Quellen Philologische Studien zur sogenannten „Friedelehe".* Berlin: de Gruyter.

Ehrhardt, Harald. 1977. *Der Stabreim in altnordischen Rechtstexten.* Skandinavistische Arbeiten 2. Heidelberg: Winter.

Einar Arnórsson. 1945. *Réttarsaga alþingis.* Reykjavík: Alþingissögunefnd.

Einzig, Paul. 1966. *Primitive Money in its Ethnological, Historical and Economic Aspects.* 2nd ed. Oxford: Pergamon.

Ejdestam, Julius. 1946. "Omfärd vid besittningstagande av jordegendom." *Svenska Landsmål* 69: 86–114.

Ekholst, Christine. 2009. *För varje brottsling ett straff: Föreställningar om kön i de svenska medeltidslagarna.* Stockholm: Historiska institutionen, Stockholms universitet.

Ekholst, Christine. 2014. *A Punishment for Each Criminal: Gender and Crime in Swedish Medieval Law.* Leiden: Brill.

Eliasson, Per and Gustaf Hamilton. 1999."'Blifver ondt att förena sigh'– några linjer i den svenska skogslagstiftningen om utmark och skog." In *Skogshistorisk forskning i Europa och Nordamerika. Vad är skogshistoria? Hur har den skrivits och varför,* ed. Ronny Pettersson, pp. 47–106. Skogs- och lantbrukshistoriska meddelanden 22. Stockholm: Kungl. Skogs- och Lantbruksakademien.

Elmevik, Lennart. 1967. *Nordiska ord på äldre kāk- och kā(k)s: En etymologisk och ljudhistorisk undersökning.* Skrifter utg. av Institutionen för nordiska språk vid Uppsala universitet 15. Uppsala: Institutionen för nordiska språk vid Uppsala universitet.

Engeler, Sigrid. 1991. *Altnordische Geldwörter.* Germanistische Arbeiten zu Sprache und Kulturgeschichte 16. Frankfurt am Main: Peter Lang.

Ericsson, Alf. 2007. *Attungen - ett medeltida fastighetsmått: En agrarhistorisk undersökning baserad på attungsbelägg i SDhk till år 1376 och Folke Dovrings kasuistik.* Uppsala: Department of Economy, Swedish University of Agricultural Sciences, http://urn.kb.se/resolve?urn=urn:nbn:se:slu:epsilon-1896

Ericsson, Alf, ed. 2008. *Jordvärderingssystem från medeltiden till 1600-talet*. Stockholm: Kungl. Vitterhets historie och antikvitets akademien.

Ericsson, Alf. 2008b. "Attungen under äldre medeltid." In *Jordvärderingssystem från medeltiden till 1600-talet*, ed. Alf Ericsson, pp. 39–63. Stockholm: Kungl. Vitterhets historie och antikvitets akademien.

Ericsson, Alf. 2012. Terra mediaevalis*: Jordvärderingssystem i medeltidens Sverige*. Uppsala: Swedish University of Agricultural Sciences, http://urn.kb.se/resolve?urn=urn:nbn:se:slu:epsilon-e-705

Esmark, Kim, Lars Hermanson, Hans Jacob Orning and Helle Vogt, eds. 2013. *Disputing Strategies in Medieval Scandinavia*. Medieval Law and its Practice 16. Leiden: Brill.

Falk, Hjalmar. 1919. *Altwestnordische Kleiderkunde mit besonderer Berücksichtigung der Terminologie*. Videnskapsselskapets Skrifter 4. Hist.-filos. Klasse. 1918 nr 3. Kristiania: Jacob Dybwad.

Fix, Hans. 1984. *Wortschatz der Jónsbók*. Texte und Untersuchungen zur Germanistik und Skandinavistik 8. Frankfurt am Main: Peter Lang.

Foote, Peter G. 1984. "Things in Early Norse Verse." In *Festskrift til Ludvig Holm-Olsen på hans 70-årsdagen den 9. juli 1984*, ed. Bjarne Fidjestøl et al., pp. 74-83. Øvre Ervik: Alvheim & Eide.

Foote, Peter Godfrey. 2003. *1117 in Iceland and England*. The Dorothea Coke Memorial Lecture in Northern Studies delivered at University College London 14 March 2002. London: Viking Society for Northern Research.

Fritzner = Fritzner, Johan. 1883–96 [repr. 1954, 1973]. *Ordbog over Det gamle norske Sprog*. 1–3. 4 Rettelser og tillegg ved Finn Hødnebø 1972. Oslo – Bergen – Tromsø: Universitetsforlaget.

"Förvaltningshistorisk ordbok." In *Svenska litteratursällskapet i Finland*, http://fho.sls.fi

Gade, Kari Ellen. 1985. "Hanging in the Northern Law and Literature." *Maal og Minne* 1985.3–4: 159–83.

Gammeltoft, Peder. 2001. *The Place-Name Element* bólstaðr *in the North Atlantic Area*. Copenhagen: C. A. Reitzel.

GAO = Brather, Sebastian, Wilhelm Heizmann and Steffen Patzold, eds. *Germanische Altertumskunde Online*. De Gruyter, http://www.degruyter.com/view/db/gao]

Gelsinger, Bruce E. 1981. *Icelandic Enterprise: Commerce and Economy in the Middle Ages*. Columbia, SC: University of South Carolina Press.

Genzmer, Felix. 1950. "Die germanische Sippe als Rechtsgebilde." *Zeitschrift der Savigny-Stiftung für Rechtsgeschichte: Germanistische Abteilung* 67: 34–49.

Gerhold, Wolfgang. 2002. *Armut und Armenfürsorge im mittelalterlichen Island*. Skandinavistische Arbeiten 18. Heidelberg: Winter.

Gísli Pálsson and E. Paul Durrenberger. 1987. "Ownership at Sea: Fishing Territories and Access to Sea Resources." *American Ethnologist* 14.3: 508–22.

Gísli Pálsson and E. Paul Durrenberger. 1996. *Images of Contemporary Iceland: Everyday Lives and Global Contexts*. Iowa City: University of Iowa Press.

Goetting, Lauren. 2006. "*Þegn* and *drengr* in the Viking Age." *Scandinavian Studies* 78.4: 375–404.

Grönberg, Lennart. 1991. *Nordisk rättshistorisk litteratur 1976–1980: En bibliografisk förteckning*. Skrifter utgivna av Institutet för rättshistorisk forskning. Serien 1: Rättshistoriskt bibliotek 45. Stockholm: Nordiska Bokhandeln.

Guðrún Ása Grímsdóttir. 2015. "A Medieval Prenuptial Agreement." In *66 Manuscripts from the Arnamagnæan Collection*, ed. Matthew James Driscoll and Svanhildur Óskarsdóttir, p. 136. Copenhagen: Museum Tusculanum.

Gunnar Jónsson. 1987. "Waldgang und Lebensringzaun (Landesverweisung) im älteren isländischen Recht: Verfahren, Erscheinungsformen und Strafgründe der Friedloslegung nach der Graugans und in den Sagas." (Unpublished doctoral thesis, University of Hamburg).

Gunnar Karlsson. 2005. "Social Institutions." In *A Companion to Old Norse-Icelandic Literature and Culture*, ed. Rory McTurk, pp. 503–17. Oxford: Blackwell.

Guth, DeLloyd J. 2002–3. "Why Pay Your Debts? Medieval Iceland's Answers." *Georgia Journal of International and Comparative Law* 31: 65–77.

Guttesen, Rolf. 1999. "On the Oldest Territorial Division of the Faeroe Islands." *Fróðskaparrit* 47: 139–52.

Göransson, Sölve. 1961. "Regular Open Field Pattern in England and Scandinavian solskifte." *Geografiska annaler* 43: 80–104.

Göransson, Sölve. 1971. *Tomt och teg på Öland: om byamål, laga läge och territoriell indelning*. Forskningsrapporter från Kulturgeografiska institutionen 27. Uppsala: Uppsala universitet.

Göransson. Sölve. 1976. "Solskifte: The Definition of a Confused Concept." In *Fields, Farms and Settlement in Europe: Papers Presented at a Symposium, Belfast, July 12–15, 1971*, ed. Ronald Hull Buchanan, Robin Alan Butlin and Desmond McCourt, 2nd ed., pp. 22–37. Holywood: Ulster Folk and Transport Museum.

Hafström Gerhard 1949a. *Ledung och marklandsindelning*. Uppsala: Almqvist and Wiksell.

Hafström, Gerhard 1949b. "Sockenindelningens ursprung." In *Historiska studier tillägnade Nils Ahnlund 23/8/1949*, ed. Åke Stille and Sven Grauers, pp. 51–67. Stockholm: Norstedt.

Hafström, Gerhard. 1951. "Hamarskipt." Skrifter utgivna av Institutet för rättshistorisk forskning. Lund.

Hafström, Gerhard, 1970. *Land och lag*. 4th rev. ed. Uppsala: Almqvist & Wiksell.

Hagland, Jan Ragnar. 2011. "Frå landskapslov til landslov." *Maal og Minne* 103.2: 52–66.

Halldór Hermannsson, 1966. *Illuminated Manuscripts of the Jónsbók*. Islandica 28. New York: Kraus.

Hansen, Lars Ivar. 2011. "Norwegian, Swedish and Russian 'taxlands' in the North." In *Taxes, Tributes and Tributary Lands in the Making of the Scandinavian Kingdoms in the Middle Ages*, ed. Steinar Imsen, pp. 295–330. Trondheim: Tapir.

Hasselberg, Gösta. 1948. "Om Smålandslagens inledningsord." *Saga och sed* 1948: 44–52.

Hasselberg, Gösta. 1953. *Studier rörande Visby stadslag och dess källor*. Uppsala: Almqvist and Wiksell.

Hastrup, Kirsten. 1985. *Culture and History in Medieval Iceland. An Anthropological Analysis of Structure and Change*. Oxford: Clarendon.

Hastrup, Kirsten. 1992. "Uchronia and the Two Histories of Iceland, 1400–1800." In *Other Histories*, ed. Kirsten Hastrup, pp. 102–20. London: Routledge.

Hastrup, Kirsten. 2006. "Closing Ranks: Fundamentals in History, Politics and Anthropology." *Australian Journal of Anthropology* 17.2: 147–60.

Haubrichs, Wolfgang. 2014. "Baiovarii, Romani and Others. Language, Names and Groups South of the River Danube and in the Eastern Alps during the Early Middle Ages." In *The Baiuvarii and Thuringi: An Ethnographic Perspective*, ed. Janine Fries-Knoblach and Heiko Steuer, pp. 23–81. Woodbridge: Boydell.

Hedeager, Lotte 2011. *Iron Age Myth and Materiality. An Archaeology of Scandinavia AD 400–1000*. London: Routledge.

Heggstad, Leiv, Finn Hødnebø, and Erik Simensen. 2012. *Norrøn ordbok*. 5th ed. Oslo: Det Norske Samlaget.

Helgi Skúli Kjartansson. 1988. "Serkneskt silfur í Grágás." In *Saga og kirkja. Afmælisrit Magnúsar Más Lárussonar*, ed. Gunnar Karlsson, Jón Hnefill Aðalsteinsson and Jónas Gíslason, pp. 43–57. Reykjavík: Sögufélag.

Helgi Þorláksson. 1991. *Vaðmál og verðlag: Vaðmál í utanlandsviðskiptum og búskap Íslendinga á 13. og 14. öld*. Reykjavík: Fjörföldun Sigurjóns.

Helgi Þorláksson. 2005. "Historical Background: Iceland 870–1400." In *A Companion to Old Norse-Icelandic Literature and Culture*, ed. Rory McTurk, pp. 136–54. Oxford: Blackwell Publishing.

Helgi Þorláksson. 2011. "Ambitious Kings and Unwilling Farmers: On the Difficulties of Introducing a Royal Tax in Iceland." In *Taxes, Tributes and Tributary Lands in the Making of the Scandinavian Kingdoms in the Middle Ages*, ed. Steinar Imsen, pp. 133–49. Trondheim: Tapir.

Helle, Knut. 2001. *Gulatinget og Gulatingslova*. Leikanger: Skald.

Helle, Knut. 1972. *Konge og gode menn i norsk riksstyring ca. 1150–1319*. Bergen: Universitetsforlaget.

Hellquist = Hellquist, Elof. 1964. *Svensk etymologisk ordbok*. 3rd ed. Lund: Gleerup.

Hertzberg, Ebbe. 1889. "Tvivlsomme ord i Norges gamle love." *Arkiv för nordisk filologi* 5: 223–44.

Hertzberg, Ebbe. 1890. "Efterskrift angaaende tvivlsomme ord i Norges gamle love." *Arkiv för nordisk filologi* 7: 262–71.

Heusler, Andreas. 1911. *Das Strafrecht der Isländersagas*. Leipzig: Duncker u. Humblot.

Hjärne, Erland. 1947. "Roden: Upphovet och namnet; Området och jarlen." *Namn och Bygd* 35: 1–96.

Hjärne, Erland. 1980–81. *Land och ledung: Ur Erland Hjärnes historiska författarskap*, ed. Gösta Åqvist. 2 vols. Skrifter utgivna av Institutet för rättshistorisk forskning. Serien 1: Rättshistoriskt bibliotek 31–32. Stockholm: Nordiska Bokhandeln.

Hobæk, Halldis. 2013. "Tracing Medieval Administrative Systems: Hardanger, Western Norway." *Journal of the North Atlantic* 5: 64–75.

Hoff, Annette. 1997. *Lov og landskab: Landskabslovenes bidrag til forståelsen af landsbrugs- og landskabsudviklingen i Danmark ca. 900–1250*. Århus: Aarhus universitetsforlag.

Hoff, Annette. 2006. *Recht und Landschaft. Der Beitrag der Landschaftsrechte zum Verständnis der Landwirtschafts- und Landschaftsentwicklung in Dänemark ca. 900–1250*. Ergänzungsbände zum Reallexikon der Germanischen Altertumskunde 54. Berlin: De Gruyter.

Hoff, Hans Henning. 2012. *Hafliði Másson und die Einflüsse des römischen Rechts in der Grágás*. Ergänzungsbände zum Reallexikon der Germanischen Altertumskunde 78. Berlin: De Gruyter.

Hollander, Lee, 1916. "Notes on the 'Nornagests þáttr'." *Publications of the Society for the Advancement of Scandinavian Study* 3.2: 105–11.

Holm, Olof. 2003 "Den norsk-svenska riksgränsens ålder och hävd: en studie av rikssamlingsprocesser och gränsbildning i mellersta Skandinavien." *Collegium Medievale* 16: 135–237.

Holmberg, Bengt. 1946. *Tomt och toft som appellativ och ortnamnselement. Studier till en svensk ortnamnsatlas*. Uppsala: Appelberg.

Holmberg, Karl Axel. 1969. *De svenska tuna-namnen*. PhD Diss. Uppsala University.

Holmbäck, Åke. 1919. *Ätten och arvet enligt Sveriges medeltidslagar*. Uppsala: Almqvist and Wiksell.

Holmbäck, Åke. 1920. *Studier över de svenska allmänningarnas historia I. Rättsreglerna för intaga av jord vid den fasta bosättningen. Uppkomsten av särskilda slag av allmänningar. Uppsala universitets årsskrift. Juridik. I*. Uppsala: Almqvist and Wiksell.

Holmblad, Lars G. 1993. *Eriksgatan från medeltid till nutid*. Stockholm: Carlsson.

Horstrup, Paul. 1963. "Snob." *Zeitschrift für deutsche Wortforschung* 19: 64–74.

Imsen, Steinar. 2009. "Den gammelnorske drapsprosessen." *Historisk tidsskrift* (Oslo) 88.2: 185–229.

Imsen, Steinar, ed. 2011. *Taxes, Tributes and Tributary Lands in the Making of the Scandinavia Kingdoms in the Middle Ages*. Trondheim studies in history. 'Norgesveldet', Occasional Papers 2. Trondheim: Tapir.

Imsen, Steinar, ed. 2013. *Legislation and State Formation: Norway and its Neighbours in the Middle Ages*. Trondheim studies in history. 'Norgesveldet', Occasional Papers 4. Oslo: Akademika.

Imsen, Steinar. 2014. "Royal Dominion in the 'Skattlands'." In *Rex Insularum: The King of Norway and His 'Skattlands' as a Political System c. 1260–c. 1450*, ed. Steinar Imsen, pp. 35–99. Bergen: Fagbokforlaget.

Inger, Göran. 1999. "Kanonisk och inhemsk rätt under biskop Brynolf Algotssons tid." *Kyrkohistorisk årsskrift* 99: 9–16.

Inger, Göran. 1999. "Skänninge möte 1248 ur rättshistorisk synpunkt." *Årsbok Kungl. Humanistiska vetenskaps-samfundet i Uppsala* 1999: 177–95.

Inger, Göran. 2011. *Svensk rättshistoria*. 5th ed. Malmö: Liber.

Iversen, Tore. 1997. *Trelldommen: Norsk slaveri i middelalderen*. Historisk insitutt, Universitetet i Bergen. Skrifter 1. Bergen: Historisk Institutt, Univ. i Bergen.

Iversen, Tore, ed. 2011. *Archbishop Eystein as Legislator: The European Connection*. Trondheim: Tapir.

Jacoby, Michael. 1986. *Germanisches Recht und Rechtssprache zwischen Mittelalter und Neuzeit unter besonderer Berücksichtigung des skandinavischen Rechts: Gegenthese zu J. Grimm und zur romantischen Auffassung im 20. Jh.* Lexemdistribution und Lexemverhalten in Textsorten und Dialekten innerhalb historischer Sprachstufen 1. New York: Peter Lang.

Janson, Svante. 2011. "The Icelandic Calendar." *Scripta Islandica* 62: 51–104.

Jesch, Judith, ed. 2002. *Scandinavians from the Vendel Period to the Tenth Century*. Studies in Historical Archaeoethnology 5. Woodbridge: Boydell.

Jochens, Jenny. 1993. "Gender Symmetry in Law? The Case of Medieval Iceland." *Arkiv för nordisk filologi* 108: 46–67.

Jochens, Jenny. 2001. "Representations of Skalds in the Sagas 2: Gender Relations." In *Skaldsaga: Text, Vocation and Desire in the Icelandic Sagas of Poets*, ed. Russell Poole, pp. 309–32. Berlin: De Gruyter.

Johansson, Marie. 1998. "Att stämma till ting: Om rättegångssystemet i Östgötalagen." *Scandia* 64: 161–93, 325–26.

Johnsen, Oscar Albert. 1912. "Ord- og sagregister." In *Norges gamle Love: Anden række, 1388–1604*, ed. Absalon Taranger, vol. 1. Christiania: Grøndahl and søn.

Jón Helgason. 1952. "Nøkur orð aftrat um kongsbókina." *Útiseti* 7: 113–15.

Jón Hnefill Aðalsteinsson. 1986–89. "The Position of Freed Slaves in Medieval Iceland." *Saga-Book* 22: 33–49.

Jón Jóhannesson. 2006. *A History of the Old Icelandic Commonwealth*. Trans. Haraldur Bessason. Winnipeg: University of Manitoba Press.

Jón Viðar Sigurðsson. 1995. "The Icelandic Aristocracy after the Fall of the Free State." *Scandinavian Journal of History* 20.3: 153–66.

Jón Viðar Sigurðsson. 1999. *Chieftains and Power in the Icelandic Commonwealth*. Trans. Jean Lundskær-Nielsen. Odense: Odense University Press.

Jón Viðar Sigurðsson. 2011a. "Kings, Earls and Chieftains: Rulers in Norway, Orkney and Iceland c. 900–1300." In *Ideology and Power in the Viking and Middle Ages*, ed. Gro Steinsland et al., pp. 69–108. Leiden: Brill.

Jón Viðar Sigurðsson. 2011b. "Skattlandet Island: Fra høvdingmakt til kongemakt." In *Nordens plass i middelalderens nye Europa: Samfunnsomdanning, sentralmakt og periferier*, ed. Lars Ivar Hansen, Richard Holt and Steinar Imsen, pp. 89–104. Tromsø: Orkana.

Jón Viðar Sigurðsson. 2012. "The Organisation of Hólar Bishopric According to Auðunarmáldagar." In *'Ecclesia Nidrosiensis' and 'Noregs veldi'*, ed. Steinar Imsen, pp. 243–59. Bergen: Fagbokforlaget.

Jón Viðar Sigurðsson. 2014. "The Making of a 'Skattland': Iceland 1247–1450." In *Rex Insularum: The King of Norway and His 'Skattlands' as a Political System c. 1260–c.1450*, ed. Steinar Imsen, pp. 181–225. Bergen: Fagbokforlaget.

Jón Viðar Sigurðsson. 2015. "Kongemakt og lokalsamfunn på Island ca. 1260–1450." *Heimen* 1: 17–24.

Jones, Gwyn. 1940. "Fjörbaugsgarðr" *Medium Ævum* IX, 155–63.

Juel, Christian. 2009. *Den Fynske Landbebyggelse 950–1350 e.kr.: En komparativ analyse af arkæologiske kilder og middelalderens landskabslove*. Specialeoversigt 2009. Copenhagen: Forhistorisk Arkæologi, Københavns Universitet.

Jurasinski, Stefan. 2002. "Reddatur Parentibus: The Vengeance of the Family in Cnut's Homicide Legislation." *Law and History Review* 20.1: 157–180.

Jörgensen, Nils. 1987. *Studier över syntax och textstruktur i nordiska medeltidslagar*. Samlingar utgivna av Svenska fornskriftsällskapet 76. Uppsala: Svenska fornskriftsällskapet.

Jørgensen, Poul Johannes. 2007. *Dansk strafferet fra reformationen til Danske Lov*, ed. Ditlev Tamm and Helle Vogt. Copenhagen: Jurist- og Økonomforbundet.

Jørgensen, Torstein. 2014. "Civil and Clerical Homicide in Late Medieval Norway." In *New Approaches to Early Law in Scandinavia*, ed. Stefan Brink and Lisa Collinson, pp. 67–87. Turnhout: Brepols.

Kadane, Joseph and Ferdinand Næshagen. 2013. "The Number of Killings in Southern Rural Norway 1300–1569." *Annals of Applied Statistics* 7.2: 846–59, https://doi.org/10.1214/12-aoas612

Kalkar, Otto. 1881–1918. *Ordbog til det ældre danske sprog, 1300–1700*. 5 vols. Copenhagen: Thiele.

Kardell, Lars. 2003. "Det medeltida skogsbruket (1200–1600)." In *Svenskarna och skogen 1. Jönköping: Från ved till linjeskepp*. Jönköping: Skogsstyrelsen.

Karras, Ruth Mazo. 1988. *Slavery and Society in Medieval Scandinavia*. New Haven: Yale University Press.

Keyser, Rudolf. 1856. *Den norske Kirkes Historie under Katholicismen*. Christiania: Chr. Tønsberg.

Kilger, Christoph . 2008. "Wholeness and Holiness: Counting, Weighing and Valuing Silver in the Early Viking Period." In *Means of Exchange: Dealing with Silver in the Viking Age*, ed. Dagfinn Skre, pp. 253–325. Kaupang Excavation Project. Publication Series, vol. 2. Norske Oldfunn XXIII. Århus: Aarhus University Press.

Kjus, Audun. 2011. *Død som straff i middelalderen*. Oslo: Unipub.

Kleiva, Ivar. 1985. *Gulatinget: Tingstader og Lovverk*. Bergen: Norsk Bokreidingslag.

KLNM = *Kulturhistorisk leksikon for nordisk middelalder fra vikingetid til reformationstid = Kulturhistorisk leksikon for nordisk middelalder fra vikingtid til reformasjonstid = Kulturhistoriskt lexikon för nordisk medeltid från vikingatid till reformationstid*. 1980–82. 2nd ed. 22 vols. Copenhagen: Rosenkilde og Bagger.

Kock, Ebbe. 1926. *Om hemföljd (förtida arv) i svensk rätt t.o.m 1734 års lag*. Lund: Ohlsson.

Kongsrud, Helge. 2011. *Det norske kanslerembetet: Kompetanse, funksjoner, arkivdannelse og overleveringsveier*. Oslo: Riksarkivaren.

Konráð Gíslason. 1881. "Nogle Bemærkinger angående Ynglingatal." *Aarbøger for nordisk oldkyndighed og historie* 1881: 185–251.

Korpiola, Mia. 2004. *Between Betrothal and Bedding: The Making of Marriage in Sweden, ca. 1200–1610*. Vantaa: Mia Korpiola.

Korpiola, Mia. 2011. *Regional Variations in Matrimonial Law and Custom in Europe, 1150–1600*. Leiden: Brill.

Krag, Claus. 2008. "The Creation of Norway." In *The Viking World*, ed. Stefan Brink and Neil Price, pp. 645–51. London: Routledge.

Kværness, Gunhild. 1996. *Blote kan ein gjere om det berre skjer i løynd: Kristenrettane i Gulatingslova og Grágás og forholdet mellom dei*. KULTs skriftserie 65. Oslo: Noregs forskingsråd.

Landro, Torgeir. 2010. "Kristenrett og kyrkjerett: Borgartingskristenretten i eit komparativt perspektiv". Bergen. PhD Diss. Universitetet i Bergen.

Larsson, Gabriela Bjarne. 2010. *Laga fång för medeltidens kvinnor och män: Skriftbruk, jordmarknader och monetarisering i Finnveden och Jämtland 1300–1500*. Serien 1: Rättshistoriskt bibliotek 66. Stockholm: Institutet för rättshistorisk forskning.

Larsson, Gabriela Bjarne. 2012. "Wives or Widows and their Representatives." *Scandinavian Journal of History* 37.1: 49–68.

Larsson, Inger. 2009. *Pragmatic Literacy and the Mediecal Use of the Vernacular. The Swedish Example.* Turnhout: Brepols.

Larsson, Inger. 2010. "The Role of the Swedish Lawman in the Spread of Lay Literacy." In *Along the Oral-Written Continuum: Types of Texts, Relations and their Implications*, ed. Slávica Rankovic, pp. 411–27. Utrecht Studies in Medieval Literacy 20. Turnhout: Brepols.

Larsson, Mats G. 1987. *Hamnor, husbyar och ledung.* Lund: University of Lund, Hist. museet.

Larsson, Mats. G. 1988. "Folkland och folkvapen." *Fornvännen* 83: 224–33.

Latham & Howlett = Latham, Ronald Edward and D. R. Howlett. 1975–2013. *Dictionary of Medieval Latin From British Sources.* 17 vols. Oxford: Oxford University Press.

Lawing, Sean. 2013. "The Place of the Evil: Infant Abandonment in Old Norse Society." *Scandinavian Studies* 85.2: 133–50.

LexMA = *Lexikon des Mittelalters.* 2013. 9 vols. Munich: Metzler.

Lindkvist, Thomas. 1979. *Landborna i Norden under äldre medeltid.* Uppsala: Almqvist and Wiksell.

Lindkvist, Thomas. 1989. "Skatter och stat i den tidiga medeltidens Sverige." In *Medeltidens födelse*, ed. Anders Andrén, pp. 171–84. Nyhamnsläge: Gyllenstiernska Krapperupstift.

Lindkvist, Thomas, 1993, 1995. *Plundring, skatter och den feodala statens framväxt: Organisatoriska tendenser i Sverige under övergången från vikingatid till tidig medeltid.* Opuscula Historica Upsaliensia 1. Uppsala: Historiska Institutionen, Uppsala University.

Lindkvist, Thomas. 1998. "Kyrklig beskattning." In *Sveriges kyrkohistoria 1: missionstid och tidig medeltid*, ed. Bertil Nilsson, pp. 216–21. Stockholm: Verbum.

Lindkvist, Thomas. 2000. "Droit et genèse de l'État dans la Suède médiévale: Royauté et communautés." In *Justice et législation*, ed. Antonio Padoa-Schioppa, pp. 251–70. Paris: Presses universitaires de France.

Lindkvist, Thomas. 2007. "The *lagmän* (law-speakers) as a Regional Elite in Medieval Västergötland." In *Lés elites nordiques et l'Europe occidentale (XIIe–XVe siècle): Actes de la rencontre franco-nordique organisée à Paris, 9–10 juin 2005*, ed. Tuomas M. S. Lehtonen and Élisabeth Mornet, pp. 67–78. Publications de la Sorbonne. Histoire ancienne et médiévale 94. Paris: Publications de la Sorbonne, https://doi.org/10.4000/books.psorbonne.33115

Lindkvist, Thomas. 2008. "Kungamakten och skatterna." In *Jordvärderingssystem från medeltiden till 1600-talet*, ed. Alf Ericsson, pp. 163–75. Stockholm: Kungl. Vitterhets historie och antikvitets akademien.

Lindkvist, Thomas. 2009a. "Bonden i lagen." *Agrarhistoria på många sätt: 28 studier om människan och jorden; Festskrift till Janken Myrdal på hans 60-årsdag*, ed. Britt Liljewall et al., pp. 57–72. Stockholm: Kungl. Skogs- och Lantbruksakademien.

Lindkvist, Thomas. 2009b. "The Hälsingelag and Hälsingland as a Political Periphery." In *Itinéraires du savoir de l'Italie à la Scandinavie : Xe–XVIe siècle: Études offertes à Elisabeth Mornet*, ed. Corinne Péneau, pp. 137–47. Paris: Publications de la Sorbonne, https://doi.org/10.4000/books.psorbonne.11544

Lindkvist, Thomas. 2010. "I stället för ättesamhälle?" In *Gaver, ritualer, konflikter. Et rettsantropologisk perspektiv på nordisk middelalderhistorie*, ed. Hans Jacob Orning, Kim Esmark and Lars Hermanson, pp. 291–300. Oslo: Unipub.

Lindkvist, Thomas. 2013. "Individ och kollektiv: Kring allmänning i Äldre Västgötalagen." In *Berättelser från markerna: En antologi om järn, skog och kulturarv; En vänbok till Gert Magnusson*, ed. Ing-Marie Pettersson Jensen, Lena Berg Nilsson and Catarina Karlsson, pp. 177–82. Norberg: Bergslagens medeltidsmuseum.

Lindkvist, Thomas. 2013. "Västergötland as a Community and the Making of a Provincial Law." In *Legislation and State Formation: Norway and its Neighbours in the Middle Ages*, ed. Steinar Imsen, pp. 55–65. Oslo: Akademika.

Lindkvist, Thomas. Forthcoming. *The Västgöta Law I* (Äldre Västgötalagen), *II* (Yngre Västgötalagen). Medieval Nordic Laws.

Lindow, John. 1976. *Comitatus, Individual and Honor: Studies in North Germanic Institutional Vocabulary*. University of California Publications in Linguistics 83. Berkeley: Univ. of California Press.

Lithberg, Nils and Wessén, Elias. 1939. *Den gotländska runkalendern 1328*. Stockholm: Wahlström and Widstrand.

Ljungqvist, Fredrik Charpentier. 2005. "Heder och sexuellt våld: En undersökning av medeltida isländska källor." In *Hedersmord: Tusen år av hederskulturer*, ed. Kenneth Johansson, pp. 47–75. Lund: Historiska Media.

Lúðvík Ingvarsson. 1970. *Refsingar á Íslandi á þjóðveldistímanum*. Reykjavík: Menningarsjóður.

Lund, George F. V. 1967. *Det ældste danske skriftsprogs ordforråd: Ordbog til de gamle danske landskabslove, de sønderjyske stadsretter samt øvrige samtidige sprogmindesmærker; Fra omtr. 1200 til 1300*. Copenhagen: Københavns Universitets Fond.

Lund, Niels, 1966. *Lið, leding og landsværn*. Roskilde.

Lundberg, Birger, 1972. *Territoriell indelning och skatt i Uppland under medeltiden*. Kungl. Vitterhets Historie och Antikvitetsakademien. Historiska serien 28. Stockholm.

Lundbye, J. T. 1933. "Danmarks veje i oltid og middelalder." In *Nordisk kultur: samlingsverk. 16. B. Handel och samfärdsel under medeltiden*, ed. Adolf Schück, pp. 200–16. Stockholm: Bonnier.

Lunden, Kare. 1999. "Money Economy in Medieval Norway." *Scandinavian Journal of History* 24.3–4: 245–65.

Lýður Björnsson. 1972–79. *Saga sveitarstjórnar á Íslandi*. 2 vols. Reykjavík: Almenna.

Lynch, Joseph H. 1998. *Christianizing Kinship – Ritual Sponsorship in Anglo-Saxon England*. Ithaca, N. Y.: Cornell University Press.

Lönnroth, Erik. 1940. *Statsmakt och statsfinans I det medeltida Sverige: studier över skatteväsen och länsförvaltning*. Göteborgs högskolas årsskrift 46:3. Göteborg: Wettergren & Kerber.

Maček, Dora. 2009. "Law Terms in Saga and Translation." In *Analecta Septentrionalia: Beiträge zur nordgermanischen Kultur- und Literaturgeschichte*, ed. Wilhelm Heizmann, Klaus Böldl and Heinrich Beck, pp. 238–55. Reallexikon der Germanischen Altertumskunde – Ergänzungsbände 65. Berlin, New York: De Gruyter.

Magnús Már Lárusson. 1956. "Biskupskjör á Íslandi." *Andvari* 81: 87–100.

Magnús Már Lárusson. 1967. *Fróðleiksþættir og sögubrot*. Reykjavík: Alþýðuprentsmiðjan.

Magnús Már Lárusson. 1971. "Á höfuðbólum landsins." *Saga* 9: 40–90.

Már Jónsson and Patricia Pires Boulhosa. 2011. "Tithe and Tribute in Thirteenth-Century Iceland." In *Taxes, Tributes and Tributary Lands in the Making of the Scandinavian Kingdoms in the Middle Ages*, ed. Steinar Imsen, pp. 151–63. Trondheim: Tapir.

Marold, Edith. 2007. "*Mansǫngr* – a Phantom Genre?" In *Learning and Understanding in the Old Norse World: Essays in Honour of Margaret Clunies Ross*, ed. Judy Quinn, Kate Heslop and Tarrin Wills, pp. 239–62. Turnhout: Brepols.

Maurer, Konrad von. 1890. "Reksþegn." *Arkiv för nordisk filologi* 7: 272–80.

Maurer, Konrad von. 1908. *Vorlesungen über altnordische Kirchenverfassung und Eherecht*. Leipzig: A. Deichert.

Maurer, Konrad von. 1910. *Altisländisches Strafrecht und Gerichtswesen*. Leipzig: A. Deichert.

Maurer, Konrad von. 1968. *Das älteste Hofrecht des Nordens: Eine Festschrift, zur Feier des vierhundertjährigen Bestehens der Universität Uppsala im Auftrage des akademischen Senates der Ludwig-Maximilians-Universität zu München verfaßt*. Aalen: Scientia-Verl.

Meissner, Rudolf. 1935. "Einleitung." In *Norwegisches Recht: Das Rechtsbuch des Gulathings*, trans. Rudolf Meissner, pp. XVIII–XXVII. Weimar.

Meissner, Rudolf. 1938. *Das norwegische Gefolgschaftsrecht. (Hirðskrá).* Germanenrechte 5. Weimar: Böhlau.

Midderhoff, Hanns. 1937. *Untersuchungen zur Stellung der germanischen Frau im altnordischen Konsens- und Fehderecht auf Grund literarischer und juristischer Quellen.* Berlin: Triltsch and Huther.

Miller, William Ian. 1983. "Choosing the Avenger: Some Aspects of the Bloodfeud in Medieval Iceland and England." *Law and History Review* 1.2: 159–204.

Miller, William Ian. 1984. "Avoiding Legal Judgment: The Submission of Disputes to Arbitration in Medieval Iceland." *American Journal of Legal History* 28: 95–134.

Miller, William Ian. 1988. "Ordeal in Iceland." *Scandinavian Studies* 60.2: 189–218.

Miller, William Ian. 1990. *Bloodtaking and Peacemaking: Feud, Law, and Society in Saga Iceland.* Chicago: University of Chicago Press.

Miller, William Ian and Helle Vogt. 2015. "Finding, Sharing and Risk of Loss: Of Whales, Bees and Other Valuable Finds in Iceland, Denmark and Norway." *Comparative Legal History* 3.1: 38–59.

MSE = Pulsiano, Phillip, ed. 1993. *Medieval Scandinavia: An Encyclopedia.* New York: Garland.

Modéer, Kjell Å. 2010. *Historiska rättskällor i konflikt: En introduktion i rättshistoria.* 3rd ed. Stockholm: Santérus.

Much, Rudolf. 1935. "Silva Caesia." *Zeitschrift für Mundartforschung* 11.1: 39–48.

Mundal, Else. 2016. "'At læra prest til kirkju'. Islandske prestar i ufridom." In *Kyrklig rätt och kyrklig orätt – kyrkorättsliga perspektiv. Festskrift till professor Bertil Nilsson,* ed. Martin Berntson and Anna Minara Ciardi, pp. 277–88. Bibliotheca theologiae practicae 97. Skellefteå: Artos.

Mykland, Knut. 1989. *Norges historie. Bind 15. Historisk atlas, oversikter, register.* Oslo: Cappelen.

Myrberg, Nanouschka. 2009. "An Island in the Middle of an Island: On Cult, Laws and Authority in Viking Age Gotland." In *From Ephesos to Dalecarlia: Reflections on Body, Space and Time in Medieval and Early Modern Europe,* ed. Elisabet Regner, pp. 101–18. Stockholm: Statens historiska museum.

Myrdal, Janken. 1999a. *Det svenska jordbrukets historia. Jordbruket under feodalismen 1000–1700.* Stockholm: Stift. Lagersberg.

Myrdal, Janken. 1999b. "Skogshistoria i ett agrarhistoriskt perspektiv." In *Skogshistorisk forskning i Europa och Nordamerika. Vad är skogshistoria? Hur har den skrivits och varför,* ed. Ronny Pettersson, pp. 125–32. Kungl. Skogs- och Lantbruksakademien. Skogs- och lantbrukshistoriska meddelanden 22. Stockholm: Skogs- och lantbruksakademien.

Myrdal, Janken. 2011. "Farming and Feudalism, 1000–1700." In *The Agrarian History of Sweden: From 4000 BC to AD 2000,* ed. Janken Myrdal and Mats Morell, pp. 72–117. Lund: Nordic Academic Press.

Myrdal, Janken and Claes Tollin. 2003. "Brytar och tidigmedeltida huvudgårdar." In *Trälar. Ofria i agrarsamhället från vikingatid till medeltid,* ed. Thomas Lindkvist and Janken Myrdal, pp. 133–68. Skrifter om skogs- och lantbrukshistoria 17. Stockholm: Nordiska museet.

Måhl, K. G. 1990. "Bildstenar och stavgardar – till frågan om de gotländska bildstenarnas placering." *Gotländskt arkiv: Meddelanden från föreningen Gotlands fornvänner* 62: 13–28.

Nationalencyklopedin, http://www.ne.se

Naumann, Hans-Peter. 1979. *Sprachstil und Textkonstitution: Untersuchungen zur altwestnordischen Rechtssprache.* Beiträge zur nordischen Philologie 7. Basel: Helbing & Lichtenhahn.

Naumann, Hans-Peter. 2003. "Andreas Heuslers Übersetzungen aus dem Altisländischen." In *Runica – Germanica – Mediaevalia,* ed. Wilhelm Heizmann and Astrid van Nahl, 466–79. Berlin: de Gruyter.

NE = *Nationalencyklopedin*

Neckel, Gustav. 1916. "Adel und Gefolgschaft: Ein Beitrag zur germanischen Altertumskunde." *Beiträge zur Geschichte der deutschen Sprache und Literatur* 41: 385–436.

Nevéus, Clara. 1974. *Trälarna i landskapslagarnas samhälle: Danmark och Sverige = Die Sklaven in der Gesellschaft der Landschaftsrechten: Dänemark und Schweden.* Studia historica Upsaliensia 58. PhD Diss. Uppsala University.

Ney, Agneta. 1998. "Människor i marginalen: Sociala definitioner i medeltida lagtexter." In *Främlingar - ett historiskt perspektiv*, ed. Anders Florén and Åsa Karlsson, pp. 105–18. Opuscula historica Upsaliensia 19. Uppsala: Historiska institutionen, Uppsala University.

Ney, Agneta. 2012. "'Uselt är att vara varg': Om vargterminologi i västnordisk litteratur och rättsuppfattning." *Historisk tidskrift* (Stockholm) 132.3: 483–89.

Niermeyer & van de Kieft = Niermeyer, Jan Frederik and C. van de Kieft. 2002. *Mediae Latinitatis lexicon minus.* Darmstadt: Wissenschaftliche Buchgesellschaft.

Nilsson, Bertil. 1989. *De sepulturis: Gravrätten i Corpus iuris canonici och i medeltida nordisk lagstiftning.* Bibliotheca theologiae practicae 44. Stockholm: Almqvist & Wiksell.

Nilsson, Bertil. 2001. "Gudsdomar i Skandinavien under vikingatid och medeltid." In *Kontinuitäten und Brüche in der Religionsgeschichte. Festschrift für Anders Hultgård zu seinem 65. Geburtstag am 23.12.2001*, ed. Olof Sundqvist, Astrid van Nahl and Michael Stausberg, pp. 503–35. Ergänzungsbände zum Reallexikon der germanischen Altertumskunde 31. Berlin, New York: de Gruyter.

Nilsson, Göran B. 2012. *Nytt ljus över Yngre Västgötalagen: Den bestickande teorin om en medeltida lagstiftningsprocess.* Serien 1: Rättshistoriskt bibliotek 69. Stockholm: Institutet för rättshistorisk forskning.

Nilsson, Göran B. 2013. "Vad man bör veta om yngre Västgötalagen." *Västgötalitteratur*: 49–62.

Nordal, Guðrún. 1998. *Ethics and Action in Thirteenth-Century Iceland.* Odense: Odense University Press.

NF = Linder, Nils, John Rosén, Theodor Westrin, Bror Ferdinand Olsson, and Bernhard Meijer, eds. 1875–99. *Nordisk familjebok: Konversationslexikon och realencyklopedi innehållande upplysningar och förklaringar om märkvärdiga namn, föremål och begrepp.* 20 vols. Stockholm: Expeditionen af Nordisk famimljebok. ["1800-talsutgåvan" available at runeberg.org]

NK = Brøndum Nielsen, Johannes, Otto von Friesen, and Magnus Olsen, eds. 1931–56. *Nordisk Kultur.* 30 vols. Stockholm: Bonnier.

Norseng, Per G. 1987. "Lovmaterialet som kilde til tidlig nordisk middelalder." In *Nordiska historikermötet: Rapporter til den XX nordiske historikerkongres, Reykjavik 1987*, ed. Gunnar Karlsson. pp. I:48–77. Ritsafn Sagnfræðistofnunar 18. Reykjavík: Sagnfræðistofnun Háskola Íslands.

Norseng, Per G. 1991. "Law Codes as a Source for Nordic History in the Early Middle Ages." *Scandinavian Journal of History* 16: 137–66.

Nørrevang, Arne. 1979. "Land Tenure, Fowling Rights, and Sharing of the Catch in Faroese Fowling." *Fróðskaparrit* 27: 30–49.

ODEE = T. F. Hoad, ed. 1986. *Concise Oxford Dictionary of English Etymology.* Oxford: Clarendon.

ODS = *Ordbog over det danske sprog: Historisk ordbog 1700–1950*, https://ordnet.dk/ods

Ólafur Lárusson. 1960. *Lov og ting: Islands forfatning og lover i fristatstiden.* Bergen: Universitetsforlaget.

Olesen, Jens E. 2000. "Middelalderen til 1536: Fra rejsekongedømme til administrationscentrum." In *Dansk forvaltningshistorie: stat, forvaltning og samfund. 1, Fra middelalderen til 1901*, ed. Leon Jesperson and E. Ladewig Petersen, pp. 4–48. Copenhagen: Jurist- og Økonomforbundets forlag.

Olsen, Olaf. 1966. *Hørg, hov og kirke: Historiske og arkæologiske vikingetidsstudier.* Aarbøger for nordisk oldkyndighed og historie. Copenhagen: Gad.

Olsson, Ingemar. 1976. *Gotlands stavgardar – en ortnamnsstudie.* Visby: Press.

Olsson, Ingemar. 1992. "Stavgardsproblemet – ännu en gång." *Fornvännen* 87: 91–97

Olsson, Mats. 1999. *Vikingatida träldom: Om slaveriets plats i Skandinaviens ekonomiska historia*. Lund Papers in Economic History 67. Lund: Department of Economic History, Lund University.

Olsson, Stefan. 2016. *Gísl. Givande och tagande av gisslan som rituell handling i fredsprocesser under vikingatid och tidig medeltid*. PhD Diss. University of Bergen.

ONP = *Ordbog over det norrøne prosasprog*. 2010–, onp.ku.dk

Orning, Hans Jacob. 2008. *Unpredictability and Presence: Norwegian Kingship in the High Middle Ages*. Leiden: Brill.

Orning, Hans Jacob. 2011. Norvegr: *Norges historie. Bind I: Frem til 1400*. Oslo: Aschehoug.

Orning, Hans Jacob. 2014. "Borgerkrig og statsutvikling i Norge i middelalderen – en revurdering." *Historisk tidsskrift* (Oslo) 2014.2: 193–216.

Orning, Hans Jacob, Kim Esmark and Lars Hermanson, eds. 2010. *Gaver, ritualer, konflikter: Et rettsantropologisk perspektiv på nordisk middelalderhistorie*. Oslo: Unipub.

Orri Vésteinsson. 2009. "Upphaf goðaveldis á Íslandi." In *Heimtur: ritgerðir til heiðurs Gunnari Karlssyni sjötugum*, ed. Guðmundur Jónsson, Helgi Skúli Kjartansson and Vésteinn Ólason, pp. 298–331. Reykjavík: Mál og menning.

Orri Vésteinsson. 2013. "What is in a Booth? Material Symbolism at Icelandic Assembly Sites." *Journal of the North Atlantic* sp5: 111–24.

Páll Sigurðsson. 2016. *Lagaþankar. Safn greina um réttarframkvæmd og lögfræði frá ýmsum tímum*. Reykjavík: Háskóli Íslands.

Pappenheim, Max. 1933. "Über die Rechtsnatur der altgermanischen Schenkung." *Zeitschrift der Savigny-Stiftung für Rechtsgeschichte: Germanistische Abteilung* 53: 35–88.

Pellijeff, Gunnar. 1967. *Lag om gård i västgötalagarna*. Nordiska texter och undersökningar 22. Stockholm: Almqvist & Wiksell.

Petersen, Sámal. 1972. "Tingstaðurin á Tinganesi." *Fróðskaparrit* 20: 71–88.

Pettersen, Gunnar I. 2013. *Priser og verdiforhold i Norge ca. 1280–1500*. Riksarkivaren. Skriftserie 39. Oslo: Riksarkivet.

Pettersson, Jonatan. 2000. "Husabyarna – en kritisk forskningsöversikt." In *En bok om husbyar*, ed. Michael Olausson, pp. 65–74. Riksantikvarieämbetet. Avdelningen för arkeologiska undersökningar. Skrifter nr 33. Stockholm: Riksantikvarieämbetet, http://urn.kb.se/resolve?urn=urn%3Anbn%3Ase%3Araa%3Adiva-5625

Phillpotts, Bertha. 1913 [repr. 2010]. *Kindred and Clan in the Middle Ages and After*. Cambridge: Cambridge University Press.

Pipping, Hugo. 1913. *Äldre Västgötalagens ordskatt: Samlad och ordnad*. Acta Societatis Scientiarium Fennicae 42.4. Helsingfors: Finska litteratursällskapet.

Pons Sanz, Sara María. 2007. *Norse-Derived Vocabulary in Late Old English Texts: Wulfstan's Works; A Case Study*. Odense: John Benjamins.

Porsmose, Erland. 1988. "Middelalder o. 1000–1536." In *Det danske landbrugs historie I. Oldtid og middelalder*, ed. Claus Bjørn et al., pp. 226–31. Odense: Landbohistorisk Selskab.

Rahmqvist, Sigurd. 1996. *Sätesgård och gods. De medeltida frälsegodsens framväxt mot bakgrund av Upplands bebyggelsehistoria*. Uppsala.

RGA = *Reallexikon der Germanischen Altertumskunde*. 1973–2008. 1–35, Register, 1–2. Berlin & New York: De Gruyter.

Ricketts, Philadelphia. 2010. *High-Ranking Widows in Medieval Iceland and Yorkshire: Property, Power, Marriage and Identity in the Twelfth and Thirteenth Centuries*. Leiden: Brill.

Rietz, Johan Ernst. 1862–67 [repr. 1962]. *Svenskt dialektlexikon: Ordbok öfver svenska allmogespråket*. Lund: Gleerups.

Riddersporre, Mats. 2001. "Skånska bolskiften – Hötofta." In *Plats, Landskap, Karta. En vänskrift till Ulf Sporrong*, pp. 64–65. Stockholm: Kulturgeografiska institutionen, Stockholms universitet.

Riddersporre, Mats. 2008. "Det skånska bolet." In *Jordvärderingssystem från medeltiden till 1600-talet*, ed. Alf Ericsson, pp. 23–38. Stockholm: Kungl. Vitterhets historie och antikvitets akademien.

Riisøy, Anne Irene. 2002. "What's on the Case-List? Legal Texts and Felonies Rediscovered." *Scandinavian Journal of History* 27.2: 77–89.

Riisøy, Anne Irene. 2005. "Kristenrettene og sosialhistorien." In *Den kirkehistoriske utfordring*, ed. Steinar Imsen, pp. 59–74. Trondheim: Tapir akademisk forlag.

Riisøy, Anne Irene. 2009. *Sexuality, Law and Legal Practice and the Reformation in Norway*. Northern World 44. Leiden : Brill.

Riisøy, Anne Irene. 2010. "Outlawry and Moral Perversion in Old Norse Society." In *Bodies of Knowledge: Cultural Interpretations of Illness and Medicine in Medieval Europe*, ed. Sally Crawford and Christina Lee, pp. 19–26. Studies in Early Medicine 1. Oxford: Archaeopress.

Riisøy, Anne Irene. 2013. "Sacred Legal Places in Eddic Poetry: Reflected in Real Life?" *Journal of the North Atlantic* 5: 28–41.

Riisøy, Anne Irene. 2014. "Outlawry: From Western Norway to England." In *New Approaches to Early Law in Scandinavia*, ed. Stefan Brink and Lisa Collinson, pp. 101–29. Turnhout: Brepols.

Riisøy, Anne Irene. 2015. "Deviant Burials: Societal Exclusion of Dead Outlaws I Medieval Norway." In *Cultures of Death and Dying in Medieval and Early Modern Europe*, ed. Mia Korpiola and Anu Lehtinen, pp. 49–81. Studies across Disciplines in the Humanities and Social Sciences 18. Helsinki: Helsinki Collegium for Advanced Studies.

Riisøy, Anne Irene. 2016. *Rings for Compensation and Fines*. Unpublished manuscript.

Rindal, Magnus. 1995. "Dei norske mellomalderlovene." In *Skriftlege kjelder til kunnskap om nordisk mellomalder*, ed. Magnus Rindal, pp. 7–20. KULTs skriftserie 38. Oslo: Noregs forskingsråd.

Robberstad, Knut. 1961. "Løgting og gildi." *Fróðskaparrit* 10: 42–46.

Robberstad, Knut. 1980. *Rettssoga*. 2nd ed. Oslo: Universitetsforlaget.

Rothenborg, Jørend Nathalie. 1988. *Tingets betydning som offentligt organ i det tidlige norske middelaldersamfund: Belyst ud fra Snorre Sturlusons Heimskringla samt de tidlige landskabslove og disses gammelgermanske baggrund.* [S.l.: s.n.]

Rosén, Jerker. 1949. *Kronoavsöndringar under äldre medeltid*. Skrifter utgivna av Kungl. Humanistiska Vetenskapssamfundet i Lund XLV. Lund: Gleerup.

Runer, Johan. 2012. "Huvudtionde, odal och prästgårdar." *Historisk tidskrift* (Stockholm) 132.4: 595–623.

Ruthström, Bo. 1988. "Oklunda-ristningen i rättslig belysning." *Arkiv för nordisk filologi* 103: 64–75.

Ruthström, Bo. 1990. "Forsaringen." *Arkiv för nordisk filologi* 105: 41–55.

Ruthström, Bo. 1993. "Öre – förslag till en alternativ etymologi." *Arkiv för nordisk filologi* 108: 94–121.

Ruthström, Bo. 1999. "Om den fornisländska terminologien för hövding och hövdingadöme." *Arkiv för nordisk filologi* 114: 89–102.

Ruthström, Bo. 2002. "Nordic language history and legal history." In *The Nordic languages*, ed. Oskar Bandle et al., pp. 344–54. Handbücher zur Sprach- und Kommunikationswissenschaft 22:1. Berlin & New York: De Gruyter.

Ruthström, Bo. 2003. Land *och fæ: Strukturellt-rättsfilologiska studier i fornnordiskt lagspråk över beteckningar för egendom i allmänhet med underkategorier*. Skrifter utgivna av Institutet för rättshistorisk forskning. Serien 1: Rättshistoriskt bibliotek 61. Stockholm: Institutet för rättshistorisk forskning.

Røsstad, Rune. 1997. *A tveim tungum: Om stil og stilvariasjon i norrønt lovmål*. Oslo: Norges forskningsråd.

Sandnes, Jørn. 2006. "Noen merknader til motstandsbestemmelse i Frostatingsloven." *Historisk tidskrift* (Oslo) 85.2: 289–98.

Sandholm, Åke. 1965. *Primsigningsriten under nordisk medeltid.* Acta Academiae Aboensis. Ser. A 29.3. Åbo: Åbo Akademi.

Sandvik, Gudmund and Jón Viðar Sigurðsson. 2005. "Laws." In *A Companion to Old Norse-Icelandic Literature and Culture*, ed. Rory McTurk, pp. 223–44. Oxford: Blackwell.

SAOB = *Svenska Akademiens ordbok*, https://www.saob.se/

Sawyer, Birgit and Sawyer, Peter. 2002. "The Good People of Scandinavia." In *Norna u istotsjnika Sud'by: Sbornik statej v-est Eleny Alexsondrovny Mel'nikovaj*, pp. 370–83. Moscow: Indrik.

Schlyter = Schlyter, Carl Johan. 1877. "Glossarium ad Corpus iuris Sueo-Gotorum antiqui = Ordbok till Samlingen af Sweriges gamla lagar." Vol. 13 of *Corpus iuris sueo-gotorum antiqui. Samling af Sweriges gamla lagar.* Lund: Gleerup.

Schulte, Michael. 2011. "Early Scandinavian Legal Texts. Evidence of Preliterary Metrical Composition?" *Nowele* 62/63: 1–30.

Schultze, Alfred. 1939. *Zum altnordischen Eherecht.* Berichte über die Verhandlungen der Sächsischen Akademie der Wissenschaften zu Leipzig. Philologisch-historische Klasse 91.1. Leipzig: Hirzel.

Schück, Adolf. 1933. "Sveriges vägar och sjöleder under forntid och medeltid." *Nordisk kultur: samlingsverk. 16. B. Handel och samfärdsel under medeltiden*, ed. Adolf Schück, pp. 229–55. Stockholm: Bonnier.

Schück, Adolf. 1949. "Svithjod och folklanden. Ett diskussionsinlägg." In *Historiska studier tillägnade Nils Ahnlund 23/8/1949*, ed. Sven Grauers and Åke Stille, pp. 8–50. Stockholm: Norstedt.

Scovazzi, Marco. 1971. "Der römische *pontifex* und die Eriksgata der schwedischen Könige." *Zeitschrift der Savigny-Stiftung fur Rechtsgeschichte: Germanistische Abteilung* 88: 198–204.

See, Klaus von. 1964. *Altnordische Rechtswörter: Philologische Studien zur Rechtsauffassung und Rechtsgesinnung der Germanen.* Hermaea 16. Tübingen: Niemeyer.

See, Klaus von. 2006. "Altnordische Rechtssprache als mittelalterliche Fachsprache. " In *Leges – Gentes – Regna: Zur Rolle von germanischen Rechtsgewohnheiten und lateinischer Schrifttradition bei der Ausbildung der frühmittelalterlichen Rechtskultur*, edited by Gerhard Dilcher and Eva-Marie Distler, pp. 159–65. Berlin: E. Schmidt.

Seggewiß, Hermann-Josef. 1978. *Goði und Hǫfðingi. Die literarische Darstellung und Funktion von Gode und Häuptling in den Isländersagas.* Frankfurt am Main: Peter Lang.

Siltberg, Tryggve. 2008. "Marklejet – Gotlands jordatal för undersåtarna." In *Jordvärderingssystem från medeltiden till 1600-talet*, ed. Alf Ericsson, pp. 85–117. Stockholm: Kungl. Vitterhets historie och antikvitets akademien.

Sjöholm, Elsa. 1988. *Sveriges medeltidslagar: Europeisk rättstradition i politisk omvandling.* Stockholm: Institutet för rättshistorisk forskning.

Sjöholm, Elsa. 1990. "Sweden's Medieval Laws: European Legal Tradition – Political Change." *Scandinavian Journal of History* 15.1–2: 65–87.

Skre, Dagfinn. 1995. "Kirken før sognet. Den tidligste kirkeordningen i Norge." In *Møtet mellom hedendom og kristendom i Norge*, ed. Hans-Emil Lidén, pp. 170–233. Oslo: Universitetsforlaget.

Skre, Dagfinn, ed. 2007. *Kaupang in Skiringssal.* Aarhus: Aarhus University Press.

SNL = *Den store norske leksikon.* 2015–, www.snl.no

Sporrong, Ulf. 1992. "hammarskifte." In *Nationalencyklopedin*, ed. Kari Marklund, vols. 26, VIII. Höganäs: Bra böcker.

Sporrong, Ulf. 2008. "Jordägande och jordvärderingssystem från medeltiden till 1600-talet – ett försök till sammanfattning." In *Jordvärderingssystem från medeltiden till 1600-talet*, ed. Alf Ericsson, pp. 241–61. Stockholm: Kungl. Vitterhets historie och antikvitets akademien.

Steen, Sverre. 1933a. "Vejene og leden i Norge. " *Nordisk kultur: samlingsverk. 16. B. Handel och samfärdsel under medeltiden*, ed. Adolf Schück, pp. 217–28. Stockholm: Bonnier.

Steen, Sverre. 1933b. "Fartøier i Norden i middelalderen." *Nordisk kultur: samlingsverk. 16. B. Handel och samfärdsel under medeltiden*, ed. Adolf Schück, pp. 282–300. Stockholm: Bonnier.

Steffen, Richard. 1945. "Gotlands indelning och organisation." In *Boken om Gotland: Minnesskrift med anledning av Gotlands återförening med Sverige genom freden i Brömsebro den 13 augusti 1645. D. 1, Gotlands historia fram till år 1645*, ed. Mårten Stenberger, pp. 226–53. Visby.

Steinnes, Asgaut. 1936. *Mål, vekt og verderekning i Noreg i millomalderen og ei tid etter*. Nordisk Kultur XXX, pp. 84–154. Oslo: Aschehoug.

Steinnes, Asgaut. 1974. *Styrings- og rettsskipnad i Sørvest-Noreg i mellomaladeren*. Oslo: Det Norske Samlaget.

Strauch, Dieter. 1998. "Wikinger." In *Dieter Strauch, Kleine rechtsgeschichtliche Schriften: Aufsätze 1965–1997; Aus Anlaß seines 65. Geburtstages*, ed. Manfred Baldus and Hanns Peter Neuheuser, pp. 366–77. Köln: Böhlau.

Strauch, Dieter. 2008a. "Geschworene statt Eisenprobe: Entwicklungen im mittelalterlichen schwedischen Prozeß." In *Nomen et Fraternitas: Festschrift für Dieter Geuenich zum 65. Geburtstag*, ed. Uwe Ludwig and Thomas Schilp, pp. 765–86. Reallexikon der Germanischen Altertumskunde Ergänzungsbände 62. Berlin, New York: De Gruyter.

Strauch, Dieter. 2008b. "Grundzüge des mittelalterlichen skandinavischen Sklavenrechts." In *Von den leges barbarorum bis zum ius barbarum des Nationalsozialismus: Festschrift für Hermann Nehlsen zum 70. Geburtstag*, ed. Thomas Gutmann, et al., pp. 224–65. Köln: Böhlau.

Strauch, Dieter. 2011. "Skandinavisches Recht: Einführung und Überblick." In *Altertumskunde – Altertumswissenschaft – Kulturwissenschaft: Erträge und Perspektiven nach 40 Jahren Reallexikon der Germanischen Altertumskunde*, ed. Heinrich Beck et al., pp. 293–316. Ergänzungsbände zum Reallexikon der germanischen Altertumskunde 77. Berlin and Boston: De Gruyter.

Strauch, Dieter. 2013. "Snorri Sturluson und der isländische Weg zum Schatzland Norwegens." In *Snorri Sturluson – Historiker, Dichter, Politiker*, ed. Heinrich Beck, Wilhelm Heizmann and Jan van Nahl, pp. 267–302. Berlin: De Gruyter.

Strauch, Dieter. 2013a. "Rechtsbücher und Gesetzbücher im Norden (*Laghman – Laghsaga –Sidveniæ*)." *Zeitschrift der Savigny-Stiftung für Rechtsgeschichte* 130: 37–77.

Strauch, Dieter. 2016. *Mittelalterliches nordisches Recht bis ca. 1500: Eine Quellenkunde*. Ergänzungsbände zum Reallexikon der germanischen Altertumskunde 97. 2nd ed. Berlin: De Gruyter.

Stuard, Susan Mosher. 1995. "Ancillary Evidence for the Decline of Medieval Slavery." *Past & Present* 149: 3–28.

Ståhle, Carl Ivar. 1988. *Studier över Östgötalagen*. Efter författarens efterlämnade manuskript utgivna av Gösta Holm. Samlingar utgivna av Svenska fornskriftsällskapet. Serie 1, Svenska skrifter 257 = 77. Uppsala: Svenska fornskriftsällsk.

Ståhle, Carl Ivar. 1958. *Syntaktiska och stilistiska studier i fornnordiskt lagspråk*. Stockholm: Almqvist & Wiksell.

Sunde, Jørn Øyrehagen. 2005. *Speculum legale: Rettsspegelen; Ein introduksjon til den norske rettskulturen si historie i eit europeisk perspektiv*. Bergen: Fagbokforlaget.

Sunde, Jørn Øyrehagen, ed. 2006. *Rettstekstar i mellomalderen: Idé og praksis*. Rettshistoriske studier 17. Institutt for offentlig retts skriftserie 2006/6. Oslo: Institutt for offentlig rett.

Sunde, Jørn Øyrehagen. 2011a. "Fiende og frende på Gulating i mellomalderen." In *Frå Gulatinget til Gulatings plass*, ed. Bjørn Solbakken, pp. 52–69. Bergen: John Grieg.

Sunde, Jørn Øyrehagen. 2011b. "Innovative Reception: Reception and Innovation Concerning Fixed Time Periods as a Criterion for the Acquisition and Loss of Rights in the *Gulating* Compilation." In *Liber Amicorum Ditlev Tamm: Law, History and Culture*, ed. Per Andersen, Pia Letto-Vanamo, Kjell Åke Modéer and Helle Vogt, pp. 217–29. Copenhagen: DJØF.

Sunde, Jørn Øyrehagen. 2014. "Daughters of God and Counsellors of the Judges of Men: Changes in the Legal Culture of the Norwegian Realm in the High Middle Ages." In *New Approaches to Early Law in Scandinavia*, ed. Stefan Brink and Lisa Collinson, pp. 131–83. Turnhout: Brepols.

Sundkvist, Olof. 2008. "Cult Leaders, Rulers and Religion." In *The Viking World*, ed. Stefan Brink and Neil Price, pp. 223–26. London: Routledge.

Sundkvist, Olof. 2015. "Custodian of the Sanctuary: Protecting Sacred Space as a Ritual Strategy for Gaining Legitimacy and Power in Pre-Christian Scandinavia." In *Rituals, Performatives, and Political Order in Northern Europe, c. 650–1350*, ed. Wojtek Jezierski et al., 113–34. Turnhout: Brepols.

Svavar Sigmundsson. 2003. "Navne på de administrative inddelinger i Island." In *Den 10. nasjonale konferansen i namngransking*, ed. Åse Wetås og Tom Schmidt, pp. 11–24. Oslo: Seksjon for namnegranskning.

Sveinbjörn Rafnsson. 1974. *Studier i Landnámabók: Kritiska bidrag till den isländska fristatstidens historia*. Lund: Gleerup.

Sveinbjörn Rafnsson. 1985. "Um Staðarhólsmál Sturlu Þórðarsonar: Nokkrar athuganir á valdsmennsku um hans daga." *Skírnir* 159: 143–59.

Sverrir Jakobsson. 2013. "From Reciprocity to Manorialism: On the Peasant Mode of Production in Medieval Iceland." *Scandinavian Journal of History* 38.3: 273–95.

Syrett, Martin. 2000. "Drengs and Thegns Again." *Saga-Book* 25: 243–71.

Söderlind, Stefan, 1989. *Leding och härad. Gård och by. En studie i medeltida svensk kameralistik och drätsel*. Uppsala: Reprocentralen.

Söderwall, K. F. 1884–1973. *Ordbok öfver svenska medeltids-språket*. 2 vols. Samlingar utgivna av Svenska fornskriftsällskapet. Serie 1, Svenska skrifter. Lund.

Sørensen, Preben Meulengracht. 1993. *Fortælling og ære. Studier i islændingesagaerne*. Aarhus: Aarhus universitetsforlag.

Sørlie, Mikjel. 1965. *En færøysk-norsk Lovbok fra omkring 1310: En studie i færøysk språkhistorie*. Tórshavn: Mentunargrunnur Føroya Løgtings.

Tamm, Ditlev. 1996. *Dansk rettshistorie*. 2nd ed. Copenhagen: Jurist- og Økonomforbundets forl.

Tamm, Ditlev. 2002a. *Retshistorie: Danmark, Europa, globale perspektiver*. Copenhagen: Jurist- og Økonomforb.

Tamm, Ditlev. 2002b. "Gulatingsloven og de andre gamle nordiske landskabslove." *Tidsskrift for rettsvitenskap* 1/2: 292–308.

Tamm, Ditlev. 2011. *The History of Danish Law: Selected Articles and Bibliography*. Law and Culture Series 5. Copenhagen: Djøf/Jurist- og Økonomforbundet.

Tamm, Ditlev, W. Schubert and J. U. Jørgensen. 2008. *Quellen zur dänischen Rechts- und Verfassungsgeschichte (12.–20. Jahrhundert)*. Frankfurt am Main: Peter Lang.

Tamm, Ditlev and Helle Vogt, eds. 2011. *How Nordic are the Nordic Medieval Laws?* Medieval Legal History 1. Copenhagen: University of Copenhagen Press.

Taranger, Absalon. 1890. *Den angelsaksiske kirkes indflydelse paa den norske*. Udgivet af Den norske historiske forening. Kristiania: Grøndahl & søns bogtrykkeri.

Taranger, Absalon. 1935. *Utsikt over den norske retts historie, 1: Innledning. Rettskildenes historie*. 2nd ed., ed. Knut Robberstad. Oslo.

Tegengren, Gunilla. 2015. *Sverige och Nordlanden: Förvaltning och nordlig expansion 1250–1550*. Kungl. Skytteanska samfundets handlingar 72. PhD Diss., University of Gothenburg, http://hdl.handle.net/2077/39337

Thunaeus, Harald. 1968. *Ölets historia i Sverige. 1, Från äldsta tider till 1600-talets slut*. Stockholm: Almqvist & Wiksell.

Tollin, Clas. 1999. *Rågångar, gränshallar och ägoområden. Rekonstruktion av fastighetsstruktur och bebyggelseutveckling i mellersta Småland under äldre medeltid*. Meddelande nr 101, Kulturgeografiska institutionen Stockholms universitet. Stockholm: Stockholm University.

Tollin, Clas. 2008. "Från avkastning till areal: olika sätt att värdera jord." In *Jordvärderingssystem från medeltiden till 1600-talet*, ed. Alf Ericsson, pp. 139–62. Stockholm: Kungl. Vitterhets historie och antikvitets akademien.

Tveito, Olav. 2005. "'Svarteboka' frå Vinje som bidrag til temaet fromhet og folklore." *Tidsskrift for Teologi og Kirke* 2005.3: 212–29.

Tveito, Olaf. 2011. *Gravskikk og kristning: En analyse i skandinavisk perspektiv 9.–11. århundre*. Oslo: Novus.

Ugulen, Jo Rune. 2008. '...alle the knaber ther inde och sædescwenne...': Ei undersøking i den sosiale samansetjinga av den jordeigande eliten på Vestlandet i mellomalderen. Phd Diss. Universitet i Bergen.

Ugulen, Jo Rune. 2012. "The *hauldr*: Peasant or Nobleman?" In *Law and Power in the Middle Ages: Proceedings from the Fourth Carlsberg Academy Conference on Medieval Legal History*, ed. Per Andersen, Mia Münster-Swendsen and Helle Vogt, 2nd ed. pp. 139–45. Copenhagen: DJØF.

Ulsig, Erik. 1981. "Landboer og bryder, skat og landgilde: De danske fæstebønder og deres afgifter i det 12. og 13. århundrede." In *Middelalder, metode og medier: Festskrift til Niels Skyum-Nielsen på 60-årsdagen den 17. oktober 1982*, ed. Karsten Fledelius, Niels Lund and Herluf Nielsen, pp. 137–65. Viborg: Museum Tusculanums Forlag.

Ulsig, Erik. 2011. *Danmark 900–1300: Kongemagt og samfund*. Aarhus: Aarhus Universitetsforlag.

Vainio, Charlotte. 2013. "Empowered Spouses: Matrimonial Legal Authority in Sweden." In *Fundamentals of Medieval and Early Modern Culture, Volume 12: Authorities in the Middle Ages; Influence, Legitimacy, and Power in Medieval Society*, ed. Sini Kangas, Mia Korpiola and Tuija Ainonen, pp. 285–306. Berlin: De Gruyter.

Venge, Mikael. 2002. *Dansk skattehistorie. Bd. 1: Danmarks skatter i middelalderern indtil 1340*. Copenhagen: Told- og Skattehistorisk Selskab.

Vestergaard, Torben Anders. 1988. "The System of Kinship in Early Norwegian Law." *Mediaeval Scandinavia* 12: 160–93.

Veturliði Óskarsson. 2001. *Middelnedertyske låneord I islandsk diplomsprog frem til år 1500*. PhD Diss. Uppsala University.

Vídalín, Páll. 1854. *Skýríngar yfir fornyrði lögbókar þeirrar, er Jónsbók kallast*. Reykjavík: Íslenzka bókmentafélag.

Vinogradoff, Paul. 1907. "Transfer of Land in Old English Law." *Harvard Law Review* 20.7: 532–48.

Vogt, Helle. 2005. *Slægtens funktion i nordisk højmiddelalderret: Kanonisk retsideologi og fredsskabende lovgivning*. Copenhagen: Jurist- og økonomforbundet.

Vogt, Helle. 2008. "*Fledføring* – Elder Care and the Protection of the Interests of Heirs in Danish Medieval Laws." *The Legal History Review* 76: 273–81.

Vogt, Helle. 2010. *The Function of Kinship in Medieval Nordic Legislation*. Medieval Law and its Practice 9. Leiden: Brill.

Vogt, Helle. 2012. "The King's Power to Legislate in Twelfth and Thirteenth Century Denmark." In *Law and Power in the Middle Ages*, ed. Per Andersen, Mia Münster-Swendsen and Helle Vogt, 2nd ed., pp. 5–14. Copenhagen: DJØF.

Vogt, Helle. 2013. "Legal Encounters in Estonia under Danish Rule, 1219–1347." In *Cultural Encounters during the Crusades*, ed. Kurt Villads Jensen, Kirsi Salonen and Helle Vogt, 237–43. Odense: University Press of Southern Denmark.

Vogt, Helle and Ditlev Tamm. 2013. "Creating a Danish Legal Language: Legal Terminology in the Medieval Law of Scania." *Historical Research* 86.233: 505–14, https://doi.org/10.1111/1468-2281.12007

Vogt, Helle and Mia Münster-Swendsen, eds. 2006. *Law and Learning in the Middle Ages: Proceedings of the Second Carlsberg Academy Conference on Medieval Legal History 2005*. Copenhagen: DJØF.

de Vries, Jan. 2000. *Altnordisches etymologisches Wörterbuch*. 2nd ed. Leiden: Brill.

Wennström, Torsten. 1933. "Fredlösheten: några rättshistoriska filologiska synpunkter." *Vetenskapssocieteten i Lund årsbok* 1933: 53–85.

Wennström, Torsten. 1936. *Tjuvnad och fornæmi: Rättsfilologiska studier i svenska landskapslagar*. Lund: Gleerup.

Wennström, Torsten. 1946. *Lagspråk och lagtexter: Rättsfilologiska studier i svenska landskapslagar.* Lund: Gleerup.

West, John F. 1975. "How Old is the Faroese grannastevna?" *Fróðskaparrit* 23: 48–59.

Widgren, Mats. 1997. "Fields and Field Systems in Scandinavia during the Middle ages." In *Medieval Farming and Technology. The Impact of Agricultural Change in Northwest Europe*, ed. John Langdon and Grenville G. Astill, pp. 173–92. Leiden: Brill.

Wijkander, Keith. 1983. *Kungshögar och sockenbildning: Studier i Södermanlands administrativa indelning under vikingatid och tidig medeltid.* Nyköping: Södermanlands mus.

Winberg, Christer. 1985. *Grenverket. Studier rörande jord, släktskapssystem och ståndsprivilegier.* Skrifter utgivna av Institutet för rättshistorisk forskning, grundat av Gustav och Carin Olin. Serien 1: Rättshistoriskt bibliotek 38. Stockholm: Institutet för rättshistorisk forskning.

Wood, Susan. 2006. *The Proprietary Church in the Medieval West.* Oxford: Oxford University Press.

Wærdahl, Randi Bjørshol. 2011. *The Incorporation and Integration of the King's Tributary Lands into the Norwegian Realm, c. 1195–1397.* Leiden: Brill.

Wærdahl, Randi Bjørshol. 2013. "Friends or Patrons? Powerful Go-Betweens in the Norwegian Realm in the High Middle Ages." In *Friendship and Social Networks in Scandinavia c. 1000–1800*, ed. Jón Viðar Sigurðsson and Thomas Småberg, pp. 93–114. Turnhout: Brepols.

Zoega, Geir T. 1975. *A Concise Dictionary of Old Icelandic.* Oxford: Clarendon Press.

Åqvist, Gösta. 1989. *Kungen och rätten. Studier till uppkomsten och den tidigare utvecklingen av kungens lagstiftningsmakt och domsrätt under medeltiden.* Skrifter utgivna av Institutet för rättshistorisk forskning, grundat av Gustav och Carin Olin. Serien 1: Rättshistoriskt bibliotek 43. Lund: Institutet för rättshistorisk forskning.

Åstrand, Björn. 2000. *Tortyr och pinligt förhör: Våld och tvång i äldre svensk rätt.* Umeå: Institutionen för historiska studier.

Åström, Adolf. 1897. *Om svensk jordäganderätt.* Stockholm: Norstedt.

Ødegaard, M. 2013. "State Formation, Administrative Areas, and *Thing* Sites in the Borgarthing Law Province, Southeast Norway." *Debating the thing in the North 1: The Atlantic Assembly Project. Journal of the North Atlantic* sp5: 42–63.

Þorkell Jóhannesson. 1933. *Die Stellung der freien Arbeiter in Island.* Reykjavík: E.P. Briem.

Þorvald Thoroddsen. 1908–22. *Lýsing Íslands.* 4 vols. Copenhagen: S. L. Möller.

Acknowledgements

Creation of the LMNL has truly been a team effort, and it would not appear as it is today without contributions from several people.

Many colleagues had significant impact on the shape of the lexicon's content, including Stefan Brink, Thomas Lindkvist, Bill Miller, Anne Irene Riisøy, Bertil Nilsson, Helle Vogt, Ditlev Tamm, Jón Viðar Sigurðsson and Annette Hoff, as well as all of the participants at our November 2015 colloquium and several others.

Our digital LMNL exists thanks to our partners at the Sheffield Digital Humanities Institute, in particular George Ionita, who developed much of the platform as it exists currently, and Mike Pidd, who leads the DHI team.

Our printed and print-on-demand LMNL has been made possible by our partners at Open Book Publishers, who were adventurous enough to take on the challenge of generating a printable volume from a database and succeeded in doing so.

Alessandra Tosi was the managing editor for this book.

Adèle Kreager performed the proofreading.

Anna Gatti designed the cover using a reproduction of Carta marina, a wallmap of Scandinavia, by Olaus Magnus, 1539, Wikimedia, public domain, https://commons.wikimedia.org/wiki/File:Carta_Marina.jpeg. The cover was produced in InDesign using Fontin (titles) and Calibri (text body) fonts.

This book is a stand-alone version of the digital resource available at https://www.dhi.ac.uk/lmnl/. The lexical content was extracted from a database hosted by the Digital Humanities Institute in Sheffield and converted into XML by Martin Keegan. Bianca Gualandi took care of converting the XML into the final typeset format (InDesign) for the creation of paperback, hardback, and PDF editions.

Luca Baffa created the digital editions—EPUB, MOBI, PDF, HTML, and XML—the conversion is performed with open source software freely available on our GitHub page (https://github.com/OpenBookPublishers).

Generous funding for the research, compilation and editing of LMNL has been provided by The Swedish Research Council. Additional funding for conversion to print and publishing was provided by The Royal Swedish Academy of Letters, History and Antiquities, Magnus Bergvalls Stiftelse, Längmanska kulturfonden and Åke Wibergs stiftelse.